OZ CLARKE'S

New Encyclopedia of Wine

OZ CLARKE'S

New Encyclopedia
of Wine

Harcourt, Inc.

Orlando   Austin   New York   San Diego   Toronto   London

CONTENTS

Requests for permission to make copies of any part of
the work should be mailed to the following address:
Permissions Department, Harcourt, Inc.,
6277 Sea Harbor Drive, Orlando,
Florida 32887-6777.
www.HarcourtBooks.com

Created and designed by
Websters International Publishers Limited,
Axe and Bottle Court
70 Newcomen Street
London SE1 1YT
www.websters.co.uk
www.ozclarke.com

Library of Congress Cataloging-in-Publication Data
Clarke, Oz
p. cm.
Includes index.
ISBN 0-15-100565-6
ISBN 0-15-602940-5 (pbk)
1. Wine and winemaking Encyclopedias.
I. Title. II. Title: New Encyclopedia of Wine.
TP546.C524 1999
641.2'2'03–dc21 99-33068

Color separations by Technographics, Singapore
and P T Repro, Multi Warner, Indonesia
Printed and bound in China

Photography Cephas Picture Library/principal
photographer Mick Rock

Editorial Director/Chief Editor Fiona Holman
Art Director/Art Editor Nigel O'Gorman
Editorial Assistant Kate Slotover
Other editorial assistance Lorna Bateson, Bill Evans,
Lesley Gilbert, Maggie Ramsay, Julie Ross
Maps Andrew Thompson
Indexer Liz Atkinson
Production Sara Granger

Page 1: Pinot Noir excels in the Carneros District of
California. These vines are at Saintsbury, one of the
best wineries in Carneros.
Pages 2–3: New Zealand's Marlborough region has
enjoyed spectacular success for quality wines since
the 1970s. Inset: Marlborough's snappy, aromatic
wines from Sauvignon Blanc brought the region
worldwide fame.

The Whitlands vineyards, located at 230m (750ft)
high up in the great Dividing Range in Victoria,
Australia, provide some of the best grapes for Brown
Brothers, the dominant producer in the King Valley.

Gamay is the only grape allowed for red Beaujolais
and produces one of the juiciest, most gulpable wines
the world has to offer. Beaujolais has that rare quality
for a red wine – it is wonderfully thirst-quenching.

A-Z OF WINES, WINE REGIONS, PRODUCERS AND GRAPE VARIETIES 54–399

Since the 1950s stainless steel has revolutionized the winemaking process. These fermentation tanks at Vergelegen in South Africa are just the sort on which many a modern winemaker relies.

Many wines are aged for a time in oak, either old or new. New oak barriques of 225 litres (50 gallons), such as these in the barrel room at Cloudy Bay in Marlborough, New Zealand, are an integral part of many fashionable wineries. As well as having the same softening effect on wine as old oak, new oak gives its own flavour to the wine. Judging the precise length of new oak aging is a matter of repeated experimentation.

INTRODUCTION

SOMETIMES I STOP and ask myself – when was the last time I had a glass of bad wine? Not wine that is out of condition, or corked wine, or wine that I've left hanging around in the kitchen for too long – but poor, stale, badly made, unattractive wine? And unless I've been extremely unlucky in the previous month or so, I won't be able to remember. The standard of basic winemaking is now so high around the world that a wine-drinker need never taste a wine that is not at very least clean, honest and drinkable. It wasn't like that ten years ago. It certainly wasn't like that a generation past.

And then, I sometimes idly try to work out how many different grape varieties from how many different wine regions of the world I've tried during a typical wine-taster's week. During every week, there will be examples of grapes that I hardly know, from regions and villages that are often still no more than names on a map for me. And it wasn't like that a generation ago either.

OK, let's be specific. This week at home I picked out a dozen bottles at random from the samples I am sent to taste. Among the more predictable wines like Australian Shiraz and Chilean Chardonnay – yet 15 years ago we wouldn't be saying they were predictable and many shops wouldn't be stocking them – was a wild and wonderful bunch that made me marvel at how wide-reaching our world of wine is now. I had a Bonarda from Mendoza in Argentina – a wonderful, perfumed red. I had a Carignan from Morocco – beefy, but good. I had a Tannat from Uruguay, a Cabernet Franc from California, a Primitivo from southern Italy, a Viognier from southern France – and so it went on. There were also bottles from Bordeaux, Burgundy, Champagne and Chianti – but they didn't hold centre stage, they didn't lord it over the other lesser known wines. Every wine in my random dozen had an equal right to be there, none was thought of as better solely because the name was famous. And if I had to say which I enjoyed the most? It was the Bonarda from Argentina – a virtually unknown grape, from a vast vineyard land that is only now waking up after a century of slumber – and it was the cheapest wine of the lot. And that is the joy of the modern world of wine.

For me, the thrilling thing about this modern world is that we now have choice – endless choice from a vast array of wines that gets bigger every year. And with choice comes excitement, challenge, but also confusion. But that's why this encyclopedia is here: to help you make sense of this cornucopia of flavours and delights that extends from the most famous and expensive wines of Bordeaux and Burgundy – the stuff of dreams rather than reality for most of us – down to the first nervous offerings of virgin vineyards from unsung valleys or the first faltering steps towards modernity from vineyards famous when the Romans stalked the land and preserved in time since then.

We, as wine-drinkers, should take some credit for this transformation. If we were not prepared to try new things, to take a bit of a risk with unknown areas and unknown grapes – winemakers would neither bother to resurrect old areas and plant new ones, nor bother to spread their

Luscious-looking Shiraz grapes caught in the early morning – still damp with dew but ripe and ready for picking in a few hours' time.

St Peter's crossed keys and an elegant blue and gold flag – simple, unassuming, yet announcing the presence of Ch. Pétrus, one of the world's most famous red wines.

That's about as stony as a soil can get! Ata Rangi produces one of New Zealand's greatest Pinot Noirs from the free-draining soils of Martinborough.

activities beyond a few universally popular grape varieties. If we weren't prepared to be adventurous, wine companies would simply flood us with a sea of Chardonnay, Sauvignon, Cabernet, Merlot and Shiraz/Syrah, gaudy labels and fantasy names bedecking wines that made no attempt to taste different or individual. And of course, this encyclopedia wouldn't be necessary either.

But it is necessary. We are in the midst of a revolution in wine that is bringing together the best of the new and the old. Traditionalists are realizing that maybe the old ways are not always the best, that they can learn something from the brash young tyros whose conversation is laced with technobabble, yet whose wines are suffused with a sweet perfumed fruit, the old-timers had never envisaged. And the modernists are quietly laying aside their reliance on cultured yeasts, scientific formulae and refrigerated stainless steel tanks, and listening with respect to the old farmers with their gnarled vines, and their quiet unhurried ways of letting a wine make itself as it will, rather than trying to impose a rigid framework on grapes used to freedom and self-expression.

The result is that the old masters in the heartland of classic wine – France, Germany and northern Italy, in particular – have surreptitiously learned the lessons of the new wave and applied them to their wines. These old classics, seasoned with techniques and attitudes from the New World, have never tasted better.

But what are these New World attitudes? They are the belief that there is never any excuse for incompetent winemaking, that effort and commitment, attention to detail, scrupulous cleanliness and hygiene in the winery, and techniques in the vineyard that have as their objective the best quality of fruit, regardless of what tradition dictates – that these attitudes make it possible to make pleasant wine anywhere that the grape will grow. Consultant winemakers frequently schooled in the Antipodes, now flood Europe in particular, and their zeal has transformed the wasteland of undrinkable plonk that used to flow from the Mediterranean basin into the European Union's infamous 'Wine Lake'. And these roaming wine wizards have also transformed communities and attitudes. After generations of complacency and neglect, areas like Portugal's Ribatejo and Alentejo, Spain's La Mancha, France's Languedoc-Roussillon and Italy's far south are throbbing with self-belief again. Eastern Europe is being dragged out of vinous chaos and resignation by New World willpower and commitment. Further afield, Mexico, Uruguay, Brazil – even Argentina and Chile – needed these travelling maestros to show them how. And the result for us? More good wine, with more different flavours, from more grape varieties and from more hills and valleys, desert oases and coastal plains, than the world has ever experienced before. It's all there for us to

Tyrrell's Vat 47 Chardonnay from the Long Flat Vineyard in the famous Hunter Valley was the first Australian Chardonnay I tasted. My wine-drinking life would never be the same again.

enjoy as broadly and deeply as we want. And this encyclopedia is here to help you along the way, covering the grapes, the places, the vintages, the people and the flavours in an easy to use A–Z format. There's a massive amount of information in here, but we've made it as easy as can be to access and, I hope, as enjoyable as possible to read.

For help with that, may I thank both my editorial team in London and our various experts around the world who have kept me up to the mark on what's happening in their areas of expertise. Without their input, this undertaking would have been far too arduous for me to do alone. How many wines can a man taste in any one day? How many vintages can he cover in any one year? So I thank my eyes, my ears and my palate in every far flung corner of the world.

THE GLOBAL PICTURE

THE WORLD OF WINE is ever expanding, as the vine has settled happily and productively in regions far from its long-established Mediterranean habitats. The proliferation of wines on the shelves of retailers today may suggest that there is not a country in the world that does not produce wine, but a glance at the map below reveals a very different picture.

For the grape to truly flourish and ripen it needs warmth and water – but not too much of either. Such conditions are found primarily between the latitudes of 30 and 50°N and 30 and 40°S. Winemaking regions also tend to hug coastal areas and river valleys. The reason for this is that water affects the climate in a number of ways. It heats up and cools down more slowly than land, keeping temperatures moderate throughout the year. Some hotter vineyard regions benefit from a cooling sea breeze or coastal fog. Sea currents also affect vine-growing: the Gulf Stream warms the western coast of Europe, while a Pacific current running down from Alaska cools some of California's fine wine regions.

The best wines are made in climates where it is only just warm enough to ripen the grape. Gradual ripening, over a long growing season, allows the grapes to concentrate their flavours in the autumn sun. In an excessively hot climate the grapes will ripen too quickly, and the flavours will be shortlived. But if it is too cold, the grapes will not ripen at all.

In the cooler regions of Europe, growers seek to maximize exposure to the sun by planting their vineyards on the sunniest, south-facing slopes. In New World regions, where the sun beats down relentlessly, many vineyards are angled away from the sun to prevent the grapes from baking in the heat. European vineyards are rarely planted more than 300m (1000ft) above sea level because it gets too cool, but some Californian and Australian vineyards are at 600m (2000ft) or more, precisely because the air is cooler.

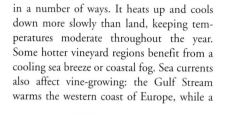

Riesling vineyards rise steeply above the river Mosel at Bernkastel-Kues, Germany, meeting the sun face on and benefiting from the heat retained by the water.

Sunshine aplenty, but at an altitude of between 400 and 500m (around 1500ft) Australia's Clare Valley produces fine cool-climate wines, including Riesling.

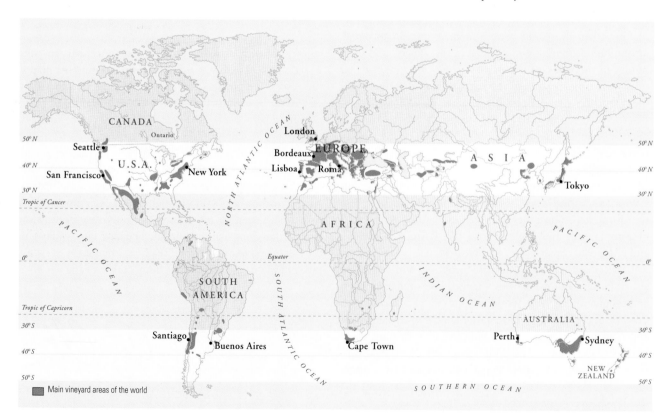

Main vineyard areas of the world

FROM VINE TO WINE

ONCE THE GRAPE'S BASIC climatic demands have been met, a number of other factors affect the flavour of the wine in the bottle you buy. Some are determined by local conditions, others can be controlled or adjusted by the winemaker. The result is an infinite number of variables, which ensure that no two wines, however similar, are absolutely identical.

Grape varieties

The most influential factor determining the flavour of the wine is the variety (or blend of varieties) of grape from which it is made.

When the great surge of interest in fine wine began to build up during the 1970s, and winemakers from all parts of the world looked for models to emulate, the styles which had most appeal were those of Bordeaux and Burgundy, and the sparkling wines of Champagne. So planting the same grape varieties that produced those wines was the first decision the new winemakers took.

In Europe, grape varieties suitable to various locations have gradually evolved over the centuries. Trial and error narrowed down the varieties that best fulfilled the demands of reliability, ability to ripen and economic yield – and these qualities did not always coincide with the best flavoured grapes. The grapes that made it through this empirical selection process were Cabernet Sauvignon, Merlot, Sauvignon Blanc and Sémillon in Bordeaux; Pinot Noir and Chardonnay in Burgundy and Champagne. These are the names that appear on the majority of wines from Australia, California and New Zealand, the new classic wine regions. California was lucky to have ancient plantings of Zinfandel/Primitivo from southern Italy, and Australia benefited from ancient Shiraz/Syrah from France.

When California's Cabernets, Australia's Chardonnays and New Zealand's Sauvignon Blancs began to gain international reputations, their presence soon became too strong to be ignored. They were not the same as the French wines they had tried to emulate – but they were often more approachable, with distinct flavours of the grapes whose names they bore, giving buyers a clear indication of what to expect.

At the same time, forward-looking winemakers, in Tuscany and elsewhere in Europe, began to use Cabernet Sauvignon and other classic grapes in areas where they were excluded from classification under traditional wine laws. Cutting through the restrictions of local regulations and the hierarchy of regional naming, they were able to make better, more internationally appealing wines.

The most famous grape varieties, names seen on the labels of thousands of wines, are the red Cabernet Sauvignon and white Chardonnay, but there are hundreds of others. Some European wines contain blends of several varieties, some of them unique to their area. Many modern winemakers, notably in southern Italy, Portugal and eastern Europe, are beginning to explore the potential of native grapes, and the new and exciting flavours they offer.

Most good winemakers will tell you that the very best they can do is bring out the full potential of the grapes. An attentive winemaker can make decent, fruity wine from unexceptional grapes and a talented one can produce stunning wine from top-quality raw materials – but no-one can make great wine from unhealthy grapes. One of the great advances of the past 30 years has been the research into clonal selection. Growers have been able to develop certain characteristics (early ripening or disease resistance, for example) within a variety. Anyone looking to plant a vineyard can now choose not only the variety but also the clone of that variety most suited to their needs.

Location and soil

The exact valley or hillside where the vines are grown may be sheltered by a forest or warmed by a lake; such local features define the mesoclimate of the vineyard. This definition is the first step in accepting the idea of terroir, the unique sense of place that the traditional winemakers of Europe believe to be the purest expression of character in a wine.

The soil that nourishes the grapes is considered by some producers, particularly in the classic French regions of Bordeaux and Burgundy, to contribute 80 per cent of the quality. Indeed, tasters sometimes claim to detect iron or flint flavours in certain wines. It is true that some grapes prefer slate (Riesling) or gravel (Cabernet Sauvignon), but

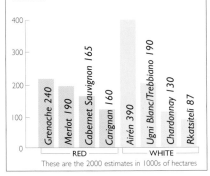

The world's most widely planted grapes
The huge traditional vineyards of Spain, the Mediterranean and the Black Sea States, planted with grapes for everyday wines and brandy, are gradually being overhauled by plantings of finer varieties.

Grenache 240	Merlot 190	Cabernet Sauvignon 165	Carignan 160	Airén 390	Ugni Blanc/Trebbiano 190	Chardonnay 130	Rkatsiteli 87	
RED				WHITE				

These are the 2000 estimates in 1000s of hectares

The terra rossa, or red earth, of Coonawarra, South Australia; this fertile topsoil over free-draining limestone is famous for producing top-quality red wines.

In Burgundy's Côte de Beaune, Pinot Noir vines are traditionally kept low (left); high training with a split canopy (right) exposes the vine to more sunlight, increasing yield.

both are free-draining soils, which supports the alternative, modernist view, that soil is simply a matter of water supply – it either holds water or allows it to drain away. In Europe's cooler, damper regions, a well-drained soil is essential, not only to prevent the vine from becoming waterlogged, but also because a drier soil will be warmer.

Most of the action takes place way below the surface, as the vine sends down deep roots in search of nutrients, but surface characteristics may also affect the ripening of the grapes. Light-coloured soils, such as chalk and limestone, reflect heat back on to the grapes, while slate and other surface stones store heat for chilly autumn evenings.

Despite the best efforts of Australian and Californian winemakers, the classic grape varieties grown in different conditions do not produce fruit with the same flavours. Their vineyards are warmer, their soil more fertile and/or drier. However, when planting their vines they are not tied by tradition: they are able and willing to experiment with a whole new range of viticultural techniques.

Viticulture

Sounds technical, but by this we mean what happens to the grapes in the vineyard. Are they planted close together to conserve heat or far apart, which not only allows cooling winds to fan the vines, but also permits mechanical cultivation? Are the vines grown close to the soil for warmth (but not so low they are vulnerable to frost) or trained high to prevent over-ripening? How hard are they pruned? How are the vineyards fertilized and irrigated (if at all)?

The first decision is whether to aim for a high or low yield. This is a simple trade-off between quantity and quality. Maximizing the number of grape bunches each vine can produce means lots of wine can be made, but lower yields result in grapes with more concentrated flavours. France's quality wine producers rely upon restraint of yield to intensify grape flavour. After careful pruning, the hostility of nature is all that is needed to limit yields in some places, but in warm and fertile valleys controlled irrigation, drainage and shade are the keys to success. A small crop will also ripen faster, so where lack of sun is a problem, yield reduction seems to make sense. But much of the best wine from America and Australia comes from vineyards where heat and sun are in plentiful supply; why restrict yield here? Depending on his or her answer to this question, the winemaker will take appropriate steps in the vineyard.

Over the generations, European producers have developed systems of pruning, trellising and training vines to suit their local conditions. In the hot, arid lands around the Mediterranean, vines are planted fairly far apart – to allow each plant a sip of the meagre water ration – and allowed to develop floppy canopies of foliage to keep the grapes cool and restrict yield. Traditional plantings on such systems in the warm, fertile conditions often found in Australia, California, South America and South Africa usually yield excellent results. However, these warm, fertile conditions would be unlikely to suit the ruthless pruning systems practised in cool, damp areas like Bordeaux and Champagne, because the vines' response would be to throw out ever more shoots and develop jungle-like foliage. The science of canopy management, developed since the 1970s, includes a range of techniques designed to prevent over-vigorous foliage from interfering with ripening.

Canopy management alters the number and position of vine shoots and bunches to maximize exposure of fruit and leaves to the sun. Techniques include winter and summer pruning, shoot thinning and leaf removal, and trellis systems that actually encourage the vine to throw a big crop and lots of foliage. Various methods have been devised to pull the leaves away from the fruit and allow the sun to reach the grapes.

Whereas irrigation is forbidden in the traditional quality vineyards of Europe, in many of the newer wine regions rainfall is in short supply and irrigation is regarded as the ultimate grape growers' tool, controlled by continual fine adjustments judged necessary by the winemaker. All young vines need water, since an overstressed young vine won't develop into a healthy plant. If you plant on a free-draining soil in a hot climate, you have to irrigate because otherwise the vine would lose so much moisture through its leaves that it wouldn't survive. If you plant on heavy fertile soils (unlike those of the great vineyards of Europe), the vines have a better chance of survival when water is in short supply and the crop can be controlled by withholding water. At a certain point in the grapes' ripening, irrigation is cut back to avoid diluting the juice. But if the weather gets very hot the grapes' ripening system will shut down – the vine needs irrigation just to keep it going.

Finally, once the grapes are ripe, the winemaker may decide to harvest at night when temperatures are cooler, so the grapes do not spoil before they get to the winery.

Consultant winemakers, such as Michel Rolland (left), share their knowledge and experience with other wineries; here he is at Casa Lapostolle, Chile.

Training techniques allow optimum ripening conditions. In his Adelaide Hills vineyard, Brian Croser of Petaluma shows the canopy held aloft by catch wires.

One of Australia's hardest-working flying winemakers, Kym Milne MW, assesses some of the wines he has made in southern Italy.

Vintage

The harvest of the grapes each year is known as the vintage. The term vintage is therefore generally used to refer to the year in which the wine was made. Not every bottle of wine declares its vintage. Inexpensive wines may be a blend of wines from different years. Producers of Champagne and other sparkling wines make a standard house style called 'non-vintage' or NV. This is meant to be the same year after year, so the rich wine from a warm year may be added to the lean wine from a colder one to maintain consistency.

Traditionally, the world's most sought-after wines come from places where the grapes are poised on a knife-edge of ripening or failing every year, like Bordeaux, Burgundy, Champagne and Germany's Mosel and Rhine valleys. These are the regions where vintages really matter, because the wines can be so different from one vintage to the next, ranging in quality from triumphant to disastrous. If the grapes are not ripe enough they will lack sugar and flavour; too ripe, and they will lack acidity, freshness and aroma. The winemaker's decision as to when to harvest can be crucial: a few days' wait for the grapes to reach optimum ripeness leaves them vulnerable to being caught in a downpour. In regions with a more predictable climate, the vintage year on the bottle is really no more than an indication of the wine's age.

In the winery

The next significant factor in the character of the wine is the winemaking process. This is the point at which the natural events of fermentation are shaped and controlled with a view to creating a particular end product. The concept of the winemaker as an interventionist who determines the character of the wine is a modern one. Earlier generations simply followed the traditions of their region; wine was more or less left to make itself.

Flying winemakers

Some of the most remarkable examples of winemaker intervention are embodied in the so-called flying winemakers. Often Australian-trained, they jet in to introduce modern regimes and impose higher standards on a winery in some generally underrated part of the wine world, and then jet off to do the same elsewhere. They may seem like gypsies, but the wines of southern France, southern Italy, eastern Europe and many other previously downtrodden regions have been transformed by their work.

THE ORGANIC APPROACH

The organic movement gains momentum every year, supported not only by altruistic environmentalists whose main concern is the future of the planet, but also by growers who are seeing a deterioration in the quality of their soil and consumers who are beginning to make the connection between what they eat and drink and their health. Organic wine, like other organic foodstuffs, is made without synthetic fertilizers, herbicides, fungicides or pesticides, or artificial preservatives. Minute traces of these chemicals, it is argued, have the potential to cause long-term health problems; another theory holds that toxic build-up may contribute to many of the food and drink allergies that are increasingly common.

Over the past 40 years or so, most crops – including grapes – have been grown with the aid of chemical fertilizers and sprays to encourage a large, disease-free, reliable harvest. Over time, the soil, forced to overproduce, will become weak and dependent on its chemical fix; chemical residues poison the tiniest micro-organisms at the start of the food chain, thus upsetting the natural balance of the ecosystem; certain vineyard pests build up a tolerance to insecticide sprays; and chemicals filter down to pollute the water table. The alternative organic techniques begin with healthy soil, nourished by compost or animal manures. Crop rotation, one of the basic tenets of organic farming, is not an option in the vineyard, but cover crops such as clover both protect the soil and provide it with nitrogen (green manure), while companion planting of vegetables, fruit, flowers and herbs create biological diversity and encourage insects, birds and animals to feed off vineyard pests.

Grape-growers face an additional hazard: their fruit is prone to mildew and black rot. Depending on local organic regulations, they may be permitted to use Bordeaux mixture (a naturally occurring chemical, copper sulphate) to combat the rot, but in practice, organic viticulture is most common in hot dry regions where fungal infections are less of a threat.

The term 'organic' can be used only on wines approved by a recognized certification body, such as the Soil Association in the UK or Ecovin in Germany. These in turn are co-ordinated by the International Federation of Organic Movements (IFOAM). A far greater number of growers follow broadly organic principles yet find the stringent regulations impracticable; they practise eco-friendly viticulture and recognize the need to reduce chemicals in the wine, but cannot subscribe to an organization that would discredit them for using chemicals in an emergency. France's Terra Vitis movement has established a charter that enshrines these principles and a growing number of producers in all regions of the country are working towards meeting its standards.

In theory, organic wines taste different. Healthier vines produce healthier grapes and the lower yield should lead to more intense flavours. Neither the soil nor the resulting wines have been 'standardized' by chemical additives, so organic wines are more honest characters, true to their roots, their region of origin, grape variety and the care in their making. In practice, some organic wines are worthy but dull, others are just plain bad, while some of the greatest wines in the world are a long way from organic.

BIODYNAMICS

Biodynamic winemakers take working with nature one stage further. They are organic, and they also use astronomy and astrology to match the vine and its growth cycles with the natural rhythms of the earth, the moon and the planets. They also practise homeopathy; plant extracts are used in minute doses to replace missing 'energies' in the soil and increase its fertility, and as sprays to protect against pests and diseases. The Demeter Association certifies biodynamic wines internationally.

VEGETARIAN WINES

Wine is made from grape juice, so why isn't it all vegetarian? The process of fining – clearing the wine – can create qualms for vegetarians, since there is no way of knowing whether a wine has been clarified with bentonite (a powdery earth), egg whites, casein or gelatin (derived from animals) or isinglass (from fish). Fining is not always necessary: given the right conditions, wine can fall bright by itself.

RED AND ROSÉ WINES

WINE IS CREATED BY fermentation – yeasts turning grape sugar into alcohol. It's as simple as that, and if you bought a few bunches of ripe grapes, squashed them, put the resulting goo into a bucket and left it somewhere warm like the airing cupboard – well, a wine of sorts would almost certainly be produced. It might taste more like vinegar, but technically it would be wine.

This simple chemical reaction has been refined by hundreds of years of experience and, more recently, by the application of high technology and microbiological know-how. It is difficult to generalize about winemaking styles and methods in countries and states as diverse as New Zealand and Texas, Argentina and Tasmania. What France or Italy may regard as old hat, the wineries of Brazil or Mexico may barely have begun to think about. At every stage, numerous fine-tunings occur and even the most technocratic winemaker indulges in little personal adjustments – in all but the drabbest corporate winemaker lurks an artist's soul – all of which affect the final character of the wine. But some techniques are standard around the globe.

Crushing

The winemaking process begins when the grapes are brought in from the vineyard. With the exception of Beaujolais and a few other wines using the 'whole bunch' method of fermentation (also called carbonic maceration, see box below), red grapes are put through a crusher to break their skins and release the juice. The crushing machine usually also removes the stems, as these have a tough, tannic taste, but with some grapes, notably Syrah, a proportion is left on to produce a firmer wine. The resulting 'must' – pulpy mush of flesh and juice and skins (which give red and rosé wines their colour) – is pumped into a big vat, ready for fermentation.

Fermentation

Fermentation is caused by the action of yeasts on the sugars in the grape juice. Yeasts are naturally present in the winery, but increasingly, cultivated yeasts are used to ensure a controlled fermentation. At this stage, in the cooler areas of Europe, the addition of sugar is permitted if the sugar content of the grapes is too low, to increase alcoholic strength, a process called chaptalization. Similarly, in very hot regions, a little acid may be added if the grapes are very ripe.

For rosé wines, the fermenting juice is drawn off the skins after a day or so and the

The fermenting juice is continually pumped over the 'cap' of grape skins in order to extract maximum colour and flavour from the skins. In France, this process is known as remontage; this is how it is done at Mas de Daumas Gassac, Languedoc-Roussillon, famous for a rich, Cabernet Sauvignon-based wine.

winemaking process then follows the same path as for white wines (see page 16).

Fermentation lasts from a few days to two weeks, depending on the yeast culture and cellar temperature. Temperature control is one of the most crucial tools available to the modern winemaker, and the introduction of stainless steel tanks and refrigeration in the 1950s were major breakthroughs in winemaking. Heat is needed to extract colour from the skins, but excess heat destroys freshness and fruit flavour, and can disrupt the fermentation process itself. Should the winemaker choose a cultured or a wild yeast? Modern cultured yeasts are controllable and produce specific results. Beneficial wild yeast strains have developed over centuries in European wine regions and quality producers are increasingly favouring these.

CARBONIC MACERATION

If you want to make a red wine that can be drunk young, with plenty of easy fruit and very little tannin, you can adopt a technique known as carbonic maceration. The method is widely used in Beaujolais, and involves placing uncrushed grapes inside a container such that the weight crushes the lowest bunches, setting off fermentation and releasing carbon dioxide which blankets the top layer and encourages the uncrushed berries at the top of the container to begin to ferment inside their skins, maximizing flavour and colour, but minimizing tannin extraction. The result is a very fruity, fresh wine for early drinking.

Throughout the process, the grape skins surge upwards, pushed by the stream of carbon dioxide released during fermentation. At the top, they form a thick 'cap' which must be mixed back in continually by punching down or pumping the juice over the cap, so that the wine can extract maximum colour and flavour and avoid air becoming trapped between the skins and the wine. Many red wines, including all those intended for long aging, are left to macerate on the skins for some days or weeks after fermentation is complete, in order to extract all the flavour, colour and tannin from the skins and pips; long maceration also softens the harsh tannins. A full-bodied red wine may macerate for seven to 28 days.

Pressing

When red wine fermentation is finished – all the sugar having been converted to alcohol – the wine is drawn off the vat, and the residue of skins is pressed, to produce a dark, tannic wine called 'press wine'. This may be used for blending purposes and added to the free-run wine to create a deeper, tougher style of wine, or it may be stored apart – it all depends on what the winemaker wants.

Malolactic fermentation

Technically, the wine is now made – but it is pretty raw stuff. To begin with, it probably has a sharp, green-apple acidity. This is reduced through a second fermentation – the 'malolactic' – which converts that tart malic acid into mild lactic acid. Almost all reds undergo this second fermentation, becoming softer and rounder in the process. It occurs naturally when temperatures rise in the spring following the harvest, but is often induced soon after the alcoholic fermentation, by raising the temperature in the cellar and by adding the appropriate bacteria.

Blending

Next the winemaker has the opportunity to alter the wine radically by blending the contents of two or more vats together. That could mean combining different grape varieties to add a whole new dimension of flavour. Some wines use only one variety, but blend grapes from different vineyards. This may be done in order to achieve a consistent style, or to balance the varying characteristics of the grapes.

Maturing

The decision on whether to mature a wine in stainless steel or oak is of enormous stylistic importance. Stainless steel (or concrete) is

Oak barrels add a new dimension to many modern wines – the wood interacts with the maturing wine, creating rich, toasty vanilla flavours. The Wolf Blass winery in Barossa Valley, South Australia, is well known for its oaky red wines, matured in these new oak barriques (small barrels).

inert and amenable to accurate temperature control, which allows the fruit flavours free rein. Small oak barrels allow controlled oxygenation and benign aging of what might otherwise be unduly aggressive wines.

If the wine is to be drunk young it is put in large tanks of stainless steel or concrete to rest a short while before bottling. Almost all rosé is treated in this way. Red wine for aging, however, is stored – often in small oak barrels (barriques) – for anything from six months to over two years. If the barriques are new or only once-used, they impart flavours of spice, herbs, perfume and vanilla as well as adding to the wine's tannic structure.

Racking

During this pre-bottling period, dead yeast cells and other solids fall to the bottom of the tank or barrel. These are separated from the wine by racking – transferring the wine to clean barrels or tanks – which may take place several times before bottling. Racking naturally mixes oxygen with the wine and this usually clears out any sulphuric or yeasty flavours. For cheaper wines, the same effect is achieved through filtration, but here some of the wine's body and flavour is lost as well. Pinot Noir, in particular, reacts badly to filtration.

Fining and filtering

With most top-quality wines, the last stage before bottling is 'fining': removing any particles held in suspension by means of a clarifying agent. The agent – which may be egg white, bentonite, isinglass or gelatin – is spread over the surface and, as it falls down through the wine, it collects all impurities with it. Most other wines are filtered; those for immediate drinking often receive quite a fierce filtration to ensure no deposit forms in the bottle. After fining, some of the best wines are also filtered, but very lightly, as preservation of their personality is all important. Many top red wines are *not* filtered – and a few are neither fined nor filtered – and so develop a harmless deposit in the bottle.

Bottling

For best results, bottling should be cold and sterile, with an inert gas like nitrogen or, for fine wines, carbon dioxide, introduced into the bottle ahead of the wine so that when the cork goes in there is no oxygen in the bottle. Some of the cheapest wines are either 'hot-bottled' or pasteurized. Both treatments involve heating the wine; they ensure its stability but they detract from its personality and make any further development impossible.

Choosing red and rosé wines

ONCE, CHOOSING WINE was a simple matter of selecting what you could afford from the limited range of classic styles that were available outside their region of origin: Bordeaux, Burgundy, Champagne and Rhône from France, Mosel and hock from Germany, Rioja and sherry from Spain and port from Portugal. Today the choice is almost limitless, as winemakers around the world are experimenting with grape varieties, blends and techniques in both vineyard and winery. They may take a classic style or use a classic grape as a starting point, but they often find that the results are very different in their new soil and climate conditions – and this is the springboard for further experiments and diversification. Choosing wine may be trickier these days – but it's far more fun, especially with a few pointers to style and taste.

Red Bordeaux-style/ Cabernet Sauvignon blends

The style may be one of the world's classics, but this example from Catena, one of Argentina's most progressive producers ❶, proves that intense, blackcurranty wines do not necessarily come only from the ancient châteaux of the Médoc. However, the red wines of Bordeaux in France are the originals. These tend to be harshly tannic at first, but they mature over 10–20 years, when the rich blackcurrant fruit is balanced by a heady scent of cedarwood, cigar boxes and pencil shavings.

If you cannot regularly indulge in fine, red Bordeaux, the Cabernet Sauvignon grape, alone or blended with Merlot or other varieties, enjoys worldwide popularity. It is sometimes made to be drinkable young, or it may be aged in oak barrels to add spice and richness. A number of super-Tuscans are based on Cabernet, with a small proportion of Sangiovese. California Cabernets are powerfully flavoursome and well structured; US Bordeaux-style blends are often described as Meritage. Chilean examples can have intense flavours and gentle tannins; Australia produces ripe-tasting Cabernets; and in New Zealand you will find blackcurrant fruit and often a taste of green leaf. Spain and Portugal both produce a few ripe but densely textured examples. Eastern Europe specializes in simple, budget-priced versions, and the southern French vins de pays made from Cabernet Sauvignon are generally good value.

Red Bordeaux-style/Merlot blends

Merlot is the dominant grape in Bordeaux's Pomerol and St-Émilion wines and appears in most Bordeaux and Bordeaux-style blends. It produces rich, juicy wines with flavours of blackcurrant, plum and mint, and is in demand wherever winemakers want to create a Bordeaux-style wine that can be drunk young. However, at its best, such as this St-Émilion Grand Cru from Ch. Angélus ❷, the wine will become richer after 10–20 years in bottle. Spain blends Tempranillo and Cabernet with good, soft-textured results.

Juicy, fruity reds/Merlot

This Merlot from the Santa Isabel estate of Viña Casablanca in Chile ❸ is typical of the style favoured by modern winemakers and wine drinkers – refreshing, full of vibrant fruit flavours, easy to drink with or without food, and with the gum-drying toughness of tannin kept to a minimum. Hungarian, Bulgarian and Romanian Merlots are simple wines in this style, Italian examples are often even softer, quaffing wines. Some California Merlot is made in this light style, as is some Zinfandel. Australia produces fruity Merlot and similar Grenache for everyday drinking, and Spain lays on the fruit in the Navarra, La Mancha and Valdepeñas regions with both the Garnacha (Spanish for Grenache) and Tempranillo grape varieties. Argentina does a good line in smooth, fruity Tempranillo, ultra-fruity Bonarda and juicy Malbec.

Juicy, fruity reds/Beaujolais

Beaujolais in France, home of the juicy, gulpable Gamay grape with its cherry-sharp fruit flavour, was the original model for this style, but to find it you need to look for a decent producer, such as this Beaujolais-Villages from Gilles Roux ❹. Elsewhere in France, Côtes du Ventoux, some Côtes du Rhône and vins de pays from all over the South fit the juicy, fruity bill, and Gamay de Touraine and Gamay d'Anjou from the Loire Valley are similar to Beaujolais, but cheaper.

Austrian Blauer Zweigelt or St Laurent and Italian Schiava/Vernatsch can be good and juicy. South Africa makes good 'young-vatted' Pinotage, like a smoky Beaujolais. Washington State Lemberger or Grenache is light and tasty.

Red Burgundy/Pinot Noir

In Burgundy the Pinot Noir grape produces some of the world's most superb wines: this one is from the vineyard of les Chaumes in the village of Vosne-Romanée ❺. Good examples are perfumed with strawberry, raspberry or cherry fruit and feel silky in your mouth. The best are frighteningly expensive and after five to ten years the initial strawberry and cherry fruit develops additional aromas of truffles, game and decaying autumn leaves. Sounds peculiar, but one taste and you'll be hooked.

France also has a lighter style in red Sancerre from the Loire Valley. California, particularly the Carneros and Russian River districts, produces Pinot Noir wines with bright, fragrant fruit; lighter styles are a speciality in Oregon. New Zealand is producing ripe, supple, stylish examples and Australia is improving fast. Chile's Pinot Noirs usually have loads of vibrant jellied fruit flavour. South Africa produces a small number of fairly impressive Pinot Noirs, though the fruit is often swamped by the flavour of oak barrels. In Germany the grape is known as Spätburgunder: the best examples, usually from Baden, are fragrant and carefully oaked. However, much commercial Spätburgunder is sweetish and thin. Switzerland's Pinots can be light and perfumed. Romania makes coarse but enjoyable budget versions.

Herby, 'dry' reds/Sangiovese

The most widely planted red grape in Italy, Sangiovese shows all the aromas and flavours typical of Italian wines: herbs, raisins, cherries and a hint of almonds. It is the main grape of Chianti and also of many super-Tuscans such as La Gioia ❻. Deeper and tougher wines come from Brunello di Montalcino and Vino Nobile di Montepulciano, lighter versions from Rosso di Montalcino and Rosso di Montepulciano. What these wines lack in initial fruity appeal is more than made up for by their success as partners for food.

The style is not the sole preserve of the Sangiovese grape: southern Italian reds from Puglia – made with grapes such as Primitivo and Negroamaro – give you the herb and raisin flavours with less aggression. Similar, somewhat fruitier flavours are found in wines made from the Barbera grape, such as Barbera d'Alba, and in top Valpolicella Classico, which uses a blend of grape varieties local to north-eastern Italy. The weird and wonderful Amarone and Recioto della Valpolicella styles made from partially dried grapes are particularly intriguing, with added dollops of chocolate and plum. Nebbiolo is the fierce grape of Piedmont, responsible for the wines of Barolo and Barbaresco. These need at least five years to mature before they reveal their complex flavours: you might find tobacco, chocolate, prunes and rose petals.

The nearest France gets to this style is in Corbières, down towards the Pyrenees. The Sangiovese grown in Argentina bears no more than a passing resemblance to its Tuscan cousins, but the Californian love affair with all things Italian has led to two styles of Sangiovese: an easy-drinking, everyday wine and a sturdier, age-worthy version, sometimes blended with Cabernet Sauvignon.

Spicy reds/Syrah or Shiraz

The grape known as Syrah in France and Shiraz in Australia is loved for its dense, heart-warming, gloriously rich flavours of berries, black pepper and chocolate, ideal for barbecues or winter evenings. Penfolds Grange, a rich Australian Shiraz ❼, is the modern archetype, and you can get good Australian examples at all price levels. The Syrah wines from the northern Rhône Valley in France known as Hermitage, Côte-Rôtie and Cornas are dark, herbal, pungent and smoky; Crozes-Hermitage and St-Joseph are generally lighter and cheaper. In the southern Rhône, where Grenache, Mourvèdre, Cinsaut and Carignan may be included in the blend, the wines of Châteauneuf-du-Pape, Gigondas and Vacqueyras can be excellent. For good value try Côtes du Rhône-Villages, or Syrah Vin de Pays d'Oc, Fitou or Minervois from southern France.

In California the Rhône grapes are high-fashion and often expensive, but Zinfandel made in the powerful style is spicy stuff at a better price. Portugal offers good value with blends of its own grape varieties from the Douro Valley, Alentejo, Ribatejo and Alenquer. In Spain, try wines from Toro and Valdepeñas. Mexico produces Petite Sirah, which is not the same as Syrah, but is made in a similar style. Chile is producing soupy, rich mouthfuls with the Carmenère grape.

Dry rosé

Bright and breezy freshness – a cool drink on a scorching day – is the point of good rosé, rather than any specific flavour. Most countries make a dry rosé, and any red grape will do, but Grenache and Cinsaut make some of the best. Grenache makes beguiling fruity rosés that pack an unexpected alcoholic punch in Lirac, Tavel and Côtes du Lubéron in the southern Rhône Valley. Spain also uses Grenache (called Garnacha here) for some tasty rosado versions of Rioja and Navarra; Gran Feudo ❽ is a good example. Good dry pinks also come from Cabernet Franc in the Loire, and Merlot and Cabernet in Bordeaux, and Pinot Noir does well in Alsace. Southern Italy is well known for fairly gutsy dry rosés, north-east Italy for delicate ones.

Sweetish rosé

California has its 'blush' Zinfandel, which is white with just a hint of pink, but is likely to be rather sweeter than you would expect. One of the best known is Mondavi's Woodbridge White Zinfandel ❾. Elsewhere the Loire Valley and Portugal produce off-dry rosés without much merit.

WHITE WINES

THE CREATION OF ANY wine begins in the vineyard, but the winemaking process proper starts with the annual grape harvest. When it comes to white wines, this involves choices: pick early and make a snappily fresh wine for quick-drinking, or pursue ripeness until the grapes fill with sugar, or, in certain parts of the world, leave the grapes to overripen and hope for an attack of the sweetness-intensifying noble rot.

In the warmer wine regions of the world, the sunshine that has ripened the grapes becomes the grapes' enemy as soon as they have been picked. White grapes are particularly vulnerable to oxidation, which spoils fruit flavours. One of the commonest solutions is to harvest at night or in the early morning when the air is at its coolest. You can then pile your grapes into a refrigerated truck if the winery is a long way away, and you can sprinkle antioxidants such as sulphur dioxide or ascorbic acid over the bunches to keep them in good condition. Some producers crush the grapes immediately and chill the resulting must at the vineyard.

Crushing

Grapes destined for white wines generally need more careful handling than those for reds. The grapes should be crushed without too much force, and may then be left to steep for a while: juice, skin, pulp, pips and all, so that maximum grape flavour can be extracted from the skins where all the varietal flavour and character lie. This 'skin contact' may be as brief as an hour or as long as a day for white wine, and will vary between grape varieties, and also according to what is likely to happen to the wine afterwards: whether it will go into a new oak barrel or a steel tank, for instance.

Pressing

If the juice is not intended to stay in contact with the skins, pressing may form part of the same process as crushing. The best quality juice emerges from the first, very gentle pressing. Further pressing will extract harsher elements from the grape's skin as well as more juice – a bottled wine may be a blend of wines from different stages of pressing, according to the winemaker's requirements.

Chardonnay grapes arriving at the Robert Mondavi Winery in the Napa Valley, California, are moved quickly but gently towards the crusher-destemmer. The juice will be handled with care and kept cool throughout the fermentation process to retain its fresh, fruity flavours in the finished wine.

Fermentation

Once the juice has settled its solids, or been filtered or centrifuged to quicken the process (although filtration will invariably remove some potential flavour as well), it is pumped into a tank – generally of stainless steel, if the objective is to make a young fresh white. A suitable yeast culture is normally added to ensure the fermentation is both efficient and controlled and, in certain cases, to create particular nuances of flavour. Alternatively, wild yeasts may be allowed to work.

The advantage of stainless steel is that it is the easiest material to keep sterile-clean, and the easiest in which to control temperature. The majority of white wines are fermented at cool temperatures to give a fruitier, fresher style, around 15–18°C (60–64°F), with the temperature kept down by running cold water or a coolant through insulated jackets or through coils within the tanks. For the finest white wines, the juice is fermented at up to 25°C (77°F) in an oak barrel, which imparts a rich, mellow flavour even to a dry wine.

Clear juice, free of sediment or any remaining yeast, with a blanket of gas on top, can be kept for some time before fermentation. This enables producers of aromatic white wines to ferment their wines in batches to put on sale at regular intervals, meaning that the wine is always as fresh as possible, and a fragrant Muscat bought a year after the harvest can be as grapy and good as though the grapes came in from the vineyards yesterday.

Malolactic fermentation

After the primary (alcoholic) fermentation, there is a second fermentation, the malolactic, in which green, appley, malic acid is turned into soft, creamy, lactic acid. Most classic whites undergo the malolactic, but as it reduces fresh-fruit character and tangy acidity it is often prevented in modern, fruit-driven whites, by the use of filtration, low temperature or sulphur dioxide.

Maturing

Use of new oak barriques (225-litre barrels) is increasingly common, not just for aging the best wines of Burgundy and Bordeaux, but also for the sturdier styles of white wine, particularly Chardonnay, from all over the

In New Zealand, as almost everywhere in the world that white wine is made, the juice is fermented in large, refrigerated, stainless steel tanks.

world. Marsanne may be aged in oak in the South of France and Australia, Macabeo (Viura) in Spain reacts well to oak, and the great Sauvignon-Sémillon dry whites of Pessac-Léognan, as well as the luscious sweet wines of Sauternes, are generally fermented and aged in oak. New oak gives a toasty, vanilla taste to wine and these days almost every bottle of Australian (or Californian) Chardonnay will have seen some oak during its fermentation and/or maturation. A final blend may consist of batches of wine which have spent time in new, one-year-old and two-year-old oak barrels, as well as some which have stayed in stainless steel. If the barrels are new, or fairly new, they give a strong, creamy or spicy character to the wine. Older barrels merely soften and round out the wine due to the slight contact with oxygen. This maturation can take up to 18 months but, in general, six months is quite long enough for a white wine.

Bottling

A wine for drinking young is generally stored in a stainless steel tank for a short time, racked off its lees if necessary, fined, filtered to produce a star-bright, stable liquid and then bottled – often at only six months old or less – to maximize its fresh, fruity character.

Ideally, the very best wines – having been matured in oak – are hardly filtered at all, since the process also removes a little of the flavour. Sterile conditions are crucial to avoid bacterial spoilage and sulphur dioxide is generally added as an antioxidant.

SULPHUR DIOXIDE

The antiseptic, antioxidant, preservative properties of sulphur dioxide make it invaluable in the winery, but an excess results in an unpleasant smell and taste in the wine, and in some people can cause an allergic reaction – or at least a headache. Before fermentation, sulphur dioxide may be used to kill off wild yeasts and bacteria to allow the flavours of the chosen cultured yeasts to prevail, although the cultured yeasts used by many modern winemakers have reduced the need for sulphur at this stage. If sulphur dioxide is added while the wine is fermenting, again, it will kill yeasts and thus halt fermentation to leave a sweet wine. It may also be added at bottling stage to kill any stray organisms and prevent spoilage. Modern winemakers have dramatically reduced the amounts of sulphur used.

MAKING SWEET WINES

White wines achieve a measure of sweetness in various ways. The great sweet wines of Sauternes and the Loire Valley, Alsace's Vendange Tardive and Sélection de Grains Nobles, Germany's Auslese, Beerenauslese and Trockenbeerenauslese, and the late-harvest wines occasionally found in Australia, New Zealand and the United States, are made from grapes that are left on the vine well after the normal harvest, so they are overripe and full of sugar; they also begin to shrivel, which concentrates the sugar.

If conditions are right, they may be attacked by a horrid-looking fungus called 'noble rot' (*Botrytis cinerea*). This sucks out the water, concentrating the sugar even more. During fermentation, the sugar is converted by yeasts into alcohol: the more sugar in the grape juice, the higher the potential alcoholic strength. But yeasts can only work in alcohol levels of up to about 15 per cent (and frequently the winemaker will add a little sulphur dioxide to stop fermentation at around 12–13 per cent). So when the yeasts stop, the rest of the grape sugar remains in the wine as sweetness – full of potential lusciousness. The distinctive flavour of botrytis is much sought after by dessert wine producers; today's winemakers have the technology to create conditions favourable to botrytis, either in the laboratory, or by spraying a fine mist of water in the vineyard.

Hungary's intensely sweet Tokaji is also made using botrytized grapes, which are added to a dry base wine.

Another method of making wine sweet is traditional in parts of Italy (where it is known as *passito* or *recioto*) and in the Jura, France (for *vin de paille*). After picking, the grapes are laid on mats or in shallow trays, or the bunches are hung from rafters. They begin to dry out, losing water, which concentrates all the other constituents, especially the sugars.

By the time the grapes are crushed they are so sweet that even after fermentation to a fair alcoholic degree some sweetness is left. For Moscato di Pantelleria, made on a small island west of Sicily, the grapes are left outdoors in the burning sun for two weeks. For Vin Santo, a speciality of Tuscany, Umbria and Trentino, the grapes may be dried indoors for four or five months.

There are lots of wines which are medium in style, vaguely sweet; for these, fermentation is stopped while there is still some sugar left unconverted to alcohol. Traditionally, this was done by pumping in sulphur dioxide to kill the yeasts, but nowadays it is much more common to remove the yeasts either by chilling the wine right down or by centrifuging it, which eliminates all the solids and leaves a stable wine, sweetness and all. It is also possible to add a little unfermented grape juice after the wine has fermented to dryness. This is the usual method for cheap German-style wines.

Finally, wine can be fortified. The grape juice is partially fermented and then neutral spirit is added which raises the alcohol level to between 16 and 24 per cent. Yeasts cannot operate at more than about 15–16 per cent alcohol, so fermentation stops and the remaining sugar stays in the wine.

Grapes hanging up to dry for Vin Santo in Tuscany. The wine will ferment and then age for several years in the small barrels (caratelli).

Choosing white wines

WHILE RED WINES MAY DISPLAY a fruity 'sweetness', they are nearly always dry. Not so whites, which range from bone dry and neutral accompaniments for seafood, to a whole gamut of perfumed or fruity dry to medium thirst-quenchers and finally to rich, luscious mouthfuls to have with – or instead of – pudding, or to sip when you're in a contemplative mood.

Bone dry, neutral whites

These are the sort of wines you might reach for on a hot day, or to accompany a plate of seafood. They will be served chilled, but it is their crisp apple or lemon acidity that makes them so refreshing and such a good match for shellfish. Neutral flavours in a white wine are an Italian speciality: Pinot Grigio (Pinot Gris) and Pinot Bianco (Pinot Blanc) are generally bone dry and light; Orvieto and Verdicchio are fairly reliable and fuller; Soave and Frascati are often mediocre, but look for Frascati Superiore or Soave Classico for better-made wines – Anselmi's Soave Classico Capitel Foscarino ❶ is one of the best. France offers Muscadet from the Loire Valley and Vin de Pays des Côtes de Gascogne from the South-West. Unoaked wines made from the Viura and Verdejo grapes in northern Spain are generally tart but good, and if you're in Portugal, proper Vinho Verde from the north-west can be neutral with a refreshing light fizz.

Classic white Burgundy

These are the wines that made Chardonnay famous in the first place: rich and succulent whites with subtle nut and oatmeal flavours and a backbone of absolute dryness. If you like this style, you've got a taste for French classics, because the best expression of it is oak-aged Chardonnay in the form of white Burgundy, most famously from the villages of Meursault ❷ and Puligny-Montrachet. The style is sometimes matched in the best examples from California, New York State, New Zealand, Australia and South Africa. Not any old examples, mind you – just the best. Italian producers in Tuscany are having a go, too.

Different flavours, but with a similar subtlety, are found in top-quality oak-aged Pessac-Léognan and Graves from Bordeaux. Here, Sémillon blended with Sauvignon Blanc gives a creamy, nutty wine with a hint of nectarines. Unoaked Semillon from the Hunter Valley in Australia develops surprisingly similar characteristics with time. All of these wines need to be kept for a few years to mature, and they don't come cheap. Less costly alternatives are the Chardonnays from Navarra and Somontano and some white Riojas, all from Spain.

Steely, dry Chardonnay

Unoaked Chablis is the adaptable Chardonnay grape in a dry, minerally style. Many growers from Chablis ❸ (in the north of the Burgundy region) and the Mâconnais (to the south) believe that oak detracts from the fruit flavours of Chardonnay, although there are producers in both regions who choose to age their wines in new oak, which brings them closer to classic white Burgundy. Chardonnay from Austria and Italy's Alto-Adige region are usually similarly dry.

Ripe, spicy Chardonnay

Upfront flavours of peaches, apricots and tropical fruits, spiced up by the vanilla, toast and butterscotch richness of new oak barrels, this is what most people mean when they talk about Chardonnay today. The style was virtually invented in Australia but it is also the hallmark of most Chardonnay in the USA and South America – it's very much a warm-climate style. In California, Au Bon Climat's Talley Vineyard Chardonnay ❹ is lush and beautifully balanced. Australian Semillon is often given a hefty dose of oak and may be blended with Chardonnay. Oaked white Rioja from Spain may be nothing like Chardonnay, but the emphasis is on the vanilla flavour.

Green, tangy Sauvignon

Sharp, grassy, love-them-or-hate-them wines, often with the smell and taste of gooseberries, nettles or asparagus. New Zealand's South Island has these tangy, mouthwatering flavours by the bucketful, as in this Sauvignon from top producer Cloudy Bay ❺. Chile makes similar, slightly softer wines, but South African versions can have real bite, as do examples from Hungary. The original Sauvignon wines are Sancerre and Pouilly-Fumé from the Loire Valley in France. These are crisp and refreshing with lighter fruit flavours

and a minerally or even a smoky edge. Modern Bordeaux Sauvignons from Entre-Deux-Mers are fresh, grassy and inexpensive, as are the vin de pays Sauvignon Blancs from elsewhere in the South of France. Really dry Portuguese Vinho Verde (the style sold in Portugal) is an aggressive alternative with a hint of fizz.

Oak-aged Sauvignons, popular in New Zealand's North Island, California (often under the name Fumé Blanc), South Africa, Australia and the Graves region of Bordeaux, add richness and peachy, apricotty flavours, making a half-way house between ripe, toasty Chardonnay and the more challenging classic Sauvignon style.

Riesling

German Rieslings from the Mosel (in green bottles) and Austrian examples made in the dry, Trocken, style have a fresh green sharpness rather like Sauvignon Blanc, with additional slaty, minerally flavours. French Rieslings from Alsace are similarly austere but with a bit more weight. New Zealand's are delicate and fresh, while Australia's have a delicious lime aroma on top of a heavier style. South Africa produces similarly perfumed styles. All these wines are at their greenest when young and develop a honeyed richness with a strange but delightful petrol aroma after a few years. This example, made in the Clare Valley by Grosset ❻, South Australia's Riesling specialist, will improve in the bottle for ten years.

Perfumy, off-dry whites

This style is the speciality of Alsace in France. Alsace Gewurztraminer wines are spicy and rich with an aroma of lychees and roses; German and Italian Gewürztraminers have a simpler floral character. Alsace Pinot Gris can be richly honeyed; Muscats are more floral with a heady, grapy scent. Aromatic dry Muscats are also made in Australia, South Africa and southern France. Irsai Oliver from Hungary and Torrontés from Argentina have a similar character. German Riesling from the Rhine (in brown bottles) can have this aromatic richness, especially in the Kabinett and Spätlese ❼ styles. France's Rhône Valley grows Viognier for the intensely apricotty and floral wines of Condrieu, and the grape is becoming popular across southern France as well as in California, Australia and South Africa. Müller-Thurgau from New Zealand or Germany provides inexpensive wines in this style.

Golden sweet whites

Many wines fall into this category – I've picked out just a few examples. In France the sweet wines of Bordeaux are at their best in Sauternes and Barsac, where the sweetness of the grapes, mostly Sémillon, is often concentrated by the effect of noble rot. Ch. d'Yquem ❽, one of the world's greatest sweet wines, can improve for 30 years or more. Some good lookalikes come from nearby Cérons and Monbazillac. California and Australia have a few intensely rich,

late-harvest Semillon and Riesling wines in the style of Sauternes.

The Loire Valley produces quince-flavoured sweeties with firm acidity from late-harvested Chenin Blanc in Coteaux du Layon and Vouvray. In Alsace, late-harvested grapes become Vendange Tardive wines, while botrytized grapes are used for the more intense Sélection de Grains Nobles.

Germany produces a few rich and delicious wines, usually from Riesling grapes, labelled in ascending order of intensity as Auslese ❾, Beerenauslese and Trockenbeerenauslese, and there's a rarity called Eiswein made from frozen grapes picked in winter which manages a thrilling marriage of fierce acidity and unctuous sweetness. Canada uses the same technique and calls it Icewine. Austria has some excellent sweet wines in the Germanic style.

Hungary's Tokaji ❿ matches acidity and sweetness with a flavour of dried fruits and smoke. Italy's sweet wines are made from dried (*passito*) grapes. Avignonesi's exotically perfumed Vin Santo ⓫ is an outstanding example, and the Veneto region has its gently honeyed, apricotty Recioto di Soave.

The aromatic, grapy Muscat lends itself to sweet wines. Spain's simple, sweet Moscatel de Valencia is incredibly good value, and Greece makes some good Muscats, especially on the island of Samos ⓬. The Muscat *vins doux naturels* from southern France are usually fortified rather than naturally sweet.

SPARKLING WINES

THE SECRET TO MAKING SPARKLING WINE is the fact that carbon dioxide is a very soluble gas. Carbon dioxide is given off during fermentation and if the fermenting wine is kept in a pressurized container – either a bottle or tank – the gas is absorbed by the wine – for as long as the pressure remains. That explains why as soon as you open a bottle of sparkling wine there is a whoosh of froth and bubbles as the pressure is released.

All the greatest sparklers are made by inducing a second fermentation in the actual bottle from which the wine will be served. It emerged from the Champagne region of northern France at the end of the seventeenth century and is now practised to great effect worldwide.

There is one major problem – the dead yeast cells form a deposit after they've finished fermenting out the sugar, leaving a nasty sludge in the container. If that container is the bottle itself, removing the sludge is difficult and expensive, but it is crucial to the Champagne method of making a wine sparkle. The natural desire of people to celebrate with fizz, but not pay a massive premium, has led to the development of simpler ways of making a wine sparkle and cleaning out its sediment.

Making the basic wine

The red grapes Pinot Noir and Pinot Meunier are popular for making sparkling wine, and the objective is to press them quickly and gently so that the juice is as pale as possible. These basic wines are then fermented out to dryness, as for white wine. Wines from different grapes and various vineyards are often expertly blended into a single style. These blends are called 'cuvées', even outside France, and many Champagnes have Cuvée in their title, which supposedly denotes the particular blend of the house.

The second fermentation

This is the first of three crucial stages of the Champagne method – creating the bubbles. The still wine is bottled with the addition of a little sugar and yeast to restart the fermentation, tightly sealed, and stored in a cool cellar for anything from a few months to several years. The second fermentation creates carbon dioxide which, since it can't escape, dissolves in the wine. To get good bubbles you want this *prise de mousse*, or 'mousse-taking', to last two or three years, longer if possible.

While this second fermentation has been creating the bubbles, it's also been depositing used-up yeast cells on the side of the bottle. But this yeasty sludge has such an attractive creamy taste that the best sparkling wines will spend a couple of years on their yeast, becoming softer and richer in flavour.

Collecting the sediment

Now, the flavour may be good and the wine may be fizzy – but no-one is going to drink it if it looks cloudy and impenetrable. First, the sludge must be dislodged from the side of the bottle. So the bottles go through a process called riddling, or *remuage* in French: they are gradually transferred from the horizontal to

Here in the Champagne house of Perrier-Jouët in Épernay, bottles of Belle Epoque Rosé vintage Champagne are held at an angle in the traditional pupitres and turned by hand.

Huge, computer-controlled gyropalettes, each holding 2720 bottles, perform the remuage automatically. These are at Domaine Chandon, owned by French Champagne house Moët et Chandon, in California's Napa Valley.

As the bottles are gradually inverted, the sediment of used yeast cells collects on the cap.

the vertical position – but upside-down – as well as being regularly turned and tapped, causing the deposit to slide down inside the glass and collect on the cork.

The process of *remuage*, or shifting the sludge, was invented in the early nineteenth century by Veuve Clicquot, the greatest of the many indomitable widows who have forged the modern Champagne industry. She devised a kind of two-sided desk with holes in it called a pupitre. Shove the bottle in the holes, go through the tilt-and-tap routine for three months and you're ready for the next stage in the Champagne method. There are mechanical pupitres now, called gyropalettes – great big metal palettes of bottles clicking and clunking the sediment on to the cork.

Removing the sediment
The *dégorgement* is literally 'removing' the sludge. It used to require a large number of men with strong wrists and fast reflexes, popping corks and ejecting sediment, but now the neck of the bottle containing the deposit is frozen and the tight, chilled pellet is whipped out on a machine production line.

Adjusting the sweetness
At this stage the wine is still totally dry, since any sugar will have been eaten up by fermentation which is also, of course, what has caused all those bubbles. After the sediment has been removed, the bottle needs to be topped up, usually with a mixture of wine and sugar syrup, the *dosage*. There are very few Champagne houses which don't add some

sugar after disgorging. Even Brut Champagnes, usually the driest a house offers, will have some sugar added back. Good New World sparklers are increasingly made from less ripe grapes, as in Champagne, but simpler, cheaper versions can be made from riper grapes, which give a less acid base wine.

Sealing the bottle
Finally, the special extra-strong Champagne cork is rammed in and secured with a wire cage to keep all those bubbles in the bottle.

Sparkling rosé and red wine
Most sparkling wine is white, but rosé is increasingly popular. This used to be made by fermenting the base wine as a rosé but it was virtually impossible to predict the eventual colour. So nowadays, almost invariably, a little red wine is added to a white sparkling base.

Sparkling red wine is rather an unusual proposition, but Australia has a rich, long-lived style made by a number of producers, using either the traditional method, or the transfer or tank methods (see below). Italy's Lambrusco, usually red, is generally made by the tank method.

Opening sparkling wine
The pressure in the bottle does the work, so all you have to do is control it. If you don't, you'll get a loud pop, a rush of foaming wine and a half-empty bottle of fizz. A cold bottle will open with a less dramatic burst than a warm one.

Tear off the foil to reveal the wire cage, place one thumb over the top of the cork and undo the cage, remembering to point the bottle away from people and breakable objects.

Grasp the cork with one hand and hold the bottle firmly with the other. Now turn the bottle slowly while holding the cork in place. The cork will start to ease out under the pressure; it should come free with a sigh rather than a bang. Holding the bottle at an angle of 45 degrees for a few moments should calm the initial rush of foam; then pour it into the waiting glass.

OTHER METHODS AND TERMS

Cuve close or tank method This involves putting wine into a pressurized tank and adding sugar and yeast to start a second fermentation. The wine is then filtered to remove the yeasty sediment and bottled under pressure. Most cheap labour-saving fizz is made this way, but it needn't taste nasty – the Italians make delicious Asti and Prosecco wine using this, or a similar method. It is also called the Charmat method after its French inventor, Eugène Charmat.

Transfer method This is like the Champagne method, without the *remuage*. The second fermentation takes place inside a bottle, but the wine is then filtered and transferred under pressure to its final bottle. The results are greatly superior to the tank method, particularly in the finesse of the bubbles. Indeed, some producers in the United States and Australia are so keen on this method they say they prefer it to the Champagne method – a lot more predictable and similar quality!

Carbonated method This is the most basic method: you simply carbonate the wine by pumping gas into it at the bottling stage. Normally what you get is a pretty vile brew with a very fleeting bubble.

Other methods There are several 'rural' or 'ancestral' methods employed in France, whereby the first fermentation continues in the bottle or rather starts again. If the sediment is not removed, the wine may be slightly cloudy. These include Blanquette de Limoux from Languedoc-Roussillon and Clairette de Die from the Rhône Valley; many Blanquette producers now use the Champagne method.

Other terms *Mousseux* implies a fully sparkling wine made in France by the *cuve close* method. *Crémant* is used for fully sparkling wine, usually made by the Champagne method, in areas other than Champagne, such as Alsace and Burgundy. *Pétillant* means lightly sparkling – frizzante is the Italian equivalent. *Perlant* means very lightly sparkling, less so than *pétillant*.

Choosing sparkling wines

SPARKLING WINES ARE MADE FOR celebrations and these days there are so many well made and inexpensive alternatives to Champagne that the merest excuse suffices to open a bottle of fizz and celebrate. The bubbles alone can create a party mood, especially if you've remembered to chill the bottle down, but good sparkling wine can have some delicious flavours as well.

Champagne styles

Good Champagne has a nutty, bready aroma and fine bubbles. Brut is usually the driest style; only a few very rare brands, often called Brut Zero, Ultra Brut or something similar, are made with no added sugar at all. Extra Dry/Extra Sec is a little gentler than Brut. The majority of Champagne is non-vintage ❶, in other words it is based on a blend of wines from several years; it improves if you store the bottles for a few months – or even a few years if you want a deeper, nutty taste – before you drink it. Vintage Champagne ❷ is made only in the best years; when mature, with at least eight or ten years in bottle, it is deep, rich and thrilling. Most major Champagne houses produce a prestige or deluxe cuvée as their top wine; this may be either non-vintage or vintage. Moët et Chandon's Dom Pérignon ❸ can be one of the world's finest, but it needs at least ten years in the bottle.

Dry sparkling wines

While other sparkling wines may be referred to colloquially as 'champagne', they are not allowed to use the French region's name on the bottle. Instead, the terms 'classic method' and 'traditional method' (made in the same way as Champagne) and 'fermented in bottle' (made by the transfer method) are seen on labels from Australia, California and New Zealand; winemakers often use traditional Champagne grape varieties such as Chardonnay and Pinot Noir to produce excellent and far less expensive versions. Much of the best is made by subsidiaries of French Champagne producers; Green Point ❹ is an Australian offshoot of Moët et Chandon.

Other good Champagne-method French fizzes include Crémant d'Alsace, Crémant de Bourgogne from Burgundy and Crémant de Loire and the sharper Saumur Mousseux from the Loire Valley. In the south, light, fresh Blanquette de Limoux and grapy Clairette de Die have their own idiosyncratic methods of production and grape varieties.

Italian sparklers made from Chardonnay and Pinot Noir are in the Champagne style, but light and creamy Prosecco is more fun and a lot cheaper. Spanish Cava is pretty good, but tends to be a bit earthy. German sparkling wine is called Sekt: the best – occasionally 100 per cent Riesling – are excellent but the rest are less successful.

Rosé and red dry sparkling wines

Pink sparkling wines, the ultimate in frivolity, can be superb. Rosé Champagne is made in all styles: Laurent-Perrier's Grand Siècle Alexandra Rosé ❺ is a vintage prestige cuvée. Good rosé is generally found wherever traditional-method sparkling wine is made: the Loire Valley, Burgundy, California and Australia.

Australian sparkling red wines made from Merlot, Cabernet Sauvignon or, preferably, Shiraz ❻ are wild things, packed with jammy fruit. You'll either love them or loathe them, but you haven't lived until you've given them a try. Italy's Lambrusco can be either red or white; for a good dry version look for one from a controlled region or DOC.

Medium and sweet sparkling wines

Champagne being a law unto itself, a bottle labelled Sec will be medium-dry; wines then increase in sweetness from Demi-sec (or Riche) to very sweet, but very rare, Doux. Some sparkling Saumur from the Loire Valley is also made in a demi-sec style. Italy's naturally sweet, scented, grapy Asti can be delightful; even better is the frizzante (semi-sparkling) version, Moscato d'Asti ❼.

FORTIFIED WINES

FORTIFIED WINES ARE WINES TO WHICH extra alcohol in the form of brandy or neutral spirit has been added at some stage during their production. In the case of port, alcohol is added during fermentation while quite a lot of the grape sugar still remains in the warm, bubbling juice. This dose of spirit stops the fermentation and so retains some of the natural sugar. This basic method is also used for Madeira and Moscatel de Setúbal from Portugal, the fortified Grenache and Muscat wines of Spain and southern France, and the Muscats of Australia and South Africa. With sherry the juice is left to ferment until all the sugar is used up. Even sweet sherries start out as dry white wine. Before the spirit is added, this is one of the world's least impressive wines. But the spirit enables it to mature for years in oak barrels – and become one of the world's greatest. Sicily's Marsala is also usually fermented to dryness, then fortified and sweetened with a blend of grape juice and 'cooked' grape syrup.

Making sherry

Fermenting and fortification

Sherry-style wines are made in two basic ways, one of which leads to bone-dry fino-type wines, the other to fuller-bodied, nutty oloroso types. Whatever the ultimate style, the juice is pressed from the skins, left to settle, then fermented right out to make a dry white wine. It is then racked and fortified with grape spirit. Fino-type sherries are fortified to no more than 15.5 per cent alcohol, olorosos up to 18 per cent.

The developing flavour

Finos then develop in a totally different way thanks to an unusual yeast called flor, which occurs naturally in all the areas that make this style of wine. The barrels for all types of sherry are filled just five-sixths full. The surface of the wine in fino barrels then grows a film of squidgy, oatmeal-white flor. While protecting the infant sherry from the air and keeping it pale in colour, flor feeds off the wine and affects its composition and flavour, in particular adding a sharp tang and memorable pungency. The tang is even more pronounced

Palomino Fino grapes, grown in the chalky soil of Jerez in Andalucía, southern Spain, make extremely dull wine, which will be transformed by the sherry process into a superb, world-class drink.

in manzanilla, a fino which is made in the coastal town of Sanlúcar de Barrameda. Flor never grows on oloroso-style wines because it will not tolerate alcohol levels over 16.2 per cent. Olorosos gradually develop in contact with the air, taking on a rich, nutty aroma. Some olorosos are sweetened at this stage.

The third major sherry style, amontillado, develops out of fino. After fino has been in barrel for six years or more, the flor begins to fade and die, and the wine comes in contact with the air, turning amber-coloured and nutty-flavoured while still retaining the pungency and tang of a fino. These are true, fine, dry amontillados. It is a pity that, in the British market especially, amontillado has come to mean nondescript, vaguely sweet sherry. Just as Germany's wine reputation was cheapened by the ubiquitous Liebfraumilch, so sherry's reputation as a great wine style was spoilt by a deluge of mediocre and non-

representative amontillado. Similar in style to amontillado are two rare styles of dry wine that fall between fino and oloroso in character: palo cortado and manzanilla pasada.

Aging

All sherries have to be wood-aged for a minimum of three years, but the finest are aged for much longer. During this time, they pass through a solera system, a traditional means of gradual blending. When sherry is needed for bottling, only about one-quarter of the wine from the most mature barrels is run off at a time. Those barrels are then filled from slightly younger ones and so on until the last barrel receives a top-up of the youngest wine. This is vital for fino, as the nutrients in the younger wines keep the flor alive, but amontillado and oloroso sherries also benefit from this continual replenishing of the stock, which helps to prevent oxidation.

This specially constructed display barrel shows flor yeast growing on the surface of the wine that will become dry fino sherry.

Making port

Fermenting and fortification

Port starts life as a dark and toughly tannic red wine, since the skins and pips must continually be mixed with the fermenting juice to extract the maximum amount of colour and tannin in the shortest possible time. Traditionally, this is done by pushing down the 'cap' of floating solids with long poles or by foot-treading in open, shallow tanks called *lagares*. Nowadays, the grapes are often fermented in autovinifiers – enclosed tanks in which the pressure of the gases produced by fermentation acts as a natural pump to spray the juice up over the skins. Top port houses are introducing mechanized *lagares* with robotic 'feet'.

The wine ferments until it has reached about 8 per cent alcohol, still containing more than half the natural grape sugar, before being fortified with raw grape spirit. This brings the alcohol level up to about 19 per cent, the yeasts die, and the wine is pressed.

Assessing and blending

Early in the year following the harvest, the young wine is tasted, its quality assessed to

Most of the famous port lodges are in Vila Nova de Gaia, at the mouth of the river Douro; here, various samples are blended to make tawny port.

ensure that the envisaged style is still appropriate, and its consequent method of maturation decided. Wines of similar style and quality are blended together and generally transported to the maturing houses, or lodges, at Vila Nova de Gaia, where they will be matured in wooden barrels, called pipes.

Racking

The wines are racked – run off any deposit and into a clean cask – about once a year for the first few years, then less frequently.

Aging

The cheapest ports (basic rubies and tawnies) are aged in wood for only about three years, but the finest old tawnies may remain in barrel for up to 40 years. As they age, the wines gradually mellow (though they remain spirity as the level of spirit is kept topped up) and turn from dense, bright red to a lighter tawny colour. Of the wines that started out a finer quality, the best are blended together in the best years to make vintage port, which is aged for just two years in wood, but needs many years in bottle before drinking. It keeps its colour much better in bottle and ends up redder and richer. Wines that are good but not of vintage quality may be kept in wood for four to six years and then sold as Late Bottled Vintage, or LBV.

Making Madeira

Fermenting and fortification

Unlike the port grapes, the different Madeira varieties are kept separate in the wineries. Sercial, Verdelho and Tinta Negra Mole grapes are pressed as for ordinary white wine, and the juice ferments without the skins. With Bual and Malmsey, however, the skins are usually left in the fermenting juice for a couple of days in order to extract more colour, tannin and aroma. The wine ferments at between 18°C and 35°C (64–77°F) in tanks or large wooden vats. Most producers add alcohol to stop the fermentation when the required sweetness level has been reached, sooner for the sweeter styles, later for the drier. Young Madeira is fortified slightly less than port, to around 17 per cent alcohol. But some producers ferment all their wines to dryness, then sweeten them with fortified grape juice.

'Cooking' the wines

Now follows Madeira's unique 'cooking' process, which gives the wines their characteristic caramelly, slightly smoked flavour. The

The aging room in the warm attic of the Madeira Wine Company's old lodge in Funchal, the island's main town.

cheaper wines go into special kettle-tanks called *estufas*, in which coils filled with hot water heat the wine to between 45°C (113°F) and 50°C (122°F) for a legal minimum of 90 days. Fine wines are left in casks for years either in hot attics above the *estufas* or in warehouses heated to 35°C–40°C (77–80°F).

Aging

Even the lowest level of Madeira – confusingly, this is often labelled Finest – must spend a minimum of 18 months in wooden casks after their time in *estufas*. Reserves have to be aged in wood for at least five years, Special Reserves for ten, and Vintages for 20 years.

Choosing fortified wines

FORTIFIED WINES RANGE FROM the very dry to the very sweet; they may be served to stimulate the appetite before a meal or to relax over after dinner. Often known as dessert wines, there is a style to suit every variation of dessert, from a handful of nuts and dried fruits to rich crème brûlée; port is a classic partner for strongly flavoured and mature cheese.

Sweet and warming

Some fortified wines are sweet and warming, tasting of raisins and brown sugar, often densely packed with spicy fruit and other flavours. Port, the rich red fortified wine of Portugal's Douro Valley, is the classic dark sweet wine and no imitator can match the finesse of the best. It is made in a number of styles: the youngest, ruby, should be deliciously fruity, but such wine is hard to find. Vintage-character port is a little older than ruby – again, it should be full of rich fruit but often disappoints. Late Bottled Vintage is produced from a single vintage and bottled, preferably without filtration, after four to six years in cask. Cheap tawny is a thin blend of ruby and white ports; the real thing develops its deep nut and fig flavours after long aging in wood (some may have spent 40 years in a wooden barrel). Vintage port, such as Taylor's **❶**, bottled at two years old, should mature slowly in the bottle for at least 15 years.

Australia and South Africa both make interesting port-style wines. The Portuguese island of Madeira produces some of the most exciting of warming fortified wines, with rich brown smoky flavours and a startling acid bite: Bual and Malmsey are the sweet ones to keep an eye out for.

Cheap sweetened 'brown' sherry is a weak parody of this style. The sweetish wines sold as amontillados are fourth-rate finos darkened and sweetened up with concentrated grape juice. Similarly, creams and pale creams are sweetened-up, low-grade olorosos and finos. The real thing – oloroso dulce – is a rare and beautiful sweet sherry with stunning concentrated flavours.

The South of France and the Rhône Valley produce *vins doux naturels* from the Muscat and Grenache grapes; despite the name these are usually fortified rather than naturally sweet. The most famous is Muscat de Beaumes-de-Venise, though Muscat de Frontignan and Muscat de Rivesaltes **❷** are cheaper alternatives. Australian sweet fortified Muscat from the Rutherglen region **❸** is rich, concentrated and dark, even treacly.

Sicily's Marsala wines, mostly sweet, are often fit only for cooking.

Dry and tangy

Some of the best Marsala, in a style known as Vergine, is unsweetened, and De Bartoli's Vecchio Samperi **❹** is actually an unfortified version, dry, intense and redolent of dates and candied citrus peel. Fortified wines can certainly be bone dry, with startling, stark, sour and nutty flavours – a taste that takes a bit of getting used to but which is well worth acquiring. The originals are the sherries from Jerez in southern Spain. Fino **❺** is pale in colour and unnervingly dry with a thrilling tang. Manzanilla, a type of fino sherry matured by the sea at Sanlúcar de Barrameda, can seem even drier, even leaner, and has a wonderful sour-dough perfume and tingling acidity. Both should be drunk as young and fresh as possible. Traditional amontillado is dark, nutty and dry, not medium-sweet as we often see it. Dry oloroso adds deep, burnt flavours and at best is one of the most haunting, lingering flavours the world of wine can offer. Palo cortado, a sherry with both fino and oloroso characteristics, is rare and dry, with a pungent bite.

Montilla-Moriles is the neighbouring region to Jerez and produces similar wines, but only the very best reach the standard of good sherry. The driest style of Madeira, Sercial **❻**, is tangy, steely and savoury. Verdelho Madeira is that bit fuller and fatter. White port, at its best, is dry and nutty-tasting; most are coarse and alcoholic. Australia and South Africa make excellent sherry-style wines though without the tang of top-class Spanish fino or manzanilla.

KEEPING AND SERVING WINE

WINE IS A LIVING THING – as it lies in its bottle over the months or years, it evolves. Red wines grow paler and develop sediment, whites darken to a honeyed brown. Wines with plenty of acid and tannin become less fierce-tasting and more approachable, and if they have the vital extra ingredient – loads of intense fruit flavour – for the true quality of the wine to be revealed, a few years in the bottle are absolutely crucial, so that the tannins can soften, the acids mellow. Older wine is not always better wine, but if a wine is worth keeping, it's worth making the effort to look after it.

Looking after your wine

Most wine is pretty resilient. A really young bottle can bounce about in the car for days, almost bake to death on the back seat in the sun, then almost freeze to death in the refrigerator and still taste reasonable – not as good as it could, but reasonable. But if the wine is at all special, there's no doubt you have a better chance of enjoying it if you treat it with at least a modicum of consideration. Indeed, if there is a general rule it is that the older a bottle of wine the more you must cherish it and expose it to the minimum amount of stress.

Most of us like to keep a few bottles in the house so we can choose a wine to suit our food or our mood. All an everyday wine requires is to be stored on its side, out of direct sunlight and away from heat sources. For the vast majority of wine the best vintage is the most recent one. Nearly all modern wine is ready to drink the moment it appears on the shop shelf, and with a few exceptions it is a huge mistake to keep any wine too long. Everyday wines simply taste more faded, stale and dull as the aging process goes on. Some bottles have guideline information on the back label, such as 'Best consumed within one year of

WINES TO KEEP

Wines from a good vintage will develop more slowly than those made in a poor year. The vintage tables on pages 400–403 give specific information; what follows are general guidelines.

Reds Cabernet Sauvignon wines are sometimes made for drinking young, but can often improve in bottle for many years. Bordeaux produces a range of Cabernet-based wines of varying aging potential. Basic wines need three years to mature and will last for another couple of years. A Classed Growth château in a good vintage will need ten years to mature, and will last for at least another ten; in a poor vintage it might mature in five years and start to fade in another five. California's Napa Valley has become Cabernet Sauvignon's second home: its wines are as varied as those of Bordeaux, drinkable after three to ten years in bottle, and capable of lasting a further 10–15 years from good producers. Most commercial Australian Cabernet Sauvignon is made to be drunk at three to six years old, although top wines can last up to 25 years.

Bordeaux's very best Merlot-based blends from St-Émilion and Pomerol need 10–15 years to reach maturity; slightly lesser wines will peak at five or six years.

In Burgundy, lesser classifications are best at three to six years; Premiers and Grands Crus will be ready after five to ten years, depending on the vintage, and the best of the lot will last 20 years or more. Elsewhere Pinot Noir should be drunk within three to five years.

Italy's Sangiovese and Nebbiolo wines vary according to the intentions of the winemaker. Some super-Tuscans and modern Barolos may be appreciated three to six years after the vintage, others, especially old-style Barolo, need at least ten years before they are approachable.

Syrah-based wines from the Rhône have good aging potential, up to 20 years in top vintages – only the best Australian Shiraz can compare. In Spain, top Ribera del Duero and Rioja take at least five years to mature, and last up to 15 years. California's Zinfandel, though usually made to drink young, sometimes has the structure to age for five to ten years.

Whites Classic white Burgundy is probably the world's longest-lived Chardonnay: a Grand Cru from Chablis or the Côte d'Or can last 20 years, although it can generally be enjoyed after three to five. Simpler white Burgundies, including those from the south of the region (Mâcon and Côte Chalonnaise), seldom develop for more than a year or two.

Dry, unoaked Chardonnay – whether it comes from Italy, the USA, Australia or elsewhere – should normally be drunk within two or three years of the vintage. Barrel-fermented or oak-aged Chardonnay has the potential to last longer – five or even ten years from exceptional producers.

Sauvignon Blanc generally makes wines to be drunk young, but in Bordeaux it is blended with Sémillon to make the great dry Pessac-Léognan and sweet Sauternes. Lesser Graves should last four years, top châteaux can improve for ten years or more. The finest Sauternes need ten years to mature and can live for decades.

Riesling can be one of the world's longest-lived grapes: a German Kabinett is immediately drinkable but good examples can improve for six to eight years; Spätlese and Auslese (and Alsace Grand Cru Riesling) should last 10–15 years or more; and the great sweet wines, German Beerenauslese, Trockenbeerenauslese and Eiswein, Alsace Vendange Tardive and Sélection de Grains Nobles, should not be drunk for at least ten years and will improve for decades.

The intensely sweet wines from the Loire, and Hungarian Tokaji, if well made, have a lifespan of 50 years or more.

Sparkling wines Non-vintage Champagne improves if kept for a year or two. Vintage Champagnes are sold at around six to eight years old, but are worth keeping for another five years. Australia's sparkling reds can also be kept for five years.

Fortified wines Most fortified wines do not evolve in the bottle, the honourable exception being vintage port, which is not ready to drink until it is about ten years old and reaches perfection after 20–40 years.

purchase' or 'This wine can be cellared for up to five years', but you won't find much of this sort of help on serious-minded wines (the ones that are best suited to long aging).

Longer term storage needs a little more thought. The traditional underground cellar has the ideal combination of even temperature, darkness, humidity and stillness, but few houses have one nowadays, so a disused fireplace, a corner of the garage, or the space under the stairs may have to do. The cooler the place is, within reason, the slower the wines will develop: somewhere between 10°C and 13°C (50°F and 55°F) is ideal. But avoiding sudden changes in temperature is the most important thing. Gradual, gentle aging is the key to bringing fine wines to maturity.

Serving temperatures
The flavour of wine is undoubtedly affected by the temperature at which it is served. It's better to serve wine slightly too cool, because you can always warm the glass in your hand. Don't do anything dramatic to change a wine's temperature like leaving it in front of the fire; sticking it in the freezer should be considered a last resort.

One rule of thumb is the cheaper the wine, the colder it should be served. Sparkling wines should be well chilled to preserve their bubbles. The cheaper the fizz, the closer to freezing! Fino and manzanilla sherry are also much better served chilled than warm.

Reds and rosés Most red wine is best served at room temperature – but that means around 15°C (60°F) or so, which is cooler than many centrally heated houses. Higher temperatures emphasize aromas while minimizing acidity and tannins: full-bodied, tannic and fine wines are therefore best at 15–18°C (60–64°F). No wine tastes at its best above a room temperature of about 20°C (68°F). As long as you don't live in a hothouse, the best way to bring red wine from cellar to room temperature is to stand the bottle in the room in which you intend to serve it a few hours before you open it.

Rosés should always be well chilled, and light, juicy, fruity reds can take a brief chilling, up to an hour, but it's not essential.

Whites Most white wines are probably best at 10–12°C (50–54°F), which they will reach after an hour or two in the refrigerator. If you've left things too late, put the bottle into an ice-bucket, empty in as much ice as you can, then fill it up with water – much more effective than ice alone.

Dry, neutral whites and tangy Sauvignon Blanc wines can take more chilling: up to two or three hours in the refrigerator.

Aromatic wines such as Riesling and Gewürztraminer, and sweet wines, start losing their perfume if you chill them for more than two hours. Chardonnay, especially good Burgundy, and Rhône whites shouldn't have more than about an hour because they begin to lose their attractive nuttiness.

Opening wine
To make this task as smooth as possible, choose a corkscrew with an open spiral and a handle that you find comfortable to use.

First remove the metal foil or plastic seal around the top of the bottle, known as the capsule. Wipe the lip of the bottle with a clean cloth if there is dirt or mould around the top of the cork.

Stand the bottle on a flat surface, press the point of the corkscrew gently into the centre of the cork and turn the screw slowly and steadily, keeping it straight. Try to stop turning before the point emerges at the bottom of the cork. Ease the cork out gently.

To remove a broken cork that is wedged into the bottle neck, drive the corkscrew in at a sharp angle and press the cork fragment against the side of the neck as you work it upwards, maintaining the angle of the corkscrew. If you're having no luck, push the cork down into the wine; it isn't pretty, but the wine will taste no worse for it.

Decanting
There are three reasons for putting wine in a decanter: to separate it from sediment that has formed in the bottle; to let it breathe; to make it look attractive. You don't need a special decanter, a glass jug is just as good.

Simply uncorking the bottle and leaving it to stand is not the same as letting it breathe, as only a tiny surface area is exposed. However, if you pour off half a glass of wine you will expose more wine to the air. Some wines do get softer and rounder after a couple of hours' decanting, and it is a good way to give very tannic red wines a more mature taste. On the other hand, decanting can kill off an old wine if you do it more than a few minutes before serving.

No wine, with the possible exceptions of vintage, single-quinta, crusted and traditional style LBV port, demands decanting. Even an old wine which has thrown a sediment can be poured out successfully from the bottle – do it slowly, avoiding any sudden movements which might make the wine slop about.

To decant, it's best to stand the bottle upright for a day or two to let the sediment settle. An hour or two before you want to drink it, open the bottle, then, with a candle or torch under the neck of the bottle, pour gently in one single motion until you see an arrowhead of sediment arrive at the lip. If you do it carefully you'll waste less than half a glass – and that can go into the gravy.

Glasses
There's one final thing – use nice big glasses which you fill to between one-third and one-half full to allow aromas to build up in the glass. A tulip-shaped glass will help to capture the aromas rather than dissipating them (such a waste!), and the glass should be clear, to show the colour of the wine.

After you've finished with them, handwash glasses in very hot water, taking care to rinse away all traces of washing-up liquid.

CORKS
The only requirements for the seal on a bottle of wine are that it should be hygienic, airtight, long-lasting and removable. Cork has stood the test of time, but it is prone to infection and shrinkage. Shrinkage is unlikely to occur if the bottle is kept on its side so the cork stays in contact with the wine and remains moist, but infected corks (sadly, common) will spoil a wine with their musty taste. Modern alternatives can give you a fresher wine. Plastic corks are now common, especially in budget wines. The best plastics have a soft texture and come in bright colours. The humble screwcap is probably as good a closure as any, and keeps wine fresh for years. It seems that its time has come, as more and more producers – especially of Riesling and Sauvignon – are switching to screwtop bottles.

TASTING WINE

TASTING WINE MEANS UNDERSTANDING what you are drinking – and enjoying it more. The ritual observed by professionals is not just showing off: there is a purpose to every stage, and it can help you to get maximum pleasure from a bottle of wine. Wine can be complex stuff, and if you just knock it back you could be missing out on a wonderful sensory experience. Instead, take a few moments to discover a little about a wine's background, appreciate its colour, and savour its scents and range of flavours.

❶ Read the label This tells you a great deal about the wine: its region of origin, age, alcohol level, sometimes its grape variety. The design – traditional or modern – can hint at the intentions of the winemaker. At a blind tasting, you will begin at the next step.

❷ Look at the wine Pour the wine into a glass so that it is about one-third full. Tilt the glass against a white background so that you can see the gradations of colour from the rim to the centre. The colour can begin to suggest the taste of the wine, with clues to grape variety, climate and age. A young red wine may have a deep purple tinge, an older one will be lighter, sometimes brick red. A very pale white will be young, fresh or neutral-tasting, a deeper yellow one will be fuller in flavour, sweeter or older (not always a good thing in white wines).

❸ Smell the wine Swirl the wine around the glass to release the aromas, then stick your nose into the glass and take a steady, gentle sniff. Register the smell in terms that mean something to you: if it reminds you of herbs, spices, strawberries, wet wool or tar, that is what makes the wine memorable.

❹ Take a sip Take a decent mouthful, so that your mouth is about one-third full, and hold the wine in your mouth for a few moments, breathing through your nose. Draw a little air through your lips and suck it through the wine to help the aromas on their way to your nasal cavity. Note any toughness, acidity and sweetness that the tongue detects, then enjoy the personality and flavour of the aromas in your nasal cavity. Now gently 'chew' the wine, letting it coat your tongue, teeth, and gums. Note the first impressions, then the taste that develops after the wine has been in your mouth for a few seconds. You can now swallow the wine or spit it out.

❺ Spit or swallow If you have to taste a number of wines in a limited time, spitting is the only way to appreciate the flavours and stay sober. Practise your technique in front of the bathroom mirror. A bucket with sawdust in the bottom makes a practical spittoon.

Assess the wine Now note your impressions. Is the wine well balanced (see box opposite)? Does the flavour linger in your mouth? A long-lasting flavour generally means a better wine.

TASTING WINE IN RESTAURANTS

Translating the above principles to a restaurant situation can save you and your guests from disappointment.
First of all, the waiter should show you the unopened bottle. The label will tell you whether it is the wine you ordered. If it is not, you are entitled to change your order, although in many modern wines the vintage is relatively unimportant. Feel the bottle to check the temperature.

The waiter should then open the bottle within your view and pour a small amount of wine into your glass. Sniff the wine and if all seems fine, take a sip. Take your time. If anything seems wrong about the wine, say so. The restaurant should replace a faulty wine without question. If you prefer to pour the wine yourself, ask the waiter to leave the bottle on the table or in an ice bucket.

Before you taste a wine, a few tell-tale signs might indicate something is wrong. A low level of wine in the bottle or a line of sediment 'baked' onto the side of the bottle suggest that it has not been stored with care. A brownish tinge – to red or white wine – may mean it is oxidized (spoilt by exposure to oxygen), in which case it will smell and taste stale, flat or sherry-like. Pieces of cork floating in the glass have nothing to do with 'corked' wine. Wine that is corked smells distinctively musty and is caused by an infected cork. The vinegary or nail-varnishy smell of volatile acidity occurs when a wine is infected by acetic bacteria. Sulphurous wines fall into two categories: a spent-match smell, from excessive use of sulphur dioxide in the winery, will usually dissipate after 30 minutes or so; a wine that smells of rotten eggs should be rejected immediately!

TASTING TERMS

The terms used by wine tasters are a useful shorthand when discussing wines, and are used throughout this and almost every other book on the subject.

Acidity All wines need acidity to be refreshing and capable of aging for any time. Too little acidity makes a wine taste lifeless, although too much makes it taste sharp.

Balance Term used to describe the relationship between the major components of wine: acidity, alcohol, fruit (and tannin in reds). In a well-balanced wine no single element dominates.

Beefy Solid, chunky red wines.

Big A full-bodied wine with lots of everything: fruit flavour, acid, alcohol and tannin.

Body Describes the impression of weight in the mouth. This is what is referred to by the terms light-, medium- and full-bodied.

Buttery Usually refers to the soft, rich, vanilla flavour imparted by new oak barrels.

Chewy Wine with a lot of tannin and strong flavour.

Clean Wine with no bacterial or chemical faults and a simple, direct flavour.

Closed Describes a wine that doesn't have much smell, but gives the impression that it will have more to offer when it matures.

Crisp Refreshing white with good acidity.

Deep A full-flavoured red or white.

Fat A heavy, sometimes clumsy wine, though if made from fully ripe grapes it can imply richness in sweet or dry wine.

Fresh The youthful aromas in a wine, and the combination of good acidity with fruit or floral flavours.

Fruit Term for the fruit element in a wine. It may not taste of grapes, but it will resemble a fruit of some kind (e.g. apple, blackcurrant, cherry) and is crucial to the flavour of most wines. Ripe fruit flavours can be confused with sweetness.

Full A wine with plenty of mouthfilling flavours and alcohol.

Grapy Quite rare flavour of the grape itself in wine. Most common in Muscat, Riesling or Gewürztraminer.

Green Unripe, or tart. This can be attractive and refreshing in light, young wine.

Hard Usually applied to reds which have an excess of tannin. In young reds, this is often necessary to facilitate aging.

Jammy Rather big, 'cooked', seemingly sweetish wines, usually red.

Length The way a good wine's flavours continue to evolve in the mouth even after swallowing.

Nutty Usually applied to dry whites (e.g. a soft Brazil or hazelnut flavour in Chardonnay, a dry richness in medium sherry or Madeira).

Oaky The slightly sweet vanilla flavour imparted by maturation in oak casks. The newer the oak the more forceful its impact on the wine.

Petrolly An attractive smell applied to mature Riesling wines, and sometimes mature Sémillon.

Prickly A wine with slight residual carbon dioxide gas. Usually attractive in light young whites, but in reds it can be a sign of re-fermentation in bottle.

Rich Wine that feels luxurious in the mouth, with sweet fruit flavours, not necessarily a sweet wine.

Ripe Lots of fresh fruit flavour dominates.

Rounded A wine in which the flavour seems satisfyingly complete, with no harshness.

Spicy Exotic fruit and spice flavours in whites, particularly Gewürztraminer, but also a peppery or cinnamon/clove perfume in some reds and whites aged in oak.

Steely Applied to good-quality Rieslings for their very dry, almost metallic flavour.

Sweet Term in dry wines for the elements of ripeness or richness which good quality can often suggest.

Tannin This substance, from the skins and pips of grapes, is what gives most red wines their tough, rather cold-tea, bitter edge. It combines with acidity to give a wine firmness. Too much tannin makes a wine bitter; low tannin makes a wine soft.

Tart Green, unripe wine with excess acidity. Can be desirable in light, dry wines.

Wine and food

Food can have a profound effect on the taste of wine: a well-matched partnership can enhance both food and wine, while an ill-chosen pair can leave a nasty taste in your mouth. The last thing we're going to do is start laying down laws about what you must or must not drink with this or that food. That's up to you. There are, though, certain points worth remembering.

Don't just match the flavour of the wine to the flavour of the food, but also take into account the body or weight of the wine: a heavy, alcoholic or oaky wine such as a spicy red Shiraz will overpower a delicate dish – a Pinot Noir would be a better bet. A rich dish can either be cut through with an acidic wine, or matched with a rich one, but either way the wine should be full in flavour so as not to taste lean and mean. A sauce needs to be considered as part of a dish; acid flavours, like lemon or tomato, need acidity in the wine – try a Sauvignon Blanc or a good Riesling.

Pastry dulls the palate, softening the flavours of the other ingredients with it; go for a more subtle wine than you might otherwise have chosen. Sweet food, including sweetish, fruity sauces, makes dry wine taste unpleasantly lean and acidic.

Red wines are not quite as adaptable as whites and rosés, largely because of their tannin. Tannin makes most fish taste metallic, and becomes more rasping with sweet things, so red wine with dessert doesn't usually work and tannic reds are unlikely to suit meat in fruity or sweet and sour sauces. However, tannin is perfect for cutting through fat, so tough reds are great with the fattier red meats and hearty stews. And the blood present in rare red meat has the knack of smoothing away all but the tougher tannins.

Juicy, Beaujolais-style reds (made from Gamay grapes) and wines based on Pinot Noir grapes have far less tannin and react differently with food. Contrary to the adage that white wine should be served with fish, these red wine grapes can go with certain fish, usually the sturdier-fleshed types such as salmon, monkfish and red mullet.

Red wine is traditionally drunk with cheese, but white is generally better. Blue cheeses, in particular, are unhappy matches for red wines, unless there's an element of sweetness, as in port.

Wine and health

A study published in 1992 highlighted the French paradox – that despite the proven link between the consumption of saturated fat and coronary heart disease, the French, whose consumption of both saturated fat and wine is high, have a significantly lower incidence of heart disease. Since then, many further studies have led most doctors in Western countries to conclude that wine in moderation – a maximum of four 120–150ml glasses a day for men, two glasses for women – can have a wide range of health benefits, particularly in reducing the risk of heart attack and stroke.

FRANCE

NEARLY ALL THE INTERNATIONALLY recognized classic wine types originate in France. All the greatest wine grape varieties are French, with the exception of Riesling. (And there's some of that in Alsace anyway.) All the methods of winemaking now accepted worldwide as the textbook procedures for the production of great wines, red or white, are based on French tradition. Not only that, but French methods of quality control, as laid out in the Appellation d'Origine Contrôlée regulations, have formed the model for such systems all over the world. The French, you see, have had 2000 years of practice at the winemaking game, ever since the Romans landed on the Mediterranean coast and settled at Narbonne, bringing with them their thirst for wine, their winemaking skills, and a tradition of law and order. And however strong the challenges from the rest of the world's vineyards, it's still going to be some time before France's supremacy is shaken.

If there is one thing which exemplifies the French wine style, it is balance – the balance between overripeness and underripeness, too much fruit flavour and not enough. And this is the result of almost 20 centuries of experimentation and refinement which continues today. Generation after generation of winemakers have patiently matched grape varieties with the most suitable soils in the most suitable sites so that appropriate ripening conditions have been found for all the great table wine grapes.

A tour of the regions

The Champagne region, in the far north, is cold and uninviting for most of the year, but in the Marne Valley and on the neighbouring slopes near the towns of Reims and Épernay, the chalky soil produces the thin acid white which is the perfect base for sparkling wine. Champagne – the world's greatest fizz – only comes from this single area of France.

The eastern frontiers of France are a series of mountain ranges and all of these produce highly individual wines. The Vosges mountains in Alsace slope into the Rhine Valley opposite Germany's Baden region, and the east-facing vineyards, warm and dry long into the golden days of autumn, produce fabulously spicy, perfumed dry white wines, unlike any other. Alsace also produces luscious sweet wines from late-picked grapes. From the Jura mountains further south come strange, unforgettably flavoured wines and from Savoie, the old alpine kingdom, come sharp, tasty and mouthwateringly good whites.

Burgundy

Inland from these mountainous redoubts is the great swathe of land which used to make up the Duchy of Burgundy. It has been famous for wine and food since Roman times and it is still the birthplace of some of the most irresistible wine flavours in the world. Burgundy built its reputation on red wines, but several of its most famous wines are white. The northernmost of these is Chablis, a stone-dry white as celebrated as any in France, from a dowdy little town between Paris and Dijon. Red wine production gets into full swing south of Dijon with the Côte d'Or – a narrow but venerated slope of southeast-facing land which produces many of the most famous wines in the world – but in extremely limited quantities. The northern section of the Côte d'Or, the Côte de Nuits, is almost entirely red wine country, while the southern section, the Côte de Beaune, can produce reds and whites of equal splendour.

South of the Côte d'Or is the Côte Châlonnaise – a less spectacular, but extremely good source of Burgundy, reds from the Pinot Noir and whites from the Chardonnay, while further south the Mâconnais exists primarily as a white wine producer of very varying quality. In nearby Beaujolais the red Gamay grape can perform brilliantly. Although it frequently doesn't.

Wines of the south

The Rhône Valley is on the whole a paradise for red wine drinkers, though the white Viognier grape makes startlingly good wine at Condrieu. On the steep, cliff-like vineyards of the northern Rhône Valley, the Syrah grape offers fragrance and fiery force with some of

The vineyards of Ch. Rouquette-sur-Mer overlook the Mediterranean town of Narbonne-Plage in Languedoc-Roussillon, a region that is currently producing some of France's most exciting wines.

France's grandest reds from Côte-Rôtie, Hermitage and Cornas. But the valley spreads out beneath the hill of Hermitage and the flavours soften too as the Grenache blends in with the Syrah, the Carignan and the Cinsaut to produce enormous amounts of easy-fruited Côtes du Rhône and much smaller amounts of concentrated, superripe Châteauneuf-du-Pape. In recent years white wines from the Marsanne and Roussanne grapes have started to make their mark.

The whole of the South of France is dominated by red wine – although Provence is more famous for its rosé and there are increasing numbers of fresh, vibrant whites. The revival in the south was sparked by the vin de pays movement – which encouraged the planting of international varieties like Chardonnay and Cabernet that weren't allowed in the traditional ACs. This 'varietal wine' movement brought about a revolution in winemaking and allowed France to present a 'New World' face. Interestingly, it is now the revivified ACs that have taken the lead in Languedoc-Roussillon, but the whole area is now buzzing with life.

The South-West, between the Pyrenees and Bordeaux, and along the valleys of the Tarn and Lot rivers, has a very varied geography and range of wines. Bergerac and its neighbours are Bordeaux in style, using the same grapes and winemaking methods. Côtes de Gascogne produces crisp fruity dry whites in the Armagnac brandy region. Madiran and Cahors have their own powerful reds, and Gaillac is best known for its sparklers and tangy whites, while Jurançon with superb sweet whites, and Irouléguy with fascinating wines of both colours round off the area with a Pyrenean accent.

Classics from the west

Bordeaux could well lay claim to the title 'red wine capital of the world'. The Merlot grape dominates the clay-rich vineyards of St-Émilion and Pomerol, while the gravelly soils of the Graves and the Haut-Médoc, especially at Margaux, St-Julien, Pauillac and St-Estèphe, provide the perfect conditions for Cabernet Sauvignon to produce a string of stunning wines. Bordeaux produces whites too, using Sémillon and Sauvignon Blanc grapes. Entre-Deux-Mers provides easy-to-drink, fruity but dry whites, but Pessac-Léognan and Graves can produce thrilling barrel-fermented dry whites, to drink young or to age. And as for Sauternes

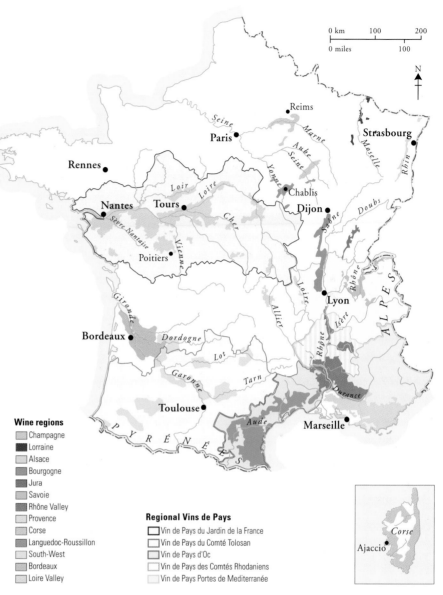

Wine regions
- Champagne
- Lorraine
- Alsace
- Bourgogne
- Jura
- Savoie
- Rhône Valley
- Provence
- Corse
- Languedoc-Roussillon
- South-West
- Bordeaux
- Loire Valley

Regional Vins de Pays
- Vin de Pays du Jardin de la France
- Vin de Pays du Comté Tolosan
- Vin de Pays d'Oc
- Vin de Pays des Comtés Rhodaniens
- Vin de Pays Portes de Mediterranée

and Barsac – their unctuously sweet, rich wines set the standard for sweet wines throughout the rest of the world, and given the unpredictable nature of their production there has been a generous number of great vintages in the last two decades.

In the Loire Valley the white Sauvignon Blanc, Chenin and Muscadet grapes produce some of France's most distinct wine styles. In the central Loire, Sauvignon creates world classics in the tangy, dry white stakes with Sancerre and Pouilly-Fumé. The ultra-dry, almost smoky green flavour has spawned imitators the world over, and made Sauvignon Blanc a superstar. Sauvignon also thrives in Touraine, but the Chenin then takes over, both at Vouvray, and further west in Anjou. Although

difficult to ripen, Chenin can produce good sparkling wines as well as dry, medium and sweet whites, all depending on the weather and the whim of the winemaker. The Cabernet Franc in a warm year makes thrilling reds at Chinon and Bourgueil. And the Muscadet grape makes – well, Muscadet, at its best an easy-going light, crisp, fresh dry white.

Between these great classic areas, there are the little backwaters of wine; the byways which usually get forgotten as the big producers surge to the fore. Well, we don't forget them. As well as covering all the major areas, in great detail, the minor areas also get their due. Great and small, famous and unknown, red, white and rosé, together they make up the magical world of France and its wines.

French wine classifications

FRANCE HAS THE MOST COMPLEX and yet the most workable system in the world for controlling the quality and authenticity of its wines, based on the belief that the soil a vine grows in, and the type of grape variety employed, are crucial to the character and quality of the wine. There are three levels above the basic Vin de Table (table wine) level.

At the top is Appellation d'Origine Contrôlée (Controlled Appellation of Origin) usually abbreviated to AOC or AC. All the great French classic wines belong in this group. The second level is Vin Délimité de Qualité Supérieure (Delimited Wine of Superior Quality), usually abbreviated to VDQS. This is a kind of junior or probationary AC.

The third category, Vin de Pays, was created to give a geographical identity and quality yardstick to wines which had previously been sold off for blending. It is a useful category for adventurous winemakers because the regulations usually allow the use of grape varieties which are not traditional to an area and are thus debarred from its AC.

There are three divisions of Vin de Pays: regional (of which there are five, covering large areas of the country – see map on page 31): departmental (each of which covers the vineyards of one *département*, such as Vin de Pays des Pyrénées-Orientales); and zonal (the smallest and most tightly controlled areas, covering a specific locality).

There are seven major areas of control in AC regulations, which are mirrored to a greater or lesser extent in the lower quality levels:

Land The actual vineyard site is obviously at the top of the list. Its aspect to the sun, elevation, drainage – all these crucially influence the grape's ability to ripen. The composition of the soil also affects flavour and ripening.

Grape Different grape varieties ripen at different rates given more or less heat and on different sorts of soil. Over the centuries the most suitable varieties for each area have emerged and only these are permitted so as to preserve each AC's individuality.

Alcoholic degree A minimum degree of alcohol is always specified as this reflects ripeness in the grapes. Ripe grapes give better flavour – and their higher sugar content creates higher eventual alcohol levels.

Vineyard yield Overproduction dilutes flavour and character, so a sensible maximum yield is fixed which is expressed in hectolitres of juice per hectare.

Vineyard practice The number of vines per hectare and the way they are pruned can dramatically affect yield and therefore quality. Minimum density and pruning methods are specified in the regulations.

Winemaking practice The things you can or can't do to the wine – like adding sugar to help fermentation, or removing acidity when the crop is unripe. Each appellation has its own particular rules.

Testing and tasting The wines must pass a technical test for soundness – and a tasting panel for quality and 'typicality'. Every year a significant number of wines are refused the AC.

Further levels of classification

You may also see words like Grand Cru, Grand Cru Classé or Premier Cru on the label. Sometimes, as in Alsace and Burgundy, this is part of the AC. But in the Haut-Médoc in Bordeaux, it represents a historic judgment of excellence. In the famous 1855 Classification 60 red wines from the Haut-Médoc – and one from the Graves (now in Pessac-Léognan) – were ranked in five tiers according to the prices they traditionally fetched on the Bordeaux market. In general, the 1855 Classification is still a remarkably accurate guide to the best wines of the Haut-Médoc. Sauternes was also classified in 1855, but Graves had to wait until 1953 for its reds and 1959 for its whites. Pomerol has no classification, though St-Émilion does – it is revised every ten years or so to take account both of improving properties and of declining ones.

These Bordeaux classifications, though obviously influenced by the best vineyard sites, are actually judgments on the performance of a particular wine over the years – something which is often as much in the hands of the winemaker as inherent in the soil. Alsace and Burgundy have a classification, enshrined in the AC, which delineates the actual site of the vineyards. So the potential for excellence is recognized as either Grand Cru (the top in both areas) or Premier Cru (the second rank, so far only in Burgundy). Ideally, this is the better method, though a bad grower can still make bad wine anywhere.

The 1855 Classification

This was created for the 1855 World Exhibition in Paris by the Bordeaux Chamber of Commerce. It included only red wines from the Haut-Médoc, one red wine from the Graves and the sweet white wines from Sauternes and Barsac. It was revised once in 1973, raising Mouton-Rothschild in Pauillac from Deuxième Cru to Premier Cru status.

Premiers Crus: Lafite-Rothschild (Pauillac); Margaux (Margaux); Latour (Pauillac); Haut-Brion (Pessac-Léognan); Mouton-Rothschild (Pauillac).

Deuxièmes Crus: Rauzan-Ségla (Margaux); Rauzan-Gassies (Margaux); Léoville-Las-Cases (St-Julien); Léoville-Poyferré (St-Julien); Léoville-Barton (St-Julien); Durfort-Vivens (Margaux); Gruaud-Larose (St-Julien); Lascombes (Margaux); Brane-Cantenac (Margaux); Pichon-Longueville (Pauillac); Pichon-Longueville-Comtesse de Lalande (Pauillac); Ducru-Beaucaillou (St-Julien); Cos d'Estournel (St-Estèphe); Montrose (St-Estèphe).

Troisièmes Crus: Kirwan (Margaux); d'Issan (Margaux); Lagrange (St-Julien); Langoa-Barton (St-Julien); Giscours (Margaux); Malescot-St-Exupéry (Margaux); Boyd-Cantenac (Margaux); Cantenac-Brown (Margaux); Palmer (Margaux); La Lagune (Haut-Médoc); Desmirail (Margaux); Calon-Ségur (St-Estèphe); Ferrière (Margaux); Marquis d'Alesme-Becker (Margaux).

Quatrièmes Crus: St-Pierre (St-Julien); Talbot (St-Julien); Branaire (St-Julien); Duhart-Milon (Pauillac); Pouget (Margaux); la Tour-Carnet (Haut-Médoc); Lafon-Rochet (St-Estèphe); Beychevelle (St-Julien); Prieuré-Lichine (Margaux); Marquis de Terme (Margaux).

Cinquièmes Crus: Pontet-Canet (Pauillac); Batailley (Pauillac); Haut-Batailley (Pauillac); Grand-Puy-Lacoste (Pauillac); Grand-Puy-Ducasse (Pauillac); Lynch-Bages (Pauillac); Lynch-Moussas (Pauillac); Dauzac (Margaux); d'Armailhac (Pauillac); du Tertre (Margaux); Haut-Bages-Libéral (Pauillac); Pédesclaux (Pauillac); Belgrave (Haut-Médoc); Camensac (Haut-Médoc); Cos Labory (St-Estèphe); Clerc-Milon (Pauillac); Croizet-Bages (Pauillac); Cantemerle (Haut-Médoc).

The 1855 Classification of Barsac and Sauternes

Premier Cru Supérieur: d'Yquem (Sauternes).

Premiers Crus: la Tour Blanche (Sauternes); Lafaurie-Peyraguey (Sauternes); Clos Haut-Peyraguey (Sauternes); Rayne-Vigneau (Sauternes); Suduiraut (Sauternes); Coutet (Barsac); Climens (Barsac); Guiraud (Sauternes); Rieussec (Sauternes); Rabaud-Promis (Sauternes); Sigalas-Rabaud (Sauternes).

Deuxièmes Crus: de Myrat (Barsac); Doisy-Daëne (Barsac); Doisy-Dubroca (Barsac); Doisy-Védrines (Barsac); d'Arche (Sauternes); Filhot (Sauternes); Broustet (Barsac); Nairac (Barsac); Caillou (Barsac); Suau (Barsac); de Malle (Sauternes); Romer du Hayot (Sauternes); Lamothe (Sauternes); Lamothe-Guignard (Sauternes).

The Classification of the Graves (since 1987 Pessac-Léognan)

This classification was carried out in 1953 encompassing only red wines. It was revised in 1959 to include white wines. Ch. Haut-Brion features both in this and the 1855 Classification. The châteaux are listed alphabetically, followed by their commune and whether they are classified for red or white wine.

Bouscaut (Cadaujac) ♥♀; Carbonnieux (Léognan) ♥♀; Domaine de Chevalier (Léognan) ♥♀; Couhins (Villenave-d'Ornon) ♀; Couhins-Lurton (Villenave-d'Ornon) ♀; de Fieuzal (Léognan) ♥; Haut-Bailly (Léognan) ♥; Haut-Brion (Pessac) ♥; Latour-Martillac (Martillac) ♥♀; Laville-Haut-Brion (Talence) ♀; Malartic-Lagravière (Léognan) ♥♀; la Mission-Haut-Brion (Talence) ♥; Olivier (Léognan) ♥♀; Pape Clément (Pessac) ♥; Smith-Haut-Lafitte (Martillac) ♥; la Tour-Haut-Brion (Talence) ♥.

The St-Émilion Classification

St-Émilion Grand Cru is a superior AC within St-Émilion, and of the several hundred Grand Cru wines a certain number are classified. The first classification was in 1954, and it was slightly modified in 1969, 1985 and 1996. The threat of re-grading can help to maintain quality.

Premiers Grands Crus Classés (A): Ausone, Cheval Blanc; **(B):** Angélus, Beau-Séjour Bécot, Beauséjour (Duffau-Lagarosse), Belair, Canon, Clos Fourtet, Figeac, la Gaffelière, Magdelaine, Pavie, Trottevieille.

Grands Crus Classés: l'Arrosée, Balestard-la-Tonnelle, Bellevue, Bergat, Berliquet, Cadet-Bon, Cadet-Piola, Canon-la Gaffelière, Cap de Mourlin, Chauvin, Clos des Jacobins, Clos de l'Oratoire, Clos St-Martin, la Clotte, la Clusière, Corbin, Corbin-Michotte, la Couspaude,

In the vintage bottle cellar at Ch. Latour, a Bordeaux Premier Cru, the cellar master holds a double magnum (equivalent to four standard bottles).

Couvent des Jacobins, Curé-Bon, Dassault, la Dominique, Faurie-de-Souchard, Fonplégade, Fonroque, Franc Mayne, les Grandes Murailles, Grand Mayne, Grand-Pontet, Guadet-St-Julien, Haut Corbin, Haut Sarpe, Lamarzelle, Laniote, Larcis Ducasse, Larmande, Laroque, Laroze, Matras, Moulin du Cadet, Pavie-Decesse, Pavie-Macquin, Petit-Faurie-de-Soutard, le Prieuré, Ripeau, St-Georges (Côte Pavie), la Serre, Soutard, Tertre-Daugay, la Tour Figeac, la Tour du Pin Figeac (Giraud-Bélivier), la Tour du Pin Figeac (J M Moueix), Troplong-Mondot, Villemaurine, Yon-Figeac.

The Crus Bourgeois of the Médoc

The Cru Bourgeois châteaux were first classified in 1932, listing 444 estates making wines of regular high quality. In 2001 the list stood at 419 estates, which between them represent about 50 per cent of the wine produced in the Médoc, as opposed to 20 per cent for the Crus Classés. A major revision in 2003 divided the châteaux into three tiers: Cru Bourgeois, Cru Bourgeois Supérieur and Cru Bourgeois Exceptionnel. The following Cru Bourgeois châteaux now produce wines of, or near to, Cru Classé standard: Angludet, Charmail, Chasse-Spleen, Citran, Haut-Marbuzet, Gloria, la Gurgue, Labégorce, Labégorce-Zédé, Marbuzet, Maucaillou, Meyney, Monbrison, de Pez, Phélan-Ségur, Pibran, Potensac, Poujeaux, Siran, Sociando-Mallet, la Tour Haut-Caussan.

Burgundy classifications

There are five levels: regional (Bourgogne); specific regional (e.g. Chablis); village or communal (e.g. Pommard); Premiers Crus; and Grands Crus. For vineyards entitled to the rank Premier Cru the vineyard name follows the village name on the label (e.g. Gevrey-Chambertin, Combe-aux-Moines). Grands Crus, the top level, are appellations in their own right, and the Grand Cru names can stand alone on the label, without a village name. The following Côte d'Or villages have Grands Crus:

Gevrey-Chambertin: le Chambertin ♥, Chambertin Clos de Bèze ♥, Chapelle-Chambertin ♥, Charmes-Chambertin ♥ incorporating Mazoyères-Chambertin ♥, Griottes-Chambertin ♥, Latricières-Chambertin ♥, Mazis-Chambertin ♥, Ruchottes-Chambertin ♥

Morey St-Denis: Bonnes-Mares ♥, Clos des Lambrays ♥, Clos de la Roche ♥, Clos St-Denis ♥, Clos de Tart ♥

Chambolle-Musigny: Musigny ♥ ♀, Bonnes-Mares ♥

Vougeot: Clos de Vougeot ♥

Vosne-Romanée: Richebourg ♥, la Romanée-Conti ♥, la Romanée ♥, la Grande Rue ♥, la Romanée-St-Vivant ♥, Richebourg ♥, la Tâche ♥

Flagey-Échézeaux: Échézeaux ♥, Grands-Échézeaux ♥. These two Grands Crus are often grouped under Vosne-Romanée as all Flagey's other wines are labelled as Vosne-Romanée.

Aloxe-Corton: Corton ♥ ♀ (divided into sub-vineyards or *climats* of which the most important are Bressandes, le Corton, Maréchaudes, Pougets, Clos de Roi, Renardes, and Rognet), Corton-Charlemagne ♀

Ladoix-Serrigny: Corton ♥ ♀, Corton-Charlemagne ♀

Pernand-Vergelesses: Corton-Charlemagne ♀

Puligny-Montrachet: Bâtard-Montrachet ♀, Bienvenues-Bâtard-Montrachet ♀, Chevalier-Montrachet ♀, le Montrachet ♀

Chassagne-Montrachet: Bâtard-Montrachet ♀, Criots-Bâtard-Montrachet ♀, le Montrachet ♀

For the Chablis Grands Crus see pages 120-122.

Alsace Grand Cru

As part of its AC, Alsace has 50 designated Grands Crus (see page 64). Among the best are: Altenberg de Bergheim, Brand, Eichberg, Frankstein, Froehn, Furstentum, Geisberg, Goldert, Hengst, Kaefferkopf, Kastelberg, Kessler, Kirchberg de Barr, Kirchberg de Ribeauvillé, Kitterlé, Mandelberg, Moenchberg, Osterberg, Rangen, Rosacker, Schlossberg, Schoenenbourg, Sporen, Zinnkoepflé, Zotzenberg.

GERMANY

GERMANY IS IN THE THROES of a revolution. It started in earnest only in the 1990s, and it has gone from strength to strength. Part of this revolution is a revival of the traditional high-quality grape varieties such as Riesling and Silvaner that used to rule the roost before upstarts like Müller-Thurgau knocked them off their perch.

But it is a rebellion as well: many of the country's best growers are rejecting the provisions of the law in order to make and sell their wines with the greatest possible flexibility, not even bothering with selling their wines under village and vineyard names. Not that the lawmakers are standing still. New classifications, both for wine styles and for vineyard sites, have come into force since the start of the 21st century – aimed at maximizing Germany's image as a quality wine producer and, at least in theory, making the wines easier to understand for customers.

German wine classifications

German wine law dates from 1971, and to wine lovers it is infamous for the confusion it has caused consumers. It grades wines according to the amount of sugar present in the grapes at harvest, on the principle that riper grapes are a sign of quality, and are found only in better vineyards, tended by better growers and in better years.

At the bottom of the ladder there is Tafelwein, or table wine. A notch above this is Landwein, which is the equivalent of the French vin de pays. Anything above this level is quality wine in EU terms. German quality wine falls into two main divisions: quality wine from a designated region, or Qualitätswein bestimmte Anbaugebiete (QbA), and quality wine from a special category, or Qualitätswein mit Prädikat (QmP). The former is Germany's everyday wine, covering everything from Liebfraumilch to the much higher quality basic wines of the finest growers. A new category, Qualitätswein garantierten Ursprung (QgU), or quality wine of guaranteed origin, indicates a QbA from a specific district, vineyard or village.

Riesling vines in the Würzgarten vineyard above the Mosel at Urzig. The river both retains and reflects heat, and the slope allows maximum exposure to the sun, helping the grapes to ripen in Germany's cool climate.

Qualitätswein mit Pradikät

It is in the second category, Qualitätswein mit Prädikat, that things get complicated. There are six Prädikat levels, each demanding a progressively higher level of sugar in the grapes. Kabinett is the lightest: Kabinett wines are usually dry or medium-dry, often very delicate and naturally low in alcohol. Spätlese, the next category, means 'late-picked', and these wines are richer and riper, sometimes dry but just as often fruity and slightly sweet. Auslese means 'selected': there may well be some noble rot on these grapes, if the year permits, and you can usually expect some sweetness. An important point here is that if any of these terms are followed by the word 'trocken' (dry) the wines will be dry. With Beerenauslese the wines become truly sweet. The term means

'berry-selected': noble-rotted grapes are picked individually for these wines, which are rare and expensive. The final category, Trockenbeerenauslese, is also rare: intensely sweet, long-lived wines made solely from individually picked, noble-rotted grapes. Eiswein ('ice wine') is just as sweet, but the sweetness is concentrated by freezing: the grapes are picked on winter mornings when the temperature is –6°C (23°F) or below, and the water in the grapes is frozen solid.

This is all well and good, but while an Auslese is undoubtedly rarer and more expensive than a Kabinett, it is not necessarily of better quality: much depends on the standards of the grower and the grape variety.

And this is why the growers are up in arms. A few have opted for making only

QmP wines, skipping the QbA category altogether, and selling anything that doesn't make Kabinett level as plain Tafelwein. Some wear Tafelwein as a badge of pride, using the freedom of the lowest of all designations to experiment with the use of new oak barriques for aging their wines (the taste of new oak is frowned upon by the authorities who grant the QbA and QmP designations). Large numbers of growers, too, are doing away with the baffling proliferation of village and vineyard names, and selling their wine simply on their company's name. Meanwhile the legislators have authorised new labelling terms which are meant to make top-quality dry wines more easily identifiable to consumers: Classic and the superior Selection. So far uptake is not exactly 100 per cent.

Quality wine regions
- Ahr
- Mittelrhein
- Mosel-Saar-Ruwer
- Rheingau
- Nahe
- Rheinhessen
- Pfalz
- Hessische Bergstrasse
- Franken
- Württemberg
- Baden
- Saale-Unstrut
- Sachsen

Quality wine regions

Germany has 13 designated quality wine regions. They are: Ahr, Mittelrhein, Mosel-Saar-Ruwer, Nahe, Rheinhessen, Pfalz, Rheingau, Hessische Bergstrasse, Franken, Baden, Württemberg, Saale-Unstrut and Sachsen, the last two being in what was East Germany. These regions are divided into Bereiche, or sub-regions, which in turn are divided into a total of roughly 150 Grosslagen – a group of vineyard sites. A single vineyard within a Grosslage is called an Einzellage and a wine from an Einzellage should, in theory, be superior to one from a Grosslage. But in Germany most vineyards are divided between more than one producer. Single ownership of a single site, as happens, for example, in Bordeaux, is rare. So standards vary enormously, and while a top vineyard name on a label may be an indication of quality, a far more reliable guarantee is the name of the grower. Nonetheless, Germany is pressing ahead with classifying its best vineyard sites as Erste Gewächse (Grand Cru sites in effect, and restricted to the Rheingau), Erste Lage (in the Mosel) and Grosse Gewächse (Premier Cru).

Wine styles

The style of the wines varies, too, from one region to another. Partly this is a question of climate and soil, partly a matter of the vines grown, and while there is obviously a change in the climate from north to south, there is a change, too, from west to east. The more easterly regions have an appreciably more continental climate – that is, a climate of extremes. And while the hardy Riesling grape, traditionally Germany's finest, produces supreme elegance and raciness in north-westerly regions like the Mosel, the Rheingau and the Pfalz, in the vineyards of Baden it is the grapes of the Pinot family – Blanc, Gris and Noir – that excel. Here, in the warmer climate of Germany's southerly regions, dry whites and reds can show fuller, softer flavours than we have come to expect from German wines, and Baden's full potential is at last being realized. Further east the winters may be too cold even for the Riesling.

The Riesling is Germany's quality flagship, and since 1996 it has overtaken the far inferior Müller-Thurgau in terms of number of hectares planted. The third most popular grape is the Silvaner, with the Kerner close behind. The Kerner is an example of a German phenomenon: new vine crossings, designed to produce good yields and to be resistant to cold and frost in the tough German climate. Their quality, in spite of the researchers' best efforts, lags behind the classic varieties, although Scheurebe can be an exception to this rule.

Germany's red wines are made mostly from Spätburgunder (or Pinot Noir), with Blauer Portugieser, Trollinger and Dornfelder also popular. And both red and white wines are year by year, region by region, grower by grower, becoming fuller, better balanced, and drier. Now, how's that for a revolution?

AUSTRIA

AUSTRIA'S VINEYARDS ARE concentrated in the east of the country, and are no respecters of national boundaries: they spill over into the Czech Republic, Slovakia, Hungary and Slovenia and take their grape varieties with them, just as they did in the days when the Austro-Hungarian Empire covered the whole region. Dry white wines predominate, made from Austria's own Grüner Veltliner and a handful of other varieties, including Riesling, Chardonnay, Sauvignon Blanc and Pinot Blanc, but Austria's great tradition for dessert wines is being revived, and some rich, powerful reds are appearing.

Wine regions

Niederösterreich
1. Wachau
2. Kremstal
3. Kamptal
4. Traisental
5. Donauland
6. Weinviertel
7. Carnuntum
8. Thermenregion

Wien
9. Wien

Burgenland
10. Neusiedlersee
11. Neusiedlersee-Hügelland
12. Mittelburgenland
13. Südburgenland

Steiermark
14. Süd-Oststeiermark
15. Südsteiermark
16. Weststeiermark

Wine regions

Austria has three main wine regions: Niederösterreich (Lower Austria), Burgenland and Steiermark (Styria); the area around Wien (Vienna) also has vineyards. While it is principally a white wine country the reds, particularly those from southern Burgenland, are improving all the time. From northern Burgenland come outstanding sweet wines. From just about everywhere these days, since fashion demands it, come first-class dry wines of body, structure and elegance – particularly Rieslings and Grüner Veltliners from regions to the west of Vienna: the Wachau especially, but also Kremstal and Kamptal. Steiermark, too, in the far south, has a very individual, sharper style of white.

The best examples are world-class and unlike any other country's top whites. Dry Austrian whites have the freshness and aromatic style of German wines, but are more full-bodied and harmonious. While the Austrians drink them as young as possible they can also age for five, ten or more years in top vintages. The 1990s saw a handful of

Dürnstein, with its Baroque monastery and ruined fortress, is one of the most famous villages of the Wachau wine region.

leading growers starting to produce world-class dessert wines. Top producers are also making rich-textured, often oaked red wines with aging potential, from native grapes such as Blauer Zweigelt and Blaufränkisch and international varieties like Cabernet Sauvignon and Pinot Noir. However, whether sweet or dry, white or red, top-quality Austrian wines are not cheap.

Austrian wine classifications

Wine quality categories are similar to those in Germany (see page 34). All Qualitätswein must come from a region specified on the label: this may be one of the 16 main wine-producing regions or a village or vineyard within the region. Like German wines, quality wines may additionally have a special category, but Austrian wine labels give a better idea of the style of the wine: Kabinett is always dry; Spätlese is usually dry; Auslese is usually a light dessert wine – although it may be dry (labelled Trocken); Beerenauslese and Trockenbeerenauslese are always sweet, and there is an additional dessert wine category, Ausbruch, between these last two styles.

However, the first Austrian appellations, know as DAC, are starting to appear, pointing to a future more aligned to French, Italian and Spanish thinking.

SWITZERLAND

IN SWITZERLAND'S COOL, alpine climate, the vineyards are concentrated around the country's lakes and rivers and are often steep and terraced – the high cost of production is one reason why Swiss wines are expensive. Perhaps surprisingly, nearly half the wines made are red; both reds and whites tend to be delicate and fresh.

Wine regions

Valais	Bern	Schaffhausen
Vaud	Jura	Thurgau
Genève	Basel	St Gallen
Neuchâtel	Aargau	Graubünden (Grisons)
Fribourg	Zürich	Ticino and Misox

Wine regions

Vaud and Valais, the French-speaking cantons that overlook Lake Geneva (Lac Léman) and the Rhône, are the sources for most of Switzerland's wine; Neuchâtel and Geneva also contribute substantially, while the Fribourg and Jura vineyards are among Switzerland's smallest. The white Chasselas (known as Fendant in Valais, Dorin in Vaud and Perlan in Geneva) is the main variety, making light, neutral, fresh wines; reds come from Pinot Noir and Gamay; rosés, under the stylistic appellation of Oeil de Perdrix ('partridge eye') are also made from Pinot Noir. The German-speaking districts of Basel, Bern, Aargau, Graubünden (Grisons in Italian), St Gallen, Schaffhausen, Thurgau and Zürich make reds and whites from the same grapes (but sometimes under different names – Pinot Noir is also known as Blauburgunder and Clevner), plus Müller-Thurgau (known as Riesling x Sylvaner) and others; the Italian-speaking canton of Ticino makes good ripe Merlot.

Swiss wine classifications

There are three major quality categories: Appellation d'Origine Contrôlée (which is granted to each canton, with the right to regulate appellations within its boundaries; each winemaking village can register its own appellation); generic indication of origin (roughly comparable with the French vins de pays); and wine with no appellation of origin (table wines, labelled 'red' or 'white').

Cantonal regulations vary according to local traditions: some stick to either canton or village appellations, others recognize Crus within the villages, or districts such as Chablais (in Vaud). The appellation also specifies grape variety or style; a well-known light red wine, Dôle du Valais, is a blend of Pinot Noir and Gamay.

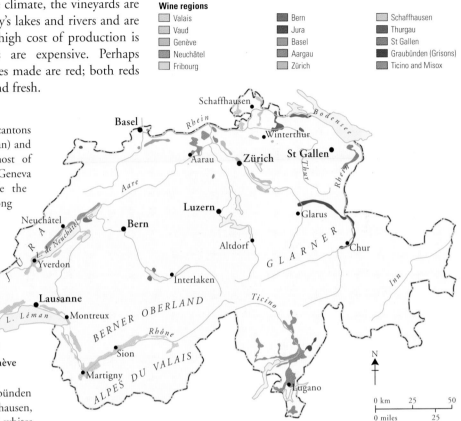

These vineyards at Sion, on the right bank of the Rhône, are in the Valais, the most intensively cultivated of Switzerland's winemaking cantons.

A big future for Swiss wine?

Very little Swiss wine is exported: put simply, domestic consumers drink all the wine the country can produce. Another big obstacle to the development of the Swiss wine industry, the nation's protectionist policy to white wine imports, was removed in 1995. During the 1990s some very interesting and innovative dry white and red wines began to be produced in the cantons of Valais, Graubünden and Ticino, which suggest that Switzerland has considerable untapped potential in both these fields. Many of these wines have been made with non-traditional grape varieties such as Chardonnay, which makes sense – cool-climate Chardonnays are often delicious. But would you ever expect to find a Swiss Syrah? And a ripe, fragrant one at that? But the Valais *does* produce Syrah in those sun-traps on the steep mountains. There is Riesling too, which is only logical when you see vertiginous vineyards with stony soils as challenging as any in Germany's Mosel Valley.

Equally interesting are rare and unusual white wines from Switzerland's indigenous vines, Amigne, Petite Arvine and Humagne Blanc. After a long period of protectionism and complacency, Swiss winemakers are beginning to create some Alpine waves.

ITALY

ITALY HAS WINES THAT ARE dry as a bone and wines that are lusciously sweet; wines that are light and dainty, and great strapping monsters; wines that are the essence of subtlety and wines that are outlandishly brash. The country stretches from Austria in the north almost to Africa in the south and houses a vast number of soil types, climates, altitudes and grape varieties, many of them strictly localized. Add to this the thousands of producers making wines in subtly different ways and it's not difficult to see that Italian wines have an almost infinite variety of flavours. And as fast as the authorities tried to classify wines, so producers created wines that didn't fit in. Well, of course, you'd expect nothing less. Creating irresistible chaos out of bureaucratic rule is one of the delights of Italy. Only now is a much improved and flexible legal framework beginning to have an effect. Whether or not the Lords of Misrule reassert their control is another matter.

Italian wine classification

The first classification system, introduced in 1963, didn't do too badly for the first 20 years, the problem is that it has had to last more than 30. Well, 'didn't do too badly' is perhaps being a little kind. From a situation of total mayhem, where almost nothing was as it seemed, a system full of good intentions was put in place. Called DOC (Denominazione di Origine Controllata) it was an Italianization of the French AC system, controlling production zones, grape varieties, yields, alcohol, aging and so on. Criteria were based upon 'local tradition and practice'. If local practices were shoddy and traditional wines dismal, that is what was enshrined. And if laws were blithely disregarded, so long as the prices remained low, no-one seemed to mind too much.

Nevertheless, requests for classification flooded in and there are now over 330 wines, some well known, like Soave, others obscure; some covering just a couple of producers, others embracing vast tracts of land. One has to presume it was an improvement on what had gone before, but clearly if top wines like Brunello di Montalcino and Barolo were being lumped together with industrial Soave and anonymous nonentities of no proven worth, a further classification was needed. And so we got the DOCG, the G standing for 'garantita', or guaranteed. Some 25 areas had the G by 2003, including some of Italy's best, but they are by no means all producing top wines. DOC was also too rigid a system to incorporate the hundreds of new, innovative wines Italians were making from atypical grapes or winemaking methods, and there was simply no place for them other than as Vini da Tavola (VdT, or table wine), theoretically the simple, everyday quaffing wine. Hence the term super-Vini da Tavola, to describe these high-priced, often brilliant anomalies.

Now there is a new law which seems to be having some effect. The basic concept of DOC(G) has been retained but now allows

The rolling hills south of Florence have been famous for their red wine for at least seven centuries. The zone is now known as Chianti Classico DOCG, and continues to produce some of Tuscany's best-known wines.

for a pyramidal structure of increasing quality within areas of decreasing size. This means DOC zones can be broken down into subzones, communes, micro-zones, estates and vineyards, with progressively more stringent controls, and can become DOCG at any stage towards the pyramid's tip. And if producers don't make use of a DOC it can cease to exist. There's also a newer category, Indicazione Geografica Tipica (IGT), toward the base of the pyramid, between DOC and VdT, which is similar to the French vin de pays.

The above paragraph describes what is possible under the new law. What is actually happening is rather different, and entrenched interests are being used to undermine much of the good it could do. But it *is* doing some good, so let's take one step at a time.

Traditions and innovations

Wine is produced in all of the country's 95 provinces, lying in 20 administrative regions, and often there are no clear divisions between one wine district and the next: changes in style are gradual. So although it is convenient to talk about, say, Tuscan reds or Friuli whites, categorizing wine styles needs a more broadbrush approach.

In broad terms, therefore, the north-east relies for quantity on its reds and quality

DOCG/DOC wine areas and main wines

Valle d'Aosta

Piemonte
1 Gattinara
2 Barbera d'Asti, Asti, Moscato d'Asti
3 Roero, Roero Arneis, Barbera d'Alba
4 Barolo, Barbaresco, Barbera d'Alba, Dolcetto d'Alba
5 Brachetto d'Acqui
6 Gavi

Liguria
7 Rossese di Dolceacqua
8 Cinque Terre

Lombardia
9 Oltrepò Pavese
10 Valtellina Superiore
11 Franciacorta
12 Lugana

Veneto
13 Valpolicella Classico, Amarone, Recioto
14 Soave Classico, Recioto
15 Breganze

Trentino-Alto Adige
16 Trentino, Trento
17 Teroldego Rotaliano
18 Alto Adige

Friuli-Venezia Giulia
19 Colli Orientali del Friuli, Collio, Friuli Isonzo

Emilia-Romagna
20 Lambrusco
21 Albana di Romagna, Sangiovese di Romagna

Toscana
22 Carmignano
23 Chianti Rufina
24 Vernaccia di San Gimignano
25 Chianti Classico
26 Bolgheri
27 Brunello di Montalcino
28 Vino Nobile di Montepulciano
29 Morellino di Scansano

Umbria
30 Torgiano Rosso Riserva
31 Orvieto
32 Sagrantino di Montefalco

Marche
33 Verdicchio dei Castelli di Jesi
34 Rosso Conero
35 Rosso Piceno

Abruzzo
36 Montepulciano d'Abruzzo

Lazio
37 Frascati Superiore

Molise

Campania
38 Taurasi

Basilicata
39 Aglianico del Vulture

Puglia
40 Castel del Monte
41 Brindisi
42 Salice Salentino
43 Primitivo di Manduria

Calabria
44 Cirò

Sicilia
45 Marsala
46 Moscato di Pantelleria

Sardegna
47 Carignano del Sulcis
48 Vermentino di Gallura

comes from the whites, mainly single-variety wines from aromatic grapes, often of French or German origin. Even so, there are some exceptional reds made in Valpolicella and Friuli, as well as some remarkable sweet wines from indigenous varieties. The north-west produces delicate sparkling white wines in Asti, but is celebrated above all for firmly structured red wines. Long aging and serious high quality come from the Nebbiolo grape, younger, zippier wines from Dolcetto, Barbera and others, and there's an overdue renewal of interest in Piedmont's native white varieties. The central Po valley is Lambrusco country. The central-west's grape is red

Sangiovese, its major wine Chianti, but it is more likely to reach its highest expression in Brunello di Montalcino – and innovation is a byword here. There is more Sangiovese across to the east too, which gives way to Montepulciano as you head south. Whites are as important, from the Trebbiano, Albana and Verdicchio varieties. Rome is Frascati, and the whole south is in the process of upheaval, changing from heavy whites and stewy reds to some excitingly promising wines made from local varieties, such as Primitivo (California's Zinfandel), Nero d'Avola, Malvasia Nera and Negroamaro; Puglia led the way but Sicily is now neck and neck.

Throughout the country there are also new-style wines, often based on Cabernet Sauvignon and Chardonnay, but also, in some exciting experiments, on Pinot Noir, Syrah, Sauvignon Blanc and Viognier. There's much use of small, new French oak barriques too – sometimes to excess, but that's the same in every country breaking out from a dull unambitious past and revelling in the joys of new oak's perfumed richness. I'm not worried. The oak obsession will pass, and then what we'll see is a diversity of flavours and styles everywhere in Italy, from chilly north to sun-soaked south that will challenge France's European supremacy of style.

SPAIN AND PORTUGAL

AS SEAFARING POWERS, the two nations of the Iberian Peninsula took their wines to the far corners of the globe; the hardiest of these, the great fortified wines of sherry, port and Madeira, survived not only the long journeys but also the test of time – they are as popular today as they have been for more than two centuries. Both countries' fortunes have waxed and waned, but they are now bringing modern versions of their historic wine styles to the world wine party.

Spain

Politically, Spain is divided into 17 autonomous regions, including the Canary and Balearic Islands, with Madrid forming an autonomy of its own, each of which produces wine at all levels. Nearly 50 per cent of the EU's vineyards lie in Spain, but that doesn't mean that Spain makes half the wine: grape yields are only half those of France, although improved viticultural practices have led to a steady increase in yields since the 1990s.

Changes have occurred at such a dizzying pace in the Spanish wine world over the past few years that many clichés no longer hold true. Chances are that the glass of co-operative red you can buy in any local bar will surprise you with a mouthful of clean, fruity wine, as a growing number of those collective wineries are joining the quality bandwagon. Smarter labels are also sprouting up.

One old cliché was that about the paucity of Spain's grape varieties: there was Palomino to make sherry and Tempranillo for all the decent reds – forget about the rest. Now Albariño has emerged as a Viognier-like star in Galicia, soon followed by its neighbour Godello. Rueda's grassy, bitterish Verdejo has made good strides, and Macabeo (Viura) is improving beyond all expectations. Among red varieties, Garnacha and Cariñena have returned to prominence, and new investment indicates that the South-East's ocean of Monastrell vines is in line for improvement. The pungent Graciano's new plantings continue in Rioja and, after Tempranillo, most of what's being planted is – in New World fashion – Cabernet Sauvignon, Merlot and Chardonnay.

Established and rising stars include the fresh, aromatic white wines from Galicia and from Rueda in Castilla y León; the reds of Priorat, Navarra, Rioja and Ribera del Duero; Cava, the DO sparkling wine – usually from Cataluña – and Andalucía's fortified wines: above all, sherry.

Spanish wine classifications

The general quality wine designation, roughly equivalent to the French AC, is Denominación de Origen (DO); there are now more than 50. In 1991 Rioja was the first region elevated to Denominación de Origen Calificada (DOCa), a new super-category for wines prepared to undergo rigorous scrutiny. Country wines fall into two categories: Vino Comarcal and the increasingly important Vino de la Tierra, which equates to the French vin de pays. Vino de Mesa is the basic table wine level, although, as in Italy, there is an increasing number of non-DO 'super-Spanish'. The presence – or lack – of a DO on the label no longer indicates a given quality level. There are some terrible Riojas and some heavenly Vinos de Mesa. Knowing the producer's name has become much more important than remembering old clichés.

Aging regulations have been standardized throughout Spain. Crianza wines must have a minimum of two years' aging before sale; red Reserva at least three years (of which one must be in oak), white Reserva at least two years (of which six months must be in oak); red Gran Reserva at least two years in oak and three in bottle, and white Gran Reserva four years' aging (of which six months must be in oak).

Portugal

For much of the past 200 years Portugal languished on the sidelines, isolated geographically (and at times politically) from the European mainstream. Globe-trotting grape varieties like Cabernet Sauvignon and Chardonnay have made remarkably few inroads into Portuguese vineyards, and grapes with unfamiliar names like the red Touriga Nacional, Baga and Trincadeira or the white Loureiro and Arinto are still Portugal's own superstars in the making.

At the ultra-modern gravity-fed winery of Abadía Retuerta in Castilla y León, the wine is treated more gently than in most wineries because rather than pumping, the barrels are set up to allow gravity to do the work.

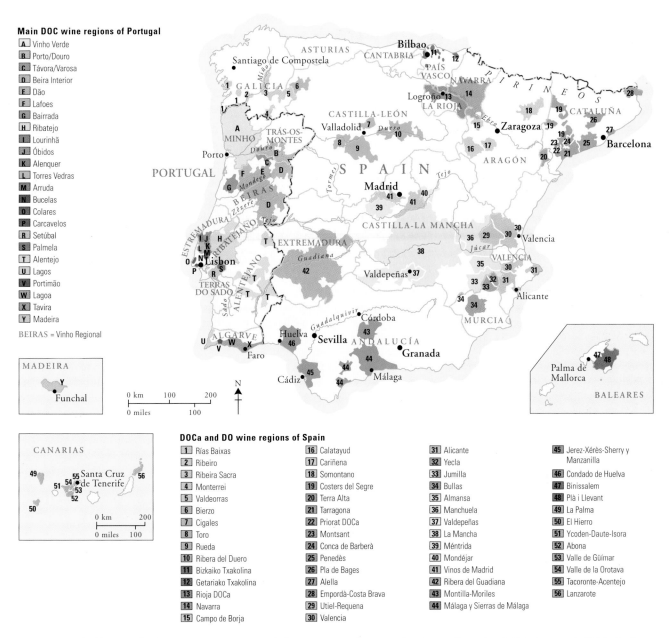

Main DOC wine regions of Portugal

- **A** Vinho Verde
- **B** Porto/Douro
- **C** Távora/Varosa
- **D** Beira Interior
- **E** Dão
- **F** Lafões
- **G** Bairrada
- **H** Ribatejo
- **I** Lourinhã
- **J** Óbidos
- **K** Alenquer
- **L** Torres Vedras
- **M** Arruda
- **N** Bucelas
- **O** Colares
- **P** Carcavelos
- **R** Setúbal
- **S** Palmela
- **T** Alentejo
- **U** Lagos
- **V** Portimão
- **W** Lagoa
- **X** Tavira
- **Y** Madeira

BEIRAS = Vinho Regional

DOCa and DO wine regions of Spain

1 Rías Baixas	**16** Calatayud	**31** Alicante	**45** Jerez-Xérès-Sherry y Manzanilla
2 Ribeiro	**17** Cariñena	**32** Yecla	**46** Condado de Huelva
3 Ribeira Sacra	**18** Somontano	**33** Jumilla	**47** Binissalem
4 Monterrei	**19** Costers del Segre	**34** Bullas	**48** Plà i Llevant
5 Valdeorras	**20** Terra Alta	**35** Almansa	**49** La Palma
6 Bierzo	**21** Tarragona	**36** Manchuela	**50** El Hierro
7 Cigales	**22** Priorat DOCa	**37** Valdepeñas	**51** Ycoden-Daute-Isora
8 Toro	**23** Montsant	**38** La Mancha	**52** Abona
9 Rueda	**24** Conca de Barberà	**39** Méntrida	**53** Valle de Güímar
10 Ribera del Duero	**25** Penedès	**40** Mondéjar	**54** Valle de la Orotava
11 Bizkaiko Txakolina	**26** Pla de Bages	**41** Vinos de Madrid	**55** Tacoronte-Acentejo
12 Getariako Txakolina	**27** Alella	**42** Ribera del Guadiana	**56** Lanzarote
13 Rioja DOCa	**28** Empordà-Costa Brava	**43** Montilla-Moriles	
14 Navarra	**29** Utiel-Requena	**44** Málaga y Sierras de Málaga	
15 Campo de Borja	**30** Valencia		

Decades of self-imposed isolation came to an end in 1986 when Portugal joined the European Union. This opened the floodgates for investment in the wine industry and new stainless steel wineries sprung up all over the country. With a number of go-ahead wine-makers (including a handful of Australians), Portugal is now well placed to take advantage of its remarkable viticultural heritage.

Although whites can be good, often dry but slightly musky, it is the reds that are pro-pelling Portugal into centre stage, fabulously fruity and perfumed, low on tannin and quite unlike any others in the world.

Portugal's wines tend to reflect a varied climate and topography. The Atlantic exerts a strong influence over the coastal wine regions and its moderating effects diminish sharply as you travel inland. As a result, crisp, crackling dry whites like Vinho Verde can be produced in close proximity to hefty reds from the Douro and rich, fortified port.

Portuguese wine classifications

There are four tiers of wine regions. The first tier, Denominação de Origem Controlada (DOC), includes all the established regions in the north of the country like Vinho Verde, Dão, Bairrada as well as the fortified wines port, Madeira and Setúbal. There are 24 in all. The second tier of small, new regions goes under the long heading of Indicação de Proveniencia Regulamentada (IPR). In theo-ry all are candidates for promotion to DOC – many have already made the leap, leaving just five languishing at IPR. The third and much more significant tier of wine regions, particularly in the south of the country, is designated Vinho Regional. Rather like the French vins de pays, these cover larger areas and the legislation permits greater flexibility in terms of grape varieties and aging require-ments. There are eight regions and a few sub-regions: Alentejano, Ribatejano, Terras do Sado and Estremadura are the names most commonly seen on labels. Wines that fall outside these three levels are classified as Vinho de Mesa (table wine).

UNITED STATES AND CANADA

FOR ALL PRACTICAL PURPOSES, American wine is California wine. But wine is everything except practical, and so growers in a dozen other states love to claim that what they grow matters just as much as anything from California, saying it tastes as good or better. California is, and will remain, the superstar, not only because of its remarkable range of soils and climates, but because nearly all of the state is a benign environment for vines. Far from California's sunny disposition, Canada has an icy image, but two areas have thawed out sufficiently to have the makings of a fine wine industry.

United States

Proponents of wine in the USA like to point out that 48 of the 50 American states grow grapes and produce wine. Well, maybe they do: the US government publishes production figures for 44 of them. However, most states grow only native varieties, or minuscule patches of imported types. In any case, they make so little wine that it never appears commercially outside the local area.

The hard fact is that California vineyards yield 95 per cent of all the grapes used for wine in the United States. The other players of any size are Washington and New York, with around 2 per cent each – which doesn't leave much for the rest.

California will continue to provide most of the wine America makes and drinks for the foreseeable future because it has both a favourable climate and vast expanses of suitable land. And California alone produces the full range of wine types familiar to drinkers of European wines. However, states other than California have the potential to bring newcomers into the fold with wines that can appeal to local pride, as has happened in Oregon, Washington and New York State. On a smaller scale, Texas and Virginia have recently demonstrated that people who never took any interest in wines from far away can be enticed to try something from just up the road.

The ironic aspect to this is that eastern states, especially New York, once prospered making wine from native grape varieties such as Concord, Isabella or Niagara. However, their flavours are so peculiar and pungent that wine drinkers familiar with European wines turn up their noses. In the south-eastern states, another native vine, the Scuppernong, yields similarly intense and peculiar flavours.

Wines from native grapes came into being after early Americans, Thomas Jefferson among them, failed in their attempts to grow French wine varieties. Native wines began to fall on hard times as soon as a modern generation of growers succeeded with European varieties.

The variables in growing conditions are staggering to contemplate. Washington State has most of its vineyards in what meteorologists call a continental climate. That translates into reliably hot, dry summers, and winters that can be – have been – bitterly cold enough to freeze hundreds of acres of vine roots to their tips. In Virginia, the problem is not freezing winters but muggy summers, favouring every sort of mould and mildew that ever attacked a leaf. New York State has some of each sort of climate.

It is startling, then, that so many states have found some sort of footing so swiftly.

USA and Canada wine regions
- US AVA and other wine areas
- Canada VQA and other wine areas

0 km   500   1000
0 miles   500

While California has grown from 150 wineries in 1960 to 240 in 1970, and today has more than 800, Oregon and Washington between them have gone from three wineries in 1970 to over 400 today. Virginia has progressed from zero to nearly 80 since 1980, and Texas is not too far off that pace.

The efforts of growers and winemakers in all of these regions have been bedevilled by a marketplace that until the 1990s wanted just two types of wine, Chardonnay as a white and Cabernet Sauvignon as a red. A new wine-loving public seems to have settled on those two varietal types as virtually synonymous with white and red. Positive reports from the medical communities about the potential beneficial aspects of wine in general and red wines in particular have created a strong interest in Merlot and more recently in Pinot Noir and Zinfandel.

Growers everywhere in the United States are learning what to grow and how to grow it well enough to make wines that compare favourably with examples from long-established regions – not just California, but France, Germany and Italy too. Unlike Europe, America has no stubborn peasant class clinging to the ways of its fathers and grandfathers. Because Prohibition removed a whole generation from vineyard and cellar, nearly all of the country's grape-growers and winemakers are university-trained.

Vintages

Making judgments about vintages in the United States is a tricky business. In California, climate conditions change so swiftly in the coastal counties that generalizations about vintages are hazardous. The division between North and Central Coast regions is very sharp indeed in some years. This much said, even the worst of years in California yield more adequate to above-average wine than poor stuff.

In most other states, with the possible exception of Oregon and Washington, weather conditions are too variable, the vineyards too far apart and their track records too short to permit even the haziest of guesses. Oregon does face some summers so cool and harvests so rainy that little or nothing ripens fully, while other sunnier years match or surpass Burgundian conditions.

US wine classifications

During the 1970s the authorities began establishing a system of appellations of origin, using the term AVA, for American

Vineyards near Calistoga, in the northern Napa Valley. This valley was the starting point for the modern California wine industry, and is now some of the most valuable vineyard land in the world.

Viticultural Area. The system remains in its infancy, limited above all by the lack of history within many of the regions it defines.

Where France and Italy, in particular, have appellation systems that specify grape varieties, density of plantings and crop levels, maximum and minimum limits of alcohol, and so on, the American version does none of these things. Still less does it attempt to distinguish shades of quality within a region. This reticence is, for the time being, wise. There remains a great deal of sorting to do before restrictions will pay greater dividends than the current liberty.

For now, all the AVA guarantees is that a minimum of 85 per cent of the wine in the bottle comes from grapes grown in the region named on the label. The use of individual vineyard names on wines is an extension of the AVA idea. Regulations require that 95 per cent of any wine using a vineyard name must be from grapes grown in that vineyard, and from within a recognized AVA.

Canada

Perhaps surprisingly, Canada has been producing wine since the early 19th century. Canadian wine has transformed itself over the past quarter century thanks to much improved vineyard practices, more suitable clones and improved technology inside the

winery. Instead of native North American grapes such as Concord, the country's most important grape varieties now hail from the *Vitis vinifera* family (which account for virtually all new plantings), the balance comprising hardy hybrids. While outstanding Icewine made from Riesling, Vidal, Gewurztraminer, Ehrenfelser, Chardonnay and even Cabernet Franc has garnered international attention, some of the most exciting new wines are dry table wines.

The bulk of the country's vineyards are located in southern Ontario and British Columbia's southern interior, with an increasing number of sites on the coast, on Vancouver Island and in Nova Scotia and Quebec. In Ontario's Niagara Peninsula, Pelee Island and Lake Erie North Shore, Chardonnay, Riesling, Vidal, Pinot Noir, both Cabernets and Merlot lead the pack. In British Columbia's Okanagan Valley and on Vancouver Island best bets include Chardonnay, Pinot Blanc, Pinot Gris and Bordeaux-style blends. New plantings of Syrah, Sauvignon Blanc and Viognier have also shown considerable promise.

Vintners Quality Alliance (VQA) is Canada's appellation and quality guarantee system. Wines are tested by chemical analysis and assessed by a tasting panel and if successful awarded a VQA seal.

SOUTH AMERICA

TROPICAL CLIMATES PRECLUDE much of South America from vine-growing, though planting at cooler, higher altitudes can overcome the problem of excess humidity. The demand for wine for domestic consumption, and for distillation into brandy, means that far more wine is made than is ever seen in world markets, but Argentina and Chile have produced wines of exceptional value for some time, and wines of international standing are now emerging from both countries.

Argentina

Up until the mid-1990s Argentine wine was only drunk in Argentina. This, despite the fact that Argentina is the world's fifth-largest wine producer (after Italy, France, Spain and the United States). The reason is that the Argentinians have traditionally consumed large quantities of wine. When domestic consumption started to drop, under attack from soft drinks and beer, Argentina began to look for export markets. It was at this stage that it discovered what Chile had discovered in the late 1970s, that the world has moved on from old-style oxidized wines. Argentina had a simple choice, continue losing market share or invest heavily to bring standards up to international levels. It opted for the latter in a big way, with much enthusiastic international participation.

Argentina is blessed with conditions that *Vitis vinifera* loves. Almost all of the vineyards are planted well inland where there is next to no ambient humidity, reducing the incidence of fungal diseases to a minimum. Altitudes of up to 2000m (6500ft) above sea level provide vast differences between day–night temperatures, and sunshine, plenty of it, helps. The only downside is precipitation: there is almost none, and what there is tends to come down either in sheets of hailstones (anathema to grapes) or in flash floods that can wipe away entire vineyards. Fortunately, the Incas solved the problem of lack of rainfall a thousand years ago by devising an incredibly intricate irrigation system using snow-melt from the Andes, including a legal framework for equitably dividing water rights, that subsequent generations have gratefully inherited.

The expanse of vineyards planted in Argentina is mind-boggling. From the beautiful Cafayate Valley high up in Salta in the north, down to the sunken and protected Río Negro Valley in Patagonia to the south, there is a huge surface area dedicated to vines. With three vast growing regions (further subdivided into an array of zones including two DOs), the province of Mendoza is the powerhouse behind Argentine winemaking: 75 per cent of all Argentine wines hail from Mendoza. San Juan, to the north of Mendoza, is another huge producing area. Further north still there is La Rioja – the Argentine province, not to be confused with La Rioja in Spain!

Argentine exports are now beginning to reflect the country's enormous production potential and are powering ahead despite economic disarray in the wake of the 2002 currency crisis. The UK, continental Europe, Scandinavia and Japan are importing ever greater quantities. Although Cabernet Sauvignon and Chardonnay are important, with excellent examples of both, Argentina is exciting because of less well-known varieties. Malbec makes sumptuous, perfumed purple-hearted reds. Tempranillo, Barbera and Syrah are good to excellent, and Bonarda is a gorgeous juicy red to eclipse Beaujolais. Torrontés is Argentina's indigenous white and has an explosive rose and nutmeg scent and delightful lime acidity. The modern era virtually starts with the 1996 vintage, and every vintage since then, even the poor 1998, has seen a quantum leap in quality.

Brazil

With the ninth-largest economy in the world, Brazil is certainly a place to sell wine. The bravest have decided to make it there as well. This is no easy task as grapes are natural prey to all kinds of rot in Brazil's climate, even down south, on the Uruguayan border, where the wine region is based. This hasn't stopped market leaders such as Moët et Chandon and Rémy-Martin, nor indeed enterprising winemakers such as Aurora, in Bento Gonçalves, from taking up the challenge. At 400m (1300ft) above sea level, Rio Grande do Sul is undoubtedly the best region you could hope to find in Brazil, with its verdant undulating hills. But don't expect miracles – it's pretty humid and unsuitable for grapes, even here, and if it wasn't for the efforts of the occasional flying winemaker and the financial muscle of the European giants, little of interest would appear.

Chile

It's unbelievable how fast Chile has leapt to the fore, in a few short years going from nervous debutante on the world stage to many modern

The Andes form a dramatic backdrop to the exciting new wine region of Tupungato, in Mendoza province, Argentina. The cool, high-altitude vineyards allow the grapes to ripen slowly, concentrating the flavours.

N

| 0 km | 500 | 1000 |
| 0 miles | | 500 |

Wine regions
- Venezuela
- Colombia
- Ecuador
- Peru
- Bolivia
- Brazil
- Uruguay
- Argentina
- Chile

where else in the world needs to graft the vine onto phylloxera-resistant rootstock.) Ally this to very fertile soils along a north-south line running more than 1000km (600 miles), regular sunshine because the Andes provide a rain shadow, but abundant Andean snow-melt to make up for the lack of rain, and Chile's description as a viticultural paradise is well deserved.

The real heartland for high-quality grapes is Aconcagua, just north of Santiago, spreading west through the Casablanca Valley. Casablanca makes Chile's greatest whites – primarily from Chardonnay and Sauvignon – as well as a few delicious reds. However, the real red core lies south of Santiago, through what is called the Valle Central or Central Valley, from Maipo in the north down through Curicó and Talca and on to the Bío-Bío river 400km (250 miles) south of Santiago. Red grapes dominate in the north and whites become more important as you head south. Every year sees new vineyards planted and further investment from overseas producers, with French and Californian interest the most intense. Chile already makes superb wine. If she stays confident in her own strengths and styles, Chile will be the wine drinkers' darling for a long time yet.

Peru

Peru has a long tradition of winemaking (albeit altar wine), dating back to the time when Spain was the colonial master. Modern winemaking is based principally in the Ica Valley, south of Lima. Despite warm days and cool nights, varietal character is usually dull. However, Tacama make a reasonable range, including Malbec for red wines and Chenin Blanc for whites.

Uruguay

Uruguay has more rainfall than its neighbour Argentina and temperatures are, in the main vineyard areas, cooler so viticulturalists have to work hard to prevent rot and disease attacking the grapes. Different training systems, for example, aid ripening and restrict disease. Tannat, a South-West French variety not normally known for its suppleness, has adapted remarkably well here, giving red wines with fruit and character. Vineyards are spread throughout Uruguay, with the majority around Montevideo. But the vineyards are mostly here because they are close to the capital city, and are usually on heavy clay soils. A second phase in Uruguay would see more suitable sites being sought – they do exist – further from Montevideo. Already Castel Pujol have headed north towards Brazil and Calvinor and Stagnari employ hot inland vineyards to good effect.

wine drinkers' darling producer. And the reason is fruit. Great big eye-boggling, palate-flooding dollops of rich ripe fruit. And that's the red wines I'm talking about. Just as Australia in the 1980s had taken the world by storm, offering jaundiced wine drinkers the joys of sunshine in bottle, so Chile in the 1990s adopted the same flavour-packed course. What Chile must beware of now is listening to advisers who try to pull her toward a leaner, more tannic red wine style under the pretence that it is more French, and therefore superior. Chile must retain her pride in the sumptuous fruit flavour of her reds and develop her own view of what is superior – and leanness of structure splashed with too much sweet oak is not the way forward.

Chile's reputation was initially built on Cabernet Sauvignon, although Merlot has become at least as important. Pinot Noir is very promising, and the rare Bordeaux grape Carmenère is rapidly assuming considerable importance because virtually all the world's surviving plantings of Carmenère are in Chile. There's a reason for that. After Europe was ravaged by the phylloxera aphid in the second half of the nineteenth century, many grapes like Carmenère were not replanted. But before phylloxera arrived in Bordeaux, cuttings of all the varieties had been shipped to Chile and planted. And phylloxera has never invaded Chile. Desert to the north, the Andes to the east and the Pacific Ocean to the west form barriers phylloxera has not overcome.

Consequently, Chile's vines grow on their own roots. (South Australia is the only other important area to be phylloxera-free; every-

AUSTRALIA

FAR TOO MANY OF US think of Australian wine as a single entity – in fact it's minutely varied. Climate is the major determinant of style, and while much of the land is desert, there are many distinctions to be made between the vineyards that extend for hundreds of miles around the coast. Early settlers found as many areas suitable for making fine wine as there are in most European countries: while Western Australia's Swan Valley was as hot as any Mediterranean vineyard, Victoria's Yarra Valley hilltops were as cool as France's chilly Champagne region, South Australia's Barossa Valley was like the Rhône Valley, yet Coonawarra, further south, was more like Bordeaux. And subtropical Hunter Valley near Sydney wasn't like anywhere really – but they planted grapes anyway. And from chaotic beginnings, by the 21st century, Australia had fashioned herself into being one of the world's most organized and imaginative wine nations.

By 1850 commercial winemaking was under way in Australia and significant markets were established in the United Kingdom. Victoria led the way before being supplanted by South Australia, and the wines had much success in international exhibitions. Australians turned away from wine in the first half of the 20th century but exports still boomed: between 1928 and 1938 inclusive, Australia exported more wine (mostly fortified, sent in barrels) to the United Kingdom than did France. For all that, the industry of today only began to take shape in the mid-1950s, when the first temperature-controlled, stainless steel fermenters were introduced. Following the Californian pattern, Cabernet Sauvignon began to rise from relative obscurity in the late 1960s, Chardonnay in the early 1980s. Now both are staples of dining tables across the globe, due to two main factors: the user-friendly style of wines and their cost-competitiveness resulting from lower land costs and viticultural efficiencies through mechanization.

What is termed the user-friendly nature of the wines reflects the Australian philosophy of retaining as much as possible of the flavour of the grape in the wine, with structural complexity of secondary importance.

Of course, broad generalizations are precisely that. Australia is a vast continent, with an immense array of climate and terroir. The grape harvest begins in late January in the hot Swan Valley (near Perth, Western Australia) and Hunter Valley (on the other side of the country, in New South Wales), and does not finish until May or even June in the coolest regions such as Tasmania. Thus Chardonnay may be voluptuously peachy/buttery or finely drawn, with intense minerally/citrus flavours; Cabernet Sauvignon may be thick with dark chocolate or as tinged with green leaf as many a respected Bordeaux – or even as pebbly as a Cabernet Franc from Chinon.

The best of Australia's original vine varieties are Semillon, Riesling and Shiraz. The

Fertile soils, temperate climate and abundant rain in winter and spring ensure high yields in the King Valley, North East Victoria, home to Avalon Vineyard.

two white wines are made in a uniquely Australian style, and good examples of both develop magnificently in bottle over 20 years or so. Semillon is sometimes aged in oak these days, but even if made without, it slowly develops a nutty toastiness which has led me, for one, to swear I can taste oak when none is present. Riesling is made crisp and dry, with the lime and passionfruit of youth slowly giving way to the classic whiff-of-petrol and lightly buttered toast aromas of age. Shiraz, the Rhône Valley's Syrah, works hard in Australia, making red wines in a variety of styles, culminating in the legendary, thrillingly rich Penfolds Grange from South Australia. The arrival of Pinot Noir and Chardonnay has sig-

nalled an immense improvement in the style and quality of sparkling wines, which were previously made from some very strange and obscure varieties. There are also now a number of Pinot Noir red wines of top quality.

Finally, there are those indigenous specialities, the luscious fortified wines of North-East Victoria, the so-called Tokay and Muscat. These magnificent wines even overshadow the sherry-styles (from fino to oloroso), and tawny and vintage port-styles, the best to be found outside Spain and Portugal.

With a fully geared up and cost-efficient export industry and all these great wines being produced to fill every niche in the market, it comes as no surprise to learn that, once more,

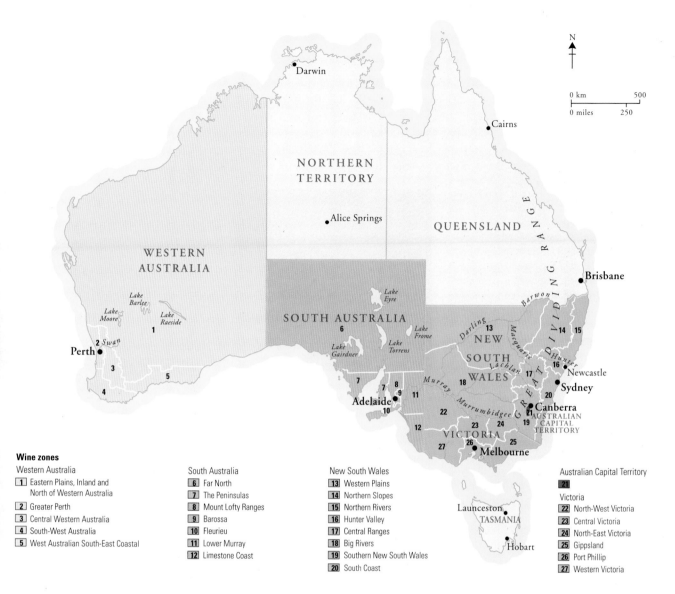

Wine zones

Western Australia
1 Eastern Plains, Inland and North of Western Australia
2 Greater Perth
3 Central Western Australia
4 South-West Australia
5 West Australian South-East Coastal

South Australia
6 Far North
7 The Peninsulas
8 Mount Lofty Ranges
9 Barossa
10 Fleurieu
11 Lower Murray
12 Limestone Coast

New South Wales
13 Western Plains
14 Northern Slopes
15 Northern Rivers
16 Hunter Valley
17 Central Ranges
18 Big Rivers
19 Southern New South Wales
20 South Coast

Australian Capital Territory
21

Victoria
22 North-West Victoria
23 Central Victoria
24 North-East Victoria
25 Gippsland
26 Port Phillip
27 Western Victoria

Australia is overtaking France as the United Kingdom's wine producer of choice. In 2002 Britain imported over 200 million litres of Aussie grog, followed by the USA at 95 million, and growing fast. These two countries are by far and way Australia's most important export markets.

Australian wine classifications

In October 1994 Australia put in place the last leg of a legislative framework covering all aspects of wine labelling; most of that framework has been extant since 1963. The 1994 legislation saw the establishment of a committee whose task it was (and is) to oversee the creation of a series of Geographic Indications (GIs) covering the whole of Australia. The first task was to divide each of the states into zones, a task that was expected to be quick

(there was no legislative requirement for any identifiable or unifying viticultural or geographical nexus for a zone) but which in fact took almost two years. Each of the main wine-producing states is divided into large chunks: Western Australia has five zones, South Australia seven, Victoria six and New South Wales eight. It is inherently improbable that zone names will make much of an impact on wine labels, with one exception: the Super Zone of South-East Australia, which effectively takes in all of the wine-producing areas of Queensland, New South Wales, Victoria, Tasmania and South Australia.

Of far greater importance are the 60-plus regions into which those zones are being divided, some of whose names are already familiar. Throughout this book you will find

the names of all but a handful of those regions, some of which are still at the interim stage with final boundaries and names to be agreed upon. One of the best known of all regions, Coonawarra in South Australia, has been the subject of a long and bitter contest over the location of the boundary involving some of Australia's most respected wine luminaries in unseemly wrangling and bickering. Other interim regions are also suffering the bluster and bullying that come when some are included and some are excluded, but in most areas the traditional Aussie belief that everyone has a right to have a go has prevailed. The market will find out the impostors, they say, and so it will. There is also provision within the legislation for subregions.

Quality, of course, is not defined by lines on maps – the wines have to *taste* special.

NEW ZEALAND

THE WINES OF NEW ZEALAND and Australia are so different that they tend to complement rather than compete with each other. Australia could never produce a wine that would come close to the pungent and distinctive Marlborough Sauvignon Blanc style, just as it would be futile for New Zealand winemakers to try to produce a wine to challenge a booming Barossa Valley Shiraz. Australia struggles with Pinot Noir; New Zealand makes it superbly. It's very much a matter of climate. New Zealand boasts of being a clean, green land: coolish climate, regular sunshine and quite a lot of rain. Australia, on the other hand, with the exception of some vineyard areas on the coast, is arid and parched by the sun.

As you look across the Tasman Sea from Australia to New Zealand, it is as if one is peering through the wrong end of a telescope at a film in fast forward motion. The industry is very much smaller, but the pace of change in New Zealand since 1984 has been frenetic, due in part to government dismantling of protective tariffs, and in part to the same invigorating winds of change as are blowing across Australia and the rest of the New World.

New Zealand is an important market for Australian wine and yet the Australians, somewhat chauvinistically, took quite a while to accept that New Zealand made anything worth drinking. A few gold medals and trophies for Kiwi whites in major Australian Wine Shows helped change their minds. But they like them now even if the UK is still the top market, and the USA is just catching on. Since 1993 exports to Australia have increased ten-fold and Australia is New Zealand's third-largest overseas market.

Wine styles

The driving forces are bracingly tangy and crystal-pure Sauvignon Blanc, fine melon-fruited Chardonnay, fragrant Riesling, and red berry Merlot from Marlborough; fleshy, fine-grained Cabernet Sauvignon and Merlot, melon and peach Chardonnay from Hawke's Bay; and even more melony and peachier Chardonnay from Gisborne just up the coast.

But, as in Australia, the viticultural map is constantly changing and expanding. Martinborough (also called Wairarapa) at the southern end of the North Island is a small region – even by New Zealand standards – with unlimited quality potential for the 'big five' grape varieties: Chardonnay, Sauvignon Blanc, Cabernet Sauvignon, Merlot, but particularly for Pinot Noir. Nelson, Waipara and especially Central Otago, source of some superb Pinot Noirs, on the South Island are flourishing. After a long period of declining vineyard acreage even Auckland is on the ascent as adventurous winemakers discover pockets of land capable of making top wine;

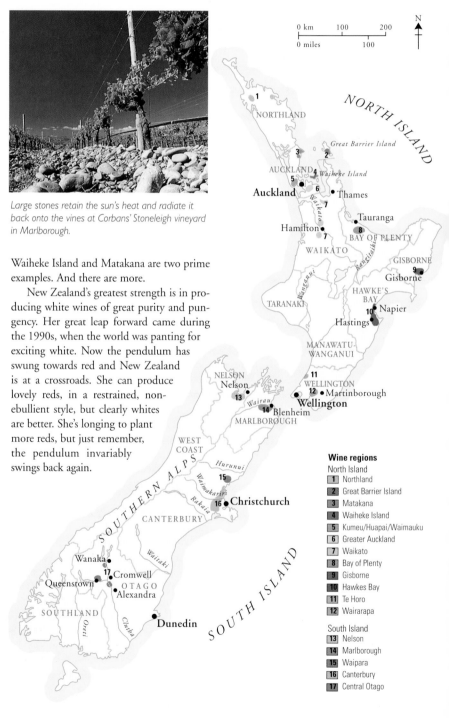

Large stones retain the sun's heat and radiate it back onto the vines at Corbans' Stoneleigh vineyard in Marlborough.

Waiheke Island and Matakana are two prime examples. And there are more.

New Zealand's greatest strength is in producing white wines of great purity and pungency. Her great leap forward came during the 1990s, when the world was panting for exciting white. Now the pendulum has swung towards red and New Zealand is at a crossroads. She can produce lovely reds, in a restrained, non-ebullient style, but clearly whites are better. She's longing to plant more reds, but just remember, the pendulum invariably swings back again.

Wine regions

North Island
1 Northland
2 Great Barrier Island
3 Matakana
4 Waiheke Island
5 Kumeu/Huapai/Waimauku
6 Greater Auckland
7 Waikato
8 Bay of Plenty
9 Gisborne
10 Hawkes Bay
11 Te Horo
12 Wairarapa

South Island
13 Nelson
14 Marlborough
15 Waipara
16 Canterbury
17 Central Otago

SOUTH AFRICA

SOUTH AFRICA IS PROBABLY the only wine industry in the world that can accurately pinpoint its birthday: 2 February 1659, a date remembered thanks to Jan van Riebeek's diary, in which he noted the first pressing of wine from Cape grapes. Carefully recorded subsequent land grants mean there's an on-going celebration of tercentenaries in the Cape winelands. The industry has gone through many ups and downs in the ensuing years. It is now taking off internationally after emerging from the economic sanctions imposed during the Apartheid era. New cool-climate areas are being developed and a replanting programme is well advanced; justifiable self-confidence is taking the place of complacency.

Producers with international experience, mainly the small independents, have been able to adapt to competing on the world stage. However, around 80 per cent of South Africa's wine is still made by the co-operatives and wholesalers, who have not been accustomed to the free market. Although much of their wine shows a modern touch, often with input from UK buyers or flying winemakers, further improvement has not kept pace with price increases. Some have converted to public companies (including KWV), to encourage their shareholders (grape farmers) to focus on quality. It may, in time, but entrenched attitudes are proving slow to change.

A huge drive to increase planting of premium varieties and introduce new ones has seen the international 'big five' – Cabernet Sauvignon, Merlot, Shiraz, Chardonnay and Sauvignon Blanc – leap from 10 per cent (in 1990) to 36 per cent, largely at the expense of Chenin Blanc, of South Africa's nearly 100,000ha (247,000 acres) of vineyards. There is a swing from white varieties to red and Shiraz has seen the most dramatic growth in recent years. Pinotage, making one of the Cape's most individual red wine styles, is on the increase, too.

There is no shortage of new, quality-oriented wineries starting up and the number of internationally recognized wines is steadily increasing, although it is tough on the small independent guys who seem to be having to create a positive image for South African wines all by themselves. The lack of a large-scale industry leader certainly doesn't help progress.

Wine regions

The majority of the vineyards are concentrated in the Western Cape, stretching 250km (150 miles) north and more like 400km (250 miles) east, with the main Stellenbosch and Paarl regions at the centre. In many ways, this spread offers an ideal climate for grape-growing, although perfectionists would have it a chillier 200km (125 miles) further south, especially the Pinot Noir fanatics. Nevertheless, new quality sites are being earmarked for future development; in particular, the cooler spots around Malmesbury up the west coast and near Hermanus on the south coast.

More international exposure, dedication to quality and, perhaps most important of all, a belief in their own ability, will see South African winemakers realize the country's true potential for great wine in the future, but the future is by no means a done deal yet.

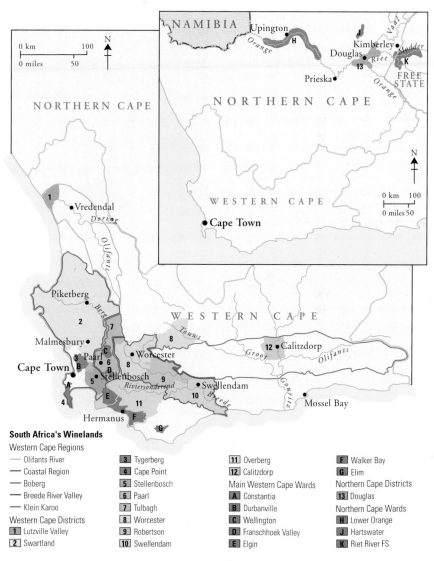

South Africa's Winelands

Western Cape Regions
- Olifants River
- Coastal Region
- Boberg
- Breede River Valley
- Klein Karoo

Western Cape Districts
1 Lutzville Valley
2 Swartland
3 Tygerberg
4 Cape Point
5 Stellenbosch
6 Paarl
7 Tulbagh
8 Worcester
9 Robertson
10 Swellendam
11 Overberg
12 Calitzdorp

Main Western Cape Wards
A Constantia
B Durbanville
C Wellington
D Franschhoek Valley
E Elgin

F Walker Bay
G Elim

Northern Cape Districts
13 Douglas

Northern Cape Wards
H Lower Orange
J Hartswater
K Riet River FS

South African wine classification

The Wine of Origin (WO) laws certify a wine's area of origin, grape variety and vintage. Origin is divided into regions, subdivided into districts and wards. As in other New World winemaking countries, there is a strong emphasis on varietal labelling: the wine must contain 75 per cent of the named variety, or 85 per cent for exported wines.

OTHER WINE REGIONS

WHEREVER GRAPES CAN BE GROWN, however inhospitable the climate, there will be a winemaker ready to rise to the challenge of producing something drinkable, pleasant – and preferably saleable. This is not just a modern phenomenon; there have always been people ready to face economic constraints, political upheaval, even war, to make wine. All they needed was someone to drink the wine – and today there are more wine drinkers than ever, eager to give anything a try.

Algeria

Sooner or later someone is going to realize the potential in Algeria's vineyards where 80 per cent of the vines are over 40 years old. If this was South Africa or Australia they'd be falling over themselves to cosset and care for the vines and proudly parade the dense exciting wines their fruit would give. But that may be asking too much in a country where Islamic influence and secular government continue to tread a knife-edge. No-one has really taken much notice of the vineyards and wineries since the French left in the 1960s. But Algeria used to be a massive player in the wine world: in 1938 it had 400,000ha (988,387 acres) of vines and during the 1950s between half and two-thirds of all international wine trade was in North African wines, with Algeria the leader! By 1990 vineyards had fallen to 102,000ha (252,040 acres) but there has been a revival and now Algeria boasts 150,000ha (370,645 acres) – by no means all of these grapes destined for wines. Most of the wine production is centred round Oran in western Algeria and there are seven Appellation d'Origine Garantie regions, with Coteaux du Mascara probably being the best of a dull bunch. Sixty per cent of the wine is red, 30 per cent white and 10 per cent rosé. Cinsaut is the main red grape, followed by Grenache, Carignan and Morrastel, all equally suited to hot climates. Farranah and Tizourine are the main white grapes.

Bulgaria

The central planners of the old Eastern bloc countries decided that Bulgaria had the potential to supply its wine needs. They were absolutely right. Vast acreages of principally red varietals were planted in easily mechanizable flatlands and well-equipped wineries were setup. In the early to mid-1980s, American investment and expertise gave the Bulgarian wine industry a new focus: Cabernet Sauvignon. This grape, in Bulgaria's warm climate, produced reliably rich, blackcurranty red wines at bargain prices.

As the economic outlook deteriorated, domestic and regional demand fell. The

Harvesting grapes at Suhindol, one of northern Bulgaria's top wine regions.

collapse of the Soviet bloc in 1989 and the muddle surrounding privatization led to a morass of uncertainty, and in the early 1990s all the reliable fruit-led pleasure of Bulgarian reds seemed to disappear.

It has taken far longer than expected for Bulgaria to recover her quality credentials and even today, the simple, mouthfilling flavours of before are difficult to find. However, investment is increasing rapidly, a new realism is persuading producers to start improvements in their long-neglected vineyards and some flying winemakers are stopping by fairly frequently. Bulgaria produces some good white wines, for example from Chardonnay and Sauvignon Blanc or the local Dimiat and Misket, but nearly all the best wines are red, either from Cabernet and Merlot, or from the local varieties of Mavrud, Gamza and Melnik.

The quality categories for Bulgarian wine are Country wines, Declared Geographical Origin wines and Controliran wines, from specific grape varieties in certain DGOs, but most wines are labelled by varietal. Wineries are named after the region in which they are located. Suhindol, Rousse, Shumen, Sliven, Svischtov and Iambol all have access to good-quality vineyards.

China

China's vineyards tend to be full of table varieties like Cock's Heart and Dragon's Eye, so anybody contemplating making Western-style wine there has a lot of planting to do. Humid conditions lead to vine disease, but most vines are on their own roots as phylloxera is almost non-existent. The first joint venture, begun in 1980, involved Rémy-Martin, and Pernod-Ricard and Torres are now in business here, too. The Huadong winery produces wines that are quite stylish.

Croatia

Croatia has suffered badly in the export market since the Balkan conflict. A number of her gutsy reds used to be sent abroad, but few are now seen. This is a pity because the coastal reds, in particular, had some foursquare character and great potential for improvement. The majority of Croatian wine is white and from inland vineyards but the 500-km (310-mile) coastal region grows Cabernet and Merlot as well as local varieties like Plavac Mali, a relative of Zinfandel. If you see wine names like Faros, Postup and Peljesac, try them.

Cyprus

This island's wine industry was for years in desperate need of modernization, and at last it seems to be happening. Large companies have been forced to take quality more seriously and early efforts with international varieties like Cabernet Sauvignon and Sémillon are impressive. There is a government scheme to uproot the worst, hottest, coastal vineyards, and the unfriendly, tannic, fruitless red Mavron grape may no longer be planted. On the minus side grapes still sit in the hot sun for hours before being processed in old wineries; the wines that emerge are generally the opposite of the fresh, fruity ones that the export market craves.

However, regional wineries are being constructed near or in the vineyards and this is helping. After the collapse of the market for sherry-style wines, the best-known export is the dessert wine Commandaria, which is seldom, alas, exciting nowadays.

England's largest vineyard, Denbies, is planted on the rolling North Downs of Surrey. With modern winemaking and attention to detail, the estate is looking to conquer export markets.

The Czech Republic

The 'velvet divorce' left this part of the former Czechoslovakia with two regions, Bohemia and Moravia, both of which produce wine. Most of the wines, since this is a distinctly chilly climate, are white, from such varieties as Pinot Blanc, Müller-Thurgau, Silvaner, Riesling, Laski Rizling, Traminer, Sauvignon Blanc and the native Irsay Oliver, but the reds, when they are good, can be very attractive, made from Frankovka (alias Germany's Limberger), St-Laurent and Pinot Noir. The quality under Communism was pretty dire, but Western investment is producing pockets of excellence. The march of privatization means that new wines from new companies are beginning to appear abroad.

England

Anyone who hasn't tasted English wine for a few years is way out of touch. There are now 1000ha (2470 acres) of vines and 115 wineries, and there is an English trademark taste developing: a delicate, hedgerow floweriness and fruit. This often comes from vine crossings that were developed in Germany and seldom succeeded in producing high-quality there: grapes like Müller-Thurgau (England's most widely planted variety), Huxelrebe, Optima and Bacchus, as well as the hybrid Seyval Blanc. The term English wine includes Welsh wine as well, but the main counties of production are Kent and Sussex in the south, with Oxfordshire, Gloucestershire, Essex, Berkshire, Surrey and Hampshire also yielding some good bottles and reliable growers. Of course, the least reliable factor is the weather. Sparkling wine would appear to have a great future in England, too.

Georgia

The Georgians don't want their wines fresh; they like them well aged in wood, preferably tannic and certainly sweet – and that's only the whites. Things are beginning to change with Georgian Wines and Spirits Co. (50 per cent owned by Pernod-Ricard) leading the way, urged on by Australian winemaker David Nelson, and of the numerous indigenous grape varieties, the dark-coloured, peppery Saperavi looks to have real potential.

Greece

The earliest fine winemaking area recorded in history, Greece lost its long-standing reputation under the Ottoman Empire. But, today, led by four major exporting companies, Achaia-Clauss, Boutari, Kourtakis and Tsantali, and supported by a large number of individual producers who have striven strongly for quality, standards have risen dramatically and fresh and fascinating wines are increasingly common. Retsina (resinated, piney-tasting white wine) is still widely available, but so, increasingly, are reds from Xynomavro, Agiorgitiko, Cabernet Sauvignon and Merlot, and whites from Assyrtiko, Robola, Chardonnay and Muscat. Native varieties are being blended with international ones to produce some superlative wines in a number of areas. Appellations to look out for include Naoussa, Nemea and Thira (Santorini).

Hungary

Hungary is the country that has so far benefited most from the collapse of the Communist bloc. Not only did it possess in Tokaji a fabled wine that had been in its pomp the most sought after in the world, but since it had always been the most progressive of the old Eastern bloc countries it found it easier to attract international finance and expertise, and projects were more likely to succeed long term than in some other countries like Moldova and Romania which suffered far greater social dislocation.

In the north-east along the Bodrog river, the Tokaj region is famous for its sweet Tokaji wine, favoured by the Russian Tsars. Most versions we see here are very sweet, but always marked by a marvellously invigorating acidity. A little to the south-west is Eger, an area whose red wine – Bull's Blood – used to be famous worldwide – and it *was* a really beefy mouthful – and where young winemakers are now resurrecting the quality red wine reputation. However, Hungary's best known region is centred on Lake Balaton in the west of the country. The volcanic slopes of the north shore, especially at Badacsony produce many of Hungary's best dry whites from grapes like Szürkebarát and Kéknyelü. Other fine whites are produced in the north at Ászár Neszmély and Mátraalja. Only 30 per cent of Hungary's wine is red, and apart from Eger, the best is from Villány near the southern border with Croatia.

India

There are plenty of vineyards in India, many of them encouraged under the Raj, but most of the grapes are not used for wine. The most successful Indian wines are those of Chateau Indage owned by entrepreneur Sham

Chougule. Bordeaux star enologist Michel Rolland advises Grover Vineyards in Bangelore and is producing fair reds.

Israel

There are big improvements here. The Golan Heights winery led the way in the 1980s with clean, fresh, varietal wines that were also kosher; now Israel's biggest producer, Carmel, has been pushed by competition into modernizing its winemaking. Small producers are making Bordeaux-style reds, with Merlot on the increase. Castel, Galil Mountain and Tishbi are newer names to look for.

Japan

Japan's wine laws allow foreign grapes, must or wine to be imported and (usually, but not always) mixed with Japanese wine to be re-labelled as Japanese. Suntory, however, makes the real thing, as does Chateau Lumière.

Lebanon

The benefit of peace in Lebanon is that we no longer have to think that Chateau Musar is Lebanon's only wine producer. Other good producers like Kefraya, Ksara and Massaya are all flexing their muscles and beginning to produce some high-quality modern wines. Above all, they're proving that areas like the Bekaa Valley are highly suited to good quality red grapes like Cabernet, Syrah, Cinsaut and Carignan. There are some good, fruity whites being made, too, from Muscat, Sauvignon and Chardonnay.

Luxembourg

Not all Mosel wine is German. Luxembourg's vineyards are based along the upper Mosel (or Moselle) and like Germany's, they produce only white wine. Unlike Germany's Mosel, the main grape varieties are Rivaner, Elbling, Riesling, Auxerrois, Gewürztraminer, Pinot Blanc and Pinot Gris. Much is made into sparkling wine, and most of the rest is on the lean side, though Riesling, Rivaner and Auxerrois can be good.

Mexico

Only about 6 per cent of Mexico's grape harvest ends up as wine, the rest being served up as table grapes, raisins or brandy. The Sierra Madre, 1500m (5000ft) above sea level in the north-east, Baja California, in the north-west and Guadalajara to the south, provide the backdrop for winemaking in Mexico. Although Mexico's wine industry can be traced back to colonial times, L A Cetto has

Vineyards at Dealul Vei in the Dealul Mare region of Romania, in the foothills of the Carpathian Mountains. The region is known above all for its red wines, from Merlot, Pinot Noir and Cabernet Sauvignon.

brought stainless steel hygiene, cold fermentation, fresh and vibrant fruit and the first decent reputation to Mexican wines. Nebbiolo and Petite Sirah have been notable successes. Other modern wineries such as Pedro Domecq (from Spain), Casa Madero, Santo Tomás and Monte Zenic give Mexican winemaking a diversity that is evident in the varieties used. You can find red wines from Cabernet Sauvignon through Barbera to Pinot Noir and Zinfandel, whites from Chardonnay to Viognier.

Moldova

Moldova could be the best of the former Soviet states in wine terms: it has the largest quantities of Western grape varieties and some pretty good wineries. It has also seen a lot of international activity; Penfolds, Hugh Ryman, Jacques Lurton and Alain Thiénot have all worked with local winemakers to produce promising whites. However, chaotic social conditions have led to many attempts being abandoned. The vineyards extend over most of the country; they are planted with, among others, Cabernet Sauvignon, Merlot, Pinot Noir and the native Saperavi for red wines, Chardonnay, Sauvignon Blanc, Aligoté, Rkatsiteli and the Romanian Feteasca Alba and Feteasca Regala for whites.

Morocco

North Africa's best reds come from here, grown in vineyards at up to 1200m (3937ft) in altitude and facing west to attract cooling breezes from the Atlantic. And there are definite signs that after two generations when the vineyards were left to stagnate upon the French departure from North Africa, investment and modernization are starting again. French wine giant Castel has planted 1200ha (2965 acres) of vines split between the main wine regions of Boulaouane and Meknès and built two large modern wineries that are already turning out good reds. There are four Appellations d'Origines Garanties but they're of no great relevance – investment and modern winemaking are.

Romania

Climatically Romania has many regions that suit the grape vine perfectly. Phylloxera played havoc with Romania's native grape varieties but led to the introduction, at the end of the nineteenth century, of grapes such as Cabernet Sauvignon, Merlot and Pinot Noir. Fortunately, many delightful native varietals also survived: Fetească Regală, Fetească Albă and Tămaîioasă Româneasca make powerfully scented white wine; Fetească Neagră is a red variety of great potential.

The Ceauçescu regime, committed to maximum agricultural output in terms of foodstuffs, consigned many vineyards to the less mechanizable hilltops, that is, to the spots that vines love best, but the country has nonetheless been held back by lack of foreign investment in modern technology, and domestic tastes are not those that might attract international palates. The establishment in 1991 of Vinexport (with British, German, Dutch and Danish capital) and more recently the investments by English company Halewood, allowed Romanian producers access to outside investment, know-how and markets.

Since then Romanian wine has experienced an important change for the better but it will only really take off when the country learns to harness the strength of its terroirs. To this end, quality areas have been delimited as DOC or the better DOCC since 1998.

Pinot Noir has made an impression outside the country because it has a faint whiff of Burgundian character, at a fraction of the price. What is even more interesting is that Romania has more Merlot than anywhere else except France.

Regions to look out for include Dealul Mare, in the valleys of the Carpathian Mountains, where good-value Pinot Noir and surprisingly good Merlot can be found. Murfatlar, on the Black Sea coast, is known for its sweet white wines, but also has Cabernet Sauvignon and some oak-aged Chardonnays that can be worthwhile. Whites predominate in Tirnave, Transylvania, but there is also some good Merlot. Iaşi, on the lowlands towards the north-eastern border, specializes in native grape varietals, especially luscious and lingering Tămâîoasă dessert wines.

Russia

The republics of the former USSR grow progressively more native grape varieties and progressively fewer Western ones the further east one travels along the Black Sea coast. Russia grows such grapes as Muscatel, Silvaner, Cabernet Sauvignon, Riesling, Aligoté, Pinot Gris and Pinot Noir, but also Rkatsiteli, Pukhjovsky and Tsimlyansky. Sparkling and still whites come from the north and west, reds from other areas.

Slovakia

Since its split with the Czech Republic in the early 1990s, Slovakia has had something of a bonus in wine terms – two-thirds of the vine-yards of the former Czechoslovakia, plus a corner of the Tokaji vineyards, most of which are in Hungary. In fact Hungary used to lease this extra bit from Czechoslovakia in exchange for beer, but now that that deal has come to an end we should begin to see Slovakian Tokaji as well as Hungarian.

The wines of the rest of Slovakia, though, are similar to those of the Czech Republic: mostly white, from Pinot Blanc, Müller-Thurgau, Roter and Grüner Veltliner, Silvaner, Traminer, Rhine Riesling, Laski Rizling, Sauvignon Blanc and Irsay Oliver, with Frankovka, St-Laurent and Pinot Noir for the reds. The reds tend to be light, since Slovakia is well to the north and the climate is cool, but when they are good they can be very attractive, and Frankovka can be very concentrated. The wines of Austria and Hungary are the nearest comparison for style.

Western investment and advice is busy turning the rather tired local style of wine into something fresh, fruity and gauged to international tastes, particularly at the Nitra State winery and the smaller Gbelce and Hurbanovo wineries.

Slovenia

Slovenia produced only 6 per cent of the wine of the old Yugoslavia, but the quality was good, and if the Slovenians are able to export it at a reasonable price we should begin to see some ripe, fresh, clean Laski Rizling, Sauvignon Blanc, Pinot Blanc, Merlot and others. And yes, fresh and clean are the operative words. The Yugoslav Laski Rizling of old, often sold under the name Ljutomer, is not a wine one would necessarily associate with that description, but the Slovenians can do a great deal better than that.

There are three wine regions: the Primorje or Littoral region, which borders Italy's Collio; the Podravje or Drava Valley, which borders Austria's Styria, and the Posavje or Sava Valley, in the south-east and east. Overall about half the wine is red and half white, and while many of the better winemakers curse their inability to afford the latest equipment, the standard of some of their wines indicates that they are doing their best in spite of their handicaps.

Turkey

Turkish wine is highly taxed and no wine is imported. The wines that are made seldom seem appealing to Western palates, since what were clearly originally fruity wines have been left in cask for far too long. Only 2 to 3 per cent of Turkey's vast grape production is turned into wine, and while there are officially some 1250 grape varieties, only 50 or 60 of them are grown on a commercial scale. Still, that's a fair number, and a few impart some earthy, spicy tastes to the wine. Western varieties tend to be grown most in the west of the country. Diren, Kavaklidere, Turasan and Doluca are using modern technology to make very drinkable wines.

Ukraine

The Ukraine has three main winemaking areas: Crimea is the most important, and there are also vineyards around Odesa on the Black Sea coast and in the Kherson region on the Dnipro. Red and white wines are made from a wide range of international and local grape varieties, and both Odesa and Crimea produce reasonable sparkling wines. The dessert wines from the Masandra winery in the Crimea have traditionally imitated the great dessert wines of the West, with 'port', 'Tokay', 'Marsala' and 'Madeira'. The greatest wines can live 100 years or more; and a large sale at Sotheby's, London, in 1990, caused quite a stir. Present day production is not up to these glorious standards. Foreign investment is trickling into the Ukraine.

Yugoslavia

The republics of the former Yugoslavia are all capable of producing wine, but the region is still struggling to regain its standards after long years of war. Traditionally, most wine made in the western Balkans is red, except in the north Serbian region of Vojvodina and the now-independent republics of Bosnia-Herzegovina, where white is in the majority, and Macedonia, where the split is equal.

Zimbabwe

One would imagine there's not much incentive to make wine in Zimbabwe, its summer rainfall being a hindrance during the December/January harvest, not to mention political upheaval. Nonetheless, vineyards were planted in the 1960s, the mix very much reflecting the influence of neighbouring South Africa, with Colombard, Chenin Blanc and Cabernet Sauvignon, as well as Sauvignon Blanc, Pinotage and Merlot. Much progress was made in the 1990s, and a flying winemaker, New Zealander Clive Hartnell has been a regular visitor at Stapleford, one of Zimbabwe's two wine producers. Mukuyu is the other. Both produce wines of varying quality, but the best are well made.

A–Z OF WINES,
WINE REGIONS,
PRODUCERS
AND
GRAPE VARIETIES

The A–Z section from page 56 to page 399 covers entries on wines, wine regions, producers and grape varieties from all over the world.

The wine, wine region and producer entries follow the same format: the heading contains information on the country, region, appellation and local classification where relevant. The grape varieties listed in these entries are divided into the colour of wine they make, indicated by a glass symbol. The symbols stand for red ♟, rosé ♟ and white ♀ wines. Where a grape variety has a local name, this appears in brackets. There are also boxed features on the world's most important grape varieties.

Many large companies, especially in the New World, have vineyards and winemaking facilities in as many as a dozen places. Because of limited space, most producers have been given only one address; the main text makes it clear what the company does and where.

If you cannot find the wine or producer you want in the A–Z, it may be described under a wine region or grape entry, so try the Index on page 407.

To help you find your way around the A–Z, wines, wine regions and producers that have their own entries elsewhere are indicated in the text by SMALL CAPITALS.

The A–Z section includes special two-page features on the world's most important wine regions, including maps and lists of related entries to be found elsewhere in the A–Z. These regional features appear alphabetically within the A–Z by local name.

Mountain ranges form a dramatic backdrop to many of the Cape vineyards in South Africa. These immaculate vineyards belong to the Plaisir de Merle estate, a showpiece winery stretching up the Paarl side of the Simonsberg range.

ABADÍA RETUERTA

SPAIN, Castilla y León, Vino de la Tierra de Castilla y León

❦ *Tempranillo, Cabernet Sauvignon, Merlot and others*

This 700-ha (1730-acre) estate on the Duero river, immediately west of RIBERA DEL DUERO, had an 800-year legacy in winemaking, but all the vines had been removed by the late 1970s. In 1988 the huge Swiss pharmaceutical firm Novartis acquired the estate and set about replanting 210ha (519 acres) with Tempranillo and French varieties and then built a futuristic, gravity-driven winery.

Since 1996 Bordeaux winemaking consultant Pascal Delbeck (from Ch. BELAIR) and enologist Ángel Anocíbar have made a number of highly individual, concentrated wines that have stunned international critics. Top wines include single-vineyard Pago Negralada (Tempranillo), PV (Petit Verdot) and Pago Valdebellón (Cabernet Sauvignon) and all the wines are certain to improve as the vineyards mature. Best years: 2001, '00, '99, '98, '97, '96.

ABRUZZO

ITALY

This region of central Italy is gloriously beautiful but little known and it might be positively obscure had its name not been included in its two major wines: Trebbiano d'Abruzzo, a dry, neutral white and MONTEPULCIANO D'ABRUZZO, usually a strapping, peppery red of real character but sometimes a rosé or lightish red called Cerasuolo. Those who complain that you can't produce good wines in southern Italy because it is too hot forget its saving grace – a mountainous backbone. Here the Apennines are at their cool-climate highest, and there is little flat land.

Controguerra is a newish DOC in the province of Teramo in the north covering a wide range of blended and varietal wines, including many international varieties such as Chardonnay, Riesling, Cabernet Sauvignon, Merlot and Pinot Noir. Encouragingly, it specifically forbids the high-yielding *tendone* system for training vines, which was widespread in the region. Colline Teramane is the first of the new Montepulciano d'Abruzzo sub-zones from which the top wines will carry the DOCG denomination.

ACACIA WINERY

USA, California, Napa County, Carneros AVA

❦ *Pinot Noir*

♀ *Chardonnay, Viognier*

Faltering after a brilliant beginning, Acacia was acquired by the CHALONE Group in 1986.

ACACIA

Acacia has been a leading producer of Pinot Noir and Chardonnay from the Carneros region since its founding in the early 1980s.

Since then, it has been a steady producer of CARNEROS Chardonnay and Pinot Noir despite supply problems created by phylloxera during the 1990s. The regular Carneros Chardonnay is restrained but attractive. Pinot Noirs, starting with regular Carneros, include the stunning DeSoto as well as a Beckstoffer Vineyard bottling. The wines have moved to a riper, meatier style of late. There is also a voluptuous Carneros Viognier and Brut fizz. Best years: (Pinot Noir) 2001, '00, '99, '98, 97, '96, '95.

ACCADEMIA DEI RACEMI

ITALY, Puglia, Manduria

❦ *Primitivo, Negroamaro, Malvasia and others*

♀ *Chardonnay*

This premium venture from the Perrucci family, long-established bulk shippers of basic wines from PUGLIA, is aimed not only at raising quality, but also at preserving ancient Puglian grape varieties and old vineyards. Quality, modern-style reds are made mainly from the local varieties Primitivo and Negroamaro and sold under various producers' names: Felline (Vigna del Feudo), PERVINI (Primitivo di Manduria Archidamo) and Masseria Pepe (Dunico). Best years: (reds) 2001, '00, '98, '97, '96.

ACKERMAN-LAURANCE

FRANCE, Loire, Anjou-Saumur, Saumur AC

❦♀ *Cabernet Franc, Grolleau*

♀ *Chenin Blanc, Chardonnay*

This is the oldest sparkling SAUMUR company, established in 1811. Until recently Ackerman, with its associated company Rémy Pannier, was a by-word for very poor wines. Fortunately there has been a marked change of policy and Ackerman has recognized that the future lies less in the traditional *négociant*'s role of wine doctor, trying to rescue other people's mistakes, but more in making their own wine from either bought-in grapes or must. A large modern winery has been built at le Puy Notre

Dame and there are projects elsewhere in the LOIRE working directly with domaines to improve their winemaking. Jacques Lurton, the flying winemaker from BORDEAUX, is involved in a number of these projects. Wines sold as Vin de Pays du JARDIN DE LA FRANCE now account for a quarter of production. In the whites, both varietals and blends are now bright, modern and fresh. All these wines are for drinking young.

TIM ADAMS

AUSTRALIA, South Australia, Clare Valley

❦ *Syrah (Shiraz), Cabernet Sauvignon, Grenache and others*

♀ *Riesling, Semillon, Chardonnay*

Every wine area needs someone like Tim Adams: a top-class winemaker, committed grape grower and, above all, passionate devotee of the region itself. CLARE VALLEY is an idyllic sylvan interlude of elegant gum trees, rustling in the breeze, and swathes of bright green vines in an otherwise arid part of South Australia. Nice place to live? The best in the world, says Adams, as he welcomes you with a rugged smile and a daunting handshake, and then proceeds to show you a string of superb wines matching modern know-how with old-fashioned sensibility to the Clare Valley style.

The richly fruity and sweetly oaked Aberfeldy Shiraz, from 100-year-old vines, spicy Fergus Grenache and straight Shiraz are outstanding reds, while Semillon, both in oaky and botrytized styles, and classic, dry Riesling are high-quality, long-lived whites. Best years: (Aberfeldy Shiraz) 2002, '01, '00, '99, '98, '97, '96, '95, '94, '93, '92.

ADELAIDE HILLS

AUSTRALIA, South Australia

The small, exciting Adelaide Hills region, with the Piccadilly Valley in the south and extending to Kersbrook and Mount Crawford in the north, is only 30 minutes drive from Adelaide. More or less east of Adelaide, the hills around Piccadilly are high, even slightly damp and they produce some exceptional cool-climate whites and exciting sparkling wines. Lenswood, a little to the north, can also produce gorgeous reds.

Powerful, dark, plummy Pinot Noir, apple, pear and citrus-tinged Chardonnay, Riesling and crisply delicate Sauvignon Blanc dominate plantings in the south, but even here some exceptional Shiraz can be found. In the north, fullish Semillon, some exhilarating spice and cherry Shiraz, Cabernet

Sauvignon and Chardonnay do well. Best years: 2002, '01, '00, '99, '98, '97, '94, '93, '91, '90. Best producers: Ashton Hills, Chain of Ponds, HENSCHKE, LENSWOOD Vineyards, Nepenthe, PETALUMA, SHAW & SMITH, Geoff WEAVER.

AGE

SPAIN, La Rioja, Rioja DOCa

❦ *Tempranillo, Grenache (Garnacha), Carignan (Cariñena, Mazuelo), Graciano*

♀ *Macabeo (Viura)*

The largest winery in the Bodegas y Bebidas portfolio and sister company to the equally widely distributed CAMPO VIEJO, now owned by Allied Domecq. The Siglo Saco red Crianza is its best known wine, probably because it comes wrapped in a hessian sack. It's fair to describe most of the AGE wines as adequate rather than exciting: they do have a reasonable level of fruit, but I'd like to see more. Best years: 2001, '00, '99, '98, '96, '95, '94.

AGLIANICO

Among the dozen or so red grapes clamouring for attention in the south of Italy, Aglianico has historically claimed top billing, although several other red varieties are now making a determined challenge. Aglianico is wholly responsible for two of the most distinguished southern reds, Taurasi (from Campania) and Aglianico del Vulture (from Basilicata), and has a good stake in a third, Falerno (from Campania).

It produces surprisingly intense and elegant wines of medium colour, firm tannin and moderate alcohol, capable of long aging. Like Nebbiolo, it has sufficient complexity to stand alone, and is ideally suited to the long growing season imposed by the mesoclimate of its classic homelands. Were the general standard of winemaking higher it might have maintained a greater supremacy over its rivals, but its exponents are all too often inclined to emphasize structure over charm. Grown mainly in Campania and Basilicata, there are also some plantings in Calabria and Puglia.

AGLIANICO DEL VULTURE DOC

ITALY, Basilicata

❦ *Aglianico*

Monte Vulture is an extinct volcano 1326m (4350ft) high, in the north of BASILICATA. The best vineyards are on volcanic soil high up on the east-facing, coolish slopes, between 400 and 600m (1300 and 2000ft) around Rionero and Barile. Despite being one of mainland Italy's most southerly DOCs, the harvest is later than in BAROLO 750km (470 miles) to the north, as Aglianico is late-ripening. Good Aglianico del Vulture is an intense, earthy wine that, with time, softens and develops rich complexity, especially if from a good vintage. From such vintages the wines may be released as Riservas, with at least five years' aging.

Growers are mostly small part-timers, selling their grapes to co-operatives or *commercianti* who make the wine, increasingly employing barrique-maturation. Best years: 2001, '00, '99, '98, '97, '95, '93, '90, '88. Best producers: Basilium, Consorzio Viticoltori Associati del Vulture (Carpe Diem), D'Angelo, Cantine del Notaio, Paternoster, Le Querce.

AHR

GERMANY

The river Ahr flows into the Rhine just south of Bonn, and the region to which it gives its name was the most northerly of all German wine regions until the two regions of the former Democratic Republic, SAALE-UNSTRUT and SACHSEN, joined the party. Ahr is also very small, with just 519ha (1282 acres) of vines, 85 per cent of which are planted with red grapes. Pinot Noir (Spätburgunder) is the main variety with 59 per cent and makes the best reds; Blauer Portugieser used to be more widely planted but the fashion for more tasty dry reds is driving it out of the region; the Riesling would surely be better if there were more interest in white wines here.

But reds are the region's acknowledged speciality, and so the Ahr goes on ignoring the logic of its northerly climate. The reds are mostly pallid, although there is an increasing move to deep-coloured, more tannic wines. The soil is generally slaty, and the best Rieslings can reflect this with a steeliness to their character and a mineral taste but they seldom compete with the finest from the RHEINGAU or the MOSEL. Average vineyard holdings in the Ahr are small; most producers take their grapes to the local co-operative.

Just one Bereich – Walporzheim-Ahrtal – covers the whole region; there is also only one Grosslage, Klosterberg. Best producers: J J Adeneuer, Deutzerhof, Meyer-Näkel.

AIGLE

SWITZERLAND, Vaud, Chablais

This village in the CHABLAIS region of the VAUD overlooks the river Rhône close to where it flows into Lake Geneva and is principally a white wine area. The Chasselas grape usually doesn't produce wines with much character, but here, where it's called the Dorin, they can be tangy and crisp. The Pinot Noir can be attractive and is fashionable in Switzerland. Best producer: Henri Badoux.

DOMAINE DE L'AIGLE

FRANCE, Languedoc-Roussillon, Limoux AC

❦ *Pinot Noir, Syrah*

♀ *Chardonnay*

Domaine de l'Aigle is probably best known for its high-quality, beautifully balanced and relatively complex Chardonnay and Pinot Noir, showing that the South of France really can excel with these varieties, especially in the cool uplands of the hills around LIMOUX – long famous for its refreshing, appley sparkler BLANQUETTE DE LIMOUX. This was the result of the efforts of Jean-Louis Denois, founder of the domaine and originally from CHAMPAGNE – though he had also worked in Burgundy, Australia, New Zealand, California and South Africa – whose arrival in Languedoc provided a much needed breath of fresh air in a complacent region.

However, his attempts to plant Riesling and Gewürztraminer, which he correctly surmised would thrive in Limoux's sunny but cool climate, led to him being prosecuted by France's wine bureaucrats who have resisted any attempt to plant supposedly 'Germanic' grapes anywhere in France except Alsace, on the German border. This absurd bureaucratic spat persuaded him to sell the domaine to Antonin RODET – a high-quality Burgundy producer – who is now focusing more on the original plan of fine Pinot Noir and Chardonnay, plus a range of smart VINS DE PAYS under the Rodet label made from bought-in grapes. Best years: (whites) 2000, '01, '99, '98, '97, '96, '95; (reds) 2000, '01, '99, '98, '97, '96.

AIRÉN

This simple-flavoured white grape covers nearly one-third of Spain's vineyards, making it the world's most planted variety, although it is now surrendering ground to red grapes. The Airén lake would be even vaster were it not for the fact that most of the vineyards are on the hot central plains of La MANCHA, where yields are tiny. Nevertheless this grape can produce fresh, decent whites. All new Airén plantings are currently banned in CASTILLA-LA MANCHA.

AJACCIO AC
FRANCE, Corsica
🍷 🍷 *Sciacarello and others*
🍷 *Vermentino, Ugni Blanc*

From the west of the island around Ajaccio and with 230ha (568 acres) under vine, this is one of the best Corsican ACs. With the shining exception of Comte Peraldi, whose excellent white shows real class in both oak-aged and non-oaked versions, the whites are still all potential and little realization, as are the distinctly orange-hued rosés. However, the reds from Sciacarello can show a bit of form even if the rather sour edge of acidity still intrudes more than it should into the fairly plummy fruit. Comte Peraldi and Clos d'Alzeto are in a different league from the others, though there are rather rustic but tasty efforts from Clos Capitoro. The reds often need two to three years in bottle to show at their best. Best years: (reds) 2002, '01, '00, '99, '98, '97, '96, '95.

ALBAN VINEYARDS
USA, California, Edna Valley AVA
🍷 *Syrah, Grenache*
🍷 *Viognier, Roussanne*

John Alban became captivated by RHÔNE wines at an early age and in 1989 he started CALIFORNIA's first estate dedicated to Rhône varietals in the Arroyo Grande district of EDNA VALLEY. The first Viognier was released in 1991. Today he offers two versions, an Estate and a CENTRAL COAST. Roussanne from estate vineyards is laden with honeysuckle scent. Syrah is also represented by two bottlings: Reva and the more expensive Lorraine. An intense Grenache rounds out the range. Best years: (Syrah) 2001, '00, '99, '98, '97, '96, '95.

ALBANA DI ROMAGNA DOCG
ITALY, Emilia-Romagna
🍷 *Albana*

Produced over a large area between Bologna and Rimini, Italy's first white DOCG (in 1987) was a political appointment that caused outrage among wine enthusiasts because of the totally forgettable flavours of most Albana

ZERBINA
This luscious passito wine with a deft touch of new oak is from one of the leading estates in the Albana di Romagna DOCG.

wine. Though also made in dry and sparkling versions, the sweet and *passito* (made from semi-dried grapes) versions are the best, notably in the form of ZERBINA's Scacco Matto. Other good producers: (passito) Celli, Leone Conti, Ferrucci, Giovanna Madonia, Paradiso, Riva, Tre Monti, Uccellina. Drink dry Albana young.

ALBARIÑO
Albariño is the top-quality white grape of GALICIA, the green and fertile region in Spain's far north-west (and just over the border around Monção in Portugal's VINHO VERDE country where it is called Alvarinho). When it's well made, Albariño wine can have complex fruity flavours of apricot, peach, grapefruit and even grape. The grapes produce relatively little juice and the wines are very fashionable, two factors which make them among Spain's most expensive whites. Newer styles (oak-fermented, late-harvest) are progressively joining the ranks of new-wave Albariño and growers in DÃO in Portugal are starting to use it, too.

ALCAMO DOC, BIANCO D'ALCAMO DOC
ITALY, Sicily
🍷 🍷 *Nero d'Avola (Calabrese), Cabernet Sauvignon, Merlot and Syrah*
🍷 *Catarratto and others*

Take the road west from Palermo and round the Gulf of Castellammare, turn inland past Alcamo and you drive through such dense hills you can rarely see more than a few hundred yards in any direction. But every single slope of every hill is dark green with vines, mainly of the Catarratto family. It is sobering to note that Catarratto is Italy's second most-grown grape, after Trebbiano which also thrives here. Small wonder, then, that white Alcamo is almost invariably a neutral and stretched wine, especially as overproduction is endemic. Only those producers whose

vineyards are at a highish altitude and who severely limit production achieve a wine of real interest, and you can count them on the fingers of one hand. Best producers: Rallo, Rapitalà, Spadafora. Drink the wines young.

ALEATICO
The Italian grape Aleatico is such an odd combination of Muscat-like aroma, style and longevity that some reckon it is a Muscat mutation. The wines are dark red, usually richly sweet, tasting of wild strawberries, red-currants and other berry fruits. They are rounded, often alcoholic, and absolutely delicious – but scarce. Aleatico is found mainly in PUGLIA, though there are outcrops by Lake Bolsena in LAZIO and recent plantings in TUSCANY. Best producers: AVIGNONESI (Tuscany), Candido (Aleatico di Puglia).

ALELLA DO
SPAIN, Cataluña
🍷 🍷 *Grenache Noir (Garnacha Tinta), Tempranillo (Ull de Llebre), Merlot, Cabernet Sauvignon, Pansa Rosáda, Pinot Noir and others*
🍷 *Xarel-lo (Pansa Blanca), Grenache Blanc (Garnacha Blanca), Chardonnay, Macabeo, Parellada, Sauvignon Blanc, Chenin Blanc and others*

This is one of Spain's smallest DOs, making mostly whites, the best of them light and fresh. Over the last two decades, vineyards have rapidly been giving way to villas as the city of Barcelona expands. The first plots to go were the prettiest, high up in the rolling hills north of the city, and these, sadly, were also the coolest and best vineyard sites. Alella's inland vineyards grow mainly Pansa Blanca (the Xarel-lo of the PENEDÈS) while the slopes that face east, seawards, grow Garnacha Blanca in the more Mediterranean climate. The co-operative produces 60 per cent of the region's wine, sold under the Marfil brand, and most of the rest comes from the reliable firms of Parxet (Marqués de Alella) and Roura. Drink the wines young.

ALENQUER DOC
PORTUGAL, Estremadura
🍷 *Camarate, Trincadeira (Tinta Amarela), Castelão (Periquita) and others*
🍷 *Arinto (Pederña), Fernão Pires (Maria Gomes), Jampal, Vital*

Vineyards set in rolling country around the small whitewashed town of Alenquer produce the best wines in Portugal's ESTREMADURA. Sheltered from the Atlantic westerlies by the Serra de Montejunto, it lies close to Lisbon north-west of the river Tagus

(Tejo). The wines are made mostly from local grapes but there is some Cabernet and Chardonnay too. Many wines are simply labelled as ESTREMADURA. Reds (mostly based on the Castelão grape, also known as Periquita) tend to be better than whites and are capable of aging for five years or so. Whites should be drunk as young as possible. Best years: (reds) 2001, '00, '99, '97. Best producers: Quinta da Abrigada, Quinta do Carneiro, Quinta de Cortezia, D F J VINHOS, Quinta de Pancas, Casa SANTOS LIMA.

ALENTEJO DOC

PORTUGAL

❢ *Tempranillo (Aragonez/Tinta Roriz), Castelão (Periquita), Trincadeira (Tinta Amarela), and others*

♀ *Arinto (Pederñā), Fernão Pires (Maria Gomes), Rabo de Ovelha and others*

The Alentejo is a huge rolling plain that takes up much of Portugal south of the river Tagus (Tejo) stretching inland from the Atlantic east to the frontier with Spain. Vineyards are not all that evident in this expansive landscape where fields of flowing corn stretch as far as the eye can see. Until the 1980s, the Alentejo's main link with the wine world was through cork from its vast cork forests.

Vines tend to be found around the outskirts of bright whitewashed towns and villages which form wine enclaves in their own right. Borba, Évora, Granja-Amareleja, Moura, Portalegre, Redondo, Reguengos and Vidigueira are all sub-DOCs of the new Alentejo DOC. But the Alentejo is all about the big picture and the whole region is now also a Vinho Regional under the name of Alentejano. Most producers tend to opt for the latter designation which allows more flexibility with grape varieties and blending.

Alentejo wines were once the butt of frequent jokes. But, with the help of EU investment, the wines have undergone such a transformation that the locals are now having the last laugh. Gleaming stainless steel wineries have been springing up all over and there is now an insatiable demand for Alentejano wines from the voracious hordes of supermarket buyers in Lisbon and Oporto. Potential is far from realized but already some of Portugal's finest reds, from evenly ripened native grapes, come from here.

In this climate where temperatures in the summer frequently soar over 40°C (104°F), it is not surprising that most of the Alentejo's reputation is based on red wines. Apart from Arinto, few white grape varieties can stand up to the sweltering daytime heat and the

The Australian winemaker David Baverstock has done much to revitalize the Alentejo region through his work at the huge Esporão estate.

wines tend to lack acidity. Nevertheless white grapes still predominate around Vidigueira and the ESPORÃO estate near Reguengos makes some fresh, subtropical dry whites. Red grapes like Trincadeira and Aragonez are much better adapted to the Alentejo scene. Alicante Bouschet (still much derided in southern France) lends ballast to many of the region's finest reds – Mouchão, a dark, concentrated red made by Herdade de Mouchão, is perhaps the best example.

Other leading producers are widely spread throughout the province. In the north around Portalegre, where the climate is somewhat more temperate, Tapada do Chaves and d'Avillez (the latter belonging to José Maria da FONSECA) make outstanding reds. In Alentejo's central plain leading producers are (in Évora) Herdade de Cartuxa, (in Borba) the large, well-run Borba co-operative along with Quinta do Carmo, Quinta do Mouro and Caves ALIANÇA (Quinta de Terrugem), (in Redondo) Herdade da Madeira/Roqueval, and (in Reguengos, the heart of winemaking in the Alentejo) ESPORÃO and the much improved Reguengos de Monsarez co-operative. Towards the Spanish border Granja-Amareleja and Moura are arid, with poor soil and there are no significant producers other than one local co-operative. Finally, the southernmost subregion is Vidigueira which has the hottest and most arid land in the whole of Portugal. CORTES DE CIMA is a welcome new producer here and working wonders with Tempranillo

(Aragonez) in irrigated vineyards. Portugal's largest wine company SOGRAPE has an estate at Vidigueira (Herdade do Peso) where they make a range of wines under the Vinha do Monte label.

J P VINHOS sources wines throughout the Alentejo and has its huge Ânforas winery at Arraiolos. The dynamic João Portugal RAMOS, one of Portugal's top consultant winemakers, also makes a smooth, spicy oakaged red at his Monte de Serrado Pinheiro estate near Estremoz in the deep south of the region. Best years: (reds) 2001, '00, '99, '97, '95, '94, '91, '90, '89.

ALEXANDER VALLEY AVA

USA, California, Sonoma County

The Alexander Valley AVA is centred on the Russian River as it cuts a long, broad swathe from SONOMA COUNTY's northerly limit at Cloverdale south to Healdsburg. It is fairly warm here with only patchy summer fog and there is a sharp contrast between the vineyards on the valley floor and those on the low hills that frame it, where the vines are often lower yielding and deliver significantly more intense flavours.

Cabernet Sauvignon is highly successful here, with lovely juicy fruit not marred by an excess of tannin and often brightened up by a refreshing green streak. Chardonnay may also be good but is often overproduced, especially from the southern area around Jimtown, and lacking in ripe, round flavours. Sauvignon Blanc can be satisfyingly grassy. Merlot ripens just that bit more fully than Cabernet and makes some of California's most attractively rich and fleshy examples. Zinfandel, made from pre-Prohibition vineyards, can be exceptional here. Of the 50 or so wineries, GEYSER PEAK and SIMI are the oldest. Best years: (reds) 2001, '00, '99, '97, '95, '94, '93, '91, '90, '88. Best producers: Alexander Valley Vineyards, Chateau Souverain, CLOS DU BOIS, Geyser Peak, JORDAN VINEYARD, Murphy-Goode, SEGHESIO, SILVER OAK, SIMI.

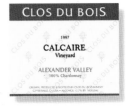

CLOS DU BOIS

One of the largest producers in Sonoma, Clos du Bois makes a speciality of Chardonnay. This barrel-fermented Chardonnay comes from the Calcaire vineyard.

ALGARVE VINHO REGIONAL
PORTUGAL

Portugal's holiday coast has a captive market among the droves of sun-worshippers who bask on the region's beaches each summer. They don't tend to bring much of the local hooch home with them though because the wines are fairly dire. The lion's share of the region's wine is red. It's pretty feeble stuff: high in alcohol and low in colour and flavour. The Algarve is sub-divided into four separate DOCs: Lagoa, Lagos, Portimão and Tavira, each based on the local co-operative. And one has to say – how did the Algarve get four DOCs when much more deserving areas have to make do with one? Did somebody say 'politics'? Anyway, of these, the wines from the Lagoa co-operative are the best.

But things are changing. Under the straightforward Vinho Regional Algarve classification D F J VINHOS now make a powerful, chunky red called Cataplana in conjunction with the Lagoa co-operative, and Sir Cliff Richard, aided by two Australians, David Baverstock (see ESPORÃO) for excellent winemaking and Dr Richard Smart for his world-famous vineyard skills, has produced a delightful soft, scented red called Vida Nova (New Life). There's no doubt that Sir Cliff's success will encourage others, but in the meantime, if you go there on holiday my advice is to drink the wines from the ALENTEJO province immediately to the north of the Algarve or stick to VINHO VERDE.

CAVES ALIANÇA
PORTUGAL, Alentejo DOC, Bairrada DOC, Dão DOC, Douro DOC and others

🍷 *Baga, Tempranillo (Tinta Roriz, Aragonez), Touriga Nacional, Trincadeira, Cabernet Sauvignon, Merlot and others*

🍷 *Baga*

🍷 *Bical, Arinto, Fernao Pires (Maria Gomes), Azal*

The family-run Caves Aliança is one of Portugal's leading wine companies and, like

CAVES ALIANÇA
Caves Aliança is leading the way in the Bairrada region, making soft, approachable red wines for early drinking instead of the traditional hard, tannic reds.

many others, has made huge improvements in the last decade or so. Its main base is at Sangalhos in the BAIRRADA region where it makes crisp, fresh whites, especially from Bical which is one of Portugal's most promising white grapes, and soft, approachable reds. Cabernet Sauvignon, a grape which performs well in Bairrada, Pinot Noir, Tinta Roriz and Chardonnay have also joined Bical in the range of Aliança's varietal wines under the Galeria label. Aliança owns large estates in the DOURO (Quinta dos Quatro Ventos), DÃO (Quintas da Garrida and das Casticeiras), BEIRAS (Quinta d'Aguiar), ALENTEJO (Quinta da Terrugem, which produces their flagship reds, and Herdade do Barranco) and BAIRRADA (Quintas das Baceladas, das Maribanas and do Vale Santo and Vinha de Sangalhos). Aliança also markets varietal Merlot, Touriga Nacional and Tinta Roriz (and a Reserva blend of all three) from Quinta da Cortezia in ESTREMADURA.

ALICANTE DO
SPAIN, Valencia

🍷 *Mourvèdre (Monastrell), Tempranillo, Grenache Noir (Garnacha Tinta) and others*

🍷 *Airén, Muscat (Moscatel), Macabeo, Merseguera and others*

Down in the hot, dry south-east corner of Spain, the Alicante DO makes mostly red wines, traditionally very dark and heavy with alcohol. Recent investment in both vineyards and wineries has led to improvements, though most of the whites (whether dry, medium and sweet) are still dull, alcoholic and best avoided. The exception is attractive Moscatel from the Muscat of Alexandria grape made by GUTIÉRREZ DE LA VEGA, in the well sited Marina Alta sub-region, right on the Mediterranean coast in among the orange groves.

The region's finest wine and a local curiosity well worth seeking out is Fondillón, a dry or medium-dry wine from the Monastrell grape with a minimum of 16 per cent alcohol, which is aged in old oak barrels, sometimes in a solera system, for at least eight years before being bottled. Unique to Alicante, it's one of Spain's best *rancio* wines with rich, nutty, toffee flavours.

Most of Alicante's vineyards are located on the cooler slopes way inland in the hills of the Vinalopó around the town of Villena near the border with MURCIA. The newish Enrique Mendoza winery has set new quality standards for the region with its reds –

mostly made with French grape varieties. Spanish wonderboy Telmo RODRÍGUEZ makes a modern style Monastrell called Almuvedre down here. Best producers: (Fondillón) BOCOPA, Salvador Poveda, Primitivo Quiles; (Moscatel) Felipe Gutiérrez de la Vega; (table wines) Enrique Mendoza, Telmo Rodríguez.

ALIGOTÉ
This French white grape – almost certainly of Burgundian origin – has a lemony tartness, with a smell when ripe rather like buttermilk soap, and sometimes a whiff of pine and eucalyptus. It gives immeasurably better wine from old vines, and many of the best Aligoté wines in Burgundy come from vines more than 50 years old. In warm years the wine can resemble a Chardonnay, especially if a little new oak is used in the winemaking.

The best known area for Aligoté is Bouzeron in the Côte Chalonnaise where the wines take the Bouzeron AC and yields are limited to 45 hectolitres per hectare, compared to 60 hectolitres elsewhere in Burgundy. However, several other Côte d'Or villages produce equally fine Aligoté from old vines, though these are only allowed to use the Bourgogne-Aligoté AC. Pernand-Vergelesses makes particularly good examples.

As well as the Côte d'Or and the Côte Chalonnaise there is some Aligoté in the Hautes-Côtes, in the Mâconnais, and in the Yonne at St-Bris-le-Vineux and Chitry-le-Fort. In all, around 500ha (1235 acres) of Aligoté is planted in Burgundy, and there are a few vines in the Rhône's Châtillon-en-Diois appellation – where the wine is rather nutty and not half bad.

Aligoté is also found in Eastern Europe – in Romania, Bulgaria and the Black Sea coast, especially in Moldova – and in Chile and California.

ALKOOMI

AUSTRALIA, Western Australia, Margaret River

❦ *Cabernet Sauvignon, Shiraz, Malbec, Merlot and others*

♀ *Riesling, Chardonnay, Sauvignon Blanc and others*

If you had stood on the porch of Merv and Judy Lange's Alkoomi property in the 1970s, you would have seen the vast expanse of gently undulating dun-coloured land that marks out a sheep station and a grain farm. That's what the Langes and everybody in the far south of Western Australia did then. But if you'd looked left, you'd have seen something totally new – a patch of leafy green vines just about to give their first fruit. The Langes were alone in seeing the potential of Frankland back in 1971 – perhaps they just wanted a bit more colour in the view from their porch – but they were truly prescient. They now have 70ha (173 acres) of vines and devote themselves full time to wine, producing very attractive whites led by Riesling and good reds led by blockbuster Blackbutt, a Bordeaux blend. And now, if you stand on the porch, you can see hardly a patch of the old dun colour as Frankland proves itself to be one of the best new vineyard sites in Australia. Best years: (Blackbutt) 2002, '01, '99, '98, '97, '96, '95, '94.

ALL SAINTS

AUSTRALIA, Victoria, Rutherglen

❦ ♀ *Syrah (Shiraz), Durif, Cabernet Sauvignon and others*

♀ *Riesling, Chardonnay, Marsanne and others*

You have to rub your eyes and think – hang on, which country am I in? There you are in the middle of the sunbaked paddocks and vineyards of Rutherglen in upstate Victoria, and yet you've just driven through ancient wrought-iron gates and are now standing on a lush green lawn gazing at what seems to be a Scottish castle! Well, it sort of is.

This magnificent red brick castellated edifice was built with misty-eyed zeal by George Sutherland Smith in 1864 to remind him of the Castle of Mey in the far north of Scotland where his family had worked for generations as carpenters. It had become something of a faded dowager waiting forlornly for a suitor by the time Peter Brown of Brown Brothers bought it in 1998, but he has quickly brought lustre back to the grand old dame with a string of super Rare Tokay and Rare Muscat releases, delicious though younger stickies under the Grand label, some powerful reds, including the Rutherglen speciality Durif, and some fair whites.

ALLEGRINI

ITALY, Veneto

❦ *Corvina, Rondinella*

One of the earliest pioneers of quality VALPOLICELLA was Giovanni Allegrini, who a few years prior to his premature death in 1983 purchased the Grola hill in Sant'Ambrogio in the heart of Valpolicella Classico for the purpose of producing fine cru wines with his new methods of planting and vinification. His modernist principles have been continued and adapted by his children, Walter, Marilisa and Franco, who now run the company. All their wines are from their own 70ha (173 acres) of vines located around Sant'Ambrogio and Fumane.

The single-vineyard La Grola and Palazzo della Torre are now sold under the regional IGT label (Veronese) – partly to further distance them from the continuing low regard in which much of Valpolicella is still held. These, and the barrique-aged La Poja made solely from Corvina, show the great potential that exists in Valpolicella. There is also outstanding AMARONE in a marvellously scented, succulent style; and an intensely fruity RECIOTO named, appropriately, Giovanni Allegrini. Best years: (Amarone) 2001, '00, '97, '95, '93, '90, '88, '85.

FINCA ALLENDE

SPAIN, La Rioja, Rioja DOCa

❦ *Tempranillo, Graciano, Grenache Noir (Garnacha Tinta)*

♀ *Macabeo (Viura), Malvasia*

The ebullient Miguel Angel de Gregorio has made his modest, young winery in the village of Briones into one of the most admired new names in RIOJA. The vineyards total 18ha (44 acres) of mostly 50-year-old Tempranillo, with a small number of other RIOJA varieties in the field blend. The bodega itself is a very modest, even basic facility. He favours big, concentrated, uncompromising wines that place him near the top of the new-wave Rioja producers. He makes a basic Allende wine and a top-end Aurus, which includes a good dollop of the rare Graciano in the blend, and Calvario. French oak is favoured. There is also a delicate, barrel-fermented white. Best years: (reds) 2001, '00, '99, 98, '97, '96.

ALOXE-CORTON AC

FRANCE, Burgundy, Côte de Beaune

❦ *Pinot Noir*

♀ *Chardonnay*

This important village nestling beneath the south-east side of the hill of CORTON at the northern end of the CÔTE DE BEAUNE produces mostly red wines. Aloxe-Corton has the largest amount of Grand Cru land anywhere in the CÔTE D'OR and its reputation is based on the two Grands Crus, Corton (mainly red wine) and CORTON-CHARLEMAGNE (white wine only) which it shares with the villages of Ladoix-Serrigny and PERNAND-VERGELESSES. The vines flow across the slopes of the hill of Corton from east to almost due west, with the highest vines nuzzling the forest-covered brow.

The large Corton vineyard is the Côte de Beaune's only red Grand Cru. The vineyards further down on the flatter land qualify for the village AC only and used to offer some of Burgundy's tastiest village wine at a fair price; nowadays the reds rarely exhibit their characteristically delicious blend of ripe fruit and appetizing savoury dryness. Although there are a number of Premier Cru vineyards, these are hardly ever named on the label, but 'Premier Cru', denoting a blend of several Premier Cru wines, is quite common.

Almost all of Aloxe-Corton's white is now sold as Grand Cru (Corton and Corton-Charlemagne); Aloxe-Corton Blanc is rare but the best can show remarkable richness of flavour and character for a dry white. Best years: (reds) 2002, '01, '99, '98, '97, '96, '95, '93, '90. Best producers: CHANDON DE BRIAILLES, M Chapuis, Marius Delarche, DROUHIN, Dubreuil-Fontaine, Follin-Arvelet, Antonin Guyon, JADOT, Rapet, Comte Senard, TOLLOT-BEAUT, Michel Voarick.

ALPINE VALLEYS

AUSTRALIA, Victoria

The splitting of North-East Victoria into five regions as part of the reorganization by the Geographical Indications committee makes eminent sense. RUTHERGLEN and Glenrowan on the warm plains produce gorgeous fortified wines and powerful reds; Beechworth is home to the stellar GIACONDA winery; then there's fertile KING VALLEY and finally Alpine Valleys, embracing the watercourses of the Buffalo, Buckland, Ovens and Kiewa rivers, all running north to join the unsightly Murray River. At the southerly end, as the valleys climb to the beautiful isolation of the Victorian Alps, vineyards are relatively cool at up to 300m (1000ft). To the north, at about 150m (500ft), the valleys open out onto the plains and conditions are much warmer – so much so that once upon a time Ovens Valley Shiraz was a famous high-octane Aussie red. Best producer: Boynton's.

ALSACE France

SOME OF THE MOST DELICIOUSLY individual white wines in France come from Alsace yet, at first sight rather than taste, you might well mistake them for German. Alsace bottles are tall, slender and green – just like the bottles from the Mosel region of Germany. The name of the producer is almost certain to be Germanic, and also, in many cases, the name of the wine – Riesling, Sylvaner, Gewurztraminer… Yet, despite the German influence Alsace is proudly, independently, French. Many of the grapes may be the same but Alsace winemakers create completely different flavours – drier, yet riper, with fuller alcohol, and almost unnervingly scented.

The key to producing wine so far north lies in the Vosges mountains – rising high to the west, they draw off the moisture from the westerly winds, leaving an east-facing slope to enjoy the second-driest climate in France. Only Pinot Noir, Alsace's lone red, has difficulty ripening here, needing exceptional summers to make red rather than rosé.

Although we now see bottles labelled according to grape type from all over the world, Alsace was the first area of France to enshrine this practice in its own wine laws. A single AC was created for the whole region – Alsace AC – and apart from the blends, called Edelzwicker, most table wines are called by the grape name used. Usually this is the only

The steep Schoenenbourg Grand Cru vineyard towers over the beautiful village of Riquewihr, a major centre of the Alsace wine trade. Riesling and Muscat have traditionally done best here, especially as late-harvested wines.

description of wine type on the label but the best 50 vineyards are designated Grand Cru. Only wines made from Riesling, Pinot Gris, Gewurztraminer, Muscat and Sylvaner are entitled to be labelled Grand Cru.

Alsace usually benefits from long, sunny autumns, so in most years it is possible to leave parcels of grapes to overripen on the vine. The resulting Vendange Tardive (late-harvested) wines tend to be very rich and intense, with a little residual sugar to balance the powerful fruit and high alcohol. Less common are the wines labelled Sélection de Grains Nobles, which are produced from even riper grapes, usually concentrated by botrytis (noble rot). These wines are rare, sweet and extremely expensive.

At the opposite end of the taste spectrum are the lively sparkling wines called Crémant d'Alsace. These are usually made from varieties with high natural acidity such as Pinot Blanc, Auxerrois and Riesling, which are picked long before they reach the high ripeness levels they would need to make decent still wines. Most Crémant is pretty good fresh fizz.

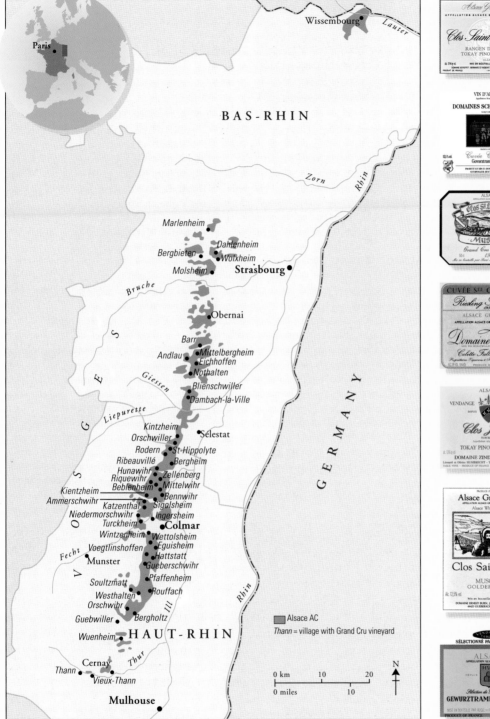

DOMAINE SCHOFFIT
The Clos St-Théobald
wines from the fabulous
Rangen Grand Cru
vineyard are full bodied
and very rich.

SCHLUMBERGER
Cuvée Christine, a
Vendange Tardive
equivalent, is one of the
top wines from this large,
family-owned domaine.

RENÉ MURÉ
From the superb
terraced vineyard of Clos
St-Landelin comes this
seductive, fruity Muscat
with heavenly perfume.

DOMAINE WEINBACH
This famous domaine's top
wine, from the Schlossberg
Grand Cru, blends the
austerity of Riesling with
depth, complexity and
seductive aromas.

ZIND-HUMBRECHT
The leading Alsace
estate produces a long
list of brilliant wines,
including many at
Vendange Tardive level.

ERNEST BURN
The Clos St-Imer is a
small terraced vineyard
on the upper slopes of
the Goldert Grand Cru
and is wholly owned by
the Burn family, whose
domaine is one of the
few in Alsace specialising
in Muscat.

HUGEL ET FILS
Hugel's rich, ripe spicy
Vendange Tardive wines
are usually capable
of lasting for 20 years
or more.

ALBERT MANN
Gewurztraminer is the most
voluptuous of all Alsace
wines and the Sélection de
Grains Nobles wines from
the Furstentum Grand Cru
can be astonishingly rich
and concentrated.

REGIONAL ENTRIES
Alsace Edelzwicker, Alsace Gewurztraminer, Alsace Grand Cru, Alsace Muscat, Alsace Pinot Blanc, Alsace Pinot Gris, Alsace Pinot Noir, Alsace Riesling, Alsace Sylvaner, Alsace Vendange Tardive, Crémant d'Alsace.

PRODUCER ENTRIES
Domaine Paul Blanck, Deiss, Hugel et Fils, Kreydenweiss, Kuentz-Bas, Schlumberger, Domaine Schoffit, F E Trimbach, Cave Vinicole de Turckheim, Domaine Weinbach, Zind-Humbrecht.

ALSACE EDELZWICKER

FRANCE, Alsace, Alsace AC

♀ *Chasselas, Sylvaner, Pinot Blanc and others*

In the mid-nineteenth century Edelzwicker was very highly regarded (*edel* means 'noble'), being a blend of the best grape varieties – Riesling, Gewurztraminer and Pinot Gris. Since ALSACE gained its AC in 1962, the tendency has been towards all the best grape varieties being vinified separately, so now Edelzwicker is generally a blend of Chasselas, Sylvaner and Pinot Blanc, beefed up with a splash or two of Gewurztraminer or Riesling. Never expensive, it can be good value and is for drinking young.

The name Edelzwicker is also giving way to wines labelled simply Alsace or Vin d'Alsace. Some producers use proprietary names for their blended wines rather than the debased Edelzwicker name, for example, HUGEL's Gentil. Best producers: Dirler-Cadé, Dopff & Irion, Éguisheim co-operative, Ehrhart, Gérard, Klipfel, Rolly Gassmann, Schoech, Schueller.

ALSACE GEWURZTRAMINER

FRANCE, Alsace, Alsace AC

♀ *Gewurztraminer*

Gewurztraminer's problem is that it is absurdly easy to enjoy. It must be wallowed in to get the best out of it. Given that ALSACE wines are renowned for their flowery spice, the 'Gewürz' (as it is often called – appropriately, since Gewürz is German for 'spice') is the most Alsatian of flavours because the smell is an explosion of roses, grapes, lychees, mangoes and peaches and the flavour is often thick with the richness of oriental fruit. Sometimes there's just not enough acidity to cope, but the effect is so luscious, you often don't mind.

It's worth emphasizing that these wines are almost always dry. The flavours are most evident in late-picked wines from hot years, but even cheap Gewurztraminer from a co-operative will be flowery, aromatic, exotic and unmistakable. Despite their low acidity, Gewurztraminer wines can be very long-lived, though they are always approachable young. Best years: 2001, '00, '99, '98, '97, '96, '95, '90, '89, '88, '85. Best producers: J-B Adam, Albrecht, Becker, Beyer, BLANCK, Boesch, Bott-Geyl, Boxler, Burn, DEISS, Dirler-Cadé, Dopff au Moulin, Ginglinger, Gresser, HUGEL, Josmeyer, Kientzler, KREYDENWEISS, KUENTZ-BAS, Landmann, Mader, Albert Mann, Meyer-Fonné, Mittnacht-Klack, Muré, Ostertag,

TRIMBACH

This Trimbach wine is a gloriously dry, full-bodied, rich and spicy example of the pink-skinned Gewurztraminer grape which is at its best in Alsace.

Rolly Gassmann, SCHAETZEL, Schleret, SCHLUMBERGER, SCHOFFIT, Sorg, Sparr, Turckheim co-operative, TRIMBACH, WEINBACH, ZIND-HUMBRECHT.

ALSACE GRAND CRU AC

FRANCE, Alsace

♀ *Riesling, Gewurztraminer, Pinot Gris or Muscat*

This appellation is an attempt, beginning with the 1985 vintage, to classify the best vineyards in ALSACE. It is fiercely resisted by some merchants, who argue that a blend from several vineyards always makes the best wines, but this just isn't so. It is the same now-discredited argument used for generations by the merchants of Burgundy who, anxious to keep tight control over their profitable share of the market, would deny a grower the right to say, 'This slope has always been special and I can show you why by offering you my version of its wine – unblended and undiluted.' At the same time, no-one would dispute that the houses that have refused to use this appellation system – notably HUGEL, Beyer and TRIMBACH – make some wines of outstanding quality. Part of their objection to the system is that too many Grands Crus were created, largely at the behest of growers with a vested interest in their existence, and that their borders were too broadly confirmed. Nonetheless, the system is clearly here to stay and, for all its deficiencies, does help identify some of the most remarkable sites. The Grands Crus vary in size from 3ha (7½ acres) to 80ha (200 acres) and are defined by broad geological principles.

At the moment 50 vineyards are classified, mostly in the southern Haut-Rhin section, though there are other sites under consideration. Only Gewurztraminer, Riesling, Pinot Gris and Muscat grapes qualify for Grand Cru status and the grape varieties must be unblended, although local authorities now also have some power to make local variations to the rules. Sylvaner is the most likely to

benefit from this change. Things look promising, especially since the minimum natural alcohol level for Grand Cru is higher (11 degrees for Riesling and Muscat, 12.5 degrees for Pinot Gris and Gewurztraminer) and the yield allowed is 55 hectolitres per hectare, as against 80 for AC wine. This alone can dramatically improve quality. However, despite a series of excellent vintages in the 1990s there are still a disturbing number of inconsequential Grand Cru wines. Here is a list of the top sites: Altenberg de Bergheim, Eichberg, Furstentum, Geisberg, Hengst, Kastelberg, Kirchberg, Rangen, Rosacker, Schoenenbourg and Vorbourg (Clos St-Landelin).

ALSACE MUSCAT

FRANCE, Alsace, Alsace AC

♀ *Muscat (Muscat Ottonel, Muscat Blanc à Petits Grains)*

ALSACE Muscat can be sheer heaven. Few wines have any taste of grape at all, but this one can seem like the purest essence of fresh grape – and yet be totally dry. It is a magical combination – the heady hothouse smell of a vine in late summer, the feel in your mouth delicate and light, yet the gentle fruit as perfumed and refreshing as the juice crunched from a fistful of Muscatel grapes.

The Muscat Blanc à Petits Grains variety used to predominate in Alsace, but its susceptibility to rot meant that producers turned increasingly to Muscat Ottonel. Now, luckily, growers are once more turning to the higher quality Muscat Blanc à Petits Grains, with good results. The two varieties cover less than 3 per cent of the vineyard area, because they are both prone to disease and often only ripen well one year in two. If you see one – snap it up, chill it for an hour, and serve it either as the perfect aperitif or as a reviving after-dinner drink. Drink young. Best producers: J-B Adam, Albrecht, Becker, Bott-Geyl, Boxler, Burn, Dirler-Cadé, Ginglinger, Kientzler, KUENTZ-BAS, Landmann, Mader, Albert Mann, Muré, Rolly Gassmann, SCHOFFIT, Schueller, TRIMBACH, WEINBACH, ZIND-HUMBRECHT.

ALSACE PINOT BLANC

FRANCE, Alsace, Alsace AC

♀ *Pinot Blanc, Auxerrois Blanc*

For an apparently simple wine, a Pinot Blanc can have an awfully complicated make-up. Usually it is a blend of Pinot Blanc and the similar, but unrelated, Auxerrois and is a soft dry white, appley, slightly creamy – the perfect wine-bar drink.

However, white wine labelled Pinot can also be made from the red Pinot Noir (and can be delicious, full and creamy) or Pinot Gris, which is sometimes used to beef up a weaker pure Pinot Blanc. The wines all share a fresh, soft, easy-drinking style and are excellent young, but sometimes also capable of aging well. Klevner or Clevner, the Alsace name for Pinot Blanc, seldom appears on a label – if it does, it generally applies to a Pinot Blanc-Auxerrois blend. Best producers: J-B Adam, Becker, Beyer, BLANCK, Bott-Geyl, Boxler, Burn, DEISS, Frick, HUGEL, Josmeyer, Kientzler, KREYDENWEISS, Mader, Albert Mann, Meyer-Fonné, Muré, Ostertag, Rolly Gassmann, Schaetzel, SCHLUMBERGER, SCHOFFIT, Tempé, TRIMBACH, TURCKHEIM co-operative, WEINBACH, ZIND-HUMBRECHT.

ALSACE PINOT GRIS
FRANCE, Alsace, Alsace AC
♀ *Pinot Gris*

Top Pinot Gris wines are frequently ALSACE's greatest wines and even the basic ones have a lovely lick of honey to soften their attractive peachy fruit. The wines used to be called Tokay d'Alsace and you may see a few labels saying 'Tokay-Pinot Gris'. Once a minor player, Pinot Gris is now firmly in fashion and covers over 11 per cent of the vineyards.

The legend is that an Alsatian soldier, de Schwendi, attacked the Hungarian fortress of Tokaj in 1565, captured 4000 vats of their Tokay wine and liked it so much that he sent his servant to fetch some Tokay vine cuttings. Now, Hungarian TOKAJI (as it is called today) is made from Furmint grapes; yet the servant brought back Pinot Gris, already well known in less distant BURGUNDY. So perhaps he really sneaked off there, and only pretended to go to Hungary. Anyway, the name Tokay stuck, but the wine is always made from Pinot Gris; and nowadays the label is supposed to say Pinot Gris in order to avoid confusion with the Hungarian Tokaji.

ZIND-HUMBRECHT
The Pinot Gris from the Clos Windsbuhl site in Hunawihr is a fabulously rich and concentrated wine from this top estate.

It is golden wine, often seeming too dark in colour for its own good. Its acidity is low, but that doesn't stop it aging brilliantly, blending a treacle, honey and raisin richness with flavours like the essence from the skins of peaches and apricots, and a slight smokiness. And, again, in Alsace this is almost always a dry wine! The Vendange Tardive styles are particularly exciting but even at the basic level you should glimpse these flavours. The wine can be drunk immediately or aged for some years. Best years: 2001, '00, '99, '98, '97, '96, '95, '90, '89, '88, '85, '83. Best producers: J-B Adam, Albrecht, Beyer, BLANCK, Bott-Geyl, Boxler, Burn, DEISS, Dopff et Irion, Dopff au Moulin, HUGEL, Josmeyer, Kientzler, KREYDENWEISS, KUENTZ-BAS, Landmann, Mader, Albert Mann, Muré, Ostertag, Rolly Gassmann, Schleret, SCHLUMBERGER, SCHOFFIT, Schueller, Sparr, TRIMBACH, WEINBACH, ZIND-HUMBRECHT; Pfaffenheim and TURCKHEIM co-operatives.

ALSACE PINOT NOIR
FRANCE, Alsace, Alsace AC
♠ ♀ *Pinot Noir*

It's bad luck on ALSACE that, although the region boasts one of the greatest cuisines in France, it can't produce the great red wines many of the dishes cry out for. You have to go south to BURGUNDY or the RHÔNE for that. The only red grape they manage to ripen in Alsace is the Pinot Noir – and then only in the warmer years. Frankly, it rarely achieves much colour or much weight, although in years like 2000 and 1996 some quite impressive specimens were made.

But, even when it is closer to pink than red, Alsace Pinot Noir often reveals a hauntingly spring-like perfume rare in a red wine, and a gentle soothing strawberry flavour that slips down pretty easily (chilling it for an hour isn't a bad idea). A lot of effort is going into making Alsace Pinot Noir a more serious proposition, which can mean aging the wine in small oak barrels with often a sizeable proportion of new oak, which is stretching things a bit since these wines rarely have the guts to cope with oak-barrel aging. In any case, the wines should be drunk for their bright, cherry-red fruit and that's the first thing to disappear if you leave the wine in an oak barrel for six months or if you leave it in the bottle for too long. Best producers: DEISS, Ginglinger, HUGEL, Koehly, KUENTZ-BAS, Mann, Muré, Rolly Gassmann, TURCKHEIM co-operative, Wolfberger.

ALSACE RIESLING
FRANCE, Alsace, Alsace AC
♀ *Riesling*

Among ALSACE winemakers Riesling is the most revered grape variety. Although it is the great grape of Germany they take positively provocative pleasure in asserting that their totally dry, yet full-bodied style is superior to Germany's lighter, sweeter product. And although Germany now makes large numbers of dry (*trocken*) styles, Alsace Riesling at its best is still that bit more substantial and interesting.

About 23 per cent of the region is planted with Riesling and this is increasing. When the wines are young they should have a steely streak of acidity, cold like shining metal splashed with lemon and rubbed with an unripe apple. As they age, sometimes after two years but sometimes not until ten years or more, a pure, strangely unindulgent honey builds up, a nutty weight balancing the acid which itself slowly turns to the zest of limes and the unmistakable wafting pungency of petrol fumes. Alsace Riesling is certainly highly individual. Vendange Tardive and special Sélection de Grains Nobles wines are mostly likely to show this style. There is a growing tendency to leave some residual sugar in the wines, which rounds them out and gives them instant appeal, but also obscures the exciting mineral steeliness of Alsace Riesling at its best. Ordinary blends can be dilute and bland, particularly since many Riesling growers overproduce. Best years: 2001, '00, '99, '98, '97, 96, '95, '90, '89, '88, '85, '83. Best producers: Adam, Albrecht, Becker, Beyer, BLANCK, Bott-Geyl, Boxler, Burn, DEISS, Dirler-Cadé, Dopff au Moulin, Ginglinger, HUGEL, Josmeyer, Kientzler, KREYDENWEISS, KUENTZ-BAS, Landmann, Lorentz, Mader, Mittnacht-Klack, Muré, Ostertag, Ribeauvillé co-operative, Rolly Gassmann, Martin Schaetzel, SCHLUMBERGER, SCHOFFIT, Sick-Dreyer, Louis Sipp, Sparr, TRIMBACH, WEINBACH, ZIND-HUMBRECHT.

ALSACE SYLVANER
FRANCE, Alsace, Alsace AC
♀ *Sylvaner*

Sylvaner used to be the most widely planted of ALSACE's grapes but now accounts for only 13 per cent of the vineyard area. It is gradually being supplanted by Pinot Blanc and Riesling, both superior non-aromatic varieties (Gewurztraminer, Pinot Gris and Muscat are the 'aromatics'). It has quite good acidity and ripens well in the northern Alsace vineyards, and down on the plain. From a good producer, young Sylvaner wine can acquire an earth and honey fullness, streaked with green apple acidity, though it often brings along a whiff of tomato, too. Best producers: Boeckel, Boesch, Dirler-Cadé, Dopff au Moulin, Kientzler, Landmann, Muré, Ostertag, Pfaffenheim co-operative, Rolly Gassmann, Schleret, SCHOFFIT, Seltz, TRIMBACH, WEINBACH, ZIND-HUMBRECHT.

ALSACE VENDANGE TARDIVE AC

FRANCE, Alsace

♀ *Riesling, Muscat, Pinot Gris, Gewurztraminer*

Vendange tardive means 'late-harvest' in French. The grapes are picked almost over-ripe, giving much higher sugar levels and therefore much more intense, exciting flavours. The wine must be made from one grape variety, and only from one of ALSACE's four noble varieties – Riesling, Muscat, Gewurztraminer or Pinot Gris. The minimum natural alcohol strength is 13.1 degrees for Riesling and Muscat and 14.4 degrees for Gewurztraminer and Pinot Gris. Fourteen degrees is quite a mouthful, and given the aromatic personality of ALSACE wines, there are some exceptional late-picked wines to be had from warm years such as 1997 and '90.

Most Vendange Tardive wines are totally dry, but usually rich and mouthfilling at the same time, and they often need five years or more to show their personality. They can be disappointingly 'shut in' at two to three years old, but then superb five years later. A growing number of these wines now contain some residual sugar, which is fine if the wine is balanced. Unfortunately there is nothing on the label to indicate the style of the wine, whether it is dry, medium-sweet or sweet.

Sélection de Grains Nobles is a further sub-category, from very late-picked grapes affected by botrytis or noble rot (the same fungus which creates the sweetness in SAUTERNES). The minimum natural alcohol here is 15.2 degrees for Riesling and Muscat and 16.6 degrees for Gewurztraminer and Pinot Gris. The actual sugar levels are often much higher in good years. Since the yeasts cannot ferment the wines much beyond 15 degrees, they are often sweet and incredibly concentrated, able to age for decades. Very little is made, and only in exceptional years such as 1998, '95 and '94, and it is always wildly expensive. Best years: (Vendange Tardive and Sélection de Grains Nobles) 2002, '01, '00, '98, '97, '96, '95, '94, '93, '92, '90, '89, '88, '85, '76.

ELIO ALTARE

ITALY, Piedmont, Barolo DOCG

♟ *Nebbiolo, Barbera, Dolcetto, Cabernet Sauvignon*

Scion of a Nebbiolo-producing family of La Morra, Elio, influenced by his trips to Burgundy, began in 1978 the process of bunch-thinning in pursuit of top-quality BAROLO, much to the horror of his father. This perceived insanity resulted in his temporary expulsion from the Cascina Nuova family estate. He later returned, introduced French oak barriques (in 1983, one of the first in Barolo) and took to horrifying just about everybody with maceration periods for Nebbiolo so abbreviated that the pulp had scarcely the time to introduce itself to the skins before it was racked away into small barrels to finish the fermentation and do the malolactic. His aim was, and is, to produce BURGUNDY-like wines, svelte in youth yet capable of aging; wines that can be drunk with pleasure at any time.

He crafts some of the most stunning of Alba's wines: excellent Dolcetto d'Alba and BARBERA D'ALBA and even finer Barolo Vigneto Arborina and new Barolo Brunate. Though a professed modernist, his wines are intense, full and structured while young, but with clearly discernible fruit flavours, thanks largely to tiny yields. He also makes three barrique-aged wines under the LANGHE DOC: Arborina (from Nebbiolo), Larigi (Barbera) and La Villa (a Nebbiolo-Barbera blend). He is one of seven producers who make a version of L'Insieme (a Nebbiolo-Cabernet-Barbera blend). Best years: (Barolo) 2001, '00, '99, '98, '96, '95, '93, '90, '89, '88, '86, '85.

ALTO ADIGE DOC

ITALY, Alto Adige

♟ *Schiava (Vernatsch), Lagrein, Pinot Noir (Pinot Nero, Blauburgunder), Merlot, Cabernet Franc, Cabernet Sauvignon and others*

♟ *Lagrein*

♀ *Pinot Blanc (Pinot Bianco, Weissburgunder), Chardonnay, Pinot Gris (Pinot Grigio, Ruländer), Gewürztraminer (Traminer Aromatico) and others*

Alto Adige, or Südtirol as it is called by the German-speaking majority, is the part of Italy north of TRENTINO that is almost in Austria (indeed it was until 1919), and enjoys official Italian/German bilingualism. Vines grow on the steep slopes of the mountains that tumble down to the Adige river (Etsch in German) and its tributary, the Isarco (Eisack), and sometimes on the narrow valley floor too.

The range of altitudes and exposures afforded by the mountains gives winemakers an unparalleled opportunity to grow a wide variety of grape types. Of the many grapes used to make varietal wines, some have their origins in Germany, some in France and a few in Italy. Red varieties, such as Lagrein, Schiava and Cabernet, grow on the lowest slopes. French whites, such as Chardonnay, Pinot Grigio and Pinot Bianco, are planted a little higher and German ones, such as Riesling, Müller-Thurgau and Sylvaner, are found on the highest slopes. The pergola *trentina* – a high trunk with an upward-angled branch following the steep angle of the slope – is the traditional training method, producing consistently high yields, but is giving way gradually to the lower *spalliera* – guyot or cordon spur – especially for quality red grapes.

Alto Adige is an historic wine region, going back some 3000 years or more. The growing area is centred on the city of Bolzano (Bozen), which stands at the crux of a Y-shaped system of valleys of which the upper right-hand branch, in the direction of Bressanone (Brixen), is constituted by the Isarco river, while the Adige descends from upper left (direction Merano/Meran) and, meeting the Isarco at Bolzano, continues on down to Salorno (Salurn) below which it enters the province of Trento. A clue to Alto Adige's success as a quality growing area is the fact that Bolzano, Italy's northernmost provincial capital, occasionally in summer records the highest temperatures in the land, beating even Palermo and Cagliari at the other end of the country.

Alto Adige's combination of climate, altitude and slope allows in its wines a wonderfully pure expression of varietal character. The region-wide DOC covers well over 30 styles of wine including varietals, blends and fizz, and production is enormous (between 30 and 40 million litres a year). Reds are almost invariably varietal and range from light and perfumed when made from the Schiava grape, to fruity and more structured from the Cabernets or Merlot, through to dark and velvety if Lagrein is used.

Although Chardonnay is seen more and more – and often barrel fermented and aged to good effect – it is Pinot Bianco (which it much resembles) that seems better adapted to Alto Adige conditions, combining creaminess with apple freshness. German grapes, like Riesling, Müller-Thurgau and Sylvaner, can be piercingly clean and pure-tasting,

ALOIS LAGEDER

Lageder is the leading private estate in the Alto Adige, making good, medium-priced varietals and star single-vineyard wines such as this classy Pinot Bianco.

while Gewürztraminer, which may well have originated in the local village of Termeno (or, more to the point, Tramin in German), is very delicate and only subtly scented.

Much of the wine comes from well-run co-operatives. Sub-zones of the Alto Adige DOC include the previously independent DOCs of Colli di Bolzano, Santa Maddalena, Terlano and Valle Isarco. All Alto Adige wines are usually drunk young, although from the best producers they will improve for two or three years and sometimes much longer.

There is also some very good sparkling wine made from Chardonnay and Pinots Bianco, Grigio and Nero. The best, using the traditional method or *metodo classico*, is from Vivaldi (under the Vivaldi Arunda label). Other best producers: Abbazia di Novacella, Caldaro co-op, Casòn Hirschprunn, Colterenzio co-op, Peter Dipoli, Giorgio Grai, Franz Haas, Hofstätter, LAGEDER, Laimburg, J Niedermayr, Ignaz Niedriest, Peter Pliger-Kuenhof, Prima & Nuova/Erste & Neue, Hans Rottensteiner, San Michele Appiano co-op, TIEFENBRUNNER, Elena Walch, Baron Widmann.

ÁLVAREZ Y DÍEZ

SPAIN, Castilla y León, Rueda DO
♀ Verdejo, Sauvignon Blanc, Macabeo (Viura)

Álvarez y Díez, the biggest private wine company in RUEDA, no longer makes traditional flor-affected, sherry-like wines, concentrating instead on pretty good modern whites. Álvarez y Díez also pride themselves in being absolutely organic.

Most interesting are the light, crisp whites for which Rueda is fast making its name. Álvarez y Díez use much more of the high-quality, flavourful Verdejo than most producers in the region, to produce soft, nutty Mantel Blanco Rueda Superior. There is also a barrel-fermented Verdejo and a finer, freshly acidic Mantel Blanco Sauvignon Blanc. Drink the wines young, within two to three years.

CASTELLO DI AMA

ITALY, Tuscany, Chianti Classico DOCG
♀ ♀ Sangiovese, Merlot, Canaiolo, Malvasia Nera, Pinot Noir (Pinot Nero)
♀ Chardonnay

This sizeable estate, purchased in 1977 by a group of Romans, is managed today by the daughter of one of them, Lorenza Sebasti, and her viticulturist/winemaker husband Marco Pallanti. Since the mid-1980s Castello di Ama has produced some of Tuscany's best CHIANTI CLASSICO and SUPER-TUSCAN wines. Pallanti has been responsible for identifying the merits of particular sections, or *vigneti,* of the 90ha (222-acre) estate and for re-grafting or re-planting them according to their optimum potential.

Today the estate is best known for its Chianti Classico crus, Bellavista (with a small percentage of Malvasia Nera) and La Casuccia (with Merlot), and especially for the super-Tuscan L'Apparita, from Merlot vines grafted in the early 1980s onto Canaiolo and Malvasia Bianca in a clay-rich 4-ha (10-acre) section of the Bellavista vineyard and trained, unusually, on the open lyre formation. L'Apparita, indeed, has become almost as famous in its genre as SASSICAIA became among Cabernet Sauvignons of the world in the 1970s, and its tremendous fruit, its power combined with elegance, has brought it glory in numerous tastings and competitions. Other super-Tuscans include a Pinot Nero (Il Chiuso) and a Chardonnay (Al Poggio). Best years: (Chianti Classico) 2001, '00. '99, '98, '97, '95, '93, '90, '88, '85.

AMADOR COUNTY

USA, California

For anyone who thinks the California wine industry has become just a little too slick and modern for their liking, it's time they took a hike into the Sierra Nevada foothills to Amador County, where the little towns established in the fervour of the Gold Rush during the 1850s are still haunted by a palpable sense of their Wild West braggadocio, where the little roads are congenitally incapable of staying straight for more than 50 yards at a time – and where some of the gnarled, blackened Zinfandel vines are over 130 years old. Amador County slumbered forgotten through most of the twentieth century, and its renaissance started cautiously in the 1970s but then took furious hold during the 1990s as California's increasingly passionate Zinfandel advocates realized that nestled into the nooks and crannies of these ancient foothills at around 400m (1300ft)

elevation were some of the last survivors of California's original plantings. These Zins are marvellously rich and briary but icy night temperatures mean thay also have appetizing acidity. Syrah and Italian varieties are also grown. White grapes are little planted. Amador now has around 25 wineries.

AMARONE DELLA VALPOLICELLA DOC

ITALY, Veneto
♀ Corvina, Corvinone, Rondinella, Molinara and others

Amarone is the dry version of ancient Recioto. It is not a recent development, as some would have it, nor is it an aberration of the classic sweet wine; it's just that this dry style has only recently come into fashion.

Amarone is made from early-picked, high-quality VALPOLICELLA grapes that are left on shallow racks in a cool, airy place after the harvest to dry for up to four or five months. The resulting shrivelled, concentrated *passito* bunches are then fermented to dryness, unlike sweet RECIOTO DELLA VALPOLICELLA – except that the wine never seems absolutely dry. Even the aromas seem to promise a wine of power and richness, while on the palate there is the sweetness of fruit and alcohol, with the promised bitterness cutting in at the end to provide a dry finish. Indeed, even the bitterness is chocolaty, with, in the best examples, a wealth of the sweet-sour cherry-fruit aromas that is so characteristic of the wines of Valpolicella. Styles vary between the classic heavyweight beasts with 16 per cent or more alcohol and (comparatively) lighter and fruitier styles around 14 per cent, the legal minimum.

At its best Amarone is not just one of the great wines of Italy but a world classic. The quality is improving every year as more and more producers join the quality-first bandwagon and the prices rise inexorably, making the whole labour-intensive exercise increasingly worthwhile. The recent construction of a huge purpose-built centre in the Valpolicella commune of Fumane, complete with automatically triggered wind-producing machines to prevent any botrytis during the drying period, is a testament to the success of Amarone. Best years: 2001, '00, '97, '95, '93, '90, '88. Best producers: Stefano Accordini, ALLEGRINI, Bertani, Brigaldara, Brunelli, Tommaso Bussola, Michele Castellani (I Castei and Cà del Pipa), DAL FORNO, Guerrieri-Rizzardi, MASI, QUINTARELLI, Le Ragose, Le Salette, Serègo Alighieri, Speri, Tedeschi, Tommasi, Villa Montaleone, Viviani, Zenato.

ANDALUCÍA Spain

ANDALUCÍA, A VAST SPREAD of eight provinces stretching right across the sunbaked south of Spain, welcomes millions of tourists each year. But relatively few of them ever stray far from the Costa del Sol. Those who do discover a land quite different from the rest of the Iberian peninsula as this was the part of Spain longest occupied by the Moors – the words 'la Frontera' tacked onto many local place names, including that of Jerez, reflects how for a full hundred years these towns were on the frontier between Christian and Moorish Spain. Whitewashed walls, cool courtyards and roof terraces on the oldest houses testify to eight centuries of Arab dominion, as do the place names, local crafts and even the inevitable flamenco dancing. Solitary farmhouses are a feature of the countryside, set in the eastern provinces among landscapes of olive trees or cereals, irrigated fruit trees or early vegetables, and in the west among fields of sunflowers, cereals and vines.

Andalucía overflows with vines, but there are far more in the west than the east. All of Andalucía's DOs lie to the west of Granada, and account for over half of the region's vineyards. But if it seems strange that the most famous wines made in such a hot climate should all be fortified – just wait until you taste the unfortified wines. It is hard to get excited by any of the bland, flavourless whites, and those are the good ones. The bad are horrific. The one small but interesting ray of light is that there are now one or two serious red wine estates establishing themselves over in the east of Andalucía, and their first results are impressive. There's absolutely no reason of soil or climate why they shouldn't be good: it's just that no one has ever though of experimenting here before.

As for the run of the mill whites, usually based on Palomino or Pedro Ximénez, thank goodness the Andalucíans evolved a way to turn their basic table wines into nectar to accompany the incessant socializing and lengthy meals. For this is a part of Spain where lunch never starts before three in the afternoon, and you consider yourself lucky if you sit down to dinner by midnight, after delicious hours of tapas – copious nibbles of olives, anchovies, fried peppers, salted almonds, squid – and glass after glass of chilled fino.

In Jerez the tulip-shaped *copita* glass would contain fino sherry, in Sanlúcar de Barrameda, manzanilla, in inland

The magnificent La Concha or 'Seashell' bodega in Jerez belongs to González Byass. Its revolutionary circular design was the work of the French engineer, Alexandre Gustave Eiffel who later went on to design the Eiffel Tower in Paris.

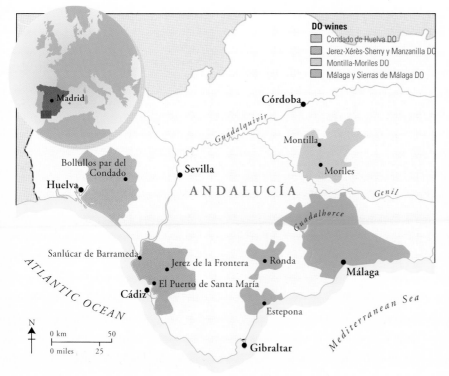

ALVEAR

The Pedro Ximénez grape, which can stand up to the withering heat of the Montilla-Moriles area, is used to make this powerful, dense, sweet fortified wine.

DOMECQ

Domecq, the oldest and largest of the sherry companies, is best known for its yeast, tangy fino sherry, La Ina.

HIDALGO

With its intense salty aroma, Hidalgo's Manzanilla La Gitana is deservedly the bestselling manzanilla in Spain.

GONZÁLEZ BYASS

Superb old sherries are the speciality of the González Byass firm – Amontillado del Duque is dry and powerful with magnificent flavour and length.

VALDESPINO

This very old-fashioned, very high-quality family business makes a range of top-class, dry sherries including the stylish, elegant Inocente Fino with its pungent, flor-influenced aromas.

Córdoba it might be Montilla, and in Málaga, down by the coast, a stiff tot of the 'mountain' wine so loved by the Victorians.

Despite the relentless, glaring heat, the sherry region, in particular, is well suited to vines. The best soil – finely grained, dazzlingly white *albariza* which sweeps right across the central growing area – contains between 60 and 80 per cent chalk and acts as a sponge, soaking up and storing the ample winter rainfall until the vines crave it in the height of midsummer. Accordingly, yields are high, for the vineyards of Jerez, all trained on wires, are among the most modern in Spain, and the Palomino Fino – the main grape for sherry – is always a generous bearer.

REGIONAL ENTRIES
Jerez y Manzanilla, Málaga, Montilla-Moriles.

PRODUCER ENTRIES
Barbadillo, Domecq, Garvey, González Byass, Hidalgo, Lustau, Osborne, Valdespino.

LÓPEZ HERMANOS

López Hermanos is by far the largest producer in the Málaga DO, making a wide range of different styles of this historic sweet wine.

LUSTAU

Based in Jerez, Lustau is renowned for its Almacenista range of very individual, dry, single-batch sherries from small private producers.

OSBORNE

From the sherry arm of Osborne, Spain's biggest drinks company, at Puerto de Santa María, comes Bailén Oloroso, a dry, rich and powerful fortified wine with a fine, nutty character.

ANDERSON VALLEY AVA

USA, California, Mendocino County

Almost overnight this small valley in western MENDOCINO COUNTY acquired a reputation for CHAMPAGNE-method sparklers. In the late 1960s these foggy hills, a few miles inland from the Pacific Ocean, had been earmarked for Gewurztraminer, Chardonnay and Pinot Noir. Then, in 1985, the famous Champagne house ROEDERER elected to locate its US operation in the valley because the weather is almost as foul as Champagne's own, or so said one of the decision-makers in the deal. The indications are that it was an excellent decision because if you look for the grape source of California's best sparklers, more and more often it's Anderson Valley. Best years: 2001, '00, '99, '98, '96. Best producers: Greenwood Ridge, HANDLEY, Lazy Creek, Navarro, Pacific Echo, ROEDERER ESTATE.

HANDLEY
Handley is one of the rising stars in California and in the cool Anderson Valley region makes a range of excellent sparkling wines.

ANDREW WILL WINERY

USA, Washington State
🍷 *Merlot, Cabernet Sauvignon, Cabernet Franc, Sangiovese, Syrah*
🍾 *Pinot Gris*

Winemaker Chris Camarda makes heady Merlots and powerful Cabernet Sauvignons at his winery on Vashon Island, west of Seattle, from a range of older vineyards from across the Cascades in eastern Washington that rank with the USA's finest. At the top are the complex Champoux Vineyard, the opulent Ciel du Cheval and the tannic, black-fruited Klipsun. Wines from the WALLA WALLA vineyards of Pepper Bridge and Seven Hills are fruitier and quicker to mature, but all the Andrew Will reds demand at least a few years' aging to show at their best. The BORDEAUX blend Sorella reveals the deftness of his winemaking, balancing ripe berry fruit, oak and glycerin in perfect proportions and is outstanding with age. I hardly ever see the white wines: I get the impression that Chris thinks wine has a duty to be red. Best years: (reds) 2001, '00, '99, '97, '96, '95, '94, '93.

CH. ANGÉLUS

FRANCE, Bordeaux, St-Émilion Grand Cru AC, Premier Grand Cru Classé
🍷 *Merlot, Cabernet Franc, Cabernet Sauvignon*

Judging by the price of the wine, you would expect Ch. Angélus to be a leading Premier Grand Cru Classé – and the rich, warm, mouthfilling flavour would confirm this. Yet it was only classified as Premier Grand Cru Classé in the 1996 revision of the ST-ÉMILION classification. This shows how the influence of an energetic owner, a talented winemaker and investment in the winery can upgrade the quality of a vineyard's wine – just as laziness, incompetence and pennypinching can dilute it. Angélus is well placed on the lower part of the *côtes* (slopes) to the west of the town of St-Émilion, but the soil is rather heavy. Until 1979 this resulted in fruity, though slightly bland wine. But in the 1980s lower yields, severe selection and new oak barrel-aging were introduced, adding a sturdy backbone and a richer concentration of fruit and increasingly gorgeous wines were made throughout the 1980s and 90s. Best years: 2001, '00, '99, '98, '97, '96, '95, '94, '93, '92, '90, '89, '88.

MARQUIS D'ANGERVILLE

FRANCE, Burgundy, Côte de Beaune, Volnay AC
🍷 *Pinot Noir*
🍾 *Chardonnay*

In the 1930s the d'Angervilles were among the first growers to bottle their own wines, and today the domaine remains one of the best in VOLNAY, the classiest of the Côte de Beaune's red wine appellations. With over half a century's experience and meticulous attention to detail, Marquis Jacques d'Angerville produces an exemplary range of elegant Premiers Crus, including Clos des Ducs, Champans and Taillepieds. All the wines should be kept for at least five years. There is also some POMMARD and MEURSAULT. Best years: (top reds) 2002, '99, '98, '97, '96, '95, '93, '91, '90.

MARQUIS D'ANGERVILLE
The Premier Cru Clos des Ducs is wholly owned by the d'Angerville family and produces a delicate and exciting wine, usually deep-coloured with a lovely, spicy nose.

CH. D'ANGLUDET

FRANCE, Bordeaux, Haut-Médoc, Margaux AC, Cru Bourgeois
🍷 *Cabernet Sauvignon, Merlot, Petit Verdot, Cabernet Franc*

The wine from this English-owned property (the Sichel family who are also part-owners of Ch. PALMER) has a delicious, approachable burst of blackcurrant-and-blackberry fruit that makes you want to drink it immediately – yet it ages superbly for up to a decade or more. Its price-quality ratio is one of the best in BORDEAUX since the wine is always of Classed Growth standard and consistent but the price is well below it – if you want to buy red wine to lay down I suggest starting with Ch. d'Angludet. Best years: 2000, '98, '96, '95, '94, '90, '89, '88.

ANJOU AC, ANJOU GAMAY AC

FRANCE, Loire, Anjou-Saumur
🍷 *Cabernet Franc, Cabernet Sauvignon, Pineau d'Aunis, Gamay*
🍾 *Chenin Blanc, Chardonnay, Sauvignon Blanc*

The large, catch-all Anjou AC covers the whole Maine-et-Loire *département*, as well as parts of Deux-Sèvres and Vienne, with a total vineyard area of 3380ha (8352 acres). The Anjou region is best known for its rosé wine (ROSÉ D'ANJOU), but it's hardly something to be proud of and the drift away from rosé by the drinking public has forced the Anjou winemakers to rethink. Increasingly the leading producers are turning their hand to reds with considerable success, particularly with Gamay, Cabernet Franc, Cabernet Sauvignon and Pineau d'Aunis grapes. There is a separate appellation for Gamay, the Beaujolais grape and using the Beaujolais method of vinification – carbonic maceration – the results for Anjou Gamay can be similar, if a bit sturdier. Best years: (top reds) 2002 '01 '00 '97 '96 '95. Best producers: (reds and rosés) M Angeli, P Baudouin, Brizé, Chamboureau, de FESLES, de la Motte, Putille, J Pithon, Richou.

Anjou Blanc accounts for over seven million bottles a year, about one-third of the total production. During the 1990s Chenin Blanc's potential as the Loire's greatest white grape was increasingly recognized. Up to 20 per cent Chardonnay or Sauvignon Blanc can be added to Anjou Blanc but increasingly producers prefer to use only Chenin. Using modern cool-fermentation methods and in the hands of the best producers, Anjou Blanc is being transformed from its mediocre former self. Anjou Blanc can cover medium-dry wines as well as dry and these are increasingly attractive – fresh, slightly honeyed and good value.

Unfortunately Anjou Blanc still has an identity crisis: it is not one style but several, and still too much is poorly made and sold very cheaply. This poses problems for producers intent on making more concentrated, 'serious' versions, some of which may have been fermented and aged in oak. Some of the better ones come from the Anjou Coteaux de la Loire sub-region. There is a small amount of sparkling dry or off-dry Anjou Mousseux. Best years: (top whites) 2002, '01, '00, '99, '97, '96. Best producers: (whites) M Angeli, Cady, de FESLES, Montgilet/V Lebreton, Mosse, Ogereau, Pierre-Bise, J Pithon, Richou, Soucherie/P-Y Tijou.

ANJOU-VILLAGES AC

FRANCE, Loire, Anjou-Saumur

♟ *Cabernet Franc, Cabernet Sauvignon*

Since the ANJOU AC is such a blanket term – and one with a fairly poor reputation – the better producers of red wines lobbied for years to get their wines upgraded. From the 1985 vintage, 46 villages have been entitled to the Anjou-Villages AC for red wine from Cabernet Franc and Cabernet Sauvignon grapes. Some extremely attractive, dry but fruity reds are being made, with better aging potential than straight Anjou Rouge.

Although some producers still make a very light Anjou-Villages which is almost indistinguishable from their straight Anjou, serious ones ensure that their Villages wine has more concentration and structure. Producers are also paying attention to ripeness and being careful not to extract too much tannin, so that their wines are more approachable, with fewer harsh tannins. The sub-appellation, Anjou-Villages Brissac, covers the area around Brissac-Quincé which has a reputation for producing the best reds. Best years: 2002, '01, '00, '97, '96, '95, '90, '89. Best producers: Brizé, P Delesvaux, Montgilet/V Lebreton, Ogereau, Pierre-Bise, Putille, Richou, Rochelles/J-Y Lebreton, Pierre Soulez.

ROBERTO ANSELMI

ITALY, Veneto

♟ *Cabernet Sauvignon*

♀ *Garganega, Trebbiano di Soave, Chardonnay and others*

The man behind the world-famous name of Anselmi is the expansive Roberto Anselmi who is rightly credited with being one of the major forces behind the revival of SOAVE, an ancient but industrially degraded wine. He entered the business in 1974 and immediately introduced French-style restricted-yield viticulture: he planted Chardonnay (heresy!), he introduced selective picking and bunch-thinning and even bought new oak barrels – probably the first in Italy to be used for white wines.

Today, Anselmi the pioneer is almost establishment, but the dynamism continues and the enthusiasm lives. Using ultra-modern methods he has honed the fruit flavours of his San Vincenzo and Capitel Foscarino and introduced small barrel-aging for his single-vineyard Capitel Croce and luscious SAUTERNES-like I Capitelli. These wines are now sold under the regional IGT – Anselmi's response to the continuing poor quality of so much Soave. Almost as revolutionary was his introduction to this region of Cabernet Sauvignon, from which he makes a sleek Bordeaux-style wine called Realdà. Best years: (I Capitelli) 2001, '00, '99, '98, '97, '96, '95, '93, '92, '90, '88.

ANTINORI

ITALY, Tuscany, Umbria, Piedmont, Puglia (Tuscan estates) ♟ *Sangiovese, Cabernet Sauvignon, Merlot, Canaiolo, Pinot Noir*

♟ *Sangiovese, Canaiolo*

♀ *Chardonnay, Grechetto, Trebbiano, Malvasia, Vermentino*

The Antinori family are proud of the fact that they have been in the wine business for over 600 years, covering 26 generations since 1385. Arguably, however, it is during the present generation, under the leadership of Marchese Piero Antinori, that the company has had the greatest influence – on the wines of TUSCANY first and foremost, but on other areas of Italy and now also abroad.

Interests further afield include Castello della Sala in UMBRIA, producing the famous Chardonnay- Grechetto blend Cervaro and sweet Muffato, PRUNOTTO in PIEDMONT, Tormaresca in PUGLIA, FRANCIACORTA's Monte Nisa, Atlas Peak in CALIFORNIA and Bátaapáti in Hungary. Their principal stronghold, however, is Tuscany where they

own 1100ha (2718 acres) and the quality of the CHIANTI CLASSICO wines like Badia a Passignano Riserva, Pèppoli, Tenute Marchese Antinori Riserva and Villa Antinori is consistently good.

Antinori were among the first to refuse to accept the now outmoded DOC system for CHIANTI in the 1970s and to experiment with Sangiovese-Cabernet blends for their two flagship SUPER-TUSCAN wines, Tignanello and Solaia from their Santa Cristina estate. From the 2001 vintage Villa Antinori is being classified as Toscana IGT instead of Chianti Classico Riserva DOCG to gve greater flexibility over blends and production methods.

Introducing small barrel-aging to Tuscany, Tignanello (Sangiovese-Cabernet) and Solaia (Cabernet-based) can be stunning wines from a top vintage. Other Tuscan wines include VINO NOBILE DI MONTEPULCIANO (La Braccesca), BRUNELLO DI MONTALCINO (Pian delle Vigne), BOLGHERI (Guado al Tasso, a Cabernet-Merlot blend) and Bramasole, a new Syrah-Merlot blend from the Cortona DOC. Piero Antinori is still brimming with energy, but is handing over power increasingly to his three daughters, Albiera, currently managing director of Prunotto, Allegra who handles international public relations and Alessia, a qualified enologist who helps on the technical side which is under the overall control of Renzo Cotarella. Best years: (Tuscan reds) 2001, '00, '99, '97, '95, '93, '90.

ANTONOPOULOS

GREECE, Peloponnese, Patras AO

♟ *Agiorgitiko, Cabernet Sauvignon, Cabernet Franc and others*

♀ *Lagorthi, Moschofilero, Chardonnay and others*

This very high-quality boutique winery with 5ha (11 acres) of vines was founded by Constantine Antonopoulos, who was sadly killed in a road accident in 1994. Both Greek and international grape varieties are planted on the estate. The fine wines include barrel-fermented Chardonnay, Cabernet Nea Dris (New Oak), a blend of Cabernets Sauvignon and Franc, and Private Collection, a promising Agiorgitiko-Cabernet blend.

ARAGÓN

SPAIN

Isolated from maritime influences by mountain ranges, Aragón's high plateaux are the epitome of the harsh and dry continental climate of most of inland Spain. Its wines have

ANTINORI
The success of Tignanello (80 per cent Sangiovese, 20 per cent Cabernet Sauvignon) in the 1970s sparked off the super-Tuscan movement outside DOC regulations that has produced many of Italy's most exciting wines.

also been typical: heavy, alcoholic, often oxidized and, as a result, the ancient reputation of its wines plummeted and bulk production became the norm. Progressively, the implantation of DO regions and the installation of better equipment has begun turning the tide.

Improvement came first to the northern SOMONTANO DO, in the foothills of the Pyrenees, with massive new investment including the planting of international grape varieties. Then, more slowly, in the other DOs: CAMPO DE BORJA (which actually adjoins the RIOJA BAJA and NAVARRA vineyards), CALATAYUD and particularly CARIÑENA. This is overwhelmingly red wine country from the Garnacha grape, with the white Macabeo grape a distant second. Tempranillo, Cabernet Sauvignon and Merlot are being planted at a brisk pace.

ARAUJO

USA, California, Napa Valley AVA

❦ *Cabernet Sauvignon, Syrah*
♀ *Sauvignon Blanc*

Boutique winery whose great coup was to buy the Eisele vineyard, traditionally a source of superb Cabernet Sauvignon under the Joseph PHELPS label. Eisele is situated in the north of the NAPA VALLEY, east of Calistoga, and was initially planted in the 1880s, largely to Zinfandel and Riesling. Cabernet Sauvignon was first planted in 1964 and throughout the 1970s and '80s special vineyard bottlings showcased the dark, mineral intensity of its fruit. Since 1991 that fruit has all been used by Araujo and the Cabernet Sauvignon is now one of California's most sought-after reds, combining great fruit intensity with powerful but digestible tannins. An attractively zesty Sauvignon Blanc and a tiny amount of impressive estate Syrah are produced as well.

ARBOIS AC

FRANCE, Jura

❦ ♀ *Trousseau, Pinot Noir, Poulsard*
♀ *Chardonnay, Savagnin*

This is the largest of the specific ACs in the JURA region. There are now 854ha (2110 acres) of vines with an annual production of just over 5 million bottles, just over half of which are reds and rosés. The chief red grape, Trousseau, usually gives hefty wines, though modern winemaking is toning things down a bit. The Poulsard grape can produce quite pleasant light reds and good, smoky rosés. Pinot Noir gives pale but tasty, perfumed reds. Some of the best wines come from the village of Pupillin.

The whites are made from Chardonnay or the local Savagnin grape. The Savagnin manages, uniquely and disconcertingly, to infect the amiable qualities of mountain vineyard dry white wine with the palate-numbing, sweet-sour properties of a really dry fino sherry. In an ordinary Arbois white wine this effect is to make you question whether the wine is 'off'.

However, there is a type of white Arbois called *vin jaune* (yellow wine), made from Savagnin, which actually develops a flor yeast growth on its surface as does fino sherry. *Vin jaune* is also made in other Jura ACs, at its best in CHÂTEAU-CHALON. The wine is left in barrel with the flor for six years, during which time it oxidizes, develops an arresting damp sourness like the dark reek of old floorboards, and yet also keeps a full fruit, albeit somewhat decayed. There is also a rare sweet *vin de paille* (straw wine) – from grapes supposedly dried on straw mats. Best years: 2001, '00, '99, '98, '97, '96, '95. Best producers: Ch d'Arlay, Aviet, Bourdy, Désiré, Dugois, J Foret, F Lornet, Henri Maire, P Overnoy, de la Pinte, J Puffeney, Pupillin co-operative, Rijckaert, Rolet, A & M Tissot, J Tissot, Tournelle.

ARCHERY SUMMIT WINERY

USA, Oregon, Yamhill County, Willamette Valley AVA

❦ *Pinot Noir*
♀ *Pinot Gris, Chardonnay, Pinot Blanc*

Founded in 1993 in the renowned Dundee Hills region of WILLAMETTE VALLEY, this winery has more than 40ha (100 acres) of vines in three estate vineyards focusing mainly on Pinot Noir. Very dark, very intense Pinot Noir is made using lots of new oak. Single-vineyard bottlings from Archery Summit Estate, Red Hills, Arcus Estate and Renegade Ridge Estate top the list and require aging for at least three years. A blended white called Vireton is also made. Best years: (Pinot Noir) 2001, '00, '99, '98, '96.

ARGIANO

ITALY, Tuscany, Brunello di Montalcino DOCG

❦ *Sangiovese, Cabernet Sauvignon, Merlot, Syrah*

The renaissance of this ancient Tuscan estate began with a mix of renewed investment and the initial involvement of wine guru Giacomo Tachis. It continues with radically refashioned BRUNELLO DI MONTALCINO Riserva that is both rich and accessible, and scintillating Solengo (a blend of Cabernet, Merlot, Sangiovese and Syrah). There is good ROSSO DI MONTALCINO, too. Best years: (Brunello) 2001, '00, '99, '97, '95, '93, '90.

ARGIOLAS
Angialis is a sweet wine with a light golden colour, elegant bouquet and rich, smooth flavours with a hint of oak. An after-dinner wine, it is also perfect with biscuits.

ARGIOLAS

ITALY, Sardinia

❦ *Monica, Grenache (Cannonau), Carignan (Carignano), Bovale Sardo, Malvasia Nera, Pascale, Merlot, Syrah*
❧ *Cannonau, Monica, Carignano and others*
♀ *Vermentino, Nuragus, Nasco, Malvasia and others*

SARDINIA may be conceived by some as being stuck somewhere in the past, but there is nothing archaic about this fully modernized company making top-quality wine from 220ha (544 acres) of vineyards. Brothers Franco and Giuseppe Argiolas are third-generation growers who had the sagacity years ago to call in the services of Italy's greatest winemaker, Giacomo Tachis.

They have been rewarded with a series of wines which regularly figure not only among the best of the island, but among the best of Italy. Top billing goes to the IGT Isola dei Nuraghi reds – Turriga, a grandiose, multi-prize-winner of a red wine made mainly from Cannonau (the Sardinian name for Grenache) which requires at least five years' aging, and Korem, a blend of local varieties plus Syrah and Merlot. Best years: 2001, '00, '99, '98, '97, '95, '93, '92, '91, '90.

ARINTO

This is one of Portugal's most promising white grapes, which succeeds in hanging on to its natural acidity, even in the scorching heat of the ALENTEJO. It is most at home in the tiny region of BUCELAS and in neighbouring ALENQUER where it is sometimes blended with the even more fiercely acidic Esgana Cão (Dog Strangler). On its own, Arinto makes fresh, fragrant grassy dry white wines which last quite well in bottle. It is also widespread in the cooler VINHO VERDE region.

DOMAINE DE L'ARLOT

FRANCE, Burgundy, Côte de Nuits, Nuits-St-Georges AC

❦ *Pinot Noir*
♀ *Chardonnay, Pinot Gris*

Jean-Pierre de Smet is that rarity in BURGUNDY, a newcomer to the region. Supported by the French insurance company AXA Millésimes (owners of Ch. PICHON-LONGUEVILLE among other BORDEAUX chateaux), he based himself at an estate in the southern part of NUITS-ST-GEORGES, a 14-ha (34-acre) property that included the large monopole vineyard Clos de l'Arlot, and made his first vintage here in 1987.

De Smet seeks elegance rather than maximum extraction. The wines are often light in colour, but rarely lack flavour, and often age surprisingly well. Although aged in 50 per cent new oak, they are rarely dominated by oak and tannin. There is also a small quantity of other wines, including ROMANÉE-ST-VIVANT, VOSNE-ROMANÉE les Suchots and BEAUNE les Grèves. One curiosity is a white Nuits-St-Georges from old vines in the Clos de l'Arlot, which include Pinot Gris as well as Chardonnay. Best years: 2000, '99, '98, '97, '96, '95, '93, '90.

DOMAINE COMTE ARMAND

FRANCE, Burgundy, Côte de Beaune, Pommard AC
♦ *Pinot Noir*
♀ *Chardonnay*

Tasting at this leading POMMARD domaine does not take very long, since the main wine comes from a single monopole vineyard, the 4.6-ha (11½-acre) Clos des Epeneaux, an enclave within the Premier Cru Épenots. This is quintessential Pommard: rich, dark, brooding, complex, and requiring quite a few years in bottle to show at its sumptuous best. There is a small amount of AUXEY-DURESSES Premier Cru red, VOLNAY Fremiets Premier Cru and Pommard from young vines in the Clos des Epeneaux, and a few rows of vines for basic BOURGOGNE GRAND ORDINAIRE white.

In 1999 Benjamin Leroux took over the winemaking from the French Canadian, Pascal Marchand, who started the vineyards' conversion to biodynamism. Marchand has moved on to run the Domaine de la Vougeraie, Jean-Claude BOISSET's new estate in NUITS-ST-GEORGES. Best years: 2000, '99, '98, '97, '96, '95, '94, '93, '91, '90.

ARNEIS

Arneis can be one of Italy's best white grape varieties, subtly intricate, releasing a fascinating array of perfumes – peaches and pears, nuts and licorice, and revealing hidden depths of complexity of flavour. Though known for hundreds of years under various names, by the early 1970s it was almost extinct and it has only found popularity as a varietal wine recently. Now encouraged by high prices achieved for the wine, it is making a strong comeback in PIEDMONT's ROERO zone, where it makes Roero Arneis; and to a lesser extent on the opposite – right – bank of the Tanaro river, around Alba. Styles vary from light and delicate and ephemeral to (occasionally) rich and powerful, sometimes oaked (often to excess), sometimes *passito*. The potential of Arneis remains exciting. There is also a little in Australia.

CH. L'ARROSÉE

FRANCE, Bordeaux, St-Émilion Grand Cru AC, Grand Cru Classé
♦ *Merlot, Cabernet Sauvignon, Cabernet Franc*

This is one of those unknown properties that swept to international prominence so quickly you had to keep checking your tasting notes to see you hadn't got the name wrong. But this small estate, situated on the western end of the *côtes*, just south-west of the town of ST-ÉMILION, really is exciting: it makes a rich, chewy and wonderfully luscious wine, with a comparatively high proportion (40 per cent) of Cabernet Sauvignon in the blend. This is a real hedonist's wine, especially in the big, broad years of 1995, '90, and '85. Drink after five years of aging or so but it may also be kept for ten years or so. Best years: 2000, '98, '96, '95, '94, '90, '89, '88, '86, '85.

ARROWOOD VINEYARDS & WINERY

USA, California, Sonoma County, Sonoma Valley AVA
♦ *Cabernet Sauvignon, Merlot, Syrah, Malbec and others*
♦ *Grenache Noir, Syrah, Mourvedre, Viognier*
♀ *Chardonnay, Viognier, Pinot Blanc, Riesling, Gewurztaminer*

CHATEAU ST JEAN's chief winemaker from its start in 1974 until 1990 during its glory years, Dick Arrowood became well known for Chardonnay and a series of late-harvest white wines, as well as familiar with a host of vineyards scattered throughout SONOMA. At Chateau St Jean he made a habit of bottling wines from single-vineyard sites. In 1986 he started his own winery which was purchased by MONDAVI in 2000. The wines have mostly been tip-top – beautifully balanced Cabernet Sauvignon, superb Merlot, deeply fruity Syrah, lovely velvety Chardonnay and crisp, fragrant Viognier. Best years: (Cabernet Sauvignon) 2001, '00, '99, '98, '97, '96, '95, '94, '91, '90.

ARTADI

SPAIN, País Vasco, Rioja DOCa
♦ *Tempranillo*

This erstwhile co-operative in Laguardia in RIOJA Alavesa (whose official name, Cosecheros Alaveses, has been totally obscured by its brand name, Artadi) now produces some of the most ambitious, striking and acclaimed wines in the fast-changing Rioja scene. The founding partners brought with them about 70ha (173 acres) of well-sited vineyards with a large proportion of old vines. Winery manager Juan Carlos López de Lacalle, now the majority owner as well, and enologist Benjamín Romeo mapped out a shrewd course, building on the success of the original young wines to introduce ever more ambitious oak-aged cuvées. Long macerations producing intense, fruit-dominated wines are characteristic of Artadi. The top wine is Grandes Añadas, first made in 1994 and only released in the best years. Viña El Pisón (from a single vineyard), Pagos Viejos and Viñas de Gain are also very good. There is also straight red and white Rioja. Best years: 2000, '99, '98, '96, '95, '94, '91.

ASCHERI

ITALY, Piedmont
♦ *Nebbiolo, Barbera, Dolcetto, Syrah*
♀ *Arneis, Muscat (Moscato), Viognier*

Winemakers in PIEDMONT for at least five centuries, the Ascheri family produces wines with plenty of weight but which are also appealingly drinkable and forward, whether it be BAROLO (Vigna dei Pola di Verduno, Sorano), Dolcetto d'Alba (Vigna Nirane), BARBERA D'ALBA (Fontanelle di La Morra) or NEBBIOLO D'ALBA. New are Syrah and Viognier sold as Montalupa Rosso and Bianco. The Cristina Ascheri MOSCATO D'ASTI is delightful. Best years: (Barolo) 2001, '00, '99, '98, '97, '96, '95, '90.

ASTI DOCG

ITALY, Piedmont
♀ *Muscat (Moscato Bianco)*

Sparkling Asti (formerly called Asti Spumante) is often portrayed as a sweet, fizzy glass of easy-gulping froth for those who find CHAMPAGNE altogether too acid, dry and serious. But that's to miss the point. The Muscat grapes that go into Asti are some of the best white grapes in Italy. And the producers have recently reduced the sugar levels so that now Asti is merely medium, but still endowed with head-spinning floral perfumes and crunchy, grapy fruit. It has pretty decent acidity and it's low in alcohol (between 7 and 9 degrees) – chilled, it's a brilliantly refreshing, reviving wine. It's also one of the few wines that can go with Christmas pudding – the Muscat fruit still sings through although it'll seem bone dry.

It is also worth remembering that traditional Asti is produced by the most natural way ever of making sparkling wine. Part way through its transformation, in large pressurized tanks called *autoclavi*, the fermentation is stopped by lowering the temperature to around 0°C (32°F), so that there is plenty of natural grape sweetness left. The bubbles are natural too, being trapped in the pressurized tanks, and since it's bottled under pressure, following very tight filtration to ensure stability, they stay in the wine until it is poured.

Many of Turin's big sparkling wine and vermouth houses (such as Cinzano, Gancia, Martini & Rossi and Riccadonna) make reliable Asti. Better still are the wines from Araldica, Bera, Contero, Giuseppe Contratto, Cascina Fonda, FONTANAFREDDA and Cascina Pian d'Or. Asti is not a wine for keeping – the fresher it is, the better.

ATA RANGI

NEW ZEALAND, North Island, Martinborough

♥ Pinot Noir, Merlot, Syrah, Cabernet Sauvignon

♀ Chardonnay, Sauvignon Blanc

Ata Rangi, meaning 'dawn sky or new beginning' is a small, high-quality winery in MARTINBOROUGH run by the Paton and Masters families. They began in 1980 with just 5ha (12 acres) of barren paddock and have gradually expanded to 33ha (82 acres). Stylish, concentrated wines include big, rich, barrel-fermented Craighall Chardonnay, seductively perfumed cherry/plum Pinot Noir and an impressive Cabernet-Merlot-Syrah blend called Célèbre. Young Vines Pinot Noir is not of the same standard, but new Syrah is exciting. A concentrated and succulent Sauvignon Blanc is a recent addition. Best years: (Pinot Noir) 2002, '01, '00, '99, '98, '97, '96.

ATLAS PEAK AVA

USA, California, Napa County

Tucked away in the south-east corner of NAPA VALLEY, this hillside appellation is named after the tallest point in the nearby mountains. Approved as an AVA in 1992, it includes 243ha (600 acres) of vineyards. The leading varieties are Cabernet Sauvignon, Chardonnay and Sangiovese. William Hill revived the area in the 1970s and developed

ATLAS PEAK VINEYARDS
California producers such as Atlas Peak are now working some of their magic on the Sangiovese grape, making both easy drinking and sturdier ageworthy versions.

its reputation for Cabernet Sauvignon. International attention came in the 1980s when Atlas Peak Vineyards, BOLLINGER and others selected it as ideal for Sangiovese – but the latest view is that it is actually better for Cabernet after all. Best years: (reds) 2001, '00, '99, '97.

AU BON CLIMAT

USA, California, Santa Barbara County, Santa Maria Valley AVA

♥ Pinot Noir

♀ Chardonnay, Pinot Gris, Pinot Blanc, Aligoté

Winemaker Jim Clendenen is a true believer in the Burgundian emphasis on *climat* or vineyard site. Clendenen works with Pinot Noir and Chardonnay from a variety of vineyard sites within fog-cooled SANTA BARBARA, and sometimes SAN LUIS OBISPO COUNTY, and takes the high-risk, anti-technological approach. In most vintages, the results have dazzled. The Chardonnays from Bien Nacido and other vineyards offer a succulent richness of fruit with warm insidious spice from new oak. A similar sweet core of (red) fruit, with floral and cherry perfume, is found in the Bien Nacido and Sanford & Benedict Pinot Noirs, but Isabelle can be best of all. Watch out for Italian varietals under the Il Podere dell Olivos label, Cold Heaven Viogniers and Vita Nova Bordeaux blends made in partnership with QUPÉ. Best years: (Pinot Noir) 2001, '00, '99, '98, '97, '96, '95, '94, '91, '90; (Chardonnay) 2001, '00, '99, '98, '97, '95, '92.

AUCKLAND REGION

NEW ZEALAND, North Island

Vineyards in this historic region now account for only 3 per cent of New Zealand's total, yet Aucklands still remains important as many of the country's largest wine companies have their headquarters here, processing grapes from all over New Zealand. The vineyards are planted in four distinct sub-regions:

Henderson, KUMEU/HUAPAI/Waimauku, WAIHEKE ISLAND and Matakana. Auckland's relatively warm temperatures favour making Bordeaux-style red wines and Waiheke Island and Matakana are increasingly exciting areas for Cabernet Sauvignon and Merlot. The development of these two sub-regions, in particular, has arrested the declining acreage in Auckland which is now experiencing a modest expansion, with over 450ha (1112 acres) in 2002. Clevedon, south of Auckland, is a fledgling area that shows promise. Chardonnay and Merlot are the main varieties here. Best years: (Cabernet Sauvignon) 2001, '00, '99, '98, '96, '94, '93. Best producers: Heron's Flight, KUMEU RIVER.

AUDE

FRANCE, Languedoc-Roussillon

A large *département* which stretches inland from Narbonne on the Mediterranean, up the Aude valley to Carcassonne and the Limoux hills, and south-west into the mountain wilderness of the CORBIÈRES. This area tended to be dismissed with a derogatory remark about wine lakes and oceans of cheap wine, but it has now emerged as one of the most exciting areas in France. The predominance of mountainous land, particularly in the vast ACs of Corbières and MINERVOIS, and the smaller ones of FITOU, LIMOUX and BLANQUETTE DE LIMOUX, means that the potential is enormous, and each vintage brings a new crop of exciting wines. Yet apart from Limoux, Blanquette de Limoux and the sweet MUSCAT DE ST-JEAN-DE-MINERVOIS, they are almost without exception red.

There is a lot of VIN DE PAYS activity in the Aude – on average nearly 200 million bottles are made a year, the majority red or rosé. About three-quarters go under the Vin de Pays de l'Aude title, France's second largest, but there are 18 zonal vins de pays, which include Coteaux de Peyriac, with a hefty 19 million bottles a year, Cité de Carcassonne, Coteaux du Miramont, Vallée du Paradis and Hauterive.

Local co-operatives and big companies such as Chantovent, Nicolas and SKALLI/Fortant de France have imaginatively pioneered Merlot, Cabernet Sauvignon, Chardonnay, Sauvignon Blanc, Sémillon, Chenin Blanc and Viognier alongside the more common varieties. The results generally show fruity reds and clean, fresh whites of pure varietal character as well as impressive barrel-fermented Chardonnays. Drink the wines pretty young.

AUSBRUCH
AUSTRIA

Today in Austria Ausbruch is a Prädikat category for dessert wines with levels of sugar ripeness between Beerenauslese and Trockenbeerenauslese. However, for the town of RUST on the bank of Lake Neusiedl in BURGENLAND it is a distinct wine style and a local speciality. For the town's leading growers it remains that: a dessert wine fermented until it has the high alcoholic content of a SAUTERNES, then aged in wooden casks, which may or may not impart an oak flavour. Best producers: FEILER-ARTINGER, Peter Schandl, Heidi Schröck, Robert WENZEL.

FEILER-ARTINGER
In the 1980s Hans Feiler began to revive the old tradition of Ausbruch, whose documented history goes back to 1617. Today Feiler-Artinger's range of Ausbruch wines are superb.

CH. AUSONE
FRANCE, Bordeaux, St-Émilion Grand Cru AC, Premier Grand Cru Classé
 Merlot, Cabernet Franc

This beautiful, tiny property (only 7ha/17 acres), situated on the *côtes* just outside the town of St-Émilion on what are arguably the best slopes in the AC, has had a troubled history. Traditionally thought of as being on a par with ST-ÉMILION's other great property, Ch. CHEVAL BLANC, few vintages between the end of World War Two and the 1980s had shown much personality, and certainly not First Growth personality.

However, a new, young winemaker, Pascal Delbeck, arrived in 1975 and during the 1980s he made a series of impressive wines that once more had the influential wine critics dancing attendance. Yet, despite a restored reputation, family quarrels and financial problems never entirely disappeared and the owner Alain Vauthier has basically made the wines since 1996, with the local wine star Michel Rolland as his consultant winemaker. The change of style is dramatic – more power, less elegance. But is it better? Production is a tiny 2500 cases per year (Cheval-Blanc makes 12,000). Best years: 2001, '00, '99, '98, '97, '96, '95, '94, '90, '89, '88, '86, '85, '83, '82.

AUXEY-DURESSES AC
FRANCE, Burgundy, Côte de Beaune
 Pinot Noir
 Chardonnay

Auxey-Duresses is rather a backwater village up in the hills behind the world-famous MEURSAULT. In times of inflated prices, it can be a crucial source of supply for those who want to drink good white BURGUNDY yet are damned if they'll pay a loony sum. It makes it all the more incomprehensible that the standard of Auxey-Duresses varies so dramatically. At its best the white is dry, soft, nutty and hinting at the kind of creaminess which should make a good Meursault. Too often, though, the wines end up rather flabby and flat. The whites make up just over half of the annual production and it's best to drink them between three and five years old. Les Duresses is the most consistent Premier Cru. Best years: (whites) 2002, '00, '99, '97, '96. Best producers: (whites) Ampeau, Dom. d'Auvenay (Dom. LEROY), Diconne, DROUHIN, J-P Fichet, Olivier LEFLAIVE, Maison LEROY, Duc de Magenta, M Prunier.

The cherry-and-strawberry-fruited reds are rather lean and recently these wines have seemed dilute or coarse. They can soften up after a few years in a bottle. Best years: (reds) 2002, '99, '98, '96, '95. Best producers: (reds) Comte ARMAND, J-P Diconne, Jessiaume Père et Fils, Duc de Magenta, M Prunier, P Prunier.

AVIGNONESI
ITALY, Tuscany, Vino Nobile di Montepulciano DOCG
 Sangiovese, Canaiolo, Cabernet Sauvignon, Merlot and others
 Chardonnay, Sauvignon Blanc, Trebbiano, Malvasia

Owned by the brothers Falvo, one of whom married into the Avignonesi family in the 1970s, this firm is often credited with leading Montepulciano's revival as one of TUSCANY's best wine zones and a new generation of Falvos is once again pushing the quality boundaries to keep Avignonesi in pole position. They produce wine from 109ha (269 acres) of vineyards spread over four farms, three (Le Capezzine, I Poggetti and newly planted La Lombarda) in the Montepulciano zone and the fourth (La Selva) near Cortona where they grow their white grapes.

Although Avignonesi's VINO NOBILE DI MONTEPULCIANO is often the best of their dry wines, for a time the international wines, Il Marzocco (Chardonnay) and Desiderio

AVIGNONESI
This is classic Vino Nobile, with fine, intense, dark berried fruit and real depth of flavour and weight, from Montepulciano's leading producer.

(previously Merlot, now Merlot-Cabernet), received more attention. However, the classic reds are very much in the lead once again and what was once a rather austere style is now rich and perfumed, very ripe and verging on the exotic (deliciously so). The VIN SANTO is the most sought after in Tuscany. There is also a rare red version from Sangiovese called Occhio di Pernice. These are both world-class and charge worldclass prices for a precious half bottle. The family's latest venture is Li Veli in PUGLIA. Best years: (Vino Nobile) 2001, '00, '99, '97, '95, '93, '90, '88.

AYL
GERMANY, Mosel-Saar-Ruwer

One of the top villages in the SAAR, Ayl produces thrilling, racy Rieslings that in a decent year are as good as anything in Germany. Its main vineyard is the Kupp, which provides some very steep slopes that make the business of making great wine as difficult as possible for the growers. The weather does the rest, refusing, in really poor years, to ripen the grapes at all and needing a really long, warm autumn to show that fine Saar wine is more than just a pipe dream. Best years: (Riesling Spätlese) 2002, '01, '99, '97, '95, '94, '93, '90. Best producers: Bischöflicher Weingüter, Peter Lauer, Dr Heinz Wagner.

BABCOCK VINEYARDS
USA, California, Santa Barbara County, Santa Ynez Valley AVA
 Pinot Noir, Syrah, Sangiovese
 Chardonnay, Sauvignon Blanc, Gewurztraminer, Pinot Gris (Pinot Grigio)

Making bold, dramatic wines is the goal of Bryan Babcock, whose family-owned Santa Ynez Valley vineyard provides him with intensely flavoured fruit. A fanatic when it comes to cluster-thinning his vines for low yields, Babcock proves his point with Reserve Chardonnays and massive Eleven Oaks Sauvignon Blancs which lean towards the ripe melon style. Highly perfumed, barrel-fermented Gewurztraminer is high drama indeed, though with the Pinot Noir, while it captures the region's typical cherry character, the amount of oak can be overly dramatic. Black Label Syrah highlights jammy black fruit and spice flavours. Best years: (Pinot Noir) 2001, '00, '99, '98, '96, '95, '94.

BABICH

NEW ZEALAND, North Island, Henderson
♥ *Cabernet Sauvignon, Merlot, Pinot Noir*
♀ *Sauvignon Blanc, Chardonnay*

A family winery, Babich has some prime vineyard land in MARLBOROUGH and HAWKES BAY but still buys in about half its fruit. Irongate Chardonnay is an intense, steely wine that needs plenty of aging, while intense, full-flavoured varietal reds under the Winemakers Reserve label show even greater potential for development. The flagship label, The Patriarch, features Chardonnay and Cabernet Sauvignon, both from Hawkes Bay. Wines from Marlborough grapes include a stylish Sauvignon Blanc, a tangy Riesling and a light, fruity Pinot Gris. Best years: (premium Hawkes Bay reds) 2002, '00, '99, '98, '96.

BACHARACH

GERMANY, Mittelrhein

This small medieval town at the southern tip of the MITTELRHEIN is the source for many of the region's best wines. Here Riesling reigns supreme, growing on precipitously steep slopes with a slate soil producing wines with MOSEL-like character but with some of the body of RHEINGAU wines. The climate is warmer here than in the Mosel, so while the wines bear a family resemblance they are fuller, with more forthright fruit aromas. Vineyard acreage is decreasing in the Mittelrhein so it is important that Bacharach's growers maintain the standards of their highly individual Rieslings. Best years: 2002, '01, '99, '98, '93, '92, '90. Best producers: Fritz Bastian, Toni JOST, Dr Randolf Kauer, Helmut Mades, Ratzenberger.

BAD DÜRKHEIM

GERMANY, Pfalz

This spa town has some good vineyards in the Michelsberg and Spielberg and is the headquarters of the dependable Vier Jahreszeiten Kloster Limburg co-operative. Best years: (Riesling Spätlese) 2002, '01, '99, '98, '97, '96, '93, '92. Best producers: DARTING, Fitz-Ritter, Pfluger, Karl Schaefer.

Baden wines owe their full-bodied dry style to the region's warm, sunny climate. Perched high above the excellent Schlossberg vineyard in the Ortenau, Schloss Ortenberg has been a wine research centre since 1950.

BAD KREUZNACH

GERMANY, Nahe

Bad Kreuznach is a busy spa town on the banks of the NAHE, and home to many well-known cellars, as well as the traditional site for the region's wine auctions. The town has 22 individual vineyard sites, most of which are planted with Riesling, which is now the biggest single grape variety in the Nahe region. The Kahlenberg and Brückes sites, both of which face south, often produce the best wines. The Steinweg and Krötenpfuhl vineyards are almost as good, and Riesling also does well in Forst, Kauzenberg, Steinberg and Narrenkappe. Best years: 2002, '01, '98, '97, '93, '90. Best producers: Anton Finkenauer, Carl Finkenauer, von Plettenberg.

BADEN

GERMANY

Baden, being the most southerly of Germany's wine regions, is also the warmest; so you would expect it to grow different grape varieties from the chillier north, and it does; or at least a different balance of varieties. But Baden is so huge that it cannot be summed up in just a few lines.

It covers about 15,866ha (39,204 acres) of vines and stretches over 400km (250 miles) from FRANKEN in the north to Bodensee (Lake Constance) on the Swiss border, The best wines are often not Riesling at all but come from the Pinot family – Blanc (Weissburgunder), Gris (Grauburgunder or Ruländer) and Noir (Spätburgunder). Fully 38 per cent of the wine is red or rosé.

Many of the Baden vineyards lie in a narrow strip tucked between the Rhine and the foothills of the Black Forest between the spa town of Baden-Baden in the north and Basel in Switzerland in the south, and 80 per cent of its wines come from here. In the north is the isolated district of Tauberfranken or Badisches Frankenland, which in all aspects except that of political administration is part of Franken; its wines are dry and earthy. To the south comes Badische Bergstrasse/Kraichgau making attractive, medium-weight white wines, particularly from Weissburgunder.

The ORTENAU, south of Baden-Baden, is one of Baden's most famous districts: the wines are complex and distinctive, from Spätburgunder and Riesling (here often called Klingelberger). Dry, minerally Riesling from the village of DURBACH is the archetype. Ortenau's neighbouring district, Breisgau, can be good, but grows a lot of Müller-Thurgau as well as the Pinot siblings Grauburgunder and Weissburgunder. Then comes Kaiserstuhl and its smaller neighbour, Tuniberg. KAISERSTUHL is the stump of a long-dead volcano, and the wines here can be among Baden's best: dry, rich and powerful. Tuniberg is slightly cooler and its wines correspondingly lighter. The speciality of Markgräflerland, between Freiburg and the Swiss border, is the Gutedal grape (better known as Switzerland's Chasselas) and, finally, Bodensee which is mainly rosé from Spätburgunder.

Baden likes to promote its wines for their dryness and vinosity, and the extra ripeness that comes from being in the south. Some of the most remarkable Baden wines are the Spätburgunders. The Baden version of Pinot Noir is undergoing a rapid transformation from the pale sweet jammy style once common to so many German reds, to a more oaky, dry, well-structured but perfumed style. Good co-operatives abound, since Baden is above all co-operative country (there are good ones at Achkarren, Bickensohl, Bötzingen, Durbach, Konigsschaffhausen and Sasbach); most make wine to a high standard, and the enormous Badische Winzerkeller, which acts as a central co-operative also produces many solid wines.

BADIA A COLTIBUONO

ITALY, Tuscany, Chianti Classico DOCG
♟ *Sangiovese, Canaiolo*
♀ *Chardonnay*

Current owners the Stucchi Prinetti family's ancestor, Florentine banker Guido Giuntini, purchased this superb thousand-year-old abbey (*badia*) at Gaiole in the middle of the nineteenth century, and it has been a leading CHIANTI CLASSICO estate since then, with 50ha (124 acres) of vineyards. The wines today are fresh and bright with the accent on fruit and ripe tannins and quality oak.

The SUPER-TUSCAN Sangioveto is the star performer and made only in the best years. With a pronounced oaky style, the wine nevertheless has good fruit depth, and needs six to ten years' aging in order to harmonize its parts and put flesh on its bones. Coltibuono RS (named after the winemaker Roberto Stucchi) is a modern Chianti Classico from Sangiovese grapes, not necessarily all from their own vineyards, and is bright and nicely balanced, with hints of quality oak (it gets just five months in barrel). The straight Chianti Classico and Riserva are 90 per cent Sangiovese, and both have something of the structure we have come to expect from Badia without sacrificing fruit. For more immediate consumption there is also a range of unoaked wines – Chianti Classico, Sangiovese, Rosato and Bianco. Best years: (Sangioveto) 2001, '99, '97, '95, '90, '88, '85.

BAGA

This Portuguese grape is rich in colour and tannins, giving dense red wines that can be bitterly astringent; it takes modern techniques to bring out its piercing blackcurrant fruit and make the wines approachable, but it can be done. BAIRRADA is its principal habitat but it also grows in substantial quantities in neighbouring DÃO and the RIBATEJO.

BAILEYS

AUSTRALIA, Victoria, Glenrowan
♟ *Syrah (Shiraz), Cabernet Sauvignon*
♀ *Muscat, Muscadelle*

This is one of the great names of North-East Victoria, long famous for its sweet fortified wines or 'stickies', making Muscat and Muscadelle (labelled Tokay in Australia) in an inimitably rich, perfumed and treacly style. Now part of the Beringer Blass empire, Baileys did not initially benefit from the change of ownership. You couldn't improve on Bailey's great stickies, but you might at least try to maintain standards. After all, this is a wine dear to my heart.

When I was playing General Perón in *Evita* in London's West End, my mother and I would repair to Leicester Square after the show and drink a bottle of Founders Muscat between us. Straight down. No nonsense. It was that good. Stickies are once again good but no longer at 'me and my mum' standards. However, the dry Shiraz reds – especially 1920s Block – are big, rich, perfumed, impressive reds.

BAILEYS
Winemakers Selection is the top level of luscious fortified wines from this old, very traditional winery at Glenrowan in North-East Victoria.

BAIRRADA DOC

PORTUGAL, Beiras
♟♟ *Baga and others*
♀ *Bical, Fernão Pires (Maria Gomes), Rabo de Ovelha and others*

Bairrada's red wines, principally from the red Baga grape, have been used for years to make some of Portugal's most impressive Garrafeiras. These wines, with startlingly rich wild-berry aromas and flavours, are often marred by excessively hard tannins which take decades to soften. Much of the region's wine is made in co-operatives which, with the benefit of newly installed stainless steel, are making ever more approachable wines, often bottled under the local Vinho Regional designation of BEIRAS. Caves ALIANÇA and SOGRAPE, two of the largest private winemakers, and an Australian, Peter BRIGHT, have also been toying with the production of softer, earlier-maturing red wine. The traditionalists (although most are by no means as traditional as they used to be) are the single-estate producers like Luís PATO (who now labels his wines as Vinho Regional Beiras, after falling out with the DOC authorities), Casa de Saima and Caves SÃO JOÃO. All three make extremely impressive wines with the capacity to develop well in bottle for about 20 years. With an Atlantic climate vintages can be very variable. Best years: (reds) 2001, 00, '97, '96, '95, '91, '90. Best producers: (reds) Caves Aliança, Quinta das Bágeiras, Quinta do Carvalhinho, Gonçalves Faria, Caves Messias, Caves Primavera, Quinta da Rigodeira, Casa de Saima, Caves São João, Sogrape, Sidónio de Sousa.

White Bairrada wines are much less interesting but with modern vinification methods they are improving fast. They should generally be drunk young. Much of the region's white still ends up in the local sparkling wine industry. Best producers: (whites) Quinta da Rigodeira, Casa de Saima, Sogrape (Quinta de Pedralvites).

BALEARES (BALEARIC ISLANDS)

SPAIN

The tourist trade happily guzzles down most of the wine produced in the Balearic Islands. Less than 800ha (1977 acres) are currently under vine, mostly on the largest island, Mallorca, which has two DOs: Binissalem, in the centre on an undulating plain and Pla i Llevant, a larger wine area to the east and south around Felanitx and Petra. The native Manto Negro and Callet grapes, plus Tempranillo, Monastrell (Mourvèdre) and Cabernet Sauvignon dominate among red varieties and the wines are usually rather alcoholic but pale. There is some dull white, from the native Moll (Prensal Blanc) as well as Macabeo, Parellada, Moscatel Romano and Chardonnay. The Anima Negra winery is turning out impressive, deep reds from Callet and shows what can be done. Best producers: Anima Negra, Franja Roja (J L Ferrer), Hereus de Ribas, Son Bordils.

CH. BALESTARD-LA-TONNELLE
FRANCE, Bordeaux, St-Émilion Grand Cru AC,
Grand Cru Classé

♟ *Merlot, Cabernet Franc, Cabernet Sauvignon,*
Malbec

This is satisfyingly reliable red Bordeaux and rightly popular. Located on the limestone plateau east of the town of St-Émilion it has been owned by the Capdemourlin family since the 1920s. Balestard demonstrates ST-ÉMILION's ability to produce numerous wines below the top rank of Premier Grand Cru Classé that are still immensely enjoyable and able to age well for 10–20 years. Vinification is traditional but the wine now enjoys partial malolactic fermentation in oak and aging takes place in 50 per cent new oak. The wine is full of strong, chewy fruit and is reasonably priced. Second wine: les Tournelles de Balestard. Best years: 2001, '00, '98, '96, '95, '90, '89, '88, '86, '85, '83.

CH BALESTARD-LA-TONNELLE
Obviously this wine has been popular for a fair old while, because the label reprints a poem which François Villon wrote back in the 15th century that describes Balestard as 'this divine nectar'.

BANDOL AC
FRANCE, Provence

♟ *Mourvèdre, Grenache, Cinsaut, Syrah, Carignan*
♀ *Bourboulenc, Clairette, Ugni Blanc, Sauvignon Blanc*

Bandol's a gorgeous place – a lovely resort town and fishing port – and add to that spectacular vineyards, cut high into the cliffs and slopes, many of which tumble down to the Mediterranean beaches. Not only this, but it still ranks as PROVENCE's top red wine.

The Mourvèdre grape, grown on terraced vineyards, is the grape that gives Bandol its character (the blend must include a minimum of 50 per cent) – gentle raisin and honey softness with a slight, tannic, plum-skins nip and a tobaccoey, herby fragrance. Other grapes, in particular Grenache, Cinsaut and occasionally Syrah, make up the blend. The reds spend at least 18 months in wood. They happily age for ten years, but can be very good at three to four. The rosés, delicious and spicy but often too pricy, should be drunk as young as possible. Best years: (reds) 2001, '00, '99, '98, '97, '96, '95, '93, '90, '89, '88. Best producers: (reds) Bastide Blanche, la

Bégude, Bunan, Frégate, le Galantin, J P Gaussen, Gros Noré, l'Hermitage, Lafran-Veyrolles, Mas Redorne, la Noblesse, de PIBARNON, PRADEAUX, Ray-Jane, Roche Redonne, Romassan, Ste-Anne, des Salettes, de Souviou, la Suffrène, Terrebrune, TEMPIER, la Tour de Bon, Vannières.

Bandol's vaguely nutty, neutral whites are not up to the red standards. However, now that Sauvignon has been legalized in the blend, some have a nice green apple fruit balancing an aniseed perfume.

CASTELLO BANFI
ITALY, Tuscany, Brunello di Montalcino DOCG

♟ *Sangiovese (Brunello), Cabernet Sauvignon, Syrah, Merlot and others*
♀ *Chardonnay, Sauvignon Blanc, Pinot Gris (Pinot Grigio), Muscat (Moscadello) and others*

I have been waiting a number of years for the vast, American-owned, high-tech Castello Banfi operation to blow my mind with wines of individuality and distinction. It still hasn't happened. The wines are good, sometimes very good, but generally lack soul, as though this relatively recent creation below the slopes of Montalcino has still not taken root in native soil. The Brunellos are good, the varietal Chardonnay (Fontanelle), Cabernet (Tavernelle) and Merlot (Mandrielle) can also be good and they're very proud of their SUPER-TUSCANS Summus (Sangiovese, Cabernet and Syrah) and Excelsus (Cabernet and Merlot). They also make GAVI and sparklers. Best years: (top reds) 2001, '99, '98, '97, '95, '93, '90.

BANNOCKBURN
AUSTRALIA, Victoria, Geelong

♟ *Pinot Noir, Cabernet Sauvignon, Syrah (Shiraz), Merlot*
♀ *Chardonnay, Sauvignon Blanc, Riesling*

From low-yielding vineyards, this small winery makes one of Australia's most famous Pinot Noirs, enormously rich Chardonnay, good Cabernet Sauvignon and idiosyncratic Shiraz, influenced by the RHÔNE's Alain GRAILLOT. The winemaker Gary Farr has worked harvests at MOREY-ST-DENIS since 1983 and is wholly committed to Burgundian practices. He creates wine of concentration, power and structure, with unmistakable varietal character. The Pinot Noirs are impressive, though I'd like a little less emphasis on 'Burgundian' gaminess and a bit more expression of his own vineyards. Despite using Burgundian techniques, their flavour is far more muscular and rich than any Burgundy you're likely to come across. All in

all, I prefer the Shiraz. Best years: (Shiraz) 2001, '00, '99, '98, '97, '95, 96, '94, '92, '91, '90, '89, '88, '86.

BANYULS AC
FRANCE, Languedoc-Roussillon

♟♀ *Grenache, Carignan, Cinsaut, Syrah*
♀ *Grenache Gris, Grenache Blanc, Macabeo, Tourbat (Malvoisie du Roussillon), Muscat Blanc à Petits Grains, Muscat of Alexandria*

This is one of those strange, rather heavy, fortified wines – *vins doux naturels* – which the French adore, generally serving it as an aperitif, but which seldom have the style and character of the fortified wines from Spain (sherry, MONTILLA, MÁLAGA) and Portugal (PORT, MADEIRA). Red and tawny Banyuls must contain at least 50 per cent Grenache Noir. There is only a tiny amount of rosé and white.

Banyuls is sometimes made fairly dry, but its strong plum and raisin flavour tastes best in a sweet version. *Rimage* styles are bottled six to 12 months after the harvest: full of fruit to drink young or age. Older tawny styles can be excellent too. BANYULS Grand Cru is at least 75 per cent Grenache, has 30 months' wood-aging and should be richer as a consequence. *Rancio* means that the wine has been intentionally oxidized and will have a tawny colour. Best stick to the red. Best producers: Casa Blanca, CELLIER DES TEMPLIERS, les Clos de Paulilles, l'Étoile, MAS BLANC, de la RECTORIE, la Tour Vieille, Vial Magnères.

BARBADILLO
SPAIN, Andalucía, Jerez y Manzanilla DO

♀ *Palomino Fino, Pedro Ximénez*

Antonio Barbadillo is the largest of the sherry companies based in Sanlúcar de Barrameda, the cool, breezy seaside home of manzanilla. It makes a huge range of good to excellent sherries in a tasty, occasionally salty

BARBADILLO
Antonio Barbadillo makes a wide range of sherries in a tasty, salty style, including Principe amontillado, a rich, elegant wine with nutty overtones.

style. Among the best are the Manzanilla de Sanlúcar, delicate and saltily tangy, the manzanilla Solear, lean and almost herbaceous, and Principe, which comes as both manzanilla (salty, dry, fino-influenced) and amontillado (an intense, rancio-style). Cuco is a very good oloroso. There is also a dry still white, Castillo de San Diego, pleasant enough in a neutral sort of way and very popular in Spain.

BARBARESCO DOCG

ITALY, Piedmont

Nebbiolo

People talk about 'BAROLO and Barbaresco', never the other way round, but there are advantages to being number two. Unless your name is GAJA, you can tend your grapes and make your wine in comparative peace. The wine is a little lighter than Barolo, so there is more chance of getting some feminine elegance into a notoriously masculine style. Barbaresco benefits from a lower minimum alcohol level (12.5 per cent) and a less stringent aging requirement of just 21 months (45 for the Riserva category), of which only nine months need be in wood. The weight of Barbaresco will depend a great deal on who makes it, but the fascinating taste of the Nebbiolo grape with its flavours of violets and raspberries, prunes and chocolates, truffles and licorice, its acidity, and its firm tannin, should always be present.

Even though the wine zone is a fairly compact 509ha (1257 acres), wine styles can differ considerably between vineyards and producers. The principal communes are Barbaresco, Neive and Treiso. Top sites include Asili, Bricco di Neive, Costa Russi, Crichet Pajé, Gallina, Marcorino, Martinenga, Messoirano, Moccagatta, Montestefano, Ovello, Pora, Rabajà, Rio Sordo, Santo Stefano, Serraboella, Sorì San Lorenzo, Sorì Paitin, Sorì Tildin.

You may need to take out a second mortgage to try the wines of Gaja, but there are many other excellent Barbaresco producers whose bottles shouldn't constitute such a drain on the finances. Best producers: Barbaresco co-operative, Piero Busso, Ceretto, Cigliuti, Stefano Farina, Fontanabianca, GAJA, Bruno GIACOSA, Marchesi di Gresy, Moccagatta, Fiorenzo Nada, Castello di Neive, Oddero, Paitin, Pelissero, Pio Cesare, Prunotto, Albino Rocca, Bruno Rocca, Sottimano, La Spinetta, Vietti. Best years: 2001, '00, '99, '98, '97, '96, '95, '93, '90, '89, '88, '86, '85, '82.

BARBERA

Barbera crops up all over the place in Italy; in Lombardy, Emilia-Romagna, Puglia, Campania, Sicily and elsewhere, but its homeland is Piedmont, particularly in the hills of Monferrato, where it is still planted on the best sites, and further west around Alba in Barolo and Barbaresco where it has to concede these to Nebbiolo. Good straight Barbera is great stuff: vividly coloured, plum-skins sweet-sour, fruit-packed, with enlivening high acidity, a low tannin level and a bone-dry, astringent finish. With carbonic maceration or in a lighter style it is at its liveliest when young; traditionally vinified with sensibly low yields, it shines when two to six years old. It also has a great affinity for barrique-aging, gaining both tannin and meaty roundness.

The grape's high acidity makes it ideal for warm climates and Mexico and Argentina make considerable use of it, but mostly as a high-acid blender. This makes sense, because much of the wine industry, particularly in Argentina, was established by Italian immigrants who would have used Barbera to freshen up blends in Italy. Argentina is now producing some excellent Barbera as a single-varietal wine, both oaked and unoaked. California has lots of Barbera and is just now beginning to appreciate its qualities. The fresh acidity, low tannin formula suits current fashions and Barbera is finding many new homes as a result, including Australia, Greece, Slovenia, Romania and Israel.

BARBERA D'ALBA DOC, BARBERA D'ASTI DOC, BARBERA DEL MONFERRATO DOC

ITALY, Piedmont

Barbera

In whichever Barbera-producing part of Piedmont one happens to find oneself, producers are always firmly convinced that theirs is the best zone, theirs the archetype. Jovial self-aggrandizement apart, there really is no such thing as a 'best' Barbera area. There are only style differences prompted by different aspects and mesoclimates. Those who go for extract and concentration, and get enthused by smokiness highlighting redcurrant fruit and balancing acidity, will choose Barbera from Alba, where top-class BAROLO and BARBARESCO producers know just how to create a wine that makes one sit up and take notice. The most modern examples are supple and generous and can be drunk almost at once. More intense, dark-fruited versions require a minimum three years' age, but might improve for as much as eight. Best years: 2001, '00, '99, '98, '97, '96, '95. Best producers: G Alessandria, ALTARE, Azelia, Boglietti, Brovia, Cascina Chicco, Ceretto, Cigliuti, CLERICO, Elvio Cogno, Aldo CONTERNO, Giacomo CONTERNO, Conterno-Fantino, Corino, Correggia, Elio Grasso, Giuseppe MASCARELLO, Moccagatta, M Molino, Monfalletto-Cordero di Montezemolo, Oberto, Parusso, Pelissero, F Principiano, PRUNOTTO, Albino Rocca, Bruno Rocca, SANDRONE, P Scavino, La Spinetta, Vajra, Mauro Veglio, Vietti, Gianni Voerzio, Roberto VOERZIO.

If, on the other hand, the preference is for the young, lively, gulpably light, sometimes *frizzante* style of Barbera, the Monferrato hills, south-east of Asti, are the place to look. Avoid the aged Superiore which apes, not always successfully, the firmer styles of Alba, be ready for a good bite of acidity (or drink it to cut a vibrant swathe through salami, cheese and other rich foods) and search out the freshest samples you can find from estates such as the exemplary Bricco Mondalino.

Barbera d'Asti stands in between Alba's weighty style and Monferrato's more frolicsome one. It can be fine drunk young or aged for a couple of years, great unoaked or resplendent after aging in barrique. Best examples can be kept for five to six years, occasionally longer. Best years: 2001, '00, '99, '97, '96, '95. Best producers: Araldica/Alasia, La Barbatella, Pietro Barbero, Bava, Bertelli, Braida, Cascina Castlèt, Coppo, Hastae, Martinetti, Il Mongetto, PRUNOTTO, Cantine Sant'Agata, Scarpa, La Spinetta, Vietti.

BARDOLINO DOC

ITALY, Veneto

Corvina, Rondinella, Molinara and others

Bardolino is one of the three famous names of the VENETO (with SOAVE and VALPOLICELLA). It can be good but, sadly, often isn't, perhaps because the light, fresh, summery style of red or rosé (called chiaretto) too easily pleases the tourists who flock to the shores of Lake Garda in the hot months. The overall standard, however, is improving. Bardolino at its best has a vibrant, ripe-cherries-and-slightly-bitter-almonds character that is usually better the younger, cheerier and less serious the wine is. However, in the hands of quality producers like Cavalchina, Corte Gardoni, Guerrieri-Rizzardi, MASI, Le Vigne di San Pietro and Zeni, more serious, weightier Bardolino can work well.

BAROLO DOCG

ITALY, Piedmont

♥ *Nebbiolo*

Barolo may be a very acquired taste, but once acquired it can become an obsession. Tough, tannic and astringent the wine may be, but there is a wonderful nugget of fruit that seems to flow round the more abrasive elements to make a remarkably alluring whole. Barolo can be as exhilarating as a summer pudding of raspberries and other berried fruits. It can be as ethereal as the scent of violets and roses. It can be earthy, truffly, smoky, deep and mysterious. It can be pruny, chocolaty, rich and seductive. Or it may be any combination of these. True, only the great Barolos can inspire the muse. And if it is a cheap example, it may well be enjoyable but it won't be revelatory.

The renowned red wine is named after a village in the steep, angular Langhe hills of southern PIEDMONT. More and more producers are extracting full benefit from the diversity of sites and making single-vineyard wines. Many winemakers of the current generation, led by Elio ALTARE, have applied new methods to make Barolo that is fresher, cleaner, better balanced and ready sooner, with greater colour, richer fruit and softer tannins yet without sacrificing Barolo's noble character. Traditionalists, committed to protracted maceration, long aging in big old oak, no hint of sweet spicy new oak barrels, still maintain that this new style of wine is not Barolo – good though it may be as international-style red wine. I disagree. Of course it's Barolo, in a modern idiom.

But there's room in Barolo for all these styles: basic and magical, cru and non-cru, traditional and new. Distinct styles of wine are made in the zone's villages. Barolo and La Morra make the most perfumed wines; Monforte and Serralunga the most hefty; Castiglione Falletto strikes the balance between the two. Barolo nowadays is frequently labelled by vineyards, though the producer's reputation often carries more weight. Best vineyards: Bricco delle Viole, Brunate, Bussia Soprana, Cannubi Boschis, Cerequio, Conca dell'Annunziata, Fiasco, Francia, Giachini, Ginestra, Monfalletto, Monprivato, Rocche dell'Annunziata, Rocche di Castiglione, Santo Stefano di Perno, La Serra, Vigna Rionda, Villero.

There is room for light vintages which are ready to drink in five years; and for brilliant heavyweights like '97 which needs ten years at least to show its best. Best years: 2001, '00, '99, '98, '97, '96, '95, '93, '90, '89, '88, '86, '85. Best producers: C Alario, G Alessandria, Altare, Azelia, Boglietti, Bongiovanni, Brovia, Ceretto, CHIARLO, CLERICO, Aldo CONTERNO, Giacomo CONTERNO, Conterno-Fantino, Corino, Luigi Einaudi, GAJA, Bruno GIACOSA, Elio Grasso, M Marengo, Bartolo Mascarello, Giuseppe MASCARELLO, Monfalletto-Cordero di Montezemolo, Oberto, Oddero, Parusso, Pio Cesare, Pira, E Pira & Figli, F Principiano, PRUNOTTO, Renato Ratti, Revello, Rocche dei Manzoni, SANDRONE, P Scavino, M Sebaste, Vajra, Mauro Veglio, Vietti, Vigna Rionda, Gianni Voerzio, Roberto VOERZIO.

BARÓN DE LEY

Barón de Ley is regarded as the leading bodega in the Rioja Baja region. The Reserva Rioja shows good balance between berried fruit and vanilla oak.

BARÓN DE LEY

SPAIN, Navarra, Rioja DOCa

♥ *Tempranillo, Cabernet Sauvignon*

♟ *Grenache Noir (Garnacha Tinta), Tempranillo, Graciano*

♀ *Macabeo (Viura)*

This relatively new estate makes all its red wine from its own 90ha (222 acres) of vineyards in the RIOJA Baja. Over half the bodega's 4000 barrels are of French Limousin oak, which the owners believe will give a more refined style of red wine. The white and rosé are made from bought-in grapes. The bodega was also one of the first to plant 'experimental' Cabernet Sauvignon in Rioja, following on NAVARRA's example. Best years: 1998, '95, '94, '91, '87, '85.

BAROSSA VALLEY

AUSTRALIA, South Australia

It was German settlers who were largely responsible for founding the South Australian wine industry here between 1840 and 1880. German place-names are more numerous than English, and brass bands and Lederhosen frequently displace rock groups and jeans.

The Barossa Valley is home to many of Australia's biggest wine companies, but due to a local predominance of low-yielding, dry-farmed vineyards most of their fruit comes from other, lower-cost areas. However, a new wave of young 'old-timers' has managed to vault Barossa from 'also ran' to mythical status during the '90s and the early twenty-first century. The reason is the phenomenally rich flavours those ancient vines can give to Barossa wines, and old-vine Barossa Shiraz, Grenache and Mataro (Mourvèdre) have now reached cult status. These are the heart of Barossa wine although old-vine Semillon also contributes its own deep, waxy yellowish style of wine, and, from the Barossa Ranges comes high quality Riesling. Best years: (Shiraz) 2001, '99, '98, '97, '96, '94, '91, '90, '88, '87. Best producers: (Shiraz) BAROSSA VALLEY ESTATE, Basedow, Bethany, Grant BURGE, Charles Cimicky, Elderton, Glaetzer, Greenock Creek, HENSCHKE, Hewitson, Jenke, Trevor Jones, Peter LEHMANN, Charles MELTON, Miranda, MOUNTADAM, ORLANDO, PENFOLDS, ROCKFORD, St HALLETT, Saltram, Three Rivers, Torbreck, Turkey Flat, VERITAS, The Willows, YALUMBA.

BAROSSA VALLEY ESTATE

AUSTRALIA, South Australia, Barossa Valley

♥ *Syrah (Shiraz), Cabernet Sauvignon, Merlot, Grenache*

♀ *Chardonnay, Semillon, Riesling*

Initially established by local grape growers as a quality co-operative and now owned half by industry giant HARDY. Its flagship reds are huge, gutsy BAROSSA beauties E & E Black Pepper Shiraz, Ebenezer Shiraz and E & E Sparkling Shiraz, all bursting with ripe plum fruit, spice and vanilla oak. Ebenezer Cabernet-Merlot and Chardonnay and intense, full-flavoured sparkling Pinot Noir are in the same range. Moculta, a second label, offers good value. Best years: (Shiraz) 2001, '99, '98, '97, '96, '94, '91, '90.

JIM BARRY

AUSTRALIA, South Australia, Clare Valley

♥ *Syrah (Shiraz), Cabernet Sauvignon and others*

♀ *Riesling, Chardonnay and others*

Formerly more of a white wine outfit, with the famous Florita vineyard as the source of perfumed, classy Rieslings. However, led by the irrepressible Barry boys, the winery is now a serious red wine player and produces one of Clare Valley's most celebrated reds – the Armagh. This is a heady, blockbusting Shiraz designed to overwhelm any palate of a sensitive disposition, but it works, and now sells for huge sums. Other reds like Cabernet Sauvignon and McCrae Wood Shiraz are also increasingly good. Best years: (Armagh Shiraz) 1999, '98, '96, '95, '93, '92, '91, '90.

BARSAC AC
FRANCE, Bordeaux
♀ *Sémillon, Sauvignon Blanc, Muscadelle*
Barsac is the largest of the five communes in the SAUTERNES AC and its sweet wines can call themselves either Barsac or Sauternes. Many producers even label their wines as Sauternes-Barsac.

Barsac lies close to the Garonne in the north of the Sauternes AC. Along its eastern boundary runs the diminutive river Ciron – source of the humid autumn mists crucial to the development of noble rot, which intensifies the sweetness in the grapes and without which you can't make truly sweet wine. The important grapes are Sémillon, which can produce syrupy, viscous wines in the best years, and Sauvignon Blanc, which adds fruit and acid balance. There is a little Muscadelle, useful for its honeyed spice in less good years.

In general, Barsac wines are a little less luscious, less gooily indulgent than other Sauternes, but from good properties they should still be marvellously heady, full of the taste of peaches and apricots and creamy nuts. Unfortunately, they're expensive, especially from the Classed Growths, of which there are ten in Barsac. Best years: 2002, '01, '99, '98, '97, '96, '95, '90, '89, '88, '86, '83. Best producers: CLIMENS, COUTET, DOISY-DAËNE, Doisy-Dubroca, DOISY-VÉDRINES, de Myrat, NAIRAC, Piada, Suau.

DOMAINE GHISLAINE BARTHOD
FRANCE, Burgundy, Côte de Nuits, Chambolle-Musigny AC
♂ *Pinot Noir*
Quality at this estate, formerly known as Barthod-Noëllat, has always been high and has, if anything, improved under the stewardship of Ghislaine Barthod. She is fortunate in possessing parcels in a number of Premiers Crus, including les Cras, Beaux Bruns, Charmes and Varoilles, and tastings

reveal subtle differences between them. The wines are rarely powerful or earthy; instead, they typify the ethereal beauty of CHAMBOLLE at its best. Their aroma can be pure raspberry, with the violet tones that are a hallmark of the village, and on the palate they are subtle, elegant and complex. Aged in about 25 per cent new oak, they are best enjoyed during their first ten years. The BOURGOGNE Rouge can be delicious. Best years: 2000, '99, '98, '97, '96, '95, '93, '90.

BASILICATA
ITALY
Basilicata is in the instep of Italy, sandwiched between CAMPANIA, CALABRIA and PUGLIA. It is Italy's poorest region and the second lowest in population. The march of progress has been slow. It is hilly and mountainous, surprisingly bleak and cold in winter. but on the other hand, the beaches along the Ionian (instep) and the fragment of Tyrrhenian (west) coasts are some of Italy's most beautiful. There's not a great deal of wine, and most of this comes from the historic Aglianico grape (AGLIANICO DEL VULTURE is the region's only DOC).

BASS PHILLIP
AUSTRALIA, Victoria
♂ *Pinot Noir, Gamay*
♀ *Chardonnay*
Winemaker Phillip Jones produces tiny quantities (around 1500 cases per year) of Australia's most eagerly sought and stylish Pinot Noirs under the standard, Premium and occasional Reserve labels, together with a hatful of Gamay and Chardonnay for home consumption. The flavour is subtle yet penetrating and incredibly long-lasting, rapidly taking on the forest undergrowth character of high-class red Burgundy. The Village is a new, less expensive Pinot Noir, but still with plenty of Bass Phillip charm. Best years: 2002, '01, '00, '98, '97, '96, '95, '94, '93, '92, '91, '89, '85.

DR VON BASSERMANN-JORDAN
GERMANY, Pfalz, Deidesheim
♂ *Pinot Noir (Spätburgunder), Merlot*
♀ *Riesling, Pinot Blanc (Weissburgunder), Pinot Gris (Grauburgunder), Chardonnay*
This PFALZ estate has a long history of making top-quality wines. The 42ha (104 acres) of vineyards, practically all Riesling, cover most of the best sites in the Mittelhaardt, including Jesuitengarten, Kirchenstück, Ungeheuer in FORST, and the Grainhübel,

Hohenmorgen and Kalkofen of DEIDESHEIM among others. Since the arrival of Ulrich Mell as winemaker in 1996, the estate has resumed making rich yet supremely balanced Riesling. Best years: 2002, '01, '00, '99, '98, '97, '96, '90, '89, '88, '86, '81, '79, '76, '71.

CH. BASTOR-LAMONTAGNE
FRANCE, Bordeaux, Sauternes AC, Cru Bourgeois
♀ *Sémillon, Sauvignon Blanc, Muscadelle*
There's no such thing as a good, cheap SAUTERNES. Good Sauternes is fiendishly expensive to make, the vineyard yield is low and the incidence of sweetness-inducing noble rot erratic and unpredictable. There is one shining exception – Ch. Bastor-Lamontagne. This 56-ha (138-acre) Sauternes property is on a good site in the commune of Preignac, just north of the great Ch. SUDUIRAUT. Year after year it produces luscious, honeyed wine at a price which allows you to wallow in the delights of high-class Sauternes without taking out a second mortgage (just). Best years: 2002, '01, '99, '98, '97, '96, '95, '94, '90, '89, '88, '86, '85, '83.

CH. BASTOR-LAMONTAGNE
Year after year this large Sauternes estate produces luscious, honeyed wine typically showing fine botrytis character and ripe apricot fruit at a reasonable price.

CH. BATAILLEY
FRANCE, Bordeaux, Haut-Médoc, Pauillac AC, 5ème Cru Classé
♂ *Cabernet Sauvignon, Merlot, Cabernet Franc*
Owned by *négociant* Émile Castéja of Borie-Manoux, this château is a byword for value-for-money – which, in the rarefied world of PAUILLAC Classed Growths, is an infrequent accolade indeed. Made in the plummier, broader Pauillac style, it should be a byword for reliability too, because since the mid-1970s the wine has been good; marked by a full, obvious blackcurrant fruit (even when very young), not too much tannin, and a luscious overlay of good, creamy, oak-barrel vanilla. As is to be expected from a good Pauillac red, this wine is sturdy enough to age well for at least 15 years, yet it is lovely to drink at only five years old. Best years: 2000, '99, '98, '96, '89, '88, '88, '85, '82.

BÂTARD-MONTRACHET AC, BIENVENUES-BÂTARD-MONTRACHET AC, CRIOTS-BÂTARD-MONTRACHET AC

FRANCE, Burgundy, Côte de Beaune, Grands Crus

♀ *Chardonnay*

Bâtard-Montrachet is a superb 11.87-ha (29-acre) Grand Cru straddling the communal border between PULIGNY-MONTRACHET and CHASSAGNE-MONTRACHET. The wines have enormous richness and grandeur, filling your mouth with flavours of freshly roasted coffee, toasted bread still hot from the stove, brazil nuts and spice – and honey, which after six to eight years becomes so strong it seems to coat your mouth. Yet despite all this, Bâtard-Montrachet is a fully dry wine; there is not the slightest hint of sugar. The richness is simply the alchemy of a great vineyard, a great grape variety – Chardonnay – and the careful, loving vinification and aging in good oak, that has given Grand Cru white Burgundy its reputation as the world's greatest dry white wine.

There are two other parts of Bâtard: 3.7ha (9.1 acres) of Bienvenues-Bâtard-Montrachet just to the north (*bienvenue* means 'welcome') and 1.6ha (4 acres) of the less opulent Criots-Bâtard-Montrachet, directly to the south and entirely within Chassagne-Montrachet. These are also great white wines, flavoursome and rich, although they are generally a little less overwhelming than Bâtard-Montrachet. All can age for a decade. Best years: 2002, '01, '00, '99, '97, '96, '95, '92, '90, '89. Best producers: Blain-Gagnard, CARILLON, DROUHIN, Fontaine-Gagnard, J-N GAGNARD, JADOT, V & F Jouard, Latour, Dom. LEFLAIVE, Olivier LEFLAIVE, Marc Morey, Pierre Morey, Michel Niellon, RAMONET, SAUZET, Verget.

DOMAINE DES BAUMARD

FRANCE, Loire, Coteaux du Layon AC

♂ *Cabernet Sauvignon, Cabernet Franc*

♀ *Chenin Blanc, Chardonnay, Verdelho*

This excellent domaine, established nearly 400 years ago, specialises in sweet wines: sensational QUARTS DE CHAUME which requires aging, as well as rich, honeyed, impeccably balanced COTEAUX DU LAYON Clos de Ste-Cathérine. There is also a fine steely, mineral-scented SAVENNIÈRES Clos du Papillon. The CRÉMANT DE LOIRE and ANJOU reds are not at the same exalted level. Best years: (Quarts de Chaume) 2000, '99, '97, '96, '95, '93, '90, '89, '88, '85, '83, 81, '78, '76, '71, '62, '59, '47.

LES BAUX-DE-PROVENCE AC

FRANCE, Provence

♂ ♀ *Grenache, Syrah, Mourvèdre, Cabernet Sauvignon and others*

This exciting AC in the south of France is showing how organic farming methods can produce spectacular results mainly due to the warm dry climate. It's a weird place, though – a desolate moonscape of tumbled rocks and gaunt cliffs between Cavaillon and Arles in the foothills of the Alpilles in the Bouches-du-Rhône *département*.

Still, the welcome is in the wines. Good fruit and intelligent winemaking produce some of the more easily enjoyable reds in PROVENCE. Fruit is what marks them out, and an incredible softness for wines that are well-structured, full and balanced, and suited to aging for several years; yet even when young they seem to soothe your palate and calm your thoughts. The most important grape is the Syrah, which here gets into its joyous, fruit-first mood. The one-time leading estate, Domaine de TRÉVALLON, is the chief exponent of the Cabernet-Syrah blend, but has been barred from the AC for exceeding the limits set for Cabernet Sauvignon. More fool the authorities, because it's still the best wine in the region. Around 80 per cent of the wine is red. Best years: (reds) 2001, '00, '99, '98, '97, '96, '95. Best producers: Hauvette, Mas de la Dame, Mas de Gourgonnier, Mas Ste-Berthe, Romanin, Terres Blanches.

CH. BEAU-SÉJOUR BÉCOT

FRANCE, Bordeaux, St-Émilion Grand Cru AC, Premier Grand Cru Classé

♂ *Merlot, Cabernet Franc, Cabernet Sauvignon*

There was a hue and cry when Beau-Séjour Bécot was demoted from the ranks of ST-ÉMILION's Premiers Grands Crus Classés in 1985. Luckily, brothers Gérard and Dominique Bécot wasted little time dwelling on the problem and the estate was reinstated in 1996, the domaine much improved and the wine back to its very best. Beau-Séjour Bécot's 16.6-ha (41-acre) vineyard is situated on St-Émilion's limestone plateau and *côtes* and is planted with 70 per cent Merlot and 15 per cent each Cabernet Franc and Cabernet Sauvignon. The wines are classically vigorous with a fine tannic structure and elegant oakiness. They improve with long aging, at least eight to ten years, from which they gain both in aroma and complexity. Best years: 2001, '00, '98, '96, '95, '94, '90, '89, '88, '86, '85.

CH. DE BEAUCASTEL

FRANCE, Southern Rhône, Châteauneuf-du-Pape AC

♂ *Grenache, Mourvèdre, Counoise and others*

♀ *Roussanne, Grenache Blanc and others*

In terms of consistency as well as quality, Beaucastel is arguably the finest estate in CHÂTEAUNEUF-DU-PAPE. Other estates may occasionally surpass Beaucastel in individual vintages, but no other estate performs so

In the north-east of the Châteauneuf-du-Pape AC, Ch. de Beaucastel's vineyards have a high proportion of the famous Châteauneuf stones or galets roulés which store daytime heat as well as retaining valuable moisture.

steadily, even making drinkable wines in the poorest of years. Beaucastel, which is owned by the Perrin family, takes a very traditional approach to the red wine, growing all 13 permitted varieties of the appellation organically and vinifying them without recourse to new oak or other modish techniques. One peculiarity is the high proportion of Mourvèdre, a grape that does not ripen easily here. But when it does it gives a density and structure to the wine that probably helps account for its remarkable ability to age. In exceptional vintages, when the Perrins are dazzled by the quality of the Mourvèdre, they bottle a small quantity of a very expensive cuvée called Hommage à Jacques Perrin.

The white wines are equally remarkable: one is produced mostly from Roussanne and partly barrel fermented, while the Vieilles Vignes bottling is made only from Roussanne and is immensely concentrated. Both wines can be enjoyed young or kept for at least ten years. Prices of these excellent wines have risen in recent years, but the Perrins also produce a fine CÔTES DU RHÔNE called Coudoulet de Beaucastel from vineyards just outside the appellation, which can give you a hint of the Beaucastel experience for half the price. There is also a range of southern reds under the Domaine Perrin label. Best years: (reds) 2001, '00, '99, '98, '97, '96, '95, '94, '93, '90, '89, '88, '85, '83, '81; (whites) 2001, '00, '99, '98, '97, '96, '95, '94, '93, '92, '90, '89, '88.

BEAUJOLAIS AC, BEAUJOLAIS SUPÉRIEUR AC

FRANCE, Burgundy, Beaujolais

 Gamay

 Chardonnay

About one-third of the Beaujolais drunk nowadays goes under the label BEAUJOLAIS NOUVEAU or Beaujolais Primeur. That's a pretty big proportion but exactly how it should be. The word Nouveau (new) or Primeur (first) on the label shows that the wine is as young as it can be, and youthful effervescence is precisely what makes Beaujolais such fun. It gushes from the bottle into the glass and down your throat with a whoosh of flavours – banana, peach and pepper fruit – typical of the Gamay grape.

This gluggable quality is usually obtained by a vinification method known as carbonic maceration. The grapes aren't pressed before fermentation; instead, they are piled into the vat in whole bunches. The skins of the grapes at the bottom of the vat gradually burst and

the juice released then begins to ferment. As the vat heats up during fermentation, the grapes on top ferment inside their skins, where the perfume and colour are concentrated. The result is loads of bright colour and orchard fruit, with minimal tannins and acids from the outside of the grape skins.

The Beaujolais AC is the basic appellation covering 22,500ha (55,600 acres) of vineyards between MÂCON and Lyon. Almost all the wine is red, though there is some rosé and a little white. In the south, towards Lyon, the wide carpet of vines produces simple AC Beaujolais, an easy-going light red wine to be drunk within months of the vintage. In the north, towards Mâcon, most of the reds qualify either as BEAUJOLAIS-VILLAGES or as a single cru. These ten crus, or villages, definitely do produce superior – and more expensive – wine: BROUILLY/CÔTE DE BROUILLY, CHÉNAS, CHIROUBLES, FLEURIE, JULIÉNAS, MORGON, MOULIN-À-VENT, RÉGNIÉ and ST-AMOUR.

The Beaujolais Supérieur AC means wine with a minimum alcoholic strength one degree higher than straight Beaujolais. Since freshness is everything, extra strength isn't really the point. Best producers: (reds) La Ronze/L & J-M Charmet, DUBOEUF, JADOT (Dom. de la Madone), P Sapin (Dom. Père Thomas), Terres Dorés/J-P Brun, Vissoux/P-M Chermette.

BEAUJOLAIS NOUVEAU

FRANCE, Burgundy, Beaujolais, Beaujolais AC

 Gamay

This is the first release of bouncy, fruity BEAUJOLAIS wine on the third Thursday of November after the harvest. The wine will normally be between seven and nine weeks old, depending on the date of the vintage – the earlier it is the better. This is as near as we'll get to how Beaujolais used to be drunk by the locals although everyone has now become a little tired of the hype surrounding

its launch. The quality is usually reasonable, since much of the best Beaujolais AC is used for Nouveau and the wine is delicious until the New Year, but thereafter, while drinkable, is likely to throw a slight sediment.

BEAUJOLAIS-VILLAGES AC

FRANCE, Burgundy, Beaujolais

 Gamay

This AC covers a grouping of 38 communes with supposedly superior vineyard sites in the north of the BEAUJOLAIS region. When carefully made from ripe grapes, Beaujolais-Villages can represent all the vivacity of the Gamay at its best. Some Villages wine is made into Nouveau and is worth keeping for six months. Many Beaujolais-Villages are now bottled under a 'domaine' name, the label indicating the name of the village. However, the larger merchants usually make up a blend from several villages. Best villages: Lancié, Perréon and Quincié. Best years: 2002, '00. Best producers: G Descombes, DUBOEUF, Manoir du Pavé, J-C Pivot, P Sapin (Dom. St-Cyr).

BEAULIEU VINEYARD

USA, California, Napa County, Napa Valley AVA

 Cabernet Sauvignon, Merlot, Pinot Noir and others

 Chardonnay, Sauvignon Blanc, Pinot Gris and others

Much of the NAPA VALLEY's early fame for Cabernet Sauvignon rested upon the wines made at Beaulieu by Georges de Latour between 1900 and 1919, and by André Tchelistcheff between 1937 and 1970. The style of BV's flagship Cabernet, Georges de Latour Private Reserve, is one of the most distinctive in CALIFORNIA, owing to its extra-ripe grapes. BV's second, less costly

Cabernet, RUTHERFORD, is lighter and ages faster. A red Meritage, Tapestry, has a hefty proportion of Merlot for instant accessibility. Recent bottlings of Chardonnay and Pinot Noir from CARNEROS and Syrah have been a pleasant surprise. Best years: (Private Reserve) 2001, '00, '99, '98, '97, '96, '95, '94, '92, '91, '90, '87, '86, '84.

BEAUNE AC

FRANCE, Burgundy, Côte de Beaune
♥ *Pinot Noir*
♀ *Chardonnay, Aligoté*

Beaune is the capital of the CÔTE D'OR and one of Burgundy's most important wine towns, as well as giving its name to the southern section, the Côte de Beaune. It is also an important appellation. Almost all the wines are red, with a delicious, soft red-fruits ripeness, no great tannin, and not much obvious acidity, plus a unique, slight minerally element which is very enjoyable. The wines age well, gaining a savoury yet toffee-rich flavour over five to ten years, but they are also among the easiest of Burgundies to drink young. There are many excellent Premiers Crus (including Boucherottes, Bressandes, Cent Vignes, Clos des Mouches, Clos du Roi, Fèves, Grèves, Marconnets, Teurons and Vignes Franches). Best years: (reds) 2002, '01, '99, '98, '97, '96, '95, '93, '90. Merchants dominate the vineyard holdings but in general seem to make a reasonable effort to produce typical wines. But there are some independent owners – such as Dom. Jacques Germain, LAFARGE, Morot and TOLLOT-BEAUT. Best merchants: BOUCHARD PÈRE ET FILS, Champy, Chanson, DROUHIN, Camille Giroud, JADOT, Jaffelin, LABOURÉ-ROI, THOMAS-MOILLARD.

Although most people think of Beaune as a red wine AC, seven per cent of the 450ha (1112 acres) of vines are planted with white varieties. Drouhin makes Clos des Mouches, an outstandingly good, creamy, nutty wine. Beaune whites age well, particularly the oaky Clos des Mouches, but are also delicious at only two years old. Best years: (whites) 2002, '01, '00, '99, '97, '96, '95.

BEAUX FRÈRES

USA, Oregon, Yamhill County, Willamette Valley AVA
♥ *Pinot Noir*

USA wine guru, Robert M Parker, Jr. is a partner in this OREGON winery, a controversial issue early on, that quickly faded after a few intense, full-bodied Pinot Noirs were released. Winemaker Michael Etzel is Parker's brother-in-law, hence the name

Beaux Frères. The wine shows tremendous blackberry fruit and new oak flavours and has attracted a cult following. A second wine, Belles Soeurs, is also good. Best years: 2001, '00, '99, '98, '97, '96, '94.

GRAHAM BECK WINES

SOUTH AFRICA, Western Cape, Robertson WO
♥ *Syrah (Shiraz), Pinotage, Cabernet Sauvignon, Merlot*
♀ *Chardonnay, Sauvignon Blanc, Viognier*

A vibrant two-cellar operation. In ROBERTSON, Pieter Ferreira concentrates on Cap Classique sparkling wine, including an elegant, rich NV Brut from Chardonnay and Pinot Noir, and a toastily fragrant, creamy barrel-fermented Blanc de Blancs. Juicy Syrah and Pinotage carry the flag for reds, while the flavourful, balanced Chardonnay does the same for still white wine; there is also a promising Viognier. Charles Hopkins runs the Franschhoek cellar: his Graham Beck Coastal range – much from old-vine STELLENBOSCH fruit – is making waves with sturdy Shiraz, The Old Road Pinotage and Cabernet Sauvignon.

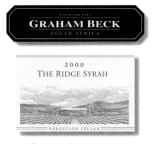

GRAHAM BECK WINES
Deep, plummy Syrah from The Ridge Vineyard on the eastern slopes of the Rooiberg is one of many excellent wines made at this dynamic winery in Robertson.

BEIRAS VINHO REGIONAL

PORTUGAL, Beira Alta, Beira Litoral, Terras de Sicó
Covering most of central Portugal, Beiras is a diverse region which stretches from the fertile coastal plain inland to the Serra de Estrela, Portugal's highest mountain range. It embraces two leading DOCs, DÃO and BAIRRADA, as well as the newer ones of Távora/Varosa, Lafões and Beira Interior.

Such a large area covers so many diverse terroirs and climates and more than 80 different red and white grape varieties are authorised for the Vinho Regional. A number of important wines are made at this level, using Portuguese red and white grape varieties, along with international ones such as Chardonnay and Cabernet Sauvignon which

are not allowed under the more restrictive DOC legislations. Cabernet Sauvignon performs well in Bairrada and is increasingly blended with the local Baga grape. The wines are generally for early drinking. Best producers: Caves ALIANÇA (Galeria), BRIGHT BROTHERS, D F J VINHOS (Bela Fonte), Figueira de Castelo Rodrigo co-op, Quinta de Foz de Arouce, Luís PATO, Rogenda, Caves SÃO JOÃO (Quinta do Poço do Lobo).

CH. BELAIR

FRANCE, Bordeaux, St-Émilion Grand Cru AC, Premier Grand Cru Classé
♥ *Merlot, Cabernet Franc*

Belair is Ch. AUSONE's neighbour on the steep, south- and south-east-facing clay limestone slopes or *côtes* just below the town of ST-ÉMILION. The fortunes of the estate were revived in the late 1970s with the arrival of winemaker Pascal Delbeck, until 1996 also responsible for the winemaking at Ausone. The estate has been run biodynamically since 1994, and effects are beginning to be felt with the soft, stylish wines on good form. Best years: 2001, '00, '98, '95, '94, '90, '89, '88, '86, '85, '83, '82.

BELLAVISTA

ITALY, Lombardy, Franciacorta DOCG
♥ *Pinot Noir (Pinot Nero), Cabernet Sauvignon, Merlot*
♀♥ *Chardonnay, Pinot Noir (Pinot Nero), Pinot Blanc (Pinot Bianco)*

Winemaker Mattia Vezzola specializes in FRANCIACORTA sparkling wines with a very good Cuvée Brut and four distinctive Gran Cuvées (including an excellent rosé). Riserva Vittorio Moretti Extra Brut, named after the company's founder and owner, is made in exceptional years. Bellavista also produces lovely still wines, including a white blend, Convento dell'Annunciata, Chardonnay Uccellanda and red Casotte (Pinot Nero) and Rosso del Sebino Solesine (Cabernet-Merlot).

BELLET AC

FRANCE, Provence
♥♀ *Folle Noire, Braquet, Cinsaut, Grenache Noir and others*
♀ *Rolle, Roussanne, Chardonnay*

Bellet is a tiny area – only 44ha (108 acres) of mainly white Rolle and red Braquet and Folle Noir vines in the hills behind Nice – whose existence was so precarious that the authorities almost withdrew its AC in 1947. However, Bellet has Nice as its home market, and after a day on the beach people don't seem to care much what their wine tastes like so long as it is supposedly rare and over-priced. There are a few good bottles, but in the chic eateries you're better off ordering a pastis or a gin and tonic. Best years: 2001, '00, '99, '98, '97, '96, '95. Best producers: Ch. de Bellet, Ch. de Crémat, Delmasso.

BENDIGO

AUSTRALIA, Victoria

Bendigo was the focus of the VICTORIA gold rush, from which much of the Victorian wine trade grew: today's figure of over 20 small-scale, high-quality wineries compare with over 100 in 1880. But this warm region is superb for red wines – the HEATHCOTE sub-region is justifiably regarded as one of Australia's greatest producers of rich, structured, dark cherry-flavoured Shiraz which lives for decades and it was recently promoted to a region in its own right. There is also good Cabernet Sauvignon, with Chardonnay the next planted variety. Best years: (Shiraz) 2001, '00, '99, '98, '97, '95, '94, '93, '91, '90. Best producers: Balgownie, Chateau Leamon, Passing Clouds, Water Wheel.

BERBERANA

SPAIN, La Rioja, Rioja DOCa

Tempranillo, Grenache Noir (Garnacha Tinta), Carignan (Mazuelo), Graciano, Mourvèdre (Monastrell)

Macabeo, Xarel-lo, Parellada

Berberana, one of RIOJA's oldest and largest bodegas, is now part of one of Rioja's largest companies, Arco Bodegas Unidas, incorporating Lagunilla, Marqués de Monistrol and MARQUÉS DE GRIÑÓN. Berberana makes a pleasant, lightly oaked Crianza and respectable Reservas and Gran Reservas. Best years: (Reserva) 1998, '96, '95, '94.

BERCHER

GERMANY, Baden, Burkheim

Pinot Noir (Spätburgunder)

Pinot Gris (Grauburgunder), Pinot Blanc (Weissburgunder), Riesling, Muscat (Muskateller), Gewürztraminer, Chardonnay

Located in the KAISERSTUHL area of BADEN, the Bercher brothers, Rainer the winemaker and Eckhardt the vine grower, are jovial perfectionists making wine for pleasure rather than analytical dissection. The high points in their large range of wines are the powerful oak-aged reds and dry Grauburgunders, which marry richness with perfect balance. Drink young or age for three to five years. Best years: (whites) 2002, '01, '99, '98, '97, '96; (reds) 2002, '01, '99, '97, '96.

BERGERAC AC, BERGERAC SEC AC, CÔTES DE BERGERAC AC, CÔTES DE BERGERAC MOELLEUX AC

FRANCE, South-West

Cabernet Sauvignon, Cabernet Franc, Merlot

Sémillon, Sauvignon Blanc, Muscadelle and others

Bergerac is the main town of the Dordogne and the overall AC for this underrated area east of Bordeaux; the region might consider itself unlucky to be denied the more prestigious BORDEAUX AC, since its vineyards abut those of Bordeaux's BORDEAUX-CÔTES DE FRANCS and CÔTES DE CASTILLON ACs, and the grape varieties are mostly the same. Indeed, for centuries Bergerac wines were sold as Bordeaux. Production is pretty sizeable – more than 72 million bottles a year, of which about 55 per cent is red, 5 per cent rosé and the rest white.

The red is like a light, fresh Bordeaux-style wine, a bit grassy but with a good raw blackcurrant fruit and hint of earth. Recent vintages have shown more ripe fruit character. A few producers make a more substantial version under the Côtes de Bergerac AC, which stipulates a higher minimum alcohol level. Bergerac rosés, often from Cabernet, can be delightful too. In general drink the most recent vintage, though a few estate reds can age for three to five years. Best years: 2000, '98, '96, '95, '90.

Production of white Bergerac Sec is dominated by the efficient local co-operative, whose wines are generally clean and slightly grassy. However, good dry white Bergerac, made under the Côtes de Bergerac regulations, can have a very tasty, strong nettles and green-grass tang to it, with a little more weight than an equivalent Bordeaux Blanc.

Just over half of Bergerac whites are sweet (mainly *moelleux* rather than *liquoreux*); the Côtes de Bergerac Moelleux AC covers sweet wines from the whole region and these should be pleasant, fruity, easily sweet, yet not exactly rich. More Sémillon-based sweet wines are made in the enclave of MONBAZILLAC and also tiny amounts in Saussignac, Rosette, Côtes de Montravel and Haut-Montravel. In recent vintages, there has been a marked increase in confidence among the independent producers and some excitingly rich wines from Saussignac and Monbazillac are the result. Best years: 2000, '99, '98, '97, '96, '95. Best producers: l'Ancienne Cure, Bélingard, Clos d'Yvigne, la Colline, Court-les-Mûts, Eyssards, Gouyat, la Jaubertie, Moulin Caresse, TOUR DES GENDRES, la Tour des Verdots, Tourmentine.

BERINGER VINEYARDS

A great name in Napa Valley wines, Beringer consistently shines with its Cabernet. The Private Reserve is Beringer's top Cabernet Sauvignon wine.

BERINGER VINEYARDS

USA, California, Napa County, Napa Valley AVA

Cabernet Sauvignon, Merlot, Pinot Noir, Zinfandel

Chardonnay, Sauvignon Blanc, Gewürztraminer, Chenin Blanc

With a long history of winemaking, Beringer, now a pivotal part of the Australian-American conglomerate Beringer Blass, is one of CALIFORNIA's leading producers, making a full range of wines from 1052ha (2600 acres) of vines in NAPA and SONOMA's Knights Valley. In particular, there is a spectacular range of top-class Cabernet Sauvignons. The Private Reserve Cabernet is one of the Napa Valley's finest yet most approachable; the Chabot Vineyards, when released under its own label, can be equally impressive. The Knights Valley Cabernet Sauvignon is made in a lighter style and is good value. Red and white Alluvium (Meritage wines) are also from Knights Valley. HOWELL MOUNTAIN Merlot from Bancroft Ranch is also one of Napa's best examples. Although best known for reds, Private Reserve Chardonnay is a serious oaky white that ages well. Beringer also owns Chardonnay specialists MERIDIAN in SAN LUIS OBISPO, CHATEAU ST JEAN in Sonoma and Stags' Leap Winery in Napa. Best years: (Cabernet) 2001, '00, '99, '98, '97, '96, '95, '94, '93, '91, '90, '87, '86, '84, '81.

BERNARDUS WINERY

USA, California, Monterey County, Carmel Valley AVA

Cabernet Sauvignon, Merlot, Pinot Noir

Chardonnay, Sauvignon Blanc

European industrialist and former race driver for Porsche, Ben Pon carved out an estate vineyard along the gentle slopes within the Carmel Valley, a sheltered corner of MONTEREY that has demonstrated fine potential for Cabernet Sauvignon. After planting 20ha (50 acres) to Cabernet with small patches of Merlot and Cabernet Franc for blending purposes, he is now building an international reputation. The top wine is Marinus, a polished, well-structured estate red. Receiving up to three years of oak aging, it has the depth to age for a decade in the bottle. There is also tasty Pinot Noir from Bien Nacido Vineyard in SANTA BARBARA and a bright, gooseberry-tinged Sauvignon Blanc from Monterey County. Best years: (Marinus) 2001, '00, '97, '96, '95, '94.

BERNKASTEL

GERMANY, Mosel-Saar-Ruwer

This medieval town on the Mosel is home to some superb Riesling vineyards. Rising 200m (656ft) above the town, and almost squeezing the houses into the river, they include the world famous Doctor vineyard. This site has an ideal aspect and very steep gradients and should provide a unique terroir but the wines are often horribly overpriced. Many wines from the neighbouring Graben and Lay sites are as good or better and cost a fraction of the price. But Bernkastel also gives its name to a Bereich and two Grosslagen, Kurfurstlay and Badstube, far larger areas that include much less distinguished vineyards. The small Badstube Grosslage covers Bernkastel's best vineyards, so the wines should be of high standard, but avoid the others which are invariably inferior. Best years: 2002, '01, '99, '98, '97, '95, '93, '90, '88. Best producers: Hansen-Lauer, Dr LOOSEN, J J PRÜM, S A Prüm, Dr H Thanisch, Wegeler.

BEST'S

AUSTRALIA, Victoria, Grampians

♛ Syrah (Shiraz), Merlot, Cabernet Sauvignon, Pinot Noir

♙ Chardonnay, Riesling

This small winery was established in western Victoria in 1866, and is the last survivor, along with SEPPELT, of the wineries established in the region, formerly known as Great Western, to slake the thirst of a society crazed by gold. Its priceless old vineyards are some of the few historic plantings left in the area, and contribute, in particular, to the wonderful, silky smooth, cherry and mint Shiraz (especially in the Thomson Family Shiraz from 130-year-old vines) which is deceptively long-lived. Tasty, clear-fruited Great Western Bin No. 0 Shiraz and Great Western Cabernet are good and the Riesling shows flashes of brilliance. Tropical-fruity, finely balanced Chardonnay is variable, delicious at best. Best years: (Thomson Family Reserve) 2001, '99, '98, '97, '96, '95, '94, '92.

Talented Ernst Loosen, in charge at the Dr Loosen estate based in Bernkastel, is one of Germany's leading organic winemakers.

BETHEL HEIGHTS

USA, Oregon, Willamette Valley AVA

♛ Pinot Noir

♙ Chardonnay, Pinot Gris, Pinot Blanc

Oregon winery with a reputation for stylish Pinot Noirs which are delicious young but can also age surprisingly well; the Southeast Block Reserve is the star. Subtle Chardonnay Reserve is gathering acclaim too, and Pinot Gris filled with citrus and mineral scents is crisp and immensely drinkable. Best years: (Pinot Noir) 2001, '00, '99, '98, '96.

CH. BEYCHEVELLE

FRANCE, Bordeaux, Haut-Médoc, St-Julien AC, 4ème Cru Classé

♛ Cabernet Sauvignon, Merlot, Cabernet Franc, Petit Verdot

This beautiful château overlooking the Gironde graciously announces your arrival in ST-JULIEN – the most concentrated stretch of top-quality vineyards in all BORDEAUX, with 80 per cent of production coming from Classed Growths. Although it is ranked only as a Fourth Growth, its quality is potentially Second. The wine has a beautiful softness even when very young, but takes at least a decade to mature into the fragrant cedarwood-and-blackcurrant flavour for which St-Julien is famous. When this occurs, Beychevelle is a sublime wine, but overcropping and underripeness inexcusably affect some vintages. Second wine: Amiral de Beychevelle. Best years: 2001, '00, '99, '98, '96, '95, '90, '89.

BEYERSKLOOF

SOUTH AFRICA, Stellenbosch WO

♛ Cabernet Sauvignon, Merlot, Pinotage

♙ Pinotage

Red-wine maestro Beyers Truter co-owns this property – recently merged with nearby Bouwland – in association with the Krige brothers of KANONKOP and a UK-based partner. The striking, supple Cabernet Sauvignon-based Beyerskloof and juicily ripe Pinotage remain as good as ever, and have been joined by a succulent, refined Pinotage-Cabernet-merlot blend called Synergy and tasty Pinotage rosé. Best years: (Beyerskloof) 2000, '99, '98, '97, '96, '95, '94, '93.

BIANCO DI CUSTOZA DOC

ITALY, Veneto

♙ Trebbiano Toscano, Garganega, Tocai and others

The existence of quality white wines from a mixed bag of varieties (no less than eight are allowed) in the south-eastern corner of Lake Garda has been documented as far back as the seventeenth century. Most wines are a slightly fuller, more interesting version of SOAVE just to the east, and, drunk young, are good value. Best producers: Cavalchina (Amadeo), Gorgo, Montresor (cru Monte Fiera), Le Vigne di San Pietro (San Pietro).

BIERZO DO

SPAIN, Castilla y León

♛ Mencía, Grenache (Garnacha Tintorera)

♙ Parellada, Doña Blanca, Malvasía, Godello

Sandwiched between the rainy mountains of GALICIA and the arid plains of CASTILLA Y LEÓN, Bierzo makes mostly commonplace reds. However, the recent arrival of Álvaro PALACIOS, of PRIORAT fame, with his inspired Corullón red sheds an entirely new and exciting light on the potential of the Mencía grape. Best producers: Pérez Caramés, Estefania, Descendientes de José Palacios, Pittacum, Prada a Tope, Dominio de Tares, Valtuille, Castro Ventosa.

JOSEF BIFFAR

GERMANY, Pfalz, Deidesheim

♛ Pinot Noir (Spätburgunder)

♙ Riesling, Pinot Blanc (Weissburgunder), Sauvignon Blanc

Gerhard Biffar runs this reliable medium-sized estate in the heart of the Pfalz, making dry and sweet Rieslings from top sites in DEIDESHEIM, RUPPERTSBERG and Wachenheim. Recent vintages have shown consistent quality. Best years: (Riesling Spätlese) 2002, '01, '99, '98, '97, '96, '93, '92.

BILLECART-SALMON

FRANCE, Champagne, Champagne AC

♀ ♂ *Pinot Noir, Chardonnay, Pinot Meunier*

If you want elegance, balance, a gently insistent creaming mousse rather than a spring tide of foam – and a character that is enjoyable young, but thrilling with a few more years' age – Billecart-Salmon is the CHAMPAGNE producer to go for. This is a small family company, based at Mareuil-sur-Ay, making just over 1.2 million bottles a year. The rosé and various vintage wines are justly famous, but it is Billecart's rare ability to produce totally consistent, totally satisfying, elegant non-vintage Champagne, year in year out, that is Billecart's most important achievement. The finest vintage wines are the stylish Blanc de Blancs, Cuvée Elisabeth Salmon Rosé and the rich, complex Cuvée N-F Billecart. Best years: 1997, '96, '95, '91, '90, '89, '88, '86, '85, '82.

BINGEN

GERMANY, Rheinhessen

This small town at the confluence of the Rhine and the Nahe is also a Bereich, the vineyards of which fall in both the NAHE and RHEINHESSEN. The best vineyard in the town is the Scharlachberg, which produces some exciting wines, stinging with racy acidity and the occasional whiff of coal smoke. Best years: (Riesling Spätlese) 2002, '01, '99, '98, '97, '96, '90. Best producer: Villa Sachsen.

BIONDI-SANTI

ITALY, Tuscany, Brunello di Montalcino DOCG

♂ *Sangiovese*

Franco Biondi-Santi's Il Greppo estate has, in less than a century, created both a legend and an international standing for BRUNELLO DI MONTALCINO, the wine which it effectively invented. The modern dynamism of the zone owes more to other producers, however, since quality has slipped over the last 20 years or so. The very expensive Riservas, with formidable levels of extract, tannin and acidity, are made only in top years and only from vines at least 25 years old. They need a minimum ten years of further aging after release before serious judgement is passed on it.

Franco's son, Jacopo, has created his own range of wines at the Montepò estate in Scansano, including Sassoalloro, a barrique-aged Sangiovese, and a Sangiovese-Cabernet-Merlot blend called Schidione, both easier-drinking wines than those from the paternal estate. Best years: (Riserva) 1999, '97, '95, '88, '85, '83, '82, '75, '71.

BLAGNY AC

FRANCE, Burgundy, Côte de Beaune

♂ *Pinot Noir*

Blagny is a tiny hamlet in the Côte de Beaune straddling the boundary of the more famous communes of PULIGNY-MONTRACHET and MEURSAULT. The appellation covers red wine only which can be fair value if you like a rough, rustic Burgundy. Matrot is the best producer in this style. Actually much more Chardonnay than Pinot Noir is grown here but this is sold as either Puligny-Montrachet, Meursault Premier Cru or Meursault-Blagny. Best years: 2002, '99, '97, '96, '95. Best producers: R Ampeau, Lamy-Pillot, Matrot.

DOMAINE PAUL BLANCK

FRANCE, Alsace, Alsace AC

♂ *Pinot Noir*

♀ *Riesling, Gewurztraminer, Pinot Blanc, Pinot Auxerrois, Pinot Gris, Sylvaner and others*

The Blanck family of Kientzheim are passionate about their wines and after a run of good vintages in the 1990s the wines have become truly exciting. Tasting here can be an exhausting experience, so many and varied are the wines. In addition to the Grand Cru bottlings, there may be other wines from individual vineyards, as well as different bottlings for old vines. Vieilles Vignes Riesling and Gewurztraminer from the Furstentum Grand Cru stand out. Riesling Schlossberg and Pinot Gris Altenbourg also offer depth and finesse. The Blancks revel in Vendange Tardive and Sélection de Grains Nobles styles when vintage conditions are right. Best years: (Grand Cru Riesling) 2002, '01, '00, '99, '98, '97, '96, '95, '94, '93, '92, '90, '89, '88.

BLANQUETTE DE LIMOUX AC

FRANCE, Languedoc-Roussillon

♀ *Mauzac, Chenin Blanc, Chardonnay*

The publicity people for Blanquette de Limoux have made great play of the claim that their product is the oldest sparkling wine in the world and that Dom Pérignon and his chums, who are supposed to have 'invented' CHAMPAGNE in northern France, pinched the idea on their way back from a pilgrimage to Spain. These wine legends are good fun, impossible to prove or disprove, and totally irrelevant to the quality of the drink, which in this case is pretty high.

Blanquette de Limoux is from a hilly region in the AUDE *département*, a surprising place to find a sharp, refreshing sparkling wine, since most whites from the Midi are traditionally flat and dull. The secret lies in the local Mauzac grape, which makes up a minimum 90 per cent of the wine and gives it its striking 'green apple skin' flavour. The Champagne method of refermentation in the bottle is used to create the sparkle, although the more rustic *méthode rurale*, finishing off the original fermentation inside the bottle, is also used, and from Mauzac alone, under the separate appellation of Blanquette Méthode Ancestrale.

For some time this very dry, lemon and apple-flavoured wine was accorded second place after Champagne among France's sparkling wines, but the improved quality of the CRÉMANT wines from the Loire, Burgundy and Alsace means this position is now hotly disputed. As a way of fighting back, a new CRÉMANT DE LIMOUX appellation was introduced in 1990 to allow producers to make slightly more 'international' style fizz. Here, a minimum of 60 per cent Mauzac must be used but 20 per cent each of Chenin and Chardonnay substantially change the flavour and create a style that isn't better, just different. Best producers: Collin, Fourn, Guinot, Martinolles, SIEUR D'ARQUES co-operative (the chief producer), les Terres Blanches.

WOLF BLASS

AUSTRALIA, South Australia, Barossa Valley

♂ *Cabernet Sauvignon, Syrah (Shiraz)*

♀ *Riesling, Chardonnay*

It's easy nowadays to lose sight of the massive importance the name Wolf Blass once held in Australian wine. Wolf Blass is a man, a diminutive, passionate bundle of energy from the BAROSSA who is the greatest wine popularizer in the history of Australia – itself the greatest popularizer in the world of wine. Back in the 1960s and '70s most Australians didn't drink table wine, so Wolf Blass set out to use the superb, ripe-tasting South Australian fruit – especially Cabernet Sauvignon and Riesling – to create crowd-pleasing wines that never welched on quality. I remember in the late 1980s still being bowled over by the irresistible mint and blackcurrant juiciness of this Cabernet and the amazing mix of sunny ripeness and lime juice aggression that marked his Riesling.

Nowadays Wolf Blass is a crucial component of the multinational company, Beringer Blass. Some of the wines are still good, but they are neither as affordable nor as unashamedly enjoyable as once they were. Riesling has probably kept its character better than most of the other styles. A recent attempt to produce varietal wines under regional labels merely goes to show that regionality is much better interpreted by small producers than by large multinationals. Best years: (Black Label) 2000, '99, '98, '96, '95, '94, '92, '91, '90, '88, '86.

BLUE MOUNTAIN

CANADA, British Columbia, Okanagan Valley VQA
♟ *Pinot Noir, Gamay*
♀ *Chardonnay, Pinot Gris, Pinot Blanc*

From the moment they opened in 1991, owners Ian and Jane Mavety met with success, establishing Blue Mountain as the quintessential BRITISH COLUMBIA estate winery. Situated on 26ha (65 acres) of rolling vineyard overlooking Vaseaux Lake, Blue Mountain has focused on a handful of varietals led by Pinot Noir and Chardonnay. Other varietals include Pinot Blanc, Gamay Noir and one of the OKANAGAN's best Pinot Gris. Two CHAMPAGNE-method sparklers complete the range of outstanding wines. Best years: 2002, '99, '98, '95.

BOEKENHOUTSKLOOF

SOUTH AFRICA, Western Cape, Franschhoek WO
♟ *Cabernet Sauvignon, Syrah*
♀ *Semillon*

Perched high in the Franschhoek mountains, this small winery, named after the surrounding Cape beech trees, captivates almost as much for its spectacular scenery as for Marc Kent's individual wines made with outstanding fruit and minimal intervention. His punchy Syrah resonates with black pepper, chocolate plum and herb savouriness. Cabernet Sauvignon is deep and powerful and built for the long term. The barrel-fermented Semillon, from 100-year-old bush vines, is as beautiful, waxy and scented as any in South Africa. The second label Porcupine Ridge range offers cheaper but excellent, more fruit-focused drinking. Best years: (Cabernet Sauvignon) 2000, '99, '98, '97.

JEAN-CLAUDE BOISSET

FRANCE, Burgundy, Nuits-St-Georges

Jean-Claude Boisset bought his first vineyards in 1964 and began a *négociant* company whose extraordinary success has enabled him to swallow up many other long-established names such as Bouchard Aîné, Jaffelin, Ponelle, Ropiteau and Héritier-Guyot in the CÔTE D'OR, Moreau in CHABLIS, Cellier des Samsons and Mommessin in BEAUJOLAIS and others elsewhere in France. Mommessin and

the top end of Moreau are beginning to show signs of life and there are a few good wines from Bouchard Aîné and Jaffelin but the quality of far too many of these wines remains mediocre. Easily the most exciting project is Domaine de la Vougeraie, a cherry-picking operation from among Boisset's now extensive vineyard holdings. These wines are in general excellent. The latest Boisset project is in Canada.

BOLGHERI DOC

ITALY, Tuscany
♟ *Cabernet Sauvignon, Cabernet Franc, Merlot, Sangiovese*
♀ *Vermentino, Trebbiano Toscano, Sauvignon Blanc*

Just inland from the Tyrrhenian coast, nestling under the coastal hills, Bolgheri is an improbably picturesque little artists' town, which traditionally has had little to do with wine but which just so happens to be the nearest commune to the SASSICAIA estate of Marchese Incisa della Rocchetta. All this is land which, not so long ago, belonged to the Gherardesca family whose various branches – ANTINORIs, Incisas, Zileris, latter-day Gherardescas themselves – have all now climbed upon the Sassicaia bandwagon, leaving just enough space for the odd peasant or incoming wine superstar to squeeze in.

In 1994 the zone extended its DOC beyond simple white and rosé to cover red wines based on Cabernet, Merlot and Sangiovese in various combinations, while creating a special sub-zone category for Sassicaia, Italy's first DOC for a single estate. The Rosso Superiore DOC covers wines from the prestigious estates of Grattamacco, Le Macchiole, ORNELLAIA, Michele Satta and Antinori's Guado al Tasso. Best years: 2001, '00, '99, '98, '97, '96, '95, '94.

The whites are based on Vermentino, Trebbiano and Sauvignon and can include small percentages of other grapes such as Chardonnay and Viognier.

GRATTAMACCO

Grattamacco was the second Bolgheri estate to produce wine commercially. Its red, from 50 per cent Cabernet Sauvignon, is increasingly refined and stylish.

BOLLINGER

FRANCE, Champagne, Champagne AC
♟ ♀ *Pinot Noir, Chardonnay, Pinot Meunier*

Far too much Bollinger gets drunk in the wrong way. It has long been the preferred tipple of the English upper classes baying for the sound of broken glass, and their more recent imitations, financial whizz-kids with more money than manners. Which is very unfair on poor old Bollinger, just about the most serious CHAMPAGNE company imaginable.

The good non-vintage (called Special Cuvée) is the best-known wine, but the company also produces a range of vintage wines (called Grande Année) which are made in a full, rich, rather old-fashioned style that you love or hate. (Bollinger is one of the few Champagne houses still to ferment its base wine in barrels.) It also produces a range of rarer vintages, including a Vintage RD (which stands for *récemment dégorgé* – recently disgorged – showing that the wine has been left in the cellars lying in bottle on its yeast for longer than usual before disgorging, picking up loads of flavour on the way) and Vieilles Vignes Françaises Blanc de Noirs, from old, ungrafted Pinot Noir vines in the village of Ay. Impressive stuff. The wines are reliably old-fashioned across the range. Best years: (Grande Année) 1996, '95, '92, '90, '89, '88, '85, '82, '79.

CH. LE BON PASTEUR

FRANCE, Pomerol AC, Bordeaux
♟ *Merlot, Cabernet Franc*

This small château right on the north-west tip of POMEROL on the border with ST-ÉMILION, has established an excellent reputation under the ownership of Michel Rolland, one of Bordeaux's leading winemakers. There are only 7ha (17 acres) of vines and the wines have been expensive in recent years, but they are always deliciously soft and full of lush fruit, reaching their peak within 10–12 years. Best years: 2001, '00, '99, '98, '96, '95, '94, '93, '90, '89, '88, '85, '83, '82.

HENRI BONNEAU

FRANCE, Southern Rhône, Châteauneuf-du-Pape AC
♟ *Grenache, Syrah, Mourvèdre, Cinsaut, Counoise, Vaccarèse*
♀ *Clairette*

Henri Bonneau has become a cult figure in CHÂTEAUNEUF-DU-PAPE, although he himself is almost reclusive. A traditionalist, his Grenache-dominated wines are bold and immensely powerful expressions of the local style. His 6ha (15 acres) include a substantial proportion of old vines, which helps explain why his wines are so dense. In a ripe vintage he doesn't destem, so the wines tend to be tannic as well as rich, and even after prolonged cask aging they usually need quite a few years in bottle. The wines that make his admirers swoon are the Réserve des Célestins and the only marginally less rich Cuvée Marie Beurrier from a tiny 0.75-ha (2-acre) site in the north-east of the appellation. Best years: (reds) 2001, '00, '98, '96, '95, '92, '90, '89, '88, '86, '85, '83, '81, '79, '78.

DOMAINE BONNEAU DU MARTRAY

FRANCE, Burgundy, Côte de Beaune, Pernand-Vergelesses

♥ Pinot Noir
♀ Chardonnay

Anyone wishing to understand why CORTON-CHARLEMAGNE is such a special and distinctive white Burgundy only need reach for a bottle from Bonneau du Martray. In most vintages the domaine's wines encapsulate the enthralling combination of power and richness that makes this such a celebrated appellation.

In 1994 Comte Jean-Charles le Bault de la Morinière took over at the family estate, one of the few in Burgundy to make only Grand Cru wine, and has thrown himself into the task with great enthusiasm. The quality of the wine derives from the 9.5ha (23 acres) of Corton-Charlemagne vineyards, which are among the largest holdings within the appellation at the top of the famous Corton hill, rather than from extravagant winemaking techniques. Only about one-third new oak is used, but the wine certainly doesn't lack complexity and it is among the most long-lived from an appellation that provides many of the grander old white Burgundies. The red CORTON (from 1.5ha/4 acres) is less exciting, but has been improving in recent years. Best years: (Corton) 2002, '01, '00, '99, '98, '97, '96, '95; (Corton-Charlemagne) 2002, '01, '00, '99, '98, '97, '96, '95, '94, '92, '90, '88, '85.

BONNES-MARES AC

FRANCE, Burgundy, Côte de Nuits, Grand Cru

♥ Pinot Noir

A large Grand Cru of 15ha (37 acres), of which 88 per cent is in the commune of CHAMBOLLE-MUSIGNY and the rest is in MOREY-ST-DENIS. This is one of the few Burgundian great names to maintain its consistency during the turmoil of the past few decades – the introduction of strict AC laws for the export trade, the see-saw of the American market, changing fashions in vineyard and cellar – which produced inconsistencies in much top Burgundy. Bonnes-Mares managed to keep its deep, ripe, smoky plum fruit, which starts rich and chewy and matures over 10–20 years into a flavour full of chocolate, smoke again, and pruny depth. Best years: 2002, '01, '00, '99, '98, '97, '96, '95, '93, '90, '89, '88. Best producers: d'Auvenay (Dom. LEROY), BOUCHARD PÈRE ET FILS, Champy, DROUHIN, DUJAC, Robert Groffier, JADOT, D LAURENT, J-F MUGNIER, ROUMIER, de VOGÜÉ, Vougeraie.

BONNEZEAUX AC

FRANCE, Loire, Anjou-Saumur, Grand Cru

♀ Chenin Blanc

A wise and prudent few are at last taking an interest in the great sweet whites of the Loire. After a gradual decline following World War Two, there are now 110ha (272 acres) planted out of a possible 130 (321) in Bonnezeaux. The whole Layon Valley, which extends south-east from the Loire near Angers, makes sweet wines (see COTEAUX DU LAYON), but Bonnezeaux and QUARTS DE CHAUME, the other Grand Cru, are potentially the best. However, much of the recent drive to improve the quality of sweet wines in the Layon has come from outside these two Grand Cru areas, which have been slightly inclined to live on their reputation. Even so, they have the lowest yields – Bonnezeaux is allowed just 25 hectolitres per hectare and often achieves only 15 hectolitres – and because they can request a higher price than their neighbours, the growers generally wait for noble rot to affect their grapes in late October, or even November, and then pick only the most shrivelled, raisiny grapes.

This is the same winemaking method as in SAUTERNES, but the flavours are different. In the Layon Valley only Chenin Blanc grapes are used, with their very high natural acidity. Consequently Bonnezeaux can seem surprisingly dry at first, because the acidity is masking the sweetness. But give it 10, 20 or even 40 years and the colour deepens to an orange gold, and the sweetness builds to an intense, yet always acid-freshened, peach, quince and apricots richness. Never quite as luscious as Sauternes, it is nonetheless unique, best drunk by itself, or perhaps with some of those peaches and apricots. It's also good with blue cheeses and rich paté, in particular *foie gras*. Best years: 2002, '01, '00,

'99, '97, '96, '95, '94, '93, '90, '89, '88, '85, '83, '79, '78, '76, '71, '64, '59, '47. Best producers: M Angeli, de FESLES, Godineau, des Grandes Vignes, Petits Quarts, Petit Val, René Renou, Terrebrune, la Varière.

BONNY DOON

USA, California, Santa Cruz County, Santa Cruz Mountains AVA

♥ Syrah, Grenache, Mourvedre, Carignane, Barbera, Zinfandel, Sangiovese, Montepulciano
♥ Grenache, Syrah, Mourvedre, Cinsaut, Marsanne
♀ Riesling, Sauvignon Blanc, Malvasia, Muscat Canelli, Viognier

Randall Grahm started out as a Francophile with a special itch to show CALIFORNIA what grape varieties from France's RHÔNE VALLEY can do. His main red, Le Cigare Volant, is an annually changing Grenache-based blend and a homage to CHÂTEAUNEUF-DU-PAPE Always open to new possibilities, Grahm has begun to bottle it with a screwcap closure and now seems happiest when it comes out more in the style of a powerful red Burgundy. Old Telegram is 100 per cent Mourvedre. Mourvedre is also used for a fine dry rosé, Vin Gris de Cigare.

Grahm sets himself at odds with New World orthodoxies and increasingly takes his cues from Europe, particularly in his quest to produce wines with greater minerality. Syrah, Zinfandel and Riesling remain among his favourites. Particularly delightful are his Ca' del Solo Italianate wines, especially a bone-dry Malvasia Bianca and a white blend, Il Pescatore, his answer to Verdicchio. He also makes a lovely Syrah from SANTA MARIA VALLEY, Cardinal Zin Zinfandel, a pure Riesling from Washington and eaux de vie. Grahm has now spread his net even wider and has three new wines from European vineyards: a MADIRAN, a Vin de Pays d'OC Syrah and a Grenache from NAVARRA. Best years: (Le Cigare Volant) 2001, '00, '99 '95, '94, '93, '92, '91, '90.

BONNY DOON
Randall Grahm is one of California's most innovative winemakers and Le Cigare Volant is his homage to France's famous red wine from Châteauneuf-du-Pape.

BORDEAUX France

BORDEAUX CARRIES A HEAVY RESPONSIBILITY, because just about every wine book describes it as the greatest wine region in the world. Is it? Well, yes, and no. It has produced many of the world's most famous red wines over the last 150 years – the great Classed Growths of Pauillac and Margaux, the sumptuous St-Émilions and exotic Pomerols, as well as many of the world's greatest sweet wines from the villages of Sauternes and Barsac. More recently it has produced a string of world-class, barrel-fermented dry whites from Pessac-Léognan. Indeed, there is probably more fine wine being made in Bordeaux now than ever before, while worldwide, each year produces a veritable flood of wines based on the principles of winemaking in Bordeaux. Based on the red Cabernet Sauvignon, Cabernet Franc, Merlot and Petit Verdot grapes; based on the white Sémillon and Sauvignon Blanc; based on trying to recreate the almost inexpressible beauty of fruit that is ripe, but not too ripe, oak that is sweet, but not too sweet, tannins that are firm, but fond, perfumes that beguile, but do not overpower, memories that linger in the brain more than the heart, satisfaction expressed with a sigh of intellectual contentment rather than a gourmand's bellowed shout for more.

This is the Bordeaux of legend – and indeed reality. But this reality is only a small proportion of the whole Bordeaux. This reality is based upon the miracle of perfectly sited vineyards on the Médoc's gravel banks, on the limestone slopes of St-Émilion, on the sticky clays of Pomerol, on the banks of the tiny river Ciron in Sauternes. Here nature conspires with a cool, damp and unpredictable climate to allow grapes to creep to a mellow ripeness as the autumn fades to winter, the harvest almost never being complete before the storm clouds hurtle in from the Bay of Biscay. On the knife-edge between ripening and failing to ripen, these top wines achieve a balance and a beauty that wines from the warmer, more reliable conditions of California's Napa Valley, Australia's Coonawarra, Chile's Maipo or South Africa's Stellenbosch seldom achieve.

But these are the top wines. Most of Bordeaux is not on gravel – it's on the various heavy clays laid down over the millennia by the Dordogne and Garonne rivers. Most of the vineyards do not have special aspects towards the sun, special protected mesoclimates hiding them from wind and rain. Most of Bordeaux, in truth, is pleasant but ordinary, it's wine unexceptional, often dull, often lacking ripeness and definition. Indeed, although Bordeaux is thought of above all as a red wine Nirvana, red grapes ripen with difficulty in the lesser vineyards which would in any case be more suited to produc-ing rosé or white. But the world wants to drink red Bordeaux. History tells 'twas ever thus.

Although the vineyards were initially established by the Romans in St-Émilion, it was the period between 1152 and 1453, when Bordeaux belonged to the English, that laid the foundation for today. Benefiting from direct access to the sea, its wines – almost all red – were enthusiastically drunk all over northern Europe, and consequently a taste for red Bordeaux – or claret as the English called it – was taken with their traders to all the other continents, in particular North America.

As a result, Bordeaux became immensely wealthy and the vineyards became dominated by large estates – called châteaux – and a powerful merchant trading elite. This system still holds today, though the prices that top Bordeaux properties can demand are now so high that many properties are now owned by commercial conglomerates rather than by the families who built their reputations. And, alongside these ritzy superstars, are the rest of the 13,000 growers who struggle to grow the remainder of the 850 million bottles produced annually.

Ch. Pichon-Longueville-Comtesse de Lalande is Bordeaux's leading 'Super-Second' wine. With vineyards on excellent land, the estate has been run since 1978 by the inspirational figure of Madame de Lencquesaing.

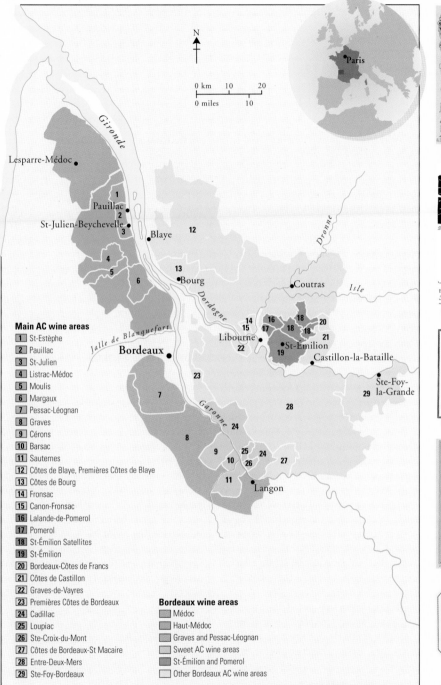

N

0 km 10 20
0 miles 10

Paris

Gironde

Lesparre-Médoc

1 Pauillac

2 St-Julien-Beychevelle

3 Blaye

12

4

5

6 13 Bourg

Coutras

Dordogne

Isle

Dronne

14 16 18
15 17 18 18 20
Libourne 21
22 St-Émilion 19
Castillon-la-Bataille

Ste-Foy-
29 la-Grande

Jalle de Blanquefort

Bordeaux

23

7

28

Garonne

24

8

9 25 24
10 26 27

11

Langon

Main AC wine areas
1 St-Estèphe
2 Pauillac
3 St-Julien
4 Listrac-Médoc
5 Moulis
6 Margaux
7 Pessac-Léognan
8 Graves
9 Cérons
10 Barsac
11 Sauternes
12 Côtes de Blaye, Premières Côtes de Blaye
13 Côtes de Bourg
14 Fronsac
15 Canon-Fronsac
16 Lalande-de-Pomerol
17 Pomerol
18 St-Émilion Satellites
19 St-Émilion
20 Bordeaux-Côtes de Francs
21 Côtes de Castillon
22 Graves-de-Vayres
23 Premières Côtes de Bordeaux
24 Cadillac
25 Loupiac
26 Ste-Croix-du-Mont
27 Côtes de Bordeaux-St Macaire
28 Entre-Deux-Mers
29 Ste-Foy-Bordeaux

Bordeaux wine areas
■ Médoc
■ Haut-Médoc
□ Graves and Pessac-Léognan
□ Sweet AC wine areas
■ St-Émilion and Pomerol
□ Other Bordeaux AC wine areas

CH. PÉTRUS
This rich, exotic, succulent wine, from almost 100 per cent Merlot, is one of the world's most expensive red wines, and often one of the greatest too, as a result of the caring genius of the Moueix family, Pétrus' owners.

CH. MOUTON-ROTHSCHILD
The most magnificently rich and indulgent of the great Bordeaux reds when young, the wine takes 15 to 20 years to open up fully to its brilliant blackcurrant and cigar box best.

CH. REYNON
This stylish white wine, from a blend of Sémillon and Sauvignon Blanc, is made by the brilliant enology professor, Denis Dubourdieu.

CH. CITRAN
This large Cru Bourgeois estate produces a wine that is usually big, plump and richly extracted with a very ripe blackcurrant and new oak bouquet.

CH. ROQUEFORT
Straight red Bordeaux wine such as this one should have a bone-dry grassy fruit and an attractive earthy edge.

CH. MARGAUX
This is the most consistently excellent and fragrantly perfumed of the great Médoc wines.

CH. D'YQUEM
At its best this sublime wine is undoubtedly one of the greatest sweet wines in the world.

AC ENTRIES
Barsac, Bordeaux, Bordeaux Clairet, Bordeaux-Côtes de Francs, Bordeaux Supérieur, Cadillac, Canon-Fronsac, Cérons, Côtes de Blaye, Côtes de Bourg, Côtes de Castillon, Entre-Deux-Mers, Fronsac, Graves, Haut-Médoc, Lalande-de-Pomerol, Listrac-Médoc, Loupiac, Margaux, Médoc, Moulis, Pauillac, Pessac-Léognan, Pomerol, Premières Côtes de Blaye, Premières Côtes de Bordeaux, St-Émilion, St-Émilion Grand Cru, St-Émilion Grand Cru Classé, St-Émilion Premier Grand Cru Classé, St-Émilion Satellites, St-Estèphe, St-Julien, Ste-Croix-du-Mont, Sauternes.

SEE ALSO
Graves & Pessac-Léognan, pages 190–191, Médoc, pages 242–243, St-Émilion & Pomerol, pages 326–327, and Sauternes, pages 336–337.

BORDEAUX AC

FRANCE, Bordeaux (see also pages 90–91)

🍷🍷 *Cabernet Sauvignon, Merlot, Cabernet Franc, Petit Verdot, Malbec*

♀ *Sémillon, Sauvignon Blanc, Muscadelle and others*

The simple Bordeaux AC is one of the most important ACs in France and, at the same time, one of the most abused. Its importance lies in the fact that it can apply to the red as well as to the dry, medium and sweet white wines of the entire Gironde *département*, the largest fine wine area in the world. Most of the best wines are allowed more specific geographical ACs, such as PAUILLAC, SAUTERNES or MARGAUX, yet a vast amount of unambitious but potentially enjoyable wine is sold as Bordeaux AC. Indeed, straight red Bordeaux – frequently known as 'claret' in Britain – is one of the most recognizable of all 'generic' wines. It often has a fresh, grassy fruit and an appetizing, earthy edge. But standards vary: much Bordeaux Rouge is pretty tannic and raw – and often overpriced.

The quality of Bordeaux Blanc, which had become a byword for flabby, fruitless, over-sulphured brews, is now remarkably good, and there are numerous pleasant, clean wines, frequently sold under a merchant's rather than a château label, which make refreshing drinking. the combination of cool fermentation in stainless steel tanks to preserve the fruit aromas of the grapes with better viticulture is the key to improved quality. Whites with less than 4 grams of sugar per litre are labelled as Bordeaux Sec or Vin Sec de Bordeaux. Many of these are 100 per cent Sauvignon Blanc wines in which case the grape name may be used on the label.

The Bordeaux AC also applies to wines made in superior appellations, but in the wrong style. White wine made in the red wine MÉDOC ACs can only be labelled as AC Bordeaux, as are red, rosé or dry white wines made in the sweet wine ACs of Sauternes and BARSAC (or BORDEAUX SUPÉRIEUR for reds). With rare exceptions (like Ygrec from Ch. d'YQUEM, and Pavillon Blanc from Ch. MARGAUX), all AC Bordeaux Blanc wines should be drunk as young as possible; good Bordeaux Rouge may cope with a year or so of aging. Best producers: (reds) Bonnet, Dourthe (Numéro 1), Ducla, Sirius, Thieuley, Tour de Mirambeau, le Trébuchet; (whites) l'Abbaye de Ste-Ferme, Carsin, DOISY-DAËNE, Dourthe (Numéro 1), d:vin, LYNCH-BAGES, Ch. Margaux (Pavillon Blanc), Premius, Reynon, Roquefort, de Sours, Thieuley, Tour de Mirambeau.

BORDEAUX CLAIRET AC

FRANCE, Bordeaux

🍷 *Cabernet Sauvignon, Merlot, Cabernet Franc, Petit Verdot, Malbec*

Bordeaux Clairet is a pale red wine, almost rosé in fact, which can be an excellent way to use red grapes that aren't quite ripe. The name 'claret', which is applied to any red wine from BORDEAUX, derives from *clairet* and a few hundred years ago all Bordeaux reds were made in a light, early-drinking style. As wine-making improved, the reds became darker and stronger, and Bordeaux Clairet almost faded away. Interestingly, a few ritzy Classed Growth properties in the MÉDOC still make a little to have with their lunch.

BORDEAUX–CÔTES DE FRANCS AC

FRANCE, Bordeaux

🍷 *Merlot, Cabernet Sauvignon, Cabernet Franc, Malbec*

♀ *Sémillon, Sauvignon Blanc, Muscadelle*

This tiny area east of ST-ÉMILION, with good clay and limestone soil, has the warmest and driest mesoclimate in BORDEAUX. Its potential is immense – at the best properties, closely controlled yields plus the use of new oak barrels give the wines a remarkable concentration of fruit, deep plum and blackberry flavours, strengthened by tannin and oak spice.

The Thienpont family, owners of Ch. Puygueraud, have long been the driving force in the AC. However, with the Côtes de Francs vineyards now maturing I feel we should be seeing more exceptional wines than the handful each vintage offers. Best years: 2001, '00, '98, '97, '96, '95, '94, '90. Best producers: (reds) les Charmes-Godard, de Francs, Laclaverie, Marsau, Moulin la Pitié, Pelan, la Prade, Puygueraud.

Less than four per cent of the three million or so bottles produced a year is white. Most of it is dry, though sweet wine is made under the Côtes de Francs Liquoreux AC.

CH. PUYGUERAUD

The flagship estate for the tiny Côtes de Francs AC makes tannic, robust and complex wines with good potential for aging.

BORDEAUX SUPÉRIEUR AC

FRANCE, Bordeaux

🍷🍷 *Cabernet Sauvignon, Cabernet Franc, Merlot, Petit Verdot, Malbec*

This appellation covers the whole of the Bordeaux region, as does the BORDEAUX AC. The difference is that Supérieur must have an extra half a degree of alcohol for red and rosé, a lower yield from the vines, and is not allowed on the market until the September following the vintage, ensuring a longer period of maturation. This makes a considerable difference to the quality, the wines generally being more concentrated and structured, sometimes with an added note of vanilla from aging in new oak barrels. Almost all the *petits châteaux* which represent affordable drinking in Bordeaux will be labelled Bordeaux Supérieur. Best producers: l'Abbaye de Ste-Ferme, Barreyre, de Bouillerot, de Courteillac, Laville, de Parenchère, Penin, le Pin Beausoleil, Reignac, de Seguin. Best years: 2002, '01, '00, '98.

BORGO DEL TIGLIO

ITALY, Friuli-Venezia Giulia, Collio DOC

🍷 *Merlot, Cabernet Sauvignon*

♀ *Tocai Friulano, Chardonnay, Malvasia Istriana, Sauvignon Blanc, Riesling Renano*

Nicola Manferrari comes from a long line of viticulturalists. On his 9ha (22 acres) or so spread over three vineyards he makes reds and whites varietally or blended (the blends changing constantly). Although most of his grapes are white, from which he produces some impressive barrel-fermented wines, like the extraordinary blend Studio di Bianco, he is perhaps most respected for his Rosso della Centa. This is a barrique-aged varietal Merlot and shows the potential of this grape in the COLLIO region. Best years: (Rosso della Centa) 2000, '99, '97, '96, '94, '93, '90.

LUIGI BOSCA

ARGENTINA, Mendoza

🍷 *Malbec, Cabernet Sauvignon, Syrah, Tempranillo, Merlot, Pinot Noir and others*

♀ *Chardonnay, Sauvignon Blanc, Viognier and others*

The Arizús founded what is now MENDOZA's oldest family wine company in 1901 – and you may see the family name on some top bottlings of wines like Petit Verdot. They have long been major vineyard owners in traditional red wine strongholds like Maipú and Luján de Cuyo, where they currently own 650ha (1600 acres). Their wines are always dense and rich, sometimes too much so, but – particularly from the El Paríso and

Carrodilla vineyards – wines made from Malbec, Cabernet Sauvignon, Syrah and Petit Verdot make a powerful statement. Finca Los Nobles Malbec-Verdot is one of the finest Malbec-based wines in Argentina. Among the whites, powerful, mineral Finca Los Nobles Chardonnay comes from very old vines at 1300m (4265ft) above sea level. Best years: (Finca Los Nobles Malbec-Verdot) 2002, '00, '97, '96, '95.

PODERI BOSCARELLI

ITALY, Tuscany, Vino Nobile di Montepulciano DOCG
♟ *Sangiovese, Cabernet Sauvignon, Merlot and others*

This estate is without question one of the zone's top producers, with 13ha (32 acres) of vineyards on the south-facing hill of Cervognano which some consider the best sub-zone for VINO NOBILE DI MONTEPULCIANO. Here Paola De Ferrari and her sons Luca and Niccolò, with guidance from the star enologist Maurizio Castelli, craft rich and stylish reds.

The vineyards, principally Sangiovese, with small amounts of Cabernet Sauvignon, Merlot and Syrah among red varieties, are being gradually replanted to superior clones at higher densities and the *cantina* re-equipped to facilitate optimum extraction from the carefully cultivated fruit. The Sangiovese-based wines are all marked by concentration of flavour and charm of aroma allied to a great finesse. Vino Nobile, Riserva del Nocio and the barrique-aged Sangiovese Boscarelli are all delicious. Best years: 2001, '00, '99, '97, '95, '93, '90, '88, '85.

BOUCHARD FINLAYSON

SOUTH AFRICA, Western Cape, Overberg WO, Walker Bay
♟ *Pinot Noir, Sangiovese, Nebbiolo and others*
♀ *Chardonnay, Sauvignon Blanc and others*

Peter Finlayson's fascination with the red Burgundy grape Pinot Noir began when he was winemaker at HAMILTON RUSSELL. So it made sense when he established vineyards next door

BOUCHARD FINLAYSON
The powerful, firm Galpin Peak Pinot Noir from cool-climate Walker Bay has elevated Cape Pinot wines to a new level of excitement.

in 1989 in partnership with leading Burgundian Paul Bouchard, unrelated to the BOUCHARD PÈRE family – who brought not only investment but also considerable Burgundian know-how – and began to realize the true quality achievable in the southern reaches of the Hemel-en-Aarde valley.

Burgundian clones and viticultural methods provide wines with a good concentration of colour, fruit and tannin. Galpin Peak, as the home-grown Pinot is called, makes a forceful argument for this cool southern tip of Africa being ideal for Pinot Noir (though the rest of the country is usually too warm for this fussy variety). Chardonnay is drawn from home vineyards and some even cooler spots. Barrel-fermented or unoaked, these wines are well-layered and balanced.

Finlayson is an inveterate experimentalist – a new Sangiovese-Pinot Noir blend reflects his love of Italian varieties, the Chardonnays (Kaimansgat and home-grown Missionvale) are full, nutty and passably Burgundian and the Sauvignon Blanc is zippy and fresh. Best years: (Pinot Noir) 2002, '01, '00, '99, '98, '97, '96, '95.

BOUCHARD PÈRE ET FILS

FRANCE, Burgundy, Beaune
♟ *Pinot Noir*
♀ *Chardonnay, Aligoté*

Important merchant and vineyard owner with vines in some of Burgundy's most spectacular sites, including 12ha (30 acres) of Grands Crus (CORTON, CORTON-CHARLEMAGNE, Chevalier-Montrachet and le MONTRACHET) and 74ha (183 acres) of Premiers Crus. The company is based in old buildings close to Beaune's town walls, and the vast Bouchard cellars are dug beneath the medieval bastions. The firm used to pride itself on being able to supply older vintages of its numerous wines.

However, by the 1970s quality had become regularly disappointing. With trembling hand, one raised a glass of MONTRACHET or Chevalier-Montrachet and, tasting it, realized it was neither worth its reputation, nor its price. In 1995 the last of the Bouchards, Jean-François, sold the company to Joseph Henriot, hitherto known as a CHAMPAGNE producer. Henriot lost no time in improving the Bouchard image. He began by throwing out or declassifying many thousands of bottles, including quite a few from the most prestigious appellations that he felt, rightly, were unworthy of the name. There is no doubt that quality improved overnight – it

BOUCHARD PÈRE ET FILS
One of the outstanding wines from this important merchant and vineyard owner is the deep, plummy red Corton which needs eight to ten years of aging.

would have been difficult for it not to – but progress has been slower than I had hoped.

As with many Burgundy producers, the basic generic wines remain poor, but the domaine wines from fabulous vineyards are just not reaching the level of those against which Henriot wishes them to be judged. They are good, but also rather lean and reserved, as though they were frightened of truly expressing themselves. Until they do, we'll never know quite how good Bouchard could be. They have also acquired the William Fèvre vineyards in CHABLIS and quality there is very good. Best years: (top reds) 2002, '01, '00, '99, '98, '97, '96.

HENRI BOURGEOIS

FRANCE, Central Loire, Sancerre AC
♟ *Pinot Noir*
♀ *Sauvignon Blanc*

This well-run grower and *négociant* business in the little village of Chavignol in the heart of SANCERRE is both one of the largest concerns and one of the top producers in this part of the LOIRE Valley. Commitment and quality are hallmarks of the Bourgeois operation, despite its size. The company is now run by Jean-Marie Bourgeois in tandem with his son, Arnaud, and Jean-Christophe, a cousin and the winemaker.

The wide list of wines, ranging from Sauvignon Vin de Pays du JARDIN DE LA FRANCE to the top non-wooded cuvée, la Bourgeoise, are always well made. Étienne Henri is vinified in oak and le MD comes from vineyards on the steep Côte des Monts Damnés overlooking Chavignol. Most of these slopes were abandoned after phylloxera and the Bourgeois were instrumental in their replanting over the past 20 years. La Demoiselle de Bourgeois is the name of their POUILLY-FUMÉ wine. Clos Henri is a new project in New Zealand, with 90ha (222 acres) in the Wairau Valley in MARLBOROUGH. Best years: (Sancerre) 2001, '00, '99, '98, '97, '96.

BOURGOGNE (Burgundy) France

THE NAME BURGUNDY (Bourgogne in French) always seems to be more suitable for red wine than white. It sort of booms: it's a rich, weighty sound, purple rather than pale, haunches of venison and flagons of plum-ripe red rather than a half-dozen oysters and Chablis.

Yet white Burgundy is nowadays at least as important as red Burgundy, possibly more so. The term Burgundy applies to a large swathe of eastern France which at one time was a Grand Duchy reaching right up to the North Sea, way down to beyond Lyon and across to the mountains guarding Switzerland and Italy. What is now left of this grandeur is some inspiring architecture – and a tradition of eating and drinking which still makes gourmets describe it greedily as the 'belly' of France. Modern Burgundy starts at Chablis in the north, stretching down through the Côte d'Or south of Dijon, the Côte Chalonnaise and on to the Mâconnais and Beaujolais. In all of these areas, except Beaujolais, white wine is of crucial importance and in two – Chablis and the Mâconnais – red wine is almost an irrelevance.

The two most important grapes are the white Chardonnay and the red Pinot Noir. Chardonnay is the grape of Chablis, of the great white wine villages of the Côte d'Or, and of the Côte Chalonnaise and the Mâconnais to the south. In each region it makes marvellously individual wines that have been copied the world over. Pinot Noir is most important in the great red wine villages of the Côte d'Or, and also in the Côte Chalonnaise. Aligoté plays a significant though second-fiddle role in the Côte Chalonnaise and Gamay excels in the Beaujolais.

Between Dijon and Chagny lies the thin sliver of land called the Côte d'Or – the Golden Slope. The northern section, the Côte de Nuits, is almost entirely red wine country with villages such as Gevrey-Chambertin, Morey-St-Denis Chambolle-Musigny, Vougeot and Vosne-Romanée producing compellingly powerful wines. The Côte de Beaune, as well as red, produces fabulously rich white wines from the villages of Aloxe-Corton, Meursault, Puligny-Montrachet and Chassagne-Montrachet.

Côte Chalonnaise whites used to be mostly made into sparkling wine, but Rully, Mercurey and Montagny are now showing they can produce lovely whites and reds without the help of bubbles. Mâconnais wines are mostly simple and refreshing, but in Pouilly-Fuissé and St-Véran a few producers are creating excellent whites. Beaujolais, a large area that tumbles up and down the granite hills between the Mâconnais and Lyon is regarded as part of Burgundy, but the style of wine is completely different, being a bright breezy gluggable red made from Gamay.

Harvesting Pinot Noir at Auxey-Duresses in the Côte de Beaune. For quality wines in Burgundy hand-picking is still the normal method used, especially for Pinot Noir grapes which are very difficult to detach from their stalks.

The various top Burgundy villages along the Côte d'Or have a great deal in common: the subsoil is limestone and most of the vineyards face east or south-east. Yet what makes great Burgundy such a fascinating wine is the subtle nuances that distinguish one fine wine from another. In the Côte de Beaune, Volnay and Pommard are neighbouring villages but the wines are totally different, Volnay being delicate and elegant, while Pommard is richer and more rustic. These nuances are conserved in the cru system which ranks all Burgundy's vineyards into a hierarchy based on the potential quality of the vineyard. A Grand Cru wine should be the finest (and most costly), followed by Premier Cru and Village wines. At the bottom of the scale are simple Bourgogne wines, which are usually from vines planted outside the boundaries of the best-known villages. Grands Crus are only found on the Côte d'Or and in Chablis. In practice, however, the track record of individual producers counts for as much, if not more, than the status of the vineyard.

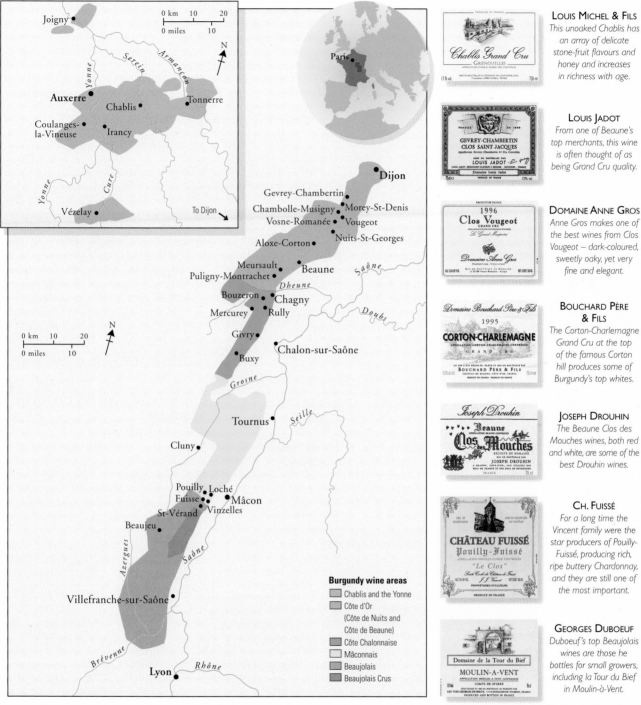

LOUIS MICHEL & FILS
This unoaked Chablis has an array of delicate stone-fruit flavours and honey and increases in richness with age.

LOUIS JADOT
From one of Beaune's top merchants, this wine is often thought of as being Grand Cru quality.

DOMAINE ANNE GROS
Anne Gros makes one of the best wines from Clos Vougeot – dark-coloured, sweetly oaky, yet very fine and elegant.

BOUCHARD PÈRE & FILS
The Corton-Charlemagne Grand Cru at the top of the famous Corton hill produces some of Burgundy's top whites.

JOSEPH DROUHIN
The Beaune Clos des Mouches wines, both red and white, are some of the best Drouhin wines.

CH. FUISSÉ
For a long time the Vincent family were the star producers of Pouilly-Fuissé, producing rich, ripe buttery Chardonnay, and they are still one of the most important.

GEORGES DUBOEUF
Duboeuf's top Beaujolais wines are those he bottles for small growers, including la Tour du Bief in Moulin-à-Vent.

REGIONAL ENTRIES

Aloxe-Corton, Auxey-Duresses, Bâtard-Montrachet, Beaujolais, Beaujolais Nouveau, Beaujolais-Villages, Beaune, Blagny, Bonnes-Mares, Bourgogne, Bourgogne-Côte Chalonnaise, Bourgogne Grand Ordinaire, Bourgogne-Hautes Côtes de Beaune, Bourgogne-Hautes Côtes de Nuits, Bourgogne Passe-Tout-Grains, Bouzeron, Brouilly, Chablis, Chablis Grand Cru, Chablis Premier Cru, Chambertin, Chambolle-Musigny, Chassagne-Montrachet, Chénas, Chiroubles, Chorey-lès-Beaune, Clos de la Roche, Clos de Vougeot, Corton, Corton-Charlemagne, Côte de Beaune, Côte de Beaune-Villages, Côte de Brouilly, Côte de Nuits-Villages, Crémant de Bourgogne, Échézeaux, Fixin, Fleurie, Gevrey-Chambertin, Givry, Irancy, Juliénas, Ladoix, Mâcon, Maranges, Marsannay, Mercurey, Meursault, Montagny, Monthelie, le Montrachet, Morey-St-Denis, Morgon, Moulin-à-Vent, Musigny, Nuits-St-Georges, Pernand-Vergelesses, Pommard, Pouilly-Fuissé, Pouilly-Loché, Puligny-Montrachet, Régnié, Richebourg, la Romanée, Rully, St-Amour, St-Aubin, St-Romain, St-Véran, Santenay, Savigny-lès-Beaune, la Tâche, Volnay, Vosne-Romanée, Vougeot.

SEE ALSO

Chablis, pages 120–121, and Côte d'Or, pages 146–147.

BOURGOGNE AC

FRANCE, Burgundy (see also pages 94–95)
🍷 🍷 *Pinot Noir, Gamay, plus César and Tressot in the Yonne*
🍷 *Chardonnay*

BOURGOGNE is the French name we have anglicized as 'Burgundy'. As a generic appellation, from CHABLIS in the north way down to BEAUJOLAIS some 290km (180 miles) to the south, it mops up all the wine with no specific appellation of its own, resulting in massive differences in style and quality.

Pinot Noir is used for most Bourgogne Rouge, except in the Yonne where the local varieties César and Tressot are used, and Gamay in the Mâconnais and Beaujolais. As for quality, well, some of the less reputable merchants buy wine from any source so long as the price is low. On the other hand, some unlucky but dedicated growers possess land only entitled to the simple Bourgogne AC yet lavish on it the same devotion as on a Grand Cru.

Red Bourgogne is usually light, overtly fruity in a breezy, upfront, strawberry and cherry way, but if the perfume is there, no-one minds if the flavour is a bit simple. It should be drunk young – two to three years' aging is quite enough – and it shouldn't be fussed over too much; just enjoy it. The better merchants' blends usually come into this category. Sometimes, however, it can be much more than this, the cherry and strawberry fruit deeper, thickened into a plummy richness, and perhaps with the creamy softness of some oak-barrel aging added in. Made from Pinot Noir, Bourgogne Rosé can be a pleasant pink wine but very little is produced.

Bourgogne Blanc may be either an elegant, classy, dry white of marvellous, nutty character or an overpriced washout, depending on how the appellation has been interpreted by the producer. Usually it will be a bone-dry wine from vineyards not considered quite good enough for a classier appellation, but vaguely in the same style. So a Bourgogne Blanc from the Yonne region will usually be light, slightly tart and refreshing, one from the CÔTE D'OR might have some of the nutty fullness of nearby MEURSAULT, while one from the Mâconnais will probably be fatter and rather appley.

If the wine is from a grower the flavours will follow regional style. However, if the address on the label is of a Côte d'Or merchant, the wine could be from anywhere in Burgundy. The best wines usually come from a single grower who has declassified some of the wine from his top label, either because it lacked the necessary concentration, or because the vines are outside the appellation boundaries. In today's world of high prices such wines may be the only way most of us can afford the joys of fine Burgundy. Best years: (reds and whites) 2002, '01, '00, '99. Best producers: (reds, growers) COCHE-DURY, Dugat-Py, J-P Fichet, Germain, LAFARGE, MÉO-CAMUZET, Pierre Morey, Patrice Rion, ROUMIER; (reds, merchants) DROUHIN, GIRARDIN, JADOT, LABOURÉ-ROI, Maison LEROY, N Potel; (reds, co-operatives) BUXY, les Caves des Hautes-Côtes. Most Bourgogne Blanc should be drunk within two years, but those matured in oak can age well. Best producers: (whites, growers) M Bouzereau, Boyer-Martenot, Coche-Dury, Henri GOUGES, P Javillier, Ch. de Meursault, Guy Roulot, SAUZET, TOLLOT-BEAUT; (whites, merchants) Drouhin, FAIVELEY, Jadot, Olivier LEFLAIVE, Rodet; (whites, co-operatives) Buxy, les Caves des Hautes-Côtes.

A ET P DE VILLAINE
The Bourgogne-Côte Chalonnaise AC is rapidly gaining a good reputation and there are some excellent producers making both red and white wines.

BOURGOGNE-CÔTE CHALONNAISE AC

FRANCE, Burgundy, Côte Chalonnaise
🍷 *Pinot Noir*
🍷 *Chardonnay*

Compared to its northerly neighbour, the CÔTE DE BEAUNE, the Côte Chalonnaise is a more traditionally rural world where the vine is merely one part of the texture of rustic life. As a result, it is the least known of all the Burgundy regions. The area was given its own generic appellation in 1990, and now accounts for 428ha (1058 acres) of vines in the Saône-et-Loire *département* around the villages of BOUZERON, RULLY, MERCUREY, GIVRY and MONTAGNY, which all also have their own ACs. The Côte Chalonnaise vineyards could almost be thought of as an extension of the CÔTE D'OR, since they are directly to the south, but they are far less cohesive. Despite the lack of renown, the area has gained enormously in importance in the last few years, particularly as a result of the spiralling price of white Burgundy. Best years: 2002, '01, '99. Best producers: X Besson, BUXY co-operative, Michel Goubard, Juillot, Venot, de Villaine.

BOURGOGNE GRAND ORDINAIRE AC

FRANCE, Burgundy
🍷 🍷 *Gamay, Pinot Noir, plus César and Tressot in the Yonne*
🍷 *Chardonnay, Aligoté, plus Melon de Bourgogne and Sacy in the Yonne*

This is the only AC to admit in its name that the wine may actually be pretty duff stuff but you hardly ever see it. Chardonnay (though anyone who uses this for 'BGO' – as the locals call it – must be nuts), Aligoté, Melon de Bourgogne (the MUSCADET grape which was supposedly banished from Burgundy generations ago for being too boring) and Sacy can be used for whites, and Gamay, Pinot Noir, César and Tressot for the reds. It's mostly sold as quaffing wine for the local bars – for which it can be perfectly suitable, especially if you add a splash of cassis.

BOURGOGNE-HAUTES CÔTES DE BEAUNE AC

FRANCE, Burgundy, Côte d'Or
🍷 *Pinot Noir*
🍷 *Chardonnay*

These wines come from 640ha (1581 acres) of vineyards in the hills behind the great Côte de Beaune slopes. If scenery could influence the end result, this lost little region of twisting country lanes, ancient trees and purest sylvan peace would surely produce ecstatic wines. However, here, the aspect of the sun is rarely ideal and the altitude, at 350–400m (1150–1300ft), is also a handicap; all the best vineyard sites on the Côte de Beaune itself are below 300m (1000ft). So don't expect wines with very ripe flavours. If the price of decent red Burgundy had not been pushed through the roof during the 1970s – forcing merchants to replant derelict vineyards – we probably would never have heard too much of this AC at all. Now, the area is reasonably prosperous and the wines are fairly good. Only in exceptional years will they attain the quality of Côte de Beaune, but in their light, raspberry-fresh way, they often give a purer view of what Pinot Noir should taste like than many supposedly classier offerings.

There's some white wine too, and the 29 villages entitled to the AC can produce pleasant, slightly sharp Chardonnay and, under the Bourgogne-Aligoté AC, some good, ultra-dry Aligoté. In really hot years the Chardonnay can even take on a dry, but discernibly nutty, taste after a couple of years in bottle, which ever so slightly reminds you of a wispy CHASSAGNE-MONTRACHET. Best years: 2002, '01, '00, '99. Best producers: D & F Clair, J-Y Devevey, les Caves des Hautes-Côtes, L Jacob, Joillot, Ch. de Mercey (RODET), Naudin-Ferrand, M Serveau.

BOURGOGNE-HAUTES CÔTES DE NUITS AC

FRANCE, Burgundy, Côte d'Or

♠ *Pinot Noir*

♀ *Chardonnay*

The relatively compact Hautes Côtes de Nuits vineyards belong to 19 villages directly behind the Côte de Nuits, and there are 570ha (1408 acres) planted, mostly with red grapes. Inevitably, altitude, averaging 400m (1300ft), is a problem and frequently the land over this height is just scrub. So ripening of the grapes is by no means guaranteed. The granting of AC to the Hautes Côtes de Nuits and Hautes Côtes de Beaune in 1961 acted as a spur, and several growers, in particular Hudelot and Thévenot, planted large estates. They were followed by the merchant houses, and the establishment of the Caves des Hautes-Côtes co-operative in 1968 gave cohesion to the area.

The wines are never weighty and are, if anything, a little leaner to start with than the Hautes Côtes de Beaune, but they do have an attractive cherry and plum flavour, sometimes with a pleasing bitter finish. Best years: (reds) 2002, '01, '00, '99. Best producers: FAIVELEY, A-F Gros, Michel Gros, A Guyon, les Caves des Hautes-Côtes, B Hudelot, JAYER-GILLES, THOMAS-MOILLARD. The whites from Chardonnay and Aligoté (under the Bourgogne-Aligoté AC) tend to be dry and flinty. In general drink young, although they will age. Best years: (whites) 2002, '01, '00, '99. Best producers: Y Chaley, Champy, J-Y Devevey, les Caves des Hautes-Côtes, B Hudelot, JAYER-GILLES, Thévenot-le-Brun, Thomas-Moillard.

BOURGOGNE PASSE-TOUT-GRAINS AC

FRANCE, Burgundy

♠ ♀ *Gamay, Pinot Noir*

Almost always red this appellation is for a mixture of Gamay with a minimum of one-third Pinot Noir in the blend. In recent years in the Côte Chalonnaise and CÔTE D'OR, as

vineyards are replanted, the percentage of Pinot Noir has increased, yielding wines of better quality. These wines should now show a good, sturdy, cherry fruit when very young, offset by a raspingly attractive, herby acidity from the Gamay, but softening over three to four years to a gentle, round-edged wine. Best years: 2002, '01, '00, '99, '98. Best producers: (growers) Bersan, Chaley, C Cornu, Rion; (merchants) Chanson, Dom. LEROY.

BOURGUEIL AC

FRANCE, Loire, Touraine

♠ ♀ *Cabernet Franc, Cabernet Sauvignon*

Bourgueil is a village just north of the river Loire between Angers and Tours. The area is unusually dry for the LOIRE Valley, favouring the ripening of red grape varieties, which explains why, in a region known for its white wines, Bourgueil is famous for red. Cabernet Franc is the main grape, topped up with a little Cabernet Sauvignon, and in hot years the results can be superb.

Although the wines can be rather peppery and vegetal at first, if you give them time – at least five years and preferably ten – they develop a wonderful fragrance which is like essences of blackcurrant and raspberry combined, with just enough earthiness to keep their feet firmly on the ground. Best years: 2002, '01, '00, '97, '96, '95, '90, '89. Best producers: (reds) Clos de l'Abbaye, Yannick Amirault, Audebert (estate wines), T Boucard, P Breton, la Butte, Caslot-Galbrun, la Chevalerie, Max Cognard, Druet, Forges, Lamé-Delille-Boucard, La Lande/Delaunay, Nau Frères, Ouches, des Raguenières.

CASLOT-GALBRUN

The Bourgueil AC makes some of the Loire Valley's best red wines and in hot years the best examples, such as this one, have a good depth of blackcurrant fruit.

BOUZERON AC

FRANCE, Burgundy, Côte Chalonnaise

♀ *Aligoté*

At one time you might have accused Bouzeron of being the most obscure wine village in the itself pretty obscure region of the CÔTE CHALONNAISE, just to the south of Burgundy's big guns in the Côte de Beaune. And you'd have been right. Not only had no

one heard of it, but it grew the barely accepted, acid-hearted Aligoté grape in a region devoted to Chardonnay. However Bouzeron had a champion – local resident Aubert de Villaine who also co-owned Burgundy's most ritzy red wine estate, the Domaine de la ROMANÉE-CONTI. He proved that you can make delightful crisp, refreshing whites out of Aligoté and his efforts were rewarded in 1998 with Bouzeron's award of its own appellation for Aligoté. There are still only 61ha (150 acres) of vineyards, tucked in behind the whimsically named Montagne de la Folie, but they're worth their appellation.

BOUZY

FRANCE, Champagne, Coteaux Champenois AC

♠ *Pinot Noir*

This leading CHAMPAGNE village on the Montagne de Reims grows the region's best Pinot Noir, which is usually made into Champagne. However, in outstanding years, a little still red wine is made. It is light, high in acid and often with a cutting, herby edge. But now and then, there is a waif-like perfume of raspberry and strawberry. Don't age it on purpose, although it can keep for several years. Best producers: Bara, Clouet, Georges Vesselle, Jean Vesselle.

BOWEN ESTATE

AUSTRALIA, South Australia, Coonawarra

♠ *Cabernet Sauvignon, Syrah (Shiraz), Merlot*

♀ *Chardonnay*

Doug Bowen is one of the most highly regarded red winemakers among the small COONAWARRA wineries. As part of his winemaking studies he prepared a report on Coonawarra's potential way back in the early 1970s, before the area was fashionable, and immediately put his money where his mouth was by setting up a vineyard and winery in 1972. His 35-ha (86-acre) estate is largely given over to a wonderfully peppery, spicy Shiraz and an elegant, discreetly herbaceous Cabernet Sauvignon. There is also a BORDEAUX-style blend. Best years: (Shiraz) 2000, '98, '97, '96, '94, '93, '92, '91.

BOYAR ESTATES

BULGARIA

♠ *Cabernet Sauvignon, Merlot, Mavrud, Gamza and others*

♠ *Cabernet Sauvignon*

♀ *Chardonnay, Dimiat, Muscat Ottonel, Ugni Blanc and others*

Established as Domaine Boyar in 1991, this company has gone on to become the leading distributor of Bulgarian wines, selling more than 65 million bottles worldwide each year. Boyar only started producing wines in 1996 and now has wineries at Iambol, Shumen, Sliven (new, state-of-the-art Blueridge) and – following its merger with Vinprom in 2000 – at Rousse. With the merger Boyar also gained control of 1000ha (2470 acres) of vineyards and its long-term strategy is to have as much control as possible in the vineyards. So far Boyar has stressed its internationalist intentions, with a range of quite attractive young reds led by Cabernet Sauvignon and Merlot, and some decent clean young whites. If Bulgaria is ever to concentrate on regional styles, Boyar is ideally placed to lead the way, but there's little sign of this so far.

BRACHETTO D'ACQUI DOCG
ITALY, Piedmont

♟ *Brachetto*

It's not always the most revered wine that gives the most delight. Brachetto d'Acqui is a case in point. From central PIEDMONT, it is a light red, with a bit of fizz, its aromas being reminiscent of Muscat with a suggestion of strawberries. The taste is light, delicate and sweet although the odd dry version exists. Drink young. Best producers: Araldica, Castello BANFI, Braida, G Marenco.

CH. BRANAIRE
FRANCE, Bordeaux, Haut-Médoc, St-Julien AC, 4ème Cru Classé

♟ *Cabernet Sauvignon, Cabernet Franc, Merlot, Petit Verdot*

Ch. Brainaire boasts 50ha (123 acres) of mature vines in several parcels dotted around ST-JULIEN, some of them up to 100 years old. After a long period of mediocrity it chose the difficult 1993 and '94 vintages to signal its renewed ambition. This was long overdue because Branaire gave me a lot of affordable pleasure from its vintages in the 1960s and '70s. Subsequent vintages have confirmed a welcome return to full, soft, chocolaty form. Second wine: Ch. Duluc. Best years: 2001, '00, '99, '98, '96, '95, '94.

BRAND'S
AUSTRALIA, South Australia, Coonawarra

♟ *Cabernet Sauvignon, Syrah (Shiraz), Merlot*

♀ *Chardonnay, Riesling*

Brand's was a famous COONAWARRA name fallen upon hard times until taken over by industry giant MCWILLIAM'S. For once the Goliath has greatly improved the David's performance, and chief winemaker Jim Brayne's influence has lifted standards dramatically. The accent is still on red wines, aided by excellent vineyards which include a precious patch of Shiraz planted in 1896, which provides the super-premium Stentiford Shiraz and shows how good Coonawarra Shiraz can be. All the reds are full flavoured and supremely honest with abundant fruit – the Cabernet at its best can epitomize the Coonawarra mulberry flavours and Special Release Merlot is among Australia's best – while the white wines have improved out of all recognition. Best years: (reds) 2001, '00, '99, '98, '97, '96, '94, '90.

CH. BRANE-CANTENAC
FRANCE, Bordeaux, Haut-Médoc, Margaux AC, 2ème Cru Classé

♟ *Cabernet Sauvignon, Merlot, Cabernet Franc*

Ch. Brane-Cantenac has been in the Lurton family hands since the 1920s and after a long drab period when the wines lacked depth and consistency returned to form in the late 1990s. Henri Lurton, a qualified enologist took over the estate in 1992 and set about restoring its reputation. Its sprawling 90-ha (210-acre) vineyard is superbly located, principally on the Cantenac plateau, the 70 per cent Cabernet Sauvignon vines being planted on poor, fine gravelly soils. Second wine: le Baron de Brane. Best years: 2001, '00, '99, '98, '97, '96, '95, '90.

CH. BRANE-CANTENAC
Recent vintages at this large estate have seen a great improvement in quality and the wine shows much of the Margaux AC's delicacy and finesse.

BRAUNEBERG
GERMANY, Mosel-Saar-Ruwer

Just upstream from BERNKASTEL lies the small village of Brauneberg, facing its precipitously steep Juffer and Juffer-Sonnenuhr vineyards on the opposite side of the river Mosel. The latter is unquestionably one of the most favourable sites in the entire MOSEL Valley. In the nineteenth century these vineyards were reckoned the best in all the Mosel, but fashion has changed: the heavy soils of Juffer and Juffer-Sonnenuhr produce heavier, fuller wines with great complexity, yet too much weight for today's conception of Mosel as something light and delicate. But they are splendid wines, so to hell with fashion. Best years: (Riesling Spätlese) 2002, '01, '99, '98, '97, '95, '94, '93. Best producers: Bastgen, Fritz HAAG, Willi Haag, Paulinshof, Max Ferd. RICHTER.

BREAKY BOTTOM
ENGLAND, East Sussex

♀ *Seyval Blanc, Chardonnay*

Small vineyard in the South Downs near Lewes that was badly flooded in 2000, forcing quirky, passionate grower Peter Hall out of his home for two whole years. Hall makes dry, nutty Seyval Blanc that becomes creamy and Burgundy-like after three to four years of aging. Sparkling Seyval Blanc is delicious, but there is a shift to fizz made from more classic varieties, with early-ripening clones of Chardonnay planted in 2002 and Pinot Noir and Pinot Meunier set to follow.

BREGANZE DOC
ITALY, Veneto

♟ *Merlot, Marzemino, Groppello Gentile, Cabernet Franc, Cabernet Sauvignon and others*

♀ *Tocai, Pinot Blanc (Pinot Bianco), Pinot Gris (Pinot Grigio), Riesling Italico, Sauvignon Blanc, Vespaiolo*

Breganze is a small wine zone north of Vicenza in gently hilly countryside scattered with the superb Palladian villas of Venice's tycoons. Wine production goes back a long time, but today the only significant historic grape is Vespaiolo, beloved of wasps (*vespe*), increasingly used for the making of one of Italy's finest stickies, Torcolato. Total production of Breganze DOC wine is modest – around 3.3 million bottles a year – at least half of which is devoted to Breganze Rosso, based primarily on Merlot, and Bianco, a dry white based on Tocai Friulano. These are supplemented by a wide range of varietals, including sometimes intense Cabernet and dry Vespaiolo. Quality production is dominated by MACULAN, and Bartolomeo da Breganze is an efficient co-operative.

GEORG BREUER
GERMANY, Rheingau, Rüdesheim

♟ *Pinot Noir (Spätburgunder)*

♀ *Riesling, Pinot Gris (Grauburgunder), Pinot Blanc (Weissburgunder)*

Medium-sized estate run by Bernhard Breuer who has gone from being one of the champions of dry German wines to an apostle of vineyard classification. His 'Premiers Crus' –

vineyard-designated wines – are powerful, concentrated, dry Rieslings from the Berg Schlossberg and Berg Rottland sites in RÜDESHEIM and the Nonnenberg in Rauenthal. The Nonnenberg is spicy, fleshy and quite quick to develop, while the Berg Schlossberg is always slow to develop; reserved in its youth but becoming a siren-like beauty when mature after six to ten years. Montosa is a blend of Rieslings from several vineyards and almost as good as the top wines.

The standard dry wines are sold under the village names of Rüdesheim and Rauenthal. There is also a barrique-aged Grauburgunder (Pinot Gris) and Spätburgunder (Pinot Noir). Breuer is now one of the top RHEINGAU names. Best years: (Berg Schlossberg) 2002, '01, '00, '99, '98, '97, '96, '94, '93, '86, '83.

BRIGHT BROTHERS

PORTUGAL, Ribatejo

♥ *Baga, Cabernet Sauvignon, Merlot, Touriga Franca, Touriga Nacional*

♀ *Fernão Pires, Chardonnay, Sauvignon Blanc and others*

The Australian Peter Bright is the driving force behind much of the wine modernization that has taken place in Portugal in the last two decades. He made his name as the winemaker for J P VINHOS until he set up his own firm in 1993. Still based in Portugal, where he has interests in the RIBATEJO, ESTREMADURA and the DOURO, he now roves the world in search of grapes for his own-label wines, most of which are varietal. He also makes a range of wines for PEÑAFLOR in Argentina.

The Fiúza-Bright operation is located in the small town of Almeirim in the Ribatejo and the Fiúza-labelled wines are made from local vineyards planted to both Portuguese and French varieties. Peter Bright also sources grapes (exclusively Portuguese varieties) from, chiefly, PALMELA and Douro for the Bright Brothers label. With the exception of the Douro red called TFN (a blend of Touriga Franca and Touriga Nacional) and a range of Reserva wines, most of his wines are for early drinking.

BRITISH COLUMBIA

CANADA

British Columbia in the far west of Canada, with most of its landscape dominated by snow-capped mountain ranges and vast forests of pine seems an unlikely place for a desert,

Here at the Fiúza winery at Almeirim in the Ribatejo Peter Bright makes beautifully focused, keenly priced wines from French grape varieties.

too. Desert? Sure. Osoyoos Lake at the southern end of the OKANAGAN VALLEY is in Canada's only desert! Which means almost no rain but also lots of sun, and even if it's not that hot, sun ripens vines (ask growers in similar conditions in Switzerland or the far south of New Zealand where snow can fall in the vineyards in midsummer). The result is that Okanagan, centred round a long, deep glacial lake lying between two mountain ranges, can produce an exciting range, mostly white but sometimes red. Similkameen Valley is also dry and high. Fraser Valley near Vancouver and Vancouver Island are cooler and damper, but do OK because of the local tourist trade.

JEAN-MARC BROCARD

FRANCE, Burgundy, Chablis AC

♥ *Gamay, Pinot Noir*

♀ *Chardonnay, Aligoté, Sauvignon Blanc*

Dynamic winemaker who has built up this 80-ha (200-acre) domaine almost from scratch over the course of 20 years. Most of his vines are in less fashionable spots of CHABLIS but the quality is uniformly fine. Except for his Premiers Crus (including Montée de la Tonnerre, Montmains) and slow-evolving Grands Crus (Les Clos stands out), all the fruit is machine-picked and vinified in steel tanks. Vieilles Vignes is usually the best of his regular Chablis. Brocard also produces a range of interesting BOURGOGNE Blancs from different soil types. Best years: 2002, '01, '99.

BROKENWOOD

AUSTRALIA, New South Wales, Hunter Valley

♥ *Syrah (Shiraz), Cabernet Sauvignon, Merlot, Pinot Noir*

♀ *Semillon, Sauvignon Blanc, Chardonnay*

Until 1982 only reds were produced here, but since that time Brokenwood's success has allowed it to spread its wings in many directions. Winemaker Iain Riggs produces classically delicate yet ageworthy, unoaked HUNTER VALLEY Semillon (with a Reserve version), a grassy, subtly oaked regional blend Semillon-Sauvignon Blanc and, more recently, a Verdelho sourced from COWRA vineyards in which it has an interest. The appropriately dark and brooding Graveyard Shiraz is one of the top half-dozen Shiraz wines in Australia, but Riggs also produces two other single-vineyard Shiraz and a regionally blended Shiraz, and powerful Cabernet Sauvignon. Cricket Pitch reds and whites are cheerful, fruity ready-drinkers.

Riggs also oversees the winemaking at Seville Estate in the YARRA VALLEY, adding supple Pinot Noir to his large repertoire, and also Chardonnay, Shiraz and Cabernet Sauvignon in very different style. Best years: (Graveyard Vineyard Shiraz) 2000, '99, '98, '96, '95, '94, '93, '91, '90, '89, '88, '86.

CASTELLO DI BROLIO, BARONE RICASOLI

ITALY, Tuscany, Chianti Classico DOCG

♥ *Sangiovese, Merlot, Canaiolo, Cabernet Sauvignon*

♀ *Chardonnay, Malvasia Toscana*

Despite the fame of the Ricasoli name in CHIANTI CLASSICO circles, this large estate in Gaiole underwent a comprehensive down-marketing over a 20-year period up until the early 1990s, when the winery was leased out to a succession of Brits and Aussies.

Rescue came in the form of young Baron Francesco Ricasoli, the 32nd Baron, along with help and advice from quality-minded people such as FONTERUTOLI's Filippo Mazzei and the now almost legendary enologist Carlo Ferrini. The new broom swept clean the cobwebs, and the pile of debts, and before anyone knew it they were putting out world-class wines like the SUPER-TUSCAN Sangiovese-Merlot blend Casalferro, as well as some very handsome and impressive Chianti Classicos and Riservas. Estate wines from a total of 227ha (561 acres), mostly Sangiovese and Merlot, are labelled Brolio; the Barone Ricasoli label is for wines made from bought-in grapes. Best years: (reds) 2001, '00, '99, '97, '95, '93.

BROUILLY AC, CÔTE DE BROUILLY AC

FRANCE, Burgundy, Beaujolais, Beaujolais cru

❡ *Gamay*

'A bottle of Brooey' doesn't sound quite serious, does it? Well, why should it? Brouilly is the largest of the ten BEAUJOLAIS crus (the top-ranking Beaujolais villages which are allowed to use their name on the label). But it's still Beaujolais: it's still made from the juicy-fruity Gamay grape; it's still supposed to make you laugh and smile – not get serious; and you're still supposed to drink it in draughts, not dainty sips.

Brouilly is the closest of the crus to the BEAUJOLAIS-VILLAGES style (a lot of growers make both wines) – the wine is very fruity and can make a delicious Nouveau. One or two growers have started using oak barrels to make an ageworthy example, but there does not seem much point in aging it. It is the most southerly of the crus and comes from vineyards around the hill of Brouilly, whereas Côte de Brouilly is the cru covering vineyards on Mont Brouilly itself. On its steep slopes the sun ripens the grapes more fully than on the flatter vineyards. This extra sun produces a full, juicy, strawberry-and-peach ripeness – a sort of 'super-Brouilly' which is good young but can age well for several years. South of Brouilly the 'Villages' and the simple 'Beaujolais' vineyards stretch away towards Lyon. **Best years:** 2002, '00. **Best producers:** (Brouilly) de la Chaize, DUBOEUF (de Nevers), A Michaud, Ch. Thivin; (Côte de Brouilly) Lacondemine, O Ravier, Ch. Thivin, Viornery.

BROWN BROTHERS

AUSTRALIA, Victoria, Rutherglen

❡ *Cabernet Sauvignon, Syrah (Shiraz), Tarrango, Graciano, Merlot, Barbera*

♀ *Chardonnay, Riesling, Pinot Gris (Pinot Grigio), Sauvignon Blanc, Chenin Blanc, Muscat of Alexandria*

This is a remarkable family company with the third and fourth generations of Browns now involved in producing and selling over half a million cases of wine per year. Brown Brothers draws on fruit from a number of vineyards in VICTORIA, in both warm and cooler, upland sites in the KING VALLEY and the mountain-top Whitlands site, and uses both familiar and unusual grapes to produce a wide choice of styles, including superb fortifieds (especially the Very Old Muscat, Port and Tokay range) and consistently good vintage fizz. Perhaps partly due to the Kindergarten winery, a 35,000-case 'winery within a winery', Brown Brothers has been

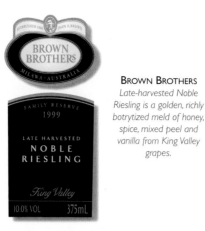

BROWN BROTHERS
Late-harvested Noble Riesling is a golden, richly botrytized meld of honey, spice, mixed peel and vanilla from King Valley grapes.

able to upgrade what was a rather ordinary range of dry table wines into a very interesting selection of good quality wines, both from well-known varietals, and such Aussie oddballs as Graciano, Dolcetto, Barbera and Tarrango.

BRÜNDLMAYER

AUSTRIA, Niederösterreich, Kamptal, Langenlois

❡ *Pinot Noir (Blauburgunder), Zweigelt, Merlot, Cabernet Sauvignon, Cabernet Franc*

🍷 *Zweigelt, Pinot Noir (Blauburgunder)*

♀ *Riesling, Grüner Veltliner, Chardonnay, Pinot Gris (Grauburgunder), Pinot Blanc (Weissburgunder)*

Willi Bründlmayer is Austria's most versatile winemaker. It was with his barrique-aged Chardonnay that he first attracted attention more than a decade ago, then his classic style dry Rieslings and Grüner Veltliners shot to the top of the Austrian class at the beginning of the 1990s. Anyone who doubts that Austria can produce world-class dry whites should experience his Riesling Alte Reben from the great Heiligenstein vineyard and his Grüner Veltliner from the Ried Lamm; magnificently concentrated, multi-faceted wines whose high alcohol is matched by superlative fruit and mineral flavours. Bründlmayer has also mastered the art of sparkling winemaking as no other in the German-speaking world, and in recent years his red wines have also gained in depth and sophistication. The finest of these is the fragrant, Burgundian-style Pinot Noir Cuvée Cécile.

Since 1996 Bründlmayer has also been a partner in and consultant for the nearby Schloss Gobelsburg estate which concentrates on dry Grüner Veltliner and Riesling, so he now works with grapes from almost 81ha (200 acres) of vines. As far as I'm concerned – the more the merrier. **Best years:** (Zöbinger Heiligenstein Riesling) 2002, '01, '99, '98, '97, '95, '94, '93, '92, '91.

BRUNELLO DI MONTALCINO DOCG

ITALY, Tuscany

❡ *Sangiovese*

Driving south from Florence through CHIANTI CLASSICO, you pass lovely Siena. Suddenly the ubiquitous vineyards disappear and not a vine is seen for miles. The surroundings seem drier, and the atmosphere gets noticeably warmer. After about half an hour a huge hill looms on the horizon with a castle on the top. This is the town of Montalcino. Ascend the hill and look out from the castle ramparts to see, in one direction, an undulating blue-grey moonscape. Yet in the other direction the land is as green and vine-clad as one might expect. It then becomes clear how unique Montalcino is.

Brunello di Montalcino is often referred to as simply 'Brunello', although this was the name of the grape, a clone of Sangiovese which got its name from the brownish hue it has when ripe. It should be a long-lived, big, rich, powerful wine with all the firm, peppery-spicy, tea-and-cinnamon, figgy character of the grape. The biggest, richest wines come from the sunbaked south-west of the area (Case Basse, Col d'Orcia, Lisini, Poggio Antico, Il Poggione, Talenti); the most elegant from the hill's north-eastern-facing scarp slope (Altesino, Caparzo); the firmest from the sheltered south-eastern slopes (BIONDI-SANTI, Cerbaiona, Costanti). Brunello has shared in the remarkable revival of Tuscan wines in general, and in good vintages they now offer Italy's most powerful but balanced expression of the Sangiovese grape. Interestingly, in *very* hot years, Brunello can get just too powerful for its own good. **Best years:** 2001, '00, '99, '98, '97, '95, '93, '90, '88, '85. **Best producers:** Altesino, ARGIANO, BANFI, Barbi, Biondi-

PIEVE SANTA RESTITUTA
Piedmont's legendary winemaker, Angelo Gaja bought this superbly sited Montalcino estate in 1994. Sugarille, from a single vineyard, is one of two Brunellos made.

Santi, Camigliano, La Campana, Caparzo, Casanova di Neri, Casanuova delle Cerbaie, Casisano Colombaio, Castelgiocondo, Centolani, Cerbaiona, Ciacci Piccolomini d'Aragona, Donatella Cinelli Colombini, Col d'Orcia, Costanti, Fuligni, La Gerla, Le Gode, Gorelli-Due Portine, Greppone Mazzi, Maurizio Lambardi, Lisini, Mastrojanni, Siro Pacenti, Pian delle Vigne/ANTINORI, Piancornello, Agostina Pieri, PIEVE SANTA RESTITUTA, La Poderina, Poggio Antico, Poggio San Polo, Il Poggione, Salvioni, Livio Sassetti-Pertimali, Talenti, La Togata, Valdicava, Villa Le Prate. The wines still have to age four years from the first of January following the vintage, but at least the minimum time in wood has been reduced from three years to two, at the behest of producers concerned that such treatment in a lesser vintage was excessive.

A separate DOC, ROSSO DI MONTALCINO, produces an increasing number of very good fruit-dominated – and more affordable – reds.

BUCELAS DOC

PORTUGAL, Estremadura

♀ *Arinto, Sercial (Esgana Cão), Rabo de Ovelha*

On the outskirts of Lisbon, the historic wine enclave of Bucelas nearly disappeared in the 1980s but has since seen a revival of interest. The DOC applies to dry white wines made mainly from the Arinto grape, which has the capacity to retain naturally high levels of acidity despite the warm maritime climate. Its partner, MADEIRA's Sercial grape, is so acidic that it is known locally as Esgana Cão ('Dog Strangler'). Caves Velhas, the mainstay of Bucelas for many years, has now been joined by several other estates including the Quinta da Murta and Quinta da Romeira. Drink young, within two or three years.

BUENA VISTA WINERY

USA, California, Sonoma County, Carneros AVA

♥ *Cabernet Sauvignon, Pinot Noir, Merlot, Zinfandel and others*

♥ *Pinot Noir*

♀ *Chardonnay, Sauvignon Blanc, Gewurztraminer and others*

Northern CALIFORNIA's oldest winery began under the ownership of Agoston Haraszthy in 1857. Sometimes called the Father of California Wine, he took his winery to exhilarating peaks and gloomy depths before he eventually went off to South America and was supposedly eaten by alligators. Today, Buena Vista's winery sits amid 405ha (1000 acres) of vineyards on slopes facing San Francisco Bay in CARNEROS. Recently, under German ownership, it was a solid performer. It has been owned by Allied Domecq since 2001 and it's too early to say what changes this will bring. The Chardonnays are vibrant with a refreshing grapefruit streak of acid from the Carneros fruit. The Pinot Noirs can be unnecessarily lean, but the Reserve wines are richer. Best years: (whites) 1998, '97, '95, '94, '92.

VIN DU BUGEY VDQS

FRANCE, Savoie

♥♀ *Gamay, Pinot Noir, Mondeuse, Poulsard*

♀ *Jacquère, Chardonnay, Altesse, Aligoté and others*

A decade or so ago these straggly little vineyards covering 300ha (741 acres) halfway between Savoie and Lyon in the *département* of Ain, made thin, lifeless whites from the Savoie grapes Altesse and Jacquère, sometimes hindered even further by Aligoté. Red varieties rarely ripened and had a distinct flavour of damp vineyards and vegetable patches. But remarkably the Chardonnay from here has become one of the trendiest quaffing wines in France. It is light, wonderfully creamy and fresh as mountain pasture. Rumour has it they make a decent fizz too. All these wines are for drinking young. Best producers: Bolliet, Cellier de Bel-Air, Crussy, Monin, Caveau du Mont July, Peillot.

REICHSRAT VON BUHL

GERMANY, Pfalz, Deidesheim

♥ *Pinot Noir (Spätburgunder)*

♀ *Riesling and others*

These are top-class, assertive PFALZ wines from a historic estate that is now leased to the Japanese Sanyo group, with lots of stainless steel for fermentation. Von Buhl can boast vines in most of the region's top vineyard sites, like FORSTer Jesuitengarten and RUPPERTSBERGer Reiterpfad; more straightforward wines are sold under the company name. The wines are rarely subtle but have full fruit and a confident Riesling character. Drink young.

BUITENVERWACHTING

SOUTH AFRICA, Western Cape, Constantia WO

♥ *Cabernet Sauvignon, Merlot, Cabernet Franc*

♀ *Sauvignon Blanc, Chardonnay, Riesling (Rhine/Weisser Riesling)*

Time slows down at this beautiful property, part of the Cape's original Constantia wine farm. The name is probably the most difficult thing to get to grips with at this estate, and the wines have undoubtedly lived up to their name (meaning 'Beyond Expectations') since the first vintage in 1985. The traditional, Old World-style wines also take time to unfold; a ripe, fruit-laden Chardonnay, penetrating, zesty Sauvignon Blanc, illustrating the region's talent for this grape, and light, racily, dry Riesling. Christine, one of the Cape's most accurate red BORDEAUX-lookalikes, promises to gain extra dimension from new, virus-free vineyards. Its fine tannins, seamless fruit and complementary barrel-maturation make this a Cape classic. Best years: (Christine) 2000, '99, '98, '96, '95, '94, '93, '92, '91.

BULL'S BLOOD

HUNGARY, Eger

♥ *Blaufränkisch (Kékfrankos), Cabernet Sauvignon, Merlot and others, including the original grape, Kadarka*

A great name and a great marketing exercise: there are umpteen legends involving the Hungarians getting the better of the invading Turks because they drank Bull's Blood (which they would have called Egri Bikavér) – a bit like Popeye and his spinach. These days it's a blend of the rather less blood-curdling Kékfrankos grape and others, instead of the original robust Kadarka. The wine is generally adequate and most comes from Hungarovin, owned by German fizz producer, Henkell. New stringent regulations should improve the quality in the two permitted regions, Eger and Szekszárd. Winemakers Tibor Gal and Vilmos Thummerer are working hard to produce something more thought-provoking.

GRANT BURGE

AUSTRALIA, South Australia, Barossa Valley

♥ *Syrah (Shiraz), Merlot, Cabernet Sauvignon, Grenache, Mourvedre, Petit Verdot*

♀ *Riesling, Sauvignon Blanc, Chardonnay, Semillon, Muscat (White Frontignac)*

Time flies; from one of the brightest of BAROSSA's bright young boys of the early 1970s, Grant Burge is now a highly mature senior citizen, with an extremely successful business based on the most extensive vineyard holdings in Barossa under single-family ownership. Generously flavoured wines are the order of the day, with heaps of American oak ladled in at every stage of winemaking but recent vintages have shown a most welcome reduction in oak. Top label is rich Meshach Shiraz and other wines include chocolaty Filsell Shiraz and Cameron Vale

Cabernet, opulent Summers Chardonnay, fresh Thorn Riesling and oaky Zerk Semillon. Shadrach Cabernet, the continually improving RHÔNE-style blend, Holy Trinity, and the excellent value Barossa Vines range are recent additions. Best years: (Meshach) 2001, '99, '98, '97, '96, '95, '94, '91, '90.

BURGENLAND

AUSTRIA

One of Austria's three principal wine regions, with 14,562ha (35,982 acres) of vineyards, Burgenland makes most styles of wine, but its speciality is the rich, sweet botrytized wines from the NEUSIEDLERSEE and Neusiedlersee-Hügelland regions on the border with Hungary. Further south the rather flat Mittelburgenland area makes mostly robust reds, from the Blaufränkisch grape. In recent years the wines have become drier, and are often blended with Cabernet Sauvignon. Good, attractive reds and mostly dry whites come from Südburgenland. Best producers: FEILER-ARTINGER, Gernot HEINRICH, Hans Igler, Juris, KOLLWENTZ, KRACHER, Krutzler, NITTNAUS, OPITZ, Peter Schandl, Ernst TRIEBAUMER, UMATHUM, VELICH, WENZEL.

ALAIN BURGUET

FRANCE, Burgundy, Côte de Nuits, Gevrey-Chambertin AC

🍷 *Pinot Noir*

In the mid to late 1980s Alain Burguet, operating out of modest cellars in the centre of GEVREY-CHAMBERTIN, was an insider's secret. Although he owned only a few hectares of village-level vineyards, he managed to craft, even in modest vintages, impressive and complex wines, especially from the parcel bottled as Vieilles Vignes Mes Favorites. In 1988 he finally acquired some Premier Cru vines in Champeaux. Today he owns 6ha (15 acres) and the wines are as stylish as ever. This is an impeccable source of Gevrey-Chambertin. Best years: 2002, '00, '99, '98, '97, '96, '95, '93, '91, '90, '88.

LEO BURING

AUSTRALIA, South Australia, Barossa Valley

🍷 *Syrah, Cabernet Sauvignon*

🍷 *Riesling, Semillon, Chardonnay*

Owned by Southcorp, Leo Buring was once unchallenged as Australia's finest producer of Riesling, notably from the EDEN and CLARE VALLEYS, though many newer wineries are now snapping at its heels. These wines mature magnificently, peaking at 10–20 years. Those from the Eden Valley retain a lime juice character and flavour all their life, while those from Clare have an added touch of toast. If you see the word 'Leonay' on the label you know it is a special bottling. Best years: 1999, '98, '97, '94, '93, '91, '90, '87, '86, '84, '79, '73, '72.

DR BÜRKLIN-WOLF

GERMANY, Pfalz, Wachenheim

🍷 *Pinot Noir (Spätburgunder)*

🍷 *Riesling, Pinot Blanc (Weissburgunder), Scheurebe, Muscat (Muskateller), Gewürztraminer*

With nearly 85.5ha (211 acres) of vineyards, this is one of Germany's largest privately owned estates. Since Christian von Guradze took over as director at the beginning of the 1990s he has transformed a sleeping giant into one of Germany's most dynamic wine producers. A champion of vineyard classification, his most revolutionary step was to introduce a stringent internal classification of the estate's wines based upon the Royal Bavarian surveyor's classification of the PFALZ vineyards from 1832. The Rieslings from the top sites are now labelled only with the vineyard name, as are Burgundian Grands Crus, and are only vinified dry. Rich, weighty and succulent, they are closer in style to top ALSACE or Austrian wines than typical German wines. The finest of these is the wine from the Kirchenstück vineyard of FORST.

The simpler Riesling wines are all sold under village names, but now even these are of very good quality. The estate's Riesling Auslese and higher Prädikat dessert wines remain among the greatest from the RHEIN. Weissburgunder is normally a supple, medium-bodied dry wine for early drinking. All the other grapes are only grown in small quantities and normally vinified dry. Best years: (Grossen Gewächse Rieslings) 2002, '01, '98, '97, '96, '95.

BURROWING OWL

CANADA, British Columbia, Okanagan Valley VQA

🍷 *Cabernet Franc, Cabernet Sauvignon, Merlot, Pinot Noir, Syrah*

🍷 *Chardonnay, Pinot Gris*

Californian Jim Wyse's Burrowing Owl winery opened in 1998 on an 11-ha (28-acre) piece of land in the heart of the Burrowing Owl vineyard in the southern part of the OKANAGAN VALLEY. It boasts the valley's first underground cellars for fermentation and barrel aging and Bill Dyer, who is also technical director at CALIFORNIA's Marimar TORRES winery, makes the wine.

Burrowing Owl initially concentrated on Cabernet Sauvignon, Merlot, Chardonnay and Pinot Gris but Cabernet Franc, Pinot Noir and Syrah have subsequently been added to the range.

CAVE DES VIGNERONS DE BUXY

FRANCE, Burgundy, Côte Chalonnaise

🍷 *Pinot Noir*

🍷 *Chardonnay, Aligoté*

This co-operative, dominating the Côte Chalonnaise far to the south of Burgundy's CÔTE D'OR, is a shining example of how the modern co-operative movement can transform a region, its reputation, and its profitability – if the will is there. The will was provided by Roger Rageot, director at Buxy from 1963 to 2000. When he arrived there, he found a demoralized, impoverished vineyard region with no identity and no self-confidence. Yet the soils were mostly excellent limestone and chalk, and the vines planted were mostly high-quality Chardonnay and Pinot Noir.

Using the great wines of the neighbouring Côte d'Or as his models over the next 30 years, by relentless pursuit of acceptable modernization and technological improvements, improved vineyard techniques, and, since 1984, the increased employment of oak barrels to ferment and mature the wines, he has made Buxy wines a byword for consistency and affordable quality.

Without Buxy's efforts, the AC MONTAGNY, of which Buxy controls 65 per cent, would never have achieved its current reputation for quality and value for money. And, almost certainly, the new BOURGOGNE-CÔTE CHALONNAISE AC would never have been created without Buxy's influence for good on the region. They've even uncovered an old vineyard called Mont-Rachet from which they produce rather a nice Chardonnay which they then sell for not a lot of money. Drink the wines within two to three years.

CAVE DES VIGNERONS DE BUXY
Clos de Chenôves is an old clos, or walled vineyard, in the southern Côte Chalonnaise and produces good, reasonably priced red and white wine.

BUZET AC

FRANCE, South-West

🍷 🍾 *Cabernet Sauvignon, Cabernet Franc, Merlot, Malbec*

🍾 *Sémillon, Sauvignon Blanc, Muscadelle*

From being an obscure appellation on the edge of the Armagnac region, Buzet has achieved fame simply by offering the public what it wants: decent flavours, decent price. The vineyards are planted with the BORDEAUX mix of grapes, and as the prices of Bordeaux wines rose in the early 1980s, Buzet produced a string of delicious, grassy-fresh, blackcurranty reds – sharp enough to be reviving, soft enough to drink as soon as they were released – and at a lower price than Bordeaux. This move into a market vacuum was helped by the fact that 95 per cent of the production is controlled by the co-operative which, luckily, knows what it is doing. There is very little rosé but the whites can be quite good. Best years: 1999, '98. Best producers: les Vignerons de Buzet co-operative, Daniel Tissot.

BYRON

USA, California, Santa Maria County, Santa Maria Valley AVA

🍷 *Pinot Noir*

🍾 *Chardonnay, Pinot Gris, Pinot Blanc*

Cool SANTA MARIA VALLEY has one of the longest growing seasons in the world and Ken 'Byron' Brown had long appreciated its potential for wine. He founded Byron in 1984 and became the first to introduce RHÔNE-style varieties to the valley. Since MONDAVI's purchase of Byron in 1990, followed by a new winery and expansion and replanting of vineyards, Ken Brown, who is still the winemaker, has been making better-than-ever Pinot Noir and Chardonnay. His Nielson Vineyard Pinot is full of spicy cherry fruit, and the Nielson Vineyard Chardonnay with mineral notes and fine balance can age for several years. The regular Chardonnay is often good value, as is a vibrant Pinot Gris. The new Io label is off to a promising start with a robust Rhône blend. Best years: (Nielson Pinot Noir) 2001, '00, '99, '98, '96, '95.

CA' DEL BOSCO

ITALY, Lombardy, Franciacorta DOCG and DOC

🍷 *Pinot Noir (Pinot Nero), Cabernet Sauvignon, Merlot and others*

🍾 *Chardonnay, Pinot Blanc (Pinot Bianco), Sauvignon Blanc*

Maurizio Zanella first began producing Italian versions of classic French wines in the early 1970s and he poured money and passion into his impressive winery, even purchasing the wood for his barriques in France, leaving it there to season for up to three years before having the barrels built by French craftsmen. Ca' del Bosco manages nearly 150ha (370 acres) of vineyards, feeding an annual production of some 950,000 bottles, of which just under half is sparkling wine, and they make some of Italy's finest and most expensive wines.

The outstanding sparkling wines include Franciacorta Brut, a non-vintage blend, Dosage Zéro, Satén and the prestige cuvée, Annamaria Clementi, which after six months in barrique spends five years in bottle on the yeasts, developing in the process an amazing complexity and tremendous wealth of flavour. The still wines include good Terre di Franciacorta Rosso and Pinero (Pinot Noir) and startlingly good Chardonnay and a Bordeaux blend, Maurizio Zanella. The best vintages of reds and whites are ready at between five and ten years. Best years: (Maurizio Zanella) 2001, '00, '99, '98, '97, '96, '95, '93, '90, '88.

CABARDÈS AC

FRANCE, Languedoc

🍷 *Cabernet Sauvignon, Cabernet Franc, Merlot, Malbec (Cot), Fer Servadou, Grenache, Syrah, Cinsaut*

Promoted to AC status in 1999, Cabardès, lying just north of Carcassonne, is the LANGUEDOC's westernmost outpost of vines and the grape varieties reflect the meeting of Mediterranean (Grenache, Syrah and Cinsaut) and Atlantic influences (Bordeaux's Cabernet Sauvignon and Merlot). At best, the wines are full-bodied, chewy and rustically attractive. Best years: 2001, '00. Best producers: Cabrol, Jouclary, Pennautier, Salitis, Ventenac.

CABERNET D'ANJOU AC

FRANCE, Loire, Anjou-Saumur

🍾 *Cabernet Franc, Cabernet Sauvignon*

This semi-sweet or *demi-sec* rosé from Cabernet is higher in alcohol than ROSÉ D'ANJOU. It is customary to stop the fermentation to leave some residual sugar and the wine is now quite fashionable in France. Drink this modern style young. It used to be made in a sweeter style from riper grapes and aged remarkably well, gaining in complexity. If you ever come across examples from the 1940s or '50s from the Domaine de Bablut, they are well worth trying. Best producers: Ogereau, Sablonettes, Terrebrune.

CABERNET FRANC

It's extraordinary how our judgment of grapes and wines is affected by what goes on in the Médoc region of Bordeaux. There, where the Cabernet Sauvignon is king, its cousin the Cabernet Franc isn't even in line for the throne: it's lucky to take up 20 per cent of a vineyard and its soft but grassy flavour does no more than calm the aggression of the Cabernet Sauvignon. Because of this we tend to think of Cabernet Franc as being an unimportant, uninteresting grape variety; yet cross the Gironde into St-Émilion and Pomerol and suddenly it takes a starring role. Many properties here have 30 per cent Cabernet Franc and two of the greatest châteaux, Ausone and Cheval Blanc, use 50 per cent and 60 per cent respectively, blending it with Merlot to add toughness and backbone to the luscious, fat Merlot fruit.

Then there's the Loire Valley. It is in cooler areas like this, or in areas where the soil is damper and heavier and where Cabernet Sauvignon cannot ripen properly, that Cabernet Franc comes into its own. The finest Anjou, Saumur and Touraine reds and rosés are likely to be Cabernet Franc: tops for reds are Saumur-Champigny, Bourgueil and Chinon, where, in a hot vintage, the wines are full of sharp, juicy, raspberry and blackcurrant fruit, and delicious.

In its other main home, the north-east of Italy, Cabernet Franc has been a mainstay of red wine production for well over a century, although these days there is a strong belief that Cabernet Franc in Alto Adige, Trentino, Veneto and Friuli is in fact an entirely different ancient Bordeaux variety called Carmenère. Cabernet Franc is grown as far south as Puglia and Sicily, where it can yield soft, fragrant wines.

Cabernet Franc's use in the New World is limited, because Cabernet Sauvignon generally ripens easily in these vineyards, but it does well in Washington State, New York State and Canada. Australia, California, Chile and Uruguay also have a few examples.

CABERNET SAUVIGNON

This grape is deservedly the world's most famous red wine grape, and is responsible for an astonishing number of the world's best red wines. It's also the grape behind an annual world-wide flood of tasty, mid-priced red wines, because it's a very easy traveller, easy to grow, easy to make into wine. Whether at the top end of the scale – the Médoc, the Napa Valley in California, Australia's Coonawarra, New Zealand's Hawkes Bay, Chile's Maipo, certain estates in Tuscany and Spain, or at the value-for-money end in all these countries as well as Eastern Europe and southern France, Cabernet Sauvignon always tastes of itself. But it is still Bordeaux that is the benchmark for Cabernet Sauvignon – curiously, perhaps, since it is always blended with other grapes there. The great clarets of the Médoc, Cabernet's heartland, are, however, usually based on at least 60 per cent, and often up to 85 per cent, Cabernet Sauvignon, and it's here that the grape shows its full glory of blackcurrant, cigar boxes, black cherries, plums and cedar, producing wines that may be firmly tannic when young, but which mellow with age – perhaps for 20 years in the greatest wines – into glorious complex harmonies.

It is such wines that many of the world's other great producers are trying to emulate. They may equal top Bordeaux in quality, but the wine's character is rarely the same. California's Napa tries hardest, and achieves wines of splendid depth and structure, with delicious flavours of black olive, black cherry and herbs. Sonoma, next door, is equally successful in a juicier, lusher way, while Washington State produces wines of power and intense blackcurrant fruit. New York State and Canadian Cabernets are usually on the green side.

In South America, Cabernet Sauvignon was responsible for the high reputation of Chilean reds and still makes many of Chile's best, pulsating with blackcurrant fruit and minty perfume, but capable of aging well. Argentina is rapidly acquiring the Cabernet knack but is still some way behind Chile.

Australian Cabernet is famous – whether it be the lean but densely structured wines of Western Australia's Margaret River, the blackcurranty, minty wines of South Australia's Coonawarra or the richer, plummier versions from the warm irrigated vineyards of the Murray Valley. New Zealand, however, has found it difficult to ripen this grape, although recent warm vintages and the development of suitable sites in Hawkes Bay and Waiheke Island, both on the North Island, are beginning to produce exciting results.

South Africa has had Cabernet planted for generations, but until recently the grapes were generally picked not entirely ripe – this was due to virus infection in the vineyards, and a liking for high-acid reds among the wine fraternity. Since the end of Apartheid, South African vineyards have been extensively replanted and wines made with a more acceptable international character – but they are still truly South African. Stellenbosch and Paarl now ripen Cabernet well but the wines retain an austere yet attractive style.

Greece has pockets of quality like Chateau Carras, Israel has the Gamla Cabernet Sauvignon from the Golan Heights, Lebanon grows good Cabernet in the Bekaa Valley and Eastern European countries all grow it, with Bulgaria, followed by Hungary, the most

consistent. All around the southern and eastern Mediterranean and Eastern Europe, especially in countries with no real wine traditions, the easy-to-grow, easy-to-make, easy-to-sell Cabernet may well become the most important quality grape.

But it is where the grape has been planted in the wine regions of western Europe, with their own established traditions, that it has caused the most controversy.

Cabernet Sauvignon in Spain, Italy, southern France and even Germany and Austria has become a bone of contention because, being the good traveller it is, it brings its own style and flavours and in so doing can all too easily overpower the local character of the region into which it has been introduced. In southern France, Cabernet has been the most important red variety in the Vin de Pays movement that has transformed the quality of basic wine in France's Languedoc-Roussillon. Its success has inspired many growers to make greater efforts with the local varieties – so, even as they complain about the international interloper, they clamber up the quality trail revealed by Cabernet's success. It has been a 'tolerated', 'experimental' variety in Rioja since the 1990s. It covers a quarter of the vineyards in Vega Sicilia, Spain's finest red wine, and the best Penedès reds are totally or principally Cabernet. The Portuguese, with their own impressive range of indigenous grapes, have proved less amenable to Cabernet than most European countries.

Cabernet Sauvignon is traditional in north-east Italy, where it makes grassy wines, and is increasingly planted in Piedmont. In Tuscany it may be made as a varietal, or used to add an international flavour to the native Sangiovese. Such wines are frequently delicious and high-quality, and that's what matters, but the debate as to whether or not such an international grape should be planted there will run for a long time yet.

CADILLAC AC

FRANCE, Bordeaux

♀ *Sémillon, Sauvignon Blanc, Muscadelle*

This rather amorphous sweet white AC, created in 1973, is situated along the northern bank of the Garonne, in the southern part of the PREMIÈRES CÔTES DE BORDEAUX AC. The area under vine varies depending on whether the producers declare their wines as Cadillac or Premières Côtes de Bordeaux, but now averages around 250ha (618 acres).

The quality of Cadillac was for many years extremely mediocre due to high yields, lack of investment and a slump in the market for sweet wines. But in the 1990s, neighbouring SAUTERNES began to regain popularity and consequent high prices with a string of good vintages, and Cadillac, though still regarded as something of a poor relation, was given the incentive – and the stuff of good vintages – to persuade growers that a bit more effort would be worthwhile.

Yields have been reduced and selective harvesting and barrel-aging have become more widespread. There is even a lobby for a 'Grains Nobles' status for more concentrated cuvées. Cadillac vineyards do get affected by the botrytis or noble rot fungus, but styles vary from fresh, semi-sweet to richly botrytized with prices varying accordingly. Best years: 2001, '99, '98. Best producers: Carsin, Cayla, du Juge/Dupleich, Manos, Mémoires, Reynon, Ste-Cathérine.

CAHORS AC

FRANCE, South-West

▪ Malbec (Auxerrois), Merlot, Tannat

After BORDEAUX, Cahors, along with MADIRAN, is the leading red wine of France's South-West, if only because it makes no attempt to ape Bordeaux and its flavours. But then, why should it? Cahors has been famous since Roman times, and was often used by Bordeaux winemakers to add colour and fruit to their wines which, two centuries ago, were nearer Bordeaux rosé than red in style.

The Cahors vineyards are on both sides of the river Lot in the Lot *département* and the whole region is about as far from hustle-bustle as can be. Only red wine is produced, with Auxerrois as the main grape (at least 70 per cent). This is called Malbec in Bordeaux, where they don't think much of it, but in Cahors it produces dark, tannic wine which when well made has an unforgettable flavour of plummy richness, streaked with fresh acidity. With age it takes on a gorgeous tangle of tastes, dominated superbly by tobacco spice, blackberry and sweet prunes. The toughest, densest wines originate from the historic valley slope vineyards. Lighter, more mainstream flavours come from new sites on the valley floor. Best years: 2000, '98, '96, '95, '94, '90, '89, '88, '86, '85. Best producers: la Caminade, Cayrou, du Cèdre, Clos la Coutale, Clos de Gamot, CLOS TRIGUEDINA, Eugénie, Gaudou, Gautoul, Haut-Monplaisir, Haute-Serre, les Ifs, LAGREZETTE, Lamartine, les Laquets, les Rigalets.

CAIN CELLARS

USA, California, Napa Valley AVA

▪ Cabernet Sauvignon, Cabernet Franc, Merlot, Petit Verdot, Malbec, Syrah

♀ Sauvignon Blanc

Don't even try to visit Cain unless you're supremely confident of your sense of direction. Situated high up SPRING MOUNTAIN in the north west of NAPA VALLEY, the road to the winery is long and tortuous as you catch yet another glimpse through the trees and swear you should have got there hours ago. But the effort is worth it, because it is a serious operation, set up to make top red wine from the five classic Bordeaux varieties. Cain Five is a fine deep red, dry but ripe and slow to age, based on the estate vines. Cain Concept is from Napa Valley benchland vines. Cain Cuvée is a pleasant glugging red, White Cain Musqué is a very floral white Sauvignon. Best years: (Cain Five) 2001, '00, '99, '97, '95, '94, '93, '91, '90, '87.

CALABRIA

ITALY

Calabria, Italy's toe, is basically two very long coastlines along the Ionian and Tyrrhenian Seas, sandwiching the southern continental section of the Apennine ridge which runs through the country from top to bottom like a giant backbone. It's pretty easy to get lost in those mountains, which make Calabria ideal bandit and mafia country. The coasts could be beautiful were it not for the tens of thousands of partially built houses – it seems every time a Calabrian in Argentina or Australia manages to save a few more dollars he sends them home to have a few more reinforced concrete pillars added to what he hopes will one day be his retirement home back in the old country.

Calabria is one of Italy's poorest regions and for a long time produced little wine of note considering its size and potential. CIRÒ, Donnici, Savuto and Scavigna reds, from the native Gaglioppo grape, and whites from Greco and Chardonnay are now much improved thanks to greater winemaking expertise. The leading producers are LIBRANDI, based in Cirò on the Ionian side, and Odoardi, based in Cosenza on the Tyrrhenian side. The main red grape is Gaglioppo, a Nebbiolo lookalike in respect of its colour and tannins, capable of making wines of considerable character and intensity. The town of Bianco has a superior form of the Greco grape which reaches its apogee as a sweet wine made from sun-dried grapes.

CALATAYUD DO

SPAIN, Aragón

▪ ♀ Grenache Noir (Garnacha Tinta), Tempranillo, Carignan (Cariñena, Mazuelo), Cabernet Sauvignon, Monastrell, Merlot, Syrah

♀ Macabeo (Viura), Grenache Blanc (Garnacha Blanca), Malvasía, Moscatel Blanco, Chardonnay

Most of Calatayud's vineyards lie up little valleys whose streams feed the Jalón river. It is attractive countryside with mountains sheltering the region to the north, east and south, but in 1990 there seemed little to justify Calatayud's promotion to DO status. However, increasing amounts of modern, fruity reds and rosés are beginning to emerge mostly from Garnacha. There are some dull whites. Calatayud Superior is for wines from 100 per cent Garnacha, from vines over 30 years old and lower yields. The San Gregorio and the Castillo de Maluenda co-operatives, along with visiting international winemakers, are leading the way.

CÁLEM

PORTUGAL, Douro, Port DOC

▪ Tempranillo (Tinta Roriz), Tinta Barroca, Tinto Cão, Touriga Nacional, Touriga Franca and others

♀ Gouveio, Viosinho, Rabigato, Malvasia Fina and others

Until 1998 Cálem, one of Portugal's leading PORT brands, was owned by the family that founded it in 1859. The company ran into financial difficulties in the mid-1990s and was bought by a local consortium. The firm's quintas, Foz and Sagrado, in the heart of the DOURO region where the river Pinhão flows into the Douro have remained with the Cálem family.

Aged tawnies (from 10 to 40 years old) and colheitas have long been a speciality of Cálem. The colheita wines are wonderful and vintage ports, particularly those from the 1960s and '70s, can be a match for the big port names. However, in the 1980s and '90s Cálem's vintage ports were disappointing and it is up to the new regime to put things right. Best years: (vintage ports) 2000, '99, '97, '94, '91, '77, '75, '70, '66, '63.

CÁLEM
Known as Old Friends in English, Velhotes Tawny is Cálem's best-selling port and one of the leading brands in Portugal and France.

CALERA WINE CO.

USA, California, San Benito County, Mt Harlan AVA

▪ ♀ Pinot Noir

♀ Chardonnay, Viognier

After Yale and Oxford, Josh Jensen continued his education in the cellars of Burgundy and in the northern RHÔNE. Learning there that legendary Pinot Noirs originate from limestone-rich slopes, he then searched out similar conditions in CALIFORNIA. In the early 1970s Jensen laid out three vineyards to Pinot Noir – Reed, Selleck and Jensen – and added a fourth, Mills, a decade later. Chardonnays, added to help pay the bills, evolved into serious contenders that have been overshadowed only by the rich, apricotty Viogniers. The Pinots, beset only by low yields, can be sensational, each unique to its vineyard site. Best years: (Pinot Noir) 2000, '99, '98, '97, '96, '95, '94, '91, '90; (Chardonnay) 2001, '00, '99, '98, '97, '96, '95.

CALIFORNIA USA

CALIFORNIA SHOULD BE INTENSELY PROUD of the fact that she was the catalyst and then the locomotive for change that finally prised open the ancient European winelands' rigid grip on the hierarchy of quality wine and led the way in proving that there are hundreds if not thousands of places around the world where good to great wine can be made. If other countries and regions have now caught up with California, and in some cases overtaken her, we should nonetheless remember that until the exploits of California's modern pioneers of the 1960s and '70s, no-one had ever before challenged the right of Europe's, and in particular, France's vineyards, to be regarded as the only source of great wine in the world.

These pioneers were men like Robert Mondavi, Warren Winiarski, Joe Heitz and others who caught hold of what was a tenuous thread of quality tradition in California, and determinedly wove their thread into the mighty hawser that is California today. But California wine very nearly did not

survive into the late twentieth century. Although founded by Franciscan missionaries in the 1770s, and although making wines of some renown by the late nineteenth century, the vine louse phylloxera had destroyed almost all the *Vitis vinifera* vines (the only ones suitable for fine wine) by 1900. Attempts to recreate the vineyards to grow quality wine were then beset by Prohibition, the Great Depression and World War II, and by the 1950s, generations of Americans had grown up with no understanding of fine wine.

Although California has conditions suitable for producing almost every kind of wine, from pale, limpid Rieslings to sturdy vintage 'port', her great strength has always been the self-confident determination of her inhabitants. This is more than ever evident today as more and more vineyards are established away from the traditional areas, and grapes other than the ubiquitous Chardonnay and Cabernet Sauvignon are planted with increasing success. A second attack by the phylloxera louse in the 1990s has meant that there has been a tremendous opportunity dramatically to improve vineyard practices and to plant varieties genuinely suitable to each mesoclimate.

The bulk of California's wine comes from the inland Central Valley. Hot and dependent on irrigation, most of the wine is inexcusably dull. Napa Valley is the most famous quality area but most of its best wines come from the cooler southern half, or from mountainside sites to the east and west of the valley. Sonoma County, to the west, is less famous but at least as fine in quality and contains top sub-regions like Russian River Valley and Dry Creek Valley.

North of these, there are good vineyards in Mendocino and Lake counties, but much of the most exciting wine comes from south of San Francisco Bay. The Santa Cruz and Gavilan mountains both produce small amounts of delicious wines. Monterey and Paso Robles, in San Luis Obispo County, after a shaky start, are producing fine wine, and the areas of Santa Maria and Santa Ynez, in Santa Barbara County, have produced some of California's finest wine to date.

Currently California has over 800 wineries and nearly 200,000ha (490,000 acres) of vineyards. Although phylloxera has forced growers to replant thousands of hectares in the North and Central Coast regions, the total land under vine in California has continued to increase rapidly. Most of the recent vineyard expansion has taken place in the Lodi region of the Central Valley and to a lesser degree, in the Central Coast counties.

The springtime flowering of wild mustard, here at Rutherford in the Napa Valley, is one of the loveliest sights in California wine country. The mustard is deep-rooted and encourages the vine to be likewise which improves its nutrition.

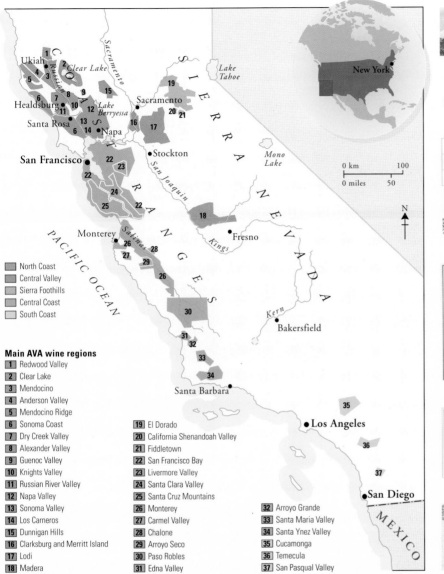

ROBERT MONDAVI
From its first vintage in 1966 Mondavi has always been associated with Cabernet Sauvignon. The Reserve wine is enormously concentrated and complex with tremendous depth.

RIDGE VINEYARDS
This dark, concentrated blackcurrant- and oak-dominated wine from the Monte Bello Vineyard is regularly one of California's top Cabernets.

MATANZAS CREEK WINERY
During the 1990s top-quality Merlot rapidly became the most sought-after wine in California. This Sonoma Valley wine is rich and elegant with concentrated blackberry and cassis fruit.

SAINTSBURY
The Reserve Chardonnay from this top winery is heavily oaked but still keeps its rich peach fruit and bright lemon acid.

SEGHESIO
The Seghesio family produces some of the best Zinfandel in California. Old Vines is a lovely, spicy, rich example.

Legend (map)

- North Coast
- Central Valley
- Sierra Foothills
- Central Coast
- South Coast

Main AVA wine regions

1. Redwood Valley
2. Clear Lake
3. Mendocino
4. Anderson Valley
5. Mendocino Ridge
6. Sonoma Coast
7. Dry Creek Valley
8. Alexander Valley
9. Guenoc Valley
10. Knights Valley
11. Russian River Valley
12. Napa Valley
13. Sonoma Valley
14. Los Carneros
15. Dunnigan Hills
16. Clarksburg and Merritt Island
17. Lodi
18. Madera
19. El Dorado
20. California Shenandoah Valley
21. Fiddletown
22. San Francisco Bay
23. Livermore Valley
24. Santa Clara Valley
25. Santa Cruz Mountains
26. Monterey
27. Carmel Valley
28. Chalone
29. Arroyo Seco
30. Paso Robles
31. Edna Valley
32. Arroyo Grande
33. Santa Maria Valley
34. Santa Ynez Valley
35. Cucamonga
36. Temecula
37. San Pasqual Valley

REGIONAL ENTRIES

Alexander Valley, Amador County, Anderson Valley, Atlas Peak, Carneros, Central Coast, Central Valley, Dry Creek Valley, Edna Valley, Howell Mountain, Mendocino County, Monterey County, Mount Veeder, Napa Valley, North Coast, Oakville, Paso Robles, Russian River Valley, Rutherford, Sacramento River Valley, St Helena, San Francisco Bay, San Luis Obispo County, Santa Barbara County, Santa Cruz Mountains, Santa Maria Valley, Sonoma Coast, Sonoma County, Sonoma Valley, Spring Mountain District, Stags Leap District.

PRODUCER ENTRIES

Acacia Winery, Alban, Araujo, Arrowood Vineyards & Winery, Au Bon Climat, Babcock Vineyards, Beaulieu Vineyard, Beringer Vineyards, Bernardus Winery, Bonny Doon, Buena Vista Winery, Byron, Cain Cellars, Calera Wine Co., Cambria Winery, Caymus Vineyards, Chalone Vineyard, Chateau St Jean, Cline Cellars, Clos du Bois, Clos du Val, Dalla Valle, Dehlinger Winery, Diamond Creek Vineyards, Domaine Carneros, Domaine Chandon, Dominus Estate, Duckhorn Vineyards, Dunn Vineyards, Far Niente Winery, Ferrari Carano Vineyards, Fetzer Vineyards, Flowers, Franciscan Vineyards, Frog's Leap Winery, E & J Gallo Winery, Grgich Hills Cellar, Handley, Harlan Estate, Hartford Court, Heitz Cellars, The Hess Collection, Iron Horse Vineyards, Jordan Vineyard, Kendall-Jackson, Kenwood Vineyards, Kistler Vineyards, Kunde Estate Winery, La Crema, Laurel Glen Vineyards, Marcassin Winery, Matanzas Creek Winery, Meridian Vineyards, Merryvale, Peter Michael Winery, Robert Mondavi Winery, Mumm Cuvée Napa, Andrew Murray Vineyard, Newton Vineyards, Niebaum Coppola Winery, Opus One, Pahlmeyer Winery, Joseph Phelps, Pine Ridge Winery, Quady, Qupé Winery, A Rafanelli, Ravenswood, Ridge Vineyards, J Rochioli Vineyards, Roederer Estate, St Francis Winery, Saintsbury, Sanford Winery, Schramsberg Vineyards, Screaming Eagle, Seghesio, Shafer Vineyards, Silver Oak Cellars, Simi Winery, Sonoma-Cutrer, Spottswoode, Stag's Leap Wine Cellars, Steele Wines, Sterling Vineyards, Sutter Home Winery, Joseph Swan Vineyards, Swanson Vineyards, Marimar Torres, Turley Cellars, Viader Vineyards, Wente Vineyards, Williams Selyem Winery.

SEE ALSO

Napa, pages 264–265.

CH. CALON-SÉGUR

FRANCE, Bordeaux, Médoc, St-Estèphe AC, 3ème Cru Classé

♥ *Cabernet Sauvignon, Merlot, Cabernet Franc, Petit Verdot*

This is the most northerly of all the MÉDOC's Classed Growths and the lowest in altitude, averaging less than 10m (30ft) above sea level. What gives Calon-Ségur Classed Growth quality is a spur of chalky, gravelly soil – usually found on higher ground in the Médoc. None of the neighbouring properties – struggling along on heavier clay soils – can produce wine that remotely matches Calon-Ségur.

Until the 1960s, Calon-Ségur used to be thought of as ST-ESTÈPHE's leading château, but has now been clearly surpassed by MONTROSE and COS D'ESTOURNEL. In the mid-1980s Calon-Ségur's problem was that its wine, though quite good, was ever so slightly dull and, at the high prices demanded by Médoc Classed Growths, dullness isn't really on. Reduced yields, more rigorous fruit selection and an increase in the percentage of new oak for aging helped produce notable wines from 1995. Second wine: Marquis de Ségur. Best years: 2000, '99, '98, '96, '95, '94, '90, '89, '86, '82.

CAMBRIA WINERY

USA, California, Santa Barbara County, Santa Maria Valley AVA

♥ *Pinot Noir, Syrah, Sangiovese and others*

♀ *Chardonnay, Chenin Blanc, Pinot Gris, Pinot Blanc, Viognier*

The biggest winery in SANTA BARBARA COUNTY, with 569ha (1405 acres) of vineyards opened for business with the 1988 vintage. Most of the production is barrel-aged Chardonnay (Katherine's Vineyard and Reserve stand out), with the remainder devoted to Pinot Noir, Syrah, Viognier and Sangiovese and also some experimental plantings. Look out for fine Julia's Vineyard Pinot Noir. Best years: (Chardonnay) 2001, '00, '99, '98, '97, '96, '95.

CAMBRIA WINERY

Julia's Vineyard is a consistently good example of Pinot Noir from Santa Maria Valley which is turning out to be one of California's top sites for the grape.

GALARDI

Terra di Lavoro is a superb example of Aglicanico and Piedirosso from northern Campania. First made in 1994 it shows the potential for excellent wine from these two local grapes.

CAMPANIA

ITALY

Campania is the region centred on Naples: bustling, chaotic, where black is the colour of the economy and theft is raised to an art form. It's the region of Sorrento, Amalfi, Ravello, Capri – 'a little piece of heaven fallen on earth' as holiday brochures smugly quote. Campania is also a geologically unstable region, where earthquakes and other terrestrial fluctuations are frequent occurrences. And it is the region of wines such as FALERNO DEL MASSICO, FIANO DI AVELLINO, Greco di Tufo, Solopaca, TAURASI and others, some of them reaching cult status, some still little known, as well as home to the finally improving Lacryma Christi del Vesuvio.

Every region has at least one grape that it can proudly claim as its own. Campania boasts a whole slew of them. The whites Falanghina, Fiano and Coda di Volpe, as well as the red Piedirosso, are virtually exclusive to the region, as are Ischia's Forastera and Biancolella. Best known are the white Greco di Tufo and the red Aglianico, which may be found elsewhere in the southern mainland but are principally associated with Campania. There is also the weird Asprinio, which produces acidic, spritzy whites from vines trained up trees to a height of 20–30m (65–100ft): an ancient Etruscan would feel quite at home. Nor should one forget the international varieties – Cabernet Sauvignon and Merlot blend with Aglianico in the famous Montevetrano estate's wine.

If Campania used to be one of Italy's most dilatory wine regions, dismissive of DOC regulations and able to make an easy living off tourists, let's not forget that it's also the area that produced the greatest wine of Roman times – Falernian – and that such a wide variety of unique grape varieties merely needs a band of committed producers to decide to exploit their potential. Just such a new generation has now arrived in Campania and the future could be as bright as anywhere in Italy.

CAMPILLO

SPAIN, País Vasco, Rioja DOCa

♥♀ *Tempranillo, Cabernet Sauvignon, Graciano*

♀ *Macabeo (Viura)*

This top-class bodega just outside Laguardia makes elegant but concentrated fruity red wines from Tempranillo with some Cabernet Sauvignon. There is also a small amount of goodish oak-aged white Crianza, and some forgettable rosé. Campillo used to be a subsidiary label belonging to FAUSTINO, but now has its own, very positive identity. The beautiful bodega is an extremely popular destination for visitors from all over the Basque country, who buy more than half the production on the spot. Best years: (Reservas) 1999, '98, '96, '95, '94.

CAMPO DE BORJA DO

SPAIN, Aragón

♥♀ *Grenache Noir (Garnacha Tinta), Macabeo, Tempranillo, Carignan (Mazuelo, Cariñena), Cabernet Sauvignon, Merlot, Syrah*

♀ *Macabeo, Moscatel Romano*

A bottle of headache pills is no longer needed if you venture south of RIOJA and NAVARRA down on to the undulating plains of Campo de Borja. Most of the wines are being turned out younger, fruitier, less astringent and somewhat less alcoholic, but 13 per cent is still considered the lightest of light. Many wines are now being sold without the traditional wood aging (and are the better and fruitier for it). Blending Tempranillo, Cabernet Sauvignon and Mazuelo with Garnacha has produced some more appetizing results. White wines have been included in the DO since 1989 and these, commendably, can be made with as little as 10.5 per cent alcohol. Best years: 2001, '99, '97. Best producers: Bodegas Aragonesas, Borsao.

CAMPO VIEJO

SPAIN, La Rioja, Rioja DOCa

♥ *Tempranillo, Carignan (Cariñena, Mazuelo), Grenache Noir (Garnacha Tinta), Graciano*

♀ *Macabeo (Viura)*

Campo Viejo, the main company in Bodegas y Bebidas, Spain's largest wine group, is huge – easily the largest producer of RIOJA. But the wines are, mostly, fairly good. The basic Rioja and Crianza are fairly forgettable but, at Reserva and Gran Reserva level, it is unusual to be disappointed.

Albor is one of the best examples of modern white Rioja, clean, appley and perfumed; the 100 per cent Tempranillo, red Viña Alcorta Reserva is even better, lean and stylish, with lively, raspberry and wild strawberry fruit. The basic Campo Viejo Gran Reservas are good, but the Marqués de Villamagna Gran Reservas are excellent, with lovely, aromatic, wild strawberry fragrance and elegant fruit. Best years: (Reservas) 1998, '96, '95, '94.

CANARIAS (CANARY ISLANDS)
SPAIN

From the times of the legendary Canary Sack of Elizabethan England, the exotic sweet wines made in the Spanish archipelago off the western African coast had notable fame, which dwindled through the years as their MADEIRA neighbours displaced them in the British market. Wine remained an important local product in the Canary Islands, where there are still more than 11,000ha (27,170 acres) of vineyards, particularly on Tenerife, Lanzarote and La Palma islands, often on precipitous slopes. Here, as in the BALEARES, tourists consume most of the production and pay high prices for it. But the seemingly disproportionate creation of new DOs has been reflected in real quality improvement.

There are no fewer than five DOs on Tenerife island alone: Abona in the southern half, and Tacoronte-Acentejo, Ycoden-Daute-Isora, Valle de la Orotava and Valle de Güímar further north. This is dry table wine country, with Negramoll the prevalent red grape variety and Listán Blanco the main white one. Wines from Viña Norte, El Lomo, Monje and Viñátigo are very original – intensely fruity and minerally at the same time. La Palma and the volcanic Lanzarote island have their own DOs, in which the rediscovered sweet Malvasía wines can reach real distinction. El Hierro DO and the two Gran Canaria DOs (Gran Canaria and Monte Lentiscal) hold much less interest.

CANBERRA DISTRICT
AUSTRALIA, New South Wales

This area is home to a handful of wineries, clustered just outside the Australian Capital Territory and the capital city, Canberra. Some seem to have a tenuous hold on the realities of life and the need for consistency; while others possess the commitment to succeed. The winters, and nights, are cold, the summer days hot and dry: virtually every grape variety is grown here, and the wine styles are extremely diverse. HARDY is pouring money into its Kamberra project here. Best years: 2001, '99, '98, '97, '96, '95, '92, '90. Best producers: Brindabella Hills, Clonakilla, Doonkuna, Helm's, Lark Hill.

VIÑA CANEPA
Full of ripe blackcurrant and black cherry fruit, Magnificum Cabernet Sauvignon is one of the top wines from this long-established Chilean winery.

VIÑA CANEPA
CHILE, Maipo Valley
♥ Cabernet Sauvignon, Merlot and others
♀ Sauvignon Blanc, Chardonnay and others

Viña Canepa was among the first bodegas in Chile to modernize, establishing one of South America's most advanced wineries in 1982 and the results were immediate in white wines at least. It was the aggressive tangy attack of their Sauvignon Blanc at a time when Chilean Sauvignons were mostly flat and dull, that along with the whites of Miguel TORRES further south, ushered in the modern era for whites in Chile.

Canepa is now equally well known for red wines as well as whites, and recent investments have seen vineyard holdings reach over 1000ha (2470 acres) as well as a new winery in COLCHAGUA, to complement Canepa's traditional base in MAIPO. Canepa also buys in grapes particularly from the Cachapoal, San Fernando and Lontué valleys. The Magnificum Cabernet Sauvignon and Private Reserve Merlot are impressive wines and the Private Reserve Chardonnay from Rancagua is balanced and ripe.

DOMAINE CANET-VALETTE
FRANCE, Languedoc, St-Chinian AC
♥ Grenache, Syrah, Mourvèdre, Carignan, Cinsaut

Marc Valette is uncompromising in his quest to make great wine: organic cultivation, low yields, a gravity-fed winery and traditional *pigeage* (foot-stomping) are just some of his methods. The wines offer a fabulously rich expression of ST-CHINIAN's Mediterranean grape varieties and clay-limestone soils. Cuvées include Mille et Une Nuits (1001 Nights) Syrah and the powerful, complex Syrah-Grenache Le Vin Maghani. Best years: (Le Vin Maghani) 2001, '00, '99, '98, '97, '95.

CANOE RIDGE VINEYARD
USA, Washington State, Columbia Valley AVA
♥ Merlot, Cabernet Sauvignon
♀ Chardonnay, Gewurztraminer

Successful WASHINGTON outpost of CALIFORNIA's CHALONE group, now with 58ha (143 acres) on the slopes of the eponymous Canoe Ridge producing reliable and tasty Chardonnay, fruit-filled Merlot and powerful Cabernet Sauvignon. Whereas most of Washington's single-vineyard reds are marked by a deep, brooding ripeness, Canoe Ridge has shown the welcome ability to produce wines which, while balanced for aging, have a bright, approachable fruit when young. Hogue Cellars and WOODWARD CANYON also produce some Cabernet from vineyards farmed by Canoe Ridge . Best years: (reds) 2001, '00, '99, '98, '97.

CH. CANON
FRANCE, Bordeaux, St-Émilion Grand Cru AC, Premier Grand Cru Classé
♥ Merlot, Cabernet Franc

Canon used to make some of the most perfect, most recognizable, most reliably rich ST-ÉMILION – reeking of that toffee-butter-and-raisins mellow ripeness which only Merlot can impart. The wine was deep, with a rich plummy fruit, and in good vintages was impressively tannic at the outset. But in the late '80s, bang in the middle of Bordeaux's golden decade, it went into one of those inexplicable declines that people blame on underfunding but which I have to suspect is more to do with the loss of the will to excel. So a string of potentially good to great vintages underachieved and it wasn't till 1996 that the decline was reversed when Canon was bought by French fashion and perfume company Chanel, owner also of Ch. RAUZAN-SÉGLA, which has pulled out all the stops to get things right. Signs are that things are now returning to form.

The vineyard is just west of the town of St-Émilion, surrounded by other First Growths. The 3.5ha (8.65-acre) vineyard of Grand Cru Classé Château Curé-Bon has recently been added to the estate. In good vintages the wine is tannic and rich at first but is worth aging for 10–15 years. Second wine: Clos J Kanon. Best years: 2001, '00, '98, '97, '96, '86, '85.

CH. CANON
Historically Ch. Canon has long been recognized as one of the top Premiers Grands Crus Classés of St-Émilion and, following a change of owners, the late 1990s have seen a welcome return to form.

CANON-FRONSAC AC

FRANCE, Bordeaux

☝ *Merlot, Cabernet Franc, Cabernet Sauvignon, Malbec*

This AC is the heart of the Fronsac region, covering 305ha (755 acres) of hilly vineyards between the villages of Fronsac and St-Michel de Fronsac. The best ones are deeply coloured, richly textured and with a firm but refined tannic structure. They age well and, after going through a rather gamy period at a few years old, usually emerge at ten years plus with a lovely, soft, Merlot-dominated flavour and a good mineral tang. Best years: 2001, '00, '98, '97, '96, '95, '94, '90, '89, '88. Best producers: Barrabaque (Prestige), Canon de Brem, Cassagne Haut-Canon, la Fleur Cailleau, Gaby, Grand-Renouil, Lamarche Canon Candelaire, Moulin Pey-Labrie, Pavillon, Vrai Canon Bouché.

CH. CANON-LA-GAFFELIÈRE

FRANCE, Bordeaux, St-Émilion Grand Cru AC, Grand Cru Classé

☝ *Merlot, Cabernet Franc, Cabernet Sauvignon*

Probably because it marries the names of two famous ST-ÉMILION châteaux – Canon and La Gaffelière, this property has itself been more famous than it deserved, especially since it is sited on relatively sandy soil at the foot of the St-Émilion slopes rather than on the slopes themselves. But when Stephan von Neipperg took over in 1985 he set about producing a wine as good as St-Émilion's best, even though his 'terroir' wasn't stellar. In both vineyard and cellar he has single-mindedly pursued quality. By the late '90s Canon-la-Gaffelière's rich, dark wine did indeed merit comparison with the top St-Émilions. Von Neipperg also owns the remarkable microcuvée LA MONDOTTE, Clos l'Oratoire, and the CÔTES DE CASTILLON property Château d'Aiguilhe. Best years: 2001, '00, '99, '98, '97, '96, '95, '94, '93, '90, '89.

CH. CANTEMERLE

FRANCE, Bordeaux, Haut-Médoc AC, 5ème Cru Classé

☝ *Cabernet Sauvignon, Merlot, Cabernet Franc, Petit Verdot*

You head out of Bordeaux on the D2, through suburbs, shrubland, damp meadows, and the occasional vineyard, and you begin to wonder if you're on the wrong road for the great wine land of the MÉDOC. Then the forests fall away and suddenly the land is thick with rows of neatly trained vines. There on the right is Château LA LAGUNE, then, on the left, Château Cantemerle, a jewel set inside its own woodland glade. Drive up the long avenue shrouded over with age-old trees and stand in front of the turretted castle. Silence. Stillness. Fairyland. Not far off.

Cantemerle was ranked last in the 1855 Classification of Bordeaux, now the wine is far better than that; rarely a blockbuster – quite right too, a fairytale château shouldn't be in the business of producing blockbusters – but always soft, easy to drink yet also surprisingly suitable for aging. Second wine: Villeneuve de Cantemerle. Best years: 2001, '00, '99, '96, '95, '90, '89, '83, '82.

CANTERBURY

NEW ZEALAND, South Island

The ever-increasing success of Canterbury as a high-quality wine region is yet another demonstration that when it comes to all the evidence telling you it's too cold to grow grapes – don't believe the experts. South Island, New Zealand in general was deemed more suitable for sheep and apples by the experts but that didn't stop a few wine-mad enthusiasts at Christchurch's Lincoln University starting vine trials in 1973. Despite their efforts, the flat windy plains around Christchurch are still only a qualified success but these early wines acted as a spur to the whole region, and Canterbury stretches both north and south of Christchurch into very different climate conditions. The mountainous Banks Peninsula to the south had vines as long ago as 1840 and now does so again, but the real Canterbury buzz is 40km (25 miles) north of Christchurch in Waipara, where soils of loess and gravel river terraces protected from sea breezes by the Teviotdale Hills produce long autumns and average summer temperatures of 2–3°C (4–6°F) warmer than those in southern Canterbury. Superb Pinot Noir, Riesling and Chardonnay could even be joined by fine Merlot and Cabernet from the warmest spots. Best years: 2002, '01, '00, '99, '98, '96. Best producers: GIESEN, Mountford, PEGASUS BAY, Daniel Schuster, Waipara West.

CAPE MENTELLE

AUSTRALIA, Western Australia, Margaret River

☝ *Cabernet Sauvignon, Syrah (Shiraz), Zinfandel*

☝ *Semillon, Sauvignon Blanc, Chardonnay*

The rammed-earth walls and local timber of one of MARGARET RIVER's leading wineries

New oak barrels are expensive but Cape Mentelle, in the Margaret River region, carefully marries fine French oak with top-quality fruit.

blend perfectly into the landscape, with its exotic native plants and a tiny rivulet meandering by.

Founder David Hohnen crafts his wines with intense care and sensitivity. He works hard to invest his Cabernet Sauvignon with the right amount of tannin to balance its full, dark fruit, and does so to such effect that I often include the wine in Bordeaux line ups – always with great success. I also love the peppery brilliance of his Shiraz and the inspired 'almost over the top' richness of his Zinfandel. Put these with top Chardonnay and excellent tangy Semillon-Sauvignon and you have one of Australia's most consistently fine wineries. Owned, along with New Zealand's CLOUDY BAY, by French luxury goods brand LVMH. Best years: (Cabernet Sauvignon) 2002, '99, '98, '96, '95, '94, '92, '91, '90.

CAPEL VALE

AUSTRALIA, Western Australia, Geographe

♥ *Syrah (Shiraz), Cabernet Sauvignon, Merlot, Malbec, Pinot Noir, Nebbiolo*

♀ *Chardonnay, Sauvignon Blanc, Riesling, Verdelho, Semillon, Viognier, Chenin Blanc*

Dr Peter Pratten's winery sources fruit from GEOGRAPHE, Mount Barker, PEMBERTON and MARGARET RIVER. Rieslings have consistently been the top wines, especially the classy Whispering Hill, while others have been variable. However, recent winemaking changes promise much more emphasis on the high-quality vineyard origins of the fruit and consequently finer, more focused wines. I'm particularly looking forward to future releases of top Shiraz and Cabernet/Merlot vintages. Best years: (Whispering Hill Riesling) 2000, '98, '97.

CAREMA DOC

ITALY, Piedmont

♥ *Nebbiolo*

Carema, north PIEDMONT's best wine, is produced almost entirely by the weekend pottering of local commuters, who part with their prized grapes to the co-operative (Cantina Sociale) or to a private producer such as the assiduous Luigi Ferrando.

It is not easy work and very little Carema is made. Viticulture is only possible because the Dora Baltea river flows swiftly through the area and keeps the air moving, therefore bringing sun to a narrow strip surrounded by cloud. Nebbiolo grown in such marginal conditions gives Carema a rare, elegant, violet-like style. Try Ferrando's Etichetta Nera (Black Label), only made in the best years, like 2001, '99, '97, '96, '95, '90, '88, '85: his normal label is

white. Or try the co-operative's reserve wine, Carema di Carema Etichetta Bianca (White Label, confusingly).

CARIGNAN

Carignan is supposed to have originated in Spain, where it is still grown in CATALUÑA, under the name of Cariñena. As Mazuelo or Mazuela, it is of marginal importance in RIOJA. It's the dominant red grape in the South of France and forms the backbone of most anonymous French vin de table, but can produce excellent juicy wines when modern methods are used on low-yield fruit from old vines.

It also pops up in SARDINIA and LAZIO, called Carignano, and in North Africa, South Africa, CALIFORNIA and Chile. What it likes best are hot, dry conditions where it can either produce deep-coloured, astringent wines that, lacking richness, aroma and flavour, are nevertheless useful in blending or, with the aid of modern winemaking, in particular the Beaujolais method of carbonic maceration, wines with a rich depth and throaty power that are good enough to stand on their own.

LOUIS CARILLON & FILS

FRANCE, Burgundy, Côte de Beaune, Puligny-Montrachet AC

♀ *Chardonnay*

♥ *Pinot Noir*

The Carillons have some 12ha (30 acres) under vine – a pretty large estate by Burgundy standards – but only the best wine is bottled under the Carillon label. The *Fils*, Jacques and François, are now in charge of winemaking. Their best wines are usually the brilliant PULIGNY-MONTRACHET Premiers Crus – les Perrières, Champ Canet and Referts – and the Bienvenues-Bâtard-Montrachet but their 'Villages' Puligny is consistently fine too. The Premiers Crus are aged in 25 per cent new oak. Carillon also produce good red wines from CHASSAGNE-MONTRACHET, MERCUREY and ST-AUBIN. Best years: 2002, '01, '00, '99, '97, '96, '95, '92.

LOUIS CARILLON ET FILS
The Carillon domaine is renowned for traditional white Burgundies of great concentration, rather than new oak. The Premier Cru les Perrières is one of their best.

CARIÑENA DO

SPAIN, Aragón

♥ *Grenache Noir (Garnacha Tinta), Tempranillo (Cencibel), Carignan (Cariñena, Mazuela), Cabernet Sauvignon, Merlot and others*

♀ *Macabeo (Viura), Moscatel Romano, Grenache Blanc (Garnacha Blanca), Chardonnay, Parellada*

This DO exemplifies the astonishing changes taking place in Spain. Where about half of the wine was once sold in bulk, the figure is now less than 2 per cent. Bottled wines still tend to be basic and alcoholic, but better harvesting and winemaking practices are reflected in an increasing amount of seriously fruity reds and fresher whites from the dominant co-operatives and the growing number of private bodegas (now about two dozen). Vineyard diversification, with Tempranillo, Cabernet Sauvignon and Merlot acreage on the upswing, is certainly helping. Best-equipped among the co-operatives is the huge Bodegas Gran Ducay, which makes pretty good, oak-aged Gran Reserva Monte Ducay reds. But the new innovator is the private Solar de Urbezo winery, whose reds are based on Tempranillo, Cabernet Sauvignon, Merlot and some experimental Syrah rather than on Garnacha Tinta. Best years: 2001, '00, '99, '98, '97, '96.

VIÑA CARMEN

CHILE, Maipo Valley

♥ *Cabernet Sauvignon, Merlot, Carmenere, Syrah, Petite Sirah, Pinot Noir and others*

♀ *Sauvignon Blanc, Chardonnay*

Carmen is one of Chile's historic wineries that managed to produce good, tasty reds long before the nationwide modernization of the 1990s ushered in the current flood of high-quality Chilean wine. However, Carmen, now under the wing of next door neighbour SANTA RITA, has adapted to the modern Chile without losing touch with its red wine tradition, and, with excellent MAIPO vineyards on hand, produces a string of top-quality Cabernets and Merlots as well as smaller quantities of varieties like Syrah, Petite Sirah and Pinot Noir. With new winemaker Pilar González in charge the quality of Sauvignon and Chardonnay is also on the rise. Carmen Nativa Cabernet Sauvignon is probably Chile's top organic wine. Best years: (Gold Reserve Cabernet Sauvignon) 1999, '97, '95, '93.

CARMENÈRE

An important but forgotten constituent of BORDEAUX blends in the nineteenth century, historically known as Grande Vidure. Planted in Chile, it was almost always labelled as Merlot until 1998 and it frequently still is. When ripe and made with care, it has rich blackberry, plum and spice flavours, with an unexpected but delicious bunch of savoury characters – grilled meat, soy sauce, celery, coffee – thrown in. A true original.

CARMIGNANO DOCG AND DOC

ITALY, Tuscany

♦ ♥ *Sangiovese, Cabernet Franc, Cabernet Sauvignon, Merlot, Canaiolo and others*

Carmignano, west of Florence, has an impeccable pedigree, from wine pots found in Etruscan tombs to citations in the 1300s. Yet it took tireless work by Conte Ugo Contini Bonacossi of Villa di Capezzana to get Carmignano accepted, first as DOC, now as DOCG. One stumbling block was the use of Cabernet to add refinement to the local Sangiovese, Bonacossi's argument centring on its traditional presence in the times of the Medici several hundred years ago. Capezzana's wine is elegant, classy, restrained and lasts well up to ten years, although 1931 is still legendary. The area also produces a young-drinking version, called Barco Reale (now DOC), a lovely rosé called Vin Ruspo and a VIN SANTO, also now DOC.

Other good producers: Ambra, Artimino, Le Farnete/E Pierazzuoli, Il Poggiolo and Villa di Trefiano, an offshoot of Capezzana. Best years: 2001, '00, '99, '98, '97, '95, '90, '88, '85. Capezzana's individual contribution to the area's renown also includes the SUPER-TUSCAN Ghiaie della Furba, a blend of Cabernet and Merlot, plus more recently Syrah. It is mellow, blackcurrantly, with plenty of weight and staying power, yet retaining a lightness of touch that gives refinement.

CARNEROS AVA

USA, California, Napa and Sonoma Counties

The grassy knolls of windy Los Carneros (meaning 'the rams' in Spanish because of the sheep farms that once reigned here) are draped like a rumpled old lion skin across the San Francisco Bay ends of both the NAPA and SONOMA VALLEYS. Much of the district is right in the path of those same wind-driven sea-fogs that chill summer tourists at Fisherman's Wharf, and they roll over these low, barren hills to cool the climate to un-CALIFORNIA-like levels. But these fogs were recognized as crucial in creating the cool climate necessary to yield fragrant Pinot Noir, finely balanced Chardonnay, lush, fruit-filled Merlot and intense, dramatic Syrah.

The combination of hot sun and clammy fogs in the low-lying Carneros region at the northern end of San Francisco Bay means that grapes grown here enjoy a very long, cool ripening period.

The weather and poor, scrubby soils combine to produce good Chardonnay and exciting Pinot Noir. And while good Chardonnay is being made elsewhere in California, the regions that have proved themselves suitable for Pinot Noir, the most difficult and temperamental red, are far fewer. Merlot and even Syrah are also doing well, but vineyard expansion is beginning to worry me. Best years: (Pinot Noir) 2001, '00, '99, '98, '97, '96, '95. Best producers: ACACIA, BUENA VISTA, Carneros Creek, DOMAINE CARNEROS, David Ramey, Rasmussen, SAINTSBURY, Truchard.

BEAULIEU VINEYARD, CLOS DU VAL, Cuvaison, Charles Krug, Robert MONDAVI and STERLING VINEYARDS also have major vineyards here and many other big Napa wineries use Carneros fruit for their Chardonnays and Pinot Noirs. The district is also important for excellent CHAMPAGNE-method sparkling wine: Domaine Carneros, DOMAINE CHANDON, Gloria Ferrer and MUMM CUVÉE NAPA have vineyards or wineries here.

CARNUNTUM

AUSTRIA, Niederösterreich

It was easy to miss Carnuntum in the old days if you were visiting Austria's vineyards. You spent most of your time on the Danube, to the west of Vienna and then headed rather nervously towards the Iron Curtain on the

Hungarian border for the sweet wine area of NEUSIEDLERSEE, fretting more about frontier guards than local scenery. But as the motorway peeled south from the Danube just east of Vienna towards the Neusiedlersee, you'd have passed by the village of Göttlesbrunn without realizing this was about to become a hotbed of Austrian winemaking in the only recently delineated area of Carnuntum. There are 891ha (2202 acres) of vines, the climate is strongly influenced by the large, shallow Lake Neusiedl as well as by the cooling breezes of the Danube and a new generation of winemakers is producing attractive whites and superb reds based on Zweigelt, Blaufränkisch and the BORDEAUX varieties. Best producers: Walter Glatzer, Markowitsch, Pitnauer.

CASA LAPOSTOLLE

CHILE, Rapel Valley

♦ *Cabernet Sauvignon, Merlot and others*
♥ *Sauvignon Blanc, Chardonnay*

Casa Lapostolle, based in the RAPEL Valley, is the newest venture of the Marnier Lapostolle family, owners of Grand Marnier, in conjunction with the local Rabat family. Their philosophy is to use French varietals and a Gallic outlook to make high-quality wines in Chile. Michel Rolland, the international star winemaker from BORDEAUX, is responsible for the towering quality of the wines, particularly the Merlot Cuvée Alexandre. The no-expense-spared winery also makes intense Sauvignon Blanc, rich, buttery Chardonnay and blackcurranty Cabernet Sauvignon, the latter two also available in the sought-after Cuvée Alexandre range. Clos Apalta is a world-class Merlot-Carmenere-Cabernet blend. Best years: (top reds) 2001, '00, '99, '98, '97, '96, '95.

CASABLANCA VALLEY
CHILE, Aconcagua Valley

I'm not sure there were any exciting white wines from Chile in the old days – I certainly never found one. And until 1982 nothing gave the impression that this situation was likely to change. That was the year Pablo Morandé, the chief winemaker for industry giant CONCHA Y TORO, trooped over the hills to the west of Santiago towards the sea, and found a barren, waterless valley, but a valley which had one priceless advantage in Chile's hot climate: it was cool. Fogs came up from the Pacific every morning, and as the sun finally burnt them off, sea breezes took their place to keep the temperature down. It could be a white wine paradise similar to New Zealand's MARLBOROUGH region, already famous for its thrilling Sauvignon Blancs. Well, that wasn't a bad comparison.

Sauvignon Blanc, followed by Chardonnay, is exactly what the Casablanca Valley became famous for, as, through the 1980s and '90s, grazing land was cleared, bore holes were sunk to find scarce irrigation water and over 3600ha (8895 acres) of vines were planted. It's only in the central to upper part of the valley that you can grow grapes – it's actually too cold at the Pacific end. But in the centre of the valley, the quality of Chardonnay and Sauvignon is undoubtedly Chile's best, and does bear a passing resemblance to the New Zealand version. Pinot Noir is also beautifully perfumed and ripe, and in the warmer, upper reaches even grapes like Carmenere, Merlot and Cabernet creep quietly towards ripeness in a vintage that may be as late as May. If frosts don't decimate the crops – and they frequently do – some of Chile's best wines come from CASABLANCA. Best years: (whites) 2002, '01, '99. Best producers: (whites) CASA LAPOSTOLLE, CASABLANCA, Concha y Toro, ERRÁZURIZ, Morandé, Veramonte, VILLARD ESTATE.

VIÑA CASABLANCA
CHILE, Casablanca Valley
🍷 *Cabernet Sauvignon, Merlot*
🍾 *Sauvignon Blanc, Chardonnay, Gewurztraminer*

In 1992 the SANTA CAROLINA winery established this winery in the CASABLANCA

VIÑA CASABLANCA
Originally famous for its white wines, Viña Casablanca produces thrilling Merlot and Cabernet using fruit from the Santa Isabel Estate.

VALLEY with the aim of bolstering its range with more aromatic white wines. Former winemaker Ignacio Recabarren established Viña Casablanca's reputation and was showered with prizes from the moment he took up the challenge here. Joseba Altuna from GUELBENZU should continue the upward march.

Viña Casablanca has 60ha (148 acres) of its own land but supplements this with fruit from 220ha (544 acres) under long-term lease. Sauvignon Blanc from Casablanca Valley has helped to redefine Chilean white wine production. Chardonnay made here is vibrant if not tropically pungent. Merlot and Cabernet from the Santa Isabel Estate are thrilling in their piercing blackcurrant fruit, but most of the best reds are from fruit harvested in other valleys, further south. Good examples are the White Label and El Bosque Cabernet Sauvignons from MAIPO. Best years: 2000, '99, '98, '97, '96.

CASSIS
FRANCE, Provence
🍷🍾 *Grenache, Cinsaut, Mourvèdre*
🍾 *Ugni Blanc, Clairette, Marsanne and others*

Cassis is really a white wine town. Rosé and reds don't figure much on the quality stakes, although they represent almost half the production. The red wine is dull at best; the rosé can be lovely and can age for a surprisingly long time – but only from a single estate such as Clos Ste-Magdeleine.

White Cassis, based on Ugni Blanc and Clairette, sometimes with Marsanne, Sauvignon Blanc and Bourboulenc to help out, is the most well-known and most overpriced white wine of the French Riviera. Could the stunning views of the vineyards rising up towards the steep cliffs, the port's daily catch of the Mediterranean's freshest fish, and the array of quayside restaurants crushed tight with trendies from nearby Marseille and Toulon have something to do with it? The wine can be fair enough if it's fresh. Best years: 2001, '00, '99, '98, '97, '96. Best producers:

Bagnol, Clos Ste-Magdelaine, Ferme Blanche, Fontblanche, Mas de Boudard, Mas Fontcreuse, Paternel.

CASTEL DEL MONTE DOC
ITALY, Puglia
🍷 *Uva di Troia, Montepulciano, Aglianico, Pinot Noir (Pinot Nero) and others*
🍾 *Bombino Nero, Aglianico, Uva di Troia and others*
🍾 *Pampanuto, Chardonnay, Bombino Bianco and others*

An arid, hilly zone inland from Bari, Castel del Monte provides the ideal habitat for the Uva di Troia grape, a gutsy, high-quality variety which can make long-lasting wine. In the hands of a top producer, Castel del Monte red can be a fragrant glassful reminiscent of rich strawberry jam, with a bitter-dry finish and fine at around three years old. Bombino Nero, on the other hand, develops less alcohol, retains good acidity and gives extract and colour quickly during fermentation, making it a natural for rosés; Castel del Monte Rosato has long been among Italy's leading rosés. New varietal reds and rosés are now appearing from Aglianico and Pinot Noir. RIVERA led the quality market with its red Riserva Il Falcone, an excellent, full-blooded southern red, with a bumped-up level of Montepulciano and a ten-year aging potential. Other good producers: Santa Lucia, Tormaresca/ANTINORI, Torrevento. Best years: 2001, '00, '99, '98, '97, '96.

The vaguely earthy whites, however, are undistinguished, but increasing amounts of varietal Chardonnay, Sauvignon Blanc and Pinot Blanc (Pinot Bianco) are being made.

CASTILLA-LA MANCHA
SPAIN

More than half of Spain's vineyard surface, or 608,000ha (1,502,350 acres) lies in the interminable, high plains of the Castilla-La Mancha region – the biggest wine region in the world, hot, dry country with poor clay-chalk soil. The DOs of the central plateau, La MANCHA and VALDEPEÑAS, make white wines from the Airén grape, and some good reds from the Cencibel (Tempranillo). Méntrida DO, the new Manchuela and Mondéjar DOs and Almansa DO make mostly rustic reds. The most ambitious wines made here are those from the groundbreaking single-estate DOs of Dominio de Valdepusa (owned by MARQUÉS DE GRIÑÓN) and Finca Élez (Manuel Manzaneque). Some of the more progressive bodegas prefer using the Vinos de la Tierra de Castilla umbrella designation.

CASTILLA Y LEÓN Spain

MANY CENTURIES BEFORE RIOJA surprised the world with delicate Bordeaux-style wines, and many centuries before La Mancha became an immense vineyard, the kingdoms of Castile and León were covered with vines as the Christian kings started reconquering the Iberian peninsula, almost entirely occupied by Arab and Berber invaders since the early eighth century. Planting vines and raising hogs were two hallmarks of advancing Christiandom, and the fortress monasteries which dotted the severe Castilian landscape in the mid-twelfth century, often run by French monastic orders, were responsible for both activities.

Good strong wines from Peñafiel, Toro or Medina del Campo became famous and were an enduring source of wealth. But the Mediterranean regions, followed by Jerez, by La Mancha, and finally by Rioja, progressively took over the markets. The nineteenth-century nationalization of the Catholic Church's assets was as much of a death blow as phylloxera was. After the louse struck, thousands of acres were replanted with the hardy but mediocre Palomino and Garnacha Tintorera grapes, and quality native varieties became almost extinct. Nothing but the supplying of cheap bulk wines seemed to remain on the horizon for Castilla y León, and vines were pulled up by the million.

The Viña Alta vineyard in Ribera del Duero belongs to Alejandro Fernández who discovered that the region's high altitude meant that the Tinto Fino grape grew thin-skinned with high levels of acidity, resulting in rich, aromatic reds.

As recently as 1980 beetroot was the main crop in Ribera del Duero, and no wine book in the world mentioned the two old kingdoms (now part of the modern Castilla y León autonomous region) as anything like a quality wine region. Yet an old isolated estate and some enterprising people from Rioja were getting ready to rekindle the flame. The Vega Sicilia estate had steadfastly proven, since the 1860s, that Ribera grapes could produce an astonishing wine if properly vinified, and by the 1970s some neighbours, led by toolmaker Alejandro Fernández, who makes the now world-famous Pesquera, had taken their cue and were following Vega's lead, making deep, dense, powerful wines from these high-altitude vineyards.

Meanwhile, the historic Rioja Alavesa firm of Marqués de Riscal had decided not to make white wines in its home region any longer, but instead to replant the native Verdejo (and later to introduce Sauvignon Blanc) on the high plateau of Rueda, where both varieties succeed now in producing aromatic, zippy modern whites. These were the sparkplugs to the revival. Success in Ribera and Rueda became the story

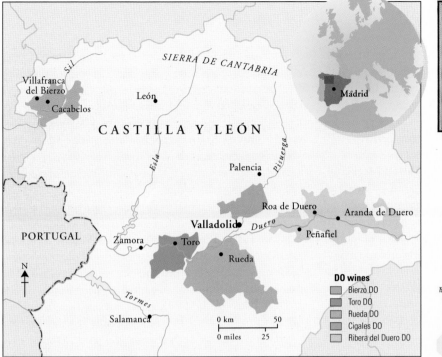

TEÓFILO REYES
From its first acclaimed vintage in 1994 this wine has shown a ripe, spicy, tobacco-influenced fruit character with excellent depth and concentration.

ISMAEL ARROYO
This bodega run by the Arroyo family in Ribera del Duero is known for its long-lived, tannic Val Sotillo Gran Reservas.

of the 1990s, and by the start of the new century the other DOs in the region (Toro, Cigales and Bierzo) were climbing aboard the bandwagon, in spectacular fashion. High altitude means a harsh continental climate here, but the valleys (particularly that of the Duero) bring just enough humidity to create some superior mesoclimates for grape-growing. The vineyard area is 52,000ha (128,500 acres), and overwhelmingly, the main varieties are native ones, though top French varieties now occupy sizeable surfaces.

ABADÍA RETUERTA
From a new vineyard on a historic site renowned for fine wine since the twelfth century, the lightly oaked Rivola wine is an aromatic blend of Tempranillo and Cabernet Sauvignon.

REGIONAL ENTRIES
Bierzo, Ribera del Duero, Rueda, Toro.

PRODUCER ENTRIES
Abadía Retuerta, Álvarez y Díez, Fernández-Tinto Pesquera, Marqués de Riscal, Mauro, Hermanos Pérez Pascuas-Viña Pedrosa, Dominio de Pingus, Vega Sicilia.

ANTAÑO
Wines labelled Rueda Superior must contain at least 85 per cent of the local Verdejo grape variety. Rueda is now Spain's top inland wine region for white wines.

VEGA SICILIA
From mainly Tempranillo with some Cabernet Sauvignon, the slow-maturing Unico is the top wine from Spain's most hallowed winery.

ALEJANDRO FERNÁNDEZ-TINTO PESQUERA
Unlike the wines from neighbouring Vega Sicilia, the Pesquera wines are made entirely from Tempranillo. The Gran Reserva is made only in the best years.

MARQUÉS DE RISCAL
Sauvignon Blanc has adapted well to the Rueda region and these whites almost single-handedly caused the renaissance of the region in the late 1970s.

CATALUÑA Spain

CATALUÑA IS ALMOST A SEPARATE COUNTRY from Spain. It has a separate language, Catalan, an immensely cultured capital, Barcelona – and a thriving separatist movement. It also has the reputation of being the hardest-working and most efficient of Spain's autonomous regions. Wine, and especially sparkling wine, has been a major source of prosperity.

The production of both sparkling wine and much of Cataluña's quality still wine is centred on the DO region of Penedès, between Barcelona and Tarragona. Cataluña has the potential to be one of the Mediterranean's most exciting wine regions, but as yet there are far too few pearls and far too many swine. A captive market in Barcelona and on the holiday beaches of the Costa Brava can't help and too many growers are used to being paid often and well for less than perfect grapes by the sparkling wine producers. There are surprisingly few well-known properties – Torres is the best-known name but is a massive merchant house not an individual domaine.

With 11 still wine DOs plus a large area overlapping these which also qualifies for the Cava DO, Cataluña scores more DOs than any other autonomous region, and 90 per cent of Catalan wine is sold with a DO. As well as Montsant, which was created in 2002, four of these DO wine areas are quite recent: Terra Alta, (1985), Costers del Segre (1988), Conca de Barberá (1989), Pla de Bages (1995). None of these initially deserved the title, though inland Costers del Segre makes some good reds and whites notably at the important estate of Raïmat, and neighbouring Conca de Barberá grows Torres' stunning Milmanda Chardonnay. But all of them have subsequently earned their spurs. There's also one new all-embracing Cataluña DO – useful for inexpensive blends from anywhere in the region.

However, it is the oldest of them all, Priorat, that has made the most spectacular strides, recovering an international lustre it last enjoyed long ago during the Middle Ages and Renaissance. The new boutique wineries in Priorat have revolutionized the map of Spain's quality wine regions which in turn has energized some smaller producers in the other southern DOs. Most of the DO regions fan out from the dusty plain of Tarragona, into the gentle slopes of Penedès, the hills of Terra Alta, Conca de Barberá and Priorat. Dotted elsewhere are only tiny Alella on the Costa Dorada above Barcelona, verdant but under-achieving Empordà-Costa

Some of Cataluña's most exciting new wine is emerging from the Priorat region. The landscape here is dramatic too and rugged mountains tower over small vineyards buried deep in the valleys and interspersed with almond and olive trees.

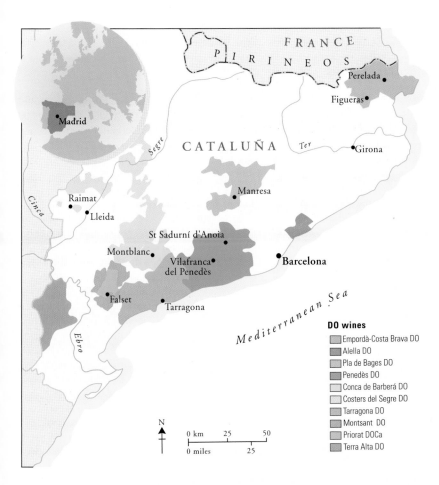

TORRES
Milmanda Chardonnay is the superstar white from Torres and Spain's first and arguably still her best coolish-climate Chardonnay.

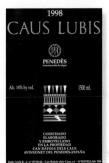

CAN RÀFOLS DELS CAUS
Some of the most exciting Penedès reds are produced from this estate. Caus Lubis is a Merlot wine and an unusual success in Spain for this variety.

COSTERS DEL SIURANA
Carles Pastrana makes stylish structured red wines, particularly Clos de l'Obac, a superripe Garnacha/Cabernet Sauvignon-based wine.

ÁLVARO PALACIOS
Álvaro Palacios is one of the top producers in Priorat. L'Ermita, from a 50-year-old Garnacha vineyard, is one of Spain's leading new cult wines.

CLOS MOGADOR
This estate helped pioneer the rebirth of Priorat in the late 1980s. The wines are high in alcohol, tannic and with natural acidity – brooding monsters built to last forever.

Brava up on the rocky northern coast with an easy local tourist market lapping up whatever is made, and the scattered patches of Costers del Segre bordering Aragón.

So far Cataluña's wines have not exhibited the same flamboyant exuberance that characterizes so much else Catalan. Priorat, with its brash, absurdly self-confident head-banging reds, has shown how thrilling Catalan wines can be.

REGIONAL ENTRIES
Alella, Cava, Conca de Barberá, Costers del Segre, Penedès, Priorat, Tarragona.

PRODUCER ENTRIES
Clos Erasmus, Clos Mogador, Codorníu, Costers del Siurana, Freixenet, Juvé y Camps, Mas Martinet, Álvaro Palacios, Raïmat, Torres.

MARQUÉS DE MONISTROL
This fresh and fruity Cava with increasing quality comes from the Marqués de Monistrol winery at Sant' Sadurní d'Anoia.

CODORNÍU
Codorníu is now the biggest Champagne-method sparkling wine company in the world and Jaume Codorníu Brut is one of Spain's best made Cavas.

JUVÉ Y CAMPS
Juvé y Camps is well-respected, ultra-traditional – and expensive. Unusually for a Catalan company, most of the grapes come from its own vineyards.

CATENA ZAPATA
Nicolás Catena has invested hugely in his top wines, Nicolás Catena Zapeta and Alta; made only in the best years, they have enormous aging potential.

CATENA ZAPATA

ARGENTINA, Mendoza
♟ *Malbec, Cabernet Sauvignon, Merlot, Bonarda*
♀ *Chardonnay, Viognier*

Catena Zapata has become such a powerful and impressive figure in the internationalization of Argentine wine that it is easy to forget that the company was at one time the leading producer of domestic bulk wine, and, though they recently divested themselves of the last of these domestic brands, they still have large interests in the anonymous hot-climate vineyards east of Mendoza city. Indeed they produce one of Argentina's tastiest. gutsiest red Bonardas there.

However, current attention is focused on Catena's vineyards in such classic areas as Lunlunta, Agrelo and the UCO VALLEY, south of MENDOZA, and the beautiful new Zapata winery in Agrelo modelled on buildings from the Mayan civilization. There's no doubt that boss Nicolás Catena is determined to prove Argentina can make world-class wines, and his top-of-the-range Catena Zapata and Catena Alta are certainly that. Also good, if a little rich in style, perhaps reflecting Catena's own wine epiphany in CALIFORNIA, are the next ranges – called Catena and Alamos. A recent attempt at a big volume brand – Argento – started out erratically but now offers good value tasty reds and whites. Two of the Catena children have local wineries – Tikal and Luca – while Nicolás himself has formed a joint venture called Caro with Ch. LAFITE-ROTHSCHILD of Bordeaux fame. Bordeaux's Cabernet married with Argentina's Malbec? That'll be a battle royal worth the wait. Best years: (Catena Zapata) 2002, '01, '00.

DOMAINE CAUHAPÉ

FRANCE, South-West, Jurançon AC
♀ *Gros Manseng, Petit Manseng*

Henri Ramonteu is synonymous with the revival in quality of the dry and sweet white wines of JURANÇON and he makes a range of astonishing wines at the 25-ha (62-acre) Domaine Cauhapé at Monein in the western Pyrenees. The dry wines, from Gros Manseng, include the fruity, aromatic Chant des Vignes and fuller, sappier Sève d'Automne. In exceptional years a dry Noblesse du Temps is made from Petit Manseng, the variety used for Jurançon's sweet wines. These are aged in new and one-year-old oak barriques and are gloriously rich and unctuous. The Symphonie de Novembre is made from late-harvested grapes picked during the first *tris* or selection and Noblesse du Temps from the second *tris*. A tiny amount of barrel-fermented Quintessence is made from extremely late-harvested grapes, often picked in January. Best years: 2001, '00, '99, '98, '96, '94, '93, '90.

CAVA DO

SPAIN
♟ *Parellada, Macabeo (Viura), Xarel-lo, Chardonnay, Grenache Noir (Garnacha Tinta), Monastrell, Trepat, Pinot Noir*
♀ *Parellada, Macabeo (Viura), Xarel-lo, Subirat (Malvasía Riojana), Chardonnay*

The word Cava is Catalan for 'cellar', and came to be applied to the CHAMPAGNE-method sparkling wines of CATALUÑA. Since all but a tiny proportion of this fizz comes from Cataluña, the Catalan name was adopted for these sparkling wines throughout Spain. There was a problem, however. The EU wine authorities insisted that any new DO should have specific geographical qualifications as well as rules relating to how the wine should be made and out of which grapes. So the Cava DO rules, declared in 1986, specified 160 authorized villages across northern Spain. Most of them are in Cataluña. These villages gained the right to the Cava DO simply because they had a long tradition of making Champagne-method wines – generally using the same grapes as their still wine neighbours.

Unfortunately, very few brands of Cava have particularly fruity, interesting flavours, DO or not. The traditional grape varieties are either dull or bland, and they don't age well, despite the fact that the Cava regulations insist upon a minimum of nine months' aging. The majority of Spanish fizz, from Cataluña, is made from Macabeo, Parellada and Xarel-lo; so, ironically, the best, fruitiest buys are usually the youngest and therefore cheapest wines. The few fizzes from La Rioja are uninspired, made from Viura, alias Macabeo. But look out especially for Cava with Chardonnay on the label (CODORNÍU or RAÏMAT and a few others). Spanish Chardonnay fizz can have lovely fruit and flowery-buttery flavours, and a softer character than Champagne – and it can benefit from a bit of aging. Best producers: Can Feixes, Can Ràfols dels Caus, Castellblanch, Castell de Vilarnau, Codorníu, FREIXENET, JUVÉ Y CAMPS, Marqués de Monistrol, Parxet, Raïmat, Raventós i Blanc, Rovellats, Agustí Torelló, Jané Ventura.

CAYMUS VINEYARDS

USA, California, Napa County, Napa Valley AVA
♟ *Cabernet Sauvignon*

Neither the late Charlie Wagner nor his son and current winery boss Chuck were ever the types to rush into anything, so when Caymus announces a new direction, you know it's not going to be a flash in the pan. Production is now limited to the two varietal Cabernets – Special Selection and NAPA VALLEY. From the 2000 vintage Special Selection Cabernet should reflect a riper fruit selection, a slightly raised alcohol level and shorter barrel-aging. These wines are dark, a bit fleshy, but always built on a solid frame of tannins and, in youth, strongly flavoured by new American oak. With age they achieve a rich fruit flavour and nicely integrated oak and the Special Selection has often been about as good as a Napa Cabernet can get. Best years: (Special Selection) 2001, '00, '99, '98, '97, '95, '94, '92, '91, '90, '87, '86, '84.

Conundrum, an exotic, deliciously scented white first made in 1989 is a hedonistic delight. It is now a separate brand with its own winery being built in MONTEREY, which is also the source of Chardonnay under the Mer Soleil label. New Belle Glos Pinot Noir is from SONOMA COAST.

DOMAINE CAZES FRÈRES

FRANCE, Languedoc-Roussillon, Rivesaltes AC
♟ ♀ *Syrah, Grenache, Carignan, Syrah, Mourvèdre, Cabernet Sauvignon, Merlot and others*
♀ *Muscat, Chardonnay, Macabeo, Rolle*

The Cazes brothers, André and Bernard, are a real powerhouse in the Roussillon and with 160ha the largest producers in the region. They produce a superb range of RIVESALTES (Vintage, Ambré, Tuilé, Aimé Cazes), some aged in barrels that were bought secondhand in 1911!, and a consistently fresh and aromatic MUSCAT DE RIVESALTES and they also produce a wide range of red and white CÔTES DU ROUSSILLON and VIN DE PAYS des Côtes Catalanes table wines. The red Canon du Maréchal is a bright fruity wine made by carbonic maceration while the white Canon is an exotically perfumed dry Muscat. The CÔTES DU ROUSSILLON-VILLAGES is a more serious wine made from Grenache, Syrah and Mourvèdre, which requires three to four years' bottle age. The latest addition to the range is the international-styled Le Credo, a Cabernet-Merlot blend aged in new oak casks. Best years: (Le Credo) 2000, '98, '96, '95, '94, '93.

CELLIER DES TEMPLIERS
FRANCE, Languedoc-Roussillon, Banyuls AC
♥ *Grenache, Carignan, Syrah, Mourvèdre*
♀ *Grenache Blanc*

The Cellier des Templiers is a serious-minded co-operative close to the Spanish border that produces an astonishing range of COLLIOURE and BANYULS. All told there are 18 Banyuls and 9 Collioures on offer, ranging in quality, style and price according to the method of production and length of aging. The vintage or *rimage* Banyuls is a smooth-textured fruit-driven wine for early drinking. Among the prestige cuvées of Grand Cru Banyuls (which receive long aging in large wooden barrels), the Viviane Le Roy, Henri Caris, Amiral Vilarem and Président Henri Vidal range from dry to sweet in style. A number of the Collioures, which are made from a varying blend of Grenache, Carignan, Syrah and Mourvèdre, come from individual estates. These include the Abbaye de Valbonne, Ch. des Abelles and Domaine du Roumani.

CENTRAL COAST AVA
USA, California

If the big quake ever does come to CALIFORNIA, we'll probably lose all the Central Coast vineyards in one fell swoop, because the region sits on the coastal side of the San Andreas fault and would probably sink into the sea. Still, while it's with us, although the region technically runs all the way from San Francisco to Los Angeles, in wine terms it usually comprises the three counties of MONTEREY, SAN LUIS OBISPO and SANTA BARBARA. These areas are characterized by mild winters, cool summers tempered by the cold Pacific and very long dry autumns reaching into December. The result is some of the most intensely flavoured fruit of any California wine region, with Chardonnay, Pinot Noir and Syrah excelling.

CENTRAL OTAGO
NEW ZEALAND, South Island

Central Otago in the far south of the South Island, boasts New Zealand's only truly continental climate, with cold winters that bring a high degree of frost risk and, in the critical late summer/early autumn ripening period, hot days with cold nights to create fantastic intensity in fruit flavours. It is now New Zealand's fastest growing wine region zooming towards a projected 1000ha (2740 acres) of vineyards in 2005.

Pinot Noir is the most planted variety and produces some of New Zealand's most scented and satisfying examples. Chardonnay ranks second, making fine, zesty, CHABLIS-style wine that often has a mineral influence. Both varieties support a growing sparkling wine production. Riesling, Pinot Gris and Sauvignon Blanc can all come up trumps in a good vintage but may fail to gain full ripeness in a cooler than normal year. Gewurztraminer produces some of the country's very best examples of the style. Best years: (Pinot Noir) 2002, '01, '99, '98. Best producers: Chard Farm, FELTON ROAD, Gibbston Valley, Mount Difficulty, Mount Edward, Peregrine, Quartz Reef, Rippon Vineyards, Two Paddocks.

MOUNT EDWARD

In only a few years Pinot Noir has become the star variety in Central Otago and now accounts for nearly three-quarters of all vineyard plantings in the area.

CENTRAL VALLEY
USA, California

If you eat a CALIFORNIA peach or pear, lemon or lime, carrot or cabbage or corn cob – it probably comes from the Central Valley – a vast monument to agro-industry that stretches parallel to the coast from the Sacramento Valley in the north to below Bakersfield in the south. And if you drink a bottle of wine that just says 'California' on the label, it probably comes from here too, because over 75 per cent of California grapes are grown here, thanks to a herculean irrigation scheme dating from the 1920s which harvests the rains of the Sierra Nevada mountains to the east and which waters the deep, fertile topsoil during the ten-month growing season.

In the north, round Lodi and Clarkesburg, there are good areas, and evidence that high-quality reds in particular are possible here. But most of the vines are in the arid south where quality is rarely a concern and vast operations like GALLO and Constellation – the world's two biggest wineries – hoover up whatever grapes are going. Some of the better brands are Delicato, R H Phillips, Sebastiani Vineyards, SUTTER HOME and Woodbridge (MONDAVI).

CÉRONS AC
FRANCE, Bordeaux
♀ *Sémillon, Sauvignon Blanc, Muscadelle*

Cérons is an enclave in the GRAVES region of Bordeaux. The AC is for white wine, both dry and sweet. Throughout the 1960s and '70s interest in sweet white wine waned and hard times hit Cérons and SAUTERNES alike. The only solution was to use the grapes to make dry wine and these, with Graves AC or Cérons Sec on the label, are now more important here than the gently sweet, mildly honeyed wines. Best years: 2001, '00, '99, '98, '97, '96, '95, '90, '89. Best producers: de Cérons, Grand Enclos du Ch. de Cérons, du Seuil.

L A CETTO
MEXICO, Baja California
♥ *Cabernet Sauvignon, Petite Sirah, Zinfandel, Nebbiolo, Malbec, Merlot and others*
♀ *Sauvignon Blanc, Chenin Blanc, Chardonnay, Viognier*

The L A Cetto winery at Tlanepantia in Baja California brought modern winemaking right up-to-date in Mexico with the use of stainless steel, temperature-controlled technology. The grapes come from the relatively cool Guadalupe Valley, about 80km (50 miles) south of the US border, and can develop reasonably good aromatic flavours. Italian Camilo Magoni makes ripe, fleshy Petite Sirah, oak-aged Cabernet Sauvignon, Zinfandel and Nebbiolo. The whites, led by Chardonnay, are at last showing balance and perfume. Drink the wines young.

CHABLAIS
SWITZERLAND, Vaud
♥ ♀ *Pinot Noir*
♀ *Chasselas (Dorin)*

South-east of Lake Geneva, this Swiss wine region specializes in whites from the Chasselas grape, here called Dorin. In the best villages like AIGLE, Yvorne and Bex, where the grapes are grown on steep terraces, it can be attractively tangy. The Pinot Noir, as well as making red, also makes a very good pink Oeil de Perdrix. Best producers: Henri Badoux, Delarze, Grognuz, J & P Testuz.

CHABLIS France, Burgundy

CHABLIS HAS MANAGED TO MAKE A VIRTUE out of the fact that in most years it barely manages to ripen its grapes, and the resulting wines have long been a byword for green, ultra-dry whites of no discernible richness and little discernible fruit. Yet that just shows how easy it is for a reputation to linger on long after it bears little resemblance to the truth. Chablis is certainly dry, but it is very rarely green or raw nowadays, and although it doesn't have the almost tropical fruit ripeness of some white wines from further south in Burgundy, it does have a gentleness and a light unassertive fruit which can make for delicious, undemanding drinking.

Also, Chablis does come from one small decidedly marginal area in the frost-prone, autumn-cool valley of the river Serein between Dijon and Paris – and from there alone. Sadly for Chablis, non-French winemakers and marketing men found the name beguiling to the eye, and extremely easy to pronounce and remember. Consequently all over the world the name Chablis has been adapted to local wines. Today, California, Australia and many other regions produce 'Chablis' versions – which are limited by one thing only – not the grape type, not by the wine style, but by the fact that they are cheap wines.

True Chablis comes only from the Chardonnay grape, comes only from the French AC region, and is always white and dry. And it is never cheap. It cannot be cheap because the vineyards are at the northern limit for fully ripening Chardonnay grapes. The Champagne region is a mere 30km (19 miles) to the north, and you only have to taste a still white Coteaux Champenois to realize how tart and thin unripe Chardonnay can be. The best Chablis vineyards – the seven Grands Crus – are tightly packed together into one south-west-facing stretch of sloping suntrap next to the town of Chablis. The best Premiers Crus are similarly angled south- to south-west to pick up every possible ray of sun and protected from cold winds by the twists and turns of the little valleys. Also the harvest is notoriously unreliable due to the risk of spring frosts, the likelihood of bad weather when the vines flower, and the probability of early winters.

You might wonder if it is worth the effort. Well, it is. New methods of frost protection are cancelling out the worst effects of a springtime relapse into winter. A better

The Chablis Grands Crus cover a magnificent south-west-facing slope above the river Serein. Les Grenouilles is in the foreground with Valmur and les Clos beyond. The famous Chablis Kimmeridgian limestone soil can be clearly seen.

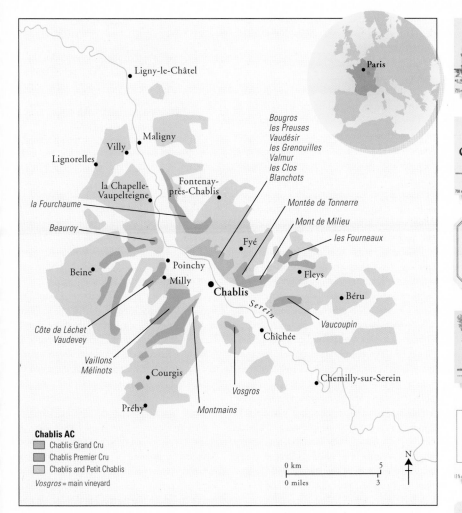

RENÉ ET VINCENT DAUVISSAT
This is one of Chablis' top domaines, specializing in concentrated, oak-aged wines.

JEAN-PAUL DROIN
The best wines here are ripe, buttery Premiers and Grands Crus which are fermented and/or aged in oak barrels.

DOMAINE LAROCHE
One of Chablis' larger négociants, Laroche produces wines that are generally light, fresh and fruity.

WILLIAM FÈVRE
William Fèvre of Domaine de la Maladière has one of the largest holdings of Grand Cru vineyards in Chablis.

LOUIS MICHEL & FILS
The prime exponents of unoaked Chablis. The wines are intensely flavoured, minerally and long-lived.

DOMAINE RAVENEAU
This small, traditional estate produces beautifully nuanced wines using both oak and stainless steel fermentation.

DANIEL-ETIENNE DEFAIX
Released later than most Chablis, these wines have a concentrated, classically austere character.

LA CHABLISIENNE
The Cuvée Vieilles Vignes is one of the best wines from this important and reliable co-operative.

JOSEPH DROUHIN
From substantial vineyard holdings in Chablis, this Beaune merchant offers good-value Chablis with a lively ripe fruit character.

understanding of the malolactic fermentation (which converts tart malic acid into softer, creamier lactic acid) means that very few wines are now harsh and green, though some may be a touch dull. And, despite Chablis' 'bone-dry' reputation, an increasing number of producers are experimenting with oak aging – resulting in full, toasty, positively rich dry whites.

In the late 1980s many producers jumped on the new-oak bandwagon, producing wines of considerable richness, but often they lacked Chablis character and at the same time never quite achieved the mellow richness of a Meursault. Today such over-oaked wines have become rare and growers use small oak barrels more judiciously, reserving them for their best Crus. The majority of producers opt for aging their wines in small oak barrels that have been used several times and lost all their vanilla spice – or in stainless steel.

REGIONAL ENTRIES
Chablis, Chablis Grand Cru, Chablis Premier Cru.

PRODUCER ENTRIES
Jean-Marc Brocard, René et Vincent Dauvissat, Jean Durup, Domaine Laroche, Louis Michel et Fils, Domaine Raveneau.

CHABLIS AC, PETIT CHABLIS AC

FRANCE, Burgundy (see also pages 120–121)

♀ *Chardonnay*

The Chablis AC covers 4400ha (10,880 acres) of land around the little town of Chablis between Dijon and Paris but only 3523ha (8705 acres) are actually planted with vines. It is Burgundy's northernmost outpost, and only Chardonnay is used to create this refined, expensive and bone dry wine.

Chablis' trouble is that it has become synonymous in many parts of the world with cheap, dry-to-medium, white-to-off-white wine from any available grape. Real Chablis couldn't be more different. It is always white and dry, often bone dry, so green-edged, so flinty that the taste reminds one of the click of dry stones knocked together. More often nowadays the dryness opens out into a broader taste, nutty, honeyed even, yet never rich, a Puritan's view of honey spice, rather than a Cavalier's.

The Chardonnay only ripens with difficulty in the Serein Valley, and there is a dreadful record of devastation by frost. Consequently the price of the wine is high. Unless it is typically stony and dry, it's too high, given the amount of good ripe Chardonnay now being produced elsewhere in the world and selling for less money. In general, drink at one to two years old, but the better wines can improve for three to five years. For best producers, see Chablis Premier Cru AC, below.

Petit Chablis means little Chablis – and that name fits the bill exactly. The Petit Chablis AC covers uninspired, rather green, unripe Chardonnay wine from the least good nooks and crannies of the Chablis region. And since the authorities have cynically 're-scheduled' most 'Petit Chablis' vineyards as 'proper' Chablis you can imagine how feeble what's left must be. The la Chablisienne co-operative or LAROCHE are the best bet for an adequate light Petit Chablis – but it's not even a bargain any more, so why bother?

CHABLIS GRAND CRU AC

FRANCE, Burgundy

♀ *Chardonnay*

This is the heart of Chablis: the vineyards of Blanchots, Bougros, les Clos, Grenouilles, Preuses, Valmur and Vaudésir comprise a single swathe of vines rising steeply above the little river Serein, facing serenely towards the south-west and able to lap up every last ray of the warm afternoon sun. It is only because of the perfect exposure, the steep elevation and the unique Kimmeridgian limestone that the

Chardonnay grapes can fully ripen and gain the fatness and strength which should mark out a Grand Cru.

Grand Cru growers, in general, have been making exceptional wines during the 1990s and 2000s, especially those who have used oak to mature their wines, adding a rich warmth to the taut flavours of the wine. There was a surge towards an excess of new oak in the '90s, but few top producers overdo it any more, preferring terroir flavours to vanilla. Prices for Chablis Grand Cru wines are high, naturally, because supplies are very limited – especially since the Grands Crus suffer more than the other vineyards from the late frosts which can decimate Chablis' crop in the spring.

There is much argument between those who use new oak to age their wines and those who don't. The anti-new oak brigade do make *le vrai* Chablis – if you're after a wine which always keeps a firm grip on that lean streak of self-denial which, even after ten years, stops a Grand Cru ever wallowing in its own deliciousness. If you use new oak barrels, the wine gains a rich, almost tropical, apricotty fruit, nuts and cream flavour, and the spicy butter of the oak completes a picture of high-quality indulgent white. And then, just when you're about to say 'this is as sumptuous as Montrachet' you find that reserved, minerally restraint clambering back to centre stage, admonishing you at the last gasp for forgetting the prim self-restraint that is the key to Chablis' character.

Never drink Grand Cru too young – it's a total waste of money. Five to ten years are needed before you begin to see why you spent so much. Best years: 2002, '00, '99, '98, '97, '96, '95, '92, '90. Best producers: J-C Bessin, Billaud-Simon, la Chablisienne, J Dauvissat, R & V DAUVISSAT, D-E Defaix, Droin, LAROCHE, Long-Depaquit, MICHEL, Pinson, RAVENEAU, Servin, Simonnet-Febvre, Vocoret.

CHABLIS PREMIER CRU AC

FRANCE, Burgundy

♀ *Chardonnay*

Almost one-fifth of Chablis' vineyards are designated Premier Cru or First Growth, one level below Grand Cru (Great Growth) in the Burgundian pecking order. There's no doubt that some of these Premiers Crus are on splendid slopes, but Chablis has been the scene of much contentious politicking over the years as 'interested' parties (those owning the relevant vineyards) have sought to upgrade Petit Chablis land to CHABLIS AC, and much straight Chablis land to the superior AC,

DANIEL-ÉTIENNE DEFAIX

The Defaix wines are known for their rich, yet bone dry yeast character, the result of spending 18 months in vat on their lees, which are stirred up for nourishment.

Chablis Premier Cru. There is little evidence yet that the 'new' Premiers Crus are doing anything except lessening the expectations of the consumer when confronted by a Premier Cru label. Of those 747ha (1846 acres) of Premier Cru vineyards, 200ha (494 acres) date from recent promotion.

So what of the good Premiers Crus? The best ones are Montée de Tonnerre, Vaillons and Monts de Milieu, just south of the Grand Cru slopes, Fourchaume, and some parts of Côte de Léchet and Montmains, both southeast-facing slopes to the west of the town of Chablis. The flavours are still dry, and are often nutty, fairly full, with a pronounced mineral streak. Whereas straight Chablis, from vines mostly grown on flatter land, is steely without any pronounced terroir flavours, a Premier Cru should show that mineral raciness which is a hallmark of fine Chablis, giving the wine a long, lingering, rangy finish. A Premier Cru should also be bigger and more intense, and if the winemaker has used wood rather than stainless steel to make his wine, it probably will have these characteristics.

But at these prices, satisfaction, unfortunately, is not guaranteed, and the sincerity of the producer is actually more important than the vineyard site. A good Premier Cru may take five to ten years of aging to show its full potential. Best years: 2002, '00, '99, '98, '96, '95, '90. Best producers: Barat, J-C Bessin, Billaud-Simon, Pascal Bouchard, A & F Boudin, BROCARD, la Chablisienne, Collet, Dampt, R & V DAUVISSAT, D-E Defaix, Droin, DROUHIN, DURUP, W Fèvre, J-P Grossot, LAROCHE, Malandes, MICHEL, Picq, Pinson, RAVENEAU, Vocoret.

CHALONE VINEYARD

USA, California, Monterey County, Chalone AVA

♂ *Pinot Noir, Syrah, Grenache*

♀ *Chardonnay, Pinot Blanc, Chenin Blanc, Viognier*

Chalone Vineyard has enjoyed near-cult status for at least three decades. Despite the death in 1998 of founder Richard Graff, this benchmark winery has remained a successful producer of full-blown but slow-developing Chardonnay and concentrated Pinot Noir, now under the guiding hand of Tom Selfridge. The winery and vineyard occupy an AVA all of their own on a gentle slope just below the Pinnacles rock face high above MONTEREY's Salinas Valley to the west.

The Chardonnays tend to have a strong note of charred wood from being fermented and aged in mostly new French barrels and have a mineral scent that may take several years to marry in. They are tart to start with, but impressively durable. Best years: 2001, '00, '99, '98, '97, '96, '95, '94, '93, '92, '91, '90. The Pinot Blancs show somewhat less of the charred wood notes and more fruit; even so, they are, if anything, a bit firmer and more tart on the palate. Chenin Blanc is made in the same style.

The Pinot Noirs are darker than most of their kin, and a good deal more tannic; they age eccentrically but superbly in the manner of a Burgundian Côte de Nuits. Best years: 2000, '99, '98, '96, '95, '94, '92, '91, '90, '88, '86. Latest releases are boutique quantities of Estate Syrah, a RHÔNE-style red called Gavilan and Viognier.

Chalone Inc. is a far-reaching organisation that also owns Edna Valley Vineyard in SAN LUIS OBISPO COUNTY, ACACIA in CARNEROS, Carmenet, high up in hills on the east side of SONOMA VALLEY and WASHINGTON STATE's CANOE RIDGE, an increasingly good producer of finely structured reds. Mid-priced CENTRAL COAST varietals are labelled Echelon.

CHALONE VINEYARD
The limestone vineyards on the arid eastern slope of Monterey's Coastal Range have an ideal cooler mesoclimate for the slow, balanced ripening required for quality Pinot Noir.

CHAMBERS

AUSTRALIA, Victoria, Rutherglen
❦ *Syrah (Shiraz) Cabernet Sauvignon, Cinsaut, Touriga*
♀ *Muscat, Muscadelle, Riesling, Gouais*

Bill Chambers is a paradox. He'd almost rather sell you plastic flagons – bring your own if you want – of dull dry basic white for

a buck or two a litre than let you give him 50, 60, 80 dollars for just a half-bottle of his Rare or Special Old Liqueur Muscats and Tokays which are among the greatest sweet wines in the world. Indeed, whenever someone has the temerity to buy some, Chambers puts the price up. But it's worth persisting. These great 'stickies' come in three grades – Rare is the top – and they are as viscous, as intense, as erotic as any wine you have ever put in your mouth and the flavour will linger for minutes, hours, days or years, depending on your mood. The Cabernet and Shiraz are good, the whites pedestrian.

CHAMBERTIN AC, CHAMBERTIN CLOS-DE-BÈZE AC

FRANCE, Burgundy, Côte de Nuits, Grands Crus
❦ *Pinot Noir*

The village of GEVREY-CHAMBERTIN has no fewer than eight Grands Crus, which between them can produce some of BURGUNDY's greatest and most intense red wine, with remarkable flavours that develop as the wine ages. Chambertin and Chambertin Clos-de-Bèze, the best Grands Crus, are neighbours on the stretch of slope at just below 300m (1000ft), running from Gevrey-Chambertin south to VOSNE-ROMANÉE, the village which produces the most sublime reds in Burgundy. The wines are basically the same, and Clos-de-Bèze can simply call itself 'Chambertin' if it wants to. 'Chambertin, King of Wines' is how the old-timers described this powerful wine and 'Emperor of Wines' might have been more apt since this was Napoleon's favourite tipple. They say he drank it wherever he went – Russia, Egypt, Italy... Waterloo? Perhaps 1815 was a bad vintage? Well, maybe, but this can be a hell of a wine, the biggest, most brooding of all.

In a good year the wine starts off positively rasping with power, the fruit all chewy damson skins and tarry tannin. But give it time, five years, maybe ten, or even 20, and Chambertin transforms itself. The scent is exotic and rich, fleetingly floral, but more likely to envelop you with the powerful warmth of

DOMAINE BRUNO CLAIR
Bruno Clair's top wine is his Chambertin Clos-de-Bèze – dense and concentrated, it has new oak, black cherries and wild floral notes in the bouquet.

choice damsons and plums so ripe they would long have fallen from the tree – add to this the strange brilliance of black chocolate, prunes, and the delicious decay of well-hung game – and you have one of the most remarkable flavours red wine can create. Due to these crus' popularity, there are many Chambertins simply not worth the high price demanded for them, but the best wines can be so good it is worth persevering. The top wines can age for a decade or more. Latricières-Chambertin, Mazis-Chambertin, Griotte-Chambertin and Ruchottes-Chambertin also produce rich, long-lived wines, while the remaining Grands Crus, Chapelle-Chambertin and Charmes-Chambertin, tend to be lighter in style. Best years: 2002, '01, '00, '99, '98, '97, '96, '95, '93, '91, '90, '88. Best producers: Denis Bachelet, BOUCHARD PÈRE ET FILS, Charlopin, B CLAIR, P Damoy, DROUHIN, Dugat-Py, FAIVELEY, R Groffier, JADOT, D LAURENT, LEROY, Denis MORTET, H Perrot-Minot, Ponsot, Rossignol-Trapet, J Roty, ROUMIER, Rousseau, Trapet, Vougeraie.

CHAMBOLLE-MUSIGNY AC

FRANCE, Burgundy, Côte de Nuits
❦ *Pinot Noir*

Chambolle-Musigny is supposed to produce the most fragrant, perfumed red wines in all Burgundy. Well, yes and no. Some bottles from the Grands Crus of BONNES-MARES or le MUSIGNY can really set the heart fluttering and from some growers the Premier Cru les Amoureuses can be of comparable quality. The names of Premiers Crus such as les Amoureuses and les Charmes, both leading sites, suggest coy, flirtatious femininity – all rustling silks and fans – and this is what many writers claim as the character of Chambolle-Musigny wines. The fact that 'Charmes' probably derives from the French for 'straw' or 'hornbeam' takes away some of the romance and the fact that most modern Chambolle-Musigny suffers from the Burgundian disease of overcropping and oversugaring the grape juice doesn't help much either. But the vineyards are well sited, just south of MOREY-ST-DENIS, and located between 250 and 300m (800 and 1000ft) up the Côte de Nuits slope and the potential for beautiful wines is unquestionably there. Best years: 2002, '01, '00, '99, '98, '97, '96, '95, '93, '90. Best producers: G BARTHOD, DROUHIN, DUJAC, R Groffier, Hudelot-Noëllat, JADOT, LEROY, Marchand-Grillot, D MORTET, J-F MUGNIER, Rion, ROUMIER, de VOGÜÉ.

CHAMPAGNE France

THE CHAMPAGNE REGION OF FRANCE has given its name to the whole concept of sparkling wine. Fizz is thought of and described as 'Champagne' even when it's made thousands of miles away from this chilly, windswept northern area. And although the hordes of imitations throughout the world relentlessly pursue a style as close as possible to that of true Champagne, they never achieve it – for one simple reason. No-one in their right mind in a country like Spain, Italy, Australia, the United States or Argentina – where sunshine to ripen the grapes is taken for granted – would ever risk planting vines in such an unfriendly, hostile environment as the stark chalklands of France's far north. It's a region where it never gets warm enough for a grape to ripen totally, where the acidity stays toothachingly high and where the thin, meagre flavour of the young still wine makes it virtually undrinkable on its own.

But this is a description of the perfect base wine for great sparkling wine. If you make sure this workhouse gruel of a wine is made from top-quality grape varieties like the white Chardonnay and the black Pinot Noir and Pinot Meunier (rosé Champagne is usually made by blending a little red wine with the white), then you can hardly go wrong – as long as you use the *méthode champenoise* (Champagne method) of winemaking to create the bubbles by a second fermentation in the bottle. It's a good thing, though, that the Romans decided to plant grapes here. It must have been warmer then, and it's unlikely that anyone would think to do it now.

'La Champagne' – the only place in the world real Champagne can come from – is mostly a charmless bitingly cold prairie land to the east of Paris. Yet centred on Reims and Épernay, and stretching down towards the northern tip of Burgundy, there are five areas where the combination of chalk soil and well-drained, protected mesoclimates allows the grapes to ripen. The Montagne de Reims is a low, wide hill curving south of Reims where Pinot Noir excels. The Côte des Blancs is a long east-facing slope, south of Épernay, almost exclusively planted with Chardonnay. This has become Champagne's most prestigious region. Although

The Premier Cru vineyards surrounding the village of Villedommange are some of the best in the Petite Montagne, an area just south-west of Reims at the western end of the Montagne de Reims.

highly regarded producers such as Krug and Bollinger use a lot of black grapes, many houses, and consumers, relish the incomparably elegant and Chardonnay-dominated wines from the Côte des Blancs. The Vallée de la Marne runs through Épernay and grows good Pinot Meunier and Pinot Noir. There are two other areas – the Aube and the Côte de Sézanne. There are very few red and white still wines made in the region; they are labelled Coteaux Champenois.

POL ROGER
Known for marvellously consistent and long-lived elegant wines, Pol Roger was Sir Winston's Churchill's favourite Champagne house.

KRUG
Krug's top Champagne is a rare and expensive Blanc de Blancs from the Clos du Mesnil vineyard in the Côte des Blancs.

ALFRED GRATIEN
Gratien's vintage Champagne is deliciously ripe and toasty when released but can age for a further ten years. Rare nowadays, Gratien still makes its base wine in wood.

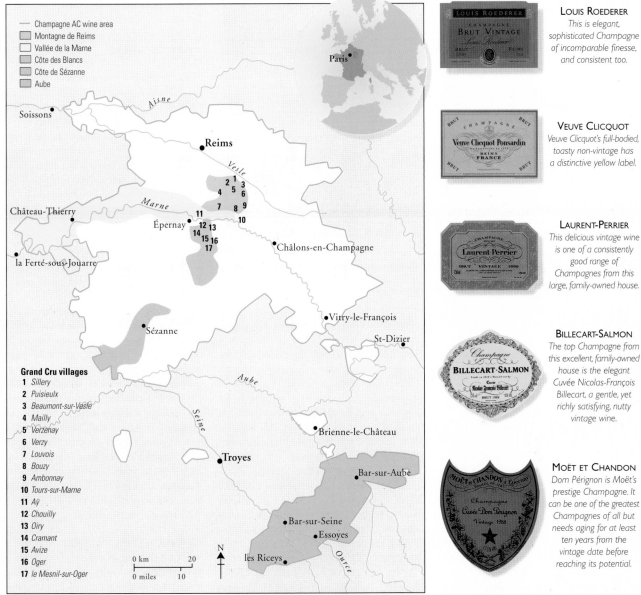

Grand Cru villages
1 Sillery
2 Puisieulx
3 Beaumont-sur-Vesle
4 Mailly
5 Verzenay
6 Verzy
7 Louvois
8 Bouzy
9 Ambonnay
10 Tours-sur-Marne
11 Aÿ
12 Chouilly
13 Oiry
14 Cramant
15 Avize
16 Oger
17 le Mesnil-sur-Oger

Map legend:
- Champagne AC wine area
- Montagne de Reims
- Vallée de la Marne
- Côte des Blancs
- Côte de Sézanne
- Aube

LOUIS ROEDERER
This is elegant, sophisticated Champagne of incomparable finesse, and consistent too.

VEUVE CLICQUOT
Veuve Clicquot's full-bodied, toasty non-vintage has a distinctive yellow label.

LAURENT-PERRIER
This delicious vintage wine is one of a consistently good range of Champagnes from this large, family-owned house.

BILLECART-SALMON
The top Champagne from this excellent, family-owned house is the elegant Cuvée Nicolas-François Billecart, a gentle, yet richly satisfying, nutty vintage wine.

MOËT ET CHANDON
Dom Pérignon is Moët's prestige Champagne. It can be one of the greatest Champagnes of all but needs aging for at least ten years from the vintage date before reaching its potential.

JACQUES SELOSSE
This fine Champagne is the result of barrel fermentation, both old and new, and biodynamic vineyards in the best bits of the Côte des Blancs.

REGIONAL ENTRIES
Bouzy, Champagne, Coteaux Champenois, Rosé des Riceys.

PRODUCER ENTRIES
Billecart-Salmon, Bollinger, Deutz, Gosset, Alfred Gratien, Charles Heidsieck, Krug, Lanson, Laurent-Perrier, Moët et Chandon, G H Mumm, Bruno Paillard, Joseph Perrier, Perrier-Jouët, Piper-Heidsieck, Pol Roger, Pommery, Louis Roederer, Ruinart, Salon, Taittinger, Veuve Clicquot.

TAITTINGER
Taittinger's prestige Blanc de Blancs Champagne has a creamy, refined elegance with a real richness after about ten years of aging.

CHARLES HEIDSIECK
Under the ownership of Rémy-Cointreau a lot of effort has gone into improving quality and this is now one of the most reliable and satisfying of all Champagnes.

BOLLINGER
This great Champagne house makes wines in a full, rich, rather old-fashioned style. The Grande Année vintage, from two-thirds Pinot Noir, is best at ten to 15 years.

CHAMPAGNE AC

FRANCE, Champagne (see also pages 124–125)

♀ ♟ *Pinot Noir, Chardonnay, Pinot Meunier*

The renown of Champagne is such that it is the only AC wine that does not have to bear the words Appellation Contrôlée on its label. Yet Champagne is more tightly controlled than most because of the insatiable thirst of the world for this most exciting of sparkling wines. Champagne is thought of as a general term for sparkling wine but in fact the AC applies only to sparkling wines (mostly white but also rosé) which have gained their bubbles by undergoing a second fermentation in the bottle from which they will eventually be served (called the Champagne or traditional method) and which come from one area, centred on Épernay and Reims, to the east of Paris. Nothing else can be true Champagne.

Grapes rarely ripen fully this far north, and the result is a light wine of very high acid, which is perfect for making sparkling wine, so long as the wine comes from good grape varieties. In Champagne it does. The Chardonnay is one of the world's greatest white grapes and here produces lovely, fragrant sparkling wines which become surprisingly creamy with a little maturity. Pinot Noir and Pinot Meunier are both high-quality red grapes, but in this northerly region their skins never develop much colour and with careful pressing the juice can be removed with virtually no coloration.

Some Champagne is made only from a single grape variety – called Blanc de Blancs when from Chardonnay, or Blanc de Noirs from Pinot Noir – but most is the result of blending the three grape varieties. Blending between the different villages is also crucial, and most Champagnes will be a blend of wines from perhaps a dozen villages from throughout the region. The villages are classified according to quality. There are 17 Grand Cru villages at the top, followed by 41 Premier Cru villages.

An increasing amount of Champagne is now made by grape growers themselves – this is usually unblended, and can be exciting when it comes from a Premier Cru or Grand Cru village. This will be clearly marked on the label. However, most Champagne is made by large merchant houses. It comes in sweet, medium, medium dry, dry, very dry (brut) and very, very dry (ultra-brut) styles. It is typically a blend of two or more years, labelled 'non-vintage', but when the vintage is good, a 'vintage' cuvée is released of wine from a single year's harvest. There are also 'de luxe' cuvées, normally vintage and supposedly the

The Côte des Blancs, where the chalky subsoil often breaks through to the surface, provides most of the finest Chardonnay grapes for the Champagne blend.

crème de la crème of Champagne. Frequently, they are more remarkable for the weirdness of their bottle shapes and high prices, than for the perfection of their flavours. Good pink Champagne has a delicious fragrance of cherries and raspberries to go with the foaming froth and should be drunk as young as possible. Best years: 2002, '99, '98, '96, '95, '90, '89, '88, '85, '83, '82. Best producers: (houses) BILLECART-SALMON, BOLLINGER, Cattier, Delamotte, Delbeck, DEUTZ, Drappier, Duval-Leroy, GOSSET, Alfred GRATIEN, Charles HEIDSIECK, Henriot, Jacquesson, KRUG, LANSON, LAURENT-PERRIER, Bruno PAILLARD, Joseph PERRIER, PERRIER-JOUËT, Philipponnat, POL ROGER, POMMERY, Louis ROEDERER, RUINART, SALON, TAITTINGER, VEUVE CLICQUOT; (Growers) Michel Arnould, Bara, Barnaut, Beaufort, Beerens, Callot, Charpentier, Chartogne-Taillet, Diebolt Vallois, Daniel Dumont, Egly-Ouriet, René Geoffroy, Gimonnet, André Jacquart, Lamiable, Larmandier, Larmandier-Bernier, Launois, Margaine, Serge Mathieu, G Michel, Moncuit, Alain Robert, Secondé, Selosse, de Sousa, Tarlant, Vilmart.

DOMAINE CHANDON DE BRIAILLES

FRANCE, Burgundy, Côte de Beaune, Savigny-lès-Beaune AC

♟ *Pinot Noir*

♀ *Chardonnay*

This is one of the rare domaines in Burgundy run by women: the Comtesse de Nicolay and her daughter Claude, who married into the

DROUHIN family. A beautiful mansion in SAVIGNY is the headquarters of a 13-ha (32-acre) estate with vineyards, more or less organically cultivated, in PERNAND-VERGELESSES and CORTON as well as Savigny itself. With the possible exception of Corton Clos du Roi and Corton Bressandes, these vineyards are not known for powerful dense wines, and the Chandon de Briailles style is one of exceptional charm, subtlety and finesse. Pernand-Vergelesses lacks the renown of Corton or even Savigny, but Chandon de Briailles makes some of the very best wines from the appellation, especially the Premier Cru Île de Vergelesses. Best years: 2002, '01, '00, '99, '98, '96, '95, '93, '90.

CHAPEL HILL

AUSTRALIA, South Australia, McLaren Vale

♟ *Cabernet Sauvignon, Syrah (Shiraz) and others*

♀ *Chardonnay, Verdelho*

Outstanding winery south of Adelaide that always manages to marry superb quality with value for money and also makes very astute use not only of local McLAREN VALE grapes but also fruit from PADTHAWAY and COONAWARRA. This allows winemaker Pam Dunsford to craft red wines of great richness which always maintain beautiful balance, particularly from Shiraz and Cabernet, as well as one of Australia's top unoaked Chardonnays and a lean but delicious Verdelho. Now owned by the Swiss Schmidheiny group who also own Cuvaison in CALIFORNIA's NAPA VALLEY. Best years: (Shiraz) 2001, '00, '98, '97, '96, '95, '94, '93, '91.

LA CHAPELLE LENCLOS

FRANCE, South-West, Madiran AC

♟ *Tannat, Cabernet Franc, Cabernet Sauvignon*

♀ *Petit Manseng, Courbu*

Patrick Ducournau is one of the leading names in the MADIRAN AC. Following in the footsteps of Ch. MONTUS he produces rich, concentrated wines with a rounded tannic structure from aging in oak barrels. He has also acquired a reputation for his patented system of controlled oxygenation, known as *microbullage*, which softens the potentially hard tannins of the Tannat grape during maturation. Two Madiran wines are produced, la Chapelle Lenclos and Domaine Mouréou. The former is a firmer, longer-aging wine, but both need a minimum five years' bottle age. There is also a small amount of sweet white PACHERENC DU VIC BILH from a blend of local varieties. Best years: (reds) 2001, '00, '99, '98, '96, '95, '94, '93, '90.

CHAPOUTIER

*FRANCE, Northern and Southern Rhône, Provence
(Northern Rhône)* ❢ *Syrah*
♀ *Marsanne, Viognier and others*

Until the late 1980s Chapoutier was a deeply old-fashioned merchant house based in Tain l'Hermitage. The wines were fairly priced, but exceedingly uneven in quality. In 1988 Michel and Marc Chapoutier took over the firm and turned the place inside out. In the vineyards yields were reduced drastically, and by the mid-1990s their own vineyards were being cultivated biodynamically, and in the cellar good-quality French oak replaced ancient chestnut casks. Michel was zealous in spreading the word about the changes he was making, but the wines have proved to be their best ambassadors. To the standard range of RHÔNE wines, they added costly single-vineyard wines such as HERMITAGE (la Sizeranne, le Pavillon), CÔTE-RÔTIE (Mordorée), CROZES-HERMITAGE (les Varonniers), and CHÂTEAUNEUF-DU-PAPE (Barbe-Rac). They also acquired properties in PROVENCE'S

CHARDONNAY

Despite some complaints about Chardonnay overkill, the Chardonnay bandwagon rolls on. Few growers who aspire to international standing can afford to be without it, and only in the most traditional non-Chardonnay areas – Bordeaux, for example – will you find winemakers happy in its absence.

There are several simple reasons. First, Chardonnay sells. That magic word on the label can make bottles walk off the shelves. Next, it's extremely versatile. Grown in cool climates, and with no oak aging, it will reveal the character of its region beneath its lemony, nutty fruit; in warmer spots it will be rich and complex, and take to new oak barrels like a duck to water, soaking up flavours of spice and cream. Last, it blends superbly with all manner of other grape varieties. In Australia some goes into partnership with Semillon; in the Loire Valley winemakers use it to soften the Chenin Blanc. And in the South of France, where it appears on its own in the vins de pays and the Limoux AC, a splash or two can also be used to perk up an otherwise dull blend of other varieties.

Chardonnay's other main incarnation is in Champagne and its lookalikes, when its tart, thin, still, cool-climate wines become graceful, complex and fascinating when made into bubbly by the Champagne method.

It's just as well it is so versatile, because there's an awful lot of it about. California alone has some 40,500ha (100,000 acres) of Chardonnay; Australia has 18,433ha (45,548 acres) and Burgundy, which in its very top vineyards can produce the sort of Chardonnays that push all the others into second place, has 9,000ha (22,240 acres). For it is here on the Côte d'Or, and further north in Chablis, that still Chardonnay wine can be better than just about anywhere else in the world. In Chablis it is chalk-dry and nutty, though often these wines are oaked as well; and from the top Côte d'Or vineyards it can reach extraordinary heights of complexity and savoury depth.

Further south it makes traditionally light and delicate, but increasingly full-bodied, discreetly oaked wines in Italy's Alto Adige, Trentino and Friuli, where the age-long confusion between Chardonnay and Pinot Blanc (Pinot Bianco) has been sorted out, with the result that there is apparently more Chardonnay and less Pinot Bianco there than anyone suspected 25 years ago. Bigger, richer, oakier and more international styles come from Tuscany, and it has invaded Soave as well, where it is now accepted officially as an optional part of the blend. In fact, Chardonnay has invaded the whole of Italy, with impressive versions coming from Piedmont (Gaja, Coppo) right down to Sicily (Regaleali, Planeta); and of course it is an essential ingredient of Italy's growing prestige *metodo classico* or Champagne-method sparkling wine industry, the zenith of which is represented by the Franciacorta DOCG in Lombardy. Chardonnay has crept into Portugal and seems to do well in the central-south of the country in the Ribatejo, Terras do Sado and Estremadura. In Austria both oaked and unoaked styles are made, a common synonym for the grape being Morillon. In Germany the area planted with the grape remains small, but some good examples come from Baden and the Pfalz.

The best Chardonnays from eastern Europe are those made in Hungary, where local winemakers were quick to learn the tricks of the trade from visiting flying winemakers. Slovakia, Bulgaria and Romania all have the potential for excellent Chardonnay but progress is slow.

California's Chardonnays have the reputation of being the biggest, beefiest and richest of the lot, and to some extent that is still true, though greater elegance and finesse have been appearing for some years now. There was even a time a few years ago when the attractive richness was being strangled, as winemakers unwisely tried to re-create lean, cool flavours from their lush, fragrant grapes. Nowadays, California's cool areas like Carneros and Russian River get the balance just right. The grape is grown in all of the USA's wine grape-growing states, but only Washington State, with a wide range of interesting styles, Oregon, with generally leaner, tarter versions, New York State – especially Long Island – Virginia and Texas produce consistent results. Canada's best Chardonnay comes from the southern Okanagan close to the Washington border and selected sites on the Niagara bench in Ontario. The style is generally bright and fruit-driven, with good supporting acid. A mix-up with imported vine material in the early 1980s saw South Africa plant large quantities of Auxerrois instead of Chardonnay. The real thing took off only in the mid-'80s but is now well represented in all the major wine areas. Time has brought more balance to the wines, which in the early days tended to be over-oaked, and a few have now achieved real complexity. Australia produces just about everything from understated complexity in a few top wines to brilliantly commercial oaky styles that sell at come-and-get-me value-for-money prices. The biggest wines here tend to come from the Hunter Valley, McLaren Vale and Barossa Valley, the leanest from cooler regions like the Adelaide Hills and Tasmania.

New Zealand's Chardonnays vary from the light and lean to the rich and tropically fruity; Gisborne, Marlborough and Hawkes Bay are the main regions. In South America, Chile, in particular, has developed its own soft, fruity style, while Argentina's style is a little broader and fuller.

COTEAUX D'AIX and in Roussillon's BANYULS, as well as land in Australia. Despite fears that the Chapoutiers might be over-extending themselves, quality has remained high. Best years: (la Sizeranne) 2001, '00, '99, '98, '96, '95, '94, '91, '90, '89, '88.

CHASSAGNE-MONTRACHET AC

FRANCE, Burgundy, Côte de Beaune

♀ *Pinot Noir*

♀ *Chardonnay*

This is the least fashionable of the great Côte de Beaune white wine villages. One explanation might be that over half the production of this supposedly white wine commune was, until quite recently, red – although the whites are better. Another explanation is that Chassagne has no restaurant, no café – not even a bar. You have to walk across the dangerously busy Route Nationale 6 into PULIGNY-MONTRACHET to find somewhere to chew the cud.

Well, that can be turned to our advantage, because the general price level in Chassagne is lower than in Puligny or MEURSAULT and the quality of the whites right now is increasingly good. This is one of the larger communes of the CÔTE D'OR: there are 339ha (838 acres) of vines in this AC, situated between Puligny and SANTENAY at the southern end of the Côte de Beaune. The commune includes some of Burgundy's greatest white wine vineyards – 3.5ha (8.6 acres) of the great MONTRACHET Grand Cru as well as 5.85ha (14.5 acres) of BÂTARD-MONTRACHET and the entire 1.6ha (4.4 acres) of the smallest white Grand Cru – Criots-Bâtard-Montrachet.

Chassagne-Montrachet has around 160ha (400 acres) of Premier Cru vineyards, and 70 per cent of the Premier Cru production is white. The Premiers Crus are not well known, but can offer big, nutty, toasty white wines. Les Caillerets, les Ruchottes, la Romanée, Morgeot, les Vergers and les Embrazées can be exciting wines – especially if aged for four to eight years. Ordinary white Chassagne-Montrachet may lack the focused excitement of the Premiers Crus, but is usually a thoroughly enjoyable high-quality Burgundy. Best years: (whites) 2002, '01, '00, '99, '98, '97, '96, '95, '92. Best producers: (whites) F d'Allaines, G Amiot, Blain-Gagnard, M Colin, Colin-Deléger, Fontaine-Gagnard, Jean-Noël GAGNARD, V GIRARDIN, F & V Jouard, H Lamy, Duc de Magenta, B Morey, M Morey, M Niellon, RAMONET.

Red Chassagne is always a little earthy, peppery and plummy, and can be enjoyable,

Chateau St Jean is a famous Sonoma Valley winery with ornate architecture and beautiful gardens. Once known almost entirely for its rich Chardonnays, St Jean now produces delicious reds too.

though hardly a bargain. The top wines can age for over a decade. Look out for the following Premiers Crus: Clos de la Boudriotte, Clos St-Jean and Clos de la Chapelle. Best years: (reds) 2002, '99, '98, '97, '96, '95, '93. Best producers: (reds) G Amiot, CARILLON, R Clerget, V Girardin, B Morey, Ramonet.

CH. CHASSE-SPLEEN

FRANCE, Bordeaux, Haut-Médoc, Moulis AC, Cru Bourgeois

♀ *Cabernet Sauvignon, Merlot, Petit Verdot*

All owners of lesser BORDEAUX properties who gaze wistfully at the Classed Growths and sulk in silent envy at the prices they can charge should look at the example of Chasse-Spleen. I first came across the wine in the '80s and marvelled at its ripe dark fruit and soothing cocoon of new oak richness – a Classed Growth in all but name. And that was exactly the point. It tasted as good as the top Médoc.

CH. CHASSE-SPLEEN *This tremendously consistent wine from the Moulis AC is right at the top of Bordeaux's Cru Bourgeois hierarchy.*

So it cost more. And nobody complained. It still tastes ripe and satisfying, and still no one complains about the price. Best years: 2001, '00, '99, '96, '95, '94, '90, '89, '88, '86.

CHÂTEAU-CHALON AC

FRANCE, Jura

♀ *Savagnin*

This tiny AC, covering 50ha (124 acres) in the centre of the mountainous JURA vineyards, is for one of the most daunting wines yet invented. *Vin jaune* (or yellow wine) offers the same kind of experience as pot-holing, hang-gliding or taking a nap on a bed of nails – pleasurable only after the initial terror subsides. It's a fierce, farmyardy white, blending oily thickness with a raw volatile acidity and a strong whiff of damp straw. It can develop a raging, sour, woody brilliance that only the very best sherries ever get. Its nearest equivalent would be an old fino sherry – both wines grow a flor yeast on their surface as they age endlessly in barrel, which imparts this strange sweet/sour intensity. Vin jaune lies in barrel for six years; during this time the wine evaporates by perhaps one-third, but is protected from oxidation by the flor. The painfully concentrated liquid is put in dumpy 62-cl *clavelin* bottles, and you can age it for, well, certainly up to 100 years. Best producers: Baud, Berthet-Bondet, Bourdy, Chalandard, Credoz, Durand-Perron, J Macle, H Maire.

CHATEAU DES CHARMES

CANADA, Ontario, Niagara Peninsula VQA

🍷 *Cabernet Sauvignon, Cabernet Franc, Pinot Noir, Gamay, Merlot*

🥂 *Chardonnay, Riesling, Vidal, Sauvignon Blanc, Auxerrois, Viognier*

Chateau des Charmes' owner Paul Bosc is a pioneer of the new ONTARIO wine industry and the estate, with 110ha (272 acres) in four sites is now the largest on the NIAGARA PENINSULA. Paul Bosc, whose family hail from the French wine region of ALSACE, was the first person to plant a vineyard in Canada solely with *Vitis vinifera* at a time when opinion was divided as to whether the vines could survive the harsh Canadian winter, let alone ripen in the short summers. Well, he'd trained as a winemaker in BURGUNDY, and he rightly reckoned Canada could match Burgundian conditions for Pinot Noir and Chardonnay. His later pioneering of super-sweet Icewine created a Canadian classic in its own right.

CHÂTEAU-GRILLET AC

FRANCE, Northern Rhône

🥂 *Viognier*

This one estate of under 4ha (10 acres), although within the CONDRIEU AC, is renowned as having its own AC, one of the smallest in France. This rare dry RHÔNE white can be remarkable stuff – all apricots and slightly soured cream, spring blossom floating on the wind and honey tinged with tangerine spice. But for less than half the price you can buy a bottle of Condrieu – same grape, same taste and no uneasy feeling that perhaps you're being taken for a bit of a ride. However, there has been some improvement since the 1995 vintage. Best years: 2001, '00, '99, '98, '95.

CHATEAU INDAGE

INDIA, Maharashtra

🍷 *Cabernet Sauvignon, Baramati, Pinot Noir, Syrah (Shiraz), Grenache, Zinfandel and others*

🍷 *Baramati, Pinot Noir, Zinfandel*

🥂 *Chardonnay, Arkavati, Chenin Blanc, Ugni Blanc, Viognier, Sauvignon Blanc, Thompson Seedless and others*

Indian mega-millionaire Sham Chougule started producing India's first CHAMPAGNE-method sparkling wine back in the 1980s, with technical assistance from Champagne's PIPER-HEIDSIECK. Dry sparklers are firm, fresh and chunky – though quality is somewhat erratic. Traditional-method Omar Khayyám is produced from a blend of Chardonnay, Ugni Blanc, Pinot Noir and Pinot Meunier. A demi-sec and a remarkably good pink fizz are also produced, plus red and white table wines. Bangalore Purple, an indigenous grape variety of India, is used in a new red blend. Joint ventures with WENTE of CALIFORNIA, the French Taillan group and others will bring in new investment, and vineyard expansion to 1000ha (2470 acres).

CHATEAU KEFRAYA

LEBANON, Bekaa Valley

🍷 *Cabernet Sauvignon, Cinsaut, Syrah, Carignan, Mourvedre, Grenache, Alicante*

🍷 *Cinsaut*

🥂 *Ugni Blanc, Viognier, Bourboulenc, Sauvignon Blanc, Clairette, Chardonnay*

One of several well-established Lebanese wineries in the Bekaa Valley which are now enjoying the bonus of peace and radically improving their wines as their domestic and export marketplace opens up. The whites are now soft and fresh, but the estate is primarily a red wine producer, making nice light modern reds like Les Bretèches, and a powerful Cabernet-Syrah plum, mint and licorice blockbuster called Comte de M.

CHATEAU KSARA

This Bordeaux blend of Cabernet Sauvignon, Merlot and Petit Verdot aged in oak for 18 months is the top red wine from this important Lebanese winery.

CHATEAU KSARA

LEBANON, Bekaa Valley

🍷 *Cabernet Sauvignon, Merlot, Cabernet Franc, Syrah, Petit Verdot and others*

🍷 *Cinsaut, Carignan, Cabernet Franc, Syrah, Grenache*

🥂 *Chardonnay, Sauvignon Blanc, Semillon, Clairette, Muscat, Gewurztraminer*

Chateau Ksara was initially the property of Jesuit monks with deep cellars first dug by the Romans. The wines have greatly improved since peace came to Lebanon, with attractive modern whites and a mix of old and new style reds led by the ripe, soft Réserve de Couvent, spearminty Ksara Cabernet Sauvignon and deep, but attractively scented Chateau Ksara. Sweet Muscat/Gewurztraminer is attractive.

CHATEAU LUMIERE

JAPAN, Honshu, Yamanashi

🍷 *Cabernet Sauvignon, Cabernet Franc, Merlot*

🥂 *Koshu, Semillon, Sauvignon Blanc*

Japanese wine law is remarkably lax about allowing imported wines to be blended and then labelled as Japanese: however, Chateau Lumiere is a rarity in that its wine genuinely is Japanese. The family of Toshihiko Tsukamoto owns Chateau Lumiere, and the tasty reds come from vineyards planted with cuttings from Ch. MARGAUX in BORDEAUX, whilst a good, sweet 'Sauternes' style is made from Semillon and Sauvignon. The standard of both red and white wines is quite high. Drink these wines young.

CHATEAU MUSAR

LEBANON, Bekaa Valley

🍷 *Cabernet Sauvignon, Cinsaut, Carignan*

🍷 *Cinsaut*

🥂 *Chardonnay (Obaideh), Semillon (Merwah)*

This winery can provide more hair-raising tales than any other: Serge Hochar made wine right through the Lebanese civil war. His vineyards were on the front line in the Bekaa Valley and the winery was over the line at Ghazir, and in some years long detours had to be made between the two to avoid the front line; in 1984 they couldn't get there at all and in 1989 the winery was shelled. Yet, with the exception of 1984 and '76, wine has been made successfully every year.

In some years the red is something like an old fashioned ST-ÉMILION, in others a northern RHÔNE, but it is never quite like either: there is always something smoky and spicy and indefinably exotic about Musar. Hochar maintains it should not be drunk until it is 15 years old, and will last until it is 30; few Musar lovers have that much patience. Since it is released at more like five years old, opinions are always divided about how good Musar is, because few have tasted a mature example. A white, from Chardonnay and Semillon lookalikes Obaideh and Merwah, and a rosé are also made. Best years: (red) 1999, '97, '95, '94, '93, '91, '90, '89.

CHATEAU ST JEAN

USA, California, Sonoma County, Sonoma Valley AVA

🍷 *Cabernet Sauvignon, Merlot, Pinot Noir and others*

🥂 *Chardonnay, Pinot Blanc, Sauvignon Blanc, Gewurztraminer, Riesling*

From the very first time I tasted Chateau St Jean – it was a Chardonnay from the early '80s – these wines seem to have epitomized a certain Californian style: rich, unctuous, mouthfilling – and I have to say, satisfying. In those days, the winery was famous for numerous single-vineyard Chardonnays. Nowadays it only makes two – Robert Young and Belle Terre – but they are still rich, ripe and mouthfilling. More effort now goes into some good reds – Cabernet, Merlot and the Bordeaux Blend Cinq Cépages. Having prospered under Japanese ownership, it is now part of Beringer Blass. Best years: (Chardonnay) 2001, '00, '99, '98, '97, '96, '95, '94, '91, '90.

CHATEAU STE MICHELLE

USA, Washington State, Columbia Valley AVA
♟ *Merlot, Cabernet Sauvignon, Syrah*
♀ *Chardonnay, Riesling, Sauvignon Blanc, Semillon and others*

WASHINGTON STATE's largest and oldest winery has carried the name of the state further and wider than any other. All the wines are soundly made though, as with many large wineries, I'd like a little more personality in some of them. The most impressive carry reserve labels or individual vineyard names. Chardonnay, Merlot and Cabernet from Cold Creek and Canoe Ridge are particularly good. Washington's initial reputation was for whites and Chateau Ste Michelle has always produced good Semillons and Sauvignons as well as fine late-harvest Riesling. The Riesling connection has been strengthened by a joint venture with German Mosel star Ernst LOOSEN which has produced a lovely Eroica Riesling as well as a thrilling, supersweet Trockenbeerenauslese. A joint venture with Italian Piero ANTINORI has produced dense impressive red Col Solare. Best years: (premium reds) 2001, '00, '99, '98, '97, '96.

CHÂTEAUNEUF-DU-PAPE AC

FRANCE, Southern Rhône
♟ *Grenache, Syrah, Mourvèdre and others*
♀ *Grenache Blanc, Clairette, Bourboulenc and others*

Châteauneuf-du-Pape is a famous name, but how many of us have ever tried a good bottle? It isn't that the wine is scarce: this 3350-ha (8275-acre) vineyard area between Orange and Avignon produces about a million cases every year – 95 per cent of them red. It's just that Châteauneuf-du-Pape ('the pope's new castle') used to be one of the most abused of all wine names: low-priced bottles appeared on every wine list, tasting thick, muddy and coarse. But now much Châteauneuf comes from single estates – it's no longer cheap, and deservedly ranks as one of France's top wines.

Châteauneuf has very strict regulations – which is apt, because it was here, in 1923, that

CH. LA NERTHE
From one of the grand estates of Châteauneuf-du-Pape, Cuvée des Cadettes is a blend of mainly old Grenache and Mourvèdre, which spends a year in new oak.

Baron le Roy of Ch. Fortia formulated the rules which became the basis of all French AC laws. A total of 13 grape varieties are permitted for the red wine – eight red and five white – though most growers only use half-a-dozen or so. Five per cent of the crop must be left on the vine at harvest to reduce the use of poor grapes. And the minimum alcohol level is France's highest – 12.5 degrees.

There are two styles of red Châteauneuf: a light style which has a delicious dusty warmth, juicy spice and raspberry fruit; and a more traditional style, which may need aging for five years or more and can last for 20. It is fat, weighty and piled high with fruit – raspberry, blackcurrant, plums – plus a chocolate-coffee-cinnamon richness and the tang of southern herbs. Acidity is low, tannin usually overwhelmed by fruit and the whole effect is a richly satisfying red. It is always worth buying an estate wine – these are distinguished by a coat of arms embossed on the bottle above the label. Best years: (reds) 2001, '00, '99, '98, '97, '96, '95, '94, '90, '89, '88. Best producers: P Autard, L Barrot, BEAUCASTEL, Beaurenard, Bois de Boursan, H BONNEAU, Bosquet des Papes, du Caillou, les Cailloux, Chante Perdrix, CHAPOUTIER, de la Charbonnière, G Charvin, CLOS DU MONT-OLIVET, CLOS DES PAPES, Font du Loup, Font de Michelle, Fortia, la Gardine, Grand Tinel, la Janasse, Marcoux, Monpertuis, Mont-Redon, la Nerthe, Pégaü, RAYAS, la Roquette, Roger Sabon, Tardieu-Laurent, P Usseglio, la Vieille-Julienne, Vieux Donjon, VIEUX TÉLÉGRAPHE, Villeneuve.

The rare white Châteauneuf, when made with modern cool-fermentation methods, can be brilliant – licorice and peach fruit, freshened up with mountain herbs and the snappy acidity of lime. The wines are good between one and two years old, although the top wines will age for five years or more. Best producers: Beaucastel, Clos des Papes, Font de Michelle, Grand Veneur, Marcoux, Rayas, St-Cosme, Vieux Télégraphe.

DOMAINE JEAN-LOUIS CHAVE

FRANCE, Northern Rhône, Hermitage AC
♟ *Syrah*
♀ *Marsanne, Roussanne*

It's not easy to assume the mantle of a world-famous father, but Jean-Louis Chave has managed it. His father Gérard made some of France's greatest reds and whites from eight different parcels on the hill of HERMITAGE, and Jean-Louis has continued the brilliant succession of vintages. He vinifies all the parcels separately, rarely destems the reds, and ages them in old barrels of various sizes before blending and bottling. In an era when so many northern RHÔNE wines are wrapping themselves in sweet new oak as a way of trumpeting their quality, the tranquil beauty of Chave's wines is a beacon of naked brilliance.

The reds begin dark, brooding and dense, but their core of black fruit, bacon fat scent and the perfume of lily stems and pepper becomes more evident as the wines age. The whites, also aged in old barrels, are a little easier to approach young than they once were but still age to an incomparable flavour of dried peaches and lime, nuts and beeswax. In great vintages such as 1998, Chave produces a barrique-aged Hermitage called Cuvée Cathelin, and also a very rare, intensely sweet *vin de paille*. In complete contrast, Chave also produces a small quantity of ST-JOSEPH which is intended to be drunk young, and is in any case usually too delicious to keep. Best years: (reds) 2001, '00, '99, '98, '97, '96, '95, '94, '91, '90, '89, '88, '86, '85, '83, '82, '81; (whites) 2001, '00, '99, '98, '97, '96, '95, '94, '93, '92, '91, '90, '89, '88, '83.

CHÉNAS AC

FRANCE, Burgundy, Beaujolais, Beaujolais cru
♟ *Gamay*

Chénas is the smallest of the BEAUJOLAIS crus and its wines only rarely have the gorgeous juicy fruit of young Beaujolais, but can make up for this with a deep, gently Burgundian flavour when mature – with a lean, dry streak of earthy reserve. Best years: 2000, '99, '98. Best producers: J Benon, G Braillon, L Champagnon, DUBOEUF (Manoir des Journets), H Lapierre, B Santé.

CH. CHEVAL BLANC

FRANCE, Bordeaux, St-Émilion Grand Cru AC, Premier Grand Cru Classé
♟ *Cabernet Franc, Merlot, Malbec, Cabernet Sauvignon*

Along with AUSONE, Cheval Blanc is the leading property in ST-ÉMILION, and likely

CHENIN BLANC

Chenin Blanc is really too versatile for its own good; as a result we don't always know what to expect, which isn't helped by the tendency of producers in its native Loire to give no indication on the label as to whether the wine is dry or medium. It can also be sparkling or sweetly honeyed and concentrated by botrytis, though these wines' distinctive flavours of lime and pear and quince can come as a surprise to those reared on the more familiar flavours of Sémillon. At a decade or two old they are complex and fascinating, but until then they can seem closed and rather dull. Vouvray and Montlouis are the places to look for semi-sweet Chenin Blanc. For truly sweet styles, try Coteaux du Layon (including Quarts de Chaume and Bonnezeaux) and Coteaux de l'Aubance.

Chenin Blanc is more familiar in its dry or sparkling incarnations. In the Loire Valley the most acidic, least ripe grapes go into the fizz, and although some examples are full of apples flecked with honey, the unripeness of much of the fruit means too often it is green and raw.

During the 1990s there has been a revolution in quality in the still wines. First the sweet wines were improved by reducing the vineyard yields and picking selectively. More recently the spotlight in Anjou-Saumur has turned to dry Chenin, and a number of growers now make very good wines. Dry Chenin, particularly in hot years, can be difficult to make because as the grape ripens sugar levels rise very rapidly. Dry Vouvray and Jasnières

can be marvellously nutty – if you allow them the five or ten years they need to soften. The medium-sweet versions from Anjou and Vouvray are probably the most underrated of the lot; unfashionable because of their style, their balanced angelica and quince fruit makes them perfect apéritifs.

Apart from some in the Aude at Limoux and in the Bouches-du-Rhône at the huge Listel winery, you need to cross the Atlantic or the whole of Africa to find Chenin Blanc in any quantities elsewhere. Chenin Blanc is the most widely planted variety in South Africa. Called Steen prior to the country's re-admittance to international markets, it is now usually called by its French name. Its main drawcard has been versatility, making anything from sherry styles, through sparkling wines to fortified desserts, although to be honest, its suitability for distillation explains its vast acreage in the Cape. The botrytis-affected sweet wines are often among the best South African interpretations.

The same spectrum applies in California. The best-balanced dry wines can come from the North Coast, and a few producers in Sonoma concentrate on quality. Washington State has done remarkably well with off-dry wines from the Yakima Valley and the occasional ice wine. South America grows a fair amount but without distinction. Chenin Blanc grows very well in the Mendoza region of Argentina but is rarely made very proficiently. Much better are the rare but very attractive Chenins from New Zealand and the exciting quince and herb examples from Western Australia.

DOMAINE DE CHEVALIER
FRANCE, Bordeaux, Pessac-Léognan AC, Cru Classé de Graves
❧ Cabernet Sauvignon, Merlot, Cabernet Franc
♀ Sauvignon Blanc, Sémillon

Domaine de Chevalier white is frequently one of the best dry whites in BORDEAUX. The red faces stiffer competition, and is far less consistently outstanding. There used to be just a low white homestead here – no grand château – but the impressive new winery makes up for all that, and the first effect has been a tightening of quality in the reds which always start out rather dry and reserved, but over 10–20 years can gain that piercing, fragrant cedar, tobacco and blackcurrant flavour which leaves you breathless with pleasure. Best years: (reds) 2001, '00, '99, '98, '96, '95, '90, '89, '88.

Just 18,000 bottles a year of the white is made, as against 95,000 of the red. The wine is both fermented and aged in oak barrels. At first the Sauvignon greenness is very marked, but after three to four years this fades and an increasingly creamy, nutty warmth takes over, building at ten years old to a deep, honeyed, smoky richness, just touched with resin, that is rarely matched in Bordeaux. Second wine: (red and white) l'Esprit de Chevalier. Best years: (whites) 2001, '00, '99, '98, '97, '96, '95, '94, '90, '89, '88.

CHEVERNY AC
FRANCE, Loire, Touraine
❧♀ Gamay, Cabernet Franc, Cabernet Sauvignon, Pinot Noir and others
♀ Sauvignon Blanc, Romorantin, Chenin Blanc, Chardonnay

Cheverny is a little-known area south of Blois covering 472ha (1166 acres) of vineyards. Although Gamay, Cabernet Franc, Cabernet Sauvignon and Pinot Noir are the main red varieties, the wines never perform as well here as they do in warmer areas. They can smell rather good – sharp and distinct – but they usually taste rather raw and acid. The rosés are a slight improvement.

White Romorantin (with its own AC, Cour Cheverny) presumably survives simply because of local traditions – it can't be because of the flavour. But Cheverny can make very attractive, light, nutty Chardonnay, fresh Sauvignon-Chardonnay blends and the CHAMPAGNE-method fizz is sharp, clean and bracing. Best producers: Cazin, Cheverny co-operative, Courtioux, Gendrier, Gueritte, du Moulin, Salvard, Sauger, C Tessier/la Desoucherie, Tue-Boeuf.

to remain so for the foreseeable future. It is a large property, right on the border of POMEROL, at the end of a billowing row of gravel humps which run north from FIGEAC. Cheval Blanc derives much of its backbone, which allows it to mature for longer than most St-Émilions, from this gravelly land; but up by the Pomerol border there are rich veins of clay, mixed with sand and iron, which give the wine its phenomenal richness and sump-

tuous fruit. Strangely for St-Émilion, Merlot is the minor grape, only 41 per cent of the blend, with 57 per cent Cabernet Franc. You might expect the wine therefore to lack some of the luscious Merlot fruit, but on the contrary, it is one of the grandest, most voluptuous, perfumed St-Émilions, easy to appreciate in its infancy, yet famously able to mature. Best years: 2001, '00. '99, '98, '97, '96, '95, '94, '90, '89, '88, '86, '85, '83, '82.

ROBERT CHEVILLON

FRANCE, Burgundy, Côte de Nuits, Nuits-St-Georges AC

🍷 *Pinot Noir*
🍾 *Chardonnay*

All of Chevillon's 13ha (32 acres) of vines are in NUITS-ST-GEORGES, and his range of Premiers Crus – les Cailles, les Perrières, les St-Georges, les Roncières and Vaucrains – are exemplary expressions of these varied sites. Les St-Georges is often the best and most complex wine. Chevillon (now working with his sons Bertrand and Denis) only uses about one-third new oak, so that the difference between the crus is not obscured. The wines are marvellously consistent, and even in modest vintages can sing of their vineyard origins: muscular, vigorous, packed with ripened fruit just as good Nuits-St-Georges should be. A small quantity of white Nuits is also produced. Best years: 2000, '99, '98, '97, '96, '95, '93.

CHIANTI DOCG

ITALY, Tuscany

🍷 *Sangiovese and others*

Chianti is an enormous region, producing practically a million hectolitres of wine, covering much of central Tuscany, most of which is divided into eight sub-districts. If a wine doesn't come solely from a sub-district, or if its producer so opts, it will have no more glorious title than Chianti, plain and simple. The denomination is often seen on the own-label Chiantis that flourish as the basic wines of the major brands. The advantages are two-fold: first, producers can buy grapes from wherever in the region suits them for consistency of quality and style; second, even if the wine is from just one of the sub-districts, labels are kept simple. Most wine sold as plain Chianti is red-purple, youthful, tasting of tea and not-quite-ripe plums with a twist of bitterness on the after-taste. It can start tiring after as little as 18 months, though usually lasts a good bit longer. Sangiovese makes up from 75 to 100 per cent of the blend. Other grapes can include a small percentage of Cabernet, Merlot or Syrah, or native varieties such as Canaiolo or Colorino.

I'll deal with six of the eight sub-districts here with basic Chianti because, for one reason or another (often because Chianti is a second or even third wine in these zones after the likes of BRUNELLO DI MONTALCINO, VINO NOBILE DI MONTEPULCIANO or CARMIGNANO), the wines are generally unremarkable. Colli Aretini is scattered in various parcels between the east of CHIANTI CLASSICO

Aging top-quality red wines in barriques is an important part of the Tuscan wine scene today. This is Fattoria di Felsina, a leading Chianti Classico estate.

and Arezzo. Invigorating acidity is the wines' hallmark. Best producer: Villa Cilnia.

Colli Fiorentini is partly sandwiched between Florence and the northern limit of the Chianti Classico zone, which it also partly envelops. Light, young quaffers and more serious, aged wines are produced here. At its best it is indistinguishable from refined Classico, at its worst very easily distinguishable indeed. Best producers: Lucignano, Malanchini, Montellori, Castello di Poppiano, Pasolini dall'Onda Borghese, la Querce, di Sammontana, San Vito in Flor di Selva, dell'Ugo.

Colli Senesi is the largest sub-district, scattered extensively south of the Classico zone, and around Montalcino and Montepulciano. The distinguishing features of the wines are rich body and high alcohol and the most distinctive wines usually come from those producers who also make good Brunello or Vino Nobile. Best producers: Amorosa, Castello di Farnetella, Castello di Monteriggioni, Chigi Saracini, Pacina, Pietraserena.

Colline Pisane is in the west of the region, south of Pisa and behind Livorno. The text-books say its wines are light and soft but a new wave of producers, like Ghizzano at Paccioli and Sangervasio at Palaia, are turning out some terrific, vibrant, powerful wines.

The slopes of Montalbano, west of Florence, between Pistoia and Empoli, lie cheek by jowl with those of Carmignano and thanks to Carmignano's winemakers some pretty attractive, if light, easy-drinking wines are

produced. Best producer: Artimino Pierazzuoli. Finally, Montespertoli, the most recently recognized sub-district and the smallest, to the west of the Colli Fiorentini is showing signs of life. Best producer: Castello Sonnino.

CHIANTI CLASSICO DOCG

ITALY, Tuscany

🍷 *Sangiovese and others*

The CHIANTI hills, that central area between Florence and Siena that was first delimited in 1716 and whose territory was last defined, a little more extensively, in 1932, is where the now world-famous name originates. The original communes were Castellina, Gaiole and Radda, all in the province of Siena, to which have been added, over the centuries, parts of Castelnuovo Berardenga and Poggibonsi (Siena) plus the whole of Greve and parts of Barberino Val d'Elsa, San Casciano and Tavarnelle Val di Pesa (Florence).

Chianti Classico is the heart of Tuscan development, experiment and innovation. While the basic grape variety (at 80–100 per cent) remains Sangiovese, traditional blending varieties like Canaiolo, Malvasia Bianca and Trebbiano have given way to international ones like Cabernet Sauvignon and, increasingly, Merlot. SUPER-TUSCANS are rife in the region: practically every estate has at least one high-priced 'fashionable' cru, in the making of which barrique-aging features heavily. In the late 1980s the Consorzio Chianti Classico launched investigations into which clones, planting densities and training systems were suitable for high-quality production in the twenty-first century. These experiments are now bearing fruit, and the implication for many growers is wholesale replanting to improve their vineyards.

Top years like 2001, '00, '99, '98, '97, '95, '93, '90 and '88 bring forth superb Classico wines and brilliant Riservas usually best at 5–10 years. The so-called *normali* or straight wines should be drunk sooner. Each year brings out even more high-quality producers – price, for once, being generally a fair guide to quality. Best producers: Castello di AMA, ANTINORI, BADIA A COLTIBUONO, Brancaia, Casa Sola, Castello di Bossi, Castello di BROLIO/Ricasoli, Cacchiano, Capaccia, Carpineto, Casaloste, Castellare, Castell'in Villa, Cecchi (Villa Cerna), Collelungo, Colombaio di Cencio, Dievole, Casa Emma, FELSINA, Le Filigare, FONTERUTOLI, FONTODI, ISOLE E OLENA, Il Mandorlo, La Massa, Melini, Monsanto, Monte Bernardi, Il Palazzino, Paneretta, Panzanello, Poggerino,

Poggiopiano, Poggio al Sole (Casasilia), Querceto, QUERCIABELLA, Castello dei RAMPOLLA, Riecine, Rignana, Rocca di Castagnoli, RUFFINO, San Felice, San Giusto a Rentennano, San Polo in Rosso, Terrabianca, Vecchie Terre di Montefili, Verrazzano, Vignamaggio, VILLA CAFAGGIO, Castello di VOLPAIA.

CHIANTI RUFINA DOCG

ITALY, Tuscany

🍷 *Sangiovese and others*

Rufina (pronounced '*Roo-fi-na*' and not to be confused with the huge producer RUFFINO which has cellars at Pontassière in the Rufina zone) has sound claims to be considered second only in the CHIANTI stakes to CHIANTI CLASSICO It is the smallest Chianti sub-district and lies east of Florence, in the foothills of the Apennine mountains. The soils are like those of the central Classico zone but most vineyards are higher and the mesoclimate is cooler, giving higher tannin and acid levels. Hence the wines age better – vintages like 1977, '75, '68 (stupendous) can still provide memorable drinking. But don't worry, good wines have emerged from recent vintages too (2001, '00, '99, '98, '97, '95, '93, '90). Best producers: Basciano, Bossi, Colognole, FRESCOBALDI, Grignano, Lavacchio, SELVAPIANA, Castello del Trebbio.

FATTORIA SELVAPIANA
This estate has always produced excellent, refined wines typical of the Chianti Rufina zone, and is now ranked as one of the top Tuscan estates.

MICHELE CHIARLO

ITALY, Piedmont

🍷 *Nebbiolo, Barbera*

🍷 *Muscat (Moscato), Cortese*

From his winery base south of Asti, Michele Chiarlo produces stylish wines from several PIEDMONT zones with an approachability that is less than common in the region. Single-vineyard BAROLOS – Cerequio is a top southeast facing site between La Morra and and Barolo – and BARBARESCOS top the list, but BARBERA D'ASTI is also good and ripe and the Rovereto GAVI has more flavour than most. The Nivole MOSCATO D'ASTI is regularly one of the freshest, grapiest examples.

CHINON AC

FRANCE, Loire, Touraine

🍷 🍷 *Cabernet Franc, Cabernet Sauvignon*

🍷 *Chenin Blanc*

This is the best LOIRE red wine. The growers of BOURGUEIL, on the opposite, northern banks of the river Loire, might dispute that, but the wonderful thing about Chinon is that, unlike most Bourgueil, it is so good young, yet can improve like Bourgueil for five, ten, 15, even 20 years to a fragrant, ethereal shadow of the great châteaux of the MÉDOC, and as such is a rare and precious delight. The Cabernet Franc here achieves a pure, startling intensity of fruit – the piercing acid/sweetness of blackcurrant juice pressed straight from the bush, sweetened and perfumed with a few drops of juice from ripe raspberries and an earthiness like fields after summer rain. About 1 per cent of Chinon is white.

There are three types of soil that give three different wines. Sandy soils, especially close to the confluence of the Loire and Vienne rivers, give light wines ready to drink young; gravel soils, along by the Vienne, give wines with more structure but still ready to drink fairly young; and, finally, limestone makes the most structured and long-lived wines. Best years: 2002, '01, '00, '97, '96, '95, '90, '89. It's always worth buying a single-estate wine. Best producers: P Alliet, B Baudry, J & C Baudry, P Breton, D Chauveau, Coulaine, COULY-DUTHEIL, Delaunay, Druet, la Grille, C Joguet, Noblaie, la Perrière, J-M Raffault, Olga Raffault, Roncée, Sourdais.

CHIROUBLES AC

FRANCE, Burgundy, Beaujolais, Beaujolais cru

🍷 *Gamay*

This is the lightest, most delicately fragrant of the ten BEAUJOLAIS crus, and is often little more than deep pink in colour with a perfume full of strawberries and flowers and just a whisper of cherries. There are only two things wrong with Chiroubles: there isn't much of it and it costs too much. At 376ha (929 acres) it is one of the smallest crus. It's expensive because the Parisians go batty about it; restaurants queue up for it, and allow their customers to pay too much for what is often only a marginally superior BEAUJOLAIS-VILLAGES. But fashions for wines always change; Chiroubles lost its chic during the 1990s and has only now begun to recover its fans. Best years: 2002, '00. Best producers: Cheysson, Méziat/Dom. de la Combe au Loup, A Passot/Dom. de la Grosse Pierre, J Passot.

BODEGAS JULIÁN CHIVITE

SPAIN, Navarra, Navarra DO

🍷 *Tempranillo, Grenache Noir (Garnacha Tinta), Merlot, Cabernet Sauvignon*

🍷 *Grenache Noir (Garnacha Tinta)*

🍷 *Chardonnay, Moscatel de Grano Menudo (Muscat Blanc à Petits Grains)*

You couldn't get much more family-run than Bodegas Julián Chivite, NAVARRA's largest wine producer: all the children of the original Julián are actively involved. The bodega started out as a coaching inn on the main road through Cintruénigo. The Chivite family began to make their own wine to sell to thirsty clients, and gradually the wine edged out the innkeeping. Progress has been rapid since the late 1980s. The 125-ha (310-acre) Señorío de Arínzano vineyard was acquired in 1988 and the nearby Granja de Legardeta (160ha/395 acres) in 1999. Chivite bought Viña Salceda in RIOJA in '96 and established 60ha (148 acres) in RIBERA DEL DUERO in 2001. The basic Gran Feudo line of wines is gradually improving, and the Reserva reds are quite dense and powerful. Colección 125 is the top range with good, if slightly dry reds, and excellent barrel-fermented Chardonnay. There is also a genuinely rich late-harvested sweet wine. Best years: (reds) 2001, '00, '99, '98 '96, '95, '94; (whites) 2001, '00, '99, '98.

CHOREY-LÈS-BEAUNE AC

FRANCE, Burgundy, Côte de Beaune

🍷 *Pinot Noir*

This is one of those tiny, almost forgotten Burgundian villages we should be thankful for, because they mean that we can still experience the flavour of good, if not great, Burgundy, without having to take out a second mortgage. The wine should not by rights be very special, as the village, with its 168ha (415 acres) of vineyards, is almost entirely on the flat valley land, just north of BEAUNE and east of the main N74 road. The general rule in the CÔTE D'OR is that decent wine only grows west of the N74, but Chorey is lucky in having several very committed property owners based there, who, although they also own much more classic land elsewhere, use their considerable skills on their local wine. Without them, Chorey's wine would merely be sold as CÔTE DE BEAUNE-VILLAGES and never heard of again. The wines can age for five to eight years, being at their best soft with a wispy strawberry fragrance. Best years: 2002, '01, '99, '98, '97, '96. Best producers: Arnoux Père et Fils, DROUHIN, Germain Père et Fils, Maillard, TOLLOT-BEAUT.

JOH. JOS. CHRISTOFFEL

GERMANY, Mosel-Saar-Ruwer, Ürzig

♀ *Riesling*

He may seem very cautious and reserved, but when it comes to wine quality Hans-Leo Christoffel does not hesitate. At his tiny estate housed in a lovingly restored seventeenth-century, half-timbered house, he makes some of the finest wines from the vineyards of ÜRZIG and ERDEN. Christoffel is a master of the MOSEL winemakers' art of balancing natural sweetness and vibrant acidity, and the hallmark of his wines is a jewel-like brilliance. His Ürziger Würzgarten Rieslings are fuller and more aromatic; those from the Erdener Treppchen sleeker, taut and muscular. All the wines will age well for five years and more. Best years: 2002, '01, '99, '98, '97, '96, '95, '94, '93, '92, '90.

CHURCHILL

PORTUGAL, Douro, Port DOC

♥ *Tempranillo (Tinta Roriz), Touriga Franca, Touriga Nacional and others*

♀ *Malvasia Fina, Gouveio, Rabigato and others*

The Grahams are synonymous with PORT but when their family company fell on hard times in 1970 it was taken over by the Symingtons (who also own DOW and WARRE). In 1981 Johnny Graham re-established his own port house, using his wife's patriotic-sounding maiden name (the company's full title is Churchill Graham).

It was the first port business to start up from scratch in 50 years. Until recently the company owned no vineyards and sourced their wines from a number of A-grade vineyards in the heart of the DOURO but they have now purchased Quinta da Gricha and Quinta do Rio, to go along with Quinta da Agua Alta, which since 1983 has been released as a single-quinta vintage port and is one of the finest in its class.

The remainder of the wines, ranging from rich, complex crusting port and LBV to a

2000
QUINTA DA GRICHA
VINTAGE PORT

CHURCHILL

First made in 1999, Quinta da Gricha is Churchill's new single-quinta vintage port. and is more approachable and fruit driven than their Vintage Port blend.

stylish vintage, go simply by the name of Churchill. With Johnny Graham's experience in the trade, it goes without saying that all are skilfully made. The white port is good but wacky, aged in wood until it is golden and nutty in style. There is also a new red Douro table wine. Best years: (vintage ports) 2000, '97, '94, '91, '85.

CIRÒ DOC

ITALY, Calabria

♥ *Gaglioppo, Trebbiano Toscano, Greco Bianco*

♀ *Greco Bianco, Trebbiano Toscano*

CALABRIA's best-known wine, Cirò has been around since the time of Ancient Greece when it was known as Cremissa and, so the story goes, was the wine given to the original Olympic champions to toast their success.

Cirò Rosso is the standard bearer, and the best chance to appreciate Gaglioppo, Calabria's most important red grape. Red Cirò has potentially excellent structure, weight and concentration of fruit, plus touches of spice and chocolate, qualities best noted in the top cru of the leading producer LIBRANDI – although their IGT wine Gravello, a blend of Gaglioppo and Cabernet, is more exciting. The ripe rosé, too, has good fruit and balance, and the white can have a lively, almost citrus character. The reds can age well, Drink the whites and rosés young. Best producers: Caparra & Siciliani, Librandi, San Francesco. Best years: (reds) 2000, '99, '97, '96, '95, '93.

CH. CISSAC

FRANCE, Bordeaux, Haut-Médoc AC, Cru Bourgeois

♥ *Cabernet Sauvignon, Merlot, Petit Verdot*

Sometimes, tasting Cissac, you feel as if you are in a time warp. The tannin is uncompromising, the fruit dark and stubbornly withheld for many years, the flavour of wood more like the rough, resinous edge of hand-hewn pine than the soothing vanilla creaminess now fashionable. Well, it is something of an anachronism. Although not included in the 1855 BORDEAUX Classification, it nonetheless doggedly refuses to accept the situation, and makes high-quality wines for the long haul by proudly traditional methods: old vines, lots of wood everywhere and meticulous exclusion of below-par wine from the final blend. The wines are deeply coloured and slow to mature. Tentative introduction of steel vats and other newer technologies from the 2000 vintage may change things. Time – and plenty of it – will tell. Best years: 2000, '98, '97, '96, '95, '94, '90, '89, '88, '86, '85.

DOMAINE BRUNO CLAIR

FRANCE, Burgundy, Côte de Nuits, Marsannay AC

♥ ♀ *Pinot Noir*

♀ *Chardonnay*

Although based at the northern end of the Côte de Nuits in MARSANNAY, the domaine's 21ha (52 acres) of vineyards cover a wide range of appellations, including GEVREY-CHAMBERTIN and VOSNE-ROMANÉE in the Côte de Nuits, SAVIGNY in the Côte de Beaune and GIVRY in the CÔTE CHALONNAISE. Bruno Clair produces a large range of excellent wines, mainly red but there is a small amount of white (CORTON-CHARLEMAGNE) and a delicious Marsannay rosé. Top wines are CHAMBERTIN Clos-de-Bèze (two-thirds of the Clair holdings date from 1912), Gevrey-Chambertin Clos St-Jacques and vineyard-designated red Marsannay. Clair's winemaker, Philippe Brun, has a light hand with the oak, and even the weightier wines are never aged in more than 40 per cent new oak. Best years: (top reds) 2002, '01, '00, '99, '98, '96, '95, '93, '90.

CLAIRETTE

This rather low-acid white grape has done a fair amount of travelling from its base in southern France: it's found in Israel, South Africa, Zimbabwe and North Africa, in all of which it makes rather dull, flabby wine that needs careful handling and is best drunk extremely young. The wine for which it is most famous, the central RHÔNE's CLAIRETTE DE DIE, in fact gains most of its attraction from additions of Muscat. Clairette's more usual role in southern France is as a blending partner to Grenache Blanc, Ugni Blanc and Terret but Chateau SIMONE in the PALETTE is a fine example of a Clairette-dominated wine.

CLAIRETTE DE DIE AC

FRANCE, Central Rhône

♀ *Muscat Blanc à Petits Grains, Clairette*

Die is one of those relaxing lost areas of France on the road to nowhere. Clairette de Die can be one of the most deliciously enjoyable sparklers in the world. Made from at least 75 per cent Muscat grapes plus Clairette, it is a lovely off-dry, light wine with a creamy bubble and an orchard-fresh fragrance of ripe grapes and springtime flowers. The wine is made to sparkle by the *méthode Dioise*. This involves fermentation in bottle, but the process (unlike in CHAMPAGNE) is arrested before all the grape sugar has been used up, and the wine is then filtered and re-bottled under pressure. As a result, the wine retains the flavour of the grape sugars as well as that heavenly Muscat scent. Crémant de Die Brut from 100 per cent Clairette grapes and made by the Champagne method isn't nearly as good. Drink young. Best producers: Achard-Vincent, Clairette de Die co-operative, D Cornillon, J Faure, J-C Raspail.

AUGUSTE CLAPE

FRANCE, Northern Rhône, Cornas AC

🍷 *Syrah*

🍷 *Marsanne*

In an appellation where some growers are trying to move CORNAS away from its dense, beetle-browed, undrinkable when young stereotype, Auguste Clape remains staunchly traditionalist.

His dark wines can be very dense in their youth, but after a few years the full, complex, smoky succulence of the Syrah grape comes to the fore. Clape's wines even manage to succeed in tough years, though they will be initially coated in tannin. The grapes are not destemmed, and all parcels are vinified separately, so as to give as many blending components as possible. Using their vineyard resources, they are able to draw on vines planted immediately post-phylloxera in the 1890s. The wines are aged in large old casks before being bottled. There are also small quantities of ST-PÉRAY and an inexpensive pure Syrah CÔTES DU RHÔNE whose fruit is usually mostly from young Cornas vines. Best years: 2001, '00, '99, '98, '97, '96, '95, '94, '92, '91, '90, '89, '88, '86, '85.

LA CLAPE

FRANCE, Languedoc, Coteaux du Languedoc AC

🍷 *Syrah, Grenache, Mourvèdre and others*

🍷 *Bourboulenc, Clairette and others*

The mountain of La Clape rears unexpectedly from the flat coastal fields south-east of Narbonne and this should alert you to the fact that these wines are not going to be flat, dull old Mediterranean hooch. The Romans planted vines in Narbonne and would have liked the look of these mountain slopes with very high sunshine yet strong maritime influence. Modern La Clape wines are full of personality. Whites based on Bourboulenc are full, fresh and herb scented. Reds, with Syrah, Grenache and Mourvèdre to the fore, have a splendid dry depth and, again, unmistakeable scent of the herb-strewn hillside. Best producers: Ferri-Arnaud, l'Hospitalet, Mire l'Étang, Négly, Pech-Céleyran, Pech Redon, Vires. Best years: (reds) 2001, '00, '99, '98, '96, '95, '93, '91, '90.

WENDOUREE

This Clare Valley winery has a cult following for its limited output of massively extracted, ageworthy reds from tiny yields and old-fashioned winemaking.

CLARE VALLEY

AUSTRALIA, South Australia

I never know quite how Clare Valley gets its 'cool climate' tag. Adelaide is seriously hot. BAROSSA VALLEY, 80km (50 miles) north is a good deal hotter still – and then there's Clare Valley, 130km (80 miles) further north towards the broiling hot heart of the continent, the last splash of green you'll see before the furious red hot earths of the outback increasingly erase even the parched remains of pastureland from your view.

But Clare does manage to be cool – bits of it – partly because it's high in Australian terms (up to nearly 1640ft/500m in places) partly because it sucks up cool maritime breezes every afternoon, and partly because on the one hand limestone and on the other hand acidic slate soils can produce fresh tangy whites even when the weather is hot. Deep dark loam elsewhere in the valley can grow big beefy reds – even when the vineyards are virtually next door to each other. Clare Valley is a paradoxical but beautiful place, able to produce some of Australia's greatest dry Rieslings as well as fine Semillon, and exciting Shiraz, Cabernet, and even crunchy Grenache and Malbec. Best years: (Shiraz) 2001, '99, '98, '97, '96, '94, '93, '92, '91, '90, '88, '86; (Riesling) 2002, '01, '99, '98, '97, '96, '95, '94, '93, '92, '90. Best producers: Tim ADAMS, Jim BARRY, Wolf BLASS, Leo BURING, Crabtree, GROSSET, KNAPPSTEIN, LEASINGHAM, MITCHELL, Mount Horrocks, PETALUMA, Pikes, Sevenhill, Taylors/Wakefield, WENDOUREE.

CLARENDON HILLS

AUSTRALIA, South Australia, McLaren Vale

🍷 *Syrah (Shiraz), Grenache, Cabernet Sauvignon, Merlot*

These aren't wines that you can approach in a technocratic frame of mind. They're such riproaring bruisers – rather like the iconoclastic owner Roman Bratasiuk – that you have

to take them for what they are – intense, brooding, massive interpretations of superb old vines, especially Grenache and Shiraz (Astralis Shiraz is his larger than life flagship wine). He also makes Chardonnay, Pinot Noir and Merlot, but they get rather lost in the rush. Best years: (Astralis) 1998, '97, '96, '95, '94.

CH. CLARKE

FRANCE, Bordeaux, Haut-Médoc, Listrac-Médoc AC, Cru Bourgeois

🍷 *Cabernet Sauvignon, Merlot*

🍷 *Sauvignon Blanc, Sémillon, Muscadelle*

Thirty years ago Ch. Clarke was just a wistful Anglo-Saxon footnote in the more scholarly books on BORDEAUX, and the vineyard looked like a bomb site. Then in 1973 along came the late Baron Edmond de Rothschild. He spent millions on it, totally redoing the vineyards and their drainage, and building imposing new installations – with sparkling new masonry, gleaming steel and reassuring piles of new oak barrels but despite all the efforts the wine never managed to escape from the earthy dryness that typifies LISTRAC. Things looked up in 1998 when Michel Rolland became a consultant, and, obviously, we Clarkes have to stick together, so here's hoping. There's also a white, le Merle Blanc and a second wine, les Granges des Domaines Edmond de Rothschild. Best years: 2001, '00, '99, '98, '96, '95, '90, '89, '88.

DOMENICO CLERICO

ITALY, Piedmont, Barolo DOCG

🍷 *Dolcetto, Nebbiolo, Barbera, Cabernet Sauvignon*

Domenico Clerico was one of the leading modernists who transformed BAROLO production during the 1980s. He produces consistently superlative Barolos (Ciabot Mentin Ginestra, Pajana, Percristina) and one of the best Barberas (Trevigne), all maximising the marriage of fruit and oak yet keeping the appetizing PIEDMONT astringency. Perhaps his most famous wine is the mould-breaking Arte, a sumptuous oaky LANGHE, mostly Nebbiolo but with additions of Barbera and Cabernet. Best years: (Barolos) 2001, '00, '99, '98, '97, '96, '95, '93, '90, '89, '88.

CH. CLIMENS

FRANCE, Bordeaux, Barsac AC, Premier Cru Classé

🍷 *Sémillon*

This is BARSAC's leading property. The 29-ha (72-acre) vineyard lies on the highest ground in the AC to the south-west of the village of Barsac, its vines coming to rather an abrupt end when they meet the A62 autoroute that runs between Bordeaux and Toulouse. This height gives Climens a particularly well-drained vineyard and helps to account for its reputation as the most elegant and refined of all Barsac properties.

The wines are rich, luscious and exotic. They may not burst with the peach and pineapple fruit of some 'sweeties', but they make up for this with an exciting syrupy sweetness, a most appetizing, toasty, nutty, dry edge and a light, lemony acidity that keeps the wine fresh. They are easy to drink at five years old, but a good vintage will be much more succulent and fascinating after ten to 15 years. There's a lovely second wine called les Cyprès. Best years: 2002, '01, '00, '99, '98, '97, '96, '95, '90.

CLINE CELLARS

USA, California, Sonoma County, Carneros AVA
♥ *Zinfandel, Syrah, Mourvedre and others*
♟ *Mourvedre, Cinsaut*
♀ *Pinot Gris, Viognier, Marsanne*

One of California's original 'Rhône Rangers', Fred Cline began as a grower overseeing a 121-ha (300-acre) old vineyard in Contra Costa County which contained Zinfandel, Carignan, Alicante Bouschet, and especially Mourvedre. Thus, armed with one of the most prized RHÔNE red varieties, he led the charge with varietal Mourvedre particularly good under Ancient Vines and Small Berries labels – and also with blended wines under the Oakley label.

This early success enabled the Cline family to move to CARNEROS to build a winery and develop adjacent vineyards with Syrah, Viognier, Marsanne and Roussanne but they've still got the old vineyards. Various Zinfandels appear each year, with the annual favourites being old vineyards such as Fulton Road and Big Break, and a Reserve labelled Jacuzzi, honouring Cline's grandfather, the famous spa manufacturer.

CLOS DU BOIS

USA, California, Sonoma County, Alexander Valley AVA
♥ *Merlot, Cabernet Sauvignon, Pinot Noir and others*
♀ *Chardonnay, Sauvignon Blanc*

Founded in 1974 by Frank Woods (hence the quirkily translated name Clos du Bois) and now owned by Allied Lyons Inc, this large winery has made a speciality of Chardonnay, including several single-vineyard versions from the estate's best vineyards, all of which have a distinct note of French oak and are barrel-fermented. The Reserve Chardonnay is concentrated but not overdone.

Even so, I have to say I've generally enjoyed the red wines more. Marlstone is a full-flavoured BORDEAUX blend and Briarcrest a classy varietal Cabernet Sauvignon; both are single-vineyard wines and both have a leafy blackcurrant freshness to balance the full-on oak. The Reserve Series also covers Merlot, Shiraz and Tempranillo as well as RUSSIAN RIVER Pinot Noir and DRY CREEK Zinfandel. Best years: (top reds) 2001, '00, '99, '97, '96, '95, '94, 91, '90, '88, '87, '86.

CLOS CENTEILLES

FRANCE, Languedoc-Roussillon, Minervois AC
♥ *Mourvèdre, Picpoul Noir, Syrah, Cinsaut, Carignan, Grenache Noir, Pinot Noir*
♀ *Grenache Blanc*

Daniel Domergue and his wife Patricia Boyer produce a range of eclectic wines at their 13-ha (32-acre) domaine in the Cévennes foothills. Fervent believers in the regional grape varieties, they produce Carignanissime, a soft, spicy wine from 100 per cent Carignan, and Capitelle de Centeilles, a big, ripe, warm-hearted wine made from 100 per cent Cinsaut – the one true Languedoc grape according to Domergue, that can age five years or more. Other good wines include Campagne de Centeilles, another Cinsaut-dominated wine, this time with a splash of Syrah, Clos Centeilles, a classic Syrah-Mourvèdre-Grenache blend, and Guigniers, made, unusually for the Midi, from Pinot Noir. Best years: 2001, '00, '99, '98, '97, '96, '95, '94, '93.

CLOS CENTEILLES
Capitelle de Centeilles is made solely from Cinsaut, the grape responsible for many of Languedoc's great wines in the 18th and 19th centuries.

CLOS ERASMUS

SPAIN, Cataluña, Priorat DOCa
♥ *Grenache Noir (Garnacha Tinta), Cabernet Sauvignon, Syrah*

Daphne Glorian's tiny estate turns out one of the most profound and personal reds in PRIORAT. In her small winery (formerly Álvaro PALACIOS' facility) she also makes a convincing second wine called Laurel. Best years: 2000, '99, '98, '97, '96, '94.

CLOS MOGADOR

SPAIN, Cataluña, Priorat DOCa
♥ *Grenache Noir (Garnacha Tinta), Cabernet Sauvignon, Syrah, Carignan (Cariñena)*

René Barbier Ferrer is the bearded, genial vinegrower-turned-winemaker who led the rebirth of PRIORAT by attracting a bunch of young friends to the then-forgotten region in southern CATALUÑA in the 1980s. In 1997 he made a big decision and changed the name of his winery from René Barbier Fill (meaning son, in Catalan) to Clos Mogador, which had been the name of his wine. He hoped to end confusions with the René Barbier firm of PENEDÈS, now a mass-market brand of the giant FREIXENET group.

It was Léon Barbier who first bought land in Priorat, back in 1870, thus sowing the seeds of his great-grandson's rediscovery. Unlike his colleagues in the area, René and his family make a single wine from their 20ha (50 acres) of old-vine Grenache and younger French varieties on hilly schist soils. His style is one of great ripeness (almost overripeness) and extraction, and a marked *sauvage* character. They are regularly among Priorat's best. Best years: 2001, '00, '99, '98, '97, '96, '95, '94, '93, '92, '91, '90.

CLOS DU MONT-OLIVET

FRANCE, Southern Rhône, Châteauneuf-du-Pape AC
♥ *Grenache, Mourvèdre, Syrah and others*
♀ *Clairette, Bourboulenc, Roussanne, Grenache Blanc*

Mont-Olivet is a classic example of a highly traditional CHÂTEAUNEUF-DU-PAPE estate. The 25ha (62 acres) of vineyards are in various locations, and about 75 per cent of them are planted with Grenache, many of the vines being very old. The style of wine is strong, dark and rich, and in good vintages can age for a very long time.

The wines are aged in large old casks – no new wood here – and bottled without fining. There is also a wine made from 100-year-old vines called Cuvée Papet. Although the Châteauneuf from Mont-Olivet can be among the finest of the appellation, there is one drawback. The Sabon brothers, who own the estate, tend to bottle the wine on demand, so some wines, especially from lesser vintages for which demand is low, can be aged for up to six years in cask, which doesn't do them any favours. Although older vintages are always for sale, it is probably better for this reason to stick to more recent years. The white Châteauneuf here is of less interest than the red. Best years: (reds) 2001, '00, '99, '98, '96, '95, '94, '93, '90, '89, '88, '85.

DOMAINE DU CLOS NAUDIN

Depending on the vintage, Foreau produces a range of styles: Brut, as shown here, Sec, Demi-Sec and Moelleux, as well as Vouvray Mousseux and Pétillant.

DOMAINE DU CLOS NAUDIN

FRANCE, Loire Valley, Vouvray AC

♀ *Chenin Blanc*

Philippe Foreau is the third generation to run this famous estate of 12ha (30 acres) purchased by his grandfather in 1923, and, while it has always been an important VOUVRAY estate, Philippe has added star quality since taking over in 1983. He runs the vineyard organically, hardly uses any new oak, never uses malolactic fermentation and never chaptalizes (i.e. adding sugar to the wine during fermentation to increase the alcohol), so the medium-dry and sweet wines are only made in years when the grapes naturally reach a high degree of ripeness. The wines are supremely ageworthy, though in their relative youth the wines are rather softer in style than the more structured Vouvrays of HUET. Best years: (Moelleux Réserve) 1997, '96, '95, '90, '89, '88, '85, '83, '78, '76, '75, '70.

CLOS DES PAPES

FRANCE, Southern Rhône, Châteauneuf-du-Pape AC

♂ *Grenache, Mourvèdre, Syrah and others*

♀ *Clairette, Roussanne, Bourboulenc, Grenache Blanc, Picpoul*

The Avril family can trace their origins back over 250 years in the town where they still have their cellars, but there is nothing antiquarian about their winemaking. Paul Avril, now joined by his son Paul-Vincent, has achieved a fine balance between traditional styles and a careful re-evaluation of practices in vineyard and winery that will best express their terroir. Thus Clos des Papes now contains more Mourvèdre than before, and yields are firmly kept in check. The red wines have a kiss of new oak, more because of the need to replace aged casks from time to time than because the Avrils want oaky flavours in the wine. The wines are robust and age extremely well. The white is one of the appellation's best, and although it is usually drunk young to enjoy its lovely fruit to the full, it can also age beautifully. Best years: (reds) 2001, '00, '99, '98, '95, '94, '90, '89, '88, '83, '81.

CLOS DE LA ROCHE AC, CLOS DE TART AC, CLOS DES LAMBRAYS AC, CLOS ST-DENIS AC

FRANCE, Burgundy, Côte de Nuits, Grands Crus

♂ *Pinot Noir*

It is strange that the little-known village of MOREY-ST-DENIS has five Grands Crus (the four named here and a sliver of BONNES-MARES) when far better-known villages like NUITS-ST-GEORGES don't have any at all. Clos de la Roche is the best and biggest. The wine has a lovely, bright red-fruits flavour when young which, from a grower like DUJAC or Ponsot, may get chocolaty or gamy as it ages. Best years: 2001, '00, '99, '98, '97, '96, '95, '93, '90, '89, '88. Best producers: DROUHIN, Dujac, Léchenaut, Dom. LEROY, H Lignier, Perrot-Minot, Ponsot, Armand Rousseau.

Clos de Tart is unusual in that it is entirely owned by one firm – Mommessin, of BEAUJOLAIS fame. The wine, light and dry at first, can develop an unexpected but delicious savoury richness. Clos des Lambrays, also under single ownership, was made a Grand Cru only in 1981. It is owned by an ambitious German proprietor, Gunther Freund.

Clos St-Denis wines are full of red fruit browning gracefully with age – but are rarely seen. Best years: 2002, '01, '00, '99, '98, '97, '96, '95, '93, '90. Best producers: Bertagna, Charlopin, Dujac, Jadot, Ponsot.

DUJAC

Clos de la Roche is one of Dujac's outstanding wines and perfectly captures the charm and complexity of Burgundian Pinot Noir at its most elegant.

CLOS ROUGEARD

FRANCE, Loire, Anjou-Saumur, Saumur-Champigny AC

♂ *Cabernet Franc*

♀ *Chenin Blanc*

This tiny domaine has had an influence out of all proportion to its size of 10ha (25 acres). Once the Frères Foucault, Charly and Nady, were viewed locally as rather bizarre curiosities. Now that there is a growing interest in making serious red SAUMUR, the Foucaults are being treated with the respect that they fully deserve.

They have always aged their SAUMUR-CHAMPIGNY in young oak barrels – this is not

a question of fashion but rather one of tradition – growers during the 1930s always ordered a few new oak barrels every year. The Foucaults use a mixture of new and second-hand barrels, the second-hand ones coming only from top properties such as Ch. MARGAUX, PÉTRUS and Domaine de la ROMANÉE-CONTI. Yields are always low – never more than 40–45 hectolitres per hectare and often lower. This means that the wines have sufficient concentration to benefit from being matured in oak.

Le Bourg is the 'basic' red cuvée, while les Poyeux is from old vines. In good vintages the domaine makes a little sweet Coteaux de Saumur, which, like the red, is capable of aging for a very long time. The Saumur Blanc, from a small parcel of old Chenin vines, shows what an extraordinary potential dry Chenin Blanc can have when it is treated seriously. Best years: (reds) 1999, '98, '96, '95, '94, '93, '90, '89.

CLOS TRIGUEDINA

FRANCE, South-West, Cahors AC

♂ *Malbec (Auxerrois), Merlot, Tannat*

♀ *Chenin Blanc, Chardonnay, Viognier*

One of the best-known domaines in the CAHORS AC, Clos Triguedina is run by Jean-Luc Baldès, the eighth generation of the family. The wines at the 60-ha (148-acre) domaine continue to be powerful and ageworthy, dominated by the Auxerrois grape (aka Malbec). The prestige cuvée, Prince Probus, is produced from 100 per cent Auxerrois and aged mainly in new oak barriques. There is also a small amount of white VIN DE PAYS produced from a blend of Viognier and Chardonnay picked in the dawn chill and a sweet Chenin. Best years: (reds) 2000, '99, '98, '96, '95, '90.

CLOS UROULAT

FRANCE, South-West, Jurançon AC

♀ *Petit Manseng, Gros Manseng, Courbu*

Charles Hours has made this one of the best addresses in JURANÇON, both for dry and sweet wines. Unfortunately, quantities from the small 7.5-ha (18½-acre) domaine are limited to around 35,000 bottles a year and demand far outstrips supply. The dry Jurançon Sec Cuvée Marie is fermented and aged in oak barriques, providing a little more perfume, weight and structure to the fruit. The sweet wine, made from Petit Manseng, is rich but perfectly balanced with a deliciously long, lingering finish. Best years: 2001, '00. '99, '98, '96, '95, '93, '90, '89.

CLOS DU VAL

USA, California, Napa County, Napa Valley AVA
♥ *Cabernet Sauvignon, Merlot, Pinot Noir, Zinfandel*
♀ *Chardonnay, Semillon, Sauvignon Blanc*

When Bernard Portet, a Frenchman from the MÉDOC, came to the NAPA VALLEY in 1972, he wanted to make Cabernet Sauvignon that was different from the heartily ripe, wooded style then in vogue in CALIFORNIA. What he sought, he said, was wine that started out with the texture of rough velvet and the flavour of fruit, then matured with the feel of silk and a fine, floral perfume. Despite these excellent intentions, the wines could be bolder and the fruit more in evidence. Portet is now moving towards a softer, fruit-driven California style. The BORDEAUX influence often gives wines that never really lose their austerity. Best years: (Reserve Cabernet) 2001, '00, '99, '97, '96, '95 ,'94, '91, '90, '87, '86, '84.

His Merlot echoes the Cabernet but with a little more obvious fruit – not enough, but a little more. His Zinfandel is richer and weightier, though still polished smoother than seems necessary for such a gutsy grape variety. Sangiovese is a step away from the Bordeaux model but Semillon, made in some years, is certainly Bordeaux in style, though a little rounder and fatter, and less perfumed than the best modern examples. Semillon-Sauvignon blend Ariadne, however, is lovely and aromatic.

CLOS DE VOUGEOT AC

FRANCE, Burgundy, Côte de Nuits, Grand Cru
♥ *Pinot Noir*

Clos in Burgundy means a vineyard enclosed by a wall, hence Clos de Vougeot is the 'walled vineyard in the village of Vougeot'. Founded by Cistercian monks in the fourteenth century, it had reached 50ha (124 acres) by the time they put a wall round it with due proprietorial pride and for more than 600 years this original boundary has stayed intact.

But the French Revolution put paid to its single ownership. The vineyard was confiscated and sold, gradually becoming fragmented until it now has 82 separate owners. This multiplicity of ownership has turned it into one of the most unreliable Grands Crus in BURGUNDY. And there's another reason. The Clos runs from the top of the CÔTE D'OR slope, next to the Grands Crus of Grands-ÉCHÉZEAUX and MUSIGNY, right down to the flat, clay soil on the N74 road – only two cars' width away from dead-end land relegated to the basic appellation BOURGOGNE. Yet it is all Grand Cru. A good owner

should be able to make great wine on the upper slopes, but these heavy, muddy lower vineyards can never produce wine of the fragrance and beauty a Grand Cru label demands. Good ones are wonderfully soft, fleshy wine, the fruit like perfumed plums backed up by a smoky chocolate richness, turning dark and exotic with age. Best years: 2002, '01, '00, '99, '98, '97, '96, '95, '93, '91, '90, '88. Best producers: B Ambroise, Amiot-Servelle, Chopin-Groffier, J-J Confuron, R ENGEL, FAIVELEY, GRIVOT, Anne Gros, Haegelen-Jayer, JADOT, Dom. LEROY, MÉO-CAMUZET, D MORTET, Mugneret-Gibourg, J Raphet, Vougeraie.

CLOUDY BAY

NEW ZEALAND, South Island, Marlborough
♥ *Pinot Noir*
♀ *Sauvignon Blanc, Chardonnay and others*

No other wine in the world has come from non-existence to global fame in such a short time as Cloudy Bay. In 1985 there wasn't a Cloudy Bay winery – that wasn't ready until 1986 – and there wasn't a Cloudy Bay vineyard – that's been evolving ever since. The 1985 Sauvignon Blanc was made in a borrowed winery from someone else's grapes and yet it immediately blew away the palates of everyone who tasted it. It almost became world famous that very first year, and within a couple of vintages it had become the most renowned Sauvignon in the world – and one of the most renowned whites of any kind. Why? Because of its explosive, palate-challenging tangy green pepper, lime and passionfruit flavours. There had never been a wine like it made before, anywhere – so modern, so appetizing – and it made New Zealand famous, the MARLBOROUGH area famous, and Sauvignon Blanc sexy and chic for the first time. Best years: 2002, '01, '00, '97.

The winery is now owned by LVMH, the luxury brands group, and the Sauvignon has many rivals but Cloudy Bay hasn't stood still. It makes very good Chardonnay and Pinot Noir, an intense barrel-fermented Sauvignon called Te Koko, as well as haunting, broodily-scented Gewurztraminer and Pelorus – one of New Zealand's best sparkling wines.

JEAN-FRANÇOIS COCHE-DURY

FRANCE, Burgundy, Côte de Beaune, Meursault AC
♥ *Pinot Noir, Gamay*
♀ *Chardonnay, Aligoté*

The wines of Jean-François Coche-Dury have become legendary, in part because they are so difficult to obtain. For many this is the

JEAN-FRANÇOIS COCHE-DURY
Jean-François Coche-Dury is a superstar, quietly turning out some of the best wines from the Côte de Beaune. Even his village-level wines are outstanding.

quintessence of MEURSAULT, bold multi-faceted wines, subtly oaked and bottled without filtration. The estate is small, with 11ha (27 acres) of vines, so production of some of the most celebrated wines, such as the magnificent Meursault les Perrières and CORTON-CHARLEMAGNE, is minuscule. But the winemaking here is so good that even the village-level Meursault or the basic Bourgogne Blanc are outstanding glasses of wine. The less acclaimed, but still very good, red wines come from VOLNAY and MONTHÉLIE. Drink them younger than the whites. Best years: (whites) 2002, '01, '00, '99, '97, '96, '95, '92, '90, '89.

COCKBURN

PORTUGAL, Douro, Port DOC
♥ *Tempranillo (Tinta Roriz), Tinta Barroca, Tinto Cão, Touriga Nacional and others*
♀ *Gouveio, Viosinho, Rabigato, Malvasia Fina and others*

Cockburn, one of the best known of all PORT shippers, sells more port in the UK than any other company. Its fortunes are largely based on Special Reserve, a rich, approachable premium ruby. Cockburn has some of the most enviable quintas in the DOURO, among them the huge Vilariça vineyard way upstream in the Douro Superior and Quinta dos Canais which faces TAYLOR's Quinta de Vargellas and is the source of a fine single-quinta port. The fact that they have control of so much of their production makes Cockburn's Special Reserve such a consistent wine.

Cockburn's more up-market ports have a slightly more patchy reputation. Although the vintage ports tend to be dense and rich in style a number of Cockburn declarations in the 1980s were not up to scratch. The 10- and 20-year-old tawnies are top-notch and the Anno LBV is on the light side but soft and raisiny. Cockburn also produces an excellent red Douro wine known as Tuella. Best years: (vintage ports) 2000, '97, '94, '91, '70, '67, '63; (dos Canais) 2000, '99, '98, '95, '92.

CODORNÍU

SPAIN, Cataluña, Cava DO
♥ *Parellada, Pinot Noir*
♀ *Macabeo, Parellada, Xarel-lo, Chardonnay*

This family-owned PENEDÈS giant is the largest CHAMPAGNE-method sparkling wine company in the world, with over 3000ha (7413 acres) of vineyards. It occupies a spectacular estate in San Sadurní de Noya, 60km (37 miles) south-west of Barcelona, complete with nineteenth-century Art Nouveau buildings which are national monuments. In general Codorníu is one of the best large volume brands of CAVA on the market – Codorníu Brut is good and widely available, but the Chardonnay-based Anna di Codorníu fizz is even better – although less easy to find outside Spain. Jaume Codorníu is also good.

Codorníu also owns the improving Penedès still wine company of Masía Bach, the RAÏMAT estate in COSTERS DEL SEGRE, Rondel, another huge Cava company, Bodegas Bilbaínas in RIOJA, as well as wineries in ARAGÓN (Nuviana), RIBERA DEL DUERO (Legaris) and Argentina (Septima). It has also purchased a 25 per cent stake in the PRIORAT property Scala Dei.

COLARES DOC

PORTUGAL, Estremadura
♥ *Ramisco*
♀ *Malvasia and others*

The tiny coastal wine enclave of Colares, north-west of Lisbon, produces one of Portugal's most historic wines. The vineyards are planted on a sandy cliff-top plateau among windswept pine groves, thickets of bamboo and scattered holiday villas. The sand, a metre or more in depth, helped to protect the roots of the vines against phylloxera in the nineteenth century and the vineyards that have survived the commercial pressures of the twentieth century are still ungrafted. Sadly, less than 50ha (124 acres) of vineyards remain. A clear distinction is therefore made between the wines from the Chão de Areia (sandy soil) and those from the Chão Rijo (hard ground).

The reputation of Colares has suffered due to some heavy-handed winemaking by the local co-operative, which held a monopoly of the region's wine production until the early 1990s. Red wines tended to be hard and astringent and whites were made in an old-fashioned oxidative manner. A number of private producers have tried to rescue Colares in recent years but so far no-one has arrested the region's decline. Judging by some of the

PAULO DA SILVA
Almost black in colour, this Colares wine starts out exceedingly tannic but is said to soften with age. Drink with at least ten years' aging..

ethereal old wines from the 1940s and '50s, Colares is clearly a region worth saving. Best producer: Paolo da Silva/Chitas.

COLCHAGUA VALLEY

CHILE, Rapel Valley

I've never completely worked out why this important vineyard area is called Colchagua Valley, because the river which has carved the valley westwards from San Fernando, close to the Andes, and away towards the Pacific Ocean is called the Tinguiririca. Hm, I see their point: Colchagua it is, and we're going to be hearing a lot more of it in the next few years.

In a country like Chile which has traditionally planted vines on the fertile valley floor, Colchagua has determinedly clambered up the untried mountain slopes to the north and south of the valley, in particular at Apalta, Ninquen and Peralillo. There are still perfectly good valley floor vines in Colchagua but this move to the hills is overdue for Chile and has brought a rapidly swelling stream of dark, intense reds using Cabernet, Syrah and Carmenere, quite unlike even the powerful reds of MAIPO. They are certain to age, and they need to age. Equally certainly they mark a significant step ahead for Chilean red quality. There are also cooler sites round San Fernando to the east, and new, warm-climate vineyards to the north-west of Peralillo at Marchihue. Best producers: CASA LAPOSTOLLE, Casa Silva, CONO SUR, MONTES, MONTGRAS, Viu Manent.

COLDSTREAM HILLS

AUSTRALIA, Victoria, Yarra Valley
♥ *Pinot Noir, Cabernet Sauvignon, Merlot, Cabernet Franc, Syrah (Shiraz)*
♀ *Chardonnay, Pinot Gris, Sauvignon Blanc*

Famous Australian wine writer James Halliday founded Coldstream Hills in 1985. In 1996 it was acquired by Southcorp, but Halliday's philosophy of understated, genuinely cool-climate flavours still holds sway. The

most famous wine is the Pinot Noir which almost obsessively avoids any hint of over-ripeness, followed by a cool, restrained but attractive Chardonnay. Reserve versions are significantly fuller-bodied Cabernet, Merlot and Shiraz all proudly show their cool-climate credentials. Best years: 2001, '00, '99, '98, '97, '96, '94.

COLLI BOLOGNESI DOC

ITALY, Emilia-Romagna
♥ *Barbera, Cabernet Sauvignon, Merlot*
♀ *Pignoletto, Pinot Blanc (Pinot Bianco), Chardonnay, Welschriesling (Riesling Italico), Sauvignon Blanc*

Most of the landscape of EMILIA-ROMAGNA is flat as a pancake, so the odd outcrops of hills bring great relief. The Colli Bolognesi are only 100m (330ft) high but the slopes are suitably angled for growing vines. The first estate to aim for quality was Enrico Vallania's Terre Rosse in the 1960s, introducing grapes such as Cabernet Sauvignon, Chardonnay and Pinot Blanc (Pinot Bianco). Tenuta Bonzara now leads the quality-minded producers, including Santarosa and Vallona.

COLLI ORIENTALI DEL FRIULI DOC

ITALY, Friuli-Venezia Giulia
♥ ♀ *Cabernet Franc, Cabernet Sauvignon, Merlot, Pignolo, Pinot Noir (Pinot Nero), Refosco, Schioppettino, Tazzelenghe*
♀ *Chardonnay, Malvasia Istriana, Picolit, Pinot Blanc (Pinot Bianco), Pinot Gris (Pinot Grigio), Ribolla, Riesling (Riesling Renano), Sauvignon Blanc, Tocai Friulano, Gewürztraminer (Traminer Aromatico), Verduzzo*

Viticulturally, the southern part of Colli Orientali or the 'Eastern Hills' is practically identical to the adjacent zone of COLLIO; only towards the north does quality tail off a little. Even so, only wine from vineyards on hilly terrain is permitted the Colli Orientali denomination. Colli Orientali's aromatic, restrained, elegantly youthful, single-varietal whites are its forte, especially Pinot Bianco, Pinot Grigio, lemony native Ribolla, Tocai Friulano and perfumed Sauvignon and Riesling, all made with balance, rather than power, in mind. The reds, with the brambly Schioppettino leading the way for native varieties and Cabernet Franc for the internationals, are improving dramatically, often offering a spicy, herbaceous tang, and good potential for aging. Best years: 2001, '00, '99, '98, '97.

The sweet wines are exciting, most notably from Verduzzo in its sub-zone, Ramandolo, and delicate Picolit making subtle, floral, honeyed wines. And since the vine suffers from a distressing-sounding affliction, floral abortion, which prevents it flowering properly, production is tiny. Best producers: Ca' Ronesca, Dario Coos, Dorigo, Dri, Le Due Terre, Livio FELLUGA, Walter Filiputti, Adriano Gigante, Livon, Meroi, Miani, Davide Moschioni, Rocca Bernarda, Rodaro, Ronchi di Cialla, Ronchi di Manzano, Ronco del Gnemiz, Scubla, Specogna, Le Vigne di Zamò, Zof.

COLLI PIACENTINI DOC

ITALY, Emilia-Romagna

♥ *Barbera, Bonarda, Cabernet Sauvignon, Pinot Noir (Pinot Nero) and others*

♀ *Malvasia, Ortrugo, Chardonnay, Pinot Gris (Pinot Grigio), Sauvignon Blanc and others*

A quirk of the regional arrangement means the boundary between EMILIA and LOMBARDY comes plumb through a prime viticultural area. The result is one district with two names: Colli Piacentini (Emilia) and OLTREPÒ PAVESE (Lombardy). Miles away (literally as well as figuratively) from the typically Emilian Lambrusco, Colli Piacentini is an umbrella DOC, covering various sub-denominations and varietal wines, sometimes a touch *frizzante*. The jewel is Gutturnio, a brilliant, raspberry, truffly, mocha blend of Bonarda with Barbera, and Ortrugo is the local oddity, a bitter-finishing white. Best producers: Luretta, Lusenti, Castello di Luzzano/Fugazza, Il Poggiarello, La Stoppa, Torre Fornello, La Tosa.

COLLIO/COLLIO GORIZIANO DOC

ITALY, Friuli-Venezia Giulia

♥ *Cabernet Franc, Cabernet Sauvignon, Merlot, Pinot Noir (Pinot Nero)*

♀ *Ribolla, Malvasia Istriana, Tocai Friulano, Chardonnay, Pinot Blanc (Pinot Bianco), Pinot Gris (Pinot Grigio), Welschriesling (Riesling Italico), Sauvignon Blanc, Riesling (Riesling Renano), Gewürztraminer (Traminer Aromatico)*

The COLLIO zone is an arc of hills squeezed up along the Slovenian border. The nearby Adriatic has a beneficial effect on the climate, keeping the area warm but well ventilated, bringing forward the growing season. Collio Goriziano (so-called after the nearby city of Gorizia) has been hailed as the cradle of the Italian white wine revolution, and while there is an element of overstatement in this, there is also an element of truth. It is certainly true that, from the 1960s and '70s on, producers like SCHIOPETTO, Vittorio Puiatti, Livio FELLUGA and Silvio JERMANN have been turning out finely crafted whites from the wealth of

The medieval town of Castell'Arquato is in the Colli Piacentini DOC, a hilly area of Emilia in the Apennine foothills and more or less an extension of Lombardy's Oltrepò Pavese DOC. The wines are also very similar.

varieties available in the zone – whites of grace and subtlety rather than of power, concentrating on pure varietal aromas in the early days, at least, rather than on those of oak. No Italian zone had ever previously managed fine white wine on such a scale.

It is also true, however, that this district, which owes as much to Austrian, French and Slavic influences as it does to Italian ones, has a strong international feel about it, and could hardly be said to be 'typical' of Italy as could, for example, the Castelli di Iesi zone in the MARCHE which today is challenging Collio for the mantle of top white wine zone in the land. Collio's answer has been to diversify. In the white department, while still turning out pristine varietals, producers are turning to ingenious blends – mixes of varieties from BORDEAUX (Sauvignon), Burgundy (Pinot Blanc or Chardonnay) and, say, ALSACE (Gewurztraminer) such as no-one in France, or anywhere else for that matter, would contemplate.

The other area of expansion in Collio of late has been into red wines. Cabernet and Merlot have been produced here for well over a century, but it is only in the last few years that Collio has been able to put flesh on the bones of its traditionally rather meagre, metallic reds while retaining the hallmark of cool understatement and restraint which the more flamboyant Tuscan reds, for example, cannot boast. Best years: 2002, '01, '00, '99, '98, '97, '96, '95. Serious producers, apart from the above-mentioned, include Borgo Conventi, BORGO DEL TIGLIO, La Castellada, Damijan, Marco Felluga, Fiegl, GRAVNER, Edi Keber, Renato Keber, Livon, Matijaz Tercic, Primosic, Princic, RUSSIZ SUPERIORE, Venica & Venica, Villa Russiz, Villanova.

COLLIOURE AC

FRANCE, Languedoc-Roussillon

♥♀ *Grenache, Syrah, Mourvèdre and others*

♀ *Grenache Blanc and others*

This tiny and beautiful coastal AC named after its local fishing port is tucked away in the Pyrenean foothills on the border between France and Spain. The wine, mainly red, is throat-warming, head-spinning stuff but not much seen elsewhere. It's capable of aging for a decade but is marvellously aggressive when young. From the 2003 vintage white will also be allowed under the AC, mainly from Grenache Blanc. Best producers: Baillaury, Casa Blanca, CELLIER DES TEMPLIERS, les Clos de Paulilles, MAS BLANC, la RECTORIE, la Tour Vieille. Best years: 2001, '00, '99, '98, '96, '95, '94, '93.

JEAN-LUC COLOMBO

FRANCE, Northern Rhône, Cornas AC

♥ *Syrah*

Until the late 1980s the northern RHÔNE was a deeply conservative place and when it came to growing grapes and making wine little seemed to have altered since the nineteenth century. Then along came Jean-Luc Colombo and changed all that. Colombo was an enologist, and thoroughly acquainted with the whole world of wine. CORNAS, in his view, was producing backward wines that had a small band of ardent followers but no wider recognition. Colombo simply applied his knowledge and skill to the local vineyards, persuading some of the growers for whom he acted as a consultant to destem their grapes and to age them in barriques, even in a proportion of new oak. Soon he purchased some vineyards of his own, which he farms organically, and began turning out a string of wines that may sometimes have lacked what most people think of as Cornas typicity, but which were extremely good in their own right.

His best wine is called les Ruchets (from 90-year-old vines and aged in 70 per cent new oak), and there are other bottlings named Terres Brûlées and la Louvée (70-year-old vines, aged in 100 per cent new oak). In the early 1990s Colombo put a few noses out of joint by charging considerably more for his wines than the other growers in Cornas, but it certainly helped this sleepy appellation to gain the attention it needed.

His activities have now spread well beyond Cornas. He makes one of the best whites – la Belle de Mai – in neighbouring ST-PÉRAY, as well as becoming increasingly involved in properties in PROVENCE, LANGUEDOC and Roussillon. Colombo also runs a *négociant* business – his whites from the southern Rhône can be delicious. Best years: (Cornas) 2001, '00, '99, '98, '97, '95, '94, '91, '90.

COLUMBIA CREST

USA, Washington State, Paterson

♥ Merlot, Cabernet Sauvignon, Syrah
♀ Chardonnay and others

Columbia Crest started life as a second label for CHATEAU STE MICHELLE but it very quickly established a personality of its own, in particular, almost from the start producing extremely good value. soft, ripe wines from Merlot and Cabernet when most wines were still struggling with the tough tannins many WASHINGTON grapes possess. The winery still does these varieties well, but also makes a good job of Syrah, Chardonnay, Riesling, Semillon and Gewurztraminer – the whites harking back to when Washington was thought of as primarily a white wine producer. Grand Estates Merlot, Cabernet, Syrah and Chardonnay are sourced from top vineyards in YAKIMA VALLEY, Wahluke Slope and

Horse Heaven Hills. There is also top sweet Semillon Icewine. Best years: (Grand Estates reds) 2001, '00, '99, '98.

COLUMBIA VALLEY AVA

USA, Washington State and Oregon

I know Columbia Valley is an AVA – an American Viticultural Area – but that's far too dry and bureaucratic a description for this vast and daunting region of WASHINGTON STATE east of the Cascades Mountains that covers 60,000 square kilometres – that's one third of the state's landmass – although only 16,600ha (41,019 acres) are actually planted with vines. The Columbia is America's second biggest river as far as volume of water goes and it has gouged out a vast bowl of valley land from the Cascade Range over the millennia, trying to reach the Pacific, and finally forcing a gap in the mountains near Richland. And its waters have transformed what would otherwise be desert into a fertile irrigated farmland, with most of the vineyards situated near the Columbia itself, and also in WALLA WALLA and the YAKIMA VALLEY.

The AVA covers all these regions east of the Cascades, as well as some in Oregon, an additional 481ha (1189 acres) on the south side of the river, though many wineries prefer to use more specific AVAs like Walla Walla. It produces 98 per cent of Washington's wine grapes: Cabernet Sauvignon is the most widely planted variety, with Merlot and Chardonnay close behind. Best years: (reds) 2001, '00, '99, '98, '97. Best producers: ANDREW WILL, Cadence, CHATEAU STE MICHELLE, COLUMBIA CREST, Matthews Cellars, QUILCEDA CREEK.

COMMANDARIA

CYPRUS, Troodos Mountains

♥ Mavro
♀ Xynisteri

This intensely sweet dessert wine never seems to be as good as its hype says it is. It comes from specified villages on the lower slopes of the Troodos mountains and is made by sun-drying the grapes on mats for about ten days, before fermentation. No fortifying alcohol is added. The best wines are made from Xynisteri only and aged in a solera system.

VIN DE PAYS DU COMTÉ TOLOSAN

FRANCE, South-West

One of France's four regional VINS DE PAYS, the Comté Tolosan covers the South-West of France, from south of BORDEAUX right down

to the Pyrenees and east into the Aveyron and Tarn *départements*. The wide range of varietal wines covers international varieties such as Chardonnay, Cabernet Sauvignon, Merlot and Sauvignon Blanc as well as blends with local varieties like Colombard, Duras, Tannat and Fer Servadou. Best producers: Cave de Crouseilles, Labastide-de-Lévis co-operative, Producteurs PLAIMONT, de Ribonnet.

CONCA DE BARBERÁ DO

SPAIN, Cataluña

♥♀ Grenache Noir (Garnacha Tinta), Trepat, Tempranillo (Ull de Llebre), Cabernet Sauvignon, Merlot
♀ Macabeo, Parellada

This small, promising DO, created only in 1989, is the highest region in CATALUÑA, therefore cooler, and capable in theory of making really fresh, aromatic wines. This is one of the CAVA DO regions, but little fizzy wine is actually made here, though as much as 80 per cent of Conca de Barberá's grapes, juice and wine is sold to the Cava firms of PENEDÈS. White grapes now account for nearly three-quarters of production and the white wines can be fresh, fruity and lemony. Concavins and the small Sanstravé winery have demonstrated the exciting potential of the region's reds. Stars of the region are the TORRES estates of Milmanda and and Grans Muralles and their impressive Chardonnay and Cabernet Sauvignon wines, respectively.

CONCHA Y TORO

CHILE, Maipo Valley

♥ Cabernet Sauvignon, Merlot, Carmenere, Syrah, Alicante Bouschet, Pinot Noir and others
♀ Chardonnay, Sauvignon Blanc and others

Concha y Toro is Chile's biggest wine producer and an increasingly impressive performer. The reds have been good for as long as I can remember, and their gentle blackcurranty flavours were some of the first I tasted from Chile. But all the wines are now greatly improved. The reds still have good fruit but are by no means merely mild mouthfuls, and the bright, fresh whites are attractively modern and refreshing. There are various quality levels, each one fairly reflecting its price. Casillero del Diablo and Marqués de Casa Concha are not expensive but very good. Amelia and Terrunyo whites and reds are first class, only outperformed by the mighty Don Melchor Cabernet and the beautiful Almaviva red, a joint venture with Bordeaux's Ch. MOUTON-ROTHSCHILD. Also involved in the Trivento project in Argentina.

CONDRIEU AC

FRANCE, Northern Rhône

♀ *Viognier*

The ugly modern village of Condrieu is the unlikely birthplace of one of the world's great white wines. To the west of Condrieu, stark, forbidding cliffs rear towards the clouds; and you can see rows of ancient vineyard terraces by no means all of them sprouting vines. Only 102ha (252 acres) of vineyards are planted – and not all clinging to the daunting rockface. In recent years, because of the great demand for this wonderful, fragrant wine, there have been new plantings on the plateau behind, which will increase, though certainly not improve, production. But we should be grateful that Condrieu has been rescued from near extinction. In 1971 a trifling 12ha (30 acres) were being cultivated.

But what a wine those original straggly patches of struggling vines produce. The Viognier is a disease-prone, shy-yielding vine found only here, at neighbouring CHÂTEAU-GRILLET, at CÔTE-RÔTIE (where it can be mixed with the red Syrah), and, in increasing amounts, in the southern RHÔNE and LANGUEDOC and the New World. A pathetic yield – rarely more than 20 hectolitres per hectare – and a propensity to rot and floral abortion (when no grapes develop from the flowers) are the reasons for this scarcity: an entire vintage has been known to produce only 19 hectolitres.

But the flavour... A fragrance of ripe apricots and juicy Williams pears, freshened by spicy flower perfumes. Yet the wine is dry. Full in your mouth, yes, almost thick and viscous – juicy apricot skins and ripe golden peaches, coated with a richness like double cream about to turn sour. These remarkable wines fade with age, and are horrifyingly expensive – but at one to three years old they are a sensation everyone should try. Best producers: G Barge, L Betton, P & C Bonnefond, du Chêne, L Chèze,

COLOMBO, CUILLERON, DELAS, P Dumazet, C Facchin, Y Gangloff, GUIGAL, Monteillet, R Niero, A Paret, A Perret, C Pichon, ROSTAING, St-Cosme, G VERNAY, F Villard.

CONO SUR

CHILE, Rapel Valley

♀ *Merlot, Cabernet Sauvignon, Pinot Noir, Syrah, Carmenere*

♀ *Chardonnay, Viognier, Gewurztraminer, Riesling, Sauvignon Blanc*

A subsidiary of CONCHA Y TORO but not in any way overshadowed. Based in Chimbarongo, near San Fernando, Cono Sur's initial fame came through Pinot Noir and recent releases using CASABLANCA fruit under the 20 Barrels label have taken it to new heights. Casablanca fruit is also becoming more important in whites with Sauvignon, Chardonnay, Viognier and Gewurztraminer beginning to shine. Cabernet and Merlot under 20 Barrels and Visíon labels are also excellent. Isla Negra offers leaner 'more European' flavours.

CH. LA CONSEILLANTE

FRANCE, Bordeaux, Pomerol AC

♀ *Merlot, Cabernet Franc*

This 12-ha (30-acre) property has some of the best land in POMEROL but has never consistently managed to reach the heights attained by its neighbours and appellation leaders Ch. PÉTRUS and CHEVAL BLANC. Nonetheless, this is sumptuous, exotic, velvety wine that blossoms beautifully after five to six years but can age much longer. As with many of these fleshy Pomerols, its popularity has rocketed in recent years and scarcity has meant the price has rocketed too. Best years: 2001, '00, '99, '98, '96, '95, '94, '90, '89, '88, '86, '85.

CONSTANTIA WO

SOUTH AFRICA, Western Cape

Constantia is the historic heart of the country's wine industry. It certainly was back in the eighteenth century, when Constantia dessert wine was famous throughout Europe and was more highly thought of than any European sweet wine except Hungarian Tokaji. Napoleon even demanded it during his exile in St Helena. The KLEIN CONSTANTIA Estate has made a commendable effort to revive this tradition by planting Muscat Blanc à Petits Grains grapes and making a high-strength, sweet Vin de Constance, but I feel they still have a long way to go before they emulate the original dessert wine.

Today, Constantia is recognized for modern, New World styles. Sauvignon Blanc has

proved particularly successful on the properties which line the slopes running down the spine of the Cape peninsula. In the main, these face south-east, so benefit from the full effect of the breezes blowing off False Bay. The soils are deep and well-drained. Virtually the only downsides are susceptibility to botrytis and, in the case of the BUITEN-VERWACHTING, Groot and Klein Constantia estates, the early disappearance of the sun behind Table Mountain making reds tricky to ripen; that, and baboons which come down the mountain and eat the grapes.

These three farms cover most of the land originally granted to Simon van der Stel in 1685 and which was divided into three on his death. A little apart, to the south, historic STEENBERG (another of the original farms) and Uitsig have lighter soils and longer sunlight. As well as elegantly intense Sauvignon Blanc and, interestingly, Semillon among the white wines, wonderfully minty expressions of Merlot, in particular from Steenberg, are showing some exciting results for red varieties in the valley. Best years: (whites) 2002, '01, '00, '99, '98. Best producers: Buitenverwachting, Constantia-Uitsig, Groot Constantia, Klein Constantia, Steenberg.

ALDO CONTERNO

ITALY, Piedmont, Barolo DOCG

♀ *Nebbiolo, Barbera, Dolcetto*

♀ *Chardonnay*

Aldo Conterno is an open, friendly man, revered as a guru by numerous younger members of the BAROLO-producing fraternity. Yet although he broke with his traditionalist brother, Giovanni, in 1969 (see Giacomo CONTERNO), Aldo could not really be accused of being a modernist. His Barolos, generally recognized as some of the absolute greatest, could perhaps best be described as of classic style without the defects, packing as he does into his finest bottles just about every nuance of which great Barolo is capable. Aldo's top cru, only produced in the best vintages, is Granbussia, a blend of vineyards on the Bussia slope which in very good years are also made separately, as Vigna Cicala and Vigna Colonello. Bussia Soprana is his mainstay Barolo, produced in every year except for truly bad ones, and it can be particularly fine in lesser years, when other wines are not made and it contains all the best grapes.

Aldo is against the use of French barriques for aging Barolo but he does use them for his LANGHE Nebbiolo, from young vines, called Il Favot. He refers to this as his sons' wine – his three boys, Franco, Stefano and Giacomo, all having followed him into the business, Stefano taking on the crucial role of winemaker. He is also in favour of barriques for Barbera and he was, indeed, one of the earliest practitioners of what's turned out to be a highly successful style. And his Chardonnay Bussiador is unmistakably oak-fermented and matured in the best Burgundian tradition. Best years: (Barolo) 2001, '00, '99, '98, '97, '96, '95, '93, '90, '89, '88, '85, '82.

GIACOMO CONTERNO
ITALY, Piedmont, Barolo DOCG
♟ *Nebbiolo, Barbera*

The elder brother referred to in the above entry (his name is actually Giovanni, Giacomo having been their father), Giovanni Conterno could not be more different in character from his extrovert sibling, Aldo. Signor Conterno (one would not call him Giovanni, nor use the familiar 'tu', although his son Roberto, now taking over, is a lot less formidable) is marginally less of a traditionalist than he was when the fraternal disputes were taking place in the 1960s, especially in respect of length of wood-aging, but he still turns out BAROLOs of heroic structure, capable of lasting a human lifetime. His top cru, Monfortino, is sought by wine collectors the world over, and even his Barolo Cascina Francia is sold out virtually before it hits the market.

The difference between these two wines lies entirely in the vinification, since only top quality grapes from the 16-ha (40-acre) property of Cascina Francia in the commune of Serralunga are used for both. Whereas the straight Barolo is macerated for three to four weeks maximum at controlled temperature, Monfortino will get a good five weeks on the skins with no attempt to keep down the temperature and will only be released after six or seven years of aging in large oak barrels. Best years: 2001, '00, '99, '98, '97, '96, '95, '93, '90, '89, '88, '87, '85, '82.

CONTINO
SPAIN, La Rioja, Rioja DOCa
♟ *Tempranillo, Graciano, Carignan (Mazuelo), Grenache Noir (Garnacha Tinta)*

Contino, part-owned by CVNE, is one of the few wines in RIOJA made from the grapes of a single estate, a 62-ha (153-acre), west-sloping vineyard in the heart of the Rioja Alavesa. The majority of the wine is from Tempranillo, with some Graciano and a tiny amount of Mazuelo and Garnacha. Top Viña del Olivo Reserva is a single-vineyard wine made in a modern style. A new winery opened for business in 2003, allowing winemaker Jesus Madrazo greater flexibility. He is a devotee of the wonderfully perfumed but devilish to grow Graciano and has introduced an interesting Graciano varietal. With staggeringly rich, blackberry fruit, the wines will improve for at least ten years. Best years: (Reserva) 2001, '00, '96, '95, '94, '85, '82, '81, '78.

COONAWARRA
AUSTRALIA, South Australia

The name, an Aboriginal word meaning honeysuckle, is the most romantic feature of Coonawarra. It is a flat, featureless dot in a flat, featureless plain in the middle of nowhere, which just happens to be Australia's best wine region for velvety rich and smooth Cabernet Sauvignon, for high-quality Shiraz (Syrah) tasting of cherry, mint and a dusting of spice, and good Chardonnay, Riesling and Sauvignon Blanc.

The magic lies in a narrow strip of land which has a layer of reddish soil – terra rossa – over a limestone base, and also in the cool climate. The best red wines are intense but never overblown and will live for 30 years or more while the whites have a real intensity of cool-climate fruit when properly made. However, an export-led boom has seen hundreds of new vineyards planted, many of which are outside the legendary terra rossa strip. I worry for Coonawarra's great reputation. Best years: (Cabernet Sauvignon) 2001, '00, '99, '98, '97, '96, '94, '91, '90, '86. Best producers: Balnaves, BOWEN ESTATE, BRAND'S, HOLLICK, KATNOOK ESTATE, Leconfield, LINDEMANS, Majella, ORLANDO, PARKER, PENFOLDS, PENLEY ESTATE, PETALUMA, WYNNS, Zema Estate.

COOPERS CREEK
NEW ZEALAND, North Island, Huapai
♟ *Cabernet Sauvignon, Merlot, Pinot Noir*
♀ *Chardonnay, Sauvignon Blanc, Riesling and others*

For a relatively small winery, Coopers Creek has always had a high profile, thanks in part to

accusations of mislabelling, but most importantly to the quality of its wines. Chardonnays come primarily from GISBORNE and HAWKES BAY, with classic peach and fig flavours and the Hawkes Bay wines filled out by nutty, spicy oak. Sauvignon Blanc from MARLBOROUGH shows wonderfully aggressive gooseberry fruit and the Riesling is delicate but fragrant. The winery works mostly with bought-in grapes, but has some of its own vineyards, too. It is on an expansion drive on both fronts and new GIMBLETT GRAVELS vineyards should produce impressive reds.

CORBIÈRES AC
FRANCE, Languedoc-Roussillon
♟♀ *Carignan, Syrah, Grenache, Mourvèdre, Cinsaut*
♀ *Marsanne, Roussanne, Grenache Blanc, Macabeo, Bourboulenc and others*

The Corbières region south of Narbonne is one of the most captivating in France and home to one of France's largest ACs. It is a wild, windswept, sun-drenched marvel of stubborn hills and delving valleys and it's hardly surprising that consistency was never the watchword in the wines. But in the new millennium a new wave of producers is creating the best ever wines from Corbières.

Partly this is due to the use of carbonic maceration, since this winemaking method, has proved itself able to tame the fierce Carignan grape which dominates vineyards here. Syrah, Grenache and Mourvèdre are on the increase, too and we're now seeing a wide range of beefy reds, often dusty to the taste but roaring with a sturdy juicy fruit, a whiff of spice and a slap of herbs. These are wines of excellent, burly quality at an excellent price to drink young. Some producers are aging wines in wood and these can be worth keeping for a few years. An indicator of the new seriousness is the push to have 11 individual terroirs recognised within the AC. Boutenac, with round stones similar to those in CHÂTEAUNEUF-DU-PAPE is one of the finest. Best years: (reds) 2001, '00, '99, '98, '96, '95, '93. Best producers: Baillat, Bel Eveque, Caraguilhes, Ch. Cascadais, Étang des Colombes, Fontsainte, Grand Crès, Grand Moulin, Haut-Gléon, Hélène, l'Ille, LASTOURS, Mansenoble, Mont Tauch co-operative, les Palais, St-Auriol, Vaugelas, la VOULTE-GASPARETS.

White Corbières is very much the minor partner, accounting for just two per cent of annual production. However, the use of modern winemaking techniques means that some interesting aromatic whites have evolved, usually for drinking young.

CORNAS AC

FRANCE, Northern Rhône

🍷 *Syrah*

Cornas is the northern RHÔNE's up-and-coming star. Fifteen years ago the region didn't really have any star, though HERMITAGE and CÔTE-RÔTIE were both making splendid wines. But the spiralling prices of red BURGUNDY and BORDEAUX encouraged wine-lovers to look elsewhere for excellence. Both Côte-Rôtie and Hermitage are now very expensive, so the spotlight turned to the very south of the northern Rhône, where the valley spreads out at Valence.

Cornas is the last roar from the great Syrah grape. You do find Syrah south of here – lots of it – but it is almost always blended with other grapes like Grenache or Mourvèdre, creating delicious flavours along the way, but they're not heartland Syrah. For this, you need to stop at Cornas. The thin terraces clinging doggedly to these granite cliffs can make the most massive of all Rhône reds.

The colour when young is a thick, impenetrable red, almost black in the ripest years. It is tough and chunky, pummelling your mouth with tannin and sheer force of personality. So you wait, five years at least – more like ten. The colour is still deep, but tingling with life; the smell is rich and opulent, blackcurrants and raspberries, heady and exotic; the taste is almost sweet, with the fruit bursting through its tannic chains; and there's the roar – pure, sensuous fruit, coating your mouth, tannin too, and herbs, and deep chocolaty warmth to sear the flavour into your memory. Prices have inevitably risen in recent years, but then so has the quality. Best years: 2001, '00, '99, '98, '97, '96, '95, '94, '91, '90, '89, '88, '85, '83. Best producers: Allemand, R Balthazar, CLAPE, COLOMBO, Courbis, DELAS, E & J Durand, Fauterie, JABOULET, J Lemencier, Lionnet/ Rochepertuis, Tain l'Hermitage co-op, Tardieu-Laurent, Tunnel, VERSET, A Voge.

DOMAINE JEAN LIONNET
This domaine offers dense, tannic Cornas in a fairly modern style with plenty of new oak aging. This Rochepertuis cuvée needs six years or so to open out.

VIN DE CORSE AC

FRANCE, Corsica

🍷🍷 *Nielluccio, Sciacarello, Cinsaut, Carignan, Grenache and others*

🍷 *Vermentino, Ugni Blanc and others*

Despite its title of Île de Beauté, this heavenly Mediterranean island has made some pretty dull wines in the past but the last decade has seen a welcome trend towards quality with producers investing in better technology and planting noble grape varieties – such as Syrah, Merlot, Cabernet Sauvignon and Mourvèdre for reds and Chardonnay and Sauvignon Blanc for whites to complement the local red Nielluccio and Sciacarello and white Vermentino. Five superior sub-regions – Calvi, Cap Corse, Figari, Porto Vecchio, Sartène – are allowed to add their name to Vin de Corse, while Ajaccio and PATRIMONIO have their own ACs. And if you're in the north, try the sweet Muscat de Cap Corse – deep, rich, grapy wines that at long last have been awarded an AC. Best producers: Arena, Catarelli, Clos d'Alzeto, Clos Capitoro, Clos Culombu, Clos Landry, Clos Nicrosi, Gentile, Leccia, Maestracci, Orenga de Gaffory, Comte Péraldi, Renucci, Torraccia.

CORTES DE CIMA

PORTUGAL, Alentejo DOC

🍷 *Tempranillo (Aragonez), Syrah, Touriga Nacional, Trincadeira and others*

The ALENTEJO is an exciting place to make red wine and the potential is vast. But it has till now been dominated by co-operatives and one or two big companies – not the best recipe for innovation. That's why the arrival of Dane Hans Kristian Jørgensen and his American wife Carrie was so important – new blood, new ideas, new vision for the region – and new grapes too, because they planted Syrah – not an authorized variety – justifiably certain that it would produce exciting wine – as it has done, even if they initially had to release this gutsy, black-fruited blockbuster under the name Incógnito. They also make excellent use of local grape varieties released under the estate labels Chaminé (the lightest), Cortes de Cima and Reserva. Aragonez is also made as a varietal. Best years: 2001, '00, '98.

CORTON AC

FRANCE, Burgundy, Côte de Beaune, Grand Cru

🍷 *Pinot Noir*

🍷 *Chardonnay, Pinot Blanc, Pinot Gris*

The vineyards occupying the sections of the Corton hill mostly facing south and east on red, iron-rich soil are the only red Grand Cru in the CÔTE DE BEAUNE. In a typically quirky example of Burgundy's appellation intricacies, there is an AC for white Grand Cru Corton too, but whereas red Corton is the greatest red wine from this hillside, white Corton is not – the CORTON-CHARLEMAGNE Grand Cru has that distinction.

Corton now has 21 sub-divisions spanning the villages of LADOIX-Serrigny to the east, ALOXE-CORTON to the south (the most important section) and PERNAND-VERGE-LESSES to the west; all can label their red wine Corton. Ideally, the wine has the burliness and savoury power of the top Côte de Nuits wines, combined with the more seductive perfumed fruit of the Côte de Beaune. Red Corton should take ten years to mature but many modern wines never make it. Best years: 2002, '01, '00, '99, '98, '97, '96, '95, '93, '91, '90, '89, '88. Best producers: B Ambroise, BONNEAU DU MARTRAY, CHANDON DE BRIAILLES, Dubreuil-Fontaine, FAIVELEY, Guyon, JADOT, Dom. LEROY, MÉO-CAMUZET, Rapet, Sénard, TOLLOT-BEAUT.

Very little white Corton is produced – some comes from Aloxe-Corton but more from Ladoix-Serrigny, at the north-east end of the hill. The best example is from the Vergennes vineyard. The Domaine Chandon de Briailles also makes white Corton in its Bressandes vineyard (a tip-top red site) from half-and-half Chardonnay and Pinot Blanc.

CORTON-CHARLEMAGNE AC

FRANCE, Burgundy, Côte de Beaune, Grand Cru

🍷 *Chardonnay*

Corton-Charlemagne, a wide strip of vineyard at the top of the hill of CORTON, part south-facing in the commune of ALOXE-CORTON, but veering round to the west in PERNAND-VERGELESSES, is by far the largest of Burgundy's white Grands Crus, at 51ha (126 acres) with an annual production of about 278,000 bottles. The name really does stem from the Emperor Charlemagne whose favourite vineyard this was – though in those days the wine was red, which left an awful mess on his flowing white beard. After a fair bit of nagging from his wife, he ripped up the red vines and planted white instead – but with the inferior Aligoté, though, not the delicious Chardonnay.

Nowadays, the vineyard is all Chardonnay and can produce the most impressive of all white Burgundies – rich, buttery, nutty, a blast of splendid golden flavours, not as perfumed as MONTRACHET – more a kind of super-MEURSAULT. Yet it is more than that, because even if it does only show its true minerally splendour after ten years or so, that slow revelation of unsuspected depths and nuances is the mark of a great wine. Best years: 2002, '01, '00, '99, '98, '97, '96, '95, '92, '90, '89. Best producers: B Ambroise, BONNEAU DU MARTRAY, BOUCHARD PÈRE ET FILS, Champy, CHANDON DE BRIAILLES, COCHE-DURY, DROUHIN, FAIVELEY, V GIRARDIN, JADOT, P Javillier, Louis LATOUR, Rapet, Rollin, ROUMIER, TOLLOT-BEAUT.

CH. COS D'ESTOURNEL

FRANCE, Bordeaux, Haut-Médoc, St-Estèphe AC, 2ème Cru Classé

Cabernet Sauvignon, Merlot, Cabernet Franc, Petit Verdot

Cos d'Estournel bears more than a passing resemblance to a Chinese temple complete with pagodas and bells. Indeed Monsieur d'Estournel was a horse dealer in the early nineteenth century who traded extensively with the Far East, and discovered his wine improved enormously if he took it on the journey with him. So he went 'oriental' in a grand manner as a way of promoting his wine. Cos d'Estournel is now one of BORDEAUX's leading châteaux and ST-ESTÈPHE's top name.

In 1998 it was sold by the Prats family to the Taillan group, owners of Ch. CHASSE-SPLEEN and GRUAUD-LAROSE. Although St-Estèphe wines are generally less perfumed than those of neighbouring PAUILLAC, because of the heavier clay soil, Cos d'Estournel makes up for this by using just under 40 per cent Merlot and through extensive use of new oak barrels. The former second wine, Ch. de Marbuzet, is now a cru in its own right. Second wine (since 1994): les Pagodes de Cos. Best years: 2002, '01, '00, '98, '97, '96, '95, '94, '93, '90, '89, '88, '86, '85, '83, '82.

COSTERS DEL SEGRE DO

SPAIN, Cataluña

Grenache Noir (Garnacha Tinta), Tempranillo (Ull de Llebre), Monastrell, Cabernet Sauvignon and others

Macabeo, Parellada, Xarel-lo, Chardonnay and others

The winemakers of the 'banks of the Segre', at the western limits of CATALUÑA, can thank the powerful CODORNÍU for their elevation to DO status in 1988. Few of the region's wines, mainly traditional whites, used to be worth a second sip, except, that is, for those of the RAÏMAT estate, subsidiary of Codorníu. But Codorníu is a powerful player in the Catalan wine scene and not only pushed through a DO containing precisely the grapes it wanted

– many of them French – but for years got away with technically forbidden activities like irrigation on the grounds that they were experimental. The quality is generally good and the prices moderate. Best years: (reds) 2001, '00, '99, '98, '96, '95, '94. Best producers: Celler de Cantonella, Castell dei Remei, Raïmat, Vall de Baldomar.

COSTERS DEL SIURANA

SPAIN, Cataluña, Priorat DOCa

Grenache Noir (Garnacha Tinta), Cabernet Sauvignon, Carignan (Cariñena), Tempranillo and others

Grenache Blanc (Garnacha Blanca), Macabeo, Xarel-lo, Muscat (Moscatel)

Carles Pastrana, the former mayor of the village of Gratallops at the heart of PRIORAT, was one of the pioneers who relaunched the region by adding some French varieties to the old Garnacha and Cariñena vines and bringing in modern winemaking. His estate has grown to 33ha (82 acres) and is one of the largest of the newer ones. He is the only grower with Tempranillo vines: the RIOJA grape is as much a foreigner in the region as Cabernet Sauvignon. This goes into his second wine, Miserere. There is also a basic Usatges red and a barrel-fermented Usatges white. The *grand vin*, Clos de l'Obac, has progressively developed a somewhat lighter, high-toned personality in relation to other Priorats. Best years: 2000, '98, '95, '94, '92.

COSTIÈRES DE NÎMES AC

FRANCE, Languedoc-Roussillon

Carignan, Grenache, Syrah and others

Clairette, Bourboulenc, Grenache Blanc and others

This large AC of around 3600ha (8896 acres) lies between Nîmes and the Rhône delta in the GARD *département*. It has very clearly allied itself to the RHÔNE, even if one might argue the region is more LANGUEDOC by nature. But then you taste the wines – the reds – powerfully influenced by Syrah, Mourvèdre and Grenache, though still with the earthy undertow of Carignan – and you realize that these are big, juicy modern reds, often perfumed, always ripe, that would be very much at home in the southern Rhône.

The rosés too are good, but the revelation is the white Costières de Nîmes. Grenache Blanc, Marsanne, Roussanne and Bourboulenc make exciting scented wines of real depth and character. Best years: 2001, '00, '99, '98, '96, '95. Best producers: l'Amarine, Grande Cassagne, Mas des Bressades, Mas Carlot, Mourgues du Grès, de Nages, de la Tuilerie, Vieux-Relais.

CÔTE DE BEAUNE AC, CÔTE DE BEAUNE-VILLAGES AC

FRANCE, Burgundy, Côte de Beaune

Pinot Noir

Chardonnay

The Côte de Beaune AC covers just 52ha (128 acres) of vineyards around the town of Beaune. The wine is almost all red. It is usually very dry to start, but has a good lean fruit which can be delicious at two to three years old. Best producers: Allexant, Vougeraie.

Côte de Beaune-Villages is the general appellation covering red wine from 16 villages in the Côte de Beaune. Most producers use their own village name but if the wine is a blend from several villages, it is sold as Côte de Beaune-Villages. It can also cover the red wine production of mainly white wine villages such as MEURSAULT. Best years: (reds) 2002, '01, '99, '98, '96. Best producers: DROUHIN, J-P Fichet, JADOT.

CÔTE DE NUITS-VILLAGES AC

FRANCE, Burgundy, Côte de Nuits

Pinot Noir

Chardonnay

Unlike CÔTE DE BEAUNE, Côte de Nuits as such is not an AC. It is simply a geographical description of the northern part of the great CÔTE D'OR. Côte de Nuits-Villages, however, is an AC specific to the villages of Corgoloin, Comblanchien and Prissey in the south of the Côte de Nuits, and Brochon and FIXIN in the north. Fixin wines may also be sold under their own name. The 310ha (750 acres) of vines in the AC are mainly red. The wines are often good, not very deep, but with a good cherry fruit, and an attractive resin-bitter edge which can go smooth and chocolaty with age. Best years: 2000, '99, '98, '97, '96, '95, '93, '91, '90, '89, '88. Best producers: (reds) de l' ARLOT, René Bouvier, JAYER-GILLES, Rion, Charles Thomas. There is only a tiny amount of white produced, and, as so often in the Côte de Nuits, the rather lean, fruitless, minerally style makes you realize why the vineyards are overwhelmingly red.

DANIEL RION ET FILS
This domaine, based in Prémeaux-Prissey, makes a wide range of excellent wines, including Côte de Nuits-Villages with impressive cherry fruit.

CÔTE D'OR France, Burgundy

THE CÔTE D'OR is Europe's northernmost great red wine area as well as one of its greatest white wine producers. The name, meaning 'Golden Slope', refers to one single stretch of vines in Burgundy, starting just south of Dijon, and fading out 48km (30 miles) later west of Chagny. It is divided into two sections. The Côte de Nuits in the north encompasses little more than 1400ha (3460 acres) of vines, since the slope is often only a few hundred yards wide. It is almost entirely devoted to red wine.

The Côte de Beaune is the southern section, beginning in the north at the famous hill of Corton. Beaune is the main town, and as the Côte progresses southwards past Volnay, white takes over from red as the most exciting wine style, until red briefly reasserts itself at Santenay where the long north-south slope of the Côte de Beaune comes to an end. The less abrupt slopes of the Côte de Beaune possess 3000ha (7410 acres) of vines.

The soil in the Côte d'Or is a mix of clay, marl and limestone. Where the marl is dominant, red wines are produced from Pinot Noir; where the limestone takes over white wines from Chardonnay are best. In the Côte de Nuits where the marl is more prevalent, the slopes are steepest, so the richness of the soil is offset by particularly efficient drainage. Further south in the Côte de Beaune the slopes are more gently inclined and more south-facing, but easy-draining limestone is much in evidence.

Over the centuries grapes growing on the best sites have consistently ripened earlier than those too high up the slope or on flatter ground at the bottom. So a minutely accurate system of vineyard classification has evolved. Top of the hierarchy are the Grands Crus or Great Growths, which are allowed to use only the vineyard name on the label without the village name. These are almost always situated at between 250 and 300m (800 and 1000ft) in elevation, and facing between south and east. With the exception of Corton in the Côte de Beaune all the red Grands Crus are situated in the Côte de Nuits. Slightly less well-situated vineyards are accorded Premier Cru or First Growth status. Their wines should still be excellent. Wines produced from vineyards with no special reputation on the bottom of the slope will usually carry just the village name.

The medieval belltower at Chambolle-Musigny, one of the most unspoilt villages in the Côte d'Or, can be clearly seen rising above the vines. More producers are now bottling their own wines here with an increase in quality generally.

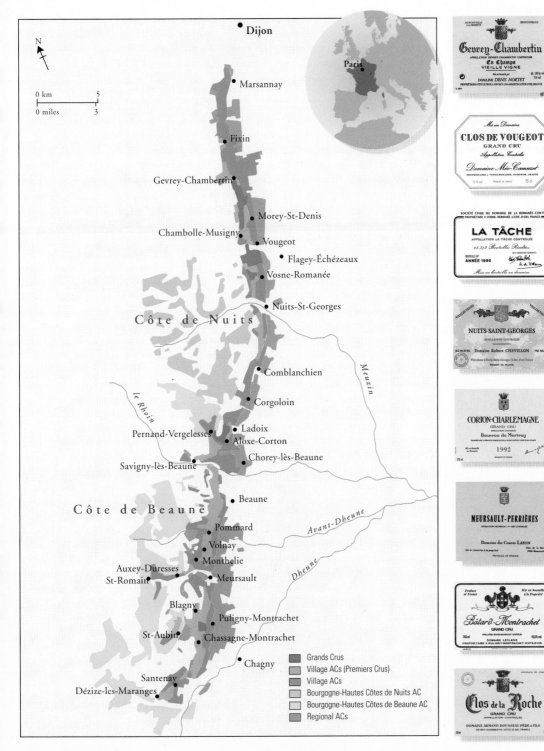

DENIS MORTET
Denis Mortet is one of the new wave stars in Gevrey-Chambertin, making impressive wines.

MÉO-CAMUZET
New oak barrels and luscious, rich fruit are the hallmarks of this quality estate based in Vosne-Romanée.

DOMAINE DE LA ROMANÉE-CONTI
La Tâche is one of the greatest red Burgundies and is wholly owned by this world-famous estate.

ROBERT CHEVILLON
Old vines and meticulous winemaking go hand in hand at this distinguished domaine.

DOMAINE BONNEAU DU MARTRAY
The Corton-Charlemagne from this historic estate is a stylish, powerful white Burgundy needing more than a decade of aging.

COMTES LAFON
Dominique Lafon is a leading producer in Meursault and one of Burgundy's best winemakers.

DOMAINE LEFLAIVE
The most famous white Burgundy estate of all has extensive holdings in some of the world's greatest vineyards.

DOMAINE ARMAND ROUSSEAU
Clos de la Roche is the best and biggest of the five Grands Crus in Morey-St-Denis.

REGIONAL ENTRIES
Aloxe-Corton, Auxey-Duresses, Bâtard-Montrachet, Beaune, Blagny, Bonnes-Mares, Bourgogne-Hautes Côtes de Beaune, Bourgogne-Hautes Côtes de Nuits, Chambertin, Chambolle-Musigny, Chassagne-Montrachet, Chorey-lès-Beaune, Clos de la Roche, Clos de Vougeot, Corton, Corton-Charlemagne, Côte de Beaune, Côte de Nuits-Villages, Échézeaux, Fixin, Gevrey-Chambertin, Ladoix, Maranges, Marsannay, Meursault, Monthelie, le Montrachet, Morey-St-Denis, Musigny, Nuits-St-Georges, Pernand-Vergelesses, Pommard, Puligny-Montrachet, Richebourg, la Romanée, St-Aubin, St-Romain, Santenay, Savigny-lès-Beaune, la Tâche, Volnay, Vosne-Romanée, Vougeot.

PRODUCER ENTRIES
de l'Arlot, Comte Armand, Barthod, Boisset, Bonneau du Martray, Bouchard Père et Fils, Burguet, Carillon et Fils, Chandon de Briailles, Chevillon, Clair, Coche-Dury, Drouhin, Dujac, Engel, Faiveley, Gagnard, Gouges, Grivot, Hospices de Beaune, Jadot, Jayer-Gilles, Comtes Lafon, Louis Latour, Laurent, Dom. Leflaive, Olivier Leflaive, Leroy, Méo-Camuzet, de Montille, Mortet, Mugnier, de la Pousse d'Or, Ramonet, de la Romanée-Conti, Roumier, Tollot-Beaut & Fils, de Vogüé.

CÔTE ROANNAISE AC

FRANCE, Loire Valley

♥ ♀ *Gamay*

Small appellation in the upper LOIRE producing mostly light reds and rosés. A new wave of producers here and in neighbouring Côtes du Forez are on a quality drive, resulting in much gutsier reds and delicious non-appellation whites. Best producers: A Demon, Fontenay, M Lutz, M & L Montroussier, R Sérol; (Côtes du Forez) Clos de Chozieux, Cave des Vignerons Foreziens, Verdier-Logel.

CÔTE-RÔTIE AC

FRANCE, Northern Rhône

♥ *Syrah, Viognier*

Côte-Rôtie – the 'roasted slope' – is the most northern vineyard area in the RHÔNE Valley, and definitely one of the oldest – there have been vines planted on these slopes for 24 centuries. Yet it is only very recently that wine drinkers have become aware that this is one of France's greatest wines. The red grape of the Rhône, Syrah, bakes itself to superripeness on these steep, south-east-facing slopes.

What marks Côte-Rôtie out from the heftier Rhône reds like HERMITAGE is its exotic fragrance, quite unexpected in a red wine. This is because a little of the heavenly scented white Viognier grape is allowed in the wine (up to 20 per cent, though five to ten per cent is more likely). The result is damson-juicy, raspberry-sweet, sometimes with a hint of apricot skins and pepper. Lovely young, it is better aged for eight to ten years. The two best slopes are called Côte Brune and Côte Blonde; they are usually blended together but some growers vinify and label them separately. There are also prestigious single vineyards such as la Landonne. Best years: 2000, '99, '98, '97, '96, '95, '94, '91, '90, '89, '88, '85. Best producers: Barge, Bonnefond, Bonserine, Burgaud, CHAPOUTIER, Clusel-Roch, CUILLERON, DELAS, Duclaux, Gaillard, Gallet, Garon, Gasse, Gerin, GUIGAL, JABOULET, JAMET, Jasmin, Ogier, ROSTAING, Tardieu-Laurent, VERNAY, Villard, Vins de Vienne.

COTEAUX D'AIX-EN-PROVENCE AC

FRANCE, Provence

♥ ♀ *Grenache, Mourvèdre, Cinsaut, Counoise, Carignan, Cabernet Sauvignon, Syrah and others*

♀ *Ugni Blanc, Bourboulenc, Clairette, Grenache Blanc, Sémillon, Sauvignon Blanc and others*

The Coteaux d'Aix-en-Provence region, covering a large area around Aix-en-Provence in the Bouches-du-Rhône *département*, was awarded its long-overdue AC in 1985. Prejudice against Cabernet Sauvignon was the cause of the delay; 95 per cent of the AC's production of 23 million bottles is red or rosé and it was the first southern French area to acknowledge that Cabernet can enhance the local varieties of Grenache, Cinsaut, Mourvèdre and Carignan.

Some quite good fresh rosé is made, but the best wines are red, and they are allowed a maximum of 30 per cent Cabernet Sauvignon in the blend. The wines are good but should do better, because some enterprising estates from neighbouring CÔTES DE PROVENCE and, in particular, from les BAUX-DE-PROVENCE, achieve richer, more succulent fruit flavours. The wines can age, but they're better young.

Traditional whites, based on Ugni Blanc, are pretty flabby mouthfuls. But cool fermentation in stainless steel tanks, early bottling and an increased use of Grenache Blanc, Sémillon and Sauvignon Blanc are now producing some pleasant, but hardly riveting, dry whites – to knock back sharpish. Best years: (reds) 2001, '00, '99, '98, '97, '96, '95. Best producers: (reds) Bas, Bastides, Béates, de Beaupré, Calissanne, Fonscolombe, Gavelles, Revelette, Vignelaure; (whites) Bas, de Beaupré, Calissanne, Fonscolombe, du Seuil.

VIN DE PAYS DES COTEAUX DE L'ARDÈCHE

FRANCE, Rhône Valley

Wines from the southern part of the Ardèche *département* in the south-west RHÔNE Valley. Look out for the increasingly good varietal reds made from Cabernet Sauvignon, Syrah, Merlot or Gamay and dry, fresh white wines from Chardonnay, Viognier or Sauvignon Blanc. Best producers: Vignerons Ardèchois, de Bournet, Colombier, DUBOEUF, Louis LATOUR, Pradel/Montfleury co-operative, St-Désirat co-operative.

COTEAUX CHAMPENOIS AC

FRANCE, Champagne

♥ ♀ *Pinot Noir, Pinot Meunier*

♀ *Chardonnay*

This AC covers still wines from the CHAMPAGNE area. The white is pale gold, but shockingly dry. The trouble is, even when fully ripe, the red Champagne grapes don't have a lot of colour or sugar, so with few exceptions (usually from the villages of BOUZY or Ay) the red is pale and rather harsh, though it often has a fresh strawberry or cherry scent. No wonder they turn 99 per cent of the region's wine into sparkling wine.

Best years: 2002, '00, '99, '98, '95, '90, '89. Best producers: Bara, BOLLINGER, Egly-Ouriet, LAURENT-PERRIER, Joseph PERRIER, Ch. de Saran (MOËT ET CHANDON).

COTEAUX DU LANGUEDOC AC

FRANCE, Languedoc-Roussillon

♥ ♀ *Grenache, Syrah, Mourvèdre, Carignan, Cinsaut*

♀ *Grenache Blanc, Clairette, Bourboulenc, Marsanne, Roussanne and others*

This increasingly successful, large AC runs approximately from Montpellier to Narbonne and produces around 73 million bottles, 78 per cent of which are red. This is one of the areas in the South of France which has become the French Australia of the 1990s, with a flood of fresh, fruity, well-made wines.

Ongoing restructuring of the appellation recognizes seven climatic sub-zones, including La CLAPE, Grès de Montpellier, PIC ST-LOUP and Picpoul de Pinet. A further refinement, with a more stringent set of rules, grades wines by terroir: these include some of the 12 villages that have historically been allowed to add their own names to the AC name, such as Montpeyroux, St-Georges d'Orques, Cabrières and La Méjanelle.

Some producers now use oak barrels to mature the best reds, and these can age for several years. In general, drink the wines young, but there is sufficient fruit in a growing number of the reds to take aging. Grenache Blanc, Bourboulenc and Clairette are the principal white varieties, with the better estates increasing plantings of Roussanne and Marsanne. Generally these are for drinking within two to three years. Best years: (reds) 2001, '00, '99, '98, '96, '95, '94, '93. Best producers: Abbaye de Valmagne, de l'Aiguelière, d'Aupilhac, Calage, Clavel, la Coste, Grès St-Paul, Haut-Blanville, Henry, Lacroix-Varel, Mas Cal Demoura, Mas des Chimères, MAS JULLIEN, PEYRE-ROSE, PRIEURÉ ST-JEAN DE BÉBIAN, Puech-Haut, St-Martin de la Garrigue, Terre Megère.

COTEAUX DU LAYON AC, COTEAUX DU LAYON-VILLAGES AC

FRANCE, Loire, Anjou-Saumur

♀ *Chenin Blanc*

It's a mixed blessing being a winemaker in one of those rare locations where the noble rot fungus, *Botrytis cinerea*, strikes. If the rot claims all your vines and you carefully pick only the most syrupy, mushy grapes, then you have the chance of making great, intensely sweet, luscious white wines. The Layon Valley does get noble rot most years – and the Chenin grape reacts well to it. But it is incredibly risky to wait into the late autumn for the fungus to develop because, all too often, rains arrive and wash away your crop. If you get SAUTERNES' prices, maybe it's worth it, but, except for its two Grands Crus – QUARTS DE CHAUME and BONNEZEAUX – no-one does here.

Over the past decade or so, there has been a quality revolution in the Coteaux du Layon and neighbouring Coteaux de l'Aubance as an increasing number of producers have striven to make significantly better wine. The secret lies in low yields and selective picking. A few producers such as Patrick Baudouin and Jo Pithon have pushed ripeness to extremes. In 1997 Pithon made a tiny amount of Cuvée Ambroisie from individually picked grapes and there was an astonishing 32° of potential alcohol. All the best producers now make a series of cuvées in ascending sweetness and levels of botrytis.

Seven villages can use the Coteaux du Layon-Villages AC and put their own name on their labels. To qualify the wines must have at least one degree more alcohol than straight Coteaux du Layon. These wines are definitely underpriced for the quality and the village of Chaume is one of the best. Best years: 2002, '01, '99, '97, '96, '95, '90, '89, '88, '85, '83, '76. Best producers: Aquilas, Baudouin, BAUMARD, Bergerie, Bidet, du Breuil, Cady, Delesvaux, Forges, Guimonière, Ogereau, Passavant, Pierre-Bise, Pithon, Joseph Renou, Roulerie, Sablonnettes, Sauveroy, Soucherie, Yves Soulez, Touche Noire.

COTEAUX DU TRICASTIN AC

FRANCE, Northern Rhône

♥ ¶ *Grenache, Syrah, Cinsaut, Mourvèdre and others*

♀ *Grenache, Clairette, Picpoul, Bourboulenc and others*

This large and fast-growing vineyard area in the southern Drôme was only created in the 1960s to cater for a flood of displaced grape-growers fleeing from North Africa after Morocco, Tunisia and Algeria gained independence from France.

Right from the start the wines have been good because the new settlers introduced modern methods – formulated to cope with the desert conditions in Africa – on to good virgin vineyard land. Reds and rosés are often quite light, but very fresh; reds are generally juicy, plummy and livened up with some peppery spice – and rarely marred by excess of tannin or acid. Only a tiny amount of white is made, but it's worth trying for a nutty but fresh drink, ideally to consume within the year. Best years: 2001, '00, '99, '98, '95. Best producers: de Grangeneuve, Lônes, St-Luc, Tour d'Elyssas, Vieux Micocoulier.

COTEAUX VAROIS AC

FRANCE, Provence

♥ ¶ *Grenache, Mourvèdre, Syrah, Cabernet Sauvignon, Cinsaut and others*

♀ *Grenache Blanc, Clairette, Rolle, Ugni Blanc, Sémillon*

A large area of some 1700ha (4200 acres) to the north of Toulon, and nudging CÔTES DE PROVENCE to the east, Coteaux Varois was promoted to AC in 1993. This was largely because a lot of growers were making great efforts, especially with new plantings of classic grapes such as Cabernet Sauvignon and Syrah, to upgrade quality. Otherwise the grapes are much the same as for CÔTES DE PROVENCE: Grenache, Cinsaut and Mourvèdre. Best years: (reds) 2001, '00, '99, '98, '97, '96, '95. Best producers: Alysses, Bremond, Calisse, Deffends, Garbelle, Routas, St-Estève, St-Jean-le-Vieux, St-Jean-de-Villecroze, Triennes.

CÔTES DE BLAYE AC

FRANCE, Bordeaux

♀ *Sémillon, Sauvignon Blanc, Colombard and others*

This AC covers dry or sweet whites from the right bank of the Gironde. Almost all of the best whites are now dry. A few sweetish wines remain, none very good, and these may be seen under the PREMIÈRES CÔTES DE BLAYE label. The most interesting wines include a fair percentage of the Colombard grape, which has far more character here than Sauvignon Blanc and Sémillon, and which produces good results with modern wine-making. Drink the wines young. Best producer: Marcillac co-operative.

CÔTES DE BOURG AC

FRANCE, Bordeaux

♥ *Merlot, Cabernet Franc, Cabernet Sauvignon, Malbec*

♀ *Sémillon, Sauvignon Blanc, Muscadelle and others*

Ch. MARGAUX, Ch. PALMER, and all the other luminaries of the MÉDOC big-time are just a tantalizing mile or two away across the Gironde, yet Bourg shares none of their glory. These seemingly perfectly placed vineyard slopes are one of BORDEAUX's forgotten areas, struggling to regain the place in the sun they used to enjoy. After all, the Romans planted vineyards in Bourg when the Médoc was merely a swamp. This is very much a red wine district; its sloping vineyards are mostly clay, but there is enough gravel to suit Cabernet Sauvignon. The good local co-operative at Tauriac and leading properties are now using new oak as they strive to upgrade their wine. They deserve to succeed as affordable good BORDEAUX is difficult to find.

The red wines are quite full, fairly dry, but with an attractive blackcurrant fruit which ensures the earthy quality doesn't dominate at all; when they are splashed with the spice of new oak, they can age to a pleasant maturity at six to ten years old. Best years: (reds) 2001, '00, '99, '98, '96, '95, '94, '90. Best producers: Barbe, Brulesé-caille, Bujan, Falfas, Fougas, Garreau, Guerry, Haut-Guiraud, Haut-Macô, Macay, Nodoz, ROC DE CAMBES, Rousset, Tauriac co-operative, Tayac.

Only a tiny amount of the wine is white, most of which is bone dry and rather lifeless.

ROC DE CAMBES
This ripe, concentrated wine, aged in 50 per cent new oak barrels, lifts the Côte de Bourg appellation on to an altogether higher plane.

CÔTES DE CASTILLON AC

FRANCE, Bordeaux

♥ *Cabernet Sauvignon, Cabernet Franc, Merlot, Malbec*

East of St-Émilion on the river Dordogne is the little town of Castillon-la-Bataille, where defeat at a crucial battle in 1453 lost the English control of Aquitaine – and their supply of BORDEAUX wine. We didn't hear much about Castillon after that until the 1980s, when the prices of decent red Bordeaux became so loony that we began searching for a few understudies able to produce decent flavours at a fair price.

Côtes de Castillon manages to be more special than simple Bordeaux Rouge because quite a few of the vineyards are a direct extension of St-Émilion's limestone escarpment. These well-sited vines give radically different flavours to the duller Castillon offerings down near the river – flavours of mint, black-currant and cedar – in miniature maybe, but these are the flavours which made the MÉDOC famous. They use a high proportion of Merlot and some estates now use new oak barrels to age the wine, which is pretty tasty at three to ten years old. Best years: 2001, '00, '99, '98, '96, '95, '94, '90. Best producers:

Domaine de l'A, d'Aiguilhe, Belcier, Cap-de-Faugères, la Clarière Laithwaite, Clos l'Église, Clos les Lunelles, Clos Puy Arnaud, Côte-Monpezat, Lapeyronie, Poupille, Robin, Veyry, Vieux-Château-Champs de Mars.

CÔTES DE DURAS AC

FRANCE, South-West

Cabernet Franc, Cabernet Sauvignon, Merlot, Malbec

Sauvignon Blanc, Sémillon, Muscadelle and others

Côtes de Duras, in the Lot-et-Garonne *département*, has a very active co-operative movement, which offers good, fresh, grassy red, rosé and white wines from traditional BORDEAUX grapes, at distinctly lower prices. There is some sweet white but it is the dry wine, often labelled Sauvignon Blanc, which is far more important – it has a strong, grassy green fruit, but a surprisingly soft, gentle texture. Drink the wines young. There are signs of the use of oak barrels down here, too. Best years: (reds) 2000, '98, '96, '95. Best producers: (reds) Amblard, Clos du Cadaret, Cours, Duras co-operative, Grand-Mayne, Lafon, Laulan, Landerrouat co-operative; (whites) Duras and Landerrouat co-operatives.

CÔTES DU FRONTONNAIS AC

FRANCE, South-West

Négrette, Cabernet Sauvignon, Cabernet Franc, Syrah and others

This is one of the most original red wine flavours in South-West France. The vineyard area isn't very big, clustered round Toulouse on dry, sun-soaked slopes. Négrette is the chief grape and the wine can be superb, positively silky in texture and combining a juicy fruit like raspberry or strawberry, coated in cream, with a lick of aniseed. They drink almost all of it in Toulouse but a little is exported and is well worth seeking out. It can age, but it's best drunk in its full flush of youth. There's a little rosé, too. Best years: 2001, '00, '99, '98, '97, '96, '95. Best producers: Baudare, Bellevue-la-Forêt, Cahuzac, la Colombière, Ferran, Flotis, Laurou, Montauriol, la Palme, Plaisance, le Roc, St-Louis.

VIN DE PAYS DES CÔTES DE GASCOGNE

FRANCE, South-West

Côtes de Gascogne is the zonal VIN DE PAYS used principally for dry white wines produced in the north of the Gers *département*. This is Armagnac country and following the decline in demand for the brandy in the 1980s a large number of producers converted

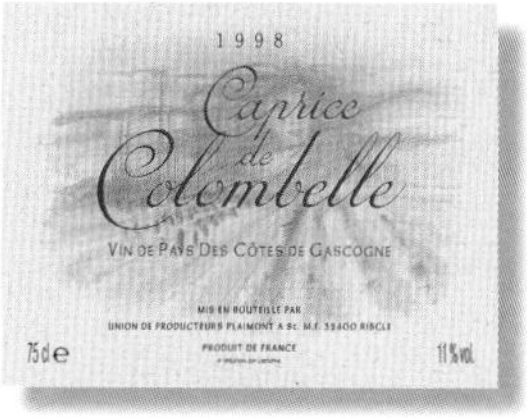

PRODUCTEURS PLAIMONT

This grouping of three Gascon co-operatives is the largest, most reliable and most go-ahead producer of Côtes de Gascogne wines.

their vineyards to the production of table wine, a saving grace for the region. Temperature-controlled vinification and stainless steel have produced extremely attractive crisp whites, mostly from Colombard and Ugni Blanc. The PLAIMONT co-operative, which accounts for over 2500ha (6170 acres) of vines, has been a particularly innovative and motivating force in recent years. Best producers: Aurin, Brumont, GRASSA (du Tariquet), de Joy, Producteurs Plaimont, St-Lannes.

CÔTES DU JURA AC

FRANCE, Jura

Poulsard, Trousseau, Pinot Noir

Chardonnay, Savagnin

The regional AC for JURA covers a wide variety of wines: dry whites, reds, rosés, *vins jaunes* and *vins de paille*. Most of the vineyards lie in the south of the region between Poligny and Lons-le-Saunier, where they spread up the mountain sides or nuzzle into thickly forested slopes. The area is wonderfully relaxing, always shadowed by the Jura mountain range, and sometimes affording spectacular vistas across the Saône Valley to Burgundy. But sadly the flavours of the wines, especially the whites, aren't of the delicate sylvan sort at all. The reason for this is the white Savagnin grape – a strange, surly creature – which admittedly does come into its own with the dark yellow, sherry-like *vin jaune*.

However, there is respite in the friendly form of Chardonnay which performs well here. Some unblended Chardonnay is now coming on to the market. It can still be infected with the strange, resiny Savagnin character, particularly when not vinified in a separate cellar; but at its best, especially from the vineyards between Poligny and Arbois, it is a particularly thirst-quenching Chardonnay. Drink the whites at one to two years old, although ones from Chardonnay can age.

Both the reds and rosés are rarely special – and can be aggressively weird. The southern part of the region can produce some lighter reds and rosés from the Trousseau and Poulsard grapes which are not too savage, while the Pinot Noir can yield rather good, light, perfumed reds. Poulsard also produces a very pale pink *vin gris*. Less than 25 per cent of Côtes du Jura AC is red or rosé. Best producers: d'Arlay, Berthet-Bondet, Bourdy, Chalandard, Clavelin, Durand-Perron, Ch. de l'Étoile, Joly, Labet, Pupillin co-operative, Reverchon, Rijckaert, Rolet, Tissot.

CÔTES DU LUBÉRON AC

FRANCE, Southern Rhône

Grenache, Syrah, Cinsaut, Mourvèdre and others

Ugni Blanc, Clairette, Bourboulenc and others

This lovely lost area to the east of Avignon and north of Aix, running along the Durance Valley and sharing the land with asparagus crops, was promoted to AC in 1988. Technically it's part of the grouping of appellations belonging to the RHÔNE Valley, but it's not really. This is PROVENCE in all but name, with the vineyards spread across the north- and south-facing slopes of the long, forested backbone of the Montagne du Lubéron, the air scented with lavender and pine needles – and, disappointingly, the beautiful location is decidedly less suited to top-quality wines than the stony expanses of the Rhône Valley itself.

As so often in Provence, the reds lack real heart – though the gravel-over-sand soils can produce bright enough fruit flavours. Interestingly, whites are showing some promise, but, since the region is dominated by co-ops, progress won't be meteoric, though the arrival of Burgundy white wine wizard Jean-Marie Guffens should give everyone a jolt. Best years: (reds) 2001, '00, '99, '98, '95. Best producers: Bonnieux co-operative, la Canorgue, la Citadelle, Fontenille, l'Isolette, la Tour-d'Aigues co-operative, Tourettes, Val Joanis.

CÔTES DE PROVENCE AC

FRANCE, Provence

Mourvèdre, Grenache, Syrah, Cabernet Sauvignon and others

Ugni Blanc, Vermentino (Rolle), Sémillon, Clairette

PROVENCE is such a hauntingly beautiful region and happily an increasing number of growers are rediscovering the magic in the soil. Rosés are becoming fruitier, and reds are emerging which, along with the powerful pine, thyme and rosemary perfumes of the rugged sun-soaked hillsides, are now displaying other scents (myrtle is one) as well as the one component previously lacking – fruit.

New plantings of better varieties (Cabernet Sauvignon, Syrah and Mourvèdre) are primarily responsible, as are cooler fermentations and lower yields. This is good news because, though the wines from this large 19,000-ha (47,000-acre) area have never been cheap, Provence's romantic overtones have seduced people into buying them. There are three main vineyard areas: the coastal strip between Ste-Maxime and Toulon, providing quaffing wine for the fashionable watering holes of the Riviera; the coastal vineyards between Toulon and Marseille, where most of the best sites qualify for the BANDOL or CASSIS ACs; and the vast sprawl north of the Massif des Maures, where quality is rarely considered.

Nearly 80 per cent of the enormous production is rosé, 15 per cent red, and most of the whites suffer from the usual southern French grape varieties of Ugni Blanc and Clairette, though these can be improved by Sémillon or, unofficially, by Sauvignon Blanc. Domaine Gavoty created waves by using the Rolle grape to make a delicious fruity white wine – and many producers have followed suit. Drink the wines very young.

Best producers: Barbanau, la Bernarde, Commanderie de Bargemore, Commanderie de Peyrassol, la Courtade, Coussin Ste-Victoire, Dragon, Esclans, Féraud, des Garcinières, Gavoty, Maîtres Vignerons de St-Tropez, Maravenne, Ott, Rabiega, Réal Martin, Richeaume, Rimauresq, Roquefort, Sorin, Élie Sumeire, Vannières.

CÔTES DU RHÔNE AC
FRANCE, *Southern Rhône*
♀ ♂ *Grenache, Cinsaut, Syrah, Carignan, Mourvèdre and others*
♀ *Grenache Blanc, Clairette, Roussanne, Marsanne and others*

Although this general AC covers the whole viticultural RHÔNE Valley, most of the wine comes from the broad southern section between Montélimar and Avignon. The chief red grape is Grenache, followed by Cinsaut, Syrah, Carignan and Mourvèdre; the last three in particular have lots of warm spicy southern personality to offer to the rich, heady flavours of Grenache.

The reds used to be marked by a rather heavy, jammy fruit and a rough, herby perfume. Modern techniques – temperature control, stainless steel installations, some carbonic maceration – have revolutionized the style, and the wines should be juicy, spicy, strawberry-fruited, very easy to drink within two years of the harvest. Single-estate wines can age considerably longer. Best years: (reds) 2001, '00, '99, '98, '95. Best producers:

(reds) Amouriers, d'Andézon, les Aphillanthes, BEAUCASTEL, Brunel, CLAPE, COLOMBO, Cros de la Mûre, DUBOEUF, Fonsalette, FONT DE MICHELLE, Gramenon, Grand Moulas, Grand Prebois, GUIGAL, Ch. d'Hugues, JABOULET, la Janasse, Lionnet, J-M Lombard, Mas de Libian, Mont-Redon, la Mordorée, Dom. la Réméjeanne, M Richaud, St-Gayan, Ste-Anne, Santa Duc, Tardieu-Laurent, Tours, Vieux-Chêne.

Interestingly, while the attention has all been on the greatly improved quality of the reds, whites have probably made even greater leaps forward. One of the first to realize the potential here was George Duboeuf of BEAUJOLAIS fame, who used early-picked grapes fermented cool in stainless steel to produce a kind of 'Rhône-Mâcon Villages'. The best producers have learned from this but also moved on to produce modern whites with good ripe Rhône fruit as well. Best producers: (whites) Chusclan co-operative, Clape, Duboeuf, Gaillard, Laudun co-operative, Dom. la Réméjeanne, Ste-Anne.

CÔTES DU RHÔNE-VILLAGES AC
FRANCE, *Southern Rhône*
♀ *Grenache, Cinsaut, Syrah, Mourvèdre and others*
♀ *Grenache Blanc, Clairette, Roussanne, Marsanne, Bourboulenc and others*

The Côtes du Rhône-Villages AC is distinguished from the CÔTES DU RHÔNE appellation by requiring a higher minimum alcohol content (12.5 per cent as opposed to 11 per cent) and a lower yield. But there's much more to the division than that.

There are 16 villages that can add their own name to Côtes du Rhône-Villages on the label; and every one of these villages does have at least some superior vineyard land. The best of the named villages, like Beaumes-de-Venise, Cairanne, Rasteau, Séguret, Sablet, Valréas and Visan, have marked personality and a raft of good producers that in other parts of France would have earned them their own appellation long ago. Cairanne has long been identified as a likely candidate for promotion to AC status, a promotion previously granted to GIGONDAS and VACQUEYRAS. If no village name is identified, then it's probable that the wine is a blend from two or more villages. These villages are dispersed among three *départements*, the Vaucluse, the Drôme and the GARD. There are a further 50 villages or so that can use the AC name but cannot put their own name on the label.

The majority of the best wines are red, exhibiting a marvellously spicy flavour, a

good smack of herbs, a reasonable amount of tannin, and a capacity to improve in bottle for up to ten years; and every one of the villages makes a contribution of some sort.

White wines used to be an afterthought, and it was only the odd example from west bank villages like Chusclan and Laudun that were accorded much respect. Well the west bank areas are better suited to white, being less exposed to the harsh afternoon sun that the reds love so much, but the revival of interest in Marsanne and Roussanne as world-class grape varieties has produced a tide of delicious, fragrant full-bodied whites.

Best years: (reds) 2001, '00, '99, '98, '95, '90. Best producers: Achiary, Alary, l'Ameillaud, Amouriers, Beaurenard, Bressy-Masson, Brusset, Cabasse, Cabotte, Cave de Cairanne, Charavin, Charbonnière, Chaume-Arnaud, Combe, Cros de la Mûre, Estézargues co-operative, Gourt de Mautens, Gramenon, Grand Moulas, Hautes Cances, JABOULET, la Janasse, l'ORATOIRE ST-MARTIN, Pélaquié, Piaugier, Rabasse-Charavin, Dom. la Réméjeanne, Richaud, ST-GAYAN, Ste-Anne, la SOUMADE, Tours, Trapadis, Verquière.

CÔTES DU ROUSSILLON AC, CÔTES DU ROUSSILLON-VILLAGES AC
FRANCE, *Languedoc-Roussillon*
♀ ♂ *Carignan, Cinsaut, Grenache, Syrah and others*
♀ *Macabeo, Malvoisie, Grenache Blanc and others*

Roussillon is the frontier area where France melts imperceptibly into CATALUÑA and Spain, somewhere high among the Pyrenean peaks. The wine you drink here is Côtes du Roussillon – red, dusty as a mountain track, but juicy as fresh orchard fruit – based on the Carignan, but increasingly helped by Cinsaut, Grenache, Syrah and Mourvèdre.

As usual in the far South of France, the Côtes du Roussillon AC – which spreads south of Perpignan to the foothills of the Pyrenees, as well as taking in a good deal of the flatter land to the north along the Agly river valley, and the most suitable vineyard sites to the west – is primarily red wine land.

Carignan is the dominant grape – and it can be juicy and full when made by the carbonic maceration method. The finer blends have a higher percentage of Grenache and Syrah. Average annual production is now 37 million bottles, 97 per cent of it red or rosé. So long as the wine is young, both red and rosé provide some of southern France's best-value drinking. Best producers: (reds) Vignerons Catalans, Casenove, CAZES, Chênes, COLOMBO, Ferrer-Ribière, Força

Réal, GAUBY, Jau, Joliette, Laporte, Mas Crémat, Piquemal, Rivesaltes co-operative, Salvat, Sarda-Malet. The whites come mainly from the unmemorable Macabeo grape but, if picked very early or almost unripe and fermented at low temperature, it can make bone-dry, lemon and aniseed-scented wine for very early drinking. More adventurous producers are using Grenache Blanc, Rolle and Roussanne and fermenting and aging in oak barrels. Best producers: (whites) Vignerons Catalans, Cazes, Chênes, Gauby, Mas Crémat, Sarda-Malet.

The Côtes du Roussillon-Villages AC – exclusively for red wine – covers the best sites around the river Agly in the northern part of the AC, where the PYRÉNÉES-ORIENTALES *département* meets the AUDE and production averages 13 million bottles a year. The wine, especially from the villages of Caramany, Latour-de-France, Lesquerde and Tautavel, which can add their names to the AC, is full, very ripe, wonderfully juicy when young but also capable of maturing for several years. Quite a few private estates are now making their mark, with some impressive wines aged in new oak. Best years: 2001, '00, '99, '98, '96, '95. Best producers: Agly co-operative, Vignerons Catalans, Cazes, Chênes, Clos des Fées, Fontanel, Força Réal, Gardiès, Gauby, Jau, Joliette, Mas Crémat, des Schistes.

CÔTES DE ST-MONT VDQS

FRANCE, South-West

♟♟ *Tannat, Cabernet Sauvignon, Cabernet Franc, Fer Servadou*

♀ *Petit Courbu, Gros Manseng, Petit Manseng, Arrufiac*

We might never have heard of this fairly obscure VDQS were it not for the decline of the Armagnac brandy industry. As volumes of Armagnac slumped, vineyard owners were left with acres of land planted with vines, but no idea what to do with them. Luckily the powerful local grouping of co-operatives – PLAIMONT – was run by a dynamic and far-sighted director who virtually made Côtes de St-Mont a fiefdom of his co-operative for sturdy, deep-tasting reds and some interesting whites. Local grapes are favoured, so reds have to be 60 per cent Tannat, and Fer Servadou is encouraged along with some Cabernets. Whites can use the Manseng varieties of JURANÇON further south, but the indigenous – and almost extinct – Arrufiac and Courbu are encouraged. These wines aren't expensive, and they're full of character. Best producer: Producteurs Plaimont.

Harvesting Grenache at Tautavel in the Côtes du Roussillon-Villages AC. Increasing use of Grenache and other superior grape varieties in many of Languedoc-Roussillon's red wine blends is bringing positive results.

VIN DE PAYS DES CÔTES DE THONGUE

FRANCE, Languedoc

They must be kicking themselves in the Côtes de Thongue, a great splash of land between Béziers and Pézenas that contains some pretty decent vineyard land. The authorities offered to classify their best sites for appellation contrôlée. With the wave of enthusiasm for VIN DE PAYS 'international' varietals sweeping the south, the growers said no thanks. Now Vin de Pays are difficult to sell and everyone wants the old southern French appellations! Ah well, Côtes de Thongue might still get their promotion and in the meantime there are some good properties whose wine is tasty and fairly-priced. Best producers: l'Arjolle, Bellevue, les Chemins de Bassac, Condamine l'Évêque, Croix Belle.

CÔTES DU VENTOUX AC

FRANCE, Southern Rhône

♟♟ *Grenache, Syrah, Cinsaut, Carignan, Mourvèdre and others*

♀ *Clairette, Bourboulenc, Grenache Blanc, Roussanne*

Côtes du Ventoux, away to the east of CHÂTEAUNEUF-DU-PAPE, is one of those ACs that has still not found its own identity. These lovely vineyards, some of which tumble down the sides of the magnificent 1910m (6260ft) Mont Ventoux, towering above the eastern side of the RHÔNE Valley, and some of which spread eastwards along the Apt Valley, have enjoyed their own AC since 1974. With the exception of a couple of single estates making good reds, the wines are usually thought of as a kind of innocuous Rhône substitute. The local co-operatives make 85 per cent of the 40 million bottles produced annually, which are then sold off anonymously to merchants. A good deal of rosé is also produced.

When well-made from a single estate, the reds have a lovely fresh juicy fruit – tasting of raspberry and spice – which is bright and breezy and undemanding; properties like Valcombe have made 'supercuvées' which are deep and impressive. The white production is less significant but, interestingly, the area was making fresh, breezy whites before Big Brother CÔTES DU RHÔNE cottoned on to the fact. Best producers: Anges, Brusset, Champ-Long, La Croix des Pins, Goult-Cave de Lumières, JABOULET, Pesquié, Valcombe, Union des Caves du Ventoux, la Verrière, la Vieille Ferme.

CÔTES DU VIVARAIS VDQS

FRANCE, Southern Rhône

♟♟ *Grenache, Syrah, Cinsaut, Carignan*

♀ *Clairette, Grenache Blanc, Marsanne*

Spread along the west bank of the Rhône where the river Ardèche joins it at Pont-St-Esprit, this is predominantly a red wine zone.

When the wines use the typical southern RHÔNE varieties – Grenache, Cinsaut, Carignan – the result is light, fresh red and rosé, for drinking young. But plantings of grapes such as Cabernet Sauvignon and Syrah are producing exciting, rich, fruity wines at irresistible prices. The whites are also improving either from local grapes or from Sauvignon Blanc and Chardonnay. Best producers: Vignerons Ardèchois, Chais du Vivarais, Vigier.

QUINTA DO CÔTTO

PORTUGAL, Douro, Douro DOC, Port DOC
♂ (Quinta da Côtto) Tempranillo (Tinta Roriz), Touriga Franca, Touriga Nacional, Sousão
♀ (Paço de Teixeiró) Avesso, Loureiro, Trajadura, Arinto (Pedernã)

The Champalimaud family are controversial. They own a vineyard in VINHO VERDE country (Paço de Teixeiró) as well as Quinta do Côtto, an estate nearby in the westerly reaches of the DOURO. Miguel Champalimaud holds forth that his supposedly inferior C/D grade PORT vineyards deserve to be just as highly rated as those further upstream, but it is his unfortified Douro wines that have really made his name.

There are two levels of red wine: the straightforward and much improved Quinta do Côtto and, in the best years, Quinta do Côtto Grande Escolha. The latter wine can seem rather unwieldy and oaky when young, but develops delicious flavours with a few years in bottle. Quinta do Côtto continues to make a small quantity of fine but rather quirky port which is fortified to a lower strength than wines from the mainstream shippers. Best years: (Grande Escolha) 2000, '97, '95, '94, '90, '87, '85.

COULY-DUTHEIL

FRANCE, Loire, Touraine, Chinon AC
♂ Cabernet Franc
♀ Chenin Blanc

This family firm is the leading grower and négociant in CHINON. Couly-Dutheil's top two properties are the Clos de l'Écho, the most famous vineyard in the region and once owned by the writer Rabelais' family, and the Clos de l'Olive. There are a number of other cuvées, including les Gravières, the lightest of their Chinons, and Baronnie Madeleine, which is mainly a blend of the best parcels of bought wine. Les Chanteaux is an attractively floral white Chinon. Couly-Dutheil's wines are always reliable but even the top cuvées and single-vineyard wines don't quite have the focus of the wines from Chinon's best independent domaines. Even so, they age

extremely well: the 1964 Clos de l'Écho remains a revelation! Best years: 2002, '01, '00, '97, '96, '95, '90, '89, '86. '85.

COUSIÑO MACUL

CHILE, Maipo Valley
♂ Cabernet Sauvignon, Merlot
♀ Chardonnay, Sauvignon Blanc, Riesling,

Cousiño Macul is Chile's most traditional wine estate and for a long time it was regarded as Chile's leading one almost as if by right. Until relatively recently, Cousiño Macul made a string of marvellous deep reds, packed with blackcurrant fruit and infused with smoke. Times have changed, and Cousiño Macul hasn't really managed to keep up with the exciting developments that now mark out Chile's top wineries. Its wines seem lumpen when compared with their peers. But things may improve. They've just sold off almost all their original vineyards, hemmed in by Santiago's suburbs, and are starting afresh further south. Good luck to them. Hopefully we'll soon be able to welcome them back to the premier league.

CH. COUTET

FRANCE, Bordeaux, Barsac AC, Premier Cru Classé
♀ Sémillon, Sauvignon Blanc, Muscadelle

This is BARSAC's largest Classed Growth property, with 38.5ha (95 acres) under vine. Traditionally a close second to Barsac's other First Growth, Ch. CLIMENS, Coutet was disappointing throughout the 1980s and early '90s. Luckily, recent vintages have shown a return to form with wines of excellent balance and concentration. Coutet blends up to 20 per cent Sauvignon with the Sémillon, producing a wine more delicate than powerful. Even so, the wines are aromatic and complex with notes of tropical fruits, honey and spicy oak. In exceptional years, a minuscule quantity of specially selected Cuvée Madame is produced – a wine that has few rivals when it comes to aroma and intensity and which can age for 15 years or more. Best years: 2002, '01, '99, '98, '97, '96, '95, '90, '89, '88.

COWRA

AUSTRALIA, New South Wales

Vines were first planted here on the western side of the Great Dividing range in 1973. The area specializes in high-quality, honey-lush Chardonnay and Cowra fruit fleshes out many big-volume brands. Best producers: Charles Sturt University, Cowra Estate, Hamiltons Bluff, Richmond Grove, ROTHBURY ESTATE, Windowrie Estate.

CRAGGY RANGE

NEW ZEALAND, North Island, Hawkes Bay
♂ Pinot Noir, Merlot
♀ Sauvignon Blanc, Chardonnay, Riesling

Exciting new venture funded by a wealthy American family and managed by brilliant viticulturist Steve Smith. Extensive vineyards in HAWKES BAY and MARTINBOROUGH are being established. Premium Hawkes Bay wines, made in small quantities, include a stylish Les Beaux Cailloux Chardonnay, a bold Cabernet-dominant blend called The Quarry and a rich Merlot-dominant blend known as Sophia. Best of the varietal range are restrained yet intense Avery Sauvignon Blanc and tangy Rapaura Road Riesling from MARLBOROUGH, plus an elegant Chardonnay and Merlot, both from the Seven Poplars Vineyard in Hawkes Bay.

QUINTA DO CRASTO

PORTUGAL, Douro, Douro DOC, Port DOC
♂ Tempranillo (Tinta Roriz), Tinta Barroca, Touriga Franca, Touriga Nacional and others

The Roquettes have quickly established their family property as one of the leading quintas in the DOURO. Situated midway between Régua and Pinhão in the heart of the region, Crasto produces both PORT and unfortified red Douro wine from grapes grown on the estate. The Douro wines, made by Australian Dominic Morris and Spaniard Susana Esteban, have become better known than the ports and Quinta do Crasto Reserva is a wonderfully supple red, softened by short aging in new oak. Depending on the year, the property also releases the occasional varietal wine made from traditional Douro grape varieties, and single-vineyard bottlings. In 2001 they bought an 80-ha (198-acre) estate right next to the Spanish border from which they plan a new red wine. When it comes to port, Crasto confines itself to a traditional LBV and a vintage port. Both are foot-trodden in stone lagares in the traditional way. Best years: (vintage ports) 2000, '97, '95, '94; (Douro wines) 2000, '99, '98.

CRÉMANT D'ALSACE AC

FRANCE, Alsace
♀♂ Pinot Blanc, Pinot Noir, Pinot Gris, Riesling and others

This CHAMPAGNE-method sparkling wine, usually made from Pinot Blanc, shot to fame when the price of Champagne rocketed and the quality slumped in the early 1980s. Enthusiasm for it has since waned but, paradoxically, the quality is better now that the opportunists have departed the fray, and annual production has increased from half a million bottles to more than 20 million in the last 15 years. But then the quality of its rival Champagne has also improved. Best producers: BLANCK, Dopff au Moulin, Dopff & Irion, Gross, KUENTZ-BAS, Muré, Ostertag, Pfaffenheim co-operative, Sparr, Stoffel, TURCKHEIM co-operative.

CRÉMANT DE BOURGOGNE AC
FRANCE, Burgundy
♀ ♂ *Chardonnay, Pinot Noir, Pinot Blanc, Gamay, Aligoté and others*

Not so long ago Crémant de Bourgogne was dismissed as raw and reedy fizz, and your first grim mouthful would have you reaching for the Crème de Cassis bottle to make a Kir Royale – for which thin, reedy fizz is ideal. But the quality nowadays is generally remarkably good – and there's absolutely no excuse for it not to be. The grape varieties are the tip-top Chardonnay and Pinot Noir, with Chardonnay usually dominating the blends, and since it's warmer in Burgundy than further north in CHAMPAGNE, the wines should have a pleasant honeyed ripeness to go along with the biscuity, yeasty but dry taste of decent bubbly. There is a growing amount of rosé in response to the fad for pink fizz which Champagne has enjoyed. Best producers: Delorme, Lucius-Grégoire, Parigot-Richard, Simonnet-Febvre; and the Bailly, Lugny, St-Gengoux-de-Scissé and Viré co-operatives.

CRÉMANT DU JURA AC
FRANCE, Jura
♀ ♂ *Poulsard, Pinot Gris, Pinot Noir, Trousseau, Chardonnay, Savagnin*

This appellation was created in 1995 and has the same strict regulations as the other Crémant ACs, such as Alsace and Bourgogne. It covers the whole of the CÔTES DU JURA and can be either white or rosé, although most is white and now replaces the ACs for ARBOIS Mousseux and sparkling l'ÉTOILE and Côtes du Jura. Best producers: Ch. de l'Étoile, de la Pinte, Pupillin co-operative.

CRÉMANT DE LIMOUX AC
FRANCE, Languedoc-Roussillon
♀ *Mauzac, Chardonnay, Chenin Blanc, Pinot Noir*

This CHAMPAGNE-method sparkling wine AC was introduced in Limoux in 1990. The wines must have a minimum of 30 per cent Chardonnay and/or Chenin Blanc, but no more than 20 per cent of each. The rest comes from the local Mauzac grape. The wines are aged on lees for a year and generally have more complexity than BLANQUETTE DE LIMOUX, but should be drunk young. Best producers: Dom. de l'AIGLE, Antech, Fourn, Guinot, Laurens, Martinolles, SIEUR D'ARQUES co-operative, Valent.

CRÉMANT DE LOIRE AC
FRANCE, Loire
♀ ♂ *Chenin Blanc, Cabernet Franc, Cabernet Sauvignon, Pineau d'Aunis, Pinot Noir and others*

If there is a way forward for sparkling LOIRE wines, Crémant de Loire should provide it. The problem with most Loire sparklers, and especially SAUMUR MOUSSEUX, is a rasping, rather fruitless acidity and an explosive bubble. The Crémant de Loire AC was created in 1975 in an effort to improve the quality of Loire sparkling wines by lowering yields – 50 hectolitres per hectare instead of the 60 allowed for Saumur – and requiring that 150kg (331lb) of grapes are used to produce one hectolitre of juice rather than the 130kg (287lb) allowed for Saumur. This means you press the grapes less hard and get much softer juice – and correspondingly softer, more refreshing, wine. Crémant de Loire is always made by the CHAMPAGNE method.

The wines now are much more attractive, with more fruit, more yeast character and a more caressing mousse. But although Crémant often outclasses sparkling Saumur and VOUVRAY, the designation hasn't fully taken off. It is generally a softer wine than Saumur and is usually good to drink as soon as it is released. Best producers: BAUMARD, Berger, Brizé, Fardeau, Gabillière, Vincent Girault, Gratien & Meyer, Lambert, Langlois-Château, Michaud, Oisly-et-Thésée co-op, Passavant.

BERGER
With a period of bottle age to develop flavour, this non-vintage Crémant de Loire is soft, round and mouthfilling. The wine is ready to drink on release.

CRIMEA
UKRAINE

The Black Sea peninsula of Crimea is part of the Ukraine, and winewise alternates effortlessly between two extremes: sparkling wine inland, and sweet dessert wines along the coast. The coastal vineyards, for which the main winery is MASANDRA, benefit from the Black Sea and the mountains and have a more temperate climate; inland the winters can be very cold and the summers hot.

The first fizz made in Russia came from the Crimea in 1799 and today the Crimea attempts to meet the seemingly insatiable demand in the former Soviet Union countries for sparkling wine. Much of it is exported further afield, too, particularly to Germany, and it's generally fair quality for what it is – which is definitely not imitation CHAMPAGNE. Some is made by the Champagne method but most is made by the tank method or the Russian Continuous, which involves pumping base wine and yeast into a series of tanks, and bottling what emerges at the other end. Sparkling Krim is made in various styles, from Brut to sweet, including a sweetish red.

CRISTOM
USA, Oregon, Willamette Valley AVA
♂ *Pinot Noir*
♀ *Chardonnay, Pinot Gris, Viognier*

Named after the owners' children, Christine and Tom, this medium-sized winery, nestled in the Eola Hills, makes fine Pinot Noir. Two of the outstanding reserve Pinot Noirs are from Marjorie Vineyard and Jessie Vineyard and part of the reason for their extra weight and complexity may be that they are made by Steve Doerner, who spent 14 years fashioning the flavours of CALIFORNIA's legendary Pinot Noir producer CALERA. Good white wines include Chardonnay from Celilo Vineyard (in WASHINGTON), Pinot Gris and Viognier. Best years: (Pinot Noir) 2001, '00, '99, '98, '97.

CROFT
PORTUGAL, Douro, Port DOC
♂ *Touriga Nacional, Touriga Franca, Tempranillo (Tinta Roriz), Tinto Cão, Tinta Barroca, Tinta Amarela*
♀ *Gouveio, Viosinho, Rabigato, Malvasia Fina and others*

2001 was a pretty important year for Croft. Having boasted for generations of being one of the oldest British PORT firms, founded in the late 1600s, with the first Croft joining the company in 1736, it languished for some time under the conglomerate wing of UDV, a part of Diageo until in 2001 Croft was bought by the Fladgate Partnership (TAYLOR and FONSECA in other words), along with DELAFORCE.

There seems little doubt that this is a move for the better. Croft ports really hadn't performed during the 1980s and '90s and one

This is Croft's beautiful Quinta da Roêda in the Cima Corgo sub-region of the Douro Valley. Sweeping over the slope in the foreground are the new-style patamares terraces, designed to allow limited mechanization.

got the feeling the owners put more effort into the big brand Croft Original pale cream sherry – not a good omen for quality port production! However, the Croft sherry business has been bought by GONZÁLEZ BYASS and now Croft, with the fine Quinta da Roêda estate at its core, should only improve. Best years: (Vintage) 2000, '94, '91, '77, '70, '66, '63, '55, '45.

CROZES-HERMITAGE AC

FRANCE, Northern Rhône

❦ *Syrah*

♀ *Marsanne, Roussanne*

Crozes-Hermitage is the largest of the northern RHÔNE ACs, with 1200ha (2965 acres) of vines spreading over the hillocks and plains behind the great hill of HERMITAGE. The last few years of Rhône wine history have been notable for the succession of rising stars, particularly in this small but high-quality northern section. Hermitage, CÔTE-RÔTIE, CORNAS and ST-JOSEPH have all been getting the showbiz treatment, but with the finite amounts of wine available from the terraced hill slopes of these ACs, and the prices they can command, people are suddenly discovering that red Crozes-Hermitage is rather better than they thought.

Ideally, it should have a full red colour, a rich blackcurrants, raspberries and earth smell,

and a strong, meaty but rich flavour. As so often with Syrah, the delicious fruit flavours have to mingle in with strange tastes of vegetables, damped-out bonfires, well-hung meat and herbs. You can drink it young, especially if the grapes were grown on flat land, but in ripe years, from a hillside site, it improves greatly for two to five years. Since the late 1990s the quality of Crozes from almost every quarter has leapt. Best years: 2001, '00, '99, '98, '97, '96, '95, '94, '91, '90, '89, '88. Best producers: (reds) Belle, CHAPOUTIER, CHAVE, Colombier, Combier, DELAS, Dumaine, Entrefaux, Fayolle, Ferraton, GRAILLOT, JABOULET, Pavillon-Mercurol, Pochon (Ch. Curson), Remizières, G Robin, Sorrel, Tardieu-Laurent, Vins de Vienne.

The white wines from Crozes-Hermitage are almost never as exciting as Hermitage whites, even though the same grape varieties are used (Marsanne and Roussanne). This is because, except on the hilly slopes at Mercurol, most of the grapes are grown on fairly flat, productive land and so the fruit lacks the astonishing concentration which marks out Hermitage. There is another reason – modern winemaking techniques. While much white Hermitage is still produced in the traditional manner, resulting in thick, gluey wines which may take ten years to open out properly, Crozes-Hermitage is now almost always

made by cool fermentation to draw out the fruit and perfume. Although Desmeure still makes a highly successful old-style white Crozes – thick with the flavour of buttered almonds and bruised apples – the best modern Crozes is now extremely fresh, with the flavour of raw nuts and apple blossom. In general, drink white Crozes young, before the floral perfume disappears. Best producers: (whites) Chave, Colombier, Combier, Dard et Ribo, Delas, Desmeure, Dumaine, Fayolle, Ferraton, Graillot, Jaboulet, Pochon, Pradelle, Remizières, Sorrel.

YVES CUILLERON

FRANCE, Northern Rhône, Condrieu AC

❦ *Syrah*

♀ *Viognier, Marsanne, Roussanne*

Yves Cuilleron took over the family estate in CONDRIEU in the late 1980s and immediately made an impression. He was one of the first growers to produce a barrel-fermented Condrieu in a late-harvest style; called les Ayguets, it is a remarkable and gorgeously aromatic wine. Cuilleron insists this is no trendy innovation, but a return to a style that was popular two centuries ago in Condrieu. His top dry cuvée is the wonderfully perfumed les Chaillets Vieilles Vignes. Cuilleron is now regularly one of Condrieu's top producers.

Although the largest single proprietor in Condrieu, with 8ha (20 acres) of vineyards in this appellation, Cuilleron soon expanded his operations by producing small quantities of excellent ST-JOSEPH and CÔTE-RÔTIE. There are three white St-Joseph wines: Coteau St-Pierre, Lyseras and le Bois Lombard, the latter being produced mostly from old vines. The red Cuvée Prestige is also made from old St-Joseph vines and is aged in 25 per cent new oak. His latest project, with two fellow growers, is a *négociant* business called Vins de Vienne. Best years: (reds) 2001, '00, '99, '98, '97, '96, '95, '94; (Condrieu) 2001, '00, '99, '98, '97, '96.

CULLEN WINES

AUSTRALIA, Western Australia, Margaret River

❦ *Cabernet Sauvignon, Merlot, Pinot Noir and others*

♀ *Chardonnay, Sauvignon Blanc, Semillon*

Cullens was one of the original pioneer wineries in MARGARET RIVER, and is still one of the quality leaders, now run by the highly talented and refreshingly opinionated Vanya Cullen, and making marvellously self-confident wines. Its complex, structured Cabernet-Merlot is generally one of Australia's best, and new release Mangan from

Malbec, Petit Verdot and Merlot is richly idiosyncratic. The Chardonnay is oaky but long-lived and partially barrel-fermented Semillon-Sauvignon is reserved, though ripe, and ages brilliantly. Best years: (reds) 2001, '00, '99, '98, '97, '96, '95, '94, '92, '91, '90, '86, '84, '82.

CURICÓ VALLEY

Chile, Valle Central

You could call the Curicó Valley the engine room of the Chilean wine industry, because all the big companies have operations down here or take significant amounts of Curicó grapes, almost all of which are used for large-volume blends rather than top cuvées. Despite being south of Santiago, Curicó is a warm area because it is largely blocked off from the cool Pacific influence by the Coastal Range of mountains. Add very fertile soil on the valley floor, giving big crops, and you have the perfect good-quality bulk provider with Cabernet, Merlot, Carmenere and Chardonnay especially successful. Best producers: Viña CANEPA, MONTES, SAN PEDRO, Miguel TORRES, VALDIVIESO.

CVNE

SPAIN, La Rioja, Rioja DOCa
♥ Tempranillo, Grenache Noir (Garnacha Tinta), Carignan (Cariñena, Mazuelo), Graciano and others
♥ Grenache Noir (Garnacha Tinta)
♀ Macabeo (Viura), Grenache Blanc (Garnacha Blanca), Malvasía

'The biggest of the smaller bodegas' is how the Compañía Vinícola del Norte de España (CVNE, pronounced 'coonay', for short) describes itself. 'And one of the best of the lot' it might justifiably add. Quality at this RIOJA bodega is extremely high.

Where CVNE is among the region's big boys is in its vineyard holdings, with over 250ha (618 acres) of its own land and full control over growing and harvesting in as many more. As well as the elegant, plummy Viña Real wines, Crianza, Reserva and Gran Reserva, there's a lovely, young, light, plummy CVNE Tinto. A prestige red called Imperial is made in the best years. The all-Tempranillo Real de Asúa is a newer wine with even loftier ambitions.

CVNE is one of the few Riojan companies to make really good, old-style, wood-aged whites. Monopole (made from 100 per cent Viura) has a fascinating custardy nuttiness from 13 months' barrel aging. Best years: (reds) 2001, '00, '99, '98, '96, '95, '94, '91, '90, '89, '87, '86, '85.

Didier Dagueneau, a much-needed quality fanatic in the Pouilly-Fumé AC, takes a sample of Pur Sang, one of his barrel-fermented Sauvignon Blanc wines.

DIDIER DAGUENEAU

FRANCE, Central Loire, Pouilly-Fumé AC
♀ Sauvignon Blanc

A rebel by nature, the mercurial Didier Dagueneau makes some of the most remarkable dry Sauvignon Blancs in the world. He preaches the use of high-density plantings, very low yields and biodynamic viticulture. Dagueneau's plain speaking (he is often critical of standards, namely over-production and poor winemaking, in his local appellation, POUILLY-FUMÉ) and his chummy relations with the media have not endeared him to his neighbours.

Dagueneau's winery, built in 1989, is one of the most striking in the region. It operates by gravity, which means that the must and the wine can be moved around the winery in the most natural way possible. He makes a number of cuvées, which include the approachable En Chailloux, the single-vineyard Buisson Renard and the barrel-fermented Pur Sang. His most famous wine is Silex, made from old vines in the flinty soil that is characteristic of part of the Pouilly vineyards. This is also fermented and aged in young oak barrels. Needless to say his wines are not cheap. Best years: 2002, '01, '00, '99, '98, '97.

DAL FORNO

ITALY, Veneto, Valpolicella DOC
♥ Corvina, Rondinella, Croatina and others
♀ Garganega, Trebbiano Toscano, Turbiana

On his small estate at Illasi, outside the VALPOLICELLA Classico area, Romano Dal Forno makes wines that were already being hailed as among the best in Valpolicella before

he started introducing new French oak barrels in 1990. Today there are those who consider him to be the quality leader in Valpolicella, with his stunning Amarone Monte Lodoletta, and liquid bombshell Recioto Monte Lodoletta. To Dal Forno must go credit for proving conclusively that great Valpolicella can be made outside the Classico area and for demonstrating how modern winemaking can be used to enhance an ancient wine without in any way compromising typicity. Best years: (Amarone) 2001, '00, '99, '97, '96, '95, '93, '91, '90, '88, '85.

DALLA VALLE

USA, California, Napa County, Napa Valley AVA
♥ Cabernet Sauvignon, Cabernet Franc

Founded by the late Gustav Dalla Valle, this beautiful hillside winery was a little slow in starting, but is now running neck and neck with NAPA's finest. On a slope overlooking the Silverado Trail, Dalla Valle developed a 10-ha (25-acre) vineyard which supplies all of the winery's needs.

In addition to its Cabernet Sauvignon, which hit full stride in 1990, there is Maya, a magnificent Cabernet Sauvignon and Cabernet Franc blend. Both will smooth out beautifully after ten years. Best years: 2001, '00, '99, '98, '97, '96, '95, '94, '93, '91, '90.

DALWHINNIE

AUSTRALIA, Victoria, Pyrenees
♥ Syrah (Shiraz), Cabernet Sauvignon, Pinot Noir
♀ Chardonnay

Dalwhinnie is consistently the best producer in the Pyrenees, drawing upon 25-year-old, low-yielding, unirrigated estate vineyards which are immaculately maintained. The quality of the grapes shines through in the carefully made wines: complex, melon and grapefruit-accented Chardonnay, almost as impressive in its way as the black cherry, berry and mint Shiraz and the sweet, cassis and chocolate Cabernet Sauvignon. Pinot Noir, made with assistance from Rick Kinzbrunner of GIA-CONDA, has also made its mark in minute quantities. Best years: (reds) 2001, '00, '99, '98, '97, '96, '95, '94, '92, '91, '90, '88, '86.

DÃO DOC

PORTUGAL, Beira Alta
♥ Touriga Nacional, Tempranillo (Aragonez/Tinta Roriz), Jaen, Alfrocheiro, Bastardo, Rufete and others
♀ Encruzado, Bical (Borrado dos Moscas), Cercial, Malvasia, Verdelho

In central Portugal, Dão has all that it takes to produce some of the country's best reds.

Mountains shelter the region from the Atlantic and yet there is sufficient rain for vines to flourish in the poor granite soils. The problem has been in the winemaking and for decades dowdy co-operatives continued to churn out hard, over-extracted reds and oxidized whites. During these dark times, only Caves São João kept the flame alight to remind everyone just how good traditional red Dão could be. Fortunately the co-operatives lost their stranglehold after Portugal joined the EU in 1986 and Dão has been on the way up ever since.

Portugal's largest wine producer, Sogrape, led the way, building a new winery in the heart of the region; Grão Vasco, the best-selling brand of Dão wine, has improved immeasurably since. Sogrape has since been joined by a new wave of single quintas, many of whom used to supply co-operatives but have now at long last decided to make and market their own wines. The redoubtable Caves São João's Porta dos Cavaleiros red is just as good as ever. Dão whites, though much improved on the days of yore, are still well behind the reds in character. Drink them young. Best years: (reds) 2001, '00, '99, '97, '96, '95, '94, '92. Best producers: (reds) Caves Aliança, Boas Quintas (Fonte do Ouro), Quinta de Cabriz (Virgilio Loureiro), Quinta das Maias, Quinta da Pellada (Tinta Roriz, Touriga Nacional), Quinta Ponte Pedrinha, Quinta dos Roques, Quinta de Sães, Caves São João, Sogrape (Duque de Viseu, Quinta dos Carvalhais).

D'ARENBERG

AUSTRALIA, South Australia, McLaren Vale
♦ *Shiraz (Syrah), Grenache, Cabernet Sauvignon*
♀ *Chardonnay, Viognier, Marsanne, Riesling, Sauvignon Blanc*

This winery first sprang to prominence in the second half of the 1960s, with a 1967 'Burgundy' (largely Grenache) which won seven trophies and 25 gold medals from major Australian wine shows, an astonishing record by the standards of the time, followed up by a 1968 Cabernet Sauvignon which won the coveted Jimmy Watson Trophy in 1969.

Things then settled down until the 1990s when Chester Osborn took over from father d'Arry, and with the help of savvy marketing (e.g. wine names like The Dead Arm Shiraz, The Coppermine Road Cabernet, The Dry Dam Riesling and The Last Ditch Viognier) and impressive winemaking that combines keen technical skill with great sensitivity for the traditional equipment that still is much

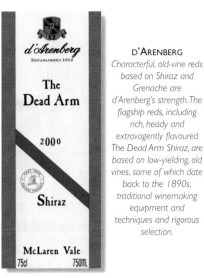

D'ARENBERG
Characterful, old-vine reds based on Shiraz and Grenache are d'Arenberg's strength. The flagship reds, including rich, heady and extravagently flavoured The Dead Arm Shiraz, are based on low-yielding, old vines, some of which date back to the 1890s, traditional winemaking equipment and techniques and rigorous selection.

in evidence at d'Arenberg, Chester has proceeded to make exceptionally lush cherry, currant, berry, spice and plum-filled reds and weighty whites, with an appropriate lick of new oak. Best years: (Dead Arm Shiraz) 2001, '00, '99, '98, '97, '96, '95, '94.

DARTING

GERMANY, Pfalz, Bad Dürkheim
♦ *Blauer Portugieser (Portugieser), Pinot Noir (Spätburgunder)*
♀ *Riesling, Pinot Blanc (Weissburgunder), Rieslaner, Scheurebe and others*

Helmut Darting is a leader of the new generation of wine growers which is transforming the Pfalz into one of Germany's most exciting regions. However, while many Pfalz growers focus on an extremely dry style, Darting's wines frequently have a mouthfilling fruit richness, and indeed almost half his production is of sweeter styles. He served his apprenticeship at the excellent Müller-Catoir estate and clearly learned his lessons well. Best years: (Riesling Spätlese) 2002, '01, '99, '98, '97, '96, '93, '92.

RENÉ ET VINCENT DAUVISSAT

FRANCE, Burgundy, Chablis AC
♀ *Chardonnay*

There are many Chablis estates with the Dauvissat name, but the most distinguished is that run by Vincent Dauvissat. Almost all the wines here are either Premier Cru (Forêt, Séchet, Vaillons) or Grand Cru (les Preuses, les Clos). The vines have an average age of 40 years. The winemaking is without frills: the must is fermented in tanks and barrels, very little new oak is used, no more than is required to replace worn-out barrels. These

wines are all that classic Chablis should be, with a great purity of fruit and a strong mineral presence. Best years: 2002, '00, '99, '98, '97, '96, '95, '92, '90, '89.

MARCO DE BARTOLI

ITALY, Sicily, Marsala
♀ *Grillo, Muscat of Alexandria (Zibibbo)*

In the early 1980s Marco De Bartoli almost single-handedly restored the credibility of Marsala as a high-class wine with his unfortified, bone dry *liquoroso* Marsala called Vecchio Samperi, even though it did not qualify for the Marsala DOC because he refused to fortify it up to the minimum 18 per cent alcohol. The main grape variety is Grillo, one of the better Marsala grapes, and the wine is aged in wooden barrels in a solera system. There is also a 20-Year-Old version.

De Bartoli, now helped by his sons Renato and Sebastiano, also produces fortified Marsala according to the modern regulations, a discreetly sweetened Superiore and Superiore Oro Vigna la Miccia, and these again are probably the best of their genre. De Bartoli is also strong on the island of Pantelleria, where he makes a delicious sweet Moscato Passito di Pantelleria called Bukkuram from sun-dried Zibibbo (Muscat of Alexandria) grapes as well as a delicious dry Muscat called Pietra Nera.

DE BORTOLI

AUSTRALIA, New South Wales (Riverina, Hunter Valley) and Victoria (Yarra Valley)
♦ *Syrah (Shiraz), Merlot, Cabernet Sauvignon, Durif*
♀ *Semillon, Chardonnay, Riesling, Sauvignon Blanc*

This winery owes its worldwide reputation to a single wine which was first made in 1982 and then largely fortuitously. What is more, the wine – a magnificent, luscious botrytis Semillon called Noble One, that even upstaged Ch. d'Yquem in some tastings – represents less than 3 per cent of De Bortoli's production, but it was of great significance, since it proved that the inland area of Riverina was not just a faceless bulk producer, but could achieve world class in this ultra-sweet 'Sauternes' style.

De Bortoli now also owns an extremely smart winery in the Yarra Valley and a new Hunter Valley operation as well as significant vineyards in Victoria's King Valley. The other Riverina wines are adequate, good value and user-friendly; the Yarra ones are some of the tastiest in the valley. Best years: (botrytis Semillon) 2000, '99, '98, '97, '96, '95, '94, '93, '90.

DE WETSHOF

SOUTH AFRICA, Western Cape, Robertson WO
♀ *Pinot Noir, Cabernet Sauvignon*
♀ *Chardonnay, Sauvignon Blanc, Riesling (Rhine Riesling)*

German-trained Danie de Wet was one of the Chardonnay pioneers in ROBERTSON and he has unerringly produced a wide range of examples that, especially at the lower end, are textbook examples of the grape. His unoaked 'Sur Lie' – fresh, melony, yeasty – is hard to rival anywhere for simple purity of Chardonnay fruit and value for money. Rhine Riesling, made in several styles, reflects his German wine education. The estate's first red grapes come from a newly planted 4-ha (10-acre) vineyard of Pinot Noir, and both this and a Cabernet are gentle, appetizing examples of red from a white wine expert.

DEALUL MARE

ROMANIA, Transylvania

Few places can be as evocative as picturesque Transylvania. The image of Germanic-style, turreted castles nestling atop hillsides overlooking pretty little villages is all true. What is equally appealing is that the wine there is improving by the vintage. Pinot Noirs from valleys that fan down the Carpathian Mountains, such as Valea Calugareasca, have reasonably focused Burgundian character and the Merlots, especially some young vatted wines, are also worth chasing. Talented young Romanian enologists are linking up with Australian winemakers in a bid to attract attention, and they surely will. Romanian oak is being used to great effect in some of the finer wines, and, when new and clean, it is giving surprising results. The Prahova winery is heading the modernization drive and new investment in Sahateni is beginning to yield good results.

DEHLINGER WINERY

USA, California, Sonoma County, Russian River Valley AVA
♀ *Pinot Noir, Cabernet Sauvignon, Syrah*
♀ *Chardonnay*

Dehlinger Winery has been a leader in RUSSIAN RIVER ever since Tom Dehlinger took over in 1985. Along with Gary Farrell, ROCHIOLI and WILLIAMS SELYEM he defined Russian River Pinot Noir, but his style has always been a little deeper, darker and richer than that of his peers, perhaps explained by his vineyards being in marginally warmer conditions down towards the Santa Rosa Creek. Tom takes his vineyards seriously, mapping each row of vines according to

health and vigour, adapting trellising and training techniques where necessary and releasing up to five different cuvées of high-quality, full-flavoured Pinot Noir. He also makes ageworthy Chardonnay. Best years: 2001, '00, '99, '98, '97, '96, '95, '94, '92, '91.

DEIDESHEIM

GERMANY, Pfalz

This village, along with FORST and Wachenheim, forms the centre of the Mittelhaardt, that part of the PFALZ with the greatest concentration of quality vineyards. Anything labelled with the Grosslage name Deidesheimer Hofstück may have come from one of the neighbouring villages. The best vineyards in Deidesheim itself are Grainhübel, Hohenmorgen, Kalkofen and Leinhöhle. Best producers: BASSERMANN-JORDAN, BIFFAR, von BUHL, BÜRKLIN-WOLF, Christmann, Wegeler. Best years: 2002, '01, '99, '98, '97, '96.

DEISS

FRANCE, Alsace, Alsace AC
♀ *Pinot Noir*
♀ *Riesling, Gewurztraminer, Pinot Gris, Pinot Blanc*

No grower in ALSACE is more fanatical about the notion of terroir than Jean-Michel Deiss. In some vintages he will bottle six or more different versions of Riesling alone. Deiss can explain the precise soil structure and meso-climatic conditions for each location, and the wines are indeed different from each other. All his wines have exemplary intensity and vigour, but the greatest Rieslings usually come from the Grands Crus Altenberg in Bergheim and Schoenenbourg in Riquewihr. Deiss claims not to be terribly interested in Pinot Gris but manages to produce sensational examples each year, nonetheless. The Vendange Tardive and Sélection de Grains Nobles wines are stunning. Prices are high, but for once they are justified by quality. Best years: (Grand Cru Riesling) 2001, '00, '98, '97, '96, '95, '94, '93, '92, '90, '89, '88.

DELAFORCE

PORTUGAL, Douro, Port DOC
♀ *Touriga Franca, Tempranillo (Tinta Roriz), Tinta Barroca, Tinta Amarela, Rufete and others*
♀ *Malvasia Fina, Rabigato and others*

Delaforce's purchase, in 2001, by the Fladgate Partnership (TAYLOR and FONSECA in simpler terms) will fundamentally change the company. And, it has to be said, the change will be for the better, because despite having a long history, Delaforce has rarely shone in

living memory, and certainly not during its ownership by the multinational Diageo group. Vintage PORTs showed some improvement in the late 1990s, but most of the over-performing port houses own top-quality quintas on which to base their vintage blends. Delaforce owns no vineyards, though it has an exclusive arrangement with the excellent Quinta da Corte. Tawnies are Delaforce's strong point, and, strangely, white port, so I'd expect the new ownership to focus on fine wines like His Eminence's Choice Tawny and quietly drop less effective lines altogether.

DELAS

FRANCE, Northern Rhône
♀ *Syrah, Grenache*
♀ *Marsanne, Roussanne, Viognier*

This long-established *négociant* house owns some of the finest vineyard sites in the northern RHÔNE, especially in HERMITAGE, yet the wines have often been lacklustre. All that began to change in 1997, after Delas was purchased by the CHAMPAGNE house of DEUTZ (now ROEDERER). A new director, Jacques Grange, who had previously worked with CHAPOUTIER and COLOMBO, didn't take long to work out what was wrong at Delas. He reorganized the cellars and discarded many of the older mustier barrels. He also reduced yields and began to select out the best parcels, especially in Hermitage, CÔTE-RÔTIE and CONDRIEU. The result is full-bodied, correct wines across the board, and some excellent top-level special selections. Best years: 2001, '00, '99, '98, '97, '96, '95, '90.

DELATITE

AUSTRALIA, Victoria, Strathbogie Ranges
♀ *Merlot, Cabernet Sauvignon, Syrah (Shiraz), Pinot Noir*
♀ *Riesling, Gewurztraminer, Sauvignon Blanc, Chardonnay, Pinot Gris*

If you neeed convincing about cool-climate vineyards in Australia, Delatite should do the trick. Even in high summer you can be standing in the middle of the ripening vines and still see the glistening snow of the Mount Buller skifields in the distance. So you'll want the wines to taste cool as well. But what does cool taste like?

Delatite Riesling, for a start, delicate as spring water, scented with flowers. Delatite Gewurztraminer, all the heady aromas of the grape intact but tasted through a filter of bride-white muslin. Or the Pinot Noir and Devil's River red BORDEAUX blend with their finely focused fruit, cut glass clarity and a sneak of minty perfume so fresh you'd never find it where the sun bakes down. A cool climate classic – if you still need persuading. Best years: (Riesling) 2000, '99, '97, '96, '94, '93, '87, '86, '82.

DELEGAT'S

NEW ZEALAND, North Island, Henderson

❧ Merlot, Cabernet Sauvignon

❧ Chardonnay, Sauvignon Blanc

New Zealand's brother and sister team, Jim and Rose Delegat, specializes in Chardonnay, Cabernet-Merlot and Sauvignon Blanc, and is one of New Zealand's most reliable and value-conscious producers. The winery uses fruit from its own vineyards and contract growers in HAWKES BAY and MARLBOROUGH. Top of the range are the Reserve wines – ripe, peachy Chardonnay and good crunchy Merlot and Cabernet. Delegat's Hawkes Bay label is for cheaper, easygoing reds and whites. The Marlborough Chardonnay and Sauvignon wines are sold under the Oyster Bay label.

DELILLE CELLARS

USA, Washington State, Woodinville

❧ Cabernet Sauvignon, Merlot, Cabernet Franc, Petit Verdot, Syrah

❧ Sauvignon Blanc, Semillon

Winemaker Chris Upchurch crafts heady, oaky, cherry-filled reds and bright, tasty whites. Using fruit from a variety of YAKIMA VALLEY vineyards, he selects his best grapes for a BORDEAUX-style blend called Chaleur Estate. A second wine, D2, is a selection of lighter barrels of Cabernet and Merlot that is ready to drink early. Chaleur Estate Blanc is an oaky Semillon-Sauvignon Blanc blend.

DENBIES

ENGLAND, Surrey

❧ Pinot Noir, Dornfelder, Pinot Meunier and others

❧ Pinot Noir, Dornfelder

❧ Müller-Thurgau, Reichensteiner, Bacchus, Ortega, Chardonnay, Seyval Blanc, Schönburger, Pinot Gris and others

This is England's most ambitious vineyard project yet, with 110ha (270 acres) of vines on the chalky North Downs near Dorking. There are some 20 varieties planted in the vineyard, but some fine white and rosé releases cannot hide the fact that much of the wine is pretty ordinary. There is also botrytized dessert wine and a CHAMPAGNE-method fizz. Marvellous Riesling, Chardonnay and Pinot Gris have been produced in tiny quantities. Drink the wines at two to three years old.

DEUTZ

Deutz makes several styles of vintage Champagne, including the weightier Cuvée William Deutz, named after one of the founders of the company in 1838.

DEUTZ

FRANCE, Champagne, Champagne AC

❧❧ Pinot Noir, Chardonnay, Pinot Meunier

By the late 1980s, the once distinguished house of Deutz had seen its reputation in decline, so there was probably a collective sigh of relief when in 1993 it was bought by one of the most quality-conscious producers in the region, Louis ROEDERER. No doubt believing that part of Deutz's problems lay in its divided attention between French and New World operations, Roederer wound down the Californian sparkling wine facility. Almost a million bottles of CHAMPAGNE are produced annually. The mainstay of the range is the Brut, made from the three Champagne grape varieties in equal proportions. A range of full-bodied vintage wines includes the outstanding Blanc de Blancs, the Pinot Noir-dominated Cuvée William Deutz and the exceptional William Deutz Rosé. Best years: 1996, '95, '93, '90, '89, '88.

D F J VINHOS

PORTUGAL

❧ Tempranillo (Tinta Roriz), Tinta Barroca, Trincadeira, Cabernet Sauvignon, Castelão, Touriga Nacional, Touriga Franca and others

❧ Fernão Pires, Chardonnay, Arinto

In the early 1990s, UK wine shippers D & F began working with one of Portugal's most innovative winemakers, José Neiva; in 1999 this relationship evolved into D F J Vinhos, who now produce some of the tastiest and best value reds in Portugal. The Bela Fonte brand includes varietal reds Baga, Jaen and Touriga Franca and a white Bical, all from BEIRAS. Other labels include Manta Preta from ESTREMADURA, Pedras do Monte and Rocha do Monte from TERRAS DO SADO, Senda do Vale from RIBATEJO, and an ALGARVE red, Cataplana. At the top end are the Grand'Arte reds, including an intensely fruity, peppery Trincadeira.

DIAMOND CREEK VINEYARDS

USA, California, Napa County, Napa Valley AVA

❧ Cabernet Sauvignon, Merlot, Cabernet Franc, Petit Verdot

On Diamond Mountain in northern NAPA, three vineyards give their names to intense, individualistic Cabernet Sauvignon bottlings. This trio – Volcanic Hill, Red Rock Terrace and Gravelly Meadow – have always been among the most expensive and talked-about CALIFORNIA Cabernets. Early vintages were tannin-laden, but since the 1990s the wines have displayed a restraint that works well with the rich fruit core. Best years: 2001, '00, '99, '98, '97, '96, '95, '94, '92, '91, '90, '87, '86.

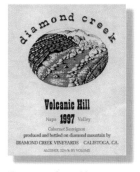

DIAMOND CREEK VINEYARDS

Volcanic Hill, a south-facing hillside vineyard on Diamond Mountain, is the warmest of the three Diamond Creek vineyards, all with different soils and different gradients.

SCHLOSSGUT DIEL

GERMANY, Nahe, Burg Layen

❧ Pinot Noir (Spätburgunder)

❧ Riesling, Pinot Gris (Grauburgunder), Pinot Blanc (Weissburgunder)

Wine writer, restaurant critic, television personality, campaigner for vineyard classification and who knows what else, Armin Diel is rightly nicknamed 'the big Diel'. After a period of stylistic oscillation, Diel came down firmly in favour of classic style Rieslings with the 1989 and '90 vintages, since which time the estate has been one of the quality leaders in the NAHE.

Although it is the Eiswein that hits the headlines, achieving record auction prices, the signature wines are the Spätlesen and Auslesen from the rocky slopes of Dorsheim's excellent Burgberg, Goldloch and Pittermännchen sites. While those from the Pittermännchen – with racy acidity and a delicate smoky tang – can easily be mistaken for top-class MOSEL wines, the wines from the Burgberg are juicy with a minerally acidity and the Goldloch Rieslings are the most noble, with a bouquet of ripe apricots.

Diel also produces barrique-aged wines from the Pinot family. These days the oak in them is much milder than during the 1980s. This, together with lower yields, has made the wines richer and silkier. Victor is the top wine of this range, a blend of Grauburgunder and Weissburgunder and capable of aging for five years and more. Best years: (Riesling Spätlese) 2002, '01, '99, '98, '97, '96, '95, '93, '90, '89.

SCHLOSSGUT DIEL
The very full-bodied and sweet Riesling Eisweins from this estate, one of the best in the Nahe region, are world famous for their thrilling intensity.

DISTELL
SOUTH AFRICA, Western Cape, Stellenbosch WO
This company, formed by the merger between Distillers Corporation and South Africa's largest merchant-producer, Stellenbosch Farmers' Winery, controls almost 30 per cent of Cape table wine production and is still finding its feet, but some of the allied individual wineries – such as Neethlingshof, STELLENZICHT and Durbanville Hills – are already performing well. The Fleur du Cap range is also improving, and other promising labels are Zonnebloem Fine Art and Pongrácz Cap Classique fizz. Two wineries in Paarl (Nederburg and Plaisir de Merle) are run separately. With better vines and a new cellar team, Nederburg is busy reinventing itself; botrytized dessert Edelkeur remains the trademark label, and is sold only through an annual auction. Plaisir de Merle, after a great start, lost its way, but signs are that it is on the way back.

CH. DOISY-DAËNE
FRANCE, Bordeaux, Sauternes AC, 2ème Cru Classé
♀ Sémillon
This is a consistently good BARSAC estate, though it uses the SAUTERNES AC, and is made almost exclusively from Sémillon. Since 1989, the wines from this 15-ha (37-acre) estate, which is neighbour to the great Ch.

CLIMENS, have been stunning – rich, powerful and bursting with tropical fruit flavours. Owner Pierre Dubourdieu's recipe for success has been low yields, successive selective picking, and vinification and aging in oak barrels. The wines are beautiful to drink young, but will age ten years or more. In 1990 and '96 an infinitesimally small amount of superrich Sauternes from individually picked botrytized grapes was produced under the label Extravagant. Best years: (sweet) 2002, '01, '99, '98, '97, '96, '95, '90, '89, '88, '86, '83.

Doisy-Daëne Sec, made essentially from Sauvignon Blanc and sold under the BORDEAUX AC, is a dry, perfumed, full-bodied white for early drinking. Best years: (dry) 2001, '99, '98.

CH. DOISY-VÉDRINES
FRANCE, Bordeaux, Sauternes AC, 2ème Cru Classé
♀ Sémillon
Next door to DOISY-DAËNE in the BARSAC AC, this is the larger of the Doisy estates and, like its neighbour, also uses the SAUTERNES AC label. Unlike most other Barsac estates, Doisy-Védrines produces a wine with more of the richness and weight of SAUTERNES from very low-yielding vines. Fermented and aged in barrel, the wines are fat and powerful, marked by new oak when young, and need eight to ten years' bottle age to be at their best. Best years: 2002, '01, '99, '98, '97, '96, '95, '90, '89, '88, '86, '85, '83.

DOLCETTO
Dolcetto is an unmistakably Italian red grape whose name means 'little sweet one' – reputedly because the grape is particularly sweet at vintage time. The wine, however, while intensely fruity, is invariably dry, and with an edge of bitterness.

Among the region's numerous Dolcetto DOCs, it is Dolcetto d'Acqui which is perhaps the most typical, generally light and fruity though always with that appetizing bitter edge and not overly serious. Dolcetto d'Asti is similar in style. Dolcetto di Dogliani is thought to represent the best quality, but Dolcetto d'Alba boasts the greatest number of high-class producers. This is not so surprising when you consider that although many Albese producers make BAROLO and/or BARBARESCO for a living, and often BARBERA too, it's actually Dolcetto they drink at practically every meal. Dolcetto di Diano d'Alba, just south of Alba, is beginning to become known as a high-quality zone. LANGHE Dolcetto tends to be less good.

Some Dolcetto is found in neighbouring LIGURIA, where it goes under the name of Ormeasco; and further afield in Australia, where Garry Crittenden at DROMANA ESTATE in VICTORIA, for one, has carried out some interesting experiments. Also found in CALIFORNIA and in Argentina.

DÔLE
SWITZERLAND, Valais
♥ Pinot Noir, Gamay
The best-known wine of the VALAIS, this is a light red blend of at least 51 per cent Pinot Noir with Gamay. The darker, richer versions with 100 per cent Pinot Noir may call themselves Pinot Noir, and anything too light for Dôle is classified as Goron, a decidedly more basic blend. Best producers: M Clavien, J Germanier, Caves Imesch, Mathier, Caves Orsat.

DOMAINE CARNEROS
USA, California, Napa County, Carneros AVA
♥ Pinot Noir
♟ Pinot Noir, Chardonnay
♀ Chardonnay, Pinot Blanc
A joint venture between the CHAMPAGNE house of TAITTINGER and Kobrand, its marketing agent, Domaine Carneros is an imposing, château-like structure presiding over green rolling hills in the centre of the CARNEROS AVA. With all eyes watching every move of this prestigious project, Domaine Carneros has developed slowly and cautiously to an impressive quality level. Under the guidance of winemaker Eileen Crane, it has earned high marks for its vintage Brut, which displays Taittinger's signature of elegance and finesse. Le Rêve is an ultra-charming vintage Blanc de Blancs. There are also three cuvées of still Pinot Noir with typical Carneros fruit and youthful charm.

DOMAINE CHANDON
AUSTRALIA, Victoria, Yarra Valley
♥ Pinot Noir, Syrah (Shiraz)
♟ Pinot Noir, Chardonnay, Pinot Meunier
♀ Chardonnay
'Anything you can do, I can do better' might well be the song sung by this Domaine Chandon to the CHAMPAGNE house MOËT ET CHANDON's other overseas subsidiaries, and in particular to the NAPA VALLEY. Since 1986 it has established itself as one of Australia's top sparkling wine producers, succeeding handsomely both in the domestic and export trade (in the latter being known as Green Point). Its various vintage sparkling wines are united by their finesse and elegance, typically with a

gentle creamy texture and flavours of citrus and ripe pear; there is also a popular non-vintage Brut and sparkling Pinot-Shiraz. Its Green Point Chardonnay and Pinot Noir table wines aren't bad either.

DOMAINE CHANDON

USA, California, Napa County, Napa Valley AVA
♀ ♀ *Pinot Noir, Chardonnay, Pinot Meunier, Pinot Blanc*

MOËT ET CHANDON's Domaine Chandon is the granddaddy of the CHAMPAGNE-owned sparkling wine houses in CALIFORNIA, located since 1975 in its own ultra-modern facility in the heart of the NAPA VALLEY. It is also the biggest, with more than 405ha (1000 acres) of vines, mostly in CARNEROS. It buys grapes from elsewhere in California to feed its second label, Shadow Creek, which is exported.

The traditional Champagne grapes of Chardonnay and Pinot Noir are the basic grape varieties used. Chandon Brut is well enough made but usually too ripe-tasting; Blanc de Noirs is smoother, with a faint copper hue. The Reserve Brut, kept for longer on its yeasts, is fuller and toastier. Étoile is an aged prestige cuvée, showing better and better with each new release, and the elegant Étoile Rosé is a charming drink. Most of the wines are not vintage dated.

DOMAINE DROUHIN OREGON

USA, Oregon, Yamhill County, Willamette Valley AVA
♀ *Pinot Noir*
♀ *Chardonnay*

After tasting OREGON Pinot Noir comparatively with red Burgundies, the well-known French *négociant* Robert DROUHIN liked its potential and in 1987 he purchased 40ha (100 acres) in the WILLAMETTE VALLEY. His daughter, Véronique Drouhin, travels to Oregon to oversee the winemaking and her talent has placed the wines among the best in Oregon. In particular, her cuvée Laurène exhibits texture and depth that few Oregon Pinot Noirs possess. In 1996 a Chardonnay from new Dijon clones was released and improves with each release. Best years: (Pinot Noir) 2001, '00, '99, '98, '97, '96, '94.

DOMAINE VISTALBA

ARGENTINA, Mendoza
♀ *Malbec, Cabernet Sauvignon, Merlot*
♀ *Chardonnay*

What happens when you blend French *savoir faire* with perfectly toned Argentine brawn? The Fabre Montmayou range is a result of just this sort of marriage. The outcome? Due to

the perfect location of the vineyards at 1150m (3770ft) above sea level in Luján de Cuyo, this pretty little bodega makes impressive Malbec. Winemaker Arnaud Meillan has a delicate touch with wood (an important skill to possess as too much oak can easily coarsen Malbec's brilliant perfumed fruit), which is particularly visible in the fine Grand Vin, a Malbec-Merlot-Cabernet blend. Chardonnay is another strong point. A separate winery at Río Negro in Patagonia makes wines under the Infinitus label. Best years: (Malbec) 2000, '99, '98, '97, '96.

DOMECQ

SPAIN, Andalucía, Jerez y Manzanilla DO and País Vasco, Rioja DOCa
♀ *Rioja: Tempranillo, Carignan (Cariñena, Mazuelo), Graciano, Macabeo (Viura)*
♀ *Grenache Noir (Garnacha Tinta)*
♀ *Jerez: Palomino Fino, Pedro Ximénez*

Pedro Domecq, now a part of Allied Domecq, is the world's biggest brandy producer and the oldest and largest of the sherry companies. Big certainly isn't bad in this case: La Ina, fresh and yeasty-tangy, is one of the best of all fino sherries and one of the lightest in alcohol. It is the second bestseller in the world, and accounts for one-third of Domecq's sherry production. Rio Viejo, a medium-bodied dry oloroso, and especially the elegant, dry, austere Botaina Amontillado Viejo are excellent. But best of all is Domecq's top range of sherries: Amontillado 51-1A, a gloriously drinkable dry amontillado, with tangy, salty concentration to the fore and toffee and hazelnut in the background; Sibarita Palo Cortado, richer, sweeter, but still with a streak of lean, iodiny concentration; and Venerable Pedro Ximénez, an alcoholic, liquid version of raisin toffee.

Domecq has invested heavily in RIOJA since the early 1970s and is now by far the biggest vineyard owner in the region. The Marqués de Arienzo Crianza is a lightish, fruity, reliable wine; the Gran Reserva is more of a mouthful. Best years: (Rioja) 1998, '97, '95, '94, '91, '89, '87, '85, '82, '81.

DOMINUS ESTATE

USA, California, Napa County, Napa Valley AVA
♀ *Cabernet Sauvignon, Merlot, Cabernet Franc, Petit Verdot*

I wasn't alone in being amazed at how fierce and beetle-browed the first Dominus releases were – the winery was co-founded by Christian Moueix, the owner of Ch. PÉTRUS in POMEROL and producer of some of

Bordeaux's most sensual reds. The trouble was, Dominus was based on the Napanook vineyard – famous for seriously tough, long-lasting reds – and the grapes it grew were mostly Cabernet Sauvignon – a combination virtually guaranteed to produce a tough wine – and it did.

That first vintage was in 1984, and clearly Christian was frustrated by Dominus' lack of progress because he took total control in 1990 and has since gradually brought his silky talents to bear on the winery's surly fruit. Recent releases are ripe and attractive, although they don't approach the nobility and interest of his Pomerol wines. Dominus ages well for at least a decade and its better vintages will easily develop for two decades. Best years: 2001, '00, '99, '97, '96, '95, '94, '91, '90.

DONAULAND

AUSTRIA, Niederösterreich

The Donauland region covers both banks of the Danube stretching from just north of Vienna west to St Polten and covers 2730ha (6745 acres) of vines. It is best known for white wines, especially from Grüner Veltliner in the Wagram area, and the region's most famous wine estate, Klosterneuburg, is the largest vineyard owner in Austria. Best producers: Karl Fritsch, Bernhard Ott, Wimmer-Czerny.

H DÖNNHOFF

GERMANY, Nahe, Oberhausen
♀ *Riesling, Pinot Blanc (Weissburgunder), Pinot Gris (Grauburgunder)*

Helmut Dönnhoff is one of Germany's greatest winemakers and obsessed with the subtle differences between wines from neighbouring vineyard sites. During the 1990s he steadily expanded his holdings in almost all the top vineyards of the Middle NAHE Valley.

Dönnhoff's most complex and refined wines come from old Riesling vines in the Niederhäuser Hermannshöhle site; the Kupfergrube of SCHLOSSBÖCKELHEIM gives the most racy and piquant wines, while the Felsenberg site makes more lavish wines with an apricotty character. From the Oberhäuser Brücke site he regularly makes some of Germany's most exciting Eisweins. Although he makes some fine dry wines, his first love is the Spätlese and Auslese wines with natural sweetness – these have extraordinary finesse and will age at least a decade, often longer. Best years: (Hermannshöhle Riesling Spätlese) 2002, '01, '00, '99, '98, '97, '96, '95, '94, '93, '90, '89, '83, '76, '71.

DOURO Portugal

AFTER THE TAGUS (TEJO), THE DOURO is the most important river in Portugal (and its importance continues over the border into Spain, where it becomes known as the Duero). It is not surprising, then, that the wine region takes its name from the river, since, without this waterway, Douro wines might never have reached the outside world. The Douro is a wild and beautiful part of Portugal. Its very poverty of natural resources has driven the inhabitants to ingenious extremes in order to wrest a living from what can only just be called soil. The part of the Douro where port can be made has the poorest soil – slate-like schist that must be broken up by digging or even dynamiting before vines can be planted. Where the slate gives way to granite, the permission to make port is withheld, limiting production to Douro table wine.

Mankind's hand is evident everywhere in the Douro landscape. In order to plant vines on the steep slopes plunging down to the Douro and its tributaries, terraces have been carved out of the slate rock. Traditional terraces are narrow, and supported by dry stone walls (one of the few ways of disposing of large boulders before the advent of proper roads and tractors). More recent planting has been undertaken with limited mechanization in mind. Some growers favour *vinha ao alta* (up and down) vineyards but the majority have opted for *patamares* or contour terraces without supporting walls.

The river has changed, too, and it is no longer a fast-flowing waterway where every journey taking wine down to Oporto (Porto) was an exciting adventure. A series of dams constructed along the river from the late 1960s has tamed the Douro's roar to a placid gurgle. The port trade is divided between the farmers who grow the grapes and the shippers who buy either grapes or young wine, though most also own some vineyards themselves. In the spring after the harvest the wine is usually taken from the wineries in the Douro Valley to Vila Nova de Gaia, facing Oporto at the mouth of the river where it is left to mature in the shippers' cellars or lodges. No longer do pipes of port make the traditional journey by boat to the lodges; instead, large tankers make the twisting road between Oporto and the Douro region hell for other motorists.

The climate in the Douro becomes hotter as you travel inland from west to east. The wet coastal climate that envelops Oporto never penetrates as far as the Douro wine region, stopped by the 1400-m (4600-ft) peaks of the Serra do Marão mountains. But there is more rainfall between Mesão Frio and Régua (the Baixa Corgo) than is good for really high-quality port, and barely enough in the very hot, eastern Douro Superior, stretching 50km (30 miles) in from the Spanish border. The prime port zone is the Cima Corgo, centred on Pinhão, an area where many of the famous port houses have their quintas (estates).

Port is one of the most tightly controlled wines in the world and the production area was demarcated in 1756. Nowadays every one of the 85,000 vineyards is given a rating (from A to F); not all the Douro's grapes qualify to be made into port – a quota is established every year (using the *benefício* system) and the rest of the grapes are made into table wines under the Douro DOC. Nearly all the best ones are red and some of them are among Portugal's most exciting new red wines. In the 1990s red Douro wines established a reputation in their own right and some now

Quinta do Crasto, enjoying a superb location overlooking the Douro river between Pinhão and Régua, is one of the new sensations of the region. Wine previously sold in bulk is now made into delicious, stylish ports and red table wines.

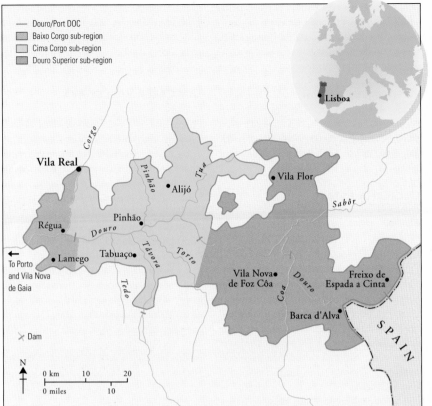

FERREIRA
First made in 1952, and only in outstanding years, Barca Velha was until the 1980s the one great traditional Douro red table wine.

QUINTA DO CRASTO
Quinta do Crasto's revival as a wine estate dates from the 1980s and the Roquette family have quickly turned it into one of the region's success stories. The scented, fruit-drenched Douro reds are almost better known than the excellent vintage port.

RAMOS PINTO
This innovative port company now owned by Roederer, the Champagne house, makes marvellous aged tawnies, particularly Quinta do Bom-Retiro.

CHURCHILL
New port company established only in 1981 makes an excellent range across the board, including single-quinta Agua Alta.

QUINTA DO NOVAL
Long famous for its extraordinary Nacional port from ungrafted vines, Quinta do Noval has recently improved the rest of its port range including the vintage.

command retail prices equivalent to LBV port. As a result, a number of producers are allocating high-quality grapes (that would have once been used to make port) for unfortified Douro wines. White grapes on the other hand have tended to lack the necessary natural acidity, although both Niepoort and Quinta do Côtto have succeeded in producing attractive, balanced, dry white wines.

REGIONAL ENTRIES
Douro, Port.

PRODUCER ENTRIES
Bright Bros., Cálem, Churchill, Cockburn, Quinta do Côtto, Quinta do Crasto, Croft, Delaforce, Dow, Ferreira, Fonseca Guimaraens, Graham, Niepoort, Quinta do Noval, Ramos Pinto, Quinta de la Rosa, Smith Woodhouse, Sogrape, Taylor, Quinta do Vesúvio, Warre.

TAYLOR
This is the aristocrat of vintage ports, and also one of the longest-lived and highest priced, from a company over 300 years old and still going strong.

FONSECA GUIMARAENS
Owned by the same group as Taylor's, Fonseca makes ports in a rich, densely plummy style. 20-Year-Old Tawny is one of the best in the Fonseca range.

WARRE
Warre's aromatic figgy vintage port is consistently one of the best produced and is made for keeping.

DOURO DOC

PORTUGAL, Douro (see also pages 162–163)

Touriga Nacional, Touriga Franca, Tinta Roriz (Tempranillo), Tinta Barroca, Tinto Cão and others

Gouveio, Viosinho, Rabigato, Malvasia Fina, Donzelinho and others

Although most people still think of the Douro region only in terms of PORT, it is being increasingly identified with unfortified wines which are now being made in their own right.

Following the outstanding success of FERREIRA's Barca Velha, along with relative newcomers like Quinta do CÔTTO, Quinta de la ROSA and NIEPOORT's Redoma, even some of the most die-hard port producers are now dabbling with reds. The grape varieties are the same as those used for port and, partly as a result of some rather heavy-handed winemaking in the past, many Douro wines used to be excessively tough and tannic. The younger generation of winemakers in the Douro (including some Australians) seems to have circumvented this problem and the recent trend has been towards full, fruit-driven reds, sometimes irresistibly scented, softened with a touch of new oak. Whites are less interesting, and are best young, but reds can improve for ten years or more. Best years: (reds) 2001, '00, '99, '97, '95, '94, '92. Best producers: (reds) Caves ALIANÇA (Foral Grande Escolha), Maria Doroteia Serôdio Borges (Fojo), BRIGHT BROTHERS (TFN), Chryseia, Quinta do Côtto (Grande Escolha), Quinta do CRASTO, Ferreira (Barca Velha, Quinta da Leda), Quinta da Gaivosa, Niepoort, Quinta do NOVAL, Quinta do Portal (Grande Reserva), Quinta da Portela da Vilariça (Touriga Nacional), Quinta de Roriz, Quinta de la Rosa, SOGRAPE, Quinta do Vale Dona Maria, Quinta do Vale Meao, Quinta do Vale da Raposa (single varietals), Vallado.

DOW

PORTUGAL, Douro, Port DOC

Tempranillo (Tinta Roriz), Tinta Barroca, Tinto Cão, Touriga Nacional, Touriga Franca and others

Gouveio, Viosinho, Malvasia Fina and others

Dow is one of a number of PORT shippers belonging to the Symington family. The Symingtons are careful to maintain a separate identity for each of their firms and Dow's wines are based on the vineyards at Quinta do Bomfim near Pinhão. They tend to be slightly drier in style than those of either WARRE or GRAHAM (the other two main companies in the Symington fold) and Dow's vintages (which start out austerely tannic) have a reputation for their extraordinary longevity. This was proved by a tasting spanning over a century of Dow's ports, which was staged to commemorate the company's bicentenary in 1998. Since 1978, Quinta do Bomfim has been released as a single-quinta wine in years when a Dow vintage is not declared. Dow also produces a good premium ruby known as Trademark, a fine range of aged tawnies and a crusted port which is notable for its richness and intensity. Best years: (Vintage) 2000, '97, '94, '91, '85, '83, '80, '77, '70, '66, '63, '60, '55, '45; (Bomfim) 1999, '98, '95, '92, '87, '86, '84.

DROMANA ESTATE

AUSTRALIA, Victoria, Mornington Peninsula

Cabernet Sauvignon, Merlot, Pinot Noir, Syrah (Shiraz), Nebbiolo, Sangiovese, Barbera, Dolcetto

Sangiovese, Nebbiolo

Chardonnay, Sauvignon Blanc, Arneis

The ever-restless Garry Crittenden, who started this model winery in 1982, is a unique combination of viticulturist, winemaker and marketer extraordinaire. He makes the more or less estate-based, high-priced Dromana Estate range; the mid-priced Schinus range; and more recently and emphatically, the Garry Crittenden 'i' range, resplendent in Italy's national colours and offering Italian varietals Sangiovese, Barbera, Dolcetto, Nebbiolo and white Arneis. The Schinus and 'i' ranges use grapes from here, there and everywhere. Best years: (Reserve Chardonnay) 2001, '00, '99, '98, '97, '95.

JOSEPH DROUHIN

FRANCE, Burgundy, Beaune

Pinot Noir

Chardonnay

This is one of BURGUNDY's most important *négociant* houses, not only because of volume – usually about 350,000 cases of wine a year – but also because, even in the darker times for quality in Burgundy, Drouhin wines maintained an integrity and personality, at, it must be said, a pretty high price.

Part of this is due to Drouhin's considerable holdings – 69ha (170 acres) in CHABLIS and CÔTE D'OR Premier and Grand Cru sites – and also because the current owner Robert Drouhin rightly saw that in a small region renowned like Burgundy, there will always be customers somewhere in the world who will be prepared to pay a premium, so long as the quality of the wine is guaranteed. Drouhin's style is fairly elegant rather than exalted and powerful. BEAUNE Clos des Mouches, MONTRACHET and the Côte de Nuits Grands Crus are particularly good, but the wines from large appellations like RULLY, ST-AUBIN and straight Chablis are also very fine. Drouhin also owns DOMAINE DROUHIN in Oregon, USA. Best years: (reds) 2002, '99, '98, '97, '96, '95, '93, '90; (whites) 2002, '00, '99, '98, '97, '96, '95.

DRY CREEK VALLEY AVA

USA, California, Sonoma County

Almost all Dry Creek's narrow valley floor is vineyard, and hillside plantings continue to expand. Red grapes have dominated this warm region since the 1870s, and the recent revival of interest in high-quality reds was exactly the boost the area needed. It persuaded growers not to rip out the considerable acreage of old Zinfandel, as well as encouraging others to plant the promising hillside sites. Interestingly the valley's initial revival probably owes more to a white wine specialist – Dry Creek Vineyard – who made a name for Sauvignon Blanc in the 1970s. Sauvignon is still the major white variety, but it's the reds that create Dry Creek chutzpah in spades. Best years: (reds) 2001, '00, '99, '98, '97, '96, '95, '94, '91. Best producers: Dry Creek Vineyard, Duxoup, FERRARI-CARANO, GALLO, Michel-Schlumberger, Nalle, Pezzi King, Preston, RAFANELLI.

DRY RIVER

NEW ZEALAND, North Island, Martinborough

Pinot Noir, Syrah

Riesling, Chardonnay, Gewurztraminer, Sauvignon Blanc, Pinot Gris

Low yields, careful selection and an uncompromising attitude to quality at this tiny winery with 10ha (25 acres) of prime vineyards, owned until recently by Dr Neil McCallum, have helped create some of the country's top Gewurztraminer and Pinot Gris, together with an intense and seductively smooth Pinot Noir, a sleek Chardonnay and powerful, long-lived Craighall Riesling. Excellent Syrah is made in tiny quantities. Best years: (Craighall Riesling) 2002, '01, '00, '99, '98, '96; (Pinot Noir) 2001, '00, '99, '96.

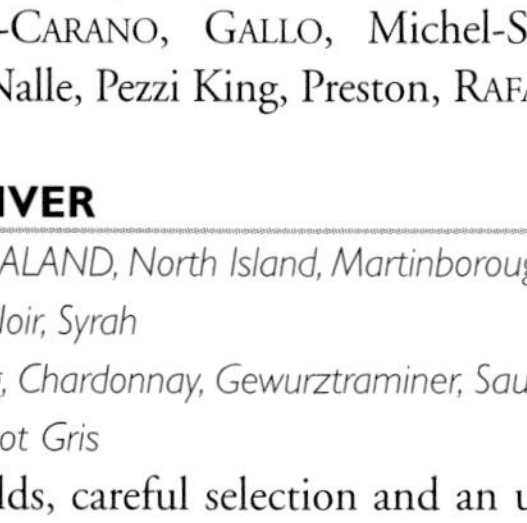

DRY RIVER

New Zealand's cult winery makes an outstanding range of wines, including strong, steely Riesling with intense citrus and lime flavours.

GEORGES DUBOEUF

Famous for his Beaujolais wines, Georges Duboeuf also specializes in good Mâconnais, including crisp, attractive St-Véran.

GEORGES DUBOEUF

FRANCE, Burgundy, Beaujolais

🍷 *Gamay*

🍷 *Chardonnay*

Easily the most important of the BEAUJOLAIS merchants, Duboeuf was responsible more than any of the others for the worldwide popularization of Beaujolais during the 1970s and '80s. His marketing flair made BEAUJOLAIS NOUVEAU a chic wine, and his winemaking and wine selection skills kept its quality high even during periods when world demand outstripped supply. Often called the 'King' of Beaujolais, Georges Duboeuf controls about 10 per cent of the region's output, and is impressive at the top and bottom ends of the market. Particular successes are Beaujolais cru wines such as MOULIN-À-VENT, FLEURIE, JULIÉNAS, MORGON and BROUILLY.

However, Beaujolais has struggled in recent years to maintain its market, and Duboeuf wisely spread his wings into the RHÔNE, the Ardèche and the LANGUEDOC from where he now sources a significant percentage of his output. As a native of the MÂCONNAIS, he is also an important producer of Mâconnais whites.

DUCKHORN VINEYARDS

USA, California, Napa County, Napa Valley AVA

🍷 *Cabernet Sauvignon, Merlot*

🍷 *Sauvignon Blanc*

Rather than try to make a name for himself in the crowded Cabernet Sauvignon market, Dan Duckhorn had the good sense to cast his lot with Merlot when he opened up shop in the late 1970s. His first Merlots – Three Palms and NAPA VALLEY – were pricy but were eagerly snapped up by wine fans jaded by an endless diet of Cabernet. But to be honest, they weren't really typically Merlot in style – you know, lush, juicy, soft-centred. I usually found them at least as hard as their neighbours' Cabernets. However, there's been a change in style and later releases are much

more enjoyably approachable. A brash but rich HOWELL MOUNTAIN Merlot is also made. Duckhorn's Cabernets, brooding and intense when young, often develop faster, and sometimes more successfully than the Merlots. Best years: (Merlot) 2001, '99, '98, '97, '96, '95, '94, '91, '90, '86. The parent Duckhorn Wine Company also produces Paraduxx, a Zinfandel-Cabernet blend, and Goldeneye Pinot Noir from a separate winery in the ANDERSON VALLEY.

CH. DUCRU-BEAUCAILLOU

FRANCE, Bordeaux, Haut-Médoc, St-Julien AC, 2ème Cru Classé

🍷 *Cabernet Sauvignon, Merlot, Cabernet Franc, Petit Verdot*

You really do get a feeling of quiet confidence as you gaze at this imposing nineteenth-century château owned by the Borie family. If this image also conjures up reliability, then this has been its reputation for many years. Until a disappointing dip in the late 1980s there hadn't been a single bad wine in more than 20 years. Ducru-Beaucaillou was thought of as the best Second Growth – and though the more showy, extrovert COS D'ESTOURNEL, LÉOVILLE-LAS-CASES and PICHON-LONGUEVILLE-COMTESSE DE LALANDE wines were also as good, many people preferred the fragrant cedar perfume, the soft, gently blackcurranty fruit and the satisfying round sensation of Ducru-Beaucaillou. Since 1994 Ducru has once again been back on form. If you want to seek out the epitome of ST-JULIEN, mixing charm and austerity, fruit and firmness, this is where you'll find it. Second wine: la Croix de Beaucaillou. Best years: 2001, '00, '99, '98, '96, '95, '94, '85, '83, '82.

DOMAINE DUJAC

FRANCE, Burgundy, Côte de Nuits, Morey-St-Denis AC

🍷 *Pinot Noir*

🍷 *Chardonnay*

In the late 1960s the young Jacques Seysses gave up a business career to devote himself to wine. He bought a small estate in MOREY-ST-DENIS, which has been gradually expanded over the years. The holdings are impressive, with Grands Crus such as CLOS DE LA ROCHE, Clos St-Denis, BONNES-MARES, Charmes-Chambertin and ÉCHÉZEAUX, as well as Premiers Crus in CHAMBOLLE-MUSIGNY and GEVREY-CHAMBERTIN.

Seysses' preoccupation with his vineyards has even extended, in a hail-damaged vineyard, to removing affected grapes with tweezers to prevent the spread of rot. During

the 1980s, when most Burgundian winemakers were seeking ever greater extraction and colour, Seysses was going in the opposite direction. He has never been one to accept conventional wisdom. To this day, he retains a high percentage of stems during fermentation, arguing that this does not, as is often thought, increase tannins, but can help reduce them. Although almost all his wines are aged entirely in new oak, which is air-dried to his specifications, he does not look for oaky flavours in his wines and thus specifies a light toast. The wines are bottled without filtration. They are deceptively light in colour, but do not lack flavour or structure and can age very well. There are few Burgundies that more perfectly capture the charm and complexity of Pinot Noir at its most elegant. Seysses also makes a small quantity of white Morey-St-Denis. Best years: 2002, '01, '00, '99, '98, '96, '95, '93, '91, '90, '89.

DUNN VINEYARDS

USA, California, Napa County, Howell Mountain AVA

🍷 *Cabernet Sauvignon*

Whether he planned it or not, Randy Dunn thrives on the mystique surrounding the HOWELL MOUNTAIN appellation and himself as a winemaker. Dunn made CAYMUS' wines between 1975 and 1985, and then retreated to Howell Mountain on the eastern side of NAPA VALLEY to work with a small Cabernet vineyard and produce his famous, perfumed but brawny Howell Mountain wine.

Grapes from the Napa Valley floor make up a somewhat softer and more accessible Napa Valley bottling which is also rich and aggressive, but which captures a fragrance rare for Napa Valley. Dark, concentrated in blackcurrant and plum fruit, his wines develop very slowly, but that hasn't stopped them achieving cult status. Best years: 2000, '99, '97, '96, '95, '94, '93, '92, '91, '90, '88, '87, '86, '85, '84, '82.

DURBACH

GERMANY, Baden

In contrast to many of Germany's wine regions, BADEN is usually thought of as being wine co-operative country, with many small growers and few lordly estates, but the village of Durbach, in the ORTENAU district south of Baden-Baden, is practically wall-to-wall private estates. Between them they make a lot of red wine, which is not so unusual for Baden, but the village also claims to have more Traminer and Pinot Blanc planted than any other village in Germany – and to confuse the issue they call the Traminer grape here 'Clevner'. Durbach is known for its Riesling, too, unlike the rest of Baden, only here it is called Klingelberger. The poor granitic soil and steep inclines suit the Riesling just fine; accordingly, it flings plenty of spice and structure into its wines. Best producers: Andreas Laible, Heinrich Männle, von Neveu, Schloss Staufenberg, Wolff-Metternich.

DÜRNSTEIN

AUSTRIA, Niederösterreich, Wachau

This irresistibly picturesque small town on the Danube still has the extensive medieval defences built with the ransom money extracted for the return of Richard the Lionheart, King of England, in 1192. Today it occupies itself with the more peaceful businesses of tourism and wine. Not only does the town boast two of the region's finest vineyard sites in the Kellerberg and Schütt, it is also home to the producer Schmidl and the remarkable co-operative, the Freie Weingärtner WACHAU.

JEAN DURUP

FRANCE, Burgundy, Chablis AC
♀ *Chardonnay*

The largest vineyard owner in CHABLIS, at least in part due to expansions in the Chablis AC of which Durup was a leading protagonist, Jean Durup is a great believer in unoaked Chablis, and his wines tend to be clean without any great complexity. Best are the Premiers Crus Fourchaume and Montée de Tonnerre. Wines appear under a variety of labels, including Domaine de l'Églantière, Ch. de Maligny and Valéry. Best years: 2002, '00, '99, '98, '97, '96, '95.

ÉCHÉZEAUX AC, GRANDS-ÉCHÉZEAUX AC

FRANCE, Burgundy, Côte de Nuits, Grands Crus
♥ *Pinot Noir*

Of all the Grands Crus in the Côte de Nuits, Échézeaux is the one with the least reputation. However, it can be a subtly powerful wine, developing a seductive raspberry and chocolate perfume as it ages. The smaller and more prestigious Grands-Échézeaux Grand Cru (so-called apparently because the rows of vines here are longer) is further down the slope immediately above CLOS DE VOUGEOT and gives deeper, richer wine, still showing a core of raspberry and chocolate fruit, but smokier in flavour, more plum-rich. It can age to a marvellous gamy, chocolaty welter of flavours over ten to 15 years. Best years: 2002, '01, '00, '99,

'98, '97, '96, '95, '93, '90. Best producers: R Arnoux, BOUCHARD PÈRE ET FILS, Cacheux-Sirugue, DROUHIN, DUJAC, R ENGEL, GRIVOT, JAYER-GILLES, Mugneret-Gibourg, Dom. de la ROMANÉE-CONTI, E Rouget.

DOMAINE DE L'ÉCU

FRANCE, Loire Valley, Pays Nantais, Muscadet Sèvre-et-Maine AC
♥ *Cabernet Sauvignon, Cabernet Franc*
♀ *Melon de Bourgogne (Muscadet), Folle Blanche, Chardonnay*

One of the finest producers of MUSCADET, Guy Bossard's biodynamically-run estate also produces GROS PLANT DU PAYS NANTAIS white, a velvety red VIN DE PAYS Cabernet blend and a refreshing sparkler, Ludwig Hahn. It is his Muscadet, though, that stands out, especially the top cuvées from different soil types: Expression de Gneiss, Orthogneiss and fuller-bodied, minerally Granite. Best years: (Granite) 2002, '01, '00, '99, '98.

DOMAINE DE L'ÉCU
Guy Bossard produces benchmark Muscadet from his biodynamically farmed domaine at Le Landreau in the heart of the Sèvre-et-Maine appellation.

EDEN VALLEY

AUSTRALIA, South Australia

After a 20-year tug of war between the ADELAIDE HILLS and the BAROSSA VALLEY, tradition and history have prevailed over geography and climate, and the Eden Valley has been joined with the Barossa Valley in the Barossa Zone, and excised from the Mount Lofty Ranges Zone. And so what? Exactly.

The fact is this undulating, windswept region produces some of Australia's best, racy, steely Rieslings as well as being home to the country's most famous single-vineyard Shiraz, HENSCHKE Hill of Grace. The style and quality of the wines are significantly affected by altitude (most vineyards are over 400m/1300ft) and by site orientation; virtually any combination can be found. Best years: (Riesling) 2001, '00, '99, '98, '97, '96, '95, '94, '92, '91, '90, '87. Best producers: Heggies, Henschke, MOUNTADAM, Pewsey Vale.

EDNA VALLEY AVA

USA, California, San Luis Obispo County

One of the coolest regions within CALIFORNIA's CENTRAL COAST, Edna Valley is a small coastal area south-east of San Luis Obispo town. Cooling ocean breezes make much of the area ideal for Chardonnay, the most widely planted variety, but more protected pockets have proved ideal for Pinot Noir as well as for Viognier and other RHÔNE grapes. Edna Valley Vineyard – a joint venture of CHALONE, which provides the winemaking skills, and Paragon Vineyards, which contributes the grapes with 240ha (600 acres) – is the biggest producer. In its relatively short history the winery has earned a substantial reputation for Chardonnays patterned directly on those of its winemaking parent, with richly toasty to outright buttery flavours coupled with attractively Burgundian, lean-limbed textures. Best years: 2001, '00, '99, '98, '97, '95, '94. Best producers: ALBAN VINEYARDS, Claiborne & Churchill, Edna Valley Vineyard, MERIDIAN, Talley.

ELGIN

SOUTH AFRICA, Western Cape

Elgin wasn't famous for wine to start with – too cold, the experts said, too wet: stick to apples and pears. So they did, and this chilly, high-altitude bowl of land perched above False Bay and looking back towards Cape Town became duly famous for apples and pears. But the quest for good cool-climate vineyard land, supported by wine wizard Neil ELLIS and local philanthropist Paul Cluver, led to plantings of Sauvignon Blanc, Chardonnay, Riesling and Pinot Noir that give wines of perfume, focused fruit and delicate texture that are among the Cape's best cool-climate offerings. Best producers: Paul Cluver, Neil Ellis, Iona.

NEIL ELLIS

SOUTH AFRICA, Western Cape, Stellenbosch WO
♥ *Cabernet Sauvignon, Syrah (Shiraz), Merlot, Pinotage*
♀ *Sauvignon Blanc, Chardonnay*

Neil Ellis is one of South Africa's top winemakers, and his goal has always been to reflect site specificity: to this end he sources grapes from far and wide. The cool, apple-orchard heights of ELGIN provide him with a penetrating Sauvignon Blanc and elegant Chardonnay. A succulent but tangy Sauvignon Blanc comes from GROENEKLOOF on the West Coast, while the warmer STELLENBOSCH area yields more Chardonnay as well as

Much of the wine from the Entre-Deux-Mers region comes from large co-operatives, but the quality has improved dramatically in recent years. However, new oak barrels for fermenting the wine are still a rarity.

Cabernet, Merlot and the latest attraction, Shiraz. All the reds are balanced and sensitively oaked. The whole winemaking operation is now carried out under one Stellenbosch roof in the picturesque Jonkershoek Valley. The attractive, modernized cellar boasts a unique cooling feature in the barrel maturation area: a waterfall and stream running through it. Best years: (reds) 2001, '00, '98, '97, '95, '94; (Chardonnay) 2002, '01, '99, '98, '97.

EMILIA-ROMAGNA
ITALY
Despite their political unity, there is a good case for considering Emilia and Romagna separately, so diverse are their wines. The vast plains of Emilia are home to the Lambrusco grape, which is actually perfectly capable of producing decent appetizing dry red, but which is usually turned into inconsequential light sweet red froth, and which flourishes on its ubiquitous high trellises in Emilia around Modena and Reggio nell'Emilia. The flatlands of Romagna also bring forth grapes in equally astonishing abundance, this time in the form of Sangiovese and Trebbiano.

In the foothills of the Apennines, however, from COLLI PIACENTINI in the west via the COLLI BOLOGNESI in the centre almost down to the Adriatic in the east there is viticulture of real and increasing worth, with quality Sangiovese rubbing shoulders with the likes of Cabernet and Chardonnay, not to mention

the indigenous Albana (see ALBANA DI ROMAGNA) and Pagadebit white grapes and red Barbarossa and Cagnina (a local name for Refosco del Terrano).

EMRICH-SCHÖNLEBER
GERMANY, Nahe, Monzingen
♀ *Riesling, Pinot Gris (Grauburgunder), Pinot Blanc (Weissburgunder), Rivaner and others*
Werner Schönleber is the leading winemaker of the Upper NAHE, making Rieslings with a crystalline clarity and intense peach and currant aromas. His top site is the Halenberg of Monzingen, which has a slate soil similar to that of the MOSEL and produces similar, if slightly bigger, wines. The Frühlingsplätzchen wines are softer and more juicy. There is good, dry Grauburgunder and Rivaner too. Best years: (Riesling) 2002, '01, '00, '99, '98, '97, '95, '94, '93, '92, '90.

ENATE
SPAIN, Aragón, Somontano DO
♀ *Cabernet Sauvignon, Merlot, Tempranillo*
♀ *Cabernet Sauvignon*
♀ *Chardonnay, Gewürztraminer*
This visually stunning winery, isolated in the foothills of the Pyrenees, is aiming to become the quality leader in the reborn region of SOMONTANO, despite its large size (400ha/1000 acres under vines and 120,000 cases produced in an average year). Enologist Jesús Artajona, who gained prestige during a prior stint with TORRES, is one of the main reasons

why Viñedos y Crianzas del Alto Aragón (Enate's official full name) has made such vast strides since its first vintage in 1992. The winery specializes in fruit-laden Chardonnays and refined, consumer-friendly reds led by the Reserva Especial, a Merlot-Cabernet Sauvignon blend. Merlot-Merlot is, as its name implies, a powerful varietal wine. The young, aromatic Gewürztraminer has been an unexpected hit. Best years: (reds) 2001, '00, '99, '98, '96, '95, '94.

RENÉ ENGEL
FRANCE, Burgundy, Côte de Nuits, Vosne-Romanée AC
♀ *Pinot Noir*
When Philippe Engel took over the family estate in 1981, he knew it was in serious need of improvements. These he has brought about, and Engel is once again one of the leading domaines in this prized corner of the Côte de Nuits. His clutch of Grands Crus includes CLOS VOUGEOT, ÉCHÉZEAUX and Grands-Échézeaux, and there is also the exceptional VOSNE-ROMANÉE Premier Cru, les Brûlées. Philippe has introduced greater grape selection at harvest, more punching down of the cap during fermentation, aging on lees, and has almost eliminated filtration. He uses a good deal of new oak, especially for the robust Grands Crus. Best years: 2000, '99, '98, '97, '96, '93, '92, '91, '90, '89.

ENTRE-DEUX-MERS AC
FRANCE, Bordeaux
♀ *Sémillon, Sauvignon Blanc, Muscadelle*
The phoenix has risen from the ashes. Thirty years ago Entre-Deux-Mers was a byword for boring, fruitless, vaguely sweet white wines of the sort that could put you off wine for life. But in the 1980s there was a dramatic about-turn, and Entre-Deux-Mers now produces some of the freshest, brightest, snappiest dry white wine in the whole of France. The AC only covers dry white wines, on average 12 million bottles annually. Red wines are produced extensively in the region but they can only use the BORDEAUX Rouge or BORDEAUX SUPÉRIEUR AC. Sweet wines are sold under the following appellations: PREMIÈRES CÔTES DE BORDEAUX, Côtes de Bordeaux-St-Macaire, LOUPIAC and STE-CROIX-DU-MONT.

The wine flavours are totally dry, grassy, appley, sometimes citrus, often with a little more weight than straight Bordeaux Blanc AC. A few properties use new oak barrels for aging, rarely for fermenting, and this adds a creamy, apricotty flavour to the wine, which can be delicious. In general, drink the wine of the latest vintage, though the better wines will last a year or two, particularly when aged or fermented in barrel. Much of the wine is made by modern co-operatives, but there are some excellent private producers too. Best producers: Bel Air, Bonnet, Castelneau, de Fontenille, Launay, Moulin-de-Launay, Nardique-la-Gravière, Ste-Marie, Tour de Mirambeau, Toutigeac, Turcaud.

ERBACH
GERMANY, Rheingau
This village in the heart of the RHEINGAU produces firm, racy and weighty wines. Some of the biggest and fullest in the region come from the Marcobrunn vineyard, a piece of land which the passer-by would probably dismiss as being obviously unsuitable for fine wine – it's at the foot of the hill, right down by the river, it's far too low, the soil too rich, it looks like a frost-trap and it probably turns to a quagmire after rain. But you would be wrong on all counts. The deep, marl soil is very well-drained and the vineyard is a sun-trap rather than a frost-trap. Part of it lies within the boundaries of the neighbouring village of HATTENHEIM. Best years: (Riesling Spätlese) 2002, '01, '00, '99, '98, '97, '96, '94, '93, '92. Best producers: Jakob Jung, Knyphausen, SCHLOSS REINHARTSHAUSEN, Schloss Schönborn.

ERBALUCE DI CALUSO DOC, CALUSO PASSITO DOC
ITALY, Piedmont
♀ *Erbaluce*
North of Turin, around the Olivetti town of Ivrea, is a strip of vineyards cultivated with Erbaluce. Its lean, flinty dry white wines and occasional sparklers, both called Erbaluce di Caluso, aren't bad, if not exactly earth shattering. But when the grapes are laid out to partially dry for up to six months before slowly fermenting, followed by aging for at least five years, a rich, sweet, citrous, gooey wine called Caluso Passito emerges, which just might make the earth quiver a bit. Drink the dry wines young. Best producers: (Caluso Passito) Cieck, Ferrando, Orsolani.

ERDEN
GERMANY, Mosel-Saar-Ruwer
The slopes behind the village of Erden are broad and gentle and planted largely with Müller-Thurgau rather than with the superior Riesling. For top Riesling, full of fire and breeding, you must swim the river and

scale the slope just where it suddenly becomes steeper opposite the village: this is the brilliant Prälat vineyard. Just above it and to the east is the Treppchen vineyard, another superb steep Riesling site, and not to be confused with the identically-named Treppchen vineyard at PIESPORT. Best years: (Riesling Spätlese) 2002, '01, '99, '97, '95, '94, '93, '90. Best producers: Joh. Jos. CHRISTOFFEL, Dr LOOSEN, Meulenhof, Mönchhof, Peter Nicolay, Dr PAULY-BERGWEILER, Heinrich Schmitges.

ERRÁZURIZ
CHILE, Aconcagua Valley
♟ *Cabernet Sauvignon, Merlot*
♀ *Sauvignon Blanc, Chardonnay*
There can be no doubt that Errázuriz is one of Chile's towering wine establishments. The combination of Ed Flaherty (formerly of CONO SUR) as winemaker and Pedro Izquierdo, viticulturist, is a red-hot one. The bodega's prime location, on the Panquehue slopes in the Aconcagua Valley, allows it to grow some of the best Cabernet Sauvignon in Chile particularly in the Don Maximiano vineyard. Its savoury yet rich Merlot and Wild Ferment Chardonnay and Pinot Noir are three of Chile's trailblazers. Syrah is their latest red flagwaver. There is also the overpriced Seña, a joint venture with MONDAVI. Best years: (reds) 2002, '01, '99, '97.

ERRÁZURIZ
Elegant Chardonnay made with wild yeast fermentation comes from the La Escultura estate in the cool-climate Casablanca Valley, Chile's top region for Chardonnay.

ESPORÃO
PORTUGAL, Alentejo, Reguengos DOC
♟ *Tempranillo (Aragonez), Trincadeira, Cabernet Sauvignon, Syrah, Touriga Nacional, Alicante Bouschet and others*
♟ *Castelão (Periquita)*
♀ *Arinto, Roupeiro, Sémillon, Antão Vaz and others*
After a chequered start in the 1970s, Herdade do Esporão has emerged as one of the ALENTEJO's leading producers. Much of its success is due to the visionary businessman, José Roquette, and the winemaker, Australian David Baverstock. Extending to around 550ha (1360 acres), Esporão boasts the largest

single vineyard in Portugal. A modern winery produces a range of red and white wines, from the young, fruity Alandra, through the middle-ranking Monte Velho to the ripe, richly-flavoured Esporão and Esporão Riserva. All are meticulously well made. Some of the best wines are varietals from Aragonez and Trincadeira, illustrating the huge potential of Portugal's indigenous grapes. Best years: (reds) 2001, '00, '99, '98, '97.

EST! EST!! EST!!! DI MONTEFIASCONE DOC
ITALY, Lazio
♀ *Trebbiano Toscano, Malvasia Bianca, Trebbiano Giallo*
This wine, from a zone in the north of LAZIO on the UMBRIAN border, no doubt owes such fame as it enjoys more to the apocryphal story about how it was discovered by some bibulous bishop in the twelfth century than to its quality, which, seeing as it is principally made from the hopelessly boring Trebbiano, will never be anything more than simple and refreshing. Best producers: Bigi (Graffiti), Falesco (Poggio dei Gelsi), Mazziotti (Canuleio).

CH. DES ESTANILLES
FRANCE, Languedoc-Roussillon, Faugères AC
♟ *Syrah, Mourvèdre, Grenache and others*
♀ *Marsanne, Roussanne, Viognier*
Michel Louison has single-handedly turned this estate into one of the top domaines in the LANGUEDOC-ROUSSILLON. Arriving from TOURAINE via Switzerland in 1976, he steadily planted Syrah, Mourvèdre and Grenache and now has 35ha (86 acres) of vines. Syrah, though, is his preferred variety and is used on its own in his top wine, the Grande Cuvée, a spicy, oaky, blackcurrant wine that needs a minimum five years' age. The Cuvée Prestige is a well-balanced blend of Grenache, Syrah and Mourvèdre, and there is also a fruity, aromatic white COTEAUX DU LANGUEDOC that is partially barrel-fermented. Best years: (reds) 2001, '00, '99, '98, '97, '96, '95.

ESTREMADURA VINHO REGIONAL
PORTUGAL
The rolling country on the Atlantic coast north of Lisbon is the most productive wine region in Portugal. For many years it was the preserve of huge co-operatives, which churned out large quantities of bland red and white wine from its 50,000ha (123,550 acres) for consumption in the nearby capital. Although Estremadura remains Portugal's

largest single wine-producing region in terms of volume, quality has now improved so much that it is the source both of good-quality high-volume brands like Ramada and also impressive brands like Manta Preta and Grand'Arte. Much of the transformation is down to roving winemaker José Neiva (of D F J VINHOS), who makes these brands. Other top wines are those from Casa SANTOS LIMA/Quinta da Boavista, sold under the names of Palha Canas and Quinta das Setencostas. The Australian Peter BRIGHT has also been making some good, spicy reds in conjunction with a co-operative in the region and there are two excellent single quintas, Abrigada and Pancas, both near the town of ALENQUER. Pancas has made excellent examples of both Cabernet Sauvignon and Chardonnay. As in much of Portugal, red tends to be better than white. All the wines from this region are ready to drink young. Best years: (reds) 2001, '00, '99, '97. Best producers: Quinta de Abrigada, Caves ALIANÇA (Quinta da Cortezia), D F J Vinhos (Grand'Arte, Manta Preta), Quinta do Monte d'Oiro, Quinta de Pancas, Companhia Agricola do Sanguinhal, Casa Santos Lima.

ETCHART

ARGENTINA, Salta and Mendoza
♦ *Cabernet Sauvignon, Merlot, Malbec*
♀ *Chardonnay, Torrontes*

Bodegas Etchart have two main centres, one in MENDOZA and another in Cafayate, SALTA, with some of the world's highest vineyards. The most interesting wines come from Salta and enologist José Luis Mounier is striving to improve the range even further. The Torrontes – drink young – is Argentina's most delicate and scented white wine. It is sometimes successfully blended with Chardonnay; you can taste the freshness of the cold but sunny uplands. Reds are a little more difficult but Malbec, in particular, has a brilliant purple hue and delightful scent of violets and taste of damsons. The wines from Mendoza lack the excitement of the Salta wines, but experimentation is going on; Argentina's first Tannat is decidedly promising.

L'ÉTOILE AC

FRANCE, Jura
♀ *Savagnin, Chardonnay, Poulsard*

L'Étoile – the star – is a lovely name for a tiny little area in the centre of the CÔTES DU JURA which has its own AC for white wines and *vin jaune* only. The local Savagnin grape is much in evidence, though less so than further north in the region, and there is a good deal of Chardonnay, either unblended – when it is light and fresh, but creamy – or blended with Savagnin, when it succeeds in soothing the savage character of that grape. The red Poulsard variety can also be part of the white wine blend. In general the wines are cleaner and fruitier than most Côtes du Jura or ARBOIS whites, and the CHAMPAGNE-method fizz, now called CRÉMANT DU JURA, can be as good as that of Pupillin in Arbois. There is also the daunting *vin jaune*, a sherry-like 'yellow' wine made from Savagnin, and the very rare sweet *vin de paille*. Best producers: Ch. de l'Étoile, Geneletti, Joly, Montbourgeau, Quintigny.

CH. L'ÉVANGILE

FRANCE, Bordeaux, Pomerol AC
♦ *Merlot, Cabernet Franc*

A neighbour to PÉTRUS and CHEVAL BLANC, l'Évangile is a top Pomerol and has a price tag to match. The Merlot-dominated wines from this 14-ha (35-acre) estate are big, rich and powerful, with layers of exotic fruit and spicy complexity. They need a minimum ten years' bottle age but good vintages will mature for 20 years or more. Since being acquired by the Rothschilds of Ch. LAFITE-ROTHSCHILD in 1990, l'Évangile has produced a string of vintages that even the great Pétrus would find hard to rival for quality and consistency. Best years: 2000, '99, '98, '96, '95, '94, '93, '90, '89, '88, '85, '83, '82.

EVANS & TATE

AUSTRALIA, Western Australia, Margaret River
♦ *Cabernet Sauvignon, Syrah (Shiraz), Merlot*
♀ *Chardonnay, Semillon, Sauvignon Blanc*

Having started life in the SWAN Valley with its Gnangara Shiraz-Cabernet, transforming the then-prevalent disdain for the Swan Valley, Evans & Tate has now moved its operations to the MARGARET RIVER, where it has grown at an exponential rate and is the winery most involved in developing the controversial Jindong region of Margaret River, a high-yielding area not approved of by traditionalists. In fact Evans & Tate take fruit from all over the region, and each vintage do a better job with it. New millennium vintages of Semillon and Chardonnay are high quality, and the Shiraz, Merlot and Cabernet are richer and riper than they used to be. Classic is a dry white with sweetness and acidity as cleverly counterplayed as salt and pepper by a three-star chef. Gnangara is a reliable red or white volume brand. Best years: (Cabernet) 2001, '00, '99, '98, '96, '94.

EXTREMADURA

SPAIN

Since 1997 a single DO, Ribera del Guadiana, has encompassed the large area (15,800ha/ 39,000 acres) which vineyards occupy on the vast plains of Extremadura – near the Portuguese border – in competition with cork trees and pastures for black-hooved Iberian pigs, Merino sheep and Retinto cattle. There is no particular geographic or climatic unity in such a large region – this is one of Europe's 'political' macro-appellations set up to counteract the market advantages which New World exporters, who are not saddled with stringent EU regulations, have enjoyed.

The newcomers are led by such established bodegas as Inviosa, whose Lar de Barros wines sell well both in Spain and abroad. Investment is leading to fast winery modernization and vineyard improvement and bringing out unexpected quality from such indigenous varieties as the white Cayetana and Pardina but the DO recognizes many varieties – local, northern Spanish and French.

THE EYRIE VINEYARDS

USA, Oregon, Yamhill County, Willamette Valley AVA
♦ *Pinot Noir, Pinot Meunier*
♀ *Pinot Gris, Chardonnay, Pinot Blanc, Muscat Ottonel*

Owner David Lett was one of the pioneers of OREGON winemaking, planting vines in 1966, and still has lessons to teach about achieving wines of finesse and restraint. His was a make-do operation to begin with – housed in an old turkey-processing plant, and equipped with cast-off tanks from dairies. It is still in the same building, but today the equipment is a little more up to date. His style of winemaking is spare; even by Oregon standards his Pinot Noirs are a shade pale, lean in texture, with understated – sometimes too understated – varietal aromas. A reserve Pinot Noir made from the South Block parcel of the original vineyard is seldom seen, but can be worth the hunt. Pinot Gris and Chardonnay are individualistic and generally successful wines – but David Lett came to Oregon to avoid the mainstream, so that's what you should expect from him. Best years: (Pinot Noir Reserve) 2002, '01, '00, '99, '98, '96, '94.

FAIRVIEW

SOUTH AFRICA, Western Cape, Paarl WO
♦ *Cabernet Sauvignon, Syrah (Shiraz), Merlot, Pinotage and others*
♀ *Viognier, Chardonnay, Chenin Blanc, Semillon and others*

Charles Back would undoubtedly be proud of his namesake and grandson, who now runs this farm with enormous energy and success, using new varieties and unconventional styles or blends which are seriously good value for money. The warm, south-west-facing vineyards favour full-bodied reds such as Shiraz, Pinotage, Cabernet Sauvignon and Merlot but the unusual Zinfandel-Cinsaut blend is invariably the richest of the lot. However, Fairview also buys in grapes and Back is very committed to the discovery of new areas – there are numerous old vineyards north of PAARL no-one has ever bothered to evaluate – and he also deals direct with the co-operatives to get hold of their old-vine fruit before it is blended away and lost.

The result is a fascinating array of wines as wide-ranging as any in South Africa. If he has made his reputation with reds, his whites are equally good – Chardonnay, Chenin, exciting Semillon and South Africa's first Viognier – a lovely rich apricotty example. He also runs the SPICE ROUTE WINE COMPANY and has created the highly successful 'Goats do Roam' brand. Back is also a leading proponent of local reform and empowerment of the local South Africans. Best years: (reds) 2002, '01, '00, '99, '98, '97, '96, '95, '93.

JOSEPH FAIVELEY

FRANCE, Burgundy, Nuits-St-Georges
♟ *Pinot Noir*
♀ *Chardonnay*

François Faiveley, who has been running this *négociant* business for over two decades, often has a worried look. I sometimes think it's because he's trying to work out how long it will take for his red wines to soften up and be ready for drinking, because despite the sky-high reputation of his wines, I find the reds almost invariably lean and unfriendly when they're released. I'm told they do soften and make lovely mature bottles, but I'm clearly not patient enough to wait. Even so Faiveley does take great pains with his whites. He was one of the first to introduce a *tapis de triage*, a moving belt on which grapes can be sorted on reception at the winery, and most of his top wines are bottled without filtration direct from the barrel. Some top wines are aged entirely in new oak.

Like many other Burgundy *négociants*, Faiveley is also the owner of some magnificent

The ruins of the medieval Ch. de Fargues loom over the vineyards owned by the Lur-Saluces family, who were until recently also owners of Ch. d'Yquem.

Grand Cru vineyards: CHAMBERTIN CLOS-DE-BÈZE, Mazis-Chambertin, CLOS VOUGEOT, CORTON Clos des Cortons and CORTON-CHARLEMAGNE, but NUITS-ST-GEORGES Premier Cru Clos de la Maréchale has now reverted to original owner J-F MUGNIER. Faiveley also owns substantial vineyards in MERCUREY and has an infectious enthusiasm for this often under-valued region – particularly for his single-vineyard bottlings. Best years: (top reds) 2002, '01, '99, '98, '97, '96, '95, '93, '90, '89; (whites) 2002, '01, '00, '99, '97, '96.

FALERNO DEL MASSICO DOC

ITALY, Campania
♟ *Aglianico, Primitivo, Piedirosso*
♀ *Falanghina*

The most fabled wine of the ancient Romans was Falernian. The nearest we can get to it is Falerno, recreated after years of patient ploughing through ancient texts by the Avallone family, whose Villa Matilde estate is now synonymous with the wine.

White Falerno is a creamy wine with perfumes of roses and raspberries and an underlying herbiness. The cru version, Vigna Caracci, is richer and more complex. Red Falerno is a delicious mix of slightly sour-tinged red fruits, cinnamon and a touch of earthiness. Even better, spicier and gutsier is Cecubo, made mainly from Piedirosso, and Villa Matilde's reincarnation of another Roman gem, Caecubum. Vigna Camarato is a

punchy, long-lived cru from Aglianico and made only in the best vintages. All the reds are improving in quality and aging capability from year to year. Best years: (reds) 2001, 00, '99, '98, '97, '96, '95. Best producers: Michele Moio, Villa Matilde (Vigna Camarato).

FAR NIENTE WINERY

USA, California, Napa County, Napa Valley AVA
♟ *Cabernet Sauvignon*
♀ *Chardonnay*

Proprietor Gil Nickel from Oklahoma paid top money for this property when he arrived in the NAPA VALLEY, and one sight of his collection of vintage Bentley cars and the most extensive and well-equipped aging cellars in the valley will show you he hasn't lost his taste for spending his money! He also lavishes money on the wines themselves. The Chardonnay is a richly oaky exotic wine no longer exactly in fashion, but still much in demand. The Cabernet is pretty tough, and though it may open up with time, I think it should have more fruit to begin with. There is also an occasional botrytized white, Dolce. Best years: (Cabernet Sauvignon) 2001, '99, '98, '97, '96, '95, '94, '92, '91, '90, '87, '86.

CH. DE FARGUES

FRANCE, Bordeaux, Sauternes AC, Cru Bourgeois
♀ *Sémillon, Sauvignon Blanc*

The most remarkable thing about Ch. de Fargues is that, even though it is classified as

a mere Bourgeois Growth, it regularly sells for more than any other wine in the AC save the great Ch. d'YQUEM. It is owned by the Lur-Saluces family, owners of Yquem for over four centuries until 1999.

The vineyard – 15ha (37 acres) on the edge of the SAUTERNES AC in the village of Fargues – is by no means ideal, and the quality of the wine is more a tribute to the commitment of the Lur-Saluces family than to the inherent quality of the estate. The vines ripen around ten days later than at Yquem, and the selection of grapes is so strict that each vine only yields two-thirds of a glass of wine. The result is that the total annual production rarely exceeds 10,000 bottles of rich, reasonably exotic wine, very honeyed, indeed almost syrupy, with something of the taste of pineapples and peaches, and a viscous feel, like lanolin, which coats your mouth. This is fine, rich wine but there are several Classed Growths which are better, and less expensive. Best years: 2002, '01, '99, '98, '97, '96, '95, '90, '89, '88, '86, '83.

FAUGÈRES AC

FRANCE, Languedoc-Roussillon

♥ ♥ *Carignan, Grenache, Cinsaut, Syrah, Mourvèdre*

Faugères was the first of the communes in the LANGUEDOC area to create a reputation of its own. For a year or two at the beginning of the 1980s it was the new buzz wine of the Paris bistros, and duly received its AC status in 1982. Luckily the wine is good and well deserves its AC. It's almost entirely red, and comes from hilly vineyards in seven little villages just north of Béziers. Annual production is over ten million bottles. What marks it out from other Languedoc reds is its ripe, soft, rather plummy flavour, its smooth rich texture and, now and then, its floral perfume. It doesn't take long to work out that this was because Faugères was one of the first Languedoc communes to pin its faith on planting as much Syrah as possible, and though it's a little more expensive than neighbouring wines, the extra money is usually worth it.

Faugères has the terrain to make good white wine too, but so far production is relatively insignificant. Until recently the whites – sold under the COTEAUX DU LANGUEDOC AC – were largely Clairette and at best crisp and light, but one or two more progressive growers have planted Bourboulenc, Grenache Blanc, Marsanne, Roussanne and Rolle, which is beginning to produce wines with a lot more character. Best years: 2001, '00, '99, '98, '96, '95, '94, '93. Best producers: Abbaye

Sylva Plana/Bouchard, Alquier, Léon Barral, Chenaie, ESTANILLES, Faugères co-operative, Fraïsse, Grézan, Haut-Fabrègues, la Liquière, Moulin de Ciffre, Ollier-Taillefer.

FAUSTINO

SPAIN, País Vasco and Rioja, Rioja DOCa, Cava DO

♥ ♥ *Tempranillo, Grenache Noir (Garnacha Tinta), Carignan (Cariñena, Mazuelo), Graciano*

♀ *Macabeo (Viura)*

High-quality Reservas and Gran Reservas are the specialities of this large, family-owned RIOJA bodega. The reds start with a delicious, fresh Viña Joven or Viña Faustina, made by fermenting the grapes uncrushed, BEAUJO-LAIS-style. The strawberry-scented Faustino V Reserva and deep, rich, spicy Faustino I Gran Reserva are good examples of their type. The whites are fair, the CAVAs pleasant, simple and honeyed. Faustino also owns Bodegas Vitorianas, makers of Don Darias and Don Hugo – oaky, vaguely Rioja-like table wines – and produces Fortius wines in NAVARRA and Condesa de Leganza wines in LA MANCHA. Best years: (reds) 1998, '96, '95, '94, '92, '91, '90, '89, '87.

FEILER-ARTINGER

AUSTRIA, Burgenland, Neusiedlersee-Hügelland, Rust

♥ *Blaufränkisch, Merlot, Blauer Zweigelt, Cabernet Sauvignon, Cabernet Franc and others*

♀ *Chardonnay, Pinot Blanc (Weissburgunder), Welschriesling and others*

Hans Feiler and his son Kurt make the finest AUSBRUCH dessert wines in RUST. Although the winery was established in the 1930s, it was only in the 1980s that Feiler began to revive the old tradition of Ausbruch.

Kurt's arrival in 1993, after a stint at BORDEAUX's famous Ch. CHEVAL BLANC, gave further impetus to reds and sweet wines. The 'Pinot Cuvée' Ausbruch, made from a blend of Weissburgunder, Grauburgunder and Neuburger, is now famous beyond Austria's borders, having already won many prizes and blind tastings. You could mistake it for a top SAUTERNES were the acidity not so fresh and animating. The whole range of Ausbruch wines since the 1993 vintage has been superb. The red wines get better and better with each vintage, Solitaire, a medium-bodied, not too tannic blend of Blaufränkisch with Cabernet Franc, Zweigelt and Merlot probably being the best. The dry whites are all clean, fruity wines for drinking when fresh. Best years: (sweet whites) 2002, '01, '00, '99, '98, '96, '95, '94, '93, '91; (Solitaire) 2001, '00, '99, '97, '95, '94.

LIVIO FELLUGA

ITALY, Friuli-Venezia Giulia, Colli Orientali del Friuli DOC

♥ *Merlot, Cabernet Sauvignon, Refosco*

♀ *Pinot Gris (Pinot Grigio), Sauvignon Blanc, Chardonnay, Tocai Friulano, Pinot Blanc (Pinot Bianco), Picolit and others*

The octogenarian Livio Felluga was a pioneer of the now fashionable FRIULI blended white wine and his estate is now run mainly by his sons, Andrea and Maurizio.

One of the largest vineyard owners in eastern Friuli, with some 135ha (334 acres) mostly in the COLLI ORIENTALI zone at Rosazzo, Felluga has for decades now been considered at the top of the quality tree not only for its white varietals but especially for Terre Alte, an exceptional unoaked blend of Tocai, Pinot Bianco and Sauvignon Blanc, only produced in good vintages.

Not that Felluga has anything against wood – the estate uses both barriques and larger barrels for maturing the reds, and its Chardonnay-Ribolla Gialla blend called Sharis is partly fermented in oak. But the accent, for Terre Alte, is on ripe fruit and sumptuousness of palate. Felluga is less well known for reds, the best of which is Sossó, a Merlot wine, both fermented and aged in barriques. And as production of most of the range is large the price of the wines are not outrageous. Best years: (whites) 2001, '00, '99, '98, '97, '96.

FATTORIA DI FELSINA

ITALY, Tuscany, Chianti Classico DOCG

♥ *Sangiovese, Cabernet Sauvignon*

♀ *Chardonnay, Sauvignon Blanc, Trebbiano Toscano*

The best thing Giuseppe Mazzocolin ever did was to fall in love with Gloria Poggiali, not only because she is a lady of exceptional quality but also because her father just happened

FATTORIA DI FELSINA
The single-vineyard Chianti Classico Riserva Vigneto Rancia is one of the greatest wines from Sangiovese, especially in a fine vintage.

to have acquired, in the mid-1960s, this large and wonderfully endowed wine estate at Castelnuovo Berardenga in the extreme south-east corner of the CHIANTI CLASSICO zone. Schoolteacher Giuseppe fell in love all over again, this time with wine, departed the classroom and has devoted himself heart and soul ever since, with the expert guidance of consultant Franco Bernabei, to making this one of the greatest wine estates in Italy.

While producing one of Italy's finest Cabernet Sauvignons in Maestro Raro, as well as one of the better Chardonnays in I Sistri, it is into his Sangiovese wines that Giuseppe pours the lion's share of his considerable enthusiasm. Felsina's straight Chianti Classico, put together by master-taster and blender Bernabei and displaying the firmness yet fruitiness conferred by the various sub-zones at his disposal (now substantially increased by the purchase of the neighbouring Pagliarese estate), is better than many estates' Riserva wine.

The 100 per cent Sangiovese Fontalloro, considered by many to be Felsina's best wine, is a veritable Classed Growth in disguise, for its breeding combined with power, and the single-vineyard Chianti Classico Riserva Vigneto Rancia is very concentrated with impressive fruit depth and marked tannin, and rich and harmonious after several years' bottle age. Best years: (Fontalloro) 2001, '00, '99, '98, '97, '95, '93, '90, '88, '85.

FELTON ROAD

NEW ZEALAND, South Island, Central Otago
♟ *Pinot Noir*
♟ *Riesling, Chardonnay*

Felton Road wasn't by any means the first CENTRAL OTAGO winery to request attention from the world's wine enthusiasts, but it was the first one to literally stand up on its hind legs and scream for attention, crying out 'You've *never* tasted a Pinot Noir like this.' And I hadn't. The Block 3 Pinot Noir had a soaring brilliance to its dark ripe fruit balanced by an acidity as taut as piano wire. Block 5 Pinot Noir was a little rounder, more earth-bound, but in the most wonderfully bucolic cherub-cheeked way. The blend of sunsoaked fruit and top C acidity was rare and thrilling, and the Chardonnays and Rieslings are exceptional too.

The vineyards are at Bannockburn – the driest area of New Zealand, one which boasts a road sign 'the Heart of the Desert'. It's a marvellous bowl of land, ringed by protective mountains, getting dawn to dusk sunshine.

FELTON ROAD
Block 3 Pinot Noir is one of the wines on strict allocation from this small winery in Central Otago that has become such a runaway success.

But there are relatively few north-facing slopes to really soak up the sun. Felton Road is on one of them. These wines are rare, expensive, but superb. Best years: (Pinot Noir) 2001, '00, '99, '98, '97.

ALEJANDRO FERNÁNDEZ-TINTO PESQUERA

SPAIN, Castilla y León, Ribera del Duero DO
♟ *Tempranillo (Tinto del País)*

In the mid-1980s, few people outside RIBERA DEL DUERO had ever heard of the Viña Pesquera wines of Alejandro Fernández. Enter an American wine merchant and some influential American wine writers, one of whom compared Viña Pesquera to one of the world's finest reds, Ch. PÉTRUS. It doesn't really taste like Pétrus, but for sheer power and perfume, there is a similarity. Now these richly coloured, firm, fragrant plummy-tobaccoey reds are among the most famous and most expensive wines in Spain. Until 1972 Alejandro Fernández ran the village smithy as well as his own agricultural machinery business. With the proceeds, he gradually built up his own vineyard holding, and constructed his own winery – even making his own vats. Oak-aging is important here – the cellar is full of American and French oak barrels, many renewed each year. The wines are 100 per cent Tinto del País (Tempranillo). Tinto Pesquera Crianza and Reserva are made every year, with Gran Reserva and Janus in the best years.

To supplement his vineyards in the village of Pesquera, Fernández bought a further 100ha (248 acres) of vineyard and built a second bodega, Condado de Haza, in the neighbouring village of Roa, which is rapidly becoming the new wine capital of the region. A further 100ha (248 acres) of Tempranillo have been planted on the recently acquired Dehesa La Granja estate near Zamora, outside the TORO DO, while El Vínculo is yet another Fernández venture in LA MANCHA DO. Best years: (Pesquera Crianza) 1999, '96, '95, '94, '93, '92, '91, '90, '89, '86, '85.

FERRARI

ITALY, Trentino, Trentino DOC
♟ ♟ *Pinot Noir (Pinot Nero), Cabernet Franc, Cabernet Sauvignon, Merlot*
♟ *Chardonnay, Sauvignon Blanc*

One of the cornerstones of high-quality CHAMPAGNE-method sparkling wine in Italy is the Trento-based firm of Ferrari (no relation, although it makes the most of the perceived connection with the motor-car – apparently Ferrari is the third commonest name in Italy). The company has nine million bottles in stock at any given time and annual sales of three million.

Grapes for the non-vintage wines are bought in from about 150 growers, many of whom have been with the firm for many decades, the cuvées being 95 per cent Chardonnay, with a touch of Pinot Nero – and more than a touch for the rosé. Minimum time spent on the yeasts is 24 months for the Brut and Rosé, rising to 30 for the Maximum Brut and 36 for the vintage Perlé, a 100 per cent Chardonnay from the firm's own vineyards, of which they have 96ha (237 acres) at highish altitudes. Top of the range is the renowned pure Chardonnay Riserva del Fondatore Giulio Ferrari. The grapes come from vineyards more than 15 years old and the wine receives between seven and eight years on the lees.

FERRARI-CARANO VINEYARDS

USA, California, Sonoma County, Dry Creek Valley AVA
♟ *Cabernet Sauvignon, Merlot, Sangiovese, Zinfandel, Petit Verdot, Cabernet Franc, Merlot*
♟ *Chardonnay, Sauvignon Blanc*

Developing 485ha (1200 acres) of vineyards spread between 18 SONOMA COUNTY sites, hotelier Don Carano started slowly as a wine producer, but he is in it for the long haul. His showcase winery in DRY CREEK VALLEY contains a vast aging cellar and an Italian villa with magnificent gardens.

The first vintages of Chardonnay gained a phenomenal amount of attention and certainly did have a ripeness and concentration that has since become much more common in modern CALIFORNIA. After a dip in quality, this winery is now back on top form and the Reserve Chardonnay has regained its former richness. The whites include a perky, stylish Fume Blanc, and the reds, Merlot, Cabernet Sauvignon, Trésor (red Meritage) and Siena (a SUPER-TUSCAN blend of Cabernet Sauvignon and Sangiovese). Best years: (reds) 2001, '00, '99, '98, '97, '96, '95, '94 ,'91.

FERREIRA
PORTUGAL, Douro, Port DOC, Douro DOC
♥ *Touriga Nacional, Tempranillo (Tinta Roriz), Tinta Barroca, Tinto Cão, Touriga Franca and others*
♀ *Gouveio, Malvasia Fina, Viosinho, Rabigato and others*

Owned by SOGRAPE, Ferreira is the best-known PORT shipper in Portugal. With two prime quintas (do Seixo and do Porto) just downstream from Pinhão, Quinta do Caêdo in the Rio Torto valley and Quinta da Leda in the DOURO Superior, Ferreira makes a complete range of ports, although it is the aged tawnies (the 10-Year-Old Quinta do Porto and 20-Year-Old Duque de Bragança) which justly earn most of the accolades. Vintage ports tend to be on the light side and relatively early maturing, although the unfiltered LBV is rich and solid.

Ferreira is just as well known for unfortified Douro reds as for port. Barca Velha, devised in the 1950s, is Portugal's uncrowned 'First Growth'. Originally made at Quinta do Vale de Meao, high in the Douro Superior, production has now transferred to nearby Quinta da Leda, although the philosophy remains the same. It is made from top-quality fruit and aged for about 18 months in new French oak. Rather like a vintage port, the wine is only released as Barca Velha in truly exceptional years. Good interim years are sold under the name Reserva Ferreirinha. Ferreira also produces other Douro reds, including Quinta da Leda and Vinha Grande. The relatively lightweight Esteva underpins the range. Best years: (Vintage) 2000, '97, '95, '94, '91, '85, '78, '77, '70, '66, '63; (Barca Velha) 1995, '91, '85, '83, '82, '81, '78.

CH. FERRIÈRE
FRANCE, Bordeaux, Haut-Médoc, Margaux AC, 3ème Cru Classé
♥ *Cabernet Sauvignon, Merlot, Petit Verdot*

MARGAUX's smallest Classed Growth, Ferrière was leased to its larger neighbour Ch. Lascombes until 1992, when it was bought by the Merlaut family of Ch. CHASSE-SPLEEN. The improvement has been startling. It is now managed by Claire Villars, and the ripe, rich and perfumed wines are among the best in Margaux. Best years: 2001, '00, '99, '98, '96, '95.

CH. DE FESLES
FRANCE, Loire, Anjou-Saumur, Bonnezeaux AC
♥ *Cabernet Franc, Gamay and others*
♀ *Chenin Blanc, Chardonnay*

Fesles has long been the leading property in BONNEZEAUX. The château is built on one of the highest spots in the area and the vineyards face south, overlooking the river Layon. Made by Jean Boivin, the 1947 wine remains a living legend. His son Jacques subsequently took over the estate and it remained in the family until it was sold in 1991 to Gaston Lenôtre, the Parisian chef and noted *pâtissier*. Soon after, Lenôtre also bought Ch. de la Guimonière and Domaine de la Roulerie (in nearby Chaume). Unfortunately, although Lenôtre was initially highly enthusiastic, he did not fully appreciate the need to take risks to make a top-quality sweet LOIRE wine and quality started to suffer. Having renovated the château and the *chai* at considerable expense, Lenôtre also started to run out of money.

In 1996 he sold out to Bordeaux *négociant* Bernard Germain and since then there has been an immediate improvement, with the 1996 wine being noticeably superior to the '95. Germain also acquired the 7-ha (17-acre) Clos de Varennes in nearby SAVENNIÈRES-Roche-aux-Moines. Germain now owns 100ha (247 acres) of vines in the region, including the excellent Domaine des Roches Neuves (SAUMUR and SAUMUR-CHAMPIGNY) run by Germain's son, Thierry. Best years: (Bonnezeaux) 2002, '01, '00, '99, '98, '97, '96, '90, '89, '76, '59, '47.

FETZER VINEYARDS
USA, California, Mendocino County
♥ *Merlot, Cabernet Sauvignon, Zinfandel, Pinot Noir*
♥ *Syrah, Zinfandel*
♀ *Chardonnay, Gewürztraminer, Sauvignon Blanc*

Barney Fetzer had ten children when he launched a small winery in MENDOCINO COUNTY's Redwood Valley in 1968. As a family, they built the enterprise from fewer than 20,000 cases a year to more than 1.3 million before it was bought by the distillers Brown-Forman in 1992. Production is now nearer four million cases, but quality has remained remarkably consistent.

Fetzer comes at three price levels: regular (Sundial Chardonnay and Eagle Peak Merlot

FETZER VINEYARDS
Well known for its drinkable, good-value wines, Fetzer makes wines from organically grown grapes under the Bonterra label, including Merlot.

are good examples of this pleasant range), Barrel Select (where the varietal flavours are a bit more concentrated) and Reserve (bigger, oakier, more limited in volume and often from some of CALIFORNIA's top vineyards). Chardonnay, Cabernet Sauvignon and Zinfandel are all good. A second label, Bel Arbor, is cheaper than the regular bottlings and is most famous for White Zinfandel. Wines made from organic grapes are labelled Bonterra, but by the 2010 vintage Fetzer intend to use nothing but organic grapes. For a four million- (and rising) case winery that's some commitment, and the recent establishment of the 240-ha (600-acre) organic Five Rivers Ranch in PASO ROBLES shows they're not joking. Overall, Fetzer gives good value for money. Best years: (Barrel Select reds) 2001, '99, '98, '97, '96, '95, '94.

FIANO DI AVELLINO DOC
ITALY, Campania
♀ *Fiano, Greco, Coda di Volpe, Trebbiano Toscano*

Fiano may be of little more than passing interest when young; but by a couple of years old it can be fabulous, with its restrained charms and subtle, but concentrated, peachy-nutty-creaminess. The classic production zone is in the Apennine hills east of Naples, around the town of Avellino. MASTROBERARDINO, which makes no fewer than three Crus, has long been the main producer but it, increasingly, is being challenged by local newcomers like Colli di Lapio, Feudi di San Gregorio, Terredora di Paolo and Vadiaperti.

CH. DE FIEUZAL
FRANCE, Bordeaux, Pessac-Léognan AC, Cru Classé de Graves (reds only)
♥ *Cabernet Sauvignon, Merlot, Cabernet Franc, Petit Verdot*
♀ *Sauvignon Blanc, Sémillon*

This is a delightful estate, with a reputation for both its red and white wines. Investment during the 1980s in the 48-ha (120-acre) estate, just south of DOMAINE DE CHEVALIER near Léognan, made it one of the most up-to-date properties in the region, but a change of ownership in 2001 has now put its reputation in question. The white wine is fermented and aged in new oak barrels and is rich, dense, balanced – and outstandingly good, whether drunk young, or aged. The red used to be equally impressive, succulent, rich and perfumed, but recent vintages seem to have lost their sensuous heart. I long for its return. Both wines are drinkable almost as soon as they're drawn from the barrel, but both should age for a decade or more. Second wine: (red and white) l'Abeille de Fieuzal. Best years: (reds) 2000, '98, '96, '95, '94, '90, '89, '88, '87, '86, '85, '83, '82; (whites) 2001, '00, '99, '98, '96, '95, '94, '93, '90, '89, '88, '85.

CH. FIGEAC
FRANCE, Bordeaux, St-Émilion Grand Cru AC, Premier Grand Cru Classé
Ⓣ *Cabernet Sauvignon, Cabernet Franc, Merlot*
You have hardly finished shaking hands with Thierry Manoncourt, the delightful though zealous owner of Ch. Figeac, before he has marched you over into the vineyards, and pointed accusingly to the north. Half-a-mile away sit the small, whitewashed buildings of CHEVAL BLANC, acknowledged as ST-ÉMILION's greatest wine. This small area, at the western end of the appellation, is called 'Graves' St-Émilion because of the high proportion of gravel soil which gives the wine its special quality. Yet who has the most gravel? Not Cheval Blanc, but Figeac. Indeed you quickly learn that Cheval Blanc used to be part of Figeac, was only sold as 'Vin de Figeac', and derives its name (meaning 'white horse') from the fact that it was there that Figeac had its stables.

Well, it's true, but Manoncourt shouldn't fret so much because Figeac's own wine is superb, but in a different way from Cheval Blanc. Figeac uses 35 per cent Cabernet Sauvignon (rare for St-Émilion) and 35 per cent Cabernet Franc – both are grape varieties which love gravel – and only 30 per cent of St-Émilion's main variety, Merlot.

The result is wine of marvellous, minty, blackcurranty perfume, with some of the cedar and cigar-smoke spice of the great MÉDOCs, and a caressing gentleness of texture. It is often more 'beautiful' than Cheval Blanc and in a smoother, more voluptuous style, though it is rarely so grand. It is lovely young yet ideally should age for 10–20 years. Second wine: la Grangeneuve de Figeac. Best years: 2001, '00, '99, '98, '95, '90, '89, '88, '86, '83, '82.

FINCA FLICHMAN
ARGENTINA, Mendoza
Ⓣ *Cabernet Sauvignon, Malbec, Merlot, Syrah and others*
Ⓦ *Chardonnay, Chenin Blanc*
For its first overseas venture, SOGRAPE, the Portuguese company famous originally for giving the world Mateus Rosé, acquired Finca Flichman, a large winery in MENDOZA in 1998. Flichman had two things to recommend such

a purchase: good vineyards in the Maipú, south-east of the city of Mendoza planted on an interesting mixture of soils, and a winery with spanking new stainless steel, rare in Argentina. Wines originally aimed at the lower end of the market are already beginning to ascend the quality scale. The wines are sold either under Flichman, the premium Caballero de la Cepa (Cabernet Sauvignon, Chardonnay, Malbec, Merlot and Syrah) or the Aberdeen Angus labels.The new ownership is beginning to pay off, especially in the quality of reds from the excellent stony Barrancas vineyards in Maipú. During Argentina's financial crisis of 2002 Flichman's international ownership was an important advantage.

FINGER LAKES AVA
USA, New York State
This important winemaking region in central NEW YORK STATE would be far too cold for vines were it not for the 11 deep, glacial Finger Lakes that temper the hard winters, protect against frost and reflect light during the summer. Even so, conditions are still marginal for grape-growing, but some excellent sparkling wine, Chardonnay, Riesling and Gewürztraminer show that it can be done, and the occasional Cabernet Franc and Pinot Noir red is light but tasty. The three biggest lakes, Keuka, Seneca and Cayuga, which now has its own AVA, have the majority of the region's total 4200ha (10,400 acres) of vines. Best producers: FOX RUN, Dr Konstantin Frank, GLENORA, LAMOREAUX LANDING, Silver Thread, Wagner, Hermann J Wiemer.

FITOU AC
FRANCE, Languedoc-Roussillon
Ⓣ *Carignan, Grenache Noir, Mourvèdre, Syrah and others*
The main Fitou area is a pocket of land around the Étang de Leucate or Salses lagoon, on the coast between Perpignan and Narbonne, but there are also some inland villages where much better, more interesting wine is made, in the heart of the CORBIÈRES hinterland, of which Tuchan is the most important. Fitou's burly, bay leaf-scented character comes from the Carignan grape, which makes a pretty stern basic brew, so there is a minimum aging requirement of nine months in wood, recently reduced from 18. The wine then ages well in bottle for five to six years at least. Best years: 2001, '00, '99, '98, '96, '95, '94, '93. Best producers: Abelanet, Bertrand-Berge, Lerys, Mille Vignes, MONT TAUCH, Nouvelles, Rochelière, Rolland, Roudène.

FIXIN AC
FRANCE, Burgundy, Côte de Nuits
Ⓣ *Pinot Noir*
Ⓦ *Pinot Blanc*
Fixin would love to be talked of in the same breath as the great villages of the CÔTE D'OR. There it sits, looking down indulgently on its great neighbour, GEVREY-CHAMBERTIN, confident in the knowledge that the Grand Dukes of Burgundy used to spend their summers here. But the wines never manage to scale the heights. They are worthy, and tannic enough to last well, but the perfume, fragrance, the mysterious mix of flavour and fantasy that marks out the greatest red Burgundies is hardly ever there. Only one-third of the vineyards are entitled to be labelled as Fixin; the rest must be sold as CÔTE DE NUITS-VILLAGES. Best years: 2001, '00, '99, '98, '96, '95, '94, '93. Best producers: Champy, Pierre Gelin, Alain Guyard, Dominique LAURENT, Naddef.

FLEURIE AC
FRANCE, Burgundy, Beaujolais, Beaujolais cru
Ⓣ *Gamay*
At its best Fleurie, the third-largest but best-known BEAUJOLAIS cru, reveals the happy, carefree flavours of the Gamay grape at their most delightful, plus heady perfumes and a lovely juicy sweetness. But, not surprisingly, demand has meant that many of the wines are now woefully overpriced and ordinary. Best years: 2002, '00, '99. Best producers: J-M Aujoux, M Chignard, Clos de la Roilette, Daumas, Depardon, Després/Dom. de la Madone, DUBOEUF (single domaines), H Fessy, Fleurie co-op, Metrat, A & M Morel, P Sapin (Dom. des Raclets), Verpoix, Vissoux/P-M Chermette.

FLOWERS
USA, California, Sonoma Coast AVA
Ⓣ *Pinot Noir*
Ⓦ *Chardonnay*
Small producer whose estate vineyard, Camp Meeting Ridge, a few miles from the Pacific Ocean, yields wines of great intensity. The Camp Meeting Ridge Pinot Noir and Chardonnay are usually made with native yeasts and offer wonderful exotic aromas and flavours. There are also vineyard-designated wines, the fruit being purchased from high quality sources like Sangiacomo. Wines from bought-in fruit use the simple SONOMA COAST designation and are also high quality. Best years: (Chardonnay) 2001, '00, '99, '98, '97, '96; (Pinot Noir) 2001, '00, '99, '98, '97, '96.

FONSECA GUIMARAENS

PORTUGAL, Douro, Port DOC

♥ *Tempranillo (Tinta Roriz), Tinta Barroca, Tinto Cão, Touriga Nacional, Touriga Franca and others*

♀ *Gouveio, Viosinho, Rabigato, Malvasia Fina and others*

Fonseca is held in the highest regard and even earns sneaking respect from many competing PORT shippers. The firm was founded in 1822 and the winemaking remains the responsibility of the Guimaraens family, even though Fonseca has been owned, since 1948, by another highly regarded shipper, TAYLOR, and is now part of the Fladgate Partnership. Fonseca's mainstay is Bin No 27, a ripe, opulent premium ruby, but the firm reigns supreme with some outstandingly fine aged tawnies and vintage ports. In great years like 2000, '97, '94, '85, '77 and '66, Fonseca manages to combine sheer power with glorious finesse. Wines from good non-declared years (like '95) use the Guimaraens label but frequently outscore fully declared wines from other shippers. Best years: (Vintage) 2000, '97, '94, '92, '85, '83, '77, '75, '70, '66, '63, '55.

JOSÉ MARIA DA FONSECA SUCCESSORES

PORTUGAL, Terras do Sado, Setúbal DOC, Palmela DOC, Alentejo DOC, Dão DOC, Douro DOC, Terras do Sado Vinho Regional

♥ *Castelão (Periquita), Touriga Nacional, Tempranillo (Tinta Roriz/Aragonez), Trincadeira (Tinta Amarela), Touriga Franca, Syrah and others*

♀ *Moscatel de Setúbal, Fernão Pires, Arinto and others*

Family owned and run, José Maria da Fonseca Successores is one of the most traditional yet innovative wine companies in Portugal. Based at Azeitão on the SETÚBAL peninsula, it is the largest producer of the sweet, fortified Setúbal wine, made mainly from Moscatel grapes. The company is best known for its brand of Periquita red, the wine that gave the nickname to the Castelão grape. Quinta de Camarate is the flagship vineyard and this produces a ripe, plummy red from Castelão and Espadeiro, together with a small amount of Cabernet Sauvignon.

Garrafeira wines, mysteriously coded as 'TE', 'RA' and 'CO', are supple and gamy. José Maria da Fonseca also has interests in the DÃO region, where it produces Terras Altas, and in the ALENTEJO, where it makes a rich, warm José de Sousa red. Wine from another estate in the northern Alentejo near Portalegre is bottled under the d'Avillez label. A sister company formerly known as J M da

Fonseca Internacional, which was hived off in the 1970s to produce Lancers Rosé and Espumante (fizz), returned to the fold in 1996. A new joint venture in the DOURO. with Cristiano van Zeller, makes promising Domini reds, as well as PORT.

TENIMENTI FONTANAFREDDA

ITALY, Piedmont, Barolo DOCG

♥ *Nebbiolo, Barbera, Dolcetto, Freisa, Grignolino*

♀ *Moscato, Gavi di Gavi, Arneis, Pinot Noir (Pinot Nero), Chardonnay*

Once the property of King Vittorio Emanuele's bastard son, Emanuele Guerrieri di Mirafiori, this estate is in the heart of BAROLO's Serralunga d'Alba commune. It has been owned since 1931 by the Monte dei Paschi bank of Siena. A relatively enormous operation – nearly 70ha (173 acres) of prime vineyards, grapes bought in from over 600 growers of Piedmont and beyond, plus an annual production of over six million bottles of which some 750,000 are Barolo and nearly four million are ASTI – Fontanafredda is one of the few giants in a land of smallholders. Biggest Barolo production by far is of the ubiquitous *normale*, rarely very inspired since Fontanafredda started making crus commercially in the early 1970s. But the traditionally crafted, single-vineyard wines – La Rosa, La Delizia, La Villa and Lazzarito – can be impressive. They need five to ten years' aging. As well as Asti, Fontanafredda makes CHAMPAGNE-method sparkling wine, including the good vintage Brut called Contessa Rosa. Best years: (Barolo) 2001, '00, '99, '98, '97, '96, '90, '89, '88, '85.

FONTANAFREDDA

As well as producing enormous quantities of straight Barolo, this large Piedmont estate makes four single-vineyard crus, including La Delizia.

CASTELLO DI FONTERUTOLI

ITALY, Tuscany, Chianti Classico DOCG

♥ *Sangiovese, Merlot, Cabernet Sauvignon*

The Mazzei family, father Lapo, sons Filippo and Francesco, owners of the Fonterutoli estate since the fifteenth century, supported by one of TUSCANY's outstanding enological consultants Carlo Ferrini, wanted to celebrate the

600th anniversary of the original Ser Lapo Mazzei's earliest inscription of the word 'Chianti', in 1398, with a bang.

In a bold gesture to show that Fonterutoli has sufficient faith in the revival of the historic CHIANTI denomination, two CHIANTI CLASSICOs have replaced the well-established Concerto (a fine SUPER-TUSCAN from Sangiovese and Cabernet) and Riserva Ser Lapo. And, indeed, the first vintages of the new wines are stunning. The amount of Cabernet Sauvignon in the new flagship Castello di Fonterutoli is only 10 per cent, so as to retain more Tuscan typicity without losing power. The grapes come from the high-quality Siepi vineyard at 260m (850ft) altitude and the Fonterutoli vineyard at 450m (1750ft). Deep coloured, with a wealth of berry fruit, dark-chocolate and coffee aromas, it has a hefty structure which will ensure considerable aging, despite the ripeness of the tannins. The only note of caution I would sound is that overuse of new oak may blunt the impressive character of the fruit. The highly sought-after Sangiovese-Merlot super-Tuscan called Siepi is still being made. Best years: (Riserva) 2001, '99, '97, '96, '95.

FONTODI

ITALY, Tuscany, Chianti Classico DOCG

♥ *Sangiovese, Cabernet Sauvignon, Pinot Noir (Pinot Nero), Syrah*

♀ *Pinot Blanc (Pinot Bianco), Sauvignon Blanc, Malvasia Bianca*

Indisputably one of Italy's high flyers and illustrative of all that's dynamic and forward-looking in CHIANTI CLASSICO today, this stunning estate has 60ha (148 acres) of vineyards south of Panzano in the heart of the zone. In 1968 the Manetti family, Florentine terracotta manufacturers, took control and Fontodi's modern era began. Sangiovese, not surprisingly, is the hub of the wheel, and Fontodi has been among the leaders in TUSCANY experimenting with different clones and planting methods.

The exemplary SUPER-TUSCAN Flaccianello della Pieve is from a single vineyard of old Sangiovese vines and there is a consistent, reliably polished Chianti Classico *normale*. The Riserva Vigna del Sorbo, a single-vineyard wine (using organic methods), brings some high-quality Cabernet into the equation at the limit of what is allowed under the Chianti regulations. There are also two more unusual varietal wines under the newer Case Via label – Pinot Nero and Syrah. Best years: (Flaccianello) 2001, '99, '98, '97, '95, '93, '90, '88, '85.

FORADORI
ITALY, Trentino, Teroldego Rotaliano DOC
🍷 *Teroldego, Syrah, Cabernet Sauvignon,*
🍷 *Sauvignon Blanc, Incrocio Manzoni, Pinot Blanc*
(Pinot Bianco)

Producer of dark, spicy, berry-fruited wines, including a regular TEROLDEGO ROTALIANO, from Teroldego, a little-known essentially rustic local grape but with a large fan club, and barrique-aged Granato. Elisabetta Foradori's interest in Syrah is producing excellent results, both in the varietal Ailanpa and the smoky, black-cherry lushness of a Cabernet-Syrah blend called Karanar. Best years: (Granato) 2001, '00, '99, '97, '96, '93.

FORST
GERMANY, Pfalz

The attractive village of Forst has a clutch of top-quality vineyards and a reputation for high quality. It can boast a list of top growers as good as any Rhineland village and vineyards of the calibre of Jesuitengarten (refinement and elegance), Kirchenstück (balance and nobility), Pechstein (racy drive) and Ungeheuer (powerful and earthy). An outcrop of black basalt above the village has for years been quarried and used in the vineyards to aid heat-retention and enrichment of the potassium-rich soil, unique in the region. Best years: (Riesling Auslese) 2002, '01, '99, '98, '97, '96, '93, '92. Best producers: BASSERMANN-JORDAN, von BUHL, BÜRKLIN-WOLF, MOSBACHER, Wegeler, J L WOLF.

FOX CREEK
AUSTRALIA, South Australia, McLaren Vale
🍷 *Syrah (Shiraz), Cabernet Sauvignon, Cabernet Franc, Merlot, Grenache*
🍷 *Verdelho, Sauvignon Blanc, Semillon, Chardonnay*

Impressive, opulent, superripe MCLAREN VALE reds are the key to this recent success

FOX CREEK

The basic Fox Creek red is almost as impressive as the Reserve wines, a hedonistic mouthful of wine with good concentration and ripeness and succulent berry flavours.

story – the winery produced its first wines in 1994 and since then Reserve Shiraz and Reserve Cabernet Sauvignon have wowed the critics; JSM (Shiraz-Cabernets) is rich and succulent; the Merlot is a little lighter but still concentrated and powerful. Vixen sparkling Shiraz is also lip-smacking stuff. The whites are comparatively ordinary, albeit fair value for money.

FOX RUN VINEYARDS
USA, New York State, Finger Lakes AVA
🍷 *Pinot Noir, Cabernet Franc, Cabernet Sauvignon, Merlot, Lemberger*
🍷 *Chardonnay, Riesling, Gewurztraminer*

A reliable producer of quality wines, including a complex ALSACE-style Gewurztraminer, an elegant Reserve Chardonnay and a delightfully quaffable semi-dry Riesling. There are also spicy, attractive reds from Pinot Noir and Cabernet Franc and, since 1996, complemented by a complex, fruit-forward red Meritage.

FRANCIACORTA DOCG, TERRE DI FRANCIACORTA DOC
ITALY, Lombardy
🍷 *Cabernet Franc, Barbera, Nebbiolo, Merlot*
🍷 *Pinot Blanc (Pinot Bianco), Chardonnay*

The Franciacorta DOCG, between Bergamo and Brescia in the centre of LOMBARDY, is known mainly for CHAMPAGNE-method sparkling wine, which at its best has an elegance and creamy, grassy classiness that is hard to upstage. It is best kept a couple of years before broaching. CA' DEL BOSCO tends to be the benchmark, especially their Cuvée Annamaria Clementi, but the Vittorio Moretti Riserva Extra Brut from BELLAVISTA is also superb. Cavalleri, La Ferghettina, Enrico Gatti and Uberti are all good producers for various styles of fizz, including in some cases a *crémant* or low-pressure fizz referred to hereabouts as Satèn; and a rosé version, which generally gets its colour from a little Pinot Noir juice in the blend.

In order to avoid confusion with the sparklers, the still wines of the zone are today grouped under the Terre di Franciacorta DOC. The reds have an unusual grape mixture that, in the right hands, is very good. From PIEDMONT, to Franciacorta's west, come Barbera, giving zest and acidity, and Nebbiolo, giving grip and backbone. From FRIULI, to Franciacorta's east, come Cabernet Franc, giving stylishness and grassiness, and Merlot, giving roundness and suppleness. There's also some decent Pinot Nero, and Ca' del Bosco

seem to have uncovered some Carmenère. The whites are less idiosyncratic, although one never quite knows whether they are pure Chardonnay or a blend. Best producers: Bellavista, Ca' Del Bosco, Fratelli Berlucchi, Guido Berlucchi, Castellino, Cavalleri, La Ferghettina, Enrico Gatti, Monte Rossa, Ricci Curbastro, San Cristoforo, Uberti, Villa.

FRANCISCAN
USA, California, Napa County, Napa Valley AVA
🍷 *Cabernet Sauvignon, Merlot, Zinfandel*
🍷 *Chardonnay*

Of all NAPA's boom-era wineries, Franciscan got off to one of the most wayward starts, and it is only since 1985 that the outfit has gained a sense of direction. Franciscan Oakville Estate wines generally have a good fruit and attractive oak perfume and are beginning to show balance, restrained fruit and skilful winemaking: Cuvée Sauvage is a stunning, limited release Chardonnay; and the Merlot offers generous plum fruit and appealing richness. Best years: 2001, '00, '99, '98, '97, '96, '95, '94.

Franciscan also owns Estancia, with vineyards in MONTEREY, ALEXANDER VALLEY and PASO ROBLES, and Mount Veeder Winery, which is gaining a good record for Cabernet Sauvignon and red BORDEAUX-blend Reserve. Quintessa, a top-quality red Bordeaux blend from a single vineyard in the RUTHERFORD AVA, is growing in importance. Franciscan is now part of Constellation Wines, the world's biggest wine group.

FRANKEN
GERMANY

It is climate that is the essential difference between Franken and Germany's other wine regions such as the RHEINGAU. The summers are hotter and the winters colder here, and the growing season is distinctly on the short side. Silvaner is the classic grape, producing understated, sturdy wines with a touch of earthiness. More recently, however, Müller-Thurgau has taken over as the principal grape in Franken which is not good news. Nor is the fondness of Franconian growers for new, frost-resistant crosses like Bacchus and Kerner, with their over-assertive aromas; subtlety is one of the great virtues of Franken wine, and it's not often found in Bacchus or Kerner. Rieslaner, however, a cross between Riesling and Silvaner, is more promising.

The wines are bottled in the distinctive flagon-shaped Bocksbeutel and are mostly dry. WÜRZBURG, the capital, is in the Bereich

Maindreieck (it is the river Main that weaves its way unsteadily through the Franken vineyards) – this is the heart of Franken, as far as wine is concerned. The other two Bereichs are Mainviereck for the region towards Frankfurt, and Steigerwald for the eastern part, where the climate is most extreme and vines are only grown in scattered warm spots, on south-facing slopes.

FRASCATI DOC

ITALY, Lazio

♀ *Trebbiano Toscano, Malvasia di Candia, Malvasia del Lazio, Greco*

When drunk in and around Rome, its homeland, Frascati goes down well enough and is drunk with anything, even with what we would consider red wine foods. There are now an increasing number of wines that are perfectly OK to going on good, and one or two which are outstanding. Best when young, Frascati should taste soft, creamy and nutty. The wine can be made from mainly either Trebbiano – great for neutral background vinous swill but not much else; or Malvasia – too prone to oxidation if not handled properly, but peachy, nutty, flavoursome and characterful. The better examples have a higher proportion of Malvasia. Best producers: Casale Marchese, Castel de Paolis, Colli di Catone, Piero Costantini/Villa Simone, Fontana Candida, Zandotti.

FREIXENET

SPAIN, Cataluña, Cava DO

(Cava) ♂ *Trepat, Grenache (Garnacha)*
♀ *Macabeo (Viura), Parellada, Xarel-lo*

When you take into account Freixenet's two sparkling wine subsidiaries, Castellblanch and Segura Viudas, the Freixenet group is the biggest CHAMPAGNE-method producer, not just in Spain, but in the world, though CODORNÍU sell more under their own label. Quality at Freixenet is sound, but most of the wines suffer from the inherent defects of Catalan CAVA – lack of true personality and an unappetizing earthiness because of the grapes used and the unnecessary aging. However, the Brut Nature can be fresh and lemony, if slightly earthy, though the Cordon Negro Brut is more of a last resort purchase on the way to a party.

Freixenet also owns Conde de Caralt, Canals & Nubiola, René Barbier (still wines), all in Spain, the Californian winery Gloria Ferrer, Henri Abelé in CHAMPAGNE, the BORDEAUX *négociant* Yvon Mau, Wingara (Deakin Estate, KATNOOK ESTATE, Riddoch Estate) in Australia and Sala Vivé in Mexico.

MARCHESI DE' FRESCOBALDI

Frescobaldi's top wine is Montesodi, a classy 100 per cent Sangiovese with real structure and depth and complex, oak-influenced flavour.

MARCHESI DE' FRESCOBALDI

ITALY, Tuscany, Florence

♂ *Sangiovese, Pinot Noir (Pinot Nero), Cabernet Sauvignon, Merlot, Canaiolo and others*
♀ *Chardonnay, Pinot Blanc (Pinot Bianco), Pinot Gris (Pinot Grigio), Trebbiano, Malvasia and others*

Frescobaldi rests its reputation on two impressive pillars: its 700-year, 30-generation experience as grape growers and winemakers; and the fact that, with nearly 1000ha (2500 acres) of vines planted in various parts of TUSCANY, it is one of the largest family-owned producers of quality wines in Europe. There are also two highly talented enologo-agronomists of Tuscan origin but with wide international experience – Lamberto Frescobaldi and Nicolò d'Afflitto.

Perhaps the most representative property is Castello di Nipozzano, in CHIANTI RUFINA, where some 200ha (500 acres) are planted principally to Sangiovese and to Cabernets Sauvignon and Franc. The principal wines here are Castello di Nipozzano, a traditional Chianti Rufina Riserva of some considerable aging ability; Mormoreto, 60 per cent Cabernet Sauvignon with Merlot and Cabernet Franc, barrique-aged (50 per cent new) for 24 months, a wine whose complexity and harmony have come on apace since d'Afflitto took over here in 1995; also what is probably the greatest of all Frescobaldi wines, Montesodi, a pure Sangiovese of exceptional refinement and breeding.

The Castello di Pomino wines are of an entirely different ilk, consisting of two-thirds whites from vines planted between 500 and 700m (1640 and 2300ft). Best known wines are the Chardonnay-Pinot Bianco blend of POMINO Bianco (one of the best-value Tuscan whites around) and Pomino Benefizio (90 per cent Chardonnay), a single-vineyard wine benefiting, to a larger extent than the Bianco, from discreet barrique-aging. Best years: (premium reds) 2001, '00, '99, '97, '95, '93, '90, '88, '85.

In recent years Frescobaldi has teamed up with CALIFORNIA giant MONDAVI to establish Luce della Vite. Luce, a Merlot-Sangiovese blend, was launched in the late 1990s to much fanfare, at a price which many consider unrealistically high. In 2002 the two companies became partners in a separate joint venture, ORNELLAIA in BOLGHERI.

FRIULI AQUILEIA, FRIULI GRAVE, FRIULI LATISANA, FRIULI ANNIA, ALL DOC

ITALY, Friuli-Venezia Giulia

♂ *Cabernet Franc, Cabernet Sauvignon, Merlot, Pinot Noir (Pinot Nero), Refosco dal Peduncolo Rosso*
♀ *Chardonnay, Pinot Blanc (Pinot Bianco), Pinot Gris (Pinot Grigio), Riesling (Riesling Renano), Tocai, Gewürztraminer (Traminer Aromatico), Verduzzo*

These flatland zones constitute the engine-room of high productivity in FRIULI. Best known and largest is Friuli Grave, followed by Aquileia, Latisana and Annia. The wines tend more towards the workmanlike than the exciting. Best producers: (Friuli Grave) Borgo Magredo, Le Fredis, Di Lenardo, Orgnani, Pighin, Pittaro, Plozner, Pradio, Russolo, Vigneti Le Monde, Villa Chiopris, Vistorta.

FRIULI ISONZO DOC

ITALY, Friuli-Venezia Giulia

♂ *Cabernet Franc, Cabernet Sauvignon, Merlot, Pinot Noir (Pinot Nero), Franconia, Refosco dal Peduncolo Rosso, Schioppettino, Moscato Rosa*
♀ *Chardonnay, Malvasia, Moscato Giallo, Pinot Blanc (Pinot Bianco), Pinot Gris (Pinot Grigio), Sauvignon Blanc, Welschriesling (Riesling Italico), Verduzzo, Gewürztraminer (Traminer Aromatico), Riesling (Riesling Renano)*

Isonzo is one of the most recent, and most surprising, of Italy's star wine zones, given that 20 years ago it was virtually unknown and yet today is turning out possibly the finest white wines in Italy.

The surprise comes from the fact that Isonzo, like the other Friuli zones of Grave, Aquileia, Annia and Latisana, is a flat plain, yet the Sauvignons from here come redolent of perfume, the Chardonnays full of body and concentrated of taste, the Pinot Grigios creamy and intense, and even some of the reds are beginning to show real distinction. Isonzo's rich topsoil with a pebbly subsoil, combined with a constant cooling breeze from the hills of nearby Slovenia, seems to be the secret. Best years: (whites) 2001, '00, '99, '98, '97. Best producers: Borgo San Daniele, Colmello di Grotta, Sergio & Mauro Drius, Masùt da Rive (Silvano Gallo), Lis Neris-Pecorari, Pierpaolo Pecorari, Giovanni Puiatti, Ronco del Gelso, Tenuta Villanova, Vie di Romans.

FRIULI-VENEZIA GIULIA Italy

THE REGION OF FRIULI-VENEZIA GIULIA, often called just Friuli for short, is the true Italian north-east. Bordered by Slovenia to the east and Austria to the north, and suffering down the centuries from innumerable wars, situated as it is on one of Europe's historic crossroads, Friuli has become a meeting place of three cultures: Slavic, Teutonic and Venetian (from the west). The atmosphere in its scattered villages and sedate towns is of diligence and collaborative dedication, yet still the region remains undeniably Italian.

The wine zones of Friuli cover much of its southern half, most of which is a flat gravel plain – the zone of Friuli Grave DOC. Quality here basically depends on the soil: the pebbly gravel gives such rapid drainage that the vines are water-stressed most of the summer, holding down yields. Even so, Friuli Grave is still responsible for its fair share of basic wine, much of it still issuing forth in large

bottles declaring 'Tocai' (white) or 'Merlot' (red). The Friuli Aquileia, Friuli Latisana and Carso DOC zones are of lesser importance, all being coastal areas where growers battle for quality on alluvial, unstable terrain. The high reputation the Friuli wines enjoy hinges on three small wine districts next to the Slovenian border: Collio (Goriziano), Colli Orientali del Friuli and Friuli Isonzo. The first two are historic rivals, despite which there is not a great deal to choose between them, the dividing line being a provincial boundary rather than soil or climate differences. Their historic pre-eminence over other Friuli DOCs is due to their situation on hill terrain. So much importance is placed on this aspect that only wines from proper hill slopes are allowed to use these highly regarded names. As for Friuli Isonzo, it was only in the last decade of the twentieth century that this plain-land shot to prominence, thanks to the efforts of a clutch of enthusiastic young growers sometimes referred to as the 'Isonzo Boys'.

There is a wide range of grape varieties grown in Friuli, a mix of local, French and German, each traditionally vinified and bottled separately. A count in 1998 revealed over 150 different combinations of zone, grape and wine style for DOC wines alone and the number continues to grow. The essence of the Friuli style has always been varietal purity, but subtlety; in other words, the understated approach. When it works, as it frequently does, the wines have an elegance and a classiness that are hard to beat. Most grape varieties are white: Germanic Traminer and Riesling rub shoulders with French Sauvignon Blanc and Chardonnay as well as with the local Ribolla, Verduzzo and Malvasia, the widely grown Pinot Grigio and Tocai, and the underrated Pinot Bianco, to name just a few. Verduzzo, in the Ramandolo sub-zone, and delicate Picolit also make excellent sweet wines.

In recent years, however, the blended white wine has become fashionable. The trend began with growers like Jermann putting together grapes as disparate as Sauvignon Blanc, Chardonnay, Ribolla, Malvasia and Picolit in the now cult wine, Vintage Tunina. Livio Felluga's Terre Alte and Josko Gravner's oak-aged Breg are two other famous examples of a style now spreading rapidly.

Red wines have traditionally trailed behind whites in the Friuli region in terms of market recognition. They, too, have been largely varietal, although here again blended wines are becoming more important, especially the ones

The vineyards of Giacomo Dri are in the alpine foothills above Nimis at the northern end of the Colli Orientali del Friuli zone. Here, around the village of Ramandolo, the native Verduzzo grape produces rich, well-balanced sweet wines.

DOC/DOCG wines
- Friuli Grave DOC
- Lison Pramaggiore DOC (also in Veneto)
- Friuli Latisana DOC
- Friuli Annia DOC
- Friuli Aquileia DOC
- Friuli Isonzo DOC
- Carso DOC
- Collio Goriziano DOC
- Colli Orientali del Friuli DOC
- Ramandolo DOCG

VIE DI ROMANS
Sauvignon Blanc is one of Friuli's success stories: Piere is the unoaked version from this leading Isonzo producer.

LIVIO FELLUGA
This classy Merlot Reserva Sossó comes from the Felluga estate which is a substantial producer by Friuli standards and effortlessly combines quality with quantity.

RUSSIZ SUPERIORE
As with most other Collio estates, Russiz Superiore produces first-class white wines, including aromatic and nutty Tocai Friulano, Friuli's main white grape.

JOSKO GRAVNER
Based in Collio, almost on the Slovenian border, Josko Gravner concentrates on making wood-aged white wines from a blend of varieties. Breg is made from no less than seven different varieties.

made in a Bordeaux-style. But among these super-premium styles that flirt with the over-oaked international flavours that can be found worldwide, we shouldn't forget that Friuli makes wonderfully refreshing simple grassy Merlots and Cabernets with no oak at all as well as a chunky but enjoyable oddity called Refosco, for when you want an oddball winter red.

LIS NERIS-PECORARI
This Cabernet-Merlot blend is proof that the Friuli Isonzo area is doing increasingly well with warm-loving red varieties.

REGIONAL ENTRIES
Colli Orientali del Friuli, Collio, Friuli Aquileia, Friuli Isonzo.

PRODUCER ENTRIES
Borgo del Tiglio, Livio Felluga, Josko Gravner, Jermann, Russiz Superiore, Mario Schiopetto.

BORGO DEL TIGLIO
Nicola Manferrari continues to keep this estate in the vanguard of Collio producers. Both whites and reds are consistently good and characterful wine.

MARIO SCHIOPETTO
Mario Schiopetto was a pioneer in Italy of high-quality, intensely concentrated whites, including impressive Pinot Bianco.

JERMANN
Silvio Jermann is one of several producers who brought a whole new image to Friulian wine. Vintage Tunina is based on late-harvested Sauvignon and Chardonnay.

FROG'S LEAP WINERY

USA, California, Napa County, Napa Valley AVA
♥ *Cabernet Sauvignon, Zinfandel, Merlot, Syrah*
♀ *Sauvignon Blanc, Chardonnay*

John Williams may have split with former partner Larry Turley and moved location to the historic Red Barn winery but he continues to earn high marks for his Sauvignon Blanc, which makes up half of the winery's output. Made entirely from RUTHERFORD fruit since the 2002 vintage, these Sauvignons offer subtle melon flavours and bracing tanginess. Williams enjoys making Zinfandel and brings out its blackberry, spicy fragrance, berry and chocolate flavours, held together by sweet oak and firm tannin, while the Cabernets keep a grassy green streak to enliven their full black cherry and blackcurrant fruit. Merlot, made in a lush fruit style, is also good. Best years: 1999, '98, '97, '96, '95, '94, '93, '92, '91, '90, '87.

FROMM WINERY

NEW ZEALAND, South Island, Marlborough
♥ *Pinot Noir, Merlot, Malbec, Syrah*
♀ *Chardonnay, Riesling*

Owner Georg Fromm, who also owns vineyards in Switzerland, believes that MARLBOROUGH offers huge potential for red wines if the vines are grown under an organic regime and more time is spent in the vineyard. Fromm claims to invest more man-hours in the vineyard than the regional average by around 150 per cent. Most of his grapes come from Brancott Valley and a north-facing hillside vineyard called Clayvin Vineyard. Results have been impressive, with an outstanding Reserve Pinot Noir, good Merlot, and a surprisingly satisfying Syrah that shows concentration and ripeness considering its cool-climate location. Much praised Chardonnay and Riesling are the main white wines. All have good aging potential. Best years: (Pinot Noir) 2002, '01, '00, '99, '98.

FRONSAC AC

FRANCE, Bordeaux
♥ *Cabernet Franc, Cabernet Sauvignon, Merlot, Malbec*

There has been significant progress in Fronsac in recent years, particularly since 1994, with Fronsac's 'rustic' tannins more firmly under control and the wines generally richer and riper. The area does have some good producers, and tucked in next to POMEROL it also has good vineyard sites. But Fronsac still hasn't really taken off. Perhaps with the present drive for quality and relatively attractive prices Fronsac's time has now come? Best years: 2001, '00, '98, '97, '96, '95, '94, '90, '89, '88, '86, '85. Best producers: de Carles, de Carolus, Dalem, de la Dauphine, Fontenil, la Grave, Magondeau, Mayne-Vieil, Moulin Haut-Laroque, Puy Guilhem, la Rivière, la Rousselle, Tour du Moulin, les Trois Croix, la Vieille Cure, Villars.

CH. FUISSÉ

FRANCE, Burgundy, Mâconnais, Pouilly-Fuissé AC
♀ *Chardonnay*

The Vincent family have been the stars of the much maligned POUILLY-FUISSÉ appellation for the best part of a generation. In a region where the wines generally seem overpriced and overhyped, the cuvées of Ch. Fuissé have been of exceptional quality. For once, the prices did not seem too much out of line with the quality in the bottle. However, recent vintages have shown a dryer, leaner style, with a dull edge replacing the exciting richness I used to admire so much. Even such erstwhile star wines as Le Clos and the Vieilles Vignes seem to have gone off the boil. Disappointing and confusing – why does an estate that was so superior discard the opulence and richness that made it famous in the first place? A second range of Mâconnais and BEAUJOLAIS wines is made under the J-J Vincent label. Best years: 2002, '99, '98, '97, '96, '95.

RUDOLF FÜRST

GERMANY, Franken, Bürgstadt
♥ *Pinot Noir (Spätburgunder), Frühburgunder and others*
♀ *Riesling, Pinot Blanc (Weissburgunder), Silvaner and others*

Though not nearly as well known as the wine estates owned by the big charitable foundations of WÜRZBURG, Paul Fürst makes some of the very best wines in FRANKEN. But red wine is his speciality in a white wine region. This works because Bürgstadt is the warmest place in Franken, allowing him to make deeply coloured, silky reds that have enough power to take some new oak. The pure Spätburgunders age much better than most German reds. Simpler, but also impressive, is Parzival, a blend of Pinot Noir and the local Domina, which is full of blackberry fruit.

The barrique-aged Weissburgunder has Chardonnay-like nuttiness and in good vintages is a big heady wine. The dry Rieslings are sleeker, but unusually aromatic for a region whose whites are generally rustic and earthy. Best years: (reds) 2002, '01, '00, '99, '98, '97, '94, '90.

JEAN-NOËL GAGNARD
One of a bewildering number of Gagnards in the village of Chassagne-Montrachet, Jean-Noël consistently makes some of the best wines.

JEAN-NOËL GAGNARD

FRANCE, Burgundy, Côte de Beaune, Chassagne-Montrachet AC
♥ *Pinot Noir*
♀ *Chardonnay*

Caroline Lestimé has recently taken up the reins from her father, Jean-Noël Gagnard. Their wines are regularly among the finest in a village that can now boast a fair number of excellent domaines. The most sought-after wine is BÂTARD-MONTRACHET, but the numerous Premiers Crus from CHASSAGNE-MONTRACHET are also of the highest standard. The whites are deservedly the best known, but there is also a good range of reds, not surprisingly, given that nearly half the vineyards in Chassagne are planted with Pinot Noir. Gagnard's whites are characterized by elegant ripe fruit, carefully judged acidity and sensitive use of oak. Best years: (whites) 2001, '00, '99, '98, '97, '96, '95.

GAILLAC AC

FRANCE, South-West
♥ ♀ *Duras, Fer Servadou, Gamay, Syrah and others*
♀ *Mauzac Blanc, L'En de l'El, Ondenc and others*

About 27 million bottles of wine are produced annually from vineyards scattered between Albi and St-Sulpice in the Tarn *département*. Mauzac, with its sharp, but attractive, green apple bite, is the main white grape, abetted by the local l'En de l'El (meaning 'out of sight' in the dialect), Ondenc, Muscadelle, Sauvignon and Sémillon. Mauzac has a very 'direct' kind of taste, so even the best whites are rather stern, but from a decent grower there is a sharp apple and licorice fruit which is extremely refreshing.

The star of Gaillac, however, is the fizz – made by either the CHAMPAGNE method or the *méthode rurale* in which the fermentation is arrested, then finished off in bottle, to create the bubbles. This Gaillac Mousseux AC can be fabulous – full of apricots and apples, honey and peaches and a sting of tobacco and pepper too. The local co-operatives make a *pétillant* (a sort of demi-semi sparkler), Gaillac Perlé AC, which is not the same thing at all. Drink all the whites as young as possible. Red Gaillac is starting to become a more serious proposition. Production has increased recently and there are now a few wines from single producers which can be exciting – sharp, peppery, tangy – and will age a bit. Best producers: Albert, Bosc-Long, Causses-Marines, Dom. d'Escausses, de Gineste, Labarthe, Labastide-de-Lévis co-operative, Mas Pignou, Plageoles, Rotier, Técou co-operative, Clément Termes, des Terrisses.

ANGELO GAJA

ITALY, Piedmont, Barbaresco DOCG

♦ *Nebbiolo, Barbera, Cabernet Sauvignon, Merlot*

♀ *Chardonnay, Sauvignon Blanc*

A legend in his own lifetime, Angelo Gaja deserves, and receives, much of the credit for dragging the wines of BARBARESCO (and of Italy) to the top of the world wine tree. He began in the family business – already the major vineyard-owner of Barbaresco – in the early 1960s, and after trips to France to study the techniques of the great winemakers, and various stormy disputes with his father began to implement his radical ideas. He introduced severe *diradamento* (thinning to reduce yields), thermo-controllable fermentation equipment, malolactic fermentation, French barriques, French grape varieties, single-vineyard production and grand cru prices.

Having shocked the old guard, he then proceeded to rock the establishment further by planting Cabernet Sauvignon in a prime Nebbiolo site in Barbaresco in the late 1970s. Then, having for 25 years worked solely with the grapes of his own estate, in the 1980s he started buying or leasing property in other blue-chip zones of Italy, starting with BAROLO, then MONTALCINO (PIEVE SANTA RESTITUTA), and most recently in BOLGHERI. A more recent chapter in this rebellious history has seen Gaja renounce the Barolo and Barbaresco DOCGs for his best wines in favour of the looser LANGHE DOC.

GAJA
Angelo Gaja is recognized as one of the world's leading winemakers. His Barolo Sperss is an outstanding wine, with tremendous depth of fruit.

His principal wines are Barbaresco plus three crus that used to be Barbaresco DOCGs but now fly under the convenience flag of Langhe Nebbiolo DOC, which denomination permits 15 per cent of other red grapes, 'recommended or authorized', in the blend, Sorì Tildìn, Sorì San Lorenzo and Costa Russi. His crus from Barolo vineyards are Sperss and Conteisa; these too are now Langhe Nebbiolo DOC. He also makes a barrique-aged Nebbiolo-Merlot-Barbera blend called Sito Moresco. His Cabernet Sauvignon Darmagi is one of the best of its type in Italy, as is his Chardonnay Gaia & Rey. Best years: (Barbaresco and Langhe Nebbiolo) 2001, '00, '99, '98, '97, '96, '95, '90, '89, '88, '85, '82, '78, '71, '61.

GALICIA

SPAIN

When phylloxera struck Spain in 1901, few wine regions were as badly hit as verdant, mountainous Galicia, in the north-western corner of the Iberian Peninsula, directly north of Portugal. And what was to follow was almost as bad: most of the vineyards were replanted with 'foreign', low-quality, high-yield grape varieties, particularly Palomino (locally called Jerez or País), Alicante Bouschet (locally called Garnacha Tintorera). This condemned the region to utter obscurity for decades. Only in the 1970s, under the leadership of a few pioneers led by retired engineer Santiago Ruiz, were native varieties gradually recovered and the interlopers axed. The seaside DO of RÍAS BAIXAS led the way. Now, 92 per cent of its 2422ha (5985 acres) under vine are occupied by the fragrant Albariño, this DO's unique – and Spain's best – white grape variety.

There are four other Galician DOs: the historic RIBEIRO, plus Monterrei, VALDEORRAS and Ribeira Sacra. The last two specialize in aromatic young red wines made with the Mencía grape, but all the regions are strong, and improving, in whites. The dominant white varieties are Treixadura and Torrontés in Ribeiro, the apricotty Godello in Valdeorras and Doña Branca in Monterrei. The wines are now mostly vinified in a modern, fresh style in well-equipped, clean wineries – although Monterrei is some way behind the other DOs. The point most in their favour is perfume. Spain's whites are largely made from neutral grape varieties, yet in Galicia these native varieties are all capable of sensuous perfume and mouthwatering fruit. Most wines are best consumed young.

E & J GALLO WINERY
Gallo Sonoma is the much publicized Sonoma operation set up to give the Gallo image a new quality sheen, and so far so good.

E & J GALLO WINERY

USA, California, San Joaquin Valley (Gallo of Sonoma) ♦ *Zinfandel, Merlot, Cabernet Sauvignon and others*

♀ *Grenache, Zinfandel*

♀ *Chenin Blanc, Colombard, Chardonnay, Sauvignon Blanc and others*

Since the merger of HARDY and Constellation, Gallo has been demoted to the world's second biggest wine company, but it's still vast. Its experimental vineyard – let alone its regular plantings – is upwards of 405ha (1000 acres); the winery's cellar of oak tanks covers 18ha (45 acres); its main blending tank holds 50,000 hectolitres (1.1 million gallons) and it has its own glass factory. For years the bulk table wine production focused on off-dry generics – 'Chablis', 'Hearty Burgundy' and their kin – and oceans of ordinary wine sold under labels such as Turning Leaf, Garnet Point and Gossamer Bay. So in solely US terms, Gallo remains virtually untouchable, though the wines don't rate so well in international terms.

Gallo of Sonoma wines, however, are in a different league. Introduced in the early 90s, Gallo of Sonoma quickly evolved into a separate brand featuring varietal wines from Gallo's extensive vineyards (809ha/2000 acres) in northern Sonoma. Leading the way are the high-priced Estate Chardonnay and Estate Cabernet Sauvignon, but there are also many good to excellent varietal wines. Tops among them are Zinfandel and Cabernet Sauvignon from DRY CREEK VALLEY and ALEXANDER VALLEY and Chardonnay from several vineyards. New vineyards in RUSSIAN RIVER VALLEY have been planted to Pinot Noir. Single-vineyard Chardonnays (Laguna and Stefani) are also fine. Ongoing vineyard acquisitions and vineyard development and the quiet introduction of 'sub-brands' like Rancho Zabaco (SONOMA COUNTY wines), Marcelina (NAPA), Indigo Hills (Mendocino) and Anapamu Cellars (CENTRAL COAST Chardonnay and Syrah) indicate we are seeing just the first fruits of a new Gallo.

GAMAY

In most of the world, the Gamay grape is considered a common kind of creature. In general, its wine is rather rough-edged, quite high in raspy acidity, and a bit raw of fruit. But on the granite outcrops of Beaujolais, Gamay has one glorious fling, producing juicy peach and strawberry-and-cherry happy juice, which at its breeziest is Beaujolais Nouveau and at its most heady and exciting is a single-domaine wine from Fleurie, Morgon or Moulin-à-Vent. Good examples can even age – to a very attractive, slightly farmyardy, gentle Pinot Noir imitation with toffee and chocolate and plums. Elsewhere in France, the Mâconnais has a lot of Gamay, the Ardèche some, the Côte d'Or has the odd plot, while both Touraine and Anjou make rather dry, occasionally pleasant, light reds and rosés. Gamay is found, too, in the South and South-West. In Switzerland it is often blended with Pinot Noir. The resulting wine is called Dôle and often tastes rather thick and dull.

For years California grew two varieties, the Napa Gamay and the Gamay Beaujolais. Then it was decided that Napa Gamay was the real Gamay, Gamay Noir à Jus Blanc, while the other was merely a weak strain of Pinot Noir. Recent studies have shown that most of what was thought to be Napa Gamay is really another variety, Valdiguié. The wineries concerned have begun using the Valdiguié name, and the style ranges from light and simple to dark and robust.

So you're pretty hard put to find any other Gamay – it's pretty much Beaujolais or nowhere if you want it to raise a smile on your lips.

GARD

FRANCE, Languedoc-Roussillon

The Gard could consider itself a bit unlucky, because of all the southern French *départements* it has the shortest coastline and what it has is merely a sliver of unprepossessing marshland just east of Montpellier – better known as the Camargue. It used to be a little unlucky in its wines, too, because although there is a decent chunk of the CÔTES DU RHÔNE AC, and TAVEL and LIRAC, inside its borders, for real RHÔNE fireworks you always had to travel east or north.

Well, things are looking up, led by the relatively new AC COSTIÈRES DE NÎMES. Until 1989 the local AC was Costières du Gard, and the wines were unremittingly dull – flat, earthy, unappetizing. But since changing its name, Costières de Nîmes has become one of the liveliest, most forward-looking appellations in France. Even little Clairette de Bellegarde AC, with just a handful of producers, is waking up.

The departmental Vin de Pays de Gard mostly applies to light, spicy and attractive reds and rosés which are fresh when young. Although technically the Gard is part of the LANGUEDOC, its modern wines, excepting some promising plots of Sauvignon and Chardonnay destined for VINS DE PAYS, are very much riding the Rhône bandwagon.

GARDA DOC

ITALY, Veneto

🍷 Cabernet Sauvignon, Cabernet Franc, Merlot, Pinot Noir (Pinot Nero), Groppello, Marzemino, Corvina, Barbera

🍷 Garganega, Pinot Blanc (Pinot Bianco), Pinot Gris (Pinot Grigio), Chardonnay, Tocai Friulano, Riesling (Riesling Renano), Welschriesling (Riesling Italico), Cortese, Sauvignon Blanc

Created in 1997, this is a large, catch-all DOC zone in the province of Verona, stretching from Lake Garda east to the farthest reaches of SOAVE via BARDOLINO and VALPOLICELLA, and taking in those parts of LOMBARDY which abut on to the lake on the west and south, in the provinces of Brescia and Mantova respectively.

Its purpose is to allow producers in those zones to do pretty well what they feel like and still remain within the DOC system, and it grew up, not as a revolutionary throwing open of the gates but as a belated official reaction to an existing system (i.e. the wine producers were already doing pretty well what they felt like).

All the above-mentioned grapes can be made into varietal wines using a minimum of 85 per cent of the variety mentioned. The DOC also allows a red blend, a white blend and a chiaretto (rosé); these latter, together with Groppello and Groppello Riserva, having the right to add the subtitle 'Classico' should they so desire. Best producers: Ca' dei Frati, Cascina La Pertica.

GARGANEGA

The prolific Garganega, Italy's fifth most-planted white variety, can be found in various parts of north-east Italy, but its historic home is the western VENETO in the provinces of Verona and Vicenza. It is a very vigorous grape which, like its mate Corvina, requires training on a long arm. Maturity occurs between the last third of September through to the middle of October, depending on altitude and the degree of ripeness desired by the producer.

That Garganega has a long tradition of high quality may come as a surprise to those who associate its wines, notably SOAVE, with industrial table wine, but grown on the slopes where yields are self-regulating Garganega can bring forth a wine of great delicacy and finesse, with a gentle angelica ripeness and even the ability to age.

GARVEY

SPAIN, Andalucía, Jerez y Manzanilla DO

🍷 Palomino Fino, Pedro Ximénez, Moscatel

Garvey's San Patricio is one of the finest finos available, and was one of the first sherry brands to prove you could lower the alcohol level of a Fino without affecting flavour or stability. Other favourites are the rich, nutty Garvey Palo Cortado, and a wonderfully treacly Pedro Ximénez. Other brands include Tío Guillermo amontillado, Ochavico nutty old oloroso, Long Life oloroso (medium sweet) and Flor de Jerez cream. Garvey still uses its beautiful old bodegas in the town of Jerez for aging its finest sherries.

GATTINARA DOCG, GHEMME DOCG

ITALY, Piedmont

🍷 Nebbiolo (Spanna), Bonarda di Gattinara, Vespolina

Gattinara lies in northern PIEDMONT, in the province of Vercelli, in the vineyard area called Coste della Sesia, which was given its own DOC in 1996. Here the Nebbiolo grape tends to a softer, plummier style than in BAROLO or BARBARESCO. At its best, Gattinara can be full-bodied and fairly powerful yet with distinct floral aromas, displaying a touch of spice and a lightly bitter finish, and drinking well from five to 15 years old or more. It can also be as tough as Barolo, and sadly it is often mediocre in quality, tending to oxidize rather rapidly. Best years: 2001, '00, '99, '98, '97, '96, '95, '93, '90, '89, '88, '86, '85. Best producers: Antoniolo, S Gattinara, Nervi, Travaglini. Other DOC zones on the right bank of the Sesia river are

Bramaterra and Lessona, whose stars have slipped considerably further into obscurity even than that of Gattinara.

On the opposite, left bank of the Sesia, north-west of Novara, the dominant if nonetheless tiny production zone is that of Ghemme, whose wine has characteristics similar to those of Gattinara while being tauter, more delicate, less earthy. The only producer of note is the Antichi Vigneti di Cantalupo (crus Collis Breclemae and Collis Carellae). Other production zones in this area are Boca, Sizzano and Fara, all DOCs of little distinction and the newer zone of Colline Novaresi.

DOMAINE GAUBY

FRANCE, Languedoc-Roussillon, Côtes du Roussillon AC
🍷 *Carignan, Grenache, Syrah, Mourvèdre and others*
🍇 *Muscat, Grenache Blanc, Macabeo, Viognier, Chardonnay*

A leading figure for the younger generation in the Roussillon, Gérard Gauby has always produced impressively powerful, concentrated wines but has now added a little finesse as well. Highlights from this 40-ha (99-acre) domaine include the firm, rich, cassis-laden CÔTES DU ROUSSILLON-Villages Vieilles Vignes and the suave, spicy la Muntada, made almost exclusively from Syrah aged in oak barriques. The whites include les Rocailles, a Vin de Pays des Côtes Catalanes Grenache Blanc, and Vieilles Vignes, a potent VIN DE PAYS blend. Best years: (reds) 2001, '00, '99, '98, '97, '96, '95, '94, '93.

GAVI DOCG

ITALY, Piedmont
🍇 *Cortese*

This white wine of southern PIEDMONT, so often dismissed as an overpriced nonentity, can sometimes rise to the occasion. It develops a subtle but engaging, delicate, steely, toasty, lemony-fruited character that impresses more and more, especially at one to two years after the vintage. Too often, though, it is drunk too young, when its acidity is still searing and seemingly ill-integrated with the wine. Usually the wine is just called Gavi; to make it seem more important the idea was hatched of calling it Gavi di Gavi. Only estates with vineyards in the commune of Gavi are permitted to do so, but since that is most of them the cachet is somewhat devalued. Best producers: Battistina, Nicola Bergaglio, Broglia, La Chiara, CHIARLO, FONTANAFREDDA, La Giustiniana, Pio Cesare, San Pietro, La Scolca, Castello di Tassarolo, Villa Sparina.

CH. GAZIN

FRANCE, Bordeaux, Pomerol AC
🍷 *Merlot, Cabernet Franc, Cabernet Sauvignon*

One of the largest châteaux in POMEROL with 24ha (59 acres), Gazin is situated on the eastern plateau next to Ch. PÉTRUS and l'ÉVANGILE. Despite the prime location on Pomerol's clay-limestone soils and with the vines in a single block, the wine from Gazin was remarkably inconsistent in the 1960s, '70s and early '80s and only really hit top form from 1988 when the estate, owned by Nicolas de Bailliencourt asked the firm of J-P Moueix to get involved. It is now one of the most improved Pomerol properties and the Merlot-dominated wines show a truly rich, ripe, unctuous character with finely woven tannins, making them delicious young but capable of long aging. Best years: 2001, '00, '98, '97, '96, '95, '94, '90, '89, '88.

GEELONG

AUSTRALIA, Victoria

It's a mark of how the Victorian wine industry was devastated by phylloxera during the nineteenth century and has never recovered its position as Australia's top producer, that Geelong which in the 1860s had 400ha (988 acres) of vines and was the most important wine region in VICTORIA – if not Australia – is hardly known today. Phylloxera arrived during the 1870s and in 1881 the Government ordered that every single vine be destroyed – and none replanted. And until 1966, when Idyll was established, none were.

But Geelong is not an easy place to grow grapes – it never was. The soils are tough, frosts are common, continual winds and frequent hailstorms can decimate a crop – most grape growers choose easier options. However Geelong has produced some exceptional wines – Prince Albert Pinot Noir, the wild and wacky Idyll reds and whites and the equally wild but somewhat more modern BANNOCKBURN. Perhaps the difficult conditions encourage idiosyncratic winemaking, because Bannockburn, though famous, is certainly not everyone's cup of tea. Scotchmans Hill is the latest winery to build a decent reputation.

GEISENHEIM

GERMANY, Rheingau

The name Geisenheim is famous on two counts. First, as a wine village with excellent vineyards, notably the Rothenberg, Kläuserweg and Mäuerchen sites. The Rothenberg is named after the vineyard's iron-rich, red slate soils which produce rich, earthy wines.

The second reason is Geisenheim's wine school, founded in 1872, where aspiring winemakers come to study, and associated research institute which is the source of all those new vine-crossings that have helped or bedevilled (depending on your point of view) German wine over the past few decades.

Vines like Optima, Kerner, Reichensteiner and Bacchus were all born here, generally as part of the search for vines that will withstand the harsher aspects of Germany's climate and still give wine with flavour and style. There are open days several times a year and a walk through the institute's experimental vineyards could give a sneak preview of German viticulture over the next hundred years. Best years: (Riesling Spätlese) 2001, '99, '98, '97, '96, '93, '90. Best producers: JOHANNISHOF, Wegeler, von Zwierlein.

GEOGRAPHE

AUSTRALIA, Western Australia, South-West Australia Zone

This is a recently created wine region, effectively representing the southern half of the previously much larger South-West Coastal Plain region, and extending from Preston Beach in the north to Busselton in the south, and inland to Collie. There are currently a dozen wineries or so, most of them around Dardanup and in the Ferguson Valley.

Geographe's coastal climate is very similar to that of northern MARGARET RIVER, but the alluvial soils are far richer, and vine vigour has to be combatted to avoid excessive yields. The interior is quite different and can get as hot as RUTHERGLEN in VICTORIA – though cold nights help to temper the heat. Grapefruit-accented Chardonnay, tangy Semillon and Sauvignon Blanc, and highly aromatic Riesling lead the white wines. Shiraz, varying from light to full-bodied, and berryish Cabernet Sauvignon are the main red styles. Best producers: CAPEL VALE, Ferguson Falls Estate, Willow Bridge Estate.

GEROVASSILIOU

Greece, Makedonia AO
🍷 *Syrah, Merlot and others*
🍇 *Malagousia, Assyrtiko, Viognier, Chardonnay*

BORDEAUX-trained Evángelos Gerovassiliou is one of Greece's most respected enologists, with 40ha (100 acres) of vineyards and a modern winery in Epanomi in northern Greece. Though he has made a considerable reputation by growing the international varieties like Chardonnay, Viognier, Syrah and Merlot – and making some excellent wines from them – he should also be respected for his efforts in preserving superb indigenous Greek varieties like the marvellously aggressive Assyrtiko and the fleshily fragrant Malagousia which he combines to great effect in the Domaine Gerovassiliou white. Fresh, modern whites include a fine Viognier that lacks a little perfume but has fantastic fruit, and barrel-fermented Chardonnay. The reds are positively RHÔNE-like – not surprising given the quality of Syrah and Grenache that he grows (he also has Merlot) and the pure Syrah and the Syrah-dominated Domaine Gerovassiliou are both very good.

GESELLMANN

AUSTRIA, Mittelburgenland, Deutschkreutz
♥ *Blaufränkisch, Blauer Zweigelt, St Laurent, Pinot Noir (Blauburgunder), Cabernet Sauvignon, Merlot, Syrah*
♀ *Chardonnay, Sauvignon Blanc, Scheurebe*

Albert Gesellmann's winemaking inspiration comes from time spent working in CALIFORNIA and South Africa, and what he learnt there enabled him to improve the colour, depth and balance of the already interesting range of red wines which his father had developed during the 1980s. Bela Rex, a rich Cabernet-Merlot blend in an almost CALIFORNIAn style is the best, followed by Opus Eximium, a blend of French and local grapes whose composition varies from vintage to vintage, but like Bela Rex also gets a dose of new oak. Best years: (reds) 2000, '99, '97, '95, '93, '92.

GETARIAKO TXAKOLINA DO (CHACOLÍ DE GUETARIA DO)

SPAIN, País Vasco
♥ *Hondarribi Beltza*
♀ *Hondarribi Zuri*

Almost all the wine from this DO (also known as Chacolí de Guetaria in Spanish) gets drunk near where it is made, in the coastal Basque country. Production is increasing and plantings have more than doubled recently to 175ha (432 acres) even though vineyards are tiny – some not even measuring 0.5ha (1.2 acres).

There are two newer, smaller Basque DOs, for the even smaller nearby Bizkaiko Txakolina (Chacolí de Vizcaya in Spanish) and Arabako Txakolina (Chacolí de Alava) in Alava province. The wine is called Chacolí in Spanish, Txakoli in Basque. The Hondarribi Zuri white grapes that constitute 90 per cent of the plantings also have optional spellings. The wine is high in acidity, with a strong fruity

flavour, but is much more sophisticated now than in the old days when it was a bit like downing mouthfuls of scrumpy cider. But in the old days alcohol levels might have been 8–9 per cent – 10.5 per cent is now the minimum for the whites. Technically the wine is much better, but I sort of miss the raw greenness of the old stuff.

GEVREY-CHAMBERTIN AC

FRANCE, Burgundy, Côte de Nuits
♥ *Pinot Noir*

Gevrey-Chambertin is an infuriating village. With its Grands Crus CHAMBERTIN and Chambertin Clos-de-Bèze, it is capable of making the most startling, intoxicatingly delicious red wines of Burgundy, yet maddeningly liable to produce a limp succession of pale, lifeless semi-reds which really don't deserve the AC at all. It's the old Burgundian problem of supply and demand. With its world-famous top vineyard, Chambertin, leading the way, all the wines – whether Grand Cru, Premier Cru or the village wines – are keenly sought-after. So production increases – Gevrey-Chambertin already has easily the biggest production on the CÔTE D'OR – less suitable land is planted (some of the Gevrey-Chambertin AC is on the plains side of the N74 road, which is generally seen as the boundary below which good wine cannot be made), and standards slip. So straightforward Gevrey-Chambertin village wine should be approached with care. On the other hand, top growers such as BURGUET, Dugat-Py and Denis MORTET make powerful and exciting wines from village parcels.

But good examples are proud, big-tasting Burgundy at its best, usually a bit chewy, jammy even, when young, but gradually getting a fascinating flavour of perfumed plums and dark, smoky chocolates after six to ten years' aging. The finest of the 26 Premiers Crus, such as Clos St-Jacques and Combe aux Moines, come close to rivalling the Grands Crus in terms of power and longevity. And as a new generation takes over, we are seeing the gradual demise of the cynicism that bedevilled the 1970s and '80s and the return of a certain muscular 'don't mess with me' pride. Best years: 2002, '01, '00, '99, '98, '96, '95, '93, '90. Best producers: Denis Bachelet, L Boillot, A Burguet, CLAIR, P Damoy, DROUHIN, C Dugat, B Dugat-Py, DUJAC, S Esmonin, FAIVELEY, Fourrier, JADOT, Philippe Leclerc, Denis Mortet, Rossignol, J Roty, Rousseau, Sérafin, J & J-L Trapet.

GEWÜRZTRAMINER

Are Gewürztraminer and Traminer synonyms for the same grape or are they two different grapes? In France's Alsace region, where the grape achieves its highest quality and its greatest fame, there's no problem. It's Gewurztraminer and that's that. In Italy, where it grows in Friuli, as far south as Calabria, and as far north as the Südtirol or Alto Adige (which is the region of the village of Tramin from which the grape takes its name) it may be called either Traminer or Traminer Aromatico (alias Gewürztraminer). Sometimes it depends on the degree of spicy flavour in the wine, the prefix 'Gewürz' meaning spice in German; there has, in times past, been some confusion with the less aromatic Rotertraminer. Or the name Traminer may just be a convenient local shorthand. In Germany it is mostly known as Traminer, and grows (albeit in small quantities) mostly in Baden and the Pfalz; the Austrians go overboard and call it Gewürztraminer, Traminer, Roter (red) Traminer or Gelber (yellow) Traminer. Australia tends to be pretty relaxed about which name it uses.

Even the less spicy sort should have something of the rose petals, tropical fruit and musk perfume that has brought fame and fortune to the Alsace versions, though some wines from Austria's Steiermark region and Italy's Südtirol can be very pared down. But that's not really what Gewürztraminer is for. It's about opulence and intensity – for which it needs good balancing acidity if it is not to turn flabby.

Most New World producers content themselves with making off-dry wines for quick drinking. Some California growers, however, are doing better things, particularly in Mendocino's Anderson Valley and Sonoma's Russian River Valley. Oregon, Texas and New York State, especially Long Island, also show promise. Chile's cooler areas can produce pale, beautifully fragrant wines. Australia's examples are usually a little fat, but New Zealand's can equal Alsace at their best.

GIACONDA

AUSTRALIA, Victoria, Beechworth
🍷 *Syrah (Shiraz), Pinot Noir, Cabernet Sauvignon*
🍷 *Chardonnay, Roussanne*

The shy, quietly spoken Rick Kinzbrunner has achieved vinous rock-star status since establishing his Giaconda winery in north-east VICTORIA in 1985. Part of the hysteria may be due to the tiny total annual production – although the vineyard has gradually doubled in size to 6ha (15 acres) – but it is hard to say whether his Burgundian looka-like, tight yet complex Chardonnay or his silky, slippery, sappy, foresty Pinot Noir is the most highly regarded wine. Best years: 1999, '98, '97, '96, '95, '92, '91, '90, '88.

BRUNO GIACOSA

ITALY, Piedmont, Barbaresco DOCG
🍷 *Nebbiolo, Barbera, Dolcetto and others*
🍷 *Arneis*

The Giacosa tradition is that of the top quality *commerciante* or merchant, buying grapes from growers with whom they have enjoyed life-long relationships. Today, with the rise and rise of the grower-bottler the company is beginning to acquire its own vineyards, starting with Falletto in the commune of Serralunga in BAROLO and Asili in BAR-BARESCO. The winemaking philosophy is updated-traditional. Bruno is very strict about what is bottled under his label: his cru Barolos and Barbarescos were all sold in bulk in 1991, '92 and '94. In top years, he bottles his Riservas under the celebrated red label. Giacosa also produces Barolo cru Collina Rionda (Serralunga) and Villero and Le Roc-che (Castiglione Falletto). In Barbaresco his most famous wine is Santo Stefano di Neive. He also makes a good sparkling Extra Brut from Pinot Noir. Best years: 2001, '00, '99, '98, '97, '96, '95, '90, '89, '88, '85, '82.

GIESEN

NEW ZEALAND, South Island, Canterbury
🍷 *Pinot Noir*
🍷 *Sauvignon Blanc, Chardonnay, Riesling and others*

The Giesen family moved from the RHINE Valley in Germany in 1980, to establish this substantial (100,000-case) winery, choosing a cool and windy climate with which they were familiar. Not surprisingly, they have succeeded best (and at times brilliantly) with non-wooded aromatic wine styles, though also with oaked Chardonnay and Pinot Noir. The botrytized Rieslings are some of the finest in the southern hemisphere. Best years: (Reserve Chardonnay) 2002, '01, '00, '98.

Giesen is Canterbury's largest winery and makes outstanding botrytized and dry Rieslings from its sunny but wind-battered vineyards.

GIGONDAS AC

FRANCE, Southern Rhône
🍷 🍷 *Grenache, Syrah, Mourvèdre, Cinsaut*

Gigondas is a large village below the craggy slopes of the Dentelles de Montmirail in the east of the RHÔNE VALLEY, with 1244ha (3074 acres) of vines. The wines have a tougher, chewier, jam-rich fruit than those from nearby CHÂTEAUNEUF-DU-PAPE; they take longer to soften and never quite set the heart so aflutter. Best years: 2001, '00, '99, '98, '97, '95, '94, '90. Best producers: la Bouïssière, Brusset, de Cassan, du Cayron, Clos des Cazaux, Clos du Joncuas, Cros de la Mûre, DELAS, des Espiers, Font-Sane, les GOUBERT, Gour de Chaule, Grapillon d'Or, GUIGAL, JABOULET, Longue-Toque, Montvac, Moulin de la Gardette, les Pallières, de Piaugier, RASPAIL-AY, Redortier, St-Cosme, de St-Gayan, Santa-Duc, Tardieu-Laurent, de la Tourade, du Trignon.

CH. GILETTE

FRANCE, Bordeaux, Sauternes AC
🍷 *Sémillon, Sauvignon Blanc, Muscadelle*

This extraordinary wine is fermented in stainless steel, then aged for 12–14 years in concrete vats before being finally released to the consumer (as Crème de Tête) a minimum of 15 years after the harvest. This method greatly reduces the oxygen contact and preserves the wine's lively fruit character. The wines have a deep golden colour, sumptuous bouquet of raisined fruits, orange zest, coffee and vanilla and a rich unctuousness on the palate with an interminable finish. The volume of wine produced from the tiny 5-ha (12-acre) vineyard is minimal. Best years: 1983, '82, '81, '79, '78, '76, '75, '70, '67, '61, '59, '55, '53, '49.

GIMBLETT GRAVELS

NEW ZEALAND, North Island, Hawkes Bay

I vividly remember my first sight of the Gim-blett Gravels. It was in 1987, on my first trip to New Zealand, and they weren't called Gimblett Gravels then. They weren't called anything. They were just that useless patch of shingle over near the Go-Kart track where even the grass won't grow. That was then.

Now they are some of the most exciting vineyard areas in New Zealand – and precisely because the soil is so poor nothing will grow. Except vines. Vines love really bad soil if they're to produce the best wine grapes, and the 700ha (1730 acres) of old river bed near Napier where the Ngaruroro River flowed until it dramatically changed course in 1876 is virtually hydroponic. But, beneath these deep gravel beds, aquifers still run, so there is loads of water for irrigation – and with that and, where the soil is *really* bare, the addition of nutrients you can grow small crops of red varieties like Merlot, Cabernet and Syrah better than almost anywhere in New Zealand. Gravel is a very warm medium for a vineyard – clay is cold – and the Gimblett Gravels during summer and autumn are 3°C (5°F) warmer than most other Hawkes Bay vineyards. When you're trying to ripen Cabernet, that makes all the difference and, though the area is still very young, the softness of texture, the perfume and the ripeness of fruit here are impressive and delicious. Best producers: CRAGGY RANGE, Esk Valley, Mills Reef, Newton Forrest, STONECROFT, Te Awa Farm, Vidal, VILLA MARIA, Unison.

GIPPSLAND

AUSTRALIA, Victoria

This fairly cool, sprawling zone, extending for 200km (125 miles) south-east of Melbourne, is principally noted for Chardonnay and Pinot Noir. Quality is erratic but some of the flavours match anything in Australia for power and intensity. Best years: 2000, '99, '98, '97, '95, '94. Best producers: BASS PHILLIP, McAlister, Nicholson River.

VINCENT GIRARDIN

FRANCE, Burgundy, Côte de Beaune, Santenay AC
🍷 *Pinot Noir*
🍷 *Chardonnay*

Girardin is very much a leader of new-wave BURGUNDY – the best grower in SANTENAY and now a thriving *négociant* as well with a new establishment in MEURSAULT. Bright, glossy reds from Santenay, MARANGES and CHASSAGNE-MONTRACHET, frequently among the best in these appellations with much brighter, riper fruit than most examples, are surpassed by excellent VOLNAY and POMMARD Grands Épenots. Chassagne-Montrachet whites (Morgeot and Caillerets) are well balanced with good fruit depth. CORTON-CHARLEMAGNE is exceptional. Best years: (reds) 2002, '01, '99, '98, '97, '96, '95.

GISBORNE

NEW ZEALAND, North Island

The Gisborne or Poverty Bay area was once a largely anonymous provider of low-cost, pleasantly fruity grapes to keep the pumps flowing for bag-in-the-box wines. The area has moved up-market (much of New Zealand's bag-in-the-box wine now comes from Australia, Chile and Spain) and labels itself 'the Chardonnay capital of NZ', although Gewurztraminer and Chenin Blanc are also successful. Improved vineyard sites and lower crop levels have done much to raise Gisborne's image. Best performers are the organic producer Millton, together with premium Gisborne-branded wines from some of the major players, such as MONTANA's Ormond Estate Chardonnay. Best years: (Chardonnay) 2002, '00, '98. Best producers: Millton, Montana, Revington.

CH. GISCOURS

FRANCE, Bordeaux, Haut-Médoc, Margaux AC, 3ème Cru Classé

♀ *Cabernet Sauvignon, Merlot, Cabernet Franc, Petit Verdot*

Ch. Giscours made a number of lovely wines in the 1960s and '70s. They started off with a rather solid, almost tarry quality but also had a heavenly perfume, just asking for a few years' maturity, and a fruit that was blackberries, blackcurrants and cherries all at once. Things tailed off disappointingly in the 1980s to a rather more typically dilute MARGAUX style of wine, and recently infighting among the owners and a scandal in 1998 concerning a vat of HAUT-MÉDOC wine that found its way into Giscours' second wine, la Sirène de Giscours, didn't exactly help. One can only hope that Giscours will be back on the rails soon, as the potential is definitely there. Best years: 2000, '99, '98, '95, '90, '86, '83, '82, '81, '79.

GIVRY AC

FRANCE, Burgundy, Côte Chalonnaise

♀ *Pinot Noir*

♀ *Chardonnay*

This is an important Côte Chalonnaise wine village with 219ha (541 acres) of vineyards,

Father and son, Walter and David Finlayson of Glen Carlou tasting a barrel sample of their acclaimed Chardonnay, which can mature for four or five years, longer than most other South African Chardonnays.

west of Chalon-sur-Saône. The red wines are generally good, not that heavy, and with a full, ripe strawberry perfume and a gently plummy flavour. White wines are much rarer – only about 250,000 bottles out of an annual production 1.5 million – and they often used to veer towards the sharp and neutral (not at all like Chardonnay should be in southern Burgundy). But in recent years the wines seem to be a little fuller and nuttier – which is much more attractive. In the 1990s about 25 vineyards were elevated to Premier Cru status. Best years: (reds) 2002, '00, '99, '98, '97, '96, '95; (whites) 2002, '00, '99. Best producers: Bourgeon, Chofflet-Valdenaire, Joblot, F Lumpp, Parize, Ragot, Sarrazin.

GLEN CARLOU

SOUTH AFRICA, Western Cape, Paarl WO

♀ *Cabernet Sauvignon, Merlot, Syrah (Shiraz), Pinot Noir and others*

♀ *Chardonnay*

Over the years, Walter Finlayson has attracted a loyal following, initially for his red wines, but since his move to this PAARL farm he has also gained recognition for excellent Chardonnay. His career started in STELLENBOSCH, on the family farm, Hartenberg (then known as Montagne); he then helped to put the Blaauwklippen estate on the map. In 1985 he began work on his own property, GLEN CARLOU on the Paarl slopes of the Simonsberg, where he has specialized in two loves, BORDEAUX and BURGUNDY. Son David is now following capably in his father's footsteps and

has reinforced the farm's already fine reputation for bold, complex Chardonnay. A good air-flow down the valley helps Pinot Noir here to turn in a surprisingly good performance on these north-facing slopes; although lightish, it has inviting ripe black cherry and raspberry flavours. These classically styled wines attracted Donald Hess of California's HESS COLLECTION and his partnership has brought renewed impetus and growth to this leading Cape producer. Best years: (Chardonnay) 2001, '00, '99, '98, '97, '96.

GLENORA WINE CELLARS

USA, New York State, Finger Lakes AVA

♀ *Cabernet Sauvignon, Merlot, Cabernet Franc, Pinot Noir*

♀ *Chardonnay, Riesling, Seyval Blanc, Pinot Blanc, Gewurztraminer*

Glenora Wine Cellars is a top-quality, large-scale producer of vinifera wines in the FINGER LAKES AVA. Its yeasty, complex sparkling wines, including a light and refreshing vintage Blanc de Blancs, are very good and a fine Riesling and attractive barrel-fermented Chardonnay are the best still wines.

GOLAN HEIGHTS WINERY

ISRAEL, Golan Heights

♀ *Cabernet Sauvignon, Merlot, Pinot Noir and others*

♀ *Cabernet Sauvignon*

♀ *Sauvignon Blanc, Chardonnay, Gewurztraminer, Riesling, Muscat Blanc à Petits Grains*

This is the winery setting the pace for all others in Israel. Its actual name is Hatzor, but it's known as Golan Heights because that's where it is located. The Golan Heights vineyards are planted up to 1200m (3940ft), and this altitude and the cool nights are the secrets of the winery's success. Using night harvesting for the white grapes and winemaking equipment and techniques derived from CALIFORNIA, the winery produces surprisingly light, fresh whites, and deep, sturdy reds that are a world away from the poor quality image of kosher wines. The range includes good Sauvignon Blanc and Cabernet Sauvignon, excellent, oaky Chardonnay and good bottle-fermented fizz. Drink the wines young. All the wines are kosher, but since the vineyards are outside the biblical Old Kingdom, the rule that says that the vineyards must lie fallow every seventh year need not be observed. The Yarden range is the best, followed by Gamla and Golan. Expansion to new vineyards in Galilee might offset any potential threat to the flagship winery as the Middle East situation evolves.

GOLDWATER ESTATE

NEW ZEALAND, North Island, Auckland, Waiheke Island

♟ *Cabernet Sauvignon, Merlot, Cabernet Franc*
♀ *Chardonnay, Sauvignon Blanc*

Every time I clamber to the top of the vine-covered hill above Goldwater's winery and look back over the sparkling blue waters and bobbing sailboats of Putiki Bay, I just think – wow, some people have all the luck. Why wasn't *I* born on WAIHEKE ISLAND, the vineyard paradise sitting in Hauraki Gulf an hour out from Auckland?

But the people who have created the modern Waiheke weren't born there either: the incomer Goldwaters were the first to establish vineyards there in 1978, and they have been at the forefront of Waiheke winemaking ever since. Their most famous wines are cedary, restrained Cabernet Sauvignon

GOLDWATER ESTATE
Intense, long-lived Cabernet Sauvignon-Merlot quickly showed the world that Waiheke Island was one of New Zealand's top red wine areas.

and Merlot and Esslin Merlot – very BORDEAUX in style – though I also like their locally grown Zell Chardonnay. A substantial part of their production is now Dog Point Sauvignon and Roseland Chardonnay, both wines from MARLBOROUGH fruit, and they have a new red wine vineyard in GIMBLETT GRAVELS. Best years: (Waiheke reds) 2002, '00, '99, '96.

GONZÁLEZ BYASS

SPAIN, Andalucía, Jerez y Manzanilla DO; La Rioja, Rioja DOCa; Cataluña, Cava DO
♀ *Palomino Fino, Pedro Ximénez*

Tio Pepe, González Byass' fino, is the top-selling sherry in the world. Unusually for such a big brand, it's also one of the very best. González Byass owns 900ha (2224 acres) of prime vineyards and also has many long-term contracts with grapegrowers. Unlike many JEREZ firms, it never buys in grape juice or ready-made wines, preferring to put all the raw material of the grapes through its own quality-oriented plant. It has enough sherry for over 70 million bottles maturing in its bodegas at any one time.

Amontillado del Duque is a fine, dry, austere, pungent and nutty wine, one of the world's great wines for a very fair price. Matusalem is a sweetened old oloroso, big, deep and pruny, majestically rich. Noe is an outstanding ultra-sweet Pedro Ximénez. And Apostoles Oloroso Viejo is medium-dry, nutty and grapy. The next step down, Alfonso Dry Oloroso, is also very good. As well as Tio Pepe, there's a cheaper fino sold under the brand name Elegante and, typically sweetened for the UK market, La Concha Amontillado, San Domingo Pale Cream and Caballero Amontillado. González Byass also owns Castell de Villarnau, a CAVA producer in PENEDÈS, and the fine Bodegas Beronia in RIOJA.

GOSSET

FRANCE, Champagne, Champagne AC
♀♟ *Chardonnay, Pinot Noir, Pinot Meunier*

There have been dramatic changes at this venerable house which can trace its roots back to 1584 and claims to be the oldest wine house in Champagne. Promoted to the now-disbanded *grande marque* grouping in 1992, it was then bought by the Cointreau family of Cognac. However, the new owners have retained the former winemaking team and show no signs of increasing annual production to more than the current 500,000 bottles. Of Gosset's two non-vintage Champagnes, the outstanding one is the Grande Réserve Brut, a

rich, sumptuous wine, composed mostly of Chardonnay and Pinot Noir. The vintage Grand Millésime has a higher Chardonnay content, and there is also a fine vintage rosé and a prestige cuvée called Celebris. Overall, these are big, bold Champagnes which may not be appreciated by those who value freshness and delicacy above all else but are fine wines for the more adventurous. Best years: 1996, '95, '93, '90, '89, '88, '85, '82.

DOMAINE LES GOUBERT

FRANCE, Southern Rhône, Gigondas AC
♟ *Grenache, Syrah, Mourvèdre, Cinsaut and others*
♀ *Viognier, Clairette, Roussanne, Bourboulenc*

Jean-Pierre Cartier began making the wines at his 23-ha (57-acre) family estate in GIGONDAS in 1974. When he and his wife took themselves off to enology and wine-tasting courses at a French university, their neighbours thought they were mad. Indeed, Jean-Pierre's spirit of inquiry and willingness to innovate still sets him apart from his more parochial neighbours; moreover, in the poor 1992 vintage he had the courage to bottle not one drop of red wine.

His reds, whether simple CÔTES DU RHÔNE or a more complex Beaumes-de-Venise or Gigondas, are always rich and deep, imposing yet lovely wines that can age very well. In the mid-1980s he enraged traditionalists by aging a special cuvée of Gigondas in barriques, largely new. Cuvée Florence went down well with his US fans, but within Europe it was more controversial. In the 1990s Cartier turned his attention to making whites as well as reds, and he is now fermenting much of his white Sablet in oak; there is also a barrel-fermented Côtes du Rhône made entirely from Viognier. Les Goubert no longer stands out within the Gigondas appellation now that other estates are matching its high standards, but it still remains an impeccable source of delicious, classic southern RHÔNE wines. Best years: 2001, '00, '99, '98, '97, '95, '94, '93, '90, '89, '88, '86, '85.

DOMAINE LES GOUBERT
Jean-Pierre Cartier makes a good range of wines at his Gigondas estate. Cuvée Florence, his top wine, spends 18 months in oak and is unfiltered.

HENRI GOUGES

*FRANCE, Burgundy, Côte de Nuits, Nuits-St-Georges
AC*

♥ *Pinot Noir*
♀ *Pinot Noir [sic.]*

Henri Gouges was one of the pioneers of fine, unadulterated Burgundies in the 1920s and '30s. But by the late '70s the estate seemed to be in decline. Fortunately, the present generation, Christian and Pierre, have made the wines once again among the very best of the appellation. Indeed, so they should be, given the excellent vineyards belonging to the family. Of the 14.5ha (36 acres) of vines, at least 10ha (25 acres) are Premiers Crus, of which the finest are St-Georges and Vaucrains. Two fascinating whites are produced from Clos des Porrets and la Perrière; they are made from an old mutation of Pinot Noir, and although white in colour and aroma, they have the body and substance of a red wine. Best years: 2002, '00, '99, '98, '97, '96, '95, '93, '90, '89.

GOULBURN VALLEY

AUSTRALIA, Victoria

Goulburn Valley is located north of the Great Dividing Range, where it becomes drier and warmer. At the southern end of the valley is the sub-region of Nagambie Lakes. Here the Goulburn River creates billabongs (or backwaters) lined with white-trunked eucalyptus trees and inhabited by an amazing variety of bird life. TAHBILK makes monumental, tannic reds, from ancient vines, while MITCHELTON produces modern, oaky wines. In the flatter and less picturesque north, the Upper Goulburn Valley, where the Goulburn joins the Murray River, irrigated white and red varietals of good quality and modest price are produced. Best producers: Tahbilk, Mitchelton. Best years: (reds) 2001, '00, '98, '97, '95, '92, '91.

GOUNDREY WINES

AUSTRALIA, Western Australia, Great Southern

♥ *Cabernet Sauvignon, Syrah (Shiraz), Merlot, Pinot Noir*
♀ *Chardonnay, Sauvignon Blanc, Semillon, Riesling*

Important winery that has led a rather topsy turvy existence since its establishment by Michael Goundrey in 1976. Perth millionaire Jack Bendat acquired it in 1992 and sales exploded from a mere 17,000 cases to 260,000 in 2002. Some of the fruit is from their own vines but much of it from further afield. The Canadian giant Vincor bought the operation in 2003 and intends to increase sales even more. Quality has actually held up reasonably well, given the expansion, and while no current

wines really shine, all are enjoyable. Riesling and unoaked Chardonnay are important here but peppery Shiraz can be good too. Fox River is a second label. Best years: (Riesling) 2001, '99, '98, '97, '96, '94, '93, '92, '91.

GRAACH

GERMANY, Mosel-Saar-Ruwer

With the village of Graach just upstream of WEHLEN we are in the heart of the MOSEL region. The soil is deep slate, fine slivers of grey rock that hold the heat and impart a whiff of smoke to the Rieslings it supports. On richer soils like these, the wines are full, honeyed, yet intense. The vineyards' southwest exposure to the sun is ideal, and there's plenty of it; the vineyards rise almost vertically from near river level to 200m (660ft). The names to look for are intensely minerally Domprobst, the more floral Himmelreich and spicy Josephshöfer. Best years: 2002, '01, '00, '99, '98, '97, '96, '95, '94, '93, '90. Best producers: Kees-Kieren, von KESSELSTATT, Dr LOOSEN, Markus Molitor, J J PRÜM, S A PRÜM, Max Ferd RICHTER, Willi SCHAEFER, SELBACH-OSTER, Weins-Prüm.

GRAHAM

PORTUGAL, Douro, Port DOC

♥ *Tempranillo (Tinta Roriz), Tinta Barroca, Tinto Cão, Touriga Nacional, Touriga Franca and others*
♀ *Gouveio, Malvasia Fina, Rabigato and others*

One of the main PORT shippers belonging to the Symington family, Graham has a house style that is usually sweeter and more florally scented than those of the other Symington companies. This is best reflected in its outstanding vintage port based on Quinta dos Malvedos. In good interim years wine from Malvedos is bottled as a single-quinta vintage port. Graham also produces some fine, aged tawnies and large quantities of LBV (filtered, unfortunately, to remove the need for decanting) which is consistently among the best in the filtered category. Six Grapes is one of the better premium rubies. Best years: (Vintage) 2000, '97, '94, '91, '85, '83, '80, '77, '75, '70, '66, '63, '60; (Malvedos) 1999, '95, '92, '90, '87, '86, '84.

ALAIN GRAILLOT

FRANCE, Northern Rhône, Crozes-Hermitage AC

♥ *Syrah*
♀ *Marsanne, Roussanne*

Alain Graillot has a background as an agro-chemist and first decided to make wine in 1985, buying in grapes for the purpose. He had gained some experience in BURGUNDY,

and adopted Burgundian techniques such as giving the red grapes a cold soak before fermentation and aging a proportion of the wine in used barriques he purchases from his friends in the CÔTE D'OR. The wines, both red and white, have been outstanding from the outset, with a richness and perfume rarely encountered in CROZES-HERMITAGE. The top red Crozes is la Guiraude. The white is made mostly from Marsanne and is partly fermented in older barrels. Graillot has a small parcel of vines in HERMITAGE, and also makes a little ST-JOSEPH. Best years: (la Guiraude) 2001, '00, '99, '96, '95, '94, '91, '90, '89.

GRAMPIANS

AUSTRALIA, Victoria

Great Western is the name by which this area has been better known, but almost 70 years of legal skirmishing between BEST'S and SEPPELT over its use made the official adoption of Grampians the only sensible solution. Syrah (Shiraz) is the great grape of the region, forming a symbiotic but subtly different relationship with the winemakers at Best's, MOUNT LANGI GHIRAN and Seppelt, ranging from cherry and mint to more spicy savoury flavours. Best years: (Shiraz) 2001, '99, '98, '97, '96, '94, '91, '90. Best producers: Best's, Mount Langi Ghiran, Seppelt.

SEPPELT

From its 70-year-old St Peters Vineyard in Grampians, Seppelt produces a benchmark red fizz, Show Sparkling Shiraz, with sweet ripe fruit and deep, spicy flavour.

CH. GRAND-PUY-LACOSTE

FRANCE, Bordeaux, Haut-Médoc, Pauillac AC, 5ème Cru Classé

♥ *Cabernet Sauvignon, Merlot, Cabernet Franc*

Don't be fooled by this wine only being a Fifth Growth. Because PAUILLAC dominated the awards of First Growths in the 1855 BORDEAUX Classification, one sometimes gets the feeling that several very exciting properties were rather unceremoniously dumped in the Fifth Growths category for appearance's sake.

However, this 50-ha (125-acre) estate owned by the Borie family of Ch. DUCRU-BEAUCAILLOU makes a classic Pauillac. It isn't as weighty and grand as better-known Pauillac wines like Ch. LATOUR and MOUTON-ROTHSCHILD, but the purity of its flavour

CH. GRAND-PUY-LACOSTE
This is classic Pauillac with lots of blackcurrant and cigar-box perfume. As the wine ages and develops, the flavours mingle with the soft sweetness of new oak.

marks it out as special. Although it begins in a fairly dense way, that's just how a Pauillac should start out; as the years pass the fruit becomes the most piercingly pure blackcurrant and the perfume mingles cedar with lead pencils and the softening sweetness of new oak. Recent wines have been splendid. Second wine: Lacoste-Borie. Best years: 2001, '00, '99, '98, '97, '96, '95, '94, '93, '90, '89, '88, '86, '85, '83, '82.

DOMAINE DE LA GRANGE DES PÈRES

FRANCE, Languedoc, Vin de Pays de l'Hérault

♥ Syrah, Mourvèdre, Cabernet Sauvignon, Counoise
♀ Roussanne, Marsanne, Chardonnay

It hasn't taken long for owner Laurent Vaillé to establish his tiny 12-ha (30-acre) domaine in Aniane as a LANGUEDOC legend – the land was bought in 1989 and the first vintage – for red – was only in 1992. With a mere 500 cases of wine produced each year, demand is high for the meticulously crafted unfiltered red made from a blend of Syrah, Cabernet Sauvignon and Mourvèdre. 1995 was the first vintage of a white which is produced in even smaller quantities and is on even stricter allocation. The vineyard is sited just down the road from the HÉRAULT's most famous property MAS DE DAUMAS GASSAC, and one senses a frisson of healthy rivalry developing. Best years: (red) 2001, '00, '99, '98, '97, '96, '95, '94, '93, '92.

GRANITE BELT

AUSTRALIA, Queensland

Situated on the western side of the Great Dividing Range, the 34 wineries of the Granite Belt constitute the epicentre of winemaking in QUEENSLAND, notwithstanding the rash of wineries forming a ring around Brisbane and which sprang up in the latter part of the 1990s. Winemaking in the Granite Belt originated with the local Italian fruit growers who used table grapes to make rough and ready jug wine, the first *Vitis vinifera* (Syrah/Shiraz) appearing in 1965. Shiraz has

proved to be the best red grape, followed by Cabernet Sauvignon, while Semillon, Chardonnay and Sauvignon Blanc have provided the best white wines. It has to be said that these are relative judgments; the principal market is the none-too-critical tourist passing through on holidays. Best producers: Bald Mountain, Ballandean Estate, Kominos, Mountview Wines, Preston Peak, Robinsons Family Vineyards, Stone Ridge, Wild Soul.

GRANS-FASSIAN

GERMANY, Mosel-Saar-Ruwer, Leiwen

♀ Riesling, Pinot Blanc (Weissburgunder) and others

This MOSEL estate, situated on the bend in the river Mosel between LEIWEN and TRITTENHEIM is not yet terrifically well known but is fast building a reputation for stylish, fragrant wines. There is a willingness to experiment which is reflected in the un-Germanic use of barriques for aging some of the wines. Gerhard Grans' best wines come from Trittenheimer Apotheke, a superb, steep vineyard site for Riesling. Eiswein is a long-standing speciality and often spectacular. Best years: (Riesling Spätlese and Auslese) 2002, '01, '99, '98, '97, '96, '95, '94, '93, '90.

YVES GRASSA

FRANCE, South-West, Vin de Pays des Côtes de Gascogne

♥ Merlot, Tannat, Cabernet Franc, Cabernet Sauvignon, Syrah
♀ Colombard, Ugni Blanc, Gros Manseng, Chardonnay, Sauvignon Blanc, Chenin Blanc, Petit Manseng

The Grassa family were one of the pioneers of crisp, snappy, fruity, dry white CÔTES DE GASCOGNE and produce a range of white wines at 11 different domaines, including the 80-ha (200-acre) Domaine du Tariquet. The different cuvées include a Colombard-Ugni Blanc blend, the Cuvée Bois for a similar blend aged in oak, a barrel-fermented Chardonnay and a late-harvested sweet white produced from Gros Manseng labelled Premières Grives. Not content with producing this excellent range of whites, the Grassas have now equipped themselves with oak vats and barrels and a system for *microbullage* in order to produce some top-flight reds under the Domaine du Mage label. There are also some good Armagnacs.

ALFRED GRATIEN

FRANCE, Champagne, Champagne AC

♀ ♥ Chardonnay, Pinot Noir, Pinot Meunier

For CHAMPAGNE, this isn't a big company, producing only 175,000 bottles a year in its backstreet cellars in Épernay (the giant MOËT

ET CHANDON, for instance, produces over 26 million a year) but whoever said you had to be big to be good? In the modern world of Champagne, where many companies are more obsessed with brand image than they are about the quality of their wines, Gratien declares its image to be the quality of the wines and absolutely nothing else.

The Champagnes are fermented in wooden casks, which is very rare nowadays, moved only by gravity since pumping is thought to bruise the wine, kept on their lees under a real cork – most other houses use crown corks similar to those on a Coca-Cola bottle – and stored appreciably longer than usual before release. The non-vintage blend is usually four years old when released for sale – many other companies sell their wine aged for little more than two years. The vintage wine is deliciously ripe and toasty when released but can age for another ten to 15 years, and is often in the slightly less fizzy, *crémant* style. There is also a non-vintage Cuvée Paradis, usually made from Chardonnay and Pinot Meunier and aged about ten years on release. Best years: 1996, '95, '91, '90, '89, '88, '87, '85, '83.

ALFRED GRATIEN
Only tiny amounts of the pricy Cuvée Paradis are made. Both this and the rosé version are non-vintage but wonderfully individual.

GRAUBÜNDEN

SWITZERLAND

Although there are only 400ha (988 acres) of vineyards between the towns of Vaduz and Chur in the Upper Rhine Valley in eastern Switzerland, they are the source for many of Switzerland's best Pinot Noirs (called Blauburgunder here). This is the result of a combination of poor slate soils and the warm Föhn winds which come over the Alps from Italy, making this one of the warmest spots in the entire country. Improved winemaking during the 1990s has given many of the wines more depth and tannin. Best producers: Donatsch, Gantenbein.

GRAVES & PESSAC-LÉOGNAN France, Bordeaux

WE MAY AT LAST BE SEEING the solution to the trauma that has affected Graves ever since the day in 1987 when Pessac-Léognan in the north of the region where all the best properties were situated, declared independence from Graves and created its own AC. The years since then have seen the remaining Graves area make a considerable effort to maximize its considerable potential and the announcement that the Graves classification of 1959 – which was, in effect, a classification solely of Pessac-Léognan– is to be re-constituted, re-appraised every ten years and opened to all the properties of the Graves will be seen as a triumph for those left behind in 1987. The whole region is still known as the Graves, but it has two ACs: Pessac-Léognan for the area closest to Bordeaux, and Graves for the rest, primarily to the south down to Langon and encircling the sweet white wine areas of Cérons, Sauternes and Barsac. The 16 Crus Classés of the Graves are at present all located in Pessac-Léognan.

The name 'Graves' means gravel, and the vineyards which now make up the new Pessac-Léognan appellation are notable for their gravelly soil. Gravelly soil is heat-retaining and quick-draining, and this, allied to a warmer climate than that of the Médoc further north, and a close proximity to the city of Bordeaux, meant that the 'Graves', as the area became

known, was for a long time the leading Bordeaux wine area. At one time the bulk of the wine made was white. However, most of this was extremely poor white wine, so it is hardly surprising that almost two-thirds of the wine now is red. However, the white wines that are now produced must be counted among France's classics. A revolution has taken place which has seen the reintroduction of hand harvesting, grape selection, gentle pressing, skin contact and fermentation and aging in new oak barrels, creating one of France's most exciting white wine regions. The major grapes are Sémillon and Sauvignon Blanc for whites and Cabernet Sauvignon and Merlot for reds.

Pessac-Léognan's gravelly soil tends to favour red wines over the rest of the Graves – in fact this appellation is home to the only Bordeaux red outside the Médoc to be awarded First Growth status in 1855 – Ch. Haut-Brion. Still, white grapes can be grown successfully on the sandier, and less well-exposed areas of the Graves AC further south towards Langon. The best estates use new oak barrels to make wines with rich, apricotty fruit and creamy vanilla spice. The

Ch. Haut-Brion was the only property outside the Médoc to be included in the great 1855 Bordeaux Classification. These barriques in the first-year chai illustrate the enormous investment required to remain in the first rank today.

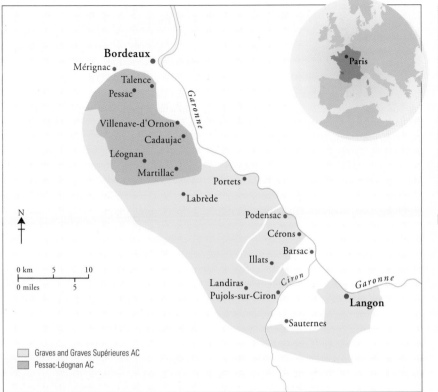

Legend:
- Graves and Graves Supérieures AC
- Pessac-Léognan AC

CH. HAUT-BRION

A wonderfully gentle, understated, yet compelling red wine and a sumptuous, memorable classic white. Both colours are of 1st Growth quality.

DOMAINE DE CHEVALIER

The red has a superb balance of fruit and oak and with ten to 20 years' aging it gains wonderful fragrant cedar, tobacco and blackcurrant flavours.

CH. SMITH-HAUT-LAFITTE

Increasingly good red but the star is the 100 per cent Sauvignon Blanc. The wine ages beautifully, becoming less pure Sauvignon and more classic Pessac-Léognan..

CH. DE FIEUZAL

This is one of the most up-to-date estates in Pessac-Léognan and the ripe, oaky wines sell at a high price. The white wine, intensely oaky and with a richly fruity flavour, is a leader among Bordeaux's new wave whites.

CH. COUHINS-LURTON

This is one of the few Pessac-Léognan estates to make its white wine solely from Sauvignon Blanc. Barrel-fermented in 50 per cent new oak, it brilliantly manages to balance Sauvignon fruit with gentle oak richness.

Graves reds have also improved, with a greater percentage of Merlot now being used in the blend.

The Graves AC only applies to reds and dry whites, but there is the little-known Graves Supérieures AC, which can be applied to sweet whites, and which sometimes comes up with tasty sweet wines at a fairly low price. However, if the Graves is to produce world-class wine, we mustn't try to force the price too low – or it won't be worth their while.

AC ENTRIES
Graves, Pessac-Léognan.

CHÂTEAUX ENTRIES
de Chevalier, de Fieuzal, Haut-Bailly, Haut-Brion, Laville Haut-Brion, la Louvière, la Mission-Haut-Brion, Pape Clément, Smith-Haut-Lafitte.

CH. LATOUR-MARTILLAC

This is now one of the most improved estates in Pessac-Léognan, for both red and white wine.

CH. MALARTIC-LAGRAVIÈRE

This is one of the few Pessac-Léognan Crus Classés whose reputation is mainly for its white wine (100 per cent Sauvignon Blanc), rather than its red.

CH. LA LOUVIÈRE

This is one of Pessac-Léognan's unclassified stars and its fine reputation is almost entirely due to André Lurton who has revitalized the estate over the last 45 years.

CLOS FLORIDÈNE

This white Graves is the equal of many Pessac-Léognan Crus Classés. From mainly Sémillon, it is barrique-fermented and aged on lees to provide added complexity.

GRAVES AC, GRAVES SUPÉRIEURES AC

FRANCE, Bordeaux (see also pages 190–191)

♥ *Cabernet Sauvignon, Merlot, Cabernet Franc*

♀ *Sémillon, Sauvignon Blanc*

South-west of the city of Bordeaux, the Graves region, which extends from the very gates of Bordeaux to south of Langon, has historically relied for its good reputation on the efforts of a small number of famous properties. Here, the soil is extremely gravelly – which is how the area came to be called 'Graves' – and the climate is slightly warmer than the MÉDOC to the north – excellent conditions for top-quality wine. Well, that all came to an end in 1987. The villages in the northern Graves formed their own AC – PESSAC-LÉOGNAN – to emphasize what they see, rightly, as their historic superiority. The Graves AC is now used mainly for wine from the less-favoured southern section. This weakened its red wine hall of fame more than the white, because much exciting white was already being created outside Pessac-Léognan, particularly in the communes of Portets, Arbanats and Illats.

For too long Graves, apart from the Classed Growths, was a byword for murky-tasting wine of no style whatsoever. However, there is a new wave of winemaking sweeping through the region. There is an increasing amount of bone-dry white, with lots of snappy freshness and a lovely apricotty flavour, as well as some richer, barrel-fermented and barrel-aged white. Add to this an increase in Merlot plantings to produce juicier reds, and a touch of spice from new oak barrels, and the Graves AC has no reason to be sorry for itself at all. Proof of this may be seen in the planned new classification of the whole Graves and Pessac-Léognan region, which will be reviewed every ten years. Best years: (reds) 2001, '00, '98, '96, '95, '90; (dry whites) 2001, '00, '98, '96, '95. Best producers: Archambeau, d'Ardennes, le Bonnat, Brondelle, de Chantegrive, Clos Floridène, Dom. la Grave, de l'Hospital, Léhoul, Magence, Magneau, Rahoul, Respide-Médeville, St-Robert, du Seuil, Vieux Château-Gaubert, Villa Bel-Air.

The Graves Supérieures AC is for white wine – dry, medium or sweet – with a minimum alcohol level of 12 degrees as opposed to 11 degrees for straight Graves. The sweet wines can, in good years, make decent substitutes for the more expensive SAUTERNES. Best years: (sweet) 2001, '99, '98, '97, '96, '95, '90, '89. Best producers: (sweet) Clos St-Georges, Léhoul.

JOSKO GRAVNER

ITALY, Friuli-Venezia Giulia, Collio DOC

♥ *Cabernet Sauvignon, Merlot*

♀ *Chardonnay, Sauvignon Blanc, Pinot Gris (Pinot Grigio), Riesling, Ribolla Gialla*

Gravner is the epitome of the moody genius, doing his own thing whether others approve or not. His thing, these days, is making blended whites for long aging, and while some of the journalists he despises dismiss them as being totally unbalanced, there are others who consider his dense, rich, concentrated Breg (a blend of Chardonnay, Sauvignon Blanc and several other varieties), involving months of oak-aging, to epitomize the best of Friulian white wines.

Certainly for weight, complexity and longevity, Breg is a remarkable wine. And there are others around the border village of Oslavia, who make similar wines. These are wines which aim to compensate in denseness and complexity for what they lack in elegance and freshness. They are not afraid of the tannins (some of the whites are even fermented, skins and all, in amphorae buried underground) or the element of oxidation derived from extensive oak treatment. Followers of the New World style may hate them, but even so, they are wines of tremendous character. As well as Breg, Gravner makes prized and high-priced Chardonnay, Sauvignon and Ribolla Gialla. As for reds, the Rosso Gravner is predominantly Merlot and Rujno, a Merlot-Cabernet Sauvignon blend.

GRAVNER

As well as some of Friuli's most interesting white wines, Gravner makes a highly personalised version of a Bordeaux-style red called Rujno.

GREAT SOUTHERN

AUSTRALIA, Western Australia

This is a vast, far-flung area along the Southern Ocean coast which includes the sub-regions of Frankland, Denmark, Porongurup, Albany and Mount Barker. Because it is so remote progress was at first very slow and often dependent on farmers

waiting to diversify crops on a bit of their land. But the quality of wine made from grapes grown at places like Forest Hill and PLANTAGANET in Mount Barker and ALKOOMI and Frankland River in Frankland was so exceptional that plantings have boomed, especially in the potentially superb Frankland region. Riesling is tremendously good down here and Chardonnay and Sauvignon Blanc are not so far behind. The pleasant surprise is the superb quality of reds, led by Shiraz, but backed up by Cabernet, Merlot and Pinot Noir. The scenery is at times spectacular, with rounded granite boulders rising from tens to hundreds of feet high in the south of Western Australia. Best years: (reds) 2001, '00, '99, '97, '96, '95, '94. Best producers: Alkoomi, Ferngrove, Frankland Estate, Gilberts, GOUNDREY, HOUGHTON, HOWARD PARK, Jingalla, Plantagenet, Wignalls King River.

GRECO, GRECHETTO

Around 2500 years ago the Greeks were responsible for importing various grape varieties into Italy, often via the port of Naples but also directly into parts of Magna Grecia – the southern mainland. These often ended up carrying a general epithet of origin – such as Greco (Greek), Grechetto (little Greek) or Aglianico (Hellenic) – rather than more precise names, even if there was little or no connection between them. Hence the confusion we have today, with two white 'Grecos', if not three, still prevalent in southern Italy, not to mention the Grechetto of Umbria.

Best known is Greco di Tufo, found in the uplands of CAMPANIA on the tufa soil around the village of Tufo, near Avellino. Most of the grapes were used by producer MASTROBER-ARDINO and its flavoursome, smoky and minerally Vignadangelo wine is still the benchmark. An increasing number of Mastroberardino's erstwhile grapegrowers, today, are taking a punt at making their own wine.

Then there is the Greco of Bianco, a small village in the extreme south of CALABRIA where the grape is grown on low, east-facing terraces overlooking the sea. Greco di Bianco is a *passito* wine with a distinct citrus/orange tang which one will seek in vain in Greco di Tufo. Further north up the same, eastern coast of Calabria is the Greco of CIRÒ, which local growers do not consider to be related to the variety at Bianco; one excellent reason for thinking this being that it tends to be rather weak in grape sugar, which Greco di Bianco certainly is not.

GRENACHE NOIR

Grenache revels in hot, dry conditions. It can produce dull, pallid, insipid wine just about anywhere, if it's allowed to overcrop, but in the southern Rhône, where it is the most important of the 13 varieties allowed in the Châteauneuf-du-Pape blend, it brings high alcohol and rich, spicy fruit to blend with the tannin and backbone of some of the other grapes. Grenache is important, in fact, throughout the South of France and Corsica. The best southern rosés, from Tavel, Lirac and Côtes de Provence in particular, are based on Grenache, usually blended with Cinsaut. In Rasteau (Côtes du Rhône) and Languedoc-Roussillon (especially Rivesaltes, Maury and Banyuls) it also makes thick, sweet, fortified reds. In the Languedoc it now often teams up with Syrah and Mourvèdre to make some of Southern France's most exciting red wines.

In Spain, where it is known as Garnacha Tinta, it is found almost everywhere: from Rioja to Penedès and La Mancha. At its best it is blended with less blowsy varieties, like Tempranillo. Or it is made into juicy *rosado* in Navarra. Only the richest and best of Garnachas, notably in Priorat, stand up to much aging. Grenache also flourishes in Sardinia, where it is called Cannonau and makes every possible style, from light to massive, dry, sweet or fortified, oaked or thoroughly stainless steel in outlook.

Grenache's other success stories are in California, where winemakers have a passion for the Rhône grape varieties, and in Australia, where it has undergone a remarkable renaissance, with the century-old, dry grown, bush-pruned vines in the Barossa Valley and McLaren Vale producing grapes that are in great demand for blending with Shiraz (and also Mourvèdre) to make rich, Rhônish dry red wines.

There is also a white version, Garnacha Blanca in Spain, where it makes big, dull wines with little flavour, and Grenache Blanc in France, which can be good when drunk very young.

GRGICH HILLS CELLAR

USA, California, Napa County, Napa Valley AVA

♥ *Cabernet Sauvignon, Zinfandel, Merlot*

♀ *Chardonnay, Sauvignon Blanc, Riesling*

Octogenarian winemaker Miljenko (Mike) Grgich and grower Austin Hills began their collaboration in 1977, hard on the heels of a Grgich-made Chardonnay from Chateau Montelena winning first place in a famous Franco-American tasting in Paris. Grgich's Chardonnay style has evolved since then, but he is still in favour of rich textures and bold flavours. The Cabernet Sauvignons, similarly, are sturdily built and full of flavour, as are the Zinfandels and Merlots. Best years: (Chardonnay) 2002, '01, '00, '99, '98, '97, '96, '95, '94, '91.

JEAN GRIVOT

FRANCE, Burgundy, Côte de Nuits, Vosne-Romanée AC

♥ *Pinot Noir, Gamay*

♀ *Chardonnay, Aligoté*

In the 1970s, Jean Grivot established this domaine, with its numerous excellent Premiers Crus in VOSNE-ROMANÉE and NUITS-ST-GEORGES, as a very reliable source of stylish and full-bodied red Burgundies. Jean's son Étienne has been in charge of the winemaking since the late 1980s, and had a few erratic years early on under the guidance of enologist Guy Accad, who believed in a prolonged cold maceration before fermentation to extract as much colour and richness as possible from the grapes. Since 1995 Étienne has settled in to a winemaking style that acknowledges the Accad years but is more inclined to traditional practices, and today the Grivot wines are truly splendid, showing both the finesse one expects from Pinot Noir at its best and the richness and power one looks for from these appellations. The domaine also owns some parcels of CLOS DE VOUGEOT and RICHEBOURG. Best years: 2002, '01, '00, '99, '98, '97, '96, '95.

GROENEKLOOF WO

SOUTH AFRICA, Western Cape

As South Africa searches avidly for cool-climate zones to grow grapes like Sauvignon Blanc and Chardonnay, the exposed slope of various outcrops running up the West Coast have come into focus. Neil ELLIS has been making an excellent Sauvignon for some years from Groenekloof near Darling, where fogs and chill breezes and the Antarctic Benguela Current ensure tangy, refreshing high acid flavours year in year out.

GROS PLANT DU PAYS NANTAIS VDQS

FRANCE, Loire, Pays Nantais

♀ *Gros Plant*

Traditionally Gros Plant is searing stuff – one of the grape's other names is Picpoul, which roughly translates as 'lip-stinger' – and, as well as in the Gros Plant vineyards around Nantes, it is also grown in the Cognac and Armagnac regions (under the name Folle Blanche or Picpoul) because its searingly high acid wine is perfect for distilling. Yet strangely, if you have a great plateful of seafood plonked down in front of you – wreathed in seaweed and still heaving with the motion of the ocean and the crunching of Atlantic rollers against the battered Brittany coast – you'll find the barefaced, eye-watering tartness of Gros Plant is surprisingly well-suited as a quaffer to cope with oysters, mussels, crab and the rest. Since they eat seafood by the bucketful around Nantes this probably explains its survival as the local white. Drink as young as possible. Best producers: Brochet, les Coins, Dom. de l'ÉCU, la Grange, Saupin.

ALOIS GROSS

AUSTRIA, Steiermark, Südsteiermark, Ratsch

♀ *Sauvignon Blanc, Chardonnay (Morillon), Pinot Blanc (Weissburgunder), Pinot Gris (Grauburgunder), Muscat (Gelber Muskateller) and others*

Alois Gross's wines are some of the most consistently impressive wines in Südsteiermark, or southern Styria. They divide into two groups: Steirische Klassik, which are vinified entirely in stainless steel for fresh fruit and crispness; and the wines with vineyard designations like Nussberg and Kittenburg that have all seen some wood, and in the case of Grauburgunder and Morillon new wood. Perhaps the best wines in this range are the extremely clean and aromatic Muskateller and the rich, nutty-buttery Grauburgunder. There is a brand new winery and Alois is now working on the challenge of producing great dry Gewürztraminer. Best years: 2002, '01, '00, '99, '98, '97, '95, '93, '92.

GROSSET

AUSTRALIA, South Australia, Clare Valley

♥ *Pinot Noir, Cabernet Sauvignon, Merlot*

♀ *Riesling, Semillon, Sauvignon Blanc, Chardonnay*

If democratic elections were held for the position of King of Riesling in Australia, Jeffrey Grosset would definitely emerge as the winner. The crystal clarity of the Polish Hill Riesling, with fragrant whispers of herb and spice, and the fractionally richer Watervale

Riesling, with a vibrant twist of lime, evolve with shimmering beauty over a ten-year period. Gaia, a Cabernet-dominant BORDEAUX blend, redolent with blackberry and sweet cassis fruit, somehow introduces finesse into a region more famous for blockbusters. His brilliant ADELAIDE HILLS trio of Semillon-Sauvignon Blanc, Piccadilly Chardonnay and Reserve Pinot Noir are as scarce as hen's teeth, but fine wines if you can lay your hands on them. Best years: (Riesling) 2002, '01, '00, '99, '98, '97, '96, '94, '93, '92, '90.

CH. GRUAUD-LAROSE
FRANCE, Bordeaux, Haut-Médoc, St-Julien AC, 2ème Cru Classé

♥ *Cabernet Sauvignon, Merlot, Cabernet Franc, Petit Verdot*

At 84ha (208 acres) of vines, Gruaud is one of the largest ST-JULIEN estates, now owned by the same family as Ch. CHASSE-SPLEEN and HAUT-BAGES-LIBÉRAL. With vineyards set a little back from the Gironde estuary, Gruaud traditionally used to exhibit a softer, more honeyed style when young than, say, the trio of LÉOVILLE estates whose vineyards slope down to the Gironde. This didn't stop the wine aging superbly and gaining a piercing, dry, blackcurrant and cedarwood aroma over 20 years or so. The vintages of the 1980s and '90s were made darker, deeper, and despite being thick with the flavours of blackberry and plums, sweetened with wood, toughened with tannin, they managed to exhibit a powerful animal scent all too often that usually, though not always, faded with maturity – if you gave the wine enough years in your cellar. Second wine: Sarget de Gruaud-Larose. Best years: 2001, '00, '99, '98, '97, '96, '95, '94, '93, '90, '89, '88, '86, '85.

GRÜNER VELTLINER
If you happen to be sitting in a café in Austria and order a quarter litre of white wine, there's a fair chance it'll be made from the Grüner Veltliner grape: fresh, cold and straight from the most recent vintage. Very nice it will be, too: slightly appley, slightly smoky and definitely with the tongue-tingling snap of white pepper. But that's only one side of Grüner Veltliner's character. When it is planted in the top-quality vineyards of NIEDERÖSTERREICH – at WACHAU on the Danube and in nearby KAMPTAL and KREMSTAL – it produces thrilling, weighty, superripe, marvellously savoury whites which are some of Europe's most intriguing and impressive wines. There's also a bit in the Czech Republic and Hungary.

Marcel Guigal is among the most famous names in the Rhône Valley, owning important vineyards in Côte-Rôtie as well as being a leading négociant.

GUELBENZU
SPAIN, Navarra

♥ *Cabernet Sauvignon, Tempranillo, Merlot, Grenache Noir (Garnacha Tinta)*

The Queiles Valley in southern NAVARRA is cooled by imposing mountains, but this is resolutely a red wine region with a warm Mediterranean influence. In the 1980s the Guelbenzu family resurrected their bodega, abandoned for a century or so. The 42ha (104 acres) of vineyards satisfy the bodega's needs. The speciality here is powerful, no-holds-barred, oak-aged reds: Guelbenzu, which is a Cabernet Sauvignon-Tempranillo-Merlot blend, and the impressive, Cabernet Sauvignon-dominated Guelbenzu Evo. Small batches of an unoaked Garnacha red, Guelbenzu Jardín, are also produced. A luxury cuvée based on old-vine Tempranillo and Merlot, called Lautus, was first made in 1995. In 2001 the the family made the momentous decision to leave the Navarra DO in order to be able to apply the Guelbenzu brand name to their new estates in Aragón and Chile. Best years: (Evo) 1999, '98, '97, '96, '95, '94.

GUIGAL
FRANCE, Northern Rhône, Côte-Rôtie AC

♥ *Syrah, Grenache and others*

♀ *Marsanne, Roussanne, Viognier and others*

If one man is venerated above all others in the northern RHÔNE, it is Marcel Guigal. Justifiably too, since it was he who dragged the region into the late twentieth century. Guigal is both a major owner in the CÔTE-RÔTIE appellation and a leading *négociant* for wines from both the northern and southern Rhône. He excels on both fronts, producing brilliant wines from his own vineyards and assembling remarkably satisfying blends from other regions. His standard CÔTES DU RHÔNE, with its high proportion of Syrah, is always one of the top generic wines of the region. But his reputation rightly rests on the trio of single-vineyard Côte-Rôties: la Landonne, la Mouline and la Turque. In 1978 he began aging these wines in 100 per cent new oak for over three years, and despite all the warnings of sceptics, the wines have aged superbly, albeit that the unique fragrance and beauty of Côte-Rôtie can be difficult to discern. More recently, Guigal has extended his magic touch to CONDRIEU, where he produces a regular bottling, and la Doriane, the special cuvée, showing a hefty whack of new oak without sacrificing typicity.

With renown has come prosperity, and the still-unassuming Guigal, rarely seen without his cloth cap, now owns the magnificent Ch. d'Ampuis, a name he has adopted for another top Côte-Rôtie wine. Guigal has also absorbed Vidal-Fleury, J-L Grippat and de Vallouit. Best years: (top reds) 2001, '00, '99, '98, '97, '95, '94, '91, '90, '89, '88, '85, '83, '82, '78.

CH. GUIRAUD
FRANCE, Bordeaux, Sauternes AC, Premier Cru Classé

♀ *Sémillon, Sauvignon Blanc*

In 1981 Guiraud was bought by a quality-obsessed Canadian, Frank Narby, who, with his son Hamilton, was bent on making great SAUTERNES. They've managed it. The 1983 was exceptional, the '86 was stunningly rich right from the start and the '90, '96 and '97 even more so. The winemaker and manager, Xavier Planty, ruthlessly selects only the best grapes, uses at least 50 per cent new oak each year to ferment and age the wine, and charges justifiably a very high price. The wine needs at least ten years to reach its peak – and top years may need 15–20. Second wine: (dry) G de Guiraud. Best years: 2002, '01, '99, '98, '97, '96, '95, '90, '89, '88, '86.

GUMPOLDSKIRCHEN
AUSTRIA, Niederösterreich, Thermenregion

This town in the THERMENREGION was the source of one of Austria's most famous wines. Then came the Austrian wine scandal of 1985, and the sort of sweet wines made here went out of fashion. Some growers turned to dry whites; others persevered with the traditional style, and there are signs that the latter might be beginning to find favour again. The traditional wine is a blend of the white Zierfandler (also known as Spätrot) and the pink-skinned Rotgipfler, and with time acquires a spicy apricot character. Best producers: Manfred Biegler, Hofer, Stefan Köstenbauer, Gottfried Schellmann, Thiel, Zierer.

GUNDERLOCH

GERMANY, Rheinhessen, Nackenheim
♀ *Riesling, Silvaner, Pinot Gris (Grauburgunder),
Rivaner and others*

During the 1990s, Fritz and Agnes Hasselbach's Rieslings from the great NACKENHEIMer Rothenberg vineyard have continually extended the possibilities of what the RHEINHESSEN can produce. These are now some of the most concentrated dry and sweet white wines you'll find anywhere in Germany. This quality and their growing reputation has rapidly pushed prices for their Beerenauslese and Trockenbeerenauslese dessert wines to stratospheric heights.

However, the Spätlese and Auslese wines, which ripple with exotic and grapefruit aromas and have a stunningly taut interplay of fruit, minerals and piercing acidity, will not break the bank. The Jean Baptiste Riesling Kabinett, which is a blend of grapes from the Rothenberg and the best vineyards of NIERSTEIN, offers some of the best value for money in top-class off-dry German wines. Grauburgunder and Rivaner are two Gunderloch specialities, both coming from old vines, the former vinified like a late-harvest ALSACE wine, the latter fermented dry. Best years: (Riesling Spätlese and Auslese) 2002, '01, '00, '99, '98, '97, '96, '95, '94, '93, '92, '90, '89.

GUTIÉRREZ DE LA VEGA

SPAIN, Valencia, Alicante DO
♀♂ *Merlot, Cabernet Sauvignon, Grenache Noir
(Garnacha Tinta), Mourvèdre (Monastrell)*
♀ *Muscat of Alexandria (Moscatel Romano)*

Felipe Gutiérrez de la Vega has been showing for over 25 years that seaside vineyards in touristy ALICANTE province have the potential to produce world-class sweet Muscat wines. He owns 10ha (25 acres) of vines on terraces that, legend says, go back to Greco-Roman times, amid the orange groves overlooking the Mediterranean in the Marina Alta sub-region. Some of the vines are grafted to red varieties, giving ample, pleasant reds and rosés. But Moscatel is his speciality: the

vine thrives here in the long, warm summers and his old vines produce a range of delicious wines sold under the Casta Diva label, including dry and semi-sweet fizzy ones.

GYÖNGYÖS ESTATE

HUNGARY, Gyöngyös
♂ *Pinot Noir*
♀ *Sauvignon Blanc, Chardonnay*

This was the first of Hungary's wineries to show that the country could, with a kick start, produce exactly the sort of crisp, fruity wines the world is thirsty for, and at affordable prices, too. Englishman Hugh Ryman was the man responsible. After the frosts of 1991 had decimated his vineyards in his stamping ground of South-West France, Ryman looked around for a new source of grapes to make up the shortfall. When he decided on Hungary, he promptly installed his own winemaker, revolutionized the winemaking and put his fingerprint on nearly all the Sauvignon Blanc there is in this part of northern Hungary. The Chardonnay was good, too. The winery was bought in 1995 by the German firm, Danubiana, that also owns St-Ursula and Ryman is no longer involved, but the modern Hungarian wine industry owes him a considerable debt for showing what was possible.

FRITZ HAAG

GERMANY, Mosel-Saar-Ruwer, Brauneberg
♀ *Riesling*

Wilhelm Haag of the Weingut Fritz Haag is a winemaker of supreme quality, with just 7.5ha (18 acres) of Riesling in some of the MOSEL's top vineyard sites, particularly BRAUNEBERGer Juffer and Brauneberger Juffer-Sonnenuhr. The Juffer-Sonnenuhr is the smaller site, and has the edge in stylishness, but all Haag's wines are terrifically elegant and concentrated. In youth they are difficult to taste, with high levels of acidity, despite an impressive overall level of ripeness that warn the drinker not to commit infanticide; with maturity they display all the fire and elegance of the best of the Mosel, but

that maturity can take 10–20 years. Winemaking is traditional, in old oak barrels, and is meticulous. Best years: (Auslese) 2002, '01, '00, '99, '98, '97, '96, '95, '94, '93, '92, '91, '90, '88, '85.

REINHOLD HAART

GERMANY, Mosel-Saar-Ruwer, Piesport
♀ *Riesling*

In good years the Riesling wines from the great amphitheatre of vines that is the PIESPORTer Goldtröpfchen vineyard tend to Baroque extravagance, often losing the delicacy typical of MOSEL wines. Theo Haart is the first winemaker to succeed in giving these wines real elegance without in any way diminishing their power. The result is some of the finest and most expressive wines in the entire Mosel region. Their blackcurrant, peach and citrus aromas and crisp acidity make them easy to enjoy young, and they age magnificently as examples such as the 1971 and '75 Auslese show. Since 1991 he has also made fine wines from the great, but overlooked, Wintricher Ohligsberg site. Best years: (Spätlese, Auslese) 2002, '01, '00, '98, '99, '97, '96, '95, '94, '93, '91, '90, '89.

HALLAU

SWITZERLAND, Schaffhausen

This is one of the best wine communes in the German-speaking Swiss canton of Schaffhausen, situated between the river Rhine and the JURA mountains. This is mainly red wine country, from Blauburgunder (Pinot Noir), and the wines are light in flavour and heavy in price; the best, though, can be good. Hallau's top vineyard is the Im Hintere Waatelebuck. Best producer: Hans Schlatter.

HAMILTON RUSSELL VINEYARDS

SOUTH AFRICA, Western Cape, Walker Bay WO
♂ *Pinot Noir*
♀ *Chardonnay*

It is mainly thanks to Tim Hamilton-Russell that South Africa has shown so much progress with Burgundy's Pinot Noir grape. When, in 1975, he found what he considered the ideal spot for this grape, and Chardonnay too, the land in Hemel-en-Aarde Valley, near the coastal town of Hermanus, had no official quota from the KWV to grow vines. This did not deter him from his quest to make Pinot Noir and Chardonnay to international standards. Today his determination has been vindicated. Now owned by his son, Anthony, HRV, as it is affectionately known, is still among the leading Pinot producers but, more importantly, has encouraged others to follow. The arrival of perfectionist winemaker Kevin Grant in 1995, and a broader selection of vine material saw some shifts in style, but, after a slight hiccup with the maiden 1999 vintage, the all new-clone Pinot Noir is showing what the Cape is capable of doing with this fickle grape. The toasty, fruitily concentrated, well structured Chardonnays are among only a few local examples which have proved they can mature over four to five years. The newer Southern Right label from a separate nearby winery focuses on Pinotage and Sauvignon Blanc from estate and bought-in grapes. Best years: (Pinot Noir) 2001, '00, '99, '98, '97, '96, '95; (Chardonnay) 2002, '01, '00, '99, '98, '97, '96, '95.

HAMILTON RUSSELL VINEYARDS
South Africa's first great Pinot Noir wine came from Hamilton Russell and it is still one of the best in the country, despite stiff competition.

HANDLEY
USA, California, Mendocino County
♥ *Pinot Noir, Pinot Meunier*
♀ *Chardonnay, Sauvignon Blanc, Pinot Gris and others*
Outstanding producer of sparkling wines, including one of CALIFORNIA's best Brut Rosés and a delicious Blanc de Blancs. But that's not all. At heart, Handley is an ANDERSON VALLEY winery, enjoying the ultra-cool climate conditions and the excellent Pinot Noir, Pinot Gris, Chardonnay, Sauvignon and, of all things, Gewurztraminer they grow there. Handley make excellent Anderson examples of all of these but also produce lusher DRY CREEK VALLEY Chardonnay. Best years: (Pinot Noir Reserve) 2001, '00, '99, '98, '96.

HANGING ROCK
AUSTRALIA, Victoria, Macedon Ranges
♥ *Pinot Noir, Syrah (Shiraz)*
♀ *Chardonnay, Sauvignon Blanc, Pinot Gris*
I don't know whether John and Ann Ellis went to see Peter Weir's classic 1975 film *Picnic at Hanging Rock* – one of the all time great atmospheric films. Even if they had, I'm not sure that spectacularly unsuccessful picnic would have had me trying to establish a vineyard on the extinct Jim Jim volcano nearby. If

you stand among the vines facing south there's the Hanging Rock dead ahead. The Rock range of wines are just good gluggers but there is also exceptional non-vintage Macedon Cuvée fizz and the mouthwatering, tangy 'Jim Jim' Sauvignon. But grapegrowing here is marginal, so they buy in grapes from elsewhere in VICTORIA too – the Heathcote Shiraz from a warm neighbouring region is a good example.

THE HARDY WINE COMPANY
AUSTRALIA, South Australia, McLaren Vale
♥ *Cabernet Sauvignon, Syrah (Shiraz), Merlot, Pinot Noir*
♥ *Grenache*
♀ *Chardonnay, Semillon, Sauvignon Blanc, Riesling, Gewurztraminer*
BRL Hardy (formed when twin RIVERLAND co-operatives Berri Estates and Renmano took over the then family-owned company of Thomas Hardy) is now Australia's second-largest wine company, newly renamed as the Hardy Wine Company, and through its merger with Constellation of the USA it is part of the official Largest Wine Company in the World. The group now includes Banrock Station, Bay of Fires, Kamberra, Berri, Renmano, Hardy, HOUGHTON, Hunter Ridge, REYNELL, YARRA BURN, Stonehaven and LEASINGHAM brands. The greatest of the Hardy wines are the Eileen Hardy Shiraz (made from basket-pressed MCLAREN VALE and PADTHAWAY grapes), Eileen Hardy Chardonnay (the ultimate grapefruit-with-melon Padthaway style), some superb 'Beerenauslese' sweet Rieslings, and the 'vintage port' – probably Australia's best PORT-style wine.

The National Trust-classified and beautiful buildings of Chateau Reynella house Hardy's corporate headquarters. There are various keenly priced labels – Tintara, Nottage Hill, Stamps of Australia and, especially, the tasty VR (Varietal Range) and VR Reserve. Best years: (Eileen Hardy Shiraz) 2001, '00, '98, '96, '95, '93, '88, '87, '81, '79, '70.

HARLAN ESTATE
USA, California, Napa County, Oakville AVA
♥ *Cabernet Sauvignon, Merlot, Cabernet Franc, Petit Verdot*
Estate in the western hills of OAKVILLE, founded by Robert Levy and BORDEAUX enologist Michel Rolland. One of California's most sought-after Bordeaux blends, Harlan Estate offers layers of ripe black fruits and heaps of new French oak. Rough upon release, the wine is built to develop for 10–20 years.

HARTFORD FAMILY WINES
USA, California, Sonoma County, Russian River Valley AVA
♥ *Pinot Noir, Zinfandel*
♀ *Chardonnay,*
The Hartford family owns and farms nine vineyards in RUSSIAN RIVER VALLEY and SONOMA COAST and almost all the wines are single-vineyard bottlings under the Hartford Court label. Very limited production Pinot Noirs (perhaps as little as 93 cases) include the stylish Marin County bottling and the massive Arrendell Vineyard. Seascape Vineyard Chardonnay has textbook cool-climate intensity and acidity. Hartford Zinfandels include Highwire and Fanucchi Wood.

HASTINGS RIVER
AUSTRALIA, New South Wales
Hastings River is an Australian rarity: a region where irrigation is not deemed necessary. The climate is relatively warm, very humid and with high summer rainfall. This means that the French hybrid Chambourcin, with its resistance to rot, is the most widely planted red grape. The region is dominated by one winery: Cassegrain. The Chardonnay is rich, generous and with peach/tropical flavours. The vivid purple of Chambourcin immediately sets it apart, suggesting that it should be drunk young while the black cherry and plum primary fruit characters are at their most expressive. Best years: 2000, '98.

HATTENHEIM
GERMANY, Rheingau
This is one of the best RHEINGAU villages for Riesling. It lies on the north bank of the Rhine between Oestrich and ERBACH, with many of its vineyards in the hills behind, including the world-famous Steinberg and part of the famous Marcobrunn, which today carries the name of Erbach. Nussbrunnen, Wisselbrunnen, Hassel, Engelmannsberg, Mannberg and Pfaffenberg are other top vineyards. Hattenheim is also the home of Kloster Eberbach, the medieval Cistercian monastery that is nowadays the site of some singularly unmonastic feasting: the German Wine Academy is based here, and runs courses for wine enthusiasts, and it is also the centre of the Rheingau's annual autumn festival, Glorreiche Rheingau Tage, a wine auction that involves hours of tasting and some gargantuan meals. Best years: (Spätlese, Auslese) 2002, '01, '00, '99, '98, '96, '95, '94, '93, '92, '90. Best producers: SCHLOSS REINHARTSHAUSEN, Schloss Schönborn.

CH. HAUT-BAGES-LIBÉRAL

FRANCE, Bordeaux, Haut-Médoc, Pauillac AC, 5ème Cru Classé

🍷 *Cabernet Sauvignon, Merlot*

I accept that Haut-Bages-Libéral is a relatively obscure little property in PAUILLAC but I don't accept that it is inferior. Although only classified as a Fifth Growth in 1855, it regularly produces deep dark reds with buckets of delicious plum and blackcurrant fruit. That's not always enough in the rarified world of Pauillac's wine politics, where austerity is often prized more than ebullience. But there's nothing wrong with the Haut-Bages vineyards – they're only separated by a little country lane from those of the great Ch. LATOUR. As the replanted vineyards mature, I'd expect to see that rich blackcurrant fruit joined by some cigarbox perfume. And then there'll be no argument about the vineyard's quality. Since 1980 the property has been part of the Taillan group, owners also of COS D'ESTOURNEL, GRUAUD-LAROSE, CHASSE-SPLEEN and FERRIÈRE. Best years: 2001, '00, '99, '98, '96, '95, '94, '90, '89, '86, '85.

CH. HAUT-BAILLY

FRANCE, Bordeaux, Pessac-Léognan AC, Cru Classé de Graves

🍷 *Cabernet Sauvignon, Merlot, Cabernet Franc*

Haut-Bailly makes the softest and most invitingly charming wines among the GRAVES Classed Growths. The 28ha (69 acres) of vines are on gravelly soil with rather more sand than usual, just to the east of the village of Léognan, and this contributes to Haut-Bailly becoming agreeably ready to drink very early. However, the wines do age fairly well and what is ready to drink at ten years old often seems magically unchanged at 20. Vintages from the 1990s have been generally splendid. Second wine: la Parde-de-Haut-Bailly. Best years: 2001, '00, '99, '98, '96, '95, '93, '90, '89, '88, '86, '85, '83, '82.

CH. HAUT-BATAILLEY

FRANCE, Bordeaux, Haut-Médoc, Pauillac AC, 5ème Cru Classé

🍷 *Cabernet Sauvignon, Merlot, Cabernet Franc*

They call this estate the 'ST-JULIEN' of PAUILLAC. It's a small property of 22ha (54 acres) of vines set back from the melting pot of brilliant wines close to the Gironde estuary, and is owned by one of St-Julien's greatest wine families – the Bories of Ch. DUCRU-BEAUCAILLOU.

Ch. Haut-Batailley gets its 'St-Julien' tag because it lacks the concentrated power of a true Classed Growth Pauillac. This doesn't matter if the wines have the perfume and cedary excitement of St-Julien, but until recently they rarely did; they were pleasant, a little spicy, but rarely memorable. Recent vintages have improved, though, with greater depth and structure and, since 1996, a return to some of the beautiful wines made in the 1970s. The wines can be drunk relatively young. Best years: 2000, '99, '96, '95, '90, '89, '85, '83, '82.

CH. HAUT-BRION

FRANCE, Bordeaux, Pessac-Léognan AC, Premier Cru Classé de Graves

🍷 *Cabernet Sauvignon, Merlot, Cabernet Franc*
🍷 *Sémillon, Sauvignon Blanc*

Haut-Brion was the first BORDEAUX property to get a write-up in the British press. In 1663, Samuel Pepys wrote that during a session at the Royal Oak Tavern he 'drank a sort of French wine called Ho Bryan; that hath a good and most particular taste that I never met with'. It was a good 50 years before other Bordeaux wines began to be known by their own château name.

One reason for this is that the excellent gravel-based vineyard which constitutes Haut-Brion is actually in the suburbs of the city of Bordeaux and so was readily accessible to visiting merchants. Haut-Brion's continued popularity is shown by the fact that when the local merchants decided to classify the top red wines of Bordeaux in 1855 all the wines they chose were from the MÉDOC – except one, Haut-Brion from the GRAVES (now PESSAC-LÉOGNAN), which was accorded First Growth status.

There's no doubt the wine deserves its lofty position. It has all the potential longevity and weight of the Médoc First Growths, and starts out tasting very like them because of the vineyard's deep gravel soil. Yet after a few years the flavour changes course; the tough tannins fade away more quickly, a gentle creamy-edged fruit takes their place and a few years' more maturity brings out all the fruit of plums and blackcurrants mingled with a heady scent of unsmoked Havana tobacco. Second wine: Bahans-Haut-Brion. Best years: (reds) 2001, '00, '99, '98, '96, '95, '94, '93, '90, '89, '88, '86, '85.

The white wine can be inconsistent, but at its best, Haut-Brion Blanc is fabulous wine, which after five to ten years blossoms out into a wonderfully lush flavour of nuts and spice, cream and a hint of apricots. Best years: (whites) 2001, '00, '99, '98, '96, '95.

CH. HAUT-MARBUZET
Exotic, opulent and powerful, this St-Estèphe wine stands out both when it is young and with as much as 20 years of aging.

CH. HAUT-MARBUZET

FRANCE, Bordeaux, Haut-Médoc, St-Estèphe AC, Cru Bourgeois

🍷 *Cabernet Sauvignon, Merlot, Cabernet Franc*

Haut-Marbuzet's 50-ha (124-acre) vineyard is sited between its more illustrious neighbours, MONTROSE and COS D'ESTOURNEL. The energetic Monsieur Duboscq treats his wine like a top Classed Growth – right up to using 100 per cent new oak for maturing it – and the great, rich, mouthfilling blast of flavour certainly isn't subtle, but certainly is impressive. The wine also ages extremely well, shaking off its cloak of oak to reveal a complex spectrum of aromas and flavours. Best years: 2001, '00, '99, '98, '97, '96, '95, '94, '93, '90, '89, '88, '86, '85, '83, '82.

HAUT-MÉDOC AC

FRANCE, Bordeaux

🍷 *Cabernet Sauvignon, Merlot, Cabernet Franc and others*

The Haut-Médoc is the southern half of the MÉDOC peninsula, stretching from Blanquefort, in the suburbs of the city of Bordeaux, north to St-Seurin-de-Cadourne. All the Médoc's finest gravelly soil is situated in this southern half, and there are six separate village ACs: MARGAUX, LISTRAC, MOULIS, ST-JULIEN, PAUILLAC and ST-ESTÈPHE. The Haut-Médoc AC covers all the areas not included in one of the specific village appellations. There are five Classed Growths within the AC, including the excellent Ch. la LAGUNE and CANTEMERLE in the south, but otherwise the wines vary widely in quality and style. They are inclined to lack a little fruit but age well in a slightly austere way. The most intense and concentrated can be cellared for ten, even 15 years. Best years: 2001, '00, '96, '95, '94, '90, '89, '88, '86, '85. Best producers: Beaumont, Belgrave, Bernadotte, Cambon la Pelouse, Camensac, Cantemerle, Charmail, CISSAC, Citran, Coufran, la Lagune, Lanessan, Malescasse, Maucamps, Sénéjac, SOCIANDO-MALLET, la Tour-Carnet, la Tour-du-Haut-Moulin, Verdignan, Villegeorge.

HAWKES BAY
NEW ZEALAND, North Island

Hawkes Bay is traditionally regarded as New Zealand's greatest red wine region, but it is only the best mesoclimates and soils that really deliver – much of the valley floor land is too heavy and is far better suited to its other major use – growing orchard fruit. But both on the valley floor – particularly inland at Ngatarawa and the newly developed and very promising GIMBLETT GRAVELS – and on various river terraces and side valleys, Hawkes Bay has proven itself, since way back in the 1890s, to be New Zealand's most versatile wine region, and when it comes to varieties like Cabernet, Merlot and Syrah, the only major area with the right conditions to ripen them regularly. Hawkes Bay, for a long period was New Zealand's biggest vineyard region, but not any more – despite more than doubling in size to over 3400ha (8400 acres), MARLBOROUGH in the South Island has grown even faster. Even so, in a world mad for good red, the Esk Valley, the river terraces of the Tukituki, the Ngaruroro (which runs down the centre of the region to the sea between Napier and Hastings) and the Tutaekuri River in Dartmoor Valley have produced impressive reds as well as fine Chardonnay and good Sauvignon Blanc, in a climate generally a little warmer than BURGUNDY in France, though cooler than BORDEAUX. It is only the exceptional warm, well-drained soil of the best sites that gets those red grapes ripe – most years but not all. Best years: (premium reds) 2000, '99, '98, '96, '95, '94. Best producers: Alpha Domus, Church Road, Clearview, CRAGGY RANGE, Esk Valley, Matariki, MATUA VALLEY, MORTON ESTATE, Newton Forrest, NGATARAWA, C J Pask, Sacred Hill, SILENI, Te Awa Farm, TE MATA, TRINITY HILL, Unison, Vidal, VILLA MARIA.

HEATHCOTE
AUSTRALIA, Victoria

A recent breakaway from the long-established BENDIGO region, and with plantings rapidly expanding, Heathcote's unique feature is the deep russet Cambrian soil, formed more than 600 million years ago, which is found on the best sites and is proving ideal for growing Shiraz. Established wineries include JASPER HILL, Heathcote and the ultra-trendy Wild Duck Creek, while BROWN BROTHERS and TYRRELL'S have extensive new vineyards. Best years: (Shiraz) 2001, '00, '97, '96, '95, '94, '91, '90.

The Ngatarawa winery is one of Hawkes Bay's top estates and the viticulture is organic, with Chardonnay and botrytized Riesling producing the best results to date.

HEDGES CELLARS
USA, Washington State, Columbia Valley AVA
🍷 *Cabernet Sauvignon, Merlot, Cabernet Franc, Syrah*
🍷 *Sauvignon Blanc, Chardonnay*

Hedges Cellars earned a reputation in the late 1980s with an affordable and approachable Cabernet-Merlot blend that was an international success. However with the maturing of their vineyards on Red Mountain, now totalling 24ha (60 acres) of the BORDEAUX red varieties as well as 2ha (5 acres) of Syrah, Hedges has adopted a far more powerful, full-throated red wine style – the core of black fruit is still there, but now draped in quite austere tannins. The whites are a milder experience. Best years: 2001, '00, '99, '98, '96.

DR HEGER
GERMANY, Baden, Ihringen
🍷 *Pinot Noir (Spätburgunder)*
🍷 *Riesling, Pinot Gris (Grauburgunder), Pinot Blanc (Weissburgunder), Silvaner, Chardonnay and others*

Joachim Heger makes some of the finest dry Weissburgunder and Grauburgunder in Germany. With each variety he makes two styles of wine: the barrique-aged one with '***' on the label and a sleeker version which only uses stainless steel during the winemaking stages.

In recent years his international-style red wines have also attracted attention and they are some of BADEN's best Spätburgunders. His yields are low – just 30–45 hectolitres per hectare. He looks for tannin, and accordingly gives the more expensive wines a 28-day maceration; the rest get about a week. And they are made in standard Burgundian style: on the skins, without the aid of thermovinification or pressurized tanks, which some Baden growers use for their red wines. Weinhaus Joachim Heger is a second label. Best years: (reds) 2002, '01, '99, '97, '96, '93, '90; (whites) 2002, '01, '99, '98, '97, '96, '94, '93, '90.

CHARLES HEIDSIECK
FRANCE, Champagne, Champagne AC
🍷🍷 *Chardonnay, Pinot Noir, Pinot Meunier*

Under the direction of brilliant winemaker, the late Daniel Thibault, the Charles Heidsieck CHAMPAGNE house went through a revolution in the 1980s. Thibault had built up stocks of reserve wines, which he blended into the revamped non-vintage Brut, renamed Brut Réserve. With 40 per cent of reserve wines in the blend, it was a terrific wine and met with well-deserved success.

Another, but more controversial innovation, was the release of Mis en Cave Champagnes in the 1990s. These carried dates, but were non-vintage wines; the dates referred to when the wine was bottled to begin its aging process. These are excellent Champagnes and far from cheap and though the consumer might be confused into thinking they were vintage wines, they shouldn't worry because the quality *is* vintage.

The outstanding wine in the Heidsieck range is the vintage Blanc de Blancs called

Blanc des Millénaires, which is wonderfully rich and biscuity. Despite a total annual production of over two million bottles, quality is high. Now owned by Rémy Cointreau. Best years: 1996, '95, '90, '89, '88, '85, '82.

GERNOT HEINRICH

AUSTRIA, Burgenland, Neusiedlersee, Gols
❡ *Blaufränkisch, Blauer Zweigelt, St-Laurent, Cabernet Sauvignon, Merlot, Syrah, Pinot Noir*
♀ *Pinot Blanc (Weissburgunder), Pinot Gris (Grauburgunder), Chardonnay and others*

Gernot Heinrich is one of the first winemakers in Austria to play the 'dynamic young winemaker' role successfully in the national media, but he is also genuinely talented in the cellar. The 'regular' whites only see stainless steel and are very fresh and zingy. In contrast, the white Pannobile is a barrique-aged blend of Chardonnay, Weissburgunder, Grauburgunder and Neuburger which packs quite a punch. However, it is his reds that are the real stars, from juicy St-Laurent, Zweigelt and Blaufränkisch up to a powerful blend called Gabarinza that sometimes includes a dollop of Cabernet or Merlot. Best years: (reds) 2000, '99, '97, '94, '93, '92.

HEITZ WINE CELLARS

USA, California, Napa County, Napa Valley AVA
❡ *Cabernet Sauvignon, Grignolino, Zinfandel*
❢ *Grignolino*
♀ *Chardonnay*

The first Heitz wine I had was pink: bone-dry pink Grignolino, rather rasping on the tongue, with the swish of herbs acting like a witch's broom to sweep away any preconceptions I'd had that California rosé was just a soft picnic wine sold in half-gallon jugs. It's such an unlikely wine to come from a winery that takes itself as seriously as Heitz, but this whimsical, almost extinct Italian variety was already planted when the decidedly non-whimsical Joe Heitz started his winery in 1961 and, just for once, sentiment took over and he kept the vines. He must have done something right, because Angelo GAJA, PIEDMONT's star winemaker, imports the wine into Italy.

But all of Heitz's mainstream reputation has come from red wine – in particular the Martha's Vineyard and Bella Oaks Cabernets which until the mid-1980s were regarded as possibly CALIFORNIA's greatest reds. They don't reach that quality level nowadays, but then Heitz Wine Cellars is now a pretty big player in NAPA, owning 140ha (350 acres) of vines, including a lot of Cabernet, Zinfandel and Chardonnay – but still keeping a plot of Grignolino for old times' sake. Best years: (Martha's Vineyard) 1997, '96, '92, '91, '86, '85, '75.

HENRIQUES & HENRIQUES

PORTUGAL, Madeira, Madeira DOC
❡ *Tinta Negra Mole*
♀ *Sercial, Verdelho, Bual, Malvasia (Malmsey) and others*

Henriques & Henriques is the largest independent MADEIRA wine producer, after the MADEIRA WINE COMPANY. Chaired by John Cossart, the wines improved greatly in the 1990s and are now of exemplary quality. The range begins with a young, dry aperitif Madeira known as Monte Seco, based on Tinta Negra Mole, and continues through 3-Year-Old, 5-Year-Old, Single-Harvest 1995 Fine Rich, 10- and 15-Year-Old wines to Century Malmsey Solera 1900 and a good range of venerable vintage wines. These include 1976 Terrantez, 1957 Boal, 1954 Terrantez, Boal and Malvasia, 1944 Sercial, 1934 Verdelho and Malvasia and four wines (one Sercial, two Boals and one Malvasia) which had lost their vintage dates before 1850 and were considered to be already old Madeiras at that time. The four Henriques 10-Year-Olds are probably the best in their class. Made according to sweetness from the four 'noble' Madeira grapes, Sercial, Verdelho, Bual and Malvasia, they have the clean, incisive, high-toned character of well-aged Madeiras and at a reasonable price.

HENRY OF PELHAM

CANADA, Ontario, Niagara Peninsula VQA
❡ *Baco Noir, Cabernet Sauvignon, Cabernet Franc, Merlot, Pinot Noir*
♀ *Chardonnay, Riesling, Sauvignon Blanc*

Henry of Pelham is a small winery with a big reputation for producing top-flight wines. Viticulturalist Matt Speck and winemaker Ron Giesbrecht work with some 60ha

HENRY OF PELHAM
The Proprietor's Reserve Riesling has intense, floral fruit flavours and is one of the top wines from this quality producer in the Niagara region.

(150 acres) of vines on the sloping hills of the NIAGARA Bench. Good sparkling wines are labelled Catharine Brut and Catharine Rosé Brut. Whites include Pinot Blanc, Sauvignon and Gewurztraminer, but Riesling and Chardonnay are the most important, in regular and reserve bottlings. Barrel-fermented Chardonnay is also released, and a top end Speck Family Reserve. Cabernet-Merlot appears in warm years, and Riesling Icewine in just about any year. Best years: (Riesling Icewine) 2001, '00, '99, '98, '97, '95.

HENSCHKE

AUSTRALIA, South Australia, Eden Valley
❡ *Syrah (Shiraz), Cabernet Sauvignon, Merlot, Pinot Noir, Grenache*
♀ *Riesling, Semillon, Chardonnay, Pinot Gris, Sauvignon Blanc, Gewurztraminer*

You cannot really understand why Henschke is so important in the world of Australian wine until you have climbed up into the hills above the BAROSSA VALLEY, tipped your cap to the tiny Gnadenberg Church and then turned and walked thoughtfully into the vineyard over the little country road. You are strolling between the vines of the Hill of Grace, some of them 150 years old, Shiraz vines, ungrafted, planted by Stephen Henschke's great-great-grandfather some time in the 1860s.

Nowadays every ancient vine in the Barossa is eagerly sought out and lovingly cosseted, but less than a generation ago few Barossa folk cared for these low-yielding wizened old vines. Stephen and Prue Henschke did. Hill of Grace Shiraz, along with PENFOLDS Grange, is now Australia's most avidly collected red – and deservedly so – for its fabulous exotic richness does seem to express a purity, the very essence of a vineyard, like few other wines worldwide. Henschke is not just Hill of Grace – Mount Edelstone Shiraz and Cyril Henschke Cabernet are two other top labels, their EDEN VALLEY Semillon and Rieslings are both exceptional, and both reds and whites from their cooler Lenswood vineyard in the ADELAIDE HILLS are subtle, modern and delicious. And over all these new endeavours, the ancient 'grandfather' vines stand looking on in silent approval. Best years: (Mount Edelstone) 2001, '00, '98, '97, '96, '94, '92, '91, '90, '88, '86, '84, '82, '80, '78.

HÉRAULT

FRANCE, Languedoc-Roussillon

The Hérault *département* was once the fountainhead of France's infamous contribution to the European wine lake. It used to produce a positive deluge of rock-bottom rot-gut every year. However, this is now the heart of the Brave New World of French winemaking, which has transformed the Midi into a high-tech, Australian-style provider of cheap, attractive, everyday table wines. This weather-beaten and ancient land, centred on Béziers and Montpellier, is the most densely planted *département* in France – and until the 1980s had the fewest ACs. Fortunately, politicians realized you can't protect sub-standard producers for ever, and during the 1980s in Hérault and the neighbouring *département* of AUDE, over 30,000ha (74,000 acres) of vines were uprooted. There is now plenty of interesting wine coming from the hills, most of it red, but as methods of cool fermentation in stainless steel take hold, and as new grape varieties come on line, the whites are improving too.

Until the 1980s, the Hérault only had one table wine AC – the dull and insipid white Clairette du Languedoc. Since then FAUGÈRES, ST-CHINIAN and the widespread COTEAUX DU LANGUEDOC (where several zones, notably Pic St-Loup, now have a well deserved reputation) have joined the AC list and are making some of the most exciting wines in the South of France. There are also a number of appellations for sweet wines in the Hérault and LANGUEDOC-ROUSSILLON's leading fortified Muscat is made at Frontignan, on the coast near Sète.

But it is the VIN DE PAYS movement that began this massive shift towards quality, either under the Hérault or more usually the Vin de Pays d'Oc title. Of the 25 zonal vins de pays in the Hérault only a few, such as Vin de Pays des CÔTES DE THONGUE, are regularly seen. Plantings of Syrah, Mourvèdre, Cabernet Sauvignon, Merlot, Chardonnay and Viognier are increasing yearly. Sémillon and Marsanne varietal wines have appeared, as well as attractively aromatic versions of Grenache Blanc, Bourboulenc, Macabeo and dry Muscat. There are two superstar properties, next-door neighbours GRANGE DES PÈRES and MAS DE DAUMAS GASSAC, On a commercial scale, the company of SKALLI, at Sète on the coast, has led the way in introducing varietal labelling in France's south and proves you can make vast volumes at a good quality level. At all levels the Hérault's vins de pays are encouraging wine merchants and producers to be innovative and to demand quality. Best producers: (Vin de Pays de l'Hérault) du Bosc, Capion, la Fadèze, la Grange des Pères, Jany, Limbardié, Mas de Daumas Gassac, Moulines.

PAUL JABOULET AÎNÉ

Jaboulet's Hermitage la Chapelle was the wine that finally brought the great red wines of the northern Rhône back into the limelight with the 1978 vintage.

HERMITAGE AC

FRANCE, Northern Rhône

🍷 *Syrah*

🍷 *Marsanne, Roussanne*

There was a time, a century or more ago, when Hermitage was regarded by many as the greatest red wine in France. And there was a time, amid the BORDEAUX and BURGUNDY fever of the early 1980s, when it was dismissed by almost all as merely a rough-and-tumble RHÔNE red. And now once again Hermitage is revered – rare, rich red wine, expensive, memorable, classic. But these words are too cold to describe the turbulent excitements of a great Hermitage. The boiling cauldron of flavours – savage pepper, herbs, tar and coalsmoke biting at your tongue, fruit of intense blackcurrant-raspberry-and-bramble sweetness – is intoxicatingly delicious, and, as the wine ages, a strange, warm softness of cream and licorice and well-worn leather blends in to create one of the greatest red-wine taste experiences.

Now, not all Hermitage achieves this eccentric but exciting blend of flavours, because the vineyard – flowing down the slopes of this bullish mound above the little town of Tain l'Hermitage on the banks of the Rhône – only covers 131ha (324 acres) and a lot of merchants will take any grapes just to have Hermitage on their list. But the best growers – using the magnificent red Syrah, and carefully blending the wines from different parts of the hill (which do give very different flavours) – can make superbly original wine, needing five to ten years' aging even in a light year; but for the full-blown roar of flavours which a hot, ripe vintage brings, then 15 years is hardly enough for the tip-top wines. Best years: (reds) 2001, '00, '99, '98, '97, '96, '95, '94, '92, '91, '90, '89, '88, '85, '83 '82, '78, '71, '70.

White Hermitage is rather less famous than the red – but the best can actually outlive the reds. Some winemakers, like JABOULET AÎNÉ, are making modern, fruity, fragrant whites – with an appetizing floral, lemon peel, licorice and apple flavour. These are lovely as young as one to two years old. But there are others – from grizzly-minded traditionalists who won't be swayed by fashion and the chance of an easy sale. They've been growing the Marsanne and Roussanne grapes on the dizzy slopes of the giant hill of Hermitage for generations, and they don't care if their wine then takes generations to mature so long as it is the 'real thing'.

The flavour of white Hermitage from producers like Jean-Louis CHAVE, Grippat or CHAPOUTIER will seem fat and oily at first, reeking of bruised apples, soured peaches and unswept farmyard rubbish; but if you give it ten years, 20, maybe twice as long, then a remarkable and welcome transformation will take place – apples and pears blend with fresh-roasted nuts, toffee, licorice, pine resin, herbs from the wild Rhône hills, mint and peaches and cream. From such sullen beginnings the glory of white Hermitage finally blazes forth. About one quarter of all Hermitage is white, totalling 140,000 or so bottles a year. Best producers: (reds and whites) A Belle, Chapoutier, B Chave, J-L Chave, Colombier, COLOMBO, DELAS (les Bessards), B Faurie, Fayolle, Ferraton, Grippat, GUIGAL, Jaboulet (la Chapelle), des Remizières, J-M Sorrel, M Sorrel, Tain l'Hermitage co-operative, Tardieu-Laurent, les Vins de Vienne.

THE HESS COLLECTION

USA, California, Napa County, Mount Veeder AVA

🍷 *Cabernet Sauvignon, Syrah and others*

🍷 *Chardonnay*

Hess Collection is actually the name of an art collection – Donald Hess is an enthusiastic modern art collector as well as vineyard owner, and has managed to combine his desire to show the public his art as well as to make fine wine at his MOUNT VEEDER winery. Some of the art is on the 'strong' side, and so is Mount Veeder – a savage terrain on steep and heavily wooded slopes in the southwestern corner of NAPA VALLEY, famous, or notorious, for aggressive, brutish red wines. Indeed, if Hess wanted to educate the public with his art, he wanted to tame the mountain with his wine, and he's managed just that with his Cabernet – the black richness of Mount Veeder fruit is still there, but the black-hearted bitterness of yore has been banished. Hess Collection Chardonnay comes from American Canyon on the eastern edge of San Pablo Bay. Hess Estates and Hess Select labels cover wines from various parts of California. Hess Collection also has partnerships in

Argentina and South Africa. Best years: (Cabernet) 2001, '00, '99, '98, '97, '96, '95, '94, '91, '90.

HESSISCHE BERGSTRASSE
GERMANY

The best place to taste the wines of Hessische Bergstrasse is in the region itself. You're unlikely to find them anywhere else, for the simple reason that there aren't many of them: 456ha (1126 acres) of vines, divided between over 1000 different growers. It is impossible, with such a small, little-known region, not to view its wines in the light of those of other regions. If Hessische Bergstrasse's Rieslings are like lesser RHEINGAUs, its Müller-Thurgaus are like lesser Müller-Thurgaus from BADEN, without the richness and finesse that the best of the latter can have, even though Hessische Bergstrasse is geographically a northerly continuation of Baden. And its Silvaners are like lesser FRANKEN Silvaners, without quite the same firmness and depth.

Even so, Hessische Bergstrasse's best wines can surpass these levels: there are powerful, well-structured wines to be had, particularly the Eisweins. Best producers: Bergsträsser Winzer, Simon-Bürkle, Staatsweingut Bergstrasse (Domaine Bensheim), Weingut der Stadt Bensheim.

HEYL ZU HERRNSHEIM
GERMANY, Rheinhessen, Nierstein
♀ *Riesling, Silvaner, Pinot Blanc (Weissburgunder) and others*

One of the finest estates in the RHEINHESSEN, Heyl zu Herrnsheim has a prime position in NIERSTEIN, right in the middle of the Rhein Terrasse. Its vines ascend steeply into the red slate Pettenthal vineyard, the Hipping, the Ölberg and the little Brudersberg vineyard, which the company owns in its entirety.

'Ecologically' farmed raw materials like these would give any winemaker a good head start; Heyl zu Herrnsheim capitalizes on them with meticulous winemaking and rigorous selection. The estate has recently been taken over by Markus Ahr, who is undertaking a modest expansion with new vines in the NACKENHEIMer Rothenberg site. Best years: (Riesling Auslese) 2002, '01, '99, '98, '97, '96, '93, '90, '89.

HEYMANN-LÖWENSTEIN
GERMANY, Mosel-Saar-Ruwer, Winningen
♀ *Riesling and others*

Before Reinhard Löwenstein began building his estate up from scratch in 1980 there was not much going on in the Lower MOSEL, an area recently renamed 'Terrassenmosel'. However, Löwenstein, a self-confessed rebel, was clearly the man to breathe life back into the giddy terraced slopes of the Röttgen and Uhlen which had been famous in the nineteenth century, and which attest their warmth by being home to vipers, lizards and various Mediterranean plants. He believes in letting the wines ferment in their own time – usually to dryness, but also, from his ripest grapes, to a powerful rich style marrying mineral intensity with sweetness. Predictable they are not, but impressive, certainly. Best years: (Riesling Auslese) 2002, '01, '00, '99, '98, '97, '95, '94, '93, '92, '91.

HIDALGO
SPAIN, Andalucía, Jerez y Manzanilla DO
♀ *Palomino Fino, Pedro Ximénez*

The three Hidalgo cousins who run this small 200-year-old company specialize with great success in manzanilla, and make all their wines from their own and other family vineyards. Besides La Gitana (one of Spain's best-selling manzanillas), they also make a good range named Mariscal, excellent Fino Especial and Miraflores, Amontillado Napoleon, Pedro Ximénez Viejo, Oloroso Viejo and single-vineyard sherries from their Pastrana site.

HILLTOP
HUNGARY, Neszmély
♂ *Merlot, Blaufränkisch (Kékfrankos), Cabernet Sauvignon*
♀ *Chardonnay, Pinot Gris, Irsai Oliver, Sauvignon Blanc, Gewürztraminer*

This dynamic company, with its showpiece winery, has been Hungary's leader in providing fresh, bright wines, especially white, at friendly prices. Based in the Ászár-Neszmély wine region, aromatic varieties such as Irsai Oliver and Gewürztraminer thrive alongside Sauvignon Blanc, Chardonnay and Pinot

HILLTOP
One of the best of the tangy, citrous Sauvignon Blancs from Hungary, Riverview is from vines grown near the Danube.

Grigio on the protected slopes between the Danube and the Transdanubian Mountains. They have 500ha (1235 acres) of white vineyards locally, but most of the grapes are still bought in from other regions. Chief winemaker Ákos Kamocsay is one of Hungary's most respected. Hilltop also produces a good but controversial TOKAJI.

HILLTOPS
AUSTRALIA, New South Wales

After a brief but successful period of viticulture towards the end of the nineteenth century, the vines disappeared in this area south of COWRA, around the town of Young, until 1975, when the late Peter Robertson decided to plant some on his large farming property. Barwang, as it was called, was acquired by MCWILLIAM'S in 1989, and since that time plantings in the region have grown from a token 13ha (32 acres) to more than 150ha (370 acres), with little end to the expansion in sight. All the vineyards are planted above the 450m (1480ft) contour line, and the dry summers and autumns provide excellent ripening conditions.

The principal wines here are stony/ minerally Chardonnay, moderately spicy Shiraz with a range of chocolate, mint, black cherry and more briary characters, and Cabernet Sauvignon, predominantly cassis/ blackcurrant but balanced with some more earthy/chocolate undertones. Best producer: Demondrille, Grove Estate, McWilliam's Barwang, Woodonga Hill.

FRANZ HIRTZBERGER
AUSTRIA, Niederösterreich, Wachau, Spitz
♀ *Grüner Veltliner, Riesling, Pinot Gris (Grauburgunder), Pinot Blanc (Weissburgunder), Chardonnay (Feinburgunder), Muscat (Gelber Muskateller)*

Franz Hirtzberger's natural charm and political skills have made him an excellent president of the WACHAU winegrowers' association, Vinea Wachau, under whom the region has taken a great stride forward.

As a winemaker he has repeatedly demonstrated the elegance and aromatic refinement of which the region's wines are capable, even with natural alcohol contents far above 13 degrees. He is helped in this by having his vines in SPITZ, at the western end of Wachau where the Danube turns south, the protective hills break up a little and the chill winds from the north find their way into the vines. It doesn't stop them ripening, but does impart to them a leaner minerally style. The majority

FRANZ HIRTZBERGER
The Hirtzberger estate at Spitz includes some of the oldest vineyards in the Wachau. This magnificent Riesling comes from the Steinterrassen site.

of his 11ha (27 acres) are Grüner Veltliner and Riesling, but he also makes fine Pinot Gris, Pinot Blanc and Chardonnay (called Feinburgunder). Best years: (Riesling Smaragd) 2002, '01, '00, '99, '98, '97, '96, '95, '94, '93, '92, '90, '88.

HOCHHEIM
GERMANY, Rheingau
This RHEINGAU village is best known for lending its name to the generic name in the UK for all Rhine wine: English attempts at pronouncing Hochheimer led to 'hockamore' and from there to 'hock' was but a short step for the abbreviating English tongue.

Still, Queen Victoria further cemented Hochheim's reputation by stopping there for a picnic in 1850 and aferwards telling the vineyard owner he could call the vineyard Königin Victoriaberg, if he wanted. He wanted alright, but all this flummery takes away from the fact that Hochheim makes some very good wine. It's archetypal Rheingau; firm, minerally, even earthy but with lovely Riesling floral scent and honeyed depth. These are long-lived, and mature beautifully. The best vineyards are the Domdechaney, the Hölle, the Kirchenstück and the Königin Victoriaberg. Best years: 2002, '01, '99, '98, '97, '96, '94, '93, '92, '90, '88. Best producers: Joachim Flick, Franz KÜNSTLER, W J Schäfer.

FÜRST ZU HOHENLOHE-ÖHRINGEN
GERMANY, Württemberg, Öhringen im Schloss
♥ Lemberger, Pinot Noir (Spätburgunder), Trollinger
♀ Riesling, Pinot Blanc (Weissburgunder) and others
WÜRTTEMBERG is primarily a red wine region so it is unusual to find an operation like this aristocratic 20-ha (50-acre) estate that majors on whites – especially Riesling. It's made fashionably dry, but the warm climate means it's ripe, not too austere. Some Riesling and Chardonnay are aged in small barriques.

The estate has sole ownership of the Verrenberger Verrenberg site. Best years: (reds) 2002, '01, '99, '97, '96, '95, '93, '92; (whites) 2001, '99, '98, '97.

HOLLICK
AUSTRALIA, South Australia, Coonawarra
♥ Cabernet Sauvignon, Merlot, Syrah (Shiraz), Pinot Noir
♀ Riesling, Chardonnay, Semillon, Sauvignon Blanc
I can't resist riling Ian Hollick. Just as he's trying to impress me with his serious Cabernets and Shirazes, I cry 'Show me your sparkling Merlot!' And he does. But you can sense this isn't the wine that a serious COONAWARRA pioneer wants to be known for. Anyway, it's a delicious red fizz. Thank you, Ian. On to the serious stuff. Hollick set up their Coonawarra vineyard in 1975. They now have 52ha (128 acres) there as well as 20ha (50 acres) in WRATTONBULLY. They've always made serious, dry reds – proper reflective Coonawarra styles, mostly based on Merlot, Cabernet and Shiraz, with a top-of-the-line range led by Ravenswood Cabernet. But they have also always championed Riesling – they don't make much white, but their Riesling, Chardonnay, Semillon and Sauvignon are good. Best years: (Ravenswood) 2001, '00, '99, '98, '96, '94, '93, '91, '90, '88.

DOMAINE DE L'HORTUS
FRANCE, Languedoc-Roussillon, Coteaux du Languedoc–Pic St-Loup AC
♥ Syrah, Grenache, Mourvèdre
♀ Chardonnay, Viognier, Roussanne, Sauvignon Blanc
Jean Orliac of the Domaine de l'Hortus spotted the potential of the PIC ST-LOUP, a sub-region of the COTEAUX DU LANGUEDOC, while rock climbing in the area in the 1970s. During the 1980s he planted Syrah, Mourvèdre and Grenache, producing his first wine in 1990 in shared cellars with Jean-Benoît Cavalier of Ch. de Lascaux. He now has his own wooden cellar building and 55ha (136 acres) of vineyard at Hortus, with a further 10ha (25 acres) for his new wine, Clos du Prieur. The Bergerie de l'Hortus Classique is a fruity, early-drinking wine matured in stainless steel vats whereas the Grande Cuvée has a higher percentage of Mourvèdre in the blend, is aged 15 months in oak, mainly new barriques, and is a more structured, powerful wine that can age five years or more. There is also a buttery, peachy, barrel-fermented white Grande Cuvée made from Chardonnay and Viognier. Best years: (Grande Cuvée red) 2001, '00, '99, '98, '97, '96, '95, '94, '93.

HOSPICES DE BEAUNE
FRANCE, Burgundy, Beaune
♥ Pinot Noir
♀ Chardonnay
When in 1443 Nicolas Rolin founded the charitable hospital in Beaune now known as the Hospices, he could never have imagined that over five centuries later it would still be thriving. Over the decades bequests have made the Hospices a major landowner in BURGUNDY, and the profits from the sale of the wines made from these mostly outstanding vineyards have sustained the Hospices financially.

The Hospices now has over 60ha (148 acres) of vines, mostly in the CÔTE DE BEAUNE. Before they are sold at the highly theatrical auction at the November weekend known as the Trois Glorieuses, the wines are vinified in new oak by the Hospices. The quality of the winemaking has increased immeasurably since 1994, partly thanks to a new winery on the outskirts of Beaune. The buyers, usually *négociants*, then remove their wine by mid-January following the auction for maturing in their own cellars. Since the wines are then subjected to the buyers' either good or bad practices the final result of an 'Hospices' wine is far more erratic than it should be. I've had great and disgraceful bottles. Inevitably, since the auction is for charity the prices paid for the wines tend to be high.

HOUGHTON
AUSTRALIA, Western Australia, Swan District
♥ Cabernet Sauvignon, Syrah (Shiraz), Merlot and others
♀ Chardonnay, Chenin Blanc, Sauvignon Blanc, Semillon, Verdelho, Riesling and others
HWB, sold outside the EU as Houghton 'White Burgundy', is one of Australia's leading white wines. It is a modestly priced blend of Chenin Blanc, Chardonnay, Verdelho, Semillon, Sauvignon Blanc and Muscadelle and made in huge quantities. Older vintages can be remarkable, and small quantities are held back for release under the Show Reserve label, which is well worth the search and the money.

As part of the giant HARDY group, Houghton has large vineyard holdings in the Frankland River sub-region of the GREAT SOUTHERN, and takes significant quantities of grapes from the PEMBERTON region and from MARGARET RIVER. Supplemented by its Moondah Brook vineyard (and brand) it produces a kaleidoscopic array of wines ranging from the monumental Jack Mann Cabernet Sauvignon (in memory of the great winemaker) and Gladstones Shiraz through to fine, subtly oaked Semillon-Sauvignon Blanc and Chardonnay, together with some startling grapefruit-and-passionfruit accented Riesling. Houghton has always been a good producer but recent focus on particular regions and their individual strengths as well as inspired winemaking is creating their best ever range of wines. Best years: (Jack Mann) 2001, '00, '99, '98, '96, '95, '94.

VON HÖVEL
GERMANY, Mosel-Saar-Ruwer, Konz-Oberemmel
♀ *Riesling*

Ebullient Eberhard von Kunow makes elegant, well-structured wines from steep vineyards in and around the village of Konz-Oberemmel on the Saar. The wines are matured in cask and have the steely acidity typical of the region, as well as, in less than ripe years, the typical distinct green apple taste. Nearly 200 years old, the estate has vineyards in some of the Saar's best vineyard sites. Notable are the Scharzhofberg – in good years, this can be a superb wine – and the solely owned Hütte vineyard in Oberemmel. Best years: (Auslese) 2002, '01, '00, '99, '97, '96, '95, '94, '93, '90, '89, '88, '85.

HOWARD PARK
AUSTRALIA, Western Australia, Great Southern
♂ *Cabernet Sauvignon, Syrah (Shiraz), Merlot, Cabernet Franc*
♀ *Riesling, Chardonnay*

After leaving an indelible mark as the maker of WYNNS' first John Riddoch Cabernet Sauvignon (in 1982) John Wade moved to the GREAT SOUTHERN region in the far south of WESTERN AUSTRALIA, setting up an immensely successful career as a contract winemaker and consultant while simultaneously establishing his Howard Park label, and ultimately the second label, Madfish. He has now moved on and Howard Park has expanded to a second winery in MARGARET RIVER, but his signature style remains – rapier-like Riesling and Cabernet-Merlot, which in top years is sublime. The Chardonnay is very nearly as impressive, and Madfish whites and reds are darlings of the smart brasserie set. Best years: (Cabernet-Merlot) 2001, '99, '98, '96, '94, '93, '92, '90, '89, '88, '86; (Riesling) 2002, '01, '00, '98, '97, '96, '95, '94, '93, '92, '91, '90, '88, '86.

HOWELL MOUNTAIN AVA
USA, California, Napa County

Both an appellation and a state of mind, Howell Mountain is a small region in NAPA's north-eastern hillsides made famous in the 1980s by DUNN VINEYARDS' massive Cabernet Sauvignon and since by various rich and dense offerings from wineries like BERINGER, DUCKHORN and La Jota. At elevations of 500–670m (1600–2200ft) above the fog zone, it has rocky, well-drained volcanic soil that is suitable for Merlot, Zinfandel, and several RHÔNE varieties, as well as Cabernet Sauvignon. Vineyard plantings have slowly grown to 240ha (593 acres). Best years: (reds) 2001, '00, '99, '98, '97, '96, '95, '94, '93, '91, '90. Best producers: Beringer, Duckhorn, Dunn, La Jota, Liparita, PINE RIDGE, VIADER.

HUADONG WINERY
CHINA, Shandong Province
♂ *Cabernet Sauvignon, Cabernet Franc, Gamay, Merlot and others*
♀ *Chardonnay, Welschriesling (Riesling Italico), Riesling, Chenin Blanc and others*

China is easily the biggest wine producer in Asia, and it is also home to thousands of different grape varieties, both native, and bred by local scientists. Attempts to grow the classic international varieties have been only partially successful not least because climatic conditions – with extreme variations of temperature inland and pervasive humidity along most of the coastline – have made it extremely difficult to ripen European grapes.

But the Shandong peninsula south-east of Beijing, has a reasonable balanced maritime climate – it already has more than 10 per cent of China's vineyards – and it also has the winery most successful at producing 'international' wine styles in China – Huadong, situated near the seaside town of Qingdao. Established in 1985, Huadong made its reputation with fresh, bright, attractive Riesling and Chardonnay. But they do also have Cabernet grapes, so, with the Chinese enthusiasm for drinking red wine to ward off heart disease, expect the reds to play an increasingly important role.

HUDSON RIVER REGION AVA
USA, New York State

The Hudson River Region north of New York City is the least known of NEW YORK STATE's wine regions, but it has a long wine history going back to the early nineteenth century and contains the USA's oldest operational winery – Brotherhood – which first crushed grapes in 1839. There are now more than 20 wineries although it's only recently, helped by the success of Millbrook near Poughkeepsie, that vinifera grapes have become important. They are able to ripen and to avoid destructive frosts because the steep-sided valley through which the Hudson flows south allows moderating maritime influences from the Atlantic to penetrate upstream.

DOMAINE HUËT
FRANCE, Loire, Touraine, Vouvray AC
♀ *Chenin Blanc*

In 2003 this uncompromisingly high-quality Vouvray estate was bought by leading TOKAJI producer István Szepsy and the Chinese-American financier Anthony Hwang. Noel Pinguet remains as winemaker and the estate will benefit from new investment and lower yields. Demi-sec and *moelleux* wines are never made here unless there is sufficient natural sweetness: the range produced each year depends wholly on the nature of the harvest. The 40-ha (100-acre) estate is run along bio-dynamic lines – one of the largest in France to wholly use this labour-intensive method. Huët owns three vineyards, le Haut-Lieu, le Mont and Clos du Bourg, all sited on some of the best land in VOUVRAY.

The wines, particularly the dry styles, can be austere when they are young but they develop a fascinating honeyed complexity with age. Even quite modest vintages can last for at least 30 years and great vintages, such as 1959 and '47, will last for a century. Best years: 2002, '01, '00, '99, '98, '97, '96, '95, '93, '90, '89, '88, '85, '76, '64, '61, '59, '47.

HUGEL ET FILS
FRANCE, Alsace, Alsace AC
♂ *Pinot Noir*
♀ *Riesling, Gewurztraminer, Pinot Blanc, Sylvaner, Pinot Gris, Muscat*

Jean Hugel is the best-known ambassador for the wines of ALSACE, although he has now delegated the daily running of his winery to the next generation, the twelfth since the firm started to make wines in Riquewihr in 1639. Lovers of sweet wines have Hugel to thank for the creation of the Vendange Tardive and Sélection de Grains Nobles styles which are now one of the glories of Alsace. At the top level (Tradition, Jubilee, Vendange Tardive and Sélection de Grains Nobles), Hugel wines remain of the highest quality, but the regular bottlings are mostly rather dull and really should have a bit more zip and style. Although Hugel owns some outstanding sites, it never uses the words Grand Cru on the label, and prefers to remain free to make up the blends as it sees fit. Best years: (Vendange Tardive Riesling) 2000, '99, '98, '97, '96, '95, '90, '89, '88.

HUNTER VALLEY
AUSTRALIA, New South Wales

The Hunter Valley is an infuriating and frustrating place which defies all logic; it would never have survived, let alone prospered, as a wine region were it not for its proximity to Sydney (less than 2 hours' drive). The soils are largely hopeless, the meagre annual rainfall has a disconcerting habit of falling in the middle of the harvest and the climate is ridiculously warm for quality grapegrowing.

Yet despite all this both the Upper and Lower Hunter Valleys regularly produce Semillon of a quality, longevity and style to be found nowhere else in the world; Chardonnay of a peachy lusciousness which propelled the valley to stardom first in Australia and then with equal panache in Europe; and Shiraz which has a freakish ability to age with extreme grace over 30 years or more.

Cabernet Sauvignon, Merlot, Pinot Noir and Verdelho are also grown in the Hunter; the reds develop a regional style with age, an amalgam of tarry, velvety, earthy, farmyardy tastes which may sound an awkward mix but often makes a strangely appealing combination, so long as the fruit is strong enough to achieve dominance over the sweat and the leather. The premium vineyards are mainly in the Lower Hunter, although ROSEMOUNT's exceptional white vineyards are in the Upper Hunter. Best years: (Shiraz) 2001, '00, '99, '98, '97, '96, '94, '91. Best producers: Allandale, BROKENWOOD, De Iuliis, Kulkunbulla, Lake's Folly, LINDEMANS, Lowe Family, MCWILLIAM'S, Meerea Park, Pendarves, Rosemount, ROTHBURY, Scarborough, TOWER, TYRRELL'S.

HUNTER'S
NEW ZEALAND, South Island, Marlborough
❦ *Cabernet Sauvignon, Pinot Noir, Merlot*
♀ *Sauvignon Blanc, Chardonnay, Gewurztraminer, Riesling, Semillon*

For the true glory of Hunter's, you have to try the Sauvignon Blanc. I should know. I was knocked backwards by the 1985 when I was judging at the *Sunday Times* Wine Festival in London. There wasn't a wine in the show like it. The other judges didn't want to make it Wine of the Show, but the public did, and this mould-breaking thriller from the South Seas became a superstar with only its third vintage. So they came back the next year and won the award again with their Chardonnay!

So what are the wines like? Well, there's nothing reserved about the Sauvignon – as sharp, as tangy, as shockingly intense as any in the world. And there's not too much reserve about the Chardonnay – its powerful dry fruit delicately wrapped in new oak richness. Maybe Riesling shows a little citrus reserve – or maybe the Gewurztraminer; but how reserved can a lovely floral Gewurztraminer be? No. For reserve I think I'd have to offer the reds – the Pinot Noir always promises much but is for me a little low key. And Miru Miru is a fine, sophisticated fizz. The spicy, oak-aged Sauvignon Blanc is good, but takes several years of bottle-aging to come together. Best years: (Chardonnay) 2002, '01, '00, '99.

IAŞI
ROMANIA

Iasi is an important university town in north-eastern Romania. It's one of the main centres of the Moldavia region, on the border with modern-day Moldova, and home to one-third of all Romania's vineyards, many of them planted with Romanian varietals. Tămîioasă Româneasca and Grasă de Cotnari are the most notable. Tămîioasă is actually Muscat Blanc à Petits Grains and here it makes some lavish, florally aromatic, penetrating dessert wines that seem capable of eternal aging – I've had deep orange, 30-year-old examples. Fetească Neagră makes deep-coloured rustic reds that can also age for donkey's years.

IDAHO
USA

Along with OREGON and WASHINGTON, Idaho is part of Pacific Northwest wine country, with some of the USA's highest vineyards. Though much smaller in acreage, at 445ha (1100 acres), and with only a handful of wineries, Idaho has produced some impressive wines during its short history. Ste Chapelle is Idaho's most important winery and uses much of the state's grapes, as well as buying in from Washington, to create sound whites, especially Chardonnay and Riesling.

IHRINGEN
GERMANY, Baden

This is the most important wine town of the KAISERSTUHL region in BADEN. The best wines come from the volcanic soil of the great Winklerberg site whose massive terraces look south-west across the Rhine plain to ALSACE and enjoy the warmest conditions of any German vineyard. Weissburgunder (Pinot Blanc), Grauburgunder (Pinot Gris) and Spätburgunder (Pinot Noir) rule here, giving big, powerful dry wines. Best years: 2002, '01, '99, '98, '96. Best producers: Dr HEGER, Konstanzer, Stigler.

INNISKILLIN WINES
CANADA, Ontario, Niagara Peninsula VQA
❦ *Pinot Noir, Cabernet Franc, Merlot, Cabernet Sauvignon*
♀ *Chardonnay, Riesling, Vidal, Pinot Grigio and others*

Donald Ziraldo and Karl Kaiser established Inniskillin as Canada's first estate winery in 1975. Today, Inniskillin churns out 140,000 cases of wine a year, with approximately an amazing 10 per cent comprising assorted Icewines, which are admired worldwide by dessert wine *aficionados*. As well as the well known Vidal Icewine, Kaiser now produces ones from Riesling, Cabernet Franc, Chenin Blanc and there is even a sparkling version.

On the drier side, the table wines are made by Philip Dowell who arrived in time for the 1999 vintage from the YARRA VALLEY. VQA premium varietal wines include single-vineyard, reserve editions and Founders' Series of Pinot Noir and Chardonnay. All the grapes come from the winery's 49ha (120 acres) or are purchased from a handful of specially selected growers spread about the NIAGARA PENINSULA. Inniskillin also has a separate winery and 9-ha (23-acre) estate in the OKANAGAN Valley. Best years: (Vidal Icewine) 2001, '00, '99, '98, '97, '95, '94.

IPHOFEN
GERMANY, Franken

This is the most important commune in the Steigerwald, in the far east of the FRANKEN region. Here, the heavy gypsum marl soils and the excellent exposure of the Julius-Echter-Berg site give the most massive, earthy, dry Rieslings and Silvaners in Franken; these are not wines for the faint-hearted! Best years: 2002, '01, '00, '99, '98, '97, '94, '93, '92, '90. Best producers: Juliusspital, Johann Ruck, Hans Wirsching.

IRANCY AC
FRANCE, Burgundy
❦ ♀ *Pinot Noir, César, Tressot*

This northern outpost of vineyards, just south-west of CHABLIS, is an unlikely champion of the clear, pure flavours of Pinot Noir, aided by the local César and Tressot. In the compact south-facing amphitheatre of 125ha (309 acres) of vineyards, the sun gives just enough encouragement to the vines to produce a delicate, clean red wine that is lightly touched by the ripeness of plums and strawberries. César, in particular, adds colour and body to the wine. Best producers: Bienvenu, J-M BROCARD, Cantin, A & J-P Colinot, Delaloge, Patrice Fort, Simonnet-Febvre.

IRON HORSE VINEYARDS

*USA, California, Sonoma County, Sonoma-Green
Valley AVA*
(Sonoma-Green Valley) ❧ *Pinot Noir*
♀ *Chardonnay*

When Forrest Tancer and Barry and Audrey
Sterling began their partnership in the late
1970s, the emphasis was on still Chardonnay
and Pinot Noir; CHAMPAGNE-method sparklers
were an amusing sideline. The latter have since
become the tail that wags the dog, enormously
successful for their delicacy and freshness of texture and flavour. The star wines are the Blanc de
Blancs and Brut Late Disgorged – superb,
nutty, creamy wines. Vineyards in the ALEXAN-
DER VALLEY provide a wide variety of grapes for
still wines including Chardonnay, Pinot Noir,
Sangiovese, Cuvée R – a rich, ripe Sauvignon
Blanc-Viognier blend – a plummy but green-
streaked Cabernet-Merlot Blend 1, and an
exotic, full-flavoured Viognier.

IROULÉGUY AC

FRANCE, South-West
❧ ❧ *Tannat, Cabernet Franc, Cabernet Sauvignon*
♀ *Petit Manseng, Gros Manseng, Petit Courbu and
others*

Tucked away up in the Pyrenean mountain
valleys, this is probably one of the most
obscure French ACs. The wines are not as
good as the scenery but the reds have
improved greatly over the years, with more
body and structure, due to greater ripeness
and oak aging being added in the 1990s. Rare
whites come from Étienne Brana and the
local co-operative. Drink these wines young –
preferably with your picnic in the meadows
by the winery at St-Étienne-de-Baigorry, just
below the snow line. The co-operative dominates production from the appellation's
200ha (494 acres) of vineyards. Best years:
(reds) 2001, '00, '98, '97, '96, '95. Best producers: Arretxea, Brana, Etxegaraya, Ilarria,
Irouléguy co-operative (Mignaberry).

ISABEL ESTATE

NEW ZEALAND, South Island, Marlborough
❧ *Pinot Noir*
♀ *Chardonnay, Riesling, Sauvignon Blanc, Pinot Gris
and others*

Michael and Robyn Tiller like to boast that
they used to supply grapes to the world-
famous CLOUDY BAY, but these same grapes
now go into their own Isabel Estate wines,
producing about 22,000 cases per year. True,
but the style at Isabel is quite different – even
the Sauvignon Blanc has an unusual richness
and the fine Chardonnay, Pinot Gris and

Pinot Noir are positively bursting with ripe
fruit. These are exciting wines, not all that
typical of the region. Best years: (Pinot Noir)
2002, '01, '00, '99, '98.

ISOLE E OLENA

ITALY, Tuscany, Chianti Classico DOCG
❧ *Sangiovese, Canaiolo, Syrah, Cabernet Sauvignon*
♀ *Chardonnay, Malvasia, Trebbiano*

This 40-ha (99-acre) estate has become
almost an emblem of modern-style, high-
quality CHIANTI CLASSICO, but has also been
as innovative, indeed iconoclastic as any other
Tuscan producer in experimenting with non-
Tuscan varieties like Syrah, Cabernet
Sauvignon and Chardonnay. Paolo De
Marchi took charge in the mid-1970s and
since then he has spared no effort to improve
every aspect of his production, despite a
quasi-permanent shortage of funds.

His standard-bearer is the straight Chianti
Classico and to maintain the quality of this
wine he will, in lesser vintages, sacrifice his
famous cru, the barrique-aged 100 per cent
Sangiovese Cepparello, for which he can
command a considerably higher price.

One of Paolo's innovations was the introduction of the RHÔNE'S Syrah grape into
Tuscan viticulture, which he will sprinkle into
the Chianti Classico blend if need be. In good
years he makes it into a varietal Syrah in the
Collezione De Marchi range, which also
includes excellent Cabernet Sauvignon and
Chardonnay. His VIN SANTO, too, is special
and one of the finest of the modern fruit-driven style. Paolo De Marchi, with his fluent,
accented English, has become one of the
greatest ambassadors of Chianti Classico
abroad. Best years: (Cepparello) 2001, '00,
'99, '98, '97, '95, '93, '90, '88.

ISOLE E OLENA
*Cepparello is Paolo De Marchi's top wine. From 100
per cent Sangiovese, it is an austere yet beautiful
rendering of Tuscany's classic red grape.*

PAUL JABOULET AÎNÉ

FRANCE, Northern Rhône, Hermitage AC
(Northern Rhône) ❧ *Syrah*
♀ *Marsanne, Roussanne*

For decades Jaboulet Aîné was one of the
most consistent of RHÔNE merchant houses,

the overall quality of its wines no doubt
boosted by the ownership of 100ha
(247 acres) of vineyards. Indeed you could
say they were the only merchant regularly
capable of supplying good quality in both
north and south Rhône wine regions. But
they began to lose their way in the 1980s,
and things weren't helped by the tragic early
death of the charismatic Gérard Jaboulet in
1997. It's not always easy to discern why a
fine company falters, but growth has coin-
cided with a time when the owners of most
of the best vineyards whose grapes they
might once have bought have started making and selling their own wines under their
own labels. There were signs at the start of
the new millennium that quality was on
the up again. Let's hope so, because Jaboulet
is an important and respected name. HER-
MITAGE la Chapelle is the most famous wine,
at its best a thrillingly intense expression of
the Syrah. CROZES-HERMITAGE Thalabert
used to be the best Crozes going, but is in the
pack nowadays. Other whites and reds from
north to south and including CÔTES DU
VENTOUX are now good rather than exciting.
Best years: (la Chapelle) 2001, '00, '99, '98,
'97, '96, '95, '94, '91, '90, '89, '88, '78.

JACKSON ESTATE

NEW ZEALAND, South Island, Marlborough
❧ *Pinot Noir*
♀ *Sauvignon Blanc, Chardonnay, Riesling*

An established grapegrower with vineyards in
MARLBOROUGH's prestigious Wairau River
Valley, Jackson Estate turned its hand to
winemaking in 1991, employing the skills of
flying winemaker Martin Shaw of SHAW &
SMITH. The range is led by tangy, nettle- and
green apple-flavoured Sauvignon Blanc that
even improves with a little age, and extends to
restrained Chardonnay and Pinot Noir and
complex traditional-method fizz. Best years:
(Sauvignon Blanc) 2002, '01, '00.

LOUIS JADOT

FRANCE, Burgundy, Beaune
❧ *Pinot Noir, Gamay*
♀ *Chardonnay, Aligoté*

One of BURGUNDY's most respected *négociant*
houses, with holdings in many of the CÔTE
D'OR's best sites, Jadot has generally kept to a
high quality level when many neighbouring
firms have slipped. Its leading white wines
are BÂTARD-MONTRACHET and CORTON-
CHARLEMAGNE, and there are first-rate reds
from BEAUNE Premier Cru sites such as Clos
des Ursules and from CORTON, GEVREY-

CHAMBERTIN and MUSIGNY. Under its brilliant winemaker, Jacques Lardière, Jadot often produces more than acceptable wines in difficult vintages. The sign of a good *négociant* is the ability to produce simpler and less expensive wines of good quality, and here too Jadot excels, with excellent wines from villages such as FIXIN, RULLY and ST-AUBIN for short-term drinking. Recent developments have included the purchase of top BEAUJOLAIS vineyards, such as Ch. des Jacques in MOULIN-À-VENT. Best years: (top reds) 2002, '01, '00, '99, '98, '97, '96, '95, '93, '90.

JOSEF JAMEK

AUSTRIA, Niederösterreich, Wachau, Joching

Riesling, Grüner Veltliner, Pinot Blanc (Weissburgunder), Muscat (Gelber Muskateller)

During the late 1950s Josef Jamek began his crusade for dry, unchaptalized wines in the WACHAU. After a period of erratic quality during the early 1990s, things have taken a decisive upturn since the arrival of his daughter Jutta, and her husband Hans Altmann. They have not made any fundamental changes, but brought new energy and ambition and the wines have taken a leap forward as a result. Top of the range are the Rieslings from the Ried Klaus of Weissenkirchen, which have a classical elegance and great aging potential. The restaurant serves Austrian cooking of the highest standard. Best years: 2002, '01, '00, '99, '98, '97, '90, '88, '86, '83, '79.

J-P & J-L JAMET

FRANCE, Northern Rhône, Côte-Rôtie AC

Syrah

Jean-Luc and Jean-Paul Jamet, the two brothers who run this small 6.5-ha (16-acre) family estate, own vineyards that are exceptionally well located on the best slopes of CÔTE-RÔTIE. The wines remain traditionally made, with no destemming, a lengthy maceration in good years, and bottling without filtration or fining. Aging takes place in casks of various sizes, and in recent vintages the brothers have introduced a modest percentage of new barriques. However, the wine is never oaky in flavour. On the contrary, the Jamet wines used to show a certain rusticity, although the style became more elegant in the 1990s. Thanks to the excellent vineyards, the Jamets usually produce a stylish and thoroughly drinkable wine even in difficult vintages. But in the great years the full smoky splendour of their wines is Côte-Rôtie at its best. Best years: 2001, '00, '99, '98, '97, '96, '95, '94, '91, '90, '89, '88, '85, '83.

The finest sherry vineyards are located on deep, snow-white albariza chalk soil which absorbs the winter rain like a sponge; this then sustains the vines during the long summer drought.

VIN DE PAYS DU JARDIN DE LA FRANCE

FRANCE, Loire Valley

Talk about a clever title for a wine: 'Country Wine from the Garden of France'. What could be more seductive or appetizing? The reality, however, is a little more mundane: this is a large and highly successful VIN DE PAYS covering most of the LOIRE Valley, whose production often exceeds 80 million bottles – mostly of white wine, from Chenin Blanc and Sauvignon Blanc, and usually fairly cheap to buy. There is an increasing amount of good Chardonnay made here, as well as one or two pricy appellation-busting reds (super-Loires?), though most reds are simple examples of Gamay or Grolleau. Best producers: Bouvet-Ladubay, Adéâ Consules, Dom. de l'ÉCU, Henry Marionnet, la Ragotière.

JASPER HILL

AUSTRALIA, Victoria, Bendigo

Syrah (Shiraz), Nebbiolo

Riesling, Semillon

If HEATHCOTE has leapt to the forefront as one of the supreme Shiraz-growing regions of Australia in the last ten years, you can hand a fair wodge of the blame to Jasper Hill. And the Laughton family, the owners, only planted their first grapes in 1975. Since then, however, the low-yield crop that goes to make up the 100 per cent Shiraz Georgia's Paddock, and the 95 per cent Shiraz Emily's Paddock (the names are those of the Laughtons' two daughters, by the way) have thrilled the relatively few wine lovers who've managed to get their hands on a bottle. What sets them apart is the startling purity of fruit, absence of intrusive oak, and enormous depth and ripeness – but it's a ripeness which, unlike some of the great Shirazes from places like BAROSSA or MCLAREN VALE, never topples into the stewy, raisiny world of overripeness. And that's why Heathcote and Jasper Hill are so special.

To be honest, in a warm, very dry area like Heathcote, I'm surprised Ron Laughton gets a crop sometimes, because he doesn't irrigate his vines and he employs non-interventionist organic principles in his vineyard. His winemaking, too, is non-interventionist, and these two 'Paddock' wines are profound and beautiful expressions of their place. Oh, I almost forgot. Jasper Hill makes a nice Riesling too, from . Everyone forgets the Riesling.

DOMAINE JAYER-GILLES

FRANCE, Burgundy, Côte de Nuits

Pinot Noir

Pinot Blanc, Chardonnay

This domaine probably makes the most impressive of all the BOURGOGNE-HAUTES-CÔTES wines, with marvellously savoury white Hautes-Côtes de Nuits. However, they also produce sensuous hedonistic ÉCHÉZEAUX and NUITS-ST-GEORGES les Damodes, oaky and exotic but fabulously true to their origins. Gilles Jayer has now taken over from his father Robert. Best years: (top reds) 2002, '01, '00, '99, '98, '97, '96, '95, '93.

JEREZ Y MANZANILLA DO
SPAIN, Andalucía
♀ *Palomino Fino, Palomino de Jerez, Pedro Ximénez, Moscatel*

Real sherry comes from Spain's south-west corner, near Cádiz. Other Spanish regions (Condado de Huelva and MONTILLA-MORILES) make similar wines, but nothing ever reaches true sherry's quality peaks. The best quality grapes from the finest *albariza* – chalk soil – vineyards generally go to make fino and manzanilla, the lightest sherries, fortified to 15.5 per cent alcohol. Both have a characteristic bread yeasty-tangy flavour (even more pronounced in manzanilla) which they develop while aging under a protective layer of flor yeast.

To the English-speaking world, amontillado and oloroso tend simply to mean 'medium' and 'sweet', and such wines sold outside Spain are generally young, cheap and unexceptional. In fact, as made and drunk in Jerez, both are bone dry, as are most of the finer versions exported. Authentic amontillados begin as finos, but are then refortified to between 16 and 18 per cent and aged until they turn tawny-brown and develop a rich, nutty flavour as well as the fino tang. Olorosos are more heavily fortified at the beginning, ending up at between 18 and 20 per cent, and age in contact with the air – without ever growing flor – into richly fragrant, dark, nutty-pruny wines. Palo cortado is an unusual, deliciously nutty, dry style somewhere in between amontillado and oloroso. Cream sherry is generally a concoction of inexpensive oloroso sweetened with concentrated grape juice, and pale cream sherry is cheap fino sweetened.

All sherry has to be aged in barrel for a minimum of three years, but all the really good ones are aged for much longer. As they age, the wines pass through a 'solera system', a complicated form of pre-blending. Only one-quarter of each barrel in the solera is ever drawn off at one time for bottling. The space is filled up with similar but younger wine from another barrel and so on, down a line of four or more. The older wine is freshened by the younger, but the younger takes on the character of the older. Best producers: BARBADILLO, DÍEZ-MÉRITO, DOMECQ, GARVEY, GONZÁLEZ BYASS, HIDALGO, LUSTAU, OSBORNE, VALDESPINO.

JERMANN
ITALY, Friuli-Venezia Giulia, Farra d'Isonzo
♥ *Pinot Noir (Pinot Nero)*
♀ *Chardonnay, Pinot Gris (Pinot Grigio), Ribolla and others*

Probably the most successful wine in modern Friulian history has, year after year, been Silvio Jermann's Vintage Tunina. In 1977 Jermann decided that the way to make a wine of unique character, avoiding the pitfalls of passing fashion, was to blend. Although the proportions may vary, the varieties used in Vintage Tunina are the same every year and, unusually, they are all picked and vinified together: Sauvignon, Chardonnay, Ribolla, Malvasia and Picolit. The fruit must be absolutely clean and ripe, Jermann's idea being to make a wine of complex aroma, with the accent on fruits and flowers, and luscious palate: you'll find peaches, tropical fruits, spices. There is absolutely no wood.

Jermann does not actually disdain the use of wood in the making of whites, as do his legendary neighbours Mario SCHIOPETTO and Vittorio Puiatti, who scorns oak-aging even for red wines. Indeed, some of Jermann's most successful white wines have been 'educated' in oak – examples being the much sought-after, barrique-fermented Chardonnay originally called 'Where the Dreams Have No End' (now, believe it or not, called 'Were Dreams, now it is just wine') and the blended Capo Martino, aged in Slavonian and Czech *botti*. Jermann also makes a range of varietal wines, of which the Pinot Bianco is perhaps the most consistently successful, and the Moscato Rosa the most unusual. Best years: 2001, '99, '98, '97, '96, '95, '94.

JERMANN
Although based in the Collio zone, Silvio Jermann produces only vino da tavola wines. His varietal whites include the very successful Pinot Bianco.

JOHANNISBERG
GERMANY, Rheingau

There are three Johannisbergs, the Bereich, the town and the Schloss, and it is the last that has brought fame to the other two. The Bereich covers the whole of the RHEINGAU. The town has other vineyards as well as its famous eponymous Schloss: there is the Klaus, the Hölle, Mittelhölle and Hansenberg among others, but none has the reputation of Schloss Johannisberg. During the 1980s and '90s, the quality of the wines from the Schloss was a rollercoaster ride, more down than up but by the end of the 1990s there were reassuring signs that the winery is on the road to recapturing past glories. Best years: 2002, '01, '99, '98, '97, '96, '93, '90. Best producers: Prinz von Hessen, JOHANNISHOF, Schloss Johannisberg.

JOHANNISHOF
GERMANY, Rheingau, Johannisberg
♀ *Riesling, Pinot Blanc (Weissburgunder)*

The Eser family currently make the finest Riesling in JOHANNISBERG and these are wines truly worthy of the town's reputation for making the most sophisticated and subtle wines in the RHEINGAU. In 1996 the Esers took a big leap into deep water by adding 4.5ha (11 acres) of vineyards in RÜDESHEIM to their 13ha (32 acres) in Johannisberg, GEISENHEIM and Winkel. These are wines of crystalline clarity and individuality. Best years: 2001, '99, '98, '97, '95, '94, '93, '92, '90, '89, '86, '83, '76, '75.

KARL-HEINZ JOHNER
GERMANY, Baden, Bischoffingen
♥ *Pinot Noir (Spätburgunder) and others*
♀ *Pinot Gris (Grauburgunder), Pinot Blanc (Weissburgunder), Müller-Thurgau (Rivaner), Chardonnay and others*

This BADEN producer specialises in new oak-aged wines. The vividly fruity Pinot Noir and Pinot Blanc are excellent, and the Chardonnay SJ is one of Germany's best examples of this varietal, and the rich, silky Pinot Noir SJ can be one of Germany's finest reds. For many years he was the winemaker at Lamberhurst in England, and in 1985 he started off with a mere 0.75ha (1.9 acres) in Bischoffingen. Best years: (Pinot Noir SJ) 2002, '01, '00, '99, '98, '97, '96, '93, '90.

JORDAN
SOUTH AFRICA, Western Cape, Stellenbosch WO
♥ *Cabernet Sauvignon, Merlot, Cabernet Franc*
♀ *Chardonnay*

Two thinks strike you about Jordan winery. Firstly, a strong sense of family – you can feel the close-knit community of the place – and secondly a quiet, thought-out determination and focus on clear but achievable objectives, which shows in the wines, in that the flavours are careful, considered, evenly balanced and polished rather than flamboyant and gaudy.

Chardonnay, Cabernet, Merlot and BORDEAUX blend Cobblers Hill are always good, but I'd just like them to let their hair down a little bit more. They have 80ha (198 acres) of increasingly mature vines at the head of the lovely Stellenbosch Kloof valley, with every conceivable aspect to the sun, and I'd like a few more of those nuances to show in the wines. Sold under the Jardin label in the USA. Best years: (Chardonnay) 2001, '00, '99, '98, '97, '96.

JORDAN VINEYARD

USA, California, Sonoma County, Alexander Valley AVA
♟ *Cabernet Sauvignon, Merlot*
♀ *Chardonnay*

When efforts to buy a BORDEAUX château were rebuffed, Colorado oil explorer Tom Jordan decided to build his own château in the ALEXANDER VALLEY. Developing 101ha (250 acres), Jordan has even achieved a touch of Bordeaux in his Cabernet-Merlot which usually has an attractive cedar and leaf-green streak – but is very un-Bordeaux-like in its lush, easy-to-enjoy texture. His attempts to create a similarly attractive Chardonnay were rewarded after he started using cool-climate RUSSIAN RIVER fruit. J fizz is an attractive mouthful now made independently by Judy Jordan's J Wine Co. Best years: (Cabernet) 2001, '00, '99, '97, '96, '95, '94, '91, '86.

TONI JOST

GERMANY, Mittelrhein, Bacharach
♟ *Pinot Noir (Spätburgunder)*
♀ *Riesling*

Owner Peter Jost has a foot in two camps: as well as vineyards at BACHARACH and Steeg in the MITTELRHEIN he also owns some at Walluf and Martinsthal, some distance away in the RHEINGAU. The Spätburgunder comes from Walluf and, like the Jost Rieslings, sees no new wood during the winemaking process; all the casks are old and neutral. Though delicious young, the Rieslings are worth aging for a few years. The reds should

be drunk young. Bacharacher Hahn Rieslings have splendidly steely and concentrated fruit. Best years: (Riesling Spätlese) 2002, '01, '99, '98, '97, '96, '94, '93, '92, '90, '89.

J P VINHOS

PORTUGAL, Setúbal DOC, Terras do Sado Vinho Regional, Alentejano Vinho Regional, Estremadura Vinho Regional
♟ *Terras do Sado/Palmela: Castelão, Tempranillo (Aragonez), Touriga Nacional, Cabernet Sauvignon, Merlot and others; Alentejo: Tempranillo (Aragonez), Alfrocheiro, Trincadeira, Syrah, Touriga Nacional and others; Estremadura: Castelão, Tempranillo (Aragonez), Tinta Miuda*
♀ *Setúbal: Moscatel de Setúbal, Moscatel Roxo; Terras do Sado/Palmela: Fernão Pires, Moscatel de Setúbal, Chardonnay and others*

J P (alias João Pires) Vinhos is the brainchild of entrepreneur António Avillez. He was aided early on by Australian winemaker Peter BRIGHT, who developed an eclectic range of wines from different parts of the country, and the 'New World' influence remains. J P's mainstay in the João Pires brand is an aromatic off-dry white based on the local Muscat grape. More upmarket wines include reds Quinta da Bacalhôa (a BORDEAUX-style blend), Tinto da Ânfora, a rich, leathery ALENTEJO red and SÓ Syrah. There is also a barrel-fermented Chardonnay, Cova da Ursa.

JULIÉNAS AC

FRANCE, Burgundy, Beaujolais, Beaujolais cru
♟ *Gamay*

Juliénas is rather a serious name; the school prefect rather than the tearaway among the BEAUJOLAIS crus. The flavour often reflects that too. It frequently lacks the happy-fruit style which we think of as Beaujolais' calling-card but what it does have is enough weight and strength to develop a distinct spiciness with age. There are 606ha (1497 acres), producing about 4.5 million bottles a year. Best years: 2002, '00, '99, '98. Best producers: G Descombes, DUBOEUF, P Granger, Ch. de Juliénas, J-P Margerand, R Monnet, Pelletier, B Santé.

JUMILLA DO

SPAIN, Murcia and Castilla-La Mancha
♟ ♀ *Mourvèdre (Monastrell), Grenache (Garnacha Tintorera), Tempranillo (Cencibel), Merlot, Cabernet Sauvignon, Syrah*
♀ *Airén, Macabeo, Pedro Ximénez, Malvasía*

Jumilla's speciality has long been big, dark, old-fashioned, alcoholic reds for blending with weedy wines from elsewhere. About 80 per cent of the wine still goes for blending, mainly

to central Europe. Monastrell, alias Mourvèdre, the main grape, has huge potential that is finally being exploited, thanks to much improved winemaking techniques and equipment. A little dull white wine is made, and some rosé. Some bodegas have been improving their facilities in recent years, installing cooling equipment and insulating tanks, so things are looking up and we are sure to see a growing flow of affordable, tasty reds. Best years: 2001, '00, '99, '98, '96. Best producers: Bleda, Casa de la Ermita, Silvano García, Induvasa (Finca Luzón), Agapito Rico, Casa de Castillo, San Isidro co-operative.

JURA

FRANCE

The Jura is a large and beautiful area of France running south along the Swiss border between ALSACE and Lake Geneva. Although many of the Jura wines have a unique character, vineyards are scattered and occupy only a tiny fraction of the region. The main regional AC is CÔTES DU JURA, with ARBOIS, CHÂTEAU-CHALON, l'ÉTOILE and CRÉMANT DU JURA the others. The region is much better known for its hills and rich pasture for cattle and also for being the home of Pernod. During the nineteenth century large quantities of absinthe were made here; Anis is the modern, tamed-down version.

JURANÇON AC

FRANCE, South-West
♀ *Petit Manseng, Gros Manseng, Petit Courbu*

Historically, Jurançon in the western Pyrenees has always been known for its sweet white wine. After a period of perilous survival, the vineyards have expanded to over 1000ha (2470 acres) and today it is an area that produces exquisite, late-harvested sweet wines and refreshing dry white Jurançon Sec. The wine is made mostly from the excellent Petit Manseng and the not-quite-so-good Gros Manseng and can be crisp and refreshing or lusciously sweet and spicy.

Dry whites can be ageworthy, but from one of the independent growers, the sweet wine can be heavenly. The growers leave the Petit Manseng grapes on the vines till late November – when they become shrivelled and thick with sugar – and then slowly ferment the juice. The wine is then left for a couple of years to age in oak barrels until it develops a lusciousness of honey, nuts and mangoes, spiced with cinnamon, cloves and ginger cut by a pure laser streak of lemon acidity. Nowadays, a greater percentage of new oak barrels is being used.

TONI JOST
The Mittelrhein's leading estate makes delicious, racy, attractively ripe Rieslings from the Bacharacher Hahn vineyard, including exotic, fruity and honeyed Auslese.

Best years: (sweet) 2001, '00, '99, '98, '96, '95. Best producers: Bellegarde, Bru-Baché, Castera, CAUHAPÉ, Clos Lapeyre, Clos Thou, CLOS UROULAT, Larrédya, de Souch.

JUVÉ Y CAMPS
SPAIN, Cataluña, Cava DO, Penedès DO
🍷 *Cabernet Sauvignon, Pinot Noir, Merlot*
🍷 *Pinot Noir*
🥂 *Parellada, Macabeo, Xarel-lo, Chardonnay*

Quality is very good in this most traditional family-owned PENEDÈS company, known for its CAVA fizz. The winemaker uses only free-run (unpressed) juice, both for the Cava, and the still white wine, which is made in much smaller quantities. With quality in mind, fermentation is done in small, temperature-controlled, stainless steel tanks. All the *remuage* is done by hand for the sparklers. Reserva de la Familia Extra Brut is the best in the sparkling wine range, soft and honeyed. The company is now self-sufficient in grapes. Apart from the traditional Penedès trio of Parellada, Macabeo and Xarel-lo, Juvé y Camps' vineyards are planted with Chardonnay, Cabernet Sauvignon and Pinot Noir, which the family uses for still wines under the Casa Vella d'Espiells and Miranda d'Espiells labels.

KAISERSTUHL
GERMANY, Baden

This wine region is one of BADEN's best. The name means Emperor's Throne and comes from an ancient volcano whose lower slopes provide some of the warmest vineyard land in all Germany. Storms frequently edge their way around this tephrite mass, leaving it as an island of sunshine. This is often too hot for Riesling, but ideal for the 'Burgunder' or Pinot family of grapes: Spätburgunder (Pinot Noir), Weissburgunder (Pinot Blanc), Grauburgunder (Pinot Gris) and also Chardonnay. In a good vintage 13 degrees of natural alcohol and the richness to go with it are easy to achieve. Best years: (dry whites) 2002, '01, '00, '99, '98, '97, '96, '93. Best producers: BERCHER, Bickensohl co-operative, Dr HEGER, K-H JOHNER, KELLER, Konigsschaffhausen co-op, Salwey.

KAMPTAL
AUSTRIA, Niederösterreich

This predominantly white wine region with 3867ha (9555 acres) of vines is centred around the pretty wine town of LANGENLOIS, just north of the town of Krems on the Danube. The majority of the wine is light- and medium-bodied dry Grüner Veltliner for drinking early, but in the hands of the region's dynamic young growers Riesling, Chardonnay and Weissburgunder (Pinot Blanc) are all capable of giving serious, intense dry wines with good aging potential. Blauburgunder (Pinot Noir), Zweigelt and St-Laurent can give good wines here, but other noble red grapes struggle to ripen fully in this coolish climate. Best years: 2001, '00, '99, '98, '97, '95, '94, '93. Best producers: BRÜNDLMAYER, Ehn, Hiedler, Josef Hirsch, Fred Loimer, Schloss Gobelsburg.

KANONKOP
SOUTH AFRICA, Western Cape, Stellenbosch WO
🍷 *Cabernet Sauvignon, Pinotage, Merlot and others*

This exclusively red wine farm is run by Johan and Paul Krige with the characterful Beyers Truter as winemaker since 1981. His wines have won many prizes both locally and internationally. Many old vines continue to yield well, including some of the first commercially planted Pinotage. Truter is one of the variety's most vociferous advocates and one of the driving forces behind the Pinotage Producers' Association, a body set up to improve the quality of the Cape's own grape. There is now plenty of competition for this farm's renowned Pinotage. Both the standard and Auction Reserve are aged in new oak.

However, the BORDEAUX blend Paul Sauer is arguably the flagship wine and its austere concentration derives much from many older vines. The varietal Cabernet Sauvignon does not seem to achieve the same punchy layers. Truter and the Kriges also join forces at nearby Beyerskloof, where Truter makes a striking Cabernet blend as well as a juicy Pinotage that is the epitome of young quaffable red. The substantial quantities made necessitate buying in grapes, although the first crop from home vineyards was harvested in 1998. Best years: (Paul Sauer) 1999, '98, '97, '96, '95, '94, '92, '91.

KANONKOP
The Bordeaux blend Paul Sauer, named after Kanonkop's founder, is the flagship wine from this exclusively red wine estate.

KANZEM
GERMANY, Mosel-Saar-Ruwer

This oft-forgotten SAAR commune has some of the best vineyards on the entire river, most notably the south-east-facing slope of the Altenberg, a Riesling 'Grand Cru' if ever there was one. The favoured conditions here result in wines with a less piercing acidity than normal for the area and a wonderful white peach bouquet. Best years: 2002, '01, '99, '97, '95, '94, '93, '90. Best producers: von KESSELSTATT, von Othegraven, J P Reinert.

KARLSMÜHLE
GERMANY, Mosel-Saar-Ruwer, Mertesdorf
🍷 *Pinot Noir (Spätburgunder)*
🥂 *Riesling and others*

Peter Geiben may look like he has just come in from the fields, and his Karlsmühle hotel may bear an unintentional resemblance to Fawlty Towers, but there is no arguing about the high quality of his Rieslings or their modest prices. Confusingly, he has two estates in the RUWER Valley: Karlsmühle, most of whose wines come from his wholly-owned Lorenzhöfer site, and Patheiger, most of whose wines are from the excellent Kehrnagel and Nies'chen sites of KASEL. There are plenty of dry wines, many of which are good, as well as superb Auslese and Eiswein dessert wines. Best years: 2002, '01, '99, '98, '97, '95, '94, '93, '90, '89.

KARTHÄUSERHOF
GERMANY, Mosel-Saar-Ruwer, Trier
🥂 *Riesling, Pinot Blanc (Weissburgunder)*

A former Carthusian monastery, but when Napoleon separated the Church from its land the current owner's ancestor moved in. The estate's considerable reputation for marvellously steely yet ripe Rieslings had sadly slumped by the 1980s, but a new generation of the family, Christof Tyrell, took charge with the 1986 vintage and has restored the estate to its former greatness. The wines, from the Eitelsbacher Karthäuserhofberg, are on top form, even at QbA level, and almost equal to the other great RUWER estate, von Schubert at MAXIMIN GRÜNHAUS. Best years: 2002, '01, '99, '97, '96, '95, '94, '93, '90, '89, '88.

KASEL
GERMANY, Mosel-Saar-Ruwer

This small village in the RUWER Valley is blessed with two of the best vineyards in the entire region and a handful of producers who turn this potential into aromatic, racy Riesling wines. Those from the Kehrnagel site are slightly leaner with more piercing acidity; those from the Nies'chen are richer and more gentle. Both have a distinctive blackcurrant (berry and leaf) aroma, and can age for a decade or more. Best years: 2002, '01, '99, '97, '95, '94, '93, '90, '89. Best producers: von Beulwitz, Bischöfliche Weingüter, KARLSMÜHLE, von KESSELSTATT.

KATNOOK ESTATE

AUSTRALIA, South Australia, Coonawarra
❢ *Cabernet Sauvignon, Syrah (Shiraz), Merlot*
♀ *Sauvignon Blanc, Chardonnay, Riesling*

Katnook is one part of the Wingara Wine Group, which owns large vineyards in COONAWARRA (as well as being the largest contract grapegrower) and Deakin Estate in the Murray Darling and it also processes a great many tonnes of grapes into juice or newly fermented wine.

The Katnook Riesling is the most powerful and concentrated of its kind in the area. The Sauvignon Blanc is that Australian rarity – a really tangy, green-tasting mouthful; the Chardonnay is long-lived and herbal with melon flavours, and the Cabernet Sauvignon after a period when the fruit was too meagre, has now recovered the dry blackcurrant intensity of fine Coonawarra Cabernet. Odyssey Cabernet and Prodigy Shiraz are the flagship reds. Best years: (Odyssey) 2000, '99, '98, '97, '96, '94, '92, '91.

KELLER

GERMANY, Rheinhessen, Flörsheim-Dalsheim
❢ *Pinot Noir (Spätburgunder)*
♀ *Riesling, Pinot Gris (Grauburgunder), Pinot Blanc (Weissburgunder), Silvaner, Rieslaner, Huxelrebe*

In the middle of nowhere up in the hill country of RHEINHESSEN the Keller family have built up one of the region's best estates. Although their Rieslings up to Auslese level lack the sophistication of those from NACKENHEIM or NIERSTEIN, they are full of fruit and beautifully made. The Riesling and Rieslaner dessert wines are spectacular, and the dry Weissburgunder and Grauburgunder perhaps the best examples of these styles in the region. Best years: (Riesling Auslese) 2002, '01, '99, '98, '97, '95.

KENDALL-JACKSON

USA, California, Sonoma County, Alexander Valley AVA
❢ *Merlot, Cabernet Sauvignon, Zinfandel, Pinot Noir, Syrah*
♀ *Chardonnay, Sauvignon Blanc*

Kendall-Jackson started in 1981 and is now one of CALIFORNIA's largest producers of barrel-fermented Chardonnay (in competition with SONOMA's CLOS DU BOIS, and NAPA's BERINGER and Robert MONDAVI). Its popular Vintner's Reserve Chardonnay, which drove the early success of the business, owes much of its crowd-pleasing style to more than a hint of sweetness – adding body and instant appeal though the trade-off is the loss of any thirst-quenching character the wine might have had.

For its other wines, notably its deluxe Grand Reserve Chardonnay, Merlot and Zinfandel, the winery is out to impress, though a certain exaggerated plumpness dilutes the focus of their fruit.

Nowadays, you may find yourself drinking a Kendall-Jackson wine without realizing it. That MATANZAS CREEK Merlot you're enjoying? It's a Kendall-Jackson wine now. The LA CREMA Pinot Noir? Kendall-Jackson. What about Yangarra Park? It's a good drop, it's Australian – and it's Kendall-Jackson's. As is Tapiz in Argentina, Calina in Chile and Villa Arceno in CHIANTI (that's Italy: real Chianti). The recent focus at Kendall-Jackson has been to acquire properties and vineyards, mostly in the USA, so that the company or the family now own 21 different labels. And only one of them is called Kendall-Jackson.

KENWOOD VINEYARDS

USA, California, Sonoma County, Sonoma Valley AVA
❢ *Cabernet Sauvignon, Zinfandel, Pinot Noir, Merlot*
❢ *Zinfandel*
♀ *Sauvignon Blanc, Chardonnay, Gewurztraminer*

When the Lee family acquired the old Pagani Brothers winery in 1970 the transformation was immediate. A friendly old rustic neighbourhood jug winery was hauled into the vanguard of CALIFORNIA winemaking, in particular leading the way with Sauvignon Blanc, a variety California has never felt truly happy with. Ripe, supple Chardonnays followed, two of them from individual vineyards called Beltane and Yulupa. The Cabernet Sauvignons tend to be tannic, especially the Jack London Vineyard and flagship Artist Series bottlings but efforts have been made to tone these down recently. Kenwood Zinfandels, several vineyard-designated, may be best of all, each one rich, juicy, spicy – and a perfect evocation of the variety's blackberry fruit. New Massara Merlot combines complexity and subtlety. Gary Heck, already a shareholder and owner of Korbel and Valley of the Moon Winery, acquired Kenwood in 1998. Best years: (Zinfandel) 2001, '00, '99, '98, '97, '96, '95, '94.

REICHSGRAF VON KESSELSTATT

GERMANY, Mosel-Saar-Ruwer, Trier
♀ *Riesling*

This huge MOSEL-SAAR-RUWER company has four estates, all planted with Riesling. Much of the wine is *trocken* or *halbtrocken* in style. With so many different vineyards to choose from, it is difficult to generalize about the house style, save to say that it is modern, focused, but on the soft side and ready for early consumption (though as with all good Mosel wine, it will age successfully). The wines from the wholly owned Josephshöfer site in GRAACH are usually the best, RK is their blend of SAAR and RUWER Riesling. Best years: (Riesling Spätlese) 2002, '01, '99, '98, '97, '96, '95, '94, '93.

KIEDRICH

GERMANY, Rheingau

This beautiful old RHEINGAU village in the hills above Eltville has a Gothic church that was restored in the nineteenth century by an Englishman, John Sutton. The vineyards are relatively high so they need a decent sunny year to produce grapes showing their full character, and in lesser years they can lack distinction. The best sites are Gräfenberg and Wasseros. Best years: (Riesling Spätlese and Auslese) 2002, '01, '99, '98, '97, '96, '95, '94, '93, '92, '90. Best producers: Baron zu Knyphausen, Robert WEIL.

KING ESTATE

USA, Oregon
❢ *Pinot Noir*
♀ *Pinot Gris*

For the first years after the establishment in 1992 of King Estate in a large clearing in the forest at Lorane near Eugene, the most significant activity was that of its nursery Lorane Grapevines, because you could grow vine rootstocks happily enough here but I wasn't at all certain you could ripen grapes. Maybe the fact that it was 8km (5 miles) outside the WILLAMETTE VALLEY AVA was a comment on the suitability of local climate and soil. Whatever, the gaudy *folie de grandeur* 'château' and its superbly equipped winery were not matched by the quality of wine from the vast vineyard (95ha/235 acres planted so far). But they did make good wine from bought-in grapes, and with strict selection in the vineyard there is also now some good Reserve Pinot Noir (the Domaine bottling is a selection of the best barrels from estate fruit) and some delightful Pinot Gris. Best years (Reserve Pinot Noir) 2001, '99, '98, '96.

KING VALLEY

AUSTRALIA, Victoria

The fertile soils and equable climate of the beautiful King Valley lured Italian farmers forming part of the post-World War Two emigration, who quickly established a thriving tobacco industry. However, in 1970, before the storm clouds had formed over tobacco-growing, two Australian farmers decided to plant vines; immediately and spectacularly successful, they were eagerly followed by their Italian neighbours.

BROWN BROTHERS played a key role in that success, and for the next 20 years the King Valley was virtually a Brown bailiwick. Since then, plantings have increased rapidly and the 14,000 tonnes produced in the region find purchasers, large and small, across Australia. Initially relatively high yields diluted the fruit character but yields are now dropping and fruit quality is greatly improving. Chardonnay, Riesling, Cabernet Sauvignon and Merlot are the most successful, and, other than Brown Brothers and Miranda, there are a number of small wineries now established in the King Valley. Best producers: BROWN BROTHERS, Dal Zotto, Miranda, Symphonia. Best years: 2000, '99, '98, '94, '92, '91.

KIONA

USA, Washington State, Yakima Valley AVA

♥ Cabernet Sauvignon, Merlot, Lemberger, Syrah, Sangiovese

♀ Riesling, Chardonnay, Chenin Blanc, Gewurztraminer

A small operation in sagebrush country, Kiona has a reputation for its barrel-fermented Chardonnay, big, full Cabernet Sauvignon and delightful dry Rieslings. However, it also deserves praise for persevering with Lemberger – making a delightful herb- and blackberry-scented wine – and for outstanding late-harvest whites, notably Chenin Blanc, Riesling and Gewurztraminer. Best years: (late-harvest wines) 2000, '99, '97.

KISTLER VINEYARDS

USA, California, Sonoma County, Sonoma Valley AVA

♥ Pinot Noir

♀ Chardonnay

Once one of the best-kept secrets within CALIFORNIA, Kistler was originally located at the end of a tortuous road high in the Maya-camas Mountains overlooking SONOMA VALLEY. While retaining this original vineyard, known as Kistler Estate, the owners moved into a bigger winery in the RUSSIAN RIVER VALLEY, and developed the Vine Hill vineyard

nearby. Winemaker Mark Bixler, working with the Kistler brothers, has earned a reputation for Chardonnays that at their best combine the depth of top California Chardonnay with the balance, finesse and nerve of fine white Burgundy. In addition to the Kistler Vineyard Chardonnay, other vineyard bottlings are Vine Hill, McCrea, Dutton Ranch, Durell and the ultra-cool-climate Camp Meeting Ridge. In the 1990s, Kistler dropped Cabernet Sauvignon production and focused attention on Pinot Noir made from Russian River Valley sites. Early vintages have yielded full flavours and balance. Best years: (Kistler Vineyard Chardonnay) 2002, '01, '00, '99, '98, '97, '95, '94, '91, '90.

KLEIN CONSTANTIA

SOUTH AFRICA, Western Cape, Constantia WO

♥ Cabernet Sauvignon, Merlot, Syrah (Shiraz) and others

♀ Sauvignon Blanc, Chardonnay, Riesling (Rhine/Weisser Riesling), Muscat Blanc à Petits Grains (Muscat de Frontignan/Muscadel)

This is part of the original CONSTANTIA estate that was famous throughout Europe in the eighteenth and nineteenth centuries for the dessert wine of the same name. Klein Constantia was the first producer in the twentieth century to resurrect a similar style of unfortified wine made from Muscat de Frontignan, and demand for this luscious Vin de Constance has led to further plantings.

In 1980, the Jooste family rescued the farm from alien vegetation and creeping urbanization and replanted the land. The first vintage (1986) yielded a striking Sauvignon Blanc, which owed much to winemaker Ross Gower's experience gained at Corbans in New Zealand; it shot the estate to fame and established a reputation for whites at least which has not dimmed since. Whites in general have performed consistently in this relatively cool region, but reds have struggled to ripen. New warmer vineyards in STELLENBOSCH should help. Best years: (Vin de Constance) 1997, '96, '95, '94, '93, '92, '91, '90.

KLEIN CONSTANTIA

With concentrated flavours of dried peach, apricot and honey, Vin de Constance is a reincarnation of a famous historic sweet wine from Muscat de Frontignan.

KNAPPSTEIN

AUSTRALIA, South Australia, Clare Valley

♥ Pinot Noir, Cabernet Sauvignon, merlot, Malbecm Syrah (Shiraz)

♀ Sauvignon Blanc, Chardonnay, Semillon, Gewurztraminer

Knappstein has now been well and truly subsumed into owner PETALUMA's group structure; to emphasize the change 'Tim' has been dropped from the label, and Petaluma stalwart Andrew Hardy took charge of wine-making in 1996. The best wine is the Riesling, often high-toned when young, but developing serenely over many years. An elegant, mildly herbal Cabernet-Merlot, faintly foresty Shiraz and premium Enterprise Cabernet Sauvignon and Shiraz are among many releases, some of which incorporate a percentage of ADELAIDE HILLS fruit, sourced via Petaluma's numerous vineyards and contracts in that area. Best years: (Enterprise) 2001, '00, '99, '98, '97.

EMMERICH KNOLL

AUSTRIA, Niederösterreich, Wachau, Unterloiben

♀ Grüner Veltliner, Riesling, Chardonnay (Feinburgunder), Muscat (Muskateller)

Three generations of Knolls, all called Emmerich, are responsible for the unique dry Riesling and Grüner Veltliner wines which this small 9-ha (22-acre) WACHAU estate produces. These are some of the most minerally and long-living white wines in all of Austria, tight and unyielding when young, but blossoming into idiosyncratic beauties with bottle age. The most extraordinary of these are the concentrated, spicy wines from the Schütt site in DÜRNSTEIN and the sleeker, but no less powerful wines from the Loibenberg site above Unterloiben. The rich dry Riesling from the Kellerberg site of Dürnstein is a new addition to the range. Best years: (Riesling Smaragd) 2002, '01, '00, '99, '98, '97, '96, '95, '94, '93, '92, '90.

KOEHLER-RUPRECHT

GERMANY, Pfalz, Kallstadt

♥ Pinot Noir (Spätburgunder), Cabernet Sauvignon, Dornfelder

♀ Riesling, Pinot Blanc (Weissburgunder), Chardonnay, Pinot Gris (Grauburgunder) and others

Bernd Philippi is the larger than life wine-making genius behind two ranges of wines. The Koehler-Ruprecht wines are made in an uncompromisingly traditional manner with wild yeast fermentations that last up to an entire year in large wooden casks. The result, particularly in the case of the Rieslings from the great Kallstadter Saumagen vineyard, is dry and dessert wines of enormous power that need several years of body-building in the bottle before they emerge as the Mr Universe of German wines. The wines sold under the Philippi name are all vinified in a non-traditional, international style. Best of these are the Spätburgunders, the closest thing to Grand Cru red BURGUNDY produced in Germany. The 'Elysium' is an YQUEM look-alike, and the Pinot Blanc and Pinot Gris are among the best barrique-aged German whites. There is great sparkling wine, too. Best years: (reds) 2002, '01, '99, '98, '97, '96, '95, '93, '90, '89, '88; (whites) 2002, '01, '00, '99, '98, '97, '96, '95, '93, '90, '89, '88.

DOMAINE KOKOTOS

GREECE, Attica, Stamata

🍷 *Agiorgitiko, Cabernet Sauvignon*

🍷 *Agiorgitiko*

🍷 *Savatiano, Chardonnay, Moschofilero*

In 1979 Englishwoman Anne Kokotos persuaded her hotelier husband to plant their estate on the northern slopes of Mount Pendeli north of Athens with vines. They now have 7ha (17 acres) of Savatiano, Chardonnay, Sauvignon and Cabernet as well as such oddballs (for Greece) as Riesling. This area was known only for bulk wine before the couple arrived, but their work has persuaded Attican growers that the traditionally derided Savatiano can make serious wine. They also make wines under the Chateau Semeli name, including Roditis from the northern Peloponnese. Best years: (reds) 2001, '00, '97, '96, '95, '92.

KOLLWENTZ

AUSTRIA, Burgenland, Neusiedlersee-Hügelland, Grosshöflein

🍷 *Blaufränkisch, Blauer Zweigelt, Cabernet Sauvignon*

🍷 *Chardonnay, Sauvignon Blanc, Welschriesling*

The town of Grosshöflein lacks the kind of centuries-old winemaking traditions that nearby RUST enjoys, but ambitious Anton Kollwentz and his charming son Andi have more than made up for this with new ideas and winemaking skills. They are best known for their Cabernet Sauvignon, which has a genuine blackcurrant and smoke character, and is probably the best example of this grape from BURGENLAND. Steinzeiler is a successful blend of Cabernet and local grapes with rich fruit, toasty oak and good tannins. Both can age very well. The dry whites tend to be a little clinical. Best is the nettle and gooseberry Sauvignon Blanc. Good dessert wines, too. Best years: 2001, '00, '99, '97, '94, '93, '90.

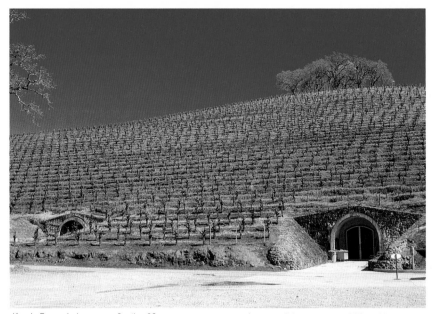

Kunde Estate belongs to a family of Sonoma grape growers who revived the winery in 1990 and became overnight successes. The magnificent aging cellars are dug into the hillside beneath a Chardonnay vineyard.

ALOIS KRACHER

AUSTRIA, Burgenland, Neusiedlersee, Illmitz

🍷 *Blauer Zweigelt*

🍷 *Chardonnay, Welschriesling, Scheurebe, Gewürztraminer (Traminer), Muscat (Muskat Ottonel), Bouvier*

'Here, like everywhere else, the best wines come from the hills,' Kracher told me, gesturing towards the vineyards of Illmitz which lie upon rises a metre or two above reed beds and ponds at the edge of Lake Neusiedl.

It might seem crazy, but his words are true, and in his hands they give some of the world's most luxurious dessert wines. The Zwischen den Seen (between the lakes) wines are vinified in old acacia barrels on their lees, while the Nouvelle Vague (new-wave) wines ferment and mature in barriques like SAUTERNES. In a great vintage like 1995, Kracher makes up to 15 different Trockenbeerenauslese wines in quantities that make his German colleagues green with envy. The Scheurebe is lusciously exotic with breathtaking acidity, the Chardonnay-Welschriesling as grand and opulent as any top Sauternes, the Traminer rich and imposing and the Muskat-Ottonel ravishingly citric. The Bouvier Beerenauslese is Kracher's cheapest dessert wine, and though less exciting has plenty of dried fruits character – the 'Grand Cuvée' is what he describes as the 'representative' wine of each vintage. He does make dry white and red but it is because of his sweeties that he has become one of the most

famous winemakers in the world. Best years: (whites) 2002, '01, '00, '99, '98, '96, '95, '94, '93, '91, '89, '86, '81.

KREMSTAL

AUSTRIA, Niederösterreich

This small wine region straddles the river Danube around the town of Krems. The best vineyards – Stein and Senftenberg in Krems – give dry white wines with a similar combination of power and elegance to those of the WACHAU. This is not surprising, since the vineyards here are also narrow terraces on steep hillsides with stony soils and the Grüner Veltliner and Riesling grapes dominate. The heavier soils elsewhere in the region give generous, juicy wines – less subtle and quicker developing. Best years: 2002, '01, '00, '99, '98, '97, '95, '94, '93. Best producers: Mantlerhof, Sepp Moser, Nigl, NIKOLAIHOF, Franz Proidl, Salomon-Undhof.

KREYDENWEISS

FRANCE, Alsace, Alsace AC

🍷 *Pinot Noir*

🍷 *Riesling, Pinot Blanc, Pinot Gris, Gewurztraminer, Muscat*

Based in Andlau, far from the more southerly heartland of Alsace, Marc Kreydenweiss is one of the region's most skilful and original winemakers, occasionally experimenting with fermentation in barriques. Although his 12ha (30 acres), which are biodynamically cultivated, only yield about 60,000 bottles each

MARC KREYDENWEISS

Mark Kreydenweiss is one of the great innovators of Alsace. Le Clos du Val d'Eleon is a remarkable blend of Riesling and Pinot Gris from a single vineyard.

year, Kreydenweiss keeps his various terroirs separate, with intriguing bottles from no fewer than three Grands Crus: Kastelberg, Moenchberg and Wiebelsberg. For some palates Kreydenweiss's style can be too austere and acidic, but with time the wines expand into full-flavoured and complex expressions of grape and soil. The rare late-harvest wines can be quite exceptional. Best years: 2000, '99, '98, '97, '96, '95, '94, '93, '90, '89, '88, '85.

KRUG
FRANCE, Champagne, Champagne AC
♀ ❦ Pinot Noir, Chardonnay, Pinot Meunier

Well, I never thought they'd do it. LVMH, the people who make Louis Vuitton luggage, Christian Dior perfume, Hennessy Cognac as well as CHAMPAGNE like MOËT and VEUVE CLICQUOT, have changed the style of Krug. I mean they can if they want, I suppose: they do own it. But why? It's still a fine Champagne, but it now tastes relatively like many of the other top fizzes instead of being gloriously, uniquely, idiosyncratically, brazenly different.

The Grande Cuvée was always weightier, more thoughtful, the kind of bottle you could open when you've just solved Fermat's last theorem rather than won a Formula One race. Now it's younger, brighter, breezier; it chortles its froth at you in the glass when you want its bubbles to spiral like the DNA double-helix. I suppose the least we could do is age the bottles a few years ourselves now, and give them a bit of gravitas through maturity. The blend is made up of as many as 50 different wines from up to 25 different villages by the way, and traditionally utilizes perhaps eight different vintages. Krug also makes fine Vintage, rosé and amazingly expensive single-vineyard Clos du Mesnil Blanc de Blancs. I do hope LVMH leaves these alone. Best years: 1990, '89, '88, '85, '82, '81, '79.

KUENTZ-BAS
FRANCE, Alsace, Alsace AC
❦ Pinot Noir
♀ Pinot Blanc, Gewurztraminer, Riesling, Pinot Gris, Muscat, Chardonnay

These wines from their own 11-ha (27-acre) estate and from contract growers can be somewhat inexpressive in their youth, but age extremely well. The Collection and Special Cuvée wines are superb. Kuentz-Bas believes in the Sigillé system, a seal of approval attached to the neck of the bottle and awarded after a locally based wine competition. Also worth looking out for are the Grand Cru bottlings from Eichberg and Pfersigberg, as well as the intense and costly late-harvest wines. Best years: 2000, '98, '97, '96, '95, '94, '93, '90, '89, '88, '85.

KUMEU/HUAPAI
NEW ZEALAND, North Island

This attractive rural area north-west of Auckland is home to 11 winemakers, although two (Kim Crawford and Selaks) do not make wine from grapes grown in their region. Heavy loam and clay soils and a high risk of autumn rain traditionally made this a relatively unfashionable area. Many of the wineries import grapes from other regions, especially GISBORNE, HAWKES BAY and MARLBOROUGH. Careful site selection and viticultural techniques have been necessary to control excessive vigour in this often damp climate. KUMEU RIVER Chardonnay and Harrier Rise Merlot clearly demonstrate the quality potential of the Kumeu/Huapai area. Best years: (reds) 2002, '01, '00, '99, '98, '96, '94, '93. Best producers: COOPERS CREEK, Harrier Rise, Kumeu River, MATUA VALLEY, NOBILO.

KUMEU RIVER
NEW ZEALAND, North Island, Kumeu
❦ Pinot Noir, Merlot, Malbec
♀ Chardonnay, Pinot Gris and others

Michael Brajkovich of Kumeu River was the first New Zealander to pass the prestigious Master of Wine exam, as well as the man who

KUMEU RIVER

Remarkably intense Chardonnay, with pronounced barrel-fermented and malolactic-influenced flavours, is one of Kumeu River's most obvious successes.

introduced many of the classic Burgundian and BORDEAUX winemaking methods into New Zealand. As a result, despite the KUMEU vineyards being located north-west of Auckland on heavy clay soils and handicapped by a humid climate, he produces some stunning wines. The Sauvignon-Semillon is good, the Pinot Gris scented and delightful, the Chardonnay, especially Maté's Vineyard, as rich and textured as any in New Zealand, and the Merlot and Merlot-Malbec blend Melba are deep, supple and seductively ripe. Best years: (Chardonnay) 2002, '00, '99, '98, '96.

KUNDE ESTATE WINERY
USA, California, Sonoma County, Sonoma Valley AVA
❦ Cabernet Sauvignon, Merlot, Syrah, Zinfandel
♀ Chardonnay, Sauvignon Blanc, Gewurztraminer, Viognier

Highly regarded vineyard owners, the Kunde family oversees over 324ha (800 acres) of vines planted along rolling hillsides in the middle of the SONOMA VALLEY. Winemakers before prohibition, they sold their grapes until easing into winemaking in the mid-1980s. With extensive aging caves, dug deep into the hillsides, plantings of 19 different grape varieties including some 120-year-old Zinfandel, and significant amounts of hillside vines that they farm without irrigation it was probably more than time that they did.

They now offer four different Chardonnays, including two single-vineyard examples, one of California's better Sauvignons, spicy Viognier, and good rich fruited reds culminating in Century Vines Zinfandel from that old Zin vineyard. Best years: (Zinfandel) 2001, '00, '99, '97, '96, '95, '94.

FRANZ KÜNSTLER
GERMANY, Rheingau, Hochheim
❦ Pinot Noir (Spätburgunder)
♀ Riesling

Founded only in 1965 by Franz Künstler, father of current owner, Gunter Künstler, this estate's rise has been meteoric. With his first vintage, 1988, Gunter Künstler proved that dry RHEINGAU Riesling could be a rich, harmonious wine with a decade and more of aging potential.

Since then he has perfected the style, making ever more concentrated wines. Those from the great Hölle site are the most impressive, with an apricot and earth character and enormous power. His classic Spätlese can also be impressive, and his Auslese and higher Prädikat dessert wines are slow-developing masterpieces. In 1996 Künstler bought the neighbouring Geheimrat Aschrott estate, considerably boosting his vineyard holdings which currently stand at 26ha (64 acres). Best years: (Riesling Spätlese trocken and Auslese trocken) 2002, '01, '99, '98, '97, '96, '94, '93, '92, '90, '89, '88.

KWV
SOUTH AFRICA, Western Cape, Stellenbosch

KWV converted from being an important grapegrowers' co-operative to a company in 1997 and the conversion was celebrated with a huge investment in the cellar and a rationalization of the wines produced. KWV retained its well-known brand name as well as its significant influence in wine wholesaling, brandy production and numerous industry support activities. They produce an icon wine called Perold, lavishly adorned with new oak, but otherwise the much-improved flagship Cathedral Cellar range are the best wines, especially the reds – bright-fruited Triptych (Cabernet-Merlot-Shiraz), rich, bold Cabernet Sauvignon and modern-style Pinotage – and a pleasingly balanced Chardonnay. The other ranges are more commercial, but have shown worrying signs of dumbing down in recent years. The dessert, sherry and often well-matured PORT-styles have maintained quality, and offer superb value, particularly the Vintage port.

LA AGRÍCOLA
ARGENTINA, Mendoza
♥ Cabernet Sauvignon, Malbec, Tempranillo, Bonarda, Merlot, Pinot Noir
♀ Chardonnay, Chenin Blanc, Viognier, Torrontes

Under its dynamic owner José Alberto Zuccardi, La Agrícola has gone from being an experimental bodega set up to help sell the high-tech irrigation equipment his father designs to being Argentina's most successful exporter. Everything is here, all the latest equipment, expertly kept vineyards, clear ideas as to where to go, an ability to absorb new ideas and a willingness to move ahead fearlessly. And José with his irrepressible enthusiasm and generosity with his time and friendship has become a kind of roving ambassador abroad for Argentine wines.

He is continually upgrading the top end of his wines – the vintage by vintage improvement of the Q (for Quality) range of barrel-aged reds shows that – but is probably more important for his work in popularizing the less well-known grapes that dominate Argentine vineyards – particularly Bonarda, Tempranillo and others. These wines are generally sold under the Santa Julia label and are deliciously juicy to drink without delay. La Agrícola's vineyards are split into two groups: 410ha (1013 acres) in Santa Rosa and 170ha (420 acres) in Maipú.

LA CREMA
USA, California, Sonoma County, Russian River Valley AVA
♥ Pinot Noir, Syrah, Zinfandel
♀ Chardonnay, Viognier

After several ownership changes, La Crema became part of the expanding KENDALL-JACKSON group in 1993. Despite its chequered history, it has continued to focus on Chardonnay and Pinot Noir grown in cool climates. It offers early-maturing wines under the SONOMA COAST appellation and limited amounts of classically structured wines from the RUSSIAN RIVER and ANDERSON VALLEYS. Grapes come from 18ha (45 acres) of its own vineyards and numerous other growers. La Crema also produces Sonoma County Syrah and Zinfandel and SONOMA VALLEY Viognier.

LA ROSA
CHILE, Rapel Valley, Cachapoal Valley
♥ Cabernet Sauvignon, Merlot, Carmenere, Malbec, Syrah, Cabernet Franc
♀ Chardonnay, Sauvignon Blanc

Founded in 1824 by Don Gregorio Ossa with a cutting brought over from France, La Rosa is clearly no newcomer to Chilean winemaking. Situated in the Cachapoal Valley, La Rosa has 600ha (1500 acres) of vineyards spread out in three smaller valleys, known as Peumo, Cornellana and La Palmería de Cocalan, where the vineyards share the land with hundreds of native Chilean palm trees. Production is climbing steadily towards a million cases a year, with the La Palmería brand, under the talented leadership of winemaker José Ignacio Cancino, in the vanguard. Unoaked Chardonnay is pure apricots and figs, and the Merlot is a delightful easy-drinking RAPEL style. Reserva and Gran Reserva wines are a step up in quality and often excellent.

LABOURÉ-ROI
FRANCE, Burgundy, Nuits-St-Georges
♥ Pinot Noir
♀ Chardonnay

This price-conscious and generally reliable *négociant* has been run with such determination by the Cottin brothers that it is now the fifth biggest wine company in BURGUNDY.

This is very laudable but in an area like Burgundy where supplies of the best grapes and wines are always limited, it has meant a loss of consistency. In each vintage, however, some wines shine, and the most likely ones are CHABLIS and MEURSAULT for the whites, and NUITS-ST-GEORGES, MARSANNAY, GEVREY-CHAMBERTIN, BEAUNE and VOLNAY for the reds. Labouré-Roi owns Domaine Manuel in Meursault. They also produce red and white varietals from the LANGUEDOC.

LACKNER-TINNACHER
AUSTRIA, Steiermark, Südsteiermark, Gamlitz
♀ Sauvignon Blanc, Chardonnay (Morillon), Pinot Blanc (Weissburgunder), Pinot Gris (Grauburgunder), Muscat (Muskateller), Welschriesling

Fritz Tinnacher and his wife Wilma Lackner never went in for all the experimenting with barrique-aging which many of their colleagues in STEIERMARK (Styria) did during the early 1990s, and their wines are none the worse for it. Here, purity of fruit, clarity and elegance are the guiding principles and result in archetypal Styrian dry whites. Most impressive are the dry and dessert Grauburgunders. Best years: 2002, '01, '00, '99, '98, '97, '95, '93, '92, '90.

LADOIX AC
FRANCE, Burgundy, Côte de Beaune
♥ Pinot Noir
♀ Chardonnay

Ladoix-Serrigny is the most northern village in the CÔTE DE BEAUNE, and one of the least known. Its best wines are usually sold as CORTON (of which 22ha/54 acres are in the commune of Ladoix), ALOXE-CORTON or Aloxe-Corton Premier Cru and the less good ones as CÔTE DE BEAUNE-VILLAGES. Even so, wine labelled with the name Ladoix does occasionally surface and can be worth a try – there are several good growers in the village and it is likely to be reasonably priced. The output is overwhelmingly red, quite light in colour and a little lean in style, but after a few years the rough edges slip away and a rather attractive soft, savoury style emerges. Best years: (reds) 2002, '01, '99, '98, '97, '96, '95. Best producers: (reds) P André, Cachat-Occuidant et Fils, E Cornu, Prince Florent de Mérode, A & J-R Nudant.

White Ladoix is very rare – they only produce 90,000 bottles each year although 6ha (15 acres) of the Grand Cru CORTON-CHARLEMAGNE are in Ladoix. It's good, a light, clean Chardonnay flavour, softened to nuttiness with a little oak aging and two or three years' maturity. Best producers: (whites) P André, E Cornu, R & R Jacob, Verget.

MICHEL LAFARGE
FRANCE, Burgundy, Côte de Beaune
✽ *Pinot Noir, Gamay*
♀ *Chardonnay, Aligoté*

The doyen of VOLNAY, Michel Lafarge has now virtually handed over to his son, Frédéric. Although he does make a MEURSAULT (perfectly OK but not thrilling) this is very much a red wine house and above all a Volnay house. These are some of the best, most typically delicate Volnays of all, notably Volnay Clos des Chênes and Volnay Clos du Château des Ducs (a monopole). BEAUNE Grèves and straightforward BOURGOGNE Rouge are also good. Top wines are accessible though on the lean side when young but can easily age up to 10 years or more. Best years: (top reds) 2002, '99, '98, '97, '96, '95, '93.

CH. LAFAURIE-PEYRAGUEY
FRANCE, Bordeaux, Sauternes AC, Premier Cru Classé
♀ *Sémillon, Sauvignon Blanc, Muscadelle*

It's fashionable to criticize the detrimental effect on quality following the takeover of a property by a large merchant, but the large Domaines Cordier company has always taken great care of its properties (they bought this one in 1913). In the 1980s and '90s their investment and commitment in this 38.5-ha (95-acre) Premier Cru in the village of Bommes made Lafaurie-Peyraguey one of the most improved SAUTERNES properties. It has made outstanding wines in great vintages since the early 1980s but has also come through well in the lesser years. Lafaurie-Peyraguey has a deep apricot and pineapple syrup sweetness, a cream and nuts softness and a good, clear, lemony acidity which give it wonderful balance for long aging. Best years: 2002, '01, '99, '98, '97, '96, '95, '90, '89, '88, '86, '85, '83.

CH. LAFITE-ROTHSCHILD
FRANCE, Bordeaux, Haut-Médoc, Pauillac AC, Premier Cru Classé
✽ *Cabernet Sauvignon, Merlot, Cabernet Franc, Petit Verdot*

This is possibly the most famous red wine in the world. This First Growth PAUILLAC of 103ha (255 acres) is frequently cited as the epitome of elegance, indulgence and expense, but it was wretchedly inconsistent in the 1960s and '70s. This has all changed in the last 25 years, with Lafite back to top form and if anything adding on extra density and structure to its legendary elegance and taking full advantage of mature vineyards; the oldest plot having been planted in 1886. The 1996 is one of the most complete Lafites in recent years and the '97 is the best of the First Growths in that difficult vintage, and the first vintages of the new millennium showed no signs of a let up.

Since Lafite often takes 15 years to weave its subtle strands into cloth of gold, and can need 30 years or more to come finally into balance, we won't know for a while yet quite how good the 'new' Lafites are going to be. But there seems every chance that they will attain that magical marriage of the cedarwood fragrance and the blackcurrant fruit, the hallmark of the great bottles of the past. Second wine: les Carruades de Lafite-Rothschild. Best years: 2001, '00, '99, '98, '97, '96, '95, '94, '90, '89, '88, '86, '85, '82.

CH. LAFLEUR
FRANCE, Bordeaux, Pomerol AC
✽ *Merlot, Cabernet Franc*

This tiny estate of only 4ha (10 acres), run by Sylvie and Jacques Guinadeu, has some of POMEROL's oldest vines, some of Pomerol's most traditional winemaking, and the wine has the potential to equal Ch. PÉTRUS for sheer power and flavour, even occasionally surpassing its celebrated neighbour for hedonistic richness and concentration. In the best years the wine starts out by exhibiting a massive, old-fashioned, unsubtle brute strength loaded with the fatness of oak and soaked in the sweet fruit of plums – unforgettable mouthfuls which, as the wines of the '80s are now demonstrating, do evolve into memorable wines eventually. The price, though, is as monumental as the wine. Best years: 2001, '00, '99, '98, '97, '96, '95, '94, '93, '90, '89, '88, '86, '85, '82.

DOMAINE DES COMTES LAFON
FRANCE, Burgundy, Côte de Beaune, Meursault AC
✽ *Pinot Noir*
♀ *Chardonnay*

The exuberant personality of Dominique Lafon seems to be reflected in his wines, which many plausibly believe to be the finest expressions of MEURSAULT you can find. They are bold and richly flavoured, almost flamboyant. The Lafons own some excellent vineyards: Clos de la Barre in Meursault, and Premiers Crus that include les Genevrières, les Charmes and les Perrières. The estate's pride and joy is the MONTRACHET, which is produced in tiny quantities. There are three red vineyards in VOLNAY, most notably in the Premier Cru Santenots, and the quality of these wines is equally exceptional. The Lafons now also own a domaine in MÂCON.

Of course, it isn't all to do with vineyard sites. Lafon is a brilliant, non-interventionist winemaker, leaving the barrels in the estate's exceptionally cold cellars to mature in their own sweet time. Grapes are harvested as late as possible, yields are very low and filtration unusual, even for the whites. Lafon uses a modest amount of new oak, up to 40 per cent, and such is their richness of fruit that the wines scarcely ever taste oaky. Even more impressive – each vineyard's wine tastes triumphantly different. And we may not have seen the best yet – the Lafon vineyards are now farmed biodynamically without any chemicals at all. Expect ever greater things. Given their concentration, it comes as no surprise that the Lafon wines, red and white, age superbly. Best years: (whites) 2002, '01, '00, '99, '97, '96, '95, '93, '92; (reds) 2002, '99, '98, '97, '96, '95, '93, '92, '91.

CH. LAFON-ROCHET
FRANCE, Bordeaux, Haut-Médoc, St-Estèphe AC, 4ème Cru Classé
✽ *Cabernet Sauvignon, Merlot, Cabernet Franc*

Guy Tesseron started improving Lafon-Rochet in the 1960s and the work has since been continued by his sons, Alfred and Michel. The effort and investment is now showing in the wines. The vineyard is a good one: 40ha (99 acres) are planted at the western end of the slopes which are also occupied by COS D'ESTOURNEL. The wines used to be considered hard and austere, a problem caused by the youthful nature of the vineyard and the high percentage of Cabernet Sauvignon planted on a part of the vineyard better suited to Merlot. The vineyard has now matured and the percentage of Merlot has been increased, resulting in wines which are more supple than in the past but which still retain a wonderful concentrated dry blackcurrant fruit, and which are not too pricy. Second wine: Numéro 2 du Château Lafon-Rochet. Best years: 2001, '00, '99, '98, '96, '95, '94, '90, '89, '88, '86, '85.

ALOIS LAGEDER
ITALY, Alto Adige, Alto Adige DOC
✽ *Cabernet Sauvignon, Cabernet Franc, Merlot, Pinot Noir (Pinot Nero), Schiava, Lagrein and others*
♀ *Chardonnay, Pinot Blanc (Pinot Bianco), Pinot Gris (Pinot Grigio), Sauvignon Blanc and others*

The current Alois Lageder, vintage 1950, is the fifth consecutive holder of that name to head this firm since 1855 and the winery is a leading producer in ALTO ADIGE. Lageder was one of the first to introduce organic methods of viticulture, restricted yields, high-density planting and other new techniques, not just into his own 17ha (42 acres) of vineyards scattered through the province, but increasingly into those belonging to the 150 growers from whom he regularly purchases grapes.

South Tyrolean producers tend to go in for a wide range of wines and Lageder is no exception. Annual production is around one million bottles, including medium-priced varietals under the Lageder label and expensive estate and single-vineyard wines that really steal the show. These are divided into three ranges: 'Classic' varietals, 17 of them no less, including the well-known Buchholz Chardonnay and Mazon Pinot Nero Riserva; single-vineyard selections, including the partially oak-fermented and/or oak-matured Haberlehof Pinot Bianco, Benefizium Porer Pinot Grigio and Lehenhof Sauvignon; and third, the estate wines which are barrique-matured whites (Tannhammer Terlaner and Chardonnay Löwengang) and reds (Cabernet Löwengang and the flagship Cabernet Cor Römigberg). Lageder also owns the Casòn Hirschprunn estate which produces Alto Adige varietals. Best years: (Cor Römigberg) 2001, '99, '98, '97, '96, '94, '93, '92, '91, '90.

LAGO DI CALDARO DOC

ITALY, Trentino-Alto Adige

Schiava, Pinot Noir (Pinot Nero), Lagrein

The wine from Caldaro, a lake surrounded by vines near the upper reaches of the Adige river, can be pleasant enough. Lightish red, it is often low in alcohol, with the smoky, strawberry-yogurt flavours of the Schiava grape. Young and fresh, it's a perfect lightweight quaffer. And there's a lake-full of it (around 120,000 hectolitres a year), so even if the Germans, Austrians and Swiss, who call it Kalterersee, continue to consume it with their customary thirst, there's still enough to go round. Only the Classico version comes from around the lake. Otherwise, vineyards stretch from north of Bolzano right down the Adige valley into TRENTINO and sadly far too many of them are overcropped.

The Superiore wine has half a per cent more alcohol and that labelled Scelto is a whole per cent higher. German speakers refer to Scelto as Auslese but Lago di Caldaro has nothing to do with sweet German Auslese wine. It is always dry – but the extra ripeness and alcohol gives it a touch more flavour. Best producers: Caldaro co-operative, LAGEDER, Prima e Nuova/Erste & Neue, San Michele Appiano co-operative, Schloss Sallegg.

CH. LAGRANGE

FRANCE, Bordeaux, Haut-Médoc, St-Julien AC, 3ème Cru Classé

Cabernet Sauvignon, Merlot, Petit Verdot

To many people, this ramshackle, lumbering estate – 109ha (270 acres) of vines at the very western borders of ST-JULIEN – didn't seem a candidate for super-stardom, but it has always had potentially one of the finest vineyards in the whole MÉDOC. The Japanese Suntory company bought Lagrange in 1983, and with the aid of inspired winemaker Marcel Ducasse, transformed the wine style in a single vintage. It is no longer an amiable, shambling wine, but instead a clear-eyed, single-minded one of tremendous fruit and increasing depth and complexity. The wines of the '80s are now delicious but the '90s wines will be even better, showing just how good this vineyard can be. Second wine: les Fiefs de Lagrange. Best years: 2001, '00, '99, '98, '96, '95, '94, '93, '90, '89, '88, '86, '85.

CHÂTEAU LAGRANGE

Particularly fine since the 1985 vintage, this St-Julien wine is rich and very concentrated with plenty of good quality tannins.

CH. LAGREZETTE

FRANCE, South-West, Cahors AC

Malbec (Auxerrois), Merlot, Tannat

Splendid CAHORS estate owned by Alain-Dominique Perrin, boss of luxury jewellers, Cartier. Since 1991, the wines have been made in a modern cellar under the eye of the roving POMEROL enologist, Michel Rolland. This would lead you to expect superripe grapes and lavish use of oak, but he's also brought back hand-harvesting, rigorous selection and gentle but intensive winemaking to extract fruit and colour without too much tannin. Moulin Lagrezette and Chevaliers Lagrezette are soft, full reds but the main wine, Château Lagrezette, is powerful and challenging. There are two 'super cuvées' – the oaky Dame Honneur from very old vines and the marvellously ripe but black-hearted le Pigeonnier made from Malbec. Perrin has also established a merchant's business called Caves de Grezette currently producing 650,000 bottles annually.

CH. LA LAGUNE

FRANCE, Bordeaux, Haut-Médoc AC, 3ème Cru Classé

Cabernet Sauvignon, Merlot, Cabernet Franc, Petit Verdot

La Lagune is just to the south of the village of Margaux, and the closest Classed Growth to the city of Bordeaux itself. The 72ha (178ha) of vineyards were renovated and replanted in the 1950s by Georges Brunet and the wine benefits from their maturity. The first wine is consistently excellent, rich and spicy, but full of the charry chestnut sweetness of good oak and with a deep, cherry-blackcurrant-and-plums sweetness to the fruit which, after ten years or more, is outstanding: always accessible, yet perfect for the long haul. Second wine: Moulin de la Lagune. Best years: 2001, '00, '98, '96, '95, '94, '90, '89, '88, '86, '85, '83, '82.

LAKE BALATON

HUNGARY, Transdanubia

The large Lake Balaton is a favourite with Hungarians as a holiday resort as much as a source of wines, but the wines used to be, and could be again, terrifically stylish and unusual. There are various wine regions clustered round its shores: Dél-Balaton to the south, and Badacsony, Balatonmellék and Balatonfüred-Csopak to the north. As well as familiar grape varieties like Sauvignon Blanc, Chardonnay, Rhine Riesling, Traminer and Rizlingszilváni (Müller-Thurgau), there are interesting native grapes, especially Kéknyelű and Szürkebarát, and it is these that could produce some splendidly fiery whites. But first of all the winemaking needs to be spruced up and outside investment brought in. First attempts by the Balatonboglár winery under the Chapel Hill name are strangely disappointing, dumbing down the area's wines rather than pointing up their character.

LALANDE-DE-POMEROL AC

FRANCE, Bordeaux

Merlot, Cabernet Franc, Cabernet Sauvignon, Malbec

Although the Lalande-de-Pomerol appellation is regarded as a POMEROL satellite, with nearly 1120ha (2768 acres) of vines, it is actually bigger than Pomerol's 800ha (1977 acres). The wines are usually full, soft, plummy and even chocolaty, very attractive to drink at only three to four years old, but aging reasonably well. They lack the mineral edge and the concentration of top Pomerols, but are nonetheless extremely attractive, full, ripe wines. They are not particularly cheap, but then nothing with the name Pomerol included in it is cheap these days. Best years: 2001, '00, '99, '98, '96, '95, '94, '90, '89. Best producers: Annereaux, Belles-Graves, Bertineau-St-Vincent, la Borderie Mondésir, Clos de l'Église, la Croix St-André, les Cruzelles, la Fleur de Boüard, Garraud, Grand Ormeau, Haut-Chaigneau, Haut-Surget, les Hauts Conseillants, Perron-la-Fleur, Sergant, la Sergue, Tournefeuille, de Viaud.

LAMBRUSCO DOC

ITALY, Emilia and elsewhere
🍷 🍷 🍷 *Lambrusco*

True Lambrusco wine should be red and makes an ideal cherry-flavoured match for the rich, buttery, cheesy sauces and the fat salami and sausages of its native lands, around Modena, where the best three sub-varieties of the Lambrusco grape are found. It should also be dry, which might come as a surprise to those who have a fondness for the cheaper versions, and should have a cork closure rather than screwcap if it's DOC-level, which it isn't when it's dirt cheap.

Major DOCs are Lambrusco di Sorbara, whose characteristics are a pronounced and elegant perfume and good acidity; Lambrusco Grasparossa di Castelvetro, more tannic than most, with fuller flavour and deeper colour; and Lambrusco Salamino di Santa Croce, whose wines are richer and fatter, although with enlivening good acidity.

It is a costly and skilled job to extract good white juice from red Lambrusco grapes, which means that good white Lambrusco can't be that cheap. And if it is dirt cheap it is probably in large part from Trebbiano instead. Best producers: Barbieri, Barbolini, F Bellei, Casali, Cavicchioli, Chiarli, Vittorio Graziano, Oreste Lini, Stefano Spezia, Venturini Baldini.

LAMOREAUX LANDING

USA, New York State, Finger Lakes AVA
🍷 *Pinot Noir, Cabernet Franc, Merlot*
🍷 *Chardonnay, Riesling, Gewurztraminer*

Although only established as recently as 1990, Lamoreaux Landing is already a major producer in the FINGER LAKES AVA, having over 48ha (120 acres) of vineyards, and is now counted as one of the most important wineries in the eastern United States. The Reserve Chardonnay, aged in new oak, and the dry Riesling are usually excellent. Merlot and Cabernet Franc are also attractive, as is good, quaffable sparkling wine.

HELMUT LANG

AUSTRIA, Burgenland, Neusiedlersee, Illmitz
🍷 *Zweigelt, Blaufränkish, Pinot Noir, Cabernet Sauvignon, Merlot*
🍷 *Riesling, Gewürztraminer, Chardonnay, Pinot Blanc (Weissburgunder), Scheurebe (Sämling 88)*

Helmut Lang is one of Illmitz's band of fiercely independent dessert wine producers. He'll make a sweet wine out of virtually anything – his dessert Chardonnay and Pinot Noir are among his best wines, though I often prefer the intensely fruity, unoaked Scheurebe (aka Sämling 88). He also produces a powerful dry Pinot Noir. While his wines are a bit hit and miss, the best are very rich, succulent and clean. His highest success rate is with Scheurebe. Best years: 2000, '99, '98, '95, '91.

LANGENLOIS

AUSTRIA, Niederösterreich, Kamptal

This town on the river Kamp just north of Krems on the Danube is one of the most important centres of quality wine production in Austria, producing large quantities of good to outstanding dry whites from Grüner Veltliner and Riesling, and some interesting Weissburgunder (Pinot Blanc) and Chardonnay. Good red wines are still rare, though Blauburgunder (Pinot Noir) shows potential. Best producers: BRÜNDLMAYER, Ehn, Hiedler, Jurtschitsch, Loimer.

LANGHE DOC

ITALY, Piedmont
🍷 *Nebbiolo, Dolcetto, Freisa and others*
🍷 *Favorita, Chardonnay, Arneis, Sauvignon Blanc*

In the mid-1990s the wise legislators of PIEDMONT decided that all the wines of their august region should be, at least, DOC. Hence the new denominations of Langhe, Monferrato and Piemonte, among others, to catch those renegades who previously had been selling their wines as vino da tavola. Varietal Nebbiolo was introduced to catch those quasi-Barolos which, their producers had decided, were not suitable to suffer the aging requirements imposed by the DOCG regulations, or which were blended in some way inconsistent with the law. The new DOC also gave growers the possibility of producing varietal Chardonnay, or Arneis and Favorita outside their previously restricted zones.

Perhaps of greatest significance, however, were the new blends, Langhe Rosso and Langhe Bianco, open to just about any grape variety provided it was 'recommended' or at least 'authorized'. In this way the legislators

opened the floodgates for wines which, while limited in number today, can be expected to multiply in future as the inventive Italian genius finds its path. Best years: (reds) 2001, '00, '99, '98, '97, '96, '95, '93, '90. Best producers: (reds) ALTARE, Boglietti (Buio), Bongiovanni (Falletto), Ceretto, CHIARLO, Cigliuti, CLERICO, Aldo CONTERNO, Conterno-Fantino (Monprà), Luigi Einaudi, GAJA, A Ghisolfi, Marchesi di Gresy (Virtus), F Nada (Seifile), Parusso (Bricco Rovella), Rocche dei Manzoni (Quatr Nas), Vajra, Gianni Voerzio (Serrapiu), Roberto VOERZIO.

LANGHORNE CREEK

AUSTRALIA, South Australia

South-east of Adelaide, the fertile, alluvial and flat river plains, coupled with the bountiful irrigation water from Lake Alexandrina and the Bremer River, have proved such an ideal combination that this is not only one of the largest, but also one of the fastest-growing, wine regions in SOUTH AUSTRALIA. Yet its history goes as far back as 1850, when Frank Potts established Potts Bleasdale Vineyards, by diverting the winter floods of the Bremer River on to his vineyards, literally submerging them in late winter; these days drip irrigation does the job far more efficiently.

While ORLANDO is the most obvious landholder producing high-quality, low-cost grapes for its various Jacob's Creek wines, Wolf BLASS has long understood the quality of the grapes that can be grown in this surprisingly cool maritime climate and Saltram's Metala is another Langhorne wine. More recently Lake Breeze has produced opulent, rich reds and Bleasdale's Shiraz quality has reminded us they were first here. Best producers: (local wineries) Bleasdale Vineyards, Bremerton, Lake Breeze, Temple Bruer.

CH. LANGOA-BARTON

FRANCE, Bordeaux, Haut-Médoc, St-Julien AC, 3ème Cru Classé
🍷 *Cabernet Sauvigon, Merlot, Cabernet Franc*

This 17-ha (42-acre) property has been owned by the Barton family since 1821. The wine is usually lighter in style than its ST-JULIEN stablemate, Ch. LÉOVILLE-BARTON, but it is still extremely impressive, reasonably priced and a gorgeous expression of St-Julien elegance. Drink after seven or eight years, although it will keep for 15. Second wine: Réserve de Léoville-Barton (a blend from the young vines of both Barton properties). Best years: 2001, '00, '99, '98, '96, '95, '90, '89, '88, '86, '85, '83, '82.

LANGUEDOC-ROUSSILLON France

THE LANGUEDOC-ROUSSILLON, also called the Midi, is a huge viticultural area that sweeps around the Mediterranean rim from the foothills of the Pyrenees to the gates of the old Roman town of Nîmes. It encompasses the *départements* of the Pyrénées-Orientales, Aude, Hérault and Gard which together provide one-third of France's vineyard acreage and an average yearly production of 18 million hectolitres of wine.

How times have changed though. Twenty years ago, the Languedoc-Roussillon was still the butt of disdain for its overproduction of *gros rouge* – cheap, rough, red wine that was sold on its alcoholic strength rather than any discernible character. Now it's the symbol of a modern, liberated, high-tech wine industry for which innovation has become the byword.

So what has wrought the changes within this vast viticultural arena? First of all a consciousness that the old days of quantity rather than quality were long gone and subsequently a move to producing clean, modern, fruit-driven wines for today's market. This has meant new investment, temperature-controlled vinification, lower vineyard yields and better grape varieties and this from the smallest producer up to the regionally powerful co-operatives.

The reorganization of the vineyards has been a key element and coupled with the creation of vin de pays, a more flexible system for regulating wine production than appellation contrôlée, has been the region's saving grace. These factors have permitted the planting of the international grape varieties Merlot, Cabernet Sauvignon, Chardonnay and Sauvignon Blanc and others like Syrah and Viognier providing wines that can compete on the world market. The Languedoc-Roussillon now produces 70 per cent of France's vins de pays of which a large percentage are varietal wines labelled as Vin de Pays d'Oc.

But vin de pays does not just mean good-value varietal wines but also the liberty to produce some highly individual, world-class wines from imaginative blends. Aimé Guibert of the Mas de Daumas Gassac estate has proved this over the years and he has now been joined by Laurent Vaillé of la Grange des Pères and other young producers.

However, if we have to thank international-style vin de pays for waking everyone up, the most exciting wines now are being made in the traditional vineyards of the ACs where the growing conditions, often on hillsides, are fantastic for the traditional warm-climate grapes – a fact acknowledged by the Romans who first planted vineyards here 2000 years ago. Increased use for reds of Syrah, Grenache and Mourvèdre has actually led to much better appreciation of Cinsaut and Carignan. Whites have been transformed by Viognier, Marsanne, Roussanne and Rolle and, in Limoux, Chardonnay. The top ACs to look for are Fitou, Corbières, Costières de Nîmes, Côtes du Roussillon, Faugères, Minervois, St-Chinian and Côteaux du Languedoc.

A movement to identify individual sub-regions within the ACs is also underway. The Coteaux du Languedoc and Corbières have both pinpointed distinct areas within their boundaries. La Livinière in Minervois has been elevated to Cru status and Tautavel now has its own identity in the Côtes du Roussillon.

Tradition in the Languedoc-Roussillon, however, still lives on with the sweet, fortified *vins doux naturels*, the whites being made from the Muscat grape and the reds from Grenache Noir. These grapes achieve very high natural sugar levels in the hot Mediterranean sun and the racy Muscat de Rivesaltes and richly complex Banyuls, France's answer to port, are two fine examples.

Nestling in the trees high up in the Gassac valley, Mas de Daumas Gassac's beautiful old stone farmhouse, or mas, is surrounded by vineyards hacked out of the natural scrub vegetation, or garrigue.

Legend:
- Languedoc
- Roussillon

Pic St-Loup = Coteaux du Languedoc Cru

AC and VDQS wine areas
1. Clairette de Bellegarde
2. Costières de Nîmes
3. Coteaux du Languedoc
4. Clairette du Languedoc
5. Faugères
6. St-Chinian
7. Minervois
8. Cabardès
9. Côtes de la Malepère VDQS
10. Limoux, Crémant de Limoux, Blanquette de Limoux
11. Corbières
12. Fitou
13. Côtes du Roussillon-Villages
14. Côtes du Roussillon
15. Collioure

Fortified wines or Vins Doux Naturels
16. Muscat de Lunel
17. Muscat de Mireval
18. Muscat de Frontignan
19. Muscat de St-Jean de Minervois
20. Maury
21. Rivesaltes and Muscat de Rivesaltes
22. Banyuls

MAS AMIEL
The best-known estate in Maury is noted for its range of traditional fortified wines which spend a year outdoors in glass bonbonnes, followed by aging in large old casks for anything up to 30 years.

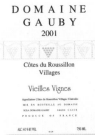

DOMAINE GAUBY
Yields are very low at this top Roussillon estate, giving wines of enormous concentration. The Vieilles Vignes, from mainly old-vine Carignan and Grenache, with a dollop of Syrah, Mourvèdre and Cinsaut, has solid tannins and ripe, berry fruit.

DOMAINE CAZES FRÈRES
This long-established estate makes outstanding Rivesaltes, including the quite powerful, sweet, rich Tuilé from Grenache.

MAS DE DAUMAS GASSAC
This inspirational property at Aniane north of Montpellier makes red wines of great power and longevity.

CH. MOURGUES DU GRÈS
François Collard is one of several young growers in the Costières de Nîmes AC aiming for quality.

REGIONAL ENTRIES
Aude, Banyuls, Blanquette de Limoux, Cabardès, La Clape, Collioure, Corbières, Costières de Nîmes, Coteaux du Languedoc, Côtes du Roussillon, Côtes du Roussillon-Villages, Faugères, Fitou, Gard, Hérault, Maury, Minervois, Muscat de Frontignan, Muscat de Rivesaltes, Vin de Pays d'Oc, Pic St-Loup, Pyrénées-Orientales, Rivesaltes, St-Chinian.

PRODUCER ENTRIES
Dom. de l'Aigle, Dom. Canet-Valette, Dom. Cazes Frères, Cellier des Templiers, Clos Centeilles, des Estanilles, Dom. Gauby, Dom. de la Grange des Pères, Dom. de l'Hortus, de Lastours, Mas Amiel, Dom. du Mas Blanc, Mas Bruguière, Mas de Daumas Gassac, Mas Jullien, les Producteurs du Mont Tauch, Dom. Peyre-Rose, Prieuré de St-Jean de Bébian, Dom. de la Rectorie, Sieur d'Arques, Skalli, les Vignerons du Val d'Orbieu, la Voulte Gasparets.

MAS BRUGUIÈRE
La Grenadière, a spicy Grenache-based red, is the top wine from this leading producer in the Pic St-Loup sub-region of Coteaux du Languedoc.

DOMAINE PEYRE-ROSE
Clos Syrah Léone, an immensely concentrated wine from incredibly low-yielding vines, has become one of the Languedoc's cult wines.

CH. DES ESTANILLES
Michel Louison has made this domaine into one of the Midi's top domaines. Syrah is his preferred variety and it plays the main role in his various Faugères cuvées.

LANSON

FRANCE, Champagne, Champagne AC

♀ ♂ *Pinot Noir, Chardonnay, Pinot Meunier*

Owners Marne-et-Champagne are the dominant force in own-label cheap CHAMPAGNE, producing 20 million bottles a year under numerous labels. Fortunately, they regard Lanson as the jewel in their crown and it has kept a very distinctive style. None of Lanson's seven million bottles produced each year undergoes malolactic fermentation. This used to mean the wines were rather aggressive on release, but the style has now been softened a little, without affecting their great ability to age. The vintage wines include the delicious, lemony Blanc de Blancs and the richly textured Noble Cuvée. Lanson's excellent vineyards were not included in its sale to Marne-et-Champagne in 1991. However, since the owners have access to equally good vineyards, quality has remained high since the takeover in 1991. Best years: 1996, '95, '93, '90, '89, '88, '85, '83, '82.

LANSON

Noble Cuvée is Lanson's prestige vintage Champagne. Made in a dry, fairly rich, powerful style, it nonetheless has an attractive softness and fruit depth.

DOMAINE MICHEL LAROCHE

FRANCE, Burgundy, Chablis AC

♀ *Chardonnay*

The urbane Michel Laroche is both an estate owner and a *négociant*, and has developed a 44-ha (109-acre) property in the LANGUE-DOC, under the Domaine de la Chevalière label, which is rapidly proving itself to be a quality leader in the South. But CHABLIS remains the focus of his activities. His 132-ha (326-acre) portfolio of Chablis vineyards includes a wide range of Premiers Crus (Beauroy, Fourchaume and Vaillons) and Grands Crus (les Clos, Blanchots and Bougros). In recent years he has moderated his use of new oak, preferring older barrels. In top vintages, Laroche releases a kind of prestige cuvée, made from selected parcels in Blanchots and called Réserve de l'Obédiencerie. Despite Laroche's fine top-level wines, it is his ability to produce large amounts of high-quality basic Chablis that I find most impressive. Best years: (Chablis) 2002, '00, '99, '96.

CH. DE LASTOURS

FRANCE, Languedoc, Corbières AC

♂ *Carignan, Grenache, Cinsaut, Syrah*

♀ *Grenache Blanc, Malvoisie, Muscat*

The first time I visited this excellent estate, scattered across the high, scrawny hills of CORBIÈRES, the manager had cooked about 100 oysters which he then proceeded to serve with his red wine – amazingly, it worked. Ah, that red. Well, he followed this with a blind tasting. They were all wonderful, they seemed to be gorgeous mature BORDEAUX. Most of them were – LATOUR, HAUT-BRION and the rest. And I chose Latour as my top wine. Except it wasn't Latour – it was 10-year-old Lastours (note the extra 's's) – and the vines weren't growing in Bordeaux and there wasn't any Cabernet Sauvignon, just lovingly tended Grenache and Carignan from a nearby chalky site down near the sea.

That 'lovingly tended' is important because Lastours is a charitable institution for the mentally handicapped, sixty of whom live there and work in the 130-ha (321-acre) vineyard and the winery, with delicious results. The rosé, the basic reds Chatellenie and Arnaud de Berre, and the top Cuvées Simone Descamps, Fûts de Chêne and the best wine, labelled simply Château de Lastours, are fine wines for their flavour and inspirational wines because of how they came about. Best years: (reds) 2001, '00, '99, '98, '96, '95, '94.

CH. LATOUR

FRANCE, Bordeaux, Haut-Médoc, Pauillac AC, Premier Cru Classé

♂ *Cabernet Sauvignon, Merlot, Cabernet Franc, Petit Verdot*

In years when the rest of BORDEAUX might as well have packed up and gone home without pressing a grape, Latour stuck to it and produced good wine. All through the 1950s, '60s and '70s Latour stood for integrity, consistency and refusal to compromise in the face of considerable financial pressure. The result was that in poor years the wine was good; in merely adequate years – like 1960, '67, '74 – the wine was excellent. In great years like 1966, '70, '75, '82, '86 and '90, Latour's personality – the sheer power of blackcurrant fruit, the temple columns of tannin daring anyone to broach a bottle before its 20th year, the full-tilt charge of cedar-dry flavours, rich, expensive, but as unconcerned with fashion and fawning as a fifteenth-generation duke – marks it as the most imperious of PAUILLAC's three First Growths. Interestingly, the 65-ha (161-acre) vineyard is on the southern side of

the AC, bordering ST-JULIEN. This might lead one to expect a lighter style of wine, but the vineyard, planted with 75 per cent Cabernet Sauvignon, 20 per cent Merlot, 4 per cent Cabernet Franc and 1 per cent Petit Verdot, generally gives as big and proudly impressive a wine as any in Bordeaux.

There have been some curiously unsatisfactory bottles from vintages like 1988, '85, '83 and '81, but this seems to have been due to management decisions rather than any fundamental decline in quality, and 1989 and '90 show the winemakers back on top again. The frosted-out 1991 vintage is remarkable, and the 1996 and '95 are truly great Latours with perhaps a little more suavity of texture than in the past, pointing the way to a fine future. Second wine: les Forts de Latour. Best years: 2001, '00, '99, '98, '97, '96, '95, '94, '93, '90, '89, '88, '86.

LOUIS LATOUR

FRANCE, Burgundy, Beaune

♂ *Pinot Noir*

♀ *Chardonnay*

Large firm of *négociants*, whose activities encompass more southerly regions such as MÂCON and the Ardèche as well as the CÔTE D'OR. Also a major owner of vineyards, with a domaine of some 50ha (124 acres), including 29ha (72 acres) of Grand Cru vineyards.

Latour is better known for its white wines than its red. The Grands Crus are aged in 95 per cent new oak, and Premier Crus in about 50 per cent. The firm has always followed a controversial procedure with its reds, subjecting the wine to a flash pasteurization for a few seconds. This means, say the Latours, that the wine needs fewer treatments subsequently, especially filtration, but there is little doubt that the red wines are generally less complex than the whites. Nonetheless, wines such as ROMANÉE-ST-VIVANT and Corton-Grancey can be very good, and age surprisingly well. However, even finer is their CORTON-CHARLEMAGNE, a perfect example of the blend of power and fruit that characterizes this large site. The simpler appellations tend to be rather bland. Best years: (top whites) 2002, '01, '00, '99, '97, '96, '95, '92.

CH. LATOUR-À-POMEROL

FRANCE, Bordeaux, Pomerol AC

♂ *Merlot, Cabernet Franc*

Luscious, almost juicy fruit, soft and ripe and very easy-to-drink wine has always been a hallmark of Latour-à-Pomerol, but the wines also have enough tannin to age well for ten years and more. Recent vintages, directed by Christian Moueix of Ch. PÉTRUS, show a beefier, brawnier style, but still with superripe softness of fruit. The vineyard covers 8ha (20 acres). Best years: 2001, '00, '99, '98, '96, '95, '94, '90, '89, '88, '85, '83, '82.

LAUREL GLEN VINEYARDS
USA, California, Sonoma County, Sonoma Mountain AVA

🍷 *Cabernet Sauvignon, Merlot, Cabernet Franc*

Owner/winemaker Patrick Campbell makes only Cabernet at his mountaintop winery. Made with a strictly non-interventionist approach, Laurel Glen's Cabernets develop a sweet blackcurrant, slightly minty perfume, wrapped in a supple, inviting texture. Laurel Glen's output is limited by Campbell's decision not to expand its 14ha (35 acres) and not to compromise on quality: declassified Cabernet goes into a fairly classy blend reflecting his musical background called Counterpoint. Any volume increase comes from vineyards elsewhere in CALIFORNIA and a project which finds him working with vineyards in Argentina and Chile. All the wines keep a bit of the Laurel Glen character, but are sold under the labels Quintana, REDS and ZaZin for old-vine Zinfandel. Terra Rosa wines (and sometimes REDS) come from South America. Best years: 2001, '99, '98, '97, '96, '95, '94, '93, '92, '91, '90.

DOMINIQUE LAURENT
FRANCE, Burgundy, Nuits-St-Georges

From modest premises, Dominique Laurent has, since the 1988 vintage, been turning out some of Burgundy's most remarkable, and costly, wines. Much has been made of his fondness for aging in '200 per cent new oak', the aim of this expensive procedure being to ensure a perfect and controlled aeration of the wines while they are in barrel.

More significant is Laurent's purchasing policy. He is a *négociant*, buying up small parcels of young wine (rather than grapes) from some of Burgundy's top domaines, insisting on very ripe fruit from low-yielding vines. By offering very high prices he ensures that he obtains the best and not surprisingly his wines have a cult following, partly because some of them are only made in minuscule quantities. While some of the wines are excessively oaky and pretty tannic, their quality is nonetheless generally outstanding although some exhibit a rather alarming level of volatility that is definitely an acquired taste. Since he does not disclose his sources, it is hard to

define the appellation character of most of the wines from his range, but he does buy wines from the same producers each year, so there should be consistency from vintage to vintage. With Michel Tardieu, he runs a similar operation in the RHÔNE Valley known as Tardieu-Laurent.

LAURENT-PERRIER
FRANCE, Champagne, Champagne AC

🥂 🍷 *Chardonnay, Pinot Noir, Pinot Meunier*

This esteemed CHAMPAGNE producer has been in the hands of the Nonancourt family since the late nineteenth century. With annual production over six million bottles, it is not surprising that quality, especially of the more basic wines in the range, can be variable, although the Brut is now less green than it often used to be. Chardonnay is the dominant grape variety, even in the regular Brut. Laurent-Perrier has a fine reputation for its full-bodied Rosé Brut, and an unusual wine in the range is the Ultra Brut, a Champagne with no *dosage*, and thus compelled to rely solely on the quality of the grapes that go into it. It's a style that takes some getting used to, but it can be one of the most pure and bracing of Champagnes. The regular vintage wines are outclassed by the superb (and very expensive) prestige cuvées called Grand Siècle. Both the white and rosé are subtle, delicate and exquisitely balanced. Best years: 1996, '95, '93, '90, '88, '85, '82.

CH. LAVILLE HAUT-BRION
FRANCE, Bordeaux, Pessac-Léognan AC, Cru Classé de Graves

🥂 *Sémillon, Sauvignon Blanc, Muscadelle*

A GRAVES Classed Growth, Laville Haut-Brion produces exclusively white wines from a 3.7-ha (9-acre) plot of land adjacent to Ch. la MISSION HAUT-BRION. Both estates, as well as HAUT-BRION across the road, are located in Bordeaux's suburbs and are owned by the American Dillon family. Unlike the majority

CH. LAVILLE HAUT-BRION
This is classic white Graves, full-bodied with rich, honeyed, complex flavours, lots of extract and super with long age (and by this I mean several decades).

of white wines in the PESSAC-LÉOGNAN AC, which have a heavy percentage of Sauvignon Blanc, Laville Haut-Brion places the emphasis firmly on Sémillon, which accounts for 70 per cent of the vineyard. This grape and an average vine age of over 50 years gives the wine an amazing aging potential as well as plenty of waxy, mouthfilling flesh and a rich, beeswaxy honeyed bouquet which is initially masked by the effect of 100 per cent new oak, but which after 10 years or so simply sweeps aside the oak to proudly dominate the wine. However, the small quantity of an average 1000 cases a year means that there is a high price tag on the wine. Best years: 2001, '00, '99, '98, '97, '96, '95, '94, '93, '90, '89, '85.

DOMAINE CONSTANTIN LAZARIDI
GREECE, Drama

🍷 🥂 *Cabernet Sauvignon, Merlot, Syrah and others*
🥂 *Sauvignon Blanc, Chardonnay, Sémillon, Assyrtiko*

This state-of-the-art, BORDEAUX-inspired winery is going from strength to strength. Winemaker Vasilis Tsaktsarlis makes good use of indigenous and international varieties to make wines ranging from the fresh gooseberry Amethystos white (Sauvignon, Sémillon and Assyrtiko) to a fascinatingly intense experimental Viognier with a stunning, oily, peach kernel finish, classy Château Julia Chardonnay and the fine Amethystos Cava, an oak-aged Cabernet Sauvignon from very low yields. Interestingly, he manages to make his international styles taste spot-on of their varietals, but wines from his Greek varieties have a powerful Greek identity, first and foremost. The next objective, starting with the red varieties, is to convert the vineyards to an organic regime.

LAZIO
ITALY

The hub of Lazio is Rome. And Rome's is the easiest image to stamp on this longish, disparate region which, at its northern end, skirts TUSCANY and UMBRIA with their enthralling scenery, their calm and cultured existence; while its southern part mingles with the laid-back, wilder, much hotter Mezzogiorno (southern Italy). A vast semi-circular ridge of hills called the Castelli Romani to the south and east of Rome is home to the most typical wines of Lazio: FRASCATI and other similar wines, for example, white Marino, Velletri, Colli Albani. They are usually dry, mostly from various combinations of tricky-to-handle Malvasia and unexciting Trebbiano, and keep both

Romans and tourists well lubricated if not exactly challenged gastronomically.

To find real Roman reds it is necessary to travel sunwards on the Autostrada del Sole until you hit the area where Cesanese is cultivated, turning out wines called Cesanese del Piglio, di Affile or di Olevano Romano. Further north, Cerveteri produces decent red blends with Montepulciano plus Sangiovese and/or Cesanese. Whites stay unswervingly Trebbiano-Malvasia blends. For something different look north by the lake of Bolsena, where there's sweet, strong, red Aleatico di Gradoli. Nearby there is also EST! EST!! EST!!!, and a little bit of the ORVIETO zone overlapping from its main home in Umbria. New reds based on Cabernet and Merlot or Sangiovese are now the region's best wines.

LEASINGHAM

AUSTRALIA, South Australia, Clare Valley
♥ Syrah (Shiraz), Cabernet Sauvignon, Malbec
♀ Riesling, Semillon

Leasingham was established in 1893, initially known as Stanley, then as Stanley Leasingham. It was acquired by HARDY in 1987, and has since gone from strength to strength.

Steely, citrous Riesling is by far the best white, particularly under the Classic Clare label, but it is the reds that have the widest reputation. Bin 61 Shiraz, Classic Clare Shiraz, Bin 56 Cabernet-Malbec and Classic Clare Cabernet Sauvignon are hefty, big-boned wines, flooded with fruit, saturated with oak, and with enough tannin and extract to stop a runaway truck. They are expensive and do particularly well in wine shows but in the real world need ten years or so to be broken in. Magnus Shiraz-Cabernet is better value. Best years: (reds) 2002, '01, '99, '98, '97, '96, '95, '94, '91, '90, '88.

L'ECOLE NO 41

USA, Washington State, Columbia Valley AVA
♥ Merlot, Cabernet Sauvignon, Syrah
♀ Semillon, Chardonnay, Chenin Blanc

If we talk of the wines of WASHINGTON STATE as a purely modern venture, the guys in historic Frenchtown might have something to say because, supposedly, a bunch of French-Canadians were growing grapes here and making wine in the early 1800s. True or not, the story's good enough for Frenchtown's present day winery named l'Ecole No 41 – the school for District 41 – and situated in the old schoolhouse. They're famous for Merlot and Cabernet, and as local WALLA WALLA vineyards have matured they use more and more

of their fruit, but their forgotten genius actually lies in whites – good Chardonnay and Chenin and exceptional Semillon, which, at Reserve and single-vineyard level, may well be the best in the USA. Best years: (top reds) 2001, '00, '99, '97, '96.

LEEUWIN ESTATE

AUSTRALIA, Western Australia, Margaret River
♥ Cabernet Sauvignon, Syrah (Shiraz)
♀ Chardonnay, Riesling, Sauvignon Blanc

Since Leeuwin's debut vintage in 1980, its Art Series Chardonnay has been one of Australia's best. Indeed, in the early days, it was *the* best, and even now is rarely overshadowed by rivals. Incredibly concentrated and long-lived, these nectarine-, melon- and grapefruit-flavoured wines, along with sophisticated but subtle savouriness and creaminess from the barrel fermentation, have all the complexity and richness of the Bayeux tapestry. Prelude Chardonnay (the bits that don't make the Art Series Chardonnay) and Sauvignon Blanc are fine wines also. The Riesling sometimes gets forgotten but undeservedly so because it is a classic citrus-scented example. But the most exciting recent development has been a seismic shift in red wine style from the lean green to a magnificent, serious, balanced but ripe MARGARET RIVER style that will match the best in the region. Best years: (Art Series Chardonnay) 2001, '00, '99, '98, '97, '96, '95, '94, '92, '91, '87, '85, '82, '81, '80.

DOMAINE LEFLAIVE

FRANCE, Burgundy, Côte de Beaune, Puligny-Montrachet AC
♥ Pinot Noir
♀ Chardonnay

Vincent Leflaive was a much respected and much loved personality in BURGUNDY for many decades. He ruled over Leflaive, one of PULIGNY-MONTRACHET's great domaines, with 22ha (54 acres) of vines almost entirely within this celebrated commune. Almost half the vineyards are in Premier Cru sites, and there are also small parcels in Bienvenues-Bâtard-Montrachet, BÂTARD-MONTRACHET, Chevalier-Montrachet and (since 1990) le MONTRACHET itself. Perhaps it was because of the high regard in which Vincent was held that few dared to declare publicly that by the late 1980s the wines seemed to lack concentration and elegance. In 1990 he retired, but his daughter Anne-Claude and nephew Olivier were in effect already running the estate. After Vincent's death in 1993, Anne-

Since taking over Domaine Leflaive in 1993, Anne-Claude Leflaive has encouraged a move to biodynamic viticulture, with encouraging results.

Claude became the sole administrator, although Olivier, who had by then developed his own successful *négociant* business, was still associated with the domaine till 1994.

Anne-Claude persuaded her team, including the domaine's respected winemaker Pierre Morey, to adopt biodynamism in the vineyards. Whether these viticultural practices are responsible for the wines' swift improvement it is hard to say, but since 1995 Leflaive has regained its place among the top producers of great white Burgundy. The wines are definitely built for the long haul and the domaine aims for a purity and precision of flavour. It achieves its objectives triumphantly, even if it takes a few years for the full glory to emerge. Best years: 2002, '01, '99, '98, '97, '96, '95, '94, '93.

OLIVIER LEFLAIVE

FRANCE, Burgundy, Côte de Beaune, Puligny-Montrachet AC
♥ Pinot Noir
♀ Chardonnay, Aligoté

For about a decade Olivier Leflaive combined two separate roles. He was a director of the revered Domaine LEFLAIVE and at the same time built up a successful *négociant* business. With the brilliant winemaker Franck Grux at his side, he was able to release each year a range of Burgundies, mostly but not exclusively white, that were as good as those of most domaines. The range was striking: from the finest Grands Crus to well-made village wines, and a generous selection of Premiers Crus from MEURSAULT, PULIGNY-

MONTRACHET and CHASSAGNE-MONTRA-CHET as well as rarer villages such as RULLY and ST-AUBIN, which offer excellent value.

Leflaive does not use a great deal of new oak, and even for the superior appellations he rarely uses more than 50 per cent though they always seem to taste fairly oaky when they're young. He now offers wine from some 60 ACs and, understandably enough, consistency is no longer what it was. But from every vintage there are some excellent cuvées, normally offered at a fair price. Leflaive has started to establish a domaine of his own, with 12ha (30 acres), including Premier Crus in Chassagne-Montrachet, purchased so far. Best years: (top whites) 2002, '01, '00, '99, '97, '96, '95.

PETER LEHMANN
AUSTRALIA, South Australia, Barossa Valley
♥ *Cabernet Sauvignon, Syrah (Shiraz), Grenache, Merlot*
♀ *Riesling, Chardonnay, Semillon, Chenin Blanc*
Peter Lehmann is a larger-than-life figure who has stood astride his beloved BAROSSA VALLEY for over 30 years and though he hasn't made the wines for some time now, they've never lost his imprint – proudly Barossa in nature, reflecting their vineyard character but also reflecting the indulgent, passionate and generous nature of Peter Lehmann himself. Though famous for red, the whites are remarkably good, in particular Chenin Blanc and Semillon and top wine EDEN VALLEY Riesling, and all age well. Reds are altogether more lush – happy-juice Grenache followed by rich, oaky Cabernet Sauvignon and Shiraz. The varietals are led by outstanding Stonewell Shiraz and extremely serious Mentor Cabernet. All the Lehmann wines feature beautiful artwork, and you'll also find mostly red blends with more fanciful names like The Seven Surveys and Eight Songs Shiraz. Best years: (Stonewell Shiraz) 2001, '99, '98, '96, '94, '93, '92, '91, '90, '89.

JOSEF LEITZ
GERMANY, Rheingau, Rüdesheim
♀ *Riesling*
Preferring to learn his lessons from practical winemaking at estates like GUNDERLOCH and LOOSEN rather than follow his wine school teaching, Johannes Leitz rapidly established himself in the early 1990s as one of the RHEINGAU's leading young winemakers with some ravishingly elegant dry and off-dry Rieslings from the top RÜDESHEIM sites (the great Berg Schlossberg and Berg Rottland), as well

as small amounts of brilliant sweet whites. Very low yields and extremely long fermentations result in concentrated wines that need time to show their best. Best years: (Riesling Spätlese) 2002, '01, '00, '99, '98, '97, '96.

LEIWEN
GERMANY, Mosel-Saar-Ruwer
Despite having the excellent Laurentiuslay site – which can produce magnificent Spätlese and Auslese wines with natural sweetness – this large wine village in the Mittel MOSEL used to be famous for quantity rather than quality. However, a new generation of winemakers has turned Leiwen into a hotbed of the Mosel Riesling revolution. Best years: 2002, '01, '99, '98, '97, '95, '94, '93, '90. Best producers: GRANS-FASSIAN, Carl LOEWEN, Alfons Stoffel, Werner & Sohn.

LENSWOOD VINEYARDS
AUSTRALIA, South Australia, Adelaide Hills
♥ *Pinot Noir, Cabernet Sauvignon, Merlot, Malbec*
♀ *Chardonnay, Sauvignon Blanc, Semillon*
Tim and Annie Knappstein established the KNAPPSTEIN winery in CLARE VALLEY but in 1981 also bought land in Lenswood. After they sold Knappstein to PETALUMA in 1992 they concentrated all their efforts on Lenswood, and further purchases have brought their distinctly cool-climate holding to 54ha (133 acres). They are best known for their tangy Sauvignon, elegant Chardonnay and perfumed Pinot Noir, but in warmer years also release a Semillon and a rich, sturdy BORDEAUX blend called The Palatine. In 2003 they sold the vineyards but will continue to produce a 'Lenswood Vineyards' label.

LEONETTI CELLAR
USA, Washington State, Columbia Valley AVA
♥ *Cabernet Sauvignon, Merlot, Sangiovese and others*
If there is one winery that has catapulted WASHINGTON into the stratosphere, it has to be Leonetti, a small cult producer of fantastically lush Merlot and superrich Cabernet. Owner Gary Figgins started it in 1978 and got into top gear immediately. Nowadays he's confident enough to experiment with different oaks and new barrels each year finding a range of ways to craft round and supple wines needing only short aging. The superlative Merlot deserves its loyal following and can be exceptionally hard to acquire. His Cabernet is almost as good. A small amount of Sangiovese is produced, and Figgins is clearly enamoured of the variety. Best years: (Cabernet) 2001, '00, '99, '98, '97, '96, '95.

CH. LÉOVILLE-BARTON
FRANCE, Bordeaux, Haut-Médoc, St-Julien AC, 2ème Cru Classé
♥ *Cabernet Sauvignon, Merlot, Cabernet Franc*
Anthony Barton, whose family has run this Second Growth ST-JULIEN since 1821, has resolutely refused to profiteer in spite of considerable pressure to do so, especially in the early to late 1980s, when every Classed Growth BORDEAUX vintage was released at a substantially higher price than the last, regardless of actual worth. But he refused to raise the prices of his wines above a level he considered fair. By 1986 he was charging only half what one or two of his more ambitious neighbours thought 'reasonable'. Yet as he freely declares, he still runs a profitable business. He knows what it costs to make fine wine, he never stints on quality, and he certainly doesn't intend to make a less than satisfactory profit. Prices in the 1990s moved with the market, but Léoville-Barton still remains reasonably priced.

This 47-ha (116-acre) estate – with 72 per cent Cabernet Sauvignon, 20 per cent Merlot, and only 8 per cent Cabernet Franc – makes dark, dry, tannic wines, difficult to taste young and therefore frequently underestimated at the outset, but over ten to 15 years they achieve a lean yet beautifully proportioned quality, the blackcurrants and cedarwood very dry, but pungent enough to fill the room with their scent. They are a traditionalist's delight. Vintages throughout the 1990s were very successful and even the off-vintages are good. Best years: 2002, '01, '00, '99, '98, '96, '95, '94, '93, '90, '89, '88, '86, '85, '83, '82.

CH. LÉOVILLE-LAS-CASES
FRANCE, Bordeaux, Haut-Médoc, St-Julien AC, 2ème Cru Classé
♥ *Cabernet Sauvignon, Merlot, Cabernet Franc, Petit Verdot*
The ST-JULIEN AC wasn't accorded a First Growth in the 1855 Classification. Any re-evaluation would change all that, because in Léoville-las-Cases, St-Julien has a property whose late owner tirelessly maximized the excellent vineyard's potential until his death in 2000. Going to meet Monsieur Delon was rather like having an audience with your headmaster at school, but these challenging tasting sessions in his cellars gave one a true understanding of the passion and commitment that is great BORDEAUX.

The 97-ha (240-acre) vineyard is the biggest of the three Léoville estates, and a neighbour of the great Ch. LATOUR. There are similarities in the wine because since 1975 las-Cases has been making wines of dark, deep concentration. Yet there is also something sweeter and more enticing right from the start – the fumes of new oak spice linger over the glass even in the wine's most stubborn adolescent sulks, and the tannins, strong though they are, have a habit of dissolving into smiles in your mouth exactly at the moment you've decided that they are just too much. Las-Cases from a good year really needs 15 years to shine. Second wine: Clos du Marquis. Best years: 2001, '00, '99, '98, '96, '95, '94, '93, '90, '89, '88, '86, '85, '83, '82.

CH. LÉOVILLE-POYFERRÉ

FRANCE, Bordeaux, Haut-Médoc, St-Julien AC, 2ème Cru Classé

♟ *Cabernet Sauvignon, Merlot, Petit Verdot, Cabernet Franc*

Until comparatively recently, Poyferré was the least good of the three Léoville properties. The 1980s saw a marked improvement, however, with a string of excellent wines made under the watchful eye of Didier Cuvelier, who has gradually increased the richness of the wine without wavering from its austere style and has significantly reduced the percentage of Merlot in the vineyard. The 1990s followed in the same vein, often ranking with the best in ST-JULIEN and achieving the epitome of St-Julien elegance. The wines need eight to ten years to blossom. Second wine: Ch. Moulin-Riche. Best years: 2001, '00, '99, '98, '96, '95, '94, '90, '89, '86, '85, '83, '82.

DOMAINE LEROY, MAISON LEROY

FRANCE, Burgundy, Côte de Nuits, Vosne-Romanée AC

♟ *Pinot Noir*

♀ *Aligoté, Chardonnay*

Until 1992 dynamic Lalou Bize-Leroy was in the enviable position of running a highly regarded *négociant* business, Maison Leroy, based in AUXEY-DURESSES and at the same time being a major partner and co-director in Domaine de la ROMANÉE-CONTI (DRC). But in the early 1990s questionable commercial

MAISON LEROY

White wine from Auxey-Duresses is not generally memorable, but Maison Leroy's example is clean and well structured, with lemon and butter aromas.

decisions led to her being ousted from the DRC, though she still owns shares. Another factor that precipitated her departure was her decision to purchase the Charles Noëllat estate in VOSNE-ROMANÉE, which, some argued, could be seen as a conflict of interest with her role at DRC.

Maison Leroy had always pursued a costly strategy of holding vast stocks of mature wines, gradually released as Madame Bize-Leroy saw fit. Although older vintages still remain available, she now focuses more on developing the superb vineyards of the former Noëllat estate, renamed Domaine Leroy. From the cellars in Vosne, she offers a range of wines from the greatest sites: CHAMBERTIN, MUSIGNY, RICHEBOURG, Romanée-St-Vivant, CLOS DE LA ROCHE and many more. She is an enthusiastic convert to biodynamism, and is fanatical when it comes to controlling yields. Her yields are always extremely low – and her wines powerfully concentrated. No expense is spared, in vineyard or winery, and most of the wines are aged in new oak. This expense, not surprisingly, is passed on to her loyal customers, and her prices rival those of the DRC. She insists that given the extremely low yields she obtains from her vines, the prices she demands are not unreasonable. Certainly, she has not lacked customers or enthusiastic reviews for her wines, which are in the starry ranks of the top tier in Burgundy. Best years: (top reds) 2002, '01, '00, '99, '98, '97, '96, '95, '90, '89.

LIBRANDI

ITALY, Calabria, Cirò DOC

♟ *Gaglioppo, Magliocco, Cabernet Sauvignon*

♟ *Gaglioppo, Cabernet Franc*

♀ *Greco Bianco, Mantonico Bianco, Chardonnay*

The brothers Antonio and Nicodemo Librandi have carved out their reputation by dint of an unremitting commitment to the improving quality in CIRÒ, their particular corner of CALABRIA. The classic Librandi wines are Cirò Rosso, from the native Gaglioppo grape, and Cirò Bianco, from the local version of Greco. An upmarket cru of Cirò Rosso, Duca San Felice, is perhaps their best wine, though in a market situation which seeks more recognizable flavours the Cabernet-Gaglioppo blend Gravello has had more success. The recently introduced Magno Megonio, made with the Magliocco grape, has had a lot of success, while the white Critone and the Rosé Terre Lontane have won considerable praise. Best years: (reds) 2001, '00, '99, '97, '96, '93, '92, '91, '90.

LIEBFRAUMILCH

GERMANY, Rheinhessen, Pfalz and Nahe

♀ *Riesling, Silvaner, Müller-Thurgau, Kerner and others*

Liebfraumilch used to be the perfect beginner's wine and was the fuel for the dramatic surge in British wine drinking in the early 1980s. It is almost always sold under a brand name or a retailer's own label; it never has a grape name on the label, and it is always a Qualitätswein. It may not be *trocken* or *halbtrocken*, and while 70 per cent of its grapes are supposed to be from the four in the list above, in practice there is no Riesling in most Liebfraumilch – Germany's finest grape is too expensive for cheap blends. The regulations say the character of the wine need only be pleasant and agreeable. The poorer, cheaper ones make you wonder just who it is who deems sulphur or oxidation to be pleasant or agreeable and Liebfraumilch is now generally regarded with mild disdain.

LIGURIA

ITALY

Flower-bedecked Liguria, 'Italy's Riviera', is a slim arc of craggy mountains, with a thin coastal strip of land, centred on Genoa. The mountains form a good barrier against the cold air from the north, and the huge mass of warm, Mediterranean water in the bay further tempers the climate, giving Liguria some of Italy's mildest winters. Most Ligurian wine comes from the Riviera Ligure di Ponente DOC, west of Genoa. The most important grapes are light, delicate, white Vermentino; floral, peachy, white Pigato; red Ormeasco (better known as Dolcetto), which also comes, called Sciac-Trà, as a deep rosé; and the succulently fruity red Rossese, particularly good from Dolceacqua. On the eastern side, the Riviera di Levante, where Colli di Luni DOC is the major wine, Vermentino is still important, but most other grapes grown here are Tuscan varieties. The exception is the tiny zone of Cinqueterre with its sought-after whites, including the sweet Sciacchetrà.

LIMESTONE COAST

AUSTRALIA, South Australia

Limestone Coast is a new name for a newly defined zone of south-east Australia, but the concept is not new. Down here in the damp cool bottom of SOUTH AUSTRALIA people have known for generations that the only bits of land that you can use to grow a crop of grapes are the thankfully numerous outcrops of weathered terra rossa limestone that litter the coast. COONAWARRA and PADTHAWAY are the most famous of these but from Mount Gambier in the south, to Robe and Mount Benson on the coast and up to WRATTONBULLY in the north, there are the remains of 14 different coastlines, all limestone, that have been created each time the seas have advanced and retreated.

Coonawarra and Padthaway are both well established but the flavours from the newer areas are exciting enough to suggest that for whites, and especially reds, Australia has found itself another star region. Whether or not it achieves superstar status depends upon whether wine companies nurture it or abuse it. Southcorp, Beringer Blass, YALUMBA, HARDY and EVANS & TATE are all involved.

LIMOUX AC
FRANCE, Languedoc-Roussillon
🍷 *Merlot, Syrah, Grenache, Malbec, Cabernet Sauvignon, Cabernet Franc, Carignan*
🍷 *Chardonnay, Chenin Blanc, Mauzac*

Limoux is probably the best white wine region in the south of France. The sparkling wines, which account for 94 per cent of production, are sold as BLANQUETTE and CRÉMANT DE LIMOUX, and the still wines as straight Limoux. This was the first AC in the Languedoc to authorize the use of Chardonnay and Chenin Blanc, which must be vinified in oak. Production is dominated by the SIEUR D'ARQUES co-operative, whose best still wine, Toques et Clochers (Chardonnay), fetches high prices at the annual charity auction. New from 2003 is a red Limoux AC, made from a minimum 50 per cent Merlot along with Syrah, Grenache, Carignan and Malbec. Best producers: Dom. de l'AIGLE, Dom. Bégude, Sieur d'Arques.

LINDEMANS
AUSTRALIA, Victoria, Murray Darling
🍷 *Syrah (Shiraz), Cabernet Sauvignon, Merlot*
🍷 *Chardonnay, Sauvignon Blanc, Semillon, Colombard*

Lindemans – a key component of the Southcorp corporation – produces around seven million cases of wine a year, including prodigious quantities of Bin 65 Chardonnay, skilfully woven together at its Karadoc headquarters in Murray Darling. However, its quality feet are planted in the LIMESTONE COAST zone in SOUTH AUSTRALIA (in COONAWARRA, PADTHAWAY and Robe) and to a lesser degree in the HUNTER VALLEY. In a fast-changing world, the supple though undoubtedly oaky, single-vineyard St George

Cabernet Sauvignon and Limestone Ridge Shiraz-Cabernet wines from Coonawarra, together with the BORDEAUX-blend Pyrus, and the similarly generously barrel-fermented and oaked Padthaway Chardonnay, keep the Lindemans flag flying high. Best years: (Coonawarra reds) 2001, '00, '99, '98, '96, '94, '91, '90, '88, '86.

LIRAC AC
FRANCE, Southern Rhône
🍷🍷 *Grenache, Syrah, Mourvèdre, Cinsaut, Carignan*
🍷 *Clairette, Grenache Blanc, Bourboulenc and others*

This excellent but underrated AC, between TAVEL and CHÂTEAUNEUF-DU-PAPE, makes wines that resemble both its more famous neighbours. There are 714ha (1764 acres) of vines producing nearly four million bottles a year, mostly red and rosé. The red has the dusty, spicy fruit of Châteauneuf-du-Pape, without achieving the intensity and power of the best examples, plus an attractive metallic streak. The rosés are breezier, more refreshing than Tavel, and can have a lovely strawberry fruit. Drink them sharpish. The reds age very well but are always delicious young. When on form, the whites can be as good as white Châteauneuf-du-Pape. Clairette is the chief grape, with other local varieties like Bourboulenc and Picpoul added. Drink it young, though, before the perfume goes. Best years: (reds) 2001, '00, '99, '98, '97, '96, '94, '91, '90. Best producers: (reds) Amido, Aquéria, Bouchassy, la Genestière, Joncier, Lafond-Roc-Épine, Maby, Mont-Redon, la Mordorée, Pélaquié, Roger Sabon, St-Roch, Ségriès, Tavel co-operative.

DOMAINE DE LA MORDORÉE
Cuvée de la Reine des Bois is a very attractive example of red Lirac – with a slightly floral, exotic nose, it has lots of ripe fruit and some herbal overtones.

LISTRAC-MEDOC AC
FRANCE, Bordeaux, Haut-Médoc
🍷🍷 *Cabernet Sauvignon, Merlot, Cabernet Franc*

This is one of the six specific ACs inside the HAUT-MÉDOC area, but does not possess any Classed Growths. All the best Haut-Médoc vineyards are on gravel soil and mainly on

ridges within sight of the Gironde estuary. Listrac, however, is set several miles inland, its 669ha (1653 acres) of vineyards fashioned on clay or outcrops of partially gravelled heavy soil, encircled by forest.

Even so, the wine can be good, although the relative lack of gravel means few of its vines have the tantalizing fragrance of top MARGAUX or ST-JULIEN wines, being nearer to ST-ESTÈPHE in style. Solid fruit, a slightly coarse tannin and an earthy flavour are the marks of most Listracs. Those owners able to invest in vineyard drainage and new oak make more attractive, balanced wines. The percentage of Merlot, better suited to the heavy soils, has also increased to provide wines with more generosity of fruit. Best years: 2001, '00, '96, '95, '90, '89, '88, '86, '85. Best producers: Cap-Léon-Veyrin, CLARKE, Ducluzeau, Fonréaud, Fourcas-Dupré, Fourcas-Hosten, Fourcas-Loubaney, Grand Listrac co-operative, Mayne-Lalande, Saransot-Dupré.

LJUTOMER
SLOVENIA, Podravje
🍷 *Laski Rizling, Furmint (Sipon), Sauvignon Blanc and others*

The Ljutomer-Ormož region in the PODRAVJE region is Slovenia's best source of whites, though anyone familiar with the feeble, branded Ljutomer (or Lutomer) wines that venture abroad would be forgiven for disagreeing. Most of the wine comes from the two co-operatives, at Ljutomer and Ormož, the latter being the bigger and better. The best wines are extraordinarily good: fresh, full Laski Rizling, balanced, rich Sipon (alias Furmint, which makes Hungary's TOKAJI), and splendid botrytis-affected dessert wines.

CARL LOEWEN
GERMANY, Mosel-Saar-Ruwer, Leiwen
🍷 *Riesling, Müller-Thurgau*

During the 1990s Karl-Josef Loewen systematically worked to make his estate one of the best in the Mittel MOSEL. He makes the best Rieslings from the excellent Laurentiuslay site of LEIWEN. His old vines here give naturally sweet Spätlese and Auslese wines with a rich peachy fruit and an intense minerally character. The second string to his bow are the firm, tight wines from the terraces of the Thörnicher Ritsch. Lighter, but with a brilliance reminiscent of the SAAR, are his Rieslings from the Maximiner Klosterlay of Detzem, which are fermented almost to dryness. Towering above all of these are his Eisweins from the Klostergarten of Leiwen. Best years: 2002, '01, '00, '99, '98, '97, '96, '95, '94, '93, '92.

LOIRE France

THE LOIRE RIVER CUTS RIGHT THROUGH the heart of France, east to west. It rises in the Ardèche gorges a mere 50km (30 miles) from the Rhône Valley and, after surging northwards, executes a graceful arc up to Orléans where it then sets off westwards for the sea. Along the way the river encompasses some of France's best-known wines – Sancerre, Anjou and Muscadet – and some of its most obscure – Jasnières, Bonnezeaux and Vin de l'Orléanais, as well as some of its most thrilling and individual wines – in particular, the sweet wines of the Layon Valley. Altogether there are about 70 different wine appellations located here, producing reds, rosés, sparkling, and the entire gamut of whites, from searingly dry to unctuously sweet.

The upper reaches of the Loire south of Nevers don't produce any wines of great consequence and there isn't much of it anyway. Sancerre and Pouilly-Fumé, regarded by many as the quintessential Sauvignon Blanc styles, are the first really important wines areas heading downstream.

The province of Touraine is a positive market garden, with vines taking their place alongside other crops, but the Sauvignon grape excels here too, and at Vouvray and Mont-louis the Chenin makes good fizz and still whites ranging from sweet to very dry. A bit of Chardonnay starts to make its presence felt, and there's some pretty decent red from Cabernet and Gamay. But the Loire's best reds are made just downstream at Chinon and Bourgueil from Cabernet Franc – they are wonderful young but also capable of staying fresh for decades.

Anjou is most famous for its rosé, though there are some tasty reds (Anjou-Villages and Saumur-Champigny are the best appellations). But the best wines are white, either sweet from the Layon Valley, and to a lesser extent, the Aubance Valley, or very dry from Savennières on the north bank of the Loire and all made from the Chenin Blanc grape. The climatic feature that allows Chenin Blanc to ripen at all along the cool Loire Valley is a generally warm, early autumn, that with luck, pushes the late-ripening Chenin to a decent level of maturity and also encourages the develop-

ment of the *Botrytis cinerea* or noble rot fungus in the grapes, which as in Sauternes, naturally concentrates their sweetness to a remarkable degree.

Saumur is one of France's chief centres for sparkling wine. The soils here are more chalky than in the rest of Anjou and this encourages a certain leanness in the wines, which along with cool ripening conditions, produces the sort of acid base wine that sparkling wine producers like. The soft local limestone (tuffeau) is ideal rock for excavating cellars to mature the sparkling wine. Many of the cellars began life as quarries for the honeyed-colour stone used to build the famous Loire châteaux.

Finally, at the western end of the Loire Valley, in the low flatland around Nantes, they make that uncomplicated light neutral white, Muscadet. A decent Muscadet *sur lie* from the Sèvre-et-Maine appellation, is an excellent bone dry but yeasty wine to accompany the superb local seafood or just a quiet seaside chat.

The vineyards around Chaume are some of the best in the sheltered Layon Valley where Chenin Blanc produces one of the world's great sweet wines. Only the most favoured sites can produce grapes with the necessary overripeness.

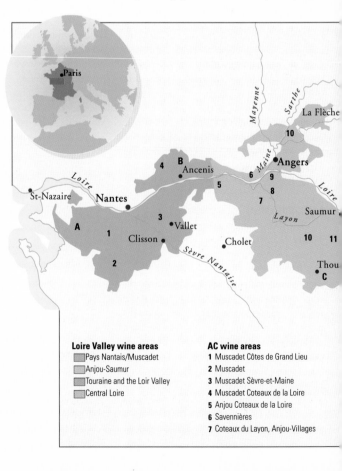

REGIONAL ENTRIES

Anjou, Anjou-Villages, Bonnezeaux, Bourgueil, Cabernet d'Anjou, Cheverny, Chinon, Coteaux du Layon, Coteaux du Layon-Villages, Crémant de Loire, Gros Plant du Pays Nantais, Menetou-Salon, Montlouis, Muscadet, Pouilly-Fumé, Quarts de Chaume, Quincy, Reuilly, Rosé d'Anjou, Rosé de Loire, St-Nicolas-de-Bourgueil, Sancerre, Saumur, Saumur-Champigny, Savennières, Touraine, Vouvray.

PRODUCER ENTRIES

Ackerman-Laurance, Henri Bourgeois, Clos Rougeard, Couly-Dutheil, Didier Dagueneau, de Fesles, Huet, Alphonse Mellot, Louis Métaireau, de Villeneuve.

Loire Valley wine areas
- Pays Nantais/Muscadet
- Anjou-Saumur
- Touraine and the Loir Valley
- Central Loire

AC wine areas
1 Muscadet Côtes de Grand Lieu
2 Muscadet
3 Muscadet Sèvre-et-Maine
4 Muscadet Coteaux de la Loire
5 Anjou Coteaux de la Loire
6 Savennières
7 Coteaux du Layon, Anjou-Villages

DOMAINE RICHOU
This sweet Coteaux de l'Aubance is a marvellous combination of richness and fresh, lime flavours.

CH. DE FESLES
In good years la Chapelle is a fabulously rich and long-lived Bonnezeaux.

JOSEPH RENOU
Sold under the Domaine du Petit Metris label, this is excellent intense Quarts de Chaume.

CLOS DE LA COULÉE-DE-SERRANT
Made exclusively from Chenin Blanc, this dry white has a fascinating honeyed, floral bouquet.

CLOS ROUGEARD
This unusual oak-fermented Saumur Blanc comes from old vines.

CHARLES JOGUET
From very old vines the Clos de la Dioterie shows dark red and black fruit with penetrating depth.

DOMAINE HUET
Le Haut Lieu is one of three excellent sites owned by this top Vouvray estate.

PASCAL COTAT
The Cotat Sancerres have a concentration of fruit that few other growers achieve.

DIDIER DAGUENEAU
Dagueneau is best known for his barrel-fermented Sauvignon Blanc called Silex, which needs several years of aging for the real style to emerge.

		VDQS wine areas	
8 Bonnezeaux, Quarts de Chaume	15 Chinon	22 Cheverny, Cour-Cheverny	A Gros Plant du Pays Nantais
9 Coteaux de l'Aubance	16 Coteaux du Loir	23 Reuilly	B Coteaux d'Ancenis
10 Anjou	17 Jasnières	24 Quincy	C Vins de Thouarsais
11 Saumur	18 Coteau du Vendômois	25 Menetou-Salon	D Vins de l'Orléanais
12 Saumur-Champigny	19 Vouvray	26 Sancerre	E Valençay
13 St-Nicolas-de-Bourgueil	20 Montlouis	27 Pouilly-Fumé, Pouilly-sur-Loire	
14 Bourgueil	21 Touraine	28 Coteaux du Giennois	

LOMBARDY
ITALY

Don't feel too sorry for Lombardy if your first sight of it is the polluted, factory-filled suburbs of Milan. Those ugly industrial expanses are pumping out wealth at a rate unmatched anywhere else in the country. But you don't have to go far to avoid the ugliness – not only is old Milan beautiful but there are numerous other fine cities like Brescia and Bergamo to enjoy. And if you stray southwards through the dull, intensely cultivated Po Valley flatlands, either keep going for the solace of the gently wooded region of the OLTREPÒ PAVESE over the River Po or, ideally, cut your losses, and hare back north, past Milan, and you'll soon be in the land of Lakes Maggiore, Como and Iseo and the fabulous Alps protecting Switzerland's southern flank.

Remarkably, this most prosperous of areas is not well endowed with famous wines. The most important area is the Oltrepò Pavese in the south-west which produces over 70 million bottles every year – but most of it goes straight down Milan's welcoming throat. Perhaps the most fascinating is VALTELLINA, way up in the mountains, where Nebbiolo, aided by some very ancient varieties as well as Merlot and Pinot Noir makes a variety of red styles. Of the rest, LUGANA is a good white near Lake Garda and there are various obscure and long-winded DOCs but the most impressive is FRANCIACORTA west of Brescia where many of Italy's finest sparklers are made as well as some very serious – and expensive – reds and whites.

LONG ISLAND AVA
USA, New York State

The Hamptons may have the bigger houses and throw the better parties, but the soil is heavier there, the climate's cooler and there's no doubt the less glitzy North Fork is where the best vineyards are – on a 19-km (12-mile) finger of land stretching from Riverhead to Southold. It has a 230-day growing season which ends with autumn conditions very similar to those of BORDEAUX. Which can be good or bad – autumn storms often blast Bordeaux just as they do Long Island – but there have been many fine wines: some Merlots and Cabernets, rather more Chardonnays and other whites so far. About 800ha (2000 acres) of vineyards have so far been planted on Long Island. Best years: (reds) 2001, '00, '98, '97, '95. Best producers: Bedell, Castello di Borghese/Hargrave, Galluccio/Gristina, Lenz, Palmer, Pellegrini, Pindar, Schneider.

DR LOOSEN

Ernst Loosen's estate has portions of some of the Mosel's most famous vineyards, including the Sonnenuhr (or Sundial) in Wehlen.

DR LOOSEN
GERMANY, Mosel-Saar-Ruwer, Bernkastel
♀ *Riesling, Rivaner*

Without in any way compromising the MOSEL's tradition for Rieslings with a naturally low alcoholic content (7.5 – 8.5 degrees) Ernst Loosen makes some of the most concentrated and complex Rieslings anywhere in the world. The definition of vineyard character is almost supernaturally clear: Dr Loosen's WEHLENer Sonnenuhr wines are the archetypal wines of this site, with tremendous elegance, peachy fruit and a very clean finish, while the bigger wines from the ERDENer Treppchen site have a herbal character which grows in intensity as they age. The ÜRZIGer Würzgarten wines really live up to their name, Würzgarten meaning 'spice garden', and the wines, from vines up to 100 years old, are packed with mineral extract.

Finest of all are the Ausleses from the Erdener Prälat site, enjoying the most favoured climate in the entire region, which have a lavish exotic fruits character and enormous intensity. Even Ernst Loosen's basic Dr L Riesling is a textbook example of regional style. In 1996 Loosen took over the WOLF estate at Wachenheim in the PFALZ. Best years: 2002, '01, '99, '98, '97, '96, '95, '94, '93, '92, '90, '89, '88, '85, '76.

LÓPEZ DE HEREDIA
SPAIN, La Rioja, Rioja DOC
♦ *Tempranillo, Grenache Noir (Garnacha Tinta), Carignan (Cariñena, Mazuelo), Graciano*
♦ *Tempranillo, Grenache Noir (Garnacha Tinta), Macabeo (Viura)*
♀ *Macabeo (Viura), Malvasia*

This endearingly old-fashioned RIOJA bodega makes wines that are fine and delicious by any standards, ancient or modern. The wines ferment and pass their early months in large wooden fermentation vats, are clarified with egg whites, and never see a filter. López de Heredia only uses Rioja Alta grapes, half of them from its own vineyards. Reds represent three-quarters of the production, and age for a considerable time in wood. The youngest red, Viña Cubillo, is soft, fine and lightly oaky, and the Viña Tondonia Tinto is elegant, strawberry-fruity and oaky. Whites are excellent too and will mature for many years: this is one of the few bodegas still making old-style, oaked white Rioja. Best is the delicious, spicily oaky, honey-and-vanilla-flavoured Viña Tondonia Blanco. Best years: (Viña Tondonia) 1995, '94, '93, '91, '87, '86, '85.

LOUPIAC AC
FRANCE, Bordeaux
♀ *Sémillon, Muscadelle, Sauvignon Blanc*

This sweet wine area is directly across the river Garonne from BARSAC. But the Loupiac growers, despite using the same grapes, can't persuade noble rot to affect their vines nearly as frequently as it does in Barsac, and they do have a far higher permitted yield – 40 hectolitres per hectare as against Barsac's 25 hectolitres. Despite this, there are some good estates producing wine which is attractively sweet, if not really gooey. Drink young, though the best can age. Best years: 2001, '99, '98, '97, '96, '95, '90, '89, '88, '86. Best producers: Clos Jean, du Cros, Loupiac-Gaudiet, Mémoires, du Noble, de Ricaud, les Roques.

CH. LA LOUVIÈRE
FRANCE, Bordeaux, Pessac-Léognan AC
♦ *Cabernet Sauvignon, Merlot, Cabernet Franc, Petit Verdot*
♀ *Sauvignon Blanc, Sémillon*

When the planned revision of the GRAVES classification comes you can take a safe bet that Ch. la Louvière will find a place in the new order. For the time being, though, it remains one of PESSAC-LÉOGNAN's unclassified stars, thanks to the efforts of dynamic owner André Lurton.

The estate is large, with 47ha (116 acres) under vine. The lion's share of this is red, planted with 65 per cent Cabernet Sauvignon and 30 per cent Merlot. The wines are well structured but attractively fruity, making them drinkable when young but with an aging potential of ten years or more. Whites plantings are 85 per cent Sauvignon, 15 per cent Sémillon and the wines tend to be vigorous and aromatic but also age surprisingly well. Second label: (red and white) L de la Louvière. Best years: (reds) 2001, '00, '99, '98, '96, '95, '94, '93, '90, '89, '88, '86, '85; (whites) 2001, '00, '99, '98, '96, '95, '94, '93, '90, '89, '88.

LOVICO SUHINDOL

BULGARIA, Northern Region
♥ *Cabernet Sauvignon, Merlot, Gamza and others*
♀ *Dimiat and others*

It shows how young the Bulgarian wine industry is that Suhindol, founded in 1909, is very much regarded as the granddaddy of Bulgarian wineries. There have been vineyards here for thousands of years, but when you remember that Bulgaria was under Turkish Islamic domination from 1396 to 1878, it makes it surprising that the Suhindol winery opened as early as 1909. The fact that it was put into pole position when the USSR triggered the planting of enormous amounts of fertile valley floor land and Suhindol's position on the Danube plain just north of the Balkan mountains meant it was perfectly placed to become one of Bulgaria's dominant wineries.

During the 1970s and '80s Suhindol Cabernet Sauvignon with its coarse but juicy blackcurrant fruit and broad, earthy but soft rustic texture, was probably Bulgaria's most famous wine. With privatization in 1991 Suhindol continued to flourish, now controlling three wineries and owning some 1500ha (3706 acres) of its own vineyards – rare in Bulgaria. Besides the Suhindol label, there are brands such as Craftsman's Creek, Copper Crossing and so on. New contracts with independent growers will eventually supply grapes from another 2500ha (6177 acres). So Suhindol is a major player, but Bulgaria as a whole has lost much of its importance and, modern though these new Suhindols are, they don't stand out like the old Cabernets once did.

LUGANA DOC

ITALY, Lombardy
♀ *Trebbiano di Lugana*

The Trebbiano di Lugana clone, like Trebbiano di Soave is a version of Verdicchio – meaning that it has far more stuffing and flavour than the usual limp offerings from normal Trebbiano. Lugana is a floral, appley white of surprising weight to be drunk young – and it mainly is, by the hordes of tourists who flock to Garda's shores every summer. It can age for a year or two. Best producers: Ca' dei Frati, Ottella, Provenza, Visconti, Zenato.

LUNGAROTTI

ITALY, Umbria, Torgiano DOC
♥ *Sangiovese, Canaiolo, Cabernet Sauvignon, Merlot, Montepulciano, Pinot Noir (Pinot Nero), Sagrantino*
♀ *Sangiovese, Canaiolo, Merlot*
♀ *Trebbiano, Grechetto, Chardonnay, Pinot Gris (Pinot Grigio)*

Lungarotti was one of the first wineries to reinstate the concept of quality in central Italy, way back in the 1970s. This was achieved not only with the wines, but with the establishment of an annual wine-tasting competition to establish the best wines of the land, called the Banco d'Assaggio – which, by the way, Lungarotti always did quite well in. Also by the painstaking assembly of one of the finest wine museums in the world, at the Lungarotti headquarters in the village of TORGIANO, near Perugia.

Lungarotti's best wine has always been Torgiano Riserva Vigna Monticchio, a Sangiovese-based blend which is aged for up to ten years, of which several are in bottle, although the DOCG regulations (which virtually only applies to this, the dominant producer) only call for three years. Second to this is the IGT Sangiovese-Cabernet blend called San Giorgio which undergoes equally impressive aging. A number of varietals and blends follow, the best of which is probably the Cabernet Sauvignon. Lungarotti is moving forward once again. Best years: (Torgiano Riserva) 1997, '95, '90, '88, '86, '85.

LUSTAU

SPAIN, Andalucía, Jerez y Manzanilla DO
♀ *Palomino Fino, Pedro Ximénez, Moscatel*

Emilio Lustau fills as many sherry bottles under supermarket own-labels as it sends out under its own name. General quality here is sound to good, but the quality of special bottlings rises to some delightful peaks. Lustau's wonderful almacenista sherries are unique. There remain about 50 smallish sherry-maturing businesses, or almacenistas, more often than not run by wealthy individuals with a career elsewhere – doctors, lawyers, cattle breeders. Lustau bottles these almacenista wines from single casks, and sells them as small-scale specialities under the joint name of Lustau and the almacenista. These can be really exceptional, complex sherries. The bodega has been part of the Caballero group since 1990.

CH. LYNCH-BAGES

FRANCE, Bordeaux, Haut-Médoc, Pauillac AC, 5ème Cru Classé
♥ *Cabernet Sauvignon, Merlot, Cabernet Franc*
♀ *Sauvignon Blanc, Sémillon, Muscadelle*

Sometimes, tasting this wonderful wine with its almost succulent richness, its gentle texture and its starburst of flavours all butter and blackcurrants and mint, you may wonder why it only has a comparatively lowly position as a Fifth Growth PAUILLAC. It can only be because the chaps who devised the 1855 BORDEAUX Classification were basically puritans. They couldn't bear to admit that a wine as openheartedly lovely as Lynch-Bages could really be as important as other less generous Growths. Well, it is. Wine is about pleasure. Great wine is about great pleasure and there are few wines which will so regularly give you such great pleasure as Lynch-Bages.

The 90ha (222 acres) of vines in the middle of the AC, near the town of Pauillac, are planted in the traditional Pauillac mix, with a lot of Cabernet Sauvignon – 75 per cent – and 15 per cent Merlot and 10 per cent Cabernet Franc. This sounds like a tough wine taking a long time to mature – but that's the magic of Lynch-Bages – rich and ripe when young, beautiful at ten years old, even more beautiful at 20 years. Second wine: Ch. Haut-Bages-Avérous. A small amount of white wine, Blanc de Lynch-Bages, has been made since 1990. Best years: (reds) 2001, '00, '99, '98, '96, '95, '94, '90, '89, '88, '86, '85, '83, '82.

MACEDON RANGES

AUSTRALIA, Victoria

With an average January temperature of 17.2°C (63°F) Macedon has a cooler climate than does Reims in northern France's CHAMPAGNE region. Without question, this region is at the sharp end of cool-climate viticulture in Australia, and self-evidently does best in

The beautiful Macedon region is one of Australia's coolest wine regions: site selection and careful matching of site and grape variety are crucial.

the warmest vintages, while it struggles with poor ripening (not with total conviction) in the normal to cool years.

The Champagne varieties (Chardonnay and Pinot Noir) dominate the plantings and also the wine styles, whether still or sparkling. Top quality fizz, densely textured, nutty, creamy Chardonnays and delicate, sappy Pinot Noirs are the leaders, although Virgin Hills, Knight Granite Hills and (sometimes) Cobaw Ridge have made convincing spicy/ leafy Shiraz and Cabernet Sauvignon, and HANGING ROCK's The Jim Jim Sauvignon is excellent. Best years: 2000, '99, '98, '97, '95, '94, '93. Best producers: Bindi, Cleveland, Cobaw Ridge, Cope-Williams, Epis, Hanging Rock, Knight Granite Hills, Rochford, Virgin Hills.

MÂCON AC, MÂCON SUPÉRIEUR AC, MÂCON-VILLAGES AC

FRANCE, Burgundy, Mâconnais

♥♥ *Gamay, Pinot Noir*

♀ *Chardonnay, Pinot Blanc*

Mâcon AC is the most basic appellation in the large Mâconnais region, directly north of BEAUJOLAIS, and accounts for just over one per cent of the 28.5 million bottles produced under the various Mâcon appellations. The AC is increasingly used for red wines, but has been usurped by the superior Mâcon-Villages AC for whites. Whatever the colour, the flavours are rarely exciting; the red usually has a 'rooty', vegetal rasp, and the rosé lacks the fresh, breezy perfume which can make pink wine such fun. Gamay reds are normally sold as Mâcon or Mâcon Supérieur and Pinot Noir reds as BOURGOGNE AC.

Mâcon Blanc used to be a cheap, bland quaffer. Now it is a rather expensive, basic quaffer, since the magic variety Chardonnay has allowed prices to boom. Quality has rarely kept pace with prices, and it is almost always worth moving up to Mâcon-Villages if you want more than simple lemony zing.

Mâcon-Villages covers the better sites in Mâcon, many of them on good limestone and should be an enjoyable fruity, fresh white wine but again, because it comes from the fashionable Chardonnay grape it is often sold at too high a price. There are 43 villages in the region entitled to the Mâcon-Villages AC, or they can add their own name, as in Mâcon-Lugny. Best villages: (in the north) Chardonnay, Igé, Lugny, St-Gengoux-de-Scissé, Uchizy; (in the south) Charnay, Prissé. The villages of Viré and Clessé and two other small ones were promoted in 1998 to their own AC, Viré-Clessé. The co-operatives, who are as strong in the Mâcon region as anywhere in France, make 75 per cent of Mâconnais wines but there are impressive numbers of private producers forcing the quality up – producers like Merlin, Thévenet and Verget have now been joined by supreme CÔTE D'OR winemaker LAFON.

The Mâcon Supérieur AC merely indicates a minimum alcohol level one degree higher than basic Mâcon. Best years: (Mâcon-Villages) 2002, '01, '00, '99. Best producers: (Mâcon-Villages) D & M Barraud, A Bonhomme, Deux Roches, E Gillet, de la Greffière, Lafon, J-J Litaud, Jean Manciat, O Merlin, Rijckaert, Roally, Robert-Denogent, Saumaize-Michelin, la Soufrandise, J Thévenet, Valette, Verget, J-J Vincent.

MACULAN

ITALY, Veneto, Breganze DOC

♥ *Cabernet Sauvignon, Merlot, Cabernet Franc, Pinot Noir (Pinot Nero)*

♀ *Chardonnay, Sauvignon Blanc, Tocai Friulano, Pinot Blanc (Pinot Bianco), Vespaiola and others*

It was in the late 1970s that Fausto Maculan, scion of a family whose wine roots in BREGANZE go back generations, decided to 'withdraw from the rat-race of low-price, high-volume production to concentrate on quality'. For decades in central VENETO this has meant using mainly French grapes, and Fausto, ever a keen observer of French methods, decided in 1984 to plant the newly acquired Ferrata hill to Cabernet Sauvignon, Chardonnay and Sauvignon Blanc (French clones) at a very dense 10,000 vines to the hectare. The resulting reds and whites have been steadily improving as the vines mature, and Pinot Noir has been added to the line-up. Fausto's quasi-obsession with the latest enological equipment has refined cellar techniques (he is particularly proud of a slow-moving belt which allows unsound or unripe grapes to be eliminated prior to crushing).

MACULAN

Acininobili is one of Italy's best dessert wines. Made from local grapes, especially Vespaiolo, the wine is intensely sweet but with good acidity.

Maculan's greatest strength, apart from Cabernet Sauvignon-Merlot blends Fratta and Brentino, and pure varietals Cabernet Palazzotto and Merlot Crosara, have always been the dessert wines, Torcolato and the outstanding botrytis-affected Acininobili, both mainly from Vespaiolo grapes.

MADEIRA DOC

PORTUGAL, Madeira

♥ *Tinta Negra Mole and others*

♀ *Sercial, Bual (Boal), Verdelho, Malvasia (Malmsey), Terrantez*

The subtropical holiday island of Madeira seems an unlikely place to find a serious wine. However, fine Madeiras are very serious indeed and can be relied upon to survive for centuries, preserving layer upon layer of complex flavour. The trouble is that not much of the island's production can be classified as 'fine' as it has mostly been made from the rather neutral Tinta Negra Mole grape, rather than the four traditional quality white grapes, Sercial, Bual (or Boal), Verdelho and Malvasia, or Malmsey. Now there are incentives to replant the vineyards with these 'noble' grapes but progress is slow (having now crept up to 15 per cent of total plantings). Any Madeira above the basic 3-year-old category should be made from one of these four varieties.

Good Sercial is a pale, incisive dry wine with searing (sometimes punishing) acidity. Verdelho tends to be medium-dry in style with a soft, peachy character when young, offset by high acidity. Bual is fuller and fairly sweet, and Malmsey, the darkest in colour, has a rich, raisiny character but due to naturally high levels of acidity is never cloying.

All the wines are fortified early on and may be sweetened with fortified grape juice before bottling. The best Madeiras are aged for years in old wooden casks, then stored in sun-baked attics. Lesser wines are subject to an artificial heating process known as estufagem which helps to simulate the effects of age, giving the wine a burnt, tangy taste. All this heating and aging before bottling means that exposure to air is unlikely to damage your bottle of Madeira once it is opened – Madeira is one wine you can enjoy, glass by glass, for months. Much the largest producer is the MADEIRA WINE COMPANY with a wide range of wines sold under various labels. The next largest (and main competitor) is HENRIQUES & HENRIQUES. Best producers: Barbeito, Barros e Souza, H M Borges, Henriques & Henriques, Vinhos Justino Henriques, Madeira Wine Company, Pereira d'Oliveira.

MADEIRA WINE COMPANY

PORTUGAL, Madeira, Madeira DOC

Tinta Negra Mole

Sercial, Verdelho, Bual, Malvasia (Malmsey), Terrantez

The Madeira Wine Company was formed from an amalgam of historic MADEIRA firms, including Blandy's, Cossart Gordon, Leacock and Rutherford & Miles. Of these, Blandy and Cossart Gordon are now the company's principal brands. The Madeira Wine Company has developed by leaps and bounds since the Symington family (of DOW, GRAHAM and WARRE PORT fame) moved in back in 1989. The Symingons now control the company although the Blandy family still retains an active involvement.

The Madeira Wine Company produces a complete range of Madeiras: from inexpensive wines destined for the large French market to venerable old vintages, cask-aged in warm attics at the São Francisco lodge in Funchal for a minimum of 20 years. Highlights in the range are the much-improved 10-Year-Old wines, particularly the nervy, medium-dry Verdelho and the rich, raisiny Malmsey. New ideas are the release of a young vintage 1994 Malmsey and Alvada, a five-year-old blend of Malmsey and Bual with a slick, ultra-modern label.

Stocks of bottled vintage Madeira include Blandy's fine, concentrated 1958 Bual and Cossart's 1908 Bual, bottled in 1985 after spending 77 years in wood! Look out for the fine, aromatic wines (10-Year-Old and vintage) made from the rare Terrantez grape.

MADIRAN AC

FRANCE, South-West

Tannat, Cabernet Sauvignon, Cabernet Franc

In the gentle Vic Bilh hills just south of Armagnac there has been a steady revival of the Madiran AC since 1953 when the vineyards had virtually died out and were down to a total surface area of only 6ha (15 acres).

The tannic Tannat vine, the main variety in Madiran, had become too degenerate to cultivate. But modern botanical science found a way of sorting this problem, and now there are 1317ha (3254 acres) of vineyards, and suddenly Madiran is popping up all over the place. Alain Brumont of Ch. MONTUS and Ch. Bouscassé has led the charge. New oak has helped the wine achieve a more attractive, less tannic style, and several of the best producers are now using it. Also helpful in reducing painful tannin levels is a system of micro-oxygenation known as *microbullage* that has been developed by Patrick Ducournau of la CHAPELLE LENCLOS and is being used to good effect, both in Madiran and other regions in France. But don't expect an easy ride. Even modern Madiran is probably France's most austere red. Best years: 2001, '00, '98, '97, '96, '95, '94, '90, '89. Best producers: d'Aydie, Barréjat, Berthoumieu, Bouscassé, Capmartin, Chapelle Lenclos, du Crampilh, Cave de Crouseilles, Laffitte-Teston, Montus, Mouréou, Producteurs PLAIMONT.

CH. MAGDELAINE

FRANCE, Bordeaux, St-Émilion Grand Cru AC, Premier Grand Cru Classé

Merlot, Cabernet Franc

This is very much a wine of two personalities. In lighter years – because of its tremendously high percentage of Merlot (90 per cent) – the wine has a gushing, tender juicy fruit, easy to drink at only four to five years old, which seems to epitomize the indulgent softness of wines from ST-ÉMILION.

However, in the grand vintages, Magdelaine changes gear. Those 11ha (27 acres) of Merlot-dominated vineyard sit on the steep slopes or *côtes* just south-west of the town of St-Émilion adjacent to the vineyards of Ch. CANON and BELAIR – a plum position for superripeness. Because the property is owned by the quality-conscious company of J-P Moueix in nearby Libourne, the grapes are left to hang until the last possible moment, then an army of pickers swoops in. Then the wine is fermented long and slow, and finally the wine is aged in predominantly new barrels for a year and a half.

And what is the result? These are dark, firmly structured wines, yet behind the tough exterior there is luscious fruit and oaky spice and as the tannin fades, a gentle glyceriny texture takes over. Great years take 15 years to mature. Best years: 2001, '00, '99, '98, '96, '95, '90, '89, '88, '85, '82, '75.

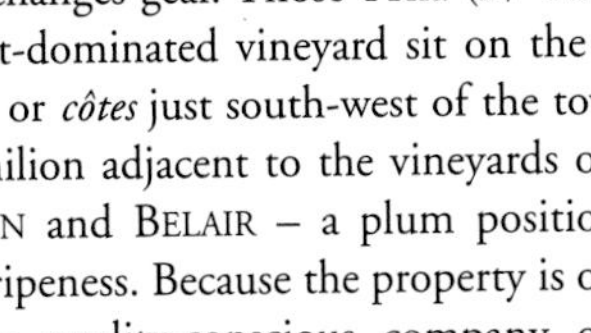

CH. MAGDELAINE

Ch. Magdelaine enjoys a classic St-Émilion location on the edge of the limestone ridge outside the town, with vineyards divided between the plateau and the slopes.

MAIPO VALLEY

CHILE, Valle Central

All the great – but beautiful – clichés of Chilean red wine are based on Maipo fruit. All those thrilling blends of blackcurrant and eucalyptus and mint that made us gasp in the 1980s and '90s were from vineyards spread east and south of Chile's capital, Santiago – although those to the east have gradually been swallowed by the expanding city. Charging out of the Andes towards the sea, the Maipo River has created a valley of infertile soils over deep rocky subsoils, with altitudes up to 740m (2430 feet). Loads of sun and cooling breezes from both east and west create fantastic conditions for Cabernet Sauvignon, Merlot, Carmenere and Syrah, though you'll also find whites led by Chardonnay. Best producers: Almaviva, CARMEN, Clos Quebrada de Macul, CONCHA Y TORO, Haras de Pirque, El Principal, SANTA CAROLINA, Santa Inés/de Martino, SANTA RITA, Tarapacá.

MAKEDONIA

GREECE

The region of Makedonia spreads right across the north of Greece, from Albania in the west to Turkey in the east. Modern Greek wine first appeared as Chateau Carras in the Chalkidiki Peninsula in the 1960s but most of the current excitement is further north, particularly at Naoussa and Goumenissa where the Xynomavro grape produces powerful, austere reds (softer in Goumenissa where blending is allowed). Nearby Amyntaio is better for whites. Later developments are at Kavala and right on the Turkish border. Best producers: Boutari, Katsaios, Kyr-Yianni, Tatsis.

MÁLAGA DO

SPAIN, Andalucía

Pedro Ximénez, Moscatel de Málaga

Most bottles of Málaga contain a curious blend of wines, juices and alcohol, which can be stunningly complex, or, more often, cloyingly sweet and boring. Alcohol ranges from 15 to 23 per cent and the label will give an indication of sweetness and colour. Production dwindled throughout the twentieth century. The minimum two-year aging period must take place in the city of Málaga, which is cooler than the inland vineyards where the wines are actually fermented. The arrival of whizzkid Telmo RODRIGUEZ is certain to boost the wine's reputation. A second DO, Sierras de Málaga, has been set up for wineries based outside the Málaga city limits. Best producers: Gomara, López Hermanos, Telmo Rodriguez.

MALBEC

In France Malbec only really produces exciting wine in Cahors (where it is known as Auxerrois), although it is planted in the Loire (where it is known as Cot) and in Bordeaux (where the St-Émilion growers call it Pressac). In Bordeaux and the Loire it can soften the other grapes, but in Cahors it makes deep, chewy, plum-and-tobacco-flavoured wine unlike any other in France.

In Argentina, Malbec (sometimes spelled Malbeck) is the most planted French varietal. It has adapted well throughout the country, and at an altitude of 1000m (2470ft) in Luján de Cuyo, Mendoza, it produces exceptional wines – deep, plummy and perfumed. Its success there has persuaded growers in Chile, Australia, California and South Africa to take a closer look.

MALVASIA

This grape, widely planted in Italy, is found in several guises, red and white. It is said to have arrived in Italy in centuries past from the port in Greece's Peloponnese peninsula called, today, Monemvasia. The general characteristic of Malvasia is an aromatic quality somewhat diverse from, and considerably less obvious than, that of Muscat.

The best sub-variety for dry white and slightly fizzy semi-sweet whites in northern Italy is the Malvasia Istriana of FRIULI, which seems to be related to EMILIA's Malvasia di Candia. The latter is also its name in FRAS-CATI, where its wines tend to be somewhat

HAUNER
On the volcanic Lipari Islands off the coast of Sicily Malvasia is used to make really tasty, apricotty-sweet wines.

flabby, with a tendency to oxidation, and where the Malvasia Puntinata or di Lazio is seen as the superior clone.

White Malvasia seems to do best in the islands off SICILY, where it is used to make *passito* or *liquoroso* style wines, as in the case of the well-known Malvasia delle Lipari. Malvasia di Cagliari and Malvasia di Bosa are two Sardinian DOCs of little commercial note although, in the latter case at least, of considerable potential quality, especially in the style called *dolce naturale*. The word *liquoroso*, in this context, indicates addition of alcohol, which helps to maintain perfumes but also to promote hangovers.

There is also Malvasia Nera, which is, generally found in southern PUGLIA and, surprisingly, in TUSCANY, where it can combine well with Sangiovese. A couple of obscure DOCs in PIEDMONT, called Malvasia di Casorzo d'Asti and Malvasia di Castel nuovo Don Bosco produce frothing, light reds. Variants of Malvasia also grow in northern Spain, where it fattens up traditional white RIOJA and Portugal. On the island of MADEIRA it produces sweet, varietal fortified wine, often known by its English name of Malmsey.

LA MANCHA DO

SPAIN, Castilla-La Mancha
♦ Tempranillo (Cencibel), Grenache Noir (Garnacha Tinta), Cabernet Sauvignon, Merlot, Syrah, Moravia Buena
♀ Airén, Macabeo (Viura), Pardilla, Chardonnay, Sauvignon Blanc

Spain's vast central plateau is the largest appellation region in the world, with more than 193,000ha (477,000 acres) of vineyard plantings. La Mancha is far too large to mean much in terms of a wine's 'origin', despite a number of common soil and climate features. The most obvious unifying factor is one that modern producers could do without: the prevalence of the white Airén grape, which still covers more than 60 per cent of the vineyards and gives, at best, cleanly neutral wines when vinified in the modern way (in stainless steel under temperature controls).

Airén is hardy and survives the region's lack of rain. It plays a major ecological role in preventing desertification, but impedes winemaking progress. When the DO regulations were altered in 1995 to allow for vineyard irrigation and the planting of new, better grape varieties there was at last an opportunity for improvement. From 1996 all

new Airén plantings were banned. In its place vineyards are being replanted with or grafted to better varieties, led by Cencibel (Tempranillo), Cabernet Sauvignon and even some Merlot and Syrah for reds, and Chardonnay and Sauvignon Blanc in whites. The Australian viticulturist Dr Richard Smart, who was active in the region, had been advocating the changes. The whites are never exciting, but nowadays are often fresh and attractive. The reds can be light and fruity, or richer – there is still some rough, old-style wine. In such a changing environment the roll-call of leading producers changes fast. Best producers: Finca Antigua (MARTÍNEZ BUJANDA), Ayuso, Vinícola de Castilla, la Magdalena co-operative, Nuestra Señora de la Cabeza co-operative (Casa Gualda), Parra Jiménez, Rodriguez y Berger (Santa Elena), Torres Filoso (Arboles de Castillejo), Casa de la Viña.

MARANGES AC

FRANCE, Burgundy, Côte de Beaune
♦ Pinot Noir

In 1989 this single AC was created to represent the villages of Cheilly-lès-Maranges, Dezize-lès-Maranges and Sampigny-lès-Maranges in the southern tip of the CÔTE DE BEAUNE. The wines are rarely exciting, being rather thin and harsh in all but the very best vintages, although they can sometimes have a pleasant strawberry perfume. In practice, most of the growers sell their wine as CÔTE DE BEAUNE-VILLAGES – a catch-all appellation applying to 16 different Côte de Beaune communes – and that is probably the best fate for most of it. Best years: 2002, '01, '99, '97, '96, '95. Best producers: B Bachelet, M Charleux, Contat-Grange, DROUHIN, V GIRARDIN.

MARCASSIN WINERY

USA, California, Sonoma County, Russian River Valley AVA
♦ Pinot Noir
♀ Chardonnay

Arguably the best-known winemaker in CALIFORNIA and, without question, the most famous consulting winemaker, Helen Turley has developed her 4-ha (10-acre) vineyard in the cool western sector of SONOMA COUNTY to supply Chardonnay and Pinot Noir for her own brand, Marcassin. Turley is noted for her signature style of winemaking that shoots from the hip in terms of ripe fruit, concentration, power and, for reds, lots of oak and rich, supple tannin. Her former clients remain among the most collectable names today – Colgin Cellars, Bryant Family, PAHLMEYER –

and she helped established her brother's Napa winery, TURLEY CELLARS. For Marcassin she has been offering single-vineyard Chardonnays from Alexander Mountain (formerly Gauer Ranch Upper Barn), Lorenzo Vineyard and Three Sisters on SONOMA COAST as well as Marcassin Vineyard. Best years: 2001, '00, '99, '98, '97, '96, '95. Her Pinot Noirs from Marcassin Vineyard and Three Sisters quickly achieved cult status for that incredible depth and restrained power.

MARCHE
ITALY

The Marche stretches, long and lean, along the Adriatic coast from Romagna to ABRUZZO, its hills, sandwiched between sea and mountain, covered seemingly ubiquitously by vines. It has always seemed a particularly blessed region – not highly populated, relatively rarely on travellers' itineraries, yet enjoying a rich patrimony of agricultural wealth, artistic and architectural splendour and touristic attractions.

The VERDICCHIO DEI CASTELLI DI JESI zone put the Marche region on the wine map. Verdicchio is grown elsewhere, too, especially further inland around Matelica, where it produces wines with a rich but steely character. These two areas are now producing some very serious examples of Verdicchio. The best known Marche red is ROSSO CONERO, based on the Montepulciano grape. Good wines from international varieties such as Cabernet, Chardonnay and Sauvignon Blanc and sold under the Marche IGT are becoming more common. Still others may add Merlot, Sangiovese or even Syrah to Montepulciano. The best include Boccadigabbia's Akronte, Oasi degli Angeli's Kurni, UMANI RONCHI's Pélago, La Monacesca's Camerte and Le Terrazze's Chaos.

MARCILLAC AC
FRANCE, South-West
🍷 🍇 *Fer Servadou, Cabernet Franc, Cabernet Sauvignon, Merlot*

Marcillac used to be a serious wine area, lost in the Aveyron *département* in the deep South-West. First the town of Rodez, then the mining town of Decazeville drank it all, but the mines closed in 1962 and it's been a struggle ever since. Yet the struggle is worth it. This is one of those almost extinct jewels that the wine world must treasure and since its award of an AC in 1990, the area under vine has actually increased. Now there are 160ha (395 acres) of vineyards. Mainly from Fer, the red is strong

and dry, rasping with herbs, grassy freshness and a slightly metallic zing and it copes remarkably well with the local Roquefort cheese. There is a little rosé. Best producers: Michel Laurens, Jean-Luc Matha, Philippe Teulier, les Vignerons du Vallon co-operative.

MARGARET RIVER
AUSTRALIA, Western Australia

This is the fastest growing of all premium regions in Australia, but it was a late starter. It wasn't until the late 1960s that a bunch of local doctors, alerted to the fact that the climate seemed uncannily similar to that of BORDEAUX, started to plant vines. And naturally they planted Bordeaux varieties, and so far most of Margaret River's top reds and whites have been from Bordeaux grapes. The most challenging wine is Semillon, with asparagus and gooseberry flavours that successfully emulate Sauvignon Blanc, which is also successful in its own right. Some of Australia's most successful Chardonnays come from here, led by LEEUWIN ESTATE. But potentially Cabernet Sauvignon and its blends do best of all, from the refined beauty of CAPE MENTELLE and CULLEN WINES to the softer MOSS WOOD and VASSE FELIX. Syrah (Shiraz) and Zinfandel also flourish. Best years: (Cabernet-based reds) 2001, '00, '99, '98, '96, '95, '94, '91, '90. Best producers: Amberley Estate, Brookland Valley, Cape Mentelle, Cullen, Devil's Lair, EVANS & TATE, Gralyn, HOWARD PARK, Leeuwin Estate, Moss Wood, PIERRO, Suckfizzle, Vasse Felix, Voyager Estate, Xanadu.

MARGAUX AC
FRANCE, Bordeaux, Haut-Médoc
🍷 *Cabernet Sauvignon, Cabernet Franc, Merlot, Petit Verdot*

Margaux is the most sprawling of the six specific ACs in the HAUT-MÉDOC, with 1409ha (3482 acres) of vines centred on the village of Margaux but also spreading through Arsac, Cantenac, Labarde and Soussans. The key to Margaux is the pale gravel banks which weave their way through the vineyards, giving little by way of nutrition but, crucially for a damp region like BORDEAUX, providing perfect drainage (supplemented by artificial drainage) so that the wines are rarely heavy and should have a quite divine perfume when they mature at seven to 12 years old. The best examples of this style are Ch. BRANE-CANTENAC, FERRIÈRE, Malescot-St-Exupéry, la Gurgue, d'Issan, Labégorce-Zédé, Ch. MARGAUX, PALMER and RAUZAN-SÉGLA.

A fuller, rounder but still perfumed style comes from the southern part of the AC, and is at its best from Ch. ANGLUDET, Cantenac-Brown, Monbrison, Siran and du TERTRE. Altogether there are 21 Classed Growths, as well as good unclassified properties, such as Ch. Siran, Angludet and Monbrison. Also good are Ch. Bel Air Marquis d'Aligre, Dauzac, Desmirail, Kirwan and, since 2000, Prieuré-Lichine and Lascombes. With a change of generation the AC now has a new dynamism and could be one of the most interesting to watch over the coming years. Winemaking techniques are also changing the style of the wines, making it more difficult to identify the archetypal Margaux. Bottles merely labelled 'Margaux' shouldn't be taken too seriously since almost all the decent stuff sports a property's name. Best years: 2001, '00, '99, '96, '95, '90.

CH. MARGAUX
FRANCE, Bordeaux, Haut-Médoc, Margaux AC, Premier Cru Classé
🍷 *Cabernet Sauvignon, Merlot, Petit Verdot, Cabernet Franc*
🍇 *Sauvignon Blanc*

After a long period of decline, Ch. Margaux fought back so successfully during the 1980s that it now lays fair claim to being the most exciting property in the whole MÉDOC. A large 81-ha (200-acre) property set back in the trees just outside the village of MARGAUX, Ch. Margaux gives a new meaning to the words perfume and fragrance in a red wine, as though an inspired *parfumeur* had somehow managed to combine a sweet essence of blackcurrants with oil from crushed violets and the haunting scent of cedarwood, then swirled them together with more earthy pleasures like vanilla, roasted nuts and plums, and spirited all these into the bottle. The surprising element is that Margaux also has evident power and structure as well. Second wine: Pavillon Rouge du Ch. Margaux. Best years: (reds) 2001, '00, '99, '98, '96, '95, '94, '93, '90, '89, '88, '86, '85, '83, '82.

There is also some white wine. The grapes don't come from the precious Margaux vineyards, but from Soussans, outside the best red wine area. There are 12ha (30 acres) of Sauvignon Blanc, which is vinified at the château, but in a separate cellar so that the red wine is not in any way affected. The result is delicious, but Pavillon Blanc must be the most expensive BORDEAUX AC by a country mile. Best years: (whites) 2001, '00, '99, '98, '96, '95, '94, '90.

MARLBOROUGH New Zealand

FLY INTO BLENHEIM AIRPORT and you begin to feel some of the excitement that the Marlborough region generates in all who visit New Zealand's largest and best-known wine region. For a start it feels like wine country. The rugged hills that adorn the superstar label of Cloudy Bay, one of the world's most sought-after wines, form a semi-circle around the valley with the distant coastline completing the ring. In summer the burnt yellow and brown hills form a stark contrast to the lush, green and well-watered valley floor. Vines surround the airport and form a patchwork quilt throughout the valley. Once the valley was used to graze sheep that picked their way between the rocks in search of precious grass. High demand for Marlborough wine has boosted vineyard prices to the point where cherry orchards and crops disappear overnight to be replaced by fields of rocky brown earth studded with bare posts and puny vine cuttings.

It is hard to believe that until 1973 few people believed that grape vines could survive Marlborough's dry summers or frosty winters. Montana Wines took an enormous risk, but one based on sound climatic and geological research, when they bought 14 farms in 1973, then planted 809ha (2000 acres) with vines, and Marlborough went from nothing to its current position of being New Zealand's largest vineyard area by far: in 2003, Marlborough's 6677ha (16,500 acres) of vines made up nearly 45 per cent of the country's total plantings. Just 30 years earlier, there were no commercial vineyards at all.

Marlborough's greatest assets are high sunshine hours, dry autumn weather, cool nights and free-draining alluvial soils littered with river boulders that retain heat and reflect sunshine. Without irrigation, however, much of the valley would be unable to support a viable wine industry. Although frost protection measures are used at the cooler northern end of the Wairau Valley frost has been a relatively minor problem. In 1990 an autumn frost stripped the leaves off vines before the red grapes had been picked, forcing growers to harvest before the grapes were fully ripe, and ever since then growers fear autumn frosts but they rarely arrive before the grapes are safely in.

Sauvignon Blanc from Marlborough has stunned the Old World with its startling, tangy intensity and this was the style that first brought the region fame worldwide – it still stuns wine drinkers when they first try it, and is still the style icon other countries – like South Africa, Australia and Chile – try to copy when they get serious about Sauvignon. Chardonnay isn't far behind although there is a still a tendency for winemakers to blur delicious tangy white peach and citrus flavours with an excess of oak. Riesling is one of Marlborough's star wines. Occasionally dry but mostly off-dry, Marlborough Riesling offers delicious lime/citrus flavours with a seductive suggestion of honey and tropical fruit in a year when botrytis affects the crop.

Great sparkling wines are made with a classic Pinot Noir and Chardonnay blend, sometimes together with a dash of Pinot Meunier. When the wines are aged long enough on their lees they are indistinguishable from good Champagne – same winemaking method, same grapes – but a good deal cheaper. People thought the cool conditions in Marlborough were tailor-made for Pinot Noir but it has been a slow starter, with rather high-cropping young vines producing too many green, pale wines. However, Wither Hills, Fromm, Isabel and a bunch of other producers are now showing serious form. Many more will follow. Cabernet Sauvignon struggles to get ripe although Merlot, in warmer years, can produce

The Richmond Range as viewed from a vineyard near the Wairau River is the scene depicted on the Cloudy Bay label (see facing page). Marlborough's most famous winery achieved cult status overnight with its 1985 Sauvignon Blanc.

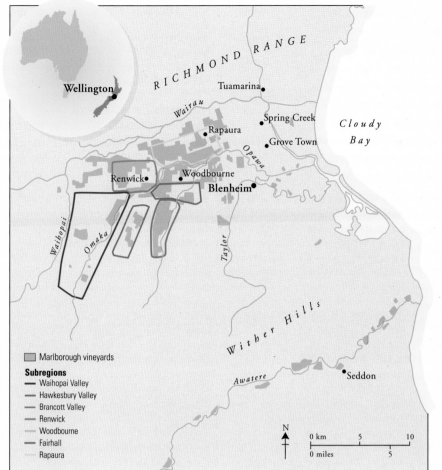

CLOUDY BAY
This is Cloudy Bay Sauvignon Blanc, New Zealand's most famous wine. The country's entire wine industry benefited from Cloudy Bay's overnight star status.

STONELEIGH
Top-selling aromatic Stoneleigh Riesling from Marlborough is now part of the vast Montana empire. Marlborough is a leading area in New Zealand for both sweet and dry Riesling.

JACKSON ESTATE
Unirrigated vineyards are used to produce classic Marlborough Sauvignon Blanc – intensely fruity, concentrated and ripe with a subtle herbaceous influence.

VAVASOUR
Based in the relatively new and exciting Awatere Valley, Vavasour has enjoyed spectacular success since its first wines were released in 1989. The Sauvignon Blanc is ripe and concentrated with all the gooseberry and lime zest attack you could wish for.

SERESIN ESTATE
This is a majestic Burgundian style of Chardonnay with oatmeal and hazelnuts and long, lingering richness.

HUNTER'S
Lean and elegant Chardonnays have helped keep this established Marlborough winery at the very top for more than a decade.

surprisingly good red. The Awatere Valley is only just over the Wither Hills Range but the mesoclimate is significantly different and it seems to manage the virtually impossible – make wines with even more intensity than the main bulk of Marlborough. Though less protected from rain, Awatere's stony river terraces offer warmer conditions when it's dry and, as well as superb Sauvignon Blanc, there's been some truly classy cedary Cabernet Sauvignon.

REGIONAL ENTRY
Marlborough.

PRODUCER ENTRIES
Cloudy Bay, Fromm Winery, Hunter's, Isabel Estate, Jackson Estate, Montana Wines, Seresin Estate, Vavasour, Wither Hills.

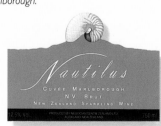

NAUTILUS ESTATE
This Champagne-method sparkling wine shows just how ideal Marlborough's cool climate and silty soils are to the production of quality fizz.

DEUTZ
Montana, New Zealand's largest wine company, makes austere, elegant Champagne-method sparkling wine with the help of the Champagne house, Deutz.

MARLBOROUGH

NEW ZEALAND, South Island (see also pages 234–235)

I can't think of anywhere else like it. Marlborough is New Zealand's most important, its largest, wine area. Yet 30 years ago there wasn't a commercial vine in the ground. It had garlic, cherry trees, and sheep – loads of those. Not until 1972 did anyone give commercial vines in Marlborough a second thought.

But that was the year a guy named Frank Yukich, desperate to expand his MONTANA Wine company but unable to afford the land prices around Auckland, realized two things. Marlborough, at the northern tip of South Island, was in a rain shadow. It wasn't hot there, but Blenheim, the little town at its heart, often gets more sunshine than any other town in New Zealand. Great for grapes. And the land was dirt cheap. So he bought. Big time. And in August 1973 he planted Marlborough's first commercial vines. Yukich's company was called Montana. Is Montana Sauvignon Blanc familiar? It's the same Montana. Every grape for what is now perhaps the most famous Sauvignon Blanc in the world comes from Marlborough. Except Montana isn't the world's most famous Sauvignon – CLOUDY BAY is. No problem. Every single grape for Cloudy Bay comes from Marlborough too. And they didn't even release their first wine till 1985.

This wide, flat, pebbly plain gouged out by the Wairau River is still expanding and has a frenetic Klondike feel about it, as local and international investors feverishly scrabble for their share. But it is a great place to grow grapes – Sauvignon definitely, Riesling, Pinot Gris, Chardonnay and Pinot Noir – great white wine, fine fizz and possibly great Pinot Noir reds too. A classic wine region, then. Yes. A *new* classic wine region. Best years: (Chardonnay) 2002, '01, '00, '99, '98, '97; (Pinot Noir) 2002, '01, '00, '99, '98, '97. Best producers: Cellier le Brun, Clifford Bay Estate, Cloudy Bay, Forrest Estate, FROMM, Grove Mill, HUNTER'S, ISABEL, Jackson, Lawson's Dry Hills, Montana, Nautilus, Saint Clair, SERESIN, Stoneleigh, VAVASOUR, VILLA MARIA, WITHER HILLS.

MARQUÉS DE CÁCERES

SPAIN, La Rioja, Rioja DOCa

♀♂ Tempranillo, Grenache Noir (Garnacha Tinta), Graciano
♀ Macabeo (Viura)

Back in the 1970s, Marqués de Cáceres was the first RIOJA bodega to produce light, fresh, fruity whites that had never seen the inside of an oak barrel – a style which all the forward-looking Rioja bodegas have since attempted to emulate.

The bodega was established in the early 1970s by Enrique Forner, a Spaniard who had long lived in France and whose family still owns Ch. Camensac in BORDEAUX. Renowned POMEROL enologist Michel Rolland is a consultant. Marqués de Cáceres Crianza reds have always been made in the fruity, not too oaky style which is now more popular with other Rioja bodegas, too. But both the Reserva and Gran Reserva styles get good oak treatment, develop a lovely wild strawberry sweetness and age well. The whites are good, fresh, herby and grassy-fruity, more reminiscent of Sauvignon Blanc than of other white Riojas. The rosés are particularly fresh and fruity, but sadly as much out of fashion here as rosés are in the rest of the world. Best years: (reds) 1999, '98, '96, '95, '94, '92, '91, '90, '89, '87, '85, '82.

MARQUÉS DE GRIÑÓN

SPAIN, Castilla-La Mancha

♂ Tempranillo, Cabernet Sauvignon, Cabernet Franc, Syrah, Petit Verdot, Grenache Noir (Garnacha) and others
♀ Verdejo, Macabeo (Viura), Sauvignon Blanc

You get something of the measure of the man when you hear him state, emphatically and simply 'Spain needs more great wines.' By that he means much of Spain needs to change its attitude about how wine is made, what it should and could taste like and where the grapes should and could be planted.

Carlos Falcó, the real life Marqués de Griñón, was a one-man whirlwind of international ambition and iconoclastic certainty when in the 1970s he planted his estate 48 km (30 miles) west of Toledo – an area of no wine tradition whatsoever – with Cabernet Sauvignon, Syrah and Petit Verdot. He also introduced New World trellising systems, was the first in Europe to install drip irrigation (in 1975) – and produced sensational wines, rich, succulent, very ripe, but fabulously true to their varietal character.

And were they true to Spain? Why not? They were grown there, they taste quite unlike anything from anywhere else. I'd say they are a prototype for a new Spain, unshackled from all its old lack of ambition and tolerance of mediocrity. These wines are now sold under the Dominio de Valdepusa label – and it has its own DO – headed by the Eméritus blend of Cabernet, Syrah and Petit Verdot. But Falcó's energies don't stop there. Since he sold a stake in his Marqués de Griñón brand – not his Valdepusa estate – to the giant Arco Bodegas Unidas/BERBERANA group he has helped them develop a range of wines from RIOJA, PENEDÈS, the DUERO and elsewhere in Spain. Best years: (Eméritus) 1998, '97.

MARQUÉS DE MURRIETA

SPAIN, La Rioja, Rioja DOCa

♂ Tempranillo, Grenache Noir (Garnacha Tinta), Graciano, Carignan (Cariñena, Mazuelo), Cabernet Sauvignon
♀ Macabeo (Viura) Grenache Blanc (Garnacha Blanca), Malvasia

Vicente Cebrián junior is steadily advancing the plan laid out by his father before his untimely death – that the Marqués de Murrieta bodega should become the leading producer of red wine not only in RIOJA but in the whole of Spain. Whether Murrieta will topple VEGA SICILIA from its pedestal of adulation is dubious, but certainly the wines are as good as ever they have been – and much more expensive. The 150-year-old bodega's vineyards, outside the village of Ygay, have been extended to 225ha (555 acres), planted 78 per cent with Tempranillo. Ygay is right at the conjunction of the three Rioja sub-regions.

The top traditional-style wine, Castillo Ygay Gran Reserva Especial, made only in top vintages, appears in two versions: 'Early Release' is aged for three or four years in barrel; the 'Historic Vintages' version remains in barrel for 20 to 25 years. Out of a total of 12,000, the bodega buys around 1000 new barrels each year – mostly made of American oak. The ambitious, sometimes spectacular Dalmau Reserva (a Tempranillo-Cabernet Sauvignon blend) marks a new foray into the realm of resolutely modern wines. Best years: (reds) 1999, '98, '96, '95, '94, '92, '91, '89, '87, '85. Bodegas Marqués de Murrieta also owns the Pazo de Barrantes estate in GALICIA, making RÍAS BAIXAS Albariño.

MARQUÉS DE MURRIETA
Castillo Ygay Gran Reserva Especial, with its splendidly ornate Art Deco style label, is made only in the best vintages.

MARQUÉS DE RISCAL

SPAIN, País Vasco, Rioja DOCa; Castilla y León,
Rueda DO

🍷 *Tempranillo, Graciano, Carignan (Cariñena,*
Mazuelo), Cabernet Sauvignon

🍷 *Tempranillo*

🍷 *Verdejo, Macabeo (Viura), Sauvignon Blanc*

Things have changed dramatically for the better in these family-owned bodegas in RIOJA
and RUEDA since the younger generation took
over the reins in 1987. The Rioja bodega,
where they make their red wine, and where
there had been major problems with dubious
barrels, has cleared out all the old wood, and
they now intend to change their barrels every
five to seven years and aim for a more modern, but still serious, style of wine.

Having had a Cabernet Sauvignon vineyard since the 1860s, this is the Rioja bodega
that has been pushing the hardest for the
variety's legalization in Rioja. It had been 'tolerated' as an 'experimental' variety in the
1990s. In 1991 a new wine, Barón de Chirel
– 45 per cent Cabernet, 55 per cent Tempranillo and aged in new oak – was launched,
modelled on the Italian SUPER-TUSCAN
blends of Sangiovese and Cabernet Sauvignon. The Marqués de Riscal Reserva and
Gran Reserva are made mainly from Tempranillo, but an important part of these
blends is the excellent Rioja red grape Graciano, which is now being replanted
throughout the region.

White wines come from Riscal's Rueda
bodega. The bright, fresh Rueda is made
mainly from Verdejo; the Sauvignon Rueda is
grassy, rounded and fruity; and the Rueda
Reserva Limousin from Verdejo is soft, oaky
and well-balanced. A 100 per cent Tempranillo de Castilla y León is made in the
Duero region. Best years: (Barón de Chirel)
1998, '96, '95, '94.

MARSALA DOC

ITALY, Sicily

🍷 *Grillo, Catarratto, Inzolia (Ansonica) and others*

🍷 *Nero d'Avola (Calabrese), Perricone and others*

Although Marsala, produced on the quasi-
African flatlands of the western tip of SICILY,
was once as highly esteemed as sherry or
MADEIRA, and can still be a great fortified
wine, until recently very little of it was. After
World War Two most Marsala producers
thought they could make a very nice living
churning out wines sweetened or flavoured in
artificial ways. While elsewhere in Italy people by the 1980s were waking up to the fact
that to survive in the modern world you

needed to aim for quality – or change jobs –
in Marsala they seemed happy to enjoy today
and let *domani* take care of itself.

When business got so bad that even they
could no longer deny reality, they revised the
law (in 1984), basically reducing the production area slightly and withdrawing the DOC
status from egg-, almond- or other flavoured
Marsalas. New titles like 'Cremovo' were
introduced for what had been called 'Marsala
all'uovo'. During the rest of the 1980s, following the efforts of the rebel Marco DE
BARTOLI along with a few other producers,
Marsala began to regain its prestige. However,
De Bartoli's objection to fortifying his best
wines up to 18 per cent alcohol tends to dis-
qualify them from using the Marsala DOC
because they are unfortified.

Finest of the traditional Marsala styles is
Marsala Vergine, an unsweetened, intense,
subtly caramelly yet dry aperitif wine made by
the solera system, which also produces sherry.
Marsala Superiore and Marsala Superiore
Riserva tend to be sweet, and can reach inter-
esting quality levels. Best producers: De
Bartoli, Florio (Baglio Florio, Terre Arse),
Pellegrino (Soleras, Vintage).

MARSANNAY AC

FRANCE, Burgundy, Côte de Nuits

🍷 🍷 *Pinot Noir*

🍷 *Chardonnay*

The village of Marsannay has some of its vineyards almost in the suburbs of Dijon. Best
known for its rosé wine, which can be pleasant if a little too austere and dry, but since
1987 Marsannay has been an AC in its own
right for reds, whites and rosés.

The red is one of the revelations of the
'new wave' in Burgundy – rarely very fleshy in
texture, but with a delightful cherry and
strawberry fragrance that is irresistible in
good examples. There is very little white wine,
but what there is isn't bad. Best years: 2002,
'01, '00, '99, '97, '96. Best producers: R Bouvier, P Charlopin, Bruno CLAIR, Collotte,
Fougeray de Beauclair, Geantet-Pansiot,
JADOT, D MORTET, J & J-L Trapet.

MARSANNE

Undervalued grape yielding rich, nutty, rather
honeyed wines in the northern RHÔNE (HER-
MITAGE, CROZES-HERMITAGE, ST-JOSEPH and
ST-PÉRAY), often with the more lively Rous-
sanne. It is also used in PIC ST-LOUP and other
LANGUEDOC wines, sometimes in conjunction
with Viognier. It performs well in Australia at
MITCHELTON and TAHBILK; there are a few

plantings in the USA; and both Italy and
Spain are giving it a go. As Ermitage, it produces some good wines in the Swiss VALAIS.

MARTINBOROUGH

NEW ZEALAND, North Island

Now generally known as Wairarapa, this wine
region at the southern tip of the North Island
sprang into prominence in the late 1980s.
Debate rages as to whether it is better suited
to Pinot Noir, Chardonnay, Cabernet Sauvignon, Merlot or Shiraz – let alone
Sauvignon Blanc, Riesling or Gewurztraminer – as this outcrop of gravelly soil,
allied to a remarkable mesoclimate in what is
otherwise, frankly, a clay-ridden and rather
damp area just east of Wellington, is producing superlative grapes from most of these
varieties – but it is as a Pinot Noir paradise
that it has achieved most fame. MARTINBOR-
OUGH VINEYARD, PALLISER, DRY RIVER and
ATA RANGI are the leaders so far, but there are
many others waiting in the wings. Best years:
(Pinot Noir) 2001, '00, '99, '98, '97, '96. Best
producers: Ata Rangi, Dry River, Martinborough Vineyard, Nga Waka, Palliser Estate,
Te Kairanga.

MARTINBOROUGH VINEYARD

NEW ZEALAND, North Island, Martinborough

🍷 *Pinot Noir*

🍷 *Chardonnay, Pinot Gris, Riesling*

Larry McKenna is the man to thank for showing just how exciting the grapes from the
MARTINBOROUGH region can be. His first
vintage here was 1986 and for many years he
almost single-handedly trumpeted the quality
of the area's wines. Claire Mulholland has now
taken over the winemaking reins, and the winery's Pinot Noir and Chardonnay wines
remain some of New Zealand's most thrilling
examples – veering between an unashamedly
Burgundian style and something intensely
South Pacific – and the Riesling and Pinot

MARTINBOROUGH VINEYARD
This impressive Chardonnay, with toasty, nutty notes
and slightly sweet fruit, is made using the whole range
of Burgundian techniques.

Gris wines are always among the best in the area. A luscious botrytized Riesling is made when vintage conditions allow. Best years: (Pinot Noir) 2001, '00, '99, '98, '97.

MARTÍNEZ BUJANDA

SPAIN, País Vasco, Rioja DOCa

♦ *Tempranillo, Carignan (Cariñena, Mazuelo), Cabernet Sauvignon, Merlot*

♦ *Grenache Noir (Garnacha Tinta)*

♀ *Macabeo (Viura), Malvasia*

Martínez Bujanda, founded in 1889, was for many years a producer of bulk wines, though right from the start the company only made wine from its own grapes. The emphasis on quality has radically increased over the years but the determination to own vineyards – rare in RIOJA, where co-operatives dominate the vineyards – has never wavered, and Martínez Bujanda now owns 480ha (1190 acres) of vines in Rioja (including the separate Finca Valpiedra estate on the River Ebro) as well as 500ha (1235 acres) in a new venture, Finca Antigua, near Toledo in LA MANCHA.

Crianza, Reserva and Gran Reserva red wines are sold under the Conde de Valdemar label, and are usually extremely attractive with wild strawberry and vanilla flavours. Basic wines are sold under the Valdemar label. Best years: (reds) 1998, '96, '95, '94, '92, '91, '90, '87, '86, '85.

MARYLAND

USA

For a long while winemaking in the state of Maryland was almost a one-man operation, as the late Philip Wagner, one of America's wine-making pioneers, spent years at his Boordy Vineyards exploring the possibilities of French-American hybrid varieties instead of native American *Vitis labrusca* grapes. In the late 1970s others began attempting to grow the classic European grape varieties. Now there is a small wine industry in the Blue Ridge foothills in central Maryland. Many of the best wines are still made from hybrids like Chambourcin and Vidal, but Chardonnay, Riesling and, surprisingly, Cabernet Sauvignon have had some success. Best producers: Basignani, Boordy Vineyards, Catoctin, Elk Run, Woodhall.

MAS AMIEL

FRANCE, Languedoc-Roussillon, Maury AC

♦ *Grenache, Syrah, Carignan, Mourvèdre*

♀ *Muscat, Grenache Gris, Macabeo*

This 155-ha (385-acre) estate located to the west of Perpignan is the largest individual

At Mas Amiel, many of the wines are aged outside for a year in the traditional manner, in glass jars or bonbonnes which are exposed to all weathers to induce a measure of oxidation in the wines known as rancio.

producer of the MAURY AC and generally the best. Reflecting the difficulty nowadays of making a living in southern France solely from fortified wine, the estate makes some pretty serious red table wine which is only allowed VIN DE PAYS status. It also makes a good sweet Muscat. However the stars are the fortified Maurys – and there is a wide range of styles. The simplest are tank-aged, the most modern are barrel-aged but the most fascinating are aged in glass demi-johns (Mas Amiel has 3000) which are put out under the powerful Roussillon sun, literally to bake, then aged in wooden vats. These come in 10 or 15-year-old styles and are well worth a try. The Vintage, produced from 100 per cent Grenache, is bottled soon after the harvest, without aging in oak casks, to guard a rich plum and cherry fruit character.

DOMAINE DU MAS BLANC

FRANCE, Languedoc-Roussillon, Banyuls AC, Collioure AC

♦ *Grenache, Mourvèdre, Syrah and others*

♦ *Grenache, Syrah, Cinsaut*

♀ *Grenache Blanc, Muscat, Marsanne and others*

The reputation of this 22-ha (60-acre) domaine is based on a range of powerful, aromatic BANYULS, but one shouldn't forget the COLLIOURE reds, especially the top crus – Clos du Moulin, Cosprons Levants and Junquets – made from varying blends of Syrah,

Mourvèdre, Grenache and Counoise. The Banyuls include a dry version, a vintage or Rimage, Rimage la Coume, Vieilles Vignes and Cuvée du Docteur Parcé. The Banyuls Hors d'Âge Vieilli en Sostréra is produced using a sherry-like solera system. There is also a white Banyuls that tastes of citrus fruit and peaches. Best years: (Collioure) 2001, '00, '99, '98, '96, '95, '94.

MAS BRUGUIÈRE

FRANCE, Languedoc-Roussillon, Coteaux du Languedoc–Pic St-Loup AC

♦ *Syrah, Grenache, Mourvèdre*

♀ *Roussanne*

One of the early pioneers of quality in the COTEAUX DU LANGUEDOC appellation, Guilhem Bruguière continues to produce consistently firm, rich, spicy wines that are redolent of the local *garrigue* or scrub. The 20-ha (50-acre) domaine was replanted in the 1970s with Syrah, Grenache and Mourvèdre and in 1992 with a little white Roussanne. The Cuvée Calcadiz, (made from young vines) part-vinified by carbonic maceration, makes light and easy drinking. The regular cuvée is vinified in a traditional manner as is the top wine, la Grenadière, which has an addition of Mourvèdre in the blend and is aged for 11 months in oak barrels. The characterful and increasingly good white Les Mûriers is soft, round and aromatic.

MAS DE DAUMAS GASSAC

FRANCE, Languedoc-Roussillon, Vin de Pays de l'Hérault

❏ ❏ *Cabernet Sauvignon, Cabernet Franc, Merlot, Malbec, Syrah and others*

❏ *Viognier, Chardonnay, Petit Manseng and others*

Trail-blazing producer of world-class red and white in the HÉRAULT *département*, Aimé Guibert was the first to prove that great wine could be made in the unheralded vineyards of France's Midi (then associated with nothing but cheap wine), where by chance he discovered perfect vineyard soil on his isolated holiday property near Montpellier. With the help of BORDEAUX experts, he planted a vineyard based largely on Cabernet Sauvignon, but also including Syrah, Pinot Noir, Merlot, Malbec, Chardonnay, Viognier, Petit Manseng, and a range of weird and wonderful varieties from the Middle East and Armenia.

There are now 40ha (100 acres) of vines set among the forest in 50 small plots and farmed organically. The first vintage was 1978 and the wine was immediately dubbed the 'LAFITE of the LANGUEDOC' – high praise, but not accurate. Certainly the red wine is made with Bordeaux in mind – Guibert is one of France's most vociferous 'anti New World' exponents – and it does need 10 to 15 years to finally soften and open out. But it would also be better if it was less Bordeaux focused and the other warmer-climate varieties in the vineyard were allowed to dominate. The white is one of the Languedoc's most scented, sensual dry whites – wonderful at one year old and sometimes wonderful at 10 times that. An occasional beautiful sweet wine rounds out the range. Best years: 2001, '00, '99, '98, '97, '96, '95, '94, '93, '90.

MAS JULLIEN

FRANCE, Languedoc-Roussillon, Coteaux du Languedoc AC

❏ ❏ *Grenache, Cinsaut, Syrah, Carignan, Mourvèdre*

❏ *Grenache Blanc, Chenin Blanc, Viognier, Clairette, Cinsaut Blanc*

In 1985 Olivier Jullien of Mas Jullien was only 20 years old when he created the domaine which now totals 15ha (37 acres). It has been a lot larger than this in the past but he has now decided that 15 hectares is the size he can handle best and his less good plots have been ripped up and replanted with trees. Similarly he has stopped making single-vineyard cuvées, and he's given up small oak barrels in favour of traditional large wooden vats. He's a real freethinker, keen to do what's best for himself and for his land, and it certainly works. There's too much new oak being used in the LANGUEDOC at the moment and it's a low-key delight to taste the restrained but deeply satisfying reds from this domaine. He also makes a fairly whacky white, a blend of several varieties. Best years: (reds) 2001, '00, '99, '98, '97, '96, '95, '94, '93, '91.

MAS MARTINET

SPAIN, Cataluña, Priorat DOCa

❏ *Grenache Noir (Garnacha Tinta), Cabernet Sauvignon, Syrah, Carignan (Cariñena)*

Josep-Lluís Pérez has led an adventurous life – there's a long trek between the young emigrant to Switzerland who worked as a barber and a taxi driver to pay for his studies to the highly trained former enology professor at Tarragona University. As a member of the band who revolutionized PRIORAT in the late 1980s he exerted considerable influence in the decision to complement traditional local grape varieties with French varieties.

From his manicured vineyards, some rather controversially located at the bottom of the valley instead of being on the more usual precipitous slopes, he and his winemaker daughter Sara Pérez Ovejero produce Clos Martinet, adding Cabernet Sauvignon, Cariñena and Syrah to the Garnacha, plus an excellent second wine, Martinet Bru. The family's joint venture with the Cavas del Castillo de Perelada and the Porrera co-operative is run as a separate company, Cims de Porrera, which produces a smashing Garnacha-Cariñena blend. Best years: 2000, '99, '98, '96, '95, '94, '93, '90.

MASANDRA

UKRAINE, Crimea

❏ *Cabernet Sauvignon, Saperavi, Mourvèdre and others*

❏ *Pink Muscat*

❏ *Sercial, Verdelho, Albillo, White Muscat and others*

The Masandra Collection contains over one million bottles of commercially available wine dating back to 1891, and library wine dating back to 1775. The winery at Masandra, on the CRIMEAN coast near Yalta, was built to supply the Russian Tsar's summer palace. It survived the twentieth century rather better than the Romanovs, and today is the central winery for the coastal Crimean vineyards. It makes no wine itself, but instead matures and bottles numerous different styles. Indeed, most of the great dessert wines of the West have been imitated here and standards have often been very high.

GIUSEPPE MASCARELLO

Barolo from the Monprivato vineyard in the commune of Castiglione Falletto is Mascarello's top wine, and consistently one of the best in the region.

GIUSEPPE MASCARELLO

ITALY, Piedmont, Barolo DOCG

❏ *Nebbiolo, Barbera, Dolcetto, Freisa*

Mauro Mascarello now runs this famous BAROLO estate. His riverside winery at Monchiero was viciously attacked by the floodwaters of 1994, but he still shows no sign of moving it up to his prime site, the superb 7-ha (17-acre) Monprivato vineyard in Castiglione Falletto. His wines have great intensity of perfume and wonderful balance despite a tendency to light colour – proof, he maintains, that they are not blended with any 'improving' grape varieties, although the wonderful primary aromas he gets in his Barolos, such a relief in a blind tasting after copious waftings of toasty oak, is proof enough. Monprivato is the principal Barolo – and in top years, a little is produced as a Riserva, Cà d'Morissio – but he also produces other good Barolo crus, as well as excellent NEBBIOLO D'ALBA San Rocco. His dense, vibrant Dolcetto d'Alba Bricco and intense BARBERA D'ALBA can be impressive. Best years: (Monprivato) 2001, '00, '99, '98, '97, '96, '95, '90, '89, '88, '85, '82, '78, '70.

MASI

ITALY, Veneto, Valpolicella Classico DOC

❏ *Corvina, Rondinella, Molinara and others*

❏ *Garganega, Trebbiano di Soave, Sauvignon Blanc*

This dynamic group run by the Boscaini family has been a leading innovator since the 1960s and is probably the best-known producer in VALPOLICELLA today. It was among the first to introduce single-vineyard AMARONE with the Mazzano and Campolongo di Torbè crus, and RECIOTO with the cru Mezzanella. During the 1960s, it was the first to re-establish the traditional *ripasso* fermentation method with its Campofiorin wine. In the 1980s Masi took the neighbouring Serègo Alighieri estate, property of the heirs of Dante, under its wing, widening its range with Amarone Vaio Armaron and Recioto Casal dei Ronchi. Today, Masi controls production in some 160ha (395 acres) in the Verona area. For decades Masi has been at the forefront of viticultural experiments and the upmarket oaky Toar, a blend of Corvina and Rondinella together with the obscure Oseleta and Dindarella, is one result of this activity. Best years (Amarone): 2001, '00, '99, '97, '95, '93, '90, '88, '86, '85, '83, '81, '79, '76, '74.

MASTROBERARDINO

ITALY, Campania

♟ *Aglianico, Piedirosso, Sciascinoso*

♀ *Fiano, Greco, Falanghina, Coda di Volpe del Vesuvio*

For years Mastroberardino was held up as the leading producer in all of south Italy, and it remains a potent force. Based just outside the town of Avellino, it was traditionally a *négociant* house, buying grapes year after year from the same growers. It was canny enough to see that the growers would become producers in their turn, as indeed has happened, and some years ago Mastroberardino began buying its own vineyards. The most important one is Radici where, at altitudes of up to 700m (2300ft), it grows the traditional Aglianico (red) and Fiano (white) grapes. TAURASI Radici DOCG, 100 per cent Aglianico, remains its top red wine.

As for the white wines – Fiano Radici, Greco di Tufo Novaserra and Falanghina Sireum – one can't help thinking that today's versions lack the concentration and complexity necessary to excel in this highly competitive and highly expensive world of wine. Perhaps the newer Fiano More Maiorum – a white of real interest with, unusually for Italian whites until quite recently, a couple of years' aging before it reaches the market – will be the beginning of a new era. Best years: (Taurasi Radici) 2001, '99, '97, '96, '95, '93, '90, '89, '88, '86, '85, '83, '82, '81, '79, '68.

MATANZAS CREEK WINERY

USA, California, Sonoma County, Sonoma Valley AVA

♟ *Merlot, Cabernet Sauvignon, Syrah*

♀ *Chardonnay, Sauvignon Blanc*

Matanzas Creek Chardonnay made an immediate impression in the late 1970s when CALIFORNIA was only just starting to work out how to make the classic wine styles. Those early Chardonnays were whoppers, but they had the indefinable quality of balance that has marked Matanzas Creek Chardonnays ever since. In the 1980s it was Merlot that made

waves – beautifully ripe and perfumed, almost floral, showing the potential of the variety that became California's most fashionable during the 1990s. Part of this was due to talented winemaking, but equally important was the situation of the vineyards in Bennett Valley with direct access to the Pacific and its cooling breezes, which gave the grapes a much longer than average ripening time. There is an extremely expensive Merlot-Cabernet blend called Journey, as well as a Syrah, mainly from Bennett Valley fruit, and a MENDOCINO Viognier. Bought by Jess Jackson of KENDALL-JACKSON in 2000. Since he also owns Bennett Valley vineyards, hopefully he won't change the style too much. Best years: (Chardonnay) 2001, '00, '99, '98, '97, '96, '95, '94, '91, '90; (Merlot) 2001, '00, '99, '97, '96, '95, '94, '93, '91, '90.

MATUA VALLEY

NEW ZEALAND, North Island, Auckland

♟ *Cabernet Sauvignon, Merlot, Pinot Noir and others*

♀ *Chardonnay, Sauvignon Blanc, Riesling, Pinot Gris*

Matua Valley deserves the credit for pioneering New Zealand's most spectacularly successful wine style, Sauvignon Blanc, which was fermented in an old puncheon, in a tin shed previously used for making 'sherry'. An innovative and adventurous approach to winemaking has seen the tin shed turn into a modern showpiece winery with row upon row of expensive new French barriques rather than a lonely old puncheon.

Matua's reputation has been based primarily on its reds, led by the Ararimu Cabernet Sauvignon-Merlot, made only in top years. The Judd Estate (GISBORNE) Chardonnay can be superb, mixing deep, syrupy orange and apricot fruit with good spicy oak. The Sauvignon Blanc from MARLBOROUGH is sold under the Shingle Peak label. Bought by Beringer Blass in 2001. Hopefully the longstanding quality ethos won't be abused. Best years: (Ararimu Cabernet-Merlot) 2000, '98, '96, '94.

CH. MAUCAILLOU

FRANCE, Bordeaux, Haut-Médoc, Moulis AC, Cru Bourgeois

♟ *Cabernet Sauvignon, Merlot, Petit Verdot, Cabernet Franc*

Don't be put off by the incongruous look of Ch. Maucaillou just next to the Grand-Poujeaux railway station in the rather backwoods BORDEAUX appellation of MOULIS. It's been described as extravagant rococo (what other kind is there?), as 'half Renaissance and half

Arcachon villa' – and it does seem out of place in this sleepy village. But the wine in no way reflects the château. It is one of the most reliably enjoyable and affordable high-quality reds in Bordeaux: the tannins, the fruit and the careful oak all classically balanced. Latest vintages have been weightier, but the balance remains. It is also a perfect example of a Moulis from the gravel banks around Grand Poujeaux. Moulis has no Classed Growths, but the châteaux located on the gravels – and the 65-ha (160-acre) Maucaillou is one of them – can deliver Classed Growth quality if they want to. Best years: 2000, '99, '98, '96, '95, '90, '89.

MAULE VALLEY

CHILE, Valle Central

The most southerly and coolest sub-region of the VALLE CENTRAL, with wet winters – Maule has three times as much rain as Santiago – and a large day/night temperature difference. Almost a quarter of Chile's vines are planted here, and although one-third of these are the low-grade País, and although white varieties (mostly Chardonnay and Sauvignon) outnumber reds by nearly two to one, there are over 7000ha (17,300 acres) of Cabernet Sauvignon, and Merlot has been successful in the cool clay soils. Cauquenes, towards the Pacific, has some very good old dry-farmed vines, as well as new plantings from producers like the Californian KENDALL-JACKSON. Best producers: (whites) J Bouchon, Calina (Kendall-Jackson), Terra Noble.

BODEGAS MAURO

SPAIN, Castilla y León, Vino de Mesa de Castilla y León

♟ *Tempranillo (Tinto Fino), Syrah, Grenache Noir (Garnacha Tinta)*

Based just downriver from the western end of the RIBERA DEL DUERO DO, Mauro is rightfully considered today as one of the 'Super-Spanish' estates outside DO regulations. Founder Mariano García, the erstwhile VEGA SICILIA winemaker, can now officially direct the operations at the small winery, which depends on its 45ha (110 acres) of vineyards around Tudela de Duero. The style of wine is full, lush, warm, with an accessibility that is perhaps due to the use of a little old-vine Garnacha and Syrah in the blends.

Térreus, a single-vineyard cuvée from the estate's oldest vineyard, the 3-ha (7½-acre) Pago de Cueva Baja, has added an extra dimension to the range. The extraordinary fruit from the 60-year-old vines is given Vega

Sicilia-like depth and complexity by García's deft hand. Even the basic Mauro is a mouthful of rich, berryish, oak-tinged pleasure. Best years: 2000, '99, '98, '97, '96, '95, '94.

MAURY AC

FRANCE, Languedoc-Roussillon
❢ *Grenache*
♀ *Macabeo, Malvoisie*

This is a *vin doux naturel* or fortified wine produced essentially from Grenache. The AC covers approximately 1700ha (4200 acres) located on high schistous soils on the borders of LANGUEDOC and Roussillon. Maximum yields are 30 hectolitres per hectare, resulting in a powerful, sweet, tannic wine that is darker and more rustic in style than BANYULS, its Roussillon cousin. Styles vary from the early bottled and fruity vintage, to the older *rancio* style where the wine has been aged for a number of years in glass demi-johns and wooden casks, under conditions of controlled oxidation. Best producers: la Coume, MAS AMIEL, Maury co-op, Maurydoré, la Pléïade, du Roy.

MAXIMIN GRÜNHAUS

GERMANY, Mosel-Saar-Ruwer, Grünhaus
♀ *Riesling and others*

Maximin Grünhaus is the name of the 34-ha (84-acre) estate on the RUWER, where Carl von Schubert makes some of Germany's greatest wines. Dating back to 966, the estate has the best, and longest, reputation of all in the Ruwer. It was a Benedictine monastery at one time, and its three vineyards (all wholly owned) are still called Bruderberg, Herrenberg and Abtsberg (in ascending order of monastic importance and quality).

Over half the wines are *trocken* and the vineyards are almost entirely Riesling. Winemaking is traditional, and the wines have a piercing intensity of flavour, steely in their fruit and stabbed through with keen Riesling acidity softened by perfume and honey. Best years: 2002, '01, '00, '97, '96, '95, '94, '93, '92, '90, '89, '88, '85, '83, '79, '76, '75, '71.

MAXIMIN GRÜNHAUS
From the best estate in the Ruwer Valley, the Riesling Spätlese from the Abtsberg site is intensely fruity, rich and elegant.

MCCREA CELLARS

USA, Washington State, Columbia Valley AVA
❢ *Syrah, Grenache, Mourvedre, Counoise*
❢ *Viognier, Syrah, Grenache*
♀ *Viognier, Roussanne*

Doug McCrea gained a reputation for his excellent Chardonnay, but it is his championing of the RHÔNE varieties that is most important. Doug McCrea has largely been responsible for identifying some of WASHINGTON's best potential sites for Rhône grapes, and for persuading the state's top grape growers to plant them. He pioneered Syrah in Washington, taking it from relative obscurity to its current popularity. His Syrahs – including Amerique, and the single-vineyard Boushey Grande Côte and Ciel du Cheval – are the best in the state. There is also a southern Rhône-style red blend, and spicy Viognier. Best years: 2000, '99, '98, '97.

MCCREA CELLARS
The range includes Washington State's best Syrahs, from several top vineyards and all aged in French oak, apart from the Amerique cuvée.

MCLAREN VALE

AUSTRALIA, South Australia

For a century McLaren Vale was known for massive ferruginous reds and mighty 'ports', prescribed by British doctors of Queen Victoria's time for their restorative powers. The region emerged as a serious quality producer in the latter part of the 1970s and '80s. Initially its rich, fat Chardonnay caught the eye, but now it is for its black cherry and plum Shiraz and its faintly spicy but always fruity Grenache that McLaren Vale is most highly regarded. The style is quite different to that of the BAROSSA, being just a little less sun-baked and full throttle, but both are now equally regarded. Best years: 2000, '99, '98, '96, '94, '92, '91, '90, '89. Best producers: Cascabel, CHAPEL HILL, CLARENDON HILLS, Coriole, d'ARENBERG, FOX CREEK, Andrew Garrett, HARDY, Kangarilla Road, Maxwell, Geoff MERRILL, REYNELL, ROSEMOUNT, Tatachilla, WIRRA WIRRA.

MCWILLIAM'S

AUSTRALIA, New South Wales, Riverina
❢ *Syrah (Shiraz), Cabernet Sauvignon, Merlot*
♀ *Chardonnay, Semillon, Colombard, Riesling*

The bulk of McWilliam's wines – and all its excellent fortifieds – come from the hot inland region of RIVERINA. However it is the smaller volume brands of this old-established family company that catch your attention most. Long-held vineyards in the HUNTER VALLEY at Mount Pleasant yield fine Shiraz and superb Semillon, particularly Elizabeth Semillon, released at five years of age, already glowing with hints of honey, butter and lightly browned toast. COONAWARRA (where it owns BRAND'S but has bought and planted extensive additional vineyards) produces top reds and Barwang, in the HILLTOPS region in NEW SOUTH WALES, exciting cool-climate reds and whites. Since 2002 McWilliam's has had a joint venture with CALIFORNIA's E & J GALLO for the Hanwood Estate brand. Best years: (Elizabeth Semillon) 1997, '95, '94, '93, '91, '89, '86, '83, '82, '81, '79.

MÉDOC AC

FRANCE, Bordeaux
❢ *Cabernet Sauvignon, Merlot, Cabernet Franc and others*

This appellation technically applies to the whole MÉDOC peninsula but is, in fact, only used for the villages in the northern half, starting north of ST-ESTÈPHE at St-Seurin-de-Cadourne. The appellation should be called Bas-Médoc – reflecting the area's downstream position on the Gironde estuary. But *bas* means low in French – and the growers didn't want the connotation of 'low' quality, especially when their neighbours in the southern part of the peninsula could already use the more attractive title 'HAUT-MÉDOC'. The fact that the 'high' Médoc wines were superior to the 'low' ones somehow eluded them.

The Médoc AC vineyards cover 5188ha (12,820 acres) and the AC applies only to red wines, which can be very attractive – dry but juicy, with a little grassy acidity to keep them refreshing. But ripeness is a problem, since there are few gravel beds in these flat, meadow-like clay vineyards, and many wines taste rather rough and earthy. The early-ripening Merlot is more important here than Cabernet. Most Médoc wines are best to drink at three to five years old, but the brilliant Ch. POTENSAC takes ten years' aging with ease. Co-operatives control about 33 per cent of the region's production. Best years: 2001, '00, '96, '95, '90, '89, '88, '86, '85, '82. Best producers: la Cardonne, d' Escurac, les Grands Chênes, Greysac, Lacombe-Noaillac, Lafon, Loudenne, les Ormes-Sorbet, Patache d'Aux, Potensac, Ramafort, Rollan-de-By, la Tour-de-By, la Tour-Haut-Caussan, la Tour-St-Bonnet, Vieux-Robin.

MÉDOC France, Bordeaux

FROM A TOTAL VINEYARD AREA of about 15,000ha (37,000 acres) the Médoc produces a good fistful of the world's most renowned red wines – great wines like Ch. Margaux, Lafite-Rothschild, Mouton-Rothschild and Latour, whose names have resonated down through the ages. Or have they? Well, they haven't resonated for that long, because until the seventeenth century this narrow lip of land running north from the city of Bordeaux was just marshland. It was dangerous and inaccessible and although there are records of the odd wine like Lafite being made in the seventeenth century, it really wasn't until the middle of the eighteenth century that Médoc wines began to establish themselves. And for that we have to thank the Dutch engineers who arrived during the seventeenth century to drain these useless marshlands, and in doing so revealed the key to great wine in the Médoc – gravel. These deep, ancient banks of gravel are often only 10–15m (33–50ft) higher than the damp clay meadowlands in between, hardly enough to notice as you drive up the Médoc's tiny roads. But every single great wine of the Médoc is grown on gravel. Nothing beyond the merely decent can grow on the heavy clays that surround the great gravelly vineyard sites.

Between the villages of Macau in the south near Bordeaux and St-Seurin-de-Cadourne in the north there are great

Ch. Pichon-Longueville in Pauillac has seen a remarkable change of fortune since its purchase by AXA-Millésimes in 1987. The fairytale turreted château has been renovated and a state-of-the art winery built.

banks of gravel, providing warm ripening conditions and perfect drainage for the Cabernet Sauvignon grape which dominates the vineyards. This whole area is called the Haut-Médoc – the Upper Médoc – and all the best wines come from here, from one of the villages with the best gravel banks – Margaux, Listrac, Moulis, St-Julien, Pauillac and St-Estèphe – each with their own appellation. Vineyards not covered by the village appellations take the Haut-Médoc AC. There are also vineyards on the low-lying land or *palus* near the estuary, which produce generic red Bordeaux AC.

Further north the land becomes flatter, verdant with pasture and dotted with quiet villages. But the gravel's place has been taken by damp clay and hence there is a preponderance of Merlot in the vineyards. The wines become fruitier, earthier and simpler. This is the Bas-Médoc – the Low Médoc. But the appellation is plain Médoc – the growers understandably felt that 'low' sounded disparaging. So long as it's a warm vintage, this is good hunting ground for some of the few value-for-money wines of the region.

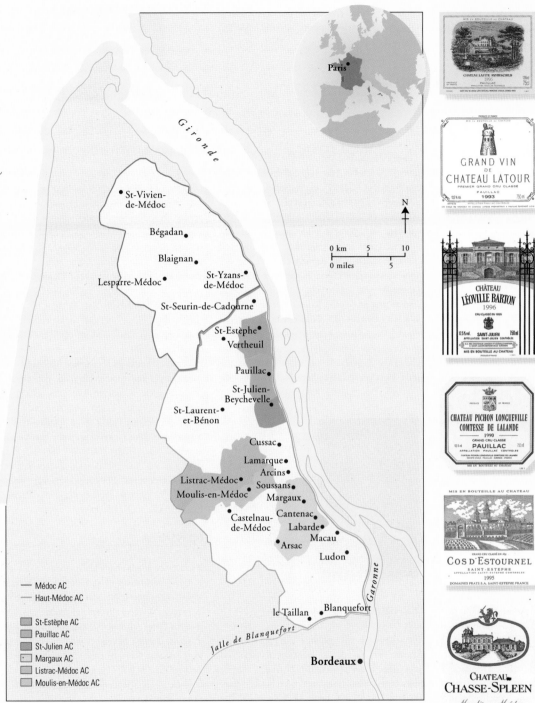

CH. LAFITE-ROTHSCHILD
Renowned for its elegant, restrained wine, this famous Premier Cru estate has seen great improvements in the last 20 years.

CH. LATOUR
Latour's great reputation is based on powerful, long-lasting classic wines. After 30 years in British hands, it returned to French ownership in 1993.

CH. LÉOVILLE-BARTON
Austere and restrained at first, this excellent traditional St-Julien wine unfolds into a purist's dream of blackcurrant and cedarwood. It has been outstanding in recent vintages.

CH. PICHON-LONGUEVILLE-COMTESSE DE LALANDE
Brilliant, classic Pauillac, this is Bordeaux's leading 'Super-Second' wine.

CH. COS D'ESTOURNEL
The undoubted leader in St-Estèphe, Cos d'Estournel is renowned for its dark, tannic, oaky wines that are classically made for long aging.

CH. CHASSE-SPLEEN
The leading Cru Bourgeois estate built up a reputation in the 1980s for its tremendously consistent and marvellously ripe, concentrated wine.

CH. SOCIANDO-MALLET
A leading Haut-Médoc estate, Sociando-Mallet makes dark, tannic wines with classic red Bordeaux flavours emerging after ten to 15 years.

AC ENTRIES
Haut-Médoc, Listrac-Médoc, Margaux, Médoc, Moulis, Pauillac, St-Estèphe, St-Julien.

CHÂTEAUX ENTRIES
d'Angludet, Batailley, Beychevelle, Branaire, Brane-Canten̄ac, Calon-Ségur, Cantemerle, Chasse-Spleen, Cissac, Clarke, Cos d'Estournel, Ducru-Beaucaillou, Ferrière, Giscours, Grand-Puy-Lacoste, Gruaud-Larose, Haut-Bages-Libéral, Haut-Batailley, Haut-Marbuzet, Lafite-Rothschild, Lafon-Rochet, Lagrange, la Lagune, Langoa-Barton, Latour, Léoville-Barton, Léoville-las-Cases, Léoville-Poyferré, Lynch-Bages, Margaux, Maucaillou, Meyney, Montrose, Mouton-Rothschild, Palmer, de Pez, Pichon-Longueville, Pichon-Longueville-Comtesse de Lalande, Pontet-Canet, Potensac, Poujeaux, Rauzan-Gassies, Rauzan-Ségla, St-Pierre, Sociando-Mallet, Talbot, du Tertre.

MEERLUST

SOUTH AFRICA, Western Cape, Stellenbosch WO
♥ *Cabernet Sauvignon, Merlot, Pinot Noir, Cabernet Franc*
♀ *Chardonnay*

Eight generations of the same family have run this farm, where vines have been grown for over 300 years. The current owner, Hannes Myburgh, has followed his father's fondness for BORDEAUX; the Cabernet Sauvignon-Merlot-Cabernet Franc blend, known as Rubicon, was one of the first such wines made in the Cape and is still one of the best.

Italian winemaker Giorgio Dalla Cia, ensconced at Meerlust since 1978, is strictly European in his approach – none of the modern gushy fruit for him. The restraint of Meerlust's reds can thus seem confusing coming from such a warm climate and New World-orientated industry. Merlot is Dalla Cia's personal obsession. Pinot Noir, benefiting from more new oak, has improved and the farm's first white, a full lemony but rich and toasty Chardonnay, immediately drew approving comments. Over the past few years, Dalla Cia's son George has shown off his distilling skills with some fruity, potent grappas. Best years: (Rubicon) 2001, '00, '99, '98, '97, '96, '95, '94, '92, '91; (Chardonnay) 2001, '00, '99, '98, '97, '96.

ALPHONSE MELLOT

FRANCE, Central Loire, Sancerre AC
♥ *Pinot Noir*
♀ *Sauvignon Blanc*

The Mellots are an old winemaking family dating back to 1513. The eldest son is always called Alphonse which clearly makes baptism easy. The eighteenth-generation Alphonse is one of the most dynamic characters in the SANCERRE region. The Mellots are both growers and *négociants* but Alphonse would now prefer to concentrate on his own vineyards, in particular, his prized 50-ha (124-acre) la Moussière to the south-west of the town of Sancerre. The white unoaked Domaine la Moussière is good 'standard' Sancerre, often with exotic fruit, while the barrel-fermented Cuvée Edmond is the flagship wine.

Until recently Mellot's red Sancerre has not been treated as seriously as the white. This has changed with the full involvement of the nineteenth Alphonse, who is now beginning to take over responsibility for the winemaking. His calling-card Génération XIX red is an impressively concentrated Pinot made with obsessive attention to detail and certainly not typical of usually lightweight red Sancerres.

Alphonse Mellot should not be confused with mainstream Sancerre producer Joseph Mellot. Best years: (Cuvée Edmond) 2001, '00, '99, '98, '97, '96, '95, '90, '89.

CHARLES MELTON

AUSTRALIA, South Australia, Barossa Valley
♥ *Syrah (Shiraz), Grenache, Mourvedre, Cabernet Sauvignon*
♀ *Grenache*

There's a bunch of young turks who have followed the lead of Peter LEHMANN in reviving the BAROSSA VALLEY's reputation as a tip-top producer of superripe, sensually scented reds – and as a consequence keeping the local growers in business and their marvellous ancient vines in the ground. Twinkly eyed 'Charlie' Melton is among the pace-setters with a rich, spicy mix of locally grown Shiraz, Grenache and Mourvedre called Nine Popes, a smashing juicy pink Rose of Virginia as well as a fizzy fantasy of a plum-red sparkling Shiraz which sells out to a frantic public in minutes. His opulently luscious Shiraz and Cabernet Sauvignon are made in the same style. Best years: (Nine Popes) 2001, '99, '98, '96, '95, '94, '93, '92, '91, '90.

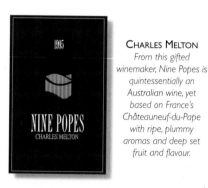

CHARLES MELTON
From this gifted winemaker, Nine Popes is quintessentially an Australian wine, yet based on France's Châteauneuf-du-Pape with ripe, plummy aromas and deep set fruit and flavour.

MENDOCINO COUNTY

USA, California

CALIFORNIA's Mendocino County is best known for its thick redwood forests and coastline. They're beautiful – the towering redwoods being thousands of years old – they actually mark the birth of Christ on the growth rings of some of these looming giants, and the coastline with its eerie fogs and pounding surf makes it easy to forget you're up there, many miles north of San Francisco, looking for California's most northerly vineyards. Well, there are two very different sorts of Mendocino County vineyards, divided by the 910-m (3000-ft) high Coastal Range. To the west of the range, heavily influenced by those sea fogs is the supercool ANDERSON

ROEDERER ESTATE
The Mendocino off-shoot of the French Champagne house Roederer is unique in California for using only grapes from its own vineyards.

VALLEY, producing delightful fragrant whites, but above all the best source of sparkling wine grapes in California. Labels like ROEDERER ESTATE make make outstanding fizz here and on the ridges of the valley, above the fogline you'll find some remarkable reds, notably Zinfandel. However, cross the Coastal Range eastwards and you come to the northern end of the RUSSIAN RIVER VALLEY. Cut off from the Pacific, it's hot here and the wines are rich and soft as a result. Most of Mendocino's 6475ha (16,000 acres) are here, in or near the river valley between McDowell Valley, in the south and Redwood Valley in the north. There's good Chardonnay, but reds like Cabernet, Merlot, Syrah and Zinfandel are more impressive. FETZER, a leader in the organic vineyard movement, is the main winery. Best years: (reds) 2001, '00, '99, '97, '96, '95, '94, '93, '91, '90. Best producers: Fetzer, Fife, Goldeneye, HANDLEY, Husch, Lazy Creek, McDowell Valley, Navarro, Pacific Echo, Parducci, Roederer.

MENDOZA

ARGENTINA

Ninety-seven per cent of Mendoza is a desert. But the remaining 3 per cent of this vast sprawling, seemingly flat plain, that tilts imperceptibly away from the Andes towards Buenos Aires, almost 900km (563 miles) to the east, is a riot of cultivation – every sort of fruit and vegetable, but above all, vines – over 140,000ha (345,935 acres) of them, mostly fanning out to the west, east and south of the city of Mendoza.

None of this would be possible without irrigation, because Mendoza, where the Andes loom magnificently above you, day and night, dawn and dusk, dominating your senses, is in a rain shadow. Rain most years totals a feeble 223mm (8.8in), much of it likely to fall in the summer as hail, which can decimate your crop in minutes. But four great rivers, led by the Mendoza River, seething with the snowmelt of the Andes peaks, surge out into the plains. Virtually every drop is taken for irrigation, using an intricate system of channels developed by the Incas and then the Huarpe tribes, enthusiastically taken up by the Spanish when they arrived here in the 1550s, and used to this day by the majority of vineyards.

There are five major Mendoza vineyard areas. North Mendoza isn't that important, but does have Malbec vines going back to 1861. East Mendoza is *very* hot and dry and is a key area for Italian grapes like Bonarda, Barbera and Sangiovese, and the Spanish Tempranillo. Historically the most important area has been the Primera Zona, around the south and west of the city. In areas like Maipú, Lunlunta, Luján de Cuyo, Las Compuertas, Perdriel and Agrelo, you'll find big plantations of marvellous ancient Malbec capable of producing heady, damson-dark scented reds, as well as fine Cabernet, Shiraz, Merlot and the fragrant white Torrontes.

130km (80 miles) south of Mendoza, but still part of the region is San Rafael, warm, dry and with the biggest hailstones in Argentina, but capable of excellent reds. And slanting northwards back towards Mendoza City, but much closer to the mountains, is the UCO VALLEY, gradually rising to 1500m (4920ft) height in Tupungato, finally so cool that even here in Mendoza, the grapes won't ripen as early frosts from the mountains bite into the fruit. This is the best place in Argentina for Chardonnay, but reds like Shiraz, Merlot, Pinot Noir, Malbec, even Tannat and Nebbiolo, also grow here, nestled tight into the flanks of the Andes. Best producers: Luigi BOSCA, CATENA ZAPATA, DOMAINE VISTALBA, Finca El Retiro, Finca La Celia, LA AGRÍCOLA, Nieto Senetiner (Cadus), NORTON, Salentein, Terrazas de los Andes.

MENETOU-SALON AC
FRANCE, Central Loire
🍷 🍷 *Pinot Noir*
🍷 *Sauvignon Blanc*

Menetou-Salon adjoins the western end of the larger and more famous appellation of SANCERRE. During the 1990s Menetou-Salon grew three-fold and there are now around 400ha (1000 acres) of vines, roughly in the proportion of 65 per cent white to 35 per cent red. The whites are very dry, but soft Sauvignon wines, with a nice hint of gooseberry and blackcurrant leaves in the taste and a pleasant chalky-clean feel. The reds quite often have a very attractive, lean but strawberry-perfumed style, and can be good and

cherry-fresh, better than many of Sancerre's offerings. Best producers: de Chatenoy, Chavet, J-P Gilbert, H Pellé, du Prieuré, J-M Roger, J Teiller, la Tour St-Martin.

MÉO-CAMUZET
FRANCE, Burgundy, Côte de Nuits, Vosne-Romanée AC
🍷 *Pinot Noir*
🍷 *Chardonnay, Pinot Blanc*

It's nice when the new generation appreciates the old. Part of this excellent estate had been leased decades ago in a share-cropping agreement to Henri Jayer, who proved himself to be arguably Burgundy's greatest red winemaker. When the lease contract came to an end the young boss Jean-Nicolas Méo had enough sense to ask Jayer to consult to the estate, and consequently the Méo-Camuzet wines, though rarely so pristine and beautiful as the old Jayer wines, are nonetheless succulent, exotic and seductive examples of top Burgundy, with particularly good wines coming from CLOS DE VOUGEOT, NUITS-ST-GEORGES and VOSNE-ROMANÉE Premiers Crus. The estate totals 14ha (35 acres) but Méo has started a micro-*négociant* business to expand production. Best years: 2002, '01, '00, '99, '97, '96, '95, '93, '90.

DOMAINE MERCOURI *1990 was the first vintage of the new era at this impressive estate. The Domaine Mercouri red is deep-coloured, powerful and marked by Refosco's typical acidity in the finish.*

DOMAINE MERCOURI
GREECE, Western Peloponnese, Korakohori
🍷 *Refosco, Mavrodaphne, Avgoustiatis, Mourvèdre*
🍷 *Roditis, Viognier*

This small, very high-quality estate in the far west of Greece was established in 1860, but its modern incarnation dates from 1989 when the fourth generation of family ownership decided to revive winemaking here. The Domaine Mercouri is a magical blend of the north Italian grape Refosco with Mavrodaphne while the flagship white – Foloï – is from Roditis. There are extensive experimental plantings of French, Italian and Greek varieties which result in some fascinating red, rosé and dry and sweet white blends.

MERCUREY AC
FRANCE, Burgundy, Côte Chalonnaise
🍷 *Pinot Noir*
🍷 *Chardonnay*

This is easily the biggest and most important of the four main Côte Chalonnaise villages; 649ha (1604 acres) of vines produce significantly more wine than any of the three other specific ACs, RULLY, GIVRY and MONTAGNY. Over half its vines are owned by merchants, so the wines are the most widely distributed of the region. Red wine production is over three million bottles a year. The flavour is usually a somewhat rustic imitation of the CÔTE DE BEAUNE, rarely very deep in colour, sometimes earthy but often with a quite attractive cherry and strawberry fruit which can take some aging. Best years: (reds) 2002, '99, '97, '96. Best producers: (reds) FAIVELEY, E Juillot, M Juillot, Lorenzon, F Raquillet, RODET, de Suremain, de Villaine.

There isn't so much white, less than 500,000 bottles a year, and the locals rather dismissively whisper that they only plant Chardonnay on ground unsuitable for Pinot Noir – but the wine can be as good as many far more expensive offerings from the more fashionable CÔTE D'OR to the north. It is quite full with a very attractive, buttery, nutty, even spicy taste. Drink at three to four years old. Best producers: (whites) Faiveley (Clos Rochette), Genot-Boulanger, M Juillot, Olivier LEFLAIVE, Ch. de Chamirey/Rodet.

MERIDIAN VINEYARDS
USA, California, San Luis Obispo, Paso Robles AVA
🍷 *Cabernet Sauvignon, Merlot, Pinot Noir, Syrah, Zinfandel*
🍷 *Chardonnay, Sauvignon Blanc, Gewurztraminer*

Meridian had a strange, almost superstar status in the late 1980s and early '90s when the world was mad for Chardonnay, and in particular for founder Chuck Ortman's Chardonnay. It's now part of the Australo-American giant Beringer Blass and the corporate dollars have allowed Ortman to invest in vineyards way down the coast from San Francisco at SAN LUIS OBISPO. From the start Meridian Chardonnay has expertly trodden the line forgotten by many of the bigger brands between quality and value for money – at both regular and reserve levels the wines overdeliver. The Meridian vineyard operation is now vast – around 2830ha (7000 acres) planted in PASO ROBLES, EDNA VALLEY and SANTA BARBARA – and it grows many varieties, including Pinot Noir, Syrah and Zinfandel, as well as Chardonnay.

MERLOT

Merlot plantings in Bordeaux these days outpace those of Cabernet Sauvignon. This never used to be the case. Merlot was always present in Bordeaux, but its fleshy, perfumed style never got as much acclaim as the elegant austerity of Cabernet Sauvignon. Then tastes began to change: suddenly the ability, nay the necessity, to age a wine for a decade or more before drinking it was far less important than the ability to take a wine off the shop shelf and drink it that night. And that's when the amount of Merlot in the vineyards of Bordeaux began to outstrip Cabernet Sauvignon. Producers also realized that Merlot was better adapted than Cabernet to heavy, clay soils.

Merlot will age, of course. Look at Ch. Pétrus: one of the most expensive reds in the world, made virtually 100 per cent from Merlot, and which has no difficulty in lasting for 20–30 years. And Merlot-dominated Pomerols generally, now in huge demand worldwide, do not exactly fall apart in your glass – in fact, they age more gracefully than many Médocs. Merlot planted in the clay-limestone soils of St-Émilion also produces wines of great 'ageability'. But Merlot does make a rounder, softer wine, which is one reason why it has always been useful in softening the hard edges of Cabernet in the Bordeaux blend.

It is used in precisely the same way in the New World, where the craze for varietal Cabernet Sauvignon is still going strong. However, alongside it is a growing realization that Cabernet Sauvignon can be too tannic from a warm climate like California and not ripe enough from somewhere cool like New Zealand. So Bordeaux-type blends are popping up all over. But equally important are the single-varietal Merlots that are the current rage. In the USA Napa and Sonoma both make good examples. Washington State is also producing rich, well-structured Merlot as are a handful of producers north of the border in British Columbia's Okanagan Valley. Further south Chile has some stunning deep, plummy Merlots. Some of New Zealand's most delicious reds are from Merlot. Merlot was welcomed with open arms by South African winemakers in the early 1980s when vines became more readily available. But only now are the best (cooler) areas being identified. The wine has made its mark both as a varietal and in blends, mainly with Cabernet Sauvignon but Pinotage and Syrah (Shiraz) have also proved interesting partners. Even Australia has fallen under Merlot's spell – but it'll need a few years to develop full Merlot know-how. Most wines so far are Cabernet blends.

In Europe, north-east Italy has a long tradition of using Merlot for its 'jug' wine, but when yields are kept down, Merlot can be just as full of blackberry and plum and fruit-cake juiciness in Italy as it is elsewhere. It makes some of Friuli's most attractive reds, and produces reasonable quality in Alto Adige and Trentino, and over the border in Switzerland's Ticino. Further south, Tuscan growers like Ornellaia (Masseto), Frescobaldi (Lamaione), Tua Rita (Redigaffi) and Castello di Ama (Vigna l'Apparita) are making world-class Merlot.

Austria, too, has Merlot, which can be very good. Merlot also floods out of eastern Europe: Bulgarian, Hungarian and Greek Merlots can all be attractive and should go on providing us with good-value drinking. Spain and Portugal, on the other hand, haven't done much with it yet.

GEOFF MERRILL
AUSTRALIA, South Australia, McLaren Vale
❦ *Cabernet Sauvignon, Syrah (Shiraz), Merlot, Grenache, Sangiovese*
❦ *Grenache*
❦ *Chardonnay, Sauvignon Blanc, Semillon*

Merrill is one of the characters of Australian wine; if he weren't a winemaker he would surely be on the comedy stage. Fortunately, his winemaking, though clearly 'showbiz' in feel, embraces the classics as well as 'end-of-pier' stuff. His Chardonnay is heavily oaked and slow maturing but worth the wait. It is lean when young and nutty and rich when mature. He also does a flowery, passionfruit and gooseberry Sauvignon Blanc to buy and gulp down with maximum speed. The Cabernet Sauvignon reflects Merrill's penchant for early picking – being zesty and crisp, with tart redcurrant flavours and low tannin but aging to a delicious blackcurrant maturity – while the Mount Hurtle Grenache, all tingling cherry and strawberry, shows his enthusiasm for pleasure in the bottle first and foremost. Merrill has also made wine in Italy, under the La Veritière label.

MERRYVALE
USA, California, Napa Valley AVA
❦ *Cabernet Sauvignon, Merlot, Pinot Noir and others*
❦ *Chardonnay, Sauvignon Blanc and others*

Merryvale makes fine wine, but its history is almost as interesting. It's situated just to the south of St Helena in the buildings of the Sunny St Helena Winery – the first winery built in NAPA after the repeal of Prohibition. It was also the first place the great Robert MONDAVI got his feet dirty in Napa because his father owned it from 1937 to 1943. The top Merryvale wines are intense Chardonnays, led by Silhouette, plus – not surprisingly, since POMEROL's Michel Rolland consults – Merlot, Cabernet and BORDEAUX-blend Profile. Starmont varietals are all from Napa Valley fruit. Best years: (Chardonnay) 2001, '00, '99, '98, '97, '96, '95.

LOUIS MÉTAIREAU
FRANCE, Loire, Pays Nantais, Muscadet de Sèvre-et-Maine AC
❦ *Muscadet*

Louis Métaireau has long stood out in MUSCADET, an appellation which has often been careless of its reputation. For many years he campaigned for real *sur lie* bottling, the wines being bottled where they were made rather than being transported elsewhere and then bottled, so losing the residual carbon dioxide which is an essential characteristic of *sur lie*. Métaireau is actually the figurehead and organizational genius of a group of *vignerons*, who cultivate their own vines and make their own wine, all sold under his name. The top cuvée is called Number 1, followed by Cuvée LM. Grand Mouton comes from a 27-ha (67-acre) vineyard owned jointly by the group. There is also a Petit Mouton and two VIN DE PAYS Melon de Bourgogne.

MEURSAULT AC
FRANCE, Burgundy, Côte de Beaune
❦ *Pinot Noir*
❦ *Chardonnay*

The wine is pale gold, glinting in the cool, bright sunlight. The powerful scent catches the aroma of spring blossoms in the courtyard and mingles tantalizingly with the sweet perfume of fresh-hewn oak casks. It is Meursault from the latest vintage, still raw and bony, but already promising the smooth-sided succulence which will make the wine cling to the memory for years to come.

Here's another wine, straw-gold but cut with green. The smell is buttery, peachy too, cream coating the fruit, with honey and hazelnuts hiding behind the richness, and the distant breakfast smells of coffee and buttered toast. Another Meursault, now perhaps two years old, already so lovely, yet still only hinting at what's to come. And one more wine weaves its magic. Deep golden, almost savoury – the rich smoke of toast and roasted almonds and a flash of cinnamon spice, the cream and melted butter of its youth now gone golden, halfway to brown – less luscious but deeper, richer – Meursault-Charmes, or Meursault-Perrières maybe, the 1995 perhaps, or even the '92. White wine perfection.

Ah, if it were all like this – but BURGUNDY being Burgundy, for every grower striving to excel there's another with his eye on the cash register, because Meursault, at 437ha (1080 acres) the biggest white wine village in the CÔTE D'OR, is also the most popular. The general standard of the wine is rather variable, though this is more the fault of greedy producers than of inferior land. There are no Grands Crus, but a whole cluster of Premiers Crus. The tiny hamlet of BLAGNY south of Meursault is allowed to sell some of its lean but classy whites as Meursault. Altogether, Meursault produces well over two million bottles a year – lovely to drink young, but better aged five to eight years. Best years: 2002, '01, '00, '99, '97, '96, '95, '92, '89. Best producers: R Ampeau, M Bouzereau, Boyer-Martenot, Coche-Debord, COCHE-DURY, DROUHIN, A Ente, J-P Fichet, V GIRARDIN, JADOT, P Javillier, F Jobard, R Jobard, LAFON, Matrot, P Morey, G Roulot.

There is a little red wine, mainly from the VOLNAY side of the village and if it comes from the Premier Cru les Santenots it can be sold as Volnay-Santenots. At the southern end of the village, especially around Blagny, reds are good, but a little hard, and sold as Blagny.

CH. MEYNEY
FRANCE, Bordeaux, Haut-Médoc, St-Estèphe AC, Cru Bourgeois
❦ Cabernet Sauvignon, Merlot, Cabernet Franc, Petit Verdot

This is one of those châteaux that has quietly but determinedly been making wines of a regular consistency and quality for a number of years. Meyney's vineyard is good – 50ha (124 acres) with 67 per cent Cabernet Sauvignon, 25 per cent Merlot, 5 per cent Cabernet Franc and 3 per cent Petit Verdot, on the same riverside plateau as the Second Growth Ch. MONTROSE. But what has made this wine so reliably fine is the uncompromising approach of Domaines Cordier, the owners – maximizing the quality and ripeness of the fruit, and ruthlessly selecting only the best vats. The result is big, broad-flavoured wine, generally a little short on nuance but with lovely dark plummy fruit that successfully evolves over 10–15 years. Second wine: Prieur de Meyney. Best years: 2001, '00, '99, '96, '95, '94, '90, '89, '88.

PETER MICHAEL WINERY
USA, California, Sonoma County, Knights Valley AVA
❦ Cabernet Sauvignon, Pinot Noir
♀ Chardonnay, Sauvignon Blanc

British-born Peter Michael expanded his country vacation home into a small vineyard and hired Helen Turley now of MARCASSIN to design his small winery and oversee his early vintages, starting with the 1987. The launch was made easy by spectacular Chardonnays which were soon joined by an estate-grown red Meritage called Les Pavots. Despite several changes of winemaker, the winery has enjoyed smooth sailing since Turley departed, and has added an intense, blockbuster Chardonnay named Mon Plaisir and equally sensational Après-Midi Sauvignon Blanc. Made in tiny quantities, Cuvée Indigène and Point Rouge are exquisite Chardonnays and le Moulin Rouge is a fine Pinot Noir from Santa Lucia. Best years: (Les Pavots) 1999, '97, '96, '95, '94, '93, '91, '90.

LOUIS MICHEL & FILS
FRANCE, Burgundy, Chablis AC
♀ Chardonnay

The CHABLIS growers are divided between those who believe the steely character of authentic Chablis is best expressed through wines that have never been near an oak barrel, and those who argue that some aging in oak, even a proportion of new oak, can lend complexity to the wine. Louis Michel is widely regarded as the finest of the producers following the no oak approach.

The estate is fairly substantial and of its 21ha (51 acres), 2ha (5 acres) are Grand Cru (Grenouilles, Vaudésir and les Clos) and 13ha (32 acres) are Premier Cru (Montmains being the largest holding). Jean-Loup Michel believes in machine harvesting, fining and filtration – anathema to many top producers – but the wines age beautifully and are wonderfully complex. Rather than imposing flavours on the wine, the Michel approach allows the specific mineral complexity of each vineyard to express itself to the full. Best years: (top crus) 2002, '00, '99, '97, '96, '95, '90.

MINERVOIS AC
FRANCE, Languedoc-Roussillon
❦ Syrah, Mourvèdre, Lladoner Pelut, Grenache, Carignan, Cinsaut and others
♀ Macabeo, Bourboulenc, Marsanne, Roussanne, Vermentino (Rolle) and others

Minervois hasn't quite got the wild 'mountain-man' reputation of CORBIÈRES. This is partly because – until recently – the wines have been relatively light, spicy, dusty and deliciously fruity but not in any way challenging, and partly because with Corbières we all dash off into those untamed sub-Pyrenean hills and are soon lost in a timeless twilight world, but with Minervois we generally stay in the AUDE valley rootling round the co-operatives and estates within easy reach of civilization.

In fact, the high, wind-swept, herb-strewn plateau of the Minervois is exciting, and offers a potential that is beginning to be exploited. But Minervois' great strength is in the admittedly boring concept of 'organization'. Big companies like Nicolas and Chantovent have worked hard with local co-operatives to produce good-quality, juicy, quaffing wine at reasonable prices, and you can now find numerous sturdy, rough-fruited reds and juicy rosés under merchant labels that come from the revitalized co-operatives. The best wines are made by the estates: full of ripe, red fruit for drinking young.

Minervois, like the rest of the LANGUEDOC, is evolving towards wines of greater quality. Since 1999, Carignan can represent only 40 per cent of the blend. A number of small domaines are now producing richer, more complex wines from blends of Syrah, Grenache and Mourvèdre aged in oak barrels.

Individuality within the AC has also been proclaimed with the raising of the village of la Livinière and several surrounding communes to cru status in 1998. There are 4560ha (11,267 acres) of the Minervois AC producing 30 million bottles a year, almost all of it red. It is best drunk young, but can age, especially if a little new oak has been used. Best years: 2001, '00, '99, '98, '96, '95. Best producers: (reds) Aires Hautes, CLOS

CENTEILLES, Coupe-Roses, Pierre Cros, Fabas, Gourgazaud, la Grave, Maris, Oupia, Piccinini, Pujol, Ste-Eulalie, la Tour Boisée, Vassière, Villerambert-Julien, Violet.

MINHO VINHO REGIONAL

PORTUGAL, Minho

Named after the rivers that surge down from the mountains in the Minho province of north-west Portugal, Rios do Minho corresponds to the VINHO VERDE DOC. The name was changed to Minho in 1999. The grapes are similar too, but the Vinho Regional category permits foreign varieties as well, including Chardonnay, Riesling, Cabernet Sauvignon and Merlot. So far there are few wines bottled under the Minho designation as most producers prefer to stick with the traditional strictures of Vinho Verde. One exception is the Quinta de Covela estate near the DOURO, which is successfully blending indigenous and international grapes.

CH. LA MISSION-HAUT-BRION

FRANCE, Bordeaux, Pessac-Léognan AC, Cru Classé de Graves

♀ *Cabernet Sauvignon, Merlot, Cabernet Franc*

This is one of those BORDEAUX properties which, by a show of hands and shouts of 'aye', could be promoted to First Growth one day. The wines are powerful – almost bullying and hectoring by nature – but, unlike those of its neighbour Ch. HAUT-BRION, never charming, and rarely with that lovely, ruminative flavour-memory which other blockbusters like Ch. LATOUR and PÉTRUS always have.

The strength of these wines lies in a dark-plums-and-chocolate fruit braided with an earthy dryness which rarely opens out before ten years and often needs 20 or more to achieve its memorable tangle of tobacco, cedar and herb garden perfumes. Since 1983 it has been under the same ownership and management as Ch. Haut-Brion but the two estates have kept their own identities. Surrounded by the Bordeaux suburbs, la Mission covers 21ha (52 acres) of vines which are sliced through by the Bordeaux-Arcachon main railway line. Second wine: la Chapelle de la Mission-Haut-Brion. Best years: 2001, '00, '99, '98, '96, '95, '94, '93, '90, '89, '88, '85.

MISSION HILL

CANADA, British Columbia, Okanagan Valley VQA

♀ *Merlot, Pinot Noir*

♀ *Chardonnay, Pinot Gris, Pinot Blanc, Riesling, Vidal*

The beginnings of Mission Hill date back to 1981, when the owner, Anthony von Mandl established the first family-owned, commercial winery in the OKANAGAN VALLEY. After years of steady growth, things changed in 1992 with the arrival of winemaker, John Simes from MONTANA in New Zealand. The cool-climate specialist has developed a series of intense, highly flavoured varietals that have propelled Mission Hill into the upper echelon of Canada's wineries. Best bets include a citrus-flavoured Chardonnay, a fresh appley Pinot Blanc and more recently, Pinot Gris. The future of Mission Hill lies in its newly expanded winery facilities and a spectacular new 89-ha (220-acre) vineyard planted to Cabernet Sauvignon, Merlot, Syrah and Viognier at the southern end of the valley in virtual desert, just north of the US border.

MITCHELL

AUSTRALIA, South Australia, Clare Valley

♀ *Syrah (Shiraz), Cabernet Sauvignon, Grenache*

♀ *Riesling, Semillon*

You could call Jane and Andrew Mitchell CLARE VALLEY oldtimers – although they won't like it – because they set up their winery in an old stone apple store way back in 1975 and since then have been a considerable force in the valley. Their reds don't quite have the intensity they used to, and their now excellent Riesling is recovering from an unexplained dip in the late 1990s, but they are definitely among the leaders once again. The Watervale Riesling is steely, the Growers Semillon rich and oaky, Growers Grenache is a lively stew of herbs and fruit and Peppertree Shiraz and Sevenhill Cabernet Sauvignon are plump, chocolaty and able to age.

MITCHELTON

AUSTRALIA, Victoria, Goulburn Valley

♀ *Syrah (Shiraz), Grenache, Mourvedre, Cabernet Sauvignon, Merlot*

♀ *Riesling, Marsanne, Viognier, Roussanne, Chardonnay*

Now part of PETALUMA, Mitchelton is the largest producer in the GOULBURN region and one which combines a high-quality range and tasty bargain-priced selection with reasonable success. RHÔNE varieties are specialities here and Marsanne is perhaps the best-known wine, but Riesling, Semillon and Chardonnay are all beautifully crafted. Reds are best in the juicy easy-drinking style. Best years: (Print Label Shiraz) 1998, '96, '95, '92, '91, '90.

MITTELRHEIN

GERMANY

The Mittelrhein region runs along the Rhine south of Bonn; the Ahr and the Mosel rivers flow into it, and the NAHE and the RHEINGAU regions bring it up short in the south. Tourists love the Mittelrhein, sailors hated it (the Rhine Gorge was home to the sirens of the Lorelei and – who knows? – may still be) and winemakers seem increasingly dissatisfied with life here: the area under vine has been declining since the 1960s and now stands at around 526ha (1300 acres). One reason is that the area has always been overshadowed by its more famous neighbours, the MOSEL and Rheingau. The vineyards are 75 per cent Riesling, and the wines are steely and fresh; ripe and good in warm vintages, distinctly lean in cool ones, but here the demands of the Sekt industry come to the rescue. J Wegeler's good Lila brand is drawn largely from Mittelrhein fruit.

The vineyards, on slaty soil, are poised on the steep slopes near the Rhine and its tributaries, mostly on the east bank in the north of the region and mostly on the west bank in the south. In the past the vineyards were terraced and highly picturesque, but these days the success of Flurbereinigung (the restructuring of vineyards into more workable units), has meant that the Mittelrhein has become more a region of sloping vineyards than it used to be. They are easier to work that way, but the change does not seem sufficient to keep the growers at work. The potential for quality is high, but there are few outstanding producers. BACHARACH is the wine centre and base of leading producer Toni JOST. The castles that dot the region were built not to make wine but to extract tolls from luckless travellers. Best years: (Riesling Spätlese) 2002, '01, '99, '98, '93, '90.

MOËT ET CHANDON

FRANCE, Champagne, Champagne AC

♀ ♂ *Pinot Noir, Pinot Meunier, Chardonnay*

If there is one company that rules our perception of CHAMPAGNE as a drink, it has to be Moët et Chandon, with its enormous production of more than 25 million bottles a year, and its domination of the Champagne market. People seem to be shooting the corks out of gigantic bottles of Moët at every first night, every film award, every glossy showbiz wedding – in fact anywhere there is likely to be a photographer who is likely to get a picture of the event – and a bottle of Moët – into the newspapers. The result is that Moët is the most famous Champagne in the world.

With all this notoriety it is little short of remarkable that the general quality of Moët is pretty good – soft, creamy, a little spicy, and

Moët et Chandon is the giant of the Champagne region. There are over 28km (17 miles) of cellars in Épernay to house its stocks of more than 100 million bottles. Underground cellars such as these are ideal for Champagne's second fermentation in the bottle which should be as cool, as slow and as long as possible.

much credit must go to their chief winemaker Richard Geoffroy. The vintage wine is consistent, and usually has a good strong style to it, though Moët is one of those houses which are apt to release a vintage rather too frequently, when some might suggest the quality of the harvest left a bit to be desired. Dom Pérignon is their world-famous de luxe cuvée, found in all the world's great nightspots. It can be one of the greatest and most refined of Champagnes, but it must be given several years' aging, even after release. Moët Rosé is one of the few rosé Champagnes that actually tastes pink. Best years: 1996, '95, '93, '92, '90, '88, '86, '85, '82.

Moët also has offshoots, all known as DOMAINE CHANDON, making sparkling wine in CALIFORNIA, Argentina and Australia, as well as operations in Spain and Brazil.

MOLISE
ITALY

A small, sparsely populated region south of ABRUZZO and north of PUGLIA on the Adriatic coast, Molise prides itself on its hard wheat, for quality pasta and long-lived bread, olive oil, honey and any number of other agricultural crops. Until the mid-1980s only one thing was missing: it suffered the ignominy of being the only region in Italy without a single DOC. Then two were awarded at once: Biferno and

Pentro. Not that this seems to have inspired many producers to raise their game, even though the potential for good wine is there. Di Majo Norante is the longest-standing exception; Borgo di Colloredo is a recent challenger – their varietal Montepulciano Molise is a pretty impressive mouthful.

MONBAZILLAC AC
FRANCE, South-West
♀ *Sémillon, Sauvignon Blanc, Muscadelle*

The leading sweet wine of the BERGERAC region, and the only one which is sometimes made in the style of SAUTERNES. At its best Monbazillac is full and honeyed, with a hefty sweetness of peaches and barley sugar. Lighter versions are likely to be very pale and resemble pleasantly drinkable sweet apples with just a touch of honey. The difference comes about largely because the botrytis or noble rot fungus, needed on the overripe grapes to concentrate sweetness, doesn't always appear here, or the growers won't take the risk of selective late harvesting to obtain grapes with noble rot. Those that do, like the owners of the sublime Ch. Tirecul-la-Gravière, produce rich, exotic wines that will happily develop over ten years or more. The price of these wines is, needless to say, higher.

A growing number of properties now make traditional rich Monbazillac but most of

the six million bottles produced each year come from the competent but unadventurous co-operative. The vineyards, covering 2500ha (6178 acres) south of Bergerac town, run up a north-facing slope to the impressive Château de Monbazillac (sadly the wine's not as exciting as the architecture). In general drink young, but a real late-harvested example can happily last ten years. Best years: 2001, '99, '98, '97, '96, '95, '90. Best producers: l'Ancienne Cure, Bélingard (Blanche de Bosredon), la Borderie, Grande Maison, Haut-Bernasse, Hébras, Theulet, Tirecul-la-Gravière, Tour des Verdots, Treuil-de-Nailhac.

CH. MONBOUSQUET
FRANCE, Bordeaux, St-Émilion Grand Cru AC
♀ *Merlot, Cabernet Franc, Cabernet Sauvignon*
♀ *Sauvignon Blanc, Sauvignon Gris*

Gérard Perse, the supermarket tycoon who also owns Ch PAVIE, bought this underachieving property on the Dordogne plain in 1993 and has transformed it into one of ST-ÉMILION's 'super-crus' with the help of consultancy from Michel Rolland. Rich, voluptuous and very expensive, the wine is 60 per cent Merlot, 30 per cent Cabernet Franc, and drinkable from three to four years, but will presumably age longer. There is also a tiny amount of white wine. Best years: 2001, '00, '99, '98, '97, '96, '95, '94.

ROBERT MONDAVI WINERY

USA, California, Napa County, Napa Valley,
Oakville AVA

(Oakville) ▮ *Cabernet Sauvignon, Merlot, Zinfandel,*
Cabernet Franc, Malbec, Sangiovese, Syrah, Petit Verdot
▯ *Sauvignon Blanc, Semillon*

You can't begin to think about the evolution of Californian wine without thinking about Robert Mondavi. In fact you can't avoid Robert Mondavi if you start to consider the whole modern world of wine across every continent because since this gravel-voiced, tightly-wound bundle of energy founded his winery in 1966 – at the ripe old age of 53, by the way – he has set out with a furious energy that frequently steps over the line into messianic zeal to prove that New World wine can be as great as Old World wine, that CALIFORNIA wine is as fine as the very best of French and that Robert Mondavi wine should sit at the same table as the first growths of BORDEAUX and the Grands Crus of BURGUNDY.

While achieving all this, Mondavi has also run some of the more ambitious programmes enquiring into the science of barrel-aging, of vineyard and vine management, of every aspect of winemaking and fermentation technology that the world has seen and – hats off to him – has made much of the research available to anyone who wanted it. And, of course, he's built up his winery, now run by his children, primarily sons Tim and Michael, into a multi-million case operation whose heart is in the elegant mission-style winery at OAKVILLE in NAPA VALLEY, but whose powerhouse is the Woodbridge winery inland in the CENTRAL VALLEY at Lodi, where the majority of Mondavi's wine is produced. However the best wines, both regular and Reserve bottlings, are made at Oakville, benefiting from the 554ha (1370 acres) of Napa and CARNEROS vineyards owned by Mondavi, particularly for Cabernet, Pinot Noir and Chardonnay – wines that Tim Mondavi stresses show at their best with food.

Mondavi also owns BYRON and ARROWOOD wineries in California and, since 2002, ORNELLAIA in TUSCANY, and is an enthusiastic partner in joint ventures: initially OPUS ONE in Napa Valley with Baron Philippe de Rothschild of BORDEAUX, then ventures with the FRESCOBALDIS of Tuscany, the Chadwicks of Chile (they own ERRÁZURIZ) and most recently ROSEMOUNT in Australia. From being a driving force in California in the 20th century, the Mondavi family shows no signs of letting up in the 21st. Best years: (Cabernet Sauvignon Reserve) 2001, '00, '99, '98, '97, '96, '95, '94, '92, '91, '88, '87, '86, '85, '84.

LA MONDOTTE

FRANCE, Bordeaux, St-Émilion Grand Cru AC
▮ *Merlot, Cabernet Franc*

La Mondotte really only exists because its owner Count von Neipperg was outraged when he was refused permission to merge these vineyards with his Grand Cru Classé CANON-LA-GAFFELIÈRE because la Mondotte wasn't classified. Petty bureaucracy, he fumed and set out to prove that the 4.5-ha (11-acre) La Mondotte could not only be better than the very good Canon-la-Gaffelière but could be one of ST-ÉMILION's greatest wines – classified or not. His efforts have been a resounding success and La Mondotte is now a rich, exotic flavour-packed leader of the so-called *garagiste* movement of tiny but excellent properties, primarily in ST-ÉMILION, but increasingly across all of BORDEAUX. Best years: 2001, '00, '99, '98, '97, '96.

LES PRODUCTEURS DU MONT TAUCH

FRANCE, Languedoc-Roussillon, Fitou AC
▮ *Carignan, Grenache, Syrah, Merlot and others*
▯ *Grenache Blanc, Muscat and others*

A big, quality-conscious co-operative producing a large range of Midi wines, from good gutsy FITOU and CORBIÈRES to rich MUSCAT DE RIVESALTES and light but gluggable VIN DE PAYS du Torgan. They have made a great success of their rather savage, herby Fitou reds, full of thyme and bay leaf scent, and are excellent leaders of the appellation with top wines Terroir de Tuchan and new les Douze demonstrating a commitment to getting the best from their growers, many of whose grapes are vinified separately. Best years: (Terroir de Tuchan) 2001, '00, '99, '98, '97.

MONTAGNY AC

FRANCE, Burgundy, Côte Chalonnaise
▯ *Chardonnay*

Montagny is a large white-only AC at the southern end of the Côte Chalonnaise. Until recently the wines were dull and listless – dry and rather lean. But then Montagny discovered the new barrel. Just a few months' aging in a new, or relatively new, oak barrel adds the nuttiness and soft spice which have been conspicuously lacking up until now, and BURGUNDY has found itself a new and much-needed, high-quality, fair-price appellation.

If you see a wine labelled Montagny Premier Cru don't be fooled. In Montagny, any white wine which reaches 11.5 degrees of alcohol – a mere half a degree more than usual – can call itself Premier Cru. Recently a more usual definition of Premier Cru was adopted, but as no fewer than 53 sites have been given this status, the words on the label remain fairly meaningless. Best years: 2002, '01, '00, '99. Best producers: S Aladame, BOUCHARD PÈRE ET FILS, BUXY co-operative, Davenay, FAIVELEY, L LATOUR, O LEFLAIVE, A Roy, J Vachet.

MONTANA WINES

NEW ZEALAND, North Island, Auckland
▮ *Pinot Noir, Merlot, Cabernet Sauvignon*
▯ *Chardonnay, Sauvignon Blanc, Riesling, Semillon*

Montana, owned by multinational Allied Domecq, produces nearly half of New Zealand's total wine output, under a range of 150 labels or so, and its philosophy has always been to make New Zealand's best wines at every price level. It has sustained an impressive export growth and accounts for almost half of New Zealand's wine exports. Grape quality is ensured through owning a high number of their own vineyards. Over 2900ha (7166 acres) of vineyards in HAWKES BAY, GISBORNE and MARLBOROUGH are owned or managed by Montana – producing about a third of all New Zealand's grapes.

The company's desire to make top-quality, CHAMPAGNE-method sparkling wine saw Montana enter into an arrangement with Champagne DEUTZ IN 1987 to produce the mellow, complex Deutz Marlborough Cuvée and the elegant, ageworthy Deutz Blanc de Blancs to complement their Lindauer range. These are some of the New World's most consistent bubblies and are Champagne in all but name. They show how brilliantly suited New Zealand is to sparkling wine production.

After a slow start Montana has become a producer of very serious single-estate Chardonnay from Marlborough and Gisborne. They were the first to plant grapes in Marlborough and the first to produce Sauvignon Blanc on a grand scale. Montana Marlborough Sauvignon Blanc is a remarkably reliable wine with aggressive gooseberry

MONTANA
Sauvignon Blanc is what made Montana famous in the 1970s and it was the Brancott Estate vineyard that provided the original grapes.

and herbaceous flavours that has become deservedly world famous . With their acquisition of Corbans in 2000 they also gained Stoneleigh who produce one of New Zealand's best Rieslings.

Montana has a joint venture with the French wine company Cordier, to refine red wine quality at their flagship Church Road Winery in Hawkes Bay. After persevering for too long with Cabernet Sauvignon in Marlborough and riding a roller-coaster between barely ripe and underripe reds Montana has embarked on a big Pinot Noir programme at Marlborough where they now produce 100,000 cases, and focused its other red production on the warmer Hawkes Bay. Worldwide, there are few if any winery giants with better overall quality than Montana.

MONTEFALCO DOC, MONTEFALCO SAGRANTINO DOCG

ITALY, Umbria

♠ Sangiovese, Sagrantino and others

♀ Grechetto, Trebbiano Toscano and others

Montefalco is arguably UMBRIA's most interesting wine. Set right in the middle of this land-locked region, between Assisi and Spoleto, it is marked out from other Sangiovese-based reds from central Italy by the addition of up to ten per cent of Sagrantino in the blend. This gives it a real boost of dark cherries, plums, prunes and licorice richness and an enlivening swipe of acidity.

Even better is Montefalco Sagrantino where, with nothing else to dilute its character, the flavours of 100 per cent Sagrantino surge out with a glorious punch. This wine ought to be an obligatory experience, though it's not easy to find. Sagrantino grapes can be semi-dried in *passito* styles, yielding an explosively concentrated *abboccato* version. Drink Montefalco at two to five years and Sagrantino with three years or more of aging. Best years: (Sagrantino) 2001, '00, '99, '98, '97, '96, '95, '93, '90, '88. Best producers: (Sagrantino) Adanti, Antonelli, A Caprai (25 Anni), Colpetrone, Terre de' Trinci.

MONTEPULCIANO

Let's get the confusion sorted out. Montepulciano, the red grape, grows widely in south-eastern Italy along the Adriatic coast, from the MARCHE right down to PUGLIA. Montepulciano is also the name of a town in TUSCANY in western Italy, which gave its name to a Sangiovese-based wine called VINO NOBILE DI MONTEPULCIANO. Whether the similarity is coincidental is a moot point but it is important to note that there is no vinous connection between the two.

Montepulciano, the grape, is most widely planted in, and ideally suited to, the conditions in ABRUZZO and, to a lesser extent, the Marche, and only occasionally is it used unblended elsewhere. It is high-yielding and, even when not restrained too much, produces a deep-coloured, rich wine, dominated by brambly fruit, with pepper and a touch of spice. When its yield is held properly in check it can be a delicious monster, filling your mouth with a surge of concentrated ripe fruit which is prevented from getting out of control by its peppery-spicy dry finish. Making wine that is almost always good and occasionally outstanding, this is one of Italy's great grapes.

Other Montepulciano-based red wines include ROSSO CONERO (Marche); Biferno, Pentro (MOLISE); San Severo (Puglia); and Cerveteri, Cori, Velletri (LAZIO); with ROSSO PICENO (Marche) containing a substantial minority of the grape.

MONTEPULCIANO D'ABRUZZO DOC

ITALY, Abruzzo

♠♀ Montepulciano, Sangiovese

Vast swathes of ABRUZZO are planted with the Montepulciano grape; in theory, at least, Montepulciano d'Abruzzo comes from the entire length of the region and stretches inland from the Adriatic coast until the Apennines rise too high for grapes to ripen.

The wine is rarely less than respectable, sometimes wonderfully concentrated with loads of character, and can be long lived. The only complaint could be that it is sometimes a little rustic for drinking without food. Red Montepulciano, brambly, peppery, spicy, is naturally deep in colour. Yet there is also a superb rosé version, called Cerasuolo, made by giving the grape juice the merest contact with its dark-coloured skins. Best years: 2001, '00, '98, '97, '95, '94, '93, '90. Best producers: Cataldi Madonna, Conteisa di Rocco Pasetti, Cornacchia, Filomusi Guelfi, Illuminati, Marramiero, Masciarelli, A & E Monti, Montori, B Nicodemi, Cantina Tollo, UMANI RONCHI, Roxan, La Valentina, Valentini, L Valori, Ciccio Zaccagnini.

MONTEREY COUNTY

USA, California

Monterey County is an extremely important grapegrowing region – it has about 16,600ha (41,000 acres) of vines, about the same as the NAPA VALLEY – but Napa Valley has ten times as many wineries. That tells you where the focus is in Monterey – on growing grapes, not making wine. One reason is that Napa has always been thought of as a desirable tourist haunt, but Monterey, 160km (100 miles) south of San Francisco and centred on the vast, pancake-flat Salinas Valley has only achieved fame through the Depression-era novels of John Steinbeck and as America's Salad Bowl. Salinas Valley is almost devoid of any visitor attraction – Soledad has a big jail, but we're talking about voluntary visitors. On the coast, Monterey itself and Carmel are hives of cultural and tourist activity but, apart from the Carmel Valley, which grows some good Cabernet and Merlot, all the Monterey wine action is in the Salinas Valley and its surrounding hills. The mouth of the valley is very cool and only useful for lettuce, but as you head up the 135-km (85-mile) long valley – often 15–25km (10–15 miles) wide too, by the way – ocean breezes fade and the climate warms up enough for first white, then red. Most of the vines are owned by growers or large companies like KENDALL-JACKSON and MONDAVI who enthusiastically use this cool climate fruit in their blends. But both at Chalone, on the north-east side, and at Arroyo Seco and in the Santa Lucia Highlands, on the south-west side of the valley, various estates grow and bottle their own wine. Best years: (reds) 2001, '00, '99, '97, '96, '95, '94, '91, '90. Best producers: BERNARDUS, CHALONE, Estancia, Heller, Jekel, Mer Soleil, Morgan, Talbott, Testarossa.

MONTES

CHILE, Curicó Valley

♠ Cabernet Sauvignon, Syrah, Merlot, Carmenere, Malbec, Pinot Noir and others

♀ Sauvignon Blanc, Chardonnay and others

It's taken Montes far longer to reach the front of the pack in Chile than it should have done, but one of the reasons may be that Aurelio Montes, the winemaker, simply refuses to make easygoing crowd-pleasing wines. He's a wine man who always seems happiest when wrestling with the most difficult vineyard terrains and the most lip staining of muscular reds, so perhaps we should applaud this simple refusal to make the kind of juicy reds that have made Chile famous over the last decade or so. Interestingly, this applies only to reds. Right from the start Montes have produced bright, fresh Sauvignon Blanc and Chardonnay, and the Montes Alpha Chardonnay year by year is full, ripe and satisfying. The reds are less easy. Basic Cabernet and Merlot are softer now than they were, but you do need to move up to Alpha, then to the Alpha M level to find wines of richness and depth. Here you'll also see the results of the Montes Alpha vineyard – *very* strong and steep: Aurelio loves it – and their use of Syrah from the slopes is impressive especially in top wine Montes Folly. Montes are also expanding into the new Marchihue area near the Pacific, and over the Andes into Argentina.

MONTEVERTINE

ITALY, Tuscany

♥ *Sangiovese, Canaiolo, Colorino*
♀ *Malvasia, Trebbiano*

The late Sergio Manetti's estate in the hills of Radda is firmly established as part of the legend of modern CHIANTI CLASSICO – even if he ceased years ago to classify his wines as DOC. The wines are all based on Sangiovese or other Tuscan varieties and the revised DOC legislation means they would all now qualify for the DOC; but in the 1970s it was their 'atypicity' which got them disqualified and which raised Sergio's ire to such extent as to make him break with all officialdom. The flagship wine, Le Pergole Torte, was and is made from 100 per cent Sangiovese, which then, absurdly, Chianti Classico was not allowed to be, and it was refined in barrique, which gave it, according to the officials, a style which lacked the roughness of the so-called 'typical' Chiantis of that time.

Today Montevertine, after years of basking in international glory, is going through a slightly lean period, the restrained style of the wine having difficulty finding favour in an age when voluptuousness of fruit and unobtrusiveness of structure are so highly prized. But with vineyards of the quality of those of Montevertine there is no reason why they should not make their way back to the top again. Best years: (Le Pergole Torte) 2001, '00, '99, '97, '95, '93, '90, '88, '85.

MONTGRAS

CHILE, Rapel Valley

♥ *Cabernet Sauvignon, Merlot, Carmenere, Syrah, Malbec, Cabernet Franc, Zinfandel*
♥ *Cabernet Sauvignon*
♀ *Chardonnay, Sauvignon Blanc, Viognier, Semillon*

MontGras are an important producer in the COLCHAGUA Valley, but we haven't seen the best of them yet because some of their vineyards are young – only planted in 1993 – and the new ones are *very* young, only being planted in 1997. It is these newer vineyards

that have excited most interest because they have been planted on Ninquén Hill in the middle of the valley and are Chile's first hilltop vines. Altogether MontGras own 435ha (1,075 acres) in valley, slope and hilltop sites of which about half are so far planted. Expect the light but attractive styles of reds and whites to deepen as the vines age.

MONTHÉLIE AC

FRANCE, Burgundy, Côte de Beaune

♥ *Pinot Noir*
♀ *Chardonnay*

Monthélie is an attractive village looking down on MEURSAULT from the north. Its steep streets and huddled houses give some clue to the wine's character, which is generally of the strong, herby, but satisfying type. Monthélie wines were historically sold as VOLNAY, the next village to the north-east. When the appellation laws were changed, Monthélie had to stand on its own two feet and trade under its own name, and it has languished in the shadows of Volnay ever since, but offers good wine at fair prices.

Most of Monthélie's 120ha (297 acres) of vines, many of them old, have an excellent south-east to south exposure, and the wines have a lovely chewy, cherry-skin fruit and a slight piney rasp which make for good-value drinking. A few rows of Chardonnay vines produce a little white Monthélie. Best years: (reds) 2002, '99, '98, '97, '96; (whites) 2002, '01, '00, '99, '97. Best producers: COCHE-DURY, Darviot-Perrin, P Garaudet, R Jobard, LAFON, Olivier LEFLAIVE, Monthélie-Douhairet, Potinet-Ampeau, G Roulot, de Suremain.

MONTILLA-MORILES DO

SPAIN, Andalucía

♀ *Pedro Ximénez, Airén (Lairén), Moscatel and others*

Montilla resembles sherry in style. It is made in the same way as sherry from fruit grown on the chalky *albariza* soils as found in JEREZ but from Pedro Ximénez rather than Palomino and less grape spirit is needed to fortify it because the grapes become riper and sweeter and produce more alcohol of their own. The wines exported – as a cheap alternative to sherry – are lighter in alcohol and go by the names Dry, Medium and Sweet (or Cream). A fast-developing trend is vintage-dated young finos and sweet wines.

Moriles is a little village in the region, reputed to make lighter, more elegant wines than Montilla itself, but in practice these

wines are rarely seen outside the immediate area, except blended with Montilla wines. In the Spanish market some outstanding Montilla-Moriles can be found at very modest prices – particularly the amontillado and Pedro Ximénez styles. Best producers: Alvear (top labels), Aragón, Pérez Barquero, Gracia Hermanos, Toro Albalá.

DOMAINE DE MONTILLE

FRANCE, Burgundy, Côte de Beaune, Volnay AC

♥ *Pinot Noir*
♀ *Chardonnay*

Hubert de Montille has long led a double life: as a Dijon lawyer and winemaker in VOLNAY, where his estate is based, although he has important holdings among Premiers Crus in POMMARD too: les Épenots, les Pezerolles and les Rugiens. The Premiers Crus in Volnay are les Taillepieds, les Mitans and les Champans.

Whereas most Burgundian winemakers routinely chaptalize their wines to ensure they have between 12.5 and 13 degrees of alcohol, Hubert de Montille is a firm believer in keeping the alcoholic level to about 12 degrees, except, of course, when the vintage produces exceptionally ripe grapes. Nonetheless, his wines age very well; indeed, they demand bottle-aging and can taste dour and almost rustic in their youth. With low alcohol, cautious use of new wood and no filtration, these wines are always expressive of their terroir. Hubert de Montille is now semi-retired and the vinification is undertaken by his children, but the practices he established are likely to continue. A small quantity of PULIGNY-MONTRACHET has been made since 1993. Best years: 2002, '00, '99, '98, '97, '96, '95, '93, '90, '89, '88, '85.

MONTLOUIS-SUR-LOIRE AC

FRANCE, Loire, Touraine

♀ *Chenin Blanc*

Montlouis is VOUVRAY's southern neighbour, just across the river Loire. But despite sharing the same grape (Chenin Blanc), the same type of soil (chalk, limestone, gravel and clay), and the same styles of wine (dry, medium and sweet whites, and CHAMPAGNE-method fizz, Montlouis Mousseux) Montlouis doesn't share its fame, and you can sense the growers' resentment and frustration in such small moves as officially renaming the appellation Montlouis-sur-Loire from 2002.

Yet the style is a little different – the dry wines leaner and the sweet wines developing quite an attractive flavour of nuts and honey, but rarely subduing the high Chenin acidity.

Only the sparkling wines (the majority of production, by the way) match Vouvray with their green appley fruit sometimes touched by honey. The still wines need aging for five or maybe ten years, particularly the sweet (*moelleux*) Montlouis, but sparkling Montlouis should be drunk young. Best years: 2002, '01, '00, '99, '98, '97, '96, '95, '90, '89. Best producers: L Chatenay, Chidaine, Deletang, Levasseur-Alex Mathur, des Liards/Berger (Vendange Tardive), Moyer, Taille aux Loups.

LE MONTRACHET AC, CHEVALIER-MONTRACHET AC

FRANCE, Burgundy, Côte de Beaune, Grands Crus
♀ *Chardonnay*

Those who love white Burgundy dream of Montrachet. There have been more adjectives expended on this than on any other wine in the world. Tasted in its infancy, it flows pale from the barrel and stings your mouth with a piercing richness far beyond youthful flavours of fruit. Later on it can be so thick in the glass it seems like syrup, and so coarse and bloated in the mouth it's almost shocking and needs ten years to sort itself out. At ten years old and more the sheer concentration of the wine is unchanged. But all the coarseness is gone, and there seems to be a richness which owes nothing to sugar, and everything to the ripest of fruits, the most tantalizing of scents, and the most fragrant of drifting woodsmoke wrapped in triple-thick cream.

Le Montrachet comes from an 8-ha (20-acre) vineyard, half in PULIGNY-MONTRACHET and half in CHASSAGNE-MONTRACHET. The land is nothing to look at – poor, stony – but there's a thick vein of limestone just below the surface, the drainage is exceptional, and the perfect south to southeast exposure soaks up the sun from dawn to dusk. If you stand among the vines of Montrachet at sunset, a dip in the hills to the west is still allowing the sun's rays to warm these grapes while all the great surrounding vineyards are in shadow.

Another Grand Cru, Chevalier-Montrachet, lies immediately above it on the slope. The higher elevation yields a slightly leaner wine that is less explosive in its youth, but good examples will become ever more fascinating over 20 years or more. Best years: 2001, '00, '99, '97, '96, '95, '92, '90, '89, '86, '85. Best producers: G Amiot, Marc Colin, DROUHIN (Laguiche), LAFON, Louis LATOUR, Dom. LEFLAIVE, RAMONET, Dom. de la ROMANÉE-CONTI, SAUZET, Thénard.

MONTRAVEL AC, CÔTES DE MONTRAVEL AC, HAUT-MONTRAVEL AC

FRANCE, South-West
♀ *Sémillon, Sauvignon Blanc, Muscadelle*

These are largely white wines from the western fringe of the BERGERAC region – though Montravel has just won itself an appellation for reds with a minimum 50 per cent Merlot. Basic Montravel is usually dry, while Côtes de Montravel and Haut-Montravel – from hillside vineyards – are sweeter, and can be exotically fragrant and delicately rich. The Montravel wines, falling uneasily between proper sweet and proper dry, are not much in fashion and so production – currently 2.6 million bottles a year – is unlikely to increase. Red wines generally use the Bergerac AC. Best years: (sweet) 2001, '00, '98, '96, '95. Best producers: le Bondieu, Gourgueil, Moulin Caresse, Perreau, Pique-Sègue, Puy-Servain, le Raz.

CH. MONTROSE

FRANCE, Bordeaux, Haut-Médoc, St-Estèphe AC, 2ème Cru Classé
♂ *Cabernet Sauvignon, Merlot, Cabernet Franc*

This leading ST-ESTÈPHE property of 68ha (168 acres) used to be famous for its dark, brooding, Cabernet Sauvignon-dominated style that only slowly revealed its blackcurrant and pencil-shavings scent. Twenty years was regarded as reasonable time to wait before broaching a bottle, and around 30 years to drink it at its prime. Then vintages of the late 1970s and early '80s underwent a sea change, becoming lighter, softer, less substantial, ready to drink at a mere ten years old. Thankfully, since 1988 this trend has been reversed, Montrose finding its former intensity along with extra richness and ripeness. The 1989 and '90 were stupendous and vintages of the 1990s have been equally good until the end of the decade when uncertainty seemed to set in again. Even so, 2000 onwards promise much. Best years: 2001, '00, '99, '98, '96, '95, '90, '89, '86.

CH. MONTUS, CH. BOUSCASSÉ

FRANCE, South-West, Madiran AC
♂ *Tannat, Cabernet Sauvignon, Cabernet Franc*
♀ *Petit Courbu, Gros Manseng, Petit Manseng, Arrufiac*

Alain Brumont has been largely responsible for the resurgence in quality in MADIRAN. A strong advocate of the Tannat grape, harvested at optimum ripeness, and the use of new oak barriques, he has introduced a richer, more refined style to these robust wines. At the 160-ha (395-acre) domaine he produces wines under two main labels: Bouscassé from vineyards on clay-limestone soils located in the Gers *département* and Montus from vineyards in the Hautes-Pyrénées *département* on gravelly soils. Among the range of wines the top of the line Bouscassé Vieilles Vignes, from vines over 50 years' old, and Montus Prestige, from vines of an average of 25 years, are both made from 100 per cent Tannat and aged for 16 months in new oak casks.

The white PACHERENC DU VIC BILH is produced in dry and sweet styles. There are three cuvées of sweet: Vendémiaire, Brumaire and Frimaire with the Petit Manseng grapes picked progressively later in respectively October, November and December. Best years: (Cuvée Prestige) 2001, '00, '99, '98, '97, '96, '95, '94, '93, '91, '90, '89, '88, '85.

MORELLINO DI SCANSANO DOC

ITALY, Tuscany
♂ *Sangiovese and others*

Scansano is a commune in that part of coastal Tuscany called the Maremma, Morellino being a local clone of Sangiovese. The name means 'little Morello' (cherry) and the aromas are reputed to put one in mind of that fruit. Morellino di Scansano, in its simple form, is indeed an easy-drinking, fruity red with appreciably less astringency than is often displayed by Sangiovese from central Tuscany. Fattoria le Pupille and Moris Farms, have demonstrated that Morellino can be a wine of fleshy yet concentrated fruit, with ripe tannins – exactly the sort of thing that appeals to pundits these days. Best years: 2001, '00, '99, '98, '97, '96, '95, '93, '90. Best producers: E Banti, Carletti/ Poliziano (Lohsa), Cecchi, Il Macereto, Mantellassi, Mazzei/Fonterutoli (Belguardo), Morellino di Scansano co-operative, Moris Farms, Poggio Argentaria, Le Pupille.

MOREY-ST-DENIS AC
FRANCE, Burgundy, Côte de Nuits
🍷 *Pinot Noir*
🍷 *Chardonnay, Aligoté*

After decades of being treated as Cinderella – squashed between CHAMBOLLE-MUSIGNY to the south and GEVREY-CHAMBERTIN to the north – Morey-St-Denis has recently been flexing its muscles, and now commands a price for its wine equal to its more famous neighbours. Certainly the vineyards deserve it. There are five Grands Crus (BONNES-MARES, Clos des Lambrays, CLOS DE LA ROCHE, Clos de Tart and Clos St-Denis) as well as some very good Premiers Crus, but the entire extent of the village's vineyards is only 142ha (352 acres) – a third of neighbouring Gevrey-Chambertin – and so the *négociants* have paid less heed to Morey, simply because there was less wine to go round.

However there is fine Morey, in particular from the Premier and Grand Cru vineyards and usually from single growers. These wines generally have a good strawberry or redcurrant fruit, sometimes a little meaty and gaining an attractive chocolate and licorice depth. Best years: 2002, '01, '00, '99, '98, '97, '96, '95, '93, '90. Best producers: Pierre Amiot, Arlaud, Dom. des Beaumonts, CLAIR, DUJAC, des Lambrays, H Lignier, H Perrot-Minot, Ponsot, Rossignol-Trapet, ROUMIER, Rousseau, Sérafin.

And there is a white Morey-St Denis. In the Monts Luisants vineyard to the north of the village, Ponsot used to produce about 3000 bottles from a weird white mutation of Pinot Noir. These vines no longer exist, and nowadays Ponsot's wine is made from

DOMAINE PONSOT
Back on form after an erratic patch in the 1980s, this domaine makes some sublime, old-fashioned wines from top vineyard sites in Morey-St-Denis.

Chardonnay and Aligoté. But it's still a strange wine, showing an almost overpowering, honeyed nutty weight, which is impressive if somewhat overbearing. Bruno Clair and Dujac also make white Morey.

MORGON AC
FRANCE, Burgundy, Beaujolais, Beaujolais cru
🍷 *Gamay*

Although MOULIN-À-VENT is the BEAUJOLAIS cru that is supposed to come closest in maturity to a fine CÔTE D'OR Burgundy, Morgon could easily lay claim to that reputation. Indeed, there is even a French verb *morgonner* to describe how the local wine begins to lose its fresh, plummy fruit after two to three years and evolves into something chocolaty, cocoa-ish and strongly perfumed with cherries or even kirsch. Sounds good? It is. But only the best wines are like this, usually from a single grower, and from the slopes around Mont du Py. You may see le Py, les Chaumes or le Clachet marked as vineyard names, and snap a bottle up if you do. Most Morgon is less special, but it still manages a soft, cherry, easy-drinking fruit. Best years: 2002, '00, '99, '98. Best producers: N Aucoeur, G Brun, DUBOEUF (Jean Descombes), M Jonchet, M Lapierre.

MORNINGTON PENINSULA
AUSTRALIA, Victoria

This is a super-trendy, fast-growing region near Melbourne where many of the 50-plus wineries make high-quality wine on a doll's house scale. The 1998 acquisition of a controlling interest in STONIER by PETALUMA has given the region an added dimension to its previous reputation as a playground for the wealthy dilettante. Land prices are high and consequently the price-quality ratio can get a bit stretched. Even so, for marvellously piercing fruit quality in Chardonnay, Riesling, Pinot Noir and Cabernet, the Peninsula has a lot to offer. The climate is ideal and the potential is excellent. Best years: (Pinot Noir) 2001, '00, '99, '98, '97, '95, '94. Best producers: DROMANA, Kooyong, Main Ridge, Moorooduc, Paringa Estate, Port Phillip Estate, Stonier, T'Gallant, Tuck's Ridge.

MORRIS
AUSTRALIA, Victoria, Rutherglen
🍷 *Syrah (Shiraz), Durif, Cabernet Sauvignon, Cinsaut, Touriga Nacional*
🍷 *Muscat, Muscadelle (Tokay), Chardonnay, Palomino*

Until his retirement in 1992 when he handed over the reins to his son David, Mick Morris

MORRIS
Morris is probably the greatest fortified wine producer in Australia. The Old Premium Tokay is remarkably luscious and has real complexity.

was the most important producer of fortified wine in the region. He made his raisiny, fortified Muscat and aromatic Tokay much as he always had in a winery as antiquated as any in the hemisphere.

The Old Premium range sits at the top of the quality tree and despite price rises they are still absolute bargains, given the age and quality of these wines, as are the Mick Morris range at the bottom, the latter selling for a song in Australia and for not that much more abroad. Why is it that the Muscat is always blamed for the hangover? Is it because it's so rich and scented and delicious you can never resist another glass, and another, until the bottle's drained. Morris has been part of the ORLANDO group since 1970.

DENIS MORTET
FRANCE, Burgundy, Côte de Nuits, Gevrey-Chambertin AC
🍷 *Pinot Noir*
🍷 *Chardonnay, Aligoté*

After Denis Mortet's father retired in 1991, this domaine was divided between Denis and his brother Thierry. Both make very good wines, but Denis's are more dramatic and have attracted greater attention. The core of his 10-ha (25-acre) estate is a range of single-vineyard GEVREY-CHAMBERTIN wines from village sites of outstanding quality with very old vines: Motrot, En Vellé and En Champs. There are also Premiers Crus such as Lavaux as well as small parcels in CLOS DE VOUGEOT, CHAMBERTIN and CHAMBOLLE-MUSIGNY.

Yields are kept low, the grapes are selected at the winery and destemmed before fermentation on the indigenous yeasts. Mortet uses a lot of new oak, up to 80 per cent, even 100 per cent on occasions, arguing that his wines have sufficient concentration and power to absorb the wood. It is hard to disagree. In fact there isn't a barrel in his cellar that is more than two years old. The wines are very dense and tannic in their youth and need patience. But those who cellar the wines will be rewarded with some of the most flamboyant expressions of the Côte de Nuits, oozing plum and blackberry fruit, with a firm underpinning of vanilla and licorice. Recent vintages show Mortet adding finesse to this deep and powerful style. the wines have acquired something of a cult following, and prices are, needless to say, high. Best years: 2002, '01, '00, '98, '97, '96, '95, '93.

MORTON ESTATE
NEW ZEALAND, North Island, Bay of Plenty
♂ Cabernet Sauvignon, Pinot Noir, Merlot
♀ Chardonnay, Sauvignon Blanc, Gewurztraminer, Riesling

Morton Estate built its reputation on blockbuster Black Label Chardonnay from its Riverview vineyard in HAWKES BAY and it is still a Chardonnay expert, though the top example is now Coniglio, a deadringer for white Burgundy made in minute quantities. Regular White Label Chardonnays are made in both Hawkes Bay and MARLBOROUGH versions. White Label Sauvignon can also come from Hawkes Bay or Marlborough.

Since the mid-1990s the winery has begun to make top-flight reds, particularly with a full-flavoured, berries and cedar Black Label Merlot-Cabernet, rich and gamy Black Label Merlot, light but tasty Black Label Syrah and perhaps the best Hawkes Bay Pinot Noir available. CHAMPAGNE-method fizz is another strength. Mill Road is the budget label. Best years: (Black Label Chardonnay) 1998, '96, '95.

MORTON ESTATE
Morton's best wines include the robust, complex Black Label Chardonnay made from grapes from the cool Riverview vineyards in Hawkes Bay.

GEORG MOSBACHER
GERMANY, Pfalz, Forst
♀ Riesling and others

This small estate makes some of the best Riesling and Scheurebe wines from the famous vineyards of FORST. They are always packed with peachy and citrus fruit, but absolutely pure and clean. Top of the range is the Riesling Erstes Gewächs from the Forster Ungeheuer site, a complex and sophisticated dry wine with an intense mineral character. However, even the estate's Kabinett wines are full of fruit and beautifully balanced. They too can age five years and more without any trouble. The estate is now run by Sabine Mosbacher-Düringer and her husband Jürgen Düringer. Best years: 2002, '01, '99, '98, '97, '96, '94, '93, '90.

MOSCATO
In Italy there are three distinct sub-varieties of the MUSCAT or Moscato grape variety making quality white wines in various regions, plus the extraordinary Moscato Rosa. In PIEDMONT the dominant type is Moscato Bianco or Moscato di Canelli, the latter named after a town in the heart of the ASTI zone from which rivers of ordinary, and increasing amounts of extraordinary, lightly sparkling wine hails. Moscato Bianco is also fairly widespread in the major islands: SARDINIA's Moscato di Cagliari, Moscato di Sorso-Sennori and Moscato di Sardegna as well as SICILY's Moscato di Noto and Moscato di Siracusa are all DOCs for Moscato Bianco.

In ALTO ADIGE, TRENTINO and the Colli Euganei sector of VENETO the sub-variety is Moscato Giallo (Orange Muscat), known to the German-speaking South Tyroleans as Goldmuskateller. The wines in Colli Euganei, best exemplified by Vignalta, may be referred to as Fior d'Arancio. In the island of Pantelleria, off the tip of Sicily, they make luscious sweet wines from Zibibbo, the local name for Muscat of Alexandria.

The wine of Moscato Rosa, or Rosenmuskateller as it is known in Südtirol (Alto Adige), is potentially a mind-blowing experience, the pale-pink liquid throwing off aromas for all the world like roses at their height of redolence. The palate, for its part, is generally sweet, though occasionally it's dry. Best producer in Alto Adige today is Franz Haas, with Graf Kuenburg, Heinrich Plattner, Laimburg and TIEFENBRUNNER in pursuit. JERMANN makes a good one in Friuli, AVIGNONESI does likewise in Tuscany.

MOSCATO D'ASTI DOCG, MOSCATO DI STREVI DOC, LOAZZOLO DOC
ITALY, Piedmont
♀ Muscat (Moscato Bianco)

Moscato d'Asti is the upmarket version of ASTI. Moscato Bianco vines seem to cover practically every hillside not already covered by Barbera in PIEDMONT's heartland, from Mango in the west to Strevi in the east, and even though the market for Asti, the inexpensive sparkling stuff which may be helped along with sugar, is declining, demand for Moscato, the much less sparkling version (maximum 1.7 atmospheres pressure), is going up by leaps and bounds as the wine world discovers the joys of this delightfully aromatic, lightweight (maximum 5.5 per cent alcohol), sweet but not cloying aperitif or dessert wine.

Production of Moscato d'Asti, and especially of Asti, is dominated by large-scale private and co-operative producers, some of which are capable of wines of real quality. Best producers: Araldica/Alasia, ASCHERI, Bava, Bera, Braida, Cascina Castlèt, Caudrina, Giuseppe Contratto, Coppo, Cascina Fonda, Forteto della Luja, Icardi, Marenco, Beppe Marino, La Morandina, Marco Negri, Perrone, Cascina Pian d'Or, Saracco, Scagliola, La Spinetta, I Vignaioli di Santo Stefano.

White Muscat is also used in Piedmont to produce a marvellously grapy *passito* wine which may go under the name of Loazzolo DOC or, if from Strevi, just a brand name such as Casarito.

MOSCATO DI PANTELLERIA DOC
ITALY, Sicily
♀ Muscat (Zibibbo)

Pantelleria is a small island off the south-west coast of SICILY, lying nearer to Tunisia in north Africa than to Sicily itself. It is rocky, with one green part covered by pine scent, small towns, weird round-domed houses called *dammusi*, terraces mostly growing capers and the wind. There's always wind, be it from south (unbearably hot), north (shiveringly cold, even in an African August), east or west. Hence Pantelleria's name, 'Island of the Winds'. The vines are Muscat of Alexandria, locally called Zibibbo and low-trained to withstand the buffeting.

The most typical Pantellerian Moscato wine is *passito*, the grapes being dried out of doors as quickly as the sun's strength allows (usually around two weeks) and at its best, like DE BARTOLI's Bukkuram, has been called liquid sunshine: and why not, with grape, raisin, oak and toffee flavours, all combining to produce a terrific luscious whole? There are numerous other styles too, some of which are rarely seen – of these the *naturale* (non-*passito*) stands out. Best producers: Benanti, D'Ancona, De Bartoli, Donnafugata (Ben Ryé), MID (Tanit), Murana, Nuova Agricoltura co-operative, Pellegrino.

MOSEL Germany

MANY OF EUROPE'S GREAT WINE REGIONS have evolved along the banks of rivers. Ease of transport of the finished product may have been one practical reason, but there are other, still more fundamental advantages that come from having an expanse of water at your feet. It mitigates the extremes of climate, which in chilly northern spots like Germany's Mosel-Saar-Ruwer region is no small point; and it reflects the sun's rays back onto the vines, giving the heat-hungry grapes a much-needed boost. Up here they need all the heat and sun they can get, because the Mosel-Saar-Ruwer is at the northerly edge of vine-growing in the northern hemisphere and it is at this point, on the margin of where the grapes will ripen, that the greatest wines can be made.

'Can' is the operative word. Not all Mosel-Saar-Ruwer wine is great; some is very poor indeed. And how are you to tell the difference? Well, not by looking for the word 'Mosel' on the label, that's for sure. The river Mosel runs for 500km (310 miles) from its source in France's Vosges mountains (where it is called the Moselle), through Luxembourg (it's

still the Moselle) and across the German border, where it becomes the Mosel. The Saar and the Ruwer rivers flow into it either side of the city of Trier; and together they join the Rhine at Koblenz. And one would hardly expect over 485km (300 miles) of river, and 10,392ha (25,678 acres) of German vineyards, to produce a consistent quality of wine.

The remarkable thing about the wine of the Mosel-Saar-Ruwer, however, is that its style is so homogeneous. There is a lightness and a delicacy that marks it out from the wine of the Rhine; a combination of fragility and intensity that reaches its long-lived peak in the estate-bottled Rieslings from the Saar and Ruwer valleys and the Middle or Mittel Mosel, with the stretch from Piesport to Erden at the heart of the latter. For this is the key to choosing fine Mosel-Saar-Ruwer: look for the name of the region's finest grape, the Riesling, and look for the names of the best growers, most of whom are listed on page 257. Vintages vary enormously, but an off-vintage from a top grower can still be a better bet than a good vintage from a poor producer.

Good growers are usually helped by having good vineyards. Site is all-important here; instead of heading straight for Koblenz, the Mosel finds itself constantly deflected by sheer walls of rock that rise high and vine-clad above the water, so it meanders back and forth, in the process revealing umpteen ideal, south-facing suntrap slopes; these are where the Riesling is king, and where the best Mosel wines come from. Lesser wines are made from Müller-Thurgau, Elbling or Kerner among other varieties. Their quality is not a patch on that of the Riesling, and at best their wines are clean and attractive.

The best parts of the Mosel-Saar-Ruwer are the Saar and the Ruwer valleys and the Mittel Mosel. Here the slopes are steepest, the soil is slate, dark and heat-absorbing, dry and instantly draining, and there is a whiff of smoke to Riesling made from grapes grown on this slate. Elsewhere in the Mosel the soil may be sandstone, marl or limestone in the Upper Mosel or Obermosel, or mixed with clay in the Lower Mosel, between Zell and Koblenz, and the slopes are usually gentler. The Saar shares the steep slopes and slate soil of the Mittel Mosel, but it is appreciably colder. If a Riesling from the Mittel Mosel has the steeliness of acidity and the ripeness of honey, the Saar in an off-vintage can have considerably more steel than honey; but in good years it triumphs. The same is true of the Ruwer: a tiny area this, but boasting a great concentration of quality.

The amphitheatre of the Goldtröpfchen vineyard high above the village of Piesport is one of the greatest sites in the Mittel Mosel, producing Rieslings with baroque fruit aromas and a firm structure.

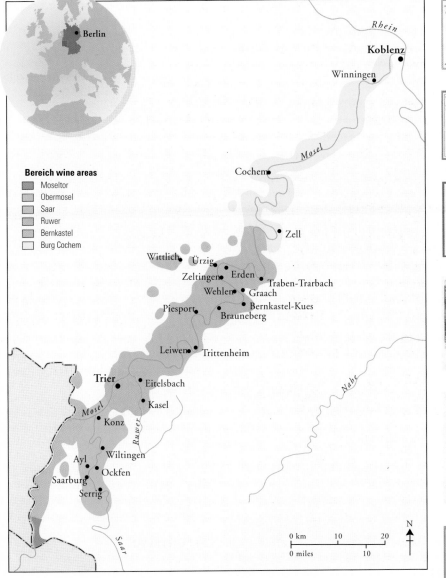

ZILLIKEN
This small estate makes classic, piercing minerally Saar Rieslings. A fashionable speciality is Eiswein from the Saarburger Rausch site.

JOH. JOS. PRÜM
This legendary Mosel estate has vines in top sites such as the famous Sonnenuhr in Wehlen.

REINHOLD HAART
Theo Haart's Rieslings from the Piesporter Goldtröpfchen site are explosively fruity yet crisp wines.

DR LOOSEN
Ernst Loosen is one of Germany's leading organic winemakers. The Prälat wines combine aromatic richness with monumental concentration.

EGON MÜLLER-SCHARZHOF
If you want the ultimate in sweet Riesling try the wines from this estate but be prepared for crazy prices.

FRITZ HAAG
For nearly 50 years Wilhelm Haag has made the finest Rieslings from the great Brauneberg vineyards.

WILLI SCHAEFER
This very small estate makes the best and most minerally wines from Graach.

REGIONAL ENTRIES
Ayl, Bad Dürkheim, Bernkastel, Brauneberg, Erden, Graach, Kanzem, Kasel, Leiwen, Ockfen, Piesport, Ruwer, Saar, Saarburg, Serrig, Trier, Trittenheim, Ürzig, Wehlen, Wiltingen, Winningen, Zeltingen.

PRODUCER ENTRIES
Joh. Jos. Christoffel, Grans-Fassian, Fritz Haag, Reinhold Haart, Heymann-Löwenstein, von Hövel, Karlsmühle, Karthäuserhof, von Kesselstatt, Carl Loewen, Dr Loosen, Maximin Grünhaus, Egon Müller-Scharzhof, Dr Pauly-Bergweiler, J J Prüm, S A Prüm, Max Ferd Richter, Willi Schaefer, Schloss Lieser, Schloss Saarstein, Selbach-Oster, Zilliken.

KARTHÄUSERHOF
This top Ruwer estate has gone from strength to strength since the mid-1980s and makes wines of concentration and character.

CARL LOEWEN
Karl-Josef Loewen is the rising star of the Mittel Mosel, making rich yet beautifully crafted Rieslings in the naturally sweet style.

HEYMANN-LÖWENSTEIN
Reinhold Löwenstein makes some of the Mosel's few exciting dry Rieslings as well as some magnificent dessert wines.

MOSS WOOD

AUSTRALIA, Western Australia, Margaret River

♥ *Cabernet Sauvignon, Pinot Noir*

♀ *Semillon, Chardonnay*

Moss Wood's finely structured, softly fleshy yet long-lived Cabernet Sauvignon is rightly revered, and peaks at seven to ten years. The Semillons, one oak-matured, the other not, are no less delicious, honeyed rather than grassy, with a long finish and capable of considerable aging. The Chardonnay can be dazzling in its peachy, butterscotch opulence, and one or two lovely, gentle Pinot Noirs have emerged. In 2000 Moss Wood bought neighbouring Ribbon Vale and so far has released very good Semillon-Sauvignon, Merlot and a Cabernet-Merlot blend. The style is quite different, but the quality is very good. Best years: (Cabernet) 2001, '00, '99, '98, '96, '95, '94, '91, '90, '85.

MOULIN-À-VENT AC

FRANCE, Burgundy, Beaujolais, Beaujolais cru

♥ *Gamay*

Moulin-à-Vent, one of BEAUJOLAIS' ten crus, would like to be a big, burly, world-famous Burgundy like CHAMBERTIN. But sadly it is in the wrong place – a good 240km (150 miles) too far south – and it grows Gamay, rather than the much more vaunted Pinot Noir. Still, the wine does in fact do a pretty good job of impersonating a fairly full, chocolaty Burgundy – slightly short on perfume, but good and rich, if you leave it for six to ten years to mature. Experiments using new oak barrels have largely been successful. Best years: 2002, '00, '99, '98, '97, '96, '95. Best producers: L Champagnon, DUBOEUF (single domaines), Ch. des Jacques, Ch. du Moulin-à-Vent, Dom. Romanesca, P Sapin (le Vieux Domaine).

MOULIS AC

FRANCE, Bordeaux, Haut-Médoc

♥ *Cabernet Sauvignon, Cabernet Franc, Merlot and others*

North-west of MARGAUX, this is the smallest of the six communal ACs in the HAUT-MÉDOC, with only 550ha (1359 acres) of vines. The best vineyards are on a gravel plateau centred on the village of Grand-Poujeaux. Much of the wine is excellent, yet rarely over-priced.

These wines are beautifully balanced, surprisingly soft behind their early tannin, and delicious to drink at five to six years old, though good examples should age for 10–20 years. Producers are increasingly using new oak to age the wines. Best years: 2001, '00,

'96, '95, '94, '90, '89, '88, '86, '85, '83, '82. Best producers: Anthonic, Biston-Brillette, Brillette, CHASSE-SPLEEN, Duplessis, Dutruch-Grand-Poujeaux, Gressier-Grand-Poujeaux, MAUCAILLOU, Ch. Moulin-à-Vent, POUJEAUX.

MOUNT LANGI GHIRAN

AUSTRALIA, Victoria, Grampians

♥ *Syrah (Shiraz), Cabernet Sauvignon, Cabernet Franc, Merlot*

♀ *Riesling, Pinot Gris*

If ever you wish to discover the taste of pepper and spice in Shiraz – and a top RHÔNE Valley wine is not to hand – take a bottle of Mount Langi Ghiran and drink it with a thick piece of rare, char-grilled rump steak. These red wines (the Cabernet Sauvignon is structurally similar but less reliably impressive) are the vinous equivalent of that steak: layers of velvety flavour and great complexity, yet broodingly, impressively dry. The Riesling is surprisingly good, perfumed, yet dry and touched with petrol and lime. And the Pinot Gris is honeyed and delightful. Recently bought by the Rathbone family from YARRA VALLEY, but winemaker Trevor Mast still remains. Best years: (Shiraz) 2001, '99, '98, '97, '96, '95, '94, '93, '90, '89, '86.

MOUNT MARY

AUSTRALIA, Victoria, Yarra Valley

♥ *Cabernet Sauvignon, Pinot Noir, Cabernet Franc and others*

♀ *Chardonnay, Sauvignon Blanc, Semillon, Muscadelle*

For some this is the leading YARRA VALLEY winery, its tiny production eagerly sought by a fanatically loyal band of followers, and its BORDEAUX-blend Cabernets are among the most European in Australia, with fragrant varietal red berry, cigar box and leafy aromas and a silky smooth, persistent flavour. They seem to reach their peak in five years, but in fact go on improving for ten or more. The Pinot Noir is nearly as good, and has an even more surprising capacity to improve with age. The white wines are not in the same class. Best years: (Quintet) 2001, '00, '99, '98, '97, '96, '95, '94, '93, '92, '91, '90, '88, '86, '84.

MOUNT VEEDER AVA

USA, California, Napa County

The first time I tried to explore Mount Veeder, it was approaching dusk. Bad idea. This densely forested, scarcely populated mountainside AVA in the south-west corner of NAPA VALLEY is a million miles away from

the glitzy valley floor you've left behind. As the coyotes begin to wail and the hungry mountain lions shuffle through the undergrowth, just remember – you could be the only human being on Mount Veeder that night. Don't be silly. Come back tomorrow. If you do, you'll find a wonderfully gaunt vineyard of about 405ha (1000 acres) dotted between the dark, forbidding forest.

These savage conditions have traditionally produced small crops of uncompromisingly brutal wines, but with an inner fruit of pure beauty. If you let the wine age – say 10 years – you'd find intense, austere, dry yet rich blackcurrant fruit matched by a haughty but magnificent cedarwood scent. In fact, the flavours of great BORDEAUX? Exactly. Something which the Napa Valley Cabernet makers have always tried so hard to emulate, but, from their rich and fertile valley vineyards' fruit have so frequently failed to do. It's really only the mountains around the Napa Valley that hold the key to those cool but beautiful flavours of Bordeaux, and Mount Veeder has them in depth. The reds also add a healthy dose of pepper and sage and thyme, sometimes tobacco and often a thrilling streak of lime peel acidity, so that you start by admiring the Bordeaux lookalike and end by realizing Mount Veeder has a brilliance all its own. The Chardonnay is very good – but it is the Cabernets, the Merlot, the Petit Verdot and the Zinfandel that sing the mountain song. Best producers: Chateau Potelle, Robert Craig, HESS COLLECTION, Lokoya, Mayacamas, Mount Veeder Winery.

MOUNTADAM

AUSTRALIA, South Australia, Eden Valley

♥ *Syrah (Shiraz), Cabernet Sauvignon and others*

♀ *Chardonnay and others*

The superbly designed Mountadam winery, perched high in the hills above the EDEN VALLEY, takes its grapes from the low-yielding estate vineyards. Wind and drought are

MOUNTADAM

Eden Valley has become one of Australia's top white grape producing areas. This rich, buttery Chardonnay with ripe tropical flavours has a worldwide reputation.

constant foes but the concentration of flavour is more than enough recompense. The Chardonnay is complex and long-flavoured; the Pinot Noir, stylish and deep; both of these wines being especially renowned for their lush fat texture; the Cabernet Sauvignon and Merlot are similarly stylish and dark-fruited if less lush; and a complex, lees-aged sparkler is a worthy addition. Eden Ridge organic and David Wynn are excellent labels for non-estate grapes. Bought in 2000 by the MARGARET RIVER winery, CAPE MENTELLE (itself owned by luxury megabrand LVMH). Best years: (Patriarch) 2000, '99, '98, '97, '96, '95, '94, '93, '91, '90, '87; (Chardonnay) 2001, '00, '98, '97, '94, '93, '92, '91, '90.

MOURVÈDRE

One of the best red grapes of the South of France, this plays a starring role in Bandol and is increasingly being used to add a little extra something to the wines of the Languedoc-Roussillon – that something being buckets of plummy, spicy fruit, a wild-herby perfume and a more solid tannic structure for aging the wine. But Bandol is underrated outside the Midi and so is Mourvèdre; a pity, because its wine is full of blackcurrants, herbs and spice with good tannic backbone. The better producers in Châteauneuf-du-Pape have, however, noted its qualities and Mourvèdre is a key component in wines like Ch. de Beaucastel.

In the New World, it had long been known as Mataro and after being dismissed for years as a junk grape, California and Australia are beginning to make exciting brawny wines from it, often blended with Syrah and Grenache in Australia. The name comes from that of the port city of Murviedro, north of Valencia, and indeed this is originally a south-eastern Spanish variety. The local name is Monastrell. There are over 65,000ha (160,615 acres) of Monastrell in Spain, but growers are only just waking up to its potential.

CH. MOUTON-ROTHSCHILD
FRANCE, Bordeaux, Haut-Médoc, Pauillac AC, Premier Cru Classé
🍷 🍾 *Cabernet Sauvignon, Cabernet Franc, Merlot, Petit Verdot*
🍾 *Sémillon, Sauvignon Blanc, Muscadelle*

Baron Philippe de Rothschild died in 1988 and so ended a remarkable era in BORDEAUX's history. For 65 years he had managed the estate, raising it from a run-down Second Growth to one of the most famous wines in the world, achieving promotion to First Growth status in 1973 – the only promotion ever effected within the traditional 1855 Classification. He did this by unremitting commitment to quality, flair, imagination and brilliant marketing.

Mouton-Rothschild is a 75-ha (185-acre) estate on the northern side of PAUILLAC, but south of Ch. LAFITE-ROTHSCHILD. The high proportion of Cabernet Sauvignon (80 per cent) and the perfectly situated gravel banks of the vineyard give a wine which, in most years, is astonishingly exotic and heavy. It manages to transform the cedarwood, cigar-box, pencil-shavings spectrum of dry, restrained fragrances into a steamy, intoxicating swirl of head-turning richness, backed up by a deep, chewy, pure blackcurrant fruit. Mouton is less tannic than the other First Growths on release but still needs 15–20 years for its sometimes rather chaotic early flavours to calm down into the blackcurrant and cigarbox brilliance for which Mouton is famous. Each year Mouton commissions a different artist to design the label, and most of the modern greats like Chagall, Miró, Picasso and Warhol have had a go. Best years: 2001, '00, '99, '98, '96, '95, '90, '89, '88, '86, '85, '83, '82, '70.

A tiny amount of white Aile d'Argent, is produced from 4ha (10 acres) of the vineyard.

Mouton-Cadet started out as a sort of 'younger brother' of Mouton-Rothschild and is now the world's most widely sold red Bordeaux. It is a correct but uninspiring Bordeaux AC, whose grapes are sourced from all over the Bordeaux region. There's also a white and rosé.

MOVIA
SLOVENIA, Primorje, Dobrovo
🍷 *Merlot, Pinot Noir (Modri Pinot), Cabernet Sauvignon and others*
🍾 *Chardonnay, Pinot Blanc, Pinot Gris and others*

Movia is the brand name adopted by Mirko and Aleš Kristančič, who have 18ha (44 acres) of vineyards, including some across the border in FRIULI. The Kristančičs were the first private producers in the PRIMORJE region to start bottling their own wine and they now export widely; Movia is the name used for the oak-fermented wines, including Merlot and Chardonnay, and Vila Marija for the lighter, fresher wines fermented in stainless steel. They also make a good dessert wine by drying the otherwise dull white Ribolla grape.

MUDGEE
AUSTRALIA, New South Wales

'A nest in the hills', the Aborigines called it, giving us the name Mudgee. And indeed it is a nest, with hills surrounding all sides, and many of the vineyards running off the flat bottom of the nest into those hills. The region is warm but generally slightly cooler than the HUNTER VALLEY thanks to the altitude (around 500m/1640ft) and the cool nights. Not surprisingly, the reds – notably Shiraz and Cabernet Sauvignon – are better than the whites, though there is some rich, buttery Chardonnay and fair to good Semillon. The reds are deep coloured, robust and taste of dark chocolate, plum and blackcurrant when young, but after seven to ten years show strong similarities with Hunter Valley reds. And it is to the big Hunter wineries that much of the wine goes. Best producers: Farmer's Daughter, Andrew Harris, HUNTINGTON ESTATE, Miramar, ORLANDO, ROSEMOUNT, Thistle Hill.

MUGA
SPAIN, La Rioja, Rioja DOCa
🍷 *Tempranillo, Grenache Noir (Garnacha Tinta), Carignan (Cariñena, Mazuelo), Graciano*
🍾 *Macabeo (Viura), Grenache Noir (Garnacha Tinta), Tempranillo*
🍾 *Macabeo (Viura), Malvasia*

Red wine production here has changed little since the bodega was founded in 1932. The reds are still fermented in huge wooden vats, then filtered off through bundles of vine prunings for aging in oak casks. The results of these artisanal methods are very good. Muga Crianza has soft, rich but elegant strawberry fruit, the Reserva, Prado Enea, is rich with strawberry-minty flavours. But the whites changed enormously during the 1990s, and are now deliciously perfumed and grassy-flavoured. The rosés are pleasantly fresh and fragrant, too. A modern, highly concentrated red (Torre Muga) and a barrique-fermented white are recent additions. Best years: (Torre Muga Reserva) 1998, '96, '95, '94.

JACQUES-FRÉDÉRIC MUGNIER

FRANCE, Burgundy, Côte de Nuits, Chambolle-Musigny AC

♦ Pinot Noir

Frédéric Mugnier now works fulltime looking after the small 4-ha (10-acre) family domaine, Ch. de Chambolle-Musigny which has exceptional sites in the CHAMBOLLE-MUSIGNY Premiers Crus les Amoureuses and les Fuées, BONNES-MARES and MUSIGNY. Apart from the Bonnes-Mares which was partially replanted in 1988, the average vine age is high and yields are low. A high proportion of new oak is used, but the wines usually have the body and structure to sustain it. Mugnier aims for a delicate, almost racy style, wines that are accessible young but capable of aging well in bottle. In 2002 the well-known NUITS-ST-GEORGES Premier Cru vineyard, the Clos de la Maréchale, reverted to the Mugniers from FAIVELEY and it will make an important contribution to the Mugnier portfolio. Best years: 2002, '01, '00, '99, '98, '97, '96, '95, '93, '90, '89.

MULDERBOSCH

SOUTH AFRICA, Western Cape, Stellenbosch WO

♦ Merlot, Cabernet Sauvignon, Cabernet Franc, Malbec, Petit Verdot

♀ Sauvignon Blanc, Chardonnay, Chenin Blanc

The partnership established between previous and founding owner, Dr Larry Jacobs, and winemaker, Mike Dobrovic in the early 1990s soon convinced wine lovers that there were many more sites in STELLENBOSCH than previously supposed which could produce top-notch Sauvignon Blanc. The sleek, gooseberry-infused Sauvignon has remained a medal-bedecked cult wine ever since. Consistent Chardonnay, oak-brushed Chenin Blanc (called Steen-op-Hout) and a barrel-fermented Sauvignon also benefit from Dobrovic's thoughtful inspiration; as does the lone red, the gentle, BORDEAUX-style blend called Faithful Hound. The new, corporate owners have sensibly avoided change for change's sake. Best years: (Chardonnay) 2001, '00, '99, '98, '97, '96, '95.

MULDERBOSCH
Faithful Hound, a Bordeaux-style blend, takes its name from a vineyard planted next to a hut where an abandoned dog lived out its last years in expectation of his master's return.

MÜLLER-CATOIR
One of the best estates in Germany today, this Pfalz producer makes sensational, full-bodied dessert wines from Rieslaner.

MÜLLER-CATOIR

GERMANY, Pfalz, Neustadt-Haardt

♦ Pinot Noir (Spätburgunder)

♀ Riesling, Scheurebe, Pinot Gris (Grauburgunder), Rieslaner and others

This PFALZ producer makes explosively powerful, dry whites – and while Müller-Catoir Rieslings are excellent, packed with fruit and endowed with a remarkable intensity and vibrancy, it is other, supposedly lesser varieties that really display the skills of winemaker Hans-Günter Schwarz. The Scheurebe is heavenly stuff, pink grapefruit coated in honey; his Grauburgunder is top-notch, and his Rieslaner (Riesling x Silvaner) dessert wines are sensational and very long lived.

He believes in minimal handling of his wines, no malolactic fermentation and as little racking and fining as possible, to allow the qualities of the individual vineyard and year to shine through. But what shines through most is the richness of the fruit and the heady perfumes. The vineyards are in Haardt, Gimmeldingen and Neustadt, amongst other places. Best years: 2002, '01, '99, '98, '97, '96, '94, '93, '92, '90, '89, '88.

EGON MÜLLER-SCHARZHOF

GERMANY, Mosel-Saar-Ruwer, Wiltingen

♀ Riesling and others

This is one of Germany's top estates and is run by Egon Müller IV. He favours a conservative style in his wines and still vinifies everything in wood, which is very rare these days in the MOSEL-SAAR-RUWER. Rigorous selection is the rule here, first of grapes then of wines. Müller's truly amazing Beerenauslese and Trockenbeerenauslese are the most expensive young wines in the world. Regular Kabinett and Spätlese wines are pricy but classic. The 8ha (20 acres) of vines are mostly in the celebrated Scharzhofberg vineyard. An intriguing new venture is Müller's involvement in developing a Riesling and Grüner Veltliner vineyard in Hungary at Béla, 50km (31 miles) north-west of Budapest near the border with Slovakia. Best years: 2002, '01, '99, '97, '95, '93, '90, '89, '88, '83, '76, '75, '71.

MÜLLER-THURGAU

This aromatic white grape, also known as Rivaner, is a cross between Riesling and Chasselas, and still covers vast amounts of land in Germany, although it is no longer the most widely planted grape variety. Although a crucial factor in the lighter flowery styles of LIEBFRAUMILCH and similar blends, it can produce quite exciting wines in the colder area of FRANKEN, and in BADEN and the PFALZ. However, its propensity to produce high yields has caused it to be planted on some of the better vineyard sites in the MOSEL, devaluing the reputation of the whole region. Austria, the Czech Republic and Slovakia have extensive plantations and with skilled growers it shows the pleasant pot-pourri of grapy freshness, spice and flowers that is Müller-Thurgau's strong point. New Zealand's ever-diminishing plantations still make some pleasant, off-dry, gently floral styles. In both England and Luxembourg it is widely planted and capable of pleasant, reasonably floral wines.

G H MUMM

FRANCE, Champagne, Champagne AC

♀ ♦ Pinot Noir, Chardonnay, Pinot Meunier

Owned by Allied Domecq, Mumm has for some time been one of the most inconsistent of the leading CHAMPAGNE houses. The once lovely Mumm de Cramant, a Blanc de Blancs from outstanding vineyards, now seems much duller than it used to be. With 212ha (525 acres) of vines, many located in Grand Cru sites, Mumm should be producing first-class Champagne, but rarely does. However, changes in the winemaking team since 1998 when Dominique Demarville became at 30, the youngest ever cellarmaster in Champagne, already seem to be having an effect. Cordon Rouge, for so long a wine whose only resemblance to Champagne was that it contained bubbles, has much improved. That's a good start: now we have to see if the young maestro can work his magic on the top cuvées. Any experiments that fail can be used to fill those big bottles they spray over each other on the Formula One winners' podium. Best years: 1996, '95, '90, '89, '88, '85, '82.

MUMM CUVÉE NAPA

USA, California, Napa County, Napa Valley AVA

♀ ♦ Pinot Noir, Chardonnay, Pinot Meunier, Pinot Gris

Mumm Napa, the CALIFORNIA offshoot of G H MUMM, made its first wines in 1983, then began substantial production in 1985. New winemaker Ludovic Dervin still pays tribute to the light, undemanding Mumm style, but in fact the Napa operation frequently produces a more successful non-vintage wine than does Mumm itself. DVX, the prestige cuvée, is in top form.

MURCIA

SPAIN

Murcia is the little-known region south of VALENCIA. It is surrounded by fabulously rich orchard land, but the vineyard regions further inland have little rainfall and summer temperatures can be suffocating. The soil is extremely poor. But this suits the late-ripening Monastrell (Mourvèdre) grape, of which there are around 33,000ha (81,550 acres): it makes for very low yields, great concentration and potentially great quality. Unfortunately, production facilities are mostly huge and basic and there are as yet few temperature-controlled vats and aging cellars in any of the three DOs in the region – Jumilla, Yecla and Bullas – but the potential is massive and progress is being made, including new plantings of Tempranillo and Syrah. Jumilla, especially, is one to watch. Best producers: Agapito Rico, Balcona, Castaño, Casa Castillo, Castillo de Luzón.

MURFATLAR

ROMANIA, Dobrogea

On the Black Sea coast of Romania, Murfatlar has long been recognized as a quality wine region. It has its own denomination and one look at the immaculate vineyards gives you an idea why. Winemaking is still influenced by domestic market requirements, and you can find some bizarre Pinot Noir wines with a fair whack of residual sugar. There is also wine aimed at international markets, though, and Pinot Gris and Chardonnay deliver rich, varietal fruit. Some oak-aged Chardonnay can be excellent value and one of Murfatlar's specialties is its botrytized Chardonnay and Pinot Gris. Cabernet Sauvignon and Merlot are potential sources of ripe, soft reds. Sparkling wines are being made too. Vie Vin is probably the most consistent producer.

ANDREW MURRAY VINEYARDS

USA, California, Santa Barbara County, Santa Ynez Valley AVA

❢ *Syrah, Grenache, Mourvedre*

♀ *Viognier, Roussanne, Marsanne, Grenache Blanc*

Andrew Murray and his restaurateur father discovered great RHÔNE wines on gastronomic tours of France and winemaker

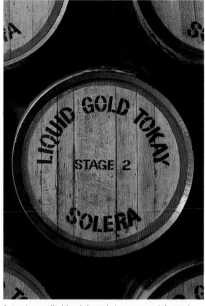

Aging in small old oak barrels is an essential step in making Australia's glorious fortified wines from the Muscat and Muscadelle (called Tokay locally) varieties.

Murray has created an impressive array of wines in their mould since his initial 1994 vintage. Rich, aromatic Viognier and Roussanne as well as several rich and juicy Syrahs, including Roasted Slope and Hillside Reserve from low yields of grapes that positively bake in their sheltered mesa vineyard in Santa Ynez. Espérance is a spicy blend patterned after a serious CÔTES DU RHÔNE. Best years: (Syrah) 2000, '99, '98, '97, '96, '94.

MUSCADELLE

This grape has nothing to do with either Muscat or MUSCADET, even though it has an aromatic muskiness that is somewhat similar to the former. In BORDEAUX it is grown in small quantities to add a pleasant, honeyed aroma to the rather neutral dry ENTRE-DEUX-MERS whites, and spice to SAUTERNES.

Where Muscadelle triumphs is in North-East VICTORIA in Australia at RUTHERGLEN and Glenrowan, where it goes under the name of Tokay. Elsewhere in the country, it may be used for table wines; here, it makes glorious, fortified wines which start off life in cask a pale golden yellow-brown, and finish it (still in cask) a dark burnt sienna with an olive green rim, and with a flavour and aroma described with various degrees of likelihood as fish oil or cough sweets, but most accurately as cold tea leaf and dried rose petals, intensely sweet in flavour but with a haunting, cleansing finish.

MUSCADET AC

FRANCE, Loire, Pays Nantais

♀ *Melon de Bourgogne (Muscadet)*

Muscadet can only come from a legally defined area at the mouth of the river Loire. The Melon de Bourgogne grape migrated from BURGUNDY in the seventeenth century – well, 'migrated' is a polite way of putting it: it was basically thrown out for making wine of quite eye-popping dullness and, fleeing west, it got to the seashore at Nantes and couldn't get any further so it settled here, in the damp flatlands round the mouth of the Loire. And it changed its name to Muscadet. To be honest, it was a good grape for the region because in those days most of the local wine was distilled into brandy and neutral white wine makes the best brandy. But when the brandy trade died, the grapes stayed – and with them their neutral dry white wine – Muscadet. There are now about 13,000ha (32,125 acres) of vines.

Muscadet is the basic appellation and can come from anywhere within the delimited area. In practice only wine from less good vineyards, mostly closer to the sea, carries the plain Muscadet AC. This is usually pretty bland wine, but does have one thing in its favour – the maximum alcoholic strength of 12 per cent. This legal maximum at least preserves a modicum of freshness in the wine. Muscadet Coteaux de la Loire, a little fuller, comes from a large area between Nantes and Angers but only accounts for 2.5 per cent of total production. The newest AC, the Côtes de Grandlieu, covers the best vineyards around the large Lac de Grandlieu, south-west of Nantes. However, the largest production of top wine comes from the extensive Muscadet de Sèvre-et-Maine AC, and this is the AC used by most quality estates.

A lot of Muscadet is dry and acid with a pretty neutral taste but a good Sèvre-et-Maine example should have a creamy softness with just enough prickle to make your tongue tingle. Look for the term *mise en bouteille sur lie*, indicating the traditional method of bottling the wine directly off its sediment or lees. This preserves some of the carbon dioxide in the wine and emphasizes a soft lees creaminess on the palate. Always drink straight Muscadet very young. Top *sur lie* Muscadets can age for several years, becoming quite full and nutty. Best years: (sur lie) 2002, '01, '00, '99, '98. Best producers: Serge Bâtard (Hautes-Noëlles), Chéreau-Carré, des Dorices, L'ÉCU, Gadais, Jacques Guindon, Herbauges, l'Hyvernière, Luneau-Papin, MÉTAIREAU, la Preuille, Quatre Routes, la Ragotière, Sauvion, Touché.

MUSCAT

There are some 200 varieties of the Muscat grape in one big, happy, grapy family, though thankfully only four of them are important for winemaking. Even so, those four can reach the extremes of wine styles: for a light, 7 per cent alcohol lightly sparkling wine to drink on a hot day in the garden, try Moscato d'Asti, from Piedmont in northern Italy. For a thick, dark brown, treacly fortified to sip on a winter's evening, try a fortified Muscat from Victoria in Australia. In between there are the elegant, dry Alsace Muscats and the lightly fortified Muscat de Beaumes-de-Venise, from the southern Rhône. Yet all these wines share the essential Muscat flavour, because whether it is light or massive, dry, sweet or fortified, that clean, grapy flavour is always there.

The aristocrat of the family is the Muscat Blanc à Petits Grains. Its numerous aliases include Gelber Muscatel, Muskateller (in Austria), Muscat de Frontignan, Muscat Blanc (in California), Brown Muscat and Muscat Canelli; it also has a pink sibling, Muscat Rosé à Petits Grains, and it is not unusual to find the two in the same vineyard. The Muscat Blanc à Petits Grains used to be, and is becoming again, the principal Muscat in Alsace, where its refinement shows well. The slightly less perfumed but hardier Muscat Ottonel (a crossbreed created in 1852) supplanted it, but the Petits Grains is on the increase again as growers begin to realize its greater quality. Further south, in the Rhône Valley, it makes sublimely grapy fizz, in the form of Clairette de Die Tradition, and the peachy, apples-and-honey, rose-scented Muscat de Beaumes-de-Venise as well as being the main grape in Languedoc's Muscat de Frontignan.

In California, as Muscat Blanc, the grape makes mostly sweetly grapy, perfumed wines, plus a few fortifieds, but Petits Grains reaches its fortified apogee in Australia's North-East Victoria, in the Glenrowan and Rutherglen regions, producing glowing, mahogany-coloured wines of extraordinary lusciousness and intensity. Here it may be called White, Red or Brown Frontignac or Frontignan, or even Brown Muscat: the grape, and the taste, are the same. Elsewhere in Australia it may be made into light, dry wines or any other style along the way; and Australia does not confine itself just to the Petits Grains variety.

The Muscat of Alexandria, otherwise known as Muscat d'Alexandrie, Moscatel, Muscatel or Zibibbo, among many synonyms, shares the perfume and grapy freshness of the Petits Grains variety, but with a streak of coarseness that tends to make its wines a little heavier, a little clumsier. In Australia it is known as Muscat Gordo Blanco, and is by far the largest single Muscat variety, contributing little to quality. Spain's principal Muscat is the Alexandrian variety, used to make aromatic, raisiny wines. In Penedès Miguel Torres grows some Petits Grains to blend into his Viña Esmeralda. Muscat of Alexandria dominates in Portugal, too, and on the Setúbal peninsula it makes Moscatel de Setúbal, very sweet, grapy-raisiny wines, usually fortified, and more recently crisp, dry wines.

In South Africa, Muscat Blanc was one of the grapes behind the historically famous Constantia dessert wine; it is the sole variety used in Klein Constantia's Vin de Constance, a modern reconstruction of that celebrated wine. The grape's more common usage, under the synonym Muscadel, is in the delicious fortified dessert wines, both white and red, which are the specialities of the warmer, inland regions. Muscat d'Alexandrie, also known as Hanepoot in the Cape, is more prolific but considered less fine than Muscat Blanc. In Tunisia, Muscat makes some of the best wines in North Africa.

Back in France, Muscat d'Alexandrie is widely planted in the South, particularly for the rather raisiny, marmalady fortified wines around Rivesaltes in Roussillon (Muscat à Petits Grains is the minor partner here).

MUSCAT DE BEAUMES-DE-VENISE AC

FRANCE, Southern Rhône
♀ *Muscat Blanc à Petits Grains*

This is the most delicious manifestation of sweet Muscat in France, and consequently the most expensive. But that's fair enough because the wine is a beauty and in the late 1970s when sweet wines looked to be in terminal decline, the phenomenal success of Muscat de Beaumes-de-Venise as a sophisticated pudding wine sparked a new interest.

Beaumes-de-Venise is an attractive village huddled up against the craggy Dentelles de Montmirail. If you ask the locals they'd probably be prouder of their gutsy red CÔTES-DU-RHONE-VILLAGES, but they've been making Muscat wine there since the Middle Ages. It's a *vin doux naturel* – a fortified wine where the fermentation is arrested by adding a slug of high-strength spirit. This preserves the flavour of the unfermented grape juice and accounts for the wine's sweet, grapy taste.

Muscat de Beaumes-de-Venise is rich, often very rich, full of the flavour of peach and grapes, orange peel, apples and honey, and with a wisp of the scent of roses left hanging in the air. But the secret is that the wine has a fruit acidity and a bright fresh feel to it which satisfies your thirst as well as stimulates your after-dinner wit. It can age, but is best drunk young to get all that lovely grapy perfume. Best producers: Baumalric, Beaumes-de-Venise co-operative, Bernardins, CHAPOUTIER, Coyeux, DELAS, Durban, Fenouillet, JABOULET, Vidal-Fleury.

MUSCAT DE FRONTIGNAN AC, MUSCAT DE LUNEL AC, MUSCAT DE MIREVAL AC, MUSCAT DE ST-JEAN-DE-MINERVOIS AC

FRANCE, Languedoc-Roussillon
♀ *Muscat Blanc à Petits Grains*

Muscat de Frontignan is the leading Muscat *vin doux naturel* on the Mediterranean coast and comes from Frontignan, a small town south-west of Montpellier in the HÉRAULT. It is supposed to be made 100 per cent from Muscat Blanc à Petits Grains, but there is probably an increasing amount of the coarser Muscat of Alexandria being used in the wine. This would go some way to explaining why much of the wine, though sweet and quite impressive, has a slightly cloying taste, like cooked marmalade, militating against the fresh grapy sweetness. The grapes are harvested as ripe as possible, partially fermented and then 'muted' by the addition of high-strength spirit. This stops the fermentation and leaves a substantial amount of the grape sweetness still in the wines. Varying between bright gold and a deep orange gold, Muscat de Frontignan is good, but not quite top class. Mireval is a less well-known, inland neighbour of Frontignan and the wines, while still sweet and ripe, can have a little more acid freshness, and quite an alcoholic kick as well.

Although the little town of Lunel, north-east of Montpellier, boastfully gives itself the title of 'la Cité de Muscat' (the city of Muscat), few people who don't actually live there would agree. Muscat de Lunel is not well known but the fairly small amounts made aren't bad with a very good raisiny flavour and less of the flat marmalady character than the better-known ones exhibit. Muscat de St-Jean-de-Minervois comes from the north-east corner of the MINERVOIS region and the wines are pleasantly sweet but not that concentrated.

Best producers: (Frontignan) Frontignan co-operative, la Peyrade, Robiscau; (Mireval) la Capelle, Mas des Pigeonniers, Moulinas; (St-Jean-de-Minervois) de Barroubio, Clos Bagatelle, Vignerons de Septimanie.

MUSCAT DE RIVESALTES AC
FRANCE, Languedoc-Roussillon
♀ Muscat of Alexandria, Muscat Blanc à Petits Grains

Rivesaltes, a small town just north of Perpignan, makes good CÔTES DU ROUSSILLON wines but its reputation is based on *vins doux naturels* – the traditional fortified wines of the South of France. The best of these is Muscat de Rivesaltes, made primarily from the Muscat of Alexandria grape; usually a big, rather thick, deep-coloured wine, not as aromatic as the best Muscats, and with a sweetness veering between raisins, honey and cooked orange marmalade. Modern producers like CAZES and de Jau are now producing more perfumed wines. Best producers: Cave de Baixas (Dom Brial, Ch. les Pins), de Casenove, Cazes, de Chênes, Fontanel, Força Réal, Jau, Lafage, Laporte, Mas Rous, MONT TAUCH co-op, Piquemal, Sarda-Malet.

MUSIGNY AC
FRANCE, Burgundy, Côte de Nuits, Grand Cru
♦ Pinot Noir
♀ Chardonnay

This extremely fine 11-ha (26-acre) Grand Cru vineyard gave its name to the village of CHAMBOLLE-MUSIGNY. Located on the slopes directly above CLOS DE VOUGEOT, it has the ability to produce red wines of such fragrance and delicacy of texture, that they have memorably been described as being 'of silk and lace', the perfume being 'a damp garden, a rose and a violet covered in morning dew'. In the hands of a few winemakers Musigny can truly be exceptional. Although very expensive, the wines show great power yet finesse. The de VOGÜÉ estate owns two-thirds of the Grand Cru and also makes a tiny amount of white. Best years: 2002, '01, '00, '99, '98, '97, '96, '95, '93, '90, '89, '88. Best producers: DROUHIN, JADOT, D LAURENT, Dom. LEROY, J-F MUGNIER, J Prieur, ROUMIER, de Vogüé, Vougeraie.

NACKENHEIM
GERMANY, Rheinhessen

This village just north of NIERSTEIN is famous as the setting for Karl Zuckmayer's play *The Jolly Vineyard* and for its Rothenberg vineyard from which some of the greatest Rieslings made anywhere on the Rhine originate. The red colour of the Rothenberg's slate soil, from which it gets its name, is so intense it can be seen from miles away. Best years: 2002, '01, '00, '99, '98, '97, '96, '94, '93, '92, '90. Best producers: GUNDERLOCH, HEYL ZU HERRNSHEIM.

NAHE
GERMANY

It can be easy to overlook the Nahe. It does not have an easily encapsulated character, unlike some German wine regions. It's relatively small, with 4385ha (10,835 acres) of vines, and many of its vineyards are scattered rather than being neatly grouped. In addition, until 1930, its wines were sold as Rhine wines, or were sent to the RHEINGAU or MOSEL for blending.

Nahe's reputation is not helped by the amount of the acceptable but unexciting Müller-Thurgau in its vineyards. But its top wines – made from Riesling – can be sublime. They have the nerve of the SAAR wines combined with some of the body of a Rheingau, though they are seldom as weighty: they have finesse, delicacy and excitement built in. But these wines come from only an 8-km (5-mile) stretch of the steepest parts of the north bank of the river Nahe south and west of BAD KREUZNACH. The Rotenfels cliff at Bad Münster sends the river momentarily hurtling south-east, and here, in a 2-ha (5-acre) patch of land at its foot, lies the fine Traiser Bastei vineyard.

Things get even better as you twist upstream past Norheim, Niederhausen, and especially, past the sweep of the river that ends in an abrupt southwards drive past SCHLOSS-BÖCKELHEIM. Here vineyards pack the northern bank – there are some good ones on the south bank too – and they grow some of Germany's greatest Riesling.

In the Lower Nahe, from Bad Kreuznach north to the Rhine at BINGEN, the wines, and the vineyards, sober down a little. There are good wines, often very good, but it's just that short stretch of river south of Bad Kreuznach that puts the Nahe into the league of Germany's great wine regions.

CH. NAIRAC
FRANCE, Bordeaux, Barsac AC, 2ème Cru Classé
♀ Sémillon, Sauvignon Blanc, Muscadelle

An established star in BARSAC, which produces a wine sometimes on a level with the SAUTERNES First Growths – not as intensely perfumed, not as exotically rich, but proudly concentrated, with a fine lanolin richness and buttery honeyed fruit. Annual production is rarely more than 15,000 bottles – sometimes less – from this 16-ha (40-acre) property. Aging in new oak casks adds spice and even a little tannin, make the wine a good candidate for aging for 10–15 years. Best years: 2002, '01, '99, '98, '97, '96, '95, '90, '89, '88.

NAOUSSA AO
GREECE, Macedonia
♦ Xynomavro

The small area of Naoussa lies west of Thessaloniki, centred on the south-eastern slopes of Mount Velia. It produces one of Greece's most individual wines, a lean but spicy red made from the native Xynomavro grape. *Xynomavro* means 'acid black' in Greek and it does take a few years for the acidity to soften and the spice to dominate. The vineyards here are fairly high, around 350m (1150ft). Best producers: Boutari, Markovitis/Chateau Pégasos, Tsantali, Vaeni Naoussa co-operative.

BOUTARI
Boutari is one of the most reliable producers of full-bodied, spicy red Naoussa wines from the local Xynomavro grape that can age well.

NAPA USA, California

TRADITIONALLY SYNONYMOUS with quality California wine, Napa County draws its wine identity, which is its only distinction these days, from its major AVA, Napa Valley, flanked on the west by the Mayacamas Mountains and on the east by the Coast Range. Most of its 230 or so wineries line the valley or overlook it from slopes and mountain perches. Over 20 major sub-areas with their own distinct mesoclimates have now been recognized, either along the valley floor or at high elevations. The most southerly and coolest AVA is Carneros, noted for Pinot Noir and Chardonnay used for both still and sparkling wines. In the mid-valley areas of Rutherford, Oakville and Yountville, Cabernet Sauvignon justifiably dominates, and its vinous hallmarks are dusty, dried sage and extra-ripe blackcur-

The bulk of grape-growing in the Napa Valley takes place on the valley floor and on the gentle slopes adjoining the floor and there is little land left that can now be converted into new space for grapes.

rant notes. Softer and more supple Cabernets and Merlots originate in the Stags Leap District AVA to the south-east and Spring Mountain to the west. In the north-east hills of the Howell Mountain AVA, Zinfandel and Cabernet develop really exciting depth and perfume. Diamond Mountain and Mount Veeder are AVAs along the Mayacamas mountain range to the west, and are best known for Cabernet Sauvignon while Spring Mountain, above St Helena, has some top estates specializing in Cabernet and Merlot reds.

DUNN VINEYARDS
Randy Dunn's Howell Mountain Cabernet is a massive wine, with ripe fruit and supreme balance that can easily age for a decade and often much longer.

JOSEPH PHELPS
Ripe, big and oaky, Insignia is one of California's top Meritage wines and is usually based on Cabernet Sauvignon with some Merlot and Cabernet Franc.

NEWTON
Newton's massive reserve-style Chardonnay, which is unfiltered and unfined, owes a good deal to the best wines of Meursault.

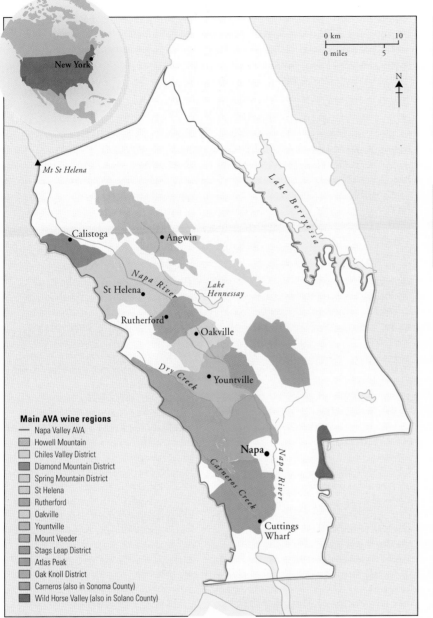

DIAMOND CREEK

Three Cabernet Sauvignon wines are made at this hillside winery, each from a vineyard planted on different soils and at different gradients. Red Rock Terrace is the most approachable of the three with vivid Cabernet fruit.

CAYMUS VINEYARDS

A Cabernet Sauvignon star for over 20 years, Caymus emphasizes a deep, ripe intense and generally well-oaked tannic style. The Special Selection can be outstanding.

STAG'S LEAP WINE CELLARS

From a winery reputed for its Cabernets, Cask 23 Cabernet Sauvignon has remarkably complex, enticing perfume and flavour and is only made in the best vintages.

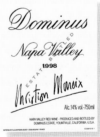

DOMINUS ESTATE

Christian Moueix of Ch. Pétrus fame has created a top Pomerol lookalike in the Napa Valley. Concentrated, with tremendous ripe fruit and lavish oak, the wine enjoyed a string of outstanding vintages during the 1990s.

JADE MOUNTAIN

This big, ripe, gamy Syrah is one of several delicious Rhône-style wines made by this winery, now part of the Chalone group.

PETER MICHAEL WINERY

Les Pavots is a Cabernet-based red from a vineyard of the same name in the Knights Valley at the north end of the Napa Valley.

Main AVA wine regions
- Napa Valley AVA
- Howell Mountain
- Chiles Valley District
- Diamond Mountain District
- Spring Mountain District
- St Helena
- Rutherford
- Oakville
- Yountville
- Mount Veeder
- Stags Leap District
- Atlas Peak
- Oak Knoll District
- Carneros (also in Sonoma County)
- Wild Horse Valley (also in Solano County)

REGIONAL ENTRIES

Atlas Peak, Carneros, Howell Mountain, Napa Valley, Mount Veeder, Oakville, Rutherford, St Helena, Spring Mountain District, Stags Leap District.

PRODUCER ENTRIES

Acacia Winery, Araujo, Beaulieu Vineyard, Beringer Vineyards, Cain Cellars, Caymus Vineyards, Clos du Val, Dalla Valle, Diamond Creek Vineyards, Domaine Carneros, Domaine Chandon, Dominus Estate, Duckhorn Vineyards, Dunn Vineyards, Far Niente Winery, Franciscan Vineyards, Frog's Leap Winery, Grgich Hills Cellar, Heitz Cellars, The Hess Collection, Merryvale, Robert Mondavi Winery, Mumm Cuvée Napa, Newton Vineyards, Niebaum Coppola Winery, Opus One, Pahlmeyer Winery, Joseph Phelps, Pine Ridge Winery, Saintsbury, Schramsberg Vineyards, Shafer Vineyards, Silver Oak Cellars, Spottswoode, Stag's Leap Wine Cellars, Sterling Vineyards, Sutter Home Winery, Swanson Vineyards, Turley Cellars, Viader Vineyards.

NAPA VALLEY AVA

USA, California, Napa County (see also 264–265)

The Napa Valley looks the way a prosperous wine region should: a mixture of flat land and hills, a river, plenty of imposing architecture in its wineries, and rows of vines everywhere. By 2002 the sprawling valley had nearly 17,400ha (43,000 acres) of vines and about 20 major sub-areas already identified, compared to barely 4047ha (10,000 acres) in the mid-1960s. The Napa Valley was built in two great, giddy waves of enthusiasm, the first in the 1880s and '90s, the second in the 1970s and '80s, when the number of wineries began to swell from a mere dozen to the 230-odd in operation today.

Napa's adaptation to Cabernet Sauvignon has been just as steady as the continuity in winemaking. By the beginning of the twentieth century, BEAULIEU and Inglenook were growing and making it as a varietal. The same vineyards at RUTHERFORD still contribute to Beaulieu's Georges de Latour Private Reserve but, like most of its neighbours, this famous vineyard was replanted in the 1990s after phylloxera struck. In the monumental replanting process, quality-minded winemakers seized the opportunity to relocate Cabernet Sauvignon and Merlot to more suitable sites and Merlot is now usually found in cooler pockets in the CARNEROS or spots immediately north of Napa city itself.

More sweeping changes occurred with Chardonnay; most Napa Chardonnay has been shifted to Carneros and other cool adjacent areas. Phylloxera also forced a few hillside vineyards to replant, but most stuck to Cabernet and other red varieties. Indeed, the hillsides and various other well-drained outcrops such as the benchlands in the western edge of the OAKVILLE and RUTHERFORD AVAs are, generally, better for reds.

As it emerges from the throes of replanting, the Napa Valley is much better aligned viticulturally not only with improved rootstocks but also with a greater overall emphasis on matching grape variety to site for improved quality. Best years: (Cabernet Sauvignon and Merlot) 2002, '01, '00, '99, '97, '95, '94, '92, '91, '90, '87, '86. The list below is just the cream of the crop. Best producers: (Cabernet Sauvignon and meritage blends) Abreu, Altamura, Anderson's Conn Valley, S Anderson, ARAUJO, Barnett (Rattlesnake Hill), Beaulieu, BERINGER, Bryant Family, Buehler (Reserve), Burgess Cellars, Cafaro, Cain Cellars, Cakebread, CAYMUS, Chateau Montelena, Chateau Potelle (VGS), Chimney Rock, CLOS DU VAL, Clos Pegase, Colgin, Conn Creek (Anthology), Corison, Cosentino, Robert Craig, DALLA VALLE, Del Dotto, DIAMOND CREEK, DOMINUS, DUCKHORN, DUNN, Elyse, Etude, FAR NIENTE, Fisher, Flora Springs, Forman, Freemark Abbey, FROG'S LEAP, Grace Family, Groth, HARLAN ESTATE, Hartwell, HEITZ, HESS, Jarvis, La Jota, Lewis Cellars, Livingston, Lokoya, Long Meadow Ranch, Long Vineyards, Markham, Mayacamas, MERRYVALE, Peter MICHAEL, Miner, MONDAVI, Monticello, Mount Veeder Winery/FRANCISCAN, NEWTON, NIEBAUM COPPOLA, Oakford, Oakville Ranch (Miner), OPUS ONE, PAHLMEYER, Paradigm, Robert Pecota, Peju Province (HB Vineyard), PHELPS, PINE RIDGE, Plumpjack, Pride Mountain, Quintessa, Raymond, Rombauer (Meilleur du Chai), Rudd Estate, Saddleback, St Clement, SCREAMING EAGLE, Seavey, SHAFER, SILVER OAK, Silverado, SPOTTSWOODE, Staglin Family, STAG'S LEAP WINE CELLARS, STERLING, SWANSON, The Terraces, Philip Togni, Turnbull, VIADER, Villa Mt Eden (Signature Series), Vine Cliff, Vineyard 29, Von Strasser, Whitehall Lane, ZD.

NAVARRA DO

SPAIN, Navarra

♦♂☿ *Cabernet Sauvignon, Graciano, Tempranillo, Grenache Noir (Garnacha Tinta), Carignan (Cariñena, Mazuelo), Merlot*
♀ *Macabeo (Viura), Chardonnay, Grenache Blanc (Garnacha Blanca), Malvasía, Moscatel de Grano Menudo (Muscat Blanc à Petits Grains)*

Though containing a slice of the RIOJA DOCa, the Navarra region's fame comes from its eponymous DO, which is one of Spain's most forward-looking. Through an ambitious research and education programme, the Navarra authorities and producers raised the quality of their wine during the 1980s, although signs of stagnation appeared in the late 1990s. Such a revival only echoes history, for in the eleventh century the powerful kingdom of Navarra included both BORDEAUX and Rioja, thus uniting three very prestigious wine regions. But, in the late 1800s, the phylloxera plague hit Navarra just as badly as it did Bordeaux and Rioja.

Although Garnacha has been Navarra's principal red grape in recent decades, almost all replanting is now with Tempranillo and already some top Tempranillo wines are rivalling those from Rioja. Other newcomers are Cabernet and Merlot – which can both be very successful blended with Tempranillo – and Chardonnay which blends well with Viura. Chardonnay must be harvested promptly, as overripe grapes can produce excessively fat, alcoholic wines. Best years: (reds) 2001, '99, '98, '96, '95, '94, '93. Best producers: Camilo Castilla (Capricho de Goya Muscat), CHIVITE, Magaña, Vicente Malumbres, Álvaro Marino, Castillo de Monjardín, Vinícola Navarra, Nekeas co-operative, Ochoa, Palacio de la Vega, Piedemonte Olite co-operative, Príncipe de Viana, Señorío de Otazu.

NEBBIOLO

This Italian red grape, even with the most modern winemaking techniques, still makes pretty insular wines. That is to say that they're not international in style: they're not drinkable young, they're not soft and fruity and they don't taste like red Bordeaux. Italophiles and other lovers of distinctive wines will regard all this as an advantage.

Nebbiolo is based in Piedmont, with some found in Lombardy's Valtellina, where its name is Chiavennasca, and it is the grape behind Piedmont's two great red wines, Barolo and Barbaresco. Barolo is not a wine to drink young. It's too tannic, too acidic and not fruity enough – but that's the chrysalis from which emerge flavours of violets, truffles, raspberries, licorice, prunes, chocolate and goodness knows what else – with time. Nebbiolo reaches its greatest heights in the south of Piedmont, around Alba. In the north the wines get less intense, more violetty but often more chocolaty, too, and apart from Carema, these northern wines may be blended with less tannic red grapes such as Bonarda and Vespolina. Nebbiolo has to be grown on south-facing slopes, but it still ripens late, sometimes even as late as November. There is plenty of fog by then, and fog in Italian is *nebbia*, hence the grape's name. In the provinces of Novara and Vercelli, in the north of Piedmont, Nebbiolo is also called Spanna.

NEBBIOLO D'ALBA DOC

ITALY, Piedmont

❦ *Nebbiolo*

Nebbiolo d'Alba is ideal if you feel like a taste of Nebbiolo but don't feel the occasion merits the power and cost of a classic wine. It is grown in lands adjacent to BAROLO and BARBARESCO but doesn't have their long aging requirement: one year is enough. Until recently, conventional wisdom had it that Nebbiolo d'Alba was a poor man's Barolo, but the late Matteo Correggia disproved that theory, his version being quite capable of taking on and beating most Barolos. Most, however, remain in the lighter mode. Best years: 2001, '00, '99, '98, '97, '96, '95. Best producers: Alario, ASCHERI, Bricco Maiolica, Ceretto, Cascina Chicco, Correggia, GIACOSA, Giuseppe MASCARELLO, PRUNOTTO, Ratti, SANDRONE, Vietti.

NELSON

NEW ZEALAND, South Island

Nelson, on the north-western tip of the South Island, is in the shadow of the large and glamorous MARLBOROUGH region but has greatly increased plantings in recent years, and won't even pause for breath at the current 398ha (983 acres), mostly in the flat Waimea Plains near Nelson city but also in the hills of Upper Moutere and even in the far north-west at Golden Bay. There are about 30 wineries, mostly small and dominated by SEIFRIED.

Chardonnay is the most widely planted and most prestigious grape variety, with NEUDORF producing what can be one of the country's best examples. Tangy, crunchy Sauvignon Blanc ranks second but it lacks the prestige of Marlborough Sauvignon and struggles to command a similar price, despite higher production costs on the smaller and often more labour-intensive vineyards. Nelson makes good to excellent Riesling in a range of mostly dry styles with strong lime flavours and a botrytis influence when the vintage allows. There is also stylish Pinot Noir. Best years: (whites) 2002, '01, '00, '99, '98. Best producers: Greenhough, Neudorf, Pomona Ridge (Pinot Noir), Ruby Bay, Seifried/Redwood Valley.

NEMEA AO

GREECE, Peloponnese

❦ *Agiorgitiko*

Hercules killed the Nemean lion and was presumably glad of a drink afterwards; and wine from Nemea, in the Peloponnese near Corinth, *has* been around for 2500 years.

The Agiorgitiko (St-George) grape, grown in vineyards between 250 and 800m (820 and 2620ft), is native to Greece and produces a big, rich wine known locally as the 'Blood of Hercules'. It can be long-lived, but like all Greek wines, so much depends on the skill of the individual winemaker. Only an example whose burly, rugged power has not been diminished by oxidation and lazy winemaking will age properly. Drink young or with short aging. Best producers: ANTONOPOULOS, Andrew P. Cambas, Gaia, KOKOTOS, Papaïannou, Skouras.

NEUCHÂTEL

SWITZERLAND

❦ ❦ *Pinot Noir*

♀ *Chasselas, Chardonnay*

One of the French-speaking Swiss cantons, Neuchâtel has vineyards that stretch in a long strip along the shore of Lake Neuchâtel, with the JURA mountains protecting their backs. The wines can be some of Switzerland's best, with some character getting into the Pinot Noir; the Chasselas is light and bone dry, often with a slight prickle. The Oeil de Perdrix Pinot Noir rosé is particularly delicate and attractive. There are three small individual appellations: Schloss Vaumarcus, Hôpital Poutalès and Domaine de Champrevèyres. Best producers: Ch. d'Auvernier, Thierry Grosjean, de Montmollin Fils, Porret.

NEUDORF

NEW ZEALAND, South Island, Nelson

❦ *Pinot Noir*

♀ *Sauvignon Blanc, Chardonnay, Riesling, Pinot Gris*

Winemaker/owner Tim Finn has made some of the most exciting and stylish Chardonnays to come from New Zealand to date, textured and complex with masses of grilled hazelnut, butter and peach flavours matching the best in Australia, yet with that unmistakable South Island New Zealand intensity of fruit. Neudorf Riesling is one of the few New Zealand examples to capture a steely, mineral character which adds extra depth to classic

NEUDORF
In New Zealand Pinot Noir is best suited to the South Island's cool conditions. Neudorf's example has a fine depth and a scented richness in the best years.

apple/lime flavours. The Pinot Noir, too, can excel with its strawberry fruit and ethereal perfume, although NELSON has a very temperamental climate and late summer rainfall is always a threat down here. Best years: (Chardonnay) 2002, '01, '00, '99, '98, '96; (Pinot Noir) 2001, '00, '99, '98, '97.

NEUSIEDLERSEE, NEUSIEDLERSEE-HÜGELLAND

AUSTRIA, Burgenland

Lake Neusiedl lies, reedy and pleasure-boat-filled, in the north of Austria's BURGENLAND, almost on the border with Hungary. Thanks to the lake, which gives just the right amount of morning humidity followed by dry sunshine, fine, sweet botrytis-affected wines are produced in remarkable quantities almost every year.

The eastern side, the district called Neusiedlersee, produces the most. Here in the south, in an area called Seewinkel around Illmitz, the effect of the lake is enhanced by umpteen tiny lakes, and botrytis will attack just about anything. In the north, around Gols and Mönchhof, red and dry white wines are made as well. The western side, Neusiedlersee-Hügelland, is more varied, in that sweet wines are mostly made in a narrow strip near the lake, with the town of RUST an important centre, and they tend to be less luscious and sweet. Elsewhere, dry, ripe whites and soft, velvety reds are produced. Best years: (sweet wines) 2002, '00, '99, '98, '96, '95, '94. Best producers: FEILER-ARTLINGER, Gernot HEINRICH, KOLLWENTZ, Alois KRACHER, NITTNAUS, Peter Schandl, Heidi Schröck, STIEGELMAR/Juris, TRIEBAUMER, WENZEL.

NEW WAVE WINES

ENGLAND, Kent

❦ *Pinot Noir, Rondo, Dornfelder, Regent*

❦ *Pinot Noir, Dornfelder*

♀ *Bacchus, Schonburger, Reichensteiner, Müller-Thurgau, Huxelrebe, Seyval Blanc*

The merger between Chapel Down and Carr Taylor (including Lamberhurst) has created a major player on the UK wine scene, with Owen Elias as chief winemaker. Grapes are from their own vineyards in Kent, and also bought in from 25 vineyards across southern England. The Chapel Down range comprises good, inexpensive sparkling wines (Brut non-vintage, Brut Rosé and Vintage). The Curious Grape range of still wines includes fruity white blends and single-varietals from Bacchus to Pinot Noir, and there's a wood-aged red, Epoch Reserve.

NEW SOUTH WALES Australia

FOR THE FIRST 170 OR SO years of viticulture and winemaking in New South Wales, the wine map was dominated by the Hunter Valley, albeit with a sideways glance at the vast sprawl of bulk production in the Riverina. But since the early part of the 1990s, the small, premium quality regions hugging the western side of the Great Dividing Range have assumed rapidly growing importance. The long-term resident was Mudgee, but it has now been joined (at a significantly higher elevation) by Orange, by Cowra, a distinctly warm region, by Hilltops, dominated by McWilliam's with its Barwang property, the Canberra District, which has recently seen the arrival of BRL Hardy, and finally, well into the foothills of the Australian Alps, Tumbarumba. Of these Mudgee, Cowra and Hilltops already stand as major producers in terms of volume, and as significant contributors to the pool of Australian premium wine. Orange, Canberra District and Tumbarumba have great quality potential, although site selection (particularly to guard against spring frosts) is essential.

The Hunter Valley remains an enigma, yet it is sharing in the near-hysterical growth of the latter part of the 1990s. Max Lake of winery Lake's Folly once said that the only thing wrong with Coonawarra (in the remote south-east cor-

In the Lower Hunter Valley the smoky blue Brokenback Range makes a dramatic backdrop to the vineyards along Broke Road near Pokolbin. These vineyards, belonging to Tyrrell's, are some of the best in the Hunter Valley.

ner of South Australia) is that it is so far from Sydney. It might equally well be said that the only thing right with the Hunter Valley is that it is only 145km (90 miles) from Sydney, Australia's most populated area.

Australian winemakers – including some in the Hunter Valley itself – have been quoted as saying that, with the level of knowledge we now have about climate, soil and the grape vines' various needs, no-one in their right mind would ever plant a vineyard in the Hunter Valley. It's far too hot and humid during the growing season for quality grapes, the spring is generally a period of drought while the autumn vintage is regularly devastated by rainstorms. Much of the soil is impenetrable 'pug' clay. But somehow the Hunter has produced some of Australia's greatest wines; and as tourism has flourished so the Hunter has duly blossomed.

In the brave new world of Geographic Indications, the four most important zones in New South Wales are Hunter Valley, Central Ranges, Big Rivers and Southern New South Wales. It

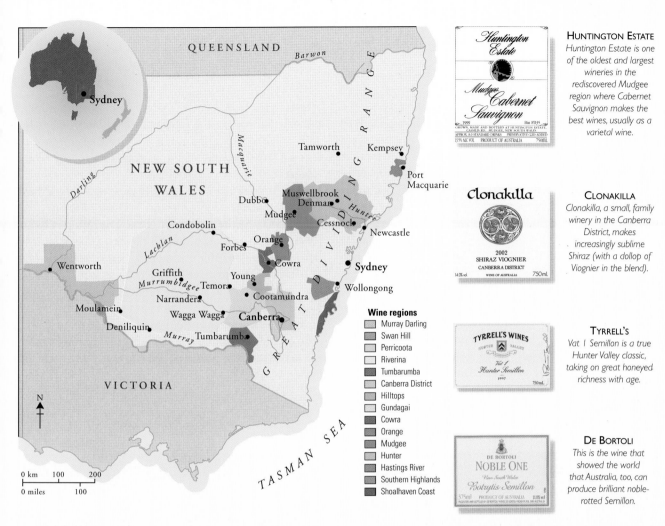

Wine regions
- Murray Darling
- Swan Hill
- Perricoota
- Riverina
- Tumbarumba
- Canberra District
- Hilltops
- Gundagai
- Cowra
- Orange
- Mudgee
- Hunter
- Hastings River
- Southern Highlands
- Shoalhaven Coast

HUNTINGTON ESTATE
Huntington Estate is one of the oldest and largest wineries in the rediscovered Mudgee region where Cabernet Sauvignon makes the best wines, usually as a varietal wine.

CLONAKILLA
Clonakilla, a small, family winery in the Canberra District, makes increasingly sublime Shiraz (with a dollop of Viognier in the blend).

TYRRELL'S
Vat 1 Semillon is a true Hunter Valley classic, taking on great honeyed richness with age.

DE BORTOLI
This is the wine that showed the world that Australia, too, can produce brilliant noble-rotted Semillon.

BROKENWOOD
The best wine from this high-profile Hunter Valley winery is the classic Graveyard Vineyard Shiraz.

ROTHBURY ESTATE
Rothbury's Brokenback Vineyard produces very low yields of Semillon, one of the Hunter Valley's classic grape varieties.

McWILLIAM'S
McWilliam's Hanwood Chardonnay proves that high volume 'brands' can deliver good flavours at a fair price.

is striking that only the Hunter Valley is on the eastern (or coastal) side of the Great Dividing Range, and no less remarkable that in a display of solidarity, the winemakers of the regions traditionally known as the Lower Hunter and Upper Hunter have agreed that their region will simply be known as the Hunter, with a host of sub-regions yet to come.

It is only when you travel west out into the hinterland that you come to the Riverina (also known as the Murrumbidgee Irrigation Area or as Griffith). Here, the high-yielding vineyards are irrigated through the growing season, and every grape variety known is propagated, chiefly feeding the bulk market. But even here the quality message is hitting home. Several companies are bottling premium lines and even trying their hand at Estate labels, and one of the world's greatest sweet wines – De Bortoli's Noble One – comes from Riverina fruit.

REGIONAL ENTRIES
Canberra District, Cowra, Hastings River, Hilltops, Hunter Valley, Mudgee, Orange, Riverina.

PRODUCER ENTRIES
Brokenwood, De Bortoli, McWilliam's, Rosemount Estate, Rothbury Estate, Tower Estate, Tyrrell's.

NEW YORK STATE USA

NEW YORK STATE IS HOME TO the oldest continuously operating winery in the USA, Brotherhood Winery established in 1839. Native and hybrid American varieties were originally cultivated in the USA along the the Hudson River. By the end of the nineteenth century, there were more than 8094ha (20,000 acres) of vineyards in New York State.

Most of this huge increase in planting took place in the Finger Lakes region. Early viticulturists believed that severe winter temperature swings (perhaps 50 degrees or more in a single day) made it impossible to grow *Vitis vinifera* grapes successfully here. Table and juice grape varieties were planted instead and it wasn't until the 1950s that vinifera grapes were cultivated by Dr Konstantin Frank, whose experience in Europe and the Ukraine had convinced him that these varieties could survive such harsh winters. He was right. Vinifera varieties find it tough in the Finger Lakes and some of them do get blasted by the harsh conditions, but all the best Finger Lakes wines are now made from classic varieties like Riesling, Gewürztraminer and Chardonnay. If the autumn is warm and dry they can make delicious fragrant dry styles. And if the weather breaks – well, they can always make Icewine – and they often do.

There are over 120 wineries and 1355ha (3350 acres) of *vinifera* vines in the seven New York State AVAs, which are split between four distinct regions. The western portion of the state falls within the Lake Erie AVA. The Finger Lakes AVA is named after the series of deep lakes below Lake Ontario. Steep lakeside slopes provide a moderating climate against severe winter cold. The newer Cayuga Lake AVA is lower in altitude and is a deeper lake creating a unique mesoclimate suitable for vinifera grapes. Riesling and Chardonnay are the trump cards here. The historic Hudson River Region AVA on steep hillsides along the river's edge starts about 65km (40 miles) north of New York City. Most of the wines here are from French hybrids, especially Seyval Blanc and Baco Noir, although Pinot Noir and Chardonnay have been planted.

Finally, there are three AVAs on Long Island, New York's most exciting area and a cool region with a long growing season that gives great concentration of fruit in a good year. The Hamptons AVA is a tiny vineyard area along the south fork

The Finger Lakes region, here at Seneca Lake, one of the best sites in the AVA, relies on the critical effects of water in tempering a climate that would otherwise be far too harsh for conventional wine grape-growing.

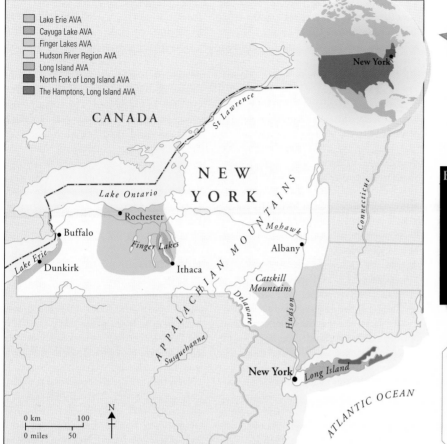

Map legend:
- Lake Erie AVA
- Cayuga Lake AVA
- Finger Lakes AVA
- Hudson River Region AVA
- Long Island AVA
- North Fork of Long Island AVA
- The Hamptons, Long Island AVA

New York

CANADA

St Lawrence

Lake Ontario

NEW YORK

Rochester

Mohawk

Buffalo

Finger Lakes

Albany

Lake Erie

Dunkirk

Ithaca

Catskill Mountains

Delaware

Hudson

APPALACHIAN MOUNTAINS

Connecticut

Susquehanna

New York

Long Island

ATLANTIC OCEAN

0 km 100
0 miles 50

N

FOX RUN VINEYARDS
Complex, Alsace-style Gewurztraminer, with its highly distinctive typical aroma of rose petals and lychees, is just one of a long list of varietal wines from this winery overlooking Lake Seneca in the Finger Lakes region.

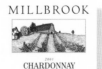

BEDELL CELLARS
Kip Bedell's wines include a Merlot Reserve which is now considered one of Long Island's top red wines. With layers of dark, concentrated black cherry and berry fruit, the wine is capable of extended aging.

LENZ
A Long Island winery going from strength to strength. The Merlot is elegant and powerful with soft, balanced tannins.

LAMOREAUX LANDING
Bold, oaky Chardonnay has helped make this Finger Lakes winery one of the most important on the East Coast.

MILLBROOK VINEYARDS
Based in the Hudson River Region, Millbrook makes stylish wines including ripe, oaky Chardonnay.

GALLUCCIO FAMILY WINERIES
Elegant, barrel-fermented Chardonnay is one of the stars at this well-regarded Long Island producer, formerly called Gristina until a change of ownership in 2000.

of Long Island bordering the Atlantic Ocean. The weather can cause havoc here and several good vintages have been ruined by hurricanes, an obstacle few other premium wine regions in the world have to face. The North Fork of Long Island is a rapidly expanding area with a maritime climate where the growing season is long enough to ripen Bordeaux varietals and provide excellent concentration of fruit in a good year. Almost all the best wines have so far been whites, but there's a tantalizing possibility of making great reds, too.

Native American and hybrid varieties, especially Concord which makes excellent grape juice but pretty duff wine, continue to dominate the East Coast vineyards. I'd like to get sniffy but I have to admit that grape jelly is sweet and perfumed and delicious on toast, and since there is an enthusiastic market for it, I can't blame farmers for growing Concord and taking the easy money. New York is not an easy place to grow vinifera grapes – even balmy Long Island is hard work – which makes the successful vinifera wines all the more impressive.

REGIONAL ENTRIES
Finger Lakes, Hudson River Region, Long Island.

PRODUCER ENTRIES
Fox Run Vineyards, Glenora Wine Cellars, Lamoreaux Landing, Millbrook Vineyards.

NEWTON VINEYARDS
USA, California, Napa County, Napa Valley AVA
♥ *Merlot, Cabernet Sauvignon, Cabernet Franc, Petit Verdot*
♀ *Chardonnay, Viognier*

Su Hua Newton's breathtaking wine estate, with its striking Chinese-style architecture and gardens, is built on the hillside overlooking the NAPA VALLEY, west of St Helena. Its main vineyards are carved onto steep slopes, with cellars tunnelled into them. Newton's Cabernet and Merlot are two of CALIFORNIA's most successful examples, showing a distinct BORDEAUX style with their ripe, black-cherry and plum fruit. New top Cabernet Le Puzzle is a dense rich red with some of the black chocolate bitter sweetness of a top Italian red. Top Merlot Epic is equally impressive – also Pinot Noir and, occasionally, Viognier. Chardonnays have regularly been among California's most refined and the top release is an unfiltered, unfined wine that owes a good deal to the best wines of MEURSAULT.

French luxury giant LVMH took a controlling interest in 2000, but the irrepressible Su Hua is still the winemaker. Best years: (Cabernet Sauvignon) 2001, '00, '99, '97, '96, '95, '94, '91, '90.

NGATARAWA
NEW ZEALAND, North Island, Hawkes Bay
♥ *Merlot, Cabernet Sauvignon, Cabernet Franc*
♀ *Sauvignon Blanc, Chardonnay, Riesling*

The Ngatarawa estate vineyards were created in 1981 by Alwyn Corban on a patch of red metal-rich soils in what has now become known as the Ngatarawa Triangle. Corban was a leader in the development of these well-drained inland sites up the Ngaruroro River valley. He makes good, lean Cabernet-Merlot blends at three levels – Stables, the mid-range Glazebrook and the top level Alwyn Reserve. The Chardonnay is similarly restrained but classy, and about one year in two he produces brilliant botrytised Noble Harvest Riesling. Viticulture is organic. Best years: (reds) 2002, '01, '98.

NIAGARA PENINSULA
CANADA, Ontario

Situated on the 43rd parallel, the Niagara Peninsula is a narrow finger of land sandwiched between the Niagara Escarpment and Lake Ontario and is the most important wine region of southern ONTARIO. In terms of sunshine hours and rainfall, the Peninsula enjoys a climate similar to Burgundy and the thermal influence of both Lake Erie and Ontario is a significant help. The vineyards begin just east of Hamilton and stretch along the south shore of Lake Ontario, all the way to Niagara Falls. Some of the best sites lie 30–50m (90–150ft) above the plain on the sloping benchland that runs along the escarpment. The most successful vinifera varieties are led by Riesling, Chardonnay and Pinot Noir. Best years: (Icewines) 2002, '00, '99, '98. Best producers: Cave Spring, CHATEAU DES CHARMES, HENRY OF PELHAM, INNISKILLIN, Konzelmann, Marynissen, Reif Estate, Southbrook, Stoney Ridge, THIRTY BENCH.

NIEBAUM COPPOLA WINERY
USA, California, Napa County, Rutherford AVA
♥ *Cabernet Sauvignon, Cabernet Franc, Merlot, Petit Verdot, Syrah, Zinfandel*
♀ *Chardonnay, Roussanne, Marsanne, Viognier*

Movie director Francis Ford Coppola entered the wine world by buying the historic estate of Gustav Niebaum (Inglenook's founder) and the surrounding organic vineyards, some of NAPA's oldest. A decade later he added the Inglenook winery and tourist centre. His pride and joy is a red meritage, Rubicon, that in its early vintages tended towards the powerful and rustic, but has since been reined in to display greater harmony and youthful appeal. It can still be aged for a decade. There is also Zinfandel Edizione Pennino and some mid-priced varietals under the Diamond Series label. Best years: (Rubicon) 2001, '00, '99, '97, '96, '95, '94, '91, '86.

NIEDERÖSTERREICH
AUSTRIA

The state of Niederösterreich or Lower Austria has a clutch of wine regions, notably the KAMPTAL, KREMSTAL and WACHAU, which have firmly established reputations for distinctive and high-quality, dry white wines. At the other extreme is the large, but comparatively unknown WEINVIERTEL region. New legislation will mean that the name Niederösterreich will start appearing on labels for the first time.

NIEPOORT
PORTUGAL, Douro, Douro DOC, Port DOC
♥ *Tempranillo (Tinta Roriz), Tinta Barroca, Tinta Cão, Touriga Nacional, Touriga Franca and others*
♀ *Gouveio, Viosinho, Rabigato, Malvasía Fina and others*

This small but very high-quality PORT company was founded in 1842 and is still family-run by Dirk van der Niepoort. Niepoort has earned a reputation for tawny ports, particularly the elegant, aromatic colheita wines (tawnies from a single year), which mature for many years in barrel before being bottled. Garrafeira ports are another speciality, wood-aged for five years, then transferred to glass demijohns for perhaps another 20 years, and finally into bottles. The vintage ports are excellent and long-lived. The company also produces a single-quinta vintage from Quinta do Passadouro deep in the Pinhão Valley. Late Bottled Vintages (unfiltered) are also extremely good and will develop well in bottle. Niepoort also produces several attractive rich DOURO reds and a pleasant white usually under the Redoma label. Best years: (Vintage) 2000, '97, '94, '92, '91, '87, '85, '83, '82, '80, '77, '70, '66, '63, '58, '55, '45, '42, '27.

NIERSTEIN
GERMANY, Rheinhessen

This famous wine town in the RHEINHESSEN is so famous that one third of the Rheinhessen basks in its reflected glory: this is the size of the Bereich Nierstein, which extends over the north-east of the region. Then there is Nierstein Gutes Domtal, a Grosslage covering 15 villages west of Nierstein itself, and including only one vineyard, Pfaffenkappe, which is technically part of Nierstein. Disgraceful, really. These Bereich and Grosslage wines have nothing to do with Nierstein's fine vineyards: they are unlikely to be more than basic, and will be from Müller-Thurgau or worse.

Nierstein itself boasts a string of steep vineyards with red slate soil, which can give richly fruity, intensely minerally Rieslings as great as any in Germany. Best years: 2002, '01, '00, '99, '98, '97, '96, '93. Best producers: Heinrich Braun, GUNDERLOCH, HEYL ZU HERRNSHEIM and St-Antony.

NIKOLAIHOF
AUSTRIA, Niederösterreich, Wachau
♀ *Riesling, Grüner Veltliner and others*

Nikolaihof is one of the WACHAU's top wine estates and Austria's leading biodynamic producer. Its owner Nikolaus Saahs and his wife Christine boast splendid, classic Rieslings and Grüner Veltliners that are several notches higher than most. The house (and chapel) are marvellous, and the courtyard is one of the most sympatico places anywhere to taste a glass of wine. Their most famous wine is the Riesling from the Steiner Hund vineyard: firm when young, it ages magnificently. Best years: (Steiner Hund Riesling Spätlese) 2002, '01, '99, '98, '97, '95, '94, '92, '91, '90, '86, '79, '77.

HANS & ANITA NITTNAUS
AUSTRIA, Burgenland, Neusiedlersee, Gols
♟ *Zweigelt, Blaufränkisch, Pinot Noir
(Blauburgunder), Cabernet Sauvignon, Merlot*
♀ *Sauvignon Blanc, Chardonnay, Welschriesling,
Neuburger*

Hans Nittnaus admits that white wine is something of a sideline for him, although his Sauvignon Blanc can have good gooseberry fruit and his Pannobile Weiss is a satisfyingly full, barrique-aged blend of Chardonnay, Neuburger and Sauvignon Blanc. The real thing for him is rip-roaring, full frontal red wine. The result used to be brutally hard monsters, but in recent years he has moderated both oak and tannin to great advantage. Best and most powerful is the Comondor, a rich plum and blackcurrant blend of Blaufränkisch and Cabernet, followed by the somewhat suppler, faster-maturing Pannobile Rot. Best years: 2000, '99, '97, '94, '93, '92.

NOBILO
NEW ZEALAND, North Island, Huapai
♟ *Merlot, Pinot Noir, Cabernet Sauvignon and others*
♀ *Sauvignon Blanc, Chardonnay, Müller-Thurgau,
Pinot Gris, Riesling and others*

I don't suppose that Croatian emigré Nikola Nobilo had this in mind when he fled the horrors of war in 1943 and planted some vines just outside Auckland (to provide his family with something to drink) but the Nobilo wine company is now part of Constellation, the biggest wine company in the world. Or perhaps Nikola wouldn't be so surprised. His family had been making wine for 300 years when he got to New Zealand, and the Nobilo boys, especially Nick, the CEO until 2000, were a super-confident, larger-than-life bunch who had built Nobilo into New Zealand's largest family-owned winery, before opting for the easy life. Importantly, they had developed good MARLBOROUGH Sauvignon and Hawkes Bay Cabernet and Chardonnay. When they bought Selaks in 1998, with their Drylands label, this cemented their strength in Marlborough. Constellation intend to nearly double production. Let's hope the quality survives.

NORTH COAST AVA
USA, California

North Coast AVA basically means pretty much anything north of San Francisco which one could describe as experiencing some kind of coastal influence. As such, it includes such great regions as NAPA and SONOMA, who would use their own AVA except in circum-

stances where they had blended wines from outside their immediate area. Given that virtually all the top-level wines in California like to boast at very least of a locality, if not an actual estate, the North Coast AVA is generally utilized for commercial blends. However, all the 15 AVAs it embraces are high quality, from ANDERSON and Potter Valleys in the north down to Sonoma and Napa Valleys and CARNEROS in the south, and North Coast on the label should mean there is no fruit from the bulk-producing regions like the Central Valley – which is something to be grateful for.

NORTON
ARGENTINA, Mendoza, Luján de Cuyo
♟ *Cabernet Sauvignon, Malbec, Merlot, Syrah,
Barbera, Sangiovese, Tempranillo, Petit Verdot, Tannat,
Cabernet Franc*
♀ *Sauvignon Blanc, Chardonnay, Semillon, Torrontes,
Chenin Blanc, Riesling*

Austrian millionaire Gernot Swarovski has ploughed a staggering fortune into Norton, based in Luján de Cuyo. Not only has he bought first-class vineyards (610ha/1507 acres) and just the right area for high-quality Malbec, he has established a high-tech winery to rival any. With single-minded perfectionist Michael Halstrick (Swarovski's step-son) in charge, I'm waiting to see major wines emerge from here but progress is slower than I'd expect, and too many of the wines seem to lack real definition. Already good are BORDEAUX blend Norton Privada, chewy Bonarda and Malbec, snappy Sauvignon and fragrant Torrontes.

NORTON
*The grape Torrontes is Argentina's white speciality,
producing aromatic, refreshing wines for drinking as
young as possible.*

QUINTA DO NOVAL
PORTUGAL, Douro, Douro DOC, Port DOC
♟ *Tempranillo (Tinta Roriz), Barroca, Tinto Cão,
Touriga Nacional, Touriga Franca and others*
♀ *Gouveio, Viosinho, Rabigato, Malvasía Fina
and others*

Quinta do Noval, one of the finest properties in the DOURO, is also the name of a PORT

shipper and belongs to the French insurance group AXA, who also have substantial wine interests in BORDEAUX. Noval is the first major port shipper to move lock, stock and barrel from Vila Nova de Gaia (the traditional home of the port business) to the Douro Valley where it has built an impressive, air-conditioned storage facility.

Noval produces a complete range of ports, all of which are of a high standard. But their most prestigious wine is their Nacional vintage port, made entirely from a 2.5-ha (6-acre) plot of low-yielding, ungrafted vines The wines are some of the most concentrated of all vintage ports, with a deep, opaque colour when young and an almost overpowering intensity of fruit.

In total there are 80ha (198 acres) planted on the estate. Noval has recently begun to produce its own unfortified DOURO wine under the Corucho label. Best years: (Nacional) 2000, '97, '94, '87, '85, '70, '66, '63, '62, '60, '31; (Vintage) 2000, '97, '95, '94, '91, '87, '85, '70, '66, '63, '60.

NUITS-ST-GEORGES AC
FRANCE, Burgundy, Côte de Nuits
♟ *Pinot Noir*
♀ *Chardonnay*

Nuits-St-Georges is one of the few relatively reliable 'village' names in BURGUNDY. The appellation, which includes the village of Prémeaux, is big, with 318ha (786 acres) of vines. Though it has no Grands Crus, there are 38 Premiers Crus (more than any other AC); many of them are extremely good. The wine can be rather slow to open out, often needing at least five years, but then it gains a lovely dry, plumskins chewiness which ages to a delicious deep figs-and-prune skins fruit, chocolaty, smoky and rather decayed. And of all the top Burgundy villages it's the one that's most likely to keep a very attractive savouriness as the wines age. Best years: (reds) 2002, '01, '00, '99, '98, '97, '96, '95, '93, '90. Best producers: de l'ARLOT, R Arnoux, J Chauvenet, R CHEVILLON, J-J Confuron, FAIVELEY, H GOUGES, GRIVOT, JAYER-GILLES, D LAURENT, MÉO-CAMUZET, A Michelot, G Mugneret, N Potel, M & P Rion, THOMAS-MOILLARD.

There are also minuscule amounts of a strange but delicious white Nuits-St-Georges, believe it or not. The few precious bottles made by Domaine Henri Gouges are the most famous whites made in the Côte de Nuits, where the red Pinot Noir is so completely dominant that the Gouges family doesn't even grow Chardonnay or Pinot

Blanc: the wines are made from a strange white mutation of Pinot Noir. Annual production is never more than 2500 bottles and often considerably less. Domaine de l'Arlot, Rion and Chevillon also make small quantities of white wine, but none to match the Gouges version for power and complexity.

NYETIMBER

ENGLAND, West Sussex

♀ ♀ *Chardonnay, Pinot Noir, Pinot Meunier*

This estate, originally named in the eleventh-century Domesday Book, was rescued by two expatriate Chicagoans, Stuart and Sandy Moss, who not only restored the rundown buildings, but, against the advice of the Ministry of Agriculture, planted vines (mostly Chardonnay) on well-drained greensand over chalk. There are now over 20ha (50 acres) of vines. First production of the CHAMPAGNE-method fizz was an exciting Chardonnay Blanc de Blancs in 1992. Subsequent vintages include Pinot Noir and Meunier in the blend. Classic Cuvée, the Chardonnay-Pinot blend, spends at least six years on its lees. Aurora Cuvée Blanc de Blancs is good too. The Mosses now only retain a consultancy role, and the wines have been less starry of late, but I very much hope the fantastic quality of their early releases will soon be repeated.

NYETIMBER
This Sussex estate quickly gained a reputation for high-quality sparkling wines and showed the potential of English wines.

OAKVILLE AVA

USA, California, Napa County, Napa Valley

This central part of the NAPA VALLEY around the town of Oakville is cooler than RUTHERFORD, which lies immediately to the north. Planted primarily to Cabernet Sauvignon, the area contains some of the best vineyards, both on the valley floor (MONDAVI, OPUS ONE, SCREAMING EAGLE) and hillsides (HARLAN ESTATE, DALLA VALLE), producing wines that display lush, ripe black fruits and firm tannins. There is also sometimes a thrilling streak of minty, eucalyptus perfume, first made famous by HEITZ Martha's Vineyard Cabernets. But how different it really is from

neighbour Rutherford will keep wine buffs happily arguing for years. Best years: (Cabernet Sauvignon) 2001, '00, '99, '97, '96, '95, '94, '91, '90.

VIN DE PAYS D'OC

FRANCE, Languedoc-Roussillon

Covering the huge area of the LANGUEDOC-ROUSSILLON, the Vin de Pays d'Oc has become the symbol of the Midi's new liberated, modern, high-tech image. It has also ballooned into a formidable commercial success and now represents 35 per cent of all French VINS DE PAYS – with a production of about 530 million bottles a year. The achievement is due in large part to the decision to produce New World-style reds and whites, using internationally successful varieties such as Merlot, Cabernet Sauvignon, Syrah, Chardonnay, Sauvignon Blanc and Viognier. Other grape varieties include Pinot Noir and the southern varieties such as Grenache, Mourvèdre, Cinsaut and Carignan for reds and rosés and Marsanne, Roussanne and Rolle for the whites.

Heavyweight local producers like SKALLI and VAL D'ORBIEU have given impetus to the movement and have been complemented by the arrival of outside investors and talented winemakers from Australia, England and Switzerland. But Vin de Pays d'Oc on the label still doesn't guarantee higher quality – there's lots of thin, poor Cabernet and Chardonnay that qualifies each year. Until they institute minimum quality standards, Vin de Pays d'Oc will still be a work in progress. Best producers: de l'AIGLE, de la Baume (whites), Clovallon, Herrick, J Lurton, Maris, Mas Crémat, Ormesson, Pech-Céleyran (Viognier), Quatre Sous, St-Saturnin, Skalli, Val d'Orbieu (top reds), Virginie.

OCKFEN

GERMANY, Mosel-Saar-Ruwer

This SAAR village boasts a good few top producers, such as the St Urbans-Hof, ZILLIKEN and Dr Heinz Wagner, but like most of the Saar, it needs a good warm year if the wines are not to turn out a bit green or raw. In such good years, however, they are immensely long-lived, never losing their cold, steely streak, but packed with piercing, full-flavoured fruit. Bockstein is the top vineyard site, planted mostly with Riesling and capable of producing some very stylish wines. Best years: 2002, '01, '99, '97, '95, '93, '90, '89. Best producers: Dr Fischer, von KESSELSTATT, St Urbans-Hof, Dr Heinz Wagner, Zilliken.

OKANAGAN VALLEY

CANADA, British Columbia

Roughly 80 per cent of BRITISH COLUMBIA's 2024ha (5000 acres) of vineyards are situated in the Okanagan Valley and plantings are increasing fast. A spectacular semi-arid region, the valley runs some 120km (75 miles) along the shores of Lake Okanagan from the town of Vernon in the north, to Penticton in the south. From here it heads south all the way to the WASHINGTON STATE border. Over 40 wineries produce a wide range of still and sparkling wines made from Chardonnay, Pinot Blanc, Pinot Gris, Gewurztraminer, Pinot Noir, Merlot, Gamay, Syrah and Cabernet Sauvignon. Though ONTARIO often hogs the limelight in Canada, I believe that many of Canada's great reds and dry whites will come from the Okanagan. Best years: (reds) 2001, '00, '98. Best producers: BLUE MOUNTAIN, BURROWING OWL, Gehringer, INNISKILLIN, MISSION HILL, QUAILS' GATE, SUMAC RIDGE, Tinhorn Creek.

OLTREPÒ PAVESE DOC

ITALY, Lombardy

♥ *Barbera, Bonarda, Pinot Noir (Pinot Nero)*

♥ *Pinot Noir (Pinot Nero)*

♀ *Cortese, Muscat (Moscato), Pinot Gris (Pinot Grigio), Pinot Noir (Pinot Nero), Welschriesling (Riesling Italico), Riesling (Riesling Renano)*

The Oltrepò ('over the Po') Pavese ('in Pavia province') is one of just two patches of LOMBARDY lying south of the lumbering Po river. Its soft, rolling hills bring blessed relief from the humidity and fog of the Po valley. Many of the wines here are single varietal and for drinking young, mainly in the bars and restaurants of nearby Milan.

Given a choice from all these varieties, the best and most typical are Bonarda, Barbera or white Moscato, or the straight Oltrepò Pavese Rosso (Bonarda with Barbera, Uva Rara, Ughetta). If from one of three sub-zones, the Rosso glories in the additional names of Barbacarlo, Buttafuoco or Sangue di Giuda. With all these, varietals and blends, reds and whites, there is a strong tendency for the wines to be a bit fizzy; that's how they like them there. Hardly surprisingly in this land where bubble is king, there's plenty of Spumante, best from Pinot-type grapes. The best wines here are good rather than great. Best years: (reds) 2001, '00, '99, '98, '97, '96, '95. Best producers: Cà di Frara, Le Fracce, Frecciarossa, Fugazza, Mazzolino, Monsupello (sparkling wines), Montelio, Vercesi del Castellazzo, Bruno Verdi.

ONTARIO

CANADA

There are several reasons to explain Ontario's dominant position in Canadian wine. Its vineyards lie between 42 and 43.5°N – which in European terms is the equivalent of CORSICA and the LANGUEDOC. That's great for summer sun but Ontario is hundreds of miles from the sea so winters should be brutal. Enter another reason – the Great Lakes – especially Lake Ontario and the shallow warm Lake Erie. They crucially temper the climate. And there's Toronto.

Now we're getting to the heart of the matter. Throughout history until literally the last few decades, vineyards were planted near the centres of population, regardless of suitability. Ontario is Canada's most populous province, with Toronto its biggest city. And just around the corner, nicely cossetted between Lakes Ontario and Erie is the NIAGARA PENINSULA. It is suited to vineyards and has produced some fine wines but the primary reason that it's there is because there was a market for its wares nearby. There are those who argue that Pelee Island, actually in Lake Erie, or the Lake Erie North shore, might be even better, but Niagara effortlessly dominates the local scene, not only for reds and whites but also for that Canadian speciality Icewine, made from grapes left to freeze on the vine as those winters (quite brutal enough, thank you) kick in.

WILLI OPITZ

AUSTRIA, Burgenland, Neusiedlersee, Illmitz

Pinot Noir (Blauburgunder), Blaufränkish, Zweigelt

Pinot Gris (Grauburgunder), Welschriesling, Scheurebe, Muskat Ottonel, Pinot Blanc (Weissburgunder), Gewürztraminer, Grüner Veltliner

Opitz is an eccentric Austrian grower from Illmitz in NEUSIEDLERSEE; as one would expect from this part of the country near Lake Neusiedl, he specializes in sweet wines. There are dry wines as well, and good reds, but even Grüner Veltliner gets turned into Auslese or Beerenauslese, and grapes (red and white) that are unaffected by noble rot are liable to become Schilfwein, or 'reed' wine, an Opitz 'original'. You'd be hard put to find much about Schilfwein in the Austrian rule book, because it is Opitz's own idea: it involves drying ripe grapes on reeds to concentrate their sugar before fermentation. The principle is similar to that of the region's Strohwein, or 'straw' wine, but the quality is higher.

WILLI OPITZ
Schilfwein, made from grapes dried on reeds from the shores of the nearby Lake Neusiedl, is one of Opitz's more unusual wines. The sweet white wine is remarkably intense.

OPPENHEIM

GERMANY, Rheinhessen

Oppenheim is in the best area of RHEINHESSEN, the Rheinfront on the Rhine banks just south of NIERSTEIN. Good, refined wines come from the Sackträger vineyard site; Herrenberg and Kreuz, part of which is in the village of Dienheim, are also distinguished. What is less exciting is the Krötenbrunnen Grosslage, which covers about 1800ha (4448 acres). It is largely either flat or very nearly flat, and is used mostly for simple QbA wines of little interest. Best years: 2002, '01, '99, '98, '97, '96. Best producers: Carl Koch Erben, Louis Guntrum, Kühling-Gillot, Staatsweingut mit Weinbaudomäne (a research institute with umpteen new crossings in its vineyards).

OPUS ONE

USA, California, Napa County, Napa Valley AVA

Cabernet Sauvignon, Cabernet Franc, Merlot and others

In 1969 the MONDAVI family and Baron Philippe de Rothschild (of Ch. MOUTON-ROTHSCHILD fame) joined together to see if a red BORDEAUX-style wine could be made that was neither purely CALIFORNIAn nor imitation Bordeaux, but a synthesis of the two. In most years this ultra-expensive wine could be legally identified as a varietal Cabernet Sauvignon, but it never has been, in order to preserve the freedom to blend in Merlot, Petit Verdot, Malbec or Cabernet Franc.

The early vintages (1979 was the first) were supple and oaky; more recent ones have perhaps been more tannic, but in general Opus One does a very good job in creating a laudable and attractive cultural hybrid that still bears witness to the warmer climate of the NAPA VALLEY, yet captures some of the clear-eyed, cedary, cool-fruited classicism of a fine PAUILLAC. At first, Opus One was priced insanely, but now with so many similarly priced competitors, the wine, which has only got better, doesn't seem quite so expensive. Best years: 2001, '00, '99, '98, '97, '96, '95, '94, '93, '92, '91, '90, '86, '85, '84.

OPUS ONE
This is a consistent, high-quality Bordeaux-style blend from the Napa Valley. Concentrated and with loads of tannin, the wine acquires delicacy and finesse with age.

ORANGE

AUSTRALIA, New South Wales

This important fruit region has diversified into wine in a big way, with a mix of small producers and a huge, single 900-ha (2224-acre) vineyard development at Molong called Little Boomey. Cabonne (owners of Reynolds) have built a large winery to process the grapes for various Reynolds brands. Altitude (between 600 and 900m/1970 and 2950ft) and cold nights are the key to the elegant yet flavoursome Chardonnays and the dry, warm autumns to the dark berry, briary, herbaceous Cabernet family – and a lovely Malbec-based rosé from Bloodwood. Best (local) producers: Bloodwood, Brangayne of Orange, Canobolas-Smith, Highland Heritage Estate, Logan.

DOMAINE DE L'ORATOIRE ST-MARTIN

FRANCE, Southern Rhône, Côtes du Rhône-Villages AC

Grenache, Mourvèdre, Syrah, Counoise

Marsanne, Roussanne, Clairette, Viognier, Muscat

In 1936 Frédéric Alary became the first grower in Cairanne to bottle his own wines. Today his descendants, the brothers Frédéric and François, are determined to keep this domaine in the forefront of southern RHÔNE estates. Although all the 25ha (62 acres) of vineyards lie within Cairanne, not all are bottled with the Villages appellation. The basic Cairanne wine, called Réserve, is made from much older vines as well as an invigorating percentage of Mourvèdre. The Cuvée Prestige has even more Mourvèdre and is intended for medium-term aging. The only wine aged in barriques is the Cuvée Haut-Coustias. The most intriguing white is the Haut-Coustias, which is pure Marsanne, fermented and aged in barrels. Best years: (Cuvée Prestige) 2001, '00, '99, '98, '97, '96, '95, '94, '90, '89.

OREGON USA

To a stunning degree, Oregon's young wine industry has put its eggs in one basket, that of Pinot Noir from the Willamette Valley, and one must search diligently to find out about Oregon Riesling and Cabernet Sauvignon as well as the other wine regions, the Umpqua and Rogue Valleys.

Though there were faint glimmerings before and after America's Prohibition in the 1920s, successful winemaking in Oregon really dates from 1972 to 1973, when the first few expatriates from California came to the Willamette Valley thinking they had found the new Burgundy. Richard Erath of Erath Vineyards and David Lett of Eyrie both planted vineyards near the town of Dundee, while William Fuller of Tualatin sought out the rolling hills a little further north near Forest Grove. By 1980, everyone had decided that Pinot Noir was the path to fame. Apart from some producers of Champagne-method sparkling wines, not one of the wineries within the adjacent counties of Washington and Yamhill has tried to make its primary reputation on another wine.

And have they found a new Burgundy in the distant Pacific Northwest? Well, what they do seem to have done is discover an area that does virtually mirror the bad side of Burgundy – poor weather at flowering, unreliable summer sunshine and heat, strong likelihood of vintage-time rain and the rest. What they have not done is to find somewhere that mirrors the Burgundian conditions that produce the greatest Burgundian wines. Too many of the Pinot Noirs have been almost self-consciously light in colour and texture, thereby aping a Burgundian myth – that all their red wines are delicate and fragrant. Many of the best modern Burgundies are in fact robust, richly textured and sensuous in a positively full-blooded way. These are the styles that Oregon should try to emulate – and indeed producers like Rex Hill and Domaine Drouhin do just that with conspicuous success.

And there is another side to Oregon. Before the Willamette pioneers had begun to operate, Richard Sommer, who had different visions, had set up Hillcrest Vineyard in the Umpqua Valley west of Roseburg. His choice was less immediately rewarded by the public clamour that attended the state's first dozen Pinot Noir vintages from the Willamette Valley. The Umpqua may have come along more slowly, but it has still come along. Oregon's other wine regions are smaller still, and even more recent. The warmer Rogue Valley has 11 small wineries, and only approximately 470ha (1168 acres) of vineyards. It has a sub-region called Applegate Valley, created in 2000, and we should see more of these micro-regions emerge over the next few years. And in the north-east corner Walla Walla, shared with Washington State, produces powerful, warm-climate wines.

Pinot Noir plantings make up about half of a vineyard total of 4896ha (12,100 acres), so it's no surprise that it remains the focus of attention. Among whites, Pinot Gris is now making waves. Eyrie and Ponzi are two of the wineries who saw the trend. Many others are following. If all of this sounds small, it is, even despite rapid expansion. All of Oregon has less than one-third the vineyard acreage of the Napa Valley alone, and its largest winery would not appear in Napa's top 20. Oregon's founding winemakers were, for the most part, undercapitalized yet idealistic refugees from California. They set strict labelling laws in place and also made smallness a prime virtue. Since the late 1980s several overseas wine companies, in particular, Burgundy's Robert Drouhin (Domaine

The Dundee Hills, an important sub-region of the Willamette Valley, is noted for its steep hillsides and red volcanic soils. Many of Oregon's leading producers for both Pinot Noir and sparkling wine are based here.

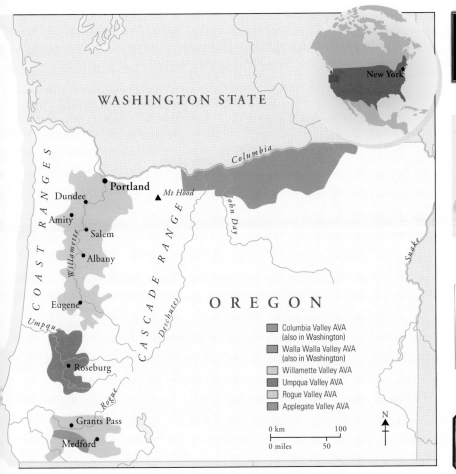

ARCHERY SUMMIT
The focus here is on deeply coloured, heavily oaked Pinot Noir. Red Hills is one of several single-vineyard wines.

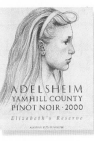

ADELSHEIM VINEYARD
Adelsheim established a reputation for excellent, generally unfiltered Pinot Noir, especially cherry-scented Elizabeth Reserve.

CRISTOM
As with most Oregon wineries, Pinot Noir is the main focus at Cristom, a bright new star on the Oregon wine scene.

BETHEL HEIGHTS
Bethel Heights' Flat Block site produces their most elegant Pinot Noir yet with a core of power.

Drouhin) and Champagne's Laurent-Perrier, have begun to invest in the Willamette Valley, spurred on by its reputation for Pinot Noir and by the relatively low cost of vineyard land. This international influence, and a clutch of fine vintages around 2000, seems finally to have persuaded Oregon to give up its Burgundian obsession – and just be the best it can be.

KEN WRIGHT CELLARS
Ken Wright has fostered single-vineyard bottlings of Pinot Noir, including one from the Guadalupe Vineyard.

REGIONAL ENTRY
Willamette Valley.

PRODUCER ENTRIES
Archery Summit Winery, Beaux Frères, Bethel Heights, Cristom, Domaine Drouhin, The Eyrie Vineyards, King Estate, Panther Creek, Ponzi Vineyards, Rex Hill Vineyards, WillaKenzie Estate, Ken Wright Cellars.

PANTHER CREEK
Along with excellent Pinot Noir, Panther Creek makes delicious Pinot Gris from Umpqua Valley grapes which ripen beautifully in southern Oregon's sunnier climate.

DOMAINE DROUHIN
The beautifully scented Laurène is capable of surpassing many of Drouhin's own top Burgundies, and is regularly one of Oregon's finest Pinot Noirs.

ELK COVE VINEYARDS
The Reserve Pinot Noirs from this winery, including La Bohème, compete with the finest in Oregon and are bottled, unfined and unfiltered.

ORLANDO

AUSTRALIA, South Australia, Barossa Valley

❦ *Syrah (Shiraz), Cabernet Sauvignon, Merlot, Grenache, Pinot Noir and others*

♀ *Chardonnay, Semillon, Riesling, Verdelho, Viognier, Sauvignon Blanc*

Owned by the French Pernod-Ricard group, Orlando Wyndham is Australia's third-biggest wine company and is responsible for some of the most valuable and well-known wine names in Australia – Coolabah boxed wines, Wyndham Estate and above all the international superstar Jacob's Creek. In 1993 Jacob's Creek became the UK's biggest brand of bottled wine – and is now a worldwide phenomenon, with sales of 5.9 million bottles.

And why the success? Wines of total consistency – consistently attractive and easy to drink, consistently reasonable in price. The basic Jacob's Creek red – loosely based on the BORDEAUX varieties from a number of different sources – and the basic white – a pleasant, soft, off-dry Semillon-Chardonnay blend – have now been supplemented by a pleasant-flavoured, pleasant-priced Chardonnay, a rather good spicy, limy Riesling, a Grenache and various Shiraz, Merlot and Cabernet permutations, as well as a sparkling Chardonnay-Pinot Noir and very classy Jacob's Creek Reserve and Limited Release wines.

There is a range of other Orlando labels – some traditional and high quality such as St Helga Rhine Riesling, St Hugo Cabernet Sauvignon and St Hilary Chardonnay, Steingarten Rhine Riesling, Lawson's Shiraz and Jacaranda Ridge Cabernet Sauvignon. Orlando also owns MORRIS (RUTHERGLEN), Russet Ridge (WRATTONBULLY), Wickham Hill (NEW SOUTH WALES), Gramp's and Richmond Grove in the BAROSSA VALLEY and Poet's Corner in MUDGEE which also produces the Montrose and Henry Lawson brands. Wyndham Estate in the HUNTER VALLEY is now showing some improvement. Best years: (St Hugo Cabernet) 2000, '99, '98, '96, '94, '92, '91, '90, '88, '86.

TENUTA DELL'ORNELLAIA

ITALY, Tuscany, Bolgheri DOC

❦ *Cabernet Sauvignon, Merlot, Sangiovese, Cabernet Franc*

♀ *Sauvignon Blanc*

This beautiful estate situated in the heart of BOLGHERI in TUSCANY's coastal area called the Maremma was developed by Lodovico ANTINORI, brother of Piero, in 1981 after he left the family firm of Antinori to strike out on his own. He is also the nephew of Marchese Niccolò Incisa della Rocchetta, the owner of the neighbouring Tenuta San Guido estate which produces the world-famous SASSICAIA. The original wine, called simply Ornellaia, is a blend mainly of Cabernet Sauvignon with Merlot, and a little Cabernet Franc. The first release was in 1985, but it was the superb 1990 that confirmed it as one of the benchmarks of Italian winemaking.

Since then Ornellaia has almost been overtaken as the winery's sexiest product by Masseto, solely from Merlot, for an allocation of which wine merchants worldwide are prepared to grovel in the dirt (not to mention buy a load of other wines which they don't want). There is also an excellent white from Sauvignon Blanc called Poggio alle Gazze; and two other red wines, Le Volte, mainly from Sangiovese with Cabernet Sauvignon and Cabernet Franc, and Le Serre Nuove, mainly Cabernet Sauvignon with some Merlot. The estate was bought by MONDAVI in 2002, so let's hope the quality remains high. Best years: (Ornellaia) 2001, '00, '99, '98, '97, '96, '95, '94, '93, '90, '88.

ORTENAU

GERMANY, Baden

The Ortenau region covers a chain of steep granitic hills facing the French city of Strasbourg across the river Rhine. You'll find some of BADEN's best Rieslings here, often under its local name of Klingelberger, and particularly in the hills around DURBACH. There is also some nice fruity Spätburgunder (Pinot Noir) red, but traditionally this area has been better at producing rosé. Best producers: Andreas Laible, Nägelsförst, Schloss Neuweier.

ORVIETO DOC

ITALY, Lazio and Umbria

♀ *Trebbiano Toscano (Procanico), Verdello, Grechetto and others*

Orvieto used to be seen mainly as a medium-dry wine with a hint of crystallized sultanas and honey in its make-up. There is even on occasion some quite delectable honeyed sweet Orvieto, made by grapes affected by noble rot. ANTINORI's Muffato della Sala is the best known and Barberani's Calcaia, Decugnano dei Barbi's Pourriture Noble and Palazzone's Muffa Nobile are also excellent. Usually, though, Orvieto is dry.

Trebbiano (locally called Procanico) at the head of the list of grape varieties isn't good news. But Grechetto is the saviour, giving a much-needed dollop of nuttiness and green fruits to the wine. With the right vineyard site in the central Classico area, low yields and proper attention Orvieto really can pull something out of the bag. Generally it's made for drinking young. Best producers: (dry) Barberani-Vallesanta, La Carraia, Decugnano dei Barbi, Palazzone, Castello della Sala/ ANTINORI, Salviano, Conte Vaselli, Le Velette; (sweet) Barberani-Vallesanta, Decugnano dei Barbi, Palazzone, Castello della Sala.

OSBORNE

SPAIN, Andalucía, Jerez y Manzanilla DO

♀ *Palomino Fino, Pedro Ximénez*

Osborne, the biggest drinks company in Spain, has the potential to make fino sherry of very high quality, based as it is in the seaside town of Puerto de Santa María (in 40 delightful whitewashed bodegas in the old town centre). Flor grows thicker here than in JEREZ, so that resultant sherries can be finer and tangier. Osborne's raw materials are good, too: two-thirds of the grapes come from its own top-quality *albariza* vineyards. Fino Quinta is light and creamy, young but pleasant. Amontillado Coquinero and rich Bailén Oloroso are properly nutty and dry.

OVERBERG WO

SOUTH AFRICA, Western Cape

South Africans are continually searching for cool vineyard positions right round their shores, but Overberg, reaching down to Walker Bay in the south, almost up to ROBERTSON in the north and encompassing the high altitude apple-cum-vineyard region of ELGIN is both the original cool region and one of the most consistently good. Apart from some vines near Cape Agulhas, Walker Bay has South Africa's most southerly vines, building on the pioneering work of HAMILTON RUSSELL near the seaside town of Hermanus. Increasing amounts of fine Pinot Noir and Chardonnay are now appearing. Elgin adds Riesling to these two, but other varieties – Sauvignon, Semillon and even Shiraz and Pinotage are also making an appearance. Best years: (Pinot Noir) 2001, '00, '99, '98, '97. Best producers: (Elgin) Paul Cluver, Neil ELLIS; (Walker Bay) BOUCHARD FINLAYSON, Hamilton Russell, Newton Johnson.

OVERGAAUW

SOUTH AFRICA, Western Cape, Stellenbosch WO

❦ *Cabernet Sauvignon, Merlot, Cabernet Franc, Syrah (Shiraz), Tinta Barroca and others*

♀ *Chardonnay, Sauvignon Blanc, Sylvaner*

It's easy to overlook this low-profile producer but if the course is set to 'steady as you go' and the wines are gently undramatic, that in no way indicates a lack of progress nor innovation. Proprietor, Braam van Velden, bottled South Africa's first varietal Merlot and first Touriga Nacional vintage port-style. His Sylvaner remains unique in the Cape, while an imaginative Pinotage-Cabernet Franc blend has resulted in a friendly, fruity combination. Van Velden's father was one of the first to experiment with small oak barrels. These are now commonplace in the cellar, where winemaker, Chris Joubert, uses them sensitively on the slow-developing Cabernet, the BORDEAUX-blend Tria Corda and increasingly elegant Chardonnay. Best years: (reds) 1998, '97, '96, '95.

PAARL WO

SOUTH AFRICA, Western Cape

Paarl's enormous historic importance was based on the giant KWV, one of the world's largest wineries, being there, along with KWV's political power. But it's a very diverse region, with many different soils and climates, though these all tend to be on the warm side.

So far only two wards have been delineated among the 17,374ha (42,931 acres) of vineyards in Paarl. Franschhoek is at the top of the Berg Valley, a beautiful region ringed by mountains where the Huguenots settled in the seventeenth century. This isn't that cool, but since Paarl is fairly hot it passes for cool. WELLINGTON is at the north side of Paarl and its importance in the old days as a 'sherry' producer tells you this is pretty warm, but excellent wineries like Linton Park and Diemersfontein can find places cool enough for top grapes. In between these, the north side of the Simonsberg mountain is proving to have some surprisingly cool sites. Wineries like GLEN CARLOU exploit them. Though less fashionable than STELLENBOSCH, Paarl is tremendously important, both for the past and the future of South African wines. Best years: (premium reds) 2001, '00, '99, '98, '97. Best producers: (Paarl) Boschendal, DISTELL

FAIRVIEW
Fairview is best known for its many wines from Rhône varieties. Goats do Roam, a spoof on Côtes du Rhône, is a blend of local Pinotage with southern Rhône grapes.

(Plaisir de Merle, Nederburg), FAIRVIEW, Glen Carlou, Rupert & Rothschild, VEENWOUDEN, VILLIERA, Welgemeend; (Wellington) Diemersfontein, Mont du Toit.

PACHERENC DU VIC BILH AC

FRANCE, South-West

♀ *Gros Manseng, Petit Manseng, Ruffiac and Courbu*

Pacherenc is local dialect for *piquets en rang* or 'posts in a line', and Vic Bilh are the local hills. So the name literally translates as 'posts in a line from the Vic Bilh hills' – a reference to the local habit of training vines very high on tall posts. Whatever the explanation it still does not do much for one's thirst. But actually the wine, sometimes medium-dry or sweet but usually dry, can have an exciting flavour of pears and apricots – especially if bottled straight off its lees. The production is tiny, but overall quality is very good. Most of the top MADIRAN estates produce excellent Pacherenc du Vic Bilh. The sweeter versions can be aged a little and the dry is for drinking young. Best years: 2001, '00, '97, '96, '95. Best producers: d'Aydie, Berthoumieu, Brumont (Ch. Bouscassé, Ch. MONTUS), du Crampilh, Damiens, Laffitte-Teston, Producteurs PLAIMONT, Sergent.

PADTHAWAY

AUSTRALIA, South Australia

SEPPELT was the first company to grow grapes here, in 1963, armed with a government soil study showing great banks of limestone; LINDEMANS and HARDY followed in 1968, and then WYNNS. The soil proved to be terra rossa over limestone, making it effectively a replica of nearby COONAWARRA. The climate is marginally warmer than Coonawarra's, but that hasn't prevented it rapidly achieving the status of one of Australia's most exciting and most reliable wine areas. Initially it was fêted as a white wine area producing stunning Chardonnay and Riesling but more recently it has produced a string of top reds, notably Shiraz. Best producers: Browns of Padthaway, Hardy, Henry's Drive, Lindemans, ORLANDO, Padthaway Estate, SEPPELT.

PAHLMEYER WINERY

USA, California, Napa County, Napa Valley AVA

❢ *Cabernet Sauvignon, Merlot, Cabernet Franc, Malbec, Petit Verdot*

♀ *Chardonnay*

Unlike many of his NAPA VALLEY colleagues, former trial attorney Jayson Pahlmeyer makes his wines in a no-frills winery which frees capital to invest in grapes, equipment and

winemaking expertise. Starting in 1986 Randy Dunn made his first few excellent vintages; in 1993 Helen Turley (see MARCASSIN) took over the BORDEAUX blend Proprietary Red and delivered a wine with layers of voluptuous flavours and an ability to age for eight to ten years; now the role has passed to Erin Green. A splendid, multi-layered, unctuous Merlot joined the roster in the late 1990s. Chardonnay continues the rich, ultra-ripe style Pahlmeyer favours. One of the reasons Pahlmeyer's red stood out was that he was one of the first to champion grapes from Coombsville in the hills east of Napa which have proved to have a very special character. Pahlmeyer has recently acquired a 89-ha (220-acre) property in the ATLAS PEAK AVA, also part of Napa, as well as a Pinot Noir property in the SONOMA COAST AVA.

BRUNO PAILLARD

FRANCE, Champagne AC, Champagne

♀ *Chardonnay, Pinot Noir, Pinot Meunier*

Bruno Paillard is one of the very few individuals who has created a new CHAMPAGNE house in the past century. He is also a major shareholder in BCC, a company owning Philipponnat among other Champagne houses. Paillard buys in the majority of its grapes and owns only a small domaine in the Côte des Blancs which supplies less than five per cent of the Chardonnay required. The non-vintage is lemony and crisp, the Réserve Privée is a Blanc de Blancs, similarly austere; the vintage Brut is a little richer, and Nec Plus Ultra is a barrel-fermented blend of seven Grands Crus from the 1990 vintage. Best years: 1996, '95, '90, '89, '88.

PAÍS VASCO

SPAIN

Were it not for the 12,000ha (29,700 acres) of RIOJA land in the Alavesa sub-region, which administratively belong to the autonomous Basque community, Spain's Basque Country (País Vasco in Castilian, Euskadi or Euskal Herria in Basque) wouldn't count for much in the wine world. But Rioja Alavesa, with powerful financial and technical assistance from the regional government, channelled through the Laguardia enological station, has made great strides recently. Dozens of small growers have been encouraged to become wine producers as well. Some of them (ARTADI, Fernando Remírez de Ganuza, Primicia, Luis Cañas, Luis Ángel Casado, Solagüen, Luberri, San Pedro) have come to join the older, élite bodegas in the area such as MARQUÉS DE RISCAL, PALACIO, CONTINO, REMELLURI or CAMPILLO. With its pale, chalky soils under the protection of the Sierra Cantabria mountains, Alavesa's terroir is much like Rioja Alta, and so are the wines.

Further north, right on the Bay of Biscay, there are 315ha (778 acres) of vineyards making pale, spritzy wines that are the Basque answer to VINHO VERDE, and can actually be very attractive when the harvest is truly ripe in hot years. They occupy three DOs – the newer Bizkaiko Txakolina and Arabako Txakolina and the larger and better known GETARIAKO TXAKOLINA, where the native Hondarrabi Zuri white is prevalent.

BODEGAS PALACIO

SPAIN, País Vasco, Rioja DOCa

🍷 🍷 Tempranillo
🍷 Macabeo (Viura)

Jean Gervais, who revolutionized this sleepy bodega in the late 1980s, sold it to the RIBERA DEL DUERO winery, Viña Mayor in 1998. Gervais introduced new Allier and Nevers oak barrels to Palacio. That, plus advice from Michel Rolland, the well-known POMEROL enologist, gave some of the younger wines a distinctly French character. The Cosme Palacio red is plummy and soft, with good, savoury oak flavour, whereas the traditional Glorioso Crianza and Reserva wines are jammier, though still full of rich, plum-pudding fruit. The Glorioso Gran Reserva is even better, rich and plummy with a fine, wild strawberry overtone. Best years: 1996, '95, '94, '91.

ÁLVARO PALACIOS

SPAIN, Cataluña, Priorat DOCa

🍷 Grenache Noir (Garnacha Tinta), Cariñena, Cabernet Sauvignon, Syrah, Merlot

The scion of an old RIOJA Baja family was ready, by his mid-20s, for an adventure somewhere else. He had already trained with Christian Moueix of Ch. PÉTRUS in BORDEAUX, he had been in the oak barrel trade and he was obsessed with making world-class wine. He was the youngest member of the group that revolutionized the PRIORAT region, and a dozen years later he is the best known of the group. In his futuristic winery he produces a top, modern Priorat blend, Finca Dofí and, from bought-in grapes, Les Terrasses which is outstanding value. But his star wine comes from the best 5ha (12 acres) of his 35ha (86 acres) of vineyards: the 50-year-old-vine L'Ermita. A powerful wine, it shares the spotlight with Peter Sisseck's PINGUS from RIBERO DEL DUERO as modern Spain's leading cult wine

and for now at least, the dubious honour of being Spain's most expensive bottle. He's also started a new project in the little known BIERZO DO producing a wine called Corullon, and he's been doing a lot of work back in Rioja as well – with his family bodega Palacios Remondo. Best years: 2000, '99, '98, '97, '96, '95, '94, '93.

PALETTE AC

FRANCE, Provence

🍷 🍷 Grenache, Mourvèdre, Cinsaut, Syrah and others
🍷 Clairette, Grenache Blanc, Ugni Blanc and others

Pine needles and resin are what you taste in the wines of Palette – a tiny AC hidden away in the pine forests just east of Aix-en-Provence. Not that the local winemakers actually employ these to make the wine, but the slopes on which the 40ha (99 acres) of vines grow are covered in pines and herbs. The rosé is herby and rather dry, and the red: well, herby again, and tough, needing several years' bottle age to even hint at a softer side.

But Palette can be proud of one achievement. Given the basic neutral bunch of southern French white grapes, Ch. SIMONE, the only producer of white Palette, has managed to squeeze more flavour out of this motley crew than any other AC. Its success must be due to Palette's limestone soil and the wine's two years' sojourn in oak barrels. Like the red, it benefits from four or five years' bottle age. Best producers: Crémade, Simone.

PALLISER ESTATE

NEW ZEALAND, North Island, Martinborough

🍷 Pinot Noir
🍷 Sauvignon Blanc, Chardonnay, Riesling, Pinot Gris

State-of-the-art winery and the largest in the Wairarapa, producing some of New Zealand's best Sauvignon (certainly the best outside MARLBOROUGH) and Riesling, with delicate Chardonnay, honeyed Pinot Gris and some impressive, rich-textured Pinot Noir (also usually one of New Zealand's best). Exciting botrytized dessert wines appear in favourable vintages. Méthode fizz is also impressive. Best years: (Pinot Noir) 2002, '01, '00, '99, '98.

PALMELA DOC

PORTUGAL, Terras do Sado

🍷 🍷 Castelão (Periquita), Alfrocheiro, Bastardo, Cabernet Sauvignon, Trincadeira (Tinta Amarela)
🍷 Arinto (Pederñã), Fernão Pires (Maria Gomes), Moscatel, Rabo de Ovelha and others

The sandy plain surrounding the hill-top town of Palmela is ideally suited to the red Periquita grape. Local winemakers J M da

FONSECA and J P VINHOS and talented interloper BRIGHT BROS produce many wines but Periquita is the mainstay for some distinctive raspberryish reds which gain in complexity with age. Caves ALIANÇA also makes a good red, 'Palmela Particular'. Best years: 2001, '00, '99, '97, '95. Best producers: Caves Aliança, Bright Bros, José Maria da Fonseca, Pegos Claros, J P Vinhos.

CH. PALMER

FRANCE, Bordeaux, Haut-Médoc, Margaux AC, 3ème Cru Classé

🍷 Cabernet Sauvignon, Merlot, Petit Verdot

Of all the properties that could justifiably feel underrated by the 1855 BORDEAUX Classification, Ch. Palmer has traditionally had the best case. Its reputation is based, above all, on its perfume. It is as though every black and red fruit in the land has thrown in its ripest scent: blackcurrant, blackberry, plum, loganberry. But Palmer can go further. Sometimes there's a rich, almost fat core to the wine; and curling through the fruit and the ripeness are trails of other fragrances – roses, violets, cedar and cigars, all in abundance. Sometimes.

There was a period in the 1960s and '70s when Palmer held aloft the banner of brilliance for the MARGAUX AC virtually single-handed. However, as properties like Ch. MARGAUX itself and RAUZAN-SÉGLA soared to new heights during the 1980s and '90s, Palmer became lighter, less substantial, its fabled perfume now struggling without the original core of sweetness. There were still some notable successes in the 1980s, like '89, but the 1990 disappointingly failed to find top gear – good but unmemorable. It wasn't until the mid-'90s that Palmer rediscovered its feet, still fragrant, but a little more broad-shouldered than before.

Named after a British major-general who fought in the Napoleonic Wars, it is a 50-ha (124-acre) site on excellent gravel right next to Ch. Margaux. The wine owes its irresistible plump fruit to the very high proportion of Merlot (40 per cent), with only 55 per cent Cabernet Sauvignon, 3 per cent Cabernet Franc and 2 per cent Petit Verdot. Second wine: Alter Ego (previously Réserve-du-Général). Best years: 2001, '00, '99, '98, '96, '95, '91, '90, '89, '88, '86, '85, '83, '82.

PANTHER CREEK

USA, Oregon, Willamette Valley AVA

🍷 Pinot Noir
🍷 Pinot Gris, Chardonnay, Melon de Bourgogne (Muscadet)

Panther Creek is not your typical OREGON winery. Admittedly 90 per cent of their output is Pinot Noir, which is *very* Oregonian – but they buy from 11 different vineyards, the majority of whose fruit ends up in vineyard-designated bottlings (the rest goes to Winemaker's Cuvée). They also go south to Oregon's Umpqua Valley to buy Merlot and Pinot Gris. They make Melon! That's the extremely neutral grape that makes Muscadet in France. Surely no one makes Melon by choice? And they cross the state line to WASHINGTON to buy their Chardonnay. And all of these, of course, are vineyard-designated. This is one of Oregon's most interesting and least parochial wineries. Oh, and there's fizz – 50-50 Chardonnay and Pinot Noir, but vineyard-designated, naturally. Best years: (Pinot Noir) 2001, '00, '99, '98, '97, '96.

CH. PAPE CLÉMENT

FRANCE, Bordeaux, Pessac-Léognan AC, Cru Classé de Graves
🍷 *Cabernet Sauvignon, Merlot*
🍾 *Sauvignon Blanc, Sémillon, Muscadelle*

This famous GRAVES Classed Growth was languishing in the doldrums until new owners Bernard Magrez and Léo Montagne arrived in the 1990s. Some fine tuning, investment in stainless steel tanks, a system of temperature control and new oak barrels and as a result since 1986 the estate has become one of the established stars of BORDEAUX.

Like Ch. HAUT-BRION down the road, Pape Clément's 30-ha (74-acre) vineyard is located on Pessac's fine, gravelly soils in the suburbs of Bordeaux, and planted to 60 per cent Cabernet Sauvignon and 40 per cent Merlot. The wines are deep-coloured, rich and powerful but elegantly aromatic and should be kept for ten years or more. In recent years Pape Clément has also produced a very fine but unclassified white wine from a further 2.5ha (6 acres) of vines. The wine is barrel-fermented in new oak casks and is rich and fullbodied with the aroma and flavour of citrus fruits, vanilla and just a hint of musk. Second wine: (red) Clémentin. Best years: (reds) 2001, '00, '99, '98, '97, '96, '95, '90, '89, '88, '86; (whites) 2001, '00, '99, '98, '96.

PARELLADA

Parellada – the most aromatic of the three major white grapes in PENEDÈS – is exclusive to CATALUÑA. Apart from Penedès, it is very important in TARRAGONA DO. It makes light, fresh, fruity wines with a floral aroma, good, fresh acidity, and, unlike most Spanish whites, is fairly low in alcohol, usually somewhere between 9 and 11 per cent. These wines are best in the spring after the harvest, and usually begin to taste dull by the following year. To preserve its aromas Parellada tends to be grown in the coolest spots, often up in the hills. It is also the most characterful constituent of Catalan CAVA and blends well with Chardonnay and Sauvignon Blanc.

PARKER COONAWARRA ESTATE

AUSTRALIA, South Australia, Coonawarra
🍷 *Cabernet Sauvignon, Merlot, Cabernet Franc, Petit Verdot*

Red wine specialist now run by Andrew Pirie (formerly of PIPERS BROOK). The top label, cheekily named First Growth in imitation of illustrious BORDEAUX reds, can be one of the best – and most Bordeaux-like – reds in Australia. It is released only in better years. The second label Terra Rossa Cabernet Sauvignon is lighter and leafier. The Merlot is among the best produced in Australia. Best years: (First Growth) 2001, '00, '99, '98, '96, '93, '91, '90.

PASO ROBLES AVA

USA, California, San Luis Obispo County

One of the older districts in the CENTRAL COAST, Paso Robles made its way from the 1880s into the 1970s with sturdy, rustic Zinfandels. In spite of its proximity to the sea, the region is among the warmest of the coastal valleys in summer because hills keep out the cool sea air, but the altitude does cool it down at night. As well as Zinfandel it has full-flavoured Cabernet Sauvignon and some good Chenin Blanc and Sauvignon Blanc. Chardonnays so far are affable though quick to age. Nebbiolo and Syrah are recent welcome additions, large commercial plantings of Merlot less so. Encouraged by the presence and also by the viticultural experiments of the Perrin family (owners of Ch. BEAUCASTEL), many growers here have developed new plantings of Syrah, Mourvèdre and related RHÔNE varieties. Best producers: Adelaida Cellars, Eberle, Justin, J Lohr, MERIDIAN, Peachy Canyon, Tablas Creek, Wild Horse.

LUÍS PATO

PORTUGAL, Beira Litoral, Beiras Vinho Regional
🍷🍾 *Baga, Touriga Nacional, Cabernet Sauvignon, Tinta Barroca*
🍾 *Fernão Pires (Maria Gomes), Bical, Cerceal, Cercealinho, Arinto*

Luís Pato is one of Portugal's star winemakers. A combination of astute marketing and good winemaking has given Pato a high profile on the home market and, consequently, most of his wines command high prices. He began making wine in 1980 when he inherited the family estate from his late father, João. After a decade or more of trial and error, Pato has

These vast vineyards belong to Meridian Vineyards, an important producer in the warm Paso Robles region of California's Central Coast which is fast gaining a reputation for the quality of its red grapes.

finally worked out a philosophy based on the French concept of 'terroir' and since 1999, he has left the BAIRRADA DO, complaining that it was too restrictive.

He reserves the sandier soils for dry whites and some lighter reds like Quinta do Ribeirinho and the heavier clay soils for full-bodied reds. His most impressive wines are solid, tannic, but rich reds from individual plots of old, low-yielding vines: Vinha Barrosa and Vinha Pan. He also has 1ha (2 acres) of ungrafted vines which yields a tiny quantity of intensely rich red wine Luís Pato has christened 'Pé Franco'. Pato's eclectic range of wines includes a deliciously creamy sparkling rosé made from the local Baga grape and an exciting white, Vinha Formal is 100 per cent Bical. *Pato* is Portuguese for 'duck' and this has inevitably become his trademark label image. Best years: (reds) 2001, '00, '97, '96, '95, '92.

PATRIMONIO AC
FRANCE, Corsica
♦ ♦ *Nielluccio, Grenache, Sciacarello, Vermentino*
♦ *Vermentino*

Patrimonio was CORSICA's first AC and is located on the south-west side of the island's finger-shaped northern cape. There are 389ha (961 acres) of vines, mainly Nielluccio for the reds and rosés and Vermentino for the whites. The best of the small band of producers have invested in modern winemaking equipment and produce fresh, fruity reds and rosés and aromatic white wines for drinking young. Patrimonio also forms part of the delimited zone for Muscat du Cap Corse, a fragrantly sweet *vin doux naturel*. Best producers: Antoine Aréna, de Catarelli, Gentile, Giacometti, Leccia, Orenga de Gaffory.

PAUILLAC AC
FRANCE, Bordeaux, Haut-Médoc
♦ *Cabernet Sauvignon, Merlot, Cabernet Franc, Carmenère, Malbec, Petit Verdot*

If there is a king of red wine grapes it probably has to be Cabernet Sauvignon. In every corner of the world where there is enough sun to ripen the fruit, it has spread to make dark, dense, rather tough but wonderfully flavoured wines. Yet its heartland remains the single village of Pauillac in the HAUT-MÉDOC region of BORDEAUX. Throughout the New World – and in much of southern France, Spain and Italy too – if you ask ambitious winemakers what model they take for Cabernet Sauvignon they will no doubt say Ch. LATOUR, LAFITE-ROTHSCHILD or MOUTON-ROTHSCHILD. These are the three Pauillac

First Growth properties, each of which, in its different way, is an ultimate expression of Cabernet Sauvignon.

There are 1183ha (2923 acres) of vines in the AC, on deep gravel banks to the north, west and south of the town of Pauillac. This makes Pauillac AC the third biggest commune in the Haut-Médoc. Sleepily huddled at the muddy edge of the Gironde estuary – with a faded promenade, boats idling, a few listless fishermen chatting on the quay – you'd never guess that for many this town is the Mecca of the red wine world.

Apart from the three First Growths, there are 15 other Classed Growth estates in Pauillac, including the world-famous Ch. PICHON-LONGUEVILLE, PICHON-LONGUEVILLE-COMTESSE DE LALANDE and LYNCH-BAGES. The wines go from terse, fretful and austere to blooming with friendly fruit, but Pauillac's uniting characteristic of blackcurrant fruit and cedar or pencil-shavings perfume – the tell-tale signs of Cabernet Sauvignon – is never far distant.

Few Pauillacs are ready young and the Classed Growths often need 20 years of aging. Best years: 2001, '00, '99, '98, '96, '95, '94, '90, '89, '88, '86, '85, '83, '82. Best producers: d'Armailhac, BATAILLEY, Clerc-Milon, Duhart-Milon, Fonbadet, Grand-Puy-Ducasse, GRAND-PUY-LACOSTE, HAUT-BAGES-LIBÉRAL, HAUT-BATAILLEY, Lafite-Rothschild, Latour, Lynch-Bages, Mouton-Rothschild, Pibran, Pichon-Longueville, Pichon-Longueville-Comtesse de Lalande, PONTET-CANET.

DR PAULY-BERGWEILER
GERMANY, Mosel-Saar-Ruwer, Bernkastel-Kues
♦ *Pinot Noir (Spätburgunder)*
♦ *Riesling and others*

This state-of-the-art MOSEL estate at BERNKASTEL belongs to Dr Peter Pauly, whose wife owns the estate of Weingut Peter Nicolay. The winemaking is designed to produce clear, clean flavours in the wines, and is one of the most modern on the Mosel.

The estate has vines in some of the best vineyard sites in the Mosel, like WEHLENer Sonnenuhr, BRAUNEBERGer Juffer-Sonnenuhr and GRAACHer Himmelreich as well as the unique Bernkasteler alte Badstube am Doctorberg, so-called to make sure no-one misses the fact the vines are right next to the famous Bernkasteler Doctor vineyard. The vast majority of the vineyards are planted with Riesling. Spätburgunder, which only accounts for about 3 per cent of the total vineyard holdings, is

planted in the Graacher Domprobst vineyard; the quality is good, and the wines have plenty of attractive varietal character. Best years: 2002, '01, '97, '95, '94, '93, '90, '89.

CH. PAVIE
FRANCE, Bordeaux, St-Émilion Grand Cru AC, Premier Grand Cru Classé
♦ *Merlot, Cabernet Franc, Cabernet Sauvignon*

Pavie has had a fairly up and down existence in the last 40 years but since being bought by rich and fanatical Gérard Perse, Pavie has shot to its highest ever level of renown. It's the second largest of the ST-ÉMILION Grands Crus (after FIGEAC) at 37ha (93 acres) enjoying a superb site on steep, south-facing slopes just to the south-east of the town of St-Émilion. Clearly it struggled with being big, because in the '60s and '70s the poor vintages were decidedly poor and the good vintages, whilst having a lovely, classically soft-centred ripeness to them, lacked that extra oomph. The '80s saw an improvement but the owners, the Valette family, couldn't keep things going in the '90s and Pavie was becoming loose-knit and ill-defined even in good vintages and when they turned in a feeble effort in the fine 1995 vintage the writing was on the wall. Perse finally bought the property in 1998 and the next three Pavie vintages displayed one of the most astonishing transformations of a property Bordeaux has seen in modern times – dense, rich, succulent wines of dramatic perfume and power. And prices. Forget the old Pavie price. That's been transformed too. Upwards. Perse has also done a similar job on neighbouring Pavie-Decesse. Best years: 2001, '00, '99, '98, '90, '89, '88, '86, '85, '83, '82.

CH. PAVIE-MACQUIN
FRANCE, Bordeaux, St-Émilion Grand Cru AC, Grand Cru Classé
♦ *Merlot, Cabernet Franc, Cabernet Sauvignon*

This has become one of the stars of the ST-ÉMILION GRAND CRU AC since the 1990s. Management and winemaking are in the hands of Nicolas Thienpont (of BORDEAUX-CÔTES DE FRANCS) and star consultant Stéphane Derenoncourt and the old vines are farmed biodynamically. Rich, firm and reserved, the wines need seven to eight years to open up and will age longer. Though quite different to its neighbours Pavie and Pavie-Decesse, it is exciting that there are now three Pavies battling it out for supremacy every vintage. Best years: 2001, '00, '99, '98, '97, '96, '95, '94, '90.

PÉCHARMANT AC

FRANCE, South-West

♥ *Merlot, Cabernet Sauvignon, Cabernet Franc, Malbec*

These are lovely red wines from a small enclave in the BERGERAC region. The soil is relatively chalky, giving wines that are usually quite light in body but with a delicious, full, piercing flavour of blackcurrants and a most attractive grassy acidity. They are rarely very tannic but are, in general, so well-balanced that good vintages can easily age ten years and end up indistinguishable from a good ST-ÉMILION. Best years: 2000, '98, '96, '95, '90. Best producers: Beauportail, Bertranoux, Costes, Grand Jaure, Haut-Pécharmant, la Tilleraie, Tiregand.

PEGASUS BAY

NEW ZEALAND, South Island, Canterbury, Waipara

♥ *Pinot Noir, Cabernet Sauvignon, Merlot, Cabernet Franc, Malbec*

♀ *Riesling, Sauvignon Blanc, Semillon, Chardonnay*

I first met Ivan Donaldson on my initial trip to New Zealand in 1987 and thought he was one of the friendliest, most intellectual, thoughtful wine people I'd met in a long while. He talked about the fantastic potential of the Waipara region north of Christchurch and how the Teviotdale Hills protected a thin stretch of land from the storms and allowed a temperature on average 2–3°C (4–6°F) warmer than in Christchurch. And I nodded, as you do. Then, ten years later, he showed me the wines he, his son Matthew and his partner Lynette Hudson had made at their new Pegasus Bay winery on some of the meanest, leanest soil hunched in behind those Teviotdale Hills – and I thought, not only is a new star wine region being born, but the region's star winery is being born too. Since then, Pegasus Bay has excelled with pinpoint Riesling, lush but refreshing Chardonnay and tremendous Pinot Noir. Their reserve level is on a musical theme – Aria Riesling, Prima Donna Pinot Noir, Maestro Bordeaux blend and even a Finale sweet Chardonnay, They're all outstanding. And I bet in ten years time the vintages will be even better. Best years: 2002, '01, '00, '99, '98.

PEMBERTON

AUSTRALIA, Western Australia

The Pemberton region neatly fills in the space between MARGARET RIVER (to the north-west) and GREAT SOUTHERN (to the south-east). Established originally with enormous enthusiasm for its perceived potential to produce high-quality, cool-climate Chardonnay and Pinot Noir, the barometer has swung more towards sparkling wine use. There are two soil types in the region: the first, and most suitable, are lateritic gravelly sands and loams of moderate fertility, and which produce the best wines. The second are the far more fertile red loams which lead to vigorous growth, excessive yields and flavour dilution. Best producers: Chestnut Grove, Mountford, Picardy, Salitage, Smithbrook.

PEÑAFLOR

ARGENTINA, Mendoza

♥ *Cabernet Sauvignon, Syrah, Malbec and others*

♀ *Chardonnay, Sauvignon Blanc*

Bodegas Peñaflor is a bit of a mystery. It seems to have everything, beautifully kept vineyards in the most enviable locations, especially one known as El Chiche on the road to Tupungato, a gigantic winery with technology to match and first-class human resources. So why doesn't it make Argentina's best wine?

One reason used to be that the owners, the Pulenta family, had fingers in so many pies that they took their eye off the ball when it came to wine. No longer. Another Pulenta (from Miami this time) bought the winery, including the upmarket TRAPICHE label and intends to concentrate on quality. Since 1997 there has been a massive turnaround and now there are significant amounts of good juicy reds as well as fairly impressive flagship Iscay, and some bright, fresh Sauvignons and Chardonnays. But I still feel some of the blends put together are just too big to express any real personality.

PENEDÈS DO

SPAIN, Cataluña

♥ ♀ *Grenache Noir (Garnacha Tinta), Carignan (Cariñena), Tempranillo (Ull de Llebre), Monastrell (Mourvèdre), Cabernet Sauvignon, Merlot, Pinot Noir and Syrah*

♀ *Parellada, Macabeo, Xarel-lo, Moscatel Romano, Chardonnay, Riesling, Gewürztraminer, Sauvignon Blanc, Chenin Blanc*

Winemaking technology in the Penedès region is way ahead of the rest of CATALUÑA, and ahead of most of Spain, largely because of the wealth and technical expertise generated by the booming CAVA industry which is largely based here. The bodegas that specialize in still wines include the famous TORRES, the trailblazer for modern Spanish wine. Co-operatives are as strong here as in the rest of Spain, but so also are the Cava companies who own one-fifth of the vineyards.

White wines predominate, and 90 per cent of these are made principally from the three local grapes, Xarel-lo, Macabeo and (best for quality) Parellada. At best, they can be fresh and pleasantly lemony-fruity. Chardonnay is now being used more widely to improve local blends. The reds made from local varieties tend to be thin, but the finest Penedès reds are made partially or entirely from the Cabernet Sauvignon grape, by Torres, Jean León and a growing group of smaller producers. Tempranillo also can produce some fairly rich flavours here. Best producers: Albet i Noya, Can Feixes, Can Ràfols dels Caus (Caus Lubis Merlot), Cavas Hill, JUVÉ Y CAMPS, Jean Léon, Marqués de Monistrol, Masía Bach, Albert Milá i Mallofré, Puig y Roca, Torres, Vallformosa, Jané Ventura.

PENFOLDS

AUSTRALIA, South Australia, Barossa Valley

♥ *Cabernet Sauvignon, Syrah (Shiraz), Merlot, Grenache and others*

♀ *Chardonnay, Riesling, Semillon and others*

For many, Penfolds and Grange, Australia's most famous red wine, are synonymous, but the modern Penfolds is actually more important for its budget-priced wines than for creating what was once called Australia's only 'First Growth'. Through a series of acquisitions Penfolds, along with LINDEMANS, WYNNS, Seaview and many others all under the umbrella name of Southcorp Wines, now dominates Australian wine production, and is the leader in full-flavoured reds at a fair price. However, it has excellent whites too; a series of ADELAIDE HILLS-sourced Semillon and Chardonnay are first rate including the so-called 'White Grange' Yattarna.

Grange is still the flagship red. The secret lies in 50- to 100-year-old, low-yielding Shiraz vines picked at peak ripeness, and in the skilled use of new American oak: a heady profusion of blackberry, cherry and vanilla aromas and flavours is supported by a structure of exceptional strength and complexity. Cabernet Sauvignon Bin 707, St Henri Claret, Magill Estate, The Clare Estate and Cabernet-Shiraz Bin 389 are the other top-ranking reds, with ripe fruit and lavish use of

PENFOLDS
Bin 707 is Penfolds' closest thing to a Cabernet Sauvignon version of Grange, its flagship Shiraz. It is very powerful, oaky and firmly structured with tremendous blackcurrant fruit richness.

new or near-new oak as cornerstones. But further down the range wines like Bins 28 and 128, Koonunga Hill and Rawson's Retreat don't have the same broad-fruited, packed-with-flavour style they used to, but over the years these reds have probably done more than any other wines to turn the rest of the world on to Aussie red. Best years: (top reds) 1998, '96, '94, '93, '92, '91, '90, '88, '86.

PENLEY ESTATE

AUSTRALIA, South Australia,, Coonawarra
♥ *Cabernet Sauvignon, Syrah (Shiraz)*
♀ *Chardonnay*

Kym Tolley comes from two wine families – the famous Tolleys and the even more famous PENFOLDs, so he was literally born with both wine and a silver spoon in his mouth. Penley Estate generated more publicity prior to producing its first wine than any other Australian winery, but after a few uncertain steps, the wine has well and truly lived up to the propaganda. Satin-smooth Cabernet Sauvignon, with highly skilled use of French and American oak, can show COONAWARRA at or near its best but he also makes Shiraz, Merlot and the traditional Coonawarra claret – a Shiraz Cabernet. He also does fine Chardonnay and lovely fizz. Best years: (Cabernet) 2000, '99, '98, '96, '94, '93, '92, '91.

HERMANOS PÉREZ PASCUAS-VIÑA PEDROSA

SPAIN, Castilla y León, Ribera del Duero DO
♥ ♀ *Tempranillo (Tinto Fino), Cabernet Sauvignon*

The immaculate Pérez Pascuas winery, in the village of Pedrosa de Duero, has modern stainless steel tanks for fermentation, the latest in filtration and bottling equipment and ranks of new oak barrels for aging. Most of the grapes (90 per cent Tinto Fino, supplemented by Cabernet Sauvignon) come from the family vineyards in one of the highest and coolest parts of the RIBERA DEL DUERO region. Viña Pedrosa is the brand name for the wines. There is a lovely, burstingly fruity Tinto Joven (young red with no oak aging).

HERMANOS PÉREZ PASCUAS
From a blend of 90 per cent Tempranillo with Cabernet Sauvignon and two years of barrique-aging, this delicious elegant wine shows just why the Ribera del Duero has become such an exciting region.

The Crianzas and Reservas have wonderful raspberry fragrance, sweet oak flavour and enough tannin to age well. The Pérez Pascuas Reserva Especial, from the estate's oldest vineyard, had its debut in 1990. Best years: 1996, '94, '91, '90, '89.

PERNAND-VERGELESSES AC

FRANCE, Burgundy, Côte de Beaune
♥ *Pinot Noir*
♀ *Chardonnay*

Pernand-Vergelesses is another of those off-the-beaten-track villages in BURGUNDY which nevertheless has a considerable slice of luck; the great hill of Corton comes round from the east, and at its western end a decent-sized chunk of it lies inside the Pernand-Vergelesses communal boundary. Red Corton from these vines lacks the richness of the wines of ALOXE-CORTON from the south- and east-facing slopes and takes longer to mature into a finely balanced, savoury-rich wine. Pernand-Vergelesses red is generally softer, lighter, very attractive young with nice raspberry pastille fruit and a slight earthiness, though good to age for six to ten years. Pernand's 127ha (314 acres) of vineyards produce about 70 per cent red wine and, apart from le CORTON, the best vineyards are Île des Hautes Vergelesses and les Basses Vergelesses, both Premiers Crus. And whereas Aloxe-Corton is often overpriced, Pernand-Vergelesses can be a bargain. Best years: (reds) 2002, '01, '99, '98, '97, '96. Best producers: (reds) Champy, CHANDON DE BRIAILLES, C Cornu, Denis Père et Fils, Dubreuil-Fontaine, Laleure-Piot, Rapet, Rollin Père et Fils.

Although a sizeable part of the white Grand Cru CORTON-CHARLEMAGNE lies within its boundaries, no-one ever links poor old Pernand with the heady heights of Corton-Charlemagne because Grand Cru vineyards don't have to use their village name, yet much of the best white Corton-Charlemagne comes from this western end. Most of the 230,000 bottles of white Pernand are made from Chardonnay, and although they're a bit lean and earthy to start with, they fatten up beautifully after two to four years in bottle. But there are also some very old plantings of Aligoté, and the wine is super – dry, deep, snappy, almost peppery and scoured with lemon peel. Best years: (whites) 2002, '01, '00, '99, '97, '96. Best producers: (whites) Chandon de Briailles, Dubreuil-Fontaine, Jacques Germain, Dominique Guyon, JADOT, Laleure-Piot, J-M Pavelot, Rapet, Rollin Père et Fils.

JOSEPH PERRIER
The Cuvée Royale Brut is a traditional Champagne blend of one third Chardonnay with the balance of Pinot Noir and Pinot Meunier.

JOSEPH PERRIER

FRANCE, Champagne, Champagne AC
♀ *Pinot Noir, Pinot Meunier, Chardonnay*

This is the sole CHAMPAGNE house left in the town of Châlons-en-Champagne, south-east of Reims, along the river Marne. In 1998 Alain Thiénot took a controlling interest in the company. The non-vintage Cuvée Royale is biscuity and creamy, the prestige Cuvée Josephine has length and complexity, but the much cheaper Cuvée Royale Brut Vintage is better value. Best years: 1996, '95, '90, '89, '88, '85, '82.

PERRIER-JOUËT

FRANCE, Champagne, Champagne AC
♀ *Pinot Noir, Pinot Meunier, Chardonnay*

This medium-sized CHAMPAGNE house, now belonging to Allied Domecq, along with MUMM, and producing about three million bottles a year, has long been a triumph of imaginative marketing which has not always been matched by the quality of the wines. Great reputations take a long time to build but can be lost in a flash and recent releases of the non-vintage, in particular, have hardly merited their fame. At its best, Perrier-Jouët is made in an understated style, emphasizing lightness and delicacy. The premium non-vintage range is called Blason de France. Most celebrated of all is the prestige cuvee La Belle Époque in its distinctive enamelled bottle. Here, too, elegance is prized over richness and body, and quality has remained pretty good. Best years: 1996, '95, '92, '90, '89, '85, '82.

PERTH HILLS

AUSTRALIA, Western Australia

This little-recognized wine region, 30km (19 miles) east of Perth, is centred around the very pretty Bickley Valley. The climate is warm by any standards being likened to Portugal's DOURO Valley by some experts. That's pretty hot and should mean a steady flow of full-bodied styles. So far the most promising grape varieties are Chardonnay, Semillon,

Shiraz and Cabernet Sauvignon. Best producers: Darlington, Hainault, François Jacquard, Plesse Brook, Scarp Valley.

PERVINI

ITALY, Puglia, Primitivo di Manduria DOC
🍷 *Primitivo, Negroamaro, Montepulciano and others*
🍷 *Negroamaro, Primitivo*
🍷 *Chardonnay*

The ancient town of Manduria, once occupied by Hannibal, is home to this dynamic winery in the heart of the Primitivo homeland. Pervini is owned by the Perrucci family and is now part of the ACCADEMIA DEI RACEMI network. For decades Pervini was a major player in the bulk-wine business but in the 1990s, it decided to add a range of fine wines, and has steadily built up an impressive network of grower-suppliers not just in Primitivo country, but in the Negroamaro lands farther south in the Salento peninsula. These fascinating wines, combining power with elegance, include Primitivo di Manduria DOC Archidamo and the Primitivo-Negroamoro blend Bizantino. Felline wines, from the Perruccis' own estate, have been very successful, too. Best years: 2001, '00, '98, '97, '96.

PESSAC-LÉOGNAN AC

FRANCE, Bordeaux (see also pages 190–191)
🍷 *Cabernet Sauvignon, Cabernet Franc, Merlot, Malbec, Petit Verdot, Carmenère*
🍷 *Sémillon, Sauvignon Blanc, Muscadelle*

The 1987 revision of the AC system in the GRAVES area south of the city of Bordeaux saw the creation of the new Pessac-Léognan AC by hiving off the area immediately to the south of the city – centred on the villages of Pessac and Léognan, but also including the communes of Talence, Cadaujac, Villenave d'Ornon and Martillac as well as four others. This is the area of Graves which includes all the Classed Growths, and has the highest proportion of the classic gravelly soil which gives the Graves its name.

The quality of the reds from this area has long been recognized. Although Cabernet is the main grape, as in the MÉDOC, a lot of emphasis is placed on Merlot, and the resulting wines can be softer than Médoc equivalents. The top half-dozen properties (such as Ch. HAUT-BRION, la MISSION-HAUT-BRION, Domaine de CHEVALIER and PAPE CLÉMENT) are superb, the others of a very high standard. They can be a little reserved in youth and need seven or eight years before extending a subtle, earthy bouquet of dark fruits and tobacco with a firm

minerally nuance. As for the whites, cool fermentation, controlled yeast selection and the use of new oak barrels for fermentation and aging of the wines, has made this one of the most exciting areas of France for top-class whites. Best years: (reds) 2001, '00, '99, '98, '96, '95, '90, '89, '88; (whites) 2001, '00, '99, '98, '96, '95, '94, '93, '90. Best producers: (reds) Brown, les Carmes Haut-Brion, Domaine de Chevalier, FIEUZAL, HAUT-BAILLY, Haut-Brion, Larrivet Haut-Brion, Latour-Martillac, la LOUVIÈRE, Malartic-Lagravière, la Mission-Haut-Brion, Pape Clément, SMITH-HAUT-LAFITTE, la Tour-Haut-Brion; (whites) Carbonnieux, Domaine de Chevalier, Couhins-Lurton, Fieuzal, Haut-Brion, Latour-Martillac, Laville Haut-Brion, la Louvière, Malartic-Lagravière, Pape Clément, Rochemorin, Smith-Haut-Lafitte.

PETALUMA

AUSTRALIA, South Australia, Adelaide Hills
🍷 *Cabernet Sauvignon, Merlot, Syrah (Shiraz)*
🍷 *Chardonnay, Riesling, Viognier*

Petaluma is the brainchild of the legendary Brian Croser, whose winemaking techniques have had the most influence on Australia's emergence as a leading wine nation.

Interestingly, Petaluma has taken many years to evolve its own wine style to the high level Croser demands, but recent vintages, in which he has finally been able to use exactly the grapes he wants from what he calls distinguished sites, in particular ADELAIDE HILLS fruit for his Chardonnay and COONAWARRA Cabernet and Merlot grapes for his red, have been stunningly good. Tiers Chardonnay rapidly became one of Australia's most expensive whites. Croser CHAMPAGNE-method sparkling wine continues to improve but still has a rather austere style. The CLARE VALLEY Riesling is at the fuller end of the Australian spectrum and requires long aging. Other wines are made under the Sharefarmers and Bridgewater Mill labels. Petaluma has acquired a number of significant producers, including MITCHELTON, KNAPPSTEIN, Smithbrook and STONIER. It was itself taken over by Lion Nathan Breweries in 2001. Best years: (Coonawarra) 2000, '99, '97, '94, '91, '90, '88.

CH. PETIT-VILLAGE

FRANCE, Bordeaux, Pomerol AC
🍷 *Merlot, Cabernet Franc, Cabernet Sauvignon*

This is not the wine to get in a blind tasting because, although this property produces one of the top POMEROL wines, the style is much

sterner and less sumptuous than that of its neighbours and you're sure to put it in the MÉDOC. This may partly be because its style was first developed by two Médoc managers, Bruno Prats, formerly of COS D'ESTOURNEL, and Jean-Michel Cazes of LYNCH-BAGES, although it has been owned by AXA-Millesimes (see PICHON-LONGUEVILLE) since 1989.

However, the soil also plays a part. There was a time when half this 11-ha (27-acre) vineyard was planted with just Cabernet Sauvignon, reflecting its gravel content, though now it is 82 per cent Merlot, 9 per cent Cabernet Franc and 9 per cent Cabernet Sauvignon. Some years are luscious and rich, but in general it is worth aging Petit-Village for eight to ten years. Vintages since 1995 have more weight and texture in the true Pomerol style. Best years: 2001, '00, '99, '98, '96, '95, '94, '90, '89, '88, '85, '82.

CH. PETIT VILLAGE

Located at the highest point of Pomerol's gravel ridge, this château makes very concentrated but somewhat austere wines with great depth of fruit.

CH. PÉTRUS

FRANCE, Bordeaux, Pomerol AC
🍷 *Merlot, Cabernet Franc*

Ch. Pétrus is a small, 12-ha (28-acre) estate with charmingly unimpressive buildings in an area that, 40 years ago, used to merit merely a paragraph or two in 'other Bordeaux wines' sections. Yet Pétrus is now one of the most expensive red wines in the world. Its AC is POMEROL, so recently acclaimed that it still has no 'classification' of quality. If it did, Pétrus would stand proud and magnificent at the very head, and for two reasons.

First, the vineyard, which is situated on an oval of imperceptibly higher land which is virtually solid clay, shot through with nuggets of iron. Only Merlot can flourish in this soil, and the Pétrus blend is almost 100 per cent Merlot. Some of these vines are remarkably old, up to 70 years of age, which is rare in Pomerol and ST-ÉMILION because the great frost of 1956 destroyed most of the vines and caused wholesale replanting. The owner of Pétrus simply waited patiently for several years while the old vines got their strength back. The result is a concentration of intensely pure fruit.

The second factor in Pétrus' quality is the caring genius of its owners, the Moueix family. They ensure that only totally ripe grapes are picked (they only harvest in the afternoon to avoid dew diluting the juice); any portion of the wine which doesn't exude Pétrus quality is rejected and the whole crop is then aged in new oak barrels. The result is a wine of powerful, viscous intensity, a celestial syrup of ripe blackcurrants, blackberries, mulberries, plums and cream, overlaid with mint and tobacco scents and the perilously earthy excitement of fresh-dug truffles. Best years: 2001, '00, '99, '98, '96, '95, '90, '89, '88, '86, '85.

DOMAINE PEYRE ROSE
FRANCE, Languedoc, Coteaux du Languedoc AC
♥ *Syrah, Grenache Noir, Mourvèdre*
♀ *Rolle, Roussanne, Viognier and others*
Don't be fooled by the soft pink name and soothing pink labels. These wines belie their appearance with a gorgeous growling terrible beauty of tannins and spices, rocks and sun-broiled fruit and hillside herbs. Brave idiosyncratic wines from a virtually hand-built winery in the midst of the LANGUEDOC scrub. The heart of the operation lies in two reds, both Syrah-based – Clos des Cistes is leavened with a little Grenache, while Clos Syrah Léone is rendered even more ferocious by the addition of Mourvèdre. There is also a less daunting white. And all the wines are stamped by organic viticulture, ultra-low yields and total absence of oak. Best years: (reds) 2000, '99, '98, '97, '96, '95, '94, '93.

CH. DE PEZ
FRANCE, Bordeaux, Haut-Médoc, St-Estèphe AC, Cru Bourgeois
♥ *Merlot, Cabernet Sauvignon, Cabernet Franc, Petit Verdot*
Sturdy fruit, slow to evolve, but mouthfilling and satisfying, with a little hint of cedarwood and a good deal of blackcurrant to ride with their earthy taste – that's ST-ESTÈPHE's forte. Ch. de Pez – for long regarded as the appellation's leading non-classified Growth, but now at least equalled by several others, including Ch. MEYNEY, Phélan-Ségur and HAUT-MARBUZET – adds a good leathery, plummy dimension in good vintages. The 24-ha (59-acre) vineyard, well-placed inland

from the Third Growth Ch. Calon-Ségur in the far north of St-Estèphe, has 45 per cent Cabernet Sauvignon, 44 per cent Merlot, 8 per cent Cabernet Franc and 3 per cent Petit Verdot. That Petit Verdot helps in warm vintages and the high proportion of Merlot is more important for providing the body and richness that de Pez usually exhibits. Owned since 1995 by the highly regarded CHAMPAGNE house Louis ROEDERER. Best years: 2001, '00, '99, '98, '96, '95, '90, '89, '88.

ROMAN PFAFFL
AUSTRIA, Niederösterreich, Weinviertel, Stetten
♥ *Blauer Zweigelt, Cabernet Sauvignon*
♀ *Grüner Veltliner, Riesling, Chardonnay, Sauvignon Blanc, Pinot Blanc*
In a very few years Roman Pfaffl has built up his estate at Stetten not only in terms of vineyard area (now totalling 31ha/78 acres), but also in reputation. His rather pretentiously named Cuvée Excellent, a blend of Cabernet Sauvignon and Zweigelt, is one of Austria's best red wines, not least because Pfaffl long ago mastered the art of moderating the tannins without sacrificing body or flavour. However, his best wines are his range of dry Grüner Veltliners, which are peppery and racy with excellent aging potential. Since 1995 a fine dry Riesling has been made, too. He also operates a 'Heuriger' tavern where you can taste the young wines. Best years: 2002, '01, '99, '98, '97, '95, '94, '93.

PFALZ
GERMANY
At 23,420ha (57,870 acres), this is Germany's second-biggest wine region, but it tops them all for climate and frequently for size of crop. It's the driest and sunniest part of the country, with the vineyards stretching in a long north-south strip between the Haardt mountains in the west and the Rhine. Mountains, river and vineyards all continue southwards after they cross the French border; the mountains change their name to the Vosges, and the vineyards become those of ALSACE.

Pfalz wines, however, are not that similar to those of Alsace. They are more flowery and less vinous; and traditionally they used to be a lot fatter and sweeter. But the region has undergone a revolution in the last few years, and while in the decades immediately after World War Two it was known for producing the RHINE's most luscious wines, wines that could turn flabby in too warm a year, now they have slimmed down, spruced up and become elegant, well structured, generally

dry, and, at their best, distinctly refined. The biggest revolution of all is taking place in the south of the region. This, even more than the rest of the Pfalz, is a land of part-time farmers who sell their wine to the co-operatives. These co-operatives themselves have improved their standards (though a lot of this wine still goes into the likes of LIEBFRAUMILCH) and there are a number of growers from hitherto little known wine villages making considerable reputations for themselves.

The best wines of the Pfalz are not always Riesling. As in Alsace, Pinot Blanc and Pinot Gris do well – here called Weissburgunder and Grauburgunder – and there is some outstanding Scheurebe, especially at the higher Prädikat levels. Good reds are made from Pinot Noir (Spätburgunder) and Dornfelder. The best vineyard sites, and the top producers, are clustered in a handful of villages in the middle of the northern Bereich, called the Mittelhaardt/Deutsche Weinstrasse. RUPPERTSBERG, DEIDESHEIM, FORST and Wachenheim are the best villages here, though the best wines, as always, are not sold under the Bereich name; there is only one other Bereich in the Pfalz, and that is the Südliche Weinstrasse; in all there are 25 Grosslagen.

JOSEPH PHELPS
USA, California, Napa County, Napa Valley AVA
♥ *Cabernet Sauvignon, Syrah, Merlot*
♀ *Chardonnay, Sauvignon Blanc, Viognier and others*
Joseph Phelps came to the NAPA VALLEY to build a winery for someone else, decided winemaking was more fun than construction, and built a place of his own in time to make a 1973 Johannisberg Riesling that happened to catch the public fancy. Since then the emphasis has shifted away from Riesling in favour of Cabernet and Chardonnay.

Most famous was the dark, iron-hard Eisele Vineyard Cabernet Sauvignon made until 1991; they still make a dense Backus Vineyard Cabernet. The Napa Valley Cabernet is less tannic, but will age. Insignia is usually based on Cabernet Sauvignon: ripe, big, oaky and since 1990, it has been a marvellous complex, supple red, and outstanding in most vintages. Phelps was also one of the first Napa wineries to experiment with Syrah, and now makes good Syrah and excellent Viognier as well as a gluggable RHÔNE red blend called Le Mistral. The latest move is towards Pinot Noir, with the purchase of land for Pinot (and some Chardonnay) on the SONOMA COAST.

Now less well known for whites, Phelps can turn out a good weighty Chardonnay, especially Ovation, and excellent sweet whites. Best years: (Insignia) 2001, '00, '99, '97, '96, '95, '94, '93, '91, '85.

CH. DE PIBARNON

FRANCE, Provence, Bandol AC
❦ ❦ *Mourvèdre, Grenache*
♀ *Clairette, Bourboulenc and others*

Comte Henri de St-Victor and his son Eric have turned Pibarnon into one of the best estates in BANDOL. The 45-ha (111-acre) vineyard is planted mainly with Mourvèdre on magnificent, rocky, terraced slopes that overlook the Mediterranean sea.

Pibarnon's red Bandol is a classic. Produced from 95 per cent Mourvèdre, it is vinified in a traditional way with the grapes fermented and macerated over a period of three weeks and the wine then aged in large oak *foudres* for 18 months. This results in a compelling flavour of sweet red-berry fruits, leather, spice and mint and firm but fine tannic texture capped by a soaring scent of the local herb-strewn hillsides. It's exciting young, but will easily age for ten years.

There is also a solid rosé made from equal amounts of Mourvèdre and Cinsaut and an average to good white made essentially from Clairette and Bourboulenc. Best years: (red) 2001, '00, '99, '98, '97, '96, '95, '94, '93, '91, '90, '89, '88, '85, '82.

PIC ST-LOUP

FRANCE, Languedoc, Coteaux du Languedoc AC
❦ *Syrah, Grenache, Mourvèdre*
♀ *Marsanne, Roussanne, Grenache Blanc and others*

Some of the best red wines in the LANGUEDOC come from the vineyards of this COTEAUX DU LANGUEDOC Cru arranged around the Pic St-Loup, a steep outcrop of limestone north of Montpellier on the borders of the GARD and the HÉRAULT. This is one of the coolest growing zones in the Midi, especially at night time leading up to the vintage. But that suits the Syrah – the dominant grape variety – and Syrah-based wines are increasingly dark and deep without losing their floral scent. Grenache and Mourvèdre are also grown. The white grapes Marsanne, Roussanne, Rolle and Viognier are clearly enjoying Pic St-Loup's cool conditions and provide some impressively fragrant flavours. Best years: (reds) 2001, '00, '99, '98, '96, '95, '93, '90. Best producers: de Cazeneuve, Clos Marie, l'Euzière, l'HORTUS, Lancyre, Lascaux, Lavabre, MAS BRUGUIÈRE, Mas de Mortiès.

F X PICHLER

AUSTRIA, Niederösterreich, Wachau, Oberloiben
♀ *Grüner Veltliner, Riesling, Muscat (Muskateller), Sauvignon Blanc*

'F X', as Austrian wine enthusiasts nickname him, is perhaps the nation's most famous producer of dry white wines. If you experience one of his incredibly concentrated Smaragd wines made from either Grüner Veltliner or Riesling you will see that there are good reasons for all the fuss. If there is a large 'M' – for 'Monumental' – or the vineyard designation Kellerberg on the label then you will have hit the jackpot.

The Rieslings are peachy and citric and the Grüner Veltliners packed with herb and exotic flavours. Dry white wine does not get any richer or more intense than this, and most of Pichler's wines age very well. His rare Muskateller is a remarkable wine, too. And he makes a BURGENLAND red called Arachon. Best years: (Riesling/Grüner Veltliner Smaragd) 2002, '01, '00, '99, '98, '97, '95, '94, '93, '92, '90.

CH. PICHON-LONGUEVILLE

FRANCE, Bordeaux, Haut-Médoc, Pauillac AC, 2ème Cru Classé
❦ *Cabernet Sauvignon, Merlot*

Somehow Ch. Pichon-Longueville (formerly known as Pichon-Baron) got left behind in the rush. Its PAUILLAC neighbour, Ch. PICHON-LONGUEVILLE-COMTESSE DE LALANDE, and its ST-JULIEN neighbours, Ch. LÉOVILLE-LAS-CASES and LÉOVILLE-BARTON, leapt at the chance offered by the string of fine vintages from 1978. These châteaux established a leadership at the top of BORDEAUX's Second Growths which now seriously challenges the First Growths for sheer quality and equals several of them for consistency.

What about Pichon-Longueville? Its 50ha (124 acres) of vineyards are regarded as superb and its mixture of 75 per cent Cabernet Sauvignon and 25 per cent Merlot is ideal for making great Pauillac. Yet it needed the arrival of Jean-Michel Cazes of Ch. LYNCH-BAGES in 1987, supported by his brilliant winemaker and a large investment by the new owners, the giant AXA-Millésimes company, to bring all this to fruition. The top wines are easily the equal of the First Growths, with an intensity of dark, sweet fruit yet structured for a very long life. Pichon-Longueville is now up there with the best 'Super Seconds'. In part this can be explained by the ruthless policy of excluding all but the best grapes – yet the

CH. PICHON-LONGUEVILLE

Since being bought by the AXA insurance group this château has transformed its quality. Recent vintages have been of First Growth standard, with firm tannic structure and rich, dark fruit.

second wine, les Tourelles de Longueville, doesn't suffer and is a fine, classic Pauillac in its own right. Best years: 2001, '00, '99, '98, '97, '96, '95, '90, '89, '88, '86, '82.

CH. PICHON-LONGUEVILLE–COMTESSE DE LALANDE

FRANCE, Bordeaux, Haut-Médoc, Pauillac AC, 2ème Cru Classé
❦ *Cabernet Sauvignon, Merlot, Cabernet Franc, Petit Verdot*

Of all the top-notch wines in the HAUT-MÉDOC, none has been so consistently exciting or beguiling as Pichon-Longueville-Comtesse de Lalande. The vineyard is on excellent land on the edge of the PAUILLAC AC that runs alongside the vines of Ch. LATOUR and LÉOVILLE-LAS-CASES in ST-JULIEN. In fact, some of the vines are actually in St-Julien; this, combined with the highest proportion of Merlot in Pauillac (35 per cent of the blend) and some old, low-yielding Petit Verdot, may account for the sumptuous, fleshy richness of the wine, and its burst of blackcurrant, walnut and vanilla perfume.

But the real cause of Pichon-Longueville-Comtesse de Lalande's sensual triumph over the usually austere Pauillac community is the inspired, messianic figure of Mme de Lencquesaing. She took over the property in 1978 and still runs the show if more from the background than before and for almost a generation led the château upwards in a wave of passion and involvement while the winemaker quietly interpreted her vision with brilliant wine after brilliant wine. This success story has run on through into the 1990s. Don't be deceived by the lush caress of the rich fruit – there's lots of tannin and acid lurking, and good examples, though wonderful at six to seven years old, will always last for 20 years or more. The second wine, Réserve de la Comtesse, is easily of Classed Growth quality, though usually lacking a little of the sheer hedonistic joy of the Grand Vin. Best years: 2001, '00, '99, '98, '97, '96, '95, '90, '89, '88, '86, '85, '83, '82, '81.

PIEMONTE (Piedmont) Italy

TUCKED AWAY UP IN THE north-west corner of Italy, up against the mighty Alps, the Piedmont region has neither coastline nor any city of the fame of Rome or Venice to attract the crowds; yet for many wine lovers a visit to the region is as de rigueur as a pilgrimage for a devout Catholic. For Piedmont is the home of Nebbiolo, Italy's most mystical grape variety, the merits of which are more hotly contested than any other, and of Nebbiolo's most prestigious wines, Barolo and Barbaresco.

The alpine foothills in north and west Piedmont often have too harsh a climate for vines, and grapes can ripen only where river valleys bring air movement and so extra sunshine. The Dora Baltea, flowing south through Ivrea, carves out the Nebbiolo zone of Carema and the area of white Erbaluce di Caluso and sweet Caluso Passito. The river Sesia

brings viticulture to the Novara and Vercelli hills, south of Lake Maggiore, in the zones of Gattinara and Ghemme.

It is the south of Piedmont, though, that harbours most of the region's wines. South-east of Turin the landscape becomes characterized by angular hills with perfectly straight rows of vines stretching horizontally across the slopes. This is the heart of Nebbiolo country, with the wine zones of Barolo and Barbaresco on either side of, and that of Roero just across the Tanaro river from, the little town of Alba, also famous for its fabulous white truffles. There, as elsewhere in the region, the late-ripening Nebbiolo is planted on the sunniest, south-facing slopes, leaving other slopes for less fussy varieties – Dolcetto, Barbera, perhaps Chardonnay. A hilltop vineyard site, called a *bricco* in dialect, is particularly prized.

Other indigenous grape varieties can be found here too, most of them only in tiny amounts and some on their way back from virtual extinction. These include Freisa and Grignolino, Pelaverga and Rouchet. All these red varieties, despite their wide differences, have a common core of austerity (especially when their wines are still young) that makes them typically Piedmontese.

White wines take very much second place in the region after reds. Apart from fashionable Gavi in the south-eastern corner, made from the Cortese grape, it was only in the 1980s that interest was shown again in the native varieties, Arneis and Favorita, as well as in imported Chardonnay. Yet the strangest thing about south Piedmont is that just next door to what are probably the harshest, most mouth-attacking reds from anywhere in Italy are the lightest, most delicate mouthfuls of grapiness you could ever hope to find – lightly sparkling Moscato d'Asti and its fully sparkling counterpart, called simply Asti.

Since 1994 Piedmont has had a regional denomination: Piemonte DOC. This is an umbrella DOC covering a wide range of grape varieties – Pinot Bianco, Pinot Grigio, Cortese, Chardonnay, Pinot Nero and Moscato for whites and Barbera, Bonarda, Grignolino and Brachetto for reds. The idea is that it acts as a catch-all for quality wines which might fail for one reason or another to be classified under a local DOC: Piedmont's wine legislators apparently think that vino da tavola, even in its trendily elevated guise, is beneath any wine produced in their region. In recent years the great Piedmont wines have become targets for collectors the world over, causing

The small village of Castiglione Falletto viewed over vineyards at Perno. Together with the village of Barolo itself, Castiglione Falletto forms the heart of the Barolo zone and includes some prime vineyards such as Monprivato.

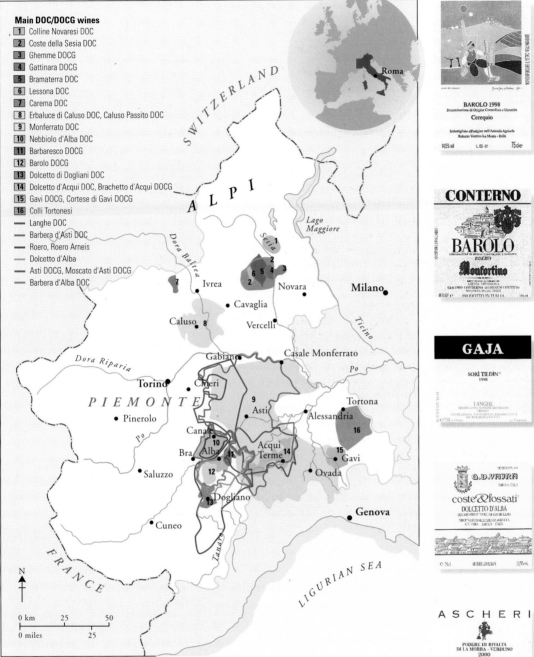

Main DOC/DOCG wines

1. Colline Novaresi DOC
2. Coste della Sesia DOC
3. Ghemme DOCG
4. Gattinara DOCG
5. Bramaterra DOC
6. Lessona DOC
7. Carema DOC
8. Erbaluce di Caluso DOC, Caluso Passito DOC
9. Monferrato DOC
10. Nebbiolo d'Alba DOC
11. Barbaresco DOCG
12. Barolo DOCG
13. Dolcetto di Dogliani DOC
14. Dolcetto d'Acqui DOC, Brachetto d'Acqui DOCG
15. Gavi DOCG, Cortese di Gavi DOCG
16. Colli Tortonesi
— Langhe DOC
— Barbera d'Asti DOC
— Roero, Roero Arneis
— Dolcetto d'Alba
— Asti DOCG, Moscato d'Asti DOCG
— Barbera d'Alba DOC

ROBERTO VOERZIO
Big and hugely concentrated Cerequio is one of several outstanding single-vineyard Barolos from this talented producer, one of the best of the new wave of Barolo producers.

GIACOMO CONTERNO
The Giacomo Conterno winery is famed for its monumental Riserva Monfortino, traditional Barolo at its best, and only released after six or seven years in large oak barrels.

GAJA
Angelo Gaja's traditional strength has always been in his single-vineyard wines from Barbaresco, now sold under the Langhe DOC.

G D VAJRA
Grapes from two sites, Coste di Vergne and Fossati, produce this super Dolcetto, one of the best from the Alba zone.

ASCHERI
Winemakers in Piedmont for at least five centuries, the Ascheri family produce a range of wines that are forward and appealingly drinkable.

prices to rocket alarmingly. But vintages have been good and quality never better, so there seems nothing much can be done. It's the old, old story of supply (in this case tiny) and demand (mushrooming).

REGIONAL ENTRIES
Asti, Barbaresco, Barbera d'Alba, Barolo, Brachetto d'Acqui, Carema, Erbaluce di Caluso, Gattinara, Gavi, Langhe, Moscato d'Asti, Nebbiolo d'Alba, Roero.

PRODUCER ENTRIES
Elio Altare, Antinori, Ascheri, Michele Chiarlo, Domenico Clerico, Aldo Conterno, Giacomo Conterno, Tenimenti di Fontanafredda, Angelo Gaja, Bruno Giacosa, Giuseppe Mascarello, Prunotto, Luciano Sandrone, Roberto Voerzio.

ELIO ALTARE
This oak-aged Nebbiolo wine is one of several modern barrique-aged Piedmontese wines from this new wave producer.

PIEROPAN

ITALY, Veneto, Soave Classico DOC

♀ *Garganega, Trebbiano di Soave, Welschriesling (Riesling Italico), Sauvignon Blanc*

No producer in Italy has been more faithful and courageous than the house of Pieropan, which for three generations kept the flag of quality flying through those years when the industrialists of Verona were churning out vast quantities of SOAVE rubbish. With outstanding vineyards at La Rocca, behind the famous castle, and at Calvarino, Leonildo Pieropan and his wife Teresita, now joined by their sons, make an excellent regular Soave Classico, as well as the two single-vineyard versions, Calvarino and La Rocca, the definitive wines of the zone.

Pieropan not only continues to fly the traditionalist flag but is more than a match for the young turks who have risen during the past ten to 20 years, claiming the 'new Soave' as their territory. Although he does not resort to using Chardonnay or Sauvignon for his dry wines, or use barriques in the making of anything but sweet wines, his Soaves have several times proved their ability to age amazingly well into their second decade.

But if the dry wines are good, Pieropan's sweet wines can on occasion be exceptional. The classic example is RECIOTO DI SOAVE Le Colombare, from Garganega grapes dried conventionally on *graticci* (racks) until the February after the harvest. There is also a Passito della Rocca, from Sauvignon Blanc, Riesling Italico and Trebbiano di Soave grapes which are dried for slightly less time on *graticci*, then fermented and aged in barrique; plus, two or three times a decade, when conditions are right, a mind-blowing late-harvest (*vendemmia tardiva*) wine from Garganega grapes left to dry on the vine until mid-December in order to develop about 40 per cent noble rot.

PIEROPAN
This wine, made from dried grapes in the millennia-old tradition of Verona, is a delightful example of a non-cloying sweet white with refreshing acidity.

PIERRO

AUSTRALIA, Western Australia, Margaret River

♀ *Cabernet Sauvignon, Cabernet Franc, Merlot, Pinot Noir and others*

♀ *Chardonnay, Semillon, Sauvignon Blanc*

Dr Michael Peterkin has an iconoclastic attitude to winemaking, and dislikes pigeon-hole descriptions of his winemaking practices and philosophy. Towering Chardonnay, very complex and rich, usually high in alcohol, is his benchmark wine and one of the most exciting in Australia; his potent Cabernets (an impressive five-varietal BORDEAUX-style blend) is equally powerful and long-lived. The Semillon-Sauvignon Blanc LTC (Les Trois Cuvées or a Little Touch of Chardonnay – take your pick) is a fruity, crisp style for early drinking. The Fire Gully range is sourced from a separate vineyard, owned and managed by Peterkin. Best years: (Chardonnay) 2001, '00, '99, '97, '96, '94, '93.

PIESPORT

GERMANY, Mosel-Saar-Ruwer

This village, in one of the steepest parts of the MOSEL, has been much devalued by having its name included in the Piesporter Michelsberg Grosslage, one of the main generic wines in Germany, churning out vast amounts of wines that are soft, light and insipid. Yet Piesport's own wines are a delight – elegant, relatively light and very stylish. Rieslings from the famous, steep Goldtröpfchen vineyard site are powerful and concentrated with intense blackcurrant, honey and peach aromas. Best years: (Riesling Spätlese) 2002, '01, '00, '99, '98, '97, '96, '95, '93, '92, '90, '89. Best producers: GRANS-FASSIAN, Reinhold HAART, Kurt Hain, von KESSELSTATT, St Urbans-Hof, Weller-Lehnert.

PIEVE SANTA RESTITUTA, CÀ MARCANDA

ITALY, Tuscany, Brunello di Montalcino DOCG

♀ *(Pieve) Sangiovese, Cabernet Sauvignon*

♀ *(Cà Marcanda) Cabernet Sauvignon, Merlot, Cabernet Franc, Syrah*

This superbly sited BRUNELLO DI MONT-ALCINO estate attracted the attention of PIEDMONT's superstar Angelo GAJA, who now owns the company. Single-vineyard bottlings of Brunello Rennina and Sugarille are very expensive, but benefit from a vigorous selection. Somewhat austere and overwhelming when young, they will repay keeping for 15 years or more, when their deep, earthy notes and concentrated red and black fruits emerge. Santa Restituta's SUPER-TUSCAN, Promis, used to be made here, but has been switched

to Gaja's more recent acquisition on the Tuscan coast at BOLGHERI, Cà Marcanda, where 65ha (160 acres) of vines have been planted on the way to an eventual 120ha (296 acres). The blend for Promis will vary from year to year; currently Merlot-based, it also includes Syrah – and Sangiovese from the Pieve Santa Restituta estate. The year 2000 was the first vintage of two new wines from Cà Marcanda: Magari (50 per cent Merlot, 25 per cent Cabernet Sauvignon, 25 per cent Cabernet Franc) and Camarcanda (50 per cent Merlot, 40 per cent Cabernet Sauvignon, 10 per cent Cabernet Franc). Best years: (Brunello) 2001, '00, '99, '98, '97, '95.

CH. LE PIN
This concentrated and elegant Pomerol, made entirely from Merlot, was first produced as recently as 1979; it now fetches huge prices at auction.

CH. LE PIN

FRANCE, Bordeaux, Pomerol AC

♀ *Merlot*

Here's a success story if ever there was one. Le Pin's first vintage was made by owner Jacques Thienpont in 1979 (before that the wine had been sold in bulk) and now it's one of the most expensive wines in the world, auction prices frequently outstripping those for Ch. PÉTRUS. The '82, only the fourth vintage, became so insanely popular that its price reached £3000/US$5000 a bottle. In 2003 the 2000 was selling for £1000/US$1650. The reasons for this sensation are twofold: scarcity and style of wine. There are barely 2ha (5 acres) of vineyard, superbly located close to Ch. TROTANOY and VIEUX-CHÂTEAU-CERTAN, which produce an average 6000 bottles a year from lowly yields of some 35 hectolitres per hectare.

The wine, 100 per cent Merlot and lavishly aged in 100 per cent new oak barrels for 12 to 18 months, is rich, lush and velvety with an almost Burgundian aroma of ripe cherries and raspberries. It's a magical experience but you have to dig deep in the pocket for the privilege of tasting it. It is best with five to ten years' age, though it will age comfortably for 20 years. Best years: 2001, '00, '99, '98, '96, '95, '94, '90, '89, '88, '86, '85, '83, '82, '81.

PINE RIDGE WINERY

USA, California, Napa County, Stags Leap District AVA

Cabernet Sauvignon, Merlot

Chardonnay, Chenin Blanc, Viognier

Founded in the 1970s, this STAGS LEAP-based winery produces most of its sizeable output from grapes sourced from other NAPA VALLEY AVAs; it now owns more than 120ha (300 acres) throughout the Napa Valley. However, its reputation was founded on its soft, supple, tantalizing Cabernet Sauvignon from Stags Leap, and its Chardonnay (one of several offered) remains one of the AVA's finest. It is being surpassed of late by a poised, delicious apple-fruited, layered CARNEROS Chardonnay. There's also a fruity, fragrant Chenin Blanc-Viognier.

The RUTHERFORD Cabernet Sauvignon captures cassis and dusty regional flavours, albeit in a tight, lean style. Both the limited volume HOWELL MOUNTAIN Cabernet Sauvignon and Andrus Reserve (a massive red BORDEAUX-style blend, made only in top years) are huge, muscular wines built to age a decade or longer. The Napa Valley Merlot has a splash of bright red cherry fruit and complex flavours. Best years: (Stags Leap Cabernet) 2001, '00, '99, '97, '96, '95, '94, '91.

DOMINIO DE PINGUS

SPAIN, Castilla y León, Ribera del Duero DO

Tempranillo (Tinto Fino), Petit Verdot

Danish winemaker Peter Sisseck, a consultant in RIBERA DEL DUERO, has created his own tiny winery in a converted shed in Quintanilla de Onésimo – very modest facilities for a venture that has made such a huge impression worldwide. From two small vineyards in La Horra and Valbuena de Duero – with old, gobelet-pruned Tinto Fino vines and a little experimental Petit Verdot which hasn't made it into the blends yet, totalling 5ha (11 acres) – he has produced one of the world's best and most expensive new wines, Pingus.

DOMINIO DE PINGUS
This cult wine, made with painstaking attention to detail from 100 per cent Tempranillo or Tinto Fino, is new style Ribera del Duero at its best.

Bunch-by-bunch selection in the vineyard, grape-by-grape destemming by hand at the winery, fermentation in oak vats, malolactic fermentation in new French oak barrels, and aging on lees without any racking for one year or more show the enormous effort that goes into the wine.

Pingus is a great, dark, concentrated red of undeniable world class. There's also a delicious second wine for export markets called Flor de Pingus, which is made from bought-in grapes. Best years: (Pingus) 2001, '00, '99, '98, '97, '96, '95.

PINOT BLANC

Pinot Blanc is a chorus member rather than a solo artiste in the white grape hierarchy of France. This grape is not the same as Chardonnay, even though the two can taste similar when the wine is young and unoaked. In Italy, however, exciting things are achieved with Pinot Bianco. In ALTO ADIGE and FRIULI-VENEZIA GIULIA it can outshine Chardonnay, it plays a major role in what is arguably TUSCANY's finest white, QUERCIABELLA's Batàr, and it is even found as far south as PUGLIA, though in those hot conditions it tends to ripen too soon to develop complexity. In LOMBARDY's FRANCIACORTA zone it plays a vital role in Italy's best sparkling wines.

When picked early Pinot Blanc is neutral and quite acid – the perfect base material for sparkling wine, and in France, where its home is ALSACE, it makes most of the local fizz, CRÉMANT D'ALSACE. With the similar-tasting Auxerrois, it is taking over the 'workhorse' role for Alsace wines from Sylvaner and Chasselas, but as a varietal Pinot Blanc produces round, fat, apple-creamy wine, positively rich in a warm year. It is also used as a minor part of the blend with Chardonnay in one or two Burgundian appellations.

It is probably taken most seriously in southern Germany and Austria where it's known as Weissburgunder and producing imposing wines with ripe pear and peach fruit and a distinct nutty character; it's also found in Slovakia and Slovenia, and many other eastern and central European areas, as well as in CALIFORNIA and OREGON, with both states experiencing a revival of interest in the varietal. BRITISH COLUMBIA's OKANAGAN VALLEY boasts more than 25 producers of cool-climate citrus-flavoured Pinot Blanc that can be stainless steel or barrel fermented. It hasn't made much impact on Australia or South Africa.

PINOT GRIS

The grapes can be anything from greyish blue to brownish pink and they are often mistaken for Pinot Noir. Another of the world's more amenable grape varieties, Pinot Gris will amiably produce whatever is required of it, ranging from crisp, refreshing whites to intense, luscious dessert wines. Even when the wine is dry and light it should have a lick of honey and spice; this increases, often becoming earthier and even a little mushroomy, as the sweetness increases. Pinot Gris is nicely susceptible to noble rot, becoming smoky, raisiny and fat.

The best dry examples come from Alsace; Germany, particularly the Baden and Pfalz regions (as Ruländer or Grauburgunder); Steiermark and Burgenland in Austria; north-eastern Italy (as Pinot Grigio); eastern Europe; Oregon in the USA's Pacific Northwest and British Columbia in Canada. New Zealand does well with Pinot Gris, as do Tasmania and southern Victoria in Australia.

Superb dessert versions come from Alsace (Vendange Tardive or the even sweeter Sélection de Grains Nobles), Germany, Austria's Burgenland and Murfatlar in Romania. As winemaking in eastern Europe improves, expect more goodies, both sweet and dry, from there.

PINOT MEUNIER

The red Pinot Meunier (or plain Meunier as it is sometimes called) is the most widely planted grape in the CHAMPAGNE region and makes up more than a third of the blend in much non-vintage Champagne, even though it is the least well regarded of the three permitted varieties (Pinot Noir and Chardonnay are the other two). Elsewhere in France, it is to be found in the LOIRE Valley where it is used in the fragile rosé, Gris Meunier d'Orléans.

In other parts of the world (from Australia through CALIFORNIA to Canada) it is usually grown as a crucial component of the sparkling wine blend and occasionally made for rosé and red wines, especially in WÜRTTEMBERG.

PINOT NOIR

This is the most capricious, ungracious, unforgiving, fascinating grape of them all – and the one that everybody wants to grow. In Burgundy, its home for a millennium or so, they still have endless problems with it, so it's not surprising that in places like Oregon, with hardly more than 20 years experience of Pinot Noir, they are only just discovering the problems.

What are the problems? For a start it's difficult to grow. It buds early and ripens early, which makes it suitable for cold climates. But its tight bunches are seriously prone to rot, it reacts to overcropping by producing wine little better than rosé, and yet because its fruit sets very irregularly, it is often pruned for extra quantity. So when it does set, you're going to overcrop, which means the juice will be pale.

Then the wines are difficult to make. The Burgundians produce the most exciting flavours by living dangerously and fermenting as hot as they dare – but if they go just a bit too far they get stewed flavours instead of the silky, ripe, vegetal strawberry and gamy tastes that are the ideal. Yet play safe and you get safe, fruity wine of no particular distinction.

The Pinot Noir that all the world wants to ape is that of the Côte d'Or, where it can produce the most startling, fascinating flavours. Can, but does not always – in fact does not probably more often than it does. Elsewhere in France, Pinot Noir makes light perfumed reds or tasty, strawberryish rosés in Savoie, Jura, the Loire – especially Sancerre – and Alsace, but its major role outside Burgundy is in Champagne. In this even cooler climate it gives pale wines which still have enough body to round out the leaner Chardonnay. It provides much of the colour in rosé Champagne, but for white Champagne it is pressed straight away and vinified like a white wine, the juice being barely coloured. This classic formula for sparkling wines, Pinot Noir, Pinot Meunier and Chardonnay, is the basis of much Champagne-method fizz around the world, including California and Australia.

In Italy only a few producers seem to have come near to cracking Pinot Noir's code as a still red: Ca' del Bosco and Bellavista in Lombardy's Franciacorta are almost there, as are Fontodi in Tuscany and Castello della Sala in Umbria; but closest of all are the growers in the Adige valley: Franz Haas, Ochsenreiter of Haderburg, and especially Hofstätter. In Germany it is most at home in Baden and the Pfalz, and the newish German fashion for dry, well-structured reds is helping its development no end; the same goes for Austria. In Germany it is called Spätburgunder, and in Austria Blauburgunder. In South Africa Hamilton Russell and Bouchard Finlayson are the most consistent producers and much Pinot Noir is now successfully used here in fizz. The real leader in the southern hemisphere is New Zealand, whose sunny but cool climate (especially in Martinborough and between Central Otago, Canterbury and Marlborough) seems well suited to the variety. The quality of Australian Pinot Noir has improved in leaps and bounds, the Yarra Valley leading the way, followed by Gippsland, Geelong, Mornington Peninsula, Adelaide Hills and Tasmania. Early Canadian results from Ontario and British Columbia are promising. Pinot Noirs from Chile have been increasingly good – scented and soft – and Río Negro in Argentina looks promising.

So far the best Pinot Noir outside Burgundy is in California. About one quarter of the Pinot Noir here is used for sparkling wine; for red wines the most promising areas are Carneros, the Russian River Valley and parts of Monterey and Santa Barbara counties.

Some years ago Oregon was being hyped as the US Côte d'Or, but when a couple of poor vintages meant that the wines failed to live up to the hype they were just as extravagantly damned. However, Oregon was chosen for Pinot Noir because it is a marginal region, and the process is a gradual one. The best wines are ripe and vegetal with a touch of silkiness. The promise is still there, and hopes have been given a boost by the performance of Domaine Drouhin.

PINOTAGE

This red grape, South Africa's speciality, is a cross between Pinot Noir and Cinsaut. It was developed in South Africa in 1925, but only introduced widely into Cape vineyards in the 1950s; it is rarely grown elsewhere (New Zealand, the US and Zimbabwe have a little).

Pinotage produces a wine with a quite distinctive flavour, likened to fresh bananas and toasted marshmallows crossed with the sweet/sour flavours of plum and redcurrant when young and usually sprinkled with coal dust. Age brings a more mellow plummy character. The abrasive, estery styles of old are being taken over by wines with cleaner, more intense fruit. Successful both in a fresh, juicy style, as well as more structured with new oak, it has attracted international attention as a novelty and is now very fashionable. On the home front, winemakers have mixed feelings about its future, although members of the Pinotage Producers' Association are active and enthusiastic promoters of the grape. Best producers (South Africa): Graham BECK (sparkling, Old Road), Bellingham (Premium), BEYERSKLOOF, Clos Malverne, Diemersfontein, FAIRVIEW, Grangehurst, Kaapzicht, KANONKOP, L'Avenir, Newton Johnson, Simonsig, SPICE ROUTE, Stony Brook, Tukulu, Uiterwyk (Top of the Hill), WARWICK; (New Zealand): BABICH.

PIPER-HEIDSIECK

FRANCE, Champagne, Champagne AC
♀ ♂ *Chardonnay, Pinot Noir, Pinot Meunier*

Traditionally a rather feeble performer, this brand has greatly improved since its purchase by Rémy and its consequent involvement with stablemate Charles HEIDSIECK, whose soaring performance is starting to rub off on Piper. Now a gentle biscuity style, with very good de luxe cuvée Rare. Popular with models, sipped through straws from quarter bottles. Best years: 1996, '95, '90, '89, '85, '82.

PIPERS BROOK VINEYARD

AUSTRALIA, Tasmania
♂ *Pinot Noir, Cabernet Sauvignon, Merlot*
♀ *Chardonnay, Riesling, Pinot Gris, Gewurztraminer*

In 1972 Andrew Pirie identified the cool Pipers Brook region of northern TASMANIA as most likely to produce wines of European style. And indeed, he has produced some of the most refined wines in Australia despite a continual battle against what, for Australia, is a very marginal climate for ripening grapes. In vintages such as 2000 and '98 the red wines come into their own, with an added dimension of fruit and a perfumed, Burgundian style that is lacking in cooler years – when the aromatic whites often excel, particularly Riesling, Pinot Gris and Gewurztraminer.

Pipers Brook has been decidedly aggressive in its expansion activities, first acquiring the important Rebecca Vineyard on the Tamar River, and then buying neighbours Heemskerk and Rochecombe, making it by far the biggest wine company in Tasmania. Andrew Pirie left in 2003 to run PARKER Estate in COONAWARRA. Second label Ninth Island. Best years: (Riesling) 2000, '99, '97, '95, '94, '93, '92, '91, '90.

BODEGA PIRINEOS
SPAIN, Aragón, Somontano DO
♟ *Moristel, Tempranillo, Merlot, Cabernet Sauvignon, Parraleta*
♟ *Tempranillo, Cabernet Sauvignon, Merlot, Grenache Noir (Garnacha Tinta)*
♀ *Macabeo, Chardonnay, Gewürztraminer*
In the 1990s, when the rich newcomers (VIÑAS DEL VERO, then ENATE) set up shop near Barbastro in SOMONTANO, ARAGÓN's coolest wine region, the old Somontano del Sobrarbe co-operative might have given up all hope of competing and reverted to bulk wines and cheap bottlings. Instead, it metamorphosed itself into a private winery, with its members holding part of the shares, changed its name to Bodega Pirineos and embarked on an ambitious investment programme.

In contrast with the newcomers, who largely rely on new plantings of foreign grape varieties, Pirineos has large, well-established tracts of the native Macabeo and Moristel grape varieties and even a little of the almost extinct, powerful, musky Parraleta. It makes light young reds from Moristel, a delightful late-harvest (*vendimia tardía*) dry Macabeo and increasingly ambitious blends of Moristel, Tempranillo and the French varieties under the Montesierra label. Top-of-the-range Señorío de Lazán Reserva is a blend of Cabernet, Moristel and Tempranillo. Prices are modest and quality exciting for a winery producing more than 200,000 cases a year. Best years: 2001, '00, '99, '98, '97, '96, '95, '94.

PRODUCTEURS PLAIMONT
FRANCE, South-West
♟ ♟ *Tannat, Fer Servadou (Pinenc), Cabernet Sauvignon, Cabernet Franc*
♀ *Gros Manseng, Petit Manseng, Arrufiac, Petit Courbu, Colombard, Ugni Blanc*
This grouping of three Gascon co-operatives (Plaisance, Aignan and St-Mont) is the largest, most reliable, and most go-ahead producer of Vin de Pays des CÔTES DE GASCOGNE and CÔTES DE ST-MONT AC. It accounts for 2500ha (6175 acres) of vineyard and produces around 24 million bottles of wine a year. Investment through the 1980s and '90s in stainless steel tanks, temperature control and new bottling equipment has provided the means to create clean, modern wines using regional grape varieties.

The whites, including the Côtes de Gascogne Colombelle, are generally crisp and fruity. The reds, in particular the Côtes de St-Mont Ch. de Sabazan, are well structured with quite rounded fruit benefiting from some oak aging and can age for upwards of five years. The co-operative also produces an average 200,000 bottles a year of MADIRAN, including the Collection Plaimont, a powerful but refined wine matured in oak barriques and capable of aging for five years or more. There is also a small amount of sweet PACHERENC DU VIC-BILH, notably the cuvée St-Albert.

PLANETA
ITALY, Sicily
♟ *Nero d'Avola, Frappato, Merlot, Syrah, Cabernet Sauvignon*
♀ *Grecanico, Chardonnay, Fiano and others*
This rapidly expanding, young and dynamic estate is run by the younger generation of the family of Diego Planeta, long one of the powers-that-be in Sicilian wine, with top PIEDMONT wine man Carlo Corino as consultant. The Chardonnay is already one of the best in southern Italy, beautifully balanced, carefully oaked; Cabernet Sauvignon Burdese is exciting, as is Syrah, and Merlot is improving every year. The rich, peppery Santa Cecilia (Nero d'Avola) is an astonishingly perfumed, juicy, yet structured wine showing just how good this native variety can be. The basic La Segreta red and white are marvellously fruity. Latest addition is a fascinating Sicilian version of FIANO DI AVELLINO, Cometa – whose scented complexity totally changed our view of the Fiano grape and which lays serious claim to being the best example of the grape currently made.

PLANTAGENET
AUSTRALIA, Western Australia, Great Southern
♟ *Syrah (Shiraz), Cabernet Sauvignon, Pinot Noir*
♀ *Riesling, Chardonnay, Sauvignon Blanc*
The senior winery in the Mount Barker sub-region of the GREAT SOUTHERN region, Plantagenet makes around 35,000 cases a year on its own account but also provides a foster home for many other producers in the region by supplying winemaking facilities.

The quality of the wine is usually very good and sometimes great: an intense, lime-and-passionfruit Riesling, a stylish, spicy oak, melon-accented Chardonnay, a riotously spicy, peppery Shiraz and a wonderfully supple and complex, cherried Cabernet Sauvignon lead the way – and all made in an unglamorous apple-packing shed. The reds in general benefit from a little aging. Omrah is the second label, with good Sauvignon Blanc, Chardonnay and Shiraz. Best years: (Cabernet Sauvignon) 2001, '98, '97, '96, '95, '94, '93, '91, '90, '86, '85.

PODRAVJE
SLOVENIA
This district in the north-east of Slovenia, adjoining Austria's STEIERMARK, can be translated as the Drava Valley, and is the home of the country's best whites. The trouble is, they tend not to get exported; the wines from the LJUTOMER-Ormož sub-region that are interesting and individual are only just starting to appear on the export markets. But as well as Ljutomer-Ormož there are other sub-regions here: Prekmurske Gorice, Radgona-Kapela, Maribor, Srednje Slovenske Gorice, Šmarje-Virštanj and Haloze. The white grapes of the Pinot family do well, as does Welschriesling (Laski Rizling), but this is best drunk on the spot. There's crisp Sauvignon Blanc, good, rich Gewürztraminer (alias Traminec), occasional Rumeni Muškat or Yellow Muscat (elegant, with great finesse) and excellent late-harvest wines. Best producers: Jeruzalem Ormož, Joanneš, Kogl, Kupljen, Ljutomer winery, Valdhuber.

POL ROGER
FRANCE, Champagne, Champagne AC
♟ ♀ *Pinot Noir, Chardonnay, Pinot Meunier*
Pol Roger is the most anglophile of CHAMPAGNE houses, and the current head of the family, Christian de Billy, would probably take it as a great compliment if you mistook him for an Englishman. Churchill was a voracious consumer of Pol Roger, and it was Pol Roger he was thinking of when he said, in the dark days of World War Two, 'In victory we deserve it, in defeat we need it.'

In 1984 Pol Roger launched a vintage de luxe Cuvée Sir Winston Churchill, a delicious, refined drink worthy of the name. However, most of the production is of the non-vintage Brut Reserve (affectionally known as White Foil), which is gentle, light and reasonably consistent. There is also a Vintage Brut which regularly equals the best of its year, a Vintage Rosé and a delicate Vintage Chardonnay. Best years: 1996, '95, '93, '90, '89, '88, '86, '85, '82.

POLIZIANO

ITALY, Tuscany, Vino Nobile di Montepulciano DOCG

♀ Sangiovese, Canaiolo, Cabernet Sauvignon, Merlot, Colorino, Mammolo

This estate of 130ha (320 acres) of vineyard was purchased by the Carletti family in 1961, but it was not until the 1980s, when the present owner Federico Carletti came on board, that it began the journey which has taken it to the highest level in VINO NOBILE DI MONTEPULCIANO and at the same time has provided the whole DOCG with welcome leadership. Carletti is a viticulturist by training, and more than most who give lip-service to the theory that 'great wine is born in the vineyard', he backs the idea in practice, supported by one of TUSCANY's great consultant agronomist/enologists, Carlo Ferrini.

'For the time being', he says, he does not believe in blending Sangiovese with the French red varieties Cabernet Sauvignon and Merlot, which he vinifies separately for the excellent SUPER-TUSCAN Le Stanze, first made in 1983. He is also strict about not making the Vino Nobile cru Vigna Asinone, in years of medium quality, preferring rather to ensure the quality of his basic Vino Nobile. The style of the Vino Nobile is deep and vibrant of colour, rich and concentrated of fruit, firm of tannic backbone but with that soft cherry-berry fruit overlaying the tannins, seemingly powerful but more thanks to concentration than to alcohol (Ferrini tries to keep the wines around 13 degrees, when from other producers it can easily climb to 14 degrees or more in good years), and ultimately remarkably elegant. There is also delicious ROSSO DI MONTEPULCIANO and MORELLINO DI SCANSONO. Best years: (Vino Nobile) 2001, '00, '99, '97, '96, '95, '93, '90.

POLIZIANO

From a blend of Cabernet Sauvignon and Merlot, Le Stanze is one of Tuscany's top Bordeaux-style wines and is packed with rich blackcurrant fruit.

ERICH & WALTER POLZ

AUSTRIA, Steiermark, Südsteiermark, Spielfeld

♀ Zweigelt, Blaufränkisch, Cabernet Sauvignon

♀ Sauvignon Blanc, Chardonnay (Morillon), Pinot Blanc (Weissburgunder), Pinot Gris (Grauburgunder), Gelber Muskateller, Gewürztraminer (Traminer) and others

Brothers Erich and Walter Polz are perhaps the most consistent wine producers in all of STEIERMARK (Styria) but maybe the most ambitious also. They make two styles of wine. Firstly Steirische Klassik, the fresh, fruity, slightly lean and sharp wines that Steiermark is famous for, stainless steel-fermented without malolactic, and the Polzes do it extremely well. But to see what makes their pulses race and their ambition surge you only have to gaze with them up the steep rock faces of their prime vineyards – Obegg, Theresienhöhe, Grassnitzberg and Hochgrassnitzberg. Wines from these steepling sites are fermented and matured in oak and the Polzes seem almost unconcerned about which varietal is used – they want you to taste the vineyard, not the grape. The result is exceptional, complex dry whites and the occasional compelling sweetie. The 2000 Trockenbeerenauslese Hochgrassnitzberg was a Chardonnay-Sauvignon blend. As I said, vineyard not varietal matters here. Best years: (Chardonnay and Sauvignon Blanc) 2002, '01, '00, '99, '97.

ERICH & WALTER POLZ

Leading Steiermark producers, Erich and Walter Polz make a wide range of dry white wines, including elegant Chardonnay under its local name of Morillon.

POMEROL AC

FRANCE, Bordeaux (see also pages 326–327)

♀ Merlot, Cabernet Franc, Cabernet Sauvignon

From being a little known AC as recently as the 1970s, Pomerol is possibly now the most famous of the BORDEAUX regions, at least in the USA. Home to Ch. PÉTRUS, and the tiny, exorbitantly priced Ch. le PIN, it has become one of the most expensive of the Bordeaux ACs across the board. But you can't tell why Pomerol is so special just by looking at the landscape – and a mere country lane divides

it from the less valuable vines of ST-ÉMILION. The unique quality lies in that soil – 784ha (1960 acres) of deep, close-packed cloddish clay, interspersed with iron, a little gravel, a little sand, but ultimately it is the clay that makes Pomerol great.

The only Bordeaux grape that relishes clay is the Merlot. Most properties have over 80 per cent in their vineyards and the result is superb, inimitable wine – richer than any dry red wine should be, sometimes buttery, sometimes creamy with honeyed spices too; often plummy, but there's blackcurrant there as well, raisins, chocolate, roasted nuts and the disturbing perfume of truffles, with mint to freshen it up. No wonder it's expensive. And if all that sounds as though the wines won't age – they will, brilliantly. Best years: 2000, '98, '96, '95, '94, '90, '89, '88, '86, '85, '83, '82. Best producers: Beauregard, Bonalgue, le BON PASTEUR, Certan-de-May, Clinet, Clos l'Église, CLOS RENÉ, la CONSEILLANTE, l'Église-Clinet, l'ÉVANGILE, la Fleur-Pétrus, GAZIN, Hosanna (previously Certan-Guiraud), LAFLEUR, LATOUR-À-POMEROL, Montviel, Nénin (since 1990), PETIT-VILLAGE, Pétrus, le Pin, de Sales, TROTANOY, VIEUX-CHÂTEAU-CERTAN.

POMINO DOC

ITALY, Tuscany

♀ Sangiovese, Canaiolo, Cabernet Sauvignon and others

♀ Pinot Blanc (Pinot Bianco), Chardonnay, Trebbiano Toscano and others

Pomino, within the CHIANTI RUFINA zone, was first mentioned in Archduke Cosimo de' Medici III's Bando, a document of 1716 defining the boundaries of the four most illustrious wines of the time. Over 90 per cent of production comes from FRESCOBALDI. though the Rosso made by SELVAPIANA is also good. Best years: (reds) 2001, '00, '99, '97, '95.

POMMARD AC

FRANCE, Burgundy, Côte de Beaune

♀ Pinot Noir

The problem with Pommard is quality control. Its easily pronounceable name made the wine very sought-after in export markets, and until the 1970s much so-called Pommard was fraudulent. Today the problem is inconsistency. Quite often you find bottles at distressingly high prices which are coarse and rough with sullen, scentless flavours; and good BOURGOGNE Rouge from the same producers in Pommard can be actually better than their Pommard. Good Pommard should have full, round, beefy flavours, a bit jammy when young but becoming plummy, chocolaty and a little meaty with age. But fruit has to be at the core of the flavour. When it's good, Pommard ages well, often for ten years or more, retaining a thick core of fruit while gradually shedding its tannin. Of the 340ha (840 acres) of vines les Rugiens Bas, les Épenots and les Arvelets (all Premiers Crus) are the best sites. Best years: 2002, '99, '98, '97, '96, '95, '93, '90, '89, '88. Best producers: Comte ARMAND, J-M Boillot, Carré-Courbin, de Courcel, Dancer, P Garaudet, M Gaunoux, V GIRARDIN, LAFARGE, Lejeune, MONTILLE, J & A Parent, Ch. de Pommard, Pothier-Rieusset.

POMMERY

FRANCE, Champagne, Champagne AC
♀ ♂ *Chardonnay, Pinot Noir, Pinot Meunier*
Pommery is a house rich in history. Madame Pommery was one of the celebrated CHAMPAGNE widows, and ran the business for three decades, developing the crucial English market, which has always retained a fondness for Pommery. Indeed, the fantastical Pommery mansion is supposed to be a homage to the English country house, but students of architecture would find the references baffling. Her descendant, Prince Alain de Polignac, is still a consultant, but Pommery is now part of the Vranken group, along with Heidsieck Monopole and Champagne Demoiselle.

The style is light and elegant and does not always show well in the form of non-vintage Brut Royal. But the vintage Brut can be delicious even in less good years, and there is an ethereal delicacy to the prestige Cuvée Louise, which, dominated by Chardonnay, is slow to evolve in bottle. With Cuvée Louise also Prince Alain has always managed good wine in difficult years. This is at least partly due to the house's stunning vineyard holdings – they have 275ha (680 acres) of Grand Cru vines, and even in the worst years some of these favoured sites will give good wine. For such a famous old house, it's a bit of a surprise to find that their best-known product could be those bright blue quarter bottles labelled POP, drunk through a straw in nightclubs and at fashionable openings the world over. Best years: 1996, '95, '92, '90, '89, '88, '85, '82.

CH. PONTET-CANET

FRANCE, Bordeaux, Haut-Médoc, Pauillac AC, 5ème Cru Classé
♂ *Cabernet Sauvignon, Merlot, Cabernet Franc*
Pontet-Canet was, until the mid-1970s, one of the most popular and widely available of

The Pommard appellation has no less than 28 Premier Cru vineyards. On the Beaune side of the village les Grands Epenots is one of the best ones.

the HAUT-MÉDOC Classed Growths. The 80-ha (198-acre) vineyard next door to Ch. MOUTON-ROTHSCHILD regularly produced the largest amount of wine of any of the Classed Growths, and no wine was château-bottled until 1972. Since 1975 Pontet-Canet has been owned by the Tesserons of Ch. LAFON-ROCHET, and we are now seeing a return to the big, chewy, blackcurrant and sweet-oak style that is typical of the great PAUILLAC wines. Recent vintages show an impressive ripeness and concentration and Pontet-Canet are one of the few top Pauillacs to keep their prices reasonable. Best years: 2001, '00, '99, '98, '96, '95, '94, '90, '89, '86, '85, '83, '82.

PONZI VINEYARDS

USA, Oregon, Willamette Valley AVA
♂ *Pinot Noir, Dolcetto*
♀ *Pinot Gris, Chardonnay, Riesling, Pinot Blanc, Arneis*
The first vineyard was planted in 1970 and Ponzi soon gained a reputation for Pinot Gris and Pinot Noir at a time when Pinot Gris – now regarded as perhaps OREGON's best white style – was seen as decidedly oddball. Dick Ponzi was an early advocate of the use of new oak for his Pinot Noir Reserve, which is a bright and boldly flavoured wine. Oregon Chardonnay production has generally fallen, but Ponzi still makes two versions: one blends older Oregon vines and new Dijon clones; the Reserve is 100 per cent Dijon clones.

Equally important, since his French-trained daughter Luisa has assumed the role of winemaker, is the production of two Italian varieties that seem as unlikely as her father's Pinot Gris once did – Dolcetto and Arneis. But I can vouch for the Arneis: it's delicious. One thing, sadly, that they've stopped making is beer. Dick Ponzi was a pioneer of the Oregon microbrewery revolution – and a smashing hoppy drop it was too.

PORT DOC

PORTUGAL, Douro
♂ *Touriga Nacional, Touriga Franca, Tempranillo (Tinta Roriz), Tinta Barroca, Tinta Cão and others*
♀ *Gouveio, Viosinho, Rabigato, Malvasia Fina, Malvasia Dorada and others*
The world regards PORT as a global wine style, but Portugal is the originator and the master. Named after Portugal's second city, Porto (Oporto in English), the port wine region (Vinho do Porto) starts out on the steep slopes of the wild and beautiful DOURO Valley and its tributaries some 70km (43 miles) inland. Grapes are one of the only crops that will grow in the inhospitable climate that gets progressively drier the further inland you travel. The hillsides have been carved over the centuries into narrow step-like terraces, each of which support a row or two of vines. Mechanization is difficult and many of the finest vineyards are still cultivated by man and mule. Few places in the world are quite so challenging for growing grapes.

Many of the larger port shippers have built modern, well-equipped wineries in the Douro but a large amount of port is still produced in the traditional manner, the grapes being trodden by foot on small private farms known as quintas. Most of the quality ports leave the Douro Valley in the spring following the vintage, and travel by tanker to the lodges (or above-ground cellars) to age in the cooler maritime environment of Vila Nova de Gaia, on the opposite bank of the river Douro from Oporto.

Ports may be either red or white and fall into two categories: wood-matured or bottle-matured. Wood-matured ports range from the youngest, most basic ruby through premium ruby (sometimes misleadingly called Vintage Character) to the finest, oldest, most delicate tawnies. All are aged in wooden vats and casks, possibly for only a few months for a component of a young ruby blend, but 20 years or more is not uncommon for a fine tawny. Colheita ports, cask-aged tawnies from a single year, also fall into this category.

The finest of the bottle-matured ports is known as vintage, which is only 'declared' by the shippers after a truly exceptional harvest. It spends a mere two years in wood before being bottled (without any treatment or filtration), where it will age for another 15 or 20 years before being ready to drink. During this time the wine throws a 'crust' or sediment in bottle and therefore requires decanting.

The best wines from great vintages like 1997, '94, '77 and '63 will continue to develop well in bottle for half a century or more. In good in-between years, many shippers bottle vintage ports from single estates or quintas. These wines tend to be slightly earlier maturing, although some independent quintas (Quinta do VESÚVIO, Quinta de la ROSA, Quinta do CRASTO) have become shippers in their own right. Best years: (vintage ports) 2000, '97, '94, '92, '91, '85, '83, '80, '77, '70, '66, '63, '60, '55, '48, '47, '45, '35, '34, '27, '12, '08, '04, 1900.

A good, relatively inexpensive alternative to vintage port is crusted or crusting port. It is usually made from a blend of wines from two or three good years, aged for a short period in cask and then bottled, like vintage port, without filtration.

The unfiltered style of late bottled vintage (LBV) port is aged for four to six years in cask before bottling. Both will develop in bottle over the medium term and need decanting. Most LBV is made in large quantities and filtered before bottling. Although considerably better than a basic ruby it is a poor substitute for vintage port or traditional, unfiltered LBV. White port (from white grapes) tends to be fairly dull unless it is given extended wood-aging, which gives the wine a 'nutty' character. Best producers: Barros (tawnies), Burmester, CHURCHILL, COCKBURN, Quinta do Crasto, DOW, FERREIRA, FONSECA, GRAHAM, NIEPOORT, NOVAL, RAMOS PINTO, Quinta de la ROSA, SMITH WOODHOUSE, TAYLOR, Quinta do Vesúvio, WARRE.

POSAVJE
SLOVENIA

This is the name of the Sava Valley, in the south-east of Slovenia, where it borders Croatia. Between half and two-thirds of the wine is red, with the local favourite an attractive, light, acidic, berry-tasting number called Cviček. It's a blend of various grapes (such as Portugalka and Žametna Črnina), all of which are traditionally grown muddled up in the vineyards. Otherwise there are light but tangy and fresh whites for drinking young as

well as a few remarkable sweet Eisweins. Best producers: Istenič, Krško, Martinčič, Pleterje monastery, Plut.

CH. POTENSAC
FRANCE, Bordeaux, Médoc AC, Cru Bourgeois
♟ *Cabernet Sauvignon, Merlot, Cabernet Franc*

What a pleasure to be able to give an unreserved thumbs-up for quality, consistency and value to a BORDEAUX wine. There are two keys to Potensac's success. First, the ridge of gravel here. These are rare in the northern MÉDOC AC where low-lying, clay-clogged meadows are the order of the day, which in a damp cool area like this means the grapes have little hope of ripening except in the better years. Gravel is warm, and drains well. And that means you can ripen your grapes and perhaps even make fine wine. Second, the 50-ha (124-acre) estate is owned and run by Jean-Hubert Delon, who runs ST-JULIEN's great Second Growth LÉOVILLE-LAS-CASES.

Of all the proprietors in the lowly Médoc AC, Delon is the one who succeeds in drawing out a richness, a concentration and a complexity of blackcurrant, vanilla and spice flavour in his wine which, during the 1980s and '90s, regularly surpassed many Classed Growths for quality. Potensac can be drunk at four to five years old, but fine vintages will improve for at least ten. Best years: 2001, '00, '99, '98, '96, '95, '90, '89, '88.

CH. POTENSAC
Potensac's success is based on quality, consistency and value for money. The wine has delicious blackcurrant fruit and considerable depth.

POUILLY-FUISSÉ AC
FRANCE, Burgundy, Mâconnais
♀ *Chardonnay*

Pouilly-Fuissé is a dry white wine from the vineyards of five villages – Pouilly, Fuissé (yes, you did see a comma, they are two different villages), Vergisson, Chaintré and Solutré in the southern Mâconnais on the border with BEAUJOLAIS – that has become faddish and expensive because of insatiable demand from the American market.

The vineyards are beautiful – clustered under the startling rock outcrop of Solutré.

Many are ideally situated to produce fine wine, but the overbearing presence of the Chaintré co-operative, and the cynical disregard for quality by many of the merchants who buy three-quarters of the wine, has meant that most growers can get a good living by simply milking their vineyards of every last grape.

Luckily, 2 or 3 per cent of the AC is in the hands of committed growers who care passionately about the quality of Pouilly-Fuissé. They restrict their yields, use only ripe grapes, employ wooden barrels to both ferment and mature their wines, and the result is wine of character and individuality – buttery, nutty, the fruit full of peach and melon and banana, and all this enriched with the spice of cloves and cinnamon and a generous splash of honey. These wines can be wonderful at two years old, but often develop beautifully for up to ten. Best years: 2002, '01, '00, '99, '98, '97, '96, '95. Best producers: D & M Barraud, Corsin, C & T Drouin, J A Ferret, M Forest, Ch. FUISSÉ, Guffens-Heynen (Verget), R Lassarat, Léger-Plumet, R Luquet, O Merlin, Robert-Denogent, Valette.

POUILLY-FUMÉ AC
FRANCE, Central Loire
♀ *Sauvignon Blanc*

'Fumé' means 'smoky' in French, and there's no doubt that a good Pouilly-Fumé wine has a strong pungent smell. The old-time wine writers used to say it had a whiff of gunflint (*pierre à fusil*) about it. In fact, the smokiness is more that fabulous, fresh yet acrid aroma of roasting coffee. The only grape allowed is Sauvignon Blanc, which is famous for its gooseberry, grassy-green, even asparagus flavours, and what gives the extra smokiness and elderflower and lychee perfume in Pouilly is that many of its vineyards – covering 1070ha (2645 acres) on slopes near the town of Pouilly-sur-Loire – are planted on a particularly flinty soil called silex.

Increasingly, Pouilly-Fumé producers are making several cuvées, especially in good years such as 2000 and '99. Often there will be a 'basic' cuvée, then a more concentrated one made from grapes from a particular vineyard or old vines. Best years: 2001, '00, '99, '98, '97, '96, '95, '90. Best producers: Dom. des Berthiers, Gilles Blanchet, Henri BOURGEOIS, A Cailbourdin, J-C Chatelain, Didier DAGUENEAU, Serge Dagueneau, Marc Deschamps, de Ladoucette, Landrat-Guyollot, Masson-Blondelet, Michel Redde, Tinel-Blondelet, de Tracy.

POUILLY-LOCHÉ AC, POUILLY-VINZELLES AC

FRANCE, Burgundy, Mâconnais

♀ *Chardonnay*

Loché and Vinzelles are two perfectly decent Mâconnais villages with the vines on the flatter land just to the east of Fuissé. Funnily enough, the growers of Vinzelles tried to organize their own AC in 1922 – long before POUILLY-FUISSÉ – but as Pouilly-Fuissé's Midas touch turned every bottling run into a money-minting extravaganza, it seemed obvious that adding Pouilly to their own names might prove profitable. That's the angle.

So does it work? Yes, Pouilly-Vinzelles and Pouilly-Loché are more expensive than equivalent wines like MÂCON-Lugny. And no, the quality of the wine – largely processed by the Loché co-operative – is not a patch on a good Pouilly-Fuissé – it's really just Mâcon-Blanc-Villages dressed up with a fancy name. Best years: 2002, '01, '00, '99. Best producers: Caves des Grands Crus Blancs, la Soufrandière, Tripoz, Valette.

CH. POUJEAUX

FRANCE, Bordeaux, Haut-Médoc, Moulis AC, Cru Bourgeois

♥ *Cabernet Sauvignon, Merlot, Cabernet Franc, Petit Verdot*

Poujeaux is one of several properties whose improving winemaking standards in the past 20 years or so have helped to nudge the MOULIS AC into the limelight. It's a big property of some 52ha (128 acres) and is beautifully located on the gravel banks around the village of Grand-Poujeaux.

Although its reputation is for dry, long-lived wines, vintages in the 1980s and '90s have been richer, more supple, with a delicious chunky fruit, new-oak sweetness and a slight scent of tobacco. This more accurately reflects the very high percentage of Merlot in the vineyard – 40 per cent, with 50 per cent Cabernet Sauvignon, 5 per cent Cabernet Franc and 5 per cent Petit Verdot. The consistency of the wines at this estate and their long aging potential – 20–30 years for good vintages – make Poujeaux a Classed Growth in all but name. Best years: 2001, '00, 98, '96, '95, '94, '90, '89, '88, '86, '85, '83, '82.

DOMAINE DE LA POUSSE D'OR

FRANCE, Burgundy, Côte de Beaune, Volnay AC

♥ *Pinot Noir*

♀ *Chardonnay*

The renown of this 13-ha (32-acre) estate was established by the late Gérard Potel, who had

a knack of producing stylish, zesty wines even in poor vintages such as 1984. The domaine's best-known wines emanated from sites in VOLNAY – Clos de la Bousse d'Or and les Caillerets – and POMMARD (les Jarollières). The estate was sold to an Australian consortium in 1997, and Gérard Potel died suddenly and poignantly on the day the sale was ratified. In 1998 La Pousse d'Or was bought by Patrick Landanger, who has made major changes to both cellar and vineyard, so the future of the domaine, in terms of quality and style, has to be somewhat uncertain. Best years: 1996, '95, '93, '91, '90, '89, '88.

CH. PRADEAUX

FRANCE, Provence, Bandol AC

♥♀ *Mourvèdre, Cinsaut, Grenache*

In every sense of the word this is a traditional domaine, which continues to produce one of the great wines from BANDOL, an appellation high above the Mediterranean. Owner Cyrille Portalis cultivates the 19-ha (47-acre) vineyard along organic lines. At the harvest the grapes are lightly crushed but not destemmed and the resulting wine then spends three or four years aging in large wooden barrels called *foudres*. This makes for a powerful, tightly textured red wine with enormous aging potential. Twenty years is not a problem for this essentially Mourvèdre-based wine.

There are usually two cuvées – La Rose Folle and Longue Garde – the second one, as the name implies, not to be taken lightly. The rosé is made from Cinsaut, Grenache and Mourvèdre. Second wine: l'Enclos de Pradeaux. Best years: (reds) 2000, '99, '98, '97, '96, '95, '93, '91, '90.

CH. PRADEAUX
This is a big, deep-hued red wine from mainly Mourvèdre which is aged for three to five years in wood to soften the Mourvèdre's tannin.

FRANZ PRAGER

AUSTRIA, Niederösterreich, Wachau, Weissenkirchen

♀ *Riesling, Grüner Veltliner*

Franz Prager was one of the pioneers of dry whites in the WACHAU from the late 1950s. Since the end of the 1980s, when his daughter Ilse and son-in-law Toni Bodenstein took over

the estate, it has gone from strength to strength. Bodenstein, who is also a director of one of Austria's largest banks, is obsessed with vineyard character, and every year his Rieslings from the Steinriegl, Achleiten and Klaus sites of WEISSENKIRCHEN are strikingly different from one another. The Steinriegl is always the sleekest and most open, the Achleiten shows seductive apricot fruit and lots of minerals, the Klaus is concentrated and severe with great aging potential. The best Grüner Veltliner is a succulent wine from the Achleiten, the site from which Bodenstein's magnificent Riesling Trockenbeerenauslese also originates.

There are only 14ha (34 acres) of vines, 75 per cent of which are Riesling. The amount of wine produced each year is tiny, but the quality is sensational. Best years: (Smaragd whites) 2002, '01, '00, '99, '98, '97, '96, '95, '93, '92, '90, '86.

PREMIÈRES CÔTES DE BLAYE AC

FRANCE, Bordeaux

♥ *Merlot, Cabernet Sauvignon, Cabernet Franc, Malbec*

♀ *Sauvignon Blanc, Sémillon, Muscadelle*

Premières Côtes de Blaye is the supposedly superior AC for reds and whites from the Blayais, a wine area of 6066ha (14,990 acres) on the opposite side of the Gironde to Lamarque in the HAUT-MÉDOC. There are definite signs of improvement in this region.

Until now the problems have been a lack of that acid bite and tannic grip which make red BORDEAUX special. The wines have been smudgy, sludgy things, jammy and sweet to taste and earthy of texture. The AC for whites permits only three grape varieties, as against seven for neighbouring CÔTES DE BLAYE. The wines can be dry, medium or even sweet, but in practice only a small amount of white wine is produced. Although vines were planted here long before they were in the MÉDOC, any wine fame the Premières Côtes de Blaye once had is long gone, and Blaye itself, a rather attractive little town, is best known for its great seventeenth-century citadel and the car ferry to Lamarque across the Gironde. However, a new generation – one-third of the growers are now under 35 – with the assistance of a technical adviser, is now producing red wines with more zip and fruit. Investment in winemaking equipment and new oak barrels along with better vineyard management have been largely instrumental in the lift in quality. Best years: 2001, '00, '98, '96, '95, '94, '90, '89, '88. Best producers: (reds) Bel Air la Royère, Haut-Bertinerie, Haut-Grelot,

Haut-Sociondo, Jonqueyres, Loumède, Mondésir-Gazin, Roland-la-Garde, Segonzac, Sociondo, des Tourtes; (whites) Haut-Bertinerie, Charron (Acacia), Cave des Hauts de Gironde, des Tourtes (Prestige).

PREMIÈRES CÔTES DE BORDEAUX AC

FRANCE, Bordeaux

♥ ♥ *Merlot, Cabernet Sauvignon, Cabernet Franc*

♀ *Sémillon, Sauvignon Blanc, Muscadelle*

The Premières Côtes de Bordeaux region has some of the most captivating scenery in BOR-DEAUX. This lovely hilly AC stretches for 60km (38 miles) down the right bank of the Garonne river. Time and again as you breast a hill you find yourself at the top of steep slopes running down to the Garonne, with an unparalleled view across the river to the famous properties of GRAVES and SAUTERNES on the opposite bank.

The Premières Côtes de Bordeaux used to be thought of as sweet white territory, especially since three communes here – CADILLAC, LOUPIAC and STE-CROIX-DU-MONT – do specialize in 'Sauternes look-alike' sweeties. But as the fashion for sweet wines faded during the 1970s, more and more growers turned to red wine with a good deal of success. Since the 1980s, plantings of white varieties have dropped by over 20 per cent to about 315ha (780 acres), while reds have rocketed to 3572ha (8830 acres). Most of this white, however, only qualifies for the Bordeaux Sec AC, since the Premières Côtes AC requires a minimum of four grams of sugar per litre. This isn't a lot, but it is too much for growers who are trying to make fashionable dry whites.

In the north, near Bordeaux, a certain amount of clairet – light red, halfway to rosé – is made for quick and easy drinking. However, as the vineyards mature, a very attractive juicy fruit quality has become evident in the reds, and – with investment in better equipment, including some oak barrels for aging – the future is already looking bright for the area, particularly as the wines represent excellent value for money in today's high-flying market. Reds and rosés are usually delicious at two to three years old, but reds should last for five to six; the whites, especially the dry ones, won't last that long. Best years: (reds) 2000, '98, '96, '95, '94, '90. Best producers: (reds) Brethous, Carsin, Chelivette, Clos Ste-Anne, Grand-Mouëys, de Haux, du Juge/Dupleich, Lamothe-de-Haux, Langoiran, Melin, Puy-Bardens, Reynon, le Sens, Suau, Tanesse.

PRIEURÉ DE ST-JEAN DE BÉBIAN

FRANCE, Languedoc-Roussillon, Coteaux du Languedoc AC

♥ *Grenache, Syrah, Mourvèdre and others*

♀ *Roussanne, Bourboulenc, Clairette, Grenache Blanc, Picpoul and others*

During the 1970s and '80s Alain Roux made this one of LANGUEDOC's ground-breaking domaines, planting Syrah, Grenache and Mourvèdre as well as growing all the 13 CHÂTEAUNEUF-DU-PAPE varieties together in one jumbled-up plot and turning out rich, spicy, powerful, if slightly rustic wines.

The quality faded in the early 1990s but has again been excellent since former wine writer Chantal Lecouty and her husband purchased the domaine in 1994. The grapes are now partially destemmed and the wine aged in barriques and 600-litre casks in order to produce a more refined tannic structure along with the intense spicy fruit. There is also a VIN DE PAYS de l'HÉRAULT L'Autre Versant from old Cabernet and Merlot vines and a barrel-fermented COTEAUX DU LANGUEDOC white. Second wine: la Chapelle de Bébian. Best years: (red) 2001, '00, '99, '98, '97, '96.

PRIMITIVO

Pundits seem satisfied that the Italian red grape Primitivo, so named because it is an early ripener, is identical to Zinfandel, both hailing from former Yugoslavia where it still exists under the name Crljenak and is related to one of Croatia's best grapes Plavac Mali.

Today Primitivo thrives in the sunbaked flatland around Manduria (east of Taranto in PUGLIA's Salento peninsula), turning out its richest, most concentrated grapes on low trained *alberello* bushes – those that remain, that is, after an ill-conceived EU vinepull scheme removed many of the oldest. No grape beats Primitivo for grape sugar, which when fermented means high alcohol levels, and indeed in Puglia the wine can achieve some frighteningly high levels of alcohol. Most of the grapes are used to bump up the weedier offerings of elsewhere in Italy and Europe (mainly France). Those that are used for Primitivo wine make, traditionally, a dark purple wine that is dry, slightly or fully sweet, even occasionally fortified, but whatever the style is a gutsy beast of 14 per cent minimum alcohol. But one producer, PERVINI, is turning out blended wines of real elegance, under the names of Bizantino (Rosso del Salento) and I Monili (Primitivo del Tarantino), both IGT wines.

Primitivo is also the grape behind the reds of Gioia del Colle, inland from Manduria.

PRIMO ESTATE

Talented winemaker Joe Grilli works wonders with an enormous range of grapes. His Joseph Moda Amarone Cabernet-Merlot uses partially dried grapes and is made in a similar way to the great Amarone wines from Valpolicella in North-East Italy.

PRIMO ESTATE

AUSTRALIA, South Australia, Adelaide Plains

♥ *Syrah (Shiraz), Cabernet Sauvignon, Sangiovese and others*

♀ *Colombard, Pinot Gris (Pinot Grigio), Riesling*

It doesn't sound promising when your driver turns off the road in the flat dusty nothing land just north of Adelaide and says 'here we are'. I've come looking for one of Australia's most talented and innovative winemakers and we've arrived on a patch of dust that looks as though it would be better growing tomatoes – which is what most of his neighbours do. But that's one reason why Joe Grilli of Primo Estate is so special.

The vineyard land around the winery isn't special, and it is very hot indeed, but Grilli coaxes marvellously lemony Colombard and spicy Shiraz-Sangiovese out of it. That's just the beginning. Under the Joseph label he produces waxy, honeyed Pinot Grigio, remarkable Cabernet-Merlot made like Italy's *amarone* from dried Cabernet grapes and a little cool-climate Merlot, and a simply stunning sparkling red containing material up to 40 years old, called just Joseph. Add in superb sweet Riesling and thrilling fortified called 'The Fronti' that he ages as hot as possible in his vineyard shed rather like they age MADEIRA – and you've got one of Australia's – and the world's – great wine originals. Oh, olive oil. He makes sumptuous olive oil from 100-year-old trees that was recently voted Australia's best. Thank goodness he doesn't play cricket. Best years: (Cabernet-Merlot Joseph) 2001, '00, '99, '98, '97, '96, '95, '94, '93, '91, '90.

PRIMORJE

SLOVENIA

This is the part of Slovenia that borders the FRIULI region of Italy and in fact straddles the COLLIO zone, so you find grapes like Tocai Friulano, Picolit, Ribolla (Rebula) and Refosco in both zones and a strong similarity

In the mountainous, isolated region of Priorat, a remote area of Cataluña, vineyards are planted in deep, slate soil on precipitous slopes. Vineyard yields here are some of the lowest in Spain.

of freshness and lightness among whites at least. There's also good Sauvignon Blanc and Merlot, but the most popular wine locally is Refosk (also called Teran), made from the red grape that over the border in Italy is called Refosco. It's lean, with razor-like acidity and cherry-like fruit, and is opaquely black. The Malvasia can be good and apricotty; the Chardonnay is fair but doesn't yet match up to the better ones from elsewhere in the world. Best producers: MOVIA, Prinčič, Santomas, Simčič, Sutor, Vinakoper.

PRIORAT DOCa

SPAIN, Cataluña
♀♂ *Grenache Noir (Garnacha Tinta), Garnacha Peluda, Cariñena, Cabernet Sauvignon, Merlot, Syrah*
♀ *Garnacha Blanca, Macabeo, Pedro Ximénez, Cariñena*

Situated inland in the south of CATALUÑA, this is one of the loveliest and wildest regions of Spain, with scrubby, craggy mountains and narrow, winding roads. Traditionally Garnacha Tinta and Garnacha Peluda were the predominant grape varieties, but Cariñena now accounts for a third to a half of most blends. Tiny yields mean Priorat (Priorato in Spanish) produces extremely concentrated, dark, intense wines. They are also inevitably alcoholic: the minimum legal strength for table wines is 13.5 per cent.

Most of the wines lately have been 'young' reds, sold at between three and four years old, but Priorat also makes some excellent *rancio*-styled wines and *generosos* – dry to sweet, penetratingly flavourful, nutty, raisiny wines, wood-aged for a minimum of five years. White wines are very scarce.

However, alongside such tradition, a revolution is taking place. A group of new producers moved into the village of Gratallops during the 1980s, planted French varieties to make blends with the native Garnacha and Cariñena, introduced modern winemaking techniques and new French oak barrels, and created a new style of Priorat which astonished the world's critics and emptied their wallets. So far, tradition and revolution seem to be good for each other. The area was promoted to DOCa in 2001. Best years: 2001, '00, '99, 98, '96, '95, '94, '93, '90. Best producers: Bodegas B G (Gueta-Lupía), Capafons-Ossó, Cims de Porrera, CLOS ERASMUS, Clos dels Llops, CLOS MOGADOR, La Conreria d'Scala Dei, COSTERS DEL SIURANA, J M Fuentes (Gran Clos), Mas Doix, Mas d'en Gil (Clos Fontà), MAS MARTINET, Álvaro PALACIOS, Pasanau Germans (Finca la Planeta), Rotllan Torra, Scala Dei, Vall-Llach.

PROSECCO DI CONEGLIANO-VALDOBBIADENE DOC

ITALY, Veneto
♀ *Prosecco, Verdiso*

Sparkling Prosecco is one of those wines the locals – such as the few Italians who live in Venice – take for granted, a little like brown ale in Newcastle, northern England. Generally, it's a simple, yeasty little number, made in a sizeable zone in eastern VENETO at the western and eastern edges of which are the towns of Valdobbiadene and Conegliano. The wine may take the name of just one of them, an option that most producers thankfully use.

At the Valdobbiadene end is a sub-zone called Cartizze, credited with producing the finest wines and so granted its own sub-denomination, Superiore di Cartizze. Prosecco di Conegliano-Valdobbiadene can be a still wine, but is usually frizzante or spumante, as Prosecco is one of those grapes that tend to produce fizz, sometimes whether you want it or not. The wine is made sparkling by a second fermentation in tank, not in the bottle as in CHAMPAGNE. All three styles of Prosecco can be dry or sweet. So there is plenty to keep label printers happy and to confuse potential customers.

When in Venice, Prosecco, with its soft, floral, appley, milky flavours will taste great. Back home it won't taste as good – you can't export atmosphere – but it will still be a refreshing glass of simple, soft wine with bubbles. Drink young. Best producers: Adami, Bernardi, Bisol, Carpenè Malvolti (the best-known name), Le Colture, Col Vetoraz, Nino Franco, La Riva dei Frati, Ruggeri & C, Tanorè, Zardetto.

PROVENCE

FRANCE
Provence is home to France's oldest vineyards but the region is better known for its beaches and arts festivals than for its wines. However, it seems even Provence is caught up in the revolution sweeping through the vineyards of southern France. The area has five small ACs (BANDOL, les BAUX-DE-PROVENCE, BELLET, CASSIS and PALETTE), but most of the wine comes from the much larger areas of the CÔTES DE PROVENCE, COTEAUX VAROIS, Coteaux de Pierrevert and COTEAUX D'AIX-EN-PROVENCE. Vin de Pays des BOUCHES-DU-RHÔNE in the west of the region is also becoming increasingly important. Provençal red wines are generally better than the whites and rosés.

J J PRÜM

GERMANY, Mosel-Saar-Ruwer, Wehlen
♀ *Riesling*
The Prüm estate, one of the important and probably the most famous of the Mittel MOSEL producers, was divided in 1911. J J Prüm has 13ha (33.5 acres) and is now the best known of several Prüms on the Mosel, making some of the region's finest Rieslings. The wines are of excellent quality, sometimes

unapproachable in youth but remarkably long-lived and rewarding to those who can be bothered to age them. The estate owns a large part of the WEHLENer Sonnenuhr vineyard as well as parts of GRAACHer Himmelreich and BERNKASTELer Lay. Best years: 2002, '01, '99, '98, '97, '96, '95, '94, '93, '90, '89, '88, '86, '85, '83, '79, '76, '71.

S A PRÜM

GERMANY, Mosel-Saar-Ruwer, Wehlen
♀ *Riesling, Pinot Blanc (Weissburgunder)*

This chunk of the original Prüm estate in the MOSEL, divided in 1911, now belongs to Dr Renate Willkomm but is still run by Raimund Prüm. Not surprisingly, it shares some vineyard sites in common with J J PRÜM, notably the WEHLENer Sonnenuhr, and GRAACHer Himmelreich and Domprobst.

J J Prüm has the greater reputation but S A Prüm should not be overlooked: the wines are made with great care, with no Süssreserve, and with extensive cask-aging. The QbA wines are sold under the estate name alone, with vineyard names only being used for the higher quality designations, a practice that is becoming quite common among the best German estates. Best years: 2002, '01, '99, '97, '95, '93, '90, '88, '86, '85.

PRUNOTTO

ITALY, Piedmont, Barolo DOCG
❗ *Dolcetto, Nebbiolo, Barbera*
♀ *Arneis, Moscato Bianco*

Following Alfredo Prunotto's retirement in 1956, Beppe Colla became the winemaker at this high-class *commerciante* establishment (buying grapes on long-term contracts from top growers). One of the quality leaders and trend-setters of the Albese region, he pioneered the concept of the single-vineyard cru, way back in the early 1960s. Meanwhile he continued to believe in blended BAROLO and BARBARESCO and maintained that great Nebbiolo and using barriques did not go together.

ANTINORI, of Tuscan fame, bought the company in 1989 and, not surprisingly, modernized practices. In 1995, after the end of Colla's consultancy, Prunotto began using French oak, 5-hectolitre *fusti* for the aging of some Barolo and Barbaresco, as well as shortening maceration time and, perhaps most important of all, purchasing new vineyards.

Despite these changes, Prunotto still remains one of the pillars of classic Piedmont reds, with wines such as the Barolo crus Bussia and Cannubi, the Barbaresco Bric Turot, NEBBIOLO D'ALBA Occhetti, and the BARBERA

PRUNOTTO
The Cannubi Barolo Cru is a perfumed, velvety Barolo with superb fruit and excellent in its well-balanced smoothness.

D'ALBA Pian Romualdo, which really shows how exciting Barbera can be given the chance. Best years: (Barolo) 2001, '00, '99, '98, '97, '96, '95, '90, '89, '88, '85.

PUGLIA

ITALY

Puglia, the heel of the Italian boot, is an elongated region which, winewise, divides into three parts. The first is in the north, a virtual extension of ABRUZZO and MOLISE, where Montepulciano and Uva di Troia feature in DOCs such as San Severo and Cacc'e Mmitte di Lucera; there is nothing here to get excited about. In the centre, around the Murge plateau, there are a cluster of DOCs of which CASTEL DEL MONTE is the least obscure.

It is from the south, however – the Salento peninsula – that the most interesting wines come. The heat of the low-lying flatlands is mitigated by sea-breezes from either side, and there is a long tradition of planting the dominant Primitivo and Negroamaro grapes to the high-quality, if labour-intensive, freestanding, bush-training system called *alberello*. Wines include Primitivo di Manduria DOC and Primitivo del Salento IGT, plus a host of Negroamaro-based wines headed, in popularity terms, by SALICE SALENTINO and including Brindisi, Copertino, Leverano, Alezio and Squinzano. The red dessert wine, Aleatico di Puglia DOC, is mostly produced south of Bari; so, too, is the key white wine of Puglia, Locorotondo DOC. International varieties like Chardonnay and Cabernet Sauvignon also feature in many of the region's IGT blends.

PULIGNY-MONTRACHET AC

FRANCE, Burgundy, Côte de Beaune
♀ *Chardonnay*
❗ *Pinot Noir and others*

If you feel a thirst coming on in Puligny-Montrachet, making a beeline for the Café du Centre won't do you much good. Although the sign is still there, the café has been closed

for years. In fact all the cafés and bars in Puligny are shut. It's a strange feeling. Puligny-Montrachet – the home of what most people reckon is the greatest dry white in the world – and yet you can't get a drink there for love or money. The reason is probably to be found in the fact that this dull little village has been declining in population for years as the mighty merchants of neighbouring Beaune buy up the land to guarantee their supplies of wine, and families whose forebears have worked the vineyards for generations must shuffle off townwards in search of work.

But the mediocrity of the village cannot dim the brilliance of its best vineyards. The pinnacle is the Grand Cru le MONTRACHET, an ordinary-looking 8-ha (19¾-acre) vineyard which manages to produce such a wine that the French author Alexandre Dumas said it should only be drunk 'on one's knees with head uncovered'.

There are three other Grands Crus, almost as good, and 11 Premiers Crus, which are still among the most exciting wines in Burgundy. These take up all the best slopes above the village, and although the flatter land is allowed the Puligny-Montrachet AC, the result is less thrilling. Good vintages need five years to show what all the fuss is about, while the Premiers Crus and Grands Crus may need ten years and can last for 20 or more. Only about 5 per cent of the AC's production is red wine. Best years: 2002, '01, '00, '99, '97, '96, '95, '92. Best producers: J-M Boillot, CARILLON, J Chartron, G Chavy, DROUHIN, A Ente, B Ente, JADOT, Larue, Louis LATOUR, Dom. LEFLAIVE (since 1994), Olivier LEFLAIVE, P Pernot, Ch. de Puligny-Montrachet, RAMONET, SAUZET.

PYRENEES

AUSTRALIA, Victoria,

The Australian Pyrenees are but a faint echo of their European counterpart, with eucalyptus trees thickly carpeting gentle slopes. From the winemaking point of view, the region got off to an erratic start. In 1962 Chateau Remy was founded to produce brandy from Trebbiano, without much success – the Trebbiano has now been replaced by Chardonnay and Pinot Noir, which now make reasonably good CHAMPAGNE-method fizz – in a region more suited to very robust reds. Luckily there are now several producers of stunning Shiraz and Cabernet as well as surprisingly fresh and tasty Chardonnay and Sauvignon Blanc. Best years: (Shiraz) 2001, '99, '98, '97, '96, '94, '91, '90. Best producers: Blue Pyrenees, DALWHINNIE, Redbank, Summerfield, Taltarni.

PYRÉNÉES-ORIENTALES

FRANCE, Languedoc-Roussillon

The Pyrénées-Orientales is the torrid, gale-scoured, southernmost French *département*, climbing up to the Spanish border in a succession of thin-aired high passes which start on the sheer cliffs above the Mediterranean, and end shrouded in clouds near Andorra.

Annual wine production is about 180 million bottles, about 45 per cent of which are VINS DE PAYS. The ACs are, first, the *vins doux naturels* – sweet, fortified wines, of which RIVESALTES and BANYULS are the best known; the dark red COLLIOURE from near the Spanish border; and CÔTES DU ROUSSILLON and CÔTES DU ROUSSILLON-VILLAGES. The extreme climate is much better suited to red than white, but there is some quite attractive Côtes du Roussillon white. The one white wine glory of the Pyrénées-Orientales – the rich and gooey MUSCAT DE RIVESALTES – is nearer a burnished gold in colour.

Unlike other southern vins de pays, there is little experimental vine planting, but a few estates, like La Barrera and Mas Chichet, are making exciting use of Merlot and Cabernet Sauvignon and the ubiquitous Chardonnay pops up here too, giving attractive, quick-maturing wines, sometimes made with a little oak. The Vin de Pays des Pyrénées-Orientales designation covers the *département*, though there are five zonal vins de pays, of which 'Catalan' is the most important. Best producers: (Vin de Pays des Pyrénées-Orientales) Vignerons Catalans, CAZES, Mas Chichet.

QUADY

USA, California, Madera AVA
❢ *Black Muscat, Tempranillo (Tinta Roriz), Tinto Cão, Tinta Amarela, Touriga Nacional*
♀ *Orange Muscat, Muscat Blanc*

Andrew Quady is one of the only true individuals to emerge from CALIFORNIA's CENTRAL VALLEY, a region synonymous with vast faceless wineries and agro-industrial vineyards stretching straight as a die as far as the eye can see. Quady worked for some of these without enthusiasm until in 1981 he set up by himself and concentrated on making sweet fortified Muscats in the style of the southern French *vins doux naturels*. Essensia is a beautifully orange blossom-scented golden wine made from…Orange Muscat. Elysium is a deep blueberry-flavoured, rose petal-perfumed wine made from Black Hamburg Muscat. He also makes low-alcohol Electra, good PORT-style wines and two exceptional Vermouths called Vya, made extra sweet or dry.

QUAILS' GATE

CANADA, British Columbia, Okanagan Valley VQA
❢ *Pinot Noir, Merlot, Foch, Cabernet Sauvignon, Gamay*
♀ *Chardonnay, Riesling, Chenin Blanc, Gewurztraminer, Chasselas, Pinot Blanc, Optima, Sauvignon Blanc*

Quails' Gate was first developed in the early 1900s when the Stewart family opened the OKANAGAN VALLEY's first nursery business to serve local orchard owners. By the mid-1950s they were growing grapes and in 1990 they opened the doors to Quails' Gate Estate Winery. In 1993 Australian winemaker Jeff Martin put Quails' Gate on the map with his fruit-driven, Limited Release varietals led by Chenin Blanc, Gewurztraminer, Riesling and a range of highly regarded Chardonnay and Pinot Noir wines. The winery has also developed a cult following for its Old Vines Foch, a Shiraz-style, blockbuster, hybrid red. The Family Reserve wines are only released in the best years. The departure of Martin opened the door for another Aussie Peter Draper, and then another, Ashley Hooper, to join the firm.

QUARTS DE CHAUME AC

FRANCE, Loire, Anjou-Saumur, Grand Cru
♀ *Chenin Blanc*

Sample a young Quarts de Chaume, and you'd never know that you were experiencing one of the world's greatest sweet wines in its infancy. Whereas most dessert wines at least taste rich right from the start, Quarts de Chaume can be rather nuttily dull, vaguely sweet in a crisp apple kind of way and acidic – above all, acidic. This is thanks to the Chenin grape – the most fiercely, raspingly acidic of all France's great grapes, frequently used to make dry whites so strangled with their own sourness they never recover. But on the gentle slopes protected by a low horseshoe of hills around the village of Chaume, the Chenin finds one of its best mesoclimates.

The vineyards slope south to the little Layon river, and if the sun shines, the grapes ripen more than any others in the LOIRE Valley. And as the mists of autumn begin to twine and curl off the river, the magic noble rot fungus concentrates the richness to as great a degree as in SAUTERNES. Pickers have to go through the vineyard several times so as to select only the grapes affected by noble rot and this contributes to Quarts de Chaume having the lowest maximum yield of any AC in France – 22 hectolitres per hectare; in many years they don't even achieve that. The winter often closes in as the pickers toil

through the vineyard for a last time, and in the following few months the wine ferments quietly until the spring.

The result is all fruit and no oak influence. And it lasts for as long as any sweet wine in the world – thanks to Chenin's acidity. It may seem dull for its first few years, but after ten years the pale gold becomes tinged with orange, the apple sweetness blends with apricot and peach…and in the full sunset glow of 20 years' maturity, honey fills out the perfume of the peach – with a bitter twist of nut kernel roughness and the dark, fascinating intensity of quince jelly. The wine may then stay in this happy state for another 20 years. Production of this classic is less than 80,000 bottles a year, and the price is now fairly high, which, frankly, is how it should be. Best years: 2002, '01, '99, '97, '96, '95, '94, '93, '90, '89, '88, '85, '83, '81, '78, '76, '70, '69, '64, '59, '47. Best producers: BAUMARD, Bellerive, Laffourcade, Pierre-Bise, Jo Pithon, de Plaisance (Rochais), Joseph Renou, Suronde.

QUEENSLAND

AUSTRALIA

You'd have to say that the problem for Queensland in growing decent wine grapes would be that it's too hot, but in the nineteenth century the complaints laid against the GRANITE BELT, Queensland's best-established quality wine area, were that it was too cold! Well, there's cold and there's cold. If you tot up the amount of heat this area below Brisbane on the NEW SOUTH WALES border gets, it's hotter than RUTHERGLEN in North-East VICTORIA whose torrid conditions are just right for making sumptuous rich fortified wines. Talking of which, if you *really* want hot, Roma, inland to the west of Brisbane, has been a wine region since 1863, and, with the exception of Alice Springs in Australia's red hot heart, that *is* the hottest vineyard in Australia. It's reputed to make Australia's best MADEIRA-style wine.

In general, it is difficult to assert that Queensland is ideally suited to the vine, when so many other parts of Australia are. But the Granite Belt thrives, admittedly helped by occupying a picturesque position south of Stanthorpe in the hills along the New England Highway that gets flooded with cash-rich tourists every year. And it's the hills that make decent wine possible. The vineyards, initially planted in 1859, are between 750 and 1000 metres (2500 and 3300ft) high, often facing away from the sun, allowing the grapes to ripen slowly so that vintage is late – mid-

March to mid-April – and some good hefty Shiraz and minerally Semillon result.

Since the 1990s several other areas have sprung up. South Burnett near Kingaroy north-west of Brisbane is now Queensland's biggest vineyard region as the locals give up dairy farming and turn to vines. Mount Tamborine near the Gold Coast has vines, and there are also vines in the Bunya Mountains, and 500km (300 miles) inland on the banks of the Balonne river near St George. So Queensland isn't a major Aussie player, and never will be, but there's a significant amount of wine that's a lot better than just tourist grog. Best producers (excluding Granite Belt): Albert River, Clovely Estate, Sirromet.

QUERCIABELLA

ITALY, Tuscany, Chianti Classico DOCG
♟ *Sangiovese, Cabernet Sauvignon, Merlot and others*
♀ *Chardonnay, Pinot Blanc (Pinot Bianco)*
In the unlikely event of there ever being a BORDEAUX-like classification of the great estates of TUSCANY, Querciabella would surely be in the running for Premier Cru status. Founded in the early 1970s by industrialist Giuseppe Castiglioni, who has today given way to his wine-enthusiast son Sebastiano, Querciabella has arrived at a point where one expects at least near perfection from every bottle produced. The CHIANTI CLASSICO has about 10 per cent of Cabernet Sauvignon and Merlot in it and is exquisitely crafted by resident enologist Guido De Santi. The top red is an illustrious SUPER-TUSCAN, Camartina, a rich and grandly elegant blend of 75 per cent Sangiovese and 25 per cent Cabernet Sauvignon and aged in new barriques, recently joined by an exciting Merlot-Sangiovese blend Palafreno. Perhaps the most surprising wine, however, is the super-Tuscan white Batàr. This is a barrique-aged blend of half Pinot Bianco-half Chardonnay of astonishing complexity and concentration, at times just a bit too much in terms of richness and oak. But am I complaining? They also own a Maremma property. Best years: (Camartina) 2001, '00, '99 '97, '95, '90, '88.

QUILCEDA CREEK

USA, Washington State, Columbia Valley AVA
♟ *Cabernet Sauvignon, Merlot, Cabernet Franc*
Begun in 1978, Quilceda Creek is a boutique winery devoted to producing fine WASHINGTON Cabernet Sauvignon. The winemaking team of Alex Golitzin, his son Paul and Marv Crum makes compelling wines – including

Red Table Wine (Cabernet Sauvignon leavened with a splash of Cabernet Franc) and tiny quantities of Merlot – which now enjoy a cult following, from grapes sourced from several Washington vineyards. They are deeply coloured, with pure varietal character, very full body and require time to show their potential. They also age gracefully for well over a decade. Best years: (Cabernet) 2001, '00, '99, 98, '97, '96, '95.

QUINCY AC

FRANCE, Central Loire
♀ *Sauvignon Blanc*
Sometimes Quincy seems to pack more unmistakable Sauvignon flavour into its bottles than any other French wine. We're supposed to find flavours of gooseberry, asparagus and nettles in SANCERRE and POUILLY-FUMÉ – but these Sauvignon wines have become so popular, and the vineyards so burdened with overproduction as a consequence, that we rarely do. Yet Quincy, from vineyards clustered along the left bank of the river Cher, just west of Bourges, always reeks of gooseberry and asparagus and nettles and, if you really want a nostril-full of unashamed Sauvignon, this intensely flavoured dry white is worth seeking out. You can age it for a year or two, but it won't improve during this period, it will merely become slightly less outrageous. Best years: 2002, '01, '00, '99. Best producers: Ballandors, H BOURGEOIS, Mardon, J Rouzé, Silices de Quincy, Troterau.

QUINTARELLI

ITALY, Veneto, Valpolicella DOC
♟ *Corvina, Rondinella, Molinara, Cabernet Franc, Cabernet Sauvignon and others*
♀ *Garganega, Trebbiano Toscano, Sauvignon Blanc and others*
The Quintarellis have been working their vineyard at Monte Cà Paletta in the commune of Negrar since 1924, and third-generation Giuseppe 'Bepi' Quintarelli still stands as a living monument to the splendour of traditional VALPOLICELLA. He is the ultimate believer in letting nature do her own thing, allowing each individual wine to make itself according to its own biochemical lights, tending to each drying berry, each gently bubbling barrel, each humble demijohn with the loving care a father would bestow upon his children. One realizes in his presence, as he draws samples from this and that barrel, that it is this attention to every detail that constitutes the difference between the great and the good in artisanal winemaking.

Undoubtedly Quintarelli's wines can be great in terms of wealth of extract and complexity of aroma (dried fruits, herbs, spices, tar, leather), and if they have to spend seven to ten years in barrel to achieve this, so be it. But being a traditionalist does not mean that he does not experiment – he makes big, bold Valpolicella Classico, famed RECIOTO and the outstanding AMARONE. He was the first, he maintains, to bring Cabernet into the Valpolicella blend, and he still makes *passito* wines from Cabernet Franc (the much sought-after wine called Alzero) as well as from Nebbiolo. His *passito* whites, from Garganega, Tocai and the local Saorin, sometimes with a high percentage of grapes which have developed noble rot as they dry, are equally amazing. Best years: (Amarone) 1997, '95, '93, '90, '88, '86, '85, '83.

QUPÉ WINERY

USA, California, Santa Barbara County, Santa Maria Valley AVA
♟ *Syrah, Mourvedre, Grenache and others*
♀ *Chardonnay, Marsanne, Roussanne, Viognier*
Winemaker Bob Lindquist shares a winery and an iconoclastic outlook with Jim Clendenen of AU BON CLIMAT. From the very beginning he has been a RHÔNE fanatic – one of the original self-styled 'Rhône Rangers' who championed the grape varieties of France's Rhône Valley against a CALIFORNIA establishment obsessed with Cabernet, Merlot and Chardonnay. Events are finally proving Lindquist right as Syrah plantings boom across the state and people realize that California's relatively warm conditions are perfect for the warm-climate varieties of the Rhône Valley. However, Lindquist has consistently sought out relatively cool conditions for his Syrah, convinced, as many other New World winemakers now are, that it can ripen brilliantly in cool but sunny regions. Some of his best wines are now based on Los Olivos fruit from the eastern part of Santa Ynez, and Bien Nacido vineyard in cool SANTA MARIA

QUPÉ
From the famous Bien Nacido vineyard, Qupé's opulent Syrah is a thrilling Rhône-like wine but with even riper blackcurrant and berry fruit.

Built in 1918, the old bodega at the Raïmat winery was Spain's first building in reinforced concrete; it was designed by Rúbio Bellver, a student of the famous Catalan architect, Antoni Gaudí.

VALLEY, where the Syrah ripens successfully right next to Pinot Noir. He now makes three reds – a delicious juicy CENTRAL COAST from warmer areas, a Los Olivos, blended with 40 per cent Mourvedre, and a Bien Nacido. He makes whites too, good Viognier and Marsanne, and a surprisingly rich, lush oaky Chardonnay at basic and Reserve levels. Best years: (Reserve Syrah) 2001, '00, '99, '98, '97, '96, '95, '94, '91, '90.

A RAFANELLI

USA, California, Sonoma County, Dry Creek Valley AVA

❢ *Cabernet Sauvignon, Zinfandel, Merlot*

Occupying a superbly located site along the upper hillsides of DRY CREEK VALLEY, the Rafanelli family's 30-ha (75-acre) vineyard was established nearly 100 years ago and they opened a commercial winery in 1974. For pure, classic Zinfandel this is the place to go. Made from old-vine, non-irrigated hillside grapes, the yield is low and the flavours – deep, lush, typical Dry Creek Valley black-cherry, blackberry fruit – are massive but don't knock you over, yet the wine is soft and easy to drink within three or four years. The quality and style have been maintained, despite an ever-increasing demand. Cut from the same cloth, the Cabernet Sauvignon shows slightly more tannin and has the structure needed to see it through a decade of aging.

RAÏMAT

SPAIN, Cataluña, Costers del Segre DO

❢ *Cabernet Sauvignon, Tempranillo, Merlot, Pinot Noir*

❢ *Cabernet Sauvignon, Pinot Noir, Chardonnay*

♀ *Chardonnay, Pinot Noir, Xarel-lo, Macabeo, Parellada*

This remarkable estate in the near-desert country of Lleida (Lérida in Spanish) province belongs to the Raventós family of the giant CODORNÍU group, who bought it in a run-down condition in 1914. The vines that now grow on over one-third of Raïmat's 2000ha (5000 acres) could not survive without irrigation – and somehow the company managed to circumvent both national and EU regulations that ban the irrigation of vines (irrigation was banned in Spain until 1999). These are no ordinary Spanish vineyards. On advice from the CALIFORNIA universities of Davis and Fresno, the vines are trained along wire trellises and much more densely planted than the traditional vineyards of Spain.

Raïmat and its Codorníu parent were the force behind the granting of a DO to several patches of land in Lleida, now collectively known as COSTERS DEL SEGRE. None of the region's other wines was really up to much, but Raïmat's wines showed what kind of quality could be achieved. There was sparkling Raïmat Chardonnay as well as a fruity, rounded and honeyed still Chardonnay; fruity, richly flavoured and heavily oaked Cabernet Sauvignon and Tempranillo and a blend of

Cabernet Sauvignon and Merlot (to which Tempranillo has now been added) sold under the name Abadía. After a brilliant start, the reds in particular have become much lighter and leaner, which is very disappointing.

The range now includes three single-vineyard Cabernet Sauvignons, a barrel-fermented Chardonnay – rich and toasty with a creamy pineapple fruit – and an oaky Merlot, plus the luxury blend, 4 Varietales. Best years: (reds) 2000, '99, '98, '97, '96, '95, '94, '92, '91, '90.

DOMAINE RAMONET

FRANCE, Burgundy, Côte de Beaune, Chassagne-Montrachet AC

❢ *Pinot Noir*

♀ *Chardonnay*

It is hard to challenge those who assert that Ramonet is the outstanding estate in the village of CHASSAGNE-MONTRACHET. As well as a fine cluster of Premiers Crus from the village (les Ruchottes, les Vergers, Morgeot, les Chaumées and les Caillerets), the family are the proud owners of choice parcels within MONTRACHET, BÂTARD-MONTRACHET and Bienvenues-Bâtard-Montrachet. The wines are invariably characterized by their depth of flavour, complexity and capacity for long aging, although there seem to be no secrets in the winery. Nor is there a heavy dependence on new oak. But the Ramonets are adamant about such matters as planting vines that bear only small berries and about low yields.

Less expensive options are the regular Chassagne-Montrachet and the ST-AUBIN. The clamour is directed at the white wines, but Jean-Claude and Noël Ramonet also make very fine reds, especially from Chassagne's Clos St-Jean. Best years: (whites) 2002, '01, '00, '99, '98, '97, '96, '95, '92, '90, '89.

JOÃO PORTUGAL RAMOS

PORTUGAL, Alentejo

❢ *Trincadeira, Tempranillo (Aragonês/Tinta Roriz), Castelão (Periquita), Touriga Nacional, Alicante Bouschet and others*

♀ *Arinto, Rabo de Ovelha, Roupeiro, Antão Vaz*

João Portugal Ramos is one of Portugal's foremost winemakers. He used to be a consultant to at least a dozen producers, including the fine Pegos Claros property in TERRAS DO SADO, but he is now making his mark with his own winery and vineyards in the ALENTEJO. Smoky, peppery Trincadeira, spicy Aragonês (Tempranillo), powerful Syrah and intensely dark-fruited Vila Santa (a blend of Trincadeira and Aragonês topped up with

Cabernet Sauvignon and Alicante Bouschet) are all superb. Marquês de Borba is the label for everyday red and white wines, though a small amount of a brilliant red Reserva is also made as well as a João Ramos Ribatejo Reserva. Best years: 2001, '00, '99, '97.

RAMOS PINTO

PORTUGAL, Douro DOC, Port DOC

❡ *Touriga Nacional, Touriga Franca, Tinta Barroca, Tempranillo (Tinta Roriz), Cabernet Sauvignon and others*

♀ *Riesling, Sauvignon Blanc, Arinto, Viosinho, Rabigato, Mistura*

Family owned until it was bought by the CHAMPAGNE house of ROEDERER in 1990, Ramos Pinto has always been a company with foresight. In the late nineteenth century it was one of the first PORT shippers to build a brand name in the lucrative Brazilian market and more recently it was a pioneer in the remote DOURO Superior, planting a vineyard on a relatively flat site at Quinta da Ervamoira. Altogether Ramos Pinto owns 185ha (460 acres) of vineyards both upstream and downstream, and these provide fruit for almost all their wine – a situation not common among the PORT houses. Ervamoira is now the source of a deliciously rich 10-Year-Old Tawny, with Quinta do Bom Retiro downstream providing the basis for a supremely refined 20-Year-Old. Vintage ports, on the other hand, have tended to be fairly light and forward, so aged tawnies are the pride of the Ramos Pinto range.

In line with its forward thinking, Ramos Pinto has expended much time and effort on its unfortified Douro wines. Another new venture is on granite soils at Quinta dos Bons Ares, where they make attractive modern red and white table wines from both indigenous and international varieties. Duas Quintas (a blend of wine from Ervamoira and Bons Ares – hence the name) is one of the leading Douro reds in both regular and Reserve styles. Best years: (Vintage ports) 2000, '97, '95, '94, '93.

CASTELLO DEI RAMPOLLA

ITALY, Tuscany, Chianti Classico DOCG

❡ *Sangiovese, Cabernet Sauvignon, Merlot, Petit Verdot*

♀ *Chardonnay, Gewürztraminer (Traminer), Sauvignon Blanc*

The late Alceo di Napoli, owner of the outstanding Castello di Rampolla estate, was undoubtedly one of the great personalities of CHIANTI CLASSICO since World War Two.

CASTELLO DEI RAMPOLLA
The Chianti Classico Riserva which includes a touch of Cabernet Sauvignon has now been superceded by a straight Classico from 100 per cent Sangiovese.

A farmer prince who worked in his vineyards, he was also a fervent believer in the importance of Cabernet Sauvignon in TUSCANY, considering Sangiovese to be a poor second cousin. By the time he died in 1991, he had planted about half his 40ha (100 acres) of vines to his favourite grape, for use in his great SUPER-TUSCAN, Sammarco, as well as for blending with his Chianti Classico Riserva, and was planning a new Cabernet cru.

He left behind some of the most superb vineyards in Tuscany – located in the golden shell of Panzano, they are visible from afar as you drive over the crest from the direction of San Donato – as well as a family mess, which was finally resolved with the second son, Luca, taking command and initiating a bio-dynamic approach in the vineyards.

With Giacomo Tachis discreetly continuing as consultant, however, it wasn't too long before Rampolla was back on top form, Sammarco, at up to 90 per cent Cabernet and 10 per cent Sangiovese, as always, receiving maximum plaudits from the pundits. There is now only a single Chianti Classico – 100 per cent Sangiovese. However, Alceo's dream has come to fruition in the form of a new wine called La Vigna d'Alceo (Alceo's vineyard), 80 per cent Cabernet and 20 per cent Petit Verdot, putting even Sammarco in the shade. Best years: (Sammarco) 2001, '00, '99, '98, '97, '95, '90, '88, '85; (Vigna d'Alceo) 2001, '00, '99, '98, '97, '96.

RANDERSACKER

GERMANY, Franken

Just south-east of WÜRZBURG, this is arguably FRANKEN's leading wine commune, thanks to a string of top vineyards – Pfülben, Sonnenstuhl, Teufelskeller and part of the Marsberg – and a hardly less impressive string of small growers. Mainly medium-bodied dry Rieslings and Silvaners, these are elegant wines in the Franken context. Best years: (Riesling Spätlese trocken) 2002, '01, '00, '99, '98, '97, '94, '93, '92, '90. Best producers: Juliusspital, Robert Schmitt, Schmitt's Kinder.

RAPEL VALLEY

CHILE, Valle Central

Rapel Valley is a rather misleading name for this vibrant, exciting part of Chile's wine scene – already producing some of its best, darkest reds – because the rivers that make up the Rapel Valley area are actually called the Cachapoal and the Tinguiririca. But they do both flow into Rapel Lake, and for the last few vineless miles to the sea, they combine to create the Rapel River – at last. But all the action is upstream of Lake Rapel. The Cachapoal is the northerly river and has two important wine zones at Requinoa and Peumo, producing primarily intense but fruity reds. The Tinguiririca Valley is usually called by the slightly snappier name of COLCHAGUA and produces Pinot Noir at the cool eastern end.

The centre of the Valley is hot and fertile and is heavily planted with vines, but it is the hillsides to the north and south that are most important since they represent Chile's first foray into the challenging world of growing grapes on hillsides as against on the traditional fertile valley floors. Fruit quality is fantastic, especially from varieties like Cabernet Sauvignon, Carmenere and Syrah. At the western end, as the river heads north towards Lake Rapel, the warm area of Marchihue is now heavily planted, mostly with reds. Best producers: Anakena, CASA LAPOSTOLLE, CONCHA Y TORO, CONO SUR, Gracia, LA ROSA, MONTES, MONTGRAS, Porta, Torreón de Paredes, Viu Manent.

DOMAINE RASPAIL-AY

FRANCE, Southern Rhône, Gigondas AC

❡ *Grenache, Syrah, Mourvèdre*

François Ay gives the impression that he doesn't greatly care what you think about his wines. He knows the wines, which all originate from his vineyards on sloping clay and limestone soils, are among the best of the GIGONDAS appellation, which is to say they are deep, rich and full-bodied. The vines are on average 30 years old, and Syrah and Mourvèdre contribute to the Grenache-dominated blend. The wines are aged in large casks, and Ay is opposed to the use of barriques for Gigondas. Treatments are minimal: indigenous yeasts ferment the wine, and fining and filtration are avoided whenever possible. The result is a ripe, harmonious wine, packed with fruit. In top years this Gigondas can take seven or eight years to reach its peak. Best years: 2001, '00, '99, '98, '97, '95, '94, '91, '90.

RASTEAU AC

FRANCE, Southern Rhône

♀ ♂ *Grenache, Syrah, Cinsaut, Mourvèdre*

♀ *Clairette, Roussanne, Bourboulenc*

Rasteau, north-east of CHÂTEAUNEUF-DU-PAPE, is an important village entitled to the CÔTES DU RHÔNE-VILLAGES AC but its reds rarely have the fresh burst of spice and raspberry which makes some of the other 'Villages' so attractive when young.

Even more old-fashioned is the Rasteau *vin doux naturel*, made from very ripe Grenache grapes which are fermented for three to four days only. Then pure alcohol is added to kill the yeasts and stop fermentation. The remaining sugar-rich juice gives a sweet, raisins-and-grape-skins flavour to the wine. It is usually red – or rather a deep tawny after some aging – but there is also a 'white', which is made by draining the juice off the skins at the start of fermentation. If it is left in barrel for several years it is then called *rancio* and tastes a bit like raspberry jam, raisins and tired toffee all mixed up, and can be curiously exquisite as an aperitif. Best producers: Beaurenard, J Bressy, Cave des Vignerons, Rabasse-Charavin, la SOUMADE, du Trapadis.

CH. RAUZAN-GASSIES

FRANCE, Bordeaux, Haut-Médoc, Margaux AC, 2ème Cru Classé

♂ *Cabernet Sauvignon, Merlot, Cabernet Franc*

This MARGAUX Second Growth has excellent vineyards, but had a poor track record until the late 1990s, when improved vineyard and winery practices began to return some personality to the wine. There really is no place in the modern BORDEAUX for underperformance from such an outstanding site and clearly the owners have finally realised this. Best years: 2000, '98, '96.

CH. RAUZAN-SÉGLA

FRANCE, Bordeaux, Haut-Médoc, Margaux AC, 2ème Cru Classé

♂ *Cabernet Sauvignon, Merlot, Cabernet Franc*

Rauzan-Ségla's much-needed new broom arrived in 1983 with Jacques Théo, who immediately declassified half the crop and produced one of BORDEAUX's best 1983s. He continued to excel throughout the 1980s. In 1994 a second new broom arrived when Rauzan-Ségla was bought by French perfume and fashion company Chanel, who implemented a massive programme of investment. The wines are marked by a rich blackcurrant fruit, almost tarry, thick tannins and weight, excellent woody spice and real concentration.

The second wine is called Ségla. Best years: 2001, '00, '99, '98, '96, '95, '94, '90, '89, '88, '86, '85, '83.

DOMAINE RAVENEAU

FRANCE, Burgundy, Chablis AC

♀ *Chardonnay*

Jean-Marie Raveneau's 8-ha (18½-acre) estate is so blessed with good sites that it produces no generic CHABLIS at all. Its Grands Crus are les Clos, Blanchots and Valmur, and the Premiers Crus Montée de Tonnerre, Chapelots, Butteaux, les Vaillons and Montmains. Although all the wines are aged for 12 months in barrels of various sizes, including the small Chablisien *feuillettes*, they are fermented in tanks, where they remain for six months before the oak-aging process begins. Raveneau is very careful not to allow any woody flavours to penetrate the wine. These are highly traditional wines, which are more austere in their youth than those from many other growers. But they age as well as any wines from Chablis, and a bottle of les Clos at ten years or more, with its magical blend of fruit and minerals, can be a memorable glass of wine. Best years: (top crus) 2002, '00, '99, '98, '97, '96, '95, '92, '90, '89.

RAVENSWOOD

USA, California, Sonoma County, Sonoma Valley AVA

♂ *Zinfandel, Merlot, Cabernet Sauvignon, Petite Sirah, Cabernet Franc, Syrah, Carignane*

♀ *Chardonnay*

Joel Peterson, one of CALIFORNIA's best-known Zin experts, established Ravenswood in 1976 and made his reputation with vineyard-designated Zinfandels from very old vines that he hunted down, usually in SONOMA and NAPA, with a positively missionary zeal. These were superb wines and earned Peterson a deserved reputation as a Zinfandel maestro, although he was also making some impressive Cabernet and Merlot. During the 1990s the winery greatly expanded, and is likely to do so even further now that it has been bought by FRANCISCAN, itself a part of the giant Constellation group.

Ravenswood still makes single-vineyard Zins – some very good – as well as County wines – those of Lodi and AMADOR COUNTY are frequently excellent, but the main wine now is the Vintners Blend, a simple red that rarely distinguishes itself. If Vintners Blend pays the bills, fair enough, but what I want to see is maintenance of quality and character in the special Old Vine Zinfandels and other reds. That's what made Ravenswood famous.

After all, this is the winery that uses as its slogan 'No Wimpy Wines'. Best years: (Zins) 2001, '00, '99, '97, '96, '95, '94, '91, '90.

CH. RAYAS

FRANCE, Southern Rhône, Châteauneuf-du-Pape AC

♂ *Grenache*

♀ *Grenache Blanc, Clairette*

Rayas became celebrated for the eccentricities of its owner as well as for the splendour of its wines. Jacques Reynaud was intensely shy, reluctant to receive visitors and even more reluctant to show them round. Reynaud died in 1997 and the estate is now run by his nephew Emmanuel.

The wine became famous for its power and concentration. Made almost entirely from old Grenache vines, the excellence of Rayas was usually attributed to the very low yields from the vineyards. More sceptical observers pointed out that the low yields were a consequence of the unhealthy condition of the vineyards. Whatever the real reason, Rayas could indeed be exceptional, although some vintages could also be deeply disappointing and not worth the very high prices demanded. The second wine, Pignan, only sporadically available, was often better value. The estate also produced superb CÔTES-DU-RHÔNE Ch. Fonsalette, with an alluring pure Syrah cuvée. Some of the whites from Rayas and Fonsalette have been rich and flamboyant; others seemed to tire fast. No doubt it will be the task of Emmanuel Reynaud to ensure that buying a bottle here is less of a lottery than it has been. Best years: (Châteauneuf-du-Pape) 2001, '00, '99, '98, '96, '95, '94, '93, '91, '90, '89, '88, '86; (whites) 2001, '00, '99, '98, '97, '96, '95, '94, '93, '91, '90, '89, '86.

REBHOLZ

GERMANY, Pfalz, Siebeldingen

♂ *Pinot Noir (Spätburgunder)*

♀ *Riesling, Pinot Blanc (Weissburgunder), Pinot Gris (Grauburgunder), Chardonnay, Gewürztraminer, Muscat (Muskateller) and others*

This estate in the southern PFALZ produces fine dry Riesling, Weissburgunder and Grauburgunder, all crystalline in their clarity, with vibrant fruit aromas. Top of the range are intensely mineral dry Riesling from the Kastanienbusch site. The barrique-aged Pinot Noir and Chardonnay are among the best of their style in Germany and I particularly like the fresh fruity Gewürztraminer and Muskateller. Best years: (whites) 2002, '01, '00, '99, '98, '97, '96, '95, '94, '93, '92, '90, '89; (reds) 2002, '01, '00, '99, '98, '97, '96.

RECIOTO DI SOAVE DOCG

ITALY, Veneto

♀ *Garganega, Trebbiano di Soave, Chardonnay*

Sweet white wine made in the SOAVE zone from dried grapes, mainly Garganega, in the same way as RECIOTO DELLA VALPOLICELLA. Garganega grapes give wonderfully delicate yet intense wines that age well for up to a decade. The best, ANSELMI's I Capitelli, is now sold as IGT Veneto. Best years: 2001, '00, '98, '97, '95, '93, '90. Best producers: Anselmi, Cà Rugate, La Cappuccina, Coffele, Gini, PIEROPAN, Bruno Sartori, Tamellini.

RECIOTO DELLA VALPOLICELLA DOC

ITALY, Veneto

♟ *Corvina, Corvinone, Rondinella, Molinara and others*

Ears in Italian are *orecchie*, in Veronese dialect, *recie*. And Recioto, a wine whose origins go back at least two thousand years, was once supposedly made solely from the 'ears' of the grape bunches – those top parts most exposed to the sun, which ripen more fully. More probably in the past, as in the present, only the most conscientious growers chose this time-consuming path, most others using the whole bunch. Recioto is basically a *passito* wine, the grapes drying for four months or more, in a well-ventilated room, before fermenting. The fermentation stops naturally before all the sugars turn to alcohol, or it is stopped by human design so that the wine, dark and strong, remains sweet.

Recioto is a far cry from ordinary VALPO-LICELLA – one could be excused for not recognizing it as a version of the same wine. But tasting its luscious, intense, bitter cherries, plums, smoke and meat stock flavours, then concentrating on the essential flavours of a top-notch Valpolicella, the common origin becomes clear. Sweet Recioto is not often seen, the trend these days heavily favouring the fermented-out, relatively dry version called AMARONE. There is a sparkling version too, which can be highly enjoyable. Recioto shows best after the meal, like PORT and, like port, the bottle can empty bewilderingly fast with predictable consequences for the next morning. Neighbouring SOAVE also makes its own version of Recioto. Best years: 2001, '00, '97, '95, '93, '90, '88. Best producers: Accordini, ALLEGRINI, Bolla (Spumante), Brigaldara, Tomasso Bussola, Michele Castellani, DAL FORNO, MASI, QUINTARELLI, Le Ragose, Le Salette, Serègo Alighieri, Speri, Tedeschi, Tommasi, Villa Monteleone, Viviani.

Two of the specialities of the Valpolicella region are Recioto and Amarone, wines made from grapes dried indoors for several months after the harvest.

DOMAINE DE LA RECTORIE

FRANCE, Languedoc-Roussillon, Banyuls AC, Collioure AC

♟ *Grenache, Carignan, Syrah*

♟ *Grenache, Carignan*

♀ *Grenache Gris, Grenache Blanc*

Since bottling their first wine in 1984 Marc and Thierry Parcé have become the undisputed specialists of vintage BANYULS and COLLIOURE. The secret of their success is the work they put into maintaining the low-yielding 22-ha (54-acre) vineyard which comprises some 30 parcels of vines, all of which are harvested and vinified separately. Among the vintage Banyuls the Cuvée Parcé Frères is full of youthful fruit while the Cuvée Léon Parcé, aged for 18 months in barriques, is richer and more structured in style, and can be kept for future pleasure. There are also a number of longer-aged traditional Banyuls.

The three cuvées of red Collioure – Col del Bast, le Seris and la Coume Pascole – are made from blends of Grenache, Carignan and Syrah and aged in *foudres* and barriques. There are also two cuvées each of white and rosé: the VIN DE PAYS de la Côte Vermeille, L'Argile, from Grenache Gris, is one of the best ROUSSILLON whites. Best years: (Coume Pascole) 2001, '00, '99, '98, '97, '96, '95, '93.

RÉGNIÉ AC

FRANCE, Beaujolais, Beaujolais Cru

♟ *Gamay*

'Lucky' is definitely what the village of Régnié and its neighbour Durette were when their combined vineyards were confirmed as the tenth BEAUJOLAIS cru in 1988. What distinguishes each cru in Beaujolais is that the wines have consistently been of a higher standard than the general run. For this reason the wines can sport their own specific AC.

The other nine crus without doubt deserve their position, but Régnié is less convincing. The soil has a high proportion of sand whereas granite typifies the best areas. The vineyards are just west of MORGON and BROUILLY, and the light, attractive wine is much closer to Brouilly in style. It does not seem to age for more than three years after bottling. In poor years the wines definitely do not rate as cru status, and even in great years like 2000 there were some unattractive attempts. Best years: 2002, '01, '00. Best producers: DUBOEUF (des Buyats), H & J-P Dubost, Gilles Roux (de la Plaigne), Rochette.

REMELLURI

SPAIN, País Vasco, Rioja DOCa

♟ *Tempranillo, Grenache Noir (Garnacha), Graciano*

♀ *Grenache Blanc (Garnacha Blanca), Roussanne, Viognier, Moscatel*

Based at Labastida in the RIOJA Alavesa, La Granja Nuestra Señora de Remelluri was the first of the modern wave of Rioja producers in the 1980s. The winemaker is no longer the charismatic Telmo RODRÍGUEZ, but quality still remains high. The red is not a wine to rush to drink, as the flavour from the organically cultivated chalk and clay hillside vineyards takes time to develop. The bodega produces tiny quanitites of a spectacular, barrel-fermented white. Best years: (Reserva) 1999, '98, '96, '95, '94, '91, '89.

RETSINA

GREECE

This Greek wine has links to antiquity. Airtight pottery sealed with a mixture of clay and resin kept the wine fresh, but also imparted a slight taste of resin to the wine. It was this flavour which, erroneously, was believed to give the wine its keeping quality. This led to the practice of adding bits of pine resin to the grape must prior to fermentation, and removing it at the first racking, as a (supposed) preservative; but the taste caught on. Today the once-massive production is falling, but white and pink retsinas (mainly from the Savatiano grape) are still found and the best can be deliciously oily and piny. The Tyrnavos winery has an interesting Muscat retsina. Best commercial producers: Boutari, Cambas, Gaia, Kourtakis, Thebes co-operative, Tsantali.

REUILLY AC

FRANCE, Central Loire

🍷 Pinot Noir, Pinot Gris

♀ *Sauvignon Blanc*

Reuilly lies west of Bourges in the featureless agricultural land which is typical of central France. There is a little rather pallid red from Pinot Noir, but the speciality here is rosé. The best ones are from Pinot Gris, very pale pink, quite soft but with a lovely, fresh, slightly grapy fruit. Sauvignon Blanc is used for the white wine, and the very high limestone element in the soil makes good Reuilly extremely dry, but with an attractive nettles and gooseberry nip to the fruit. Drink all Reuilly wines young. Best years: 2002, '01, '00, '99. Best producers: Henri Beurdin, Gérard Bigonneau.

DOMAINE HENRI BEURDIN
Pinot Noir is the grape used for red wines in the Central Loire. This example from Reuilly has floral and cherry character and becomes more complex with a little age.

REYNELL

AUSTRALIA, South Australia, McLaren Vale

🍷 Shiraz (Syrah), Cabernet Sauvignon, Merlot

♀ *Chardonnay*

The National Trust-classified and beautiful buildings of Chateau Reynella house the corporate headquarters of the HARDY WINE COMPANY. A limited range of Basket Pressed Shiraz, Basket Pressed Merlot and Basket Pressed Cabernet Sauvignon are released under the Chateau Reynella label (Reynell is used inside Australia), all exhibiting awesome power, concentration and depth of blackberry/blackcurrant fruit. They're more tannic nowadays than they used to be, but the old vines, some dating back to the 1930s, give so much intensity to the fruit that a little tannin and a heavy hand with the oak doesn't do too much harm. Best years: (reds) 2001, '00, '98, '96, '95, '94.

REX HILL VINEYARDS

USA, Oregon, Willamette Valley AVA

🍷 Pinot Noir

♀ *Chardonnay, Pinot Gris, Sauvignon Blanc, Riesling, Pinot Blanc and others*

Rex Hill Vineyards makes fine Pinot Gris and Pinot Noir, including many single-vineyard bottlings from over 90ha (225 acres) of vineyards. The Pinot Noir Reserve is a big, full-bodied wine with rich, intense black cherry fruit that ages gracefully. Lynn Penner-Ash handed over the winemaking reins to Aron Hess in 2002.

RHEINGAU

GERMANY

This is not Germany's largest wine region – at 3205ha (7920 acres) it is dwarfed by the RHEINHESSEN, and even the NAHE can outdo it – but it competes with the MOSEL for the greatest fame. Partly it's because the Rheingau village of HOCHHEIM has had its name mangled and abbreviated in the English language as 'hock', the term for all Rhine wine, and partly it is because of the concentration of high-profile aristocratic estates in the region. It is also, of course, because of the quality of its wine, because Rheingau Riesling from a top vineyard is outstanding – a combination of power, concentration, elegance and breed that will improve in bottle for years. The whole region comes under a single Bereich named, confusingly, after the Rheingau's most famous village, JOHANNISBERG.

Inevitably, the wines of the Rheingau are not all of a style. Those of the western stretch of the river, from Lorch on the border with the MITTELRHEIN east to RÜDESHEIM, are lighter and often have a touch of slatiness, and Assmannshausen is famous throughout Germany for its Pinot Noir (Spätburgunder) reds. Those from the eastern end, from Wiesbaden along the river Main to Hochheim and beyond, are earthier but frequently attractively ripe.

It is the central stretch of vineyards, between Rüdesheim and Wiesbaden, that produces the epitome of Rheingau Riesling. The river here is broad, more than half a mile

WEINGUT JOHANNISHOF
This historic estate in Johannisberg, the Rheingau's best known wine village, makes elegant, top-quality Rieslings, from sites in both Johannisberg and Rüdesheim.

across, and this not only helps to stabilize the temperature but reflects the sun back on to the grapes. Many of the big estates here have been resting on their laurels for years, but the most hopeful sign has been the recently approved classification of the top vineyards. Best years: (Riesling Spätlese) 2002, '01, '99, '98, '97, '96, '93, '90.

RHEINHESSEN

GERMANY

This is the largest of the German wine regions at 26,330ha (65,060 acres), but often the least distinguished; these gentle, rolling vineyards hemmed in by the Rhine on two sides have become associated with LIEBFRAUMILCH and its cousins on the blended wine shelf, NIERSTEINer Gutes Domtal and Bereich Nierstein. It's a shame, because although there is a lot of land planted with vines here that could never produce anything of character, and although the name of Nierstein, one of the region's most famous villages, has been so utterly devalued, there are some excellent estates, and even in the hinterland there are growers beginning to strive for quality.

The best area of the Rheinhessen, though, is the Rheinfront, a stretch of nine villages along the banks of the Rhine: from north to south these are Bodenheim, NACKENHEIM, Nierstein, OPPENHEIM, Dienheim, Ludwigshöhe, Guntersblum, Alsheim and Mettenheim. The vineyards here are on steeper slopes descending to the river. As with any wine area, it should not be supposed that quality is uniformly high, but Rieslings from good growers in Nierstein and Nackenheim, in particular, can be absolutely delicious, full, perfumed, and balanced. As always, it's a question of seeking out the good growers.

But many Rheinhessen vineyards are nowhere near the Rhine at all. There are smaller rivers weaving their way through this gently undulating countryside, to be sure, but even the best parts of the Rheinhessen are not the places to look for Rheingau-style austerity and power. The Riesling is a minority grape variety (although it dominates the best sites), and is generally found on the heavier marl. The Silvaner wines can be among the Rheinhessen's better offerings, particularly if they are vinified dry. There are three Bereiche (Nierstein, BINGEN and Wonnegau), and a total of 24 Grosslagen – the most famous, and most abused, is Gutes Domtal, on whose infamy Nierstein's historically high reputation has foundered. Best years: (Riesling Spätlese) 2002, '01, '00, '99, '98, '97, '96, '93, '90.

RHEIN (Rhine) Germany

THE RHINE IS THE QUINTESSENTIAL RIVER of German wine. It rises in the Swiss Alps and ambles westwards, more or less along the Swiss border, before crossing into Germany at Basel, and no sooner is it there than the vineyards start. The river heads northwards, keeping company (though not always closely) with the vineyards of Baden, the Pfalz, Rheinhessen; until it makes a steep westward turn at Mainz and the great vineyards of the Rheingau tumble right down to the very river banks. As the river turns north into the Mittelrhein, the vines cling to the crazily steep banks as far north as they dare, and to the west of them is the tiny Ahr region, but then the river is on its own. On its journey the Rhine travels from one extreme of German wine to the other; from Baden's substantial, ripe reds and whites to the Mittelrhein's steely Rieslings; it also demonstrates just how much German wine is totally unlike the unfortunate stereotype of a wine that is sweetish, white and dull.

Down in the south, the wines of Baden are mainly dry. They can afford to be: this is Germany's warmest wine region, and if the wines resemble any others it is the well-built dry wines of Alsace, just over the Rhine to the west. A little further downstream, in the Pfalz, the wines, particularly in the south, are changing rapidly. The Pfalz used to be a warm, gently hilly region of fat, soft wines which in a hot year veered into blowsiness; now they're elegant, sharp-suited and a whole lot drier. Rheinhessen wines are generally rather soft, perhaps slightly earthy and without the nerve or depth of a good Rheingau.

The Rheingau is the land of aristocratic estates and aristocratic wines. It is no surprise that in Germany's new vineyard grading system, the only Erste Gewächs (equivalent to the French classification of Grand Cru) should be found here. At their best the wines have fire and concentration and a marvellous, tense balance of acidity; and just across the river, in the Nahe, there are wines of complexity that often combine the fullness of the Rheingau with the steeliness of the Mosel. Going north again, the small region of Mittelrhein yields lean but tangy wines that are mostly Riesling and regrettably unfashionable. In the Ahr most of the wines are pale red, but there is as yet little incentive to improve quality.

This view of the Rhine looks from the great sweep of vines in the Hipping vineyard south to the village of Nierstein. This stretch of vineyards rising directly from the river is the heart of the Rheinfront along Rheinhessen's eastern border.

In the Rheingau the Charta organization was at the forefront of popularizing a drier style of German wine. It has now merged with the VDP (Verband Deutscher Prädikats- und Qualitätsweingüter), another voluntary grouping of like-minded growers: they impose strict conditions of quality on their members, and the VDP initials and eagle symbol or Charta's embossed double-windows on their bottles should be a reassuring sign for consumers.

H DÖNNHOFF

Helmut Dönnhoff produces the finest Rieslings from the famous Nahe vineyards of Niederhausen, Schlossböckelheim and Oberhausen.

SCHLOSS REINHARTSHAUSEN

This large Rheingau estate has several first-class vineyard sites in both Hattenheim and Erbach and makes both good Riesling and Sekt.

GUNDERLOCH

The great Rothenberg site, which soars above the Rhine at Nackenheim, gives some of richest and sweetest Rieslings made on the entire Rhine.

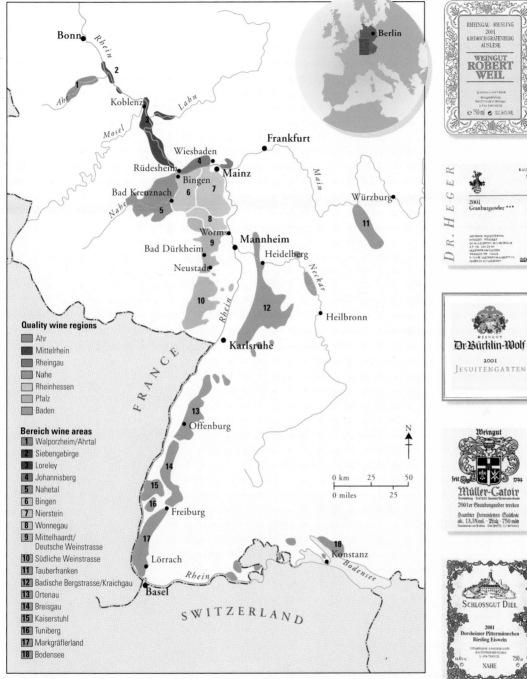

Quality wine regions

- Ahr
- Mittelrhein
- Rheingau
- Nahe
- Rheinhessen
- Pfalz
- Baden

Bereich wine areas

1. Walporzheim/Ahrtal
2. Siebengebirge
3. Loreley
4. Johannisberg
5. Nahetal
6. Bingen
7. Nierstein
8. Wonnegau
9. Mittelhaardt/ Deutsche Weinstrasse
10. Südliche Weinstrasse
11. Tauberfranken
12. Badische Bergstrasse/Kraichgau
13. Ortenau
14. Breisgau
15. Kaiserstuhl
16. Tuniberg
17. Markgräflerland
18. Bodensee

ROBERT WEIL
The top wines from this Rheingau estate are classic concentrated and very rich Rieslings from the Kiedricher Gräfenberg site.

DR HEGER
Joachim Heger makes some of Baden's best dry Weissburgunder and Grauburgunder wines at Ihringen, in the Kaiserstuhl region, which is supposedly Germany's warmest village.

DR BÜRKLIN-WOLF
Today Bürklin-Wolf once again stands in the first rank of Pfalz estates. The village of Forst has long been regarded as the best in the Pfalz and Jesuitengarten is one of its greatest vineyards.

MÜLLER-CATOIR
From little-known Pfalz vineyards Müller-Catoir produce wines of a piercing fruit flavour and powerful structure from a long list of varieties, including Grauburgunder (Pinot Gris).

SCHLOSSGUT DIEL
Sensational Riesling Eiswein, and among the best in Germany, is the top wine from this well-known Nahe estate.

FRANZ KÜNSTLER
Since taking over the estate in 1988, Gunter Künstler has been one of the leading producers of Rheingau Riesling.

REGIONAL ENTRIES

Ahr, Bacharach, Bad Kreuznach, Baden, Bingen, Deidesheim, Durbach, Erbach, Forst, Geisenheim, Hattenheim, Hessische Bergstrasse, Hochheim, Ihringen, Johannisberg, Kaiserstuhl, Kiedrich, Liebfraumilch, Mittelrhein, Nackenheim, Nahe, Nierstein, Oppenheim, Ortenau, Pfalz, Rheingau, Rheinhessen, Rüdesheim, Ruppertsberg, Schlossböckelheim.

PRODUCER ENTRIES

Dr von Bassermann-Jordan, Bercher, Josef Biffar, Georg Breuer, von Buhl, Dr Bürklin-Wolf, Darting, Schlossgut Diel, H Dönnhoff, Emrich-Schönleber, Gunderloch, Dr Heger, Heyl zu Herrnsheim, Johannishof, Karl-Heinz Johner, Toni Jost, Keller, Koehler-Ruprecht, Franz Künstler, Josef Leitz, Georg Mosbacher, Müller-Catoir, Rebholz, Schloss Reinhartshausen, Schloss Vollrads, Robert Weil, J L Wolf.

RHÔNE France

IT'S ONE OF THOSE TRICK QUESTIONS: 'What is the most northerly wine grown in the Rhône Valley?' Tricky indeed. It isn't even in France – it's in the Valais high up in the Swiss Alps. We always forget that the Rhône starts out as a Swiss river, ambling through Lake Geneva before hurtling southwards into France and out into the Mediterranean.

Well, as far as the AC Côtes du Rhône is concerned, we are in France. This appellation starts below Vienne, just south of Lyon, but nowhere near Switzerland, and finishes just south of Avignon. Below this the river sprawls out and fragments into marshlands which soon become the wild Camargue swamps. 'Côtes du Rhône' does, after all, mean 'Rhône slopes', or at least 'Rhône banks', and south of Avignon, there isn't much of either. But between Avignon in the south and Vienne in the north there's enough excitement to show the Rhône as one of France's greatest, most diverse wine regions.

This central section of the valley splits naturally into two parts. The north doesn't produce much wine, but the little that does appear is of a remarkable individuality. On the vertigo-inducing slopes of Côte-Rôtie at Ampuis, the Syrah grape produces sensuously fragrant, long-lasting reds, while at Tain-l'Hermitage the great hill of Hermitage produces what they used to call France's 'manliest' wine. St-Joseph and Crozes-Hermitage also make excellent reds, while Cornas, a few miles south, makes a marvellous monster red too. The white Viognier grape yields perfumed, pungent wine at Condrieu and the tiny AC, Château-Grillet.

There is a gap as the valley widens and flattens, and the slopes give way to vast expanses of land, rising a little into the hills both east and west but, in general, flat, with vines sweltering under the sun. Most of these vineyards are either Côtes du Rhône or Côtes du Rhône-Villages, reds, whites and rosés, but there are also various specific ACs. Red Gigondas is to the east, huddled under the jagged fangs of the Dentelles de Montmirail hills on ridges of thin, stony soil which descend into the valley floor. This is also the home of luscious, golden Muscat de Beaumes-de-Venise. South-west are Lirac and Tavel. But the best-known wine name of all is south of Orange – Châteauneuf-du-Pape, which has long been one of the most celebrated wines of France.

The steeply terraced vineyards on the famous hill of Hermitage overlook the town of Tain l'Hermitage and the Rhône far below. The steep granite hill has excellent exposure to the sun and is possibly the oldest vineyard area in France.

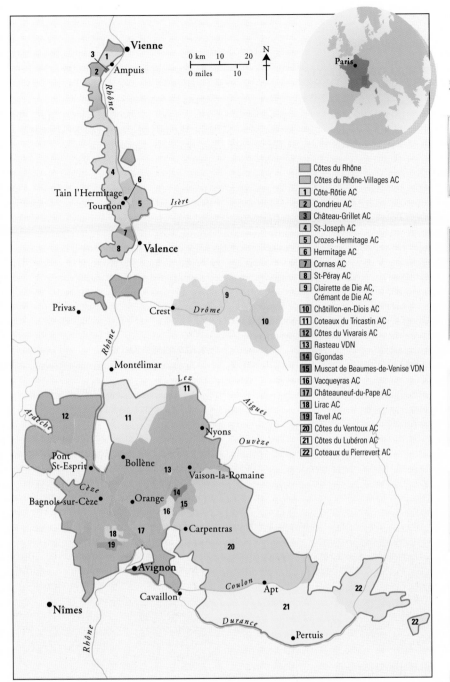

Côtes du Rhône
Côtes du Rhône-Villages AC
1 Côte-Rôtie AC
2 Condrieu AC
3 Château-Grillet AC
4 St-Joseph AC
5 Crozes-Hermitage AC
6 Hermitage AC
7 Cornas AC
8 St-Péray AC
9 Clairette de Die AC,
Crémant de Die AC
10 Châtillon-en-Diois AC
11 Coteaux du Tricastin AC
12 Côtes du Vivarais AC
13 Rasteau VDN
14 Gigondas
15 Muscat de Beaumes-de-Venise VDN
16 Vacqueyras AC
17 Châteauneuf-du-Pape AC
18 Lirac AC
19 Tavel AC
20 Côtes du Ventoux AC
21 Côtes du Lubéron AC
22 Coteaux du Pierrevert AC

GUIGAL
The brilliant Marcel Guigal produces wines from his company's own vineyards in Côte-Rôtie under the Ch. d'Ampuis label.

CHAPOUTIER
This négociant company specializes wines from both the northern and southern Rhône, including a range of exciting wines from Hermitage.

GEORGES VERNAY
The leading Condrieu estate produces excellent wines, including opulent, rich Les Terrasses de l'Empire.

AUGUSTE CLAPE
The top estate in Cornas is very traditional, making dense tannic wines with rich roasted fruit.

JEAN-LOUIS CHAVE
This red Hermitage is one of the world's great wines, a savoury, complex expression of the Syrah grape at its best.

DOMAINE DE L'ORATOIRE ST-MARTIN
This estate based in Cairanne makes exciting Côtes du Rhône-Villages.

CH. DE BEAUCASTEL
The exquisite white Vieilles Vignes is a powerful white Châteauneuf-du-Pape made from 100 per cent Roussanne.

CH. DE FONSALETTE
The Reynaud family of Ch. Rayas, Châteauneuf-du-Pape's most famous estate, make rich, full-bodied Côtes du Rhône at Ch de Fonsalette.

REGIONAL ENTRIES
Château-Grillet, Châteauneuf-du-Pape, Clairette de Die, Condrieu, Cornas, Côte-Rôtie, Coteaux du Tricastin, Côtes du Lubéron, Côtes du Rhône, Côtes du Rhône-Villages, Côtes du Ventoux, Côtes du Vivarais, Crozes-Hermitage, Gigondas, Hermitage, Lirac, Muscat de Beaumes-de-Venise, Rasteau, St-Joseph, St-Péray, Tavel, Vacqueyras.

PRODUCER ENTRIES
de Beaucastel, Henri Bonneau, Chapoutier, Dom. Jean-Louis Chave, Auguste Clape, Clos des Papes, Clos du Mont-Olivet, Jean-Luc Colombo, Yves Cuilleron, Delas, Dom. les Goubert, Alain Graillot, Guigal, Paul Jaboulet, Joseph Jamet, Dom. de l'Oratoire St-Martin, Dom. Raspail-Ay, Rayas, René Rostaing, Dom. de St-Gayan, Dom. la Soumade, Georges Vernay, Dom. de Vieux Télégraphe.

RÍAS BAIXAS DO

SPAIN, Galicia

♥ *Caiño Tinto, Espadeiro, Loureira and others*

♀ *Albariño, Loureira Blanca, Treixadura and others*

The best of GALICIA's five DOs, Rías Baixas is making increasing quantities of Spain's best whites (apart from a few Chardonnays in the north-east). The magic ingredient is the characterful Albariño grape, making dry, fruity whites with a glorious fragrance and citrus tang. But popularity has brought an eightfold increase in vineyards since 1988, and not every bottle will be all it's cracked up to be. Drink young or with short aging. Best producers: Agro de Bazán, Martin Códax, Quinta de Couselo, Granxa Fillaboa, Adegas Galegas, Lagar de Fornelos (La RIOJA ALTA), Lusco do Miño, Lázaro, Pazo de Barrantes, Pazo de Señorans, Salnesur, Santiago Ruiz, Terras Gauda.

RIBATEJO DOC

PORTUGAL

♥ ♀ *Baga, Camarate, Castelão (Periquita), Trincadeira (Tinta Amarela), Cabernet Sauvignon, Tinta Miúda*

♀ *Arinto (Pederñã), Fernão Pires (Maria Gomes), Rabo de Ovelha, Tália, Trincadeira das Pratas and others*

Portugal's second-largest wine region straddles the river Tejo (Tagus) upstream from Lisbon as far as the towns of Tomar and Chamusca, both of which are sub-DOCs of the new Ribatejo DOC (there are six sub-DOCs in all). The Vinho Regional is now called Ribatejano. Vineyards in the fertile flood plain are being uprooted in favour of less vigorous soils away from the river. White wines predominate but some good reds are beginning to emerge. Best producers: (reds) Quinta da Alorna, BRIGHT BROTHERS, Casa Cadaval, Quinta do Casal Branco, D F J VINHOS, Caves Dom Teodosio, Quinta do Falcao, Falua, Fiuza, Quinta Grande, Horta da Nazaré, Quinta da Lagoalva, Quinta de Santo Andre.

RIBEIRO DO

SPAIN, Galicia

♥ *Caiño, Garnacha Tintorera, Ferrón and others*

♀ *Treixadura, Godello, Palomino, Torrontés and others*

An enchanting wine region in north-west Spain. Even though it's only 60 km (37 miles) inland, it's far dryer than the rainsoaked regions like RÍAS BAIXAS but still gets a healthy drenching of 800–1000mm (32–39in) a year. It has fantastic local varieties (Loureira, Treixadura, Torrontés, Godello and Albariño) which, with the dramatic recent improvement in winemaking technology and skills, are determinedly pushing out the inferior Palomino. Fresh fruity reds are

becoming more common. The quality drive is being led by private producers – particularly Alanís, Emilio Rojo, Vilerma, Viña Mein.

RIBERA DEL DUERO DO

SPAIN, Castilla y León

♥ ♀ *Tempranillo (Tinto Fino), Grenache Noir (Garnacha Tinta), Cabernet Sauvignon, Merlot, Malbec*

Ribera del Duero reds, at best richly aromatic, well balanced and very fine, have become cult items, and consequently extremely expensive. The VEGA SICILIA estate has been renowned since the nineteenth century for its powerful, complex, lengthily wood-aged wines, made partly from the French grapes Cabernet Sauvignon, Merlot and Malbec, and partly from the local Tinto Fino. But it took the discovery of Alejandro FERNÁNDEZ's Pesquera bodega by the American critic Robert Parker for the outside world to recognize the region's potential.

Ribera del Duero means 'the banks of the Duero' (which flows on to become the Douro, Portugal's PORT river). The gentle, often pine-covered hills around the valley lie 700–800m (2300–2625ft) above sea level, near the upper limit for vines, and this helps explain the wines' intense flavours. Most of the grapes are Tinto Fino, but other bodegas have followed Vega Sicilia and planted Cabernet and Merlot. They make an excellent blend with Tempranillo, and are ideally suited to oak-aging. The DO also includes the occasional rosé. Best years: 2001, '00, '99, '96, '95, '94, '91, '90, '89, '86, '85. Best producers: Alión (Vega Sicilia), Arzuaga, Balbás, Hijos de Antonio Barceló, Briego, Félix Callejo, Cillar de Silos, Convento San Francisco, Hermanos Cuadrado García, Dehesa de los Canónigos, Hacienda Monasterio, Matallana, Emilio Moro, Pago de los Capellanes, Pago de Carraovejas, Parxet, Pedrosa, Pesquera, PINGUS, Protos, Rodero, Telmo RODRIGUEZ, Hermanos Sastre, Tarsus/Bodegas y Bebidas, Valderiz, Valduero, Valtravieso, Vega Sicilia, Winner Wines.

RICHEBOURG AC

FRANCE, Burgundy, Côte de Nuits, Grand Cru

♥ *Pinot Noir*

This 8-ha (20-acre) Grand Cru, one of Burgundy's most famous and most expensive, at the northern end of the village of VOSNE-ROMANÉE, produces a rich, fleshy wine, its bouquet all flowers and sweet, ripe fruit and its flavour an intensity of spice and perfumed plums which fattens into chocolate and figs and cream as it ages. Most domaine-bottlings are exceptional. Best years: 2002, '01, '00, '99, '98, '97, '96, '95, '93, '91, '90, '89, '88, '85.

Best producers: GRIVOT, Anne Gros, A-F Gros, Hudelot-Noëllat, LEROY, MÉO-CAMUZET, Domaine de la ROMANÉE-CONTI.

MAX FERD RICHTER

GERMANY, Mosel-Saar-Ruwer, Mülheim

♀ *Riesling and others*

This MOSEL grower makes wines with great individuality and even the most basic Riesling is an excellent example of the grape – and good value too. There are vines in such superb vineyards as WEHLENer Sonnenuhr, GRAACHer Himmelreich, Graacher Domprobst and BRAUNEBERGer Juffer. Mülheimer Helenenkloster is where Richter attempts to make an Eiswein every year. Or nearly every year: he didn't manage 1999 and wild boar ate the whole crop in 1991, but then Germans have always maintained that Riesling goes with wild boar. There is good Riesling-based Sekt too. Best years: (Riesling Spätlese) 2002, '01, '99, '98, '97, '96, '95, '94, '93, '90, '89, '88.

RIDGE VINEYARDS

USA, California, Santa Clara County, Santa Cruz Mountains AVA

♥ *Cabernet Sauvignon, Zinfandel, Petite Sirah, Syrah, Grenache, Carignan (Carignane)*

♀ *Chardonnay*

Ridge is one of CALIFORNIA's most outstandingly original wineries, started by a group of scientists from nearby Stanford University who hankered after the sylvan lifestyle. The current winemaker, Paul Draper, pursues a positively nineteenth-century, low-tech winemaking style (though backed by impressive technology, just in case). The main wines are Cabernet Sauvignon – the remarkable Monte Bello – and Zinfandels from various parts of California. These wines are now lighter than they used to be, the tannins less evident, but they still easily have enough stuffing to put together a series of shocking, intense, unexpected flavours, both when the wines are young and after long aging. Best years: (Monte Bello) 2001, '00, '99, '98, '97, '95, '94, '93, '92, '91, '90, '87, '85, '84.

RIDGEVIEW ESTATE

ENGLAND, West Sussex

♀ ♥ *Chardonnay, Pinot Noir, Pinot Meunier*

Christine and Michael Roberts are emulating CHAMPAGNE every step of the way at their South Downs vineyard. Bloomsbury and Belgravia blends of Chardonnay, Pinot Noir and Pinot Meunier are produced under the Cuvée Merret label. There is also delicious Fitzrovia rosé, Pinot Noir-based Cavendish, and the new vintage Knightsbridge Blanc de Noirs.

RIESLING

Riesling may not be the world's most popular white wine grape, but there are many who would say it is the best, capable of surpassing in quality even the ubiquitous Chardonnay. It is not, however, so easy to understand. Riesling is a demanding grape. Its wine can be greenly acidic, but with age (and great, classic Riesling must have bottle age) it mellows, the acidity providing the backbone for honeyed fruit that often develops a nose and flavour described as 'petrolly', and tasting a million times more delicious than it sounds.

But it is also the victim of many a misconception. For a start, many of the cheap and nasty wines from eastern Europe that incorporate Riesling or Rizling in their titles are not from the Riesling grape at all. Riesling is not automatically sweetish: the cheap sugar-water that pours out of German wine factories has done an efficient job in blackening the name of even the finest German wines, but is virtually never made from Riesling grapes. Fashionable taste in Germany and Austria is for dry Rieslings, and the Rieslings of Alsace and Italy's Alto Adige (Südtirol) have long been vinified dry. But when the Riesling does make sweet wines from grapes affected by noble rot, they are dessert wines to remember: racily acidic, richly honeyed and complex, and generally needing years to show at their best. The Beerenauslesen, Trockenbeerenauslesen and Eiswein of Germany and Austria and the dessert Rieslings of Australia, New Zealand and California and the Riesling Icewine of Canada can be exceptional.

The Riesling by which all other Riesling is measured comes from Germany, and in particular from the Rhine and Mosel. In the Mosel it is light and delicate; in the Rheinhessen softer, in the Rheingau bigger and well-structured, in the Pfalz broader but still firm. It is Germany's second most widely planted grape behind the Müller-Thurgau, accounting for just over 20 per cent of the vineyard area.

Hot climates produce Riesling that is fat and blowsy, sometimes keeping a reasonably simple fruit, but often ending up tasting like diesel fuel. In Australia all the best Rieslings come from regions blessed with cold nights, which yield wines that have a fresh, limy streak of acidity and, frequently, a delightful floral perfume. The Clare Valley makes impressively austere examples, Eden Valleys are gentler, more floral but still impressively citrus, as are those from Western Australia's Margaret River and Frankland regions. In the USA, cool-climate Washington State, Oregon and New York State are all making a name for the grape but some of the best examples may yet come from further north in Canada. New Zealand's Rieslings continually promise to be beautifully floral and light but rarely so far deliver and tend to be most exciting when botrytis-affected and sweet.

Riesling isn't a major player in warm South Africa. Only the Elgin and Constantia regions have regularly succeeded with dry versions. Best examples are in the botrytis-affected, dessert styles.

In Europe, Rieslings to rival those of the Rhine and Mosel come from Austria's Wachau, Kamptal and Donauland regions in Niederösterreich, and usually have higher alcohol than their German equivalents. Alsace Rieslings are also fuller and higher in alcohol, particularly when grown on one of the Grand Cru sites. In Italy's Alto Adige the wines are often very light, steely-fresh and bone dry for drinking young. Jermann, in Friuli, makes a good varietal called Afix. No-one in Italy, however, is getting anywhere near the quality levels attained further north. Slovenia and Croatia have some good dry examples.

Synonyms for the true Riesling include Riesling Renano (in Italy), Rhine Riesling (in Austria and Australia) and Johannisberg or White Riesling (in the USA). The grape variously called Welsch Riesling, Laski Rizling, Olasz Rizling or, in Italy, Riesling Italico, is not the true Riesling at all.

CH. RIEUSSEC

FRANCE, Bordeaux, Sauternes AC, Premier Cru Classé
♀ *Sémillon, Sauvignon Blanc, Muscadelle*

Apart from the peerless Ch. D'YQUEM, Rieussec is often the richest SAUTERNES. The 75ha (185 acres) of vineyards, on high ground just inside the commune of Fargues, lie alongside Yquem and, since the property was bought in 1984 by the Rothschilds of Ch. LAFITE-ROTHSCHILD, one wondered if they were going to try to challenge the pre-eminence of Yquem. Fermentation in barrel was reintroduced from 1995, adding extra glycerol and complexity to the marvellous trio of 1997, '96 and '95 and greater intensity to wines that are already super-rich, but not only affordable to the super-rich – which is more than one can say for Yquem. There is a dry wine called 'R' which is pretty dull. Second wines: Clos Labère, Ch. de Cosse. Best years: 2002, '01, '99, '98, '97, '96, '95, '90, '89, '88, '86, '85, '83.

RIO GRANDE DO SUL

BRAZIL

The beautiful, green, rolling landscape of Rio Grande do Sul is the site of Brazil's wine industry. Near the border with Uruguay, it is as close to winemaking country as Brazil can manage. The fight against predators, fungal as well as creepy crawly, is a constant one, so winemaking can be relatively expensive. There are two main sub-regions, Serra Gaucha and the more recently established Frontera, near the Uruguayan border, growing varieties such as Cabernet Sauvignon, Chardonnay, Trebbiano, Cabernet Franc, Merlot and Petite Sirah. MOËT ET CHANDON, Provifin (a Moët subsidiary making large quantities of sparkling wine), Martini & Rossi and Pedro DOMECQ are the major producers.

RÍO NEGRO

ARGENTINA

A handful of brave winemakers are ploughing a lonely furrow in the beautiful, cool-climate, fruit-growing Río Negro Valley at the northern end of Patagonia, on the same latitude as New Zealand's South Island and almost as isolated. Time will tell if wine wins over the current lucrative crops of plums, pears and cherries. Humberto Canale is the largest quality producer, and DOMAINE VISTALBA (under the Infinitus label) and Bernardo Weinert also have interests here. Malbec, Merlot, Syrah, Pinot Noir, Sauvignon Blanc, Chardonnay and Torrontés are all grown with considerable success. Canale has massively modernized its plant to tremendous effect. Others are sure to follow.

LA RIOJA Spain

JUST BECAUSE YOU SEE A SIGN by the roadside welcoming you to La Rioja, there's no reason to believe that you've arrived in the Rioja DOCa, even if the car window does give you an uninterrupted vista of vines. La Rioja, the autonomous region, has quite different boundaries from Rioja, the Denominación de Origen Calificada. Not all the vines that grow in the autonomous region are entitled to the name Rioja. And the Rioja DOCa stretches way out into Navarra, where vines yield priority to asparagus, artichokes and spicy red peppers, all flourishing in the fertile soil, while an important part of the DOCa (Rioja Alavesa) lies inside the boundaries of the Basque country (País Vasco) and there are some western patches in Castilla y León.

But there is a certain logic to the Rioja DOCa region taken as a whole. Named after the Rio or River Oja, a tributary of the River Ebro, the region is centred on the Ebro Valley and, for much of its length, is bounded to the north and south by dramatic chains of mountains, particularly the Sierra de Cantabria. (Take a half-hour drive north of Logroño, the wine capital of the region, through cornfields and vineyards, and you'll suddenly find yourself amid rough-hewn mountains of spectacular beauty, dotted with half-deserted villages.) But when you get down to the three official sub-

The Marqués de Riscal bodega was a pioneering firm in Rioja in the 1860s – this is their fermentation cellar built in 1883 – and in Rueda in the 1970s and is still up there in Rioja's top rank making classic pungent red wines.

regions of Rioja – Rioja Alta, Rioja Alavesa and Rioja Baja – it soon becomes evident that the characteristics of the three regions are less clear-cut than sometimes suggested and many Riojas are a blend of wines from two or more of these regions.

The Rioja Baja (mostly in Navarra), accounts for 30 per cent of the Rioja DOCa. Enjoying a Mediterranean climate, it is hot and dry, and much of its silt or clay soil on the flat valley floor is too fertile for good-quality grapes. The resulting wines are fatter and more alcoholic – generally from the Garnacha Tinta, which survives better than the Tempranillo in these hot conditions. The difference between Rioja Alavesa (20 per cent of the Rioja area) and Rioja Alta (the most important quality area with 50 per cent of the vines) is less significant in wine terms, because the division was simply drawn along the border of the Basque province of Alava.

The most aromatic Tempranillo red wines come from grapes grown on the yellow limestone clay which occurs all over the Rioja Alavesa and extends well into the Alta region; Tempranillo flourishes here in the limestone, producing

REMELLURI
The wines from this organic estate have considerable extract and structure as well as fruit and will age well.

LA RIOJA ALTA
One of the very best of the old-established Rioja producers, La Rioja Alta makes almost entirely Reservas and Gran Reservas.

CVNE
From a new, ultra-modern winery, CVNE's top wine, Imperial Gran Reserva, is long-lived and impressive.

ARTADI
This former co-operative now produces some ambitious and highly acclaimed Riojas under the brand name Artadi. Pagos Viejos is made from very old vines.

MARQUÉS DE RISCAL
The exotic Barón de Chirel wine is made only in selected years and predominantly from Cabernet Sauvignon.

BODEGAS RODA
This company applies Catalan winemaking skills to two old-vine Rioja wines, called Roda I and Roda II, with exciting results.

grapes with high acidity and a good concentration of flavours. However, a lot of the Alta soil is very similar to the silt and clay of the Baja and consequently grows Garnacha. But, unlike the Baja, both the Alta and the Alavesa regions have climates in which the hot, Mediterranean weather is moderated by cooler breezes from the Atlantic Ocean.

REGIONAL ENTRY
Rioja.

PRODUCER ENTRIES
AGE, Allende, Artadi, Barón de Ley, Berberana, Campillo, Campo Viejo, Contino, CVNE, Faustino, López de Heredia, Marqués de Cáceres, Marqués de Murrieta, Marqués de Riscal, Martínez Bujanda, Muga, Bodegas Palacio, Remelluri, La Rioja Alta, Roda.

BODEGAS BRETÓN
The single-vineyard Dominio de Conté shows the demanding Rioja traditions of long barrel-aging from low-yielding old vines at their best.

BODEGAS PALACIO
Benefiting from the advice of Michel Rolland, the Pomerol winemaker, Palacio's top wine, Cosme Palacio quickly became a cult wine in Spain.

MARTÍNEZ BUJANDA
This is a rich and intense, buttery, barrel-fermented white entirely from the Viura grape and the first single-vineyard white in modern Rioja.

RIOJA DOCa

SPAIN, La Rioja, Navarra and País Vasco (see also pages 314–315)

🍷🍾 *Tempranillo, Grenache Noir (Garnacha Tinta), Carignan (Cariñena, Mazuelo), Graciano*

🍷 *Macabeo (Viura), Garnacha Blanca, Malvasía de Rioja*

In the 1970s, when Rioja first became popular outside Spain, people learned to expect oaky-flavoured reds smelling and tasting of vanilla – partly because there were a lot of new oak barrels in use, and partly because flavour merchants were doing a roaring trade in bottles of dark, gooey oak essence.

All that changed in the 1980s, as the regulations tightened and those serried ranks of once-new barrels, oaky taste long gone, had now become flavourless containers. Red Riojas today are almost always less vanilla-oaky, sometimes more positively fruity, and only 40 per cent of Riojas are oak-aged. But some of the best bodegas are turning to expensive new oak again, following a worldwide change in fashion – and they can afford it, because Rioja prices soared at the end of the 1980s and again at the end of the 1990s. Traditional white Riojas were also oak-aged, but this style became unpopular during the 1980s. However, some bodegas now make barrel-fermented creamy whites. In 1991, Rioja became the first region to be granted Spain's superior quality status, Denominación de Origen Calificada (DOCa).

Though more than three-quarters of the grapes in this extensive 57,000ha (140,850-acre) wine region are produced by small-scale growers, the big Rioja firms bottle and sell most of the wines. The two major grapes for red Rioja are Tempranillo, with an elegant, plummy character that develops well with age in barrel and bottle into wild strawberry and savoury flavours, and Garnacha Tinta, whose fat, jammy-fruit flavours fade fast. Of the minor grapes, Graciano has recently become more popular because its flavour, spicy and aromatic, is excellent but unfortunately it is far more capricious to grow than Rioja's other vines. Cabernet Sauvignon is also creeping into the vineyards under the pretext of experimentation. It can make fine wine and must have a strong chance of becoming officially accepted in the Rioja grape mix. Best years: 2001, '96, '95, '94, '91, '89, '87, '86, '85, '83, '82, '81, '78. Best producers: (reds) ALLENDE, Altos de Lanzaga (Telmo RODRÍGUEZ), ARTADI, BARÓN DE LEY, BERBERANA, Bodegas Bilbaínas, Bretón, CAMPILLO, CAMPO VIEJO, CONTINO, El Coto, CVNE, DOMECQ, FAUSTINO, LÓPEZ DE HEREDIA, MARQUÉS DE CÁCERES, MARQUÉS DE GRIÑÓN, MARQUÉS DE MURRIETA, MARQUÉS DE RISCAL, Marqués de Vargas, MARTÍNEZ BUJANDA, Montecillo, MUGA, PALACIO, REMELLURI, Fernando Remírez de Ganuza, La RIOJA ALTA, Riojanas, RODA, Benjamin Romero (Contador), Señorío de San Vicente; (whites) Campo Viejo, CVNE, López de Heredia, Marqués de Cáceres, Marqués de Murrieta, Martínez Bujanda, Riojanas.

LA RIOJA ALTA

SPAIN, La Rioja, Rioja DOCa

🍷 *Tempranillo, Grenache Noir (Garnacha Tinta), Graciano and others*

🍷 *Macabeo (Viura), Malvasía de Rioja*

Although La Rioja Alta only makes a tiny per cent of RIOJA's total production, it sells almost one-fifth of all the Reserva and Gran Reserva wine made in the region.

In the past decade, it has made massive investments and wood-aging is still one of the major hallmarks of this traditional bodega. The Reservas Viña Alberdi and Viña Arana contain about 90 per cent Tempranillo and are light, elegant wines. The other Reserva, Viña Ardanza, is a fuller, richer wine, with about 75 per cent Tempranillo and a higher proportion of Garnacha Tinta. Gran Reservas labelled with the numbers 904 and 890 are produced only in the best years, and, for Gran Reserva 890, the wine has to be truly exceptional. Barón de Oña Reserva is a lovely Alavesa style.

La Rioja Alta is also the owner of the Lagar de Fornelos winery in GALICIA, which makes a tangy white called Lagar de Fornelos, from 100 per cent Albariño, in the RÍAS BAIXAS DO. Best years: (Gran Reserva 890) 1987, '85, '82, '81, '78.

RIVERA

ITALY, Puglia, Castel del Monte DOC

🍷 *Uva di Troia, Montepulciano, Aglianico, Primitivo and others*

🍾 *Bombino Nero*

🍷 *Bombino Bianco, Pampanuto, Chardonnay, Sauvignon Blanc and others*

One of southern Italy's most dynamic producers, Rivera is situated in the Murge uplands of central PUGLIA, in the area called Rivera. Rivera, owned by the de Corato family, started experimenting with non-traditional varieties like Sauvignon Blanc, Chardonnay and Aglianico as far back as the 1950s while aiming simultaneously to get the best out of local grapes like Bombino and Montepulciano. Today, Rivera's greatest wine is probably still the full rich, red Riserva Il Falcone, made from Uva di Troia and Montepulciano grapes. But hard on its heels is the Aglianico Rosso under the Cappellaccio label. The range also includes a Primitivo called Triusco, two 100 per cent Chardonnays, a Sauvignon Blanc, and a rosé – Puglia's traditional wine – produced from the local Bombino Nero grape.

RIVERINA

AUSTRALIA, New South Wales

Also called the Murrumbidgee Irrigation Area (MIA), this isolated area is one of the engine-rooms of the Australian wine industry since the hot, dry summers and abundant irrigation water mean consistently big crops and low production costs. This area is now desperate to upgrade its image, and many of the large wineries are starting to produce high end wines – the reds in particular being good.

Following DE BORTOLI's invention of their super-sweet botrytis Semillon Noble One in 1982 the other Riverina wineries each produce good to excellent examples. Yet when all's said and done, Riverina is still a flat, dusty, hot, featureless piece of land miles from anywhere well suited to good quality bulk production – and that's largely what it will have to continue doing. Semillon, Trebbiano, Chardonnay and Syrah (Shiraz) dominate the plantings but other grapes like Durif and Petit Verdot do well. Best producers: Casella, Cranswick Estate, De Bortoli, Gramp's, Lillypilly, McWILLIAM'S (also important for fine fortifieds), Miranda, Westend.

WESTEND
The hot, dry Riverina region has quickly established a reputation for botrytis-affected Semillon wines. This gently honeyed wine is from Westend, one of several Riverina wineries making huge efforts to improve quality in an area better known for producing vast quantities of cheap, everyday wines.

RIVERLAND

AUSTRALIA, South Australia

The Riverland produces around a third of the Australian grape harvest. Most ends up in wine boxes, but magic can occur in the hands of the best producers. The most important of Australia's vast irrigated vineyard areas stretches along the serpentine loops of the Murray River and many of the country's most successful brands of wine have a base of Riverland fruit. White wines from Chenin Blanc, Chardonnay, Colombard and Riesling have been the region's forte, but there are good, though unsubtle, juicy reds as well. The red wine boom has seen large amounts of soft but unambitious Cabernets, Shirazes, Mataros and Grenaches from Riverland as well as exotic but high quality reds like Petit Verdot which makes stunning wine here. Best producers: Angove's, HARDY (Banrock Station, Berri Estates, Renmano), Kingston Estate, YALUMBA (Oxford Landing).

RIVESALTES AC

FRANCE, Languedoc-Roussillon

❢ ❢ *Grenache*

♀ *Grenache Blanc, Macabeo, Malvoisie*

The fame of Rivesaltes, a small town just north of Perpignan, lies in its being the home of some of France's best fortified wines or *vins doux naturels*. The most famous and best of these are deep and gold, from the Muscat grape (see MUSCAT DE RIVESALTES). If stored for several years in barrel to produce a maderized *rancio* style the red wines acquire an attractive barley sugar, burnt toffee taste in addition to Grenache's original plummy grapiness and can age well.

The Rivesaltes AC covers 90 communes in the PYRÉNÉES-ORIENTALES *département* and nine in the AUDE, and about 19 million bottles are produced a year. There is also a growing interest in table wines, and some decent whites and fruity 'Nouveau' style reds are made. Best producers: de Casenove, CAZES, des Chênes, Fontanel, Força Réal, GAUBY, de Jau, Joliette, Laporte, Rivesaltes co-operative, Sarda-Malet, Terrats co-operative, Trouillas co-operative.

ROBERTSON WO

SOUTH AFRICA, Western Cape

What do vines, horses and roses have in common? A love of limestone soils, which, although uncommon elsewhere in the Cape, abound in this hot inland area, where all three thrive. About 130km (80 miles) from Cape Town, Robertson is separated from mainstream PAARL and STELLENBOSCH by imposing mountain ranges. It also marks the start of the country's dry interior and irrigation is the norm. The dominant plantings of Colombard and Chenin Blanc give evidence of the area's standing as a distilling region.

Today Robertson is also well known for attractive, reasonably priced Chardonnay and tangy Sauvignon Blanc. In pursuit of a regional blend, serendipity decreed the matching of Chardonnay and Colombard; this has resulted in some good wines. Many of the Cape's excellent fortified Muscadels and Jerepigos also come from here. Red varieties have hardly had a look in until recently, but producers such as Graham BECK, Robertson Winery and Van Loveren are showing that Cabernet, Merlot and Shiraz have exciting potential. Best producers: Graham Beck, Bon Courage, DE WETSHOF, Robertson Winery, SPRINGFIELD ESTATE, Van Loveren, Zandvliet.

CH. ROC DE CAMBES

FRANCE, Bordeaux, Côtes de Bourg AC

❢ *Merlot, Cabernet Sauvignon, Cabernet Franc, Malbec*

François Mitjavile of Ch. TERTRE-RÔTE-BOEUF has applied enthusiasm and diligence to this 10-ha (25-acre) property nestled in an amphitheatre above the town of Bourg facing the Gironde since he purchased it in 1988. Benefiting from plenty of old vines, the ripe dark wines make you realize why the Romans planted the Bourg slopes when they first arrived and make you wonder why the region has languished so long. Best years: 2001, '00, '99, '98, '97, '96, '95, '94, '93, '91, '90, '89.

J ROCHIOLI VINEYARDS

USA, California, Sonoma County, Russian River Valley AVA

❢ *Pinot Noir*

♀ *Sauvignon Blanc, Chardonnay*

For years one of the best-kept secrets among winemakers was the high-quality grapes grown by the Rochioli family on their 45-ha (110-acre) vineyard in the RUSSIAN RIVER VALLEY. Producers like Davis Bynum, WILLIAMS SELYEM and Gary Farrell kept winning prizes and garnering lavish praise and it was only bit by bit that people realized that, especially when it came to Pinot Noir, an awful lot of these top examples were coming from the vineyards of Rochioli. Well, the Rochiolis had been farming the Russian River Valley since 1938, their grapes had been making wines since the 1970s – and in 1983 they decided they'd move into winemaking as well.

They've always made a famous but controversial Sauvignon – controversial because it actually tasted like Sauvignon should – tangy and sharp – and that style didn't go down too well in California. They also make a cultish Chardonnay, but it is the rich, smooth, dark Pinot Noir that made Rochioli's name – whether the wine was made by themselves or their famous neighbours. Best years: (Pinot Noir) 2002, '01, '00, '99, '98, '97, '95.

ROCKFORD

AUSTRALIA, South Australia, Barossa Valley

❢ *Syrah (Shiraz), Grenache, Cabernet Sauvignon, Mataro*

❢ *Alicante Bouschet*

♀ *Semillon, Riesling, Muscat Blanc (White Frontignac)*

Wonderfully nostalgic wines from Robert O'Callaghan, a great respecter of the old vines so plentiful in the BAROSSA VALLEY and supporter of the farmers who grow them. He also delights in using antique machinery. Masterful Basket Press Shiraz, EDEN VALLEY Riesling, Moppa Springs (a Grenache-Shiraz-Mourvedre blend) and cult sparkling Black Shiraz, are all redolent of another age, not only in the way they are made, but, fancifully, in the way they taste. Best years: (Basket Press Shiraz) 2001, '00, '99, '98, '96, '95, '92, '91, '90, '86.

RODA

SPAIN, La Rioja, Rioja DOCa

❢ *Tempranillo, Grenache Noir (Garnacha Tinta)*

Roda is an acronym for the Barcelona family, Rotllan-Daurella, which has launched one of the most impressive new bodegas in RIOJA. The winery is in the heart of the historic Railway Station section of Haro, surrounded by the great classic bodegas. Some 60ha (148 acres) of vineyards were planted in the late 1980s and '90s in top Rioja Alta sites, but the grapes are being sold to other producers until the vineyards are more than 15 years old. In the meantime, some very old plots have been leased near Haro, and their fruit goes into some of the densest, most aromatic Riojas made today. They are made in utterly traditional style, including fermentation in oak vats, but new French oak barrels are used for aging. The top Roda I cuvée is mostly Tempranillo, while Roda II contains one-quarter Garnacha and is ready sooner. On top of it all, Cirsion is an exceptional, old-vine blend that is rivalling PINGUS and Álvaro PALACIOS' L'Ermita in Spanish tastings. Best years: 2000, '99, '98, '95, '95, '94, '92.

ANTONIN RODET

FRANCE, Burgundy, Côte Chalonnaise, Mercurey

♀ *Pinot Noir, Gamay*

♀ *Chardonnay, Aligoté*

Rodet is a large *négociant* house based in MERCUREY, and indeed wines from their Ch. de Mercey and Ch. de Chamirey are usually excellent examples of the Mercurey AC and Ch. de Rully of the neighbouring RULLY AC. But in recent years Rodet has bought other domaines, which operate with varying degrees of independence, although still overseen by the parent company. The best known of these is the MEURSAULT estate of Jacques Prieur, of which Rodet became co-owner in 1988. Domaine Jacques Prieur has a most enviable portfolio of vineyards, with holdings in MONTRACHET and MUSIGNY for a start. Since about the 1997 vintage the domaine has made a series of smashing wines.

In 1989 Rodet bought half of the Ch. de Mercey, with 65ha (161 acres) of vineyards in Mercurey and the HAUTES-CÔTES DE BEAUNE; it bought the whole estate in 1998. Finally, in 1996 Rodet bought the Domaine des Perdrix in Prémeaux, adjoining NUITS-ST-GEORGES, an estate with Premier Cru sites in Nuits as well as vineyards in VOSNE-ROMANÉE, including the ÉCHÉZEAUX Grand Cru. The best wines from the Rodet estates are labelled Cave Privée. Rodet is still, with FAIVELEY, the major player in the Côte Chalonnaise, and its wines from these villages are inexpensive and very well made. Rodet now also has a foothold in LIMOUX in the LANGUEDOC (see Domaine de l'AIGLE). Best years: (reds) 2002, '99, '98, '97, '96, '95; (whites) 2002, '01, '00, '99, '97, '96.

TELMO RODRÍGUEZ

SPAIN

The former winemaker for REMELLURI has now formed a 'wine company' that is active throughout Spain. With a team of enologists and viticulturists, it forms joint ventures with

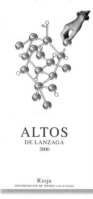

ALTOS
DE LANZAGA
2000

Rioja
DENOMINACIÓN DE ORIGEN CALIFICADA

TELMO RODRÍGUEZ
Altos de Lanzaga, a Rioja wine from 90 per cent Tempranillo with the rest Graciano and Mazuelo, is one of a string of exciting reds from this talented producer who works all over Spain.

local growers and manages the whole winemaking process. The results are often spectacular. Top wines: Molino Real (Sierra de MÁLAGA), Alto Matallana (RIBERA DEL DUERO), Altos de Lanzaga (RIOJA), Dehesa Gago Pago La Jara (TORO), Viña 105 (CIGALES), Basa (RUEDA).

ROEDERER ESTATE

USA, California, Mendocino County, Anderson Valley AVA

♀ ♀ *Pinot Noir, Chardonnay*

After a long and exhaustive search for a suitable site, this CALIFORNIA outpost of the CHAMPAGNE house of ROEDERER developed 140ha (346 acres) of vineyards in the cool western corner of the ANDERSON VALLEY. This site was chosen for its climatic similarity (meaning dicey and cool) to Champagne, and indeed the harvest is late and the yields are low. Chardonnay and Pinot Noir are used here as they are in Champagne.

Maintaining the same emphasis on owning and controlling grape sources as the parent company, Roederer Estate succeeded from the start with its Brut, a crisp bubbly full of complex yeasty character, yet more austere than the California competition. Introduced in 1994 as a limited edition prestige wine, L'Ermitage offers a creamy complexity and refinement and is an extraordinary rich bubbly by any standard. It would take well to aging, but is too attractive to often be given that opportunity. A gorgeous, decadent Brut Rosé is also available.

There used to be a lot of discussion as to whether the Californian versions of fizz could ever really match the French equivalents. Roederer have shown, by discovering the right grapes sources and by consummate winemaking that, yes, indeed they can. Best years: (L'Ermitage) 1997, '96, '94, '92, '91.

LOUIS ROEDERER

FRANCE, Champagne, Champagne AC

♀ ♀ *Pinot Noir, Chardonnay, Pinot Meunier*

This company has long had a reputation of some of the most serious winemaking in CHAMPAGNE. Obviously the word's got around, because the chief problem with Roederer is to try to find a bottle which is mature enough for you to experience its full splendour. But despite that, the quality is consistently good, and the green edges which afflict so much over-young Champagne are soothed and softened here by the cool creaminess of the yeast and the evidence of reserve wines used in the blends.

As well as the excellent non-vintage and pale rosé, it also makes a big, exciting Vintage, a rare but delicious vintage Blanc de Blancs, and the famous Roederer Cristal, a de luxe cuvée which comes in a clear bottle originally designed for the Russian Tsars. At the moment 'Cris' is the ultimate cool drink among the major rap artists. Until that fashion passes, I don't think the rest of us'll be seeing much of the stuff. Louis Roederer makes the best non-dry Champagnes on the market, too. They need aging to show their class, but can be rich and honeyed and not at all cloying – unlike most sweet Champagnes, which are generally feeble stuff. Best years: 1996, '95, '93, '90, '89, '88, '86, '85.

ROERO DOC, ROERO ARNEIS DOC

ITALY, Piedmont

♀ *Nebbiolo, Barbera*

♀ *Arneis, Favorita*

This is a zone of hills similar in shape (if rather more abrupt) to those of BAROLO and BARBARESCO, just across the river Tanaro, but divided between soils that resemble those of the famous neighbours – on which are grown the red Nebbiolo and Barbera – and lighter, sandier soils on which growers today tend to plant the white Arneis and Favorita. The Nebbiolo wines are classified simply as Roero DOC, the Barberas as BARBERA D'ALBA, the Arneis as Roero Arneis DOC and Favorita falls under the LANGHE DOC.

There is, to be sure, a certain overlap of styles, so alongside the fuller reds which are in the process of being developed (top producers are Correggia and Malvirà), there are a number of much lighter ones which accentuate the aromatic and youthful-fruity character of Nebbiolo. Now that the Roero has been 'discovered' it seems to have been designated Alba's prime area for experimentation with alternative – i.e. international – grape varieties: Syrah and Viognier as well as Cabernet and Merlot, Chardonnay and Sauvignon, are all being attempted here. But Roero is best known today, and rightly, for its whites, especially the recently resurrected Arneis, whose nutty, peachy, pear and apples aromas make it unique among Italian whites. Best years: (reds) 2001, '00, '99, '98, '97, '96. Best producers: (Arneis) Araldica/Alasia, Brovia, Cascina Chicco, M Correggia, Delletto, GIACOSA, Malvirà, Angelo Negro, PRUNOTTO, Vietti, Gianni Voerzio; (reds) G Almondo, Ca' Rossa, Cascina Chicco, M Correggia, Delletto, Funtanin, F Gallino, Malvirà, Monchiero Carbone, Angelo Negro, Porello.

Aubert de Villaine in the cellar at Domaine de la Romanée-Conti, the largest owner of Vosne-Romanée's Grands Crus. The wines are fabulously scented and rich in texture – and generally Burgundy's most expensive.

LA ROMANÉE AC, ROMANÉE-CONTI AC, ROMANÉE-ST-VIVANT AC

FRANCE, Burgundy, Côte de Nuits, Grands Crus
🍷 *Pinot Noir*

These are three of the six Grands Crus in the BURGUNDY village of VOSNE-ROMANÉE. La Romanée is the smallest AC in France, covering a touch over 0.8ha (2 acres), but this tiny little scrap of magic dirt doesn't produce wines of the class of the other Vosne Grands Crus. While the wines made by its neighbour Domaine de la ROMANÉE-CONTI are all rich flavours and exciting perfumes, la Romanée, wholly owned by the Comte Liger-Belair, is strangely lean and glum. For many years the wine has been cellared and distributed by BOUCHARD PÈRE ET FILS, whose change of ownership in the mid-1990s signalled a step up in quality for la Romanée which, by the end of the 1990s was being realized. Best years: 2001, '00, '99, '98, '97, '96.

Romanée-Conti is the pinnacle of red Burgundy for many extremely wealthy Burgundy lovers. The wines can be released at virtually any price – the 1996 was £650 (US$1040) a bottle – and yet you must still fight off the competition to buy a single bottle. The wine has a remarkable, satiny texture, its bouquet shimmering with the fragrance of sweet-briar and its palate an orgy of wonderful scents and exotic opulence which has been known to strike wine writers dumb. But not many of us can comment on that, because the vineyard, wholly owned by the Domaine de la Romanée-Conti, is only 1.8ha (4.4 acres) and only produces 7000 bottles in a good year – one reason why the prices are so high. Best years: 2001, '00, '99, '98, '97, '96, '95, '93, '91, '90, '89, '88, '85, '78.

Of Vosne's great Grands Crus, Romanée-St-Vivant is the one which has proved most troublesome to love of late. The wine doesn't seem so rich as it used to, and there is even a rather gruff, rough edge which isn't easy to interpret. Perhaps it is simply that this 9.3-ha (23-acre) vineyard, by far the largest of Vosne's Grands Crus and scrunched up to the houses of Vosne-Romanée below the RICHEBOURG Grand Cru, is no longer having to pander to the instant gratification market and at 10–15 years these wines will show the keenly balanced perfume and brilliance of which the vineyard is capable. I hope so. Even so, they are rarely as long-lived as those from Romanée-Conti. Best years: 2001, '00, '99, '98, '97, '96, '95, 93, '91, '90, '89, '88. Best producers: l'ARLOT, R Arnoux, S Cathiard, J-J Confuron, DROUHIN, Hudelot-Noëllat, JADOT, Domaine LEROY, Domaine de la ROMANÉE-CONTI, THOMAS-MOILLARD.

DOMAINE DE LA ROMANÉE-CONTI

FRANCE, Burgundy, Côte de Nuits, Vosne-Romanée AC
🍷 *Pinot Noir*
🍷 *Chardonnay*

The Domaine de la Romanée-Conti (or DRC as it is also known) is unique in BURGUNDY, since every one of its wines is a Grand Cru. As an estate it is a twentieth-century creation, having been shaped by the grandfather of the present owner Aubert de Villaine, who took in as partners the Leroy family. The estate's policy was to sell off lesser vineyards in exchange for outstanding ones. The partnership persisted until an almighty row broke out in 1992, which led to the ousting of Lalou Bize-Leroy, who left in order to develop further her own Domaine LEROY. Her place at DRC was taken by Henri Roch.

Aubert de Villaine insists there are no secrets to DRC's eminence. The vineyards are top quality and are cultivated pretty much along organic principles; yields are low, though not fanatically so, and the grapes are picked as late as possible to ensure optimal ripeness. Vinification is traditional, with no cold soak, and a fairly high fermentation temperature. The wine is aged in new oak for up to 18 months and bottled without fining or filtration. Of the six VOSNE Grands Crus, the finest are usually RICHEBOURG, la TÂCHE, and ROMANÉE-CONTI itself, although the other three, ÉCHÉZEAUX, Grands-Échézeaux and Romanée-St-Vivant can also be superb. In addition the DRC produces small quantities of incredibly expensive MONTRACHET.

The question is always asked: are the DRC wines worth the very high prices demanded for them? In realistic terms, the answer has to be no: there are other wines in each vintage that can usually rival the DRC range in intensity and quality. Twenty years ago that was not the case, and the DRC wines were unmatched for their splendour and longevity and no other estate had a comparable track record. Today there are other domaines practising the kind of perfectionism in vineyard and winery that once made the DRC unique. Quality hasn't slipped at the domaine, and if anything, the wines are better than ever. But quality has risen elsewhere too. Nonetheless, the DRC wines are of rare beauty and in the eyes of many, the most perfect imaginable expression of Pinot Noir in all its subtlety and complexity. In top years, the wines last for decades, and these great Grands Crus can also succeed in vintages written-off by other domaines. Best years: (reds) 2001, '00, '99, '98, '97, '96, '95, '93, '90, '89, '88, '85, '78.

QUINTA DOS ROQUES

PORTUGAL, Beira Alta, Dão DOC

🍷 *Touriga Nacional, Tinta Roriz and others*

🍷 *Alfrocheiro*

🍷 *Encruzado, Malvasia, Bical*

Now the Dão's finest producer, the wines of two estates with quite different characters are made here. Quinta dos Roques red is ripe and supple, while Quinta das Maias is a smoky, peppery red. The top wines are the dos Roques Reserva, made from old vines and aged in 100 per cent new oak, and Touriga Nacional. Both estates also have a decent dry white, especially Roques Encruzado. Best years: 2001, '00, '97, '96.

QUINTA DE LA ROSA

PORTUGAL, Douro, Port DOC, Douro DOC

🍷 🍷 *Tempranillo (Tinta Roriz), Tinta Barroca, Tinto Cão, Touriga Nacional, Touriga Franca and others*

🍷 *Gouveio, Viosinho, Rabigato, Malvasia Fina and others*

Unhitching themselves from a mainstream PORT shipper, the Bergqvist family have quickly established La Rosa as one of the leading independent quintas in the DOURO, proud of only using their estate grapes for all their ports. It makes a full range, from a good mid-weight vintage, through traditional LBV, 10-Year-Old Tawny, a robust premium ruby called 'Finest Reserve', to basic ruby and tawny and a wood-aged, dry white port.

Unlike the port shippers, La Rosa works on a similar basis to a French château, declaring a vintage port in all but the worst years. At the time of writing, 1993 is the only year to have been bypassed since its first vintage port in 1988. Although port comes first, with the help of winemaker David Baverstock (of ESPORÃO and Quinta do CRASTO), La Rosa also makes a firm, fragrant Douro red and Vale da Clara and Dourosa reds from non-estate grapes. Best years: (Vintage ports) 2000, '97, '96, '95, '94, '92, '91.

ROSÉ D'ANJOU AC

FRANCE, Loire, Anjou-Saumur

🍷 *Cabernet Franc, Cabernet Sauvignon, Pineau d'Aunis, Malbec (Côt), Gamay, Grolleau*

Varying from off-dry to reasonably sweet, most Rosé d'Anjou is made by the local co-operatives and *négociants* and to a price point. Production is gradually declining as individual producers prefer to make ROSÉ DE LOIRE or CABERNET D'ANJOU instead, and it is now difficult to sell. Annual production is still around 18 million bottles. Best producers: M Angeli, de Montgueret, de la Sansonnière, de Tigné, des Trottières.

ROSÉ DE LOIRE AC

FRANCE, Loire, Anjou-Saumur and Touraine

🍷 *Cabernet Franc, Cabernet Sauvignon, Pineau d'Aunis, Pinot Noir, Gamay, Grolleau*

This is a catch-all appellation covering ANJOU, SAUMUR and TOURAINE. It can be made from a range of grapes but Cabernet must make up a minimum of 30 per cent. These rosés are generally dry and can be very attractive young, with lovely red fruit aromas and flavours and enough acidity to make them refreshing. Drink within a year. Best producers: des Hautes Ouches, de Passavant, St-Arnoud, des Trottières.

ROSÉ DES RICEYS AC

FRANCE, Champagne

🍷 *Pinot Noir*

This is a real oddball still rosé, from les Riceys in the very south of the CHAMPAGNE region, and made only in the ripest years. The wine is a strange sort of dark golden pink, and tastes full and rather nutty. Only about 7500 bottles are made a year and it's expensive. Although usually drunk young, it can age surprisingly well. Best producers: Alexandre Bonnet, Devaux, Guy de Forez, Morel.

ROSEMOUNT ESTATE

AUSTRALIA, New South Wales, Hunter Valley

🍷 *Syrah (Shiraz), Cabernet Sauvignon, Merlot, Pinot Noir*

🍷 *Chardonnay, Semillon, Sauvignon Blanc, Riesling*

Rosemount first challenged Australia, and then took on the world, with a small but very talented winemaking and management team, and with success following success. Its vineyard holdings now include prime land in the Upper HUNTER VALLEY, MUDGEE, COONAWARRA, McLAREN VALE and the ADELAIDE HILLS, while its grape-purchasing tentacles extend into every worthwhile nook and cranny of South Eastern Australia.

All of this has meant a proliferation of labels and for a time seemed to defy the usual logic of increasing demand meaning declining quality by maintaining their character and individuality. In 2001 the business merged with Southcorp and since then ambitious plans for rapid expansion have led to the inevitable loss of personality in the wines and a fear that the vast Rosemount/Southcorp giant has become too big for anybody's good. Roxburgh Chardonnay (Upper Hunter), Mountain Blue Shiraz-Cabernet (Mudgee), Balmoral Syrah (McLaren Vale) and Show Reserve Cabernet Sauvignon (Coonawarra) are some of the flagships, and there's a mighty armada of flotsam and jetsam following behind, with the Diamond Label range at its core. Best years: (Balmoral Syrah) 2001, '00, '98, '97, '96, '94, '92, '91, '90.

ROSSESE DI DOLCEACQUA DOC

ITALY, Liguria

🍷 *Rossese*

Right by the French border in the far west of Italy's rocky and riotously colourful Riviera of Flowers, Rossese di Dolceacqua continues to turn out small quantities of its own, much sought-after, fragrant wine, although it is contained within the new Riviera Ligure di Ponente zone, which also grows the Rossese grape. Rossese di Dolceacqua is a delight when young and just as good, and much softer, after a couple of years. Most of it comes from tiny, artisanal producers. Best producers: Cane, Enzo Guglielmi, Lupi, Maccario, Castello di Perinaldo.

ROSSO CÒNERO DOC

ITALY, Marche

🍷 *Montepulciano, Sangiovese*

Rosso Cònero is the MARCHE's best red wine, primarily because it is made almost entirely from the gutsy Montepulciano grape and the general level is pretty reliable, although a few bottles taste as if the grapes had been crushed by a steamroller. This area near the Adriatic coast is towards the northern limit of where the Montepulciano grape will thrive, so its almost voluptuous brambly fruit gets a sharper edginess along with its pepper and spice. The name of the DOC comes from a particular type of cherry tree (called Cònero by the Greeks) that grows on the stony white soil of its peaks. Best years: 2001, '00, '98, '97, '95, '90. Best producers: Fazi Battaglia, Garofoli (Grosso Agontano), Lanari (Fibbio), Leopardi Dittajuti, Malacari, Enzo Mecella (Rubelliano), Moroder (Dorico), Le Terrazze (Sassi Neri, Visions of J), UMANI RONCHI (Cúmaro), La Vite (Adeodato).

ROSSO DI MONTALCINO DOC

ITALY, Tuscany

🍷 *Sangiovese*

BRUNELLO DI MONTALCINO is a big, serious, slow-maturing wine that needs years of aging before it can be sold. In other words, the high price aside, it is a wine that one wouldn't want to drink every day. Plus the fact that producers would expire of cash flow strangulation if they only had their big wine to sell.

Hence Rosso di Montalcino, which is basically a less intense, fresher version of

Brunello that can be sold after only one year. But what it loses in mature complexity, Rosso often gains in youthful excitement. It is affordable too. Any recent vintage is worth a gamble, because even in poor vintages responsible growers will sell what would otherwise have been Brunello as Rosso. Some Rossos today are, however, made along Brunello lines except for the aging, and these deserve greater attention – an example is Caparzo's La Caduta. Best years: 2001, '00, '99, '98, '97, '95. Best producers: Altesino, ARGIANO, Caparzo, Casanova di Neri, Ciacci Piccolomini d'Aragona, Col d'Orcia, Collemattoni, Costanti, Due Portine-Gorelli, Fuligni, M Lambardi, Lisini, Siro Pacenti, Agostina Pieri, Poggio Antico, Il Poggione, Poggio Salvi, Salicutti, San Filippo-Fanti, Talenti, Valdicava.

ROSSO DI MONTEPULCIANO DOC

ITALY, Tuscany

🍷 *Sangiovese, Canaiolo*

This wine was conceived on the same lines as ROSSO DI MONTALCINO, but has been less of a success in its own right. For one thing, VINO NOBILE producers do not have to wait four years for their principal wine to be saleable. For another, Vino Nobile is rather nearer in style to the second wine, creating a certain confusion in the minds of producers and consumers alike. The upshot is that no-one has taken on the Rosso di Montepulciano DOC with the enthusiasm that has greeted its colleague from that other hill town of the province of Siena, and it has yet to establish a recognizable style. Best years: 2001, '99, '98, '97. Best producers: La Braccesca/ANTINORI, La Ciarliana, Contucci, Dei, Del Cerro, Il Faggeto, Fassati, Nottola, POLIZIANO, Salcheto, Valdipiatta, Val di Suga, Villa Sant'Anna.

ROSSO PICENO DOC

ITALY, Marche

🍷 *Sangiovese, Montepulciano and others*

This wine is made in most of the southern MARCHE as a fruitier and less interesting version of ROSSO CÒNERO, with the fluctuations in quality one might expect from such a basic beverage. But the Superiore version, from a zone near the ABRUZZO border, is distinctly better. For once the word 'Superiore' does not just imply slightly higher alcohol, but rather a more traditional and suitable terroir in the spirit of 'Classico'. Best years: 2001, '00, '98, '97, '95, '94, '93, '90. Best producers: Boccadigabbia (Villamagna), Le Caniette, Laurentina, Saladini Pilastri, Velenosi.

RENÉ ROSTAING

René Rostaing is a meticulous winemaker who makes several outstanding Côte-Rôties, including a darkly dense cuvée from the la Landonne lieu-dit.

RENÉ ROSTAING

FRANCE, Northern Rhône, Côte-Rôtie AC

🍷 *Syrah*

🍷 *Viognier*

By profession René Rostaing is a legal academic and a property dealer, but I can't see how he has much time for selling houses since he has now become one of CÔTE-RÔTIE's top producers as well as being the creator of a delightfully scented, crystal clear CONDRIEU. Altogether, he has 7.4ha (18 acres) of Côte-Rôtie, with vines in some of the best sites, and just 1ha (2.5 acres) of Condrieu. He used to make four different Côte-Rôties, but has now cut the number to three: a fine, much-improved Classique, a rich, beefy la Landonne and a fragrant yet juicy Côte Blonde, made even more sumptuous by the inclusion of 5 per cent Viognier. These wines are now bottled unfiltered, and though gorgeous young, age with distinction. Best years: (top crus) 2001, '00, '99, '98, '95, '94, '91, '90, '88, '85.

ROTHBURY ESTATE

AUSTRALIA, New South Wales, Hunter Valley

🍷 *Syrah (Shiraz), Cabernet Sauvignon, Merlot, Pinot Noir*

🍷 *Chardonnay, Verdelho, Semillon, Sauvignon Blanc*

The king is dead, and neither queen, prince or princess to follow him. Following its acrimonious acquisition by Beringer Blass, the wine division of Fosters, Len Evans has left Rothbury for good, but is busily creating a new, multi-faceted empire in the HUNTER VALLEY (see TOWER ESTATE). Rothbury meanwhile is making some effort to redefine and reposition itself and its products, with modest success. The imposing winery is still there, and the Fosters Group now owns one of the largest direct mail wine businesses in the world, into which the Rothbury Estate Society direct mail club naturally fits. Soulless stuff, perhaps, but properly handled, keeps shareholders happy.

DOMAINE GEORGES ROUMIER

FRANCE, Burgundy, Côte de Nuits, Chambolle-Musigny AC

🍷 *Pinot Noir*

🍷 *Chardonnay*

Although this well-known estate is based in CHAMBOLLE-MUSIGNY, its holdings of 11.8ha (29 acres) are quite dispersed. There are Grands Crus in GEVREY-CHAMBERTIN, a monopole Premier Cru in MOREY-ST-DENIS called Clos de la Bussière, and vines in CLOS DE VOUGEOT and CORTON-CHARLEMAGNE. But Chambolle remains Roumier's heartland, and their BONNES-MARES and MUSIGNY are as exquisite as any. Yields are invariably low, which partly accounts for the wines' intensity.

The domaine has enjoyed a high profile under the energetic Christophe Roumier. The winemaking is a blend of traditional and innovative techniques: there is a cold soak before fermentation, maceration at relatively high temperatures, and aging in a moderate proportion of new oak. The wines fetch deservedly high prices but Christophe Roumier is so adept at teasing out the best that any vineyard has to offer that even his basic BOURGOGNE Rouge is often equal to other growers' Premiers Crus, and Clos de la Bussière is not only excellent but good value. Best years: (reds) 2002, '01, '00, '99, '98, '97, '96, '95, '93, '90, '89, '88.

ROUSSANNE

This is the better of the two major white grapes of France's northern RHÔNE Valley (Marsanne is the other). Both may be added, in small quantities, to the red wines of HERMITAGE as well as making whites in their own right. Roussanne makes fine, delicate wines which, however, are often too delicate to stand up on their own; without the body-building addition of Marsanne they fade rapidly. It is also one of the improving white varieties being planted in the LANGUEDOC-ROUSSILLON, where there are now some interesting examples made with barrel fermentation and oak aging. It is increasingly being planted in the southern Rhône, and a truly outstanding (if costly) example is the Vieilles Vignes from CHÂTEAUNEUF-DU-PAPE's Ch. de BEAUCASTEL.

ROYAL TOKAJI WINE COMPANY

HUNGARY, Tokaj-Hegyalja

🍷 *Furmint, Hárslevelü, Muscat*

I have to say, one of the things I most enjoy about this company is how it states its address on its letterhead as 'London and Mád'. But there's method in it; Mád is one of the Tokaji region's top three villages, and the Royal Tokaji Wine Company was the first international company to take advantage of the collapse of communism by establishing a headquarters there in 1989. Since then there has been a deluge of international interest in Tokaji – which historically has been one of the greatest and most famous sweet wines in the world. One of Royal Tokaji's most important achievements has been to resurrect the Vineyard Classification of 1700 and to produce five separate vineyard bottlings as well as their regular blends. Best years: 1999, '96, '95, '93, '91.

RÜDESHEIM

GERMANY, Rheingau

This RHEINGAU town should not be confused with that of the same name in the NAHE. It has some of the steepest vineyards in the Rheingau, particularly those west of the town. A few years ago they were intricately terraced, but Flurbereinigung, the radical restructuring of vineyards to make them more economic and easier to work, has done away with the terraces. The best vineyard sites include the Berg Schlossberg and Berg Rottland. The wines are big, ripe and powerful. Best years: (Riesling Spätlese) 2002, '01, '00, '99, '98, '97, '96, '94, '93, '90. Best producers: Georg BREUER, JOHANNISHOF, Josef LEITZ.

RUEDA DO

SPAIN, Castilla y León
♀ *Verdejo, Palomino, Macabeo (Viura), Sauvignon Blanc*

Rueda is capable of making some of Spain's best whites for two reasons. First, the predominant grape variety, the Verdejo, has more character and flavour than most Spanish white grapes, making fresh, fruity, nutty wines with lots of body. Second, the Verdejo's potential is maximized here because of the altitude – between 700 and 800m (2300 and 2625ft) above sea level – and consequent big temperature drops on summer nights, which enable the grapes to retain their aromas. Rueda was once famous for its sherry-style wines but the light, fresh whites are now far more important here.

The full, fresh Rueda Superior by MARQUÉS DE RISCAL is the benchmark wine for this new style. Indeed it was this RIOJA bodega which created the new style, from scratch, after opening its Rueda subsidiary in the 1970s. Marqués de Riscal also introduced the Sauvignon Blanc grape and made the first

modern barrel-fermented Verdejo. All these developments relaunched a moribund region. Best producers: ÁLVAREZ Y DÍEZ, Antaño (Viña Mocén), Belondrade y Lurton, Cerrosol (Doña Beatriz), Hermanos Lurton, Marqués de Riscal, Bodegas de Crianza Castilla La Vieja (Palacio de Bornos Vendimia Seleccionada), Javier Sanz Cantalapiedra, Viñedos de Nieva, Viños Sanz, Ángel Rodríguez Vidal (Martínsancho).

RUFFINO AND A & A FOLONARI

ITALY, Tuscany, Chianti Rufina DOCG
♣ *Sangiovese, Colorino, Merlot, Cabernet Sauvignon, Pinot Noir (Pinot Nero) and others*
♣ *Sangiovese*
♀ *Chardonnay, Pinot Gris (Pinot Grigio), Trebbiano Toscano, Malvasia and others*

The Folonari family – owners of Ruffino since 1913, though they split in two parts recently, the other half now being called A & A Folonari, produce not just millions of bottles of what is arguably the world's most famous CHIANTI but also various crus at different levels of quality. Top CHIANTI CLASSICO is their Riserva Ducale and its superior version, Riserva Ducale Oro. On a similar level is the VINO NOBILE DI MONTEPULCIANO Lodola Nuova, while BRUNELLO DI MONTALCINO Il Greppone Mazzi can be put on a par with 'Oro', though retaining a structure and a character typical of good Brunello.

Probably the best wine under the Ruffino label in recent years has been the SUPER-TUSCAN Romitorio di Santedame which was 40 per cent Sangiovese until the 1997 vintage – now Merlot – with the balance made up of Colorino, one of TUSCANY's more obscure but, when vinified correctly, most exciting grapes. The Sangiovese version was full of the wild cherry and blackberry aromas of the Tuscan hills with firm acidity and ripe tannins at a level capable of improving and aging for years.

Il Pareto, the top wine from A & A Folonari, is a tremendously full, complex (berry fruit, raisin, dark chocolate and coffee, toast and spice, long sweet finish) Cabernet designed successfully to impress at international level. But perhaps the most famous of what were Ruffino's, now A & A Folinari's, crus is Cabreo Il Borgo, 70 per cent Sangiovese with 30 per cent Cabernet Sauvignon, and much hailed since its first appearance in 1983: in good years, this wine has tremendous concentration and richness of fruit and is perhaps more muscular than subtle, but very modern, and endowed with considerable aging potential. The twin white, Cabreo La

Pietra, a barriqued Chardonnay complete with *bâtonnage*, is equally impressive for concentration and wealth of fruit, although it hasn't yet developed a memorable personality.

RUINART

FRANCE, Champagne, Champagne AC
♀♣ *Chardonnay, Pinot Noir*

Age isn't everything, but Ruinart is the oldest surviving CHAMPAGNE house, having been founded in 1729. Today it is part of the giant LVMH group, but has managed to maintain its own identity; nor has production risen significantly: a manageable two million bottles are produced each year.

'R' de Ruinart is the standard range, and comes in both non-vintage and vintage versions. Although Pinot dominates the 'R' wines, it's a close thing, and Chardonnay makes up a generous proportion of the blend. Quality here is very consistent, and the vintage 'R' is a fine biscuity mouthful. Ruinart's pride and joy, however, is the Dom Ruinart Champagne, exceptional in both its manifestations: Blanc de Blancs and Rosé. What makes the Blanc de Blancs unusual is that much of the fruit comes not from the Côte des Blancs but from the Montagne de Reims, which may account for the richness of the wine. In 1998 Ruinart launched L'Exclusive, blending a number of different vintages in an expensively packaged magnum to celebrate the millennium. Best years: 1996, '95, '93, '92, '90, '88, '86, '85, '83, '82.

RULLY AC

FRANCE, Burgundy, Côte Chalonnaise
♣ *Pinot Noir*
♀ *Chardonnay*

This is an example of a little-known wine village hauling itself up by the bootstraps. Rully is the northernmost of the individual Côte Chalonnaise ACs (though BOUZERON, with its special AC for Aligoté, is further north still), and in reputation is more of a white wine village than a red; two-thirds of the wines produced are white. Rully is one of the few areas in BURGUNDY where there is room for expansion, with some very promising steep slopes facing east to south-east, recently planted and coming into full production.

The vines of Rully, covering 300ha (740 acres), once provided thin light base wine for the village's thriving fizz industry, which meant the village had no real reputation for its still wines. This all changed in the 1970s and '80s as the prices of both red and white Burgundy from the CÔTE D'OR, just a few miles to the north, began to go crazy – not only was there a lot of new planting in Rully, but the bubbly-makers began to bring in their base wines from elsewhere, leaving Rully's own vineyards to capitalize on a sudden demand for good-quality, reasonably priced Burgundy. Red Rully is light, with a pleasant strawberry and cherry perfume. There could be a bit more body in the wines, but at two to four years they can be very refreshing. You may see Premier Cru on some labels but such epithets have little importance here, and several of the best vineyards are not Premiers Crus. Best years: (reds) 2002, '01, '00, '99. Best producers: (reds) A Delorme, Dureuil-Janthial, Duvernay, de la Folie, H & P Jacqueson, de Rully (RODET).

Rully has always made fairly light whites, due to its limestone-dominated soil, but in recent vintages the wines have become fuller, rather nutty, their appley acidity jazzed up by an attractive hint of honey. As some growers also begin to use oak barrels, we should start to see an increasing amount of exciting wine, at a price nearer to a MÂCON Blanc-Villages than a MEURSAULT. Some wines sport the name of a vineyard – probably one of the 19 Premiers Crus, but, as usual here in the Côte Chalonnaise, the term Premier Cru doesn't mean a lot. Best years: (whites) 2002, '01, '00, '99. Best producers: (whites) d'Allaines, Michel Briday, J-C Brelière, DROUHIN, Dureuil-Janthial, Duvernay, FAIVELEY, V GIRARDIN, JADOT, Jaffelin, Olivier LEFLAIVE, de Rully (Rodet), de Villaine.

RUPPERTSBERG

GERMANY, Pfalz

This little village lies to the south of DEIDESHEIM, its famous neighbour in the PFALZ; it marks the southern end of the Mittelhaardt, the stretch of the Pfalz which used to make all the greatest Pfalz wines but which is nowadays increasingly challenged by talented producers in virtually unknown villages further to the south.

Luckily the move towards making weighty but dry white in the Pfalz suits Ruppertsberg perfectly, with most of the vineyards here being flat or gently sloping up towards the Haardt Mountains and their protective forests, and with vine-friendly loam and sandstone soils. The pedigree of the wines is good, too, with growers like von BASSERMANN-JORDAN, von BUHL, BÜRKLIN-WOLF, Dr Kern and J Wegeler having vines in sites like Reiterpfad, Hoheburg, Gaisböhl and Spiess. Although the fashion here is for full dry whites there is a tradition also for magnificent sweet wines up to Trockenbeerenauslese level. Best years: 2002, '01, '99, '98, '97, '96.

RUSSIAN RIVER VALLEY AVA

USA, California, Sonoma County

It's the fog that makes Russian River Valley special. In most parts of the wine world, a great bank of fog blotting out the sunshine for several hours a day would be seen as an excellent reason for *not* planting a vineyard there. And until the 1980s the fog that rolls up from the Pacific most days, through Guerneville and on up to Healdsburg, with a particular partiality to heavy mists in July and August, was the reason that most of the Russian River concentrated on apples, dairy farming, poultry and horticulture.

But the 1980s brought the realization that cool climate conditions might produce more aromatic, elegant, balanced wines than hot climate conditions. Most of CALIFORNIA errs on the side of hot and the one thing that can cool most of the coastal areas down is this daily influx of fog and chill breezes from the Pacific. In particular, this is of vital importance for grape varieties like Pinot Noir and Chardonnay that only thrive under relatively cool conditions, and for the sparkling wine industry which *has* to have cool climate grapes. So, suddenly, Russian River became a desperately trendy vineyard region, quickly proving its worth as the area most of the famous SONOMA-CUTRER and KISTLER Chardonnays came from and following this up with great Pinot Noirs from ROCHIOLI and WILLIAMS SELYEM and fine sparkling wine from IRON HORSE.

At the slightly warmer Healdsburg end of the AVA Zinfandel and Merlot have also been successful. There are two sub-AVAs. Green Valley, lying just to the south of the Russian River, is significantly affected by fog and chill winds and has proved to be one of California's best cool-climate regions. Marimar TORRES is one of the top estates here. To the east, Chalk Hill is considerably warmer and rarely affected by fog. Its wines are good but atypical and there are now moves afoot to remove it from the Russian River AVA, thereby limiting the AVA to areas affected by the river fogs. If this is achieved it will be the first time an AVA has been re-defined. Since almost all the original AVAs were based on political not vinous considerations, this could set a vital precedent, allowing the AVAs to become real vineyard-sensitive appellations, not just political lines drawn arbitrarily on a map. Best years: 2002, '01, '00, '99, '97, '95, '94, '93, '91, '90. Best producers: Davis Bynum, DEHLINGER, De Loach, Dutton-Goldfield, Gary Farrell, Iron Horse, Rochioli, Sonoma-Cutrer, Rodney Strong, Joseph SWAN, Marimar TORRES, Williams Selyem.

RUSSIZ SUPERIORE

ITALY, Friuli-Venezia Giulia, Collio DOC

Cabernet Sauvignon, Cabernet Franc, Merlot

Tocai Friulano, Pinot Blanc (Pinot Bianco), Pinot Gris (Pinot Grigio), Sauvignon Blanc and others

The Felluga family acquired this historic FRIULI estate in the 1960s and they make their top range of wines here, including good varietal Cabernet Franc and Merlot. There are also, more predictably, some first-class COLLIO whites in the form of Pinot Bianco, Pinot Grigio, Sauvignon and Tocai Friulano. The same family controls the separate winery of Marco Felluga, at Gradisca d'Isonzo, which produces a worthy rival to Rosso degli Orzoni called Carantan. Best years: 2001, '00, '99, '97, '95, '93.

RUST

AUSTRIA, Burgenland, Neusiedlersee-Hügelland

It would be hard for the town of Rust, in the NEUSIEDLERSEE-HÜGELLAND on the western shore of Lake Neusiedl, to be any prettier. It has painted baroque houses, it has Buschenschanken (watering holes) galore, it has mellow old churches and it even has storks. Unfortunately all these delights attract the tourists, and Rust in summer has coaches lined up like cows at a milking parlour.

Rust has plenty of good winemakers, producing some of Austria's best sweet wines. These come from vineyards running in a narrow strip near the lake, which is broad and shallow and offers a perfect mesoclimate for the development of the noble rot fungus. Dry reds and whites come from other Rust vineyards further back from the lake, but Rust's

PETER SCHANDL
Peter Schandl is one of the leading producers of Ausbruch, a unique botrytized sweet wine from Rust. This one comes from Pinot Gris.

own speciality is AUSBRUCH, a sweet wine made by adding non-botrytized must to nobly rotten must. The best ones are closer to SAUTERNES in style than German sweet wines, with less fruit flavour than the German examples and perhaps less waxy weight than Sauternes, but with great complexity and power. Best growers: FEILER-ARTINGER, Bruno Landauer, Peter Schandl, Heidi Schröck, Ernst TRIEBAUMER, Robert WENZEL.

RUSTENBERG

SOUTH AFRICA, Western Cape, Stellenbosch WO
♥ Cabernet Sauvignon, Syrah, Merlot and others
♀ Chardonnay, Sauvignon Blanc, Viognier and others

It takes guts – and a deep pocket – to drop out of the market for three vintages, but this is what owner Simon Barlow did when problems arose with some wines of the early 1990s. In the meantime, the farm has undergone a complete revamp, from vineyards to a new cellar skilfully inserted into the skeleton of the old dairy. All the new buildings have certainly not destroyed the ambience of this magnificent old farm and national monument in the Simonsberg foothills of STELLENBOSCH. New varieties, many reflecting the worldwide interest in RHÔNE grapes, are being introduced and a nursery has been established to propagate the farm's own vines.

To complement all this activity, the farm has now bounced back with some fine wines. Starting level is the competitive Brampton label, which includes fruit from Simon Barlow's farm on the Helderberg; this range concentrates on varietal fruit – the Sauvignon Blanc is a top example of the modern tangy Cape style. The premium, classically styled Rustenberg wines include the individual Five Soldiers Chardonnay and the flagship wine called Peter Barlow, 100 per cent Cabernet. Beautifully oaked and balanced, these are wines with excellent aging potential; they also assured Rustenberg a flying start into the twenty-first century. Best years: (Peter Barlow) 2001, '99, '98, '97, '96; (Five Soldiers) 2001, '00, '99, '98, '97.

RUTHERFORD AVA

USA, California, Napa County
With the OAKVILLE District as its southern boundary and ST HELENA to the north, Rutherford lies in the middle section of the NAPA VALLEY. Made famous decades ago by Cabernet Sauvignon grown by BEAULIEU and Inglenook (now called NIEBAUM-COPPOLA), Rutherford's terroir was said to contribute a dried herb, earthy character called 'Rutherford dust'. Most of the historic vineyard sites and many of the new cult producers are found along the western foothills.

Vineyard redevelopment in the 1990s left no doubt that Cabernet Sauvignon is the preferred variety in Rutherford, with a smattering of Merlot and a patch or two of Chardonnay still to be found. Total plantings of around 2700ha (6650 acres) include such famous vineyards as Bella Oaks, Inglenook and Bosché. Best years: (Cabernet) 2001, '00, '99, '97, '96, '95, '94, '93, '92, '91, '90, '86. Best producers: Beaulieu, Cakebread, Flora Springs, Freemark Abbey, Niebaum-Coppola, Quintessa (FRANCISCAN), Staglin Family.

RUTHERGLEN AND GLENROWAN

AUSTRALIA, Victoria
Steeped in history – just drive through the main street of Glenrowan or visit MORRIS, BAILEYS or Fairfield, or read about Ned Kelly and his last stand – these regions (they are being split like Siamese twins under the Geographic Indications scalpel) produce Australia's most remarkable wines: the fortified Tokays (read Muscadelle) and Muscats (read Muscat Blanc à Petits Grains, a brown clone the Australians often call Brown Frontignac). Wrinkled, raisined and incredibly sweet grapes are harvested very late in the season, and barely allowed to ferment before alcohol is added, the fermentation stopped and the long period of barrel-aging commenced – still aided by storage in broiling conditions underneath the ceiling of the corrugated iron wineries, a system borrowed directly from the MADEIRA 'cooking' approach. Suitably monumental and long-lived reds are also made, most notably from Shiraz. Best producers: (Rutherglen fortifieds) ALL SAINTS, Buller's, Campbells, CHAMBERS, Morris, Stanton & Killeen.

RUWER

GERMANY, Mosel-Saar-Ruwer
The Ruwer produces the most ethereal wines in Germany, so wispy, fragile, yet fragrant, so water pale and so low in alcohol that you will be excused for wondering if they are really wine at all. Well, they are. Ruwer Rieslings are indeed delicate and, in warm years, surprisingly soft, but they make a heavenly drink to sip as the sun fades on a hot summer's day. And it's entirely right they should be so charmingly insubstantial, because the Ruwer, which joins the Mosel just below Trier, is a mere trickle of water rather than a river or even a stream. Surprisingly there are a couple of world-class vineyards here too, which can make intense fragrant Riesling – Maximin Grünhaus and Karthäuserhofberg – but most of the other vineyards, even the best from the villages of KASEL and Waldrach, produce wines that are gentle and delicate in the extreme. Best years: 2002, '01, '99, '97, '95, '94, '93, '90, '89. Best producers: von Beulwitz, KARLSMÜHLE, KARTHÄUSERHOF, von KESSELSTATT, MAXIMIN GRÜNHAUS.

SAALE-UNSTRUT

GERMANY
The Saale and the Unstrut are both rivers, and together they make up one of the wine regions of the former East Germany. There are only 650ha (1605 acres) under vine and these are Germany's most northerly vineyards. Frost can be a serious problem, and this, together with low rainfall, poor vine clones and gaps in the vineyards where replanting has not been possible, makes for low yields averaging 34 hectolitres per hectare, compared with around 100 hectolitres per hectare in the former West Germany. The soil is limestone or gypsum marl and the wines light with plenty of acidity. Nearly the whole production is divided between the State Domaine at Naumburg and the larger Freyburg co-operative, with 500 members. There are also now a few private growers. The other large producer in the region, the Rotkäppchen Sektkellerei at Freyburg, imports the base wine for its fizz from abroad. Best producers: Lützkendorf, Pawis.

SAAR

GERMANY, Mosel-Saar-Ruwer
The glory of Saar wines lies in their thrilling, bracing acidity. Though the river Saar runs into the Mosel from above Trier, and the little valley at first sight seems an amiable sylvan kind of place, don't be fooled. On the Mosel, the towering cliffs and the serpentine twists and turns of the river protect the vineyard sites from the elements and provide numerous south- to west-facing suntraps. The Saar Valley doesn't offer such protection, although it does have many superb steep south- to west-

facing vineyards in villages like WILTINGEN, AYL and OCKFEN. Consequently in cool years it's positively cold in the windswept Saar and the predominantly Riesling grapes simply don't ripen. But in hot years, the Saar always manages to retain this almost shocking acidity and a chill glint of mineral even as the floral scent and honey seduce your palate. Best years: 2002, '01, '99, '97, '95, '94, '93, '90, '89. Best producers: Bischöfliche Weingüter, von HÖVEL, von KESSELSTATT, Egon MÜLLER-SCHARZHOF, SCHLOSS SAARSTEIN, van Volxem, Dr Wagner, ZILLIKEN.

SAARBURG
GERMANY, Mosel-Saar-Ruwer

The most important town on the stretch of the SAAR Valley where vines are still grown is dominated by its medieval castle. Less well-known than this and the cable car that pulls in the tourists are the excellent vineyards, most notably the Saarburger Rausch. Best years: 2002, '01, '99, '97, '95, '94, '93, '91, '90, '89. Best producers: Dr Wagner, ZILLIKEN.

SACHSEN
GERMANY

If the vineyards of Sachsen somehow survived economic crises, the Nazis, the destruction of central Dresden in 1945 and half a century of Communism, then it was because of the patriotism of the people of Saxony who remembered their country's great past. Until Saxony was cut down to size at the Vienna Congress in 1815 it was a great European power with a thriving wine industry.

The best vineyards, now totalling 445ha (1100 acres), are on steep terraces above the river Elbe just north-west of Dresden around Meissen. They have been replanted with good vine material during the 1990s and are starting to yield good wines. Best are the dry Riesling, Pinot Gris (Grauburgunder) and Traminer, all of which can have astonishing power along with the crisp acidity you would expect from a region north of the 51° latitude. Best producers: Schloss Proschwitz, Schloss Wackerbarth, Klaus Zimmerling.

SACRAMENTO RIVER VALLEY
USA, California

The Sacramento River Valley and Delta spreads across the northern end of CALIFORNIA's CENTRAL VALLEY, source of most of California's bulk wine. But the Sacramento River and its AVAs Clarksburg and Lodi benefit from coastal breezes while the rest of the Central Valley doesn't. The result is greatly

superior fruit and some genuinely interesting reds and whites. Best producers: Bogle, Fiddlehead, Lucas, MONDAVI Woodbridge, Peirano, St Amant.

CH. ST-AMAND
FRANCE, Bordeaux, Sauternes AC, Cru Bourgeois
♀ *Sémillon, Sauvignon Blanc, Muscadelle*

This is one of the few non-Classed Growth properties that manages to produce big, rich, classic SAUTERNES – and which doesn't charge the earth. The 22-ha (54-acre) estate is in the commune of Preignac – right next to the little river Ciron, whose autumn mists have so much to do with the formation of the noble rot fungus on the grapes. Recent vintages have been less consistent. The second wine is Ch. la Chartreuse. Best years: 2001, '99, '98, '97, '96, '90, '89, '88, '86, '83.

ST-AMOUR AC
FRANCE, Burgundy, Beaujolais, Beaujolais cru
♀ *Gamay*

What a lovely name – the 'Love Saint'. Obviously this BEAUJOLAIS cru has missed its vocation: it ought to be a honeymoon retreat. The calf-eyed couples would certainly find it quiet: there isn't even a village inn. So perhaps the inhabitants are better off making a particularly juicy, soft-fruited Beaujolais, ready to drink within the year, but lasting well for two or three. St-Amour is just inside the Saône-et-Loire *département* (all the other Beaujolais crus are in the RHÔNE *département*) and so is theoretically in the Mâconnais. With 317ha (783 acres) of vineyards it lies at the northernmost limits of Beaujolais' granite subsoil and produces wines of great intensity of colour that may be initially harsh, requiring a few months to soften. There is no co-operative at St-Amour, and several *négociant* wines are better than average. Best years: 2002, '00, '99, '98. Best producers: des Billards/Loron, DUBOEUF (des Sablons), des Duc, J-P Ducoté.

ST-AUBIN AC
FRANCE, Burgundy, Côte de Beaune
♀ *Pinot Noir*
♀ *Chardonnay*

St-Aubin is not actually on the CÔTE D'OR's Golden Slope but in its own cleft, just up the hill from PULIGNY-MONTRACHET, which means that prices are comparatively low, and despite recent replanting, there are lots of old vineyards producing quite big, chewy-fruited reds. There is a fair bit of old Gamay – which can't be used for the St-Aubin AC, but which makes the local Gamay-Pinot Noir blend,

BOURGOGNE PASSE-TOUT-GRAINS particularly tasty here. In fact most of the 237ha (585 acres) of vineyards are on good east- to south-east-facing slopes, and two-thirds of them are classified Premiers Crus. Les Frionnes and les Murgers des Dents de Chien are two of the best. Best years: (reds) 2002, '01, 99, '98, '96.

The white wines combine lean, racy fruit with a delicious toasty, biscuity perfume from a little oak aging, making these wines as good as many CHASSAGNE-MONTRACHETs or MEURSAULTs. They're delicious young, but are better after five years' aging. Perhaps St-Aubin is in fact the patron saint of the white BURGUNDY lover with limited means, because these delicious wines are never overpriced. Best years: (whites) 2002, '01, '00, '99. Best producers: (reds and whites) d'Allaines, Bernard Bachelet, D & F Clair, M Colin, DROUHIN, JADOT, Lamy-Pillot, Larue, Olivier LEFLAIVE, B Morey, H Prudhon, RAMONET, Roux, G Thomas.

ST-CHINIAN AC
FRANCE, Languedoc-Roussillon
♀♀ *Grenache, Lladoner Pelut, Syrah, Mourvèdre, Carignan, Cinsaut*

Along with FAUGÈRES, this was the first of the red wines of the HÉRAULT *département* to break away from the pack and start making a name for itself back in the 1980s. In the hill villages set back from the coast, the rocky slopes can produce strong, spicy reds with a great wodge of turbulent fruit and fistfuls of hillside herbs far removed from the run of the Hérault mill – particularly when carbonic maceration has been used at least partially.

About 19 million bottles of St-Chinian are produced annually from around 2977ha (7355 acres) of vines in the hills above Béziers. Grenache, Syrah and Mourvèdre are increasingly taking the place of the traditional Carignan. The wines can be drunk very young but age happily for two to three years. The best most fiery St-Chinian comes from the steep schist slopes close to the mountains. If you head off to the south and west the landscape suddenly becomes less rugged, the vineyards flatter and the tiny villages more complacent. There are good limestone soils here, but the wines, unsurprisingly, are more mellow and soft. Best years: 2001, '00, '99, '98, '96, '95, '94, '93. Best producers: Borie la Vitarèle, CANET-VALETTE, Cazal-Viel, Clos Bagatelle, Combebelle, M Fonsalade, des Jougla, la Madura, Mas Champart, Moulin de Ciffre, Moulinier, Navarre, Rimbert; the Berloup, Roquebrun and St-Chinian co-operatives.

ST-ÉMILION & POMEROL France, Bordeaux

THE RIGHT BANK OF THE DORDOGNE RIVER in Bordeaux is dominated by the Merlot grape, and the greatest right bank wines are those of St-Émilion and Pomerol. Indeed, the hilltop citadel of St-Émilion, huddled into clefts of rock above the vineyards and looking out over the valley, is the most ancient wine region in Bordeaux. Over 1800 years ago the Romans were planting the steep south-facing slopes just outside the town, and several leading properties, like Ch. la Gaffelière and Ch. Ausone (named after the Roman poet Ausonius to whom the vineyards once belonged), can trace their records as far back as the second century.

The finest St-Émilion vineyards with most of the famous names and all but two of the Premiers Grands Crus Classés lie on the steep sites round the town, on the *côtes* or 'slopes'. But there is also an enclave to the west of the town, towards Libourne, called the *graves* where two of St-Émilion's greatest estates – Ch. Cheval Blanc and Ch. Figeac – are situated. The *graves* refers to a gravel ridge, which is more suited to Cabernet Sauvignon than other parts of St-Émilion, on a plateau which is otherwise noted for its heavy clay soil.

The clay soil comes into its own in Pomerol, which begins right next to Cheval Blanc and continues westward to the outskirts of Libourne, and means that Merlot is the dominant grape here. There are no fancy buildings here, no signs of affluence and renown, just an almost monotonous stretch of vineyards, yet one of the world's most expensive red wines – Ch. Pétrus – is made in a tiny, inconspicuous building in the heart of Pomerol. Here, on the highest part of the Pomerol plateau, the soils are 90 per cent clay mixed with gravel, and the compact blue clay limits vigour in the vine, regulates water supply and dictates that almost 100 per cent Merlot is used. The resulting wine with an unctuous richness of fruit, exotic aromas and a firm but fine structure is echoed by numerous other modest-looking, mainly family-owned properties crammed into the tiny area. None is as great as Pétrus, not even the micro-property le Pin whose wines have

Below the beautiful town of St-Émilion, the Roman town at the centre of Bordeaux's most historic region, is a labyrinthine network of ancient cellars used by some of the châteaux for aging their wines.

from time to time outstripped Pétrus in price, but many Pomerols give more than just a suggestion of the power and succulence which make Pétrus so dazzling.

CH. CHEVAL BLANC
This is the leading St-Émilion estate and likely to remain so for the foreseeable future, fully justifying its ranking as an 'A' category Premier Grand Cru Classé.

CH. FIGEAC
This is one of the better Premiers Grands Crus Classés and like Cheval Blanc Figeac uses a high proportion of Cabernet in the blend.

CH. ANGÉLUS
Excellent wines in the 1980s, an energetic owner and talented winemaker brought well-deserved promotion for this estate to Premier Grand Cru Classé in 1996.

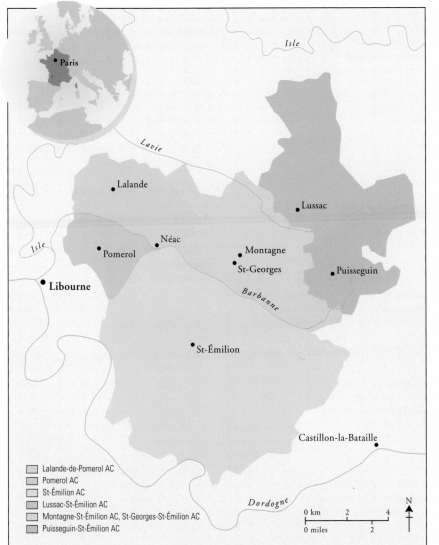

CH. DE VALANDRAUD
This tiny estate has only existed since 1991 yet the immensely rich and concentrated wine has already become one of the most expensive in Bordeaux.

LA MONDOTTE
Newly launched in 1996, this is a remarkable micro-cuvée from a vineyard belonging to Ch. Canon-la-Gaffelière.

CH. DE BARBE-BLANCHE
The Cuvée Henri IV is a good example of a lighter St-Émilion wine from one of its satellite appellations.

CH. GAZIN
Situated next door to the legendary Ch. Pétrus, Ch. Gazin is one of the most improved Pomerol properties of recent years. Traditionally succulent and sweet-textured, the wine is now showing real richness and a very individualistic character.

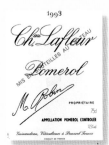

CH. LAFLEUR
Using some of Pomerol's most traditional winemaking techniques, this tiny estate makes wines that seriously rival those from Ch. Pétrus for sheer power, tannic structure and hedonistic richness and concentration.

CH. DES ANNEREAUX
This is one of the better estates from Pomerol's neighbour, Lalande-de-Pomerol and in top years, the wine is very Pomerol-like – plump and plummy with a certain opulence.

Both Pomerol and St-Émilion have 'satellite' appellations which employ hyphenated versions of the more famous names. Though they are never as good as the top wines, Lalande-de-Pomerol, in particular, produces many excellent lush, soft reds. North of St-Émilion a group of small appellations (Lussac, Puisseguin, St-Georges and Montagne) all produce sturdy but attractively fruity reds. It's difficult to gauge quite how exciting the vineyards could be because these appellations are dominated by co-operatives which, good though they are, don't push individuality to the limit.

AC ENTRIES
Lalande-de-Pomerol, St-Émilion, St-Émilion Grand Cru, St-Émilion Grand Cru Classé, St-Émilion Premier Grand Cru Classé, St-Émilion Satellites.

CHÂTEAUX ENTRIES
Angélus, l'Arrosée, Ausone, Balestard-la-Tonnelle, Beau-Séjour Bécot, Belair, le Bon Pasteur, Canon, Cheval Blanc, la Conseillante, l'Evangile, Figeac, Gazin, Lafleur, Latour-à-Pomerol, Magdelaine, Pavie, Petit-Village, Pétrus, le Pin, Trotanoy, Vieux-Château-Certan.

ST-ÉMILION AC, ST-ÉMILION GRAND CRU AC

FRANCE, Bordeaux (see also pages 326–327)
❦ *Merlot, Cabernet Franc, Cabernet Sauvignon, Malbec (Pressac), Carmenère*

If William the Conqueror had decided to take some BORDEAUX wines to England with him when he laid low poor old Harold at the Battle of Hastings in 1066, there's a good chance his triumphant tipple would have been St-Émilion, because the Brits have been drinking it very happily for over 800 years. And it became so popular so quickly because the one thing that marks the flavour of St-Émilion is a gorgeous softness, a buttery, toffeeish sweetness and a fruit whose flavour owes more to the dark, chewy richness of raisins in a fruit cake, than to the leaner, more demanding tastes of the wines of the GRAVES and MÉDOC.

The St-Émilion ACs are centred on the Roman town of St-Émilion on the right bank of the Dordogne, east of Bordeaux. The vines cover 5492ha (13,570 acres) in eight different communes, although the best vineyards lie within the boundaries of the St-Émilion commune itself. It is a region of smallholdings, with over 1000 different properties, the smallest being Ch. le Couvent actually in the town of St-Émilion. Consequently, the co-operative (the Union des Producteurs) is of great importance, and vinifies over 20 per cent of the entire St-Émilion crop to a consistently pretty high standard.

St-Émilion AC is the region's basic AC, accounting for roughly 37 per cent of the production, much of this handled by the co-operative. St-Émilion Grand Cru AC is St-Émilion's top quality AC. Geographically, it has the same delimitations as St-Émilion AC, but a lower yield and higher minimum degree of alcohol are demanded as well as a supplementary tasting examination before a wine will be granted the AC certificate. It includes St-Émilion's classified wines. Undoubtedly, with its more qualitative approach, the best wines fall into this AC, including the unclassified but highly priced micro-crus, like de VALANDRAUD and la MONDOTTE, that made an appearance in the 1990s. Best years: 2001, '00, '98, '96, '95, '90, '89, '88, '86, '85. Best producers: (Grand Cru AC – unclassified) Barde-Haut, Bellefont-Belcier, Destieux, Faugères, Fleur-Cardinale, Fombrauge, la Gomerie, Gracia, MONBOUSQUET, la Mondotte, Moulin St-Georges, Quinault l'Enclos, Rol Valentin, TERTRE-RÔTEBOEUF, Teyssier, de Valandraud.

CH. PAVIE-MACQUIN
Great strides were made at this estate in the late 1980s. The vineyard is run on biodynamic lines and the wine is now delicious and sumptuous.

ST-EMILION GRAND CRU CLASSÉ

FRANCE, Bordeaux, St-Émilion Grand Cru AC
❦ *Merlot, Cabernet Franc, Cabernet Sauvignon, Malbec (Pressac), Carmenère*

This is the first category of ST-ÉMILION's two-tier system of classification. The St-Émilionnais were late in devising an order of grading for their châteaux, introducing the first classification in 1955, exactly 100 years after the famous 1855 classification of the MÉDOC. Châteaux are nominated for two categories, St-Émilion Grand Cru Classé and St-Émilion Premier Grand Cru Classé. But there is an original aspect to the arrangement, which is that the classification is reviewed every ten years or so. Hence, there were new classifications in 1969, 1985 (following postponement) and most recently in 1996, when 55 châteaux were attributed with the title St-Émilion Grand Cru Classé. Obviously, with such a large number of properties, styles and quality levels of wine vary considerably but the best ones can age for 10–15 years. Best years: 2001, '00, '98, '96, '95, '90, '89, '88, '86, '85. Best producers: l'ARROSÉE, BALESTARD-LA-TONNELLE, CANON-LA-GAFFELIÈRE, Clos de l'Oratoire, la Clotte, la Dominique, Grand Mayne, Grand Pontet, Larmande, Pavie-Decesse, Pavie-Macquin, Soutard, la Tour Figeac, TROPLONG-MONDOT.

ST-ÉMILION PREMIER GRAND CRU CLASSÉ

FRANCE, Bordeaux, St-Émilion Grand Cru AC
❦ *Merlot, Cabernet Franc, Cabernet Sauvignon, Malbec (Pressac), Carmenère*

The elite category of the ST-ÉMILION classification, the Premiers Grands Crus Classés are further divided into two grades – 'A' and 'B' – with only the much more expensive CHEVAL BLANC and AUSONE in grade 'A'. There are 11 'B' châteaux, with ANGÉLUS and FIGEAC the outstanding names. Since the inauguration of the classification in 1955 Angélus is the only château to be added to the original list of 12, receiving promotion in 1996. BEAU-SÉJOUR

BÉCOT was demoted in 1985 and then re-elected again in 1996. Most of the wines drink superbly with 10–15 years' aging but much depends on the vintage and château. Ausone and Cheval Blanc occasionally last half a century or more. Best years: 2001, '00, '99, '98, '96, '95, '90, '89, '88, '86, '85. Best producers: Angélus, Ausone, Beau-Séjour Bécot, Beauséjour, BELAIR, CANON, Cheval Blanc, Clos Fourtet, FIGEAC, la Gaffelière, MAGDELAINE, PAVIE.

ST-ÉMILION SATELLITES

FRANCE, Bordeaux
❦ *Merlot, Cabernet Franc, Cabernet Sauvignon, Malbec*

There are four satellite ST-ÉMILION ACs, in descending size, Montagne-, Lussac-, Puisseguin- and St-Georges-St-Émilion, totalling 3971ha (9812 acres), lying a few miles north of the town of St-Émilion in gently hilly countryside. The wine can be tasty, if a little solid, and is normally drunk within four years of the vintage. Some of the best may keep up to ten years. The important co-operative at Puisseguin produces a large percentage of the wines of Lussac and Puisseguin. Best years: 2001, '00, '98, '96, '95. Best producers: (Lussac) de Barbe-Blanche, Bel-Air, Bellevue, du Courlat, de la Grenière, Lyonnat, Mayne Blanc, des Rochers, Vieux-Château-Chambeau; (Montagne) Calon, Corbin, Croix Beauséjour, Faizeau, des Laurets, Montaiguillon, Négrit, Roc de Calon, Rocher Corbin, Roudier, Vieux-Château-St-André; (Puisseguin) Bel-Air, Branda, Durand-Laplagne, Fongaban, Guibeau-la-Fourvieille, des Laurets, la Mauriane, Producteurs Réunis, Soleil; (St-Georges), Calon, Griffe de Cap d'Or, Macquin St-Georges, St-André-Corbin, Ch. St-Georges, Tour-du-Pas-St-Georges, Vieux-Montaiguillon.

ST-ESTÈPHE AC

FRANCE, Bordeaux, Haut-Médoc
❦ *Cabernet Sauvignon, Cabernet Franc, Merlot and others*

The wines of St-Estèphe are frequently accorded only grudging praise. Yet, in its old-fashioned, tweeds-and-plus-fours way, St-Estèphe is the most reliable and the least over-priced of the HAUT-MÉDOC's specific ACs. It is a large AC at 1250ha (3088 acres), but the most recently established of the great Haut-Médoc areas, partly because the gravel soil which gives all the finest wines in PAUILLAC, ST-JULIEN and MARGAUX is much less prevalent here – clay clogs your shoes as you wander these vineyards. It also has a cooler climate than the other main villages and the vines may ripen a week later than those in Margaux. This means that most of the properties have a fairly high proportion of the earlier-ripening Merlot, though Cabernet Sauvignon is still the leading grape. St-Estèphe has only five Classed Growths, due partly to the clay soils, and partly to the late development of the area – many vineyards were not fully established by 1855. Several non-classified properties consistently make fine wine of Classed Growth quality.

St-Estèphe wines are not the most likeable wines straight off. They have high tannin levels, and a definite earthy scratch in their texture. Give them time, however, and those sought-after flavours of blackcurrant and cedarwood do peek out – but rarely with the brazen beauty of a Pauillac or a St-Julien. There is some evidence of a softer style of winemaking, but although this is fine for the lesser properties, for the leading châteaux the end result is a bit half-hearted and St-Estèphe's best efforts are still in the brawny mould, demanding 10–20 years of aging. Best years: 2001, '00, '96, '95, '94, '90, '89, '88, '86, '85, '83, '82. Best producers: CALON-SÉGUR, COS D'ESTOURNEL, Cos Labory, HAUT-MARBUZET, LAFON-ROCHET, Lilian-Ladouys, Marbuzet, MEYNEY, MONTROSE, les Ormes-de-Pez, de PEZ, Phélan-Ségur.

ST FRANCIS WINERY
USA, California, Sonoma County, Sonoma Valley AVA
♥ *Cabernet Sauvignon, Merlot, Zinfandel and others*
♀ *Chardonnay*

In the 1980s St Francis quickly moved out of the shadow cast by its neighbour CHATEAU ST JEAN on the strength and individuality of its Merlot. Today it has evolved into a 300,000-case-a-year winery offering a modest range of high-quality wines. Aged in both American and French oak barrels, Merlot, so soft, supple and fruity, remains its calling card. The SONOMA VALLEY Reserve reds are ripe, supple yet more powerful and intense than most. After buying vineyards in the 1990s, the winery has dramatically improved its Cabernet Sauvignons, and the impressive Reserve is full of cassis fruit and deep, rich flavours. New vineyards are responsible for the wonderful, intense Old Vine Zinfandel, which is occasionally bested by the winery's special Pagani Ranch Zinfandel, a powerful, thick, velvety wine.

The Chardonnays should not be ignored, with the Reserve usually having plenty of depth and oak to rise far above the ordinary.

DOMAINE ST-GAYAN
FRANCE, Southern Rhône, Gigondas AC
♥ *Grenache, Syrah, Mourvèdre*
♀ *Viognier, Bourboulenc, Clairette, Grenache Blanc*

The Meffre family have inhabited this region since the fifteenth century, and St-Gayan remains very much a family business, with Jean-Pierre Meffre and his wife Martine representing the current generation. The high quality of the wines probably originates with the very old vines, up to a century old, which are planted on one-third of the estate's 37ha (91 acres). Yields are low, and the wines are aged initially in tanks and then large casks. St-Gayan is not a blockbuster GIGONDAS but an elegant, soft-textured wine that can be drunk fairly young. With age it shows intriguing leathery, earthy aromas. There is also a Gigondas Cuvée Fontmaria. Other wines include CHÂTEAUNEUF-DU-PAPE, CÔTES DU RHONE-VILLAGES-Rasteau and -Sablet, and CÔTES DU RHÔNE. Best years: (Gigondas) 2001, '00, '99, '98, '97, '96, '95, '93, '90.

ST HALLETT
AUSTRALIA, South Australia, Barossa Valley
♥ *Syrah (Shiraz), Cabernet Sauvignon, Grenache*
♀ *Chardonnay, Semillon, Riesling*

St Hallett made its reputation in much the same way as Peter LEHMANN. When the BAROSSA VALLEY wineries were all being taken over by multinationals whose accountants immediately said – these Barossa grapes are too expensive, let's use something cheaper – St Hallett, in the shape of larger-than-life boss Bob McLean stood up and said 'Barossa grapes may be expensive, but they're exceptional: we'll use nothing else.' In 1988 when McLean took over, this act of faith in Barossa was of massive significance. Nowadays, everyone appreciates how good Barossa fruit is and they fall over themselves to pay top dollar for it. But then, McLean and Lehmann were offering a lifeline to grapegrowing families

ST HALLETT
One of the Barossa Valley's best red wines is Old Block Shiraz from St Hallett. Full of ripe tannins, the wine is made from very old vines.

who'd been in the valley since the 1850s. St Hallett makes a whole raft of reds and whites – good Semillon and excellent EDEN VALLEY Riesling lead the whites – but it is the reds that are St Hallett's best – especially its rich, proud, dense Shirazes: Faith, Blackwell, and, above all, one of Australia's most famous – Old Block – made from vines that are never younger than 60 years old and have often passed the century mark. Now owned by Lion Nathan brewers (as is PETALUMA), so keep your fingers crossed. Best years: (Old Block) 2001, '99, '98, '96, '94, '93, '91.

ST HELENA AVA
USA, California, Napa County

Napa City may be the biggest town in the NAPA VALLEY, but there's no doubt that St Helena, up towards the head of the valley, is the spiritual heart of the wine community. It's a very attractive, somewhat touristy town with many of the valley's best restaurants and shops. However, it doesn't have the best vineyards: these are mostly further south in OAKVILLE, RUTHERFORD and STAGS LEAP, or on the mountainsides to the north-west and south-east of the valley.

One reason is that the valley floor narrows at St Helena before turning westwards to Calistoga, but the bonus is that the St Helena AVA covers the mountain slopes up to 152m (500ft), and there are a number of good sites both on the hills and on the foot of the slopes, including such cult wines as SPOTTSWOOD and Grace Family. It's getting fairly warm up at St Helena, so nearly all the best wines are red. Several major wineries are based here, including SUTTER HOME, BERINGER and Louis M Martini.

ST-JOSEPH AC
FRANCE, Northern Rhône
♥ *Syrah*
♀ *Marsanne, Roussanne*

If ever the Syrah grape wished to show the smiling side of its nature in the northern RHÔNE, it would have to be at St-Joseph. Most of the wines are an absolute riot of rich, mouthfilling fruit with an irresistible blackcurrant richness. The AC used to be limited to the granite slopes of half-a-dozen right-bank villages centred on Mauves, just south of HERMITAGE, and all the best wine still comes from there. But, inexplicably, it was extended in 1969 to take in another 20 communes on flat land north of Tournon and Tain l'Hermitage. This wine isn't anything like as good, although it's still a nice drink. Latest news is that they're thinking of tightening things up again. Brilliant at only one to two years old, the wine can age for up to ten if the vines are from the area around Mauves, but you'll gradually lose that wonderful fruit, so drink it before five years old. Best years: (reds) 2001, '00, '99, '98, '97, '96, '95, '94. Best producers: CHAPOUTIER, J-L CHAVE, du Chêne, L Chèze, J-L COLOMBO, Courbis, Coursodon, CUILLERON, DELAS, E & J Durand, Florentin, P Gaillard, Gonon, GRAILLOT, B Gripa, GUIGAL, JABOULET, du Monteillet, Paret, A Perret, P Pichon, St-Désirat co-operative, Tain l'Hermitage co-operative, Tardieu-Laurent, du Tunnel, F Villard.

At their best, the St-Joseph whites have an astonishing flavour halfway between the peach and apricot headiness of a CONDRIEU and the buttery richness of a good MEURSAULT. The old-style wines are made from low-yielding vines around Tournon and Mauves, matured in old oak and capable of lasting 20 years. When well made, they are rich, heavy, scented with sandalwood, woodsmoke and peaches, and tasting of toast and brazil nuts draped in butter caramel. Best years: (whites) 2001, '00, '99, '98, '97, '96, '95. Best producers: du Chêne, L Chèze, Courbis, Cuilleron, Delas, E & J Durand, Ferraton, P Finon, Florentin, P Gaillard, B Gripa, Guigal, Jaboulet, du Monteillet, A Perret, Trollat, F Villard.

ST-JULIEN AC
FRANCE, Bordeaux, Haut-Médoc
🍷 *Cabernet Sauvignon, Cabernet Franc, Merlot and others*

If someone said to me, 'show me the perfect red Bordeaux, the quintessence of restrained cedarwood perfume and lean but mouthwatering blackcurrant fruit' – St-Julien is where I would look. Of all the HAUT-MÉDOC ACs St-Julien has the perfect balance between substance and delicacy, between opulence and austerity, between the necessary brashness of youth and the lean-limbed genius of maturity. Although the great PAUILLACs are the models

for winemakers across the world, if it were the perfect BORDEAUX they sought to emulate, St-Julien should be their target.

There's not very much of it: at 900ha (2248 acres) it is the smallest of the four main Haut-Médoc communal appellations, but almost all of it is vineyard land of the highest class, on gravelly outcrops near the Gironde estuary, and 85 per cent of the land is taken up by 11 Classed Growths. The Second Growths, Ch. LÉOVILLE-LAS-CASES, DUCRU-BEAUCAILLOU and LÉOVILLE-BARTON are the leaders, and not far behind are BRANAIRE, GRUAUD-LAROSE, LAGRANGE, LANGOA-BARTON, LÉOVILLE-POYFERRÉ and ST-PIERRE. Also making excellent wine are BEYCHEVELLE, Gloria and TALBOT. Best years: 2001, '00, '99, '98, '97, '96, '95, '94, '90, '89, '88, '86, '85, '83, '82.

ST-NICOLAS-DE-BOURGUEIL AC
FRANCE, Loire, Touraine
🍷🍷 *Cabernet Franc, Cabernet Sauvignon*

This enclave inside the BOURGUEIL area covers 1000ha (2470 acres) of vines, as opposed to 1350ha (3336 acres) for Bourgueil. As with Bourgueil, Cabernet Franc is usually the sole grape, sometimes with a little Cabernet Sauvignon. St-Nicolas has a higher proportion of gravel soils than Bourgueil, otherwise there is little to distinguish between them. It probably owes its existence to a forceful mayor of the village in the 1930s, who insisted that his village deserved an AC of its own.

Almost all the wine is red and the best has the piercing raspberry and blackcurrant flavours of nearby Bourgueil and CHINON. But they are prone to be a little tannic and have an earthy background which is pleasant enough if the fruit is there. Drinkable at two to three years, they will last seven to ten years from warm vintages. Best years: 2002, '01, '00, '97, '96, '95, '90, '89. Best producers: Y Amirault, M Cognard, P Jamet, F Mabileau, J-C Mabileau, Taluau-Foltzenlogel, Vallée.

ST-PÉRAY AC
FRANCE, Northern Rhône
🍷 *Marsanne, Roussanne*

A century ago St-Péray was the producer of France's most famous fizz – after CHAMPAGNE, of course. Sparkling wine is supposed to be lively, vivacious, witty stuff – but this is the hot RHÔNE Valley, and it seems extremely unlikely that the remaining 59ha (146 acres) of vineyards can produce the light, acid wine favoured by fizz-makers. Well, they can't. The Marsanne and Roussanne grapes make big

round wines which undergo the Champagne method and turn out as – big round wines with fizz in them. Most of it goes no further than the local bars and restaurants. There is a little still white, usually dry and stolid, but occasionally more exciting. The wine can have a lovely golden feel of nuts and honey and fruit brushed with the spice of apricots and quince, with a flicker of orange peel at the end. This is Marsanne at its best, but it's rare. Best years: 2001, '00, '99, '98, '97, '96, '95. Best producers: S Chaboud, CLAPE, J-L COLOMBO (la Belle de Mai), DELAS, de Fauterie, B Gripa, J Lemencier, Lionnet, J-L Thiers, A Voge.

CH. ST-PIERRE
FRANCE, Bordeaux, Haut-Médoc, St-Julien AC
🍷 *Cabernet Sauvignon, Merlot, Cabernet Franc*

After a century of anonymity, Ch. St-Pierre (previously St-Pierre-Sevaistre) has stepped forward to claim its place in the sun. It used to be undervalued, and in years like 1979, '81, '82 and '86 you got superb quality at half the price of the better-known ST-JULIENs. It isn't a big property, only 17ha (42 acres), but the vines, close to BEYCHEVELLE, are well sited and old. The wine often lacks the startling beauty of the best St-Julien, but makes up for this with a lush feel and full, almost honeyed flavour – plums and blackberries and soft vanilla backed up by unassertive but effective tannins. It is often ready quite young. Top vintages can easily improve for 20 years. Best years: 2001, '00, '99, '98, '97, '96, '95, '94, '90, '89, '88, '86, '83, '82.

ST-ROMAIN AC
FRANCE, Burgundy, Côte de Beaune
🍷 *Pinot Noir*
🍷 *Chardonnay*

St-Romain is better known for barrels than wine, since François Frères, barrel-makers to the Domaine de la ROMANÉE-CONTI and other top estates, are based here. Actually there isn't much room for vines, since St-Romain is at the rocky head of a little side valley running up through AUXEY-DURESSES, and the difficult growing conditions mean there are more trees than vines. Part of the problem is altitude: up here the grapes ripen fully only in the warmest years. Only 135ha (333 acres) of vines are cultivated, and the poor geology results in its being the only AC in the Côte de Beaune without any Premiers Crus. In fact, but for a certain historical reputation for quality, St-Romain would have had to be happy with the lowly BOURGOGNE-HAUTES-CÔTES DE BEAUNE AC.

CH. TALBOT
A superb Fourth Growth St-Julien, Ch. Talbot has a reputation for consistency. The wine is chunky, soft-centred but capable of aging extremely well for 10–20 years.

The reds often have a slightly unnerving earthiness which can verge on the resinous, but they also have a firm, bitter-sweet cherrystone fruit and can age very well for five to seven years. Best years: (reds) 2002, '00, '99, '98, '97, '96. Best producer: (reds) A Gras.

The white tastes more like a CHABLIS than a Meursault, although Meursault is only a few miles away. The wine is flinty dry, hinting at ripeness but held back by a rather herby, stony personality which can be quite refreshing. It should age well for a good five years or more. Best years: (whites) 2002, '00, '99, '97. Best producers: Bazenet, H & G Buisson, Chassorney, A Gras, Jaffelin/BOISSET, Olivier LEFLAIVE, P Taupenot, Verget.

ST-VÉRAN AC

FRANCE, Burgundy, Mâconnais
♀ *Chardonnay*

Until 1971 the Mâconnais had one star white AC – POUILLY-FUISSÉ – and then merely a welter of MÂCON-VILLAGES; in the south, there was also a certain amount of BEAUJOLAIS Blanc shared with the Beaujolais communes of Leynes and St-Vérand (yes, there is a 'd'). It was clear, however, that these two villages – and five others tightly grouped round the Pouilly-Fuissé AC – were far better than the general run, more closely resembling the classier examples of Pouilly-Fuissé than the normally anonymous glut of Mâcon-Villages. So in 1971 they were given their own AC – St-Véran covering 590ha (1458 acres) – and it immediately came to be thought of as a Pouilly-Fuissé understudy. That's fair in price terms – St-Véran is always cheaper – but a real stylistic difference has emerged.

Oak is very rarely used, revealing the gentle Mâconnais Chardonnay at its clearest and best – very fresh but with a richness combining bananas, apples, pineapples, peaches and even musky grapes, softened with a yeasty creaminess. The wines don't gain a great deal from aging more than a year. Best producers: D & M Barraud, G Chagny, Corsin, Deux Roches, B & J-M Drouin (Dom. des Gerbeaux), DUBOEUF, Ch. FUISSÉ, G Guérin, Lassarat, Merlin, Saumaize-Michelin, J C Thévenet, J-L Tissier, Verget.

STE-CROIX-DU-MONT AC

FRANCE, Bordeaux
♀ *Sémillon, Sauvignon Blanc, Muscadelle*

Historically, this is the best of the three sweet wine ACs (LOUPIAC and CADILLAC are the others) that gaze jealously across at SAUTERNES and BARSAC from the other –

The Taurino estate is one of the leading producers in Salice Salentino, Puglia. Here Francesco Taurino is tying up Chardonnay vines.

wrong – side of the Garonne river. The views are magnificent as the vines tumble down what look to be perfectly sited, south-west-facing slopes.

But to make great sweet wine, sunshine and a great view aren't enough; you must have the clammy, humid autumn days that encourage the noble rot fungus to shrivel your grapes and concentrate their sugar. The little river Ciron running through Sauternes creates these conditions, but the wide Garonne is far less likely to waft morning mists towards Ste-Croix-du-Mont. Even so, the vines do occasionally produce splendidly rich wines, but more often the wine is mildly sweet – very good as an aperitif but not really luscious enough for dessert. Best years: 2001, '99, '98, '97, '96, '95, '90, '89, '88. Best producers: Crabitan-Bellevue, Loubens, Lousteau-Vieil, Mailles, du Mont, du Pavillon, la Rame.

SAINTSBURY

USA, California, Napa County, Napa Valley AVA
♦ ♀ *Pinot Noir*
♀ *Chardonnay*

CARNEROS fruit was already well-known when Richard Ward and David Graves founded Saintsbury in 1981, but virtually all the decent wine was being made by wineries away from the district. Carneros needed a focal point – and Saintsbury provided it. Determined to produce stellar Chardonnay and Pinot Noir from the start, they have never wavered. Using

a mixture of bought-in fruit and, more recently, estate fruit, they produce two excellent Chardonnays and three Pinots – Garnet, Carneros and Reserve in ascending order of perfume, richness and complexity which have, if anything, got better while production has expanded. There's also a seriously expensive Brown Ranch bottling to round off an impressive selection. This wine is released on 23rd October each year in celebration of the birthday of noted wine connoisseur and author George Saintsbury, after whom the winery is named. Best years: (Pinot Noir Reserve) 2001, '00, '99, '98, '97, '96, '95, '94, '91.

DUCA DI SALAPARUTA/CORVO

ITALY, Sicily, Vino da Tavola
♦ *Nero d'Avola, Nerello Mascalese, Perricone*
♀ *Inzolia, Trebbiano, Catarratto*

Corvo is the trading name of the Casa Vinicola Duca di Salaparuta, whose giant-size, state-of-the-art winery near SICILY's northern coast transforms grapes culled from every corner of the island. The standard red and white have for decades constituted a reliable if unexciting choice on the wine lists of more second-rate Italian restaurants around the world than one could possibly imagine. The winery has decided, though, to nail its banners to the mast with four other higher quality wines. White Colomba Platino has a high proportion of aromatic Inzolia, making it markedly more fragrant than the ordinary white. The reds, Duca Enrico and Terre d'Agala, are based on Nero d'Avola. Aged in barriques, these two serious reds need four to five years to soften their tannins. A similarly oaked Inzolia white, Bianca di Valguarnera, completes a fine foursome.

SALICE SALENTINO DOC

ITALY, Puglia
♦ ♦ *Negroamaro, Malvasia Nera, Aleatico*
♀ *Chardonnay, Pinot Blanc (Pinot Bianco), Sauvignon Blanc and others*

The best known wine of that southern tip of PUGLIA, the Salentino peninsula, is the deep-coloured, richly fruity red from the commune of Salice Salentino. It is made principally from the Negroamaro variety which, centuries ago, made the crossing from Greece, where it still thrives as Xynomavro, tempered with a dash of the perfumed Malvasia Nera. Generally the 'black bitterness' of its name is attenuated by a dose of soft, aromatic Malvasia Nera and the wine needs several years to settle down before it comes good. Several other local DOCs (Alezio, Brindisi,

Copertino, Leverano, Lizzano, Nardò and Squinzano) are similar in style, some of them including Montepulciano in the blend.

The Salice Salentino DOC extends to an excellent rosé, from the same grapes, and to a rare but potentially lip-smacking aromatic sweet red from the Aleatico grape. The whites are distinctly less interesting. Best years: (reds) 2001, '00, '98, '97, '96. Best producers: Candido, Casale Bevagna, Due Palme, Leone De Castris, TAURINO, Vallone, Conti Zecca. Some of the best wines fall outside the DOC: Cappello di Prete and Duca d'Aragona (Candido), Notarpanaro and Patriglione (Taurino) and Graticciaia (Vallone).

SALON

FRANCE, Champagne, Champagne AC
♀ *Chardonnay*

Salon is truly unique: a CHAMPAGNE produced from a single grape variety from a single village, Mesnil, and from a single vintage, whereas most Champagne is the result of blending the three grape varieties and blending between wines from different villages of the region, often up to a dozen. Moreover Salon is made in a most uncompromising way, aging for many years on its lees before disgorgement and release.

In some years no wine is produced at all, and the grapes, which come from very old vines, are offered to the neighbouring house of Delamotte which, like Salon, is part of the LAURENT-PERRIER group. The style is monumental, austere, powerful and penetrating. This is indeed one of the few Champagnes that can truly be enjoyed with any number of dishes during a meal. Moreover, it has such richness and breadth that it is possible to consume Salon in a non-dosé (unsweetened) version, as is sometimes done at the winery when unreleased vintages are pulled from the cellar and disgorged. Production is minimal – about 80,000 bottles in any declared vintage – and prices very high, but you do get a lot of flavour for your money. Best years: 1995, '90, '88, '85, '83, '82, '79, '76, '73, '71, '69, '66, '64, '61.

SALON
Few Champagnes can match Salon for depth and power. The fine fruit richness becomes increasingly apparent with age.

SALTA

ARGENTINA

The Cafayate Valley in the province of Salta is Argentina's most northerly and remote wine area. Set in the most beautiful, crisp and clean mountain countryside imaginable, with vineyards being planted at over 2000m (6562ft), although most of the wines are sited at about 1700m (5577ft), it is a natural home for the scented, delicate Torrontes. Malbec from here is sensuous, supple and fragrant and has a fantastic, vibrant purple colour because of the intense sunshine – Cafayate gets 350 days of sun a year – matched by ice-cold Andean night times – daytime temperatures can be as high as 38°C (100°F) but they usually drop back to 12°–15°C (53°–59°F) at night. Enormous investments are being made in new vineyards, to complement what Pernod Ricard has already committed at Bodegas ETCHART. Salta, though still in rather a rudimentary state, could become a crucial part of the Andean wine scene, offering scent and sensuality rather than power. There are three main producers: Etchart, Michel Torino and an independent member of the Etchart family, but more plantings are under way as communications improve, new roads are built, and an airport is opened.

SAN FRANCISCO BAY AVA

USA, California, San Francisco, San Mateo, Santa Clara, Alameda, Contra Costa, Santa Cruz, San Benito counties

San Francisco has had a reputation for being one of the USA's great centres of good food and good wine since the Gold Rush days – well, not necessarily *good* food and wine in the 1840s and '50s – herculean eating and drinking, more like. But it has rarely been paid much heed for the wines made in its immediate locality: nearly all the action has been north in SONOMA and NAPA counties and beyond, or south, from SANTA CRUZ right down the coast to SANTA BARBARA, the reason being, quite simply, these wines were better.

Since 1999, however, there has been a San Francisco Bay AVA – largely at the behest of important producers in little-known Livermore Valley, across the Bay, who felt, quite rightly, that the chance to put world-famous San Francisco on their labels would make it a lot easier to sell their wine abroad. The AVA covers the first five counties listed above (to the east, south and west of the Bay) plus parts of Santa Cruz and San Benito. You could argue that all share a certain maritime influence. Or you could argue that doesn't San Francisco Bay AVA look nice on the label.

J LOHR
Hilltop Cabernet is an excellent example of a medium-bodied, approachable Cabernet Sauvignon from Paso Robles where it is one of the most important varieties.

SAN LUIS OBISPO COUNTY

USA, California

Historic PASO ROBLES is by far the most important AVA in San Luis Obispo. With its hot, dry climate it has long been Zinfandel country and the once heady, rustic style has been toned down a little as more wineries establish themselves. There is also good Cabernet and Syrah. West of Paso Robles, York Mountain is a small, cool AVA near the ocean. Further south, both EDNA VALLEY (fine Chardonnay and Pinot Noir) and Arroyo Grande (excellent Chardonnay, Pinot Noir and Zinfandel) are influenced by maritime cool. Vineyard acreage in San Luis Obispo has increased by 72 per cent in the last decade, one of the most dramatic increases in the USA. Best years: (reds) 2001, '00, '99, '98, '97, '95, '94. Best producers: Claiborne & Churchill, Creston, Eberle, Edna Valley, Justin, J Lohr, MERIDIAN VINEYARD, Norman, Saucelito Canyon, Savannah-Chanelle, Seven Peaks, Talley, Wild Horse.

SAN PEDRO, SANTA HELENA

CHILE, Lontué Valley
(San Pedro) ♥ *Cabernet Sauvignon, Merlot, Carmenere, Syrah (Shiraz), Pinot Noir*
♥ *Cabernet Sauvignon*
♀ *Sauvignon Blanc, Chardonnay, Semillon, Riesling, Viognier*

San Pedro is one of the oldest and largest Chilean wineries and produced little of note before Jacques Lurton arrived as consultant in 1994. He dramatically improved things during his tenure, in particular bringing a leafy blackcurrant freshness to the reds and a tangy acidity to the Sauvignon Blanc. Quality is now good and improving. Labels to look for are 35 South, Castillo de Molina Reserve, and 1865. New top of the range Viña Totihue is a joint venture with ST-ÉMILION's Ch. Dassault.

The Santa Helena winery is under the same ownership but hasn't shone recently. However a major management and winemaking shakeup in 2002 should revitalize the label.

SANCERRE AC

FRANCE, Central Loire

🍷 🍷 *Pinot Noir*
♀ *Sauvignon Blanc*

The omni-thirsty Henry IV of France is on record as saying that if all his subjects were to drink Sancerre there'd be no more religious wars. Louis XVI said much the same thing a short while before the French Revolution proved otherwise. And then, in the 1970s, some Paris journalists (always on the lookout for a new fad wine) noticed the high mound of Sancerre rising above the Loire, tasted the wines from its steep chalk and flint vineyards, and tore back to Paris with the news – Sancerre was the super-freshest, ultra-modernest white wine in France. Sancerre-mania broke out – first with the white, which can indeed be a wonderful, refreshing drink, tasting of nettles, asparagus and gooseberries, and a whiff of brewing coffee, and then with the rather less exciting reds and rosés. This is excellent news for the growers, but Sancerre is consequently rarely a bargain.

But even so, a Sancerre from a village like Bué, Chavignol, Verdigny or Ménétréol, made by a good grower in a coolish vintage, and drunk before it is two years old, can be one of the most deliciously refreshing French whites. The top wines can last for five years or so. The wines are now more consistent than those of neighbouring POUILLY.

Pre-phylloxera Sancerre was largely a red wine area. In modern times the emphasis has been on Sauvignon, with Pinot Noir often relegated to the least good sites. Now it accounts for just 14 per cent of annual production (and the rosé just over 5 per cent). There is increased emphasis on the reds and, although quality is still very variable, there are some concentrated, serious wines being made that benefit from three or four years' aging, as well as light, charming quaffers. The rosé is usually very dry, sometimes with a hint of fruit. Best years: 2002, '00, '99, '98, '97, '96, '95, '90. Best producers: F & J Bailly, Balland-Chapuis, H BOURGEOIS, H Brochard, R Champault, F Cotat, L Crochet, Delaporte, Gitton, P Jolivet, Serge Laloue, A MELLOT, J Mellot, P Millérioux, H Natter, A & F Neveu, R Neveu, V Pinard, H Reverdy, J Reverdy, Reverdy-Ducroux, J-M Roger, Vacheron, André Vatan.

LUCIANO SANDRONE

ITALY, Piedmont, Barolo DOCG

🍷 *Nebbiolo, Barbera, Dolcetto*

Sandrone learned the art of making great BAROLO as winemaker at Marchesi di Barolo.

He began producing wine from his own grapes in the late 1970s, and increasing fame induced him in the late 1990s to set up on his own. Today, his cru Cannubi Boschis and blend Le Vigne, wines at their best miraculously combining power and concentration with elegance, are almost impossible to obtain even at high prices. Generally associated with the Barolo modernists, Sandrone uses French oak *tonneaux* for aging his Barolo and barriques for his BARBERA D'ALBA. The unoaked Dolcetto is another impressive mouthful of sheer fruit.

SANFORD WINERY

USA, California, Santa Barbara County, Santa Ynez Valley AVA

🍷 *Pinot Noir*
♀ *Chardonnay, Sauvignon Blanc*

If the Santa Ynez Valley, a cool, foggy little gap in the Coastal Range, has found fame as one of the USA's greatest sites for Pinot Noir – it is substantially due to Richard Sanford, who, along with Michael Benedict, spent the five years from 1971 to 1976 planting vines on a 45-ha (112-acre) north-facing slope that became known as Sanford and Benedict vineyard and which quickly proved to be a source of stunning Pinot Noir. However, most of the best wines from this vineyard were made by other wineries until 1990 when Sanford took over the management of the site and has since used its fruit for top Pinot Noirs and Chardonnays. He generally releases three versions of Pinot Noir, the rich, ripe La Rinconada being the top wine, as well as two Chardonnays, a classically restrained Estate bottling from three different vineyards and a richer, creamier Barrel Select. He also produces a pretty wild, barrel-fermented Sauvignon Blanc. Best years: (Pinot Noir) 2001, '00, '99, '98, '97, '96, '95, '94.

SANFORD
Sanford makes deep, lush, velvety smooth Pinot Noir from Santa Ynez Valley fruit and these wines can be some of the best Pinot Noirs outside Burgundy.

SANGIOVESE

Almost certainly of Tuscan origin, Italy's most-planted grape variety (100,000ha/ 247,100 acres) is by far the most important one in central Italy. Indeed, it is planted in at least 16 of Italy's 20 regions, not to mention in several other countries, notably California and Argentina. Along with Barbera, Sangiovese is indisputedly the nearest Italy gets to an 'international' grape variety.

Sub-varieties and clones abound, even within small areas, sometimes graced with exotic or parochial names like San Zoveto (the first recorded name, in the year 1600), Sangioveto (central Tuscany and Elba), Brunello (Montalcino, though for fear of Californian rip-offs the name no longer applies to a grape but only to a wine), Prugnolo Gentile (Montepulciano) and Romagnolo (Romagna), all of which have greater marketing than ampelographical significance. The fundamental distinction is between Sangiovese Grosso and Sangiovese Piccolo, the adjectives mainly referring to berry size, but the reality is that over a period of time within a given area it becomes difficult, if not impossible, to distinguish between them. Perhaps the main point to remember is that Sangiovese is a highly adaptable variety, capable of changing radically, even morphologically in terms of leaf shape, bunch character and berry size, according to its immediate environment – much more so than Merlot or Cabernet Sauvignon varieties.

In California, Sangiovese was a late arrival, despite the number of immigrant Italian wine families. Winemakers are trying out various styles of wine, from simple and tart to super-Tuscan versions blended with Cabernet Sauvignon and aged in small oak barrels but it has proven to be very difficult to find the right soils and climate for it. Australia has only recently become interested in Sangiovese, but early signs are good.

Argentina's Sangiovese was brought to the country by waves of Italian immigrants and it ripens fully here to produce an attractive fruity wine.

SANTA BARBARA COUNTY

USA, California

This coastal county north-west of Los Angeles is where many politicians and Hollywood stars retire, usually to large ranches. It is also where some of CALIFORNIA's most distinctive Pinot Noir and Chardonnay grapes now grow.

Vineyard development did not begin in earnest until the late 1960s, and today there are 4450ha (11,000 acres) of vineyards centred on SANTA MARIA VALLEY in the north and Santa Ynez Valley in the south with the promising enclave of Los Alamos sandwiched in between. Both valleys are dramatically affected by the offshore fogs and ocean breezes, and it is too cold to ripen grapes at the mouth of either valley. But for every mile you travel inland the temperature rises, making it firstly suitable for Pinot Noir, then Chardonnay, Sauvignon, Syrah, Merlot and even Cabernet. And somewhere among all this are wedged some delightful Rieslings and Gewurztraminers. Santa Ynez Valley has more small vineyards and lifestyle properties whereas the drabber landscape of Santa Maria means its vines are largely shared between three big farms, with Bien Nacido the most famous, especially for the pioneering of RHÔNE varieties, Syrah and Viognier. Best years: (Pinot Noir) 2001, '00, '99, '98, '97, '95, '94. Best producers: AU BON CLIMAT, BABCOCK, Beckmen, BYRON, CAMBRIA, Foxen, Hitching Post, Longoria, Andrew MURRAY, Fess Parker, QUPÉ, SANFORD, Whitcraft, Zaca Mesa.

SANTA CAROLINA

CHILE, Maipo Valley

♥ Cabernet Sauvignon, Merlot, Syrah, Carmenere, Pinot Noir

♀ Sauvignon Blanc, Chardonnay

Santa Carolina celebrated its determination to enter the modern wine world in 1994 in the most dramatic fashion possible. It took out all the ancient wooden vats that had been storing wine for generations and burnt them in a vast bonfire. This was long overdue and the stainless steel tanks and new oak barrels that now pack the winery have allowed for a dramatic change of direction towards freshness, fruit and balance, often enhanced by new oak aromas. They use grapes from MAIPO and San Fernando but have been extremely influential in developing the CASABLANCA Valley. Indeed VIÑA CASABLANCA is a sister winery. Tangy Sauvignons and mellow Chardonnays are partnered by serious single-vineyard Merlots and Cabernets.

SANTA CRUZ MOUNTAINS AVA

USA, California, San Mateo, Santa Clara and Santa Cruz counties

A sub-region of the CENTRAL COAST AVA, most of which is wild, lonely forest highlands between the San Andreas Fault and the ocean. There are only 283ha (700 acres) of vines, and long-lived Chardonnays and Cabernet Sauvignons are the most notable wines; the most famous is the stunning Monte Bello Cabernet from RIDGE, who also grow excellent Merlot and Chardonnay. Small amounts of impressively robust Pinot Noir are also produced here by David Bruce and Mount Eden. Best producers: BONNY DOON, David Bruce, Clos La Chance, Kathryn Kennedy, Mount Eden Vineyards, Ridge, Santa Cruz Mountain Vineyard.

SANTA MARIA VALLEY AVA

USA, California, Santa Barbara and San Luis Obispo counties

You certainly don't visit Santa Maria for the lifestyle. The city of Santa Maria gets blanketed by impenetrable fog for 87 days a year, most of these in the summer and autumn, when you might want to be working on your tan. But those fogs and the brisk Pacific winds that blow when the fog has cleared are the key to why Santa Maria is an excellent area for vines. It's too cold and damp down by the sea, but 10–15km (6–9 miles) inland as the fogs get burnt off by the sun and the breezes soften sufficiently so that they merely cool the vines rather than rip them from their roots, you get a magic combination of consistently sunny days (post fog) but reliably cool temperatures because of the maritime breezes. The result is excellent Chardonnay and Pinot Noir as well as remarkably good Syrah and Viognier on the large and impressive Bien Nacido Ranch. Best producers: AU BON CLIMAT, BYRON, CAMBRIA, Foxen, Lane Tanner (Pinot Noir), Longoria, QUPÉ.

SANTA RITA

CHILE, Maipo Valley

♥ Cabernet Sauvignon, Merlot, Carmenere

♀ Sauvignon Blanc, Chardonnay

When Chile returned to democratic rule at the end of the 1980s, Santa Rita was the first winery to make an immediate impression on the export markets with its succulent juicy reds masterminded by Chile's first modern winemaking maestro Ignacio Recabarren. Despite flirting with a leaner more BORDEAUX style once or twice since, Santa Rita has such good vineyard sources primarily in MAIPO for

reds, but also in MAULE, RAPEL and, important for whites, CASABLANCA, that it always returns to a style humming with the rich ripe quality of its grapes. Whites are greatly improved, and there's a dark, juicy Casablanca Pinot Noir, but the true joys are the Cabernets and Merlots, both alone, and blended with Carmenere or Syrah, that appear under such labels as Triple C and Floresta. Casa Real is the most famous Santa Rita wine. If it were less self-consciously European in style it might also be the best Santa Rita.

SANTENAY AC

FRANCE, Burgundy, Côte de Beaune

♥ Pinot Noir

♀ Chardonnay

You can almost taste the CÔTE DE BEAUNE winding down in the red wines of Santenay, yet the large village is an important one, and there are good wines. The vineyards to the north-east, well-angled to the morning sun, give the best wines – rarely heavy and sometimes a little stony and dry, but reasonably fruity and reasonably priced. Occasionally a full, rather savoury style appears from a Premier Cru vineyard like les Gravières, on the border with CHASSAGNE-MONTRACHET. It is worth aging Santenay for at least four to six years. Most Santenay white is drunk locally, since the village has a casino and a spa to boost demand. Best years: (reds) 2002, '01, '99, '98, '97, '96. Best producers: R Belland, D & F Clair, M Colin, J Girardin, V GIRARDIN, Monnot, B Morey, L Muzard, Prieur-Brunet, Roux Père et Fils.

SANTORINI AO

GREECE

This small, volcanic Aegean island produces high-quality piercingly dry whites, both oaked and unoaked, mainly from the highly individual and very acidic Assyrtiko grape. Additionally there is vinsanto, a fascinating sweet wine of great antiquity, originally the Greek Orthodox Church communion wine, made from sun-dried grapes. Best producers: Argyros, Boutari, Gaia/Thalassitis, Sigalas.

CASA SANTOS LIMA

PORTUGAL, Estremadura, Alenquer DOC

♥ Tinta Miúda, Preto Martinho, Castelão, Camarate, Trincadeira, Alicante Bouschet, Merlot, Cabernet Sauvignon, Syrah, Alfrocheiro, Tempranillo (Tinta Roriz), Touriga Franca, Touriga Nacional, Pinot Noir

♀ Moscatel, Arinto, Fernão Pires, Chardonnay

A beautiful estate north of Lisbon producing an expanding range of wines from a host of varieties, both native and international. Espiga reds and whites are light, fruity and tasty, but for more character look to the spicy red and creamy, perfumed white Palha-Canas, or to red and white Quinta das Setencostas. New reds sold under the Casa Santos Lima label include Touriz (from DOURO varieties) and varietal Touriga Nacional, Touriga Franca, Trincadeira and Tinta Roriz. There is also a promising peachy, herby Chardonnay.

CAVES SÃO JOÃO
PORTUGAL, Beira Litoral, Bairrada DOC, Dão DOC
🍷 *Bairrada: Baga, Castelão (Periquita), Moreto; Dão: Touriga Nacional, Jaen, Bastardo*
🍷 *Bairrada: Fernão Pires (Maria Gomes), Bical; Dão: Arinto, Dona Branca, Barcelo, Encruzado*

Wines from this resolutely traditional family firm have long been among the best in both BAIRRADA and DÃO. The Frei João Bairrada and Porta dos Cavaleiros Dão reds are both rich and complex, the Reservas (with cork labels) particularly so, and develop impressively with age. Even the white wines have real character and age well in bottle. Much of the wine is bought in from local growers and co-operatives and aged in neat, cobwebby cellars in the heart of the Bairrada region at São João de Anadia. Selection is paramount. It is perhaps paradoxical for such a traditional firm that São João's latest venture has been to plant Cabernet Sauvignon on the family's own estate at Quinta do Poço do Lobo.

SARDEGNA (SARDINIA)
ITALY

Traditional Sardinian wines are big, fat and strong: some dry, and a fair number sweet and sticky. But there are also plenty of light, fresh wines, red, white and rosé, from all over the island, mostly from the important co-operatives who still control most of the island's wine production. This huge, hilly island was ruled by the Spanish for many years and grapes of Spanish origin dominate production. The major red grape, Cannonau, is none other than Spain's Garnacha. Native grapes include Nuragus and Vernaccia. Best producers: ARGIOLAS, Gallura co-operative, Santadi co-operative, SELLA & MOSCA.

SASSICAIA
ITALY, Tuscany, Bolgheri Sassicaia DOC
🍷 *Cabernet Sauvignon, Cabernet Franc*

Sassicaia, from the Tenuta San Guido estate at BOLGHERI near the Tuscan coast, started the Cabernet Sauvignon craze in TUSCANY. The first commercial release of the wine, in 1968, astounded everyone with its wonderfully seductive, fruit-dominated, blackcurrant and mint flavours. The archetypal SUPER-TUSCAN, it was also the first of the big-gun VINO DA TAVOLAs to be absorbed into the DOC system when it was awarded its very own sub-zone status in 1994, under the simultaneously created Bolgheri DOC.

Devised by the BORDEAUX-loving Marchese Mario Incisa della Rochetta, father of the present incumbent Niccolò, Sassicaia was conceived along cru classé lines, with the help of Bordeaux's Professor Émile Peynaud and Italy's most renowned enologist, Giacomo Tachis, formerly of ANTINORI. Aged for 18 months to two years in French barriques and another year at least in bottle before release, the blend is Cabernet Sauvignon with a touch of Cabernet Franc. Older vintages have demonstrated that Sassicaia ages brilliantly and from a good vintage it continues to blossom for 20 years or more. Some say the greatest year ever was 1985, but 2001, '99, 98, '97, '95, '90, '88, '84, '83, '82, '81, '78, '75, '71 and '68 are all memorable.

HORST SAUER
GERMANY, Franken, Escherndorf
🍷 *Pinot Noir (Spätburgunder) and others*
🍷 *Müller-Thurgau, Silvaner, Riesling and others*

His wines from the late 1990s shot the ebullient and energetic Horst Sauer to stardom. His dry and off-dry Rieslings and Silvaners are a revelation of focus and fiery intensity matched by gorgeously juicy fresh fruit for a region renowned for blunt, earthy wines. His late-harvest wines are unchallenged in the region and his super-sweet wines are some of the best in Germany: they will easily live a decade, sometimes much more. Best years: 2002, '01, '00, '99, '98, '97.

SAUMUR AC
FRANCE, Loire, Anjou-Saumur
🍷 *Cabernet Franc, Cabernet Sauvignon, Pineau d'Aunis*
🍷 *Chenin Blanc, Chardonnay, Sauvignon Blanc*
🍷🍷 *(sparkling) Chenin Blanc, Chardonnay, Sauvignon Blanc, Cabernet Franc, Cabernet Sauvignon, Pineau d'Aunis*

You only have to taste the basic still white wine of Saumur to realize why most of it is rapidly transformed into sparkling wine – it is generally thin, harsh stuff, often showing off the Chenin Blanc grape at its graceless worst. But producers like Jean-Pierre Chevallier (Ch. de VILLENEUVE), Philippe Vatan (Ch. du Hureau), the Foucault brothers at CLOS ROUGEARD and Thierry Germain, as well as the St-Cyr-en-Bourg co-operative, are now showing how complex properly ripe and well made dry Chenin wine can be. Fortunately, the important local *négociant*, ACKERMAN-LAURANCE, has also realized that there is no future in poor wines. Up to 20 per cent Chardonnay can now be added to the blend.

The Saumur region is also a fairly important producer of rather sharp reds, mainly from Cabernet Franc and lighter than those from the SAUMUR-CHAMPIGNY AC. There is a little reasonable dry to off-dry Cabernet rosé. There is also a little sweet white Coteaux de Saumur in good years. Best years: (whites) 2002, '01, '00, '99, '97, '96. Best producers: Clos Rougeard, Collier, Filliatreau, Gaillard, du Hureau, Langlois-Château, R-N Legrand, la Paleine, Roches Neuves, St-Just, VILLENEUVE, Yvonne.

Sparkling Saumur has been made by the CHAMPAGNE method since 1811. Usually called Saumur Brut rather than Mousseux, it is a reasonable cheap alternative to Champagne, made mainly from Chenin Blanc. Adding Chardonnay and Cabernet Franc to the blend makes it softer and more interesting. It is usually only made as a non-vintage wine and there is also a small amount of rosé. Best producers: (sparkling) Bouvet-Ladubay, GRATIEN & Meyer, Grenelle, la Paleine, la Perruche, St-Cyr-en-Bourg co-operative.

SAUMUR-CHAMPIGNY AC
FRANCE, Loire, Anjou-Saumur
🍷 *Cabernet Franc, Cabernet Sauvignon, Pineau d'Aunis*

The vineyards for the best red wine in the SAUMUR region are found on a chalk and limestone plateau above the river Loire. Cabernet Franc is the dominant grape, and in hot years the wine can be superb, with a piercing scent of blackcurrants and raspberries easily overpowering the earthy finish. There are two styles of Saumur-Champigny: one is a light, early quaffer while the other, one of the best reds in the Loire, is more concentrated and may have had some wood aging. An increasing number of producers make several cuvées of differing weight and concentration. Technically Pineau d'Aunis is allowed but this is now very rare. Best years: 2002, '01, '00, '97, '96. Best producers: Clos Rougeard, Clos des Cordeliers, Filliatreau, des Galmoises, du Hureau, R-N Legrand, de Nerleux, la Perruche, Rétiveau-Rétif/Dom. des Champs Fleuris, Roches Neuves, de Targé, St-Vincent, VILLENEUVE, Yvonne.

SAUTERNES France, Bordeaux

IT SEEMS STRANGE TO THINK that not long ago the names Sauternes and Barsac had come to suggest sweet gooey wines without much character, to be passed off on anyone who doesn't like dry wines. This implies that they are easy and cheap to produce, and incapable of achieving any memorable personality. Nothing could be further from the truth – these are the best sweet wines in the world. The production of fine sweet white wine is an exhausting, risk-laden and extremely time-consuming and expensive affair, requiring nerves of steel, a huge bank balance, and just the right mix of grape varieties, vineyard sites and quite idiosyncratic local climatic conditions. It so happens that Bordeaux has half a dozen localities where, to a greater or lesser extent, the vineyards and the climate get the balance right.

Greatest of these areas are Barsac and Sauternes. Just north of the town of Langon, the little river Ciron sidles up from the south to join the larger river Garonne. On the Ciron's east bank lie the vineyards of Sauternes and on its west bank those of Barsac. Adjoining Barsac to the north is Cérons, whose speciality is a light sweet white, but increasingly Cérons vineyards are now producing reds and dry whites (which are not allowed the Cérons AC). On the opposite bank of the Garonne river are the areas of Cadillac, Loupiac and Ste-Croix-du-Mont whose speciality is also sweet white wine, but whose vineyards rarely produce anything with the concentration of a good Sauternes.

Sauternes and Barsac produce the most exciting sweet wines because their vineyards enjoy humid conditions ideal for the onset of 'noble rot' or *pourriture noble* which is caused by the fungus *Botrytis cinerea* which settles on the skins of the grapes, feeding off the water inside. This dramatically reduces the amount of juice, but what is left is extra concentrated in sugar and flavour. Noble rot occurs only in the autumn months, if at all, and needs a mixture of humidity and warmth to take root. On warm autumn days, fogs rise off the river in the mornings, only to be driven away later in the day by the sun's heat – the perfect combination. Cérons and the ACs on the Garonne's right bank get these condi-

Distinguished as a Premier Cru Classé in the famous 1855 Bordeaux Classification, Ch. d'Yquem is still recognized as the world's greatest sweet wine. Its richness and astonishingly exotic flavour mean it is constantly in demand.

tions to a much lesser degree than they do in Sauternes and Barsac. Noble rot usually strikes well into the autumn so the possibility of storms are an ever-present threat for the growers, since a couple of days' heavy rain can dilute the juice and bloat the grapes. In some years the whole crop can be ruined this way.

Another complication is that noble rot does not strike consistently. On one bunch, some grapes may be totally rotted, some may be partially affected and some untouched. So the pickers have to go through the vines time after time snipping off only the most affected bunches, or sometimes only the most rotted single grapes on a bunch! Needless to say, anything so labour-intensive is very expensive, and takes a lot of time, sometimes dragging on for more than two months –

CH. DE FARGUES

This small property making fine, rich wine is owned by the Lur-Saluces family, formerly of Ch. d'Yquem, and run with similar perfectionist zeal.

CH. LAFAURIE-PEYRAGUEY

From a property now returned to cracking form, this is wonderfully balanced, beautifully rich Sauternes, usually scented with new oak to great effect.

CH. COUTET

Barsac's largest Cru Classé property makes sweet wines that are aromatic and complex with added concentration in recent vintages.

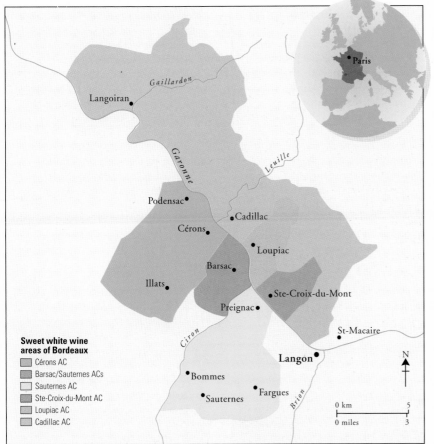

Sweet white wine areas of Bordeaux
- Cérons AC
- Barsac/Sauternes ACs
- Sauternes AC
- Ste-Croix-du-Mont AC
- Loupiac AC
- Cadillac AC

CH. LA TOUR BLANCHE
Thanks to dynamic direction and a generous investment in new oak for both fermentation and aging, this wine now has the rich unctuousness of great Sauternes.

CH. DOISY-VÉDRINES
From the commune of Barsac, this rich, intensely fruity wine is one of the most reliable Sauternes, and usually fair value, too.

CH. NAIRAC
The influence of fermentation and aging in new oak casks produces a concentrated oaky style of Sauternes.

CH. RAYNE-VIGNEAU
Huge investments have brought impressive results at this great Sauternes property which enjoys arguably the finest soil and mesoclimate after Ch. d'Yquem.

CH. RABAUD-PROMIS
At last, vintages since the mid-1980s have shown a long-awaited return to First Growth quality and the wines are rich and opulent but with fine balancing acidity.

and only the top châteaux, whose wines command the very top prices, can afford to do this.

When you realize that a single vine may produce as little as one glass of wine, as against the bottle or more that a producer of dry wine could expect, it becomes painfully obvious that we've been underestimating – and underpricing – these great wines for far too long.

AC ENTRIES
Barsac, Cadillac, Loupiac, Ste-Croix-du-Mont, Sauternes.

CHÂTEAUX ENTRIES
Bastor-Lamontagne, Climens, Coutet, Doisy-Daëne, Doisy-Védrines, de Fargues, Gilette, Guiraud, Lafaurie-Peyraguey, Nairac, Rieussec, St-Amand, Suduiraut, la Tour Blanche, d'Yquem.

CH. SUDUIRAUT
Often regarded as a close runner-up to Yquem, the wines are now back on top form after new owners arrived in 1992.

CH. GILETTE
This remarkable property ages its wines in concrete tanks for 20 to 30 years before releasing them.

CH. CLIMENS
The leading estate in Barsac, using rigorous selection to keep yields low, makes rich, elegant wines with a light, lemony acidity ensuring wonderful freshness.

CH. RIEUSSEC
Situated on a hill adjacent to Ch. d'Yquem, Rieussec has a reputation for producing the richest, most succulent wine of Sauternes.

SAUTERNES AC

FRANCE, Bordeaux (see also pages 336–337)
♀ *Sémillon, Sauvignon Blanc, Muscadelle*

What marks out this small enclave of vineyards on the left bank of the Garonne is the particular susceptibility of its grapes to go rotten before they are picked in the autumn.

That doesn't sound very encouraging so I'll explain. If you ripen a grape fully during a good summer, it will have enough sugar to convert to a lot of alcohol during fermentation, but the wine will be dry. For a really sweet wine you need to have so much sugar in the grapes that the yeasts ferment out as much as they can, yet you are still left with masses of unfermented sugar to provide rich concentration. That's where the 'rot' comes in. There is a particular sort of rot (called 'noble') which attacks grapes and, instead of ruining the flavour, eats into the skin, then sucks out the water in the grape, leaving behind most of the sugar, which then gets more and more concentrated, and may end up twice as strong as in a normally ripe grape with perhaps 25 degrees of potential alcohol in the sugar. Since yeast can't convert more than about 14–15 degrees to alcohol, all the rest remains as sweetness. The result is a wine of high alcoholic strength and deep, mouth-coating richness, full of flavours like pineapples, peaches, syrup and spice.

In some vintages the 'rot' doesn't develop, and then it is not possible to make intensely sweet wine, although it may still be sold as Sauternes. This can be a pleasant, adequately sweet drink, especially from a château that uses modern methods of cryo-extraction to concentrate the sugar. It is always expensive, though, because the permitted yield is extremely low at 25 hectolitres per hectare – less than half that of a HAUT-MÉDOC red – and because production is labour intensive, the grapes being selectively picked. Sometimes pickers make up to seven or eight passages or *tris* through the vines. The top wines are also fermented and aged in new oak barrels. Good vintages should age for five to ten years and often twice as long. Best years: 2002, '00, '99, '98, '97, '96, '95, '90, '89, '88, '86, '83. Best producers: BASTOR-LAMONTAGNE, Clos Haut-Peyraguey, Cru Barréjats, DOISY-DAËNE, DOISY-VÉDRINES, de FARGUES, GILETTE, GUIRAUD, Haut-Bergeron, les Justices, LAFAURIE-PEYRAGUEY, Lamothe-Guignard, de Malle, Rabaud-Promis, Raymond-Lafon, Rayne-Vigneau, RIEUSSEC, Sigalas-Rabaud, SUDUIRAUT, la TOUR BLANCHE, d'YQUEM.

SAUVIGNON BLANC

This is a grape that wears its heart on its sleeve. Its wine is sharp, green and tangy, reeking of lime zest and passionfruit, gooseberries and crushed nettles and blackcurrant leaves, clear, clean and refreshing. It seldom has any great complexity, whether it is sweet or dry, oaked or unoaked. That description is of classic Sancerre or Pouilly-Fumé from France's Loire Valley, the benchmark areas for Sauvignon wine – until New Zealand came along.

It is also grown by the mile in Bordeaux, but has never been so popular, for the simple reason that instead of tasting of fresh gooseberries it was liable in the past to taste of old socks. But the spread of cold fermentation worked wonders, and the average Bordeaux Blanc Sec, made entirely or mostly from Sauvignon Blanc, while lacking the pungency of the Loire wines, is at least these days likely to be clean and fresh, even if dull. In the northern Graves area of Pessac-Léognan where white wines are made from a majority of Sauvignon Blanc, fermentation and aging in new oak barrels has provided a rich, citrus, tropical fruit and vanilla slant to the variety.

Like Sémillon, it is susceptible to noble rot, and the addition of between 10 and 40 per cent Sauvignon Blanc in the blend for Sauternes and Barsac freshens up the wine no end, adding crucial zip. It is often similarly employed in the New World but most Sauvignon Blanc, however, is made dry. Regional characteristics come through strongly, with California producing wines that are melony or sweetly grassy, sometimes asparagus-like in flavour. The northern Napa Valley produces the most melony Sauvignons while the southern Napa and Sonoma wines are grassier. Robert Mondavi coined the now-popular New World synonym for Sauvignon Blanc: his dry Fumé Blanc is aged in new oak and shows a distinctly rounder character, more vanilla and less grass.

Chile's first releases of so-called Sauvignon Blanc were surprisingly feeble until winemakers realized that most of what they thought was Sauvignon Blanc in the vineyards was actually the inferior Sauvignonasse. Now top Chilean releases, especially from the Casablanca Valley, are the real tongue-tingling thing. Argentina finds Sauvignon more difficult but early picking and cool fermentation has produced some good results.

In Australia Sauvignon Blanc tends to be broad, generous and tropical-fruit-flavoured, sometimes gooseberryish and often aged in oak. It seldom approaches the pungency of the New Zealand examples – because these have really shown the world what can be done with the grape, particularly in the Marlborough region of South Island. Cloudy Bay may be the cult wine but it is by no means the only one: New Zealand Sauvignon Blancs may be brilliantly gooseberryish or tropically fruity; they are often highly aromatic, generally full in texture, strong in acid and quite unmistakable.

South Africa has had Sauvignon Blanc since the 1920s but only since the early 1990s has it made an impression. Firstly the cool Constantia region produced some zesty, leafy examples, then Robertson followed suit and in recent years there has been a string of excellent green-streaked, generally unwooded examples from coastal vineyards to the north and east of Cape Town.

The occasional good example emerging from eastern Europe shows that these countries, too, could do good things with the grape. Austria produces clean, acidic versions, particularly from Steiermark, under the pseudonym of Muscat-Sylvaner. Sauvignon has been present in Italy for well over a hundred years, but it is only recently that producers, mainly in Friuli and Alto Adige, have begun making high-class wine. Recently, too, the grape has begun to spread south. Sauvignon Blanc is playing a growing role in Spain, mostly in Rueda and Cataluña, where it usually produces sharply aromatic wines.

DOMAINE ÉTIENNE SAUZET
FRANCE, Burgundy, Côte de Beaune, Puligny-Montrachet AC
♀ *Chardonnay*

A producer with a reputation for rich, full-flavoured white Burgundies, made in an opulent, fat style, but recently showing more classical restraint. Sauzet owns prime sites in PULIGNY-MONTRACHET (including the Premiers Crus les Champs Canet, les Combettes, les Perrières and les Referts) and CHASSAGNE-MONTRACHET, as well as small parcels of vines in BÂTARD-MONTRACHET and Bienvenues-Bâtard-Montrachet, and supplements grapes from its own 8ha (19 acres) of vineyards with bought-in supplies. Best years: 2002, '00, '99, '97.

SAVENNIÈRES AC
FRANCE, Loire, Anjou-Saumur
♀ *Chenin Blanc*

Savennières is often hailed as the crowning dry wine glory of the Chenin grape – and there are two Grand Cru vineyards which further enhance this theory. But as frequently happens with Chenin, the wine is so rough and unfriendly when young, and the maturation period is so painfully slow – often lasting eight years or more – that it is difficult to embrace Savennières' undoubted quality in an entirely wholehearted way. The AC's 124ha (306 acres) are on perilously steep slopes on the north bank of the Loire, opposite the little river Layon, and annual production veers between 225,000 and 600,000 bottles – the wide variation is caused by a particularly capricious mesoclimate. In cooler years much of the wine is declassified to Anjou AC. Young Savennières is gum-judderingly dry but the wines do get there in the end. Even if it takes a decade or two, honey begins to soften the steel, and the creaminess of nuts soothes the gaunt herb-harsh dryness. But even at the peak of maturity, there'll still be an acid freshness.

The two Grand Cru vineyards have their own ACs. They are Savennières-Coulée-de-Serrant, a 7-ha (17-acre) plot which makes the subtlest and most refined wine; and another vineyard of 19ha (47 acres), Savennières-Roche-aux-Moines, whose wines are lighter, but also extremely good. Coulée-de-Serrant is also important as the property of Nicolas Joly whose messianic fervour for bio-dynamic methods of grapegrowing has influenced growers all over France. Best years: 2002, '01, '00, '99, '97, '96, '95, '93, '90, '89, '88, '85, '83, '82. Best producers: Dom. des

DOMAINE DES BAUMARD
As part owners of the Clos du Papillon, the Baumard family produce fine Savennières, combining accessibility with elegance and a typical ability to age.

BAUMARD, Clos de Coulaine, Clos de la Coulée-de-Serrant, Clos de Varennes, Closel, d'Épiré, des Forges, aux Moines, Monnaie, Pierre-Bise, P Soulez, P-Y Tijou.

SAVIGNY-LÈS-BEAUNE AC
FRANCE, Burgundy, Côte de Beaune
♥ *Pinot Noir*
♀ *Chardonnay, Pinot Blanc*

Although Savigny-lès-Beaune is off the main 'Côte de Beaune', in the side valley through which the Autoroute du Soleil now leaps, its communal boundaries are far flung, spreading right down to BEAUNE, and across to ALOXE-CORTON. The vines follow the cleft in the hills, facing both north-east and south to south-east. This less than perfect aspect does show in the red wines, which are usually fairly light with a rough minerally streak, but there can also be a very pleasant strawberry fruit flavour. There are nearly 20 Premiers Crus: the richest wines tend to come from les Marconnets and les Narbantons; the most elegant include les Lavières and les Vergelesses, and Aux Guettes and les Serpentières are firm but stylish. From a top producer all these Premiers Crus are worth paying extra for. Best years: (reds) 2002, '01, '99, '98, '97, '96, '95, '93. Best producers: S Bize, Camus-Bruchon, Champy, CHANDON DE BRIAILLES, B Clair, M Écard, J-J Girard, P Girard, V GIRARDIN, L Jacob, D LAURENT, Domaine LEROY, C Maréchal, J-M Pavelot, TOLLOT-BEAUT.

Savigny whites aren't terribly impressive when young, but manage to show a bit of dry, nutty class after three or four years.

J-M PAVELOT
J-M Pavelot is one of the most important domaines in Savigny. The red Aux Guettes enjoys a fine balance between ripe fruit, delicate tannin and good length.

VIN DE SAVOIE AC
FRANCE, Savoie
♥ ♥ *Mondeuse, Gamay, Pinot Noir*
♀ *Roussette (Altesse), Jacquère, Chardonnay, Roussanne and others*

Apart from CRÉPY and SEYSSEL, which have their own ACs, most Savoie wines are simply labelled Vin de Savoie AC, sometimes with the name of a village. The best of these are Abymes, Apremont, Arbin, Chignin, Cruet and Montmélian. The vines here have to contend with holiday chalets, ski-lifts and fairly intense agriculture – so they tend to spring up all over the region, wherever there's a south-facing slope not yet nabbed for a ski run. There are around 1800ha (4450 acres) of vineyards altogether, producing about 15 million bottles a year, most of it white wine. You can age the wines for a year or two, especially those with some Chardonnay in them, but then they lose their thrilling snap of tangy fruit. Roussette de Savoie is an appellation for wines made exclusively from the Roussette grape, locally called Altesse, and these can age for several years.

There is some good sparkling wine made, but most of that comes under its own appellation at Seyssel, although Ayze, south-east of Geneva, also has a reputation for it. The best reds are made from the Mondeuse grape; plummy, chewy wines capable of aging. Best producers: P Boniface, Bouvet, Dupasquier, Jacquin, Magnin, C Marandon, Monin, Neyroud, Perret, A & M Quénard, R Quénard, de Ripaille, Rocailles, C Trosset.

SAXENBURG
SOUTH AFRICA, Western Cape, Stellenbosch WO
♥ *Syrah (Shiraz), Cabernet Sauvignon, Merlot, Pinotage and others*
♀ *Sauvignon Blanc, Chardonnay and others*

After a few false starts in its modern renaissance, this Kuils River property finally found top gear with the 1991 vintage. Its success is in no small part due to the symbiotic partnership between the philosophical owner, Swiss businessman Adrian Bührer, and his decidedly non-mainstream Afrikaaner winemaker, Nico van der Merwe. They make a successful pair in both hemispheres; van der Merwe is also in charge of winemaking at Bührer's other property, Ch. Capion, neighbour to MAS DE DAUMAS GASSAC in the LANGUEDOC. Red wines are the STELLENBOSCH property's real forte, with a rip-roaring Saxenburg Shiraz Select, one of South Africa's priciest reds. Private Collection Shiraz is very good and a lot cheaper, as are Cabernet,

Merlot and Pinotage. Whites are modern and fresh. Most intriguing members of the range are the Grand Vin Blanc and Grand Vin Rouge, each a happy blend of wines from Ch. Capion and Saxenburg. Best years: (premium reds) 2000, '99, '98, '97, '96, '95, '94, '93.

WILLI SCHAEFER
GERMANY, Mosel-Saar-Ruwer, Graach
♀ *Riesling*

Schaefer's naturally sweet Riesling Spätlese and Auslese from the great Domprobst vineyard in GRAACH are classic, MOSEL wines. The balance of piercing acidity and lavish fruit are every bit as dramatic as Domprobst's precipitous slope. They are made in tiny quantities and are extremely long-lived, as is the sensational Beerenauslese produced in exceptional years. Best years: (Riesling Spätlese and Auslese) 2002, '01, '00, '99, '98, '97, '96, '95, '94, 93, '92, '90, '89, '88, '83, '76, '71.

SCHEUREBE

Scheurebe is a white crossing of Silvaner with Riesling found in Germany, especially in the RHEINHESSEN and the PFALZ, and Austria, where it is known also as Sämling 88. It produces some good, rich Prädikat wines, especially at the top levels of Trockenbeerenauslese and Eiswein. The dry wines, though, especially in the hands of a lesser winemaker, can be a bit dodgy: 'catty' can be the kindest way of describing some of them. It's generally assertive and lacks subtlety, but a few good producers are making some serious, and seriously enjoyable, wines packed with honey and the fruit of the pinkest of pink grapefruit.

MARIO SCHIOPETTO
ITALY, Friuli-Venezia Giulia, Collio DOC
♂ *Merlot, Cabernet Franc, Cabernet Sauvignon, Refosco dal Peduncolo Rosso*
♀ *Tocai Friulano, Pinot Blanc (Pinot Bianco), Pinot Gris (Pinot Grigio), Sauvignon Blanc, Malavasia*

The late Mario Schiopetto was admired as the father of modern Friulian viniculture, and hence of modern Italian white wine. He began in the 1960s in his modest plot in Capriva del Friuli, where his two sons and his daughter continue to produce intensely concentrated wines of impeccable character.

There is a wide range of COLLIO wines, including outstanding Sauvignon Blanc and Pinot Bianco (cru Amrità, Sanskrit for deathless) as well as excellent Pinot Grigio, but the real speciality is Tocai Friulano. Merlot and the Cabernets are blended for the red vino da tavola, Rivarossa.

SCHLOSS LIESER
This Auslese from the Niederberg Helden site, the top site in Lieser, is full of ripe peach, exotic fruit and vanilla flavours.

SCHLOSS LIESER
GERMANY, Mosel-Saar-Ruwer, Lieser
♀ *Riesling*

Schloss Lieser and its excellent Niederberg Helden vineyard had fallen on hard times and were virtually unknown until Thomas Haag, the son of Wilhelm Haag from BRAUNEBERG's famous Fritz HAAG estate, took over running this estate in 1992. Within a remarkably short space of time quality improved in dramatic leaps and bounds and Schloss Lieser joined the first rank of Middle MOSEL producers with fine dry Auslese and higher Prädikat dessert wines with great purity of flavour. All are best with five or more years in bottle. Best years: 2002, '01, '99, '98, '97, '96, '95, '94, '93.

SCHLOSS REINHARTSHAUSEN
GERMANY, Rheingau, Erbach
♂ ♀ *Pinot Noir (Spätburgunder)*
♀ *Riesling, Pinot Blanc (Weissburgunder), Chardonnay and others*

The most aristocratic estate of an aristocratic region, Schloss Reinhartshausen belonged to the Hohenzollern family who ruled Germany until 1918 and is now owned by a consortium of Frankfurt businessmen. The winery is in the village of ERBACH, with vines in the vineyard sites of Marcobrunn, Schlossberg, Rheinhell and others, and at other top RHEINGAU villages. The wines are rich and quite full, though often made dry. The estate is known for its experiments with Chardonnay, and there is a good Weissburgunder-Chardonnay blend as well as pretty passable fizz, made using the CHAMPAGNE method. Best years: 2002, '01, '99, '98, '97, '96, '95, '94, '93, '92, '90, '89.

SCHLOSS SAARSTEIN
GERMANY, Mosel-Saar-Ruwer, Serrig
♀ *Riesling, Pinot Blanc (Weissburgunder) and others*

This SAAR property, run by Christian Ebert, places an emphasis on QbA and Kabinett wines: Ebert makes Spätlese and Auslese in the best years, and they can be terrifically

powerful and concentrated. There is also the occasional Eiswein. But this is after all the Saar and there's no shortage of acidity: when young the wines can be pretty lean. There is a vineyard called Schloss Saarsteiner, and this estate is the sole owner. Of late the wines, good as they are, have not been as exciting as they once were. Best years: 2002, '01, '99, '97, '95, '93, '92, '90, '89, '88, '86, '85.

SCHLOSS VOLLRADS
GERMANY, Rheingau, Winkel
♀ *Riesling*

When the great prophet of dry German Riesling, Erwein Graf Matuschka-Greiffenclau, commited suicide in the summer of 1997 the future of this famous historic RHEINGAU estate hung in the balance. However, Dr Rowald Hepp, previously director of the Staatlicher Hofkeller in WÜRZBURG and the Rheingau State Domaine, was appointed director by Matuschka's bank in 1999 and the vintages since then have been increasingly good. Best years: 2002, '01, '00, '99.

SCHLOSSBÖCKELHEIM
GERMANY, Nahe

The village of Schlossböckelheim is home to the ex-State Domaine of Niederhausen-Schlossböckelheim, now going under the unromantic name of Gutsverwaltung Niederhausen-Schlossböckelheim. The village's best vineyard sites are the famous steep Kupfergrube, planted on a rocky hillside over the workings of an old copper mine, and Felsenberg; these are vineyards with ideal exposure to the sun and produce long-lived Rieslings. Good wines also come from the Mühlberg and Königsfels sites. Best years: 2002, '01, '00, '99, '98, '96, '95, '94. Best producers: Dr Crusius, DÖNNHOFF, Gutsverwaltung Niederhausen-Schlossböckelheim.

SCHLUMBERGER
FRANCE, Alsace, Alsace AC
♂ *Pinot Noir*
♀ *Riesling, Gewurztraminer, Pinot Gris, Pinot Blanc, Sylvaner, Muscat*

Looming above the town of Guebwiller are the mighty flanks of the steep vineyards that contain the Grands Crus of Kitterlé, Kessler, Saering and Spiegel, where Schlumberger is easily the most important producer. Indeed, with 140ha (346 acres) of vineyards under cultivation, this is the largest estate in ALSACE.

The Schlumberger style is always broad and rich, and often better suited to Gewurztraminer, Pinot Gris and Pinot Blanc than to

Riesling, though the Saering Rieslings can be very fine. The Schlumberger family have acquired an intimate knowledge of the vineyards and their characteristics, and these wines illustrate as well as any in Alsace the true diversity of terroirs that make the region so fascinating. The full-blown sumptuous style of these wines may not be to everyone's taste, but they are an impressive expression of Alsace at its most lush. Although they come across as low in acidity, they age extremely well. The Vendange Tardive and Sélection de Grains Nobles from Gewurztraminer and Pinot Gris are impressive and surprisingly elegant, but very expensive. Best years: 2001, '99, '98, '97, '96, '95, '94, '93, '92, '90, '89, '88, '85, '83.

DOMAINE SCHOFFIT

FRANCE, Alsace, Alsace AC
🍷 *Pinot Noir*
🍷 *Pinot Gris, Riesling, Gewurztraminer, Pinot Blanc and others*

One of the two main owners of the outstanding Rangen Grand Cru vineyard at Thann, at the southern end of Alsace. This is a remarkable vineyard, rescued from dereliction by ZIND-HUMBRECHT in 1977, with whom Schoffit shares the site. The dark, volcanic soils of this suntrap give magnificent wines that often taste more of their intensely minerally birthplace than of their grape variety, and Schoffit's Clos St-Théobald wines, especially the thrillingly austere Riesling, are outstanding examples, usually needing at least five or six years to show all their class. Most of Schoffit's wine, however, comes from completely different soils, since the estate is based in Colmar where the vineyards are generally thought of as too flat for quality production. Schoffit disproves this with a range of delightfully fruity wines. Best years: (Clos St-Théobald Riesling) 2001, '00, '99, '98, '97, '96, '95, '94.

SCHRAMSBERG VINEYARDS

USA, California, Napa County, Napa Valley AVA
🍷🍷 *Chardonnay, Pinot Noir, Flora and others*

Starting in 1965, the late Jack Davies at Schramsberg was the first Californian to prove that great sparkling wine was possible in the Golden State. He used the traditional CHAMPAGNE varieties of Chardonnay and Pinot Noir and techniques culled from French sources. Since the first releases in the early 1970s, the quality has been exceptional. Mirabelle Brut and Querencia are non-vintage dated and there are a number of vintage cuvées, including Blanc de Blancs, Blanc de Noirs and the Blanc de Noirs-style Reserve, all of them strongly marked by the flavours of yeast and toast; the vintage-dated Brut Rosé is a traditional dry rosé; the dessert-sweet Crémant uses a CALIFORN-IAn white grape called Flora as its base. The prestige cuvée is named J Schram: in some vintages, it can dazzle, and in most it is very good. Vintage-dated wines can be drunk with up to ten years' age.

SCREAMING EAGLE

USA, California, Napa County, Oakville AVA
🍷 *Cabernet Sauvignon, Merlot, Cabernet Franc*

Real estate agent Jean Phillips first produced a Cabernet Sauvignon from her valley floor vineyard – measuring just 0.9ha (2.2 acres) – in 1992. Made in very limited quantities, the wine is CALIFORNIA's most sought-after Cabernet each vintage and sells for hundreds of dollars a bottle on release, thousands per bottle at auction with a little bottle age. Made by Heidi Peterson-Barrett, winemaker for Grace Family Vineyards and Paradigm, the Cabernet Sauvignon is a huge, brooding wine that displays all the lush fruit of OAKVILLE.

SEGHESIO

USA, California, Sonoma County, Alexander Valley AVA
🍷 *Zinfandel, Sangiovese, Barbera, Pinot Noir, Petite Sirah and others*
🍷 *Pinot Gris (Pinot Grigio), Arneis*

Having grown grapes in SONOMA COUNTY for a century, the Seghesio family is today known for its own Zinfandel. The whole range, from Sonoma County to the single-vineyard San Lorenzo and Cortina, displays textbook black fruit and peppery spice. Sangiovese, from 1910 vines, is one of the best in the state. Also look for the crisp Italian whites such as Pinot Grigio and Arneis.

SEIFRIED ESTATE

NEW ZEALAND, South Island, Nelson
🍷 *Pinot Noir, Merlot, Cabernet Sauvignon, Merlot, Malbec and others*
🍷 *Sauvignon Blanc, Chardonnay, Gewurztraminer, Riesling*

Hermann Seifried had made wine in Europe and South Africa and had worked for the New Zealand Apple and Pear Board before setting up the Seifried Estate in Nelson which now has 110ha (272 acres) of vines. Since then he has dominated the region with his technically flawless whites, especially from the German varieties. The lime-flavoured Riesling and spicy lychee Gewurztraminer are especially good, with the Late Harvest wines outstanding. During the 1990s he developed a coastal vineyard called Rabbit Island for Sauvignon and Chardonnay and his latest venture is a vineyard on stony soils at Brightwater for red varieties, including experimental Shiraz and Zweigelt. Old Coach Road is an entry-level label. Best years: (whites) 2002, '01, '00, '99, '98.

SELBACH-OSTER

GERMANY, Mosel-Saar-Ruwer, Zeltingen-Rachtig
🍷 *Riesling, Pinot Blanc (Weissburgunder)*

This estate is the source of some benchmark MOSEL Riesling – nervy, racy and maturing to flavours of honey and petrol. Some of the vines are over a hundred years old and ungrafted, which makes them quite genuinely pre-phylloxera, the wines are matured in traditional oak casks and the natural grape sweetness is always discreet. The vineyards, at BERNKASTEL, WEHLEN, GRAACH and especially ZELTINGEN, are top-notch. Best years: 2002, '01, '00, '99, '98, '97, '96, '95, '94, '93, '92, '91, '90, '89, '88, '85.

SELLA & MOSCA

ITALY, Sardinia, Alghero DOC
🍷 *Grenache Noir (Cannonau), Cabernet Sauvignon, Carignan (Carignano), Merlot, Sangiovese and others*
🍷 *Grenache Noir (Cannonau), Cabernet Sauvignon, Carignan (Carignano), Sangiovese*
🍷 *Vermentino, Torbato, Sauvignon Blanc and others*

For decades this large company has been the leading private player in the SARDINIAn wine field, turning out wines at ever-increasing levels of quality. Fresh whites from Torbato, Vermentino and Sauvignon are matched by modern tasty reds from Cannonau and Carignano as well as good Cabernet Marchese di Villamarina and Cannonau-Cabernet blend, Tanca Farrà.

Their most idiosyncratic wine, however, is the sweet, red dessert Anghelu Ruju, made from Cannonau grapes which, after picking,

SELLA & MOSCA
Apart from the rich, port-like Anghelu Ruju, this much-modernized old firm produces a large range of sleek, modern wines, including powerful Tanca Farrà, a blend of the local Cannonau with Cabernet Sauvignon.

are left outside to dry on cane mats for some three weeks. There being plenty of heat left in the sun at that period, the already rich grapes concentrate their sugars to such an extent that the wine can approach 18 per cent alcohol with plenty of natural sweetness remaining. And as if that's not enough spirit is then added for good measure to stop all the sugar fermenting out. The wine is then matured five years in large oak barrels before release as a magnificent, heady sweet red wine. Best years: (Marchese di Villamarina) 2001, '00, '97, '95, '93, '92, '90.

FATTORIA SELVAPIANA

ITALY, Tuscany, Chianti Rufina DOCG

❢ *Sangiovese, Cabernet Sauvignon, Merlot*

❢ *Pinot Blanc (Pinot Bianco), Trebbiano, Malvasia*

With FRESCOBALDI and Basciano, Selvapiana is one of the few estates of the Rufina district, east of Florence, to be regularly included by pundits as among the finest of TUSCANY. Owned by one of the great gentlemen of Chianti, Francesco Giuntini, and run by his adopted son Federico Masseti-Giuntini with the very active consultancy of enologist Franco Bernabei, its wines always have a richness and ripeness of fruit to cover that inbuilt CHIANTI RUFINA structure which other Rufina wines achieve only sporadically.

The top wine, the 100 per cent Sangiovese Chianti Rufina Riserva Bucerchiale, is only produced in good to great years, when the grapes are not needed to boost the standard Chianti Rufina which is regularly the most classic example of the austere yet intriguing Rufina style, needing several years of aging to open out and show its personality. The Chianti Rufina Riserva Fornace, which includes Cabernet Sauvignon and Merlot in the blend, while very well made, is more international in flavour. In general the Selvapiano style is one of the most intrinsically Tuscan among the leading estates. Another recent venture times is the promising red POMINO called Petrognano.

On the other side of the coin, since World War Two Selvapiana has held back some bottles of the best vintages. So, if your credit card can handle it and you're sure your willpower can stop you splurging on every significant vintage since the war, you can still buy wines there going back to 1947 – and they're still good! Selvapiana VIN SANTO, too, is a classic, and so is the olive oil, if you like your oil seriously green and spicy. Best years: (Bucerchiale) 2001, '00, '99, '96, '95, '93, '91, '90, '88, '85.

SÉMILLON

Sémillon is grown all over the place but only in two places does it really have star status and in one of these, Bordeaux, it needs a little help from its friends. Sauternes and Barsac were the regions to give it fame in the first place. But with a couple of exceptions in Bordeaux – the dry Ch. Rahoul in Graves and the sweet Ch. Doisy-Daëne in Barsac, both of which are more or less 100 per cent Sémillon, virtually all France's best Sémillon-based wines are blended with Sauvignon Blanc. They complement each other perfectly, the weighty, smooth, waxy Sémillon needing that 20 per cent or so of Sauvignon Blanc to liven it up. The great dry whites of Pessac-Léognan have a greater proportion of Sauvignon.

Sémillon's susceptibility to rot makes it invaluable in Sauternes. This is one of the few places in the world where rotten grapes are essential – providing that it is the right sort of rot, *Botrytis cinerea*, occurring only at a particular time, once the grapes are ripe. Then the fungus shrivels and concentrates the grapes, sucking the water out and leaving behind it a concentrated, thick, sugary goo, the base material for some of the most complex dessert wines in the world. Sémillon is also used for dessert wines in California and Australia, where they tend to be chunkier and more intensely sweet, but Australian examples, in particular, can be world class and the best can age.

The sweet Australian Semillons are made in the Riverina region, but great dry Semillons are also made, particularly in the Hunter Valley. The traditional way of making Semillon here is to bottle it young and green and lemony, and then not touch it for perhaps five to ten years. What emerges then is all restrained mellowness, creamy texture and a unique flavour of nutty biscuits and lime. There are also good Australian examples of Semillon-Sauvignon blends.

SEPPELT

AUSTRALIA, Victoria, Grampians

❢ *Syrah (Shiraz), Pinot Noir, Cabernet Sauvignon*

❢ *Chardonnay, Riesling, Semillon*

Another member of the Southcorp family, Australia's most all-embracing wine company, Seppelt has led the way in Australia in creating good CHAMPAGNE-method fizz, made from Pinot Noir and Chardonnay: Drumborg (from very cool vineyards in the far south of Victoria) and Salinger are its leading labels, while Great Western, Queen Adelaide and Fleur de Lys are good value. Seppelt's other fizzy speciality is sparkling Shiraz – deep mulberry red and foaming full of fun – a brilliant madcap wine.

In still wines Seppelt makes some of Australia's best Shiraz from GRAMPIANS fruit, and a variety of fine Chardonnay and Semillon. But it is the Seppelt fortified wines from the historic Seppeltsfield winery in the BAROSSA VALLEY that truly shine. The Seppelt efforts at recreating classic European 'port' and 'sherry' styles, personified by the 100-year-old Para Vintage Tawny port, are frequently magnificent as are their entirely Australian-inspired Liqueur Muscats and Tokays.

SERESIN ESTATE

NEW ZEALAND, South Island, Marlborough

❢ *Pinot Noir, Pinot Meunier and others*

❢ *Sauvignon Blanc, Chardonnay, Pinot Gris, Riesling and others*

Seresin has star quality. You can feel the showbiz about the impressive modern winery. And you can taste it in the lush, rather hedonistic style of the wines made from vines grown in 44ha (110 acres) of old riverbed terrace land about as far westwards up the Wairau Valley as you can go before getting into serious frost problems as the valley cools down.

Well, the showbiz shouldn't be a surprise because the owner is Michael Seresin, an internationally successful New Zealand filmmaker who thought about buying an estate in TUSCANY but then, in 1992, came back to his roots and founded Seresin. He installed a fairly ritzy winemaker, globetrotter Brian Bicknell who up until then had been making some seriously good wines at ERRÁZURIZ in Chile. The lush wine style will not diminish over the years, since the vineyard, already organic, is going one step further and becoming biodynamic. Sauvignon Blanc, wooded and unwooded, two Chardonnays and a Pinot Noir are the top bottlings, but there's also good Pinot Gris and Riesling, and they made one Cabernet and two Malbecs before ripping out the vines. Since they also have some Sangiovese and Montepulciano growing there, don't count out further surprises in the next really hot MARLBOROUGH vintage.

SERRIG

GERMANY, Mosel-Saar-Ruwer

This is the last wine commune as you travel up the Saar from its confluence with the MOSEL just above Trier and it makes the most extreme of all SAAR wines. Serrig's Rieslings have precisely the piercing steeliness for which the Saar is famous and in a great vintage the wines can shine with an astonishing brilliance, even though you may have to wait five to ten years for the beauty to shine through. The downside of this is that in a poor year they are very lean and tart. Best years: 2002, '01, '99, '97, '95, '94, '93, '90, '89. Best producers: Bert Simon, SCHLOSS SAARSTEIN.

SETÚBAL DOC

PORTUGAL, Terras do Sado
♀ *Muscat (Moscatel de Setúbal), Moscatel Roxo, Tamarez, Arinto, Fernão Pires*

The fishing port of Setúbal lends its name to an unctuous fortified wine made mainly from different types of Moscatel grown on the surrounding hills. The wine is called Moscatel de Setúbal when made from at least 85 per cent Moscatel, and Setúbal when it's not. Prolonged maceration on the grape skins for up to six months following partial fermentation and fortification powerfully accentuates the aroma and grapy richness.

Setúbal varies in style according to age. Younger wines (bottled after spending around five years in wood) are orange-brown in colour with a spicy-raisiny character. Older wines (with 20 or more years in wood) are darker with butterscotch and molasses flavours. J M da FONSECA maintain stocks of old wines in wood, some of which date back

to the nineteenth century. I can vouch for wines from the 1955 and the '38 vintages being outstanding. Deep in the cellars there are also wines dating from the time when casks of Setúbal were shipped (like MADEIRA) across the equator and back. These are bottled as Torna Viagem (return journey). Fonseca also makes a small quantity of wine from the rare Moscatel Roxo (red Muscat). Best producers: J M da Fonseca, J P VINHOS.

SEYSSEL AC

FRANCE, Savoie
♀ *Molette, Roussette (Altesse)*

Seyssel is the best known of the SAVOIE wine villages, mainly because it is the headquarters of the region's sparkling wine industry. Real Seyssel Mousseux – a featherlight, water-white fizz, the lovely sharp peppery bite of the Molette and Altesse grapes smoothed out with a creamy yeast – is tasting even better than in its previous heyday over a generation ago. The wines are often released with a vintage date and are worth seeking out as an ideal summer gulper. There is a little still white Seyssel AC, from the Altesse grape: very light and slightly floral. Best producers: Mollex, Varichon & Clerc.

SEYVAL BLANC

This white hybrid grape is grown in France, Canada and in NEW YORK STATE, but has so far produced its finest wines in England, where its resistance to disease and ability to continue ripening in a damp autumn means it crops reliably in an unreliable climate. It consistently produces some of England's best wines, light, flowery, nettly and crisp when young, but capable of developing a full, nutty, Burgundian depth with age.

SHAFER VINEYARDS

USA, California, Napa County, Stags Leap District AVA
♂ *Cabernet Sauvignon, Merlot, Syrah, Sangiovese*
♀ *Chardonnay*

So where do you find out what the red wines of SARDINIA are particularly good for? Shafer Vineyards, that's where. (And Sardinian reds are good at keeping people alive; there are a remarkable number of wine-drinking centenarians on the island today.) And where do you find out how many rodents a pair of barn owls will eat during the rearing season? Shafer Vineyards, of course (and the answer is – a thousand).

In an era when many NAPA VALLEY wineries go to absurd lengths of self-glorification to

promote their wine, John and Doug Shafer take a different view. They send out a welcome stream of quirky, humorous and downright useful facts and figures to the waiting world, and then quietly let us know about how their wines are doing at the same time.

They're doing very well. I tasted the original Shafer wine, a 1978 Cabernet, in the mid-1990s – and was thrilled by its sweet fruit and serious but approachable character – at over 15 years old. From making only 1000 cases in 1978, Shafer now produces 32,000 cases from a total of 69ha (170 acres) of vineyards but quality is as high as ever. Red Shoulder Ranch Chardonnay is one of CARNEROS' best; the straight Cabernet and above all the Hillside Select, from their Stags Leap Estate, is superb: deep, ripe but muscular stuff. They also produce a Napa 'SUPER-TUSCAN' Sangiovese-Cabernet called Firebreak, and their latest venture is Relentless Syrah, with a splash of Petite Sirah – again, from their excellent Stags Leap vines. All in all, Napa could do with a few more Shafers. Best years: (Cabernet Hillside Select) 2001, '00, '99, '98, '97, '96, '95, '94, '93, '92, '91, '90, '84.

SHAW & SMITH

AUSTRALIA, South Australia, Adelaide Hills
♂ *Merlot, Syrah (Shiraz)*
♀ *Sauvignon Blanc, Chardonnay, Riesling*

Michael Hill-Smith MW (Australia's first Master of Wine) and his cousin, peripatetic winemaker Martin Shaw, founded a vibrant, internationally focused business in 1989 making one of Australia's first truly tangy Sauvignon Blancs, a trail-blazing unoaked Chardonnay, and an utterly convincing, complex pear, citrus, nut and cream-influenced Reserve Chardonnay. Since completing a new winery in 2000, and with 28ha (69 acres) of ADELAIDE HILLS vineyards coming on line, the Reserve Chardonnay is now from their Woodside site and renamed M3 Vineyard. They've also started on Merlot, and want to get moving next on Riesling and Pinot Noir. And I'm sure they will.

SHAW & SMITH
This Adelaide Hills winery makes wines of great definition and flavour, including tangy, fresh Sauvignon Blanc for drinking as young as possible.

JOSÉ MARIA DA FONSECA
Moscatel has been growing on the slopes of Setúbal since the Roman times. Trilogia is a limited-release blend of three outstanding 20th-century vintages (1900, 1934 and 1965) of Moscatel from José Maria da Fonseca, one of Portugal's most go-ahead wineries.

SICILIA & SOUTHERN ITALY

ON A FIRST VISIT TO SICILY (Sicilia in Italian) the island can seem harsh and barren. Travelling through the interior seems to take forever, with not a sign of habitation, just an endless succession of mountainous rocks. The lack of enchantment will not last long, however. Those craggy lumps soon stop looking bleak and start to appear austerely magnificent. And when finally one discovers the island's proudly maintained villages, vivid colours and flowers are everywhere and in the countryside the stunning straw-coloured swathes of wheat (Sicily was once called the bread-basket of Europe) make a vivid contrast with the vistas of olive trees with their silver-grey leaves glistening under the burning sun.

The Sicilians haven't worried too much in the past about bringing their wines into the DOC net. Many of the island's most important wines, such as Corvo, Regaleali and Terre di Ginestra, have made their names on their own merits, and producers have been able to adapt their techniques and grape blends freely with experience. Even some of the DOCs that do exist are so obscure as to be practically unobtainable.

Despite generally accepted wine lore that cooler climates are better for white wines, hotter zones for reds, Sicily's greatest success has been with its light, crisp whites from indigenous grapes such as Catarratto or Inzolia, which suit its climate perfectly. They're found mainly in the west of the island. Reds have taken longer to find their feet, not because the local varieties such as Nero d'Avola, Nerello Mascalese, Frappato and Perricone, are inferior but because there was a reluctance to take up modern winemaking techniques quite as enthusiastically. Part of this was the esteem given by some to wines that are *marsalesi* (Marsala-like) and therefore what would today be dismissed as oxidized and faulty. But the past few years have seen some amazing developments, particularly with Nero d'Avola, Sicily's best and most original grape.

Marsala is one of Italy's most famous wines, and, theoretically, one of the world's great fortified wines, but, despite an upturn in its fortunes, there's still a lot produced that is nowhere near great now. The real dessert-wine gems come instead from the islands off Sicily: Moscato di Pantelleria from Pantelleria to the south-west towards Tunisia, and Malvasia delle Lipari from the Aeolian (or Lipari) archipelago to the north-east. They are gems not just because they are (when properly made) delicately sweet and delicious but because they are the true heritage of Sicily, especially the *passito* versions, the most typical.

'Mezzogiorno' is the general if unofficial name applying to Italy's South, as 'Midi' applies to France's South, and they mean the same thing: midday (i.e. the land of the overhead sun at noon). This is a huge area which has suffered over the centuries in a variety of ways – politically and economically. Winewise the Mezzogiorno has been a producer of enormous volumes of full-bodied bulk blenders for sale at low, low prices to other parts of Italy and Europe, notably France and Germany. It is only relatively recently – within the last 20 years or so – that the Mezzogiorno has begun to follow the Midi's lead and sell some of the millions of hectolitres in bottle. The potential is for a massive market in value-for-money reds and whites, although, while a good beginning has been made in some parts of Puglia and Sicily, a lot of work remains to be done to catch up with the Midi. The real ace – or aces – in the hand of the South are its traditional grape varieties, some of which have real personality and quality. In addition the international varieties have proved that they can achieve real quality, not to say excellence, in southern Italy.

The potential for quality in southern Italy has been shown by recent progress with fresh, dry whites, especially from Pinot Bianco, seen here on the Rivera estate in Puglia, and Chardonnay, as well as with the more famous red wines.

N

0 km 50 100
0 miles 50

Roma

APPENNINI

Bari

ADRIATIC SEA

PUGLIA

Napoli

Brindisi

Ischia

CAMPANIA

Potenza

Taranto

Lecce

Capri

BASILICATA

Salerno

TYRRHENIAN SEA

CALABRIA

Cosenza

IONIAN SEA

Lipari Islands

Palermo

Messina

Reggio di Calabria

SICILIA

Vallelunga Pratameno

Catania

Pantelleria

Siracusa

Campania
Puglia
Basilicata
Calabria
Sicilia

Main DOC/DOCG wines

1 Falerno del Massico DOC
2 Solopaca DOC
3 Aglianico del Taburno/Taburno DOC
4 Sannio DOC
5 Taurasi DOCG
6 Greco di Tufo DOC
7 Fiano di Avellino DOC
8 Vesuvio DOC
9 Campi Flegrei DOC
10 Ischia DOC
11 Capri DOC
12 Costa d'Amalfi DOC
13 Aleatico di Puglia DOC

14 San Severo DOC
15 Moscato di Trani DOC
16 Castel del Monte DOC
17 Murgia DOC
18 Gioia del Colle DOC
19 Locorotondo DOC
20 Brindisi DOC
21 Primitivo di Manduria DOC
22 Salice Salentino DOC
23 Squinzano DOC
24 Copertino DOC
25 Leverano DOC
26 Alezio DOC

27 Aglianico del Vulture DOC
28 Cirò DOC
29 Melissa DOC
30 Donnici DOC
31 Savuto DOC
32 Scavigna DOC
33 Greco di Bianco DOC
34 Faro DOC
35 Malvasia delle Lipari DOC
36 Etna DOC
37 Moscato di Siracusa DOC
38 Cerasuolo di Vittoria DOC
39 Marsala DOC
40 Alcamo, Bianco d'Alcamo DOC
41 Contessa Entellina DOC
42 Moscato di Pantelleria DOC

REGIONAL ENTRIES

Aglianico del Vulture, Alcamo, Basilicata, Calabria, Campania, Castel del Monte, Cirò, Falerno del Massico, Fiano di Avellino, Marsala, Moscato di Pantelleria, Puglia, Salice Salentino, Taurasi.

PRODUCER ENTRIES

Accademia dei Racemi, Argiolas, Marco De Bartoli, Librandi, Mastroberardino, Pervini, Planeta, Rivera, Duca di Salaparuta, Sella & Mosca, Conte Tasca d'Almerita, Taurino.

LIBRANDI

Chocolaty, black cherry-fruited Gravello, from a blend of Gaglioppo and Cabernet Sauvignon, is one of the leading wines from this exciting Calabrian producer.

COSIMO TAURINO

Patriglione is an increasingly famous, wonderfully harmonious and complex red made from late-picked, old-vine Negroamaro along with 10 per cent Malvasia Nera.

TASCA D'ALMERITA

Conte Tasca d'Almerita's large estate in inland Sicily, with high-altitude vineyards, makes some of Italy's most admired wines, including Rosso del Conte, from 90 per cent Nero d'Avola.

PLANETA

This rapidly expanding, dynamic company produces a wide range of wines from both international and native Sicilian varieties. Burdese is one of Sicily's finest examples of Cabernet Sauvignon.

FEUDI DI SAN GREGORIO

Aromatic Fiano di Avellino is one of southern Italy's most interesting native white grape varieties. This estate produces a straightforward version as well as a partly botrytized, late-picked version.

LES VIGNERONS DU SIEUR D'ARQUES

FRANCE, Languedoc-Roussillon, Limoux AC

🍷 *Grenache, Cabernet Sauvignon, Merlot and others*

🍷 *Syrah, Cinsaut*

🥂 *Mauzac, Chardonnay, Chenin Blanc, Sauvignon Blanc*

This dynamic co-operative accounts for some 6000ha (14,800 acres) of vineyard and around 80 per cent of the production in the LIMOUX area west of Carcassonne. It pioneered the cultivation of Chardonnay in the South of France and has had its members' vineyards classified into four climatic zones. A range of barrel-fermented Chardonnays, labelled Toques et Clochers, are produced from the four zones: Océanique, Méditerranéen, Haute Vallée and Autan. These exhibit quite different characters and show how supremely suited Limoux is to Chardonnay and, I suspect, a whole host of other cool climate varieties. To show what can be done, the co-op now makes a range of red and white varietal VINS DE PAYS. Sieur d'Arques also produces 90 per cent of all sparkling BLANQUETTE DE LIMOUX and CRÉMANT DE LIMOUX as well as small quantities of *méthode ancestrale*, a local sparkling wine. Most wines are ready to drink on release.

SILENI

NEW ZEALAND, North Island, Hawkes Bay

🍷 *Merlot, Cabernet Franc, Pinot Noir*

🥂 *Chardonnay, Semillon*

Established in 1997 by millionaire Graeme Avery and now comprising 106ha (262 acres) of vines, this spectacular winery brings a touch of the NAPA VALLEY excess to HAWKES BAY – but taste the quality of the wines and some of the grandeur of Sileni makes sense. The wines are at three levels: Cellar Selection for good basic reds and whites; Estate Selection for excellent oaky Chardonnay, nutty Semillon and fine, deep Merlot-Cabernet. And then there's EV – Exceptional Vintage. Dense but delicious oaky Merlot and Merlot/Cabernet Franc are the current flagships, but EV Pinot Noir and Chardonnay should follow. You can almost taste the wealth in these wines, but a rich man's folly it is definitely not.

SILVER OAK CELLARS

USA, California, Napa County, Napa Valley AVA

🍷 *Cabernet Sauvignon, Cabernet Franc, Petit Verdot*

Only Cabernet Sauvignon has ever been made here since the late Justin Meyer, an ex-monk, began the winery in 1972. The style of winemaking favours a lengthy aging regime – three

years in cask and one in bottle – for ultra-softness and suppleness. There are two Cabernets – ALEXANDER VALLEY and NAPA VALLEY – both aged in American oak and managing to be approachable when young but capable of sustained aging, even in the weaker years. The Alexander Valley Cabernet reverberates with irresistible berry fruit and velvety oak spice, the Napa Valley is still rich, but more powerful and wrapped round with typical Napa tannins. Best years: (Napa Valley) 2001, '00, '99, '97, '96, '95, '94, '93, '92, '91, '90, '87, '86, '85.

SIMI WINERY

USA, California, Sonoma County, Alexander Valley AVA

🍷 *Cabernet Sauvignon, Merlot, Zinfandel and others*

🥂 *Chardonnay, Sauvignon Blanc, Semillon*

Simi has been tossed and turned from one ownership to another since being founded in 1876, and its reputation has likewise see-sawed. The first wines were made in San Francisco by the Simi brothers who moved to SONOMA VALLEY in 1881. Eighteen-year-old Isabelle Simi took over the winery in 1904 and ran it till 1970, after which it had a succession of owners, until being acquired by Constellation Wines in 1999.

Along the way it acquired some extremely good vineyards in ALEXANDER and RUSSIAN RIVER VALLEYS and, in Zelma Long, one of CALIFORNIA's most high-profile winemakers. Long arrived in 1979 and was particularly effective in producing a string of superb Chardonnays, making the best of the estate fruit – full-bodied, ripe but savoury in a positively Burgundian way. She also produced top-quality Sauvignon Blanc. For a long time Simi reds seemed underripe and lean in comparison, but Alexander Valley is good red wine country and the Cabernet Sauvignon and Shiraz, as well as a DRY CREEK Zinfandel, are all now fine wines. Long has now left Simi and until 2003 New Zealander Nick Goldschmidt was the hands-on winemaker, exhibiting a sure hand with both reds and whites from this historic winery. Best years: (reds) 2001, '99, '97, '95, '94, '91, '90.

SIMI
Sendal is Simi's Bordeaux-style blend of Sauvignon Blanc and Semillon and is a richly fruity but well-balanced wine.

CH. SIMONE

FRANCE, Provence, Palette AC

🍷 🍷 *Grenache, Mourvèdre, Syrah, Cinsaut and others*

🥂 *Clairette, Grenache Blanc, Ugni Blanc, Muscat*

This extraordinary domaine in the eastern suburbs of Aix-en-Provence is to all intents and purposes the AC PALETTE, the 17ha (42 acres) of vineyard representing 80 per cent of the area under vine. The Rougier family has not been swung by fashions, remaining loyal to local grape varieties and traditional winemaking. The white is made essentially from Clairette, fermented and aged in barrel. It is rich, full, dry, complex and balanced but needs at least four to five years' aging and can age for ten years or more. The rosé is a fairly robust wine, best drunk with a little age and with food. The old-style red, with its leather and prune flavours and sometimes delicate constitution, is made from 13 varieties and undergoes a long aging in old wood. All three wines are likely to show aromas from the pine trees growing all round the property.

CH. SIMONE
A special mesoclimate near Aix-en-Provence, some very old vines and traditional winemaking all combine to make these robust wines. Even the rosé seems designed to age.

SION

SWITZERLAND, Valais

Sion is the centre of the VALAIS wine industry and also of industry generally in this beautiful part of the Upper RHÔNE Valley. Chasselas (known here as Fendant) dominates the vineyards, followed by Pinot Noir and Gamay for the light red blend called Dôle, but more exciting grape varieties, ranging from the traditional Petite Arvine and Sylvaner (here called Johannisberg) to Syrah and Chardonnay, produce more interesting wines. Best producers: Robert Gilliard, Mont d'Or.

SKALLI

FRANCE, Languedoc-Roussillon, Vin de Pays d'Oc

🍷 🍷 *Cabernet Sauvignon, Merlot, Syrah, Grenache*

🥂 *Chardonnay, Sauvignon Blanc, Grenache Blanc*

Fortant de France is the trade name for the wines of Robert Skalli, who is the most important wine producer in the South of France, and who is also credited with transforming the Midi from the much-derided spring of the

European wine lake into one of the world's most exciting wine regions. He has done this by using New World methods of winemaking, by cajoling the local growers to modernize their wineries and to plant international grape varieties – and by labelling his wines with the grape variety under the catch-all VIN DE PAYS d'OC label. There are three basic ranges – an unoaked range that concentrates on pure fruit flavours, a subtly oaked range of varietals and a top 'collection' range, baptized F – along with the Robert Skalli label for both top varieties and southern French appellations. Skalli also owns properties in the LANGUEDOC and CORSICA and in 2000 bought the RHÔNE merchant Bouachon.

CH. SMITH-HAUT-LAFITTE

FRANCE, Bordeaux, Pessac-Léognan AC, Cru Classé de Graves

 Cabernet Sauvignon, Merlot, Cabernet Franc

 Sauvignon Blanc, Sauvignon Gris, Sémillon

The property is one of the region's biggest at 55ha (136 acres), producing about 230,000 bottles of red and 58,000 bottles of white a year. The vineyard is primarily planted for the reds with 55 per cent Cabernet Sauvignon, 35 per cent Merlot and 10 per cent Cabernet Franc. The soil is good and gravelly on a swell of ground to the north of Martillac. The property has undergone a revolution since the arrival of new owners, Daniel and Florence Cathiard, in 1990 who restored the vineyards and modernized winemaking facilities. Only the red wine is classified but until the 1990s it was rather lean and uninteresting. A reduction in yields, careful tending of the vineyard, severe selection and aging in new oak barrels, has resulted in wine of an additional concentration, structure and elegance. From the 1994 vintage it can be ranked with the best in the PESSAC-LÉOGNAN AC. Best years: (reds) 2001, '00, '99, '98, '96, '95, '94, '90, '89.

The whites have been in the forefront of BORDEAUX's white wine revolution. Using barrel fermentation and maturation in new oak, today the château stands as a shining example to others in the region of what investment and commitment can do to a wine. So far only 9ha (22 acres) of land are planted with white grapes, which are almost all Sauvignon (there is a little Sémillon and Sauvignon Gris). The white is not classified since there were no white grapes at all when the Graves Classification was decided in 1959, but it surely deserves classification today. Second wine (red and white): les Hauts de Smith. Best years: (whites) 2001, '00, '99, '98, '96, '95, '94, '93, '92.

Ch. Smith-Haut-Lafitte's vines are superbly located in a single block on a gravel hillock – the gravel soils provide excellent natural drainage and the pebbles retain heat which helps to ripen the grapes.

SMITH WOODHOUSE

PORTUGAL, Douro, Port DOC

 Touriga Franca, Touriga Nacional, Tempranillo (Tinta Roriz), Tinta Barroca, Tinto Cão and others

 Gouveio, Viosinho, Rabigato, Malvasia Fina and others

One of six PORT firms belonging to the Symington family (the others are DOW, GRAHAM, WARRE, Quarles Harris and Gould Campbell) Smith Woodhouse is often rather unfairly thought of as a second-tier shipper. The fact is that in years like 1977, '83 and '85 its vintage ports frequently match the very best.

Unlike Dow and Graham, Smith Woodhouse is not attached to any particular quinta (although the company does own the small Quinta Madalena in the Torto Valley). Smith Woodhouse wines therefore tend to be a finely tuned exercise in blending. It is true that much of the company's output is inexpensive standard tawny, but Smith Woodhouse is also the source of some excellent value-for-money port. The company has created a niche for itself with its unfiltered LBV, which is only released when the wine is ready to drink, having spent four years in barrel followed by between six and ten years in bottle. The result is a very agreeable poor man's vintage port. Best years: (Vintage port) 2000, '97, '94, '91, '85, '83, '80, '77, '70, '63; (Madalena) 1999, '98, '95.

SOAVE DOC, SOAVE CLASSICO DOC, SOAVE SUPERIORE DOCG

ITALY, Veneto

 Garganega, Pinot Blanc (Pinot Bianco), Trebbiano di Soave, Chardonnay

The reason why the recently changed laws governing Soave have elevated some, called 'Superiore', to DOCG status while leaving others, including some of the better Classicos, behind in DOC, are too Byzantine to explain here. Suffice it to say that the flat land or *pianura* generally yields plonk and that most of the good stuff comes from the Classico hills – and in this region you need sloping vineyards for high-quality fruit. This is why so much Soave, DOCG or otherwise, remains innocuous swill with little more than an almondy hint and a slightly bitter finish. Not only innocuous, but also monothematic, not surprisingly given that 80 per cent of production is controlled by the local co-operative and bottled for various companies under different labels or sold in bulk to them.

Soave growers who have dedicated themselves to quality in recent years include ANSELMI (who introduced the international taste in Soave with Chardonnay and the use of barriques, and who has pulled his wines out of the DOC system altogether in protest at the botched laws, as he sees them), Ca' Rugate, La Cappuccina, Coffele, Gini,

Inama, PIEROPAN, Portinari, Prà, Suavia and Tamellini. Even the big producers like Bertani, MASI and Pasqua/Cecilia Beretta are coming up with cru Soaves from particular vineyards which are streets ahead of the norm. But, remember, if you want flavour the grapes must come from the Classico zone.

CH. SOCIANDO-MALLET

FRANCE, Bordeaux, Haut-Médoc, Haut-Médoc AC, Cru Bourgeois

♟ *Cabernet Sauvignon, Merlot, Cabernet Franc, Petit Verdot*

This established star estate holds lonely vigil over the last really decent gravel outcrop of the HAUT-MÉDOC at St-Seurin-de-Cadourne. The château is presided over by the beady-eyed, furiously passionate owner, Monsieur Gautreau, and the results are impressive – dark, brooding, tannic, dry, but with every sign of great, classic red BORDEAUX flavours to come if you could hang on for 10–15 years.

So hats off to Monsieur Gautreau for his dedication and for believing in his wine, which now easily attains Classed Growth quality – it achieves Classed Growth prices too. Up to 100 per cent of the oak barrels used to mature the wine are new; this is an unusually high percentage and really very rare for a non-Classed Growth. Second wine: la Demoiselle de Sociando-Mallet. Best years: 2001, '00, '99, '98, '97, '96, '95, '94, '93, '90, '89, '88, '86, '85, '83, '82.

SOGRAPE

PORTUGAL, Bairrada DOC, Dão DOC, Douro DOC, Vinho Verde DOC, Alentejo Vinho Regional

♟ *Alentejo: Tempranillo (Aragonez), Trincadeira, Moreto, Castelão (Periquita); Bairrada: Baga; Dão: Touriga Nacional, Bastardo, Jaen and others; Douro: Tinta Roriz, Touriga Franca, Touriga Nacional and others*

♟ *Mateus Rosé: Baga and others*

♀ *Bairrada: Maria Gomes, Bical, Rabo de Ovelha and others; Dão: Encruzado, Bical (Borrado das Moscas) and others; Douro: Viosinho, Malvasia, Gouveio and others; Vinho Verde: Alvarinho, Loureiro, Paderná and others*

This huge company (the largest wine producer in Portugal) is still in the private hands of the Guedes family. It was established on the back of the ubiquitous Mateus Rosé, which developed into one of the world's most successful wine brands. Originally made in the DOURO (at a winery close to the palace depicted on the label), Mateus is now mostly produced at a high-tech winery in the BAIRRADA region. Even though the Portuguese

don't actually drink it themselves, Mateus still accounts for the lion's share of Sogrape's sales.

Since the early 1980s Sogrape has been very active in other areas of Portugal and the company has built up a huge portfolio of wines. It now owns both FERREIRA and Offley PORT shippers and produces unfortified red and white Douro wines under the Vila Regia and Sogrape Reserva labels. Sogrape has also bought land in the VINHO VERDE region, where it produces four different wines: the fresh, fruity, off-dry Gazela; Chello, an authentically dry Vinho Verde; the crisp Quinta de Azevedo; and an aromatic Alvarinho named Morgadio da Torre.

Sogrape has also developed new styles of wine in Bairrada (the white Quinta de Pedralvites is exemplary), but it is in the DÃO region where the company has really made the running with a brand new winery for Grão Vasco, the best-selling brand of peppery red and crisp dry white Dão. Sogrape has expanded its range of Dão wines to include some impressive oak-aged reds and whites: Duque de Viseu and Quinta dos Carvalhais (based on Touriga Nacional). The best reds can age for five years or more.

No longer confined exclusively to northern Portugal, Sogrape has made a successful foray into the ALENTEJO, where a supple, fleshy red wine, Vinha do Monte, captures the warmth of the southern sun. Sogrape also has interests in Argentina, where it purchased FINCA FLICHMAN in 1997 and in 2002 bought sherry and port specialist Sandeman.

FELIX SOLÍS

SPAIN, Castilla-La Mancha, Valdepeñas DO

♟ *Tempranillo (Cencibel), Cabernet Sauvignon, Grenache Noir (Garnacha Tinta)*

♟ *Tempranillo (Cencibel), Airén, Cabernet Sauvignon*

♀ *Airén, Macabeo*

Felix Solís is by far the biggest wine company in VALDEPEÑAS and, according to the brothers

who own it, the largest in the whole of Castilla-La Mancha. It makes – at the top of the range – some of the very best wines of Valdepeñas and some of the best-value wine in Spain. In this predominantly white wine area, Solís has planted its own 500ha (1235 acres) of vineyards with red Cencibel (Tempranillo), plus the inevitable experimental plantations of Cabernet Sauvignon. The Viña Albali Reservas tend to be more impressive than the Gran Reservas, with a lovely oaky nose and good, meaty fruit. Until recently, the white wines have not been its strong point, but the latest examples are also delicious, particularly the aromatic Viña Albali Early Harvest Blanco.

SOMONTANO DO

SPAIN, Aragón

♟ *Moristel, Tempranillo, Grenache Noir (Garnacha Tinta), Parraleta, Cabernet Sauvignon, Merlot, Pinot Noir and others*

♀ *Macabeo, Grenache Blanc (Garnacha Blanca), Chardonnay, Gewürztraminer*

Somontano means 'under the mountain', and that is just where this enchantingly pretty region is, isolated from other DO areas up in the green foothills of the central Pyrenees. Its altitude keeps the temperature bearable, while the mountains protect it from cold winter winds. Most of the recent plantations have been Cabernet Sauvignon, Chardonnay, Tempranillo, Merlot, Pinot Noir and Gewürztraminer, which now form the backbone of new-age Somontano wines. Chenin Blanc and Riesling, also planted in the 1980s, were subsequently excluded from DO recognition and had to be grafted with other varieties – mostly the successful Merlot. Best

years: (reds) 2001, '99, '98, '97, '96, '95, '94.
Best producers: ENATE, PIRINEOS, VIÑAS DEL
VERO (Blecua).

SONOMA COAST AVA

USA, California, Sonoma County

A huge appellation defined on its western
boundary by the Pacific Ocean, that attempts
to bring together the coolest regions of
SONOMA COUNTY. It encompasses the
Sonoma part of CARNEROS and overlaps parts
of SONOMA VALLEY and RUSSIAN RIVER VAL-
LEY. At the heart of the appellation are
vineyards on the high coastal ridge only a few
miles from the Pacific. Intense Chardonnays
and Pinot Noirs are the focus. Best years:
2001, '99, '98, '97, '96, '95, '94. Best producers: FLOWERS (Camp Meeting Ridge),
HARTFORD COURT, KISTLER (Hirsch Pinot
Noir), Littorai (Hirsch Pinot Noir), MAR-
CASSIN, W H Smith, Wild Hog.

SONOMA COUNTY

USA, California

Unlike the compact and easy-to-access NAPA
VALLEY wine region, Sonoma is a big, sprawling
area that includes dozens of mesoclimates and
soil types. The climates range from the warm
areas in the northern ALEXANDER VALLEY to the
cool, often foggy and chilly regions in the
south-west corner of the RUSSIAN RIVER VAL-
LEY, Green Valley and CARNEROS.

Historically, its pioneering producers sent
their wines to Napa wineries for blending and
bottling, and in all honesty, Sonoma was
identified with cheap jug wines until the wine
boom finally occurred here. The wine boom
demonstrated just why the big companies
were so keen on Sonoma fruit – the wines had
a succulence and gentle power quite unlike
those of neighbouring areas like Napa. After
playing second fiddle for years to Napa Valley,
Sonoma County began to come alive in the
1970s when it was home to 24 wineries. It
has grown to over 200 producers today. With
room available for further vineyard expansion, its current 17,000ha (42,000 acres) of
vines already surpasses plantings in Napa. It
is now the leader in Chardonnay and Pinot
Noir acreage, and makes some of the best
of each. Fortunate to have numerous pre-
Prohibition vineyards still in production,
Sonoma also enjoys a well-deserved reputation for Zinfandel.

Among Sonoma's AVAs, the warm DRY
CREEK VALLEY is practically synonymous with
intensely fruity Zinfandel, and there is also
some lively, succulent Sauvignon Blanc. The

SONOMA-CUTRER

*The Les Pierres, from a single vineyard in the Sonoma
Valley, is the most complex and richest of the three
Chardonnays made by Sonoma-Cutrer.*

neighbouring Alexander Valley, after some
uninspiring early vintages, is now on track for
producing big-bodied, lush and lightly tannic
Cabernet Sauvignon and large-scale Merlot.

Sharing the Carneros District with Napa,
Sonoma County also has the Russian River
Valley as a prime region for concentrated, balanced Chardonnay. Improving steadily since
the mid-1980s, Russian River Pinot Noir has
come along to challenge the New World's best
regions and growers in BURGUNDY have also
taken note of the velvety smooth, black-
cherry-fruited Pinots from better sites within
this AVA. Other AVAs are SONOMA VALLEY,
Knights Valley, Chalk Hill, Green Valley,
SONOMA COAST, Wild Horse, Sonoma
Mountain and Rockpile. Even though it lacks
real precision and AVA status Sonoma
County is often used on labels by producers
who own vineyards in several of these AVAs.
Sonoma's best-known wineries are the two big
players in the Chardonnay category –
KENDALL-JACKSON and GALLO – but it is also
home to many outstanding small wineries
such as KISTLER, MATANZAS CREEK, LAUREL
GLEN VINEYARDS, Peter MICHAEL, MAR-
CASSIN, Marimar TORRES and others.

SONOMA-CUTRER

*USA, California, Sonoma County, Russian River Valley
AVA*

♀ *Chardonnay*

Sonoma-Cutrer was established in 1981 to do
just one thing: make Chardonnays of distinction from individual vineyards. Les Pierres,
from the SONOMA VALLEY, leads with depth
and age-worthiness and The Cutrer, from
RUSSIAN RIVER VALLEY, challenges it. Russian
River Ranches is blended from grapes from
five vineyards owned by Sonoma-Cutrer and
doesn't get anywhere near the other two wines
for quality. Now owned by Brown Forman
distillers, the wines are no longer that distinctive but are still among America's most
successful high-end Chardonnays.

SONOMA VALLEY AVA

USA, California, Sonoma County

Sonoma Valley has one of the longest and the
most romantic histories of any wine district in
CALIFORNIA. Franciscan missionaries planted
vines almost as soon as they arrived in 1825.
Mariano Vallejo took over the vineyard when
the Mexican government secularized the
town a few years later, and – after the revolt
that made California part of the United States
– he stayed on as a winemaker.

Long and narrow, the valley runs exactly
parallel to the NAPA VALLEY, which lies to the
east, on the other side of the Mayacamas
Mountains. While Napa grows steadily
warmer south to north, Sonoma hits its
warmest spot more or less at its mid-point. In
the south it overlaps the CARNEROS AVA,
allowing some vineyards to use either name.
In the east is a sub-appellation, Sonoma
Mountain, known for Cabernet Sauvignon.
In general, Sonoma fruit produces reds and
whites that are softer and more approachable
than Napa wines, but often of similarly high
quality. The best varieties are Chardonnay
and Zinfandel, with Cabernet and Merlot
from hillside sites also good. Best years:
(Zinfandel) 2001, '00, '99, '98, '97, '96, '95,
'94. Best producers: ARROWOOD, Carmenet,
CHATEAU ST JEAN, B R Cohn, Fisher, Gund-
lach-Bundschu, KENWOOD, KUNDE,
Landmark, LAUREL GLEN, MATANZAS CREEK,
RAVENSWOOD, ST FRANCIS, Sebastiani.

DOMAINE LA SOUMADE

FRANCE, Southern Rhône, Rasteau AC

♦ *Grenache, Syrah, Cabernet Sauvignon, Merlot,
Mourvèdre, Petit Verdot*

André Romero is not a grower who makes
many concessions to those touting the virtues
of lighter, slimmer wines from the southern
RHÔNE. His 24ha (59 acres) of vines are well
situated and the grapes routinely reach high
ripeness levels, which are translated into alcohol levels of 14 degrees or more. Romero
expects his clients to keep his wines for a few
years for their tannins to harmonize. As well as
the regular CÔTES DU RHÔNE-VILLAGES-
Rasteau, there are other cuvées, not all made
each year: Prestige, Confiance, partially aged in
new oak barrels, and Fleur de Confiance, from
100 per cent Grenache. Some of his Grenache
vines are nearly a hundred years old. All these
wines show the depth and complexity resulting
from old vines and low yields. Romero is also
a leading producer of RASTEAU, the local fortified wine or *vin doux naturel*. Best years: 2001,
'00, '99, '98, '97, '95, '94, '90, '89.

SOUTH AUSTRALIA Australia

SOUTH AUSTRALIA IS not only the engine-room but also the standard bearer for Australian wine. Thanks to the massive irrigated Riverland plantings that spread relentlessly along the banks of the Murray River, the state generally provides over half of Australia's wine. But thanks to many of Australia's most famous wine companies producing some of the country's most thrilling flavours, in the regions of Clare, Barossa, McLaren Vale and Coonawarra, for many people South Australia wine *is* Australian wine.

All the biggest Australian wine companies are either based in South Australia, or have substantial operations there. Lindemans may have its main winery at Karadoc in north-western Victoria, but its principal vineyards are in Coonawarra and Padthaway. Seppelt may have a major presence in the Grampians region in Victoria, but its most visible asset is at the end of the palm-tree-lined approach to the historic Seppeltsfield Winery in Barossa, and some of its most valuable vineyards are in Padthaway. Penfolds, Hardys and Orlando are South Australian through and through, as are Wolf Blass and Yalumba. Only the tie up of the Southcorp group (Penfolds, Lindemans and others) with New South Wales-based Rosemount breaks this pattern.

The focal point of this activity is the Barossa Valley, an easy hour's drive north of Adelaide, where almost all Australia's major players have operations. However, they largely use cheaper, high-yield fruit from the Riverland, and at one time it looked as though Barossa, one of Australia's first and best grape-growing regions, might merely become a processing centre for grapes from elsewhere. But there is a new pride in the region and its history these days; new vineyards have been established and old ones revitalized. It remains, in particular, a producer of ultra-typical, full-bodied Australian reds, with voluptuously sweet, rich fruit reaching its zenith in Penfolds Grange.

The contrast comes in the East Barossa Ranges. The climate here is very much cooler: Riesling performs superbly in the windswept Eden Valley. The red wines are tighter, yet still generously proportioned in the hands of a maker such as Stephen Henschke. Going south to the Adelaide Hills, the climate becomes cooler still. Sauvignon Blanc, Chardonnay and Pinot Noir thrive as the numerous small vineyards vie for space with Adelaide's inhabitants intent on a home in the Hills. North of the Barossa is the Clare Valley, theoretically too warm for delicate wines yet a regular producer of limey Riesling and intense Shiraz and Cabernet Sauvignon.

The next important area is McLaren Vale south of Adelaide. Here the wineries, most of them small and sitting cheek by jowl among ominously encroaching housing, are

The Hill of Grace vineyard north of Keyneton in the Eden Valley is one of Australia's most famous Shiraz vineyards. Owned by Henschke the Shiraz vines are over 100 years old and produce tiny yields of fantastic flavoured fruit.

producing a surprising range of white and red wines united by the generosity of their flavour. Glowing, buttercup-yellow Chardonnay fills the mouth with peaches and cream and Sauvignon Blanc with gooseberries and passionfruit – yet traditionally McLaren Vale is famous for dark-chocolate-flavoured reds and concentrated, pungent 'vintage ports'.

Finally, there are the vast open expanses of the Limestone Coast Zone, visually boring, but of ever increasing importance. Coonawarra and Padthaway need no herald, but the emerging regions of Wrattonbully, Robe, Mount Benson and Bordertown point the way for the future. Limestone-laced soils, plentiful underground water, and a moderately cool climate all contribute to the making of elegant, premium wines from the classic core of grape varieties, led by the cassis, blackberry and mulberry Cabernet Sauvignon of Coonawarra. During the years ahead plantings in these new regions are bound to increase significantly.

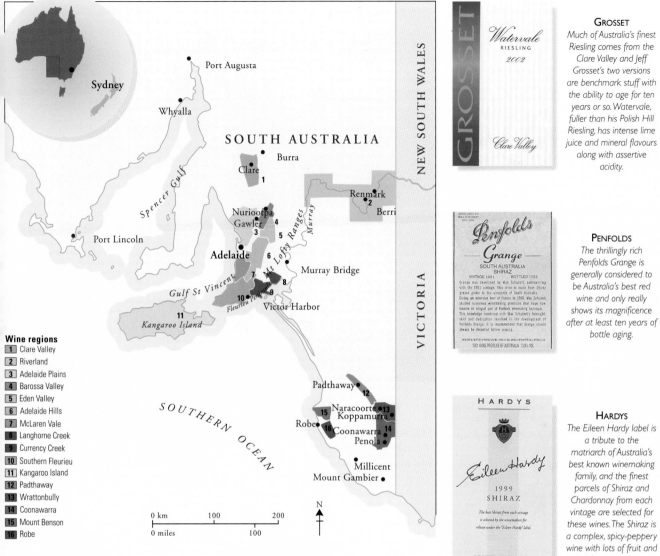

SOUTH AUSTRALIA

NEW SOUTH WALES

VICTORIA

Sydney

Port Augusta

Whyalla

Port Lincoln

Spencer Gulf

Burra

Clare **1**

Renmark **2**

Berri

Nuriootpa
Gawler **4**

3

5

Adelaide

Mt Lofty Ranges

Murray

7

6

Gulf St Vincent

10

8

9

Murray Bridge

Fleurieu Peninsula

Victor Harbor

11 Kangaroo Island

Padthaway **12**

15 Naracoorte
Koppamurra **13**

Robe

16 Coonawarra **14**
Penola

Millicent

Mount Gambier

SOUTHERN OCEAN

N

0 km   100   200
0 miles   100

Wine regions

1 Clare Valley
2 Riverland
3 Adelaide Plains
4 Barossa Valley
5 Eden Valley
6 Adelaide Hills
7 McLaren Vale
8 Langhorne Creek
9 Currency Creek
10 Southern Fleurieu
11 Kangaroo Island
12 Padthaway
13 Wrattonbully
14 Coonawarra
15 Mount Benson
16 Robe

GROSSET

Watervale RIESLING 2002 Clare Valley

Much of Australia's finest Riesling comes from the Clare Valley and Jeff Grosset's two versions are benchmark stuff with the ability to age for ten years or so. Watervale, fuller than his Polish Hill Riesling, has intense lime juice and mineral flavours along with assertive acidity.

PENFOLDS

The thrillingly rich Penfolds Grange is generally considered to be Australia's best red wine and only really shows its magnificence after at least ten years of bottle aging.

HARDYS

The Eileen Hardy label is a tribute to the matriarch of Australia's best known winemaking family, and the finest parcels of Shiraz and Chardonnay from each vintage are selected for these wines. The Shiraz is a complex, spicy-peppery wine with lots of fruit and oak influence, now made mainly from McLaren Vale grapes.

REGIONAL ENTRIES

Adelaide Hills, Barossa Valley, Clare Valley, Coonawarra, Eden Valley, Langhorne Creek, Limestone Coast, McLaren Vale, Padthaway, Riverland, Wrattonbully.

PRODUCER ENTRIES

Tim Adams, Barossa Valley Estate, Jim Barry, Wolf Blass, Bowen Estate, Brand's, Grant Burge, Leo Buring, Chapel Hill, Clarendon Hills, D'Arenberg, Fox Creek, Grosset, Hardys, Henschke, Hollick, Katnook Estate, Knappstein, Leasingham, Peter Lehmann, Lenswood Vineyards, Charles Melton, Geoff Merrill, Mitchell, Mountadam, Orlando, Parker Coonawarra Estate, Penfolds, Penley Estate, Petaluma, Primo Estate, Reynell, Rockford, St Hallett, Seppelt, Shaw & Smith, Veritas, Geoff Weaver, Wendouree, Wirra Wirra, Wynns, Yalumba.

HENSCHKE

Hill of Grace, a stunning wine with dark, exotic flavours, comes from a single plot of low-yielding Shiraz, first planted in the 1860s (see photo facing page).

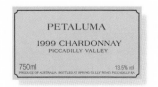

PETALUMA
1999 CHARDONNAY
PICCADILLY VALLEY
750ml   13.5% vol

PETALUMA

Made by the talented Brian Croser, Petaluma's Chardonnay from the cooler Adelaide Hills is recognized as one of Australia's best.

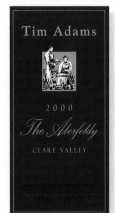

TIM ADAMS

Wines with exceptional depth of flavour are the hallmark here. The peppery Aberfeldy Shiraz is a remarkable wine from 90-year-old vines growing near Wendouree in the Clare Valley.

SPICE ROUTE WINE COMPANY

SOUTH AFRICA, Western Cape, Swartland WO
❢ *Merlot, Syrah, Pinotage and others*
♀ *Chenin Blanc and others*

High-profile operation owned by Charles Back, of FAIRVIEW. Initially the wines were made by young Cape whizzkid Eben Sadie, but he's now running his own Sadie Family Wines – and making smashing stuff. New whizzkid Charl du Plessis understands that Spice Route wine should be powerful, adventurous and memorable. Excellent Syrah and Pinotage top the Flagship Range, while the Standard Range boasts exuberant, bold versions of Shiraz, Pinotage, Chenin, Semillon, Sauvignon Blanc and several others.

SPITZ

AUSTRIA, Niederösterreich, Wachau

Spitz is the last important wine commune as you travel west through the WACHAU up the Danube. The climate is cooler here than further east due to the proximity of the Jauerling Mountain and the way in which the massive cliffs at DÜRNSTEIN block the flow of warm 'Panonian' air streams from the Hungarian plain. However, some of the most exciting and aromatic late-harvested Wachau wines can be produced here. Best producers: Donabaum, Franz HIRTZBERGER, Josef Högl, Karl Lagler, Freie Weingärtner WACHAU.

SPOTTSWOODE

USA, California, Napa County, Napa Valley AVA
❢ *Cabernet Sauvignon, Cabernet Franc*
♀ *Sauvignon Blanc, Semillon*

In the 1970s the Novak family revived its adjacent pre-Prohibition 16-ha (40-acre) vineyard and planted BORDEAUX varieties, first red then white. In 1982 Spottswoode began an enviable record for sturdy but sweet-fruited and violet-scented Cabernet Sauvignon. Tony Soter, the then winemaker, is a master at maximizing the character of different vineyards' Cabernets, and his skill was crucial in allowing Spottswoode and many other NAPA wineries to discover their potential in the 1980s and 1990s. Today, with a completely replanted vineyard and Soter now a consultant, the Novaks, mother Mary and daughters Beth and Lindy, maintain high standards. The recent Cabernets are more supple and inviting in their youth, but destined to age well for at least a decade. The Sauvignon Blanc, partially barrel-fermented and enhanced by a generous splash of Semillon, is an enticing mouthful of melon fruit and lovely figs, balanced by a touch of oak.

The dramatic rocky peak of Stag's Leap in the hills on the eastern side of the Napa Valley, has given its name to the picturesque Stags Leap District, which has built up a reputation for distinctive Cabernet Sauvignon.

SPRING MOUNTAIN DISTRICT AVA

USA, California, Napa County

The beautiful Spring Mountain District begins west of St Helena at the foothills above 150m (500ft) and continues on up to the top of the ridge separating NAPA VALLEY from SONOMA VALLEY at about 640m (2100ft). Although its pioneering winery, Stony Hill, is a Chardonnay specialist with an interest in Riesling and Gewurztraminer, the area which enjoys long summer days but cooler temperatures than on the valley floor is best suited today to red varieties such as Cabernet Sauvignon, Merlot, Petite Sirah and Syrah. These reds dominate the 161ha (400 acres) presently planted to vines. Pierce's Disease took its toll in the 1990s and many vineyards have had to be replanted. Best years: (reds) 1999, '98, '97, '95, '94, '92, '91, '90. Best producers: Barnett, CAIN, Keenan, NEWTON, Stony Hill, Togni.

SPRINGFIELD ESTATE

SOUTH AFRICA, Western Cape, Robertson WO
❢ *Cabernet Sauvignon, Cabernet Franc, Merlot, Petit Verdot*
♀ *Chardonnay, Sauvignon Blanc*

Abrie Bruwer's approach is strictly hands-off in his efforts to capture his vineyard's terroir and it's some terroir – rocky and impoverished, but blessed with great swathes of limestone – white grapes' favourite soil. This really shows in the aggressive, mouthfilling flavours of his Sauvignon Blanc, especially in the forbidding but delicious Life from Stone Sauvignon. He also believes in wild yeasts – and ancient winemaking methods – which show in his Méthode Ancienne Cabernet and Chardonnay – thick, jolting flavours, sometimes unnerving – and not all the vintages succeed! But mostly they are magnificent and certainly unique.

STAGS LEAP DISTRICT AVA

USA, California, Napa County

Cabernet Sauvignon has been the focus in this small but beautiful sub-AVA in the south-eastern NAPA VALLEY ever since its

STAG'S LEAP WINE CELLARS
This winery was one of the first in the Stags Leap District and it soon established a reputation for velvety, well-structured Cabernet Sauvignon.

vineyards were replanted in the early 1970s. CLOS DU VAL and STAG'S LEAP WINE CELLARS soon produced impressive Cabernet Sauvignons, and other wineries have since followed suit.

The AVA consisting of 1093ha (2700 acres), only half of which is planted so far, is a bit generous in its boundaries because of pressure from some large local residents, but the heart of the district threads its way east from the Napa River up increasingly steep slopes to the foot of a towering basaltic palisade. The combination of shading hills, alluvial soils, west-facing exposure and morning fogs can yield Cabernets and Merlots with sweeter fruit flavours and more perfume than those from the valley floor, which lies to the west. There is also estimable Zinfandel (Clos du Val) and above-average Chardonnay (S Anderson). Best years: 2001, '00, '99, '98, '97, '95, '94, '92, '91, '90. Best producers: Chimney Rock, Clos du Val, Hartwell, PINE RIDGE, SHAFER, Silverado, Robert Sinskey, STAG'S LEAP WINE CELLARS, Stags' Leap Winery.

STAG'S LEAP WINE CELLARS

USA, California, Napa County, Stags Leap District AVA

♟ *Cabernet Sauvignon, Merlot, Petit Verdot*
♀ *Chardonnay, Sauvignon Blanc*

As an upstart winery back in 1976, Stag's Leap put CALIFORNIA on the international wine map when its Cabernet Sauvignon bested BORDEAUX's biggest names in the now-famous Paris tasting. Famous French tasters categorically chose the best red on show swearing it was a top Bordeaux. But it wasn't. It was Stag's Leap 1973 Cabernet made from vines only planted three years before. The New World had arrived, thanks to Stag's Leap.

No flash in the pan, Stag's Leap has gone on to develop an impressive record for its various Cabernet Sauvignons. The deluxe limited edition is the Cask 23 Cabernet, a supple, ultra-voluptuous wine made only in exceptional vintages. Of similar quality is the SLV Reserve, a sturdy, classically sculpted, yet supple Cabernet from the original parcel of the Stag's Leap Vineyard. Made in slightly larger volume is the fine Fay Vineyard Cabernet Sauvignon which I often find to be the equal of Case 23 and SLV, and this is complemented by the NAPA VALLEY Cabernet Sauvignon. There's also good Chardonnay from Arcadia vineyard in southeastern Napa and as prices are high for the top wines, thankfully a pleasant, reasonably priced second label called Hawk Crest. Best years: (Cabernet Sauvignon) 2001, '00, '99, 97, '96, '95, '94, '93, '92, '91, '90.

STEELE WINES

USA, California, Lake County

♟ *Pinot Noir, Syrah, Zinfandel, Merlot and others*
♀ *Chardonnay, Pinot Blanc, Sauvignon Blanc and others*

Veteran winemaker Jed Steele was the mastermind behind the KENDALL-JACKSON popular style of wine that made the winery king of Chardonnay in the 1990s. Starting his own winery after a long dispute with Mr Jackson, Steele returned to his first love, Zinfandel.

Now ensconced in Lake County, he offers a range of Zinfandel from some of the oldest vineyards in MENDOCINO and Lake counties. He has recently turned his many talents to Chardonnay from several vineyard sources such as Sangiacomo, Durell and DuPratt, and offers Pinot Noir from Sangiacomo's CARNEROS vineyard, from Bien Nacido Vineyard in SANTA MARIA VALLEY and from other growers. Balancing ripe fruit and oak, Steele's Chardonnays and Pinot Noirs develop nicely with three to four years of aging. Shooting Star is a second label offering lower-priced wines. Steele has encouraged Lake County growers to develop Syrah and plans to make Syrah part of his primary roster in the future. A tasty oddity is Blue Franc from Lemberger grapes.

STEENBERG

SOUTH AFRICA, Western Cape, Constantia WO

♟ *Cabernet Sauvignon, Merlot, Syrah (Shiraz)*
♀ *Sauvignon Blanc, Semillon*

The oldest farm in CONSTANTIA is seeing great results from total vineyard replanting in the early 1990s and proving that it may also be the best of the Constantia producers, not only because of the high quality of the winemaking but because its wines are the closest to the cooling influence of False Bay. The result is superb consistency from year to year, which is something most other Constantia wineries find difficult. This is most obvious in the Sauvignon Blanc Reserve, firmly established as one of South Africa's best, which is smoky and flinty with underlying fruit richness; straight Sauvignon is also exc ellent, pinging with zesty upfront fruit. Semillon is likewise impressive. An irresistible, minty Merlot has been joined by BORDEAUX-blend Catharina and exciting, smoky Shiraz. Best years: (whites) 2002, '01, '00, '99, '98, '97.

STEIERMARK

AUSTRIA

This region (Styria in English), is divided into three areas: West-, Süd- and Süd-Oststeiermark. Steiermark has the distinction of being Austria's favourite wine region: its lean, austere style of wine proved a perfect antidote to the scandal-tainted sweet wines of the 1980s, and fashion has stayed with Styria ever since, inexorably raising the prices.

Of the three areas, Südsteiermark has the most vineyards (1740ha/4300 acres). It also has the best wine, particularly from Chardonnay (here called Morillon), Sauvignon Blanc, Pinot Blanc and Gelber Muskateller. Weststeiermark's speciality (with 430ha/1062 acres of vines) is a light, acidic rosé wine called Schilcher, made from the local Blauer Wildbacher grape. Drink it young and fresh. Try it if you find yourself in the region, but don't bother bringing it home: it'll probably curdle in your luggage. Most wine from the Süd-Oststeiermark (1115ha/2755 acres of vines) is sold in the local taverns or *Heurigen*. Best producers: GROSS, LACKNER-TINNACHER, E & W POLZ, E & M TEMENT, Winkler-Hermaden.

STELLENBOSCH WO

SOUTH AFRICA, Western Cape (see also pages 354–355)

East of Cape Town, this wine region is the most important in South Africa. Nearly half of all South Africa's quality red varieties (Cabernet Sauvignon, Cabernet Franc, Pinot Noir, Merlot and Shiraz) are planted in the Stellenbosch region and many of the country's finest red wines come from here. Some very fine whites are also made – one-third of the country's Sauvignon Blanc is planted in Stellenbosch and selected sites, such as those at THELEMA and MULDERBOSCH, consistently turn out Sauvignon of international standing. There are plenty of excellent Chardonnays too, although the winemaker's influence still often overrides that of the vineyard. Stellenbosch is the base for industry giant DISTELL, South Africa's largest wine company. Best producers: BEYERSKLOOF, Delaire, De Trafford, Eikendal, Neil ELLIS, Ken Forrester, Grangehurst, Hartenberg, JORDAN, KANONKOP, L'Avenir, Le Bonheur, Le Riche, Lievland, Longridge, MEERLUST, Meinert, Morgenhof, MULDERBOSCH, Neethlingshof, OVERGAAUW, RUSTENBERG, Rust en Vrede, SAXENBURG, Simonsig, Stellenbosch Vineyards, STELLENZICHT, THELEMA, Uiterwyk, VERGELEGEN, WARWICK ESTATE, Waterford.

STELLENBOSCH South Africa

THE PICTURESQUE WINE REGION OF STELLENBOSCH can be likened to a vast amphitheatre, the towering mountains represent the curve of seats, the vine-clad slopes and valley the stage and False Bay its backdrop. No wonder it struck Simon van der Stel, after whom the town is named, as an ideal spot for farming and settlement. That was in 1679; in the intervening centuries, the area has established itself as the hub of South Africa's wine industry and producer of many of the country's finest red wines. The town itself boasts many national monuments, thousands of oak trees (introduced by van der Stel) and an ever-increasing number of restaurants, never sufficient it seems to cope with residents, a university population and flocks of tourists.

As might be expected of a region covering more than 16,500ha (40,900 acres), there are many different climates and soils, one to suit each of the major grape varieties currently available and probably all the new ones starting to make an appearance. This diversity and versatility is partly due to the fact that the region's boundaries were originally drawn up along all-inclusive political rather than climatic lines. But the most famous wines traditionally from Stellenbosch were Cabernet Sauvignon – and they still are.

The historic Vergelegen estate at Somerset West lies on the western foothills of the Hottentots Holland mountains and benefits as much from the cooling breezes from Walker Bay as from those of nearby False Bay.

Stellenbosch boasts the greatest concentration of wineries of any region in the Cape and was the first region in South Africa to develop a wine route for tourists. The burgeoning number of wineries has encouraged producers in smaller, more homogenous areas within the region to recognize they have a certain similarity of style. These have mostly been demarcated as wards, where criteria for inclusion features, *inter alia*, topography and mesoclimate. There is, however, no restriction on grape varieties planted, viticultural nor winemaking practices. It is becoming noticeable that varieties that do particularly well within a ward are being promoted by the producers. Bottelary is known for red wines, Shiraz in particular but also Merlot and Cabernet Sauvignon. Stylistically, the red wines of Simonsberg-Stellenbosch are big and muscular, while those of the Helderberg, not yet legally a ward, but a continuous stretch of mountain close to the cooling influence of False Bay with its maritime breezes produces finely focused reds and racy whites.

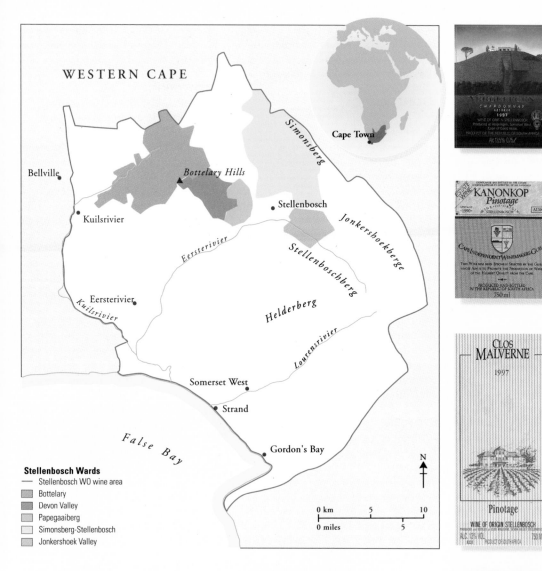

WESTERN CAPE

Cape Town

Bellville

Kuilsrivier

Bottelary Hills

Stellenbosch

Simonsberg

Jonkershoekberge

Eersterivier

Stellenboschberg

Eersterivier

Kuilsrivier

Helderberg

Louensrivier

Somerset West

Strand

False Bay

Gordon's Bay

N

Stellenbosch Wards
— Stellenbosch WO wine area
Bottelary
Devon Valley
Papegaaiberg
Simonsberg-Stellenbosch
Jonkershoek Valley

0 km   5   10
0 miles   5

VERGELEGEN
The stylish barrel-fermented Chardonnay Reserve is one of the leading wines from this stunning estate with its new, state-of-the-art octagonal winery built on top of a hill.

KANONKOP
Kanonkop has long produced South Africa's best-known Pinotage wine from mostly old bush vines. The Estate wine is vividly coloured with intense fruit and some new oak.

CLOS MALVERNE
The Pinotage grape, South Africa's own local variety, can produce powerful, flavoursome, opulently plummy wines, some of them world-class. Clos Malverne makes a speciality of the variety but now usually blends it with Cabernet Sauvignon and Merlot, to avoid any bitterness and astringency, two common Pinotage faults.

REGIONAL ENTRY
Stellenbosch.

PRODUCER ENTRIES
Beyerskloof, Distell, Neil Ellis, Kanonkop, Meerlust, Mulderbosch, Overgaauw, Rustenberg, Saxenburg, Stellenzicht, Thelema, Vergelegen, Villiera, Warwick Farm.

SAXENBURG
Shiraz is the signature variety at this historic estate founded in 1693. The headily scented, burly Private Collection Shiraz often attracts the highest prices for Shiraz at South Africa's famous Nederburg Auction.

THELEMA
From vineyards located high up in the Simonsberg range, Gyles Webb makes first-rate Chardonnay with fine spicy, toasty oak and ripe peachy, lemony fruit.

PLAISIR DE MERLE
Located on the Paarl side of the Simonsberg, this estate is best known for its red wines, including finely tuned Merlot with a touch of oak.

MEERLUST
Rubicon was one of the Cape's first Bordeaux-style reds and continues to be among South Africa's top few wines of this style.

STELLENZICHT
SOUTH AFRICA, Western Cape, Stellenbosch WO
♥ *Cabernet Sauvignon, Syrah, Merlot, Pinotage and others*
♀ *Sauvignon Blanc, Chardonnay, Semillon*

Winemaker Guy Webber aims for fruit and perfume rather than power in his wines, which he achieves more often than not at least partly due to the input from talented young consultant from BORDEAUX, Pascal Chatonnet. This would certainly help explain his success with a silky, lemony Semillon Reserve and a snappy, gooseberryish Sauvignon. Now famous for rich chocolaty Syrah from the delightfully named Plum Pudding Hill vineyard but there is also a good Stellenzicht Bordeaux blend and high-quality easy-drinkers under the Golden Triangle label. Best years: (Syrah) 2000, '99, '98, '97, '95, '94.

STERLING VINEYARDS
USA, California, Napa County, Napa Valley AVA
♥ *Cabernet Sauvignon, Pinot Noir, Merlot*
♀ *Chardonnay, Sauvignon Blanc and others*

Situated just south of Calistoga the striking Sterling winery, built in the style of a Greek island village, is a famous local landmark. The new winemaking team of Rob Hunter and Greg Fowler of MUMM CUVÉE NAPA is beginning to improve quality and consistency after a long, drab period and several changes of ownership. Merlot is the focus here, led by Three Palms Vineyard and Reserve, both impressively packed with ripe, dense fruit. Reserve Cabernet is generally good, and the regular bottling is improving, as is Winery Lake Pinot Noir, from a famous CARNEROS property. The Winery Lake Chardonnay delivers honey and apple fruit in an elegant package. Best years: (Three Palms) 2001, '00, '99, '97, '96, '95, '94.

STIEGELMAR/JURIS
AUSTRIA, Burgenland, Neusiedlersee, Gols
♥ *Pinot Noir, St Laurent, Blaufränkisch, Cabernet Sauvignon, Merlot, Zweigelt*
♀ *Chardonnay, Sauvignon Blanc, Muskat Ottonel*

Georg Stiegelmar built an international reputation for his winery and his son Axel continues to build upon it. Though the NEUSIEDLERSEE is above all a sweet wine area the Stiegelmar wines are generally dry. He makes good Chardonnay, Weissburgunder and Gewürztraminer but I find his reds the most interesting. St Laurent is a local grape and makes delicious juicy wines. Pinot Noir is also delightful here and the two varieties are blended into the St Georg Reserve. More

challenging is Ina'mera Reserve, a powerful blend of Cabernet, Merlot and Blaufränkisch. There is a Buschenschank (watering hole) in Gols where the wines may be tasted.

STONECROFT
NEW ZEALAND, North Island, Hawkes Bay
♥ *Cabernet Sauvignon, Merlot, Syrah*
♀ *Chardonnay, Gewurztraminer*

Dr Alan Limmer, an analytical chemist, is an enthusiastic promoter of the GIMBLETT district of HAWKES BAY and long time champion of New Zealand's ability to grow Rhône varieties like Syrah. Deep gravel beds provide free drainage and accelerate the ripening process by reflecting the sun's rays and retaining heat in the large river stones that litter the vineyard. Stonecroft pioneered quality Syrah in New Zealand and its lead has encouraged others, particularly in Hawkes Bay and on WAIHEKE ISLAND. They've even produced a Zinfandel and it's not bad! The winery makes intensely floral Gewürztraminer, a weighty Chardonnay with strong tropical fruit and an occasional delicious sweet wine. Best years: 2002, '01, '00 (whites only), '99, '98, '96.

STONIER
AUSTRALIA, Victoria, Mornington Peninsula
♥ *Pinot Noir, Cabernet Sauvignon*
♀ *Chardonnay*

Its not often that you conduct your first tasting of a winery's product lying on your back in the rolling surf trying to keep the salt water out of the glass. But that's how it was with Stonier. I arrived to taste, but Tod Dexter, the talented winemaker, is a surfie too. 'The surf's up,' he said, and I just knew that something as mundane as an Englishman asking him how long he kept his Chardonnay in barrels wasn't going to keep him from the waves. So we both went. I was hopeless. He was elegance personified.

And I don't know if it was the brine still sticking to my lips, but the Chardonnay with its lovely melon and cashew freshness and the Reserve, deeper, lusher but still with a classy Burgundian savouriness, tasted fantastic. The Pinot Noirs depend more on the vintage in the cool part of VICTORIA south of Melbourne, and can be a little green in colder years, but delightful at standard and Reserve level when the sun shines. They also make a rather green-streaked Cabernet and since 1999 a Stonier Cuvée fizz. This may be due to the influence of PETALUMA, who bought the company in 1997. With 20ha (50 acres) of vines and at 18,000 cases, it's the largest

winery on the Peninsula and one of the best. Best years: (Reserve Chardonnay) 2001, '00, '99, '98, '97.

STONYRIDGE
NEW ZEALAND, North Island, Waiheke Island
♥ *Cabernet Sauvignon, Merlot, Cabernet Franc, Malbec, Petit Verdot, Syrah*

Owner Stephen White believes the vinous world starts at BORDEAUX and finishes at WAIHEKE ISLAND – well, almost. The vineyards look like those of Bordeaux and, frequently the wine tastes like really good Classed Growth MÉDOC from a ripe year. Which is some compliment but no more than the boisterous Stephen White would expect. He worked in the famous Bordeaux vineyards of d'ANGLUDET, PALMER and Prieuré-Lichine (so did I, but not at the same time, and, I bet, not half as seriously as Stephen did). That's an important point about Stephen. He loves to give off this aura of sex, booze and rock 'n roll, which he does most convincingly, but he is one of the most serious wine producers in New Zealand. And it shows in the wines.

The top wine is labelled Larose and is a superb, Bordeaux-style red and one of New Zealand's most expensive wines. The second label is Airfield – and it's a good Bordeaux-style red. If you want to try anything non-Bordeaux from Stonyridge, you'll have to turn up at the winery itself where you'll be able to indulge in such delights as Row 10 Chardonnay and Syrah/Grenache. The vines are organically farmed. Best years: (Larose) 2002, '00, '99, '98, '96, '94, '93, '91.

CH. SUDUIRAUT
FRANCE, Bordeaux, Sauternes AC, Premier Cru Classé
♀ *Sémillon, Sauvignon Blanc*

Suduiraut has often been described as a close runner-up to SAUTERNES' clear leader d'YQUEM, because the wine has a viscous ripeness that coats your mouth as if the whole were wrapped in melted butter and cream. Add to this a delicious fruit, like pineapples and peaches soaked in syrup, and you can get some idea of the expansive lusciousness of which Suduiraut is capable. After a long period in the 1970s and '80s when, despite many excellent vintages, Suduiraut didn't excel, the property was bought by insurance giant AXA in 1992 and by the end of the decade it was back snapping at Yquem's heels. The 90-ha (222-acre) estate usually produces about 132,000 bottles a year. Best years: 2002, '01, '99, '98, '97, '96, '95, '90.

SUMAC RIDGE

CANADA, British Columbia, Okanagan Valley VQA
 Merlot, Cabernet Sauvignon, Pinot Noir, Cabernet Franc
 Gewurztraminer, Pinot Blanc, Chardonnay, Sauvignon Blanc

Sumac Ridge's founder, Harry McWatters, opened the doors of Sumac Ridge in 1980 and later played a key role in building the BRITISH COLUMBIA Wine Institute and establishing Canada's national Vintners Quality Alliance (VQA) wine laws. Sumac produces one of the valley's finest Gewurztraminers, a fine Pinot Blanc, and one of the country's best CHAMPAGNE-method sparklers – Steller's Jay Brut. A vineyard acquisition in the southern part of the OKANAGAN VALLEY is expanding the production of red wine, including both blended (Meritage) and varietal wines from Cabernets Sauvignon and Franc, Merlot and Pinot Noir.

SUNBURY

AUSTRALIA, Victoria

Two of VICTORIA's most historic wineries are located in this region, only 20 minutes' drive north of Tullamarine Airport. Goona Warra was built in 1863, and Craiglee the following year. After a hiatus in the first half of the 20th century, viticultural life has returned to Sunbury, and Craiglee is producing one of Australia's best cool-climate Shiraz wines – harking back to its famous 1872 vintage, which a number of lucky connoisseurs have been able to taste after a cache was unearthed at the winery. The key to the modern Shiraz is the intensity of the black cherry, spice and licorice flavours enveloped in fine tannin. Best years: 2000, '99, '98, '97, '94, '93. Best producers: Craiglee, Goona Warra, Wildwood.

SUPER-TUSCAN

ITALY, Tuscany

The super-Tuscan phenomenon started life as a high-class VINO DA TAVOLA revolt against prevailing restrictive DOC laws, in particular in CHIANTI CLASSICO; today, the laws are in the process of being altered to bring most examples back into the DOC fold, under denominations such as the revised Chianti Classico, SANT'ANTIMO or, failing that, IGT TOSCANA.

Basically there are three types of super-Tuscan: 100 per cent Sangiovese; 100 per cent French red grapes such as Cabernet, Merlot, Syrah or Pinot Noir, separately or as a blend; and Italian grapes (read Sangiovese) and French (usually Cabernet or Merlot) blended. The wines will be barrique-aged and will be at

Riserva quality level at least. Prototypes are usually considered to be MONTEVERTINE's Le Pergole Torte of the first type; of the second, SASSICAIA; and of the third, ANTINORI's Tignanello or Solaia. The law is determined that the strays will be brought back into the fold and already a vino da tavola that does not satisfy the admittedly flexible laws of IGT has no right to state a grape variety, a provenance or a vintage on the label. The first two one could do without, but not being able to state a vintage condemns a wine to looking cheap.

SUTTER HOME WINERY

USA, California, Napa County, Napa Valley AVA
 Cabernet Sauvignon, Zinfandel, Merlot, Pinot Noir
 Zinfandel, Merlot
 Chardonnay, Sauvignon Blanc, Chenin Blanc, Gewurztraminer

Though its home is the NAPA VALLEY, Sutter Home made its name in the 1970s for its robust AMADOR COUNTY Zinfandels. Yet it was an experiment in 1972 that produced a mere 200 cases of sweetish, pinkish 'white' Zin-fandel that changed the face of American wine. By the mid-1980s this had mushroomed to 1.4 million cases and now White Zinfandel sales are nearer four million cases a year. Some experiment, but many believe that this surge in demand saved numerous old Zinfandel vineyards from extinction during a period no-one wanted their big, briary reds. At least the White Zinfandel producers bought the grapes and made it worthwhile leaving the old vines in the ground. Now the real rich, dark red Zinfandel is once more fashionable. Maybe we *should* thank Sutter Home after all. Profits have enabled the Trinchero family, the savvy owners, to purchase other wineries such as Monteviña and to develop vineyards north of Sacramento for successful low-priced wines. They now have over 1255ha (3100 acres) of vineyard, much of it farmed organically.

SWAN DISTRICT

AUSTRALIA, Western Australia

The Swan District boasts the oldest Australian winery in continuous production: Olive Farm, started in 1830. It is also Australia's hottest important wine region, and was initially famous for 'ports' and 'sherries' but is now mostly a white wine region, the most important varieties being Chenin then Verdelho and Chardonnay and Muscatelle. There is some Cabernet and Shiraz. Best producers: Paul Conti, HOUGHTON, Lamont, Sandalford, Upper Reach, Westfield.

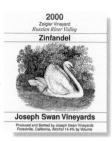

JOSEPH SWAN VINEYARDS
Old-vine Zinfandel is still a speciality of this winery. The Zeigler Vineyard, located in the heart of the Russian River Valley, was planted in the 1920s.

JOSEPH SWAN VINEYARDS

USA, California, Sonoma County, Russian River Valley AVA
 Pinot Noir, Zinfandel, Syrah and others
 Pinot Gris, Chardonnay

Joseph Swan made legendary Zinfandel in the 1970s and was one of the first winemakers to age Zinfandel in French oak. In the 1980s he turned to Pinot Noir which is now probably the winery's best offering. Since Swan's death in 1989, his son-in-law, Rod Berglund, has proved a worthy successor. Best years: (Zinfandel) 2001, '99, '98, '97, '96, '95, '94, '93.

SWANSON VINEYARDS

USA, California, Napa County, Oakville AVA
 Merlot, Cabernet Sauvignon, Syrah
 Pinot Gris (Pinot Grigio)

Swanson Vineyards has the surprisingly rare distinction of being founded by a wine merchant. Businessman Clarke Swanson was the owner of legendary British wine shipper Averys of Bristol in 1985 when he acquired a property in OAKVILLE and followed this by buying the nearby Schmidt Ranch which had some old Syrah vines. Swanson now own 56ha (140 acres) and make a good range of rich but attractive balanced reds, all from their own grapes. Swanson is best known for its Merlot, although there is also a Syrah and Cabernet-based Alexis and Pinot Grigio. Best years: (reds) 2001, '97, '96, '95, '94, '92.

SYLVANER

This grape may not be exciting (it is generally rather acidic and appley), but it is found all over Germany and Central Europe, where it is often spelled as Silvaner. Germany's FRANKEN makes some good examples. In France it is planted only in ALSACE, and even there it is giving way to Pinot Blanc as the workhorse grape, which has similarly big yields but with the added attraction of good creamy flavours.

SYRAH

Syrah, the great red grape of the northern Rhône in France, leapt from relative obscurity in the 1980s to worldwide fame during the '90s – but it largely achieved this using an entirely different name, Shiraz. This was because, though it makes such stupendous wines as Hermitage and Côte-Rôtie in the Rhone Valley, the name of the grape is never on the label. It was Australia's rapid ascent to global popularity during the '90s that catapulted Shiraz into pole position as the quality alternative to Cabernet Sauvignon, because in Australia it is the name of the grape variety on the label in capital letters that is important, rather than the vineyard region. Why the Australians call the Syrah Shiraz isn't clear – although the Iranian city of Shiraz is given as one possible birthplace of the grape as long ago as 600BC – but the grape is the same, and it makes many of the most thrilling, enthralling and unique wines to come out of Australia. And since, during the 1990s, the New World dictated terms more than the old, the name Shiraz spread round the world faster than the name Syrah. Still, the original wines to make the grape famous are from France, so let's go back there.

In the northern Rhône ACs of Hermitage, Côte-Rôtie, Cornas, St-Joseph and, in milder form, Crozes-Hermitage, it makes dark, concentrated wine, thick with tannin and hot with jammy fruit and pepper and tar that, between five and ten years after its birth, undergoes a transformation. The tar and pepper subside into a smoky, leathery perfume, while the tannins drop away to reveal a wonderful sweet fruit – blackberries, blackcurrants, raspberries, violets and plums – the black chewiness of dark treacle and licorice, the slightly bitter edge of pine. Further south in the Rhône Valley, and in the Languedoc, Syrah is used to add a dark juicy fruit and a floral perfume to many more mundane reds. It is showing powerful form in Spain, and both Italy and Greece have succeeded with it, as, amazingly, has Switzerland!

The most famous – or infamous – Australian example of Shiraz was from New South Wales' Hunter Valley, where a tarry 'sweaty saddle' pong was thought of as true varietal style. Nowadays far more exciting examples are made elsewhere – in particular in South Australia, where Clare, Barossa and McLaren Vale produce wines of enormous power but heady, giddy sweetness as well. Victoria and Western Australia also do fine versions and even New Zealand has a couple of examples.

South Africa's love affair with Cabernet Sauvignon hindered Shiraz's development there, but recent examples have shown good, quite rich style. California, too, was late getting going with the grape. Washington State is making a 21st-century bid for Syrah stardom with extensive recent plantings. Countries such as Mexico, Chile and Argentina are ideally suited to Shiraz and we'll see some exciting flavours from them in the coming years.

another era in Australian wine, while the white Marsanne – a rarity in itself – was served to the young Queen Elizabeth in 1953. The Shiraz and Cabernets have mouth-ripping tannin but enough flesh and fruit to persuade you that the 20- to 30-year wait will be worthwhile. Best years: (1860 Vines) 1998, '97, '96, '95, '94, '92, '91, '90, '87, '86, '82.

TAITTINGER

FRANCE, Champagne, Champagne AC
♀ ⚇ *Pinot Noir, Chardonnay, Pinot Meunier*

This is one of the few large independent CHAMPAGNE houses. For many years it was infuriating that the delicious, top-of-the-line Comtes de Champagne Blanc de Blancs was one of the most memorable wines produced in Champagne and the Comte de Champagne rosé elegant and oozing class, while the non-vintage Brut – the affordable one – was dull and lifeless. Well, there's been a change of direction. The non-vintage is now soft, honeyed, much better balanced between fresh acidity and spice, and showing a relatively high percentage of Chardonnay. Best years: 1996, '95, '92, '90, '89, '88, '86, '85, '82, '79.

CH. TALBOT

FRANCE, Bordeaux, St-Julien AC, 4ème Cru Classé
⚇ *Cabernet Sauvignon, Merlot, Petit Verdot, Cabernet Franc*
♀ *Sauvignon Blanc, Sémillon*

Talbot is a superb Fourth Growth which regularly makes wine above its ranking. It's a very big estate – 102ha (252 acres) – occupying a single chunk of land bang in the middle of the ST-JULIEN AC. The wine is big, soft-centred but sturdy, capable of aging extremely well for 10–20 years, going from rather rich, almost sweet beginnings to a maturity of plums, blackcurrants and cigar-box scent. A small amount of white BORDEAUX, Cailloux Blanc de Talbot, is also produced from mainly Sauvignon Blanc. Second wine: Connétable de Talbot. Best years: 2001, '00, '99, '98, '96, '95, '90, '89, '88, '86, '85, '83, '82.

TARRAGONA DO, TERRA ALTA DO, MONTSANT DO

SPAIN, Cataluña
⚇ ⚇ *Grenache Noir (Garnacha Tinta), Mourvèdre (Monastrell), Carignan (Cariñena), Samsó, Cabernet Sauvignon, Merlot, Syrah, Tempranillo (Ull de Llebre), Pinot Noir and others*
♀ *Macabeo, Xarel-lo, Parellada, Grenache Blanc (Garnacha Blanca), Chardonnay, Muscat of Alexandria (Moscatel de Alejandría), Sauvignon Blanc and others*

LA TÂCHE AC

FRANCE, Burgundy, Côte de Nuits, Grand Cru
⚇ *Pinot Noir*

Along with ROMANÉE-CONTI, la Tâche is at the very peak of VOSNE-ROMANÉE's Grands Crus, and similarly owned by Domaine de la ROMANÉE-CONTI. But there's a lot more la Tâche – 6.1ha (15 acres) as against 1.8ha (4.4 acres) – and annual production is generally around 24,000 bottles. The vineyard's position is superb, just yards south of Romanée-Conti, fractionally more southeast, at the perfect altitude of between 250 and 300m (800–1000ft). The wine is not only a sensation for the palate, but also for the brain and the heart, because this is the most sensuous and emotional of all Burgundy's great reds. Best years: 2002, '01, '00, '99, '98, '97, '96, '95, '93, '90, '89, '88, '85, '78.

TAHBILK

AUSTRALIA, Victoria, Goulburn Valley
⚇ *Syrah (Shiraz), Cabernet Sauvignon*
♀ *Marsanne, Viognier, Chardonnay, Riesling*

The Tahbilk winery is one of the gems of the wine industry in Australia. Largely unaltered since its construction in the 1870s, and still possessing a block of Shiraz vines planted in 1860 (whose wine is released under the 1860s Vines label), Tahbilk's reds are reminders of

These southern Catalan DOs are trying to catch a ray of the spotlight now shining on their neighbour PRIORAT. The DO was essentially awarded to Tarragona to upgrade its trade in alcoholic bulk wines with southern France and, later, it became an important supplier of base wines for CAVA. Terra Alta was for a long time mainly white wine country and home of the de Muller vineyard which made the Vatican's communion wine.

First, producers in the favoured Falset sub-region of Tarragona, the one closest to Priorat (and with thin soils over granite bedrock that approach Priorat's slate for quality), began producing similar big, fruity, deep red wines. Cabernet Sauvignon, Merlot and Syrah were extensively planted. The local co-operative, Celler de Capçanes, led the charge with a dazzling array of wines. So successful were they that the Falset sub-region has been promoted to the new Montsant DO.

In turn, the smaller family bodegas in Terra Alta awoke from their slumber and began turning out some of the more interesting, markedly Mediterranean whites in Spain. Fast improvement in winemaking was apparent, yet much remains to be done, particularly by the predominant co-operatives. Best years: 2000, '99, '98, '97, '96, '95, '94. Best producers: (Montsant) Josep Anguera Beyme, Celler de Capçanes; (Terra Alta) Vinyes i Cellers Clua, de Muller, Bárbara Forés, Gandesa co-operative, Vinos Piñol.

TARRAWARRA

AUSTRALIA, Victoria, Yarra Valley

🍷 *Pinot Noir, Syrah (Shiraz), Merlot*

🍷 *Chardonnay*

Local wits call Tarrawarra Disneyland; certainly until DOMAINE CHANDON came along it was the YARRA's only answer to the NAPA VALLEY. Multi-millionaire owners Marc and Eva Besen and their son Daniel have spared no expense on the winery, where winemaker Clare Halloran fashions a rich, slow-maturing Chardonnay. Her dense, dark plum Pinot Noir is high quality but equally slow to mature. New less pricy 'Tin Cows' label includes Merlot and Shiraz. Best years: (Pinot Noir) 2001, '00, '99, '98, '97, '96, '94, '92.

CONTE TASCA D'ALMERITA

ITALY, Sicily

🍷 *Nero d'Avola, Cabernet Sauvignon, Merlot, Pinot Noir, Perricone*

🍷 *Nero d'Avola, Nerello Mascalese*

🍷 *Inzolia, Catarratto, Grecanico, Varieta Tasca (Grecanico), Chardonnay, Sauvignon Blanc*

Regaleali, bang in the uplands of central SICILY, must be one of the last bastions of old-style Sicilian aristocracy. Run by Count Lucio Tasca d'Almerita and his family, this huge estate has 360ha (890 acres) of vineyards. Both red and white wines have been acclaimed as the best in Sicily, though all are classified as VINO DA TAVOLAS, and new arrivals in the area certainly rival, and may outclass these wines. The altitude of the site helps, and the fact that it is kept from over-heating by breezes and night-time mists.

The relatively simple Regaleali red and white are always highly reliable. The top red is Rosso del Conte, all punchy plums, coffee and tobacco flavours from selected late-picked Nero d'Avola grapes. Nero d'Avola also forms the base of newer blends using Cabernet (Cygnus) or Merlot (Novantasei). There is also the white, Nozze d'Oro from the Sicilian Inzolia grape whose lemony, leafy, herby taste is like a non-sweetened and non-spirity vermouth. In recent years international grapes, especially Chardonnay and Cabernet Sauvignon, have been planted and the resulting varietal wines are of great concentration and intensity.

TASMANIA

AUSTRALIA

Cool-climate Tasmania supplied the grape vines which established the wine industries in both VICTORIA and SOUTH AUSTRALIA; wine was sold on a commercial scale in Tasmania before those states' vines were even planted, but vine-growing declined by 1860, then ceased until 1956.

Now vines (925ha/2285 acres) are grown in a number of areas in Tasmania – except for the mountains in the west – but as yet results with different grapes are erratic. What is certain is the outstanding potential for high-acidity base wine for CHAMPAGNE-method sparkling wine. PIPERS BROOK's fizz Pirie is exceptional, the racily biting Jansz sparkling wine started in collaboration with ROEDERER is now owned outright by YALUMBA, and various vineyards have been planted solely to supply sparkling base wine. However, delightful still Pinot Noir can be produced, especially on the East Coast, Chardonnay is often good, and Riesling and Gewurztraminer are a delight. Best years: (Pinot Noir) 2001, '00, '99, '98, '97, '95, '94, '93, '92, '91. Best producers: Elsewhere Vineyard, Freycinet, HARDY (Bay of Fires), Stefano Lubiana, Moorilla, Notley Gorge, Pipers Brook, Spring Vale, Wellington.

TAURASI DOCG

ITALY, Campania

🍷 *Aglianico and others*

Taurasi, from well-drained, cool, hilly country well inland of Vesuvius, is often held up as the great red wine of southern Italy that exemplifies the glories of the Aglianico grape. Yet it can be disappointing, and consecutive vintages can be remarkably different, too. Most wine is sold at three years old, four if a Reserva; so don't worry, just tuck the bottle away somewhere for a few years because it really needs to age. If you lack the patience, try leading producer MASTROBERARDINO's more stylish, single-vineyard, Radici, or Caggiano's Salae Domini. Best years: 2001, '00, '98, '97, '96, '94, '93, '92, '90, '89, '88. Best producers: A Caggiano, Feudi di San Gregorio, Mastroberardino, S Molettieri, G Struzziero, Terradora di Paolo.

TAURINO

ITALY, Puglia, Salice Salentino DOC

🍷 *Negroamaro, Malvasia Nera*

🍷 *Negroamaro*

🍷 *Chardonnay*

Of the several producers of the Salentino peninsula who have emerged nationally and internationally over the past few years, most of them under the winemaking tutelage of Dr Severino Garofano, Taurino is the one which has enjoyed the highest profile.

The principal wines are red, indeed almost black, and the main grape is Negroamaro, which needs several years of aging. The range of wines is typical of the Salento area, ranging from the rich, late-picked red called Patriglione, a dark and brooding wine full of coffee, dark chocolate and raisiny fruit tones, to the relatively light, summery *rosato* – a must for any producer down here – called Scaloti, via the elegant red Notarpanaro, produced from old vines as is Patriglione, and the firm's standard-bearer, SALICE SALENTINO Rosso Riserva which has an average production of nine million bottles a year.

TAURINO

Some of the best warm, aromatic reds from southern Italy include a consistently good Salice Salentino Rosso Riserva from Taurino.

TAVEL AC

FRANCE, Southern Rhône

🍷 *Grenache Noir, Cinsaut, Clairette and others*

The Tavel AC applies only to rosé wine, but one that boasts a hefty degree of alcohol as well as a big, strong, dry taste. The Tavel vineyards, west of Orange, are fairly extensive at 950ha (2347 acres). Grenache Noir is the dominant grape and gives ripe juicy flavours to the young wine, unfortunately frequently diluted by Cinsaut. Altogether nine grapes are allowed, but Grenache and Cinsaut are the important ones. The best producers allow the grapes to soak with the juice for a few hours before fermentation to add colour as well as perfume and flavour, but too frequently Tavel is very pale orange-pink and decidedly short on perfume and freshness. Drink young. Best producers: d'Aquéria, la Forcadière, Genestière, GUIGAL, Montézargues, de la Mordorée, Vignerons de Tavel, Trinquevedel.

TAYLOR

PORTUGAL, Douro, Port DOC

🍷 *Touriga Franca, Tempranillo (Tinto Roriz), Touriga Nacional, Tinta Barroca, Tinta Amarela and others*

♀ *Gouveio, Viosinho, Rabigato, Malvasia Fina and others*

This three-hundred-year-old PORT house is regarded by many as the best. It is now the flagship brand of the Fladgate Partnership, along with CROFT, DELAFORCE and the superb FONSECA. Its vintage ports are famous for their richness, perfume and longevity. Taylor owns a number of fine properties in the DOURO including Quinta de Terra Feita, Quinta do Junco and Quinta de Vargellas, which provide the backbone for the vintage ports. The wine from Vargellas has a particularly memorable fragrance and is bottled as a single-quinta vintage port in good interim years. Best years: (Vargellas) 1998, '96, '95, '91, '88, '87, '86, '82, '78, '67, '64, '61. Wine from old Vargellas vines may be bottled separately under the Vinha Velha (Old Vineyard) Vintage Port label (1995 is the only year so far).

Taylor's rather pukka image extends to the remainder of its wines, including a ripe LBV (filtered, unfortunately, but still fairly good) and First Estate, an upmarket premium ruby. Aged tawnies can also be extremely good, particularly the 40-Year-Old Tawny – one of the few wines in this sub-category to combine both freshness and the complexity of age. Taylor's White Port (which can make a long drink with tonic) is called Chip Dry. Best years: (Vintage) 2000, '97, '94, '92, '85, '83, '80, '77, '75, '70, '66, '63, '60, '55, '48, '45, '27.

TE MATA

NEW ZEALAND, North Island, Hawkes Bay

🍷 *Cabernet Sauvignon, Merlot, Cabernet Franc, Syrah*

♀ *Chardonnay, Sauvignon Blanc, Viognier*

New Zealand has changed so fast around the turn of the millennium. So many new stars hurtle across the wine sky that it's easy to forget one of the wineries that did more than any other to establish the claims of Cabernet and Chardonnay in New Zealand and which, rather than resting on its award-strewn laurels, is now embarking on an ambitious programme of expansion. Te Mata's mouldbreaking 1980 Cabernet from vines on the slopes of Te Mata Peak, was a revelation of blackcurrant fruit and cedary perfume, BORDEAUX in all but name and since then under the top Coleraine or second Awatea label, a string of high-quality wines have emerged. Elston Chardonnay was and still is a beautiful oatmealy Burgundian wine that takes happily to ten years' aging. Bullnose Syrah is an intense peppery red and Cape Crest is a wooded Sauvignon. New vineyards at Woodthorpe in the Dartmoor Valley will bring increased volume and expansion of wine styles. Best years: (Coleraine) 1998, '96, '95, '94, '91.

E & M TEMENT

AUSTRIA, Steiermark, Südsteiermark, Ehrenhausen

♀ *Sauvignon Blanc, Chardonnay (Morillon), Pinot Gris (Grauburgunder), Muscat (Gelber Muskateller), Gewürztraminer (Roter Traminer), Welschriesling*

Manfred Tement's wines are STEIERMARK's most dramatic and concentrated. Even weedy Welschriesling is capable of giving an exciting wine in his hands. However, it is for other things that wine lovers worldwide idiolize him. The serious wines are divided into two ranges: Steierische Klassik, which is made without any new oak, and the vineyard-designated wines which are made in a mix of new and used barrels. Best of all are intense Sauvignon Blanc and the powerful, toasty Morillon fermented and aged in new oak. Best years: (Morillon Zieregg) 2002, '01, '99, '97.

DOMAINE TEMPIER

FRANCE, Provence, Bandol AC

🍷🍷 *Mourvèdre, Cinsaut, Grenache and others*

♀ *Clairette, Ugni Blanc, Bourboulenc*

Owned by the Peyraud family since 1834 but currently run by Daniel Ravier, Tempier has been consistently one of the best BANDOL estates for a number of years. The 28ha (69 acres) of vines are planted in tiny parcels spread through three communes, allowing different cuvées to be made. These contain varying amounts of Mourvèdre, but rarely less than 60 per cent. The standard wine is the Bandol Classique, followed by the Cuvée Spéciale and then the individual vineyard sites: la Migoua, la Tourtine and the 95 per cent Mourvèdre Cabassaou from 40-year-old vines. These wines have a rising crescendo of power, volume and structure and need a minimum four to five years' age and probably eight years for the Cabassaou. The rosé is one of Provence's best. There is a tiny amount of white. Best years: 2001, '00, '99, '98, '97, '96, '95, '93, '92, '90, '89, '88.

TEMPRANILLO

Spain's best native red grape is grown widely over the northern and central parts of the country. It goes by different names in different regions: Tempranillo in Rioja and Navarra, but Tinto Fino or Tinto del País in Ribera del Duero, Tinto de Toro in Toro, Cencibel in La Mancha and Valdepeñas, and Ull de Llebre or Ojo de Liebre (hare's eye) in Cataluña.

Tempranillo performs best in the cooler regions: Ribera del Duero, the Rioja Alavesa and Alta, and the higher parts of Penedès. Here, it can make elegant wines with good colour and balancing acidity, and wild strawberry and spicy, tobaccoey flavours. It is enhanced by blending – usually with Garnacha, Graciano and Mazuelo in Rioja, and Cabernet Sauvignon in Navarra, Penedès and other parts of Spain. It can be made into lovely young, fruity wines, yet is suitable for aging in oak barrels.

In Portugal as Tinta Roriz it is the most planted red variety in the Douro, where it is used both for port and unfortified wine. It is also increasingly important in the Alentejo.

Elsewhere it is fairly widely planted in Argentina, and Mexico has some fair examples. It's in California, so far without distinction, but Australia is taking it seriously and, interestingly, both southern France and Italy are planting more of it.

TEROLDEGO ROTALIANO DOC

ITALY, Trentino

🍷 *Teroldego*

The Italian red grape Teroldego is planted virtually exclusively on the gravelly soil of the Campo Rotaliano plain in TRENTINO between Mezzocorona and Lavis. Teroldego is called the 'Prince' of Trentino red wines, prized for its elegance, complexity and harmony but when overcropped, as the vine too often is, it can be very ordinary, at best a pleasant leafy wine for early drinking. The wine may be red, rosé or Superiore, the latter qualifying as Riserva after two years of aging. Nowadays the undisputed top producer is Elisabetta FORADORI. Best years: 2001, '00, '99, '97. Best producers: Barone de Cles, M Donati, Dorigati, Endrizzi, Foradori, Conti Martini, Mezzacorona (Riserva), Cantina Rotaliana, A & R Zeni.

TERRAS DO SADO VINHO REGIONAL

PORTUGAL, Terras do Sado

From a wine point of view the SETÚBAL Peninsula, south of Lisbon, is now officially called Terras do Sado. The warm maritime climate is well suited to viticulture and a number of different grape varieties flourish in the area, particularly the red Castelão. The Setúbal area has long been famous for sweet fortified wines from Moscatel. Many of the better reds, mostly based on Castelão, come from the PALMELA DOC further inland. There are three innovative producers here – J M da FONSECA, BRIGHT BROS and J P VINHOS who have helped put the area on the map. Most of the vineyards are concentrated in the north of the region on the limestone slopes of the Serra da Arrabida and the sandy soils along the northern side of the Sado estuary. Most wines are for drinking young. Best years: 2001, '00, '99, '97, '96, '95. Best producers: (reds) Caves ALIANÇA, Bright Brothers (Reserva), D F J Vinhos, José Maria da Fonseca, Hero do Castanheiro, J P Vinhos, Pegões co-operative, Pegos Claros.

CH. DU TERTRE

FRANCE, Bordeaux, Haut-Médoc, Margaux AC, 5ème Cru Classé

🍷 *Cabernet Sauvignon, Cabernet Franc, Merlot, Petit Verdot*

This 50-ha (124-acre) vineyard is well sited atop a knoll (*tertre* means 'knoll') on the highest ground in the AC, with extremely gravelly soil. The mixture of 65 per cent Cabernet Sauvignon, 20 per cent Cabernet Franc, 10 per cent Merlot and 5 per cent Petit Verdot could be expected to produce hard, difficult, slow-maturing wine, but in fact du Tertre shows wonderful fruit, with strawberries, blackcurrants and mulberries apparent right from the start. There is tannin too, certainly, but also a glyceriny ripeness coating your mouth and a marvellous cedar, strawberry and blackcurrant scent building up after a few years. It's usually delicious at five to six years old, but will happily age 10–15 years. Hopefully du Tertre's new ownership (1998) will provide the necessary impetus for further improvement. Best years: 2001, '00, '99, '98, '97, '96, '95, '94, '90, '89, '88, '86, '85, '82.

CH. TERTRE-RÔTEBOEUF

FRANCE, Bordeaux, St-Émilion Grand Cru AC

🍷 *Merlot, Cabernet Franc*

François Mitjavile was way ahead of his time when he took this unheralded little 5.7-ha (14-acre) property by the scruff of the neck in the 1980s and proved that so-called lesser 'terroirs' could produce wines to equal or indeed eclipse those of the ancient 'Classed Growth' hierarchy of ST-ÉMILION. St-Émilion is now flooded by these micro-crus, often called 'garagiste' wines because their tiny volumes could be vinified in your garage – and some of them were! These wines are marked by tiny yields, intense concentration of fruit and lavish use of new oak. Some examples became mere parodies, but Tertre-Rôteboeuf is actually on a beautiful little amphitheatre slope of limestone clearly ideally suited to quality grapegrowing and Mitjavile is a thoughtful and passionate wine man. It shows in the excellent wine. Best years: 2001, '00, '99, '98, '97, '96, '95, '94, '90, '89, '88, '86, '85.

TEXAS

USA

Vineyards came to Texas during the wine boom of the 1970s, as they did to most parts of the USA and it is now the fifth largest wine-producing state in the USA. This success has been something of a surprise to many who cast glances across the mostly parched landscapes – seemingly fit only for cowboy movies – and thought, 'No, never'. Never say 'never' when it comes to Texas.

There is no place like Texas to hide 1335ha (3300 acres) of anything. The most significant areas are the Texas High Plains AVA (Lubbock and surrounds), Trans-Pecos (centred on Midland), largely because of a University of Texas-Cordier joint venture called Domaine Cordier, and the Hill Country (north and west of Austin). The rest of the vineyards are scattered through the state. The major varieties are Cabernet Sauvignon, Chardonnay, Sauvignon Blanc, Chenin Blanc and Merlot. The state currently has 49 wineries and production will soar as the new vines mature. The oldest winery, Llano Estacado, has had the most impressive track record, especially for its Chardonnays. Fall Creek has made several of the worthiest reds to date, particularly from Carnelian grapes. Thunderstorms are a menace, capable of destroying entire crops in minutes. To be honest, Texas wines are still a fair amount of sizzle, and not an awful lot of steak. Best producers: Alamosa, Becker, Cap Rock, Fall Creek, Llano Estacado, Messina Hof, Pheasant Ridge.

THELEMA

SOUTH AFRICA, Western Cape, Stellenbosch WO

🍷 *Cabernet Sauvignon, Merlot, Syrah (Shiraz) and others*

🍷 *Sauvignon Blanc, Chardonnay and others*

From the first vintage in 1987, this former fruit farm has shown that South Africa can make world-class wine. The priority here is always quality fruit; these high mountain vineyards have won as many awards as the wines. The owner/winemaker Gyles Webb brings a very international perspective to wine: he has travelled to most of the world's major wine regions and tastes widely. He also calls on the viticultural expertise of Californian, Phil Freese. Both Cabernet Sauvignon and Merlot have intense rather BORDEAUX-style fruit and good structure with a distinctive hint of mint. Barrel-fermented Chardonnay has juicy yet firm, nutty, limy complexity; the Sauvignon Blanc bursts with vigour and tangy fruit, while the Riesling is delicate and dryish. Best years: (Cabernet Sauvignon) 2000, '99, '98, '97, '96, '95, '94, '93, '92, '91; (Chardonnay) 2001, '00, '99, '98, '97, '96.

THERMENREGION

AUSTRIA, Niederösterreich

This area used to be called GUMPOLDSKIRCHEN und Vöslau (after its two famous wine villages) but Gumpoldskirchen's sweetish whites went out of fashion following Austria's diethylene glycol scandal in the 1980s, and the new wine law paid tribute to the local thermal spas. Today Thermenregion, with 2332ha (5762 acres) produces far more dry wines than sweet, though Gumpoldskirchen still produces traditional wines. In the north of the region there is a lot of Rotgipfler and Zierfandler, both white; in the south there is more red, generally fairly light, cherryish wine from Blauer Portugieser. Best years: (sweet whites) 2000, '99, '98, '96, '95. Best producers: Biegler, Fischer, Hofer, Johanneshof, G Schellmann, Stadlmann.

THIRTY BENCH WINERY

CANADA, Ontario, Niagara Peninsula VQA
♟ *Merlot, Cabernet Sauvignon, Cabernet Franc, Pinot Noir*
♟ *Vidal, Cabernet Franc*
♀ *Riesling, Chardonnay, Gewurztraminer and others*

Thirty Bench has three winemakers – which might seem excessive until you realize one is a physician specializing in cholesterol control, one's a Professor of Geography and Economics and the third runs a busy winemaking shop, and none of them have a lot of time to spare. Or to argue, it seems, because the 12-ha (30-acre) Thirty Bench vineyard, on the Beamsville Bench, has made a remarkable reputation, in particular for Icewine but also for Dry Riesling and Chardonnay and reds from Pinot Noir, Merlot and the Cabernets.

THIRTY BENCH
Close to 80 per cent of production at Thirty Bench on the Niagara Peninsula is Riesling, including an elegant, almost Germanic style Icewine full of lychees, pear and apricot aromas.

DOMAINE THOMAS-MOILLARD

FRANCE, Burgundy, Côte de Nuits, Nuits-St-Georges
♟ *Pinot Noir*
♀ *Chardonnay*

This is the label for wines from the family-owned vineyards of the *négociant* house Moillard-Grivot. The best wines, including ROMANÉE-ST-VIVANT and BONNES-MARES, are very fine, in an old-fashioned, long-lived, robust style. Other good reds include NUITS-ST-GEORGES Clos de Thorey, BEAUNE Grèves and VOSNE-ROMANÉE Malconsorts. Red and white BOURGOGNE HAUTES-CÔTES DE NUITS stand out at the simpler end of the range. Best years: (top reds) 2002, '01, '00, '99, '98, '97.

THREE CHOIRS

ENGLAND, Gloucestershire
♟ *Regent, Rondo, Triomph, Pinot Noir*
♟ *Pinot Noir, Regent*
♀ *Seyval Blanc, Phoenix, Reichensteiner, Siegerrebe, Bacchus and others*

Along with THAMES VALLEY, Three Choirs is one of the leaders of quality English wine. There are 30ha (75 acres) of vines between the three cathedral cities of Gloucester, Hereford and Worcester, where the Three Choirs music festival takes place every summer. The wine ranges from a CHAMPAGNE-method fizz from Seyval Blanc and Pinot Noir through to a white New Release – available to coincide with each year's BEAUJOLAIS Nouveau – to Late-Harvest Siegerrebe when the vintage permits, and surprisingly good tangy Bacchus.

TICINO

SWITZERLAND

Merlot was introduced into this Italian-speaking Swiss canton in the late nineteenth century, and has flourished ever since. It can make juicy, attractive wines which generally sell at what for Switzerland are reasonable prices; the letters VITI on the label are held to be a guarantee of quality. Recent vintages have seen some impressive oaked examples. Other grapes, generally a mixture of Italian varieties, are blended into Nostrano, a cheaper everyday wine. Best years: 2000, '97, '96. Best producers: Agriloro, Guido Brivio, Gialdi (Sassi Grossi), Daniele Huber, Rovio Ronco, Tamborini, Christian ZÜNDEL.

TIEFENBRUNNER-SCHLOSS TURMHOF

ITALY, Alto Adige, Alto Adige DOC
♟♟ *Cabernet Sauvignon, Cabernet Franc, Lagrein and others*
♀ *Gewürztraminer (Traminer Aromatico), Chardonnay, Pinot Gris (Pinot Grigio), Pinot Blanc (Pinot Bianco) and others*

Schloss Turmhof has been the Tiefenbrunner home for over 150 years. The current owner Herbert Tiefenbrunner is probably the longest-serving *Kellermeister* in Italy, celebrating his 60th anniversary in that role in 2003; and while, today, he has yielded much ground to his son Christof, he can still be found wearing his cellarmaster's blue apron whenever you turn up for a tasting.

The house of Tiefenbrunner, having a thriving in-house tourist trade in the form of busloads of Austrians and Germans, offers a vast range of wines covering every South Tyrolean possibility – red, white and pink

wines from Germanic, French and local varieties, from its own 20ha (50 acres) of vines and also from bought-in grapes. Somehow it manages to keep track of it all, turning out excellent wines under both the Linticlarus and Castel Turmhof labels. Feldmarschall von Fenner is a steely, elegantly perfumed Müller-Thurgau.

TOCAI FRIULANO

Unrelated to Hungary's TOKAJI wine and ALSACE's Tokay-Pinot Gris, the Italian white grape Tocai produces the white 'jug wine' of the plains of FRIULI in north-east Italy. It is also one of Friuli's prized native varieties but only when pruned hard does the resulting wine have enough stuffing to allow its alluring, broad, nut-cream, oily, appley, slightly figgy character to emerge. It flourishes throughout Friuli and in central and eastern VENETO. A few Californians are trying to prove Tocai has a bright future there too. Best producers: Borgo San Daniele, BORGO DEL TIGLIO, Dorigo, Drius, Livio FELLUGA, JERMANN, Edi Keber, Miani, Princic, Paolo Rodaro, Ronchi di Manzano, Ronco del Gelso, RUSSIZ SUPERIORE, SCHIOPETTO, Specogna, Le Vigne di Zamò, Villa Russiz.

TOKAJI

HUNGARY, Tokaj-Hegyalja
♀ *Furmint, Hárslevelü, Muskat Ottonel (Muskotály)*

This potentially wonderful, and historic wine, drunk by Russia's Tsars, comes from a small hilly area of north-east Hungary. To make Tokaji Aszú, those grapes affected by botrytis (or *aszú*) are separated from the rest, and collected in a wooden tub, or *puttonyos*; their free-run juice is called *essencia*, and makes the finest Tokaji of all. The grapes are then mashed to a pulp and added to a 140-litre cask, or *gönc*, of dry wine. The result can, accordingly, be described as 2, 3, 4, 5 or 6 Puttonyos, depending on how much pulp was added (two is never made and six only in good years). There is also Szamorodni, which is Tokaji from which the *aszú* grapes were not separated out; it can be sweet (*édes*) or dry (*száraz*).

A wave of Western investment since Hungary's independence, notably from Spain and France, precipitated a new range of more modern styles and higher quality. There is considerable variation between vintages; Tokaji should be sold ready to drink but can last a very long time. Best years: 2000, '99, '97, '93. Best producers: Disznókö, Château Megyer, Oremus, Château Pajzos, ROYAL TOKAJI WINE CO, István Szepsy, Tokaji Kereskedöház.

DOMAINE TOLLOT-BEAUT & FILS
FRANCE, Burgundy, Côte de Beaune, Chorey-lès-Beaune AC

🍷 Pinot Noir

🍷 Chardonnay

This family-owned estate became well known in the USA before World War Two, and has also enjoyed a firm following in the UK. Most of the vineyards are fairly modest – in ALOXE-CORTON, CHOREY and SAVIGNY – but there are also impressive holdings in BEAUNE (Clos du Roi and Grèves) and CORTON, both red and white. The wines are rarely in the first rank, but they are very well made, nicely balanced, stylishly oaked and very reasonably priced. Even the basic village wines have a gentleness of fruit and a charming slightly sweet oaked texture. The Cortons are particularly good value, combining high quality with modest prices; and at the other end of the price scale, the Premier Cru Savigny Champs Chevrey is worth seeking out. Best years: (reds) 2002, '01, '99, '98, '97, '96, '95.

TORGIANO DOC, TORGIANO RISERVA DOCG
ITALY, Umbria

🍷🍷 Sangiovese, Canaiolo and others

🍷 Chardonnay, Pinot Gris (Pinot Grigio), Welschriesling (Riesling Italico) and others

This famous UMBRIAN wine zone near Perugia is effectively dominated by one producer, LUNGAROTTI. The red Riserva wine was elevated to DOCG status in 1990, with a requirement that it be aged for at least three years, although Lungarotti gives its Vigna Monticchio nearer to ten. In 1990 the Torgiano DOC was revised to include various wines: Rosso, Cabernet Sauvignon, Pinot Nero, Rosato, Bianco, Chardonnay, Pinot Grigio, Riesling Italico and Spumante. The principal wine is the Rosso, best known under the Lungarotti brand name of Rubesco.

TORO DO
SPAIN, Castilla y León

🍷 Tempranillo (Tinta de Toro), Grenache Noir (Garnacha Tinta), Cabernet Sauvignon, Merlot

🍷 Verdejo, Malvasía

Bordering RUEDA to the north-west and bisected by the Duero river, Toro became a DO in 1987 and for years it had only one winemaking star, originally known as Bodegas Porto, now as Bodegas Fariña. Fariña's reds are big and fairly alcoholic, but well made, fruity and oaky – and reasonably cheap. General standards in Toro are on the up, however. The flat Toro countryside is lower, hotter and drier than nearby RIBERA DEL DUERO and yields are very low indeed. The reds tend to be darker, more tannic, more alcoholic, lower in acidity and less fine but bursting with flavour (but also vastly cheaper). When VEGA SICILIA, MAURO, Sierra Cantabria and other reputed wineries launched subsidiaries in Toro it became obvious that this region had become one of Spain's new stars. There is a tiny amount of rosé and white. Best producers: Alquiriz (Vega Sicilia), Dos Victorias, Frutos Villar (Muruve), Quinta de la Quietud, Telmo RODRÍGUEZ, San Román, Vega Saúco, Vega de Toro/Señorío de San Vicente (Numanthia).

TORRES
SPAIN, Cataluña, Penedès DO

🍷 Tempranillo, Grenache Noir (Garnacha Tinta), Carignan (Cariñena), Cabernet Sauvignon and others

🍷 Grenache Noir (Garnacha Tinta), Carignan (Cariñena)

🍷 Parellada, Gewürztraminer, Sauvignon Blanc, Xarel-lo, Macabeo, Chardonnay and others

Since his return from studying wine in France in 1971, Miguel Torres has worked relentlessly on the family wines, as well as masterminding vineyards in CALIFORNIA and Chile (see Miguel TORRES).

Bodegas Torres is now Spain's largest independent wine company with 600ha (1483 acres) of vines, mostly Parellada and Tempranillo, but also including French varieties. About half its grape needs (mostly the local Catalan varieties) are bought from local growers. Viña Sol is an excellent snappy quaffing white, Viña Esmeralda is a spicy, off-dry blend of Muscat Blanc à Petits Grains and Gewürztraminer, Waltraud is a floral, fragrant Riesling, and Fransola is a rich, grassy, oaky Sauvignon Blanc and Parellada blend. His top white wine achievement has been the lovely, rich, barrel-fermented Chardonnay from the company's Milmanda vineyard in neighbouring CONCA DE BARBERÀ.

Red wines include Tres Torres and Gran Sangredetoro, Coronas (Tempranillo), soft, oaky Gran Coronas (Cabernet and Tempranillo) and Viña Magdala (Pinot Noir and Tempranillo). A single-vineyard wine, Mas La Plana, is made from Cabernet Sauvignon. The Grans Muralles vineyard in Conca de Barberà, with only old Catalan varieties, and new vineyards in PRIORAT are the latest initiatives. Quality of the whites is very high, but reds are frequently disappointing. Best years: (Mas la Plana) 1996, '95, '94, '91, '90, '88, '87, '83, '81, '79, '76.

MARIMAR TORRES
Named in honour of the late patriarch of the Torres family, the Don Miguel Vineyard provides Chardonnay and Pinot Noir for Marimar Torres' estate wines.

MARIMAR TORRES
USA, California, Sonoma County, Sonoma-Green Valley AVA

🍷 Pinot Noir

🍷 Chardonnay

Sister of Miguel TORRES, Marimar selected a cool vineyard site in the far west of SONOMA COUNTY. Adhering to the European concept of viticulture (vines packed tightly together for stress and low yields) she has planted 23ha (57 acres) of vines. Concentrated, but closed-in when young, her Chardonnays blossom with two to three years' aging. Along with typical cherry fruit and spice, her Pinot Noirs are becoming more complex with each vintage, showing a chalky, mineral side that adds charm and intrigue. Her latest venture is a *very* cool vineyard out towards the coast – and she has 0.2ha (0.5 acres) of Parellada to remind her of CATALUÑA – but it *never* ripens. Best years: 2001, '00, '99, '98, '97, '95, '94.

MIGUEL TORRES
CHILE, Curicó Valley

🍷🍷 Cabernet Sauvignon, Merlot, Carignan (Cariñena)

🍷 Sauvignon Blanc, Riesling, Gewurztraminer, Chardonnay

Miguel TORRES' place in the firmament of great winemakers would have been assured had he never left Spain – but seduced by Chile's near-perfect viticultural conditions and no phylloxera he then set about transforming winemaking there. When he arrived in 1979, winemaking was as it had been more or less for a century, sleepy and slapdash. He led the way with technical innovation and it did not take long before all of Chile, and then Argentina, had copied him. His fame is well-founded, although his wines in Chile no longer command the high ground. His Manso de Velasco premium Cabernet, made from very old vines, is fine wine as is his Cordillera from old Carignan. His Sauvignon Blanc is bone dry and suitably aggressive. Best years: (Manso) 2000, '99, '97, '95.

TOSCANA (Tuscany) Italy

This evocative Tuscan scene of vines interspersed with olives and the occasional cypress grove is of La Rancia vineyard near Castelnuovo Berardenga which belongs to a leading Chianti Classico producer, Fattoria di Felsina.

FOR MANY PEOPLE CENTRAL TUSCANY represents Italy. Steep rolling hills in all shades of green, tall cypresses, delicate olive trees, sturdy vines and pretty stone houses all combine to form a captivating scene. Wine is central to the culture – the vine has been cultivated here for nearly 3000 years and Tuscan wines today include some of Italy's best. The atmosphere in Tuscany is a heady mix of respect for wine traditions, regard for quality and enthusiasm for innovation.

Central to Tuscany – and not just geographically – is Chianti. Barely a generation ago it typified the worst of Italian wine: cheap, acidic and sold in a wicker-covered flask aptly called a *fiasco*. Now the *fiaschi* are gone, yields have plummeted, white grapes have all but gone from the blend and new investment has massively improved producers' understanding of the Sangiovese grape. High-calibre Chianti is now abundant, mainly in the Classico zone but also in Rufina, a small area east of Florence. And prices have soared.

Most Chianti producers are deeply wedded to Sangiovese, some using nothing else for their Chianti and many making a separate super-Tuscan solely from the grape. There are also numerous Sangiovese/Cabernet Sauvignon super-Tuscans and a few based either on Cabernet Sauvignon or Merlot, grapes that have also infiltrated into a number of Chiantis. Almost all these wines are barrique-aged.

But Tuscany is far more than just Chianti. Brunello di Montalcino and Vino Nobile di Montalcino to the south, and Carmignano to the west, all show Sangiovese at its classiest and Morellino di Scansano from the south-west in the Maremma emphasizes its chewy fruit. A fast-developing area for high-quality reds is the coastal zone, from Pisa to south of Grosseto. In the northern section, mainly in the province of Livorno, French varieties thrive in the communes of Bolgheri and Montescudaio. Farther south, the boom is on in areas like Scansano, mainly based on Sangiovese, which there comes that bit riper and plummier than from the higher vineyards of central Tuscany.

Striking whites come mainly from the native Vernaccia and imported Chardonnay and Viognier, sometimes barrique-aged. In the coastal areas there is an increasingly impressive resurgence of white wines based on Vermentino, often associated more with Sardinia and Liguria. The traditional Trebbiano and Malvasia are rapidly giving way to higher-quality varieties, except in the case of Vin Santo where they work beautifully.

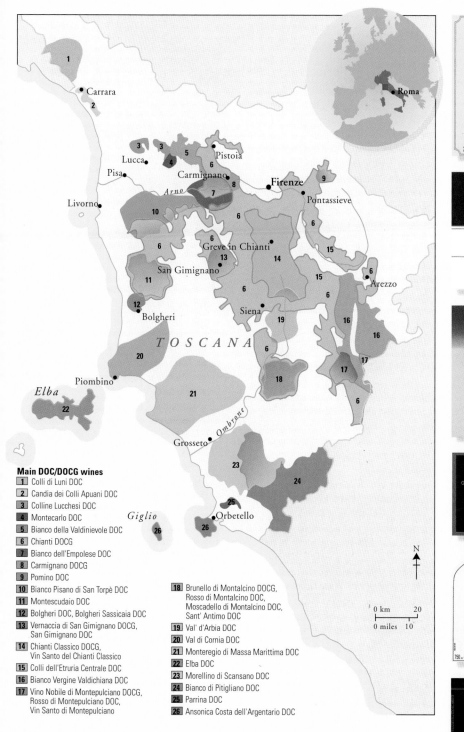

Main DOC/DOCG wines

1. Colli di Luni DOC
2. Candia dei Colli Apuani DOC
3. Colline Lucchesi DOC
4. Montecarlo DOC
5. Bianco della Valdinievole DOC
6. Chianti DOCG
7. Bianco dell'Empolese DOC
8. Carmignano DOCG
9. Pomino DOC
10. Bianco Pisano di San Torpè DOC
11. Montescudaio DOC
12. Bolgheri DOC, Bolgheri Sassicaia DOC
13. Vernaccia di San Gimignano DOCG, San Gimignano DOC
14. Chianti Classico DOCG, Vin Santo del Chianti Classico
15. Colli dell'Etruria Centrale DOC
16. Bianco Vergine Valdichiana DOC
17. Vino Nobile di Montepulciano DOCG, Rosso di Montepulciano DOC, Vin Santo di Montepulciano
18. Brunello di Montalcino DOCG, Rosso di Montalcino DOC, Moscadello di Montalcino DOC, Sant' Antimo DOC
19. Val' d'Arbia DOC
20. Val di Cornia DOC
21. Monteregio di Massa Marittima DOC
22. Elba DOC
23. Morellino di Scansano DOC
24. Bianco di Pitigliano DOC
25. Parrina DOC
26. Ansonica Costa dell'Argentario DOC

REGIONAL ENTRIES

Bolgheri, Brunello di Montalcino, Carmignano, Chianti, Chianti Classico, Chianti Rufina, Morellino di Scansano, Pomino, Rosso di Montalcino, Rosso di Montepulciano, Sassicaia, Super-Tuscan, Vernaccia di San Gimignano, Vin Santo, Vino Nobile di Montepulciano.

PRODUCER ENTRIES

Castello di Ama, Antinori, Argiano, Avignonesi, Badia a Coltibuono, Castello Banfi, Biondi-Santi, Boscarelli, Castello di Brolio, Felsina, Castello di Fonterutoli, Fontodi, Frescobaldi, Isole e Olena, Montevertine, Ornellaia, Pieve Santa Restituta, Poliziano, Querciabella, Castello dei Rampolla, Ruffino, Selvapiana, Villa Cafaggio, Castello di Volpaia.

SASSICAIA

Since the first release of the 1968 vintage, this wine has consistently proved itself to be one of the world's great Cabernets. It was recently granted a special DOC under the Bolgheri appellation.

FONTODI

The Flaccianello della Pieve super-Tuscan is from a single vineyard of old vines and has shown the world what the Sangiovese grape can achieve on its own.

CASTELLO DI AMA

From this model Chianti Classico estate L'Apparita is the greatest of Tuscany's burgeoning, high-quality Merlots. It commands a phenomenal price and is almost impossible to obtain.

CAPEZZANA

This increasingly fine wine is another Tuscan mould-breaking red from Capezzana in the Carmignano zone.

RIECINE

This tiny, high-altitude estate in Gaiole has long made outstanding Chianti Classico, Reserva and La Gioia from low yields.

BIONDI-SANTI

This estate helped forge the international reputation of Brunello di Montalcino.

AVIGNONESI

Long years in small barrels have made this wine one of the most sought-after Vin Santos, the traditional dessert wines of Tuscany.

CH. LA TOUR BLANCHE

FRANCE, Bordeaux, Sauternes AC, Premier Cru
Classé

♀ *Sémillon, Sauvignon Blanc, Muscadelle*

In the 1855 classification of BORDEAUX wines la Tour Blanche was classified first of the First Growths just behind Ch. d'YQUEM but until the mid-1980s it rarely justified this status. Now, thanks to a major re-think in the vineyards and the winery and a generous investment in new oak barrels for fermentation and aging, the wines are again among the best in the AC, rich and unctuous with a generous but elegant underpin of oak. The 34-ha (84-acre) estate, which is owned by the French Ministry of Agriculture, is planted with 77 per cent Sémillon, 20 per cent Sauvignon Blanc and 3 per cent Muscadelle, the latter adding a little exotic fruitiness to the blend. Second wine: les Charmilles de la Tour Blanche. Best years: 2002, '01, '99, '98, '97, '96, '95, '90, '89, '88, '86.

CH. TOUR DES GENDRES

FRANCE, South-West, Bergerac AC

♂ ♀ *Merlot, Cabernet Sauvignon, Cabernet Franc,*
Malbec (Cot)

♀ *Sémillon, Sauvignon Blanc, Muscadelle*

This is now the benchmark domaine in the BERGERAC AC. Owner Luc de Conti vinifies with as much sophistication as is found in the BORDEAUX Crus Classés. The 40-ha (100-acre) domaine is split evenly between red and white wines. The white Cuvée des Conti is Sémillon with a dash of Muscadelle, vinified in vat and aged on lees, while the Moulin des Dames is a blend of 60 per cent Sémillon with Sauvignon Blanc and Muscadelle, fermented and aged in 70 per cent new oak barrels.

The top red, Moulin des Dames, comes from a 6-ha (15-acre) *clos* heading towards biodynamic farming and is made mainly from Cabernet Franc and aged for 18 months in 60 per cent new oak barrels. The la Gloire de Mon Père is mainly Merlot. The wines are best drunk with between three and four years' age but will surely age if you want them to. Best years: (la Gloire de Mon Père) 2001, '00, '99, '98, '97, '96, '95, '94, '90, '89, '88.

TOURAINE AC

FRANCE, Loire

♂ *Gamay, Cabernet Franc, Malbec (Cot), Cabernet*
Sauvignon, Pineau d'Aunis, Pinot Noir

♂ *Grolleau, Pineau d'Aunis*

♀ *Sauvignon Blanc, Chenin Blanc, Chardonnay*

Touraine is the most interesting of the LOIRE's wine regions. All the best wines have their own specific appellations – the red ACs are CHINON, BOURGUEIL and ST-NICOLAS-DE-BOURGUEIL; the chief white ACs are VOUVRAY, MONTLOUIS and Jasnières. However, there is still a large amount of wine, which merely qualifies for the Touraine AC, covering a large area of the Loire Valley to the east and west of Tours, the region's capital.

The red grapes used reflect Touraine's position on the Loire, between the wine cultures of BORDEAUX and BURGUNDY. The Loire grapes Grolleau and Pineau d'Aunis are used for rosé only, whereas the Bordeaux grapes Cabernet Sauvignon, Cabernet Franc and Malbec (here known as Cot), the Pinot Noir from Burgundy and the Gamay from BEAUJOLAIS are used for rosés and reds. Although most of the reds are from Gamay and in hot years can be juicy, rough-fruited wines, the best are often made from Cot, especially if the vigneron has old vines. Touraine Tradition is a blend of Cabernet, Cot and Gamay. In the Touraine-Amboise AC, this is called Cuvée François I.

Fairly good white wines come from the Chenin (often called Pineau de la Loire here), but the best are from Sauvignon. Dry, tangy, with a light apple-and-gooseberry fruit and a flicker of nettly acidity, Sauvignon de Touraine can be a good SANCERRE substitute at half the price.

There are three villages which can add their names to Touraine AC on the label. Touraine-Amboise is a surprisingly good red from Cabernet or Cot, made in an area of high chalk cliffs on the south bank of the river. Gamay can be used if it is blended with the other two varieties. Touraine Azay-le-Rideau is pink or white – the rosé, based on the Grolleau, is adequate and can be raspingly dry or slightly sweet; the whites, dry and off-dry, are fair in quality. Touraine-Mesland, to the west of Blois, produces reds from Gamay which can be Touraine's best wines from this grape. The rosé is fair.

Touraine whites should be drunk young, in the year following the vintage, though Chenin Blanc can last longer. Best years: (reds) 2002, '01, '00, '97, '96. Best producers: (reds and rosés) Ch. de Chenonceau, Clos de la Briderie, Corbillières, J Delaunay, Robert Denis, Ch. Gaillard, Marcadet, Marionnet/la Charmoise, Pavy, Roche Blanche; (whites) des Acacias, Ch. de Chenonceau, Marcadet, Marionnet/la Charmoise, Michaud, Octavie, Oisly-et-Thésée co-operative, Pibaleau, Pré Baron, J Preys, Roche Blanche.

TOURIGA NACIONAL

This has long been one of Portugal's leading red grapes, having found its way into most of the finest ports as it contributes deep colour and tannin to the blend. As a result of Portugal's long overdue viticultural sort-out in the 1980s, Touriga Nacional is being increasingly revered for unfortified red wines, not only in the Douro, but also in Dão, Estremadura and Terras do Sado.

Aside from port, its full potential can be seen in a growing number of varietal wines like the impressive Touriga Nacional from Quinta dos Roques in Dão. The wines tend to be solid, foursquare, but multi-textured if softened by some new oak aging. The only problem is that it is difficult to grow and can therefore be properly described as a winemaker's rather than a viticulturalist's grape. Indeed, even inside Portugal there are hundreds of different strains, yielding wines that range from pale and insipid to dense, damsony and perfumed with violets. Few other countries so far have taken much note of this grape, but Australia, with its fortified wine tradition, is making some progress.

TOWER ESTATE

AUSTRALIA, New South Wales, Hunter Valley

♂ *Pinot Noir, Merlot, Syrah (Shiraz), Cabernet*
Sauvignon

♀ *Semillon, Verdelho, Sauvignon Blanc, Riesling,*
Chardonnay

Len Evans is a flamboyant, irrepressible Welshman-cum-Australian who virtually created the Australian wine boom of the 1960s and '70s single-handed. Or that's what *he* says. He was certainly Australia's best known wine man and for many years ran ROTHBURY ESTATE in the HUNTER VALLEY. His latest venture, in partnership with a syndicate that includes British superchef Rick Stein, focuses on sourcing top-notch grapes from their ideal regions. So, there is powerful, stylish COONAWARRA Cabernet, top-flight BAROSSA Shiraz, fine floral CLARE Riesling, fruity ADELAIDE HILLS Sauvignon Blanc and Chardonnay and classic Semillon, Shiraz

Verdelho and Chardonnay from the HUNTER VALLEY. Volume is limited to 1000 cases per wine. Len, old chum, these wines had better be good.

TRAPICHE

ARGENTINA, Mendoza

❦ *Cabernet Sauvignon, Malbec, Syrah, Pinot Noir and others*

♀ *Chardonnay, Sauvignon Blanc*

Trapiche continues to produce enjoyable Chardonnay, unoaked and oaked, some good snappy Sauvignon Blanc, some fairly rich Malbec and some interesting Syrah. Trapiche is the quality trademark for the giant PEÑAFLOR group, and as such has access to grapes from some of MENDOZA's best vineyards. Now that POMEROL wizard enologist, Michel Rolland is acting as consultant, Trapiche should be able to make the best use of these resources.

TRÁS-OS-MONTES VINHO REGIONAL

PORTUGAL

This remote wine region covers the entire north-east corner of Portugal. It is bounded on one side by mountains (hence the name meaning 'behind the mountains') and on the other by Spain. Soils are poor, mostly based on either granite or schist, and the climate becomes progressively more arid nearer Spain. There is a sub-division called Terras Durienses, which covers some of the southern part of the region. The range of grape varieties is similar to the DOURO's but also includes foreign grapes such as Cabernet Sauvignon and Sauvignon Blanc. Apart from a few Douro-based reds, the wine is rarely found outside the region. Best producers: Quinta de Cidrô (Chardonnay), RAMOS PINTO (Bons Ares), Valle Pradinhos.

TREBBIANO

This white grape takes neutrality to extremes. From its base in central Italy it has spread so far that only the border regions of PIEDMONT, VALLE D'AOSTA and FRIULI-VENEZIA GIULIA escape its insidious influence. But while it tastes of very little, it yields huge quantities. There are numerous different sub-varieties, Trebbiano Toscano being the most common and least distinguished. Trebbiano di Lugana or Trebbiano di Soave, on the other hand, does have plenty of character.

Perhaps Trebbiano's greatest attribute is its ability to retain acidity at high productivity levels which, together with its neutrality,

make it a good stretcher for both white and red wines.

In France there's plenty of Trebbiano, under the name of Ugni Blanc, but it has no more character there. This is fine for distilling Cognac and Armagnac, but there's VIN DE PAYS wine to be tried as well from these regions: generally it's light and sharp and sometimes oaked, but some CÔTES DE GASCOGNE is fruity and snappy. In Australia it used to be planted in places like the HUNTER VALLEY to provide acidity for reds, but now it mostly fills wine boxes in which the actual flavour comes from the Muscat Gordo Blanco grape.

TRENTINO

ITALY

Trentino is essentially the province of Trento, the southern half of the Trentino-Alto Adige region, whose northern half, ALTO ADIGE, fiercely retains its Austrian character. Viticulturally and culturally, the province splits at the city of Trento. To its north, the wines are almost indistinguishable from Alto Adige's; white wines are in the ascendant (except for TEROLDEGO ROTALIANO) and the feel of the place is Austrian. To the south, the atmosphere is irrefutably Italian; the Adige river valley gradually widens out and the climate becomes less sub-Alpine. The wines are softer and broader, and full reds are more important, while the overcropping found all over the region cannot be so easily disguised. Wine classifications do not reflect this division, unfortunately.

The Trentino DOC covers a wide range of red (Cabernets Franc and Sauvignon, Lagrein, Marzemino, Merlot and Pinot Noir/Pinot Nero) and white varietals (Chardonnay, Orange Muscat, Müller-Thurgau, Nosiola, Pinot Blanc/Pinot Bianco, Pinot Gris/Pinot Grigio, Welschriesling/Riesling Italico, Riesling/Riesling Renano and Gewürztraminer/Traminer Aromatico) and stretches along the river valley the entire length of the province, as do the Casteller and Valdadige DOCs. Other Trentino specialities include the rare blend Sorni, some elegant VIN SANTO and some excellent CHAMPAGNE-method sparkling wine. Best producers: N Balter, N Bolognani, La Cadalora, Castel Noarna, Cavit co-operative, Cesconi, De Tarczal, Dorigati, FERRARI, Graziano Fontana, FORADORI, Letrari, Longariva, Conti Martini, Maso Cantanghel, Maso Furli, Maso Roveri, Mezzacorona, Pojer & Sandri, Pravis, San Leonardo, Simoncelli, E Spagnolli, Vallarom, La Vis co-operative.

DOMAINE DE TRÉVALLON

FRANCE, Provence, Vin de Pays des Bouches-du-Rhône

❦ *Cabernet Sauvignon, Syrah*

♀ *Marsanne, Roussanne, Chardonnay*

Excluded by self-serving bureaucrats from les BAUX-DE-PROVENCE AC since the 1994 vintage for having too much Cabernet Sauvignon in its 20-ha (50-acre) vineyard, Domaine de Trévallon is still the revelation of Provence. Eloi Dürrbach's tradition-busting blend of Cabernet Sauvignon and Syrah aged in oak casks or *foudres* provides a rich palette of flavours combining blackberry, blackcurrant and plum with the laurel and thyme of the surrounding *garrigue*. The wines are best drunk with a minimum of five years' aging but improve with longer keeping. A tiny amount of intense, elegant white is produced from a blend of Roussanne and Marsanne and a dash of Chardonnay fermented and aged in new oak barrels. Best years: (reds) 2001, '00, '99, '98, '97, '96, '95, '94, '93, '90, '89, '88.

ERNST TRIEBAUMER

AUSTRIA, Burgenland, Neusiedlersee-Hügelland, Rust

❦ *Blaufränkisch, Cabernet Sauvignon, Merlot*

♀ *Chardonnay, Sauvignon Blanc, Welschriesling, Pinot Blanc (Weissburgunder)*

Known as ET to his loyal Austrian followers, Triebaumer makes his best wines from indigenous Blaufränkisch grown in the Marienthal site of RUST and this is one of Austria's most famous and influential reds. Old vines and an obsession with extracting everything the grape has to give result in very deep-coloured, powerful wines with an intense blackberry-mulberry character and substantial tannins. His other Blaufränkisch wines are also impressive, but mature more quickly. His Cabernet-Merlot blend is another power pack. Drink these on release or after a few years' bottle aging. The dry whites are crisp and fresh rather than exciting, but the AUSBRUCH wines from various grape varieties have loads of alcohol and stacks of flavour. Best years: (reds) 2000, '99, '97, '94, '93, '92, '90, '86.

F E TRIMBACH

FRANCE, Alsace, Alsace AC

♟ *Pinot Noir*

♟ *Riesling, Gewurztraminer, Pinot Gris, Pinot Blanc, Muscat, Sylvaner*

Decades ago, it would seem, the Trimbach family decided on the style of the wine they were going to make, and have stuck to that resolution ever since. Despite the fact that Trimbach produces close to a million bottles each year, the style has remained utterly consistent and the quality exemplary, in particular keeping to a lean, elegant style while many Alsace producers are veering towards a richer, blowsier character.

No wine typifies the assertive, minerally Trimbach style more vividly than the Riesling from Clos St-Hune, an enclave within the Rosacker Grand Cru. It is hard to disagree with those who claim that this is ALSACE's finest Riesling and even in poor vintages it can be compellingly good, though it is often unapproachable in its youth. But the range is excellent across the board. Riesling is always exceptional, both the bone-dry generic bottling and the steely, long-lived Cuvée Frédéric Émile. Pinot Gris is especially good here and the Gewurztraminer Cuvée de Seigneurs de Ribeaupierre is often first-rate. Vendange Tardive and Sélection de Grains Nobles wines from Pinot Gris can be sensational. Best years: (Clos Ste-Hune) 1998, '97, '96, '95, '93, '92, '90, '89, '88, '85, '83, '81, '76.

TRINITY HILL

NEW ZEALAND, North Island, Hawkes Bay

♟ *Cabernet Sauvignon, Cabernet Franc, Merlot, Syrah, Tempranillo, Pinot Noir and others*

♟ *Sauvignon Blanc, Chardonnay, Viognier and others*

Talented ex-winemaker of MORTON ESTATE, John Hancock, is one of three partners in this exciting new HAWKES BAY winery. Hancock is a passionate fan of the GIMBLETT GRAVELS district of Hawkes Bay, where Trinity Hill has established its 33ha (81 acres) of vineyards. A stylish and moderately complex Cabernet-Franc-Merlot-Shiraz blend is made from grapes purchased from growers in the Shepherd's Croft vineyard in Hawkes Bay, while a steely, dry Riesling is produced from MART-INBOROUGH grapes.

Gimblett Road is the winery's top label featuring an elegant, nutty Chardonnay and three ripe, concentrated reds: Cabernet Sauvignon, Cabernet Sauvignon-Merlot and Syrah. Gimblett Road wines are hot prospects for long-term aging while the others should be enjoyed within a few years of release.

TRITTENHEIM

GERMANY, Mosel-Saar-Ruwer

This important Mittel MOSEL commune has a string of excellent vineyard sites – Apotheke, Altärchen, Felsenkopf and Leiterchen – which produce very elegant Rieslings. For some years there were few exciting wines produced though, because of the high-yield policy pursued by most of the local growers. However, during the late 1990s this changed significantly for the better. Best years: 2002, '01, '00, '99, '98, '97, '95, '93, '90. Best producers: Ernst Clüsserath, Clüsserath-Weiler, GRANS-FASSIAN, Milz-Laurentiushof.

CH. TROPLONG-MONDOT

FRANCE, Bordeaux, St-Émilion Grand Cru AC, Grand Cru Classé

♟ *Merlot, Cabernet Franc, Cabernet Sauvignon*

Owned by the Valette family, Ch. Troplong-Mondot is one of a group of supposedly second-division ST-ÉMILION GRANDS CRUS CLASSÉS – Ch. CANON-LA-GAFFELIÈRE was another – who ripped up the rule book at the beginning of the 1990s and began making dense, intense reds quite unlike anything they'd ever done before. Contentiously denied promotion to the rank of Premier Grand Cru Classé in 1996, it has been making structured, mouthfillingly, unfiltered red wines for more than a decade now. Best years: 2001, '00, '99, '98, '97, '96, '95, '94, '90, '89, '88, '86, '85.

CH. TROTANOY

FRANCE, Bordeaux, Pomerol AC

♟ *Merlot, Cabernet Franc*

Trotanoy puts itself up as Ch. PÉTRUS' main challenger for the title 'King of Pomerol' but, in general, it has to be content with the role of crown prince.

The wine is tremendous stuff, though, and another example (along with Ch. Pétrus, LAFLEUR, LATOUR-À-POMEROL and a gaggle of others) of the brilliant touch of the late Jean-Pierre Moueix and his son Christian. The Jean-Pierre Moueix company owns this 8-ha (19-acre) property to the west of Pétrus on slightly more gravelly soil, and though the plantings of 90 per cent Merlot and 10 per cent Cabernet Franc do give a rich, massively impressive, Pétrus-like wine, they are also likely to have a tempering of leather and tobacco scents, and just lack the magic mingling of sweetness, spice and perfume which makes Pétrus so memorable. Best years: 2001, '00, '99, '98, '97, '96, '95, '94, '93, '90, '89, '88, '82.

CAVE VINICOLE DE TURCKHEIM

FRANCE, Alsace, Alsace AC

♟ *Pinot Noir*

♟ *Gewurztraminer, Pinot Blanc, Riesling, Pinot Gris, Sylvaner*

Unlike most regions of France, ALSACE is studded with good-quality wine co-operatives, and none has performed more consistently over the years than Turckheim. The growers have vineyards in some outstanding sites, including the Brand, Hengst and Sommerberg Grands Crus. By and large even the generic bottlings are soundly made and attractive, although the special bottlings, notably the Grands Crus, show much more complexity. Turckheim also succeeds with varieties such as Pinot Noir and Sylvaner, which can often be dull in Alsace. There is also attractive rosé and CRÉMANT D'ALSACE.

TURLEY WINE CELLARS

USA, California, Napa County, Napa Valley AVA

♟ *Petite Sirah, Zinfandel*

♟ *Viognier, Marsanne, Roussanne*

After many successful years with FROG'S LEAP, co-founder Larry Turley started his own brand and his former partner Larry Williams continued with Frog's Leap at another site. Assisted during the first two vintages by his famous sister, winemaker Helen Turley, Larry pursued his interest in making Zinfandel and Petite Sirah from several old, low-yielding, head-pruned vineyards. Small amounts of white are made from the adjacent vineyard. In recent vintages, he has made Zinfandels from as many as six individual vineyards and up to four single-vineyard Petite Sirahs. Made in small-case lots, Turley's red wines are highly concentrated, with intense fruit, scarily high alcohol levels and sometimes some residual sugar. Though likely to be consumed young by their avid fans, the Zinfandels develop some harmony with four to five years of aging. Turley experimented with Zinfandels from old vineyards in Contra Costa County and Lodi and liked the results well enough to add Zinfandels from these appellations to his ever-expanding roster. Best years: (Zins) 2001, '00, '99, '98, '97, '96, '95, '94.

TYRRELL'S

AUSTRALIA, New South Wales, Hunter Valley

♟ *Syrah (Shiraz), Pinot Noir, Cabernet Sauvignon*

♟ *Semillon, Chardonnay, Verdelho, Sauvignon Blanc*

Tyrrells has changed out of all recognition since the first time I bowled up as a cub reporter and asked the famously curmudgeonly Murray Tyrrell – What's your most successful wine? 'Blackberry nip,' he growled before lurching off to do something more important than talk to me. That gruff exterior masked one of the great innovative characters of the HUNTER VALLEY, the man who introduced Chardonnay to the valley – his 1971 Vat 47 revolutionized attitudes to Chardonnay with its magnificent golden waxy depth – whose Pinot Noir had prime ministers of Australia on their knees begging for a case, and whose Shiraz and Semillon were – and still are – some of Australia's classics.

Murray's gone now – though happily the higgledy piggledy old winery building is still there – but son Bruce has transformed a great classic wine company into a highly successful modern winery, offloading the 'Long Flat' brand but keeping up the big-volume 'Old Winery' label, adding vineyards in McLAREN VALE, LIMESTONE COAST and HEATHCOTE and yet maintaining the standard of the great old-numbered Vat Tyrrell classics of Semillon, Chardonnay and Shiraz.

UCO VALLEY
ARGENTINA, Mendoza

This valley, in the Andean foothills, is an old secret of Argentine viticulture, newly rediscovered. With vineyards over 1000m (3200ft) above sea level, clearly white wines are going to be important, and the Chardonnays, especially from the Tupungato area, are Argentina's best. Reds are also showing fascinating flavours, with Merlot, Malbec, Syrah and Pinot Noir promising to be exceptional. Already most major Argentine producers source at least some of their white grapes from here, but the massive influx of investment – much of it European – marks this out as being one of Argentina's future stars. Best producers: CATENA ZAPATA, La Celia, Salentein, Terrazas de Los Andes.

UMANI RONCHI
ITALY, Marche, Rosso Conero DOC
Montepulciano, Sangiovese, Cabernet Sauvignon, Merlot, Lacrima di Morro
Verdicchio, Bianchello e Trebbiano, Chardonnay, Sauvignon Blanc

One of the leading producers in the MARCHE, which has been improving year by year since being acquired in 1970 by the Bernetti family from Gino Umani Ronchi. Both the red and white wines are made to a high standard, each in their own winery. Among the reds are the two ROSSO CONERO crus, Cúmaro and San Lorenzo, though their thunder has to some appreciable extent now been stolen by the much lauded blend called Pélago. On the

white side, VERDICCHIO DEI CASTELLI DE JESI not surprisingly reigns supreme, the two crus, Plenio Riserva and Casal di Serra, vying with each other for top honours. Among other whites are a Verdicchio-Chardonnay blend called Osimo and a Sauvignon Blanc called Tajano, plus a dessert wine, Maximo. Best years: 2001, '00, '98, '97, '95, '94.

UMATHUM
AUSTRIA, Burgenland, Neusiedlersee, Frauenkirchen
Blauer Zweigelt, St Laurent, Blaufränkisch, Pinot Noir, Cabernet Sauvignon, Syrah
Sauvignon Blanc, Pinot Gris (Grauburgunder), Welschriesling, Chardonnay, Gewürztraminer (Traminer)

It is not by chance that Josef Umathum's 1992 St Laurent wine beat all the BURGUNDY Grands Crus to win the International Wine Challenge Pinot Noir Trophy. The wine, from St Laurent, a mutation of Pinot Noir, is so Burgundian in style that even an expert would be fooled (I was; I was a judge!!). His winery, with its vaulted barrique cellar, could also be in Burgundy and looks a bit lost among the flat vineyards of Frauenkirchen. That does not matter because Umathum makes a string of superb reds, most notably the powerful, tannic Zweigelt-Blaufränkisch blend from the minerally Ried Hallebühl site, that needs five years to reveal its considerable spicy depths. The Zweigelt-Blaufränkisch-Cabernet blend from the Ried Haideboden site is more supple, but hardly less impressive. The Pinot Noir Unter den Terrassen has become Austria's best example of that grape. Best years: 2000, 99, '97, '94, '93, '92.

UMBRIA
ITALY

'The green heart of Italy' is what the publicity posters call the region of Umbria. And it is Italy's geographical heart, midway between Florence and Rome, and it is green – and predominantly remote and hilly. The hilliness of Umbria is reflected in the names of some of its wines: Colli del Trasimeno (meaning the Hills of Trasimeno, from around Lake Trasimeno), Colli Altotiberini (in the north, along the course of the upper river Tevere, or Tiber, which flows through the region on its way to Rome) and Colli Perugini (south of Perugia).

These light red and white wines are pleasant but far more impressive are TORGIANO, a tiny area just south of Perugia; MONTEFALCO, with its brilliant red Sagrantino grape, between Assisi and Spoleto in mid-Umbria; and ORVIETO in the south-west

on the border of Lazio, producing one of Italy's best known whites and with more than its fair share of quality-conscious producers.

ÜRZIG
GERMANY, Mosel-Saar-Ruwer

The village of Ürzig faces ERDEN across the Mosel, each vying with the other for the steepest slopes; Erden's best vineyards are on the same side of the river as Ürzig's, all squeezed between mountains and water. The soil at Ürzig is a mixture of red slate and red sandstone, and the name of the Würzgarten site, which means 'spice garden', gives a clue as to the wine's style: rich, racy and aromatic, concentrated and characterful. Best years: 2002, '01, '00, '99, '98, '97, '96, '95, '94, '93. Best producers: Bischöfliche Weingüter, J J CHRISTOFFEL, Dr LOOSEN, Mönchhof.

UTIEL-REQUENA DO
SPAIN, Valencia
Bobal, Tempranillo, Grenache Noir (Garnacha Tinta), Cabernet Sauvignon, Syrah, Merlot
Macabeo, Chardonnay, Merseguera, Planta Nova

Utiel-Requena – remote, high country west of Valencia city – is the source of some of Spain's best rosé. Made principally from Bobal, and with modern methods it is now often light, fresh and fragrant. There are also good reds with a strong, herby character using an ever greater proportion of Tempranillo, and the emergence of some high-quality, fairly-priced, creamy RIOJA look-alikes is encouraging. Like other Valencia DOs, Utiel-Requena also makes strong, dark red tinto *doble pasta*, made with a double dose of colour and tannin-rich skins. Whites can be fresh, but are never very characterful. Best producers: Vicente Gandía Pla, Bodegas Palmera (L'Angelet), Schenk, Torre Oria, Vinival.

VACQUEYRAS AC
FRANCE, Southern Rhône
Grenache, Syrah, Cinsaut, Mourvèdre
Clairette, Grenache Blanc, Bourboulenc, Roussanne

Vacqueyras was the most important and consistently successful of the southern RHÔNE's CÔTES DU RHÔNE-VILLAGES communes, where Grenache is the chief red grape variety, and was promoted to its own AC in 1989. The village itself is rather a large one, liable to be raucous with visitors in summer and silent as a tomb in winter, and lies on the flat land just south of GIGONDAS.

However, the terraced vineyards of Vacqueyras sweep up towards the jagged, dramatic-looking Dentelles de Montmirail

The Valais vineyards high above the Rhône Valley are some of the most spectacular in the world. The vines seem to climb up every available mountainside in the search for sun and shelter.

and produce red wines of a lovely dark colour, a round, warm, spicy bouquet and a fruit that happily mixes plums and raspberries with the wind-dried dust of the South. Lovely at two to three years, good producers' reds from good vintages will age well for ten years or more. The whites and rosés are beginning to show an appealing perfume and fruit in recent vintages. Best years: 2001, '00, '99, '98, '97, '96, '95, '94. Best producers: des Amouriers, de la Charbonnière, Clos des Cazaux, Couroulu, DELAS, Font de Papier, la Fourmone, la Garrigue, JABOULET, de Montmirail, Montvac, Sang des Cailloux, Tardieu-Laurent, Ch. des Tours, Vacqueyras co-operative, Verquière.

LES VIGNERONS DU VAL D'ORBIEU

FRANCE, Languedoc-Roussillon

This growers' association is France's largest wine-exporting company, selling in excess of 20 million cases of (mostly uninspiring) wine a year. Membership includes several of the Midi's best co-operatives (Cucugnan, Cuxac, Ribauté and Montredon) and individual producers (Dom. de Fontsainte, Ch. la VOULTE-GASPARETS). It also owns Cordier (BORDEAUX) and Listel. Also marketed by Val d'Orbieu are Château de Jau and the excellent BANYULS and COLLIOURE estate, Clos de Paulilles. Its range of blended wines (Cuvée

Chouette, Chorus, Pas de Deux, Elysices, Réserve St-Martin and la Cuvée Mythique) are a judicious mix of traditional Mediterranean varieties with Cabernet Sauvignon or Merlot and show welcome signs of ambition to raise quality.

VALAIS

SWITZERLAND

🍷 *Pinot Noir, Gamay and others*

🍷 *Chasselas (Fendant), Sylvaner, Riesling and others*

From a wine perspective, this is by far the most interesting and innovative of the Swiss cantons; it's also the most famous. Most of the Valais' vineyards are crowded onto the north bank of the Rhône between Sierre and SION before the river turns north-west and flows on into Lake Geneva. This is one of the sunniest parts of Switzerland and most of the vines are on terraces perched high on the Alpine slopes, angled towards the sun, and since they are possibly the driest in Switzerland, irrigation is necessary. Most of the 22,700 grapegrowers take their grapes to the local co-operatives or merchants so the wines are usually sold by grape name or style.

Chasselas (here called Fendant) is the most planted grape variety and it makes light, dry whites, sometimes with a touch of *pétillance*. DÔLE, a blend of Pinot Noir and Gamay, is the Valais red speciality. But tucked away in odd corners are other vines: Malvoisie

(better known as Pinot Gris), Marsanne (here called Ermitage), Amigne, Arvine, Humagne (white and red), Païen and Rèze as well as international interlopers like Chardonnay and Syrah. Best producers: M Clavien, J Germanier, R Gilliard, Caves Imesch, Didier Joris, Mathier, Dom. du Mont d'Or, Raymond, Zufferey.

CH. DE VALANDRAUD

FRANCE, Bordeaux, St-Émilion Grand Cru AC

🍷 *Merlot, Cabernet Franc, Cabernet Sauvignon, Malbec*

This is the very heart of the 'garagiste' movement, because Jean-Luc Thunevin, the ex-disc jockey and bank clerk who has brilliantly raised this tiny property from obscurity to superstardom did make his first vintages, starting in 1991, in a backstreet garage in St-Émilion. Valandraud is now a rich, densely structured but wonderfully hedonistic wine that drapes its flavours over your palate like velvet, and is made from an increasing number of parcels of land around the ST-ÉMILION AC. Thunevin stands as spokesperson for the 'garagistes' when he calls his wine 'hand-sewn'. With no money, the original garagistes achieved concentration, and memorable intensity in their wines, by obsessive attention to detail. There are many such wines now, especially in St-Émilion, and some are not made by poor men but by multimillionaires, but the spirit of the garage resides at Valandraud with Jean-Luc Thunevin.

VALDEORRAS DO

SPAIN, Galicia

🍷 *Mencía, Garnacha Tintorera (Alicante), Gran Negro, Merenzao, Albarello*

🍷 *Godello, Doña Blanca, Palomino, Moscatel de Grano Menudo*

The Valdeorras vineyard area has declined to 1300ha (3200 acres), but quality is better, since almost half are now planted with the outstanding native Godello grape, which almost became extinct in the 1970s. The red Mencía is also making a comeback. The land is barren and mountainous, and the inhabitants have little alternative to growing vines. Production is dominated by two co-operatives, Barco de Valdeorras and La Rua, both of which have upgraded their winemaking equipment recently, and are able to make good wines – as long as they can get good grapes from their members. But the strong Godello revival has been spearheaded by a few private bodegas: Godeval, Joaquín Rebolledo, Santa Marta, A Tapada.

VALDEPEÑAS DO

SPAIN, Castilla-La Mancha

♥ ♂ *Tempranillo (Cencibel), Grenache Noir (Garnacha Tinta), Cabernet Sauvignon*

♀ *Airén, Macabeo*

Some of Spain's best red wine bargains come from this hot, dry undulating country in the south of the great central plains. More Cencibel (Tempranillo), the region's best grape, has been planted recently, along with some Cabernet Sauvignon.

The most common style of Valdepeñas is Clarete, a pale red made with a legal minimum of 20 per cent Cencibel and the rest the characterless white Airén and very popular in Spain. These wines can easily shoot up to a headache-inducing 15 per cent of alcohol (though the best modern ones are now kept at around 12.5 per cent), but colour and flavourwise this is feeble stuff. The best reds contain only red grapes. Some rosés and whites are now made by modern methods, and are simple, fresh and fruity. Best producers: Miguel Calatayud, Los Llanos, Luís Megía, Real, Félix Solís, Casa de la Viña.

VALDESPINO

SPAIN, Andalucía, Jerez y Manzanilla DO

♀ *Palomino Fino, Pedro Ximénez*

Until recently family-owned, this old-fashioned sherry company makes wines of very fine quality in limited quantities. Most unusually nowadays, Valdespino still ferments most of its wines in wooden casks (rather than stainless steel) and blends from myriad individual wines. The best-known wine is the lovely, classic Fino Inocente. Other wines include Tio Diego, a good, subtle amontillado; a richly flavourful, amontillado-style Palo Cortado Cardenal; dark, dry, immensely concentrated Amontillado Coliseo; dry, nutty-tangy Don Tomás Amontillado; complex, malty, raisiny Don Gonzálo Old Dry Oloroso; and, for the sweet-toothed, a dense, demerara-and-raisin flavoured Pedro Ximénez Solera Superior. The bodega has been bought by the José Estévez group and future developments are uncertain.

VALDIVIESO

CHILE, Curicó Valley

♥ *Cabernet Sauvignon, Merlot, Cabernet Franc, Malbec*

♀ *Chardonnay*

Valdivieso are one of those companies that seemed to resist modernizing for as long as possible, and then, when it was obvious which way Chile was heading, it modernized in a headlong rush. I remember my first meeting with the serried ranks of the owners, the Mitjans family – a powerful commercial clan in Santiago – and each time I querulously raised my voice to criticize their frankly undistinguished wines, I could feel the hackles of the whole room rise. But they had an excellent winemaker with extensive Australian experience, and gradually they released their grip on wine styles. Since then there has been a flood of usually good and sometimes excellent reds and whites led by top-of-the-line multi-vintage red blend Caballo Loco. My chief criticism is their rather liberal application of oak to some of the wines. They are also Chile's leading sparkling wine producer.

VALENCIA DO

SPAIN, Valencia

♥ *Mourvèdre (Monastrell), Tempranillo, Grenache Noir (Garnacha Tinta), Garnacha Tintorera, Bobal, Cabernet Sauvignon, Merlot, Pinot Noir and others*

♀ *Merseguera, Macabeo, Moscatel, Malvasía, Planta Fina, Chardonnay*

Down in the south-east, this is one of Spain's big exporting wine regions. Much of the wine is made in co-operatives, but it is the five modern, private companies, Vinival, Schenk, Vicente Gandía Pla, Valsangiacomo and Egli, that do most of the foreign trade. Valencian wines are reasonably cheap and can be good value if well made. They are unlikely to be great wines, however, though better grape varieties are improving flavours. Most of the wines are white, and mainly made from the unimpressive Merseguera grape, with some reds and rosés made largely from Garnacha Tinta and Garnacha Tintorera, and from the Monastrell in the south of the region.

Moscatel de Valencia is perhaps the region's most successful drink; a lusciously sweet, grapy combination of Moscatel juice and wine alcohol. Minimum legal alcohol levels were recently reduced to a sensible 11 per cent. Best producers: Vicente Gandía Plá, Los Pinos, Celler del Roure, Schenk/Murviedro, Cherubino Valsangiacomo (Marqués de Caro).

VALENTINI

ITALY, Abruzzo, Montepulciano d'Abruzzo DOC

♥ ♂ *Montepulciano*

♀ *Trebbiano d'Abruzzo*

Edoardo Valentini is a gentleman farmer with a large estate planted to a variety of crops under the shadow of the Apennines' highest peak, Gran Sasso. The vineyards comprise 120ha (297 acres) of vines, Montepulciano and Trebbiano d'Abruzzo, as is the norm in this region. But Valentini is an almost fanatical perfectionist, making wine to sell under his label from only 5 per cent of the total crop (he sells the rest to a local co-operative), and since he never knows until vintage time where the 5 per cent will come from the whole lot get looked after as if they were in the vineyard of Ch. LATOUR.

The secret of Valentini's hugely successful red MONTEPULCIANO D'ABRUZZO and white Trebbiano d'Abruzzo (he also makes a pink Cerasuolo) is in the fruit quality – although he would maintain, no doubt with some truth, that the secret is also in the winemaking methods, which are as artisanal and non-interventionist as possible. Best years: 2001, '99, '97, '95, '93, '90, '88, '85, '77.

VALLE D'AOSTA DOC

ITALY, Valle d'Aosta

♥ *Gamay, Nebbiolo, Petit Rouge, Pinot Noir (Pinot Nero), Vien de Nus, Petite Arvine, Dolcetto and others*

♂ *Nebbiolo, Petit Rouge*

♀ *Blanc de Morgex, Muscat (Moscato), Müller-Thurgau, Pinot Gris (Pinot Grigio), Pinot Noir (Pinot Nero), Chardonnay, Malvasia and others*

The long Aosta Valley, down-river from the ski resort of Courmayeur, has been divided into a string of sub-denominations, comprising numerous wine styles, all belonging to the Valle d'Aosta DOC. From west to east these are Blanc de Morgex et de La Salle (white, from Blanc de Morgex grapes); Enfer d'Arvier, Torrette (both red, from Petit Rouge); Nus (white and *passito* from Pinot Grigio, but this local sub-variety is often called Malvoisie); Nus Rosso (red, from Vien de Nus); Chambave (white and *passito* from Moscato); Chambave Rosso (red, from Petit Rouge); Arnad-Montjovet and Donnaz (both red, from Nebbiolo).

There are also varietal sub-denominations, for Gamay (red), Müller-Thurgau (white) and Pinot Nero (red and also white, if the grape juice is quickly removed from the dark skins). To make it even more confusing, wine labels may be in either Italian or French and some styles only exist in minute quantities. Excellent producers do not abound, but there is a remarkably good wine school in Aosta, the Institut Agricole Régional, whose top wine, from a wide range, is a Cabernet-Merlot blend called Vin du Prévôt. Best producers: R Anselmet, C Charrère/Les Crêtes, La Crotta di Vegneron, Grosjean, Institut Agricole Régional, Onze Communes co-operative, Ezio Voyat.

VALLE CENTRAL (Central Valley) Chile

IN 1990 CHILE SOLD $50 MILLION of wine on the export markets of the world. By 2002 this figure had soared to over $600 million. The powerhouse behind this dramatic rise is the Valle Central, or Central Valley. Extending southwards from the capital, Santiago, the Valle Central widens and undulates as it dips into the deeper river valleys that criss-cross it east to west draining the Andes into the Pacific Ocean. Rivers like the Lontué, Rapel and Maipo flow down from the majestic Andes and wash silt and volcanic debris through their dramatic valleys. The mineral-rich deposits left behind, the by-product of the tumultuous growth of the Andes, have created slopes and valleys with excellent viticultural potential. The only slight problem is that although the Pacific Ocean provides ambient humidity, there isn't enough rainfall to sustain widespread farming, so over a thousand years ago the Incas devised a sophisticated irrigation system for harnessing the water in the rivers and it's only now that this 'flood' system is gradually being replaced by modern 'drip'.

Viticulture came to Chile with Spanish colonization and soon Chile was supplying wine to much of Spanish America. Immigrants brought vines with them and eventually French varietals began to show their liking for the conditions. Development continued slowly until the mid-1970s, when Miguel

The Central Valley climate is strongly influenced by the Andes mountains that tower above the flat valley floor. The combination of cool nights and hot days in the vineyards during the growing season enhances grape acidity and flavour.

Torres arrived from Spain with the first stainless steel technology on the continent. It wasn't long before most other bodegas copied him, and the modern Chilean wine revolution was underway. There has been no stopping it since. Chile is now a leading exporter of wine to the USA, after France, Italy and Australia. New vineyards have been planted in just about every suitable spot. Good-value Cabernet Sauvignon, with attractive blackcurrant, green pepper and fresh mint aromas led to nicely focused, aromatic Sauvignon Blanc. Deep, luscious and friendly Merlots followed. Then, we were introduced to the concept of Carmenère, an old Bordeaux grape variety that performs brilliantly in Chilean conditions.

The latest development is super-premium reds, blends to die for. This generally involves outside investment – like Mondavi with Errázuriz, Ch. Mouton-Rothschild with Concha y Toro and Bruno Prats and Paul Pontallier of Bordeaux who have set up Viña Aquitania. The prices are always high – sometimes silly – especially when the wines end up tasting more international than Chilean.

Central Valley sub-regions
- Maipo Valley
- Rapel Valley
- **1** Cachapoal Valley
- **2** Colchagua Valley
- Curicó Valley
- **3** Teno Valley
- Maule Valley
- **4** Tutuvén Valley
- **5** Claro Valley
- **6** Loncomilla Valley

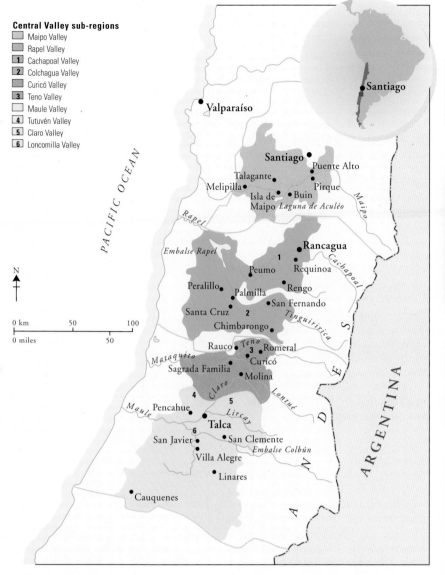

LA ROSA
La Rosa makes a range of Merlots from the stunningly beautiful La Palmeria vineyard in the Cachapoal Valley.

CASA LAPOSTOLLE
Merlot does particularly well in the Colchagua Valley and Clos Apalta is a world-class Merlot-Carmenère-Cabernet Sauvignon blend from this dynamic winery based in the valley.

CONCHA Y TORO
Powerful Don Melchor Cabernet Sauvignon leads a long list of reds at Concha y Toro, Chile's largest wine producer.

VIÑA CARMEN
Wine Maker's Reserve red (a blend of mainly Cabernet Sauvignon along with four other varieties) is one of the best wines from this sister winery to Santa Rita.

REGIONAL ENTRIES
Colchagua Valley, Curicó Valley, Maipo Valley, Maule Valley, Rapel Valley.

PRODUCER ENTRIES
Viña Canepa, Viña Carmen, Casa Lapostolle, Concha y Toro, Cono Sur, Cousiño Macul, La Rosa, Montes, MontGras, San Pedro, Santa Carolina, Santa Rita, Miguel Torres, Valdivieso.

SANTA RITA
This large, old Chilean winery was revitalized in the late 1990s and powerful new red blends such as Triple C (Cabernet Franc, Cabernet Sauvignon and Carmenere) show real flair.

VALDIVIESO
This successful company is best known for its smooth Pinot Noir but it also makes a wide range of other wines, including traditional-method fizz.

MONTGRAS
This wonderfully equipped new winery in the Colchagua Valley is building a reputation for red wines. The Reserva Merlot is oaky but shows good fruit intensity.

VALLEY VINEYARDS

ENGLAND, Berkshire
🍷 *Pinot Noir*
🍷 *Pinot Noir, Pinot Gris*
🍷 *Schönburger, Reichensteiner, Würzer and others*

Valley Vineyards based at Stanlake Manor in the Berkshire village of Twyford near the Thames, played an important role in the 1980s and 1990s by proving that far higher quality was possible in English wine than was being achieved if both the vineyard management and winemaking were put on an up-to-date, professional basis. It didn't do any harm that the vineyard owner Jon Leighton and the winemaker, John Worontschak, were both Australians of the 'you gotta have a go' school. Keeping crop levels low on their 10-ha (16-acre) vineyard, they showed you can ripen grapes such as Pinot Noir in England for table wine and fizz, and with very precise winemaking they have produced top fizz, fragrant whites, rosés and reds as well as England's best oak-aged whites. To supplement volume, the Valley Vineyard also buys in grapes from vineyards across southern England.

VALPOLICELLA DOC

ITALY, Veneto
🍷 *Corvina, Corvinone, Rondinella and others*

This wine can range in style from a light, cherryish red to the rich PORT-like RECIOTO and AMARONE Valpolicellas. Originally grapes for Valpolicella were grown on the hillsides of a series of parallel valleys north-west of Verona near Lake Garda. As time went by plantings gradually spread onto less hilly and even unashamedly flat countryside. But demand continued apace and the temptation became ever stronger to squeeze as much production as possible from the grapes. So Valpolicella became an over-extended area with the vines giving a far too generous yield. The original Valpolicella zone was given the Classico tag, but the coincidence of the Valpolicella name was enough to bring even Classico crashing in terms of price and, consequently, of quality.

Nonetheless, it is a mistake to think that good Valpolicella comes only from the Classico zone, and that everything from the extended zone is rubbish. On the contrary, there are some outstanding wines from the eastern sector (DAL FORNO, arguably the greatest contemporary producer, is in Illasi; Bertani, high-priests of traditional Amarone della Valpolicella, is in Valpantena). The overproduced stuff comes not from the east *per se*, but from the plains where the vines give absurdly high yields.

Young Valpolicella, made for drinking with a year or so of aging, can be lovely: light and fresh, fully packed with its typical bitter morello cherries flavour. But much commercial Valpolicella is sold at two or three years old, often already tired as it is too insubstantial to age properly. It is better to find a Ripasso wine, the most traditional style of Valpolicella, strengthened by a re-fermentation on the flavour-soaked lees of the *passito* wines. It picks up richness, weight and structure and its bitter cherries flavour gets augmented by chocolate – altogether a much more serious proposition. It is not easy to distinguish from the label which wines are made in this style and whether from the best grape, Corvina, but the designation Valpolicella (Classico) Superiore can be a pretty reasonable clue. Best years: 2001, '00, '97, '95, '93, '90, '88. Best producers: S Accordini, ALLEGRINI, Bertani, Brigaldara, Brunelli, Tommaso Bussola, M Castellani, Dal Forno, Guerrieri-Rizzardi, MASI, Mazzi, Pasqua/Cecilia Beretta, QUINTARELLI, Le Ragose, Le Salette, Serègo Alighieri, Speri, Tedeschi, Villa Monteleone, Viviani, Zenato, Fratelli Zeni.

VALTELLINA DOC, VALTELLINA SUPERIORE DOCG

ITALY, Lombardy
🍷 *Nebbiolo (Chiavennasca), Pinot Noir (Pinot Nero), Merlot and others*

Valtellina is an Alpine wine, produced in the south-facing, steep Adda valley, just below the Swiss border. It is only the air movement caused by the river and the heat trap of the valley that enable the grapes to reach ripeness. When they do, in the hands of a skilled winemaker, Valtellina is one of the most elegant and refined incarnations of Nebbiolo, locally called Chiavennasca. The predominant flavour is violetty with some raspberry and walnuts, quite soft, although Nebbiolo's characteristic tannin is still around.

Valtellina Superiore is a cut above the normal version, made from 90 per cent Nebbiolo as opposed to 80 per cent for straight Valtellina, and with a lower vineyard yield. It is produced in one or more of four sub-districts: Sassella (the best), Grumello, Inferno and Valgella. Best years: 2001, '00, '99, '98, '97, '95, '93, '90, '88, '85. Best producers: La Castellina, Enologica Valtellinese, Fay, Nino Negri, NERA, Rainoldi, Conti Sertoli Salis, Triacca.

Sfursat or Sforzato wines are lightly *passito*, enough to get the alcohol up to 14 per cent, although the wine remains dry, like AMARONE DELLA VALPOLICELLA. Some think

NINO NEGRI
The best Valtellina wines are made under the Superiore DOCG. Nino Negri's Le Tense wine comes from the Sassella sub-district.

Sfursat is the best type of Valtellina. It's just a question of whether you prefer the big and butch to the subtle and elegant.

VASSE FELIX

AUSTRALIA, Western Australia, Margaret River
🍷 *Cabernet Sauvignon, Syrah (Shiraz), Merlot and others*
🍷 *Semillon, Chardonnay, Sauvignon Blanc and others*

One of the original wineries responsible for MARGARET RIVER rocketing to fame in the 1970s, with decadently rich Cabernet Sauvignon and Shiraz and owned since 1987 by the wealthy Holmes à Court family. The winemaking style has continued along the lines of lush fruit and generous use of oak, and the flagship red and white Heytesbury take this style even further. Best years: (Heytesbury) 2001, '99, '98, '97, '96, '95.

VAUD

SWITZERLAND
🍷 *Gamay, Pinot Noir*
🍷 *Chasselas (Dorin) and others*

Most of the vineyards along Lake Geneva's northern shore are in the Vaud canton, with the region of CHABLAIS being famous for its tangy Chasselas. Lavaux is probably the best region and includes the village of Dézaley, Vaud's top appellation and famous for surprisingly powerful, minerally wines from Chasselas. Other regions are La Côte, Côte de l'Orbe-Bonvillars and Vully, all with high-altitude vineyards. Nearly all Vaud wine is white from Chasselas, here called Dorin; reds are from Pinot Noir or Gamay, either separate or blended. Best producers: Henri Badoux, Louis Bovard, Conne, Delarze, Dubois Fils, Grognuz, Massy, Obrist, Pinget, J & P Testuz.

VAVASOUR

NEW ZEALAND, South Island, Marlborough
🍷 *Pinot Noir*
🍷 *Sauvignon Blanc, Chardonnay, Riesling*

I've been thrilled by the tremendous zesty attack and tangy fruit of the MARLBOROUGH whites ever since I first tasted them way back in the 1980s. And then, in the early 1990s, I tasted Vavasour and knew immediately that here was a winery that was going to take tongue-tingling tanginess to an altogether new level. And the reason for this citrous onslaught was that the grapes didn't come from the usual Marlborough source of the Wairau Valley, but from another smaller valley through the Wither Hills to the south – the Awatere Valley.

Vavasour was the first winery in the Awatere Valley, situated majestically on a bluff overlooking the river, and since its first vintage in 1989 has defined the brilliantly austere yet aromatic style of Sauvignon from Awatere, whose soils in general are very low in fertility, whose rainfall is minimal, and where the difference between day and night temperatures is so marked that even after a perfect midsummer day you'll need a jersey when you go out at night. Chardonnay and Riesling are also delicious and there has been a string of good Pinot Noirs. Dashwood is an alternative label, usually incorporating more Wairau Valley fruit. Best years: (Sauvignon Blanc) 2002, '01, '00.

VEENWOUDEN

SOUTH AFRICA, Western Cape, Paarl WO
🍷 Merlot, Cabernet Sauvignon, Cabernet Franc, Malbec, Syrah (Shiraz)
♀ Chardonnay

International opera singer Deon van der Walt and his brother Marcel, an ex-golf pro turned winemaker, continue to raise the roof at this tiny cellar – the wines regularly command the highest prices at auction. Three reds are based on BORDEAUX varieties: sumptuous, well-oaked Merlot, firm and silky-fruited Veenwouden Classic and Vivat Bacchus. A tiny quantity of fine Chardonnay is also made. New Thornhill Shiraz is milder, but promising. Best years: (Merlot, Classic) 2000, '99, '98, '97, '96, '95, '94, '93.

VEENWOUDEN

The Veenwouden wines, including this Merlot, are made in a traditional style but with beautifully ripe fruit, from low yields and aged in new oak for up to two years.

Spain's most expensive red wines, rich, fragrant, complex and very slow to mature, come from the Vega Sicilia bodega in the Ribera del Duero region. This estate was the first in Spain to grow French grape varieties.

VEGA SICILIA

SPAIN, Castilla y León, Ribera del Duero DO
🍷 Tempranillo (Tinto Fino), Cabernet Sauvignon, Merlot, Malbec

Even the King of Spain is on strict allocation for Vega Sicilia, Spain's most expensive wine. The large estate has been famed since the nineteenth century for its rich, fragrant, complex and long-lasting wines. Prices have always been extremely high, vying with those for top BORDEAUX. Vega Sicilia was the first bodega in Spain to make extensive use of the Bordeaux grape varieties. and over one quarter of the vines are now Cabernet Sauvignon.

Apart from the extraordinary richness of the grapes, one of Vega Sicilia's main hallmarks has been unusually long wood-aging. Depending on the vintage, the top red, Único, was traditionally given up to ten years in large wooden vats and oak barrels – both new and old, American and French. If these wines were still richly alive and complex after treatment that would kill most other great wines, how much greater would they be if given more time in bottle and less in wood?

So from the 1982 vintage, the aging process has been gradually reduced to only five to six years in wood (including only a few months in new oak). Now at least half of the pre-release aging is spent in the bottle and though the wine-making approach has been greatly modernized, the result is a certain loss of individuality. Valbuena is the label for a five-year-old wine from a specified vintage and the Alión label, from a separate winery, is for powerful modern, Tempranillo reds, aged for 18 months in new French oak. Vega Sicilia's new Alquiriz winery makes some of the most distinctive wines in TORO. Best years: (Único) 1990, '89, '86, '85, '83, '82, '81, '80, '79, '76, '75, '74, '70, '68.

VELICH

AUSTRIA, Burgenland, Neusiedlersee, Apetlon
♀ Chardonnay, Neuburger, Muscat (Muskat Ottonel), Gewürztraminer (Traminer), Welschriesling
Roland Velich makes by far the best Chardonnay in Austria; his Tiglat Chardonnay is neither too alcoholic nor too heavily oaked. Instead, the old vines planted on stony soil give the wine a waxy-nutty character and great Burgundian savoury elegance. The slightly less refined Chardonnay from the Darscho vineyard is almost as good. The spectacularly concentrated Welschriesling Trockenbeerenauslese is the best sweet wine. Best years: (Tiglat Chardonnay) 2002, '01, '00, '99, '97, '95, '93, '92; (sweet whites) 2002, '00, '99, '98, '96, '95, '94, '91.

VENETO Italy

THERE IS NEVER ANY SHORTAGE OF WINE in the Veneto, Italy's third-largest wine-producing region and number one in respect of DOC wines. The province of Verona alone produces more than enough to satisfy the entire region. Some of the best-known and mostly widely available Italian wine names come from there: Soave, Valpolicella and Bardolino. But a passing acquaintance with those three wines plus a random dip into the wines of the more easterly Piave and Lison-Pramaggiore zones or the central Colli Berici and Colli Euganei, and one could be excused for thinking that the good folk of the Veneto are far more concerned about how much wine they are making than how good it is. While drinkable enough, the average Veneto wine can hardly be described as exciting. Too many of the vineyards are on its extensive plains and too many DOCs provide for over-abundant yields, resulting in wines that, even when decently made, lack real flavour. The bigger problem is that many of them are *not* decently made. The Merlot that grows on the Veneto plains in vast profusion gives cheap, simple wines that must rate as just about the lightest reds that Merlot pro-

duces anywhere in the world. And the bulk producers of Soave and Valpolicella, including some very well-known companies, should be ashamed by the appalling quality of their ordinary blends. But then the DOC authorities should be ashamed of themselves for allowing such debasing of traditionally fine wine names as Soave and Valpolicella in the name of politics and profit.

The Veneto, however, doesn't lack potential once wine-making is in the hands of quality-conscious producers, who make the most of any nearby hills and prune vines ruthlessly to keep yields down (thereby ensuring better quality). Soave Classico and Valpolicella Classico (the Classico zones cover the better hill sites), each with a number of estates committed to quality, produce an increasing amount of first-class wines, which bear no resemblance to cheap commercial offerings. Real Soave Classico is a full, broad white, beautifully balanced and developing a delightful richness of nuts and honeysuckle with age. Real Valpolicella Classico, especially one dominated by the excellent Corvina grape, manages to provide cherry-rich fruit, as well as a delightful bitter-sour twist. And the remarkable red Amarone (rich, yet bitter) and Recioto (rich and sweet) wines of Valpolicella and the sublime Recioto di Soave are among Italy's finest wines. Breganze produces an eclectic range of high-quality dry and sweet wines. Even the rarely seen Colli Berici and Colli Euganei, areas with a number of single-varietal wine styles (Cabernet, Merlot, Pinot Bianco, Tocai, the exotically named Fior d'Arancia), have glorious hilly terrain, which so far only a very few producers fully exploit.

The Veneto wines of Lake Garda are young, cherry-fresh red Bardolino and white Bianco di Custoza. The hilly, southern part of the Bardolino zone overlaps that of Bianco di Custoza. This has two advantages. Bianco di Custoza usually comes from only the slopes best suited for white wine, and Bardolino only from slopes better for red; and producers are used to making white wines, hence they make a marvellous crisp, fresh, pale rosé, Bardolino Chiaretto.

There is no doubt about the wine to drink in Venice. Although nearby Piave has eight wines from different grape varieties to choose from (red Raboso is especially invigorating), and next-door Lison-Pramaggiore has even more, Venice is the place for Prosecco. Lorryloads of bottles of this light, fruity fizzy stuff, from the grape of the same name, trundle down from north of Treviso to keep both Venetians and tourists happily lubricated.

The best vineyards in the Valpolicella DOC are situated on the steep slopes of the various valleys. Some of the most famous wines come from the valley of Fumane in the Classico zone.

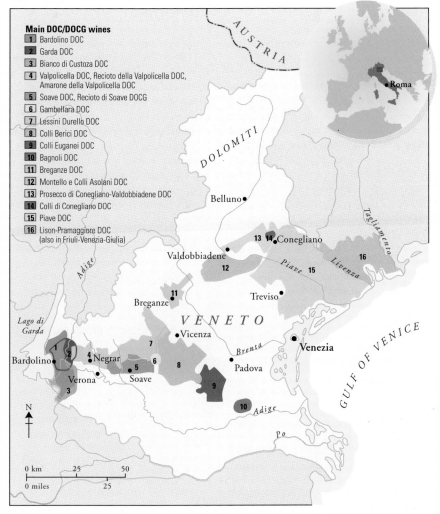

Main DOC/DOCG wines

1. Bardolino DOC
2. Garda DOC
3. Bianco di Custoza DOC
4. Valpolicella DOC, Recioto della Valpolicella DOC, Amarone della Valpolicella DOC
5. Soave DOC, Recioto di Soave DOCG
6. Gambellara DOC
7. Lessini Durello DOC
8. Colli Berici DOC
9. Colli Euganei DOC
10. Bagnoli DOC
11. Breganze DOC
12. Montello e Colli Asolani DOC
13. Prosecco di Conegliano-Valdobbiadene DOC
14. Colli di Conegliano DOC
15. Piave DOC
16. Lison-Pramaggiore DOC (also in Friuli-Venezia-Giulia)

MASI
One of the driving forces in Valpolicella, Masi is constantly experimenting with new wines. Osar is a new red blend from two local varieties, Oseleta and Corvina, the main Valpolicella grape.

PIEROPAN
Pieropan's La Rocca, made solely from Garganega, is one of Soave's benchmark wines. Slightly steely and austere at first, it develops richness and flavour with time.

ALLEGRINI
This high-profile producer in Valpolicella Classico is concentrating increasingly on quality. La Poja, the flagship wine, is an elegant oak-aged red made solely from late-harvested Corvina, Valpolicella's best quality grape from the top of the La Grola hill.

REGIONAL ENTRIES
Amarone della Valpolicella, Bardolino, Bianco di Custoza, Breganze, Prosecco di Conegliano-Valdobbiadene, Recioto della Valpolicella, Recioto di Soave, Soave, Valpolicella.

PRODUCER ENTRIES
Allegrini, Roberto Anselmi, Dal Forno, Masi, Pieropan, Quintarelli.

NINO FRANCO
One of the best producers of both still and sparkling Prosecco is Nino Franco.

QUINTARELLI
These distinctive handwritten labels herald some of the most remarkable wines in Valpolicella. This is complex, powerful and benchmark Amarone.

ANSELMI
Made by Roberto Anselmi, one of the star producers in Soave, I Capitelli is a gently honeyed wine with a rich, smooth texture.

DAL FORNO
Romano Dal Forno's Amarone della Valpolicella from the Monte Lodoletta vineyard is a voluptuous wine of massive structure, deep ruby colour and spicy bouquet.

VERDICCHIO

Home for the white Verdicchio grape is the MARCHE in central Italy and it has been since the fourteenth century. Verdicchio's name derives from the word *verde* (Italian for 'green') as the grapes, even when ripe, remain strongly greenish in colour. The wine, too, has a greenish tinge to its pale straw colour when young. Verdicchio produces one of the most refreshing white wines, with high natural acidity which keeps it crisp. This acidity also makes it a natural for sparkling wine. The grape is also amenable to unconventional treatments such as late-picking or aging in large oak casks, and it can improve with a few years of bottle age. Its yield may not be reliable but it is hardy. For all these reasons many consider Verdicchio to be one of the best of Italy's native white grape varieties.

VERDICCHIO DEI CASTELLI DI JESI DOC, VERDICCHIO DI MATELICA DOC

ITALY, Marche
♀ *Verdicchio, Trebbiano Toscano, Malvasia*

Castelli di Jesi (named after the river Esino and nothing to do with Jesus) is a sizeable wine region inland from the port of Ancona, specializing in whites from the local Verdicchio grape. It became famous by using an amphora-shaped bottle but the wine was never more than cheap and cheerful and in today's quality-first environment, wineries are striving to lose the 'amphora' image.

In fact Verdicchio, the grape, is one of Italy's finest and the Castelli di Jesi DOC is capable of offering some very serious white wine, with, at its best, tremendous concentration and richness of mouthfeel and the ability to age, in the right conditions, for several years. The number of top producers seems to grow every year. Best producers: (Jesi) Brunori, Bucci, Colonnara, Coroncino, Fazi Battaglia, Garofoli, Mancinelli, Terre Cortesi Moncaro, Monte Schiavo, Santa Barbara, Sartarelli, Tavignano, UMANI RONCHI, Fratelli Zaccagnini. All these wines, though varying in style, have a dry nuttiness and a rich-sharp salty edge that the old wines lacked. Sparkling Verdicchio (especially from Le Terrazze) is one of Italy's most tasty fizzes.

Verdicchio di Matelica, from a smaller region further inland towards the Apennines, at a somewhat higher altitude, produces excellent wines that tend to have a more acid bite and rather more obvious fruit and perfume. Best producers: Belisario, Bisci, Enzo Mecella, La Monacesca.

VERDUZZO

This north-eastern Italian grape makes some pretty lively dry whites but is more famous for its sweet wines. Best suited to COLLI ORIENTALI in FRIULI, as it spreads west into the VENETO it makes wines that are drier and more bitingly fresh. Sweet Verduzzo is richly honeyed – runny honey – and floral, with an enlivening backbone of acidity. It can be aged, but it is really best when young and fresh.

VERGELEGEN

SOUTH AFRICA, Western Cape, Stellenbosch WO
♂ *Cabernet Sauvignon, Merlot, Syrah (Shiraz), Cabernet Franc*
♀ *Sauvignon Blanc, Chardonnay, Semillon*

With a bit more luck we could be regaling outselves with vertical tastings of Vergelegen wines going back decades, because more than a few people regard this windswept hilltop winery just north of Somerset West on False Bay as one of South Africa's finest. And Vergelegen was founded in 1700. Yes, but before it was bought by gold and diamonds giant Anglo-American in 1988, it had been owned by teetotallers, who relished ripping out the vines.

In any case Vergelegen's reputation is inextricably bound up with that of iconoclastic winemaker André van Rensburg and he's only been there since 1998. In double quick time he's made worldclass Sauvignon Blanc, Chardonnay and excellent Cabernet, Cabernet Franc-Merlot, as well as fine barrel-fermented Sauvignon-Semillon Vergelegen white, and dark, impressive BORDEAUX-blend Vergelegen red. Shiraz is new and delicious. So is it one of South Africa's finest? With van Rensburg in charge, without a doubt.

VERITAS

AUSTRALIA, South Australia, Barossa Valley
♂ *Syrah (Shiraz), Cabernet Sauvignon, Merlot, Mourvedre (Mataro), Grenache*
♀ *Semillon, Riesling, Chardonnay*

In vino veritas (In wine there is truth), say the Binder family. There's certainly truth in the bottom of a bottle of Hanisch Vineyard Shiraz or Heysen Vineyard Shiraz, both blindingly good wines. The Shiraz-Mourvedre (known locally as Bulls' Blood as a reminder of Rolf Binder's Hungarian roots) and Shiraz-Grenache blends are lovely big reds; the Cabernet-Merlot is also good. Under the Christa-Rolf label, Shiraz-Grenache is good and spicy with attractive, forward black fruit. A move to a new winery in 1999 hasn't affected the quality.

VERMENTINO

SARDINIA's best dry whites generally come from Vermentino which is thought to have originated from Spain in the Middle Ages. Light, dry, perfumed and nutty, the best of these tend to come from the north of the island, where in Gallura Vermentino now has its own DOCG.

It is also found along the Tyrrhenian coast from LIGURIA's Ponente down to TUSCANY's Maremma. Further north in PROVENCE it is called Rolle and is the main grape of BELLET, a full-bodied white. It is important in CORSICA (as Malvoisie de Corse) and is now permitted and is on the increase in LANGUEDOC-ROUSSILLON where it blends happily with other local grapes. Best producers: (Sardinia) ARGIOLAS, Capichera, Cherchi, Piero Mancini, Pedra Majore, SELLA & MOSCA; Gallura, Santadi and Vermentino co-operatives.

VERNACCIA

The word Vernaccia means something along the lines of 'belonging to here', which goes some way to explaining why there are at least three grape varieties in Italy called Vernaccia (four if you reckon Alto Adige's Vernatsch or Schiava to be a variation on the theme), none bearing any relation to any of the others.

Vernaccia number one is an ancient white variety from Tuscany and grown mainly around the famous hill town of San Gimignano. Here, it makes wines that are white, dry and anything from lean to rich. The word Vernaccia on its own almost always refers to the wine from San Gimignano.

Vernaccia number two is also a white grape but this time from the central west of Sardinia, just north of Oristano. The outstanding, oxidized, almost sherry-like wines can be strong and dry or fortified (dry or sweet).

Vernaccia number three is a red grape variety and comes from the central-southern Marche, around Serrapetrona. The wines it makes here are usually sparkling and can be either dry, semi-sweet or sweet.

VERNACCIA DI SAN GIMIGNANO DOCG

ITALY, Tuscany

♀ *Vernaccia di San Gimignano, Chardonnay*

San Gimignano, the 'town of towers', is such a popular tourist destination that it wouldn't have been at all surprising if Vernaccia di San Gimignano had degenerated to a tourist gimmick of no intrinsic quality. Yet very few of San Gimignano's wine producers have fallen into this profitable but short-sighted trap.

Traditionally, the wines were golden in colour, rich, broad and often oxidized. The modern wave of winemaking brought in pale, tight, lean, crisp wines, which were perhaps too restrained. Now some estates are slackening the reins, resulting in salty, creamy, nutty, tangy wine, with, in the hands of masters like Teruzzi & Puthod, a buttery richness that lasts a good three years or so. Chardonnay is now allowed in the blend (up to 10 per cent). Best producers: Cà del Vispo, Le Calcinaie, Casale-Falchini, V Cesani, Montenidoli, G Panizzi, Il Paradiso, Pietrafitta, La Rampa di Fugnano, Guicciardini Strozzi-Cusona, Teruzzi & Puthod, Casa alle Vacche, Vagnoni.

DOMAINE GEORGES VERNAY

FRANCE, Northern Rhône, Condrieu AC

♀ *Syrah*

♀ *Viognier*

It's not unreasonable to say that the genial Georges Vernay saved CONDRIEU from extinction in the dark days of the 1960s when the vineyards had dwindled to a mere 12ha (30 acres) but he obstinately went on making his wines of such perfumed beauty that fashion would surely catch up with them again. And it did. Now Condrieu is one of the most sought after and expensive French whites and Vernay is still the leader. His son Luc now makes the wines from the 7ha (17 acres) of vineyards in Condrieu, and he also produces CÔTE-RÔTIE and ST-JOSEPH.

There are a number of different Condrieus. The regular bottling is aged for six months, while the others are aged for 12 months before bottling. Coteau de Vernon is a single vineyard, as is the Chaillées de l'Enfer, which is often the most impressive wine. Vernay believes in late-bottling to keep the aromas fresh, although conventional wisdom would favour the opposite approach. Wines from young vines, both white and red, are usually bottled as vin de pays, ensuring that only the best wines are released under the precious Condrieu name. Vernay produces about 100,000 bottles a year,

VESUVIO DOC

ITALY, Campania

♀ ♀ *Piedirosso*

♀ *Coda di Volpe, Verdeca and others*

Red wines based on Piedirosso and whites from Coda di Volpe and Verdeca. The evocative name Lacryma Christi del Vesuvio merely demonstrates the wine is half a degree stronger. There are also rare sparkling and liquoroso versions of Lacryma. Best producers: Cantine Caputo, Cantina Grotta del Sole, MASTROBERARDINO.

QUINTA DO VESÚVIO

PORTUGAL, Douro, Port DOC

♀ *Touriga Nacional, Touriga Franca, Tempranillo (Tinta Roriz), Tinta Barroca, Tinto Cão and others*

♀ *Gouveio, Viosinho, Rabigato, Malvasia Fina, Donzelinho*

One of the largest and most stately properties in the DOURO, Quinta do Vesúvio belonged to the FERREIRA family until it was bought by the Symington family (owners of DOW, GRAHAM and WARRE) in 1989. Quinta do Vesúvio is now a PORT wine producer in its own right and, in all but the poorest years, the property bottles a rich, minty, spicy single-quinta vintage port that sells for a high price. It is best with ten years' aging. Best years: 2000, '99, '98, '97, '96, '95, '94, '92, '91, '90.

QUINTA DO VESÚVIO
The Symington family showpiece in the Upper Douro is a consistent top performer and this brilliant port is best with ten years of aging.

VEUVE CLICQUOT

FRANCE, Champagne, Champagne AC

♀ ♀ *Pinot Noir, Chardonnay, Pinot Meunier*

Widows have featured prominently in the affairs of the CHAMPAGNE houses, but when someone talks of 'The Widow' in Champagne, they are sure to be talking of the Widow Clicquot or Veuve Clicquot. Not only was she Champagne's dominant figure at the beginning of the nineteenth century, but she invented the winemaking process of *remuage* – the last stage in the process needed to obtain clear Champagne.

Modern Veuve Clicquot Champagne can, but doesn't always, live up to the Widow

VEUVE CLICQUOT
Veuve Clicquot's prestige cuvée is called la Grande Dame after the original widow. With real refinement, it is a fairly rich and full-bodied Champagne.

Clicquot's original high standards. The non-vintage Champagne is full, toasty, slightly honeyed and quite weighty for a sparkling wine and is only marred by inconsistency. There is also a vintage which resembles the non-vintage but is even fuller, and a prestige cuvée, la Grande Dame, which usually manages to be exquisite and impressive at the same time. Best years: 1996, '95, '93, '91, '90, '89, '88, '85, '82.

VIADER VINEYARDS

USA, California, Napa County, Howell Mountain AVA

♀ *Cabernet Sauvignon, Cabernet Franc, Syrah, Petit Verdot*

Born in Argentina, Delia Viader developed an 11-ha (28-acre) vineyard along the steep, rocky slopes of HOWELL MOUNTAIN employing top vineyard man David Abreu and top winemaking consultant Tony Soter to help her. Since these two are probably the NAPA VALLEY's most talented and sensitive consultants, her determination got off to the best possible start with a good first vintage in the difficult year of 1989.

Since then her wines have become some of the best in Napa, without ever indulging in the palate-bashing self-parody that marks out some of the cult wines. Viader also produces V – a Petit Verdot-dominated red, and Howell Mountain Syrah. Her latest venture is a 5-ha (12-acre) vineyard in the BOLGHERI region of TUSCANY. Best years: 2001, '00, '99, '98, '97, '95, '94, '93, '92, '91, '90.

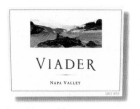

VIADER VINEYARDS
Delia Viader uses 40 per cent Cabernet Franc to temper the Cabernet Sauvignon and it clearly works as the result is deep, serious, but velvet in texture.

VICTORIA Australia

Located only a few kilometres from the sea, Stonier's Winery is the leading producer in the cool-climate, windy Mornington Peninsula region and not surprisingly, Chardonnay and Pinot Noir are the main specialities here.

IN 1890 VICTORIA'S VINEYARDS produced well over half of Australia's wine, yet by 1960 there were only four wineries in the state outside North-East Victoria: Tahbilk, Osicka's, Best's and Seppelt Great Western. Today, there are almost 300 licensed winemakers. From being on its knees, Victoria is now bursting with new wineries and new regions. Tomorrow, who knows?

There are 19 wine regions in Victoria, most of them grouped within a radius of 200km (125 miles) from Melbourne. The outposts are the distinctly chilly Henty near Portland in the far west, the bountifully mass-producing Murray Darling extending around Mildura in the furthest north-west corner, and Rutherglen and Beechworth in the north-east. In between, virtually every kind of wine style and climate is covered, though most of Victoria's most famous wines are from relatively small wineries, in relatively cool areas.

Indeed, Victoria is the state of the small winery. True, it is home to Lindemans' vast Karadoc winery (the company's operational headquarters, producing 8 million cases a year) in the Murray Darling region; but, apart from that, most of the wineries, even those owned by the large national groups, are small- to medium-sized operations.

The small wineries are primarily red wine producers, though there is exciting Chardonnay, Sauvignon, Riesling and Gewurztraminer, and even Marsanne in small quantities. Red wine production is focused on the Grampians-Pyrenees-Bendigo-Heathcote-Goulburn Valley belt of Central Victoria. Here you find dark, blood-red Shiraz, sometimes spicy, sometimes with a distinctly minty character. Cabernet Sauvignon is similarly intense and concentrated, once again with mint running into dark berry and blackcurrant flavours. The wines have weight and power, ranging from the almost silky smoothness of those produced by Best's or Seppelt through to the tannin and long-lived astringency of the young reds of producers such as Taltarni and Tahbilk.

Nearer Melbourne, Yarra Valley, the Mornington Peninsula and Geelong are all very cool regions, with a maritime climate. A total of 90 wineries here produce elegant, crispy fruit wines, with Chardonnay, Pinot Noir and the Cabernet family the centre of attention. While Australia still has to convince the sceptics about the intrinsic merits of its best Pinot Noir, it is from these regions that the best Pinots come.

The Gippsland zone (see page 47) is a rambling, flat region with cool but very dry growing conditions. Cooler still is the Strathbogie Ranges region where grapes can actu-

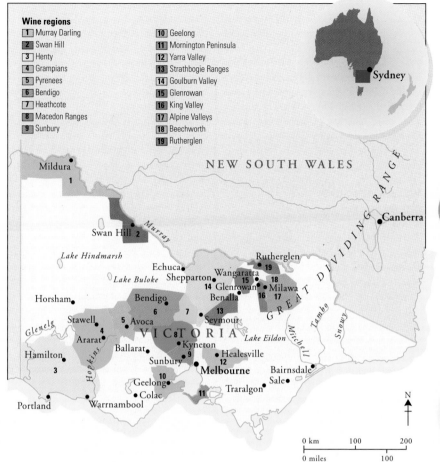

Wine regions

1. Murray Darling
2. Swan Hill
3. Henty
4. Grampians
5. Pyrenees
6. Bendigo
7. Heathcote
8. Macedon Ranges
9. Sunbury
10. Geelong
11. Mornington Peninsula
12. Yarra Valley
13. Strathbogie Ranges
14. Goulburn Valley
15. Glenrowan
16. King Valley
17. Alpine Valleys
18. Beechworth
19. Rutherglen

CHAMBERS
Bill Chambers is one of the characters of the Australian wine industry. His speciality is remarkably powerful liqueur Muscat and Tokay.

JASPER HILL
Highly regarded and eagerly sought after, these Shiraz wines have immense richness and structure.

GIACONDA
Beautifully balanced and packed with fruit sweetness, this wine nevertheless clearly has Burgundy as its role model.

MORRIS
This historic Rutherglen winery makes some of the most magnificent Australian fortifieds, including Liqueur Muscat.

TAHBILK
Enjoying a distinct honeysuckle aroma, the Marsanne from this wonderfully old-fashioned family company is a regional benchmark.

MOUNT MARY
This classic Yarra estate takes Bordeaux as its role model. Quintet is based on all five red Bordeaux varieties.

ally struggle to ripen. The North-East, centred on Rutherglen and Glenrowan, produces Australia's distinctive fortified Muscats and Tokays. It is also the home of some massive red wines: Morris's Durif and Shiraz from Campbells and Baileys still produce echoes of the past. But these days the most interesting wines are more likely to be those from the slopes of the King and Alpine Valleys regions, which produce much of Brown Brothers' white table wines and which, in the future, will provide the grapes for Orlando's sparkling wine.

Two of Australia's top sparkling wine producers are based in central Victoria: Seppelt in the Grampians and Yellowglen near Ballarat.

REGIONAL ENTRIES
Alpine Valleys, Bendigo, Geelong, Gippsland, Goulburn Valley, Grampians, King Valley, Macedon Ranges, Mornington Peninsula, Pyrenees, Rutherglen and Glenrowan, Sunbury, Yarra Valley.

PRODUCER ENTRIES
All Saints, Baileys, Bannockburn, Bass Phillip, Best's, Brown Brothers, Chambers, Coldstream Hills, Dalwhinnie, Delatite, Domaine Chandon, Dromana Estate, Giaconda, Hanging Rock, Jasper Hill, Lindemans, Mitchelton, Morris, Mount Langi Ghiran, Mount Mary, Seppelt, Stonier, Tahbilk, TarraWarra, Yarra Burn, Yarra Ridge, Yarra Yering, Yellowglen, Yering Station, Yeringberg.

BANNOCKBURN
The experience of several vintages spent at Domaine Dujac in the Côte de Nuits is reflected in Gary Farr's Pinot Noir.

VIEUX-CHÂTEAU-CERTAN

The high level of Cabernets Franc and Sauvignon make this Pomerol wine relatively slow-developing and tannic, becoming supremely complex with age.

VIEUX-CHÂTEAU-CERTAN

FRANCE, Bordeaux, Pomerol AC

♀ Merlot, Cabernet Franc, Cabernet Sauvignon

Traditionally the position of runner-up to Ch. PÉTRUS in POMEROL has always been occupied by Vieux-Château-Certan, but le PIN and TROTANOY now dispute this title. But whereas they often seem to ape Pétrus, Vieux-Château-Certan means to be different.

It is owned by the Thienpont family and, although it is only just down the road from Pétrus, its soil is different, mixing sand and gravel with its clay. But most importantly it has only 60 per cent Merlot as against Pétrus' virtually 100 per cent. The rest of the 13.5-ha (33-acre) vineyard is 30 per cent Cabernet Franc and 10 per cent Cabernet Sauvignon, and it is this unusually strong presence for Pomerol of Cabernet which makes Vieux-Château-Certan drier, leaner, less sumptuous. The slow-maturing wine gradually builds up over 15–20 years into an exciting 'MÉDOC' blend of blackcurrant and cedarwood perfume just offset by the brown sugar and roasted nuts of Pomerol. Best years: 2001, '00, '99, '98, '96, '95, '90, '89, '88, '86, '85, '83, '82.

DOMAINE DU VIEUX TÉLÉGRAPHE

FRANCE, Southern Rhône, Châteauneuf-du-Pape AC

♀ Grenache, Mourvèdre, Syrah and others
♀ Clairette, Grenache Blanc, Bourboulenc, Roussanne

The Brunier family have been managing this extremely well run and consistent estate since 1898. Most of the 70ha (173 acres) of vineyards lie in the eastern part of the CHÂTEAUNEUF-DU-PAPE AC, where the grapes ripen earlier than elsewhere. Many of the vines are over 60 years old, which accounts for the wine's consistent richness. The winery, unlike many in the region, is modern and well equipped, and this is reflected in the wines, which are full of fruit, not unduly tannic and accessible young, though they do age well. In the 1990s the pro-

portion of Mourvèdre increased, giving the red wine more backbone. In 1994 a second winery, Vieux Mas des Papes, was introduced, further enhancing the quality of the main wine. The white Châteauneuf includes a portion of barrel-fermented Roussanne and is usually delicious. Annual production is quite high, at about 220,000 bottles. The Bruniers also own another Châteauneuf estate, Domaine la Roquette and part-own Domaine les Pallières in GIGONDAS. Best years: (reds) 2001, '00, '99, '98, '97, '96, '95, '93, '90, '89.

VILLA CAFAGGIO

ITALY, Tuscany, Chianti Classico DOCG

♀ Sangiovese, Cabernet Sauvignon

You can't get a much better site for your vineyard in CHIANTI CLASSICO than Villa Cafaggio's 30ha (74 acres) bang in the middle of Panzano's golden shell with such star properties as FONTODI, Castello dei RAMPOLLA and La Massa as your neighbours. Panzano is the point at which the clay-dominated soils of Chianti's northern zones give way to the much superior *galestro*, a friable shaly soil that suits the Sangiovese perfectly. Cafaggio wines have got better and better during the 1990s and early 2000s, partly due to owner Stefano Farkas' planting of top Sangiovese clones during the 1990s, but also due to his early inclusion of Cabernet Sauvignon in the vineyard and his unashamed enthusiasm for new oak barrels. The Chiantis and SUPER-TUSCAN San Martino (Sangiovese) and Cortaccio (Cabernet) are rich, ripe and high quality.

VILLA MARIA

NEW ZEALAND, North Island, South Auckland

♀ Merlot, Cabernet Sauvignon, Syrah and others
♀ Sauvignon Blanc, Chardonnay, Riesling, Gewurztraminer and others

George Fistonich, the founder and co-owner of the Villa Maria-Vidal-Esk Valley group, has always been a doughty streetfighter, several times knocked down by economic disasters

VILLA MARIA

The Terraces is one of New Zealand's top red Bordeaux-style blends and only produced in exceptional years. The wine has an unusually high percentage of Malbec (39 per cent) with Merlot and Cabernet Franc making up the rest of the blend.

yet always struggling back to his feet. The results are now plain to see. Villa Maria is by far the largest independently owned winery in New Zealand (and second largest overall behind MONTANA), as well as scooping more medals and trophies in local and international wine competitions than any other New Zealand winery.

Villa Maria is equally effective in both North and South Island, with particularly fine Sauvignon and Chardonnay from MARLBOROUGH, and superb Merlot and Cabernet-based reds from HAWKES BAY. Along with sister labels, Vidal and Esk Valley, the company makes some of the best and most fairly priced wines in all New Zealand at regular, reserve and single-vineyard level. What other New Zealand wine company can claim to make some of the country's best Sauvignon Blanc, Chardonnay, Riesling, BORDEAUX-style reds as well as botrytis-affected sweet wines? And as many of New Zealand's larger companies have consolidated or been bought up, Villa Maria becomes more defiantly independent and its wines seem to improve in response to the challenge. From the 2003 vintage all its wines have been bottled with screwcaps. Best years: (Hawkes Bay reds) 2002, '00, '99, '98.

VILLARD ESTATE

CHILE, Casablanca Valley

♀ Pinot Noir, Cabernet Sauvignon, Merlot
♀ Chardonnay, Sauvignon Blanc

Frenchman Thierry Villard has had a peripatetic wine career. I first met him not in France but in Australia, where he was working for ORLANDO. But he has put his roots down in Chile, especially in the CASABLANCA VALLEY, where he has created one of Chile's first and most successful boutique wineries. He makes excellent Sauvignon Blanc, Chardonnay and Pinot Noir from Casablanca fruit but also uses MAIPO fruit for his tasty Merlot and Cabernet wines. He also periodically makes a stunning sweetie, El Noble, from botrytized Sauvignon Blanc.

VILLARD ESTATE

Chile's Casablanca Valley quickly established a reputation for Chardonnay and this buttery wine with loads of tropical and citrus fruit is one of the best.

CH DE VILLENEUVE
This leading Saumur estate is equally successful with reds and whites. Le Grand Clos, the top red, comes from old Cabernet Franc vines.

CH. DE VILLENEUVE

FRANCE, Loire, Anjou-Saumur, Saumur AC
♥ *Cabernet Franc*
♀ *Chenin Blanc*

During the 1990s, Jean-Pierre Chevallier established Villeneuve as a leading SAUMUR estate. His success comes from his work in the vineyard and he is a passionate believer in the quality of Chenin Blanc. Across the board he is moving towards organic viticulture, as well as adopting biodynamic principles for some parts of his vineyard. The results are clear to see. When rot threatens the vintage, as it often does in the LOIRE VALLEY, his grapes remain healthy and he is able to leave them on the vine to ripen properly while his neighbours rush to save their crop, albeit unripe.

There are three SAUMUR-CHAMPIGNY reds: the estate cuvée; the Vieilles Vignes, which has some barrel aging; and le Grand Clos, which is aged in newer oak for about 18 months. These last two big wines need bottle age to show their best, and even the 'basic' cuvée is more than usually concentrated.

Chevallier is equally successful with his dry Saumur whites, made entirely from Chenin Blanc. The straight Saumur is wonderfully floral, often with some rich exotic fruit and crisp acidity in the finish. Les Cormiers, from old, single-vineyard vines, is both fermented and aged in new oak. This needs to age and is one of the best examples of how complex ambitiously made Chenin Blanc can be.

VILLIERA

SOUTH AFRICA, Western Cape, Stellenbosch WO
♥ *Pinotage, Merlot, Cabernet Sauvignon, Syrah (Shiraz), Pinot Noir and others*
♀ *Chenin Blanc, Sauvignon Blanc, Riesling, Chardonnay and others*

Villiera is now best known as a top producer of Cap Classique (CHAMPAGNE-method) fizz, but the Grier family have been running this estate for 20 years now. I first came across them because of their excellent Bush Vine Sauvignon Blanc, years before South African Sauvignon was as universally acclaimed as it is now. In fact Villiera produces the whole gamut of wine styles, from fine whites to deep ripe reds, with Merlot-Pinotage and BORDEAUX-blend Cru Monro especially good, a decent 'Port' and, of course, the fizzes. Heading the sparkling range is top-quality vintage Monro Brut which, when released with enough age, as the 1995 was, is impressive stuff. Best years: (Cru Monro) 2000, '99, '98, '97, '96, '95, '94.

VIN DE PAYS

FRANCE

There's no doubt about it. The 'New World' is alive and well in France. But it isn't living in the famous regions of BORDEAUX or BURGUNDY, CHAMPAGNE or CHÂTEAUNEUF-DU-PAPE. It's living in the forgotten byways and backwaters of French wine regions that until recently had never made decent wine.

Until 20 years ago all the most famous French wines had come from various renowned ACs, hallowed by time and tradition. But the 1980s brought the wines of Australia, CALIFORNIA, New Zealand and Chile rushing to the front of the world stage and enthused a whole generation of winemakers with the idea that anyone with passion, commitment, some decent grape varieties and some money to invest in good equipment could make great wine. As for the French idea of a sacred terroir, there was no such thing in Australia or New Zealand. There were simply places where you could grow good grapes and places where you couldn't. And in most of France it was exactly the same. Most French vineyards had been condemned for generations simply to produce basic table wine, usually from mediocre grape varieties, because they fell outside the AC boundaries.

Then came the lead set by the Californians, Australians and New Zealanders in taking the great French grapes and creating 'varietal' wines – wines that were first and foremost dependent on the actual grape variety for the flavour. Previously no-one outside the ACs had had the confidence to strike out for quality. Now it became clear that the names of the producer and the grape variety were sufficient to sell wine at a decent price and of an exciting quality.

Of course, this being France and the EU, there has to be some kind of legal framework. And this is provided by the vin de pays category of wines. 'Country wines', the direct translation, implies that these are the traditional wines of the country districts of France which have been enjoyed for centuries by the locals. The reality is a little different and the vast majority are impressively modern.

The name vin de pays was conceived as a category of French wine only in 1968, with improvements made to the concept in 1973. Until then, in many parts of the country – especially the far south – there was a serious problem of overproduction of very mediocre wine and no incentives available to the grower to improve quality since all the wines were consigned to the anonymity of the blending vats of various shippers and merchants. The aim was to encourage quality, and to provide a specific guarantee of geographical origin for the wines. In this the vin de pays system follows the example set by the two top quality tiers in French wines, with similar guidelines based on geographical origin, yield of grapes per hectare, minimum alcohol level and choice of grape varieties, though the controls are looser and generally a wider choice of grape varieties is permitted, including those not 'native' to the region.

There are three geographical categories, each one becoming more specific. Vins de pays régionaux cover a whole region, encompassing several *départements*. There are five of these and any wine made in the region concerned may qualify. The most important is Vin de Pays d'OC, which accounts for 33 per cent of all vin de pays and which is France's principal source of 'varietal' wines. Vins de pays de département cover the wines of a whole *département*. There are approximately 40 of these. Vins de pays de zone is the most specific category, and relates only to the wines of a specific community or locality. There are about 100 of these but many are unknown outside their region.

Overall, the LANGUEDOC-ROUSSILLON region is the leading vin de pays producer, accounting for around 80 per cent of the production. Yield is higher than for ACs since the vins de pays can as yet rarely command high prices, and alcoholic strength is generally

LES VIGNERONS DU VAL D'ORBIEU
La Cuvée Mythique is an attempt to make a deep, ageworthy wine using the traditional Languedoc varieties of Mourvèdre, Carignan and Grenache spiced up with Syrah.

lower. The grape varieties are specified to eliminate the worst sorts, but the crucial element here is that excellent varieties excluded from a region's ACs but capable of producing high-quality wine are included. Consequently, for example, we are seeing excellent white Chardonnay and Sauvignon Blanc and red Merlot and Cabernet Sauvignon from the Languedoc-Roussillon – varieties which had previously been virtually unknown there. These varieties, along with Syrah, Grenache and Cinsaut, now represent nearly 50 per cent of plantings in the Languedoc-Roussillon, with other noble varieties like Pinot Noir and Viognier also to be found. Increasingly, vins de pays are labelled with the grape variety – and these are now the source of some of France's best-value flavours. Lower yields and better winemaking has also enabled less fashionable grape varieties, like Carignan, to make a comeback in a minor way as a 'varietal' wine. Whereas vins de pays are generally regarded as good value, some producers have pushed the bounds with lower yields and aging in new oak barrels to produce higher quality but more expensive wines. The pioneer of this up-market style is Aimé Guibert of MAS DE DAUMAS GASSAC.

VIN SANTO

ITALY, Tuscany, Umbria and Trentino-Alto Adige
♀ *Malvasia, Trebbiano, Sangiovese*

The 'Holy Wine', where the grapes were traditionally left to dry until Holy Week, just before Easter, is called Vino Santo in TRENTINO, Vin Santo elsewhere. Unlike most *passito* wines, the grapes for Vin Santo are usually dried hanging in bunches in airy barns; only occasionally flat on straw mats. After crushing, the juice is put into very small barrels (traditionally 50 litres), called *caratelli*, often together with the mother yeast or *madre* left in after the previous wine's racking, and it ferments very slowly for several years. Indeed, the wine stays sealed in the *caratelli* long past the period of fermentation; three to six years is not unusual. The white juice deepens to gold. The barrel is then opened, the wine tasted, and if deemed good enough goes into the blend for bottling. In each barrel, a little *madre* is left behind for next time.

Making Vin Santo is such an artisanal process that everyone's ideas on how to make it differ. It may be dry, sweet or anything in between. Modern producers have for the most part eschewed the oxidized style that might remind one of sweet sherry and look instead for vibrant if raisiny fruit. The best

Vin Santo comes from AVIGNONESI which includes Grechetto in the Malvasia-Trebbiano blend more usual in TUSCANY, and keeps it for eight years in *caratelli*. Other good Tuscan producers: Castello di AMA, Basciano, Bindella, Cacchiano, Capezzana, Fattoria del Cerro, Corzano & Paterno, FONTODI, ISOLE E OLENA, Romeo, San Felice, San Gervasio, San Giusto a Rentennano, SELVAPIANA, Villa Sant'Anna, Villa di Vetrice and VOLPAIA. UMBRIA's star is from Adanti (made predominantly from Grechetto) and Trentino's (made from Nosiola) comes from Pisoni. Beware of versions declaring themselves to be *liquoroso* – they are fortified and usually pretty nasty.

Vin Santo, in Tuscany, is seen as a post-prandial or as a mid-afternoon pick-me-up, and can be taken with *cantuccini*, those hard, sweet biscuits baked with almonds, often deliciously dunked into the wine.

VIÑAS DEL VERO

SPAIN, Aragón, Somontano DO
♥ *Merlot, Cabernet Sauvignon, Pinot Noir, Tempranillo, Garnacha, Moristel, Syrah*
♦ *Tempranillo, Moristel, Cabernet Sauvignon*
♀ *Chardonnay, Gewürztraminer, Macabeo*

With strong backing from the Aragón regional government, Viñas del Vero was created from scratch in the late 1980s as a giant bodega with important vineyard holdings (550ha/1360 acres) destined to exploit the cool SOMONTANO region's potential and make quality wine at all price levels. With the able enologist Pedro Aibar deftly controlling

VIÑAS DEL VERO
The top white, Clarión, is an age-worthy, partly barrel-fermented blend whose components are doggedly kept a secret, but probably include an unusual blend of Chardonnay, Gewürztraminer and the local Macabeo.

a sizeable annual production of 500,000 cases in his high-tech winery, that goal was reached by the late 1990s, when everything from unoaked young Tempranillo to the top wines was uniformly good. Fine vintages in 1994, '95 and '96 helped the top reds reach their full potential, especially Gran Vos, a Merlot-Cabernet blend with a dollop of Pinot Noir. Blecua is a separate subsidiary producing top-notch reds only.

VINHO VERDE DOC

PORTUGAL, Minho and Douro Litoral
♥ *Amaral, Borraçal, Alvarelhão, Espadeiro, Padeiro, Pedral, Rabo de Anho, Vinhão*
♀ *Alvarinho, Arinto (Paderña), Avesso, Azal, Batoca, Loureiro, Trajadura*

Vinho Verde is one of Portugal's most distinctive wines. It translates as 'green wine' but Vinho Verde may be either red or white. The 'green' refers to the need to drink the wines young as opposed to the designation Vinho Maduro ('mature wine'). Few Vinhos Verdes are vintage dated as the wines are usually from the most recent harvest.

The relatively cool, damp maritime climate of north-west Portugal conspires with high yields to produce grapes that are naturally low in sugar and high in acid. Most wines therefore have natural alcohol levels of no more than 10 per cent and many white Vinhos Verdes are slightly sweetened for export to balance the rasping acidity. Red wines are best kept for the local food. Nearly all the wines have a slight *pétillance* which results from carbon dioxide being injected into the wine before bottling. At its best it is a crisp, dry white to drink ice cold on a hot summer's day. A number of single estates (quintas) are now producing fuller-flavoured varietal Vinhos Verdes from Loureiro or Alvarinho grapes. Best producers: Quinta de Alderiz, Quinta da Aveleda, Quinta da Baguinha, Encostas dos Castelos, Quinta da Franqueira, Monção co-operative (Deu la Deu Alvarinho, Muralhas de Monção), Muros de Melgaço (Alvarinho), Quintas de Melgaço, Palácio de Brejoeira, Dom Salvador, Casa de Sezim, Soalheiro, SOGRAPE (Gazela, Quinta de Azevedo), Quinta do Tamariz (Loureiro).

VINO NOBILE DI MONTEPULCIANO DOCG

ITALY, Tuscany
♥ *Sangiovese (Prugnolo Gentile), Canaiolo and others*

Vino Nobile, unlike its rival BRUNELLO DI MONTALCINO, is a wine with a centuries-old tradition of quality, but it has had its ups and downs. At present it is well on the way to coming out of a very deep depression lasting most of the middle part of the twentieth century, when it descended to the level of ordinary CHIANTI, itself at a pretty low ebb. During the 1990s there were energetic efforts to raise quality and today there are several wineries equal with the best of TUSCANY.

The vineyards are located at 250 to 600m (820 to 1970ft) on the sides of a massive hill, atop which sits the narrow, cobbled, steeply sloping streets of Montepulciano itself. Exposures are excellent, the climate more benign than in CHIANTI to the north.

The principal grape variety is Sangiovese, here called Prugnolo Gentile, supported by Canaiolo, with the optional addition of other international grapes such as Cabernet Sauvignon, Merlot and others. The wine must be aged for two years before release, three years for Riserva. This puts its image somewhere between CHIANTI CLASSICO and Brunello di Montalcino, and the truth is that Vino Nobile has not yet decided exactly who it is. But there are some excellent producers and every year Vino Nobile's identity becomes clearer. Best years: 2001, '00, '99, '97, '95, '93, '90, '88. Best producers: AVIGNONESI, Bindella, BOSCARELLI, La Braccesca/ANTINORI, Le Casalte, La Ciarliana, Contucci, Dei, Del Cerro, Fassati, Il Macchione, Nottola, Palazzo Vecchio, POLIZIANO, Redi, Romeo, Salcheto, Trerose (Angelini), Valdipiatta.

VINOS DE MADRID DO

SPAIN, Madrid
♟ ♟ *Tempranillo (Tinto Fino), Grenache Noir (Garnacha), Merlot, Cabernet Sauvignon*
♀ *Albillo, Malvar, Airén, Macabeo (Viura), Torrontés, Parellada*

With five centuries of winemaking behind them, perhaps it's surprising that Madrid's wine producers gained their DO only as recently as 1990. The DO covers three areas, all to the south of the capital, with 11,750ha (29,000 acres) of vineyards. Arganda del Rey, the eastern zone, produces most of the DO's white wines, as well as the best reds – made from Tinto Fino as opposed to the Garnacha used in the other two areas south-west of Madrid, Navalcarnero and the more promising, mountainous San Martín de Valdeiglesias. Quality remains average throughout the DO but the top winemakers are finally producing a few serious reds. Best producers: Ricardo de Benito, Francisco Casas, Jesús Díaz, Jeromín.

VIOGNIER

You may well wonder how Viognier became one of France's leading grape varieties when there are less than 750ha (1850 acres) planted in its Rhône Valley homeland. Ah, but never mind the quantity, taste the wine – if you can find any. The vine is an incredibly poor yielder, producing less than any other mainstream dry white variety, and the two tiny Rhône vineyards – Château-Grillet and Condrieu – which make 100 per cent Viognier wines are some of the rarest labels in the world. It has one of the most memorable flavours of any white grape because it manages to blend the rich, musky scent of an overripe apricot with the breeze-blown perfume of springtime orchard flowers. Autumn and spring in one glass. Taste the wine and you'll swear it's sweet but it isn't. It's strange but also very special.

Viognier also traditionally occurs in Côte-Rôtie, just north of Condrieu, where it can be blended with Syrah to make one of France's greatest red wines. Can be, but few growers have more than 5 per cent of Viognier today.

But it is on the increase in the Ardèche, southern Rhône and Languedoc-Roussillon, where it is having runaway success as a varietal wine and to add elegance and aroma to blends. California has a rapidly growing number of exciting producers and Australia, New Zealand, South America and South Africa are getting in on the act too. Viognier can also be found in Italy, Spain and Greece.

VIRGINIA

USA
The eastern state of Virginia was the first of the original thirteen colonies to try its hand with imported wine grape vines from Europe in the seventeenth century. The trouble was the phylloxera vine louse destroyed vines as fast as they were planted. President Thomas Jefferson tried as hard as anyone at his Monticello Estate, but failed just as ignominiously.

By 1960 there were only 6.5ha (16 acres) of vines left in Virginia. Since then there's been a remarkable revival – there are now 810ha (2000 acres) of vines, more than 80 wineries, and pretty decent whites and reds, led by Chardonnay, Riesling, Cabernet Franc and Merlot, but including such unlikely bedfellows as Barbera and Viognier. Wineries to look for are Barboursville, Horton, Meredyth and Prince Michel.

ROBERTO VOERZIO

ITALY, Piedmont, Barolo DOCG
♟ *Nebbiolo, Barbera, Dolcetto, Merlot*

One of the best of the new wave of BAROLO producers that came to prominence in the late 1980s. Dolcetto, called Priavino, is successful, as is Vignaserra – barrique-aged Nebbiolo – and the outstanding new BARBERA D'ALBA Riserva Vigneto Pozzo dell'Annunziata. Barriques are also used for fashioning his Barolo, but such is the quality and concentration of fruit coming from densely planted vineyards that the oak does not overwhelm. Single-vineyard examples made in the best years are Brunate, Cerequio, La Serra and new Riserva Capalot. Best years: (Barolo) 2001, '00, '99, '98, '97, '96, '95, '93, '91, '90, '89, '88, '85.

COMTE GEORGES DE VOGÜÉ

FRANCE, Burgundy, Côte de Nuits, Chambolle-Musigny AC
♟ *Pinot Noir*
♀ *Chardonnay*

One of the oldest estates in BURGUNDY, de Vogüé is celebrated for its MUSIGNY Vieilles Vignes, which at its best can be one of the most breathtakingly yet sumptuous elegant wines in all of Burgundy. Those unable to afford its astronomic price should settle for one of the 'lesser' wines: the BONNES-MARES or exquisite CHAMBOLLE-MUSIGNY les Amoureuses. De Vogüé has substantial holdings in all these vineyards – including 77 per cent of Musigny itself – so these wines are produced in generous quantities.

It is no secret that in the 1980s the wines slipped well below the standards set in the '40s and '50s. However, since the arrival of the taciturn François Millet as winemaker in the late 1980s there has been a marked improvement. The 1990 Musigny was magnificent and subsequent vintages have shown this was no fluke. The wines are once again quintessential elegant Chambolle, yet they never lack depth or concentration. Best years: (Musigny) 2002, '01, '00, '99, '98, '97, '96, '95, '93, '92, '91, '90.

VOLNAY AC

FRANCE, Burgundy, Côte de Beaune

♦ *Pinot Noir*

Until the eighteenth century, Volnay produced BURGUNDY's Nouveau wine, much the same way as BEAUJOLAIS does now. The wine was extremely pale and was snapped up for high prices. The soil has a fair bit of chalk and limestone, particularly in the higher vineyards – normally the cue for planting white vines, but there isn't a white vine in Volnay's 215ha (530 acres) of vineyards.

There are, in fact, two main styles of Volnay. One is light, perfumed in a delicious cherry and strawberry way, sometimes even lifted by a floral scent. However, there are also wines of tremendous, juicy, plummy power, particularly from the lower vineyards like les Champans and les Santenots (which is actually in MEURSAULT but is called Volnay-Santenots). Volnay is drinkable at three to four years old, but unless the wine is very light this is usually a pity, because lovely flavours can develop between seven and ten years. Best years: 2002, '99, '98, '97, '96, '95, '93, '91, '90. Best producers: R Ampeau, d'ANGERVILLE, J-M Boillot, J-M Bouley, Carré-Courbin, COCHE-DURY, V GIRARDIN, LAFARGE, LAFON, Dom. Matrot, MONTILLE, N Potel, J Prieur, Roblet-Monnot, J Voillot.

CASTELLO DI VOLPAIA

ITALY, Tuscany, Chianti Classico DOCG

♦ *Sangiovese, Merlot, Cabernet Sauvignon, Pinot Noir (Pinot Nero), Syrah and others*

♀ *Trebbiano Toscano, Malvasia, Chardonnay, Sauvignon Blanc and others*

The wines from this beautifully preserved hamlet perched high up in the hills of CHIANTI CLASSICO in the commune of Radda, are known for their elegance and perfume rather than power and opulence. This is to some extent consistent with the altitude of the vineyards – at between 450 and 600m (1500–200ft) they are some of the highest in Chianti – and with the nature of their soil, which has a marked sandy component.

The top wines are the stylish SUPER-TUSCANs Coltassala and Balifico. The former is a barrique-aged, mainly Sangiovese wine whose intense cherry-fruit and floral aromas are joined by hints of vanilla. Balifico is a blend of Sangiovese topped up with Cabernets Sauvignon and Franc, combining gentle soft-fruit aromas (strawberry, loganberry) with the same fine-grained tannins that grace the Coltassala. The Chianti Classicos, both the *normale* and Riserva, have less of the

CASTELLO DI VOLPAIA

Coltassala is a top-quality super-Tuscan from Sangiovese with a drop of Mammolo. The bouquet has a classic trace of ripe blackcurrants and vanilla.

concentration and intensity of the super-Tuscans but share the tendency to gracefulness, while achieving relatively early drinkability.

VOSNE-ROMANÉE AC

FRANCE, Burgundy, Côte de Nuits

♦ *Pinot Noir*

They call it the greatest village in Burgundy – simply because it has an incomparable clutch of six red Grands Crus at its heart. There are 183ha (452 acres) of vineyards of which just under 27ha (67 acres) are the Grands Crus RICHEBOURG, LA TÂCHE, LA ROMANÉE, Romanée-Conti, Romanée-St-Vivant and La Grande Rue. This village total includes the wines from the village of Flagey-Échézeaux, whose Grands Crus ÉCHÉZEAUX and Grands-Échézeaux have separate appellations.

However, a village's reputation is not just made on its Grands Crus. There are 46ha (114 acres) of Premiers Crus which match Grands Crus from other villages in quality. Best of these are les Malconsorts and les Suchots. And the fact that all of Vosne-Romanée's other AC land is on the slopes to the west of the N74 road, rather than slipping across to the inferior plains beyond, also helps to keep the wine quality high.

The mix of exciting, red-fruit ripeness with a delicious tangle of spices and smoke that finally ages to the deep, decaying pleasures of prunes, brown sugar and chocolate, moist autumn dampness and well-hung game – all these make Vosne-Romanée red one of the world's really exciting experiences. In good years the wines should have at least six years' age – 10–15 would be even better. Lighter years still need five to eight years. Best years: 2002, '01, '00, '99, '98, '97, '96, '95, '93, '91, '90. Best producers: R Arnoux, Cacheux-Sirugue, Sylvain Cathiard, Champy, B CLAIR, B Clavelier, R ENGEL, GRIVOT, Anne Gros, A-F Gros, Haegelen-Jayer, F Lamarche, LEROY, MÉO-CAMUZET, Mugneret-Gibourg, Rion, Dom. de la ROMANÉE-CONTI, E Rouget, THOMAS-MOILLARD.

VOUGEOT AC

FRANCE, Burgundy, Côte de Nuits

♦ *Pinot Noir*

♀ *Chardonnay*

Most people are accustomed to seeing CLOS DE VOUGEOT rather than plain Vougeot on a label. But there are 16ha (40 acres) of Vougeot vines outside the famous walled Clos, producing annually about 70,000 bottles of wine, divided six to one in red's favour. It's not bad stuff – full and slightly solid to start but gaining a really good chocolaty richness with a few years age – and it's a lot cheaper than Clos de Vougeot – but then, what isn't? The Premiers Crus Clos de la Perrière, les Cras and les Petits Vougeots are best. The Clos Blanc de Vougeot vineyard was first planted with white grapes in 1110. Best years: (reds) 2002, '01, '00, '99, '98, '97, '96, '95, '93, '91, '90, '89, '88. Best producers: Bertagna, Chopin-Groffier, C Clerget, Vougeraie.

CH. LA VOULTE-GASPARETS

FRANCE, Languedoc-Roussillon, Corbières AC

♦ *Carignan, Grenache, Mourvèdre, Syrah*

♀ *Grenache Blanc, Rolle, Macabeo*

A leading light in CORBIÈRES, la Voulte-Gasparets produces two top wines from hillside vineyards on the 46-ha (114-acre) estate. The top wines, the Cuvée Reservée and Romain Pauc, are both made from 60 per cent Carignan, 30 per cent Grenache and 10 per cent Syrah, but whereas the vines for the Cuvée Reservée average 20 to 40 years, those for Romain Pauc average 45 to 90 years and are much lower yielding, giving the wine an extra edge of concentration and intensity. Romain Pauc is also aged for longer in barriques, 10 per cent of which are renewed yearly. These wines require four to five years of aging in bottle, whereas the generic Corbières, both red and white, are for drinking young. Best years: (Romain Pauc) 2001, '00, '98, '96, '95, '93, '91.

VOUVRAY AC

FRANCE, Loire, Touraine

♀ *Chenin Blanc*

Chenin's excruciatingly high acidity is both the main problem with young Vouvray, and also the reason why the best ones last 50 years. The grapes in this decidedly one-grape town grow in 2000ha (4940 acres) of picturesque vineyards east of Tours, on a limestone and chalk clay soil – which yields intensely flavoured juice, but in cool years creates even more acidity. Unripe grapes traditionally go to make Vouvray Mousseux AC, produced by the CHAMPAGNE method and usually of a high standard. The best sparkling Vouvray is the semi-sparkling *pétillant* but sadly it remains a little known local speciality.

However, the still wines are more exciting. They can be dry – in which case they'll start out bitingly sharp, but round out beautifully into a dry buttermilk and nuts flavour after about ten years. And they can be sweet *(moelleux)* with occasional noble rot, producing wines of quince and honey-soft sweetness but ever-present acidity. Vouvray's greatest role is as a medium-dry *(demi-sec)* wine. Cheap Vouvray has spoilt our appreciation of this style, but when it is properly made from a single domaine, it will slowly, perhaps over 20 years, build up an exciting, smoky peach, pears and quince fullness. Best years: 2002, '01, '99, '97, '96, '95, '93, '90, '89, '88, '85, '83, '78, '76, '75, '70. Best producers: Aubuisières, Bourillon-Dorléans, Champalou, CLOS NAUDIN, la Fontainerie, Gaudrelle, Gautier, Haute Borne, HUET, Pichot, F Pinon, Taille aux Loups, Vigneau Chevreau.

WACHAU

AUSTRIA, Niederösterreich
The beautiful Wachau region west of Vienna is just one brief 32-km (20-mile) long kink in the great River Danube, but as the river forces its way through the high wooded hills it creates pockets of steep stony soil on which grapegrowers have built narrow terraces for more than 1000 years, producing slender amounts of white wines that rival the finest in the world. Altogether there are 1390ha (3435 acres) of vines. The dominant grape is the Grüner Veltliner, which makes marvellously savoury, peppery, broad-shouldered whites, but Wachau Rieslings can be even better, ranging from impressively dry to irresistibly sweet and never losing a thrilling streak of minerality, however ripe the fruit gets. Several other excellent whites include Chardonnay, Muscat and Pinot Gris. Smaragd is a local term for fully ripe dry whites.

The top Wachau wines are usually labelled with the name of a vineyard site and some of the best of these are Singerriedel and Tausendeimerberg in SPITZ, Achleiten in WEISSENKIRCHEN, Kellerberg in DÜRNSTEIN and Loibenberg in Unterloiben. Best years: 2002, '01, '00, '99, '98, '97, '95, '94, '93, '92, '90, '88, '86, '83, '79, '77. Best producers: F HIRTZBERGER, Högl, Emmerich KNOLL, NIKOLAIHOF, F X PICHLER, PRAGER, Freie Weingärtner WACHAU.

FREIE WEINGÄRTNER WACHAU

AUSTRIA, Wachau, Dürnstein
♀ Pinot Noir (Blauburgunder), Zweigelt
♀ Grüner Veltliner, Riesling, Pinot Blanc, Müller-Thurgau, Muscat (Gelber Muskateller), Chardonnay
This co-operative winery regularly produces some of the WACHAU's best white wines, even though it takes the grapes from fully 600ha (1480 acres) of vineyards. Of course, with production on this scale there are bound to be some simpler wines, but everything sold under the main label depicting the baroque 'Kellerschlössel' is good to first class.

Top of the range are the Smaragd wines from the region's top sites in SPITZ, WEISSENKIRCHEN, DÜRNSTEIN, Oberloiben and Unterloiben which are sold under the Domäne Wachau label. These are powerful, concentrated dry wines which can age magnificently. Best years: 2002, '01, '99, '98, '97, '96, '95, '93, '92, '91, '90.

WAIHEKE ISLAND

NEW ZEALAND, North Island
GOLDWATER established the first vineyard on this small island in AUCKLAND Harbour and made the first Waiheke wine in 1982. Now there are nearly 120ha (300 acres) of vines and more than 30 winemakers on this fashionable island. Waiheke boasts a hotter, drier climate than Auckland and mostly free-draining clay/loam soils of moderate to low fertility. Cabernet Sauvignon represents nearly one-third of Waiheke's production although it is always blended with at least one partner, usually more.

Although the island is regarded as probably New Zealand's best BORDEAUX-style red wine region there is growing interest in Chardonnay, possibly in response to market demand rather than the island's ability to make great white wine. Syrah is growing in popularity, with the first small release from STONYRIDGE suggesting that the variety has a future there. Best years: (reds) 2002, '00, '99, '98, '96. Best producers: Fenton, Goldwater, Obsidian, Stonyridge, Te Whau.

WALLA WALLA VALLEY AVA

USA, Washington State and Oregon
A sub-appellation of the vast COLUMBIA VALLEY AVA, this is unusual in that it encompasses vineyards in both south-east WASHINGTON and north-east OREGON. It is now one of the fastest growing AVAs in the USA with 325ha (800 acres) already planted and more to come. There are over 50 wineries, but 22 have only been producing since 1999. There's a real goldrush feel to this clearly exciting area, especially since many of the recent plantings are of Washington's new sexy variety, Syrah. Best producers: CANOE RIDGE, Dunham Cellars, L'ECOLE NO 41, LEONETTI CELLAR, Pepper Bridge Winery, WOODWARD CANYON.

WARRE

PORTUGAL, Douro, Port DOC
♀ Touriga Franca, Touriga Nacional, Tempranillo (Tinta Roriz), Tinta Barroca, Tinto Cão and others
♀ Gouveio, Viosinho, Rabigato, Malvasia Fina and others
Warre is the oldest British PORT shipper, having been founded in 1670. Although the family still retain a link, the company is owned (along with DOW and GRAHAM) by the Symingtons. Its style of port is usually somewhere between the dry austerity of Dow and the richness of Graham. Warre's vintage ports, based on the company's Quinta de Cavadinha vineyard, combine perfumed opulence with the substance and structure to last. Wine from Cavadinha is also bottled as a single-quinta vintage port in good interim years and, like SMITH WOODHOUSE, which also belongs to the Symington family, Warre produces an unfiltered, bottle-matured LBV. One of Warre's greatest triumphs is Warrior, a rich, dense premium ruby port which is consistently the among the very best in its class. Best years: (Vintage) 2000, '97, '94, '91, '85, '83, '80, '77, '70, '66, '63; (Cavadinha) 1999, '98, '95, '92, '90, '88, '87, '86, '82, '78.

WARWICK ESTATE

SOUTH AFRICA, Western Cape, Stellenbosch WO
♀ Cabernet Sauvignon, Merlot, Cabernet Franc, Pinotage
♀ Chardonnay, Sauvignon Blanc
Warwick Estate, beautifully situated on the pass between STELLENBOSCH and PAARL, has always aimed high. Cabernet Sauvignon vines were planted soon after Stan Ratcliffe bought the property in 1964, and after several trips to Europe, Norma Ratcliffe decided on a strongly BORDEAUX-oriented winemaking style which saw her complex Bordeaux blend Trilogy, as well as Merlot and Cabernet Franc, make the Estate's reputation. These wines have now been joined by Three Cape Ladies – a Cabernet-Merlot-Pinotage blend – as well as Chardonnay, Sauvignon and Old Bush Vines Pinotage. Now run by son Michael, the estate has been farmed organically for ten years. Best years: (Trilogy) 2000, '99, '98, '97, '96, '95, '94.

WASHINGTON STATE USA

WASHINGTON STATE IS DIVIDED neatly into two by the high, ever-snowy Cascade Range, as is Oregon, its neighbour to the south. On the west is the cool, often rainy Puget Sound basin, where sun is at a premium and on the east is the dry, generally sunny Columbia River basin where irrigation is an absolute necessity. Washington's grape growers and wine-makers have almost exactly reversed the Oregon experience. While their southern neighbours have their vines in the cool west and lean heavily to grape varieties developed in Burgundy, Washingtonians grow the great majority of their vines in the warm east and they favour vine types native to Bordeaux, most particularly Semillon for whites and Cabernet Sauvignon and Merlot for reds though there is good Chardonnay, and Syrah/Shiraz may yet prove the best reds.

A pair of Washington wineries began to make varietal table wines from vinifera grapes in the late 1960s but the real blossoming did not come until the 1970s. Ever faster growth has come since then, and the roster of wineries now numbers over 200, and wine vine plantings total 11,330ha (28,000 acres).

Washington has won recognition for its red wines from Merlot and Cabernet Sauvignon, and Syrah has come from nowhere to be the state's third red grape after a tidal wave of plantings in the late 1990s. Washington Chardonnays match up favourably with California's when the wines are young, being in general a little lighter, less lush. Pinot Gris, Gewurztraminer and Riesling (Washington's original star grape variety) are on the increase and growers are showing a lot of interest in Syrah's Rhône counterpart, Viognier. Semillon can be the USA's best when barrel-fermented.

Producers in Washington have begun the process of carving their state into various growing regions. The foremost one is the semi-arid Yakima Valley, a long, straight slice from the eastern foothills of the Cascades down to the Yakima River's confluence with the Columbia River near an urban centre called Tri-Cities (Pasco, Kennewick and Richland). The Yakima Valley holds a little more than half of Washington's vineyards, along with far larger plantings of dozens of

The Yakima Valley is a prosperous agricultural region and densely planted with vineyards. Mechanical harvesting, here at Covey Run, one of the Yakima's largest producers, is the only practical way of harvesting such large quantities of grapes.

other crops. A small area to the south-east of Yakima now holds the separate Red Mountain AVA. The Walla Walla Valley east of the Columbia River is the other specific growing region. These AVAs and all other grape-growing regions in eastern Washington fall within the umbrella Columbia Valley AVA, which also includes a big slice of land in northern Oregon. Most eastern Washington vineyards not in the Yakima or Walla Walla Valleys lie near the Columbia River between Vantage and the Tri-Cities or along the Snake River east of Tri-Cities. No one region in Washington has established itself yet as notably more adapted to any one grape variety than its neighbours, though Walla Walla and Red

LEONETTI CELLAR

This small winery based in the Walla Walla Valley makes outstanding Merlot and Cabernet Sauvignon. The wines are immense with concentrated fruit.

QUILCEDA CREEK VINTNERS

This tiny winery has built a cult following in Washington because of its big, rich Cabernet Sauvignon that ages gracefully for well over a decade.

DELILLE CELLARS

Using fruit from some of Yakima Valley's top vineyards, Chaleur Estate is the premium red wine here where the goal is to make top-quality Bordeaux-style blends.

THE HOGUE CELLARS
This long-established winery has added peppery Syrah to its large range of wines. Syrah, along with the other Rhône varieties, is a relative newcomer to Washington State and acreage has increased substantially since the late 1990s.

Mountain have both made a series of impressive reds from Cabernet, Merlot and Syrah.

Many of the state's most important wineries (for example Chateau Ste Michelle, Columbia Cellars and Arbor Crest) are in or near the cities of Seattle and Spokane, well placed to serve their local markets. In western Washington there are just a handful of vineyards.

ANDREW WILL WINERY
First made in 1994, Sorella is one of the winery's top wines. A Bordeaux blend, the wine balances ripe berry fruit and oak with an elegant texture.

REGIONAL ENTRIES
Columbia Valley, Walla Walla Valley, Yakima Valley.

PRODUCER ENTRIES
Andrew Will Winery, Canoe Ridge Vineyard, Chateau Ste Michelle, Chinook Wines, Columbia Crest, DeLille Cellars, Hedge Cellars, Kiona, Leonetti Cellar, McCrea Cellars, Quilceda Creek Vintners, Woodward Canyon Winery.

L'ECOLE No 41
This is a consistent producer of both reds and whites, including Apogee, a Bordeaux-style blend from the Pepper Bridge Vineyard in Walla Walla Valley.

COLUMBIA CREST
Columbia Crest now has its own extensive quality vineyards to draw on for its top wines, Grand Estates Merlot and Chardonnay.

CHATEAU STE MICHELLE
The international acclaim achieved by this pioneering winery for its enormous range of wines has created the market for Washington State wines.

WOODWARD CANYON WINERY
Big, barrel-fermented Chardonnay with layers of new oak is the trademark of this renowned winery. The Celilo Vineyard blend is top of the range.

KIONA
A family operation in sagebrush country, Kiona has a growing reputation for its marvellous fruit. The Late-Harvest White Riesling has clean, pure fruit flavours and heady perfume.

GEOFF WEAVER

Geoff Weaver's small, high-quality vineyard produces Sauvignon Blanc jammed with intense varietal character and lovely fruit sweetness.

GEOFF WEAVER

AUSTRALIA, South Australia, Adelaide Hills
♦ *Pinot Noir, Cabernet Sauvignon, Merlot*
♀ *Sauvignon Blanc, Chardonnay, Riesling*

In a way you need to go up into the ADELAIDE HILLS with Geoff Weaver in the bright early morning and sit with him idly, silently, contemplating his lovely vineyards to really understand him and his wines. He is now a winegrower and an artist – he creates his own labels – and someone who is truly content in his low-key calling, making excellent tangy Sauvignon Blanc and Riesling and smoothly honed Chardonnay and Pinot Noir. Then ask him for his history, and he'll tell you he was one of the most powerful winemakers in Australia in 1992, heading HARDY's winemaking, responsible for 10 per cent of all Australia's grapes. And I knew him then too. He wasn't happy then. He is now.

WEHLEN

GERMANY, Mosel-Saar-Ruwer

The great south-south-west-facing Wehlener Sonnenuhr or 'Sundial' vineyard is directly across the river from the village of Wehlen, a part of the curving wall of slate that towers over the Mosel river from BERNKASTEL down to ERDEN and just beyond. There have been vines planted in the Sonnenuhr supposedly since the ninth century and the steep, rocky site with its stony, grey slate soil imparts steely intensity and fire to the wines – archetypal MOSEL, archetypal Riesling.

The fame of Wehlen, in fact, rests on this one 65-ha (160-acre) vineyard. It has others, on the same side of the river as the town, and Klosterberg is good – but nothing can compete with Wehlener Sonnenuhr. Best years: 2002, '01, '00, '99, '98, '97, '96, '95, '94, '93, '92, '90. Best producers: Kerpen, Dr LOOSEN, Markus Molitor, J J PRÜM, S A PRÜM, Max Ferd RICHTER, SELBACH-OSTER, Wegeler, Dr Weins-Prüm.

ROBERT WEIL

GERMANY, Rheingau, Kiedrich
♦ *Pinot Noir (Spätburgunder)*
♀ *Riesling*

Renamed Robert Weil from Dr Weil after its purchase by the Japanese drinks giant Suntory at the end of the 1980s, this estate has since soared to the pinnacle of the RHEINGAU. Huge investments in the most modern cellars in the region and director Wilhelm Weil's fanaticism for quality are the reasons. The Auslese and higher Prädikat wines are among the finest Riesling dessert wines in Germany. Prices may be high, but these wines have a pristine clarity, great concentration and enormous aging potential. The only vineyard designation used is the KIEDRICHer Gräfenberg, one of the Rheingau's undisputed 'Grands Crus'. The best bottlings from this site get the additional 'Gold Cap' designation and are sold through auction. All other wines are sold under just the estate name. There is a tiny amount of Spätburgunder (2 per cent). Best years: 2002, '01, '99, '98, '97, '96, '95.

DOMAINE WEINBACH

FRANCE, Alsace, Alsace AC
♦ *Pinot Noir*
♀ *Riesling, Gewurztraminer, Pinot Gris, Pinot Blanc, Muscat, Sylvaner, Chasselas*

There's a lot to be said for matriarchy if the Weinbach estate in Kaysersberg is typical of it. Mme Colette Faller plus daughters run this impeccable estate. Visitors are ushered into a drawing-room, and one of the Fallers will enter from time to time bearing a bottle for tasting, beginning with classic Rieslings and Pinot Gris and culminating, perhaps, with a celestial Sélection de Grains Nobles. The cuvées, such as Cuvée Théo, are often named after family members. Fortunately everything's good, and most of the wines are superb, lean, classic, exceptionally balanced and can be aged for many years. Grapes are picked as late as possible and many of the most elegant come from the Grand Cru Schlossberg. The Cuvée Ste-Catherine is usually picked on or around 25 November: St Catherine's Day. These are expensive wines but they are hand-crafted and of the highest quality. Best years: (Grand Cru Riesling) 2001, '00, '99, '98, '97, '96, '95.

WEINERT

ARGENTINA, Mendoza
♦ *Malbec, Cabernet Sauvignon, Merlot*
♀ *Chardonnay, Sauvignon Blanc*

In a way Weinert was the first famous modern winery in Argentina. Based on an old winery bought and re-named by Brazilian Bernardo Weinert in 1975, it made its name with thick, richly textured yet decidedly old-style reds. One famous red – the Malbec Star 1977 – yes 1977 – was aged for 20 years in big vats before bottling. I never particularly liked those big old bruisers. There's a new Swiss winemaker and signs are that these beefy old reds are lightening up and modernizing a little.

WEINVIERTEL

AUSTRIA, Niederösterreich

Stretching north and east of Vienna, this is easily Austria's largest wine region, with 15,892ha (39,268 acres) of vineyards, a third of Austria's total. Most of the wine made is light, crisp Grüner Veltliner for everyday quaffing. Only in a few corners, such as the Mailberg Valley close to the border with the Czech Republic (with reds from Zweigelt and Blauer Portugieser), Falkenstein (known for fragrant Riesling) and around Korneuburg (rich, spicy wines from Grüner Veltliner and Riesling), close to Vienna, do the wines rise to greater things.

In 2003 the Weinviertel was the first region to implement the new Austrian DAC appellation system, based on a wine's origin not its grape variety. The Weinviertel DAC covers typical wines made from Grüner Veltliner, which covers 50 per cent of the region's vineyards and more than 400 producers from the region now offer such wines. Best producers: Diem, Graf Hardegg, PFAFFL, Setzer, Zull.

WELLINGTON WO

SOUTH AFRICA, Western Cape

It's only recently that Wellington has appeared on the labels of South African wines. Not that it wasn't making any – Wellington has been an important producer for at least a century, and one of the Cape's first wine co-operatives was formed at Wellington in 1906. But the vast majority of its grapes ended up in bottles labelled PAARL 'sherry'. I remember them – they were a very good sherry imitation, but as that

DIEMERSFONTEIN

Diemersfontein is a new label using high-quality fruit grown on excellent Glen Rosa soils on cool, high slopes well above the broiling valley floor.

Famous for its great Rieslings, the steep Sonnenuhr vineyard at Wehlen in the Mittel Mosel is named after its prominent sundial, built in 1842 for the vineyard workers.

Today, Wente owns 810ha (2000 acres) of vineyards in the small Livermore AVA, almost half the total, and 324ha (800 acres) in Arroyo Seco in MONTEREY, where it pioneered grapegrowing. Its prestige wines are labelled Wente Vineyard Reserve and include Riva Ranch Chardonnay from Monterey, Cabernet and Merlot from Livermore Valley and Reliz Creek Pinot Noir from Arroyo Seco in Monterey. Syrah is a new and encouraging addition. CHAMPAGNE-method sparkling wines are also made, but Chardonnay and Cabernet are the bread-and-butter wines.

Eric Wente, the current head of the firm, is deeply involved with efforts to avoid urban sprawl consuming what remains of Livermore Valley's agricultural land. And he's a fanatic for far-flung, joint ventures – I last met him in the Maharashtra hills above Mumbai in India.

WENZEL
AUSTRIA, Burgenland, Neusiedlersee-Hügelland, Rust
🍷 *Pinot Noir, Blaufränkisch, Merlot*
🍾 *Furmint, Sauvignon Blanc, Pinot Gris (Ruländer), Gelber Muskateller*

Robert Wenzel makes the most traditional AUSBRUCH in RUST, which is effectively to say the best in Austria; his dry wines are pretty stylish too, with bags of character.

He was the first grower in Rust to replant Furmint, which was always traditional here (it is the principal grape variety in Hungary's great sweet TOKAJI wines). The Ausbruch wine spends a long time in cask and the results are totally different to a Trockenbeerenauslese: less grapy and with a touch of tangy *rancio*. The grapes are botrytized, as they are with Trockenbeerenauslesen, but fresh grapes or must are added to help the fermentation along. Robert has begun to hand over the reins to his son, Michael and other members of the family. Best years: (Ausbruch) 2000, '98, '95, '93, '91.

---

market dried up, it took Wellington a while to work out what to do next. Wellington is at the north end of Paarl so doesn't benefit from the sea breezes, and on the valley floor it is decidedly hot – a reason its easy-ripening Chenin Blanc was so popular for sherry. But there are also very good vineyard zones which weren't exploited in the old days. There's a whole hillside of mostly east-facing Glen Rosa red soil that is proving excellent for black grapes, and the Groeneberg has high, east-facing and *very* cool slopes also producing exciting red wines. Best producers: Diemersfontein, Mont du Toit.

WENDOUREE
AUSTRALIA, South Australia, Clare Valley
🍷 *Syrah (Shiraz), Cabernet Sauvignon, Mourvedre, Malbec, Mataro*
🍾 *Muscat of Alexandria*

Wendouree must rank at the very top of the vinous national treasures of Australia. The stone winery was constructed by A P Birks in 1895, and much of the second-hand equipment he obtained for the winery is still in use. Then there are the 100-year-old vines planted in a truly unique pocket of the CLARE VALLEY, with a magic combination of climate and soil. And for the past 20 years there has been the fierce guardianship of Tony and Lita Brady, and the winemaking skills of Stephen George.

If you want the most profound and timeless red wines, which need 25 years before they begin to unfold, and with another 50 years' life thereafter, forget all the new pretenders and come to Wendouree, where patient, exhaustive pursuit of ultimate quality has been going on without any fanfare for 100 years. Actual composition of the wines released each year varies, and is usually a mix of blends and varietals. There is also excellent medium-sweet Muscat and an inspired Vintage Port. Best years: (reds) 2001, '99, '98, '96, '95, '94, '92, '91, '90, '86, '83, '82, '81, '80, '78, '76, '75.

WENTE VINEYARDS
USA, California, Alameda County, Livermore Valley AVA
🍷 *Cabernet Sauvignon, Merlot, Zinfandel, Pinot Noir, Syrah*
🍷 *Zinfandel*
🍾 *Chardonnay, Pinot Gris (Pinot Grigio), Riesling, Sauvignon Blanc*

Wente was founded in 1883 by Carl Wente who believed the Livermore Valley had great potential for white wines: the gravelly soils reminded him of the GRAVES region in BORDEAUX. A little empire was built on the strength of Wente's whites, with the Bordeaux varieties of Sauvignon Blanc and Sémillon used for the quality wines.

WENZEL
The Wenzel family is one of the leading producers of Ausbruch dessert wines, an Austrian speciality traditionally made from Furmint. Furmint is particularly susceptible to the botrytis or noble rot fungus which occurs regularly each autumn in the vineyards of Rust on the western shore of Lake Neusiedl.

WESTERN AUSTRALIA Australia

IT'S THE SHEER VASTNESS of Western Australia that hits you first. That and the emptiness. If you approach Perth, the one centre of population, from the north or the east, you can gaze from the plane window in vain for any signs of life. Any township, any road or railway, any river even, or lake – and the searing orange soils glare back at you, offering nothing and no-one. Since the state covers well over a third of Australia's landmass, yet boasts a population of a mere 1.9 million, you begin to understand how isolated the few inhabitants must feel. The export markets of Asia are closer to Perth than the domestic markets of the rest of Australia to the east. Yet Western Australia can lay fair claim to being one of the originators of vineyards in Australia. Though New South Wales, where the first fleet arrived in 1788, was the first to plant vines, Western Australia wasn't far behind – and was way ahead of South Australia and Victoria. Olive Farm had vines planted in 1829 on the banks of the Swan River just outside Perth, and since it is still going today, counts as the oldest operating winery in Australia. And it must have been reasonably decent stuff they made in the Swan Valley, because towards the end of the nineteenth century the valley had more wineries than any other Australian region. And until the 1970s there was only one wine that regularly found its way out of the local market – Houghton's White Burgundy – now renamed Houghton's HWB for export markets and still selling worldwide – all the rest was drunk locally.

Of course, it may have been the heat. The Swan has the hottest climate of any serious Australian wine region, having summer temperatures that can soar to 45°C (113°F), low humidity and virtually no summer rain at all. If this sounds like a place where you should be making port and sherry-style wines – you're right. And yet, remarkably, many of the most successful Swan wines are white. This is probably because of the happy chance of grape varieties. Chenin is the leading variety, and prides itself on retaining acidity, whatever the heat.

Even so, despite the continual success of large companies like Houghton and Sandalford – who both, by the way, source much of their fruit from elsewhere – the winds of fashion are blowing most of our attention way to the south – to the Margaret River and Great Southern regions. The conditions couldn't be more different from the Swan District – cool, temperate, often compared to Bordeaux or Burgundy rather than to the baking Douro Valley of Portugal. And the wines are totally different too.

The Margaret River area was established by a variety of local medics and one or two Perth bigwigs in the late 1960s and 1970s after a visiting expert had noted remarkable similarities between its climate and that of Bordeaux. Indeed, it has less frost risk, more summer sunshine and less risk of vintage rain than Bordeaux – it's like Bordeaux in a really nice, warm year. With this in mind, Cabernet and Merlot regularly produce stunning results, but so too do Shiraz, Pinot Noir, Chardonnay, Sauvignon Blanc, Semillon and Riesling – and even Zinfandel. A dog's dinner, then? Not at all. Just another of these remarkable Australian regions that seem to be able to take the grapes of anywhere from northerly Germany to southern Italy – and achieve brilliant results with them all.

Being even more isolated than the Margaret River in Australia's most isolated wine-growing state, the Great Southern region has made haphazard progress, but there's no doubting that this relatively cool remote region can produce smashing wine – and again it manages to excel with such wildly different varieties as Cabernet, Shiraz, Pinot, Chardonnay, Sauvignon and Riesling. Frankland River and Mount Barker in particular are producing wines of scintillating fruit and intensity.

Harvesting Zinfandel at Cape Mentelle in the Margaret River. Associated mainly with California, Zinfandel is planted commercially in only a few regions in Australia which is a pity as Cape Mentelle's example has lots of chewy fruit.

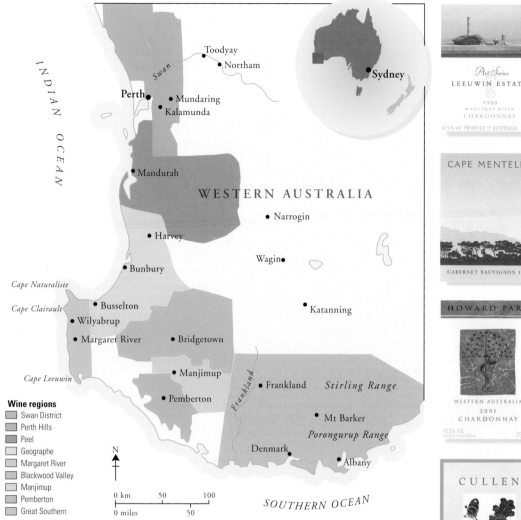

LEEUWIN ESTATE
Many rate this premium Chardonnay from the Art Series as the finest in the whole of Australia. Very oaky when young, the wine becomes complex and full-bodied with impressive richness.

CAPE MENTELLE
This leading Margaret River winery makes superb, cedary Cabernet Sauvignon that benefits from up to ten years' aging after bottling.

HOWARD PARK
Expensive but superb, long-lived wines, including a supremely classy Chardonnay, come from this dynamic winery on the south coast near Denmark.

CULLEN WINES
This is one of the original and best Margaret River wineries. The Cabernet/ Merlot blend is deep, well-structured and scented, and even better now that the Reserve version is no longer being made.

Wine regions
- Swan District
- Perth Hills
- Peel
- Geographe
- Margaret River
- Blackwood Valley
- Manjimup
- Pemberton
- Great Southern

REGIONAL ENTRIES
Geographe, Great Southern, Margaret River, Pemberton, Perth HIlls, Swan District.

PRODUCER ENTRIES
Alkoomi, Cape Mentelle, Capel Vale, Cullen Wines, Evans & Tate, Goundrey Wines, Houghton, Howard Park, Leeuwin Estate, Moss Wood, Pierro, Plantagenet, Vasse Felix.

MOSS WOOD
Cabernet Sauvignon is the wine upon which Margaret River's reputation was founded. This wine is silky smooth, rich but structured.

EVANS & TATE
Chardonnay is one of the Margaret River's most successful wine styles.

CAPEL VALE
Classy Whispering Hill Riesling, with bright citrous fruit, is one of the best wines at Capel Vale, by far the largest and oldest winery in the Geographe region.

HOUGHTON
Houghton's flagship wine was created in honour of Jack Mann, one of Australia's most innovative winemakers who did 51 consecutive vintages with the company.

WIEN
AUSTRIA

Vienna, or Wien, is proud of its claim to have more hectares of vines (680ha/1680 acres) than any other capital city; but we are not talking about the city centre here. Vienna's vineyards are mostly on the outskirts, in the semi-rural villages that get choked with tourists every summer: Grinzing, Stammersdorf and Nussdorf are the main centres, and in Grinzing the tourists must outnumber the locals by several to one. The traditional wine of Vienna is Gemischter Satz, a blend of whatever varieties were mixed up in the vineyard; these days the vines are separated according to variety and Vienna's best are the Grüner Veltliner, Rhine Riesling, Weissburgunder (Pinot Blanc), Chardonnay, Welschriesling, Gewürztraminer and Neuburger. Riesling from the steep, south-facing slopes of the Nussberg rises well above these everyday levels. Best years: 2002, '01, '00, '99, '97, '95, '94, '93. Best producers: Bernreiter, Kierlinger, Franz Mayer, Schilling, Fritz WIENINGER.

FRITZ WIENINGER
AUSTRIA, Wien

🍷 Pinot Noir (Blauburgunder), Cabernet Sauvignon, Merlot, Zweigelt

🍸 Chardonnay, Grüner Veltliner, Riesling

Fritz Wieninger is one of the best winemakers in the WIEN region, and he also runs one of its best *Heurigen* (wine taverns) in Stammersdorf close to his vines on the slopes of the Bisamberg. His top wines, such as the barrique-fermented Grand Select Chardonnay, a big mouthful of butter and pear, and the Pinot Noir, which in a good vintage has intense cherry aromas and plenty of soft tannins, have been influenced by his experiences in CALIFORNIA, as has his powerful Cabernet-Merlot blend. And for everyday he makes bright Riesling and Grüner Veltliner, and Trilogie, a juicy red blend.

WILLAKENZIE ESTATE
USA, Oregon, Yamhill County, Willamette Valley AVA

🍷 Pinot Noir, Gamay, Pinot Meunier

🍸 Pinot Gris, Pinot Blanc

Not many wineries actually name themselves after a soil type but this one, with 41ha (102 acres) of vineyards, is named after the sedimentary WillaKenzie soils that in the Chehalem mountains of the WILLAMETTE VALLEY encourage grapes to ripen up to two weeks before nearby areas on different soils. Certainly WillaKenzie Estate's Pinot Noirs

WILLAKENZIE ESTATE
WillaKenzie is a Pinot Noir specialist and releases several different cuvées each vintage, based on different vineyards and different clones.

are lush and the Pinot Gris and Pinot Blancs viscous and ripe, but this may also be due to an impressive gravity-flow winery and a near-organic approach in the vineyard. There are several different Pinot Noir releases, reflecting different vineyard sites and clones, and a proportion of WillaKenzie wines are now released under screwtop. Best years: (Pinot Noir) 2002, '01, '00, '99, '98.

WILLAMETTE VALLEY AVA
USA, Oregon

By far the most developed of OREGON's wine regions, the Willamette Valley grew more swiftly than its competitors because early acclaim for Pinot Noir grown here brought a continuous stream of new hopefuls to augment the small handful of pioneers.

The valley is a long one, beginning south of Eugene and extending all the way north to Portland, where the Willamette empties into the Columbia River. Low, forested hills form its west boundary; the rock-ribbed, snow-capped Cascade Mountains limit it on the east. Rain is both a salvation and a curse. It helps keep the climate cool, but sometimes drowns both the flowering vines and the harvest. Hail is not unknown, nor are spring frosts. All this makes Willamette winemakers believe they have found America's CÔTE D'OR, though Oregon's soils do not much resemble Burgundy's and it is the bad, not good, climatic conditions that are more similar. Even so, the resemblances are enough to have caused Robert DROUHIN of BURGUNDY to buy land and plant vines here with considerable success (see DOMAINE DROUHIN).

Washington County, west and south-west of Portland, is home to Montinore Vineyards, Oak Knoll Winery, PONZI VINEYARDS and Shafer Vineyard Cellars (not to be confused with NAPA VALLEY's SHAFER VINEYARDS). The more heavily planted Yamhill County flanks

Washington County to the south. Wineries include Adelsheim Vineyard, Amity Vineyards, ARCHERY SUMMIT, BEAUX FRÈRES, Cameron Winery, CRISTOM, Domaine Drouhin, Domaine Serene, Elk Cove Vineyards, Eola Hills, Erath, The EYRIE VINEYARDS, PANTHER CREEK, REX HILL VINEYARDS, St Innocent, Sokol Blosser Winery, Torii Mor Winery, WILLAKENZIE ESTATE, Ken WRIGHT and Yamhill Valley Vineyards. From here, vineyards and wineries tail off all the way to Eugene, 190km (120 miles) south of Portland, and include good Pinot Noir from BETHEL HEIGHTS and Tyee Wine Cellars. To hear people talk, Pinot Noir is the main game – almost the only one. The majority of the state's 2610ha (6450 acres) of this variety grow in the Willamette. In fact Chardonnay and Riesling dominated at the start, and it is Pinot Gris which is currently and quite rightly capturing the wine-drinking public's imagination. Speculation that CHAMPAGNE-method sparkling wines could prove best of all Willamette's wine styles have not really been borne out, despite good fizz from Argyle. Best years: (reds) 2002, '01, '00, '99, '98.

WILLIAMS SELYEM WINERY
USA, California, Sonoma County, Russian River Valley AVA

🍷 Pinot Noir, Zinfandel

🍸 Chardonnay and others

Founders Ed Williams and Burt Selyem took a threadbare, low-budget operation and converted it into one of CALIFORNIA's top names. Emphasizing cool-climate, oak-aged blockbuster Pinot Noir, their non-interventionist winemaking style developed a cult following, especially for the single-vineyard Pinots from ROCHIOLI, Allen and Olivet Lane vineyards.

After moving to a larger facility in 1990, they added Zinfandel and Chardonnay, and both were well received by fans of big, upfront wines. With annual production averaging only 2500 cases, the winery had such a faithful fan club that it was selling Pinot Noir for the price of $100 a bottle (tops for California Pinot Noir). However, the physical toil persuaded the partners to sell the winery which, after a heated bidding war, was acquired in 1998 by John Dyson, who owns NEW YORK STATE's MILLBROOK WINERY. Not much seems to have changed. I detect a bit more interest in SONOMA COAST vineyards like Hirsch and Summa, but the successful formula of rich fruit and toasty oak remains. Best years: (Pinot Noir) 2001, '00, '99, '98, '97, '96, '95, '94.

WILTINGEN
GERMANY, Mosel-Saar-Ruwer

This town is the heart of the SAAR region and has the Saar's most famous vineyard (the great Scharzhofberg) and one of Germany's top estates, making some of the world's greatest dessert wines (Egon MÜLLER-SCHARZHOF).

The Saar is a cool, even chilly region, where in most years the wines will be lean and acidic, mellowing after a few years to be sure, but without the ripeness and richness that can make wines great. But when the weather obliges with a long warm autumn with plenty of sun, then everything changes. Then the wines have a knife-edge excitement which few can match – and even in the Saar, few can match the Müller-Scharzhof wines. This estate produces Wiltingen's, and the Saar's, best wines, especially from the steep slopes of the Scharzhofberg vineyard. Other great wines come from von HÖVEL, von KESSELSTATT and van Volxem. The Kabinett wines can be drunk young but everything will benefit from bottle age; the Auslese need ten years to reach their peak. Best years: 2002, '01, '99, '97, '95, '94, '93, '90, '89.

WINNINGEN
GERMANY, Mosel-Saar-Ruwer

The last major wine commune before the Mosel flows into the Rhine at Koblenz has the best vineyards in the 'Terrassen-Mosel', as this lower part of the MOSEL Valley is called. As the name suggests, the vines cling to narrow terraces along the steep, rocky, valley sides, and in Winningen's excellent Röttgen and Uhlen sites the terraces are literally like steps climbing up to heaven. Best years: 2002, '01, '00, '99, '98, '97. Best producers: HEYMANN-LÖWENSTEIN, von Heddesdorff, Knebel, Richard Richter.

WIRRA WIRRA
AUSTRALIA, South Australia, McLaren Vale
Syrah (Shiraz), Cabernet Sauvignon, Grenache, Petit Verdot, Merlot
Cabernet Franc, Grenache, Petit Verdot
Chardonnay, Riesling, Semillon, Sauvignon Blanc, Semillon, Viognier

The modern day Wirra Wirra winery was not established until 1969, but the viticultural and winemaking links of the family of proprietor Greg Trott – a wonderfully eccentric and much-loved figure, usually called 'Trottie' – go back to the nineteenth century.

Recent years have seen rapid expansion of this already impressive winery. Its best white wines are tropical gooseberry Sauvignon

WIRRA WIRRA
The delicious Angelus Cabernet Sauvignon was one of the first Cabernet wines to draw attention to the McLaren Vale region.

Blanc and sculpted Chardonnay, but its stellar acts are the Church Block Cabernet blend and the superpremium, chocolaty RSW Shiraz and The Angelus Cabernet Sauvignon, whose blackcurrant, berry, cedary aroma and impressive depth of fruit are partly due to an addition of COONAWARRA grapes to the blend. The Cousins is a pretty decent fizz. Best years: (The Angelus) 2001, '00, '99, '98, '97, '96, '95, '92, '91, '90.

WITHER HILLS
NEW ZEALAND, South Island, Marlborough
Pinot Noir
Sauvignon Blanc, Chardonnay

This high-flying, quality-focused winery is one of the best in the MARLBOROUGH region. In 2002 it was taken over by the giant Australian liquor group Lion Nathan Breweries; the talented founder/winemaker Brent Marris stays until 2005. A trio of stylish Marlborough wines – concentrated, pungent Sauvignon Blanc, fine, fruit-focused Chardonnay and vibrant Pinot Noir – allows Wither Hills to concentrate only on wines that perform with distinction in this region. Expect little change, at least while Marris remains at the helm.

J L WOLF
GERMANY, Pfalz, Wachenheim
Pinot Noir (Spätburgunder)
Riesling, Pinot Gris (Grauburgunder)

For years this estate, based in one of the most beautiful of many imposing PFALZ villas, made mediocre wines in spite of having old vines in many of the region's top sites. When Ernst Loosen from the Dr LOOSEN estate in the MOSEL arrived for the 1996 vintage he catapulted Wolf straight into the first rank of Pfalz estates, with a string of concentrated dry and naturally sweet Rieslings, even if some leading Pfalz winemakers complained that the wines taste too like Mosels! Me, I'm not complaining. The extra zest and refreshing acidity that Loosen added is something the Pfalz has lacked for ages. Best years: 2002, '01, '00, '99, '98, '97, '96.

WOODWARD CANYON WINERY
USA, Washington State, Walla Walla AVA
Cabernet Sauvignon, Merlot and others
Chardonnay

The excellent toasty Chardonnay Reserve has been the banner wine here since the first vintage in 1981. However, the greatly increased interest in WASHINGTON red wines has been mirrored by more reds here – a variety of blended and single-vineyard Cabernets full of ripe dark fruit lead the way, along with Merlot, Syrah, Pinot Noir, and red and white BORDEAUX blends. Best years: (Cabernet Sauvignon) 2001, '00, '99, '98, '97, '96.

WORCESTER WO
SOUTH AFRICA, Western Cape

Any of us who've tasted basic South African wine will probably have tasted Worcester wine, because this is the Cape's biggest vineyard region. Yet nearly all of the grapes here have traditionally been used for brandy, or for padding out the large-volume brands of different merchants. Worcester has about 20 per cent of the Cape's vines and produces 25 per cent of her wine, most of it in one of the 19 co-operative cellars in the region. The vineyards are generally on the fertile alluvial valley floor, but more plantings are now taking place on the hillsides, and individual bottlings from the co-ops or from the handful of private estates are becoming more common.

WRATTONBULLY
AUSTRALIA, South Australia

Every country is entitled to a practical joke, and this is Australia's. Instead of taking the name Koppamurra (first choice), Naracoorte Ranges (second choice), Joanna (third choice) or one or two others, and at the end of interminable wrangling, this important grape-growing region has, at least for the time being, christened itself Rat and Bully – sorry, Wrattonbully – under the GI legislation. With over 2000ha (4940 acres) of vines and annual production of over 10,000 tonnes of grapes it deserves better. Koppamurra Wines is the long-term resident winery; Heathfield Ridge Wines a newly constructed, large, grape-purchasing winery serving part of the needs of the many major Australian companies drawing grapes from this region – notably HARDY, Beringer Blass and YALUMBA. Situated just south of PADTHAWAY, Wrattonbully is equally at home producing generous yields of Sauvignon Blanc and Chardonnay on the one hand and Cabernet Sauvignon, Shiraz and Merlot on the other.

KEN WRIGHT CELLARS

USA, Oregon, Yamhill County, Willamette Valley AVA
❧ *Pinot Noir*
♀ *Chardonnay, Pinot Blanc*

Ken Wright specializes in single-vineyard Pinot Noirs. The collection of wines includes Carter, Canary Hill, Elton, Guadalupe, McCrone and Shea vineyards. Ripe fruit and lots of new wood make these wines impressive at an early age. His Celilo Vineyard Chardonnay (from WASHINGTON fruit) is excellent and a small amount of Pinot Blanc is also made. Best years: (Pinot Noir) 2002, '01, '00, '99, '98, '97.

WÜRTTEMBERG

GERMANY

Red wines are Württemberg's speciality. Two-thirds of its 11,336ha (28,010 acres) of vines are planted with red varieties, of which the Trollinger is far and away the most popular. In spite of the region's warm climate the red wines are seldom very dark in colour, seldom tannic and sometimes sweetish which is the way the locals like them. But during the 1990s there has been something of a red wine revolution here, with some powerful, oaky serious reds making better use of the many excellent sites. The climate is warm in the summer, but it is cold in the winter and so vineyard site selection is as important here as anywhere else in Germany.

The main white grape, the Riesling, can sometimes lack the startling acidity of other German regions because malolactic fermentation, which has the effect of softening the taste of the wine, is traditional here. Württemberg's other speciality is rosé, here called Schillerwein. This is a mix of red and white grapes; a rosé made just with red grapes, in the more usual way, may be called Weissherbst.

There are three Bereichs: Remstal Stuttgart in the south, which encompasses the car-making centre of Stuttgart; Württembergisch Unterland in the centre, which takes in most of the vineyards; and tiny Kocher-Jagst-Tauber in the north, specializing in white wines. Best years: (reds) 2002, '01, '99, '97, '93. Best producers: Graf Adelmann, Beurer, Ernst Dautel, Drautz-Able, Karl Haidle, Graf Neipperg, Albrecht Schwegler, Wöhrwag.

WÜRZBURG

GERMANY, Franken

The cultural, political and viticultural centre of FRANKEN, Würzburg is one of Europe's great wine cities. It is worth visiting for the historical monuments alone, which include Balthasar

Although semi-arid, the Yakima Valley has produced some of Washington State's most distinctive wines. Kiona Vineyards is located in the barren Red Mountain sub-region where little grows except for sagebrush and vines.

Neumann's Baroque palace, the Residenz. However, the three large wine estates owned by charitable foundations – the Bürgerspital, the Juliusspital and the Staatliche Hofkeller – are also good reasons to make the pilgrimage. Some Rieslings can be great but the real star is Silvaner. Best years: 2002, '01, '00, '99, '97, '94, '93, '90. Best producers: Bürgerspital, Juliusspital, Staatlicher Hofkeller, Weingut am Stein.

WYNNS

AUSTRALIA, South Australia, Coonawarra
❧ *Cabernet Sauvignon, Syrah (Shiraz), Pinot Noir*
♀ *Chardonnay, Riesling and others*

Wynns is not only the largest COONAWARRA producer but also – despite being owned by the giant Southcorp, whose track record on quality is not thrilling – one of Coonawarra's best producers. Aromatic, limy Riesling sells for a song, yet performs like a thoroughbred in the cellar, building complexity for five years at least. Chardonnay is becoming increasingly subtle and complex. The spicy, peppery Shiraz is one of the best-value reds in Australia; the Black Label Cabernet Sauvignons provide enormous flavour at five years, peaking at 10 to 12 years. Top of the line John Riddoch Cabernet is packed with concentrated fruit and capable of aging for a generation. The top Shiraz is called Michael and is powerful oaky stuff. Best years: (John Riddoch) 2000, '99, '98, '96, '94, '91, '90, '88, '86, '82.

XAREL-LO

This low-quality white Spanish grape is the curse of CAVA, though few producers would admit it. Most Catalan Cava (and that means most Spanish Cava) is made from a blend of Xarel-lo with the somewhat higher-quality Macabeo and even better Parellada. While none of these three is capable of retaining its fruitiness and freshness throughout the lengthy aging periods to which much Cava is subjected, Xarel-lo takes on a particularly unfortunate earthy flavour within a very short time. Some of the best PENEDÈS producers wisely choose to leave it out of their blends. When scrupulously made as still wine, young Xarel-lo can show an attractive gooseberries-and-cream character, though it can easily become over-alcoholic and coarse, or just bland. It is exclusive to CATALUÑA, but it grows there in such profusion that it ranks as Spain's sixth most-planted white grape variety. In Alella it is the principal grape and is known as Pansá Blanca – and makes quite decent wine.

YAKIMA VALLEY AVA

USA, Washington State

The Yakima Valley is a curious place, a sort of linear oasis that is also one of North America's great food baskets. Nothing looks easy here, nor is it. Hard in the lee of the Cascade Mountains, the valley gets so little rain that any unirrigated land resembles desert. The Yakima's summer climate is hot, with more than a few days of 37°C (100°F) temperatures. In winter, the thermometer can stay below –17°C (0°F) for days on end.

Yet, as well as the apples and apricots and beans and hops strung along the south-facing slopes of the Rattlesnake Hills and irrigated by canals hacked into the hillside, are vines that year by year yield some of the USA's most consistently impressive wines, especially Sauvignon Blanc, Semillon, Cabernet, Merlot and Syrah. These, plus Chardonnay, Chenin Blanc, Riesling, a delightful red called Lemberger and even some Grenache, are the most successful.

Altogether there are about 4455ha (11,000 acres) of wine grapes in the Valley, and despite it being the pioneer of vinifera grapes in WASHINGTON, it is nowadays rather outshone by newer areas like WALLA WALLA. One sub-region, however, is deservedly famous – Red Mountain, at the eastern mouth of the Valley, where vineyards like Klipsun have created a formidable reputation for mighty reds. Top wineries include Chinook, HEDGES, Hogue and KIONA.

YALUMBA
AUSTRALIA, South Australia, Barossa Valley
Cabernet Sauvignon, Syrah (Shiraz), Pinot Noir, Merlot, Petit Verdot, Sangiovese
Riesling, Chardonnay, Sauvignon Blanc, Semillon, Viognier, Pinot Gris

Owned by the Hill-Smith family, Yalumba is one of the most successful of Australia's independent wine companies and manages to operate on several levels, all with considerable success. In particular, it has managed to have a smash hit with its sparkling wine portfolio, led by huge-selling, enjoyable Angas Brut. Oxford Landing has developed a good reputation as a keenly priced range of varietal wines and the new 'Y' series of varietals is good, as are the high-quality 'hand-picked' labels. The Signature, The Menzies and Octavius embody a rather more traditional but high-quality approach.

Yalumba also operates three separate estates – Hill-Smith Estate, Pewsey Vale and Heggies – all producing good, single-vineyard wines from the northern end of the ADELAIDE HILLS with particular emphasis on slow-maturing wines from Riesling, Semillon and Chardonnay. They also own Nautilus in Marlborough, New Zealand, and Jansz in Tasmania. Best years: (The Signature red) 2000, '99, '98, '97, '96, '95, '93, '92, '91, '90.

YAMANASHI
JAPAN
If you believe the legend, Japanese grape-growing was started in Yamanashi prefecture, between Tokyo and Mount Fuji, in 718AD precisely, by the Buddha Nyorai whose statue stands at Zenkoji temple to this day. Certainly most of Japan's wineries and more than a quarter of her vines are in Yamanashi, but conditions are very difficult – freezing winters, monsoon summers and an annual risk of typhoons. These humid conditions mean the vines are usually trained on an overhead pergola system that allows the grapes to keep reasonably dry, but gives high yields of dilute grapes. Koshu is the main wine grape, although there are some plantings of Merlot, Cabernet and Chardonnay. The majority of the grapes, however, are hybrids or American *Vitis labrusca*. The Japanese boom in wine-drinking means the big companies like Mercian and Suntory are putting enormous efforts into improving the grapes, but nature makes their life as difficult as possible.

YARRA BURN
AUSTRALIA, Victoria, Yarra Valley
Pinot Noir, Syrah (Shiraz), Cabernet Sauvignon
Chardonnay, Sauvignon Blanc, Semillon

Acquired by BRL HARDY in the mid-1990s, along with two of the largest independent YARRA VALLEY vineyards, much of the wide range of fruit goes to making Hardy's top-end sparkling wines and (in varying proportions) its Eileen Hardy Chardonnay. Bastard Hill Chardonnay and Pinot Noir (yes, the name is real, coming from the terrifying degree of slope of the up-and-down vineyards) are the best two Yarra Burn wines. Best years: 2002, '00, '99, '98, '97, '94.

YARRA RIDGE
AUSTRALIA, Victoria, Yarra Valley
Pinot Noir, Cabernet Sauvignon, Merlot
Chardonnay, Sauvignon Blanc

Founded in 1983, Yarra Ridge enjoyed a meteoric rise in production and reputation, then was acquired by Beringer Blass. Yarra Ridge made its reputation with a trail-blazing, tangy, tropical gooseberry Sauvignon Blanc, but as volume grew rapidly, it lost its edge and indeed moved outside the YARRA VALLEY for its grape sources. Pinot Noir, however, is the main focus, and the Reserve in particular, based on mature vineyards tucked into the Christmas Hills, is a ripe, smooth-textured wine. Chardonnay is also good. Best years: 2002, '00, '99, '98, '97, '96, '95.

YARRA VALLEY
AUSTRALIA, Victoria
If Australia's table wines were world-renowned at the end of the nineteenth century, it was Yarra Valley vines that provided the grapes for her greatest triumphs. Yet for the first half of the twentieth century, this beautiful valley on the outskirts of Melbourne was used for grazing cattle and at the end of the 1960s there were just 1.2ha (3 acres) of vines planted. By 2000 there were over 486ha (1200 acres) of vineyards, a figure still on the rise, with around 50 wineries and millions of dollars of foreign investment pointing up the fabulous potential of Yarra Valley vineyards.

As it is slightly cooler than BORDEAUX, yet warmer than BURGUNDY, and with a much more regular rainfall pattern than either of these two regions, which provides essentially dry summers and autumns, it is Pinot Noir and Chardonnay that have shown the most exciting flavours so far. Cabernet Sauvignon – especially blended with the earlier-ripening Cabernet Franc – Merlot and Malbec can be good, if sometimes a little grassy. Yarra Valley Shiraz is interesting, Sauvignon Blanc good, and the occasional botrytis-affected sweet wines can be luscious.

However, not surprisingly considering the success of the two CHAMPAGNE grapes (Pinot Noir and Chardonnay) here, it is as a provider of sparkling wines that the Yarra Valley's most regular triumph has so far been seen – Green Point Vineyards (DOMAINE CHANDON), founded in 1985, makes some of Australia's best fizz. Best years: (reds) 2002, '00, '99, '98, '97, '94, '92, '91, '90, '88. Best producers: Arthur's Creek, COLDSTREAM HILLS, DE BORTOLI, Diamond Valley, Domaine Chandon/Green Point, Métier, MOUNT MARY, St Huberts, Seville Estate, TARRAWARRA, YARRA BURN, YARRA RIDGE, YARRA YERING, YERING STATION, YERINGBERG.

YARRA YERING
AUSTRALIA, Victoria, Yarra Valley
Cabernet Sauvignon, Syrah (Shiraz), Pinot Noir and others
Chardonnay, Viognier

Bailey Carrodus makes the richest, deepest, most complex and (for many years) least understood reds in the YARRA VALLEY, hiding their laurels under the enigmatic labels Dry

YARRA YERING
Bailey Carrodus uses unusual winemaking methods to create extraordinary wines from his exceptional vineyards. Dry Red Wine No 2 is a delicious, perfumed Shiraz blend with ripe, sweet, berried fruit.

Red Wine No 1 (a BORDEAUX blend) and Dry Red Wine No 2 (a RHÔNE-style wine based on Shiraz but including some white Viognier). Carrodus believes that great wine is made in the vineyard, and practises benign neglect (except for a generous purchase of new oak barrels each year) in his winemaking, allowing vintage variation full play. The result is red wines crammed full of personality, which make the blood race despite sometimes upsetting the purists. They may not always fit into a mainstream style based solely on varietal flavours – but so what? You don't buy Yarra Yering in a spirit of complacent certainty but rather in a lather of uncertain anticipation.

His latest mould-breaking wines are a delicious, idiosyncratic Pinot Noir and a Chardonnay strongly reminiscent of old-fashioned PULIGNY-MONTRACHET. Yarra Yering also releases some peppery Shiraz under the Underhill label and a few cases of frighteningly expensive Merlot. Best years: (No. 1) 2001, '99, '98, '97, '96, '94, '93, '91, '90, '89, '86.

YELLOWGLEN

AUSTRALIA, Victoria, Ballarat

Pinot Noir

Chardonnay, Semillon

Yellowglen just does sparkling wine. Visiting its winery just outside Ballarat in VICTORIA for the first time, I remember thinking – isn't this a bit hot to be growing grapes for fizz? Well, yes it is, and Yellowglen has never been the subtlest of wines, but it was created as a marketing venture – not a wine venture – and that included having a winemaker from CHAMPAGNE. It's now a highly successful operation, sourcing its grapes from far and wide yet still playing on its homespun Ballarat roots and its Champenois winemaker.

YERING STATION

AUSTRALIA, Victoria, Yarra Valley

Pinot Noir, Cabernet Sauvignon, Syrah (Shiraz), Merlot, Cabernet Franc and others

Chardonnay and others

Historic Yering Station is now a vibrant, modern winery/restaurant complex whose chief claim to fame is a successful joint venture for fizz with the French CHAMPAGNE house of Devaux. And beneath all the glitz lie the very first vineyards to be planted in the State of Victoria way back in 1838. The grapes were hardly top drawer – Black Muscat and something called 'Sweet Water', but in the 1850s they obtained cuttings from Ch. LAFITE-ROTHSCHILD in BORDEAUX and by 1861 Yering Station had won the 'best vineyard in Victoria' award. So the pedigree is there, and the modern wines are good – fine toasty Yarrabank fizz, good Pinot Noir and Chardonnay and – perhaps reflecting those old Ch. Lafite Cabernet vines – one of Yarra Valley's ripest Cabernets.

YERINGBERG

AUSTRALIA, Victoria, Yarra Valley

Cabernet Sauvignon, Pinot Noir, Cabernet Franc, Merlot, Malbec

Chardonnay, Marsanne, Roussanne

From Guillaume, Baron de Pury, formerly of Neuchâtel in Switzerland and cousin of the first Governor of VICTORIA, Charles la Trobe, the ownership of Yeringberg has passed in direct succession to his grandson, Guill de Pury. The once-large vineyards are now reduced to a token 3ha (7.4 acres), and de Pury makes a little wine for his health's sake in the unbelievably well-preserved wooden winery, built in 1885. The wines rival those of YARRA YERING for depth and richness. Best years: 2001, '00, '99, '98, '97, '96, '94, '92, '91, '90, '88, '86, '85.

CH. D'YQUEM

FRANCE, Bordeaux, Sauternes AC, Grand Premier Cru

Sémillon, Sauvignon Blanc

If we're talking about total commitment to quality and a no-compromise approach to winemaking, many people rate Yquem – the supreme sweet wine of SAUTERNES – as the greatest wine in Bordeaux and maybe even in France. In 1855, when BORDEAUX was busy classifying wine, Yquem was accorded a sort of 'first of firsts' position as against the other famous First Growths like Ch. MARGAUX, LATOUR and, of course, several other top Sauternes. Ch. d'Yquem's title was Premier Cru Supérieur or Great First Growth. It was the only wine accorded the title, and this shows that Yquem was regarded as supreme all those years ago – and its position hasn't changed since then.

The vineyard is large – 103ha (255 acres), planted with Sémillon (80 per cent) and Sauvignon Blanc (20 per cent) – but production is tiny, an average of 95,000 bottles per year. Only fully noble-rotted grapes are picked – often berry by berry. This means that the pickers may have to go through the vineyard as many as eleven times, selecting the grapes by hand; it's a slow process and can also mean that the vintage doesn't finish until the freezing winter days of December.

Noble rot concentrates the juice but radically reduces the volume produced. Although the Sauternes AC allows a yield of 25 hectolitres per hectare – which is already very low – at Yquem the yield is more like 8 hectolitres. This works out at a glass of wine per vine (a great red wine estate might easily produce a bottle of wine per vine). This precious liquid gold is then fermented in new oak barrels and left to mature for three-and-a-half years, before bottling and eventual release.

If the wine isn't outstanding, it simply isn't released as Yquem. In 1972, '74 and '92 the entire crop was declassified and in 1978, 85 per cent of the wine was refused the château label. The result is a frantically expensive wine, which is nonetheless in constant demand, because for sheer richness, for exotic flavours of vanilla, pineapple, melons, peaches and coconut, enveloped in a caramel richness so viscous and lush your mouth feels coated with succulence for an eternity after swallowing the wine; for all that, and for its ability to age a decade, a generation, or a century even, when the wine will be deep, dark brown, barely glinting with gold, and will taste of orange chocolate, butterscotch, barley sugar and caramel... no wine in the world can touch Yquem. The takeover in 1999 by LVMH after 406 years of ownership by the Lur-Saluces family should not affect its supreme quality. In certain years a rather brilliant bone dry white Bordeaux (called 'Ygrec') is made from equal amounts of Sémillon and Sauvignon Blanc. Best years: 1997, '96, '95, '94, '93, '91, '90, '89, '88, '86, '83, '82, '81, '80, '79, '76, '75, '71, '70, '67, '62.

ZELTINGEN

GERMANY, Mosel-Saar-Ruwer

This is a Mittel MOSEL town between ÜRZIG and GRAACH, but without quite the fame of either. Sonnenuhr and Schlossberg are its best-known vineyards. Its growers claim, with some reason, that Zeltingen's Sonnenuhr vineyard is every bit as good as nearby

SELBACH-OSTER
This historic estate is the best producer in Zeltingen and the source of some benchmark Mosel Riesling, including elegant sweet wines from the Sonnenuhr site.

WEHLEN's. Zeltingen Sonnenuhr can have great elegance and the site seems particularly good for sweet wines; it has a worthy champion in SELBACH-OSTER. The Schlossberg vineyard is good at putting muscle into dry wines. Best years: 2002, '01, '99, '97, '95, '94, '93, '90. Best producers: Markus Molitor, J J PRÜM, Selbach-Oster.

ZERBINA

ITALY, Emilia-Romagna, Albana di Romagna DOCG
♟ *Sangiovese, Cabernet Sauvignon, Merlot*
♀ *Trebbiano di Romagna, Albana di Romagna,*
Sauvignon Blanc

Of all the Italian wine regions which promise greater things in the future, Romagna, and specifically the lower slopes of the Apennines between Bologna and Cesena, probably ranks as number one. And by common consent, the top estate is Zerbina, owned by Cristina Giminiani.

Her wines are at such a high general level, indeed, as to make it difficult to choose between them. There's the Sangiovese di Romagna Superiore Riserva Pietramora, which single-handedly puts the lie to the myth that Sangiovese from Romagna is nothing but bulk table wine, as does the barriqued Sangiovese di Romagna Torre di Ceparano. The Cru Marzieno is also Sangiovese, but this time blended with Cabernet Sauvignon. Then there is the wonderful dessert wine Scacco Matto which, again almost single-handedly, justifies the DOCG status of the all-too-often derided ALBANA DI ROMAGNA. If Zerbina can reach these heights in much maligned Romagna, why not others? And, in fact, a few are, notable among which are Castelluccio (Vittorio Fiore's property), Drei Doña, Tre Monti and San Patrignano, where Riccardo Cotarella has been enologist for the past few years. Best years: 2001, '00, '99, '97, '95, '93, '90.

FORSTMEISTER GELTZ ZILLIKEN

GERMANY, Mosel-Saar-Ruwer, Saarburg
♀ *Riesling*

This old-established estate at SAARBURG is soaring to even greater heights under its current owner, Hans-Joachim Zilliken. The vineyards are in some of the best spots on the SAAR and winemaking is traditional, using only old oak casks, giving elegant, racy wines that are often lean in youth. Those from the Rausch vineyard, with its notable weathered grey slate and diabase soil, are often particularly long-lived. There are also vines in the Bockstein vineyard at OCKFEN. The estate

makes a speciality of Eiswein, producing one most years, which is unusual because it can only be harvested if temperatures reach –8°C (19°F) or lower. A new dry Riesling wine called Butterfly is attracting a lot of attention. Best years: 2002, '01, '99, '97, '95, '94, '93, '91, '90, '89, '88, '85, '83, '79, '76.

ZIND-HUMBRECHT

FRANCE, Alsace, Alsace AC
♟ *Pinot Noir*
♀ *Riesling, Gewurztraminer, Pinot Gris, Pinot Blanc,*
Muscat

There are many connoisseurs convinced that this estate is the source of the very finest ALSACE wines. They are certainly among the richest and most powerful. Léonard Humbrecht, who established the reputation of the 30-ha (74-acre) estate, is now semi-retired, and his son Olivier (the first French Master of Wine) runs the property. The estate has vines in four Grands Crus – Rangen, Hengst, Goldert and Brand – but also produces a whole range of single-vineyard bottlings from individual sites the Humbrechts consider outstanding. These include Clos Windsbuhl for Riesling and Clos Jebsal for Pinot Gris.

The Humbrechts are fanatical about low yields that will permit a full expression of the estate's varied terroirs, and this allows them to produce Vendange Tardive and Sélection de Grains Nobles wines even in vintages such as 1991 and '92 that were not especially good for

late-harvested wines. In terms of concentration and richness, these wines are beyond compare, but the very ripe grapes often result in residual sugar remaining in the wines, which may not be to everyone's taste. Best years: 2001, '00, '99, '98, '97, '96, '95, '94, '93, '92, '90, '89.

ZÖBINGEN

AUSTRIA, Niederösterreich, Kamptal

This village, close to the wine centre of LANGENLOIS, has one of Austria's greatest Riesling vineyards, the steep, terraced Heiligenstein. It produces wines with less opulence and more elegance than those from the top sites in the nearby WACHAU, and with astonishing aging potential. Best producers: BRÜNDLMAYER, Ehn, Hiedler, Jurtschitsch, Loimer.

CHRISTIAN ZÜNDEL

SWITZERLAND, Ticino, Beride
♟ *Merlot, Cabernet Sauvignon*
♟ *Merlot*
♀ *Chardonnay*

Although German speaking and with vineyards in the Italian-speaking province of TICINO, Zündel has an uncompromisingly French approach to winemaking. That may seem eccentric, but his Orizzonte (Horizon), Cabernet-Merlot blend is the region's most impressive red wine. Its big blackberry and plum fruit is well supported by spicy oak and it has enough tannin to need three or four years in bottle to give its best.

ZINFANDEL

Zinfandel may be the Primitivo grape of southern Italy, but it has followed the example of many of its compatriots and made good in the New World.

So much so that Primitivo is now becoming highly regarded in Puglia in Italy's far south, especially when the wine is well-oaked. A little Zinfandel is found in South Africa, Australia, Mexico and Chile, New Zealand has a patch – and there's even a Zinfandel vine on the hill of Hermitage in the Rhône Valley, but it is unshakably associated with California, where at times it seems cursed by its very versatility. Here it makes sweetish 'blush' or rosé wines, labelled White Zinfandel, fruity Beaujolais-style reds, headily alcoholic reds with enough tannin

to cure leather, and – last but not least – fortified wines styled after ruby or vintage-character ports. It can be cheap and cheerful or it can appear as pricy, classy, single-vineyard bottlings from top winemakers. Some is even made properly sweet, and that's some mouthful.

Except for the big burly styles found in Amador County, Sonoma County has an edge over the rest of California, especially in the Sonoma Valley and Dry Creek Valley AVAs and other fairly cool areas. But good vineyards are pretty well scattered, and the largest plantings are further inland in the Lodi AVA in San Joaquin County. Excellent vineyards exist, too, in parts of San Luis Obispo County, notably around Paso Robles. After a long period of being unfashionable, there is now renewed interest in full-blooded red Zinfandels as the craze for Cabernet wines wanes.

VINTAGES French Wines

Vintage guides are only relevant to wines which have personality and individuality – to the top five or ten per cent of any one country's wine. Any mark given to a vintage is a broad generalization to steer you towards the best bottles – there are brilliant wines made in difficult years and disappointing wines in brilliant years. The highest marks are for vintages where the ripeness of the grapes is best balanced by the acidity of the juice – and, for red wines, the proper amount of tannin, giving wines which have the potential to age.

HOW TO READ THE CHART

Numerals (1–10) represent an overall rating for each year

▲ = not ready ● = just ready ★ = at peak ▼ = past its best ○ = not generally declared

	02	01	00	99	98	97	96	95	94	93

BORDEAUX

The following ratings apply only to the top châteaux in each area. Vintages can vary a lot within the large Bordeaux region – a great year in Sauternes is not necessarily the same for the Médoc, but progress in the vineyard and at the winemaking stage, rather than changes in the climate, have ensured that disastrous vintages are now a thing of the past. Red Bordeaux is one of the longest-lived wines in the world, thanks to the dense fruit and tannins of the Cabernet and Merlot grapes and to its excellent balance and well-made wines from good vintages are still in the prime of life at 20–30 years. The sweet white wines from Sauternes, with high levels of sugar and alcohol, can be some of Bordeaux's longest-lived wines, the very best lasting over 50 years.

	02	01	00	99	98	97	96	95	94	93
Margaux	7 ▲	7 ▲	9 ▲	8 ▲	7 ▲	6 ●	8 ▲	8 ●	7 ●	6 ●
St-Julien, Pauillac, St-Estèphe	8 ▲	8 ▲	10 ▲	7 ▲	7 ▲	6 ●	9 ▲	8 ▲	7 ●	6 ●
Graves/Pessac-Léognan (reds)	7 ▲	8 ▲	9 ▲	7 ▲	8 ▲	6 ●	8 ▲	8 ●	6 ●	6 ●
Graves/Pessac-Léognan (whites)	8 ▲	8 ▲	8 ▲	7 ▲	9 ▲	5 ●	8 ●	8 ●	8 ★	6 ★
St-Émilion, Pomerol	6 ▲	8 ▲	9 ▲	7 ▲	9 ▲	6 ●	7 ●	9 ●	7 ●	6 ★
Sauternes, Barsac	8 ▲	10 ▲	6 ▲	8 ▲	7 ▲	9 ●	9 ●	7 ●	5 ★	4 ▼

BURGUNDY

Red Burgundy is desperately unreliable so the vintage has been rated according to what can be expected from a decent domaine. Better vintages may be drunk young for their impressive fruit but become immeasurably more complex in their second decade. Wines from light vintages should be drunk before they are ten years old. Chardonnay is a hardy grape that generally ripens early and is seldom subject to rot so white Burgundy is generally more reliable than red and top examples, fermented as well as aged in oak, are some of the longest-living white wines in the world.

	02	01	00	99	98	97	96	95	94	93
Chablis	8 ▲	5 ●	9 ▲	7 ●	7 ●	7 ★	10 ▲	8 ★	7 ▼	6 ▼
Côte de Nuits	9 ▲	7 ▲	7 ▲	9 ▲	7 ▲	8 ▲	9 ▲	8 ●	5 ▼	9 ●
Côte de Beaune (reds)	8 ▲	6 ▲	5 ●	9 ▲	7 ▲	7 ●	9 ▲	8 ★	4 ▼	8 ●
Côte de Beaune (whites)	8 ▲	7 ▲	8 ▲	8 ●	5 ★	8 ★	8 ▲	9 ★	6 ▼	6 ▼
Mâconnais (whites)	8 ▲	8 ▲	7 ★	7 ★	8 ★	8 ★	9 ▼	8 ▼	7 ▼	7 ▼
Beaujolais Crus	7 ●	5 ★	9 ★	8 ★	8 ★	7 ▼	6 ▼	9 ▼	5 ▼	7 ▼

	02	01	00	99	98	97	96	95	94	93

LOIRE

With so many different climates to be found in the vineyards of the Loire any vintage assessment is a broad generalization. In general Loire wines should be drunk young within a year of two of the harvest but the best wines in fine vintages will age well, in particular the Cabernet Franc reds and the sweet Chenin whites. With their high sugars and relatively high acids, the sweet wines can keep for many decades – a sweet Vouvray reaches maturity at around 12 years old and will last for a century. Hot summers are rare in the Loire Valley but when they do occur, as in 1996, they always produce great wine.

Region	02	01	00	99	98	97	96	95	94	93
Bourgueil, Chinon and Saumur-Champigny	8▲	7▲	6●	6●	6★	8★	10★	8★	5★	6★
Anjou/Vouvray (sweet whites)	8▲	7▲	6▲	7●	7●	9●	9●	9●	6★	6★
Sancerre (whites)	8▲	7●	8★	7★	7★	9★	8★	8★	6▼	6▼

RHÔNE

In the warmer southern half of France, the Rhône Valley suffers fewer really difficult vintages than cooler parts of the country, though rain and rot can still be a problem, as they were in 2002, and in the southern Rhône too much sun can shrivel the grapes. The Syrah-based reds of the northern Rhône take to aging well – Hermitage and Côte-Rôtie are the longest living and slowest maturing of these wines and good vintages need a decade or so to loosen up. Southern Rhône reds can age but mature sooner – even the top Châteauneufs are ready by eight years. White wines, especially those from the South, should be drunk young; the exceptions are white Hermitage and Château-Grillet.

Region	02	01	00	99	98	97	96	95	94	93
Côte-Rôtie	4▲	8▲	9▲	9▲	9▲	6●	7●	9●	7●	4★
Condrieu	6●	8★	9★	9▼	8▼	7▼	9▼	8▼	8▼	5▼
Hermitage (reds)	5▲	8▲	8▲	8▲	9▲	8●	8●	9●	7●	3★
Hermitage (whites)	4▲	9▲	8▲	8▲	9▲	7▲	9▲	8▲	7●	5★
Châteauneuf-du-Pape (reds)	3▲	8▲	8▲	8▲	9▲	6●	7●	8●	8●	6★
Châteauneuf-du-Pape (whites)	5●	8★	8★	8▼	8▼	7▼	7▼	8▼	7▼	6▼

ALSACE

Alsace's very dry climate gives it an advantage over the rest of France in that the vintages are very rarely rained-off. Simple Alsace wines are best drunk within two to four years of the harvest. Wines from the best Grands Crus and *lieux-dits* can be kept longer, as can the late-picked Vendange Tardive wines and the botrytized Sélections de Grains Nobles. I have selected Riesling for the chart below as it is the most long-lived grape in Alsace and the only one that really needs at least five years to show its true complexity. Alsace's other noble grape varieties (Muscat, Gewurztraminer and Pinot Blanc) are more or less successful in different vintages. Muscat is best drunk young while Gewurztraminer and Pinot Gris should have enough natural sugar and concentration to last for a decade or more.

Region	02	01	00	99	98	97	96	95	94	93
Alsace Riesling Grand Cru	6▲	7▲	7●	7●	9●	9★	8★	8★	5★	6★

CHAMPAGNE

Most Champagne is non-vintage and is ready to drink when released for sale. In this cold, northerly region it is blending (of different vintages and vineyards) that produces the most consistently elegant and ripe wine. Vintage wines are usually only 'declared' in the best years, several years after the harvest. A few Champagne houses will make vintage Champagne virtually every year and in times of high demand some less-than-great years may be selected. Good vintage Champagne will improve for a few more years after release, reaching true maturity at ten years old and tasting well after 15 years or so.

Region	02	01	00	99	98	97	96	95	94	93
Vintage Champagne	8▲	2○	6▲	7▲	8▲	6●	9●	8●	5○	7★

VINTAGES Rest of the World

HOW TO READ THE CHART

Numerals (1–10) represent an overall rating for each year

▲ = not ready ● = just ready ★ = at peak ▼ = past its best ○ = not generally declared

	02	01	00	99	98	97	96	95	94	93
ITALY										

Though vintages are of considerable importance for the best Italian wines, winemaking methods of individual producers differ so widely within the same wine zones that these ratings are only approximate.

	02	01	00	99	98	97	96	95	94	93
Barolo/Barbaresco	5 ▲	9 ▲	9 ▲	9 ▲	8 ▲	9 ●	10 ▲	8 ●	6 ★	7 ★
Chianti Classico Riserva	5 ▲	9 ▲	7 ▲	9 ▲	7 ▲	10 ●	6 ★	8 ★	6 ★	8 ★
Brunello di Montalcino/ Vino Nobile di Montepulciano	5 ▲	9 ▲	8 ▲	9 ▲	8 ▲	10 ▲	6 ★	8 ★	6 ★	8 ★
Amarone della Valpolicella	5 ▲	7 ▲	9 ▲	7 ▲	7 ▲	10 ●	6 ★	10 ★	6 ★	8 ★

GERMANY

Since 1988 German vintages have been mostly at least good, often very good or outstanding and fine Rieslings have been made in most regions. Germany's cool climate means there can be substantial variation between vintages in both style and quality but at the top estates improved viticulture and rigorous selection means poor Riesling vintages are a thing of the past.

	02	01	00	99	98	97	96	95	94	93
Mosel Riesling	7 ▲	10 ▲	6 ▲	8 ▲	7 ●	8 ●	6 ●	9 ●	7 ★	8 ★
Rheingau Riesling	7 ▲	8 ▲	6 ▲	7 ●	8 ▲	7 ●	8 ▲	7 ●	7 ●	8 ●
Pfalz Riesling	6 ▲	7 ▲	5 ▲	7 ●	9 ▲	7 ●	8 ▲	5 ★	7 ★	8 ★

SPAIN (red wines)

Spain's relatively even climate makes for less exaggerated vintage differences than in northern Europe. Many Spanish wines have traditionally been released when ready to drink, although this is changing slowly and an increasing number are now released early and need further bottle aging.

	02	01	00	99	98	97	96	95	94	93
Priorat	5 ▲	7 ▲	7 ▲	7 ▲	6 ★	7 ★	7 ★	8 ★	6 ★	6 ★
Ribera del Duero	4 ▲	8 ▲	7 ▲	8 ▲	7 ●	6 ●	9 ★	8 ★	9 ★	4 ▼
Rioja (red)	6 ▲	8 ▲	7 ●	6 ●	6 ●	7 ●	8 ★	8 ★	9 ★	5 ▼

PORTUGAL (red wines)

Port is one of the great vintage wines though a vintage is only declared in exceptional years.

	02	01	00	99	98	97	96	95	94	93
Alentejo and the South	5 ▲	8 ●	9 ●	8 ●	6 ●	8 ★	6 ★	8 ★	7 ★	5 ▼
Dão and Bairrada	5 ▲	8 ▲	9 ▲	7 ●	6 ●	8 ★	8 ★	7 ★	7 ★	4 ▼
Douro	5 ▲	7 ▲	9 ▲	8 ▲	6 ●	8 ★	7 ★	8 ★	9 ★	3 ▼
Port	6 ○	7 ○	9 ▲	7 ○	6 ○	8 ▲	7 ○	7 ○	10 ▲	2 ○

	02	01	00	99	98	97	96	95	94	93

AUSTRIA

Riesling is responsible for many of the country's finest dry white wines. Austrian Rieslings are drunk young in Austria but the best examples from the Wachau can improve for six or eight years.

Wachau Riesling	8 ▲	8 ●	7 ●	8 ●	7 ●	9 ●	6 ★	8 ★	7 ★	8 ★

USA

There are major weather variations in both California and the Pacific Northwest and vintage ratings are bound to be general.

	02	01	00	99	98	97	96	95	94	93
Napa Cabernet	7 ▲	8 ▲	8 ●	9 ●	6 ★	8 ★	7 ★	8 ★	9 ★	7 ★
Sonoma Chardonnay	7 ▲	8 ●	8 ●	9 ★	6 ★	8 ★	7 ★	8 ★	7 ★	7 ★
Carneros Pinot Noir	8 ▲	9 ▲	9 ●	8 ●	9 ★	8 ★	8 ★	8 ★	9 ★	7 ▼
Santa Barbara Pinot Noir	7 ▲	8 ▲	7 ★	9 ★	6 ★	8 ★	7 ★	8 ★	8 ★	7 ★
Oregon Pinot Noir	8 ▲	8 ▲	9 ●	9 ●	8 ●	5 ★	7 ★	5 ▼	9 ▼	7 ▼
Washington State Cabernet Sauvignon	8 ▲	7 ▲	9 ▲	9 ▲	8 ●	8 ●	9 ●	8 ●	9 ★	7 ▼

AUSTRALIA

In most instances in Australia the skill of the winemaker is more important than the vintage.

	02	01	00	99	98	97	96	95	94	93
Coonawarra Cabernet	8 ▲	7 ▲	9 ▲	8 ▲	10 ▲	7 ●	9 ●	5 ★	8 ★	7 ★
Hunter Semillon	8 ▲	7 ▲	9 ▲	8 ▲	10 ▲	8 ●	9 ●	7 ★	8 ★	7 ★
Barossa Shiraz	9 ▲	10 ▲	8 ▲	8 ▲	10 ▲	8 ●	10 ●	7 ★	9 ★	7 ★
Clare Riesling	9 ▲	8 ●	7 ▲	6 ●	9 ●	7 ★	8 ★	8 ★	7 ★	6 ★
Margaret River Cabernet Sauvignon	7 ▲	10 ▲	8 ▲	10 ▲	8 ▲	7 ▲	9 ▲	10 ●	9 ★	6 ★

NEW ZEALAND

As winemaking expertise improves more New Zealand wines are showing some capacity for aging.

	02	01	00	99	98	97	96	95	94	93
Marlborough Sauvignon	8 ★	8 ★	9 ★	8 ★	5 ▼	8 ▼	9 ▼	3 ▼	8 ▼	4 ▼
Hawkes Bay Cabernet	9 ▲	7 ▲	8 ▲	8 ▲	10 ▲	7 ●	8 ●	7 ★	8 ★	5 ▼
Martinborough Pinot Noir	8 ▲	8 ●	7 ★	7 ★	9 ★	8 ★	8 ★	6 ▼	7 ▼	6 ▼

SOUTH AFRICA

Most of South Africa's ageworthy red wines come from the Stellenbosch area. Most whites are for drinking young.

	02	01	00	99	98	97	96	95	94	93
Stellenbosch Cabernet	6 ▲	9 ▲	8 ▲	7 ●	8 ●	9 ●	6 ★	9 ★	8 ★	5 ▼
Stellenbosch Chardonnay	8 ●	8 ●	6 ★	7 ★	7 ★	8 ★	6 ▼	8 ▼	6 ▼	8 ▼

GLOSSARY

Acidity Naturally present in grapes; gives red wine an appetizing 'grip' and whites a refreshing tang. Too much can make a wine seem sharp but too little and it will be flabby.

Aging Essential for fine wines and for softening many everyday reds. May take place in vat, barrel or bottle, and may last for months or years. It has a mellowing effect on a wine but too long in storage, though, and the wine may lose its fruit.

Alcoholic content Alcoholic strength, sometimes expressed in degrees, equivalent to the percentage of alcohol in the total volume.

Alcoholic fermentation Biochemical process whereby yeasts, natural or added, convert the grape sugars into alcohol and carbon dioxide, transforming grape juice into wine. It normally stops when all the sugar has been converted or when the alcohol level reaches about 15 per cent.

American Viticultural Area (AVA) American appellation system introduced in the 1980s. AVA status requires that 85 per cent of grapes in a wine come from a specified region. It does not guarantee any standard of quality.

Appellation d'Origine Contrôlée (AC or AOC) Official designation in France guaranteeing a wine by geographical origin, grape variety and production method. When used loosely in a general wine context it means any legally defined wine area.

Assemblage Final blending of fine wines, especially Bordeaux wines and Champagne.

Auslese German and Austrian quality wine category for wines made from grapes 'selected' for higher sugar levels. The wines will be generally sweet.

Barrel aging Time spent maturing in wood, normally oak, during which the wines take on flavours from the wood.

Barrel fermentation Oak barrels may be used for fermentation instead of stainless steel to give a rich, oaky flavour to the wine.

Barrique The *barrique bordelaise* is the traditional Bordeaux oak barrel of 225 litres (50 gallons) capacity, used for aging and sometimes for fermenting wine.

Beerenauslese German and Austrian quality wine category for wines made from berries 'individually selected' for higher sweetness. The wines are sweet to very sweet.

Bereich German for region or district within a wine region.

Bin number Australian system used by wine companies to identify batches of wine.

Blanc de Blancs White wine, especially Champagne, made only from white grapes. Blanc de Noirs is white wine from black grapes.

Blending The art of mixing together wines of different origin, styles or age, often to balance out acidity, weight etc.

Bodega Spanish winery or wine firm.

Botrytis *Botrytis cinerea* fungus which, in warm autumn weather, attacks white grapes, shrivels them and concentrates the sugars to produce quality sweet wines, as in Sauternes. Also called 'noble rot'.

Brut Term for 'dry', usually seen on Champagne labels and sparkling wines in the New World. In Champagne the term 'Extra Dry' is, in fact, slightly sweeter.

Canopy management Adjustments to alter the exposure of a vine's fruit and leaves to the sun, to improve quality, increase yield and help to control disease. Simpler measures include leaf trimming, early fruit culling and more general pruning.

Carbonic maceration Winemaking method traditional to Beaujolais and now widely used in warm wine regions all over the world. Bunches of grapes, uncrushed, are fermented whole in closed containers to give well-coloured, fruity wine for early drinking.

Cava Spanish Champagne-method fizz.

Cask Wooden (usually oak) barrel used for aging and storing wine. Known in France as *foudres*, Germany as *fuders* and Italy as *botti*.

Chai Bordeaux term for the building in which wine is stored.

Champagne method Traditional way of making sparkling wine by inducing a second fermentation in the bottle in which the wine will be sold.

Chaptalization Addition of sugar during fermentation to raise a wine's alcoholic strength. More necessary in cool climates where lack of sun produces insufficient natural sugar in the grape.

Château A wine-producing estate. Applied to all sizes of property, especially in Bordeaux.

Claret English term for red Bordeaux wine.

Clarification Term covering any winemaking process (such as filtering or fining) that involves the removal of solid matter either from the must or the wine.

Classico Italian heartland of a zone from where its best wines come.

Climat French term meaning a specifically defined area of a vineyard, often very small.

Clone Propagating vines by taking cuttings produces clones of the original plant. Vine nurseries now enable growers to order specific clones to suit conditions in their vineyards. Through this clonal selection it is possible to control yield, flavour and general quality.

Clos Term for a vineyard that is (or was) wall-enclosed; traditional to Burgundy.

Cold fermentation Long, slow fermentation at low temperature to extract maximum freshness from the grapes. Crucial for whites in hot climates.

Corked/corky Wine fault derived from a cork that has become contaminated, usually with Trichloranisole or TCA, and nothing to do with pieces of cork in the wine. The mouldy, stale smell is unmistakable.

Commune A French village and its surrounding area or parish.

Cosecha Spanish for 'vintage'.

Côtes/Coteaux French for 'slopes'. Hillside vineyards generally produce better wine than low-lying ones.

Crémant Champagne-method sparkling wine from French regions other than Champagne, e.g. Crémant de Bourgogne.

Crianza Spanish term used to describe both the process of aging a wine and the youngest official category of matured wine. A Crianza wine is aged in barrel, tank and/or bottle for at least two years.

Cross, Crossing Grape bred from two *Vitis vinifera* varieties.

Cru French for 'growth'. Used to describe a wine from a single vineyard.

Cru Bourgeois In Bordeaux, a quality rating immediately below Cru Classé.

Cru Classé Literally 'Classed Growth', indicating that a vineyard is included in the top-quality rating system of its region.

Cuve close Less expensive method of making sparkling wine where the second fermentation takes place in closed tanks, not in bottle as in the Champagne method.

Cuvée Contents of a *cuve* or vat. The term usually indicates a blend, which may mean different grape varieties or simply putting together the best barrels of wine.

Demi-sec Confusingly, it means medium tending to sweet, rather than medium-dry.

Denominación de Origen (DO) The main quality classification for Spanish wine. Rules specify each region's boundaries, grape varieties, vine-growing and winemaking methods.

Denominaçao de Origem Controlada (DOC) Portugal's top quality classification. Rules specify each region's boundaries, grapes, vine-growing and winemaking methods.

Denominacíon de Origen Calificada (DOC) Spanish quality wine category one step up from DO. So far only the Rioja DO has been promoted to DOC.

Denominazione di Origine Controllata (DOC) Italian quality wine classification for wines of controlled origin, grape types and style.

Denominazione di Origine Controllata e Garantita (DOCG) Top Italian quality wine classification meant to be one notch above DOC.

Domaine Estate, especially in Burgundy.

Einzellage German for an individual vineyard site, which is generally farmed by several growers. The name is normally preceded by that of the village, e.g. Wehlener Sonnenuhr is the Sonnenuhr vineyard in the village of Wehlen.

Eiswein Rare German and Austrian wine made from grapes harvested and pressed while still frozen, thus concentrating the sweetness. Known as icewine in Canada.

Élevage French term covering all wine-making stages between fermentation and bottling.

Embotellado de/en Origen Spanish term for estate-bottled.

Engarrafado na Origem Portuguese term for estate-bottled.

Enologist Wine scientist or technician.

Espumoso Spanish for 'sparkling'.

Estate-bottled Wine made from grapes grown on the estate's vineyards and then bottled where it has been made. In France, this is indicated on the label as *mis en bouteilles* followed by *au domaine, au château*.

Fermentation See Alcoholic fermentation, Malolactic fermentation.

Filtering Removal of yeasts, solids and any impurities from a wine before bottling.

Fining Method of clarifying wine by adding coagulants, traditionally egg-whites, to the surface. As these fall through the wine they collect impurities.

Flor Special film of yeast that grows on the surface of certain wines when in barrel, especially sherry. Protects the wine from air, and imparts a unique taste.

Flying winemaker Term coined in the late 1980s to describe enologists, many of them Australian-trained, brought in to improve quality in many of the world's under-performing wine regions.

Fortified wine Wine which has high-alcohol grape spirit added, usually before the initial alcoholic fermentation is completed, thereby preserving sweetness.

Frizzante Italian term for lightly sparkling wine.

Garrafeira Portuguese term for high-quality wine with at least half a per cent of alcohol higher than the required minimum, that has had at least three years' aging for reds, and at least one year for whites.

Geographical Indication (GI) Australian term to indicate the origin of a wine.

Gran Reserva Top quality, mature Spanish wine from an especially good vintage, with at least five years' aging (cask and bottle) for reds, and four for whites.

Grand Cru 'Great growth'; the top quality classification in Burgundy, used less precisely in Alsace, Bordeaux and Champagne.

Grand vin Term used in Bordeaux to indicate a producer's top wine. Usually bears a château name.

Hectolitre (hl) 100 litres; 22 imperial gallons or 133 standard 75-cl bottles.

Hybrid Grape bred from an American vine species and European *Vitis vinifera*.

Indicaçao de Proveniência Regulamentada (IPR) Official Portuguese category for wine regions aspiring to DOC status.

Indicazione Geografica Tipica (IGT) A quality level for Italian wines (roughly equivalent to French vin de pays) in between vino da tavola and DOC.

Kabinett Lowest level of German QmP wines.

Late harvest Late-harvested grapes contain more sugar and concentrated flavours; the term is often used for sweetish New World wines.

Lees Coarse sediment – dried yeasts, etc. – thrown by wine in a cask and left behind after racking. Some wines stay on the lees for as long as possible to take on extra flavour.

Liquoroso Italian term for wines high in alcohol, often – but not always – fortified.

Malolactic fermentation Secondary fermentation whereby sharp, appley malic acid is converted into mild lactic acid and carbon dioxide; occurs after alcoholic fermentation. It is encouraged in red wines, softening them and reducing their acidity, but often prevented in whites to preserve a fresh taste, especially in wines made in warm regions, where natural acidity will be lower.

Maturation The beneficial aging of wine.

Meritage American, primarily Californian, term for red or white wines made from Bordeaux grape varieties.

Mousseux French term for sparkling wine.

Must The mixture of grape juice, skins, pips and pulp produced after crushing (but prior to completion of fermentation), which will eventually become wine.

Négociant French term for merchant or shipper who buys in wine from growers, then matures, maybe blends and bottles it for sale.

Noble rot See Botrytis.

Nouveau, novello French and Italian terms for new wine. Wine for drinking very young, from November in year of vintage.

Oak Traditional wood for wine casks. During aging or fermenting it gives flavours, such as vanilla and tannin, to the wines. The newer the wood, the greater its impact. French oak is often preferred for aging fine wine. American oak is cheaper but can give strong vanilla overtones.

Oechsle German scale for measuring must weight; in effect, it indicates the level of sweetness in the juice. Each quality category has a minimum required Oechsle degree.

Oxidation Over-exposure of wine to air, causing bacterial decay and loss of fruit and flavour. Often characterized by a rather sherry-like aroma.

Passito Italian term for dried or semi-dried grapes, or strong, sweet wine made from them.

Pétillant French for semi-sparkling wine.

Phylloxera Vine aphid (*Phylloxera vastatrix*) which devastated viticulture worldwide in the late 1800s. Since then, the vulnerable European *Vitis vinifera* has been grafted on to phylloxera-resistant American rootstocks. Phylloxera has never reached Chile and parts of Australia, so vines there are ungrafted and can live up to twice as long.

Prädikat The grade, based on must weight, that defines top-quality wine in Germany and Austria. The grades are, in ascending order of ripeness in the grapes, and therefore sweetness: Kabinett, Spätlese, Auslese, Beerenauslese, Eiswein, Ausbruch (for Austria only) and Trockenbeerenauslese.

Premier Cru 'First growth'; the top quality classification in Bordeaux, but second to Grand Cru in Burgundy. Also used in other parts of France, not always with the same precision.

Prohibition 18th Amendment to the US

Constitution, passed in 1920, banning alcoholic beverages; the measure ruined most wineries, but some survived making grape juice, communion and medicinal wines. Repealed in 1933.

Qualitätswein bestimmter Anbaugebiete German wine classification (abbreviated to QbA) for 'quality wine from designated regions' – the middle level, for fairly ordinary wines, though some good experimental wines can also be QbA.

Qualitätswein mit Prädikat German wine classification (abbreviated to QmP) for 'quality wine with distinction' (the top level), which is further subdivided into the various categories of Prädikat.

Quinta Portuguese farm or wine estate.

Racking Gradual clarification of a quality wine as part of the maturation process. The wine is transferred from one barrel to another, leaving the lees or sediment behind. Racking also produces aeration necessary for the aging process, softens tannins and helps develop further flavours.

Rancio Style of wine that is deliberately oxidized; either naturally strong or fortified, it is aged in the sun in glass bottles, earthenware jars or wooden barrels.

Récoltant French for 'grower'. They may make their own wine or sell the grapes to a merchant.

Reserva In Spain, quality wine from a good vintage with at least three years' aging (cask and bottle) for reds, and two for whites. In Portugal it designates wine that has an alcohol level at least half a per cent higher than the minimum for the region.

Réserve The term should indicate the wine has been aged longer in oak but many New World producers use it freely on their wine labels to indicate different wine styles or a special selection rather than a better wine. It has no legal meaning. Other similar terms are Private Reserve and Special Selection.

Ripasso Valpolicella wine refermented on the lees of Amarone della Valpolicella to give extra richness.

Riserva Italian term meaning wines aged for a specific number of years according to DOC(G) laws.

Rootstock The root stump of the vine on to which the fruiting branches are grafted. Most rootstocks are from phylloxera-resistant American vines.

Rosado, rosato Spanish (or Portuguese) and Italian for pink wine or rosé.

Sec French for 'dry'. When applied to

Champagne, it actually means medium-dry.

Second wine Wine from a designated vineyard which is sold separately from the main production, under a different name. Usually lighter and quicker-maturing than the main wine.

Sekt German term for sparkling wine.

Solera Blending system used for sherry and some other fortified wines. When mature wine is run off a cask for bottling, only a quarter or so of the volume is taken, and the space is filled with similar but younger wine from another cask, which in turn is topped up from an even younger cask, and so on.

Spätlese German quality wine category for wines made from 'late-picked' grapes.

Spumante Italian for sparkling wine.

Sugar Naturally present in grapes. Transformed during fermentation into alcohol and carbon dioxide.

Sulphur Sulphur is commonly used during vinification as a disinfectant for equipment; with fresh grapes and wine as an anti-oxidant; and added as sulphur dioxide to the must to arrest or delay fermentation.

Supérieur French term for wines with a higher alcohol content than the basic AC.

Superiore Italian term for wines with higher alcohol, maybe more aging too.

Super-Tuscan English term for high-quality non-DOC Tuscan wine.

Sur lie French for 'on the lees', meaning wine bottled direct from the fermentation vat or cask to gain extra flavour from the lees. Common with quality Muscadet, white Burgundy, similar barrel-aged whites and, increasingly, commercial bulk wines.

Tafelwein German for 'table wine', the most basic quality designation.

Tannin Harsh, bitter element in red wine, derived from grape skins, pips, stems and from aging in oak barrels; softens with time and is essential for a wine's long-term aging.

Terroir A French term used to denote the combination of soil, climate and exposure to the sun – that is, the natural physical environment of the vine.

Trocken German for 'dry'. Applied to new-style German wines made dry in an effort to make them better matches for food.

Trockenbeerenauslese German quality wine category for wines made from noble-rotted single grapes – the highest level of sweetness.

Varietal The character of wine derived from the grape; also wine made from, and named after, a single or dominant grape

variety and usually containing at least 75 per cent of that variety. The minimum percentage varies slightly between countries and, in the USA, between states.

Vendange tardive French for 'late harvest'; grapes are left on the vine after the normal harvest time to concentrate the flavours and sugars.

Vieilles vignes Wine from mature vines.

Vin Délimité de Qualité Supérieure Second category of French quality control for wines, below AC, abbreviated to VDQS.

Vin de paille Wine made by drying the grapes on straw (*paille*) before fermentation. This concentrates the sugar in the grapes: the resulting wines are sweet but slightly nutty. Mostly from the Jura region of France.

Vin de pays French for 'country wine'. Although it is the third and bottom category for quality in the official classification of French wines, it includes some first-class wines which don't follow local AC rules.

Vin doux naturel (VDN) French sweet wine fortified with grape spirit. Mostly from Languedoc-Roussillon.

Viña Spanish for 'vineyard'. Often loosely used in names of wines not actually from a vineyard of that name.

Vinification The process of turning grapes into wine.

Vino da tavola Italian for 'table wine'. Quality may be basic or exceptional. Many wines formerly sold as vino da tavola are now IGT.

Vintage The year's grape harvest, also used to describe the wine of a single year.

Viticulture Vine-growing and vineyard management.

Vitis vinifera The species of vine, native to Europe and Central Asia, responsible for most of the world's quality wine, as opposed to other species such as the native American *Vitis labrusca*, which is still used in the eastern USA to make grape juice and sweetish wines but which is more suited to juice and jelly manufacture.

Wine of Origin (WO) South African equivalent of Appellation Contrôlée.

Yeast Organism which, in the wine process, causes grape juice to ferment. In the New World it is common to start fermentation with cultured yeasts, rather than rely on the natural yeasts present in the winery, known as ambient yeasts.

Yield The amount of fruit, and ultimately wine, produced from a vineyard, generally ranging between 40 and 100 hectolitres per hectare.

INDEX

Numbers in **bold** refer to main entries. Numbers in *italic* refer to photograph and label captions.

Acknowledgments

Regional consultants
Nicolas Belfrage MW, Stephen Brook, Jim Budd, Bob Campbell MW, Anthony Gismondi, James Halliday, Harold Heckle, James Lawther MW, Angela Lloyd, Richard Mayson, Dan McCarthy, Maggie McNie MW, Stuart Pigott, Norm Roby, Victor de la Serna.

Photographs of Oz Clarke by Stephen Bartholomew 6, 21, 27, 28. Photographs of bottles by Steve Marwood 14, 15, 18, 19, 22, 25. All other photographs supplied by Cephas Picture Library. All photographs by Mick Rock except: Jerry Alexander 352; Nigel Blythe 8 (left), 308; Andy Christodolo 4 (left), 9 (left), 198, 218, 229, 370, 376; David Copeman 24 (below); Bruce Fleming 106, 128, 264; Bruce Jenkins 6 (right); Kevin Judd 2–3, 3, 5 (right), 6 (left), 48, 185, 234, 392; Herbert Lehmann 306; Steven Morris 10 (left), 372, 380; R & K Muschenetz 43, 44, 111, 396; Alain Proust 5 (left), 54–55, 186, 354; Ted Stefanski 212.